Personality Theory

A Multicultural Perspective

by

Mark D. Kelland, Ph.D.

Professor of Psychology
Lansing Community College

2014

ISBN: 1495225925
ISBN 13: 978-1495225925

Dedication

This book is dedicated to my children

Samuel & John

Acknowledgments

I would like to thank Donna Kelland for reading most of the chapters in this book, and for providing very helpful comments regarding both the content and the general approach used in the writing. Her expertise in psychology proved helpful on numerous occasions. I would also like to thank Chenika Martinez, Minister Danny Martinez, and Professor Isaac Addai for reviewing the appendix on African perspectives on personality.

Special thanks to Michele Sordi, without whom this project might never have started.

Most of the chapters in this book were reviewed by colleagues around the country. This was done anonymously, while the book was under contract with another publisher. Once I parted ways with my former publisher, I had no access to the names of those reviewers. Though they shall remain anonymous, I hope they know how much I appreciate their input during the writing of this book.

Some of the images in this book are the property of the author, and he thanks the subjects in those photographs for giving permission to use images of them.

The photographs on the cover of this book are a collection of family photographs belonging to the author.

I would also like to thank

Sunny,

who was often by my side while I was writing this book.

[Image by Mark Kelland]

Table of Contents

Preface

There are several personality textbooks which claim to be comprehensive, but they clearly aren't. Primarily, those textbooks focus on Western psychology. A couple of personality textbooks have ventured into the realm of topics such as Yoga, Buddhism, or Sufism, but either do so only superficially, or at the expense of traditional topics of great relevance to Western psychology. So how does one go about writing a truly comprehensive textbook on personality, while at the same time keeping the book from becoming overwhelmingly long? That was the challenge I set for myself.

As I was writing this book, and receiving some professional reviews along the way, a concern that several reviewers raised was the emphasis on religion/spirituality in this book, particularly in the last two chapters. My response is that psychology has been afraid of religion/spirituality for far too long. It is a major factor in *many* people's lives, and affects their personality development as children and their personality growth (or lack thereof) as adults. Indeed, over the decades since Freud first proposed a comprehensive theory of personality development, there have been many psychologists who embraced spirituality (if not religion, per se). So the last two chapters can be included in one's course, or not. If not, they are still available for those students who have an interest in broadening their knowledge of personality.

And yet, I still consider this book to be incomplete. Perspectives based on an African worldview, contained in Appendix B, are certainly deserving of an entire chapter. However, my knowledge on the subject is limited, and the material does not conform to traditional ways in which psychologists study personality. Indeed, traditional ways of studying personality in Africa have a somewhat dubious history. There are also other distinct cultures that may share commonalities, such as the Native Americans in both North and South America, and the Aborigines in Australia. Although I have made an effort in this book to address the personality development and structure of many non-Western people around the world, there is still a lot of research to be done by those who study personality.

I have also included what I hope are thought-provoking review/discussion questions. I like to teach my courses in something of a seminar style, with a lot of discussion and debate. When the theories presented in this book are applied to one's real life experiences, the material takes on a relevance that is often neglected in college courses. Personality is fundamental to who we are, thus it is fundamental to everything we do and every minute of our lives. The study of personality is a vast and complex field, but that just makes it all the more fascinating.

Mark Kelland
April, 2010

Preface #2

Although this is a second edition, it has only minor additions to the first version. Since I am no longer working with an academic publisher (by my own choice), rather than calling it the second edition I have changed the name slightly so I can simply publish it anew. Since I like to focus on the historical basics in the field of personality, it was not necessary to add lots of new material. However, should anyone be using this book for academic purposes, such as a professor teaching a class, they can certainly bring new articles into their classroom to supplement this book. I encourage them to do so, and make their class their own. Students are inspired by professors who really love the material they teach.

Mark Kelland
January, 2014

Chapter 1 - Introduction

When you first think of personality, what comes to mind? When we refer to certain people as being "personalities," we usually mean they are famous, people like movie stars or your favorite band. When we describe a person as having "lots of personality," we usually mean they are outgoing and fun-loving, the kind of person we like to spend time with. But does this tell us anything about personality itself? Although we may think we have an understanding of what personality is, professional psychologists always seek to move beyond what people think they know in order to determine what is actually real or at least as close to real as we can come. In the pursuit of truly understanding personality, however, many personality theorists seem to have been focused on a particularly Western cultural approach that owes much of its history to the pioneering work of Sigmund Freud.

Freud trained as a physician with a strong background in biomedical research. He naturally brought his keen sense of observation, a characteristic of any good scientist, into his psychiatric practice. As he worked with his patients, he developed a distinctly medical model: identify a problem, identify the cause of the problem, and treat the patient accordingly. This approach can work quite well, and it has worked wonderfully for medical science, but it has two main weaknesses when applied to the study of personality. First, it fails to address the complexity and uniqueness of individuals, and second, it does not readily lend itself to describing how one chooses to develop a healthy personality.

The diversity that is the human experience can be seen in the faces of the people around us. [Image by Mark Kelland]

Quite soon in the history of personality theory, however, there were influential theorists who began to challenge Freud's perspective. Alfred Adler, although a colleague of Freud's for a time, began to focus on social interest and an individual's style of life. Karen Horney challenged Freud's perspective on the psychology of women, only to later suggest that the issue was more directly related to the oppression of women as a minority, rather than a fundamental difference based on gender. And there were Carl Jung and Carl Rogers, two men profoundly influenced by Eastern philosophy. Consequently, anyone influenced by Jung or Rogers has also been influenced, in part, by Eastern philosophy. What about the rest of the world? Have we taken into account the possibility that there are other, equally valuable and interesting perspectives on the nature of people? Many fields in psychology have made a concerted effort to address cross-cultural issues. The primary purpose of this textbook is to address some of these different cultural perspectives, and to compare them to, and contrast them with, the traditional Western perspectives. In addition, we will examine the relationships between the traditional approaches as well. In particular, the final section of this book introduces a number of paths developed throughout history to help people choose how to live their lives. Although each path is intimately identified with a religious perspective, the paths themselves represent more of a style of life. As we examine these perspectives, you will see that they are all quite similar in their essential elements, making it clear that the principles involved transcend religious culture. My hope is that when you have read this book, you will have a broad understanding of the field of personality, and an appreciation for both what we have in common and what makes us unique, as members of our global community.

Definitions and Descriptions of Personality

It would seem to make sense that we should begin our study of personality by defining the term. Unfortunately, there is no single definition that fits the variety of theories that have been developed in the field of personality research. Most psychologists agree that the term personality comes from the Latin word **persona**, a term referring to the masks worn by actors performing ancient Greek plays. Often there were not enough actors available to play all of the roles in a play, so they would wear these masks to let the audience know that they were playing different roles. But are our personalities just masks? Freud certainly considered the unconscious mind to be very important, Cattell considered source traits to be more important than surface traits, and Buddhists consider the natural world (including the self) to be an illusion. Adler believed the best way to examine personality is to look at the person's style of life, and Rogers felt that the only person who could truly understand you is yourself. What definition could possibly encompass all that?

Still, we need a working definition as a starting point for discussion. Borrowing loosely from Allport's definition of personality, personality can be viewed as the dynamic organization within an individual of various psychological factors that determines the person's characteristic thoughts and behaviors. In simpler terms, a variety of factors blend together to create each person, and as a result of those factors the individual is most likely to think and act in somewhat predictable ways. However, given the complexity of human life, those predictions may prove to be elusive. Theodore Millon (1996, 2004; Millon & Grossman, 2005), a renowned clinician and theorist in the field of personality disorders, has sought a definition of personality broad enough to encompass both normal and abnormal personality. Millon describes the modern view of personality as a complex pattern of psychological characteristics that are deeply embedded, largely unconscious, and resistant to change. These intrinsic and pervasive traits arise from a complex matrix of biological dispositions and experiential learning, and express themselves automatically in nearly every aspect of the individual's unique pattern of perceiving, feeling, thinking, coping, and behaving (e.g., Millon, 1996).

Another challenge we face in defining personality is how we approach the question in the first place. Traditionally, there have been two basic approaches to the study of personality: the **nomothetic** perspective and the **idiographic** perspective. The nomothetic perspective seeks to identify general rules that pertain to personality as a **construct** (a working hypothesis or concept used to identify something we can describe but not see, such as IQ or the self). Thus, it can be rather abstract, and often fails to appreciate the uniqueness of individuals. In contrast, the idiographic perspective focuses specifically on the individuality and uniqueness of each person. Although the idiographic approach often seems more appealing to students, especially since it enhances their self-esteem by considering them as individually important, it is difficult for any theory of personality to encompass research that treats only one person at a time. Such a theory would naturally suffer from problems of generalizability, and may be useful for therapists working with one patient or client at a time, but it will not be particularly useful for enhancing our overall understanding of personality in general. It is important to note, however, that many early personality theories were based on individual case studies, and this critique is one that we will see several times in this book.

As is often the case in psychology, the best approach may be to attempt blending the nomothetic and idiographic perspectives, seeking the generalizability of the nomothetic perspective's general principles on personality and personality development - while maintaining an appreciation for the idiographic perspective's recognition of the value of an individual's unique character. Millon (1996) suggests an integrative approach to defining personality. Not only would an integrative approach combine the nomothetic and idiographic perspectives, it would also help to bring together the two broad traditions of clinical and applied psychology. Clinical psychologists are compelled by the nature of their work with patients, or clients, to try to understand the individual. Thus, they need to follow a more idiographic approach. In contrast, applied psychologists (e.g., experimental psychologists) are more construct-focused, and find the nomothetic approach more appealing and useful for developing generalizable theories on the nature of various aspects of personality. If personality can be defined in a satisfactory way by an integrative approach, then clinicians may benefit more from applied research, and experimental psychologists may see their work more directly applied in clinical settings where it may help people in our society.

In order to better understand how some of the different disciplines within the field of psychology contribute to our definition of personality, let's take a brief look at some of the widely recognized factors that come into play:

Discussion Question: The nomothetic and idiographic perspectives approach personality in very different ways. Do you believe that your personality can be described in a way that might also be used to describe the personalities of other people (maybe your friends), or do you feel it is necessary to describe each person as an individual?

Psychodynamic Factors

The very word "psychodynamic" suggests that there are ongoing interactions between different elements of the mind. Sigmund Freud not only offered names for these elements (id, ego, and superego), he proposed different levels of consciousness. Since the unconscious mind was very powerful according to Freud, one of the first and most enduring elements of psychodynamic theory is that we are often unaware of why we think and act the way we do. Add to that the belief that our personality is determined in early childhood, and you can quickly see that psychological problems would be very difficult to treat. Perhaps more importantly, since we are not aware of many of our own thoughts and desires, it would difficult or even impossible for us to choose to change our personality no matter how much we might want to.

Most psychodynamic theorists since Freud have expanded the influences that affect us to include more of the outside world. Those theorists who remained loyal to Freud, typically known as neo-Freudians, emphasized the ego. Since the ego functions primarily in the real world, the individual must take into account the influence of other people involved in their lives. Some theorists who differed significantly from the traditional Freudian perspective, most notably Alfred Adler and Karen Horney, focused much of their theories on cultural influences. Adler believed that social cooperation was essential to the success of each individual (and humanity as a whole), whereas Horney provided an intriguing alternative to Freud's sexist theories regarding women. Although Horney based her theories regarding women on the cultural standing between men and women in the Victorian era, to a large extent her theory remains relevant today.

Learning and Cognitive Factors

As a species, human beings are distinguished by their highly developed brains. Animals with less-developed nervous systems rely primarily on instinctive behavior, but very little on learning. While the study of animals' instinctive behavior is fascinating, and led to a shared Nobel Prize for the ethologists Nikolaas Tinbergen, Konrad Lorenz, and Karl von Frisch, animal behavior remains distinctly limited compared to the complex learning and cognitive tasks that humans can readily perform (Beck, 1978; Gould, 1982). Indeed, the profound value of our abilities to think and learn may be best reflected in the fact that, according to Tinbergen's strict definition of instinct (see Beck, 1978), humans appear not to have any instinctive behavior anymore. Yet we have more than made up for it through our ability to learn, and learning theory and behaviorism became dominant forces in the early years of American psychology.

John B. Watson and B.F. Skinner are among the most famous and influential of American psychologists. Learning about their groundbreaking research on classical and operant conditioning is standard fare in psychology courses. More recently, Albert Bandura has enjoyed similar popularity and respect in the field of social learning theory. Anyone who has children knows full well how eagerly they observe us and mimic our actions and speech. An important aspect of the learning perspective is that our personalities may develop as a result of the rewards and/or punishments we receive from others. Consequently, we should be able to shape an individual's personality in any way we want. Early behaviorists, like Watson, suggested that they could indeed take any child and raise them to be successful in any career they chose for them. Although most parents and teachers try to be a good influence on children, and to set good examples for them, children are often influenced more by their peers. What children find rewarding may not be what parents and teachers think is rewarding. This is why a social-cognitive approach to learning becomes very important in understanding personality development. Social-cognitive theorists, like Bandura, recognize that children interact with their environment, partly determining for themselves what is rewarding or punishing, and then react to the environment in their own unique way.

As suggested by the blend of behaviorism and cognition that Bandura and others proposed, there is a close association between behaviorism and the field of cognitive psychology. Although strict behaviorists rejected the study of unobservable cognitive processes, the cognitive field has actually followed the guidelines of behaviorism with regard to a dispassionate and logical observation of the expression of cognitive processes through an individual's behavior and what they say. Thus, the ability of human beings to think, reason, analyze, anticipate, etc., leads them to act in accordance with their ideas, rather than simply on the basis of traditional behavioral controls: reward, punishment, or associations with unconditional stimuli. The success of the cognitive approach when applied to therapy, such as the techniques developed by Aaron Beck, has helped to establish cognitive theory as one the most respected areas in the study of personality and abnormal psychology.

Biological Factors

Although humans may not exhibit instinctive behavior, we are still ultimately a product of our biological makeup, our specific DNA pattern. Our individual DNA pattern is unique, unless we happen to be an identical twin, and it not only provides the basis for our learning and cognitive abilities, it also sets the conditions for certain aspects of our character. Perhaps the most **salient** of these characteristics is **temperament**, which can loosely be described as the emotional component of our personality. In addition to temperament, twin studies have shown that all aspects of personality appear to be significantly influenced by our genetic inheritance (Bouchard, 1994; Bouchard & McGue, 1990; Bouchard et al., 1990). Even such complex personality variables as well-being, traditionalism, and religiosity have been found to be highly influenced by our genetic make-up (Tellegen et al., 1988; Waller et al., 1990).

Sociobiologists and evolutionary psychologists also emphasize the role of genetics and adaptation over time. Sociobiologists consider how biological factors influence social behavior. For example, they would suggest that men are inclined to prefer multiple sexual partners because men are biologically capable of fathering many children, whereas women would be inclined to favor one successful and established partner, because a woman must physically invest a year or more in each child (a 9-month pregnancy followed by a period of nursing). Similarly, evolutionary psychologists consider how human behavior has been adaptive for our survival. Humans evolved from plant-eating primates, we are not well suited to defend ourselves against large, meat-eating predators. As a group, however, and using our intellect to fashion weapons from sticks and rocks, we were able to survive and flourish over time. Unfortunately, the same adaptive influences that guide the development of each healthy person can, under adverse conditions, lead to dysfunctional behaviors, and consequently, psychological disorders (Millon, 2004).

Discussion Question: Some research suggests that personality is largely determined by genetics. Do you see similarities in your personality as compared to your parents, grandparents, brothers, sisters, etc.? Do you think that your environment, things like your community, your friends, television, movies, the Internet, etc., are more influential than your biological inheritance from your parents?

Inherent Drives

Freud believed that we are motivated primarily by psychosexual impulses, and secondarily by our tendency toward aggression. Certainly it is necessary to procreate for the species to survive, and elements of aggression are necessary for us to get what we need and to protect ourselves. But this is a particularly dark and somewhat animalistic view of humanity. The humanistic psychologists Carl Rogers and Abraham Maslow believed in a positive view of people, they proposed that each of us contains an inherent drive to be the best that we can be, and to accomplish all that we are capable of accomplishing. Rogers and Maslow called this drive **self-actualization**. Interestingly, this concept is actually thousands of years old, and having spent time in China, Rogers was well aware of Buddhist and Yogic perspectives on the self.

Somewhat related to the humanistic concept of self-actualization, is the existential perspective. Existential theorists, like Rollo May, believe that individuals can be truly happy only when they find some meaning in life. In Eastern philosophical perspectives, coming from Yoga and Buddhism, meaning in life is found by realizing that life is an illusion, that within each of us is the essence of one universal spirit. Indeed, Yoga means “union,” referring to union with God. Thus, we have meaning within us, but the illusion of our life is what distracts us from realizing it.

Discussion Question: Do you feel that you are driven to accomplish something great, or to find some particular meaning in life? Do you believe that there might be pathways to guide you, particularly spiritual or religious pathways?

Sociocultural Influences

Culture can broadly be defined as “everything that people have, think, and do as members of a society” (Ferraro, 2006a), and appears to be as old as the *Homo* genus itself (the genus of which we, as *Homo sapiens*, are the current representatives; Haviland et al., 2005). Culture has also been described as the memory of a society (see Triandis & Suh, 2002). Culture is both learned and shared by members of a society, and it is what the makes the behavior of an individual understandable to other members of that culture. Everything we do is influenced by culture, from the food we eat to the nature of our personal relationships, and it varies dramatically from group to group. What makes life understandable and predictable within one group may be incomprehensible to another. Despite differences in detail, however, there are a number of cultural universals, those aspects of culture that have been identified in every cultural group that has been examined historically or ethnographically (Murdock, 1945; see also Ferraro, 2006a). Therefore, if we truly want to understand personality theory, we need to know something about the sociocultural factors that may be the same, or that may differ, between groups.

In 1999, Stanley Sue proposed that psychology has systematically avoided the study of cross-cultural factors in psychological research. This was not because psychologists themselves are biased, but rather, it was due to an inherent bias in the nature of psychological research (for commentaries see also Tebes, 2000; Guyll & Madon, 2000; and Sue, 2000). Although some may disagree with the arguments set forth in Sue's initial study, it is clear that the vast majority of research has been conducted here in America, primarily by American college professors studying American psychology students. And the history of our country clearly identifies most of those individuals, both the professors and the students, as White, middle- to upper-class men. The same year, Lee et al. (1999) brought together a collection of multicultural perspectives on personality, with the individual chapters written by a very diverse group of authors. In both the preface and their introductory chapter, the editors emphasize that neither human nature nor personality can be separated from culture. And yet, as suggested by Sue (1999), they acknowledge the general lack of cross-cultural or multicultural research in the field of personality. Times have begun to change, however. In 2002, the American Psychological Association (APA) adopted a policy entitled "Guidelines on Multicultural Education, Training, Research, Practice, and Organizational Change for Psychologists (which is available online at www.apa.org/pi/multiculturalguidelines/homepage.html). The year 2002 also saw a chapter in the prestigious *Annual Review of Psychology* on how culture influences the development of personality (Triandis & Suh, 2002). In a fascinating article on whether psychology actually matters in our lives, former APA president and renowned social psychologist Philip Zimbardo (2004) identified the work of Kenneth and Mamie Clark on prejudice and discrimination, which was presented to the United States Supreme Court during the *Brown vs. Board of Education of Topeka, KS* case (which led to the end of school segregation in America) as one of the most significant impacts on American life that psychology has contributed to directly (see also Benjamin & Crouse, 2002; Keppel, 2002; Pickren & Tomes, 2002). Finally, an examination of *American Psychologist* (the principle journal of APA) and *Psychological Science* (the principle journal of the American Psychological Society) since the year 2000 reveals studies demonstrating the importance of cross-cultural research in many areas of psychology (see Table 1.1). So, although personality theorists, and the field of psychology in general, have been somewhat slow to address cross-cultural and diversity issues, in more recent years psychologists appear to be rapidly gaining a greater appreciation of the importance of studying human diversity in all its forms.

As mentioned in the opening paragraphs of this chapter, one of the primary goals of this book is to incorporate different cultural perspectives into our study of personality theory, to take more of a global perspective than has traditionally been done. Why is this important? It is actually very easy to point out the answer to that question. The United States of America has less than 300 million people. India has nearly 1 billion people, and China has over 1 billion people. So, two Asian countries alone have nearly 7 times as many people as the United States. How can we claim to be studying personality if we haven't taken into account the vast majority of people in the world? Of course, we haven't entirely ignored these two particular countries, because two of the most famous personality theorists spent time in these countries when they were young. Carl Jung spent time in India, and his theories were clearly influenced by ancient Vedic philosophy, and Carl Rogers spent time in China while studying to be a minister. So it is possible to draw connections between Yoga, Buddhism, psychodynamic theory, and humanistic psychology. Sometimes this will involve looking at differences between cultures, and other times we will focus on similarities. At the end of the book I hope you will appreciate not only the diversity of personality and personality theory, but also the connections that tie all of us together.

Discussion Question: Do you notice cultural differences around you every day, or do you live in a small community where everyone is very much the same? What sort of challenges do you face as a result of cultural differences, either because you deal with them daily or because you have little opportunity to experience them?

Introduction

Some Basic Questions Common to All Areas of Personality Theory

In addition to the broad perspectives described above, there are a number of philosophical questions that help to bring the nature of personality into perspective. Thinking about how these questions are answered by each theory can help us to compare and contrast the different theories.

Is our personality inherited, or are we products of our environment? This is the classic debate on nature vs. nurture. Are we born with a given temperament, with a genetically determined style of interacting with others, certain abilities, with various behavioral patterns that we cannot even control? Or are we shaped by our experiences, by learning, thinking, and relating to others? Many psychologists today find this debate amusing, because no matter what area of psychology you study, the answer is typically both! We are born with a certain range of possibilities determined by our DNA. We can be a certain height, have a certain IQ, be shy or outgoing, we might be Black, Asian, White or Hispanic, etc. because of who we are genetically. However, the environment can have a profound effect on how our genetic make-up is realized. For example, an abused child may become shy and withdrawn, even though genetically they were inclined to be more outgoing. A child whose mother abused alcohol during the pregnancy may suffer from fetal alcohol syndrome, the leading cause of preventable mental retardation, even though the child was genetically endowed with the possibility of being a genius. So the best perspective may be that our genetic make-up provides a range of possibilities for our life, and the environment in which we grow determines where exactly we fall within that range.

Are we unique, or are there common types of personality? Many students want to believe that they are special and truly unique, and they tend to reject theories that try to categorize individuals. However, if personality theories were unique to each person, we could never possibly cover all of the theories! Also, as unique as you may be, aren't many people, like your friends, similar to you? In order to understand and compare people, personality theorists need to consider that there are common aspects of personality. It is up to each of us to decide whether we are still willing to find what is unique and special about each separate person.

Which is more important, the past, present, or future? Many theorists, particularly psychodynamic theorists, consider personality to be largely determined at an early age. Similarly, those who believe strongly in the genetic determination of personality would consider many factors set even before birth. But what prospects for growth does this allow, can people change or choose a new direction in their life? Cognitive and behavioral theorists focus on specific thoughts, beliefs, and behaviors that are influencing our daily lives, whereas existential theorists search for meaning in our lives. Other theorists, such as the humanists and those who favor the spiritually-oriented perspectives we will examine, consider the future to be primary in our goals and aspirations. Self-actualization is something we can work toward. Indeed, it may be an inherent drive.

Do we have free will, or is our behavior determined? Although this question seems similar to the previous one, it refers more to whether we consciously choose the path we take in life as compared to whether our behavior is specifically determined by factors beyond our control. We already mentioned the possibility of genetic factors above, but there might also be unconscious factors and stimuli in our environment. Certainly humans rely on learning for much of what we do in life, so why not for developing our personalities? Though some students don't want to think of themselves as simply products of reinforcement and punishment (i.e., operant conditioning) or the associations formed during classical conditioning (anyone have a phobia?), what about the richness of observational learning? Still, exercising our will and making sound choices seems far more dignified to many people. Is it possible to develop our will, to help us make better choices and follow through on them? Yes, according to William James, America's foremost psychologist. James considered our will to be of great importance, and he included chapters on the will in two classic books: *Psychology: Briefer Course,* published in 1892 and *Talks to Teachers on Psychology and to Students on Some of Life's Ideals,* which was published in 1899. James not only thought about the importance of the will, he recommended exercising it. In *Talks to Teachers...,* he sets forth the following responsibility for teachers of psychology:

> But let us now close in a little more closely on this matter of the education of the will. Your task is to build up a character in your pupils; and a character, as I have so often said, consists in an organized set of habits of reaction. Now of what do such habits of reaction themselves consist? They consist of tendencies to act characteristically when certain ideas possess us, and to refrain characteristically when possessed by other ideas (p. 816).

Table 1.1: Sampling of Cross-Cultural Research in Select Psychology Journals Since the Year 2000	
Attachment	Chao, 2001; Gjerde, 2001; Kondo-Ikemura, 2001; Posada & Jacobs, 2001; Rothbaum et al., 2000; Rothbaum et al., 2001; van Ijzendoorn & Sagi, 2001
Child Development	Callaghan et al., 2005; Goldin-Meadow & Saltzman, 2000; Lal, 2002
Cognitive Dissonance	Kitayama et al., 2004
Cognition and Creativity	Antonio et al., 2004; German & Barrett, 2005; Hong et al., 2000; Leung et al., 2008; Norenzayan & Nisbett, 2000; Tomasello, 2000
Conflict and Perceptions of Safety	Eidelson & Eidelson, 2003; Graham, 2006; Juvonen et al., 2006; Van Vugt et al., 2007
Cooperation	Wong & Hong, 2005
Cultural Research and Cultural Competency in Psychotherapy	Goldston et al., 2008; Heine & Norenzayan, 2006; Leong, 2007; Matsumoto & Yoo, 2006; Smith et al., 2006; Sue, 2003; Vasquez, 2007; Whaley & Davis, 2007
Education	Tucker & Herman, 2002
Emotion	Elfenbein & Ambady, 2003; Frijda & Sundararajan, 2007; Hejmadi et al., 2000; Tsai, 2007
Globalization, Nationality, Race Relations	Arnett, 2002; Heine et al., 2008; Henry & Hardin, 2006; Inglehart et al., 2008; McCrae & Terracciano, 2006; Sue, 2004; Tropp & Pettigrew, 2005
Family Dynamics	Dudley-Grant, 2001; Halpern, 2001; Kameguchi & Murphy-Shigematsu, 2001; Kaslow, 2001
Goal-Seeking Behavior	Elliot et al., 2001; Markus et al., 2006
Intelligence	Daley et al., 2003; Sternberg, 2004
Learning	Gurung, 2003; Li, 2003; Li, 2005; McBride-Chang & Treiman, 2003; Tweed & Lehman, 2002; Tweed & Lehman, 2003
Memory	Cohen & Gunz, 2002; Fivush & Nelson, 2004
Neural Substrates of Attention	Hedden et al., 2008
Perception and Spatial Representation	Bar-Haim et al., 2006; Cohen & Gunz, 2002; Dobel et al., 2007; Feng et al., 2007; Ji et al., 2001; Kitayama et al., 2003; Leung & Cogen, 2007; Maass & Russo, 2003; Miyamoto et al., 2006
Self, Self-esteem, Social Perspective	Perunovic & Heller, 2007; Wang, 2006a,b; Wu & Keysar, 2007; Yamagishi et al., 2008; Yamaguchi et al., 2007
Stress Responses	Taylor et al., 2007

Table 1.2: Brief Comparison of Factors Influencing Personality	
Psychodynamic Factors	Emphasis is on the unconscious mind, interactions between elements of the mind, early childhood experiences, stages of development, defense mechanisms, etc.
Learning and Cognitive Factors	Emphasis is on environmental stimuli and/or thought patterns that predictably influence behavior; focus is on observable behavior or identifiable thoughts.
Biological Factors	Emphasis is on genetic factors, which set ranges within which the individual may develop. This approach does not ignore the environment, but genetic factors (e.g., inborn traits and temperament) may cause different environmental influences to be experienced in similar ways, or conversely, may cause similar environmental influences to be experienced in different ways.
Inherent Drives	Humanistic psychologists focus on self-actualization; existentialists and spiritually-oriented psychologists focus on the search for meaning in one's life.
Sociocultural Influences	Cross-cultural and multicultural psychologists remind us that all of the above categories must be considered in terms of the rich diversity that is the human experience. Addresses both the differences between and the similarities among groups of people around the world.

Personality as a Discipline within the Field of Psychology

As difficult as it may be to define personality, it is important to know something about it. Personality is probably the most important field in psychology. Understanding who we are as individuals, and why we think certain thoughts and do certain things is the starting point for addressing clinical issues, abnormal psychology, and health psychology, it is the ultimate goal of studying human development, and it is the point from which we begin to address social psychology. Without an appreciation of the individual, without concern for each person, these other areas of psychology become little more than academic subjects.

Personality as a Common Thread in the History of Psychology

Most historians identify the starting point of the modern field of psychology with the experimental psychologists, particularly the establishment of Wilhelm Wundt's laboratory in Leipzig, Germany in 1879. Personality theorists, however, were not far behind. Freud, Adler, and Jung were all beginning to work in the field of psychiatry (they were medical doctors) in the late 1800s as well. If one wants to put an official date on the start of modern personality theory, it would most likely be 1900, the year in which Freud published "*The Interpretation of Dreams* (Freud, 1900/1995)." Since Freud's theories were based on his work with patients, this date is also the beginning of a relationship between personality theory, abnormal psychology, and psychotherapy, a relationship that continues today. Early psychodynamic theorists were also influential in developmental psychology and school psychology. Freud began his theory of personality with a proposed series of developmental stages: the five psychosexual stages. Erik Erikson, another well known psychodynamic theorist, is probably better known as a developmental psychologist for his eight-stage theory of psychosocial crises. Adler considered the early years of childhood so important that he felt parents and teachers should have access to training and counseling in the schools. With the endorsement of the minister of education, Adler and his colleagues established child guidance centers in many public schools.

As psychodynamic theory dominated the European scene in the early 1900s, America was largely influenced by behaviorism. Behavioral theorists also considered personality within their domain, suggesting that personality is learned. John B. Watson boasted that he could use behavioral principles to direct any child into any given career path. B.F. Skinner constructed an advanced version of his famous "Skinner Box," which was typically used to train rats or pigeons, to raise and care for children during the early years of life. As behaviorism continued to develop, social learning theorists focused on a rich mixture of imitation, observation of the rewards and punishment experienced by others, expectations, and personal assessment of the value of potential rewards and punishers.

Against this backdrop of psychodynamic theory and behaviorism, Rogers and Maslow became the leading advocates of a new and openly positive view of human development, referred to most commonly as humanistic psychology. This new field emphasized self-actualization, though self-actualization itself does not appear to have been a new concept. It closely resembles the enlightenment described by Yoga and Buddhism (each of which is thousands of years old), though Yoga and Buddhism ultimately reject the existence of the self. Is there a relationship between Eastern philosophical perspectives and humanistic psychology? Rogers had traveled throughout Asia, particularly in China, and Maslow had studied with renowned psychodynamic theorists who were fascinated by Buddhism (such as Horney), so both were well acquainted with the basics of Eastern philosophical thought.

Closely related to the behavioral perspectives, cognitive theories of personality are also prominent in psychology. Today, the use of non-invasive brain imaging techniques (e.g., functional magnetic resonance imaging), which function in real time, have made the study of cognitive processes one of the most exciting areas of psychological research. Studying cognition is hardly new, however, since the earliest studies of consciousness can be traced to William James in the late 1800s. Still, what James was able to study over 100 years ago is completely different than what modern cognitive neuroscientists are able to study today. Nonetheless, if we can find something in common between the studies of over a century ago and the research of today, perhaps we will really begin to understand the complexity and diversity of personality.

Positive Psychology and Spirituality: New Directions in the Field of Personality

In 1998, Martin Seligman, then president of APA and author of *What You Can Change & What You Can't* (1994), urged psychologists to rediscover the forgotten mission of psychology: to build human strength and nurture genius. Seligman called this new area Positive Psychology (for thorough overviews see Compton, 2005 or Peterson, 2006). In 2000, *American Psychologist* published a special edition on happiness, excellence, and optimal human functioning (*American Psychologist, Vol. 55*, Number 1, 2000; with an introduction by Seligman & Csikszentmihalyi, 2000). The general goal of positive psychology is to find ways in which psychological research can help people to be happier, and to lead more fulfilling lives. Positive psychology can also serve as a focus for psychologists to become more appreciative of not only human nature, but also of the potential for the field of psychology itself to benefit all people (Sheldon & King, 2001). Table 1.3 offers a sampling of the wide range of interest in positive psychology that exists today.

Young children enjoy helping even younger children. Positive psychology encourages us all to study and promote such behavior. [Image by Mark Kelland]

Closely related to positive psychology is the concept of resilience. Many individuals face difficult or traumatic challenges in life, and yet some manage to maintain stability in their lives in spite of these unfortunate circumstances. How exactly these individuals maintain stability and a positive direction in their lives is not always clear, and there may be a variety of different ways that individuals respond to such extreme stress (Bonanno, 2004, 2005a; Masten, 2001; for commentary on the first article see also Bonanno, 2005b; Kelley, 2005; Linley & Joseph, 2005; Litz, 2005; Maddi, 2005; Roisman, 2005). Among the important factors, particularly for our perspective here, is the ability to maintain positive emotions and to pursue self-enhancement

(Bonanno, 2004, 2005; Masten, 2001). Throughout history, a variety of cultures have given rise to spiritual pursuits that help to guide the development of individuals in positive directions. We will cover some of these spiritual paths in the last section of this book, taking just a brief look here at the relationship between spirituality, positive psychology, and personality.

It appears that spirituality is an essential attribute of human nature. It has been recognized for some time that religious ritual is a cultural universal (Murdock, 1945; see also Ferraro, 2006a). More than simply a cultural universal, however, spirituality appears to be a natural consequence of child development. Deborah Kelemen (2004) brought together a number of different theories, and was able to demonstrate that young children, around the age of 5 years old, have both the ability and the inclination to explain the world around them in terms of an intentional act by a supernatural being. Thus, Kelemen suggests that young children are what she calls "intuitive theists." Surprisingly, this tendency appears to continue into adulthood, since even college students studying evolution exhibit a tendency to think of evolution as a purposeful agent itself, an agent that guides further evolution according to a thoughtful plan (Kelemen, 2004).

Table 1.3: Selection of Books and Articles Related to Positive Psychology Published Since the Year 2000

Books on Positive Psychology	Compton, 2005; Snyder & Lopez, 2005
Human Strengths and Virtues	Aspinwall & Staudinger, 2003; Fowers, 2005
Happiness and Well-Being	Cloninger, 2004; Hampson, 2008; Hsee et al., 2008; Huppert, 2009; Inglehart et al., 2008; Molden et al., 2009; Seligman, 2002; Siegel, 2007
Articles on Academic Excellence and Creativity	Lubinski & Benbow, 2000; Simonton, 2000; Winner, 2000
Cognition and Motivation	Baltes & Staudinger, 2000; Lyubomirsky, 2001; Peterson, 2000
Coping	Folkman & Moskowitz; 2000; Vaillant, 2000
Economics	Diener, 2000; Diener & Seligman, 2004; Myers, 2000; Smith et al., 2005
Emotions, Happiness, Well-Being	Dolan & White, 2007; Ekman et al., 2005; Fredrickson, 2001; Fredrickson & Joiner, 2002; Fredrickson & Losada, 2005; Kesebir & Diener, 2008; Kim & Moen, 2001; Napier & Jost, 2008; Oishi et al., 2007; Robinson et al., 2004; Weiss et al., 2008
Enjoying a Good Life	Bauer & McAdams, 2004a,b; Bauer et al., 2005a,b; Schneider, 2001
Evolution	Buss, 2000a; Massimini & Fave, 2000
Physical Health	Cohen & Pressman, 2006; Ray, 2004; Salovey et al., 2000; Taylor et al., 2000
Relationships	Myers, 2000
Self-Determination	Ryan & Deci, 2000; Schwartz, 2000
Therapeutic Intervention	Ahmed & Boisvert, 2006; Joseph & Linley, 2006; Seligman et al., 2005
Youth Development	Larson, 2000

Introduction

The relationship between psychology and religious/spiritual pursuits has a long and interesting history. One of William James' most famous books is *The Varieties of Religious Experience: A Study in Human Nature* (James, 1902/1987), and around the turn of the century in 1900 psychologists of the day actually used religion in the popular press to help engender respect for the new field of psychology (Pickren, 2000). Since the more recent turn of the century there have been a number of books and articles published connecting psychology, spirituality, religion, and psychotherapy (see Table 1.4). Thus, a topic that was viewed as important at the beginning of the field of psychology, but was then pushed aside as unscientific, is once again become an area of interest and importance. Although spirituality is certainly not synonymous with positive psychology, it does appear to be an important factor in positive psychology.

Numerous studies have shown that individuals who are actively spiritual have higher levels of well-being and fewer serious problems in their lives (see Compton, 2005; Myers, 2000; Seligman, 2002; Seligman & Csikszentmihalyi, 2000). The recently published *Handbook of Positive Psychology* has two chapters devoted specifically to spiritual pursuits and their benefits (Pargament & Mahoney, 2005; Shapiro et al., 2005). Peterson and Seligman (2004) have identified spirituality as one of the twenty-four specific character strengths that have consistently emerged across history and culture. Indeed, they believe that spirituality "is the most human of the character strengths as well as the most sublime…People with this strength have a theory about the ultimate meaning of life that shapes their conduct and provides comfort to them" (pg. 533; Peterson & Seligman, 2004). In the last section of this book we will examine a number of spiritual approaches to life, each of which suggests a path for positive development. Despite being associated with very different religions, which range from 1,400 years old to perhaps more than 5,000 years old, these spiritual paths have much in common. Perhaps this should not be surprising, as it may help to explain the inherent nature of children to be "intuitive theists" and the universality of religious ritual in human culture.

Table 1.4: Selection of Recent Books and Articles Relating Spirituality to Psychology

Books on psychology seen through the eyes of faith	Myers & Jeeves, 2003
Relationships between meditation, mindfulness, Buddhism and psychology	Brantley, 2003; Dockett et al., 2003; Helminiak, 2005; McQuaid & Carmona, 2004
Spiritual counseling from a variety of perspectives	Brach, 2003; Brazier, 1995; Mruk & Hartzell, 2003; Richards & Bergin, 2000, 2004, 2005; Sperry & Shafranske, 2005; Weiner et al., 2005; Williams et al., 2007
Multicultural clinical assessment	Dana, 2000; Suzuki et al., 2001
Articles on the religious roots of individualism vs. collectivism	Burston, 2001; Lynch, 2001; Lynch Jr., 2001; Margolis, 2001; Sampson, 2000
Childhood Development of Faith	Kelemen, 2004
Shamanism	Krippner, 2002
The relationships between spirituality, religion, and health	Ginges et al., 2009; Hill & Pargament, 2003; Kier & Davenport, 2004; McCormick, 2004; Miller & Thoresen, 2003; Miller & Thoresen, 2004; Powell et al., 2003; Rayburn, 2004; Richmond, 2004; Seeman et al., 2003; Seybold & Hill, 2001; Wallace & Shapiro, 2006

> **Discussion Question:** Do you believe that psychology should work to develop itself as a field that focuses on helping people to develop in positive ways? Can spirituality or religion be helpful, or might they present more problems?

Methods of Studying Personality

In all types of research, we need to consider two closely related concepts: **hypothesis** vs. **theory**. An hypothesis can loosely be defined as an educated guess about some relationship or circumstance that we have observed, and the purpose of the hypothesis is to explain what we have experienced and to provide a starting point for further research. When a set of observations seems to come together, especially as the result of testing our hypotheses, we might then propose a theory to bring those observations together. However, a theory is not necessarily our end point, since the theory itself may generate new hypotheses and more research. In this way, all scientific endeavors continue to develop, expand, clarify, change, whatever the case may be, over time. As a result, we have many different personality theories, since different theorists have viewed the human condition differently, and they have also used different techniques to study personality.

A variety of methods have been used to study personality. Much of the early research was based on clinical observations, which were not done according to strict experimental methods. Today, ethical restrictions on the types of research we can conduct with people limit our ability to re-evaluate many of those classic studies. So we are left with a field that is rich in theory, but somewhat poor in the validation of those theories. Of course some personality theorists have approached personality in a more scientific manner, or at least they have tried, but that has limited the questions they have been able to ask. Since a detailed analysis of experimental psychology and research design is beyond the scope of this textbook, we will only cover this topic briefly (though it may come up again within individual chapters).

Case Studies

Many of the best-known personality theorists relied on case studies to develop their theories. Indeed, it was after seeing a number of patients with seemingly impossible neurological complaints that Freud began to seek an explanation of psychological disorders. Basically, the case study approach relies on a detailed analysis of interesting and unique individuals. Because these individuals are unique, the primary criticism of the case study approach is that its results may not generalize to other people. Of greater concern, is the possibility that early theorists chose to report only those cases that seemed to support their theories, or perhaps they only recognized those elements of a patient's personality that fit their theory? Another problem, as mentioned above, is that two different theorists might view the same cases in very different ways. For example, since Carl Rogers worked initially with children, he found it difficult to accept Freud's suggestions that even children were motivated primarily by sexual and aggressive urges. Consequently, Rogers sought a more positive view of personality development, which led to the establishment of the humanistic perspective. Thus, the case study approach can lead to very different conclusions depending on one's own perspective while conducting research. In other words, it can easily be more subjective than objective, and psychologists who focus on our field as a scientific discipline always strive for more objective research.

Correlational Designs

When conducting correlational research psychologists examine the relationships that exist between variables, but they do not control those variables. The measure that is typically used is the **correlation coefficient**, which can range from –1.0 to 0.0 to +1.0. A value close to zero suggests that there is no relationship between the variables, whereas a value closer to –1.0 or +1.0 suggests a strong relationship, with the direction of the relationship determining whether the value is positive or negative. It is important to remember that the strength of the correlation is determined by how far the correlation coefficient is from zero, not whether it is positive or negative. For example, we would most likely find a positive correlation between the number of hours you study for a test and the number of correct answers you get (i.e., the more you study, the more questions you get right on the test). On the other hand, the exact same data will give us a negative correlation if we compare the number of hours you study to the number of questions you get wrong (i.e., the more you study, they fewer questions you get wrong). So the way in which you ask the question can determine whether you have a positive or negative correlation, but it should not affect the strength of the relationship.

Since the investigator does not control the variables in correlational research, it is not possible to determine whether or not one variable causes the relationship. In the example used above, it certainly seems that studying more would lead to getting a better grade on a test. But consider another example: can money buy happiness? There is some evidence that wealthy people are happier than the average person, and that people in wealthy countries are happier than those in poorer countries. But does the money affect happiness? Certainly a million dollars in cash wouldn't help much if you were stranded on a desert island, so what can it do for you at home? People with money can live in nicer, safer communities, they have access to better health care (so they may feel better physically), they may have more time to spend with their family and friends, and so in many ways their lives might be different. We can also look at the correlation the other way around; maybe happy people get more money. If you ran a company, and were going to hire or promote someone, wouldn't you want to find someone who is friendly and outgoing? Wouldn't you look for someone who other people will enjoy working with? So, maybe happy people do find it easier to be successful financially. Either way, we simply can't be sure about which variable influences the other, or even if they influence each other at all. In order to do that, we must pursue experimental research.

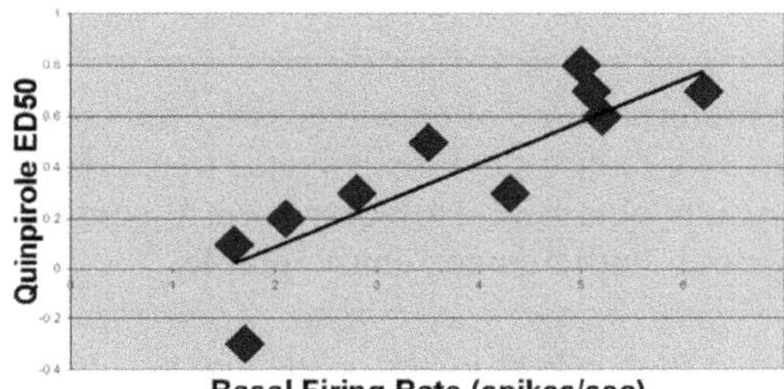

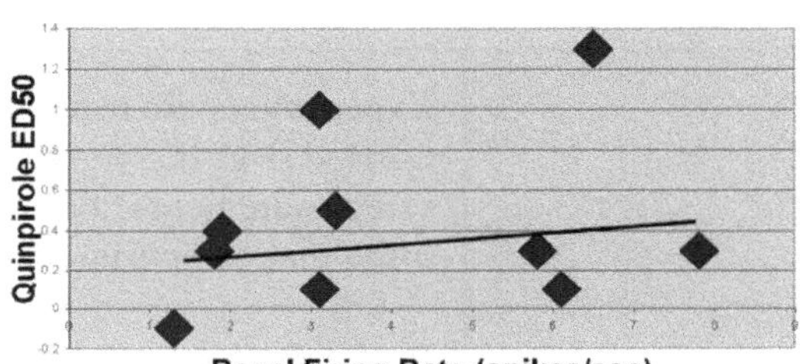

In these figures, adapted from research conducted by the author (Kelland et al., 1989), we see two correlations reported in an actual study. In the figure on the left, we can see a significant positive correlation between the firing rate of dopamine neurons in the rat brain and the dose of the drug quinpirole needed to inhibit those cells. In the figure on the right, we can see that the correlation is eliminated (the dose of quinpirole needed is not related to the firing rate of the cell) following administration of the drug MDMA (more commonly known as Ecstasy!). [Image by Mark Kelland]

Experimental and Quasi-Experimental Designs

The experimental design is usually preferred within psychology, as with any other science. The goal is to control every aspect of the experiment and then manipulate a single variable, thus allowing us to attribute the results to that single manipulation. As a result, experiments allow us to make cause-and-effect statements about the relationships between the variables.

A simple experiment begins with defining the **independent variable**, the factor that will be manipulated, and the **dependent variable**, the factor that will be measured. Ideally, we then select our subjects in a random fashion, and assign them randomly to a **control group** and an **experimental group**. The experimental group is then exposed to the independent variable, whereas the control group is not. If we have successfully controlled all other variables through random selection of subjects (i.e., all subjects in a specified population have an equal chance of being selected for the study) and random assignment to the control and experimental groups (so that hopefully each group has an equal representation of gender, races, age, intelligence, personal habits, etc.), we should see a difference in the dependent variable that was caused by the independent variable.

Unlike the natural sciences, however, we can seldom control human behavior in the precise ways that true experimental designs require. For example, if we want to study the effects of prenatal exposure to cocaine on personality development, we certainly cannot ask pregnant women to use cocaine. Unfortunately, there are pregnant women who abuse cocaine and other illegal drugs. Therefore, we can try to identify those women, and subsequently study the development of their children. Since a variety of other factors led these women to abuse illegal drugs, we lose the control that is desired in an experiment. Such studies are called quasi-experimental, because they are set up *as if* we did an experiment, and can be analyzed in similar ways. The quasi-experimental approach has many applications, and can provide valuable information not available otherwise, so long as the investigators keep in mind the limitations of the technique (for the classic discussion of this design see Campbell & Stanley, 1963).

Table 1.5: Research Designs in the Study of Personality

Case Studies	Focus is on a detailed examination of unique and interesting cases. May provide a great deal of information, but due to the individual nature of the case that information may not generalize to others.
Correlational Designs	Focus is on how variables change in relation to each other. However, since there is no control over that change, we cannot determine whether one variable affects the other, or vice versa, or even if the change is due to some unidentified outside factor.
Experiments	Experiments are usually the preferred type of research, since the control exerted over the variables involved allows the investigator to make cause-and-effect statements about the results obtained. However, ethical considerations often make experimental research with humans unacceptable.
Quasi-Experiments	When individuals choose to put themselves in situations that psychologists could not ethically create, a situation arises in which the consequences can be studied *as if* an experiment was done. These are not true experiments, however, since the investigator cannot be sure of all the variables that led the individuals to put themselves in such situations to begin with.
Cross-Cultural and Multicultural Research	In an effort to control the conditions of their research, psychologists try to work with clearly defined groups. Unfortunately, that means their results may not generalize to other groups of people. Cross-cultural and multicultural psychologists remind us that, in a truly global world, we must strive to address both the differences and the similarities that characterize human nature.

Cross-Cultural Approaches to the Study of Personality

Cross-cultural approaches to studying personality do not really represent a different type of research, but rather an approach to research that does not assume all people are influenced equally by the same factors. More importantly, cross-cultural psychologists recognize that seemingly common factors may, in reality, be quite different when viewed by people of very different cultures. The most obvious problem that arises when considering these issues is the potential difference between cross-cultural and multicultural research. Cross-cultural research is based on a comparison of cultures; two well-known categorizations are Eastern vs. Western perspectives and the somewhat related topic of individualistic vs. collectivistic cultures. However, a multicultural approach tells us that we must consider the true complexity of the human race. What is "Eastern," is it Asia, China, Japan, does it include India, and what about Muslim groups of people? Should Buddhism be viewed as an Eastern perspective or a religious perspective? This book will address a variety of spiritual paths toward positive psychological development, but none of the associated religions are indigenous to Africa, so will our discussions be complete? The list goes on and on, because there are so many different cultures in the world. And finally, is it practical to really try coming up with a theory of personality that can encompass all the different groups of people throughout the world? Only by pursuing an understanding of different cultures can psychology truly be considered a global science, and that pursuit has only just begun. Since we have a long way to go, the future is ripe for new students to pursue careers in psychology and the study of personality.

> **Discussion Question:** Do you consider psychology to be a science? Has psychology successfully applied the scientific method to the study of mind and behavior, particularly the study of personality and personality development?

Application of Personality Theory - Assessing Personality

As in the section above on research methods, an extensive discussion of personality assessment is beyond the scope of this textbook. However, this is such an important issue that we will look at it briefly here, and then will take a closer look in some of the chapters throughout the rest of the book. There are a number of excellent handbooks available on psychological assessment (e.g., Goldstein & Hersen, 1990; Groth-Marnat, 2003), including two that focus on cross-cultural and multicultural assessment (Dana, 2000; Suzuki et al., 2001).

Personality assessment most commonly occurs in a clinical setting, when an individual is seeking help for some problem, whether it is an adjustment disorder or a potential mental illness. Assessing personality goes beyond this singular role, however. Certainly a clinical psychologist would be using personality assessment in order to understand a patient's symptoms, provide a diagnosis (if appropriate), and recommend a preferred course of therapy. Similarly, school psychologists use assessment to identify any possible learning disorders and/or adjustment issues as they pertain to the educational environment. But other psychologists use personality assessment for a variety of reasons as well. Industrial/organizational psychologists use personality assessment to identify preferred candidates for particular jobs, career counselors use these assessments in order to provide valid recommendations regarding the choice of a career path, and research psychologists use assessment in their ongoing efforts to correlate certain personality types to observable behavior or other measures. Thus, the assessment tools used to describe and/or understand personality have a wide range of potential applications.

Reliability, Validity, and Standardization

A particular personality assessment is of little value if it has no reliability or validity and if it is not presented in a standardized format. **Reliability** refers to the likelihood that a test will give essentially the same result on different occasions, or that two versions of the same test will give similar results. **Validity** refers to whether a test actually measures what it purports to measure. **Standardization** refers to the manner in which a test is given, which must be the same for every person receiving the test if there is to be any value in comparing the results among different people.

Determining the reliability and validity of a test can be a long and complicated process, involving a variety of statistical methods to confirm the results. During this process the psychologist(s) developing the test will also typically establish norms. **Norms** are consistent ways in which particular groups score on a test. For example, on measures of aggressiveness the "normal" level for men may be quite different than the "normal" level for women. Standardization is quite a bit simpler to establish, since the test can include precise instructions dictating the manner in which it is to be given.

Assessing Personality with Objective Tests

The most famous self-report inventory is the **Minnesota Multiphasic Personality Inventory** (or **MMPI**). The MMPI is also probably the most widely used psychological test in the world, and it has stood the test of time (it is currently in its second version, a 1989 revision of the 1943 original). The current version consists of 567 true-false questions, which address not only normal personality traits, but psychopathology and the accuracy of the test-taker as well. The test has several built in "lie" scales, in case a person were trying to fake a mental illness (e.g., if they were trying to fake an insanity defense to avoid responsibility for a crime) or minimize any symptoms they may actually be experiencing. The questions themselves range from rather simple (e.g., I enjoy drama.) to rather strange (e.g., I am a prophet of God.), but when put all together they provide a highly valid assessment that can easily be scored by computer (hence the popularity of the test, for both reasons).

NOTE: Those are not actual questions from the MMPI, but they are based on real questions. The MMPI is an empirically based instrument. That is, interpretations are based on the pattern of responding obtained by various psychiatric samples. Since the standard MMPI was developed for adults and is rather lengthy, an abbreviated version was developed for use with adolescents: the MMPI-A.

A number of alternatives to the MMPI have been developed. The California Psychological Inventory has been available almost as long as the MMPI and, more recently, the Personality Assessment Inventory has become popular. Another important test is Millon's Clinical Multiaxial Inventory (the MCMI), which was developed in accordance with Millon's own theories on personality development and personality disorders (see Appendix A). The MCMI was designed with certain advantages in mind, including being relatively short compared to the MMPI and being connected with a specific clinical theory. However, since the test was designed specifically to distinguish amongst psychiatric populations, it is not as useful when assessing "normal" individuals (Keller et al., 1990; Groth-Marnat, 2003).

Behavioral assessment and thought sampling are techniques designed to gain an appreciation of what an individual actually does and/or thinks on a day-to-day or moment-to-moment basis. In each case, observers are trained to make precise observations of an individual at precise times. This provides a statistical sample of the individual's actual behavior and/or thoughts over time. Naturally the only person who can record an individual's thoughts is that person himself or herself, but as long as they are carefully informed of the procedure and are fully cooperating, the technique works fine. When applied correctly, the great value of these techniques is that they are truly objective, in other words, they record *actual* behaviors and *actual* thoughts.

Assessing Personality with Projective Tests

The two most famous projective tests are the **Rorschach Inkblot Technique** and the **Thematic Apperception Test** (or **TAT**). Both tests involve the presentation of ambiguous stimuli in an attempt to draw out responses from a patient, responses reflecting impulses and/or thoughts that the patient may not even be aware of (i.e., the patient projects their own thoughts and feelings onto the ambiguous stimuli, even if those thoughts and feelings are subconscious).

The Rorschach Inkblots are just that, inkblots on a piece of paper that can look like most anything. An individual being tested is first asked to say what each inkblot looks like, and then they are asked to explain how they saw what they identified. The answer to a single inkblot is not particularly informative, since any one inkblot may remind the person of some particular thing. However, as the patient goes through all 10 inkblots, trends should become apparent to the psychologist that reflect the dominant issues affecting the personality of the patient (again, even if those issues are subconscious and not available to the conscious awareness of the patient). Initially, the Rorschach was reviewed unfavorably and then ignored. Rorschach became depressed, and died only 9 months after the test was published. Eventually, however, the test became more and more popular, and today is certainly one of the most widely recognized psychological tests. However, studies comparing the Rorschach and the MMPI have shown the latter to be far more valid. In an effort to improve both the reliability and validity of the Rorschach technique, there is now a standardized scoring system.

The TAT is similar to the Rorschach, except that it involves actual pictures of people (although they are still very ambiguous drawings) and the patient is asked to tell a story about the people in the picture. There is no objective scoring system for the TAT, so reliability and validity remain arguable, and the test is more famous than popular as an assessment tool. However, it has been shown to have high validity for certain specific research studies, such as studies on the need for achievement, and continues to serve a function in clinical formulations.

Clinical Interviews

As valuable and informative as the well-established psychological tests are, there is certain vital information that simply cannot be addressed with most tests, such as: a person's appearance, their attitude, facial expressions, ability to communicate with another person, etc. In addition, tests often lead to further questions, or the need for clarification or explanation. In order to address such issues, both in general and in greater detail, clinical interviews are an essential part of the overall personality assessment. Although the results of an interview are somewhat subjective, when viewed in the context of the psychologist's clinical experience, along with results of an assessment tool, they provide psychologists with a much more complete understanding of the person whom they are evaluating.

> **Discussion Question:** Have you or anyone you know ever had psychological testing (don't forget standardized tests of knowledge and intelligence in school!)? If you are at all familiar with psychological testing, for any reason, what effect did it have on you (or someone you know)?

Critical Thinking in Psychology

Critical thinking is always important in psychology, but given the complexity of individual personalities, the many different theories, and the variety of approaches for studying and assessing personality, it is particularly important for our consideration here. Although we often think of the word *critical* as something negative, when we talk about critical thinking in psychology we are actually talking about being open-minded to many possible answers, but arriving at a most likely answer in a reasoned and logical fashion. Critical thinking is a skill, but unfortunately one that all too often isn't taught (Halpern, 1996, 2007; Sternberg, 2007).

A typical approach to teaching critical thinking is to use examples of false claims and systematically deconstruct the manner in which they are made to appear true, while at the same time discussing the psychological processes involved in decision making (see, e.g., Halpern, 1996; Ruscio, 2006). John Ruscio has done a nice job of organizing his discussion around four areas pertaining to the tactics of pseudoscientists who would intentionally mislead us: 1) deception, the methods they use to deceive us; 2) self-deception, the types of evidence that lead us toward unwittingly deceiving ourselves; 3) psychological tricks, a variety of tricks that create and sustain unwarranted beliefs; and 4) the decision-making process and the ethical concerns of pseudoscientific practices. Ruscio (2006) has also provided a handy list of the characteristics of pseudoscience:

1. Outward Appearance of Science
2. Absence of Skeptical Peer Review
3. Reliance on Personal Experience
4. Evasion of Risky Tests
5. Retreats to the Supernatural
6. The Mantra of Holism
7. Tolerance of Inconsistencies
8. Appeals to Authority
9. Promising the Impossible
10. Stagnation

While it may seem tempting for you to take for granted that you do not need to apply critical thinking to the theories presented in this book, that could present something of a problem for you. Many of these theories disagree with one another. Although the major theories have all been proposed by famous and respected theorists, some critics claim they were not developed scientifically, and the spiritual paths that will be discussed in the last section of the book have many skeptics. As you consider each theory, there are some critical thinking skills you can keep in mind. What is your goal as you evaluate a theory? What do you know and how are you drawing conclusions? If your class is having a debate or a discussion what is being said, how is it being said, and how are the arguments being analyzed? Are certain conclusions probable; are you, or others, overconfident in your conclusions? Have you considered alternatives? Practicing these, and other, skills can help to develop your critical thinking abilities (Halpern, 2007). Finally, consider this "simple" definition of critical thinking offered by Diane Halpern:

> Critical thinking is the use of those cognitive skills or strategies that increase the probability of a desirable outcome. It is used to describe thinking that is purposeful, reasoned, and goal directed - the kind of thinking involved in solving problems, formulating inferences, calculating likelihoods, and making decisions, when the thinker is using skills that are thoughtful and effective for the particular context and type of thinking task. (pg. 6; Halpern, 2007)

> **Discussion Question:** When you hear someone make a claim, whether it is something scientific or a commercial advertisement, do you tend to believe it, or do you apply critical thinking to evaluate whether the claim is likely to be true?

Overview of the Approach of This Textbook

This textbook has been written with three main goals in mind, beyond simply presenting the classic theories found in most personality textbooks. First, I want to introduce you to multicultural perspectives on personality development, occasionally drawing on work that was done by the classic theorists, but is often overlooked. Second, I have attempted to tie the non-traditional perspectives into the established theories, as well as compare and contrast the development of the traditional theories themselves, in a way that should help you make sense of the broad field of personality theory. Finally, exercises and discussions questions have been included in an effort to help you connect these theories and perspectives to your own life.

In addition to basic information on a particular theory or perspective, each chapter will typically contain three learning aids to help accomplish these goals. As each chapter begins, there will be a biography of the theorist(s) or a brief history of the perspective, and then there will be a learning aid called "Placing *What'sTheirName* in Context." This feature will be partly historical and partly theoretical, but the goal will be both to connect the theory to those we have already discussed and to those still to come. Somewhere within the body of the chapter there will be another learning aid that may vary between two topics: either "Connections Across Cultures" or "*Theory X* Related to Personality Disorders." The first of these mid-chapter features will address some particular aspect of the theory in a multicultural context. It is all too easy for each of us to see things only from our own cultural perspective. This is natural, and there is nothing inherently wrong with it. Many people, however, are actively working toward the globalization of our society, and in order for globalization to be successful we need to be able to appreciate other people and other cultures. What better way to begin than by studying their personality, who they are and how they became who they are. While there may very well be common aspects of personality across cultures, there are certainly differences as well. The second of these mid-chapter features will address the theory within a clinical context, particularly with regard to abnormal personality development. Finally, at the end of the body of each chapter there will be a learning aid called "Personality Theory in Real Life." Rather obviously, these will be examples to help you apply certain aspects of the personality theory being discussed to everyday examples, hopefully in ways that you can relate to your own life. In chapters covering more than one topic these features may be repeated to provide better coverage of the material in the chapter.

Personality Theory in Real Life: Making the Connection Between Your Life and Personality Theory

In this chapter we do not have a particular theory or perspective within which to consider your own life. So, let's try considering your life in any way you want. I do want you to consider one basic question, though. Who are you? You might also ask yourself what makes you the person you think you are. Try writing down some of your thoughts. Writing the ideas down helps to force you to really pay attention to your thoughts, rather than just casually thinking about the questions without going into any detail. When you are done, take a look at what you have written. Ask yourself again, "Is that really me?" You may want to write down your new thoughts after evaluating what you have written.

Then try something that may be very interesting, but possibly a little unnerving. Ask a friend or relative, someone you think really knows you well, and have them write down some ideas on who you are. Don't bother them, or distract them, while they are doing this. Let them have the time they need to do it. Then look at what they have written, and once again ask, "Is that really me?" Finally, compare what you wrote and what they wrote. Is there a difference, and if so, is it a big difference?

Whether the different descriptions of who you are or, in other words, the descriptions of your personality are the same or different, how do you feel about that? Some may find comfort in learning that others see them as they see themselves. Some may be confused if others see them quite differently than they see themselves. There are no right or wrong answers here, it is just an exercise to help you begin thinking about how psychologists study personality. As we move through the various theories and perspectives presented in this textbook, it will provide a starting point from which you can hopefully learn something interesting about yourself and about the people you interact with every day.

Review of Key Points

- There is no simply definition of personality. The nomothetic approach focuses on personality as a construct, while the idiographic approach emphasizes the uniqueness of individuals.
- A wide variety of theoretical perspectives influence how psychologists view personality, including psychodynamic factors, learning/cognitive factors, biological factors, inherent drives, and sociocultural influences.
- The various personality theories also address questions related to nature vs. nurture, whether individuals are unique or whether there are types of personality common to all people, the relative importance of the past, present, and future, and the significance of free will.
- An important trend in psychology today is the emphasis on positive psychology, and the potential for the field of psychology to contribute in positive ways to society.
- A variety of research designs have been used by personality theorists. Historically, many famous theorists relied on case studies. When possible, however, many psychologists prefer the experimental design, since only true experiments allow psychologists to make case-and-effect statements. More recently, some psychologists have begun to focus on cross-cultural and multicultural approaches to studying personality.
- A wide variety of personality tests have been developed, both objective and projective tests. Since it often proves difficult to establish the reliability and validity of some personality tests, a clinical interview is an essential step in forming an opinion regarding someone's personality (especially if there is a question of mental illness).
- Critical thinking is purposeful, reasoned, goal-directed thinking aimed at evaluating claims that are made as being true.

Review of Key Terms

construct	Minnesota Multiphasic	salient
control group	Personality Inventory	self-actualization
correlation coefficient	(MMPI)	standardization
critical thinking	nomothetic	temperament
dependent variable	norms	Thematic Apperception Test
experimental group	persona	(TAT)
hypothesis	reliability	theory
idiographic	Rorschach Inkblot	validity
independent variable	Technique	

Annotated Bibliography

Compton, W. C. (2005). *An introduction to positive psychology*. Belmont, CA: Thomson Wadsworth.
Peterson, C. (2006). *A primer in positive psychology*. New York, NY: Oxford University Press.

Compton's review of the field of positive psychology has been prepared as a college textbook for courses on this topic. As such, it is both readable and informative, and it includes its own lists of recommended readings in each chapter. Peterson's excellent primer also provides a thorough overview of positive psychology and lists many valuable resources.

James, W. (1899/1992). Talks to teachers on psychology and to students on some of life's ideals. In G. E. Myers (Ed.), *William James: Writings 1878-1899* (pp. 705-887). New York, NY: The Library of America.

William James is considered by many to be America's preeminent psychologist. I am constantly amazed at how things he wrote over 100 years ago still seem relevant today. *Talks to Teachers on Psychology...* makes for wonderful reading for both psychology students and professors, and provides a marvelous link to the history of our field. This collection of William James' writings, along with a companion volume, is readily available from sources such as Amazon.com.

Myers, D. G. & Jeeves, M. A. (2003). *Psychology: Through the eyes of faith*. New York, NY: HarperCollins.

David Myers (a well known introductory psychology textbook author) and Malcolm Jeeves present in this book an interesting perspective on the relationships between the so-called "science" of psychology and people of Christian faith. These open-minded authors have done a wonderful job of describing the compatibility of psychology, science, and faith. A full range of topics in psychology is covered, but each section is fairly brief. Thus, the book is a relatively quick and easy read. The book is not superficial, however, since the authors occasionally include logical twists that challenge assumptions and give the reader much to think about.

Seligman, M. E. P. (2002). *Authentic happiness: Using the new positive psychology to realize your potential for lasting fulfillment*. New York, NY: The Free Press.

Martin Seligman transformed a prestigious career in basic research involving animals (he proposed the concept of learned helplessness as a model for depression) into a career proposing that psychology work toward supporting the positive development of individuals. This book brings together Seligman's earlier work in positive psychology and presents pathways for individuals to move beyond self-improvement toward improved relationships in all aspects of their lives, including love, **raising** children, and their career.

Peterson, C. & Seligman, M. E. P. (2004). *Character strengths and virtues: A handbook and classification*. New York, NY: Oxford University Press.

This tour-de-force is impressive in both size and content. Working on behalf of the Values in Action Institute, with a veritable Who's Who list of advisors and numerous contributors, Peterson and Seligman have presented an extraordinary analysis of what it means to be "of good character."

Chapter 2 - Personality, Culture, and Society

In the first chapter we briefly examined the concern of many psychologists that the field of psychology has been slow to embrace the value of cross-cultural research (see Lee et al., 1999; Sue, 1999; Triandis & Suh, 2002). This concern is by no means new. In 1936, Ralph Linton wrote that "different societies seem to show differences in the relative frequency of occurrence of the various psychological types" (pg. 484), and in 1973, Robert LeVine suggested that "this is a moment at which even those who are skeptical about the value of culture and personality study might consider stretching their curiosity in this direction" (pg. ix). Throughout this textbook we will examine a number of theorists who emphasized studying cultural differences as a significant part of their careers and, often, their personality theories as well.

However, it remains true that cross-cultural studies in psychology have only recently moved closer to the mainstream of psychological research and clinical practice. As of 2002, the American Psychological Association has "Guidelines on Multicultural Education, Training, Research, Practice, and Organizational Change for Psychologists" (www.apa.org/pi/multiculturalguidelines/homepage.html). To cite just a few examples of the range of current interest in cross-cultural psychology, we now have a *Dictionary of Multicultural Psychology* (Hall, 2005) and books on the relationships between culture, mental illness, and counseling (Axelson, 1999; Castillo, 1997), as well as on the relationships between race, class, and the social and personal development of women (Jordan, 1997b; Pack-Brown, Whittington-Clark, & Parker, 1998). There are also major new texts on African American psychology (Belgrave & Allison, 2006) and racism, prejudice, and discrimination in America (Miller & Garran, 2008; Whitley & Kite, 2006).

The fact that studying cross-cultural factors in personality has always been present in the careers and theories of certain individuals, while not becoming a mainstream focus of attention, is more than just an historical curiosity. By emphasizing biological factors (i.e., genetics), Freud's theory did not allow for cultural differences. Behavioral theorists emphasized environmental factors, a seemingly cultural approach, but they did not allow themselves to address factors beyond immediate scientific control. Thus, they defined with great precision the role of reinforcement, punishment, discriminative stimuli, etc., while not allowing for the richness of cognition and cultural experiences. Likewise, cognitive theorists clung to the scientific approach of the behaviorists, rather than embracing the potential of sociocultural perspectives. In other words, because strict Freudian theorists, as well as behavioral and cognitive theorists, believed that their theories applied to all people equally, they typically chose not to address differences between people. Thus, those who wished to bring sociocultural perspectives on the development of personality into the field of personality theory faced a degree of direct opposition. And yet, their perseverance is now being fulfilled.

In this chapter, we will briefly examine some of the issues facing personality psychologists who wish to examine personality development in a sociocultural context. The United States, Canada, and Western Europe represent only about one tenth of the world's population. Ralph Linton, a renowned anthropologist with an interest in cultural influences on personality (see Linton, 1945), also edited a book entitled *Most of the World: The Peoples of Africa, Latin America, and the East Today* (Linton, 1949). Thus, it is essential that we consider the influence of different cultures around the world if we are going to claim that we have really examined human personality in all its variations.

Cultural Studies in the Field of Psychology

Since the 1990s, a number of general books on psychology and culture have been available (e.g., Brislin, 2000; Lonner & Malpass, 1994; Matsumoto, 1994, 1997; Matsumoto & Juang, 2004; Okun, Fried, & Okun, 1999; Price & Crapo, 2002; Segall et al., 1990). Although all of these books address topics such as the "self" and person-perception, and other various aspects of personality, only a few of them devote an actual chapter or section to the topic of personality itself (Matsumoto & Juang, 2004; Price & Crapo, 2002; Segall et al., 1990), and in each case the topics are fairly specific. There is, however, some older literature on the relationships between culture, society, and personality. We will examine that research in the second part of this section. First, let us examine some of the general principles of incorporating cross-cultural perspectives into the study of personality.

The Challenges of Cultural Research

The first problem faced by those who are interested in the study of culture and personality is the question: what exactly is to be studied? At the most basic level, there are two types of research. **Cross-cultural research** typically refers to either parallel studies being conducted in different cultures, or similar concepts being studied in different cultures. In contrast, **intercultural research** is the study of individuals of different cultures interacting with one another (Brislin, 2000; Matsumoto & Juang, 2004; Segall et al., 1990). As you will see in later chapters, some personality theorists consider interpersonal relationships to be the only true domain for studying individual personality. While most of the research done in psychology has been cross-cultural, as the world becomes more and more of a global community the opportunity for, and importance of, intercultural research is rapidly expanding.

Another fundamental problem with the study of culture is our attention to it, or rather, the lack of attention we pay to something that is so deeply ingrained in our daily lives. Richard Brislin suggests the following exercise: write down three answers for someone from a different culture who asks "What should I know about your culture so that we can understand each other better?" (pg. 10; Brislin, 2000). Because we simply take our cultural influences for granted, it proves quite difficult for us to think that they need to be identified or explained. For example, freedom of speech is a cherished right in America. Consequently, we often speak our minds. If I am upset about some new college policy, I might say very negative things about the administration of our college, even about particular administrators. It does not mean I intend to be disrespectful, or that I dislike those individuals, or that I won't say positive things about them when I agree with the next new policy. It is simply an expression of one of the great freedoms in our society: the right to speak out. However, someone from a different culture, particularly a collectivist culture, might be shocked at my apparent disrespect toward my "superiors."

The next important issue is the difference between **emic** and **etic** tasks or behaviors. Simply put, emic tasks are those that are familiar to the members of a given culture, whereas etic tasks are common to all cultures. In an elegantly simple, yet revealing study, Irwin, Schafer, & Feiden (1974) demonstrated these phenomena in two cultures: American undergraduates and Mano rice farmers (from Liberia). The American college students were consistently better at performing the Wisconsin Card Sort, a well-known psychological test measuring cognitive reasoning skills, which relies on geometric shapes and color. The Mano farmers, however, were consistently better at sorting different categories of rice. Thus, the ability to sort items into categories appears to be an etic task (most likely common to all humans, regardless of culture), whereas the more specific abilities to sort by geometry and color (common to American college students) or type of rice grain (common to Mano farmers in Liberia) is an emic task that requires familiarity. Thus, if we made a judgment about the Mano farmers' cognitive abilities based on the Wisconsin Card Sort, we would clearly be making a mistake in comparing them to Americans, due to the unfamiliarity of the particular task.

Another important aspect of cross-cultural research, which may involve applying our understanding of etics and emics, is the issue of **equivalence**. Is a concept being studied actually equivalent in different cultures? In other words, does a concept mean the same thing in different cultures, is the comparison valid? For example, an etic related to intelligence is the ability to solve problems. So how might we compare different cultural groups? Would the speed with which they solve a problem make sense as a measure of intelligence? Such an answer would be emic, and therefore valid, in America (where we typically value independence and competition). However, among the Baganda of Uganda, slow and careful thought is the emic. Among the Chi-Chewa of Zambia, the emic is responsibility to the community, i.e., solving the problem in order to best get along with other people. Thus, the speed at which people solve problems is conceptually equivalent, since it is the way in which people in each culture identify those individuals who are considered intelligent (Brislin, 2000). However, we cannot compare the actual speed of reporting a solution to others, as this is viewed quite differently in each culture.

One particular type of equivalence that raises a very interesting problem is that of **translation equivalence**. Psychologists often want to use tests developed in their own language with people of a different culture who speak a different language. Translating a test from one language to another can be a difficult task. The best way to assess translation equivalence is through **back translation**. In this procedure, one person translates the test, or survey, into the foreign language, and then a different person translates the foreign language test back into the original language. The original test can then be compared to the back translated test to see how closely they are worded. Ideally they would be identical, but this is seldom the case. To give you a simple example, when I was in graduate school, we had a student from Taiwan join our research group. One day I asked her to translate my last name, Kelland, into a Chinese character. When she had done that, I asked her how she would translate that particular Chinese character into English for someone who was not Chinese. She translated the character as Kwang. Despite the first letter, I hardly consider Kwang to be a reasonable translation of Kelland, but she didn't seem to think of this as much of a problem (perhaps revealing another cultural difference!). When the process of back translation is used successfully, which may involve working back and forth with the translations, it has the effect of **decentering** the test from the original language. Specifically, that means that the test should be free of any culturally emic references or aspects that interfere with the translation equivalence of the different versions of the test (Brislin, 2000; Matsumoto & Juang, 2004).

While the list of issues pertaining to cross-cultural research goes on, let's consider just two more specific issues: **cultural flexibility** and **cultural response sets**. Cultural flexibility refers to how individuals are willing to change, or adapt, in situations in which they know there are cultural differences. For example, American businesspeople can stand about 15 minutes of small talk before getting down to business. Their Japanese counterparts, in contrast, consider it important to get to know their business partners, and they are comfortable with hours of conversation about a variety of topics. This would, of course, be an important consideration for anyone studying the relationship between individual personality and success in business situations in this intercultural setting. Cultural response sets refer to how a given culture typically responds. If a given culture is more reserved, and they are asked to rate the importance of some value in comparison to how a more open culture rates that value, a difference in the rating may reflect the cultural difference in responding, rather than the degree to which people in each culture value the variable being measured (Brislin, 2000; Matsumoto & Juang, 2004).

Finally, in light of these challenges, it may be particularly important to conduct **cross-cultural validation studies**. Rather than testing hypotheses about specific cultural differences, cross-cultural validation studies are used to examine whether a psychological construct that was identified in one culture is meaningful and equivalent in another culture (Brislin, 2000; Matsumoto & Juang, 2004). For example, as we will see in Chapter 7, Erik Erikson did not feel confident in proposing his eight stages of development (the psychosocial crises) until he had confirmed his observations in two separate Native American tribes. He was able to gain the trust of these groups, and thus able to closely observe their child-rearing practices, thanks to the anthropologists who introduced him to the tribes they had been studying for a long time.

Anthropologists have done much more for psychology than merely introducing some psychologists to cultural issues and unique cultural groups. Some of them have had their own interests in personality. Many anthropologists, as well as some psychologists, have relied on **ethnographies** to report detailed information on the customs, rituals, traditions, beliefs, and the general way of daily life of a given group. They typically immerse themselves in the culture, living for an extended period of time with the group being studied (this helps get past the anxiety of being observed or any lack of cultural flexibility). Comparing the ethnographies of different groups can help guide cross-cultural psychologists in determining the likelihood that their cross-cultural studies are valid (Matsumoto & Juang, 2004; Segall et al., 1990).

Discussion Question: Translating psychological tests into different languages is often a problem for cross-cultural psychologists. Americans have a reputation for only knowing English, whereas people in other countries often speak more than one language. Do you know a foreign language well enough to actually communicate with someone in another country? How important do you think it is to learn another language as part of understanding their culture?

Placing Cross-Cultural Studies in Context: Blending Psychology with Anthropology

As the field of psychology entered the twenty-first century, there was a groundswell of interest in cultural factors as they pertain to all areas of psychology. In the field of personality, as well as in other areas, there have always been individuals with an interest in culture and society, but they tended to remain as individuals. Although they were often admired for their unique interests and ideas, the major emphasis in psychology was on the scientific method and data that had been obtained in carefully controlled situations, and then analyzed with similar, exacting precision.

Culture, as difficult as it is to define, was left largely to anthropologists and sociologists.

Anthropologists, in particular, were not as shy about addressing the domain of psychology, and a number of anthropologists crossed over into the study of psychology to such an extent that they are often mentioned even in the introductory psychology textbooks. But given that their primary interest was in anthropology, they did not form detailed personality development theories of the type presented in this (or other) personality textbooks. In this chapter, however, we will take a look at some of the ideas presented by the renowned anthropologist Ralph Linton, and his occasional colleague Abram Kardiner, a psychoanalyst with an associate appointment in the same anthropology department as Linton. In addition to their books, students of personality with a strong interest in cultural influences on personality will also find the works of Ruth Benedict and Margaret Mead of great interest.

The Influence of Culture and Society on Personality

Many psychology textbooks mention a few famous anthropologists, such as Ruth Benedict and Margaret Mead, whose research included work on child development and personality. However, less well-known in the field of psychology is the renowned anthropologist Ralph Linton, who paid particular attention to personality development in relation to culture and society. Linton also collaborated with Abram Kardiner, a founding member of the New York Psychoanalytic Institute (and who was analyzed by Sigmund Freud himself in 1921-1922). Linton and Kardiner freely acknowledged the connections between anthropology and psychology, noting the influence of Benedict and Mead, Franz Boas (recognized as the father of American anthropology and mentor to both Benedict and Mead), and the psychoanalysts Anna Freud, Erich Fromm, Karen Horney, and Wilhelm Reich (Kardiner, 1939; Kardiner, Linton, DuBois, & West, 1945; Kardiner & Preble, 1961).

Linton described personality as existing on three levels. First, personality can be described based on either its content or its organization. The organization, furthermore, can be examined in terms of its superficial organization or its central organization. The central organization of personality gives the whole personality its distinctive character, and includes the most invariant aspects of personality, such as the degree of introversion/extraversion, or other aspects of temperament (Linton, 1936, 1945). Although these temperamental attributes are present at birth, they do not comprise personality *per se*. The superficial organization of personality, however, is based on the goals and interests of the individual, and incorporates the individual's experiences in life within the context of the central organization. In this regard, the superficial organization should not be confused with something transient or insignificant. It is "superficial" only in the sense that it is on the surface of the personality, and the goals and interests of the person are based on the content of personality that represents their life experiences as they are organized within the personality. The goals and interests themselves, which incorporate the content of personality, are determined almost entirely by the culture in which the individual is raised. According to Linton (1936), the process of integrating the individual's experience within the context of one's temperament (or "constitutional qualities") forms a "mutually adjusted, functional whole."

A critical question, of course, is whether cultural experiences can affect the central organization. Linton (1936, 1945, 1955) believed that no matter how an individual receives the cultural characteristics of their society, they are likely to internalize them, a process known as **enculturation**. One of the main reasons that enculturation is so influential in every aspect of the person's being, is that it pervades every aspect of the society in which the person lives. Thus, even someone who is considered a rebel, most likely exists within a range of rebellion that is possible within that particular culture. This is directly related to the apparent reality that cultures do give rise to certain types of personality. Making the matter even more complicated, or simpler depending on one's perspective, is the role of status within a culture. Thus, although a given culture or society, or one's own temperament, may influence personality in one direction, a particular social class might influence personality in a different direction. An individual born into a given class, whose personal constitution does not fit that class, may develop what Linton called a **status personality**, i.e., a persona that fits with societies expectations for the individual in certain settings. For example, someone born into an upper middle class family involved in business, who is personally rather introverted and withdrawn, may present a confident and outgoing personality when working, and only upon returning home do they revert to their natural inclination to be shy and quiet.

One of the most interesting points made by Linton is that individuals with complimentary personalities are also mutually adjusted. The most obvious example is that of the gender roles of men and women. Men are expected, in many cultures and societies, to be the dominant member of the family, as well as the "bread-winner." Conversely, women are expected to be submissive, and to remain home and care for the household and the children. In this way, the men and women together complete the necessary tasks for family life without entering into conflict (at least in theory!). In some cultures, these gender roles are quite relaxed with regard to the sex of the individual. Amongst the Comanche (a Native American tribe), men whose personalities were not at all suited to being warriors assumed a special role, that of ***berdache*** (Linton, 1936). The *berdache* wore women's clothes, and typically fulfilled a woman's role, but they were treated with somewhat more respect than women (in keeping with the patriarchal nature of the society). Some were homosexuals (though not all), and even married. This was generally accepted, and any disapproval these relationships received was directed toward the warrior husband, not the *berdache*!

Abram Kardiner, a psychoanalyst who collaborated with Linton, shared the same general perspective on the relationship between personality and culture, and attempted to put the relationship into psychological terms. He distinguished between the **basic personality**, or **ego structure**, which he considered to be a cultural phenomenon, and the individual's **character**, which is their unique adaptation to the environment within their cultural setting. Thus, each individual develops a unique character, but only within the constraints of the culturally-determined range of potential ego structure (Kardiner, 1939). The process of personality development, within a cultural setting, results in what Kardiner called a **security system**. The security system of the individual is the series of adaptations that serve to ensure the individual's acceptance, approval, support, esteem, and status within the group. Thus, for each person within a given cultural group, their basic personality is formed through an ongoing interaction with the very culture in which that person needs to be (and, hopefully, will be) accepted as a member. Both of Kardiner's major books, *The Individual and His Society* (Kardiner, 1939) and *The Psychological Frontiers of Society* (Kardiner, et al., 1945), offer extraordinary examples of detailed anthropological studies of a wide variety of cultures followed by psychoanalytic evaluations of the functions served by various aspects of the cultural practices of those people.

Robert LeVine, like Kardiner, was an anthropologist and psychoanalyst with a strong interest in personality (LeVine, 1973, 1974). He begins by asking the question of whether there are differences in personality between different cultural groups. If there are not, then any analysis of the nature or causes of those alleged differences is meaningless. If there are differences, can we then point to specific evidence that the environment can elicit changes in those differences? The answer is yes to both, and as one example LeVine points to the dramatic **acculturation** of rural immigrants from underdeveloped areas of Europe and Asia who emigrated to industrialized countries, such as the United States, and within two or three generations had radically altered not only their basic ways of life, but also their social class (moving from traditional peasantry to the middle-class; LeVine, 1973). LeVine also continued Kardiner's approach of using a psychoanalytic perspective to evaluate and compare the nature of different cultures, and he proposed the term **psychoanalytic ethnography**. In an effort to justify the use of psychoanalytic ethnography, LeVine argues that there are enough common elements in the nature of all people and cultures to provide for valid comparisons of the differences between those same people and cultures (LeVine, 1973).

One of the most striking discussions of the relationship between culture and the potential for personality development was offered by Pitirim Sorokin, the founder of Harvard University's sociology department and a colleague of the trait theorist Gordon Allport (see Chapter 13). Sorokin points out that culture can have a dramatic influence on the biological substrates of personality. For example, through the use of contraception, abortion, etc., many potential individuals are never born. Conversely, if such measures are prohibited, many unwanted children are born. In addition, cultural rules and norms against sexual intercourse and/or marriage between certain age groups, races, social classes, families, religions, etc., directly influence the potential for genetic variation within and across different groups of humans (Sorokin, 1947). Indeed, Sorokin took such a broad view of the role of society and culture in the environmental universe of each individual, that he described trying to understand sociocultural phenomena by locating them in terms of **sociocultural space** and **sociocultural distance**. The concept of sociocultural distance has taken on new meaning since Sorokin proposed it over 50 years ago. Today, anyone can travel around the world in a matter of hours or days, and many people do so regularly. Technology and globalization have dramatically reduced the distance between people, and consequently brought their cultural differences into contact with one another. Efforts to study cultures and societies alter the location of sociocultural phenomena within our own universe of personal development. In other words, by studying the relationships between society, culture, and personality, we are altering the meaning and influence of those relationships, hopefully for the better.

As a final note, although this section has highlighted the influence of anthropologists and sociologists on cross-cultural research in the study of personality, there has also been an influence from psychology on these investigators. As noted above, both Abram Kardiner and Robert LeVine were psychoanalysts. In addition, Kardiner acknowledges having learned a great deal from a professor named John Dollard. Dollard was a sociologist who had studied psychoanalysis and who collaborated with Neal Miller (a psychologist trained in learning theory) in an effort to apply classical learning theory to psychodynamic theory (see Chapter 10). Dollard contributed a chapter to one of Linton's books, and was cited by both LeVine and Sorokin (who was, again, also a colleague of Allport). Given such an interesting interaction between the fields of psychology, anthropology, and sociology over half a century ago, it seems surprising that psychology is only now emphasizing the value of focusing on cultural influences on personality development.

Discussion Question: Have you ever had an interest in ethnography? When you begin to learn something about another culture, how much does it interest you? How influential do you think your culture has been in your own personal development?

Different Cultural Factors Affecting Personality

Since culture pervades every aspect of our lives, the number of cultural factors that we might examine in the study of personality is quite large. However, there are a few major factors that stand out, and that have been the subject of significant research in the field of psychology. Thus, we will take a brief look at four major factors that will come up repeatedly throughout this book: **religion**, **race**, **gender**, and **age**.

Religion as a Cultural Influence

> ...religion in its turn exerts the most decisive influence upon all groups and systems of culture, from science and the fine arts to politics and economics. Without knowing the religion of a given culture or group - their systems of ultimate values - one cannot understand their basic traits and social movements. (pg. 228; Sorokin, 1947)

The essential importance of religion was also recognized by Abram Kardiner and Robert LeVine, both of whom, as noted above, studied anthropology and psychoanalysis (see Kardiner, et al., 1945; LeVine, 1973). As we will see in the next chapter, the recognized founder of psychoanalysis, Sigmund Freud, also placed great emphasis on the influence of religion and religious symbolism (though he did not believe in God).

Religion/spirituality appear to be the most significant cultural factors affecting people's lives and personal development. Islam, Buddhism, Taoism, Yoga, Christianity, and Judaism, taken together, represent the religious or spiritual traditions of some 5 to 6 billion people, most of the world's population. Shown are some of the author's copies of the Holy Bible, Holy Quran, Discourses of the Buddha, Yoga-Sūtra, Bhagavad Gita, and the Tao Te Ching. [Image by Mark Kelland]

Despite the importance of religion, as perhaps the most significant cultural factor, there is variation in the extent to which formal religious beliefs and practices are a part of the routine life of people in different cultures (see Matsumoto & Juang, 2004). Since most psychologists were not emphasizing cultural factors as an essential aspect of the early development of the field (leaving that to anthropologists and sociologists), and given Freud's powerful and convincing arguments against religion (see Chapter 3), it is not surprising that psychology has not focused on the influence of religion on personality. But that is changing, and despite the role that religion has played in many political battles and outright war (as has been the case in the Middle East for thousands of years!), religion and spirituality are also recognized as potentially favorable aspects of psychological development in general, and personality development in particular, in the field of positive psychology (Compton, 2005; Peterson, 2006; Peterson & Seligman, 2004; Snyder & Lopez, 2005). Given the importance of religion as a cultural determinant, and the emphasis on culture in this book, we will examine the influence of religion on personality development throughout this textbook.

The Question of Race and Ethnicity as Cultural Influences

> At the very outset we must face three possible alternatives as we consider the concept of race: 1) there *is* such a thing as race in mankind; 2) there is *not* such a thing as race in mankind; 3) even if race in mankind exists, it can have no significance save as people think of it and react to their conception of it. (pg. 38; Krogman, 1945)

Although religion may be the most significant cultural factor, the concept of race has probably existed even longer, and it is certainly the most visually obvious factor. But is it really? The fact is that there is no clear answer to the question of what actually constitutes race (Krogman, 1945; Linton, 1936, 1955; Sorokin, 1947). Although most people quickly think of three major races (White, Black, and Asian), and many of us would add a fourth category (Latino), studies have suggested that there may actually be as many as thirty-seven distinct races (see Matsumoto & Juang, 2004). In addition, genetic studies have suggested that there is more inter-group variation than there is between-group variation, further suggesting that race is nothing more than a social construction. As an alternative to race, some people use the term **ethnicity**, which identifies groups according to commonalities such as nationality, culture, or language. This fails to solve our problem, however, since the concept of ethnicity suffers from the same problems as the concept of race (Brislin, 2000; Matsumoto & Juang, 2004; Miller & Garran, 2008; Whitley & Kite, 2006).

Although the terms race and ethnicity are often used interchangeably with culture, they are quite different. The United States, for example, has large populations of people from different races, ethnic groups, religions, and nationalities, but they all contribute to the greater cultural identity of "American." Indeed, the very concept of America as a "melting pot" defies the use of racial or ethnic characterizations of the American people. This argument goes both ways, of course. We cannot simply refer to people who live within the boundaries of the United States as American, and expect that they are similar in every other cultural respect. Although this may seem rather confusing, that is exactly the point. Critical thinking must always be applied to personality theories and their application in broad ways. This does not mean they are not useful, just that we must be careful in our interpretations of people's behavior and personality if they are from another culture.

Although ethnicity and race may be of questionable value as cultural factors, there are two critically important issues that arise from them. A common problem in cross-cultural research is that of **ethnocentrism**, the belief that one's own culture has the right beliefs and practices, whereas other cultures have wrong beliefs and practices (Matsumoto & Juang, 2004; Whitley & Kite, 2006). Such value judgments interfere with the objectivity of cross-cultural research, and can have negative effects on intercultural communication. The other, very serious problem is that of **racism**. As noted in the quote above, race is very real if people believe in it and act according to their perception of it. We will examine racism later in the textbook. For now, consider the following quote from a recently published book entitled *Racism in the United States: Implications for the Helping Professions*:

> Racism has evolved as a persistent part of the human condition. Its obstinacy and intractability are frustrating and at times baffling. We live in a world in which most nations have signed United Nations declarations of human rights and claim to be democracies, yet racial and ethnic conflict abound. (pg. xvii; Miller & Garran, 2008)

Gender and Culture

Gender has been the subject of a wide range of studies, from pop-psychology books like *Men Are From Mars, Women Are From Venus* (Gray, 1992) and *Self-Made Man: One Woman's Journey into Manhood and Back Again* (Vincent, 2006) to such ominous sounding titles in academic psychology as *The Longest War: Gender and Culture* (Wade and Tavris, 1994). In 2005, the president of Harvard University suggested that one of the reasons there were so few women in math and science fields was that they lacked the intrinsic aptitude. The subsequent uproar led to the end of his presidency at Harvard, and a renewed effort to examine the reasons why few women succeed in math and science careers. An extensive study, led by former APA President Diane Halpern came to no specific conclusions, due to the complex interactions of a variety of factors, but in so doing made it clear that no blame can be placed directly on inherent/genetic ability (Halpern, et al., 2007; see also Barnett, 2007).

Gender is a distinctly cultural term, representing the behaviors or patterns of activity that a given culture or society expects from men and women. It is perhaps most commonly used to address differences between males and females, with an underlying assumption that sex differences lead to gender differences. However, apparent sex differences may actually be cultural gender differences, and cultures and societies exert significant influence on **gender roles** from a very early age (Brislin, 2000; Matsumoto & Juang, 2004; Stewart & McDermott, 2004). Still, some cultural factors may also have a basis in biological reality. For example, males are typically larger and stronger than females, so it makes sense for males to do the hunting and fight the wars. Women become pregnant and then nurse the infants, so it makes sense for them to provide early childcare. How this led to man have greater control and prestige in society, however, remains unclear, especially since that is not universally the case (Wade & Tavris, 1994). In addition, older men often become involved in childcare after their hunting/warrior days are behind them, further complicating the issue.

Among the differences between men and women that seem to be fairly common across cultures, and which may stem from sex differences, are aggression and emphasizing relationships. Men are typically more aggressive, and women seem to focus more on relationships with other people. In accordance with these tendencies, women typically defer to men, particularly in situations that may be confrontational. It also leads to conflict between men and women due to their difficulties communicating, hence the popularity of John Gray's book suggesting that men and women are from completely different planets. Given the status of men, the challenges that these gender differences create for women were not typically given a great deal of attention. However, Karen Horney (see Chapter 8) and more recently the women of the Stone Center Group (see Chapter 9) have made great strides in changing that situation. Not only have the members of the Stone Center Group provided a number of collected works on the psychology of women (Jordan, 1997b; Jordan, Kaplan, Miller, Stiver, & Surrey, 1991; Jordan, Walker, & Hartling, 2004), there are also textbooks devoted exclusively to the subject (e.g., Matlin, 2004).

Aging within a Cultural Context

Age is used as routinely as sex to divide the people in a society. All societies recognize at least three age groups: child, adult, and old. Childhood is typically further divided into young childhood and adolescence. Each group has different rights, responsibilities, roles, and status (Linton, 1936; Sorokin, 1947). Sometimes, these can come into conflict. For example, among the Comanche, as with most Plains tribes in North America, the adult male was expected to be a warrior, whereas the old man was respected for his wisdom and gentleness. Transitioning from being a warrior to being an old man was very difficult, and Comanche men often hoped to die in battle in order to avoid the transition. Those who were forced to make the transition became very dangerous adversaries for the young men transitioning from childhood to adulthood, and often the old men would kill the young men when they could (out of sheer envy). Moving even beyond old age, into death, there are many societies in which the dead remain in the minds of the community members, and deceased relatives and heroes are even worshipped. In some cultures, the relationship with those who are dead is a very important part of daily life (Linton, 1936).

Throughout history, as societies have changed, so have the ways in which they treated and cared for (or did not care for) aged individuals. Although modern industrialization is correlated with a significantly longer lifespan, such dramatic cultural changes favor the young people who can more readily adapt to the changes. In addition, industrialized societies typically shift some of the responsibility of caring for the aged from the family to the state. Curiously, this removes the responsibility of caring for aged persons from the very family whom those aged individuals had cared for and raised themselves! The one area in which aged members of the community are likely to retain their leadership status is religion, and the rituals associated with it (Holmes, 1983; Johnson & Thane, 1998; Schweitzer, 1983).

David Gutmann, an early gerontologist with an interest in the effects of aging on personality, has focused his career on studying men in four cultures: a typical American population (to the extent that there is such a thing), the Navajo in the United States, both Lowland and Highland Maya in Mexico, and the Druze in Israel (see Gutmann, 1987, 1997). One of the most interesting realities that he begins with is the recognition that the human species is the only one in which aged individuals remain active long past their reproductive prime. What possible evolutionary advantage does this offer our species? Gutmann believes that our elders fill unique roles in society, thus providing essential benefits to the extended family and the community, particularly for the young. Indeed, Gutmann points out that it is uniquely human to favor the ends of the lifespan, both childhood and old age, over the middle of the lifespan, when reproductive fitness is at its biological peak. As we noted above, however, the transition into old age is not always easy, and this leads to some unique changes in personality associated with aging.

The beginning of old age is marked by the maturity of one's children, such that the adult individual no longer needs to provide care for their children. Thus, both men and women can begin to express those aspects of their personality that were set aside in order to mutually facilitate raising children. Consequently, there is often a relaxing, or even reversal to some extent, of gender roles. A particularly significant change for men who no longer have the physical strength to be warriors (or to engage in the physical labor of their community) is the manner in which they seek mastery over their lives. Young men have the ability to seek **active mastery**, they strive toward autonomy, competence, and control. Older men must seek **passive mastery**, through adaptation and accommodation. The oldest men must rely on **magical mastery**. The world becomes one of potential providers and potential predators. They rely on primitive defense mechanisms, and wish fulfillment becomes synonymous with reality. Their relationship to the world is marked by feelings of vulnerability (Gutmann, 1987, 1997). It is easy to see how they would rely heavily on religion, and the promise of a supernatural being for protection and eternal reward, thus inclining them toward an involvement in religious practice that would naturally lead to a degree of respect, or at least acknowledgement, as religious leaders. Of course, the degree to which a society provides for its oldest members, such as through retirement benefits, would have a significant effect on this aging process. Nonetheless, Gutmann found evidence for these changes in mastery style amongst men in mainstream America as well as in the Navajo, Maya, and Druze cultures.

Discussion Question: To what extent have religion, race, gender, and age been important factors in your personal development (either currently, or in the past)? Which do you expect will be the most important in your future development?

Addressing the Degree of Cultural Integration

Adding to the complexity of culture's role in shaping our personalities are two important factors. First is the degree to which an individual is integrated into their culture, and vice versa. As Sorokin points out, it is exceedingly rare that an individual is either totally integrated into their culture or not integrated into it at all (Sorokin, 1947; see also Kardiner, et al., 1945; Linton, 1936). Thus, culture provides a framework within which individual variation is possible, but at the same time there will always be some consistent basis for understanding the people within a given culture. This becomes particularly important when considering cross-cultural research, since it may be reasonable to make some general assumptions about an individual from another culture, but we must also be prepared for their own unique variation as a person in that cultural group.

A second important factor is that cultural phenomena do not exist in isolation. Both gender and race/ethnicity, for example, influence how one adapts to the aging process (see, e.g., Arber, Davidson, & Ginn, 2003; Barrow, 1986; Calasanti & Slevin, 2001; Cool & McCabe, 1983; Holmes, 1983). Gender also interacts with race/ethnicity in determining one's reactions to group psychotherapy (Pack-Brown, Whittington-Clark, & Parker, 1998) and/or adapting to life as a minority student on a majority campus (Levey, Blanco, & Jones, 1998). Religion is considered to be such an important factor in the African American community that its role has been the subject of special interest (see, e.g., Belgrave & Allison, 2006; Taylor, Chatters, & Levin, 2004). Obviously many more examples can be found, the point being that as an individual develops, with multiple cultural factors influencing them, and each factor being integrated to a great or lesser degree, the potential for individual personality differences is extraordinary, even when the overall effect of the specific culture, or society, is to guide its members toward certain underlying tendencies that become characteristic of that culture's members.

Discussion Question: Are you, or is anyone you know, distant or unintegrated with your family's culture or that your community? If so, what sort of problems does that create for your identities? If none, does your cultural integration provide a sense of integrity?

Culture and Diversity

The importance of studying culture can be found in the diversity of people both around the world and within our own communities. For example, although many communities may be quite limited in terms of religion and race/ethnicity, nearly all communities have a mixture of gender and age. Although religion, race/ethnicity, gender, and age may be the major factors that have traditionally been studied in the field of psychology, in the instances where culture was studied, it is important to remember two additional points. First, there are other cultural factors that may be very important for certain individuals and/or select groups of people, and second, people can be excitingly (or frustratingly, depending on your point of view) unique in their individuality.

One area of diversity that has been receiving more attention as a cultural factor affecting the lives of many people is that of physical disability. In the past, although it was recognized that individuals with physical disabilities experience basically the same personality development processes as other people, disabilities were considered to be specific conditions that isolated the disabled person from their surroundings (Barker et al., 1953; Pintner et al., 1941). Over time, as more research became available on the psychology of people with disabilities (e.g., Goodley & Lawthorn, 2006; Henderson & Bryan, 1984; Marks, 1999; McDaniel, 1976; Roessler & Bolton, 1978; Stubbins, 1977; Vash, 1981; Wright, 1983), perspectives on how to study these individuals changed as well. In 2004, the Society for Disability Studies adopted preliminary guidelines for developing programs in disability studies. They emphasize challenging the previously held view that disabilities are individual deficits or defects that can or should be fixed by "experts." Rather, they recommend exploring models that examine cultural, social, political, and economic factors which integrate personal and collective responses to difference (the society's website is www.disstudies.org).

There are several chapters in this book where we will address the biological aspects of personality development, including the mind-body connection. Whereas a few academic authors have made passing mention of the value of exercise, self-defense training, and spirituality in coping with physical disabilities (Nardo, 1994; Robinson, 1995; Sobsey, 1994), one particularly interesting area in which culture, physical disability, the mind-body connection, positive psychology, and spirituality all come together is martial arts training (see Kelland, 2009, 2010). A number of notable martial arts experts actively encourage people with disabilities to practice the physical, psychological, and spiritual aspects of these ancient exercises (such as Grandmaster Mark Shuey Sr. of the Cane Masters International Association, Master Jurgen Schmidt of the International Disabled Self-Defense Association, and Grandmaster John Pellegrini of the International Combat Hapkido Federation), and several books are available on this subject (McNab, 2003; Robertson, 1991; Withers, 2007). We will revisit this topic later in the book, but for now consider the diversity of cultures and personal interests that come together when, for example, a disabled American living in the modern world pursues the spiritual and physical development associated with an ancient, Asian practice of self-development.

When considering the life of an individual like Shawn Withers, the son of a Maine fisherman, who suffered a massive stroke at the age of 20, but then went on to earn a black belt in Kenpo Karate and then developed his own style known as Broken Wing Kenpo (Withers, 2007), broad descriptions of personality theory and cultural perspectives fall short of giving us an understanding of the person. Thus, some researchers, like Dan McAdams (McAdams, 1985, 2006; McAdams et al., 2001), have emphasized the need for studying a narrative framework within which we not only live our lives, but actually create them:

> ...like stories in literature, the stories we tell ourselves in order to live bring together diverse elements into an integrated whole, organizing the multiple and conflicting facets of our lives within a narrative framework which connects past, present, and an anticipated future and confers upon our lives a sense of sameness and continuity - indeed, an *identity*. As the story evolves and

> our identity takes form, we come to *live* the story as we *write* it, assimilating our daily experience to a schema of self that is a product of that experience. (pg. v; McAdams, 1985)

Although this textbook will cover broad personality theories and cultural perspectives, there are also reflective elements and discussion questions included to help you try to address your own narrative stories. In addition, there are biographies at the beginning of each chapter on the major theorists, which although they are not personal narratives, will nonetheless give some insight into the sort of person that theorist was, and hopefully, how their life and their personal experiences helped to shaped the personality theory they developed.

Culture and Mental Illness

Although this book focuses on normal personality development, one cannot escape the fact that most of the famous personality theorists were clinicians who were trying to understand how their patients/clients had developed psychological disorders. So, our understanding of personality development grew hand-in-hand with our understanding of psychological disorders. The *Diagnostic and Statistical Manual of Mental Disorders* began addressing the importance of culture in the 4th edition, and more recently it has taken a dramatic step forward with the publication of the DSM's 5th edition (American Psychiatric Association, 2000, 2013).

The DSM-V includes a section on *Emerging Measures and Models*, one chapter of which is called *Cultural Formulation*. Although the DSM-IV began to present an outline for cultural formulation, the DSM-V includes two valuable sets of questions that have been field-tested to help clinicians assess the cultural identity of a patient/client and how that cultural identity may affect the diagnosis and treatment of any potential psychological disorder. The first set of questions is the basis for the Cultural Formulation Interview, and the second set comprise the Cultural Formulation Interview - Informant Version (which is given to someone who is knowledgeable about the life circumstances and potential clinical problems of the patient/client).

In our increasingly global and multicultural world it is more and more likely that therapists will encounter individuals from different cultural backgrounds than their own. Thus, in order for the therapist to fully understand the individual and the context of their psychological distress, the therapist must be aware of and attentive to possibly significant cultural differences. Failure to do so might result in what Iijima Hall (1997) has described as **cultural malpractice**!

A Final Challenge

As important as it is to keep cultural factors in mind when studying personality, the unfortunate reality is that the major personality theories in psychology, as we recognize psychology today, have arisen within Western intellectual settings. Thus, we do not have corresponding systems of personality theory that arose in other cultures that we might compare to the theories we do have. This somewhat limits our perspective on cross-cultural personality theory to attempts to apply our Western theories to people of other cultures. This limitation should not, however, keep us from considering these issues. It is merely an inconvenience that you should keep in mind as you consider the theories present in this textbook. Should your career lead you into the field of psychology, perhaps you will be one of the people to help develop and advance some theory that moves beyond this limitation.

Another concern has to do with the nature of this textbook, and personality courses in general. Although we have emphasized anthropology and sociology in this chapter, this is a psychology textbook. Nonetheless, culture is an all-encompassing factor in the development and psychology of both individuals and the groups in which they live. Indeed, in *Personality and Person Perception Across Cultures*, Lee, McCauley, & Draguns (1999) boldly state that "human nature cannot be independent of culture" (pg. vii). Thus, it is essential that we learn as much as possible about culture. As an encouragement for studying other cultures, Ralph Linton had this to say:

> The ability to see the culture of one's own society as a whole, to evaluate its patterns and appreciate their implications, calls for a degree of objectivity which is rarely if ever achieved...Those who know no culture other than their own cannot know their own...Even such a master as Freud frequently posited instincts to account for reactions which we now see as directly referable to cultural conditioning. (pp. 125-126; Linton, 1945).

Personality Theory in Real Life: Examining Your Own Cultural Background

I consider myself to be an American. But what does that actually mean? I know a few tidbits about my ancestors that are quite interesting. One of my ancestors, a great aunt, was on the Titanic when it sank (like most women and children, she was one of the survivors). I am directly descended from John Howland and Elizabeth Tilley, who came to America on the Mayflower, in the year 1620. Actually, John Howland fell overboard in the middle of the Atlantic Ocean during rough seas, but was saved when he grabbed a rope trailing in the water and was then pulled back aboard! Among John Howland and Elizabeth Tilley's other direct descendants (and, therefore, my distant relatives) are the U. S. Presidents Franklin D. Roosevelt, George H. W. Bush, and George W. Bush, the renowned poets Ralph Waldo Emerson and Henry Wadsworth Longfellow, and the founder of the Mormon church, Joseph Smith. This lineage does not, however, come down through the Kelland name, as the Kellands came to America later. If you add one more generation, John Howland's brothers include among their descendants U. S. Presidents Richard Nixon and Gerald Ford, as well as British Prime Minister Winston Churchill. The other side of my family was primarily German, and when they first came to America they settled in Kansas and became well-respected wheat farmers.

What do you know about your cultural background? Are you proud of your background in a way that has shaped your life? For example, knowing one of my ancestors was on the Mayflower helped to kindle in me an ongoing interest in history. If you don't know much about your family's history, who might you turn to for information? Try it; you may learn something fascinating.

Review of Key Points

- It is important for the field of psychology to consider both cross-cultural and intercultural research.
- Emic tasks are familiar to the members of a given culture, whereas etic tasks are common to all cultures.
- In cross-cultural research, it is important to determine whether a concept is equivalent in each culture being studied.
- One of the most important considerations for the equivalence of psychological tests is the issue of translation equivalence. This can be addressed by examining back translations of the test(s) being used.
- Back translation helps to decenter a psychological test from the cultural influence of the original language/culture.
- Cultural flexibility and cultural response sets determine the range within which members of different cultures respond. Thus, one must have some understanding of these factors for a given culture when attempting to interpret cross-cultural or intercultural research.
- Cross-cultural validation studies specifically examine whether a given cross-cultural study makes sense within the context of a research project.
- Ethnographies provide detailed information on the daily lives and habits of the members of a given culture. They are often conducted by anthropologists, and can be of great value to cross-cultural psychologists.
- Anthropologists, such as Ralph Linton, believe that personality develops on multiple levels. Central organization involves the biological aspects of personality (such as temperament), whereas the superficial organization is profoundly influenced by culture.
- The process of enculturation involves internalizing cultural norms, and may be able to influence the central organization of individuals, as well as the superficial organization.
- When an individual's basic personality contradicts that which their social class expects of them, they may develop a status personality.
- Complimentary personalities, such as those seen in typical gender roles, tend to be mutually adjusted.
- The psychoanalyst Abram Kardiner, who worked with Linton, distinguished between the culturally-determined basic personality, or ego structure, and the individual's character, which is their unique adaptation to the environment given their inherent tendencies and personal experiences.
- According to Kardiner, personality development within a cultural setting provides a security system.

- Acculturation can lead to changes both in individuals and in entire cultures.
- The anthropologist/psychoanalyst Robert Levine proposed the term psychoanalytic ethnography to describe the work done by researchers like himself and Kardiner.
- The sociologist Pitirim Sorokin described personality development within one's entire cultural universe, referring to sociocultural phenomena in terms of their sociocultural space and sociocultural distance.
- Religion appears to be the single most significant cultural factor.
- Race and ethnicity are complex, and are hard to consider as cultural factors because they cannot easily be defined. Nonetheless, as individuals think about them in their own ways, they often give rise to ethnocentrism and, potentially, racism and discrimination.
- Although sex is a biological distinction, gender roles are an influential cultural factor that is applied from very early in life. Certain aspects of gender roles likely reflect some of the underlying biological differences between males and females.
- All societies recognize distinct age groups, and treat those age groups differently. However, there is great variation in the status of each age group, which often leads to conflict.
- Old age is of particular interest, since the human species is the only in which individuals remain active long past their reproductive prime.
- One of the common cross-cultural factors facing old men is the transition in how they seek master in their lives. Only young men can expect to be successful seeking active mastery, whereas older men seek passive master and then magical mastery.
- In addition to sometimes dramatic differences between cultures, individuals within a culture also differ in the extent to which they integrate different aspects of their culture into their own lives.
- Sometimes cultural phenomena interact, making for interesting, yet complex, situations. For example, religion has played an important role in the cultural identity of African Americans throughout their history in America.

Review of Key Terms

acculturation active mastery age back translation basic personality *berdache* character cross-cultural research cross-cultural validation studies cultural flexibility cultural malpractice	cultural response sets decentering ego structure emic enculturation equivalence ethnicity ethnocentrism ethnographies etic gender gender roles	intercultural research magical mastery passive mastery psychoanalytic ethnography race racism religion security system sociocultural space sociocultural distance status personality translation equivalence

Annotated Bibliography

Brislin, R. (2000). *Understanding culture's influence on behavior, 2nd Ed.* Belmont, CA: Wadsworth Thomson.

Matsumoto, D. & Juang, L. (2004). *Culture and psychology, 3rd Ed.* Belmont, CA: Wadsworth/Thomson Learning.

Segall, M. H., Dasen, P. R., Berry, J. W., & Poortinga, Y. H. (1990). *Human behavior in global perspective: An introduction to cross-cultural psychology.* Boston, MA: Allyn and Bacon.

Each of these books offers an excellent overview of cross-cultural research in the field of psychology. Despite numerous similarities in the material covered, each book has its own unique approach to studying this diverse and still forming field of study.

Linton, R. (1936). ***The study of man: An introduction.*** **New York, NY: D. Appleton-Century Company.**
Linton, R. (1945). ***The cultural background of personality.*** **New York, NY: Appleton-Century-Crofts.**

At the time of his death, in 1953, Ralph Linton was recognized as one of the leading anthropologists in the world. In these two books, Linton describes the broad range of the field of cultural anthropology and the study of the human race, as well as the influence of culture on personality development.

Kardiner, A. (1939). ***The individual and his society: The psychodynamics of primitive social organization.*** **New York, NY: Columbia University Press.**
Kardiner, A., Linton, R., DuBois, C., & West, J. (1945). ***The psychological frontiers of society.*** **New York, NY: Columbia University Press.**
LeVine, R. A. (1973). ***Culture, Behavior, and Personality.*** **Chicago, IL: Aldine Publishing Company.**

Abram Kardiner and Robert LeVine studied anthropology and psychoanalysis. As such, there were uniquely qualified to study the influence of culture on personality development, and to analyze those cultural influences within a psychodynamic perspective. Together, these books offer an excellent example of what can be accomplished when different disciplines come together to address a question of common interest.

Sorokin, P. A. (1947). ***Society, culture, and personality: Their structure and dynamics – A system of general sociology.*** **New York, NY: Cooper Square Publishers.**

As the founder of Harvard University's sociology department, Pitirim Sorokin was an important and influential individual in the history of the field of sociology. This lengthy book covers a broad range of topics in sociology, with an emphasis on the relationships between society, culture, and individual personality development. In addition, Sorokin takes the unique perspective of considering personality development within the context of the individual's entire "universe" of experience.

Lee, Y.-T., McCauley, C. R., & Draguns, J. G. (Eds.). (1999). ***Personality and person perception across cultures.*** **Mahwah, NJ: Lawrence Erlbaum Associates.**

As the title implies, this collection of articles offers a wide variety of perspectives on personality. Included are chapters on the value of studying culture in relation to personality and how to incorporate such information into formal cross-cultural training programs.

Belgrave, F. Z. & Allison, K. W. (2006). ***African American psychology: From Africa to America.*** **Thousand Oaks, CA: Sage Publications.**
Taylor, R. J., Chatters, L. M., & Levin, J. (2004). ***Religion in the lives of African Americans: Social, psychological, and health perspectives.*** **Thousand Oaks, CA: Sage Publications.**

African American culture has been of particular interest in the United States for some time. These comprehensive texts carefully examine the nature of African American psychology and the special role that religion has played in their culture.

Gutmann, D. (1987). ***Reclaimed powers: Toward a new psychology of men and women in later life.*** **New York, NY: Basic Books.**
Gutmann, D. (1997). ***The human elder in nature, culture, and society.*** **Boulder, CO: Westview Press.**

David Gutmann focused his career on the personality changes that occur as adults become old, with particular emphasis on changes that appear to be consistent across different cultures. These two books summarize much of his research and the theories he developed.

Chapter 3 – Sigmund Freud

Sigmund Freud is unquestionably the most famous person in the fields of psychiatry and psychology, and one of the most famous individuals in modern history. He is of particular importance for this subject because he was probably the first person to address psychological problems by examining the individual's personal development in detail. As he developed his psychodynamic theory, and the treatment known as psychoanalysis, he attempted to carefully observe and listen to his patients in order to determine not only how and why they had become the person they were, but also whether those developmental processes might be common to all people. This careful approach to studying psychological conditions was likely the result of Freud's substantial scientific research in anatomy and physiology earlier in his career.

But why is Freud so famous? Much of his theory may not seem relevant today, and it's hard to imagine how anyone could ever have come up with the theory of penis envy. And yet Freud remains extraordinarily influential. There are at least three good reasons for Freud's enduring influence and popularity. First, Freud was first! No one before him had established a cohesive theory of the development of personality, especially a theory that attempted to explain both normal and abnormal development. Thus, most theories developed since then have been viewed as extending, modifying, or opposing Freud's psychodynamic theory. Second, key elements of Freud's theory are generally accepted in psychology and psychiatry, such as the existence of unconscious elements of our mind that can affect our thoughts and behaviors and both the normal and abnormal roles of psychological defense mechanisms. The final factor contributing to Freud's lasting influence is somewhat more complicated. Psychodynamic theory was not well received at first. In fact, the emphasis on childhood sexuality was ridiculed and scorned by many in the medical profession. However, Freud was determined, and he did not let the rejection of others deter him from continuing his studies. In addition, there were several very famous and influential individuals who supported his efforts. Thus, Freud found the motivation to persevere, and the rest, as they say, is history.

A Brief Biography of Sigmund Freud, M.D.

Sigismund Schlomo Freud was born on May 6th, 1856, in the small, industrial town of Freiberg in Moravia (today it is known as Pribor in the Czech Republic). Freud never used the name Schlomo, his paternal grandfather's name, and he shortened his first name while at the University of Vienna. His family life was unusual, and somewhat complicated. His father, Jakob Freud, was 40 years old when he married Freud's mother, Amalia Nathanson. She was 20 years younger than Jakob Freud, and several years younger than Jakob's son, Emanuel, from an earlier marriage. One of Freud's first friends was a nephew who was a year older than Freud!

Jakob Freud was never particularly successful in business. The industrial importance of Freiberg was declining, so the young family left and eventually settled in Vienna, Austria (Jakob's sons from his first marriage, Emanuel and Philipp, emigrated to England). At this point Jakob and Amalia Freud had two children, Sigmund and his sister Anna (a brother born between them, Julius, died at 7 or 8 months of age). Shortly after arriving in Vienna, however, they had five more children during the years 1860-1866: Rosa, Marie, Adolfine, Pauline, and Alexander. This resulted in continued financial difficulties, which appears to have been painful for the young Freud (Gay, 1998). There were also personal difficulties that made it difficult for Freud to enjoy a close relationship with his father. Jakob Freud once told his son a story about being abused by an Austrian Christian, a man who knocked Jakob Freud's hat into the muddy street and then ordered the "Jew" to get off the sidewalk. When Freud asked his father how he had responded, his father said he simply stepped off the sidewalk and picked up his hat. Freud was very disappointed by what he apparently perceived as weakness in his father (Gay, 1998). There was also an embarrassing episode involving his father's brother, Josef. Josef Freud was convicted and sent to jail for trading in counterfeit money. This caused a great deal of concern for Jakob Freud, who might have been involved in the illegal scheme along with his sons, Emanuel and Philipp (Gay, 1998; Jones, 1953).

Still, Jakob Freud did try to be a good father. His children were generally successful, and he remained active and supportive in the lives of his children and grandchildren. The story mentioned above, when Jakob Freud tried to impart some "fatherly" wisdom to his son, may not have had the intended effect, but it demonstrates that he cared about teaching his son some of life's lessons. On Freud's thirty-fifth birthday his father sent his "dear son" a copy of the family's Philippson Bible (this Bible contains the Old Testament, which is the only testament in the Jewish faith), which Freud had often studied as a young child (Gay, 1998; Jones, 1953; Nicholi,

2002). The inscription written by Jakob Freud in the Bible ended with a description of the gift "as a token of love from your old father" (see Jones, 1953; Nicholi, 2002). When Jakob Freud died, Freud wrote to a friend that his father's death had profoundly affected him, leaving him feeling uprooted. He described the death of one's father as "the most important event, the most poignant loss, in a man's life" (see Nicholi, 2002). The death of his father appears to have stimulated Freud's self-analysis, the writing of *The Interpretation of Dreams* (Freud, 1900/1995) and the formulation of his theory of the Oedipus complex (Nicholi, 2002). Jakob Freud was also remembered quite fondly by his grandson Martin, the eldest son of Freud (M. Freud, 1983).

Freud's relationship with his mother was also complex. Amalia Freud is described as young (which she was, compared to Jakob), attractive, and energetic. She always took great pride in her son, and was a strong and positive influence throughout his life. Later in life he wrote that "A man who has been the indisputable favorite of his mother keeps for life the feeling of a conqueror, that confidence of success that often induces real success" (see Jones, 1953). During Freud's self-analysis, around the year 1897, he uncovered profound memories from his earliest years. Sometime between the ages of 2 ½ and 4 years old, Freud accidentally saw his mother naked. This event awakened a powerful desire in Freud. Shortly after recovering this memory, he remembered the deep jealousy he had felt when his brother Julius was born, shortly before Freud was 2 years old. So jealous was Freud, that he remembered welcoming the death of his infant brother (see Gay, 1998; Jones, 1953). Each of these incidents certainly had an impact of Freud's theory of the Oedipus complex. Surprisingly, however, during the first 2 ½ years of Freud's life he actually spent very little time with his mother, since he was being raised by a nursemaid. Keep in mind that his mother became pregnant again, then his brother Julius became ill and died, and then his mother became pregnant again, finally giving birth to his sister Anna, all by the time Freud was 2 ½ years old.

Freud's nursemaid has been described as an old and ugly woman, but Freud loved her and dreamed about her later in life (see Gay, 1998; Jones, 1953; Nicholi, 2002). The nursemaid was a devout Roman Catholic, and she regularly took Freud to church with her. Despite his young age (less than 2 ½ years old), Freud would come home from church and preach to his family about God. Even though his family was Jewish, they did not practice their faith with much devotion, and it must have been quite interesting to listen to the sermons of their little boy. Why then, as we will see, did Freud come to reject religion and spirituality? It turns out that this relationship ended abruptly. Freud's half brother Philipp accused the nursemaid of petty theft, and she was sent to prison. At this time Freud's mother was confined with his recently born sister, so Freud was suddenly denied access to both his mother and his nursemaid. It has been suggested that because he was abandoned so suddenly, and at such a critical time (Freud was 2 ½ years old at this time), by his Roman Catholic nursemaid, that his anger and disappointment led to his ultimate rejection of the spiritual worldview and his antagonism toward the Catholic church (Gay, 1998; Jones, 1953; Nicholi, 2002).

Freud's Early Career in Basic Research (Pre-Psychiatry)

Freud was very successful in school from an early age. At the Gymnasium, which is the term for a preparatory school in countries such as Germany and Austria, he was first in his class for 7 years. This led to a variety of special privileges, including seldom being required to take any examinations (Freud, 1952). It also led to privileges at home. According to his sister Anna, Freud always had his own room to study in, no matter how difficult the family's financial situation (Gay, 1998). As he prepared for college, Freud initially wanted to study law. However, after learning about Darwin's theory of evolution and hearing Goethe's essay on nature, he decided to become a medical student (Freud, 1952).

In 1873, Freud entered the University of Vienna. Initially he suffered greatly from prejudice and discrimination against him because he was Jewish. Believing that he was expected to feel inferior and alien because he was Jewish, he nonetheless persevered. As a result of these experiences, later in life he was prepared for dealing with the considerable resistance that occurred in response to his theories (Freud, 1952). His first research project in medical school came at the suggestion of Professor Carl Claus. Prof. Claus was interested in a report that the Polish scientist Simone de Syrski had identified structures that might represent the testes of the male eel. This was a question that had been studied for centuries without success. After dissecting some 400 eels, Freud appeared to have confirmed Syrski's findings. The research was not definitive, however, and Freud found little satisfaction in the publication of his work (Gay, 1998; Jones, 1953). He was, however, about to find satisfaction, in the physiological laboratory of Ernst Brücke.

Brücke was a renowned physiologist, anatomist, histologist, and more. Freud had great respect for his newfound mentor, referring to him as Master Brücke and describing him as "the greatest authority I ever met." In Brücke's laboratory Freud "found rest and full satisfaction at last" (Gay, 1998; Jones, 1953). The research he conducted under Brücke's guidance was impressive. Brücke put Freud to work studying the anatomy of the spinal cord and its neurons. At that time, the structure of neurons was not understood. Freud modified the histological staining methods being used in Brücke's laboratory, and eventually developed a gold chloride method of staining nervous system tissue around the year 1880 (Jones, 1953). This was one of the first uses of a heavy metal stain on nervous system tissue. The silver nitrate method of staining neurons had been developed by Camillo Golgi a few years earlier, in 1873, but it was not until 1888 that Santiago Ramon y Cajal first reported on the structure of the brain using Golgi's technique. For this research, Golgi and Ramon y Cajal shared the Nobel Prize for Medicine in 1906 (Finger, 1994). If Freud had not left basic research for a career in medicine, he might have ended up famous just the same.

Freud did eventually leave the university, however, and began a career in medicine at the General Hospital in Vienna. Part of the reason for leaving and beginning his medical career was that he had met Martha Bernays, the woman who would become his wife, and he needed to begin earning enough money to support a wife and family. First, however, he needed to establish himself in his career. At the General Hospital he met and worked with the eminent Theodor Meynert, who, among other accomplishments, was the first to correctly suggest that Parkinson's disease resulted from abnormal functioning of the basal ganglia (Finger, 1994). This stimulated Freud's continued interest in anatomy and brain function, and in 1891 Freud published a book entitled *On Aphasia*. You may remember from introductory psychology that the two primary speech centers in the human brain are Broca's area (speech production) and Wernicke's area (speech reception), and that damage to these areas results in Broca's aphasia or Wernicke's aphasia. Carl Wernicke had also been a student of Meynert, but Freud's book on aphasia was especially critical of Wernicke (Finger, 1994). This put both men firmly in the middle of the debate on structuralism vs. functionalism as it pertains to the activities of the human brain (see Finger, 1994). Although Meynert suggested that Freud should devote himself to studying the anatomy of the brain, Freud had had enough of this sort of work in Brücke's laboratory. Instead, Freud's interest turned toward the diseases of the brain (Freud, 1952). With the help of a recommendation by Brücke, Freud was awarded a Traveling Fellowship, which allowed him to afford a trip to Paris to study at the prestigious Salpetriere. He intended to study under Jean-Martin Charcot, one of the world's foremost neurologists of his day, and the man who named Parkinson's disease after the physician James Parkinson (Finger, 1994).

Freud was largely ignored when he arrived at the Salpetriere, since he was just one of a crowd of foreign visitors. As luck would have it, one day he heard Charcot expressing regret that Charcot had not heard from his German translator in some time, and he wished someone could be found to translate his latest lectures into German. Freud wrote to Charcot, offered to do the job, and was accepted. From that point on he became a member of Charcot's inner circle, and was active in all aspects of the work at the clinic (Freud, 1952). One of the main topics Freud studied with Charcot was the use of hypnosis in the study of hysteria. Freud discussed the earliest conceptions of his psychodynamic theory with Charcot. Charcot was supportive and agreed with Freud's fledgling ideas, but Charcot's interests remained firmly in the field of neurology, not in psychology or psychiatry (Freud, 1952).

Upon returning to Vienna and settling down as a practicing physician, Freud was finally able to marry Martha in 1886 (he was 30 years old, and she was 25). They had six children: Matilde, Martin, Oliver, Ernst, Sophie, and Anna. According to his son Martin, Freud was a loving and generous father (M. Freud, 1983). He was also very supportive of his children. As Martin became disillusioned with the study of law, he turned to his father for advice:

> …It had always been his hope that one of his sons would become a lawyer. Thus he watched, and I think guided, my first faltering steps in my law studies with the greatest concern.
>
> He agreed that my first studies were dull and boring, but he assured me that one day I would find a teacher with an impressive personality, perhaps a man of genius, and that I would become deeply interested and carried away by his lectures…
>
> Father always expressed himself with great clarity and, when advising me at so critical a time in my life, he added to his normal clarity of expression a natural tenderness and concern… (M. Freud, 1983; pg. 161)

Martin did become a lawyer and, after Martin served as an officer in the Austrian army during World War I, his father helped him to establish his practice.

Finally, any discussion of Freud's early research career would not be complete without mentioning what Ernest Jones, Freud's official biographer, called "the cocaine episode" (Jones, 1953). In his last autobiographical book (Freud, 1952; originally published in 1925 in a collection of medical autobiographies) he makes only passing reference to studying cocaine, reporting another near miss in his research career. He had begun studying cocaine while he was away from Vienna, and an opportunity arose to return home for vacation and an opportunity to see his fiancé Martha. As he prepared to leave, he suggested to a couple of colleagues that they examine the effectiveness of cocaine as an anesthetic for use in eye diseases. While Freud was visiting Martha, one of his colleagues, Carl Koller, confirmed the local anesthetic properties of cocaine and became famous for it. Afterward, Freud noted that "it was the fault of my fiancé that I was not already famous at that early age," but he insists that "I bore my fiancé no grudge for her interruption of my work" (Freud, 1952). Something quite fascinating is that Freud's interest in cocaine was initially based on the possibility that its euphoric properties might be used to alleviate the problems associated with withdrawal from morphine. A close and long-time friend, Ernst von Fleischl-Marxow had become addicted to morphine because of the extreme pain of an infection, and Freud hoped that cocaine would help. Freud himself began using cocaine to boost his own mood. He sent some to Martha with the recommendation that she try it (there is no evidence that she ever did), and he even began sending cocaine to friends, colleagues, and his sisters. Eventually, however, Freud realized that cocaine was not helping his friend; indeed von Fleischl-Marxow became addicted to cocaine instead of morphine. Freud eventually deeply regretted his research on cocaine, especially since the one positive result of that research had garnered fame for a colleague while Freud was on vacation (Gay, 1998; Jones, 1953).

Freud's Psychiatric Career

Many people believe that psychoanalysis was developed by Freud during the early years of his medical practice in Vienna. Freud, however, would disagree. He insisted that psychoanalysis was begun by the Viennese physician Josef Breuer (Freud, 1914/1995), a close friend and mentor of Freud. The basis of psychoanalysis lay in a patient that Breuer had seen as early as 1880, and had treated with hypnosis. This case, and the use of hypnosis as part of the "cathartic procedure" developed by Breuer, was the original inspiration for Freud's interest in hypnosis and his trip to Paris to study the technique with Charcot. When Freud returned to Vienna, he asked Breuer to tell him all of the details of this case, which involved a young woman. This famous patient, known as Anna O., was described by Breuer in the book coauthored by the two men (Freud & Breuer, 1895/2004). As Freud used Breuer's techniques with his own patients, however, he began to realize that something was lacking. Hypnosis did little to reveal the underlying causes of the hysteria that their patients were experiencing. Since Freud was every bit the scientist, he needed to know more about why he was able to help some patients. He eventually replaced hypnosis with his own techniques of free association (early 1890s) and, eventually, dream analysis (essentially done in 1896, but not published until 1900). This was the point at which psychoanalysis, in the sense that we think of it today, was born (Freud, 1914/1995, 1952).

As Freud's ideas diverged from those of Breuer, the two parted ways. Freud then developed the aspect of psychodynamic theory that led to his near total rejection by the German and Austrian medical communities: the primacy of childhood sexuality. This theory was so difficult for others to accept that Freud spent nearly 10 years working on psychoanalysis in isolation. However, Freud claims that the concept of a sexual etiology for the neuroses was not really his idea, it had been superficially suggested by Breuer, Charcot, and a highly respected Viennese gynecologist named Chrobak (Freud, 1914/1995). During those years of isolation Freud began to define other major aspects of psychodynamic theory, such as: resistance, repression, conflict, and unconscious impulses.

Around 1902, Freud began to find support for his theories among a select group of physicians. Shortly thereafter a group of psychiatrists in Zurich, Switzerland, which included Eugen Bleuler (the man credited with identifying both schizophrenia and autism as we define them today) and his assistant Carl Jung, began "taking a lively interest in psychoanalysis" (Freud, 1952). In 1909 Freud and Jung were invited to America, where they were warmly received, and psychoanalysis became well-established in America and Canada. By the 1910s it was reported that psychoanalysis was being championed in Austria, Switzerland, the United States, Canada, England, India, Chile, Australasia (the region), France, Italy, Sweden, Russia, Hungary, Holland, and Norway (where the first textbook on psychiatry that included psychoanalysis was written) (Freud, 1914/1995). Germany proved quite resistant, although the renowned Karl Abraham practiced psychoanalysis in Berlin.

Perhaps it was inevitable that all of this success should eventually lead to conflict. Two major groups, whose members differed significantly in their views on psychodynamic theory and psychoanalysis, broke away from the main psychoanalytic groups. They were led by Alfred Adler (see Chapter 4) and Carl Jung (Chapter 3). In his first autobiography, Freud is not exactly kind to these two men. He goes to great length to dismiss Adler's theories as mistaken, and he flatly rejects Jung's perspective:

> Of the two movements under consideration here, Adler's is undoubtedly the more important. Though radically false, it is, nevertheless, characterized by consistency and coherence, and it is still founded on the theory of the instincts. On the other hand, Jung's modification has slackened the connection between the phenomena and the instinctive-life; besides as its critics (Abraham, Firenze, and Jones) have already pointed out, it is so unintelligible, muddled and confused, that … it is impossible to know how one can arrive at a correct understanding of it... (Freud, 1914/1995; pg. 940).

It is curious to speculate whether Freud's isolation for so many years may have led to the profound possessiveness he later expressed regarding psychoanalysis as his technique, and his alone, in *The History of the Psychoanalytic Movement*:

> ...For psychoanalysis is my creation; for ten years I was the only one occupied with it, and all the annoyance which this new subject caused among my contemporaries has been hurled upon my head in the form of criticism. Even today, when I am no longer the only psychoanalyst, I feel myself justified in assuming that nobody knows better than I what psychoanalysis is… (Freud, 1914/1995; pg. 901)

Freud's Final Years

Freud's final years were somewhat tumultuous. The Nazis had taken over Germany and Austria, and they were rapidly preparing for World War II. Being Jewish, Freud's life was in danger; indeed, at least three of his sisters were murdered in the concentration camps, most likely in Auschwitz (M. Freud, 1983). Freud, however, had influential friends, including European royalty and wealthy individuals with ties to the British and American governments. The American secretary of state, Cordell Hull, took word of the situation to President Franklin Roosevelt, and following Roosevelt's instructions, Hull had the American ambassador to Germany intervene on Freud's behalf (Gay, 1998; Jones, 1957). Freud also received substantial help and comfort from Marie Bonaparte, H.R.H. the Princess George of Greece, including the payment of a ransom in order to secure permission for Freud to leave Austria (M. Freud, 1983). Finally, in May 1938, Freud, his wife Martha, and their daughter Anna left together for England, along with Freud's dog. They were all received quite warmly in London, except for the dog. She was quarantined for six months (M. Freud, 1983).

Freud, however, had already been ill for many years, and was suffering a great deal of pain due to cancer. He was also in his eighties. Nonetheless, Freud continued to work, and he completed *An Outline of Psychoanalysis* (1938/1949) and *Moses and Monotheism* (1939/1967) while living in London. But the end was near, and the cancer was progressing rapidly. In September 1939, Freud asked his doctor, Max Schur, to remember an agreement the two had made not to prolong Freud's life unnecessarily. Freud asked Schur to discuss his condition with Anna Freud. Anna Freud at first resisted, but eventually submitted to the inevitable, and Schur administered a series of morphine injections that proved fatal. Sigmund Freud died on September 23, 1939 (Gay, 1998; Jones, 1957).

In the funeral oration delivered by Ernest Jones, Jones remembered that three qualities had particularly impressed him upon first meeting Freud: first, "his nobility of character;" second, "his direct and instinctive love of truth;" and third, "his courage and inflexible determination." Jones also said that a "great spirit has passed from the world…for Freud so inspired us with his personality, his character and his ideas that we can never truly part from him…" (Jones, 1957). Prior to the escape from Austria, Freud had expressed a sincere desire to "die in freedom." He loved England, where he was able to accomplish that goal. In reference to England and the funeral ceremony, Jones said:

> He died surrounded by every loving care, in a land that had shown him more courtesy, more esteem and more honor than his own or any other land, a land which I think he himself esteemed beyond all others. (pg. 247; Jones, 1957).

Placing Freud in Context: Connecting Personality Theories

Sigmund Freud was one of the greatest minds of modern times. He was the first person to provide a comprehensive theory of personality and personality development, and he did so in what he considered to be a logical and scientific manner. Since he was first, however, how can we place him amongst the other great psychologists? As I contemplated the importance of Freud to the history of psychology, I looked back at my own graduate school training. The textbook assigned for my graduate history of psychology course was *Theories and Systems of Psychology* by Robert Lundin (1979). In the chapter titles, Lundin mentions only three psychologists by name: Wilhelm Wundt, the founder of experimental psychology; William James, America's preeminent psychologist; and Sigmund Freud. Since Freud's name is also mentioned in the title of the chapter devoted to his followers, Freud actually has two chapters devoted to his influence. I also looked at *A History of Psychological Theories* by Ross Stagner (1988), who was an esteemed faculty member in the psychology department at Wayne State University in Detroit and author of one of the first personality textbooks (Stagner, 1937). Stagner mentions six individuals in the titles of his twenty-two chapters, and once again Freud is among them. In addition, the well-known psychological historian Ludy Benjamin includes a chapter on the correspondence between Freud and Jung in *A History of Psychology in Letters* (1993). There are actually numerous books published on the correspondence between Freud and a variety of other people, and thousands of those letters have been published. These are just a few examples of how deeply Freud is recognized as a major figure in the history of psychology.

Another testament to the legacy of Freud is how enduring some of the issues he addressed have proven to be. In the early years of the twenty-first century there has been a growing conflict between religion and society. In the United States the concept of separation of church and state has been challenged perhaps most aggressively in our schools, with issues such as praying at school sporting events and the teaching of creationism in science classes. In other countries, religious fundamentalists often stand in opposition to the establishment of democratic governments. Increasing globalization does not seem to be bringing people together, but rather bringing people into competition and conflict. Freud used the knowledge he had learned in his studies on psychoanalysis to address such major societal issues. He presented his ideas in books such as *The Future of an Illusion* (1927/1961) and *Civilization and its Discontents* (1930/1961), and he hoped that by advancing our knowledge of the human psyche we could help to continue the development of the human species and civilization. The recognition that problems like these still plague humanity suggests that we have a long way to go. But brilliant men like Sigmund Freud have helped to provide us with a basis for moving forward.

Basic Concepts

It is not easy to read the earliest writings of Freud on psychoanalysis. Following his years of working in isolation, Freud published four books in a span of 5 years: *The Interpretation of Dreams* (1900/1995), *Psychopathology of Everyday Life* (1904/1995), *Three Contributions to the Theory of Sex* (1905/1995), and *Wit and Its Relation to the Unconscious* (1905/1995). Each of these books clearly reflects their author: a genius, educated in Europe, and writing in a style well suited to the late 1800s/early 1900s. Not only are these books intellectually challenging, but even the English translations are sprinkled with lines in German, French, and Latin. In 1917, however, Freud published a series of lectures he had given at the University of Vienna during the years 1915-1917. His *Introductory Lectures on Psycho-Analysis* (1917/1966) describes the essential aspects of his theory in neatly organized lectures that are much easier to grasp than his earlier work. Shortly before he died, Freud presented a very brief outline of his theories in the aptly named *An Outline of Psycho-Analysis*

(1938/1949). In what seems to be a logical approach to the study of Freud's work, we will begin with the general theory and then address the psychoanalytic method. Keep in mind, however, that Freud actually worked the other way around: first he developed his modifications of Breuer's cathartic method and began treating patients (actually, treating patients contributed to his development of the methods), and then he developed his theoretical perspectives in order to explain what had already proved successful.

Hysteria and Psychic Determinism

The term **hysteria** generally refers to a condition in which psychological trauma or stress is converted into physical symptoms and/or excessive emotional behavior. Today, this condition is typically referred to as a **conversion disorder** (DSM-V; American Psychiatric Association, 2013). However, Freud meant to use the term in a rather broad sense, and he applied it to a collection of disorders that are not officially recognized today: the **neuroses** (relatively mild mental illnesses, often associated with stress, but which do not result in a loss of contact with reality).

Freud and Breuer (1895/2004) believed that their clinical observations revealed a number of key elements that provided the early framework for **psychodynamic theory** and **psychoanalysis**. In each case, the symptoms exhibited by their patients were connected to some earlier psychological trauma. This connection was not always obvious, however, and often could not be remembered by the patient. When the patient was helped to remember the traumatic event, the symptoms were typically relieved, a process known as **catharsis**. In order to help patients remember, Breuer and Freud (as well as Charcot and a few others) relied primarily on hypnosis. What intrigued Freud and Breuer was the observation that these traumatic memories seemed to last for a very long time without getting weaker, even though they were not conscious memories. What seemed to matter most was whether there had been an energetic reaction to the emotional event when the memory was formed. In order for the trauma to be released, there needed to be a cathartic event strong enough to adequately dissipate the energy associated with the formation of the traumatic memory.

Both Freud and Breuer recognized that this was only the beginning of this new field of clinical research. Although they were somewhat satisfied that they had described the nature of hysterical symptoms, and that they had moved further than Charcot, they recognized that they were no closer to understanding the internal causes of hysteria and the neuroses. This would become the work of Freud alone, at least for a number of years.

The concept of **psychic determinism** arises naturally from these early observations. Freud believed that all behavior and thought is the result of psychological connections created during previous experiences, nothing happens by accident or chance. The fact that we might find it difficult to recognize the connections between some emotion or behavior and a previous incident does nothing to minimize the reality of those connections, it just presents a challenge for the psychoanalyst. In *Psychopathology of Everyday Life*, Freud (1904/1995) described how psychic determinism results in many common problems, certainly the most famous of which is the "**Freudian slip**." A Freudian slip is an instance where someone says something wrong, but it actually reflects the persons true feelings. Freud attributed the following example to Dr. Brill:

> While writing a prescription for a woman who was especially weighed down by the financial burden of the treatment, I was interested to hear her say suddenly: "Please do not give me *big bills*, because I cannot swallow them." Of course, she meant to say *pills*. (italics in the original, pg. 50; Freud, 1904/1995)

Discussion Question: Consider psychic determinism and what it means for your own life. Do you believe that *everything* you think and do is predetermined by earlier experiences? And what would that mean for your ability to change and grow?

Freud's Theory of Instincts

Freud used the term instinct in a way that does not fit with the technical term instinct as defined by Tinbergen (see Beck, 1978). It has been suggested that the German word *trieb* should not have been translated as instinct, and actually referred to something more like a *drive* or *impulse*. Freud was not concerned with specific behaviors, but rather with general categories of behavior. As a former scientist, Freud never left his interests in biology behind. When Freud referred to the psyche, or mind, he considered both its physical elements, the brain and the rest of the nervous system, and its mental elements, primarily our consciousness (which is made possible by the structure and function of the brain). Given our basic biological nature, and our genetic make-up, we inherit basic instincts essential to our survival: both our individual survival and the survival of our species. In recognition of the general rule in nature that all systems are comprised of opposing forces (attraction and repulsion) Freud hypothesized a life instinct and a death instinct.

Freud gave the life instinct the name **Eros**. Each organism has available to it energy to act within its environment. The energy associated with Eros is called **libido**. Libido has been mistakenly associated with the concept of a sexual impulse. What Freud was really referring to was a general survival impulse, both individual and species survival. While it is true that the survival of our species depends on sexual reproduction, there are many aspects of our behavior that are not directly related to sex. For example, we might have many friends, but our sexual interests are typically limited to only a few (it is our culture that encourages us to limit our interests to only one person). From an evolutionary perspective, of course, friends and others within our social group helped to protect us from predators and enemies. Similarly, the love and care we provide for our children are essential to the survival of our species, but are not usually associated with sexual acts. Incest appears to be one of the most common cultural taboos, and Freud found this to be a fascinating observation amongst primitive societies, which could not be expected to know anything of Western ideas of morality (Freud, 1913/1995). So it becomes apparent that the impulse to survive, Eros and its associated libido, involves many types of behavior, of which sexual intimacy is just one.

Libido is limited. We have only so much energy to devote to the many aspects and responsibilities of our lives. **Cathexis** refers to the attachment of libidinal energy to some psychical phenomenon. This is what Freud and Breuer meant by an energetic reaction to some experience. When we are attracted to someone, we connect some of our libidinal energy to that relationship. That energy is no longer available to us for other relationships, or to deal with the daily stress of our lives. If we have previously connected libidinal energy to some traumatic event, which might require a great deal of libidinal energy, it may prove difficult to maintain the level of energy we desire for our new relationship. As a result, that relationship, indeed all of our relationships, may suffer.

Although the libido is limited, it has the important characteristic of mobility (Freud, 1938/1949). In other words, it can switch from one task to another as necessary. At least, that is how it is supposed to work under normal conditions. Sometimes, however, problems arise, such as the failure to satisfy the needs that occur during a particular **psychosexual stage of development** (see below). When this occurs, the libido can become **fixated** on particular psychological objects. These fixations can last a lifetime, interfering with continued normal development and the individual's ability to live a healthy adult life.

Freud also proposed a destructive instinct, which is sometimes referred to as the death instinct. The energy associated with the death instinct is aggressive, but Freud never gave names to either the death instinct or its associated aggressive energy. This was never an important aspect of Freud's theories, but he did address it in some detail in the book *Beyond the Pleasure Principle* (Freud, 1920/1961). In this book, Freud makes one thing very clear: the life instinct is far more influential than the death instinct. The primary role of the death instinct is protective. This may sound strange, but he considered the developing organism, even well before birth, as a fragile being assailed on all sides by threatening stimuli (both external stimuli and internal psychical stimuli). The death instinct creates a shell of inert tissue (figuratively, if not also literally), which protects the developing organism from harm.

Although Freud did not include the death instinct among his major concepts, other psychologists have. The **neo-Freudian** theorist Melanie Klein found evidence of the death instinct in the aggressive fantasies of children, and Wilhelm Reich's concept of armoring is reminiscent of Freud's description of the theoretical shell protecting the developing organism. Regarding aggression itself, there are many different forms, including predatory aggression, self-defense, defense of one's young, learned aggression, etc. The noted animal behaviorist and Nobel Laureate Konrad Lorenz wrote extensively on aggression, and he proposed a very Freudian perspective in which instinctive aggressive energy builds up and lashes out, unless an opportunity for catharsis arises first (see Beck, 1978).

At first it might seem strange that Freud suggested the role of the death instinct is to create a protective shell around the core of the developing nervous system, but the important question is whether we can find any evidence of it. Daniel Goleman, in *Emotional Intelligence* (1995), suggests a similar theory. The primitive role of emotion is evident in the brain regions devoted to emotion, which are common to many species other than humans. As the mammalian brain evolved, structures were added to the reptilian brain, culminating in the neocortex of the cerebral hemispheres. The cerebral hemispheres are necessary for the cognitive functions that are characteristic of humans. Still, we retain the emotional structures that developed first, and our rational thoughts can easily be hijacked by emotional reactions (Goleman, 1995, 1998). Perhaps the most important brain region involved in the processing of emotional information is the **amygdala**. Jerome Kagan has suggested that if the amygdala is overly sensitive a child will avoid external stimuli, leading to a life of shyness, and vice versa (cited in Goleman, 1995). The development of brain structures that process emotion and allow for cognitive processing well beyond the primitive and most basic emotions sounds very much like what Freud had proposed regarding the role of the death instinct. This is not to suggest that either the amygdala or some portion of the neocortex is the anatomical location of the death instinct, but the evidence that such functions exist within the brain lends support to Freud's concept. According to Goleman, the ability to work with emotional intelligence is essential to one's well-being in life, and fortunately emotional intelligence can be trained and strengthened (Goleman, 1995, 1998).

Discussion Question: Compare Freud's concept of a life instinct and a death instinct, and consider the choices you make in life. Do you make choices that provide an opportunity to grow and change, or do you get caught up in pointless, even self-defeating, activities? If you make bad choices, where do you think those choices come from?

The Development of Libido and Psychosexual Function

Freud's most controversial theories related to sexual function and its role in personality development. Even more controversial than that initial statement was his suggestion that the sexual life of every person begins at birth. It is important, of course, to remember that Freud did not mean intimate sexual behavior when he talked about sexual impulses, but rather a general life impulse. He made an important distinction between "sexual" and "genital." By sexual he was referring to a wider concept of obtaining pleasure from different regions of the body, whereas genital refers to the act of reproduction, which comes into play following puberty.

Freud was well aware of this controversy during the early days of psychoanalysis, and many of his books make a special point of defending the theory of infantile sexuality. As mentioned in the biography, he actually attributed the initial observations of the role of sexuality in the development of neuroses to Breuer, Charcot, and Chrobak (Freud, 1914/1995). As he reflected on the history of psychoanalysis, Freud described how he and others before him had not intended to address infantile sexuality, but it proved unavoidable after extensive experience with psychoanalysis. In other words, Freud kept encountering infantile sexuality, and eventually he concluded that it was both universal and far too important to ignore. Therefore, he felt he could not allow old prejudices against recognizing or discussing the relevance of sexuality to interfere with the development of psychoanalysis (see Freud, 1938/1949).

Freud also defended his theory of sexuality in logical ways. In his initial work on this topic, *Three Contributions to the Theory of Sex* (1905/1995), Freud specifically argued against the prevailing views that sexuality develops at puberty for the purpose of attracting a man and a woman to each other for the ultimate purpose of reproduction. He noted that there are individuals who are attracted to members of their own sex, that there are those who engage in sexual acts that disregard the genitalia (e.g., fetishes), and there are undeniable examples of children who become interested in their genitalia and obtain some excitation from them. Finally, in his *Introductory Lectures...* (Freud, 1917/1966) he declared his position quite clearly:

> To suppose that children have no sexual life – sexual excitations and needs and a kind of satisfaction – but suddenly acquire it between the ages of twelve and fourteen, would (quite apart from any observations) be as improbable, and indeed senseless, biologically as to suppose that they brought no genitals with them into the world and only grew them at the time of puberty. (pg. 385).

Levels of Consciousness

From the very beginning of psychoanalysis, Freud and Breuer (1895/2004) recognized that their patients were often unaware of the connections between their symptoms and earlier traumatic events, and they might not even recall the events themselves. And yet, as described above, the memory of those events remained strong. How can a memory be strong but not remembered? The answer lies in the theory that there are different levels of consciousness. Freud described three levels of consciousness: the **conscious**, the **preconscious**, and the **unconscious**.

The conscious mind is our awareness, the knowledge that we exist and are alive. As you read this book you are conscious of it, when you talk to a friend you are aware of what they are saying and how you will respond (unless, of course, you respond with a Freudian slip!). Although the conscious mind is usually identified with our personality, and Freud recognized that people viewed consciousness as nothing more or less than the defining characteristic of the mind, his clinical experience with psychoanalysis made it impossible for him to accept the identification of the conscious mind with the mental mind (Freud, 1917/1966).

The unconscious mind, according to Freud, is the true psychic reality, and all conscious thought has a preliminary unconscious stage. And yet, the unconscious mind is truly inaccessible. In *The Interpretation of Dreams* (1900/1995), Freud wrote about the unconscious mind that:

> …in its inner nature it is just as much unknown to us as the reality of the external world, and it is just as imperfectly communicated to us by the data of consciousness as is the external world by the reports of our sense-organs. (pg. 510)

How then does the unconscious mind affect our personality? Between the unconscious and conscious minds there is an intermediary: the preconscious. Technically, the preconscious mind is part of the unconscious, but only through the preconscious mind can the impulses arising in the unconscious enter into our conscious awareness. Freud distinguished between the two by theorizing that the unconscious cannot enter into consciousness, but if certain rules are followed, the preconscious can enter into consciousness (but perhaps only after being censored; Freud, 1900/1995).

Freud also made two important points regarding these levels of the mind. First, the unconscious, preconscious, and conscious minds are not located in different regions of the brain. Instead, the level of consciousness of any particular psychical phenomenon depends on the cathexis of libidinal energy (or perhaps energy related to the death instinct) and repression (see *Anxiety* and *Defense Mechanisms* below). If the memory of a traumatic event is significantly repressed, it will remain in the unconscious, if not, it may enter into consciousness through the preconscious. Yet it has remained the same memory within the same memory structure of the brain. Freud also distinguished between the mind and reality, particularly between the unconscious mind and reality. He did, however, remind his readers that they would do well to remember that psychic reality is a special form of existence, though not to be confused with material reality (Freud, 1900/1995).

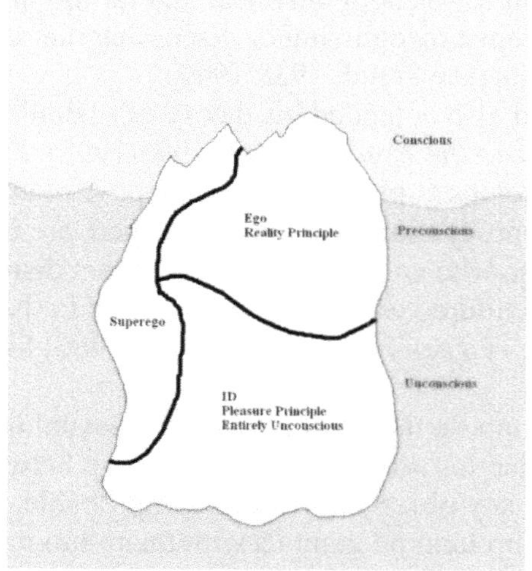

The levels of consciousness and the structures of the mind, as proposed by Freud. The iceberg analogy should actually be attributed to Theodor Lipps, whose work on the unconscious mind and humor was cited extensively in Freud's early books. [Image by Mark Kelland]

Structure of Personality

It is no accident that our discussion of the **id**, **ego**, and **superego** follow immediately after our discussion of the levels of consciousness. In *The Ego and the Id* (which also discuss the superego, despite not including it in the title; Freud, 1923/1960), Freud begins with a chapter on consciousness and what is unconscious, then follows with a chapter on the ego and the id, and then a chapter on the ego and the superego. It is difficult to discuss the two concepts, levels of consciousness and the **psychical apparatus** (a term Freud used for the id, ego, and superego), without intertwining them. In addition, these three structures begin as one, the ego develops from the id, and later the superego develops from the ego. As with levels of consciousness, it is inappropriate to think of the id, ego, and superego as actual structures within the brain, rather they are **constructs** to help us understand the psychodynamic functioning of the mind. Freud acknowledged this lack of understanding, and went so far as to say that even if we could localize them within the brain we wouldn't necessarily be any closer to understanding how they function (Freud, 1938/1949).

Id, Ego, Superego

The oldest aspect of the psyche is the id, which includes all that we inherit at birth, including our temperament and our instincts. The only goal of the id is to satisfy instinctual needs and desires; therefore, it acts according to the **pleasure principle**. It knows nothing of value judgments, no good, no evil, and no morality at all. It does not change or mature over time. According to Freud, there is nothing in the id except instinctual cathexes seeking discharge (Freud, 1933/1965). The energy associated with these impulses, however, is different from other regions of the mind. It is highly mobile and capable of discharge, and the quality of the discharge seems to be disregarded. This is a very important point, because it means that the id does not need to satisfy its desires in reality. Instead, they can be satisfied through dreams and fantasy.

Because the id demands satisfaction, and knows nothing of restraint, it is said to operate as a **primary process**. Since it can be satisfied in unreal ways, if we examine phenomena such as fantasies and dreams we can uncover the nature of the id. It was during his studies on dream-work that Freud developed his understanding of the primary process of the id (Freud, 1923/1960). Actually, we can only know the id through psychoanalysis, since it exists entirely within the unconscious mind. Therefore, we need a **secondary process** structure in order for the mind to interact with the external world. This structure is found in the ego.

The ego arises from the id as an intermediary between the id and the external world. The ego functions according to the **reality principle**, and tries to bring the external world to bear on the impulses of the id. In other words, as the id demands satisfaction it is hindered by the reality of our environment, our societal and cultural norms. The ego postpones satisfaction until the time or the circumstances are appropriate, or it may suppress the id impulses altogether (Freud, 1938/1949). Freud believed that the ego is associated with perception (of reality), in the same way that the id is associated with instinct. The id is passionate, whereas the ego represents reason and common sense. But the id has the energy, the libido, to demand its satisfaction in some way, and the ego can only derive its energy from the id. Freud likened the ego to a horseback rider on a horse named id. The rider cannot always control the far more powerful horse, so the rider attempts to transform the will of the horse as if it were the rider's own will (Freud, 1923/1960).

The ego develops in part because it is that portion of the mind impacted by sensory input from the external world. Therefore, it resides partially in the conscious mind, and must serve three tyrannical masters: the id, the external world, and the superego (which we will discuss below). The goals of these three masters are typically at odds with one another, and so the ego's task is not an easy one (Freud, 1933/1965). The ego approaches this task by monitoring the **tension** that exists within the mind. This tension arises from internal and external stimuli making demands upon the mind, lowering this tension is felt as pleasurable, and increasing the tension is unpleasant. The id demands immediate reduction of tension, in accordance with its pleasure principle, whereas the ego seeks an appropriate reduction of tension, in accordance with its reality principle. A key point, of course, is that the ego also seeks pleasure. It does not try to deny the impulses of the id, only to transform or delay them. But why does the ego even bother to do that? There are times when pursuing pleasure can get us in serious trouble, but there are also times when we make choices because they seem right to us. These decisions, based on justice, morality, humanism, whatever term you choose, are mediated by the superego.

According to Freud, the superego is heir to the **Oedipus complex** (which we will discuss below), and arises as the child abandons their intense attachment to their parents. As a replacement for that attachment, the child begins to identify with their parents, and so incorporates the ideals and moral values of their parents and, later, teachers and other societal role models (Freud, 1933/1965). According to this view, the superego cannot fully develop if the child does not resolve the Oedipus complex, which, as we will discuss below, cannot happen for girls (Note: In addition to further discussion below, the issue of a more balanced female psychology will be discussed again in later chapters). The superego functions across all levels of the conscious and unconscious mind.

The superego takes two forms: an **ego-ideal** and a **conscience**. Freud considered the term ego-ideal as an alternative to the term superego, and it is not until we incorporate the development of conscience that we can recognize ego-ideal and conscience as different aspects of the superego. Indeed, it might be more appropriate, if one reads *The Ego and the Id* carefully (Freud, 1923/1960), to consider the ego-ideal and conscience as consecutive transformations of that portion of the ego that becomes known in general as the superego. The development of the superego is a complicated process, and seems to derive from the development of the ego itself. For an infant, the attachment to the parents and identification with them is not recognized as something different. The ego is weak, and can do little to restrain the id. As the child grows, the erotic nature of the love for the mother is slowly transformed into identification; the ego grows stronger, and begins to become associated with being a love-object itself. When the ego is capable of presenting itself to the id as an object worthy of love, narcissistic libido is generated and the ego becomes fully formed (Freud, 1923/1960). In other words, the child becomes an individual, aware that they are separate from their parents. There is still an intense attachment to the mother, however, which stems from the early days of breast feeding. The child must eventually lose this intense attachment to the mother, and begin to more fully identify with either the father (for boys) or the mother (for girls). As noted above, this final transformation from attachment to identification should occur during the Oedipus complex, and the ego-ideal arises within the context of the child knowing "I should act like my father" (for boys) or "I should act like my mother" (for girls).

Although the ego-ideal could represent the culmination of development, Freud believed that one more step came into play. Because of the difficulty the child encounters during the loss of the intense, erotic desires of the Oedipus complex, Freud felt there was more than simply a residue of those love-objects in the mind. He proposed an energetic **reaction-formation** against the earlier choices. Now, the child incorporates concepts of "I must *not* act like my father or mother." Under the influences of authority, schooling, religion, etc., the superego develops an ever stronger conscience against inappropriate behavior. This conscience has a compulsive character and takes the form of a categorical imperative (Freud, 1923/1960). This conscience is our knowledge of right and wrong, and early on it is quite simplistic. There is right and there is wrong (as with Kohlberg's earliest stages of moral development; Kohlberg, 1963).

Discussion Question: Do you feel that your behavior is being driven by the unconscious impulses of the id? Do you believe that your moral development (your superego) is the result of internalizing your parent's views of what is right or wrong? How close are your values to those of your parents?

Anxiety

We have already taken a look at the challenge faced by the ego in trying to balance the demands of the id, the superego, and the external world. What happens when the demands of these conflicting elements become too much for the ego to deal with? Simply put, we get scared, we experience fear and **anxiety** as a signal that there is some impending danger. Only the ego can experience anxiety, even if the underlying cause begins with the id or superego. Anxiety arises primarily from libido that has not been utilized. For example, if we are frustrated from fulfilling some id impulse, such as needing to go to the bathroom in the middle of a great movie, the libido cathexed to that impulse grows. This creates tension and the corresponding unpleasant feelings. As the id demands satisfaction, but the ego cannot figure out how to satisfy the id (and you really don't want to miss the good part of the movie), the fear arises that the id will satisfy itself. Most of us would consider the possibility of going to the bathroom in our pants while at a movie a real danger to our self-esteem, and we could be arrested if we simply went to the bathroom right there in the movie theater. As the ego is reduced to helplessness in its inability to find a reasonable outlet for the impulse of needing to go to the bathroom, anxiety serves the useful and important purpose of warning the ego that the impulse *must* be satisfied in order to avoid the danger (Freud, 1926/1959). And in support of Freud's view regarding our sexual nature, who would deny the great pleasure felt upon finally getting to the bathroom?

Freud described three general types of anxiety. Realistic anxiety involves actual threats to our physical safety. It is similar to fear, in that there is a real and external object that could harm us, but it differs from fear in that we may not be aware of a specific danger. For example, after the famous book *Jaws* (Benchley, 1974) was made into a movie (the kind of movie that you don't want to miss the good scenes) many people became anxious about swimming in the ocean, even though there were no specific sharks for them to fear. Still, there are sharks in the ocean, so it might be reasonable to experience some anxiety. Sometimes we are anxious about a real danger, but the anxiety we experience is completely out of proportion in relation to the threat. This suggests that there is an element of neurotic anxiety accompanying the realistic anxiety (Freud, 1926/1959).

Neurotic anxiety generally arises from an internal danger, the threat that unacceptable id impulses will break through and be acted on by the individual. The ultimate danger that exists is that we really will be harmed as a result of our actions. Therefore, Freud considered there to be a close association between neurotic and realistic anxiety (Freud, 1926/1959). For example, if we are being harassed by a bully, our aggressive id impulse might be to respond by killing this bully. Of course, that could result in going to prison or having the bully's friends kill us. So the anxiety that our violent id impulse might break out and influence our behavior is associated with the real danger posed by the consequences of that behavior, if it should happen to occur. Therefore, our neurotic anxiety is composed, in part, of our internalized realistic anxiety.

In a similar way, moral anxiety arises from conflict between our ego and the constraints imposed on it by the superego. Since the superego arises from the internalization of our parent's teaching us what is or is not appropriate behavior, we again have an association between the internal threat of the superego and the real, external threat of being punished by our parents. Therefore, as with neurotic anxiety, the precursor to our moral anxiety is realistic anxiety, even if our fears are based on our psychological impressions of a situation as opposed to an actual danger (e.g., the fear of castration; Freud, 1926/1959, 1933/1965). Freud (1933/1965) described the relationships this way:

> Thus the ego, driven by the id, confined by the super-ego, repulsed by reality, struggles to master its economic task of bringing about harmony among the forces and influences working in and upon it; and we can understand how it is that so often we cannot suppress a cry: 'Life is not easy!' If the ego is obliged to admit its weakness, it breaks out in anxiety – realistic anxiety regarding the external world, moral anxiety regarding the super-ego and neurotic anxiety regarding the strength of the passions in the id. (pgs. 97-98)

Freud also described an overall pattern to the development and expression of anxiety and its useful role in life. In early childhood we experience traumatic situations in which we are helpless. Remember that Freud believed that psychic reality is every bit as significant as actual reality (Freud, 1900/1995), so the nature of these traumatic events is subject to individual perception. As the child's capacity for self-preservation develops, the child learns to recognize dangerous situations. Rather than waiting passively to be threatened or harmed, an older child or an adult will respond actively. The initial response is anxiety, but anxiety is a warning of danger in anticipation of experiencing helplessness once again. In a sense, the ego is recreating to the helplessness of infancy, but it does so in the hope that now the ego will have at its command some means of dealing with the situation. Therefore, anxiety has hopefully transformed from a passive response in infancy to an active and protective response in later childhood and/or adulthood (Freud, 1926/1959).

Discussion Question: What makes you anxious, and how do you respond to those feelings?

Defense Mechanisms

We will cover **defense mechanisms** only briefly in this chapter. Although Freud talked about a wide variety of defense mechanisms during his career, he left it to his daughter Anna to literally write the book on *The Ego and the Mechanisms of Defense* (Anna Freud, 1936/1966). Freud himself discussed primarily two defense mechanisms: **repression** and **regression**. The recognition of these defense mechanisms was essential to the development of psychoanalysis, and they are the only two defenses mentioned by Freud in *The History of the Psychoanalytic Movement* (1914/1995). The purpose of these defense mechanisms is to protect the ego during the early years of life, when the ego has not adequately developed in its ability to control the libidinal impulses of the id. Thus, defense mechanisms serve a useful function at first, but later prove inadequate when the re-animation of the sexual life is reinforced following puberty (Freud, 1938/1949). Similarly, in adult life, defense mechanisms are useful in the short-term, but since they do not deal with problems directly they must eventually prove inadequate.

Freud identified repression as one of the key elements establishing psychoanalysis as unique from the cathartic method he had been working on thanks to the contributions of Josef Breuer (Freud, 1914/1995). Indeed, according to Freud, his own contributions that transformed Breuer's cathartic method into psychoanalysis were repression, **resistance**, infantile sexuality, and dream analysis for the understanding of the unconscious mind. The value of repression cannot be underestimated:

> The theory of repression is the pillar upon which the edifice of psychoanalysis rests. It is really the most essential part of it, and yet, it is nothing but the theoretical expression of an experience which can be repeatedly observed whenever one analyses a neurotic without the aid of hypnosis. One is then confronted with a resistance which opposes and blocks the analytic work by causing failures of memory. This resistance was always covered by the use of hypnosis; the history of psychoanalysis proper, therefore, starts with the technical innovation of the rejections of hypnosis. (pg. 907; Freud, 1914/1995)

The resistance Freud is referring to here is the defense mechanism of repression, which is the means by which the ego refuses to associate itself with an unacceptable instinctual impulse generated by the id. The ego is able to keep the "reprehensible" impulse from entering into the conscious mind (Freud, 1926/1959). But an important question arises: What then happens to this impulse seeking satisfaction? There are several possibilities, and Freud himself considered the answer to be rather complex. One thing that might happen is that the ego attempts to shift the libido cathexed to the impulse toward release as anxiety (Freud, 1926/1959). However, anxiety is unpleasant, and the id demands satisfaction in accordance with its pleasure principle. Therefore, this procedure is doomed to failure (and, therefore, the development of neurosis). There are, of course, alternatives that can occur prior to the failure of this initial defense. The ego may find some acceptable alternative to the impulse through the other defense mechanisms, such as **sublimation** or reaction-formation.

Regression can be seen when an individual engages in behavior typical of an earlier stage of development. As Freud and Breuer tried to work out the causes of their patient's neuroses by using the cathartic method, they repeatedly found that they could not help their patients by focusing on the actual event that had led to a crisis. Instead, their patients inevitably made associations between the traumatic event and earlier experiences. Initially, these earlier experiences went back to puberty, and ultimately they went back to early childhood. Although Breuer favored some physiological explanation of this phenomenon, Freud insisted that it was psychological, and he termed the process regression (Freud, 1914/1995). According to Freud:

> This regressive direction became an important characteristic of the analysis. It was proved that psychoanalysis could not clear up anything actual, except by going back to something in the past. (pg. 903)

Psychosexual Stages of Development

Above, we examined the basic development of libido and psychosexual function. Freud also believed that psychosexual function developed in a series of stages that occur in two waves. The first three stages occur during early childhood, from infancy to about the age of 5. Freud referred to this early period as the **pregenital phase** (Freud, 1905/1995). There is then a **latency period**, which lasts until puberty, after which the final stage, the **genital stage**, is realized and the individual is capable of physically mature reproductive functioning. These stages are typically presented as if they are exclusive and sequential. Although it is true that they are sequential, they are not entirely exclusive. Therefore, it is possible for the stages to overlap (Freud, 1938/1949). However, it remains true that during a particular stage one region of the body will be dominant, and most of the libido will be focused on that region (see Jarvis, 2004). For the sake of simplicity, we will treat the stages as if they occur one after another.

Sigmund Freud

The Psychosexual Stages

The first phase of psychosexual development begins at infancy with the **oral stage**. According to Freud, the mouth is the first region of the body to become an **erotogenic zone**, and this lasts for approximately the first year of life. During this time the mouth makes libidinal demands on the mind. In other words, the region of the mouth demands that the mind direct adequate libidinal energy to satisfy the desires of the oral region. Although this serves the purpose of sustaining the infant by satisfying its nutritional needs, Freud believed that the infant's persistent sucking belied a need for satisfaction that was far greater than simply taking care of physiological needs. He believed that the infant needed to satisfy its desire for psychological pleasure independent of nourishment, and this was the basis for arguing that the behavior was sexual (in the larger, life-oriented perspective on sexuality).

Evidence for this stage is easy to see, and such commonplace observances contributed to Freud's thinking. Infants suck almost continuously, even when not being fed. They suck their thumbs, they can be comforted with pacifiers, as they become older they put everything they can get their hands on into their mouths. If they cannot satisfy this need, they may become fixated in the oral stage. As a result of this oral fixation, when an older child or adult becomes frustrated or overwhelmed, they may regress and engage in oral behavior. This occurs because the fixation of libido on the oral region during infancy results in a deficiency of the libidinal energy needed to cope with some stressful period of adulthood. This oral behavior can take many forms, such as: overeating, smoking, drinking too much (of course, this usually refers to drinking alcoholic beverages), or just talking excessively.

During the second stage of psychosexual development, the **anal stage**, the anus becomes the focus of the libido, and the child derives pleasure from the ability to both retain and expel feces. Initially, the pleasure associated with evacuating the bowels is felt within the child, something Freud referred to as the **autoerotic** nature of sexual development (Freud, 1917/1966). Soon, however, the child learns that the world can be an inhibiting place, that greater pleasure can be derived only if the child defecates when and where others consider it to be appropriate. This realization occurs as a result of the most significant parent-child interaction during this stage of development: toilet training. If the parents are either too strict or begin too early the child may develop the traits of an anal character (Jarvis, 2004). These traits include excessive orderliness, stubbornness, and parsimony, each of which results from denial of the child's anal pleasure during toilet training. Orderliness, or tidiness, serves as a denial of taking pleasure in defecating, and stubbornness carries over from the child's assertion of their right to defecate at will (Jarvis, 2004). Parsimony, or being stingy, stems from the child's association of the feces with money. According to Freud (1917/1966):

> He feels no disgust at his feces, values them as a portion of his own body with which he will not readily part, and makes use of them as his first 'gift,' to distinguish people whom he values especially highly. (pg. 390)

Freud was by no means unaware of how strange this part of his theory seemed. Immediately following the above quote, he went on to say the following, and remember that his *Introductory Lectures on Psycho-analysis* were actual lectures delivered to students at the University of Vienna:

> I know you have been wanting for a long time to interrupt me and exclaim: 'Enough of these atrocities! You tell us that defecating is a source of sexual satisfaction, and already exploited in infancy! That feces are a valuable substance and that the anus is a kind of genital! We don't believe all that…' No, Gentlemen. You have merely forgotten that I have been trying to introduce the facts of infantile sexual life to you in connection with the facts … that for a large number of adults, homosexual and heterosexual alike, the anus does really take over the role of the vagina in sexual intercourse? (pg. 391)

So Freud was simply trying to address very real issues that he, and others, had observed in their clinical practices. His years of working in isolation had prepared him for dealing with disapproval, and he was not going to be shy about studying things that might make others uncomfortable.

The **phallic stage**, in which the libido focuses on the genitalia, represents the culmination of infantile sexuality. Although it typically occurs between the ages of 3 to 5 years old, it sets the stage for adult sexuality.

Therefore, it is a very important period. According to Freud (1905/1995), this stage will "leave behind the profoundest (unconscious) impressions in the person's memory; if the individual remains healthy they determine his character and if he becomes sick after puberty, they determine the symptomatology of his neurosis." There are two critical aspects of this stage: the first involves the **castration complex** and **penis envy**, and the second is the Oedipus complex. Technically, the Oedipus complex subsumes castration anxiety, but it is important to consider these aspects separately. In *Three Contributions to the Theory of Sex* (Freud, 1905/1995), the book that obviously focuses on the sexual aspects of psychoanalysis, Freud discussed the castration complex and penis envy, but not the Oedipus complex. Although he discussed the Oedipus legend in his earlier books, he did not use the term Oedipus complex until 1910 (see Jarvis, 2004). The other reason for considering the major aspects of this stage separately is the difference between boys and girls. Penis envy is obviously something that only girls can experience and, according to Freud, the Oedipus complex is something that only boys can experience. Girls experience something similar to the Oedipus complex, but their efforts are in vain, and this has a permanent, negative effect on their character (Freud, 1938/1949). For more discussion on the latter point, see the section below on Freud's perspective on the female psyche.

As we begin to address the castration complex and penis envy, it is important to realize that Freud's phallic stage is entirely focused on the penis, for both boys and girls. As the libido becomes focused on the genitals, a boy begins to manipulate his penis. He experiences no shame, and even enjoys displaying his body (Freud, 1905/1995). As a counterpart to this joy in his own sexuality, children are often curious about seeing other children's bodies. This creates a very different experience for boys and girls. When boys see a girl's body, they believe the absence of a penis means that the girl has been castrated. This leads to a fear of the same thing happening to them, and creates castration anxiety, which in adulthood can lead to a castration complex. When girls see a boy's body they are fully prepared to recognize the penis, and they become envious of it. Indeed, this envy can become strong enough that the girl wishes she was a boy (Freud, 1905/1995). Since she cannot be a boy, she begins to seek an alternative, either her father or a child of her own.

As Freud continued to develop his theory of the phallic stage, he included a broader perspective beyond the castration complex: the Oedipus complex. A boy's first love object is his mother, the one who feeds him and attends to all of his needs. This is only natural. As his libido becomes focused on his genitalia, however, this takes on the sexual desire that became so controversial. Keeping in mind that Freud did not believe that children understand the adult reality of their desires (much of it is unconscious), he described their behaviors as obvious evidence of their desire: boys talk about loving and marrying their mother, they persistently pursue being in her presence when she is dressing, they want to be in bed with her at night, etc. (Freud, 1917/1966). This eventually leads to conflict with the father, and with it the castration anxiety described above. Since there is no satisfactory resolution, given that the father is much more powerful than the child, the boy is compelled to give up the Oedipus complex, to repress it. In the healthiest condition, the Oedipus complex is completely destroyed in the id, and gives rise to a severe superego (Freud, 1933/1965). This repression, or destruction, of the Oedipus complex allows the boy to transition into the latency period.

It seems only natural that a boy's first love would be his mother. [Image by Jordan Whitt]

For girls, the Oedipus complex takes a very different course. A girl's first love object is also her mother, since again it is the mother who provides most of the childcare. Once the girl realizes that she does not have a penis she develops penis envy, and she must undertake a change in her love object to her father, the one who can provide her with the desired penis. The mother is then seen as a rival for the father's penis, and indeed as someone who has already received all that the girl wants from her father. This can intensify feelings of hostility toward the mother. Consequently, she may enter into the Oedipus complex feeling that it is a refuge or safe haven. However, the girl does not fear castration, since she has no penis to begin with, and without the fear of castration leading to repression of the Oedipus complex there is no motivation for the girl to move into the latency period (Freud, 1933/1965). Freud believed that girls remain in the Oedipus complex, and thus the phallic stage, for an indeterminate period of time, and that they cannot ever completely resolve it. Adding one more point of controversy, the only way in which girls can shift from an initially masculine situation (the mother as love object) to a feminine situation (the father as love object) is if they replace their penis envy with the desire for a child, given the ancient symbolic equivalence between the penis and giving birth (Freud, 1933/1965).

Following the oral, anal, and phallic stages there is a period of latency, during which progress is at a standstill. There are, however, some interesting things that happen during this period. The child knows that they are still incapable of procreation (even though this knowledge may be unconscious), so they begin to turn away from their sexual desires. They begin to view sexual impulses with disgust and shame, and to consider them immoral (Freud, 1905/1995). Although their education has much to do with this, Freud believed that it is also a natural occurrence. To compensate, the child (or the child's mind, as this again may be entirely unconscious) engages the defense mechanism of sublimation: the conversion of the unacceptable sexual impulses into activities that are socially acceptable (such as school work or sports). Another important consequence of this mental activity is that we forget our infantile sexual impulses, something Freud called **infantile amnesia**. Infantile amnesia is critical to the whole theory of the development of neuroses and the technique of psychoanalysis (Freud, 1938/1949), and it is one of the main reasons that many adults insist upon denying the possibility of infantile sexuality in the first place.

With the onset of puberty, the individual enters the final stage of psychosexual development: the genital stage. If the challenges of the earlier stages have been resolved in a satisfactory way, the individual is finally capable of appropriate and mature intimacy and sexual behavior. All of the psychodynamic processing that has taken place is not gone, however. According to Freud (1938/1949), even normal people have some of the following factors included in their final psychosexual organization: some libidinal cathexes are retained, others are taken into sexual activity as preliminary acts (such as foreplay), and still others are excluded from the organization either by repression or sublimation.

Freud's Perspective on the Female Psyche

I would like to begin this section by being fair to Freud. First and foremost, there were no other theories on the development of personality for Freud to consider as he developed his own theory. Second, most of the patients Freud saw were women, and apparently he needed to explain how it was that so many of his patients were women and not men. There were certainly other possible explanations than those offered by Freud, but it has been easy for others to look back and criticize him with the benefit of new and different ideas. One must also keep in mind that Freud was a basic scientist for many years, and he put a lot of emphasis on details. It is an undeniable, biological fact that men are male and women are female! Freud believed that psychology could never truly understand sex and gender differences unless we could understand why so many species exists as two different sexes in the first place (Freud, 1933/1965). Nonetheless, having acknowledged this, Freud's theory does, unfortunately, describe women as the products of an incomplete and frustrated male development.

Freud believed that the development of the feminine psyche was more difficult and complicated than that of the masculine psyche for two main reasons, neither of which is faced by boys during their development. Initially, there are basic biological differences, both anatomically and in terms of temperament. Girls are typically less aggressive, defiant, and self-sufficient; they also seem to have a greater need for affection, and as a result become more dependent and pliant. However, Freud disregarded these differences, feeling that they were insignificant compared to individual differences between boys and girls (Freud, 1933/1965). Through much of the first wave of infantile sexuality, particularly the oral and anal stages, there is no difference between boys and girls. Even during the early portion of the phallic stage there is no difference between the sensations boys experience via the penis and the sensations girls experience via the clitoris. The first difference, however, arises from the need for girls to shift the focus of their libido from the clitoris to the vagina, particularly with regard to the importance of the latter for sexual activity leading to procreation. The second difference is the need for the girl to shift the focus of her libido from the mother to the father as she enters the Oedipus complex. This shift in the love object is not easy, and the outcome is not pleasant.

Freud proposed that the young girl's attraction to her father at the beginning of the Oedipus complex is not simply a shift in the libido, but involves a rejection of the mother who had been the previous love object. The girl's rejection of her mother is accompanied by hostility, and can end in hate. The hate can be profound and last the girl's entire life, even if it is carefully compensated for later in life (Freud, 1933/1965). The reason for this hostility toward the mother arises from the castration complex and penis envy. Whereas a boy fears being castrated, the girl believes that she already has been, and the mother is responsible. The girl then develops an overwhelming desire to have a penis, the so-called penis envy, but it simply cannot be. Even when a girl is old enough to understand the basic biology of sex differences, she still retains an unconscious feeling of having been wronged and a considerable cathexis of libido remains (Freud, 1933/1965). It is interesting to note that Freud acknowledges that it is difficult to see these processes in action if one simply observes young girls. However, in his clinical practice he saw patients whose neuroses amplified these processes, and following psychoanalysis the underlying basis of this developmental stage seemed evident to Freud.

Table 3.1: A Summary of the Psychosexual Stages

Stage	Approximate Age Range	Essential Elements
Oral Stage	Birth through the first year	The mouth is the source of erotic pleasure; this helps to obtain nourishment, but babies also put everything else they get their hand on into their mouths
Anal Stage	From age 1 to 3 years old	The anus is the source of erotic pleasure; toilet training is the major task of this stage (and as any parent can tell you, a most interesting experience!)
Phallic Stage	From age 3 to 5 years old	The genitals are the source of erotic pleasure; boys may fear castration, girls develop penis envy; boys resolve the Oedipus complex due to the motivation provided by their castration anxiety; since girls are not motivated by castration anxiety, they lack the motivation to completely resolve the Oedipus complex
Latency Period	From age 6 to puberty	At the beginning of this period infantile amnesia hides our earlier experiences from us; recovering them is the major task of psychoanalysis
Genital Stage	From puberty throughout adulthood	If the earlier stages were resolved successfully, then normal adult life proceeds; if not, a neurosis may develop; according to Freud, women cannot resolve the Oedipus complex, so they must have some psychological deficiencies relative to men

How then is a girl to resolve the Oedipus complex and achieve a healthy, adult personality? As described above, she can't! In Freud's own words:

> The girl, after vainly attempting to do the same as the boy, comes to recognize her lack of a penis or rather the inferiority of her clitoris, with permanent effects on the development of her character; as a result of this first disappointment in rivalry, she often begins by turning away altogether from sexual life. (pg. 26; Freud, 1938/1949)
>
> In these circumstances the formation of the superego must suffer; it cannot attain the strength and independence which give it its cultural significance, and feminists are not pleased when we point out to them the effects of this factor upon the average feminine character. (pgs. 160-161; Freud, 1933/1965).

Another important observation that came to Freud in his early psychoanalytic practice was the recognition that almost all of his female patients reported having been seduced by their fathers (which, if true, is an inaccurate way of saying they were sexually assaulted by a child molester). This led Freud to propose a **seduction theory**, which was the basis for first proposing the role of sexual trauma in the development of neuroses. This sexual trauma did not have to be as severe as rape, but it was considered significant nonetheless (see Jarvis, 2004). Later, however, Freud came to the conclusion that these seductions occurred only in the fantasies of the young girls. Indeed, Freud described the fantasy of a young girl being seduced by her father as the typical expression of the Oedipus complex in women (Freud, 1933/1965). Freud was criticized for theorizing that young girls fantasized about being seduced by their fathers, and Breuer ended his pursuit of understanding sexual trauma when faced with the same conclusion (Freud, 1914/1995). Today, however, Freud is criticized more for having turned away from what may have been his most startling discovery, the prevalence of sexual abuse (see Jarvis, 2004).

Connections Across Cultures: Male/Female Differences

We don't normally think of men and women as being different cultures, but this has become a more popular approach to understanding their differences (e.g., see Brislin, 2000; Ferraro, 2006a; Haviland, 2005; Matlin, 2004). As we consider gender differences it is, of course, important to avoid stereotyping individuals. Nonetheless, the reality of cultural expectations related to sex and gender, some of which have a basis in the development of the human species, has led to some interesting research in both professional and popular psychology. As mentioned in Chapter 1, psychology has often been portrayed as a discipline focusing on White, European males. However, research on the psychology of women continues to expand, it has begun to address the specific differences of women of color, and it has led to the establishment of specific men's studies as well (Matlin, 2004). The latter point is an important one, since the earlier emphasis on White males was more circumstantial than intentional. For our purposes, I would like us to consider some of the interesting popular work on male/female differences.

In 1992, John Gray first published a very popular book entitled *Men are From Mars, Women are From Venus.* This book openly addresses the different ways in which men and women typically communicate and express their emotions. He offers practical advice on how men and women should react, or perhaps not react, to one another in everyday interactions. In his introduction to the paperback edition, Gray (2004) emphasizes how important it is *not* to try changing your partner. To expect members of the opposite sex to become more like yourself sends a message that they are not good enough as they are. He also notes that not all men or women will fall into the typical gender roles, so it is important not to stereotype. What is important, according to Gray, is that we recognize the general differences that exist between men and women and keep them in mind when we communicate with each other. If we can, then hopefully we can avoid conflicts that need not be inevitable. It might sound simple, but Gray clearly struck a chord in couples and individuals across America. He wrote numerous follow-up books, including *Mars and Venus on a Date* (1997) and the parenting guide *Children are From Heaven* (1999), each of which became #1 New York Times Bestsellers like the original. There is an interesting website (www.marsvenus.com), there are workshops and counseling centers based on Gray's work, and workplace seminars based on *Mars and Venus in the Workplace* (2002). Clearly, relationship problems based on the differences between men and women are of great interest to people in our society today. As harshly as Freud has been criticized for his views on the differences between men and women, he was certainly on to something. Perhaps that's part of the reason why even those who criticize Freud continue to talk about him.

More recently, Norah Vincent (2006) spent 18 months masquerading as a man, and then wrote about her experiences in *Self-Made Man.* Ms. Vincent spent a substantial amount of time working to look and act like a man. She consulted a professional make-up artist (especially to help with her "beard"), a voice coach, and a personal trainer to help her build muscle mass in her arms and shoulders. She even went to a sex shop and purchased a prosthetic penis, just to help make sure that her appearance was as convincing as possible. Using the name Ned, she then traveled around the country, to five different states, and attempted to pass for a man in a variety of settings. She played on a men's bowling team, went to strip clubs with "other" men, spent time in a monastery, got a job as a salesman, and joined a men's group. One of the most interesting aspects of her masquerade involved dating. Curiously, it was not really difficult for her to consider dating women, because she happens to be a lesbian. But she was not prepared for how often she would be rejected when trying to meet women! Maybe that's why she wrote: "It was hard being a guy. Really hard." In fact, she found the entire experience quite disturbing. As a woman, she had always been viewed as very masculine. But when pretending to be a man, she was seen as very effeminate. She felt that her masculinity was constantly being judged, both by men and women. And the constant pressure to be a "real man" was overwhelmingly stressful. As she concluded her book, talking about the camaraderie of the men on the bowling team, she observed that:

> Making this removed comforting contact with men and feeling the relief it gave me as my life as a man went on was not a sign of having joined the overclass, for whom superiority is assumed and bucking up unnecessary. It was more like joining a union. It was the counterpart to and the refuge from my excruciating dates, which were often alienating and grating enough to make me wonder whether getting men and women together amicably on a permanent basis wasn't at times like brokering Middle East peace.
>
> I believe we *are* that different in agenda, in expression, in outlook, in nature, so much so that I can't help almost believing, after having been Ned, that we live in parallel worlds, that there is at bottom really no such thing as that mystical unifying creature we call a human being, but only male human beings and female human beings, as separate as sects. (pgs. 281-282; Vincent, 2006)

As an indication of how popular this topic continues to be, shortly after Ms. Vincent published her book she was interviewed on the popular news/comedy show *The Colbert Report* on Comedy Central. I guess it's important to keep smiling as we struggle through the many challenges of male/female relationships.

Freud's perspectives on women have created a great deal of negativity toward him and his theory, particularly among women. But should we judge Freud so harshly? It was common in the society in which he lived to consider women as the "weaker sex." In his practice, most of the patients he saw were female, so he needed his theory to explain why most of the people with psychological disorders were women (at least, that's what he thought). Granted he had made fundamental errors by not realizing that men might be avoiding help for psychological problems because of the culture and by not recognizing that women might be suffering from oppression caused by men, but since there were no other theories to compare his own ideas to, it is easy to condemn him. However, those theorists who began to address the cultural issues, like Adler and Horney, had Freud's theory for comparison. Horney in particular also had a growing body of research on anthropology and sociology to draw on. So as much as Adler and Horney may have disagreed with Freud, he still laid the foundation for their work and the work of many others.

Psychoanalysis

Most psychologists today make a distinction that Freud seldom, if ever, made. We refer to all theoretical perspectives related to the views of Sigmund Freud as psychodynamic theories, reserving the term psychoanalysis for the therapeutic method developed by Freud. Freud simply referred to both his theories and his therapy as psychoanalysis. This may well have resulted from the fact that Freud began as a therapist, and only developed his theories in order to explain why certain approaches worked and others did not. It may also have something to do with the fact that Freud's personality theories came first, and so there was no need in his mind to distinguish his views from the work of others. Whatever the reason, for our purposes we will use the term psychoanalysis to refer to the therapeutic method developed by Freud, which was uniquely different from the techniques already in use by people such as Breuer and Charcot. I would also like to note that many of the references in this section cite the book co-authored by Freud and Breuer (1895/2004). However, the citations come from a portion of the book written by Freud alone, and in which he takes personal credit for the work. Therefore, we need to acknowledge that although the book is published as the work of both men, it contains mostly each man's individual work, and only the "Preliminary Statement" is co-authored by Freud and Breuer. This point is by no means a small one, because it was at this point in their careers that the two men went their separate ways.

As mentioned above, Freud came to believe that the use of hypnosis, which had been championed by Breuer and Charcot, was unable to get at the root causes of patient's neuroses. He also learned through experience that psychoanalysis could only be effective if he was able to go back into the early childhood of his patients and uncover the unconscious conflicts and repressions that led to their neurotic behaviors. In order to accomplish this goal, Freud relied primarily on **free association** and **dream analysis**. In the history of psychoanalysis, there have been those who believed that psychoanalysis officially began when Freud rejected hypnosis and introduced free association (Freud, 1914/1995). Free association is often used, of course, during the interpretation of dreams, so the two techniques are not mutually exclusive. With regard to the value of interpreting dreams, Freud wrote perhaps his most famous line: "...the interpretation of dreams is the *via regia* [royal road] to a knowledge of the unconscious element in our psychic life." (pg. 508; Freud, 1900/1995).

Free Association – Freud's Therapeutic Breakthrough

Free association grew out of a need that resulted from problems implementing Breuer's cathartic method. The first problem was that many patients could not be hypnotized. With the patients that Freud could not hypnotize, especially those who would not even allow him to try hypnotizing them, Freud tried a technique of pressing them to remember. This technique also came up short, and Freud recognized a need to work around the patient's resistance (which we will examine in more detail below). The first technique that Freud developed involved pressing his hand against his patient's forehead and asking them to say whatever thought, no matter how seemingly irrelevant, came first into their consciousness (Freud & Breuer, 1895/2004). Freud himself described this technique as a trick, one that disconnects the patient's attention from his conscious searching and reflecting. However, trick or not, Freud found the technique to be indispensable. The thoughts that came to the forefront of consciousness, those believed to be easily accessible via the preconscious, were likely to be connected to the underlying associations responsible for the neurotic patient's symptoms. Freud used this technique of free association quite successfully. As early as 1892, he treated a patient known as Fräulein Elisabeth von R. by relying entirely on free association (Freud & Breuer, 1895/2004).

Still, Freud did make some modifications in the technique. Two other methods used to begin the free association were to have the patient think of a number or a name at random. Of course, Freud did not believe that it was possible for anything in the mind to occur at random, and by continuing the association brought up by that first name or number, Freud could help his patient to arrive at the true unconscious associations that were the root of their problems (Freud, 1917/1966). He also used free association during the interpretation of dreams, and often found it helpful to examine which part of the dream the patient chose to begin making free associations (Freud, 1933/1965). Freud also considered psychoanalysis to be effective with children, but cautioned that a child's lack of psychological development limited their ability for free association. Other psychodynamic theorists worked more extensively with children, however, including Adler, Anna Freud, and Klein.

The classic image of psychoanalysis involves a patient lying on a couch while the psychoanalyst listens and searches for themes that reflect the unconscious conflicts causing psychological distress. [Image by Robert Hufstutter]

Sigmund Freud

The Elements of Dream Analysis

For someone who considered dreams to be the royal road to the unconscious mind, it is no surprise that Freud's first book of his own was *The Interpretation of Dreams* (Freud, 1900/1995). The value of this work never diminished, and Freud devoted a chapter to dream interpretation in one of his last books: *An Outline of Psycho-Analysis* (Freud, 1938/1949). In the latter book, published only a year before Freud died, he wrote:

> The only thing that can help us are states of conflict and uproar, when the contents of the unconscious id have a prospect of forcing their way into the ego and into consciousness and the ego puts itself once more on the defensive against this invasion. ...Now, our nightly sleep is precisely a state of this sort, and for that reason psychical activity during sleep, which we perceive as dreams, is our most favourable object of study. In that way, too, we avoid the familiar reproach that we base our constructions of normal mental life on pathological findings; for dreams are regular events in the life of a normal person... (pg. 38)

Freud described our recollection of a dream as a façade, a covering that hides the underlying process of the dream. Thus, a dream has both **manifest content** and **latent content**. The manifest content (or the dream-content) of a dream is what we actually remember when we wake up. The latent content (or the dream-thoughts), however, is the true underlying meaning of the dream, the unconscious material from the id desiring satisfaction. Freud described the process by which the latent content is transformed into the manifest content as the **dream-work** (Freud, 1900/1995). Studying the nature of the dream-work, the way in which the unconscious material from the id forces its way into the ego but is transformed by the ego's opposition to the impulse, allows us to understand what is known as **dream-distortion** (Freud, 1938/1949). The importance of dream-distortion becomes clear when we consider the purpose of dreams. Freud believed that all dreams represent our true desires. Therefore, all dreams can be viewed as wish fulfillment. Although some dreams can be very anxiety-provoking, and certainly do not seem to represent our wishes and desires, this is the result of the distortion. If we successfully analyze the dream and identify its latent content, then Freud believed we would recognize the true wish-fulfillment nature of even anxiety-provoking or frightening dreams (Freud, 1900/1995).

When we sleep, the ability of the ego to repress or otherwise redirect the unacceptable impulses of the id is paralyzed. The id, then, is afforded "a harmless amount of liberty" (Freud, 1938/1949). But the ego is still the seat of consciousness, and still exerts some influence over the expression of the id impulses. And so the dream is distorted, transformed into something less threatening to the ego, particularly into something not threatening enough to wake the person up. To summarize this situation, when we are asleep the ego is less able to restrain the id. Consequently, the impulses of the id intrude in the preconscious and then into the conscious mind. This provokes anxiety and threatens to wake us up. However, the dream transforms the id impulse into the fulfillment of a wish, and we are able to continue sleeping. As Freud described it:

> We shall be taking every experience into account if we say that a dream is invariably an attempt to get rid of a disturbance of sleep by means of a wish-fulfillment, so that the dream is a guardian of sleep. (pg. 46; Freud, 1938/1949)

Does it seem reasonable to say that all dreams are wish fulfillment? Certainly some dreams clearly fulfill our wishes and desires, at least through fantasy. Such dreams do not require any analysis. Other dreams, however, seem to make no sense at all. The id and the unconscious mind are not logical at all, contradictory ideas easily coexist side by side, and Freud even referred to the unconscious mind as the "Realm of the Illogical" (pg. 43; Freud 1938/1949). As these latent impulses are transformed into manifest content, it can be very difficult to separate them and make sense of a given dream. The dream-work itself, the very process of distorting or transforming the latent content into the manifest content in order to disguise the meaning of our dreams, involves a variety of factors, including: **condensation**, **displacement**, the use of **symbolic representation**, and **secondary elaboration** (Freud, 1900/1995).

According to Freud, condensation refers to the tendency to create unity out of a variety of dream elements that we would keep separate if we were awake. So, a single element of the manifest content of a dream might represent a number of latent thoughts. Thus, the analysis of a dream could be much longer than the dream itself. Displacement is not unrelated to condensation according to Freud, and refers to the switching of libidinal energy from one object to another, such that the important object of a dream might seem inconsequential, and vice versa. In other words, the apparent focus of the dream is probably not the actual focus of the dream. This does not simply suggest that we might substitute one person for another in a dream, it also happens that we might represent various elements through symbols. Once again, these symbols are employed by dreams to disguise the representation of latent content. As important as Freud considered symbols to be in a dream, he did not support the idea that dream dictionaries can identify universal meanings of dream symbols. It is only through the associations relevant to a specific dreamer that we can make sense of a dream's symbolism (Freud, 1938/1949). Finally, as the dream is actually presented to the conscious mind, the ego ensures that the material is acceptable by performing what Freud termed the secondary elaboration. As with any perception, the ego fills in gaps and connections, but also misunderstands the true nature of the dream. As a result the secondary elaboration can offer little more than a smooth façade for the dream. Also, the secondary elaboration may only be partial, or even absent (Freud, 1933/1965). All of these processes together form the manifest content of the dream, resulting in something that might be difficult to understand, but which is within the reach of a determined psychoanalyst.

Discussion Question: Have you ever analyzed your own dreams? Were you able to discover any revelations after considering a dream in greater depth, even though it made no sense at first?

The Therapeutic Process

Initially, Freud began with a fundamental belief in the effectiveness of catharsis, the discharge of pent-up emotion that follows the recall and re-experiencing of traumatic memories (see Jarvis, 2004). If only a patient can recognize the unconscious association between an early traumatic event and their current symptoms, then the symptoms should be relieved. As Breuer and Freud noted in the introduction to their book:

> For we found, at first to our great surprise, that the individual hysterical symptoms disappeared immediately and did not recur if we succeeded in wakening the memory of the precipitating event with complete clarity, arousing with it the accompanying affect, and if the patient then depicted the event in the greatest possible detail and put words to the affect. Remembering without affect almost always fails to be effective… (pg. 10; Freud and Breuer, 1895/2004).

One can see from this description, however, that the process of psychoanalysis is not easy. There must be a clear recognition of the initial traumatic event, in detail, with all of its original emotional impact, and the patient must then be willing to talk about the event in relation to their current problems.

As we have already seen, the first obstacle is resistance, the patient's reluctance to experience the anxiety associated with recovering repressed material. The more severe the symptoms, the more severe the resistance is likely to be. Even when a little trick is successful, such as pressing on the forehead to break the patient's concentration and allow free association, in serious cases the self remembers its intentions (which are often unconscious motives) and resumes its resistance (Freud & Breuer, 1895/2004). Because of this challenge, Freud believed that the therapist must be patient. Resistance that has been constituted over a long period of time can only be resolved slowly, step by step. In addition to the intellectual role of the therapist, there is an important emotional role as well. In some cases, Freud found that only the personal influence of the doctor could successfully break down the patient's defense mechanisms.

A large part of the reason that psychoanalysis can be so difficult has to do with how the unconscious mind exists. Freud believed that memory of a traumatic event exists as a pathogenic nucleus within multiple layers of pathogenic psychical material of varying resistance. The outer layers may be easy to uncover, but as one progresses into the deeper layers, resistance grows steadily. Adding to the challenge, the associations between layers do not simply go deeper, they can travel at odd angles, in something of a zigzag fashion, or branch out in multiple ways (Freud & Breuer, 1895/2004). Because multiple associations may exist between a patient's neurosis and the underlying traumatic event, it is critical to address all of the psychical material that comes to bear on the current condition of the patient. Even if the therapist rightly knows the basis for the patient's problems:

> …there is no point at all in advancing directly to the nucleus of the pathogenic organization. Even if it were possible for us to guess this, the patient would not know what to do

with the elucidation given to him and would not be altered by it psychically. (pg. 293; Freud & Breuer, 1895/2004)

As suggested above, a different kind of obstacle arises when the relationship between the doctor and the patient has been damaged somehow. Freud considered this to be a likely occurrence in serious cases of analysis. Freud described three ways in which the doctor/patient relationship can suffer. The first case involves the patient feeling estranged, neglected, undervalued, insulted, or if they have heard negative things about the doctor. Freud considered this problem to be fairly easily handled through good communication, although he noted that good communication can be difficult with hysterical patients. The second situation involves patients who fear that they will become too dependent on the therapist and that they will lose their independence. This can lead to new resistances. As an example, Freud described patients who complained of headaches when he pressed on their forehead, but really they were just creating a new hysterical symptom to mask their aversion to the belief that they were being manipulated or controlled. The final problem that commonly disturbs the relationship between the therapist and the patient is known as **transference** (Freud & Breuer, 1895/2004). Transference occurs when the patient reacts as if the therapist were an important figure from the patient's childhood or past, and transfers onto the therapist feelings and reactions appropriate to that person from the past. Although transference can interfere with the therapeutic process, it also offers advantages. The power conferred on the therapist by transference affords him an opportunity to re-educate the patient, correcting the mistakes of the parents, and it leads patients to reveal more about themselves than they might have if they had not developed such a connection to the therapist (Freud, 1938/1949).

Following transference, it is also possible for **countertransference** to occur. Countertransference refers first to an unconscious influence of the patient on the therapist, after which the therapist directs their own emotional states back onto the patient. In Freud's circle of analysts their own psychoanalysis was conducted in large part to eliminate the influence of this distorting effect. Today, there are some therapists who view countertransference as a useful means to gain a deeper perception about what is going on in their patient's mind (see Jarvis, 2004).

Is Psychoanalysis Effective?

The effectiveness of psychoanalysis as a treatment for psychological disorders has been a source of ongoing debate. In 2006, a select task force, established by the presidents of five major psychoanalytic organizations, published the *Psychodynamic Diagnostic Manual* (PDM Task Force, 2006). Included within the PDM is a section on research, including meta-analytic studies on the effectiveness of psychoanalysis on patient populations in the United States (Westen et al., 2006), the United Kingdom (Fonagy, 2006), and Germany (Leichsenring, 2006). Each of these chapters emphasize the difficulty in empirically evaluating the effectiveness of psychotherapy, and even more so comparing the effectiveness of different psychotherapeutic approaches. Nonetheless, for a variety of psychological disorders, there is evidence supporting the efficacy of psychoanalytic treatments. Both Fonagy (2006) and Leichsenring (2006) identify another area of research that needs to be continued: there is *not* just one type of psychoanalysis. Thus, continued research on the efficacy of psychoanalytic treatments should address the relative efficacy of different styles of psychoanalytically based therapies.

Religion and Spirituality

In the last section of this book, we will look at spiritual philosophies that provide positive guidelines for personal development and living one's life. Freud had rather strong feelings about religion, and simply put, he did not approve! Freud actually considered religion to be an obstacle to the further development of civilization, and of the "three powers" that oppose a scientific worldview (art, philosophy, and religion), "religion alone is to be taken seriously as an enemy" (Freud, 1933/1965). In his first and last books reviewing psychoanalysis Freud makes almost no mention of religion (Freud, 1917/1966, 1938/1949), a rather conspicuous absence. In between, however, he wrote two books thoroughly condemning religion and societies depending on it.

In *The Future of an Illusion* (Freud, 1927/1961), Freud describes the role that religion has played in establishing and maintaining inequitable civilizations. According to Freud, the primary purpose of civilization is the gathering of wealth and, then, its distribution. This distribution is almost always unfair, and leads to the establishment of a small group of wealthy elite and a much larger mass of lower classes. The challenge for the wealthy elite is to maintain this unfair distribution, without the unreasonable use of force. The use of force will ultimately fail, since the instinctual demands for pleasure by the masses (driven by their id impulses) will drive them to take whatever they want from each other and from the wealthy. And the masses have power in numbers! Religion has served civilization by providing a controlling force over these instinctual demands, incorporated directly into the psyche of each individual by means of the development of the superego. The problem, however, lies in the fact (according to Freud) that there is no God, it is all an illusion. Thus, in *Civilization and Its Discontent* (Freud, 1930/1961), Freud states that the "religions of mankind must be classed among the mass-delusions…" that are used to provide people with a certain degree of happiness and protection against suffering, in spite of the reality of an unfair and uncertain world.

In his last completed book, *Moses and Monotheism* (Freud, 1939/1967), Freud flatly rejects the entire basis for Judaism and Christianity. Based on archaeological evidence, Freud claims that Moses was not Jewish, but rather an Egyptian. Furthermore, he argues that the monotheistic religion that provides the basis for Judaism, Christianity, and Islam (the Abrahamic religions) was a discredited Egyptian religion established by the pharaoh Amenhotep IV. When Amenhotep IV died, and Egyptians who still followed the traditional religion of Egypt came back into power, Moses led the Jewish people out of Egypt so that he would have followers to whom he could teach the religion he hoped to maintain. Since Moses was a hero to the Jewish people, Freud claims that they rewrote the story to say that Moses was Jewish and that their one true God had been revealed to them long before they entered Egypt (Freud, 1939/1967).

Freud attacked the very foundation of Judaism, claiming that Moses was not Jewish, but rather an Egyptian who conceived the idea of a monotheistic religion by himself. [Image from Wikimedia Commons]

If religion is nothing more than an illusion, where does it come from, and what is the danger of it? According to Freud, the development of religion is analogous to the development of each individual. Basically, God is symbolic of our relationship with our own father. In his *New Introductory Lectures…* (Freud, 1933/1965), Freud neatly lays out this relationship. Religion serves to provide us with an understanding of the origins of the universe and life, it offers us hope for protection and ultimate happiness, and it lays down moral guidelines for living our lives. Similarly, our fathers give each of us life, they protect us when we are young, and they teach the rules and morality of our culture. Although the establishment of religions by our primitive ancestors may be quite understandable, Freud used rather harsh language when referring to religion. He wrote that "…our wretched, ignorant and downtrodden ancestors…" "…were far more ignorant than we are…" (Freud, 1927/1961). In his opinion, ancient religious books are the product of "fraud" from a time when "man's ignorance was very great…," and he includes the Bible and the Qur'an in that category (Freud, 1933/1965). He considered religion to be the antithesis of science and art, the two highest achievements of man (Freud, 1930/1961). Even when addressing more modern times, he compares the political oppression by the Russian Bolsheviks, with its prohibition of thought (punishable by death), as "just as ruthless as was that of religion in the past…doubts of its correctness are punished in the same way as heresy was once punished by the Catholic Church" (Freud, 1933/1965). And in anticipation of his views being challenged, Freud wrote that his considerations "will impress only that minority of readers familiar with analytical reasoning and able to appreciate its conclusions" (Freud, 1939/1967). The danger in all of this, according to Freud, is what might happen if people become aware of this illusion and fraud. If people become aware that there is no God, if they discover that no one else believes, then there may be a violent reaction as a result of the inherent hostility toward civilization by the masses (Freud, 1927/1961). Accordingly:

> …either these dangerous masses must be held down most severely and kept most carefully away from any chance of intellectual awakening, or else the relationship between civilization and religion must undergo a fundamental revision. (pg. 39; Freud, 1927/1961)

And yet, in spite of such harsh condemnation of religion, Freud was at times fascinated by individuals who expressed deep spiritual experiences. While in college, Freud was profoundly impressed by the religious philosopher Franz Brentano, a former Catholic priest. Freud wrote to a friend that he could not refute any of Brentano's theistic arguments, and he referred to Brentano as a "remarkable man" (cited in Nicholi, 2002). Much later in life, Freud discussed an alternative to his earlier analysis of the basis for religion. He had sent a copy of *The Future of an Illusion* to a friend who was well versed in traditional Yoga. This friend, named Romain Rolland, described for Freud an "oceanic" feeling, a sense of eternity and limitlessness. Freud was unable to discover such feelings within himself, and expressed a general dissatisfaction with scientific investigations of such phenomena. Today, however, neuroscientists are using real-time brain imaging techniques, such as functional magnetic resonance imaging (fMRI), to study the alterations in brain activity unique to meditative states and, in particular, positive emotions (e.g., see Barinaga, 2003; Goleman, 1988, 2003; Mathew, 2001). Although Freud obviously had no knowledge that such studies would someday be possible, he did acknowledge that experiences like the "oceanic" feeling might form the basis for religious sentiments in the human species (Freud, 1930/1961). Yet another friend encouraged Freud to practice Yoga, particularly meditation, to experience these altered states of mind for himself. It is unclear whether Freud ever attempted to meditate, but he does make mention of his friend's belief that meditation may reveal a primordial state of mind, perhaps even deeper than that of the id and the unconscious with which Freud had occupied his career (Freud, 1930/1961). Freud even went so far as to suggest that if we could somehow achieve a complete reduction, an extinction, of the tension between our instinctual needs and the constraints imposed by reality and the superego that we might achieve "nirvana" (Freud, 1938/1949).

How might we reconcile the seeming contradiction between Freud's harsh attitude toward religion with his apparent fascination with mystical spirituality and deeply spiritual individuals? Freud believed that religion had failed society. Religion has ruled human civilization for thousands of years, and yet, "We see that an appallingly large number of people are dissatisfied with civilization and unhappy in it…In every age immorality has found no less support in religion than morality has…" (Freud, 1927/1961). Also, it is undeniable that death awaits each of us, and Freud was definitely concerned with death. In 1909 Freud met William James (Freud, 1952). James asked Freud to carry the bag James had with him and to walk on; James said he would catch up after dealing with an attack of angina pectoris. James died of heart disease a year later. Freud wrote that "I have always wished that I might be as fearless as he was in the face of approaching death." Freud was also concerned about how his own death might affect his mother, who lived to a ripe old age. Martin Freud noted that "Grandmother Amalia…looked for some time as if she would live forever, and my father was terrified by the thought that she might survive him and, in consequence, have to be told of his death." (M. Freud, 1983). Perhaps we should not be surprised that someone who was so thoughtful regarding death, someone who proposed a death instinct, might be inclined to have some concern regarding what happens after one's life comes to an end.

As gloomy as Freud's perspective may seem at first, he remained hopeful regarding the future of humanity. He considered religion to have been just one step in the development of our species, and that science had reached a point where it could move us ahead another step. When addressing the belief of many people that we were created in the image and likeness of God, a god who must also have created evil and the Devil (other theologians have come to a different conclusion on this point; see, for example, *Mere Christianity* by C. S. Lewis [1952]), Freud suggested that we bow to the deeply moral nature of mankind, which has overcome this difficulty (Freud, 1930/1961). He acknowledged the positive role that religion has played in redirecting and transforming some of our sexual impulses into impulses experienced as love. Indeed, the purpose of civilization itself is to serve Eros, the life instinct, by combining individuals into "families, then races, peoples and nations, into one great unity, the unity of mankind" (Freud, 1930/1961). But the natural aggressive instinct, the death instinct manifested as the hostility of the individual for civilization, opposes the establishment of civilizations. Thus, the meaning of the evolution of civilizations becomes clear:

> It must present the struggle between Eros and Death, between the instinct of life and the instinct of destruction, as it works itself out in the human species. This struggle is what all life essentially consists of, and the evolution of civilization may therefore be simply described as the struggle for life of the human species. And it is this battle of the giants that our nurse-maids try to appease with their lullaby about Heaven. (Freud, 1930/1961)

Discussion Question: Freud believed that religion has failed to resolve the difficulties that many people face, that it has outlived its usefulness, and that God is only an illusion anyway. Does this fit with your view of the world in which we live?

Personality Theory in Real Life:
The Things We Do Are Not Really Surprising!

It isn't difficult to apply Freud's theories to everyday life. Only a few years after publishing his landmark book on dream analysis, Freud published *Psychopathology of Everyday Life* (1904/1995). One year later, he published *Wit and Its Relation to the Unconscious* (1905/1995). So Freud clearly intended his theory to address all aspects of life, and he was well aware that jokes and laughter are as much a part of life as any of the darker aspects of psychoanalysis (with concepts such as demanding id impulses and the death instinct).

As mentioned earlier in the chapter, the most famous example of a simple, everyday psychopathology is the famous Freudian slip. A very humorous example of a Freudian slip can be found on the Wikipedia website (http://en.wikipedia.org): "Excuse me, but I'm having doubts about your theories, Dr. Fraud." There are, of course, a variety of other mistakes we commonly make when we talk. We often forget names, words, the order of phrases and sayings, and these errors can carry over into reading and writing as well as speaking. Of course, Freud believed that these mistakes are neither random nor just the result of forgetfulness. Rather, they represent psychological processes leading to the expression of one's real feelings and beliefs. An interesting example that often comes to mind is a quote by former Vice-President of the United States Dan Quayle. The Honorable Mr. Quayle intended to quote the slogan of the United Negro College Fund: A mind is a terrible thing to waste. Instead, he said "What a waste it is to lose one's mind." Since "losing one's mind" is slang for becoming mentally ill, it might be argued by some that the vice-president had revealed a negative attitude toward minority groups. We should always be very careful, of course, to avoid analyzing situations with only the bare minimum of information. Without the implication of the slang meaning of "losing one's mind" and some alleged unconscious intentions, Vice-President Quayle's statement seems like nothing more than a simple mistake. Haven't we all made mistakes like this that were very embarrassing at the time? I don't know if it's good or bad, but Vice-President Quayle made a variety of other infamous comments that can easily be found on the Internet, suggesting that his only issue was a penchant for making mistakes in ordinary speech. However, people seem to find such mistakes quite interesting. An Internet search for embarrassing quotes will locate a wide variety of examples like the one above, but they are not always attributed to the same person. Some of the same embarrassing quotes have been attributed to whoever happens to be the current political target of the person posting the webpage. So obviously a lot of people enjoy the embarrassment of others, but be careful about attributing any quote you locate on a random webpage.

Of course, any time a famous person like Vice-President Quayle makes that big a mistake, the late-night comedians are all over it! And that brings us to *Wit and Its Relation to the Unconscious* (Freud, 1905/1995). In this early book, Freud discussed jokes and witticisms in great detail. He actually considered wit-work, the process of forming a joke or witty remark, as being essentially the same thing as dream-work. Thus, the examination of how an individual uses humor on a daily basis might reveal a great deal about their personality. The following is one of the jokes Freud included in his book for analysis. It takes a little thought, since it is in a category that Freud referred to as sophistic faulty thinking (Freud described over 20 types of joke):

> A gentleman entered a shop and ordered a fancy cake, which, however, he soon returned, asking for some liqueur in its stead. He drank the liqueur, and was about to leave without paying for it. The shopkeeper held him back. "What do you want of me?" he asked. "Please pay for the liqueur," said the shopkeeper. "But I have given you the fancy cake for it." "Yes, but you have not paid for that either."

"Well, neither have I eaten it." (pg. 634)
The next time you think of a really good joke or something really funny to say, or the next time you hear a joke that really makes you laugh, take a minute or two to consider what that laughter might be saying about who you really are.

A Final Note

An important aspect of Freud's theory is his belief that development occurs in a series of predictable stages. This belief is not common to all of the theories we will cover in this textbook. Furthermore, stage theories are likely to be influenced by **cultural relativism**, the perspective that the significance of an idea or concept is determined by how it is valued within a given culture. Noted psychologists who have offered such a developmental perspective include Vygotsky and Bronfenbrenner, and it has been suggested that an approach incorporating cultural relativism may be of particular importance when studying the development of African Americans and other minority groups (Belgrave & Allison, 2006; Howard-Hamilton & Frazier, 2005). For example, it has been noted that religion is a very important aspect of African American, Hispanic American, and Asian American culture (Axelson, 1999; Belgrave & Allison, 2006; Taylor, Chatters, & Levin, 2004), and we have just examined how little Freud cared for religious or spiritual matters. Other psychologists, however, gave significantly more consideration to cultural influences (e.g., Adler, Horney, and the Stone Center Group). We will examine their contributions in later chapters.

Review of Key Points

- Early in his career, Freud felt that hypnosis could not help to understand why hysteria developed or why some patients got better with treatment. Psychoanalysis grew out of his desire to understand psychological processes better.
- The terms hysteria and neurosis are no longer recognized as technical terms. Hysteria would commonly be called a conversion disorder today, and the neuroses refer to a variety of disorders.
- Catharsis refers to the release of pent-up emotion that occurs when a patient remembers a traumatic event
- Psychic determinism is the concept that all thoughts and behaviors have some basis in prior experience, nothing happens by accident or chance.
- Each person is driven by a life force known as Eros. The energy associated with this life force is called libido.
- Cathexis refers to the attachment of libido to some psychical phenomenon. Since libido is limited, experiencing numerous traumatic events can leave a person with limited resources to cope with normal life.
- Freud believed that individual development is driven by sexual impulses that begin at birth. However, when Freud referred to sexual impulses he was really referring to the life force Eros.
- Freud described three levels of consciousness: the unconscious, the preconscious, and the conscious minds.
- Personality has three basic components according to Freud: the id, the ego, and the superego. The id is the oldest and most basic component, and the source of all sexual impulses and libidinal energy. The id acts according to the pleasure principle.
- The ego arises from the id, and acts according to the reality principle. It tries to balance the desires of the id with the constraints of the superego and the real world.
- The superego arises from the ego as we internalize the rules and customs of society. As it develops it takes two forms: the ego-ideal and the conscience.
- When we are conscious of the ego being unable to restrain the impulses of the id we experience anxiety. The threat can be real, or primarily psychological. Freud emphasized that psychological reality can be every bit as important actual reality.
- When faced with anxiety, we resort to defense mechanisms. The defense mechanisms first proposed by Freud were repression and regression.

Sigmund Freud

- There are four psychosexual stages, separated by a latency period. The oral, anal, and phallic stages occur during early childhood. Following the latency period and puberty, the genital stage represents physically mature reproductive functioning.
- During each psychosexual stage, a different region of the body becomes an erotogenic zone. The child's recognition of these sexual feelings belies the autoerotic nature of sexual development.
- The most dramatic development occurs during the phallic stage. It is in this stage that the Oedipus complex occurs, with its potential for the castration complex or penis envy.
- Infantile amnesia occurs naturally, according to Freud, and is the reason that we do not remember these psychosexual processes from our childhood.
- Freud's perspective on the development of girls has been problematic since its inception. He considered the female psyche to be the result of an incomplete and frustrated male development.
- Freud's initial contributions to therapy were the development of free association and dream analysis, leading some to suggest that this was point when psychoanalysis was created.
- In analyzing dreams, Freud distinguished between the manifest and latent content. The difference results from distortion that occurs during the dream-work.
- The analysis of a dream can be quite complex, since information might be condensed, displaced, represented symbolically, and finally it all undergoes a secondary elaboration.
- The challenge faced by a psychoanalyst is the nature of the unconscious mind. It exists as layer upon layer with different degrees of resistance. Only through patience can the psychoanalyst overcome this resistance and help the patient.
- During the process of psychoanalysis itself the psychoanalyst may encounter transference and experience countertransference.
- Freud acknowledged that religion had served a useful role in the history of humanity, but he firmly believed that there is no God. He felt we have grown beyond the ignorance of our ancestors, and the observations of psychoanalysis could explain how religion had arisen. He believed that the future of humanity was being hindered by clinging to these ancient and meaningless beliefs.

Review of Key Terms

amygdala	Eros	pregenital phase
anal stage	erotogenic zone	primary process
anxiety	fixated (fixation)	psychical apparatus
autoerotic	free association	psychic determinism
castration complex	Freudian slip	psychoanalysis
catharsis	genital stage	psychodynamic theory
cathexis	hysteria	psychosexual stages
condensation	id	reaction-formation
conscience	infantile amnesia	reality principle
conscious	latency period	regression
construct	latent content	repression
conversion disorder	libido	resistance
countertransference	manifest content	secondary elaboration
cultural relativism	neo-Freudian	secondary process
defense mechanism	neurosis (pl. neuroses)	seduction theory
displacement	Oedipus complex	sublimation
dream analysis	oral stage	superego
dream-distortion	penis envy	symbolic representation
dream-work	phallic stage	tension
ego	pleasure principle	transference
ego-ideal	preconscious	unconscious

Sigmund Freud

Annotated Bibliography

Freud, S. (1917/1966). ***Introductory lectures on psycho-analysis.*** **New York, NY: W. W. Norton & Company.**

One can almost see and hear Dr. Freud presenting these lectures to the medical students at the University Vienna as you become absorbed in this book. These well-crafted presentations are thoroughly engaging, and present in clear terms the basic essentials of psychoanalysis as defined by Freud himself.

Freud, S. (1933/1965). ***New introductory lectures on psycho-analysis.*** **New York, NY: W. W. Norton & Company.**

Freud, S. (1938/1949). ***An outline of psycho-analysis.*** **New York, NY: W. W. Norton & Company.**

These books followed the style of the earlier *Introductory Lectures*… Over time Freud advanced and modified aspects of his theories, thus providing the basis for his *New Introductory Lectures*… His outline of the theory, one of his last publications, is a very brief and easily read review of the most basic information on psychoanalysis.

Freud, S. (1914/1995). The history of the psychoanalytic movement. In A. A. Brill (Ed.), ***The basic writings of Sigmund Freud*** **(pp 899-945). New York, NY: The Modern Library.**

Freud, S. (1952). ***An autobiographical study.*** **New York, NY: W. W. Norton & Company.**

Written by Freud himself, these books provide an extraordinary and indispensable view of the man and his theories. Due to interesting circumstances, they were presented in reverse order. Freud first wrote about the history of the psychoanalytic movement. Some years later, when asked to provide an autobiography for a compilation on renowned doctors, Freud wrote more extensively about the early portion of his life and career (partly in order to avoid repeating what he had already written about the psychoanalytic movement).

Freud, S. (1927/1961). ***The future of an illusion.*** **New York, NY: W. W. Norton & Company.**

Although Freud had addressed religion in earlier works, it was in this book that Freud presented religion as an obstacle to the further development of mankind and society. More than just an attack on religion, however, Freud suggests that the knowledge obtained through the discovery of psychoanalysis can help us to understand the origins of religion. Accordingly, we can use that knowledge to help us transition to a future in which we are not blinded by meaningless faith in illusory religions. At least, that's what Freud believed.

Gay, P. (1998). ***Freud: A life for our time.*** **New York, NY: Norton & Co.**

In one of the best-known biographies of Freud, the author has done an excellent job of thoroughly covering Freud's life. Though the book is somewhat lengthy, it is by no means as challenging as the three-volume official biography written by Ernest Jones.

Freud, M. (1983). ***Sigmund Freud: Man and father.*** **New York, NY: Jason Aronson.**

Martin Freud does not try to cover the history of his father's work, which had already been done by his father. Instead, Martin Freud offers a marvelous view into the life of Sigmund Freud as a loving and devoted family man. It is, naturally, a unique perspective.

Goleman, D. (1995). ***Emotional intelligence: Why it can matter more than IQ.*** **New York, NY: Bantam Books.**

In this highly successful book, Dr. Goleman presents a modern perspective on human emotion, which fits well with Freud's concept of unconscious id impulses driving our behavior. From an evolutionary perspective, he presents the brain-based mechanisms of emotion that we share with other species. However, he also begins to address how we might recognize our emotional hijackings, and how we might then begin to control our negative emotional reactions.

Nicholi, A. M. (2002). ***The question of God: C. S. Lewis and Sigmund Freud debate God, love, sex, and the meaning of life.*** **New York, NY: Free Press.**

In this thought-provoking book, Dr. Nicholi, a psychiatry professor at Harvard University, compares the scientific worldview advocated by Freud to the spiritual worldview advocated by the renowned Christian author C. S. Lewis. The issue of whether Freud or Lewis was right is, of course, left unanswered. Nonetheless, the investigation is fascinating.

Gray, J. (2004). ***Men are from Mars, women are from Venus: The classic guide to understanding the opposite sex.*** **New York, NY: Quill.**
Vincent, N. (2006). ***Self-made man.*** **New York, NY, Viking.**

These popular psychology books present very interesting perspectives on male-female relationships and gender roles. Both are easy and enjoyable to read, and help to show us how psychological theories really do apply to everyday life.

Chapter 4 - Carl Jung

Carl Jung brought an almost mystical approach to psychodynamic theory. An early associate and follower of Freud, Jung eventually disagreed with Freud on too many aspects of personality theory to remain within a strictly Freudian perspective. Subsequently, Jung developed his own theory, which applied concepts from natural laws (primarily in physics) to psychological functioning. Jung also introduced the concept of personality types, and began to address personality development throughout the lifespan. In his most unique contribution, at least from a Western perspective, Jung proposed that the human psyche contains within itself psychological constructs developed throughout the evolution of the human species.

Jung has always been controversial and confusing. His blending of psychology and religion, as well as his openness to different religious and spiritual philosophies, was not easy to accept for many psychiatrists and psychologists trying to pursue a purely scientific explanation of personality and mental illness. Perhaps no one was more upset than Freud, whose attitude toward Jung changed dramatically over just a few years. In 1907, Freud wrote a letter to Jung in which Freud offered high praise:

> ...I have already acknowledged...above all that your person has filled me with trust in the future, that I now know that I am dispensable like everyone else, and that I wish for no one other or better than you to continue and complete my work. (pg. 136; cited in Wehr, 1989)

In 1910, hoping that others would also support Jung, Freud wrote to Oskar Pfister:

> I hope you will loyally support Jung, I want him to acquire the authority that will entitle him to leadership of the whole movement. (pg. 136; cited in Wehr, 1989)

However, in a dramatic shift just three years later, Freud wrote to Jung:

> I suggest to you that we completely give up our private relationship. By this I lose nothing, since for a long time I have been bound to you emotionally only by the thin thread of previously experienced disappointments. ... Spare me the supposed "duties of friendship." (pg. 136; cited in Wehr, 1989)

Later, in 1922, Freud thanked Oskar Pfister for his help in trying to eliminate Jung's influence on the psychoanalytic community:

> With your ever more thorough and ever more clearly demonstrated dismissal of Jung and Adler, you have for a long time given me great satisfaction. (pg. 136; cited in Wehr, 1989)

Who was this man who inspired such profound confidence from Sigmund Freud, only to later inspire such contempt? And were his theories that difficult for the psychodynamic community, or psychology in general, to accept? Hopefully, this chapter will begin to answer those questions. As evidence of his character, and in contrast to Freud, Jung did not turn his back on his former mentor. Following Freud's death in 1939, and later in 1957, Jung wrote the following:

> [Freud's work was]...surely the boldest attempt ever made on the apparently solid ground of empiricism to master the riddle of the unconscious psyche. For us young psychiatrists, it was a source of enlightenment... (pg. 29; cited in Wehr, 1989)

> ...Despite the resounding censure I suffered at the hands of Freud, I cannot, even despite my resentment toward him, fail to recognize his importance as a critical analyst of culture and as a pioneer in the field of psychology. (pg. 39; cited in Wehr, 1989)

A Brief Biography of Carl Jung

At the beginning of his autobiography, entitled *Memories, Dreams, Reflections*, Jung (1961) described his life as "a story of the self-realization of the unconscious." Jung believed that our personality begins with a collective unconscious, developed within our species throughout time, and that we have only limited ability to control the psychic process that is our own personality. Thus, our true personality arises from within as our collective unconscious comes forth into our personal unconscious and then our consciousness. It can be helpful to view these concepts from an Eastern perspective, and it is interesting to note that "self-realization" was used in the name of the first Yoga society established in America (in 1920 by Paramahansa Yogananda).

Carl Gustav Jung was born on July 26th, 1875, in the small town of Kesswil, Switzerland, into an interesting and notable family. His grandfather of the same name had been a physician, and had established the psychiatric clinic at the University of Basel and the "Home of Good Hope" for mentally retarded children. At an early age he had been imprisoned for over a year, for the crime of having participated in a demonstration supporting democracy in Germany. Rumored to be an illegitimate son of the great Johann Wolfgang von Goethe, though there is no convincing evidence, the elder Carl Jung died before his namesake grandson ever knew him. Nonetheless, Jung was greatly influenced by stories he heard about his grandfather. His maternal grandfather, Samuel Preiswerk, was the dean of the Basel (Switzerland) clergy and pastor of a major church. He was one the first people in Europe to suggest a restoration of Palestine to the Jews, thus establishing himself as a forerunner to the Zionists. Samuel Preiswerk also believed that he was regularly surrounded by spirits (or ghosts), something that likely had quite an influence on Jung's theories (Jaffe, 1979; Wehr, 1989).

Jung's father, Johann Paul Achilles Jung, married Emilie Preiswerk in 1874. Johann Jung was a scholar of Oriental languages, studied Arabic, and was ordained a minister. In addition to being a pastor at two churches during Jung's childhood, Johann Jung was the pastor at Friedmatt, the insane asylum in Basel. During Jung's early childhood he did not always have the best of relationships with his parents. He considered his mother to be a good mother, but he felt that her true personality was always hidden. She spent some time in the hospital when he was three years old, in part due to problems in her marriage. Jung found this separation from his mother deeply troubling, and he became mistrustful of the spoken word "love." Since his father was a pastor, there were often funerals and burials, all of which was very mysterious to the young Jung. In addition, his mother was considered a spiritual medium, and often helped Jung with his later studies on the occult. Perhaps most troubling of all, was Jung's belief that his father did not really know God, but rather, had become a minister trapped in the performance of meaningless ritual (Jaffe, 1979; Jung, 1961; Wehr, 1989).

An only child until he was 9, Jung preferred to be left alone, or at least he came to accept his loneliness. Even when his parent's guests brought their children over for visits, Jung would simply play his games alone:

> ...I recall only that I did not want to be disturbed. I was deeply absorbed in my games and could not endure being watched or judged while I played them. (pg. 18; Jung, 1961)

He also had extraordinarily rich and meaningful dreams, many of which were quite frightening, and they often involved deeply religious themes. This is hardly surprising, since two uncles on his father's side of the family were ministers, and there were six more ministers on his mother's side. Thus, he was often engaged in religious discussions at home. He was particularly impressed with a richly illustrated book on Hinduism, with pictures of Brahma, Vishnu, and Shiva (the Hindu trinity of gods). Even at 6 years old, he felt a vague connection with the Hindu gods, something that once again would have an interesting influence on his later theories. These dreams led Jung into deep religious speculations, something he considered to be a secret that he could not share with anyone else (Jaffe, 1979; Jung, 1961; Wehr, 1989).

Jung's school-age years were a mixture of experiences. He enjoyed school, in the sense that it was easy for him and he found other children to play with. However, he also began studying Latin with his father and taking divinity classes. He found the classes on religion terribly boring, and the more he got to know his father, the less he believed that his father understood either God, religion, or spirituality. It didn't help that he was well-aware of the continued turmoil in his parent's marriage. In a cave in the garden he tended a fire that he meant to keep burning forever, and although he allowed other children to help gather the wood, only Jung himself could tend the fire. At the age of 11 he began attending the Gymnasium in Basel (something like an advanced high school). The other children were quite wealthy, and Jung became aware of how poor they were. Although this led him to feel some compassion for his father, the Gymnasium created a number of problems. Jung simply did not understand mathematics, his divinity classes became unbearably boring, and so, school itself became boring. This led to a severe neurosis at the age of 12 (Jaffe, 1979; Jung, 1961; Wehr, 1989).

Jung had been knocked down by another boy on the way home from school. He hit his head on a rock, and was nearly knocked out. He was so dizzy that others had to help him, and he suddenly realized that he did not have to go to school if he was ill. Consequently, he began having fainting spells any time he was sent to school or to do his homework. He missed 6 months of school due his psychological problems, and Jung loved the opportunity to spend his days exploring the world in any way he wished. He was eventually diagnosed with epilepsy, though Jung himself knew the diagnosis was ridiculous. One day he heard his father expressing great fear to a friend about what would become of Jung if he were unable to earn his own living. The reality of this statement was shocking to Jung, and "From that moment on I became a serious child." He immediately went to study Latin, and began to feel faint. However, he consciously made himself aware of his neurosis, and cognitively fought it off. He soon returned to school, recognizing "That was when I learned what a neurosis is" (Jaffe, 1979; Jung, 1961; Wehr, 1989).

As he continued through school, his personal life continued to be quite strange. He began to believe that he was two people, one having lived 100 years earlier. He also had heated religious debates with his father. Fueling his courage during these debates was his belief that a vision had led to his understanding of true spirituality:

> One fine summer day that same year I came out of school at noon and went to the cathedral square. The sky was gloriously blue, the day one of radiant sunshine. The roof of the cathedral glittered, the sun sparkling from the new, brightly glazed tiles. I was overwhelmed by the beauty of the sight, and thought: "The world is beautiful and the church is beautiful, and God made all this and sits above it far away in the blue sky on a golden throne and …" Here came a great hole in my thoughts, and a choking sensation. I felt numbed, and knew only: "Don't go on thinking now! Something terrible is coming, something I do not want to think, something I dare not even approach. Why not? Because I would be committing the most frightful of sins. What is the most terrible sin? Murder? No, it can't be that. The most terrible sin is the sin against the Holy Ghost, which cannot be forgiven. Anyone who commits that sin is damned to hell for all eternity. That would be very sad for my parents, if their only son, to whom they are so attached, should be doomed to eternal damnation. I cannot do that to my parents. All I need do is not go on thinking." (pg. 36; Jung, 1961)

However, Jung was not able to ignore his vision. He was tormented for days, and spent sleepless nights wondering why he would have to think something unforgivable as a result of praising God for the beauty of all creation. His mother saw how troubled he was, but Jung felt that he could not dare confide in her. Finally, he decided that it was God's will that he should face the meaning of this vision:

> I thought it over again and arrived at the same conclusion. "Obviously God also desires me to show courage," I thought. "If that is so and I go through with it, then He will give me His grace and illumination."
>
> I gathered all my courage, as though I were about to leap forthwith into hell-fire, and let the thought come. I saw before me the cathedral, the blue sky. God sits on His golden throne, high above the world - and from under the throne an enormous turd falls upon the sparkling new roof, shatters it, and breaks the walls of the cathedral asunder. (pg. 39; Jung 1961)

Jung was overjoyed by his understanding of this vision. He believed that God had shown him that what mattered in life was doing God's will, not following the rules of any man, religion, or church. This was what Jung felt his own father had never come to realize, and therefore, his father did not know the "immediate living God." This conviction that one should pursue truth, rather than dogma, was an essential lesson that returned when Jung faced his dramatic split with Sigmund Freud.

When Jung decided to enter medical school, he did not leave his interest in strange spiritual matters behind. His cousin Helene Preiswerk led séances in which she would fall into a trance and channel strange spirits. The climax of these trances was often a mandala (a mandala is a geometric figure that represents wholeness, completeness, and perfection), which she would dictate to Jung, and then attempt to translate what was told to her by the spirits. Eugen Bleuler urged Jung to publish his studies on occult phenomena (remember that Bleuler defined schizophrenia), which Jung did, under the title *On the Psychology and Pathology of So-called Occult Phenomena.* Another important event that occurred early during Jung's medical training was the death of his father. The church had no provisions for the family of a deceased minister, but one of his uncles loaned Jung the money he needed to continue his studies. Upon completing medical school, he joined Dr. Bleuler in Zurich at the Burgholzli Mental Hospital, and soon became the first assistant physician. The Burgholzli clinic was a renowned institution. Bleuler was considered one of the two most influential psychiatrists of the day, and the clinic had come to prominence under his predecessor Auguste Forel, who was the first person to formally publish the theory that neurons communicate through synaptic junctions (though just how was not well understood at the time; Finger, 1994). Jung worked hard at Burgholzli, as Bleuler expected nothing less. He also spent some time in France, at the internationally recognized Salpetriere hospital, where he met Pierre Janet. Janet is a curious figure in the history of psychoanalysis. He claimed that he developed everything good in psychoanalysis, and that everything Freud developed was bad. Janet also apparently suggested that only the corrupt city of Vienna could be the source of a theory that traces the development of personality to sexual urges (Freud, 1914/1995). Jung spoke favorably of what he learned from Janet; Freud soundly rejected Janet's claims, but did grudgingly acknowledge that Janet did some important work on understanding neuroses (Freud, 1914/1995; Jung, 1961).

In 1906, Jung sent Freud a copy of his book *The Psychology of Dementia Praecox* (an earlier term for schizophrenia), which Freud found quite impressive. The two met in February, 1907, and talked for nearly 13 straight hours. According to Jung, "Freud was the first man of real importance I had encountered…no one else could compare with him." Very quickly, as evidenced in the letters quoted at the beginning of this chapter, Freud felt that Jung would become the leader of the psychoanalytic movement. In 1909, Jung's psychoanalytic practice was so busy that he resigned from the Burgholzli clinic, and he traveled to America with Freud. During this trip the two men spent a great deal of time together. It quickly became evident to Jung that he could not be the successor that Freud was seeking; Jung had too many differences of opinion with Freud. More importantly, however, Jung described Freud as neurotic, and wrote that the symptoms were sometimes highly troublesome (though Jung failed to identify those symptoms). Freud taught that everyone was a little neurotic, but Jung wanted to know how to cure neuroses:

> Apparently neither Freud nor his disciples could understand what it meant for the theory and practice of psychoanalysis if not even the master could deal with his own neurosis. When, then, Freud announced his intention of identifying theory and method and making them into some kind of dogma, I could no longer collaborate with him; there remained no choice for me but to withdraw. (pg. 167; Jung, 1961)

Clearly Jung could not accept a dogmatic approach to psychoanalysis, since he believed that God Himself had told Jung not to follow any rigid system of rules. Even worse, this was when Jung first published his "discovery" of the collective unconscious. Freud wholly rejected this concept, and Jung felt that his creativity was being rejected. He offered to support Freud in public, while extending honest opinions in so-called "secret letters." Freud wanted none of it. Almost as quickly as their relationship had grown, it fell apart (Jaffe, 1979; Jung, 1961; Wehr, 1989).

The loss of his relationship with Freud, following the loss of his father, led Jung in a period of personal crisis. He resigned his position at the University of Zurich, and began a lengthy series of experiments in order to understand the fantasies and dreams that arose from his unconscious. The more he studied these phenomena, the more he realized they were not from his own memories, but from the collective unconscious. He was particularly curious about mandala drawings, which date back thousands of years in all cultures. He studied Christian Gnosticism, alchemy, and the *I Ching* (or: *Book of Changes*). After meeting Richard Wilhelm, an expert on Chinese culture, Jung studied more Taoist philosophy, and he wrote a glowing foreword for Wilhelm's translation of the *I Ching* (Wilhelm, 1950). These extraordinarily diverse interests led Jung to seek more in-depth knowledge from around the world. He traveled first to North Africa, then to America (to visit Pueblo Indians in New Mexico), next came East Africa (Uganda and Kenya), and finally India. Jung made every effort to get away from civilized areas, which might have been influenced by other cultures, in order to get a more realistic impression of the local culture, and he was particularly successful in this regard in meeting gurus in India (Jaffe, 1979; Jung, 1961; Wehr, 1989).

Through it all, he continued his work in psychology. He had developed his concept of psychological types, one of his most significant contributions, and published his work shortly after the break with Freud. He continued to develop his own form of psychoanalysis. Jung's family was also an important part of his life. He had married Emma Rauschenbach in 1903. They had four daughters and one son, followed by nineteen grandchildren and many great-grandchildren. Emma Jung was very supportive of her husband, especially during the more turbulent periods of his career (including the break with Freud), and she was no stranger to his work. She had done some analytical work with Freud herself, she wrote essays on Jung's concept of *anima* and *animus*, and she was the first president of the Psychological Club of Zurich. When his wife Emma died in 1955, Jung wrote in a letter that the loss had taken a lot out of him, and that at his age (80 years old) it wasn't easy to recover. Yet two years later, he began dictating his autobiography to Aniela Jaffe. Looking ahead to the end of his life, Jung said:

> The world into which we are born is brutal and cruel, and at the same time of divine beauty. Which element we think outweighs the other, whether meaninglessness or meaning is a matter of temperament. If meaninglessness were absolutely preponderant, the meaningfulness of life would vanish to an increasing degree with each step in our development. But that is - or seems to me - not the case. Probably, as in all metaphysical questions, both are true: Life is - or has - meaning and meaninglessness. I cherish the anxious hope that meaning will preponderate and win the battle.
>
> When Lao-tzu says: "All are clear, I alone am clouded," he is expressing what I now feel in advanced old age. Lao-tzu is the example of a man with superior insight who has seen and experienced worth and worthlessness, and who at the end of his life desires to return into his own being, into the eternal unknowable meaning. The archetype of the old man who has seen enough is eternally true. (pp. 358-359; Jung, 1961)

Carl Jung died at home in 1961, in Kusnacht, Switzerland, at the age of 85. As psychologists today examine more deeply the relationship between Eastern and Western perspectives, it may be that Jung's legacy has yet to be fulfilled.

Discussion Question: Even as a child, Jung had vivid dreams that he believed were giving him insight and guidance for the future. Have you ever had dreams so vivid, dreams that left such a powerful impression on you, that you felt they must have some special meaning? How did you respond, and what consequences, if any, followed your responses?

Placing Jung in Context: A Psychodynamic Enigma

Carl Jung holds an extraordinary place in the histories of psychiatry and psychology. Having already been an assistant to the renowned psychiatrist Eugen Bleuler, he went to Vienna to learn more about the fledgling science of psychoanalysis. He became Freud's hand-picked heir to the psychoanalytic throne, and was one of the psychiatrists who accompanied Freud to America. Later, however, as he developed his own theories, he parted ways with Freud. Freud eventually came to describe Jung's theories as incomprehensible, and Freud praised other psychiatrists who also opposed Jung's ideas.

The most dramatic contribution that Jung made to psychodynamic thought was his concept of the collective unconscious, a mysterious reservoir of psychological constructs common to all people. Jung traveled extensively, including trips to Africa, India, and the United States (particularly to visit the Pueblo Indians in New Mexico), and he studied the cultures in those places. He also observed many basic similarities between different cultures. Those similarities led Jung to propose the collective unconscious. How else could so many significant cultural similarities have arisen within separate and distant lands? Jung did not reject the concepts already developed by Freud and Adler, including the dynamic interaction between the conscious mind and the personal unconscious, but he extended them in order to connect them with his own theory of our underlying collective unconscious. As strange as this theory seemed to Freud, and Freud wondered whether it even made sense to Jung, such a concept is not difficult to understand from an Eastern perspective.

Initially Jung's theories had more influence on art, literature, and anthropology than they did on psychiatry and psychology. More recently, however, cognitive-behavioral theorists have begun to explore mindfulness as an addition to more traditional aspects of cognitive-behavioral therapies. As psychologists today study concepts from Yoga and Buddhism that are thousands of years old, Jung deserves the credit for bringing such an open-minded approach to the modern world of psychotherapy. Many famous and influential people admired Jung's work, including psychiatrist Viktor Frankl, psychologist Erich Fromm, the authors Hermann Hesse and H. G. Wells, and Nobel Laureate (Physics) Wolfgang Pauli (for a number of interesting testimonials see Wehr, 1989). In addition, Jung's discussion of how the libido has transformed throughout the evolution of the human species sounds very much like sociobiology, which was not an established field until the 1970s. Clearly Jung did not simply dabble in a wide range of ideas, but rather, he had an extraordinary vision of the complexity of the human psyche.

Basic Concepts

In order to distinguish his own approach to psychology from others that had come before, Jung felt that he needed a unique name. Freud, of course, had chosen the term "psychoanalysis," whereas Alfred Adler had chosen "individual psychology." Since Jung admired both men and their theories, he chose a name intended to encompass not only their approaches, but others as well. Thus, he chose to call his approach **analytical psychology** (Jung, 1933).

Analytical psychology, as presented by Jung, addresses the question of the psyche in an open-minded way. He laments the overly scientific approach of the late 1800s and efforts to explain away the psyche as a mere epiphenomenon of brain function. Curiously, that debate remains with us today, and is still unanswered in any definitive way. Jung did not accept the suggestion that the psyche must come from the activity of the brain. This allowed him to consider the possibility of a collective unconscious, and fit well with his acceptance of the wisdom of Eastern philosophers. Indeed, Jung suggests that psychology will find truth only when it accepts both Eastern and Western, as well as both scientific and spiritual, perspectives on the psyche (Jung, 1933).

Dynamic Psychic Energy

Jung believed in a dynamic interaction between the conscious and unconscious minds, in a manner quite similar to that proposed by Freud. However, as we will examine below, his concept of the psyche included elements of an unconscious mind that transcends the individual, and may be considered a combination of the spirit, or soul, and one's thoughts and sensations. This inner psychic realm is capable of affecting the brain and its functions and, therefore, can influence one's perception of external reality. In addition, Jung thought of the libido somewhat differently than Freud. Although Jung considered sexuality to be an important aspect of the libido, primarily he thought of libido as a more generalized life energy (Douglas, 1995; Jarvis, 2004). Jung believed that as the human species evolved, the nature of sexual (or survival) impulses transformed. For example, early in human evolution we needed, as do other species, to be able to attract mates for procreation. Over time, these attraction behaviors generalized to behaviors such as art or music. Thus, a Freudian might say that creating music is a sexual act, but according to Jung "it would be a poor, unaesthetic generalization if one were to include music in the category of sexuality" (Jung, 1916/1963).

An important element of Jung's conception of the psyche and libido is found in the nature of opposites. Indeed, all of nature is composed of opposites:

> ...The concept of energy implies that of polarity, since a current of energy necessarily presupposes two different states, or poles, without which there can be no current. Every energic phenomenon...consists of pairs of opposites: beginning and end, above and below, hot and cold,

> earlier and later, cause and effect, etc. The inseparability of the energy concept from that of polarity also applies to the concept of libido. (pg. 202; Jung, 1971)
>
> ...opposites are the ineradicable and indispensable preconditions of all psychic life... (pg. 170; Jung, 1970)

In accordance with this view, Jung felt that the psyche sought balance, much like the concept of **entropy** from the field of physics. Entropy, in simple terms, is a thermodynamic principle that all energy within a system (including the universe) will eventually even out. Jung applied this principle to motivation, believing that we are driven forward through our lives in such a way that we might reduce the imbalance of psychic energy between opposing pairs of emotions (such as love and hate; Jarvis, 2004; Jung, 1971). Borrowing concepts from physics was certainly not a strange thing for Jung to do. As mentioned in Chapter 3, Freud's theories were motivated in part by advancements in science and Darwin's theory of evolution. Jung was personally acquainted with the Nobel Prize winning physicist Wolfgang Pauli, and the two published essays blending psychology and physics in a book entitled *The Interpretation of Nature and the Psyche* (Jung & Pauli, 1955). However, entropy and motivation are focused forward in time. Such an orientation toward the future marks another distinction between the theories of Freud and Jung.

Jung did not simply study symbolism, such as that in dreams, to uncover evidence of past repression. Jung believed that dreams could guide our future behavior, because of their profound relationship to the past, and their profound influence on our conscious mental life. Jung proposed that dreams can tell us something about the development and structure of the human psyche, and that dreams have evolved with our species throughout time. Since consciousness is limited by our present experience, dreams help to reveal much deeper and broader elements of our psyche than we can be aware of consciously. As such, dreams cannot easily be interpreted. Jung rejected the analysis of any single dream, believing that they belong within a series. He also rejected trying to learn dream analysis from a book. When done properly, however, dream analysis can provide unparalleled realism (see Jacobi & Hull, 1970; Jung, 1933):

> ...I cannot prove in every case that dreams are meaningful, for there are dreams that neither doctor nor patient understands. But I must regard them as hypothetically meaningful in order to find courage to deal with them at all...We must never forget in dream-analysis, even for a moment, that we move on treacherous ground where nothing is certain but uncertainty...When we take up an obscure dream, our first task is not to understand and interpret it, but to establish the context with minute care. What I have in mind is not a boundless sweep of "free associations" starting from any and every image in the dream, but a careful and conscious illumination of those chains of associations that are directly connected with particular images. (pp. 11-12; Jung, 1933)

In the final analysis, there is a particular challenge to understanding what dreams point to, and that is the situation under which a therapist typically learns of someone's dreams: in therapy. Jung suggested that if therapists could continue to observe the journey of one's dreams after therapy was successful, then the therapist, and possibly the client as well, might begin to more clearly understand the meaning and direction of the dreams. Still, dreams themselves are about both health and sickness, in keeping with Jung's principle of opposites. As such, Jung wrote that "dreams are the natural reaction of the self-regulating psychic system." The theory of entropy allows for an imbalance of energy in a closed-system. We may think of our conscious mind as just such a closed system. When we dream, however, the ongoing effort of our psyche to balance itself takes over, and the dreams counteract what we have done to imbalance our psychological selves. Thus, it is within the context of dreams, not the details, that meaning is to be found (Jung, 1959a, 1968).

Discussion Question: Jung believed that the source of our motivation was a psychological drive to achieve balance (the effect of entropy on the psyche). Have you ever felt that you were being pushed or pulled in the wrong direction, or in too many directions at once, and simply wanted to achieve some balance in your life? In contrast, have there been times that your life was unfulfilling, and you needed something more in order to feel whole?

The Unconscious Mind

Perhaps Jung's most unique contribution to psychology is the distinction between a **personal unconscious** and a **collective unconscious**. The personal unconscious is not entirely different than that proposed by Freud, but is more extensive. In addition to repressed memories and impulses, the personal unconscious contains undeveloped aspects of the personality and material arising from the collective unconscious that is not yet ready for admission into conscious awareness. The personal unconscious is revealed through clusters of emotions, such as those resulting in a particular attitude toward one's father or other father figures, which Jung referred to as a **complex** (Douglas, 1995; Jarvis, 2004). In this sense, a complex is not synonymous with a psychological problem, as the term is often used today, but rather any general state of mind common to certain situations. In this context, it is quite similar to the **schemas** discussed by cognitive theorists.

Jung arrived at his theory of complexes as a result of his research into schizophrenia, under the direction of Dr. Bleuler. Bleuler had assigned Jung the task of studying the **Word Association Test**, a test in which a list of 100 words is read to the patient, and the therapist watches for evidence of emotional arousal, such as pauses, failures to respond, or physical acts. In addition, Jung noticed that even with schizophrenic patients, the patterns of word association were often centered on a particular theme. That theme could then be regarded as a complex (which, again, could be either positive or negative). Sometimes, complexes remain unresolved, such as one's feelings about parents, if the parents have died. In relatively healthy individuals, these unresolved complexes could result in dreams, visions, or similar phenomena pertaining to the object(s) of the unresolved complex. These complexes might even become personified. In the extreme situation of personified complexes, such as in a person suffering from schizophrenia, the patient cannot distinguish the personification of the unresolved complex from the seeming reality of being another person. Hence, the schizophrenic "hears" voices in their head, "spoken" by someone else. As Jung further investigated the nature and themes of complexes in psychiatric patients, he found common themes that could not always be attributed to the patient's personal history. And so, he began to form his concept of the collective unconscious (Douglas, 1995; Jarvis, 2004; Jung, 1959b, 1961; Storr, 1983).

> …from the standpoint of the psychology of the personality a twofold division ensures: an "extra-conscious" psyche whose contents are *personal*, and an "extra-conscious" psyche whose contents are *impersonal* and *collective*. The first group comprises contents which are integral components of the individual personality and could therefore just as well be conscious; the second group forms, as it were, an omnipresent, unchanging, and everywhere identical *quality or substrate of the psyche per se*. This is, of course, no more than a hypothesis. But we are driven to it by the peculiar nature of the empirical material…
>
> Whereas the contents of the personal unconscious are acquired during the individual's lifetime, the contents of the collective unconscious are invariably archetypes that were present from the beginning. (pp. 7-8; Jung, 1959c)

Thus, according to Jung, the collective unconscious is a reservoir of psychic resources common to all humans (something along the lines of psychological instinct). These psychic resources, known as **archetypes**, are passed down through the generations of a culture, but Jung considered them to be inherited, not learned. As generation after generation experienced similar phenomena, the archetypal images were formed. Despite cultural differences, the human experience has been similar in many ways throughout history. As such, there are certain archetypes common to all people. According to Jung, the most empirically valid archetypes, and therefore the most powerful, are the **shadow**, the **anima**, and the **animus** (Jung, 1959c).

Jung described the shadow as "the inferior and less commendable part of a person," and "a moral problem that challenges the whole ego-personality" (Jung, 1940, 1959c). It encompasses desires and feelings that are not acceptable to society or the conscious psyche. With effort the shadow can be somewhat assimilated into the conscious personality, but portions of it are highly resistant to moral control. As a result, we tend to project those thoughts, feelings, or emotions onto other people. When they have moved beyond one's control, such as when we lose our temper, these projections isolate the individual from their environment, since they are no longer approaching situations realistically. Jung described the circumstance as tragic when people continue to ruin their lives, and the lives of others, because they cannot see through the illusion of how their shadow has been projected, and consequently interfered with their ability to live a healthy life (Jung, 1959c).

The shadow is not, however, entirely evil. Rather, Jung described it as un-adapted and awkward, much like a child trying to function in the company of adults. Trying to entirely suppress the shadow is not the appropriate solution, since the shadow is driving us forward in our efforts to achieve balance between the unconscious and conscious realities. In other words, just as a child may act inappropriately while trying to grow up, the shadow may cause inappropriate behavior in opposition to the accepted rules of society. Nonetheless, it is important for us to have that driving force pushing us toward self-development (and the development of the human species), so that we don't simply live a life of passivity and/or reaction to outside events. It is the shadow that pushes us forward (Jacobi & Hull, 1970; Jung, 1961).

Although many people emphasize the differences between men and women, psychologically their common traits can readily be observed. Jung described the anima as the female aspect of the male psyche, and the animus as the male aspect of the female psyche. Jung intentionally addresses this difficult concept in mythological terms, but he also makes it clear that this is a natural phenomenon for each person, and not a substitute for one's mother (in the case of the anima) or father (in the case of the animus). While the presence of a feminine aspect within the male psyche and the presence of a masculine aspect within the female psyche have some positive benefits, such as making it possible for men and women to relate to one another, the unfortunate reality is often the opposite. In 1959(c), Jung described the difficulties that men and women have relating to family and friends of the opposite sex, due to fundamental differences in style. Although men may contain the anima, they are still primarily masculine, whereas women, despite the animus, are still primarily feminine. As with the shadow, relationship problems can arise from the anima or animus when we allow our archetypal image to be projected onto others. As Jung himself noted, many men project a desired image onto a woman that would require her to be a sexually vivacious virgin, something of a contradiction in terms. Thus, over time, such a man's relationships may suffer as a result of his learning more about the real life of his companion, even though she has done nothing but be herself (Jung, 1940, 1959c).

Jung did not place a limit on the number of possible archetypes, and he described quite a few in his writings. It did not matter to Jung whether archetypes were, in fact, real. In a perspective quite similar to cognitive theorists, he wrote that "insofar as the archetypes act upon me, they are real and actual to me, even though I do not know what their real nature is" (Jung, 1961). One of the more important archetypes is the self, which represents the integration of the whole personality. Indeed, Jung described the self as the goal of all psychic development. A special type of image often associated with the self, and with Jung himself, is the **mandala**. A mandala is a geometric figure that represents wholeness, completeness, perfection (Jung, 1958). They also tend to be symmetrical, representing the natural balance of opposites. Although they typically have religious or spiritual significance, it is not required. Jung was very interested in mandalas, and from 1916 to 1918 he draw a new one every morning (Wehr, 1989). Mandalas can appear in dreams as an image of wholeness, or in times of stress they may appear as compensatory images (Douglas, 1995). Their potential healing ability stems from their connection between the uniqueness of our present consciousness and the depths of our primordial past:

> ...The psyche is not of today; its ancestry goes back many millions of years. Individual consciousness is only the flower and the fruit of a season, sprung from the perennial rhizome beneath the earth; and it would find itself in better accord with the truth if it took the existence of the rhizome into its calculations. For the root matter is the mother of all things. (pg. xxiv; Jung, 1956)

Jung often drew unique mandalas. [Image from Wikimedia Commons]

It is important to note that archetypal images are considered to be ancient. Although we talk about them as if they are still forming, and that may well be possible, the fact is that there were countless human generations long before recorded history. Jung has referred to archetypes as primordial images, "impressed upon the mind since of old" (Jung, 1940). Archetypes have been expressed as myths and fables, some of which are thousands of years old even within recorded history. As the eternal, symbolic images representing archetypes were developed, they naturally attracted and fascinated people. That, according to Jung, is why they have such profound impact, even today, in our seemingly advanced, knowledgeable, and scientific societies.

Table 4.1: Common Archetypes in Jung's Theory of the Collective Unconscious*	
Self	Integration and wholeness of the personality, the center of the totality of the psyche; symbolically represented by, e.g., the mandala, Christ, or by helpful animals (such as Rin Tin Tin and Lassie or the Hindu monkey god Hanuman)
Shadow	The dark, inferior, emotional, and immoral aspects of the psyche; symbolically represented by, e.g., the Devil (or an evil character such as Dracula), dragons, monsters (such as Godzilla)
Anima	Strange, wraithlike image of an idealized women, yet contrary to the masculinity of the man, draws the man into feminine (as defined by gender roles) behavior, always a supernatural element; symbolically represented by, e.g., personifications of witches, the Greek Sirens, a *femme fatale*, or in more positive ways as the Virgin Mary, a romanticized beauty (such as Helen of Troy) or a cherished car
Animus	A source of meaning and power for women, it can be opinionated, divisive, and create animosity toward men, but also creates a capacity for reflection, deliberation, and self-knowledge; symbolically represented by, e.g., death, murderers (such as the pirate Bluebeard, who killed all his wives), a band of outlaws, a bewitched prince (such as the beast in "Beauty and the Beast") or a romantic actor (such as Rudolph Valentino)
Persona	A protective cover, or mask, that we present to the world to make a specific impression and to conceal our inner self; symbolically represented by, e.g., a coat or mantle
Hero	One who overcomes evil, destruction, and death, often has a miraculous but humble birth; symbolically represented by, e.g., angels, Christ the Redeemer, or a god-man (such as Hercules)
Wise Old Man	Typically a personification of the self, associated with saints, sages, and prophets; symbolically represented as, e.g., the magician Merlin or an Indian guru
Trickster	A childish character with pronounced physical appetites, seeks only gratification and can be cruel and unfeeling; symbolically represented by, e.g., animals (such as Brer Rabbit, Wile E. Coyote or, often, monkeys) or a mischievous god (such as the Norse god Loki)
*For more information read *The Integration of the Personality* (Jung, 1940), *Aion: Researches Into the Phenomenology of the Self* (Jung, 1959c), and *Man and His Symbols* (Jung, et al., 1964).	

Discussion Question: What is your impression of the concept of archetypes? Think about mythic heroes and gods, or concepts of motherhood or being a father. Can you identify commonalities between different cultures, now or throughout time, which seem to suggest themes that are common to all people?

Connections Across Cultures: Symbolism Throughout Time and Around the world

Near the end of Jung's life, he was asked to write a book that might make his theories more accessible to common readers. Jung initially refused, but then he had an interesting dream, receiving advice from his unconscious psyche that he should reconsider his refusal:

> …He dreamed that, instead of sitting in his study and talking to the great doctors and psychiatrists who used to call on him from all over the world, he was standing in a public place and addressing a multitude of people who were listening to him with rapt attention and *understanding what he said*… (pg. 10; John Freeman, in his introduction to *Man and His Symbols*, Jung et al., 1964)

Jung then agreed to write the book that became known as *Man and His Symbols*, but only if he could hand-pick the co-authors who would help him. Jung supervised every aspect of the book, which was nearly finished when he died. Written purposefully to be easily understood by a wide audience, the book presents an astonishingly wide variety of symbolism from art, archaeology, myth, and analysis within the context of Jung's theories. Many of the symbols were represented in dreams, and symbolic dreams are the primary means by which our unconscious psyche communicates with our conscious psyche, or ego. It is extraordinary to see how similar such symbolism has been throughout time and across cultures, even though each individual example is unique to the person having the dream or expressing themselves openly.

Symbols, according to Jung, are terms, names, images, etc. that may be familiar in everyday life, but as symbols they come to represent something vague and unknown, they take on meaning that is hidden from us. More specifically, they represent something within our unconscious psyche that cannot ever be fully explained. Exploring the meaning will not unlock the secrets of the symbol, because its meaning is beyond reason. Jung suggests that this should not seem strange, since there is nothing that we perceive fully. Our eyesight is limited, as is our hearing. Even when we use tools to enhance our senses, we still only see better, or hear better. We don't comprehend the true nature of visual objects or sounds, we only experience them differently, within our psychic realm as opposed to their physical reality. And yet, the symbols created by our unconscious psyche are very important, since the unconscious is at least half of our being, and it is infinitely broader than our conscious psyche (Jung et al., 1964).

Jung believed that the symbols created in dreams have a deeper meaning than Freud recognized. Freud believed that dreams simply represent the unconscious aspects of one's psyche. Jung believed, however, that dreams represent a psyche all their own, a vast and ancient psyche connected to the entire history of humanity (the collective unconscious). Therefore, dreams can tell a story of their own, such as Jung's dream encouraging him to write a book for a common audience. Thus, his dream did not reflect some underlying neurosis connected to childhood trauma, but rather, his unconscious psyche was pushing him forward, toward a sort of wholeness of self by making his theories more readily accessible to those who are not sufficiently educated in the wide variety of complex topics that are typically found in Jung's writings. By virtue of the same reasoning, Jung considered dreams to be quite personal. They could not be interpreted with dream manuals, since no object has any fixed symbolic meaning.

What makes the symbolism within dreams, as well as in everyday life, most fascinating, however, is how common it is throughout the world, both in ancient times and today. In their examination of symbols and archetypes, Jung and his colleagues offer visual examples from: Egypt, England, Japan, the Congo, Tibet, Germany, Belgium, the United States, Bali, Haiti, Greece, Switzerland, Spain, Italy, Cameroon, Java, France, Kenya, India, Sweden, Russia, Poland, Australia, China, Hungary, Malaysia, Borneo, Finland, the Netherlands, Rhodesia, Israel, Saudi Arabia, Scotland, Ireland, Brazil, Monaco, Burma, Bolivia, Cambodia, Denmark, Macedonia, and Peru, as well as from Mayan, Celtic, Babylonian, Persian, Navaho, and Haidu cultures. There are also many Biblical references. It would be safe to say that no one else in the history of psychology has so clearly demonstrated the cross-cultural reality of their theory as is the case with Carl Jung.

Of course, as with dreams, many of these symbols are unique to the culture in which they have arisen. Therefore, it takes a great deal of training and experience for a psychotherapist to work with patients from different cultures. Nonetheless, the patterns represent the same basic concepts, such as self, shadow, anima, animus, hero, etc. Once recognized in their cultural context, the analyst would have a starting point from which to begin working with their patient, or the artist would understand how to influence their audience. One important type of art that relies heavily on cultural images and cues is advertising. Cultural differences can create problems for companies pursuing global marketing campaigns. Jung's theory suggests that similarities in how we react to certain archetypal themes should be similar in different countries, but of course the images themselves must be recognizable, and we may still be a long way from understanding those fundamental images:

> ...Our actual knowledge of the unconscious shows that it is a natural phenomenon and that, like Nature herself, it is at least *neutral*. It contains all aspects of human nature – light and dark, beautiful and ugly, good and evil, profound and silly. The study of individual, as well as of collective, symbolism is an enormous task, and one that has not yet been mastered. (pg. 103; Jung et al., 1964)

Personality Types

One of Jung's most practical theories, and one that has been quite influential, is his work on **personality types**. Jung had conducted an extensive review of the available literature on personality types, including perspectives from ancient Brahmanic conceptions taken from the Indian Vedas (see below) and types described by the American psychologist William James. In keeping with one of Jung's favorite themes, James had emphasized opposing pairs as the characteristics of his personality types, such as rationalism vs. empiricism, idealism vs. materialism, or optimism vs. pessimism (see Jung, 1971). Based on his research and clinical experience, Jung proposed a system of personality types based on **attitude-types** and **function-types** (more commonly referred to simply as attitudes and functions). Once again, the attitudes and functions are based on opposing ways of interacting with one's environment.

The two attitude-types are based on one's orientation to external objects (which includes other people). The **introvert** is intent on withdrawing libido from objects, as if to ensure that the object can have no power over the person. In contrast, the **extravert** extends libido toward an object, establishing an active relationship. Jung considered introverts and extraverts to be common amongst all groups of people, from all walks of life. Today, most psychologists acknowledge that there is a clear genetic component to these temperaments (Kagan, 1984, 1994; Kagan, Kearsley, & Zelazo 1978), a suggestion proposed by Jung as well (Jung, 1971). Of course, one cannot have an orientation to objects without consciousness, and consciousness cannot exist without an **ego**. For Jung, the ego is a complex, so it is associated with both the conscious psyche and the personal unconscious. According to Jung, "it is always in the center of our attention and of our desires, and it is the absolutely indispensable centre of consciousness" (Jung, 1968).

Jung's four functions describe ways in which we orient ourselves to the external environment, given our basic tendency toward introversion or extraversion. The first opposing pair of functions is **thinking** vs. **feeling**. Thinking involves intellect, it tells you *what* a thing is, whereas feeling is values-based, it tells what a thing is *worth* to you. For example, if you are trying to choose classes for your next semester of college, perhaps you need to choose between a required general education course as opposed to a personally interesting course like *Medical First Responder* or *Interior Design*. If you are guided first by thinking, you will probably choose the course that fulfills a requirement, but if you are guided by feeling, you may choose the course that satisfies your more immediate interests. The second opposing pair of functions is **sensing** vs. **intuition**. Sensing describes paying attention to the reality of your external environment, it tells you that something *is*. In contrast, intuition incorporates a sense of time, and allows for hunches. Intuition may seem mysterious, and Jung freely acknowledges that he is particularly mystical, yet he offers an interesting perspective on this issue:

> ...Intuition is a function by which you see round corners, which you really cannot do; yet the fellow will do it for you and you trust him. It is a function which normally you do not use if you live a regular life within four walls and do regular routine work. But if you are on the Stock Exchange or in Central Africa, you will use your hunches like anything. You cannot, for instance, calculate whether when you turn round a corner in the bush you will meet a rhinoceros or a tiger - but you get a hunch, and it will perhaps save your life... (pg. 14; Jung, 1968)

The two attitudes and the four functions combine to form eight personality types. Jung described a so-called cross of the functions, with the ego in the center being influenced by the pairs of functions (Jung, 1968). Considering whether the ego's attitude is primarily introverted or extraverted, one could also propose a parallel pair of crosses. Jung's theory on personality types has proven quite influential, and led to the development of two well-known and very popular instruments used to measure one's personality type, so that one might then make reasoned decisions about real-life choices.

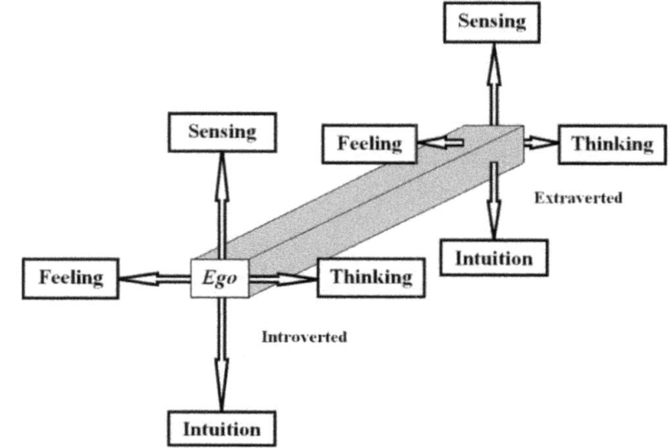

Jung proposed a "cross of the functions," in which the ego sits at the center of the opposing pairs of functions (Jung, 1968). When the attitudes of introversion and extraversion are included, one can represent Jung's view as parallel crosses of the functions. [Image by Mark Kelland]

Discussion Question: Jung described two attitudes (introversion-extraversion) and four functions (thinking-feeling, sensing-intuition) as the primary basis for psychological types. Think about yourself and/or some of your close friends and family members. Can you use the eight types described by Jung to get a reasonable impression of the people you know, or does Jung's theory seem to fall short?

In 1923, Katharine Briggs and her daughter Isabel Briggs Myers learned of Jung's personality types and became quite interested in his theory. After spending 20 years observing individuals of different types, they added one more pair of factors based on a person's preference for either a more structured lifestyle, called **judging**, or a more flexible or adaptable lifestyle, called **perceiving**. There were now, according to Briggs and Myers, sixteen possible personality types. In the 1940s, Isabel Myers began developing the **Myers-Briggs Type Indicator** (MBTI) in order to help people learn about their personality type. To provide just one example of an MBTI profile, an individual who is extraverted and prefers sensing, thinking, and judging (identified by the initials ESTJ) would be described as: "Practical, realistic, matter-of-fact. Decisive, quickly move to implement decisions. Organize projects and people to get things done...Forceful in implementing their plans" (Myers, 1993; Myers & McCaulley, 1985; see also the website for the Myers & Briggs Foundation, at www.myersbriggs.org). While it is relatively easy to find shortcut tests or variations of the MBTI online, if one plans to make any meaningful decisions based on their personality type they should consult a trained MBTI administrator. What sort of decision might one make? The MBTI has become a popular tool for looking at career choices and workplace relationships. A number of popular books, such as *Do What You Are* (Tieger & Barron-Tieger, 2001) and *Type Talk at Work* (Kroeger, Thuesen, & Rutledge, 2002), are available that provide information intended to help people choose satisfying careers and be successful in complex work environments. In addition to its use in career counseling, the MBTI has been used in individual counseling, marriage counseling, and in educational settings

(Myers, 1993; Myers & McCaulley, 1985; Myers & Myers, 1980). Another popular instrument, based once again on Jung's theory and compared directly to the MBTI, is the **Keirsey Temperament Sorter**. David Keirsey uses plain language in an effort to make personality types easy to comprehend. Setting aside introversion vs. extraversion, he has identified eight character portraits: mentors, organizers, monitors, operators, advocates, engineers, conservators, and players. When Keirsey adds extraversion and introversion back into the mixture, he can identify one's personality type even more clearly: monitors become either supervisors (E) or inspectors (I), players become performers (E) or composers (I), engineers become inventors (E) or designers (I), etc. As with the MBTI, Keirsey provides concrete recommendations regarding how one might use the results of his temperament sorter to make decisions about one's choices in life (Keirsey, 1987).

Table 4.2: Jung's Eight Personality Types*

Type	Description
Introverted Thinking	Focused on own internal thoughts and ideas, do not communicate well, can be highly conflicted and will lash out at critics, generally stubborn and do not get along well with others
Introverted Feeling	Tend to be silent, inaccessible, and melancholy, have deep emotions but hide them and appear cold and reserved on the surface, tend to be suspicious of others, most are women
Introverted Sensing	Guided by subjective impression of real-life objects, often express their sensations through artistic endeavors, the objective world may seem make-believe and comical
Introverted Intuitive	Tend to be peculiar and lack contact with reality, may be completely misunderstood even by those who are close to them, may seem like a mystical dreamer and seer on one hand but just a cranky person on the other, may have vision but lack convincing power of reason
Extraverted Thinking	Seek intellectual conclusions based on objective reality, seek to influence others, suppress emotion, can be rigid and dogmatic (tyrannical when others penetrate their power province)
Extraverted Feeling	Feelings harmonize with objective situations, can be highly emotional, will avoid thinking when it proves upsetting, most are women
Extraverted Sensing	Immersed in realism and seek new experiences, whole aim is concrete enjoyment, most are men
Extraverted Intuitive	Always seek new opportunities, may seize new opportunity with enthusiasm and just as quickly abandon it if not promising, has vision, often found among business tycoons and politicians, but have little regard for welfare of others

*For more information read *Psychological Types* (Jung, 1971).

Personality Development

Jung believed that "everyone's ultimate aim and strongest desire lie in developing the fullness of human existence that is called personality" (Jung, 1940). However, he lamented the misguided attempts of society to educate children into their personalities. Not only did he doubt the abilities the average parent or average teacher to lead children through the child's personality development, given their own personal limitations, he considered it a mistake to expect children to act like young adults:

> It is best not to apply to children the high ideal of education to personality. For what is generally understood by personality - namely, a *definitely shaped, psychic abundance, capable of resistance and endowed with energy* - is an adult ideal...No personality is manifested without *definiteness*, *fullness*, and *maturity*. These three characteristics do not, and should not, fit the child, for they would rob it of its childhood. (pp. 284-285; Jung, 1940)

This is not to suggest that childhood is simply a carefree time for children:

> No one will deny or even underestimate the importance of childhood years; the severe injuries, often lasting through life, caused by a nonsensical upbringing at home and in school are too obvious, and the need for reasonable pedagogic methods is too urgent...But who rears children to personality? In the first and most important place we have the ordinary, incompetent parents who are often themselves, all their lives, partly or wholly children. (pg. 282; Jung, 1940)

So, if childhood is a critical time, but most adults never grow up themselves, what hope does Jung see for the future? The answer is to be found in midlife. According to Jung, the middle years of life are "a time of supreme psychological importance" and "the moment of greatest unfolding" in one's life (cited in Jacobi & Hull, 1970). In keeping with the ancient tradition of the Vedic stages of life, from Hindu and Indian culture, the earlier stages of life are about education, developing a career, having a family, and serving one's proper role within society:

> Man has two aims: The first is the aim of nature, the begetting of children and all the business of protecting the brood; to this period belongs the gaining of money and social position. When this aim is satisfied, there begins another phase, namely, that of culture. For the attainment of the former goal we have the help of nature, and moreover of education; but little or nothing helps us toward the latter goal... (pg. 125; Jung, cited in Jacobi & Hull, 1970)

So where does one look for the answers to life? Obviously, there is no simple answer to that question, or rather, than are many answers to that question. Some pursue spiritual answers, such as meditating or devoting themselves to charitable causes. Some devote themselves to their children and grandchildren, others to gardening, painting, or woodworking. The answer for any particular individual is based on that person's **individuation**.

Individuation is the process by which a person actually becomes an "individual," differentiated from all other people. It is not to be confused with the ego, or with the conscious psyche, since it includes aspects of the personal unconscious, as influenced by the collective unconscious. Jung also described individuation as the process by which one becomes a "whole" person. To some extent, this process draws the individual away from society, toward being just that, an individual. However, keeping in mind the collective unconscious, Jung believed that individuation leads to more intense and broader collective relationships, rather than leading to isolation. This is what is meant by a whole person, one who successfully integrates the conscious psyche, or ego, with the unconscious psyche. Jung also addresses the Eastern approaches, such as meditation, as being misguided in their attempts to master the unconscious mind. The goal of individuation is wholeness, wholeness of ego, unconscious psyche, and community (Jung, 1940, 1971):

> Consciousness and the unconscious do not make a whole when either is suppressed or damaged by the other. If they must contend, let it be a fair fight with equal right on both sides. Both are aspects of life...It is the old play of hammer and anvil: the suffering iron between them will in the end be shaped into an unbreakable whole, the individual. (pg. 27; Jung, 1940)

Jimmy Carter was a successful farmer, Governor of Georgia, and President of the United States. As president he brokered a peace treaty between Egypt and Israel that earned him a Nobel Peace Prize nomination. Despite such an illustrious life to that point, he has, perhaps, done even more good since then. After devoting himself to a wide variety of social and political activities focusing on peace and justice, including personally building houses with Habitat for Humanity, the Honorable Mr. Carter received a well-earned Nobel Peace Prize in 2002. [Presidential portraits are in the public domain.]

Discussion Question: Jung identified the first half of life as a time to take care of the biological needs of the species (e.g., raising children). It is in the second half of life, according to Jung, that one looks within oneself for the guidance and motivation to fulfill the needs of society and one's culture.

Jungian Analysis

Jung was deeply moved by his ability to help patients, and he took the process of analysis very seriously. This is not to say, however, that he considered a specific process to be necessary. He was suspicious of theoretical assumptions, he focused on each individual in therapy, and was just as likely to adapt Adlerian techniques as he was to adapt Freudian techniques. In fact, he considered general professional experience to be an important aspect of one's ability to be a good analyst. He did consider training to be very important, and that it should include medical training. He was not opposed to lay analysts (those with a Ph.D., rather than an M.D.), but felt that they should be supervised by a psychiatrist (Jung, 1961).

He built his general system of psychotherapy on four tenets: the psyche is a self-regulating system, the unconscious has creative and compensatory components, the doctor-patient relationship is crucial, and personality growth takes place throughout the lifespan. In addition, the process of psychotherapy involves four stages: **confession**, **elucidation**, **education**, and **transformation** (see Douglas, 1995). The confession and elucidation stages involve the patient recounting elements of their personal history, dreams, and fantasies, followed by the analyst bringing attention to symptoms, transferences, and attempting to help the patient gain insight on both intellectual and emotional levels. The education stage then involves moving the patient into the realm of an individual, hopefully as an adapted social being. Education focuses mostly on the persona and the ego, whereas confession and elucidation serve the role of exploring the personal unconscious. The education stage also involves trying to provide the patient with realistic options for changing their behavior. The final stage, transformation, was described by Jung as being similar to self-actualization. Also like self-actualization, not every patient (or person) makes it to this stage. Addressing the archetypal image of the self, the image of wholeness, requires working with the whole range of the conscious, personal unconscious, and collective unconscious psyches. The final goal is to inspire the patient to become a uniquely individual self without losing a sense of responsible integrity (the collectiveness inherent in the collective unconscious; see Douglas, 1995).

Since Jung did not want to be tied to any specific technique(s), he incorporated a variety of techniques as appropriate for each patient. Like Freud, Jung experimented with hypnosis early in his career, but discarded the technique as ineffective. He used dream analysis regularly, but did not consider each dream to be necessarily important. Instead, he looked for patterns in dreams over time, particularly recurring dreams. Jung taught his patients to get in touch with their own unconscious psyche through an active imagination technique. This meditative imagery procedure is somewhat similar to that of the Buddhist mindfulness techniques taught by Gotama Buddha some 2,600 years ago, but involves much more active cognition. Jung's active imagery technique was also extended into actual physical activity. Jung found it helpful, especially with particularly withdrawn patients, to have them act out their thoughts and feeling. Jung would even mimic their movements to help himself better understand what his patients were trying to communicate (Douglas, 1995). The importance of physical states, as reflective of psychological states, was developed in more detail in the somatic psychology theories of Wilhelm Reich. In addition, Jung extended his therapeutic approach to group therapy, family and marital therapy, art therapy, child therapy, and the recurrent nightmares of patients suffering from post-traumatic stress. Through it all, Jung paid special attention to complexes, as representative of the psychic processes of the patient. Once an analyst understands both the symptoms and the complexes of the patient, Jung believed, the analyst has found the key to treatment (Douglas, 1995).

Like Freud, Jung felt that analytical psychology could serve a greater purpose beyond just helping individuals, so he turned his attention to society in several of his books. In *Modern Man in Search of a Soul* (Jung, 1933), Jung addressed the spiritual problems of our times. A modern person, according to Jung, is one who is whole, aware of their conscious psyche and their unconscious psyche (both personal and collective). Though such people are few and far between, Jung believed he saw evidence of a need for understanding the unconscious psyche. One obvious piece of evidence was the rise of psychology as a discipline at the beginning of the twentieth century. However, in contrast to Jung's personal preference, psychology has largely moved away spiritual pursuits, with its preference for a scientific evaluation of the human mind. Religion, in Jung's opinion, has also moved away from spirituality, in favor of the dogma of human rules and regulations. Jung believed that we can learn a great deal from Yoga and Buddhism in terms of blending psychology and spirituality in order to understand the whole nature of human beings. In *The Undiscovered Self* (Jung, 1957), Jung continues this argument in a more personal way. He suggests that modern psychological approaches to "self-knowledge" are at best superficial, and don't address the real psychic processes that lead to individuality. As a general condemnation of our obsession with science, he questions any theory based on statistical averages, since those averages say very little at all about the unique units being studied, whether they are people or some other object. In *Civilization in Transition* (Jung, 1964), the tenth volume of Jung's collected works, he addresses the problems of American psychology, and what all Westerners can learn from the ancient wisdom of India about studying our own unconscious psyche. The importance of understanding the true and complete nature of our psyche is that until we do we cannot live our lives to the fullest:

> Our souls as well as our bodies are composed of individual elements which were all already present in the ranks of our ancestors. The "newness" in the individual psyche is an endlessly varied recombination of age-old components...Once the past has been breached, it is usually annihilated, and there is no stopping the forward motion. But it is precisely the loss of connection with the past, our uprootedness, which has given rise to the "discontents" of civilization and to such a flurry and haste that we live more in the future and its chimerical promises of a golden age than in the present, with which our whole evolutionary background has not yet caught up. (pp. 235-236; Jung, 1961)

A Final Note on Carl Jung

It can be something of a challenge to view Jung's work as psychological. It lends itself more readily to, perhaps, the study of the humanities, with elements of medieval pseudo-science, Asian culture, and native religions (an odd combination, to be sure). With titles such as *Aion: Researches into the Phenomenology of the Self* (Jung, 1959c) and *Mysterium Conjunctionis: An Inquiry into the Separation and Synthesis of Psychic Opposites in Alchemy* (Jung, 1970), Jung is not exactly accessible without a wide range of knowledge in areas other than psychology. **Alchemy** was of particular interest to Jung, but not in terms of turning base metals into gold (alchemy is a strange mixture of spirituality and chemistry). Rather, Jung believed that psychology could find its base in alchemy, and that it was the collective unconscious that came forth in the ongoing human effort to understand the nature of matter (Jaffe, 1979; Jung, 1961; Wehr, 1989). He even went so far as to write about flying saucers, the astrological seasons of time, and the prophesies of Nostradamus (Jung, 1959c; Storr, 1983).

And yet, Jung addressed some very important and interesting topics in psychology. His theory of psychological types is reflected in trait descriptions of personality and corresponding trait tests, such as Cattell's 16-PF and the MMPI. The value Jung placed on mid-life and beyond, based largely on the ancient Vedic stages of life, suggests that one is not doomed to the negative alternative in Erikson's final psychosocial crises. So Jung's personal interests, and his career as a whole, straddled the fence between surreal and practical. He may always be best-known for his personal relationship with Freud, brief as it was, but the blending of Eastern and Western thought is becoming more common in psychology. So perhaps Jung himself will become more accessible to the field of psychology, and we may find a great deal to be excited about in his curious approach to psychodynamic theory.

Personality Theory in Real Life: Synchronicity - Coincidence or an Experience with Mystical Spirituality?

Many people are deeply religious and many others consider themselves to be just as deeply spiritual, though not connected to any specific religion. As important as religion and spirituality are in the lives of many people, psychology has tended to avoid these topics, primarily because they do not lend themselves readily to scientific investigation. Jung certainly did not avoid these topics, and he studied a wide range of spiritual topics. For example, he wrote the foreword for Richard Wilhelm's translation of the *I Ching* (Wilhelm, 1950), he wrote psychological commentary for a translation of *The Tibetan Book of the Great Liberation* (Evans-Wentz & Jung, 1954), he discussed the psychology of evil in *Answer to Job* (Jung, 1954), he wrote about Gnostic traditions at length (see Segal, 1992), and one of the volumes of his collected works is entitled *Psychology and Religion: West and East* (Jung, 1958). In addition to his varied spiritual interests, Jung became interested in psychological phenomena that could not be explained in scientific terms. Such phenomena do not necessarily require a spiritual explanation, but in the absence of any other way to explain them, they are often thought of in spiritual terms. One such topic is **synchronicity**.

Jung uses the term synchronicity to describe the "coincidence in time of two or more causally unrelated events which have the same or a similar meaning" (Jung & Pauli, 1955). In particular, it refers to the simultaneous occurrence of a particular psychic state with one or more external events that have a meaningful parallel to one's current experience or state of mind. I would like to share with you two experiences of synchronicity from my own life. Having a Ph.D. in physiological psychology, and having spent a number of years conducting biomedical research, it seems rather strange to be sharing experiences that can be classified as extrasensory perception, or ESP. Jung also found it difficult to address this topic:

> …If I have now conquered my hesitation and at last come to grips with my theme, it is chiefly because my experiences of the phenomenon of synchronicity have multiplied themselves over the decades…As a psychiatrist and psychotherapist I have often come up against the phenomena in question and could convince myself how much these inner experiences meant to my patients. In most cases they were things which people do not talk about for fear of exposing themselves to thoughtless ridicule. I was amazed to see how many people have had experiences of this kind and how carefully the secret was guarded. So my interest in this problem has a human as well as a scientific foundation. (pp. 5-6; Jung, in Jung & Pauli, 1955)

<u>Synchronicity Experience #1</u>: In February, 1992, our first son, Mark David Kelland, Jr., died at birth. Later that year, I was traveling across the country, taking a whole week to get to a neuroscience convention in California, and I decided to hike up Wheeler Peak, the highest point in New Mexico (13,161 feet). I arrived a little late in the day, but decided I had enough time to make the climb and get back down off the ridge before dark. I just made it, but still had a few miles to go on the jeep trail down to the parking lot. Along the way, I stopped and looked back up at Wheeler Peak. I turned off my flashlight, and in the dark I could just make out the outline of the mountain against the night sky. I prayed to God for a sign that our son was in Heaven. The instant I said "Amen," a brilliant shooting star streaked across the sky and descended behind Wheeler Peak! I took it to be the sign I had asked for.

<u>Synchronicity Experience #2</u>: While growing up, we lived next door to Bill and Jackie O'Reilly, who co-owned the corner drugstore in the center of Foxborough, MA. When I was

young I mowed their lawn in the summer and shoveled their driveway in the winter. When I was old enough to get a regular job, I asked Mr. O'Reilly for a letter of recommendation for a job at the local newspaper. He declined, saying he wanted me to work at their drugstore. But he didn't say anything else, until Mrs. O'Reilly told him to give me a job. So, I worked at the drugstore from the age of 15 to 20 years old. I even began college at the same school they had attended: the Massachusetts College of Pharmacy. Although I changed schools and switched my major to psychology, I was always hopeful that the O'Reilly's would be proud of me. Unfortunately, Bill O'Reilly died a week after I graduated from college. Jackie O'Reilly retired and sold their building, and the old corner drugstore in the center of town ceased to exist.

Eventually I moved away, pursued my career in psychology, got married and had children, and visits to Massachusetts became few and far between. One night, about 25 years after I had worked at the drugstore, I had a very vivid and moving dream. I was standing in the center of Foxborough, looking at the building where the drugstore had been. I was overwhelmed by a profound sense of sadness, sad that things must change with time and cannot remain the same, no matter how much we may long for the past. I awoke from that dream astonished by its sense of reality and its emotional impact. The next morning my mother called me, and told me that Jackie O'Reilly had died during the night! Was it merely a coincidence that I dreamt about O'Reilly's Pharmacy and felt the sadness of watching time pass away, while Jackie O'Reilly was in reality passing away, or was it something more? There can be no scientific explanation. I searched my mind for anything that might have coincidentally caused me to think about the drugstore the day before, but nothing came to mind except for an alternative explanation, which was not at all scientific. Had Jackie O'Reilly's spirit passed by and said goodbye, on her way to the great beyond?

In the quote cited above, Jung wrote that he was amazed by how many people have had experiences of synchronicity. The questions I would pose to you are quite simple. Have you ever experienced synchronicity? If you have not, do you consider it possible that such events occur as something more than simple (if improbable) coincidence?

Before dismissing synchronicity as non-scientific, keep in mind the circumstances that led Jung to this theory. In addition to personally knowing Wolfgang Pauli, Jung also knew Nils Bohr and Albert Einstein (both of whom, like Pauli, had won a Nobel Prize in physics). Although these men are considered among the greatest scientists of modern times, Einstein perhaps the greatest, consider some of their theories. For instance, Einstein proposed that time isn't time, it's relative, except for the speed of light, which alone is always constant. In recent years, experimental physicists have exceeded the speed of light, broken Heisenberg's Uncertainty Principle (which, by definition, couldn't be broken), and proposed that it might be possible to get something colder than absolute zero. How can we accept things that cannot be observed or proved as scientific, while rejecting something that Jung and many others have observed time and time again? Jung was impressed by the possibility of splitting atoms, and wondered if such a thing might be possible with the psyche. As physics suggested strange new possibilities, Jung held out the same hope for humanity (Progoff, 1973).

Regardless of whether the strangest of Jung's theories are ever proven right or wrong, at the very least they provide an opportunity for interesting discussions! There also happens to be another well-known person in the history of psychology who has experienced synchronicity and who talked about many of her patients having had out-of-body and near-death experiences: Elisabeth Kubler-Ross. In her book *On Children and Death* (Kubler-Ross, 1983), Kubler-Ross describes even more serious concerns than Jung about discussing this topic, but as with Jung, she has also met many, many patients who have had these experiences:

> …I have been called every possible name, from Antichrist to Satan himself; I have been labeled, reviled, and otherwise denounced…But it is impossible to ignore the thousands of stories that patients - children and adults alike - have shared with me. These illuminations cannot be explained in scientific language. Listening to these

experiences and sharing many of them myself, it would seem hypocritical and dishonest to me not to mention them in my lectures and workshops. So I have shared all of what I have learned from my patients for the last two decades, and I intend to continue to do so. (pg. 106; Kubler-Ross, 1983)

Discussion Question: Jung studied and wrote about topics as diverse as alchemy, astrology, flying saucers, ESP, the prophecies of Nostradamus, and synchronicity. Does this make it difficult for you to believe any of his theories? If you don't believe anything about any of these topics, are you still able to find value in other theories proposed by Jung?

Review of Key Points

- As a child, Jung was introduced to a wide variety of cultural and religious perspectives from around the world. As a result of these experiences, he was open to many different perspectives throughout his career.
- Jung had extremely vivid dreams, many of which he interpreted as visions (or unconscious communications) intended to guide his actions.
- Jung called his approach "analytical psychology" in order to distinguish it from Freud's "psychoanalysis" and Adler's "individual psychology."
- An important starting point for Jung's theories was the concept of entropy, which proposes an eventual balance of all energy. Jung applied this concept to the psychic energy present in the conscious and unconscious psyches.
- Jung proposed two distinct realms within the unconscious psyche, the personal and the collective.
- According to Jung, the personal unconscious is revealed through its complexes.
- Jung advanced the Word Association Test as a means of examining the complexes contained within the personal unconscious.
- The collective unconscious communicates through archetypal images. Jung believed the most readily observed archetypes are the shadow, the anima, and the animus.
- Another important archetype is the self, the representation of wholeness and the completed development of the personality. The self is often symbolically represented by mandalas.
- Jung developed a framework for recognizing particular personality types. He proposed two attitudes, introversion and extraversion, and four functions, thinking, feeling, sensing, and intuition.
- Jung's type theory provided the basis for some practical personality tests. The Myers-Briggs Type Indicator and the Keirsey Temperament Sorter are both well-known in the field of psychology.
- Jung believed that everyone's ultimate goal is to fully develop the potential of their personality. Jung called this process individuation.
- Development during the first half of life involves the natural aims of survival and procreation. The second half of life offers the opportunity to seek cultural development and the fulfillment of one's self.
- Jungian analysis follows a basic series of stages, involving confession, elucidation, education, and transformation. However, Jung suggested it was better to avoid being locked into a rigid procedure. As a result, he utilized many different techniques, based on each individual patient.
- As Freud had before him, Jung developed a grand vision of how analytical psychology might help society as a whole. One unique proposition was that the Western world had much to learn from Eastern cultures.
- Jung's interest in topics such as alchemy and extrasensory perception did not sit well with colleagues seeking to establish psychology as a scientific discipline. This opposition to Jung remains quite strong today, though Western psychology is broadening its perspective.

Review of Key Terms

alchemy analytical psychology anima	feeling function-types hero	persona personal unconscious personality types

animus archetypes attitude-types collective unconscious complex confession education ego elucidation entropy extravert	individuation introvert intuition judging Keirsey Temperament Sorter mandala Myers-Briggs Type Indicator perceiving	schemas self sensing shadow synchronicity thinking transformation trickster wise old man Word Association Test

Annotated Bibliography

Jung, C. G. (1961). *Memories, dreams, reflections.* New York, NY: Vintage Books.

This is Jung's autobiography, written quite late in his life (actually, he dictated it to his colleague Aniela Jaffe). Since it is a personal description of his life, covering nearly all 85 years, it offers an incomparable view of this extraordinary and complex man.

Jung, C. G. (1959c). Aion: Researches into the phenomenology of the self, 2nd Ed. In Sir H. Read, M. Fordham, G. Adler, & W. McGuire (Eds.), *The collected works of C. G. Jung, Vol. 9* (333 pp.). Princeton, NJ: Princeton University Press.

Jung, C. G. (1940). *The integration of the personality.* London, England: Kegal Paul, Trench, Trubner & Co., Ltd.

These two books contain many of the basic principle of Jung's theory of personality. *Aion: Researches into the Phenomenology of the Self* provides information on the ego, archetypes, the self, and symbolism. It also incorporates many of Jung's ideas on alchemy and Gnosticism. *The Integration of the Personality* focuses on the ultimate goal of individuation, including a case history.

Jung, C. G. (1971). Psychological types. In Sir H. Read, M. Fordham, G. Adler, & W. McGuire (Eds.), *The collected works of C. G. Jung, Vol. 6* (608 pp.). Princeton, NJ: Princeton University Press.

In this book, Jung described a wide variety of approaches to studying the different types of personality, including literary, philosophical, and psychological perspectives. He then proceeds to offer his own theory, going over each attitude and function, and then their combinations, in great detail.

Jung, C. G., von Franz, M.-L., Henderson, J. L., Jacobi, J., & Jaffe, A. (1964). *Man and his symbols.* Garden City, NY: Doubleday & Company.

As described in the chapter, this book represented a project undertaken late in Jung's life, and completed shortly after his death. Jung's goal, in collaboration with four of his most trusted colleagues, was to provide an understandable description of his theories of the collective unconscious and symbolism. The book includes a fascinating array of images from around the world, including many archeological images from civilizations that no longer exist.

Jacobi, J. & Hull, R. F. C. (1970). *C. G. Jung - Psychological reflections.* New York, NY: Harper & Brothers.

There are a number of excellent collections of Jung's writings. This book is particularly enjoyable because it offers brief and specific perspectives by Jung on a variety of issues of everyday interest, including sections on the soul, dreams, men and women, self-realization, good and evil, West and East, and God. It also offers numerous perspectives on each topic, so one gains a good impression of Jung's viewpoint without having to wade through his own extensive and complex books.

Jaffe, A. (1979). C. G. Jung - Word and image. Princeton, NJ: Princeton University Press.
Wehr, G. (1989). ***An illustrated biography of C. G. Jung.*** **Boston, MA: Shambhala.**

Each of these biographies is relatively brief, while still being complete. They also include many graphic images of Jung, his life, and examples of symbols that are representative of his theories. Each book offers an excellent window into the life of Carl Jung in readable and concise formats.

Keirsey, D. (1987). ***Portraits of Temperament.*** **Del Mar, CA: Prometheus Nemesis Book Company.**
Myers, I. B. (1993). ***Introduction to type: A guide to understanding your results on the Myers-Briggs Type Indicator, 5th Ed.*** **Palo Alto, CA: Consulting Psychologists Press.**

These two books represent the most practical applications of Jung's theory on psychological types. The Myers-Briggs Type Indicator may well be the most widely administered psychological test used in non-clinical settings. Keirsey's Temperament Sorter is also quite well-known. There are a number of books by Isabel Myers that go into more detail, but this booklet provides a quick and easy introduction to the work she began with her mother.

Chapter 5 - Alfred Adler and Harry Stack Sullivan

Alfred Adler was an early member and president of the Vienna Psychoanalytic Society, but he never considered himself a follower of Sigmund Freud. He strongly disagreed with Freud's emphasis on sexual desire in the development of personality, focusing instead on children's striving for superiority and the importance of social relationships. He began to address the psychology of women as a cultural phenomenon, as opposed to Freud's view that women are fundamentally incapable of developing a complete and healthy personality. Adler also addressed issues of education, an individual's unique perspective on the world, and family therapy. Adler provided a perspective in which the striving of individuals to improve themselves is an essential characteristic of personality development. Most importantly, he believed that personal improvement and success are best achieved in cooperation with others, and that culture is an important factor in determining how that can be accomplished.

It has been suggested that Adler may have had an even greater influence on the overall development of psychiatry and psychology than Freud himself, and that theorists such as Sullivan, as well as Karen Horney and Erich Fromm, should be recognized as neo-Adlerians, not neo-Freudians (Ellis, 1973; Kaufmann, 1992; Mosak, 1995; Watts, 1999). Indeed, a reviewer of one of Karen Horney's books once wrote that Horney had just written a new book by Adler (see Mosak, 1995). Albert Ellis suggested that Adler set the stage for the cognitive/behavioral psychotherapies that are so popular today (Ellis, 1973). Late in life, Adler encouraged the wife of a good friend to write his biography, and he gave Phyllis Bottome, who was herself a friend of Adler, a great deal of assistance (Bottome, 1957). He wanted to be understood. Perhaps, however, she came to understand him too well:

> Adler was at once the easiest of men to know, and the most difficult; the frankest and the most subtle; the most conciliatory - and the most ruthless. As a colleague he was a model of generosity, accuracy and wholehearted integrity, but woe betide that colleague who dared to presume upon his generosity; or who was himself guilty of inaccuracy; or who failed in common honesty!
>
> Adler never again worked with a person whom he distrusted; except when that person was a patient. (pg. 13; Bottome, 1957)

Adler also had the ability to make an impression on people who did not know him. When Raymond Corsini, a well-known psychologist in his own right, was 21 years old, he was invited by a friend to hear Adler speak at the City College of New York. During the question period that followed the lecture, an angry woman called Adler stupid, and berated one of the observations he had discussed. The young Corsini shared Adler's perspective, and Corsini looked forward to hearing Adler's "crushing reply." However, something quite different occurred:

> He seemed interested in the question, waited a moment, then in the most natural and careful manner, completely unruffled by her evident antagonism, spoke to her very simply…
>
> He seemed so calm, so reasonable, so precise, and so kind, I knew we were in the presence of a great man, a humble and kind person, one who repaid hostility with friendship. (pg. 86; Corsini cited in Manaster, et al., 1977)

Harry Stack Sullivan extended Adler's focus on the individual and social interest, believing that each of us can be understood only within the context of our interpersonal relationships. Like Freud, Sullivan focused intently on developmental stages, though he recognized seven of them, and believed that the primary purpose of development was to form better interpersonal relationships. In regard to his interest in relationships he can be closely associated with Adler, who believed that social interest, and its resulting social interaction, was the best way for an individual to overcome either real inferiority (such as in the case of a helpless newborn) or feelings of inferiority that might develop as part of one's personality. Unlike Freud and Adler, however, Sullivan was born in America. Thus, he should be considered one of the most important figures in American psychology, particularly within the field of psychodynamic theory.

Brief Biography of Alfred Adler

Alfred Adler was born on February 7, 1870, on the outskirts of Vienna. The second of six children, the family was fairly typical of the middle-class. His father was a corn-merchant, and did well in his business. While Adler while still quite young the family moved out into the country, where they kept cows, horses, chickens, goats, rabbits, and they had a very large garden. Adler was particularly fond of flowers when he was a toddler, and the move out of Vienna had the consequence of protecting him from his bad habit of stealing flowers from the garden of the Palace of Schonbrunn, which belonged to the Kaiser! Despite the seemingly idyllic setting, and the family's financial comfort, Adler did not have a happy childhood. The two main reasons for this were his sibling rivalry with his older brother and the unfortunate fact that he seemed to be surrounded by illness and death (Bottome, 1957; Manaster, et al., 1977; Sperber, 1974).

His older brother seemed to be an ideal child, and Adler felt he could never match his brother's accomplishments. Even late in life, Adler told Phyllis Bottome with a sigh "My eldest brother…he was always ahead of me…he is *still* ahead of me!" (pg. 27; Bottome, 1957). As for his younger brothers, however, one felt the same sort of jealousy of Adler himself, whereas the youngest brother adored Adler. As for the illness and death, he suffered from rickets (a vitamin D deficiency) and spasms of his vocal cords, both of which made physical activity very difficult during his early childhood years. He was often forced to sit on a bench while watching his older brother run and jump. As he recovered, he joined his brother and the other local children in playing in a large field. Despite the fact that there were very few vehicles at the time, and those that were there moved very slowly, Adler was run over twice! Fortunately, he was not injured seriously. One of his younger brothers, however, had died suddenly when Adler was 4, an event that deeply affected him. And when Adler was 5, he came down with a serious case of pneumonia. After he had been examined by the doctor, Adler heard the doctor tell his father that there was no point in caring for Adler any more, as there was no hope for his survival. Adler was stricken with terror, and when he recovered he resolved to become a doctor so that he might have a better defense against death (Bottome, 1957; Manaster, et al., 1977; Sperber, 1974).

On the lighter side, most of the family was musically gifted. One of his brothers played and taught the violin, and one of his sisters was an excellent pianist. Despite the throat problems Adler had in early childhood, he developed a beautiful tenor voice. He was often encouraged to set aside his interest in science and pursue a career as an opera singer. Adler's parents encouraged the musical interests of their children, and took advantage of the marvelous musical culture available in Vienna at the time. Adler attended every opera and play that was running, and even by the age of 4 years old could sing entire operettas (Bottome, 1957; Manaster, et al., 1977; Sperber, 1974).

Although Adler spent a great deal of time reading, he was not a particularly good student. His worst subject was math, until he finally had a breakthrough one day. When the instructor and the best student in class failed to solve a problem, Adler raised his hand. Everyone in the room, including the instructor, laughed out loud at him. However, he was able to solve the problem. After that, he did quite well in math, and overall he did well enough to enter the University of Vienna. He studied medicine, as he had planned since being a young child, and graduated in 1895. Almost nothing is known of his time spent at the University of Vienna. Afterward, he briefly practiced ophthalmology, but then switched to general practice, a field in which he was very popular amongst his patients. He also became active in socialist politics, where he met his future wife: Raissa Timofeyewna Epstein (Bottome, 1957; Manaster, et al., 1977; Sperber, 1974).

Raissa and Alfred Adler had three daughters and one son between the years 1898 and 1909. The family lived rather simply, but they always had enough to meet their needs. Their daughter Alexandra and son Kurt both became psychiatrists. Alexandra Adler described her relationship with her father as close and positive, and she considered it a privilege to follow in his footsteps, whereas Kurt Adler said that everyone in the family felt respected as an individual and that no one had to search for their identity (see Manaster, et al., 1977).

In his general practice, Adler began to see psychiatric patients. The first was a distant cousin who complained of headaches. Adler suggested that no one ever has *only* a headache, and asked if her marriage was happy. She was deeply offended, and left in a huff, but 2 months later she filed for divorce. As he saw more psychiatric patients, Adler treated each case as unique, and followed whatever therapy seemed most appropriate for the particular patient. This was the beginning, of course, of Individual Psychology. Adler was so popular in this regard that his biographer had the following experience herself when leaving a message for Adler:

> 'Are you sure', she asked the clerk at the desk, 'that Professor Adler will get this message directly he comes in?' [sic] 'Adler?' the clerk replied. 'If it's for him you needn't worry. He always gets all his messages. You can hardly keep the bell-boys or the porter out of his room. They'll take *any* excuse to talk to him, and as far as that goes, I'm not much better myself!' (pg. 54; Bottome, 1957)

In 1900, Sigmund Freud gave a lecture to the Vienna Medical Association on his recently published book *The Interpretation of Dreams* (Freud, 1900/1995). The audience was openly hostile, and Freud was ridiculed. Adler was appalled, and he said so publicly, writing to a medical journal that Freud's theories should be given the consideration they deserved. Freud was deeply flattered, he sent his thanks to Adler, and the two men met. In 1902, Adler was one of four doctors asked to meet weekly at Freud's home to discuss work, philosophies, and the problem of neurosis. These meeting evolved into the Psychoanalytic Society. Adler and Freud maintained their cooperative relationship for eight years, and in 1910 Adler became the president of the International Psychoanalytic Association and co-editor of the newly established *Zentrallblatt fur Psychoanalyse* (with Freud as Editor-in-chief). During the preceding 8 years, however, the differences between Freud and Adler had become increasingly apparent. By 1911 he had resigned from the both the association and the journal's editorial board. Although Freud had threatened to resign from the journal if Adler's name was not removed, leading to Adler's own decision to resign from the journal, Freud urged Adler to reconsider leaving the discussion group. He invited Adler to dinner to discuss a resolution, but none was to be found. Adler is said to have asked Freud: "Why should I always do my work under your shadow?" (pg. 76; Bottome, 1957). The Psychoanalytic Society debated whether or not Adler's views were acceptable amongst the members of the society. The no votes counted fourteen, and the yes votes counted nine. Freud's supporters had won a small majority, and the nine other members left to join Adler in forming a new society, which in 1912 became the Society for Individual Psychology (Bottome, 1957; Manaster, et al., 1977; Sperber, 1974).

During the years in which Adler was still active in the Psychoanalytic Society he had begun his studies on organ inferiority and the inferiority complex, and after the split with Freud he focused his career on psychiatry (giving up his general medical practice). During World War I he served in the Army as a physician, and he continued his observations on psychiatric conditions as he helped injured servicemen. Following the war the Austrian Republic began to emphasize education and school reform. Adler established his first child guidance center in 1922, and by the late 1920s there were thirty-two clinics in Vienna alone (as well as some in Germany). The clinics were intended to help train teachers to work with special needs children, but Adler felt it was important to help the children themselves as well. In 1930, Adler brought together a number of his colleagues, including his daughter Alexandra, and published *Guiding the Child: On the Principles of Individual Psychology*. This volume contains twenty-one chapters on the work being conducted in the Vienna child guidance clinics (including one chapter by Adler, and two by his daughter; Adler, 1930a). In addition, Adler taught at an adult education center and at a teacher training college. Adler continued to be so popular that after a long day of work he would settle in at the Cafe Siller and carry on friendly conversations until late at night.

In 1926, Adler made his first visit to America. Becoming a regular visitor, he lectured at Harvard and Brown Universities, in Chicago, Cincinnati, Milwaukee, and several schools in California. In 1929, he was appointed a visiting professor at Columbia University, and in 1932 he was appointed as the first chair of Medical Psychology in the United States, at Long Island Medical College. All of his child guidance clinics were closed when the fascists overthrew the Austrian Republic in 1934, and Alfred and Raissa Adler made New York their official home. In the spring of 1937 he began a tour of Europe, giving lectures and holding meetings. As he traveled to Aberdeen, Scotland on May 28th, he collapsed from a heart attack and died before he reached the hospital.

One of the enduring questions about Adler's career was the nature of his relationship with Freud. As mentioned above, it was the very popular Adler who defended Freud's early theories, and helped Freud to gain recognition in psychiatry (remember that Freud was well known as an anatomist and neurophysiologist). And yet, it is often suggested that Adler was a student or disciple of Freud. According to Abraham Maslow, Adler was deeply offended by these suggestions:

> I asked some question that implied his discipleship under Freud. He became very angry and flushed, and talked so loudly that other people's attention was attracted. He said that this was a lie and a swindle for which he blamed Freud entirely. He said that he had never been a

> student of Freud, or a disciple, or a follower…Freud, according to Adler, spread the version of the break which has since been accepted by all - namely, that Adler had been a disciple of Freud and then had broken away from him. It was this that made Adler bitter…I never heard him express personal opinions of Freud at any other time. This outburst must, therefore, be considered unusual. (pg. 93; Maslow cited in Manaster, et al., 1977; see also Kaufmann, 1992)

Placing Adler in Context: Perhaps the Most Influential Person in the History of Psychology and Psychotherapy

To suggest that anyone may have been more influential than Freud, let alone a contemporary of Freud, is difficult to say. And yet, if we look honestly at the accomplishments of Alfred Adler, and the breadth of his areas of interest, we will see that the case can be made. When Freud first proposed his psychodynamic theory, with its emphasis on infantile sexuality, Freud was often mocked, or simply ignored. It was the popular Dr. Adler's defense of Freud, and Adler's favorable review of the interesting nature of Freud's theories, that helped Freud find an interested audience. As supportive as Adler was, he had his own theories from the very beginning of their association, and Adler's Individual Psychology has a certain logical appeal, without the corresponding controversy generated by Freud.

Infants are inferior, and we all try to gain control over our environments. Thus, the basic inferiority/striving for superiority concept seems self-evident. Likewise, the inferiority complex is one of the most widely recognized and intuitively understood concepts in the history of psychology. Suggesting that each person adopts a style of life that helps them to pursue their goals also again makes perfect sense, and the suggestion that we have within us a creative power to form our style of life is a decidedly hopeful perspective on the human condition.

Adler's influence within the psychodynamic field has been widely recognized, if not adequately advertised. When he split with Freud, nearly half of the psychoanalytic society left with him. His emphasis on social interactions and culture provided a framework within which theorists such as Karen Horney and Erich Fromm flourished. Adler's emphasis on child guidance, and including school teachers as being just as important as parents, must have had an important influence on Anna Freud (though she would never have admitted it). Within the child guidance centers, Adler was one of the first (if not the first) to utilize family therapy and group psychotherapy, as well as school psychology. It was within such an environment, influenced also by Maria Montessori, that Erik Erikson evolved into the analyst and theorist he became.

Adler's influence also extended well beyond the psychodynamic realm. His scheme of apperception set the stage for the cognitive psychology and therapies that are so popular (and effective) today. He is recognized by many as the founder of humanistic psychology, though it was Rogers, Maslow, and the existentialists Viktor Frankl (Frankl worked closely with Adler for a time) and Rollo May who clearly split from psychodynamic theory into new schools of psychology.

Given this extraordinary influence, it is surprising that Adler is not widely recognized as belonging amongst the greatest theorists and clinical innovators in the history of psychology and psychiatry. The honor is certainly well deserved.

Adler's Individual Psychology

Adler developed the concept of **Individual Psychology** out of his observation that psychologists were beginning to ignore what he called the **unity of the individual**:

> A survey of the views and theories of most psychologists indicates a peculiar limitation both in the nature of their field of investigation and in their methods of inquiry. They act as if experience and knowledge of mankind were, with conscious intent, to be excluded from our

> investigations and all value and importance denied to artistic and creative vision as well as to intuition itself. (pg. 1; Adler, 1914/1963)

To summarize Individual Psychology briefly, children begin life with feelings of **inferiority** toward their parents, as well as toward the whole world. The child's life becomes an ongoing effort to overcome this inferiority, and the child is continuously restless. As the child seeks **superiority** it creatively forms goals, even if the ultimate goal is a fictional representation of achieving superiority. Indeed, Adler believed that it is impossible to think, feel, will, or act without the perception of some goal, and that every psychological phenomenon can only be understood if it is regarded as preparation for some goal. Thus, the person's entire life becomes centered on a given plan for attaining the final goal (whatever that may be). Such a perspective must be uniquely individual, since each person's particular childhood feelings of inferiority, creative style of life, and ultimate goals would be unique to their own experiences (Adler, 1914/1963).

The suggestion that seeking to overcome one's inferiorities is the driving force underlying personality development is, of course, a significant departure from Freud's suggestion that development revolves around seeking psychosexual gratification. Another important difference is that Adler did not distinguish between the conscious and unconscious minds as Freud had:

> The use of the terms "consciousness" and "unconsciousness" to designate distinctive factors is incorrect in the practice of Individual Psychology. Consciousness and unconsciousness move together in the same direction and are not contradictions, as is so often believed. What is more, there is no definite line of demarcation between them. It is merely a question of discovering the purpose of their joint movement. (pg. 56; Adler, 1929a)

Inferiority and Compensation

In 1907, Adler published his classic *Study of Organ Inferiority and Its Psychical Compensation*, which was translated into English 10 years later (Adler, 1917). This was primarily a medical article on the consequences of **organ inferiority**, in which Adler looked at how the nervous system helped the body to adapt to physical infirmities that resulted from, literally, inferior organ development. For example, it is often suggested that people who are blind develop better hearing. However, social psychologists have demonstrated that the social environment can profoundly affect our sensitivity to external stimuli. The reason for this is probably just what Adler described as the primary means through which the brain can compensate for any deficiency: by bringing attention to the processes necessary for compensation. Thus, if a person has difficulty seeing, they pay more careful attention to hearing, as well as to the other senses. However, this is not a perfect system, and it can also lead to over-compensation. As a result, a wide variety of physical symptoms can result from the psyche's efforts (including unconscious efforts) to compensate for some problem. As noted by Freud, hysterical symptoms are typically manifested as physical problems. According to Adler, underlying these physical symptoms, even when they are caused solely by the psyche, there must be some organ inferiority within the body (Adler, 1917).

Adler did not limit his theory of organ inferiority to medical problems or neurotic symptoms, but rather, he expanded the theory to incorporate all aspects of life. **Compensation** refers to the typical manner in which a person seeks to overcome challenges. For example, if one breaks their arm, they learn to function with a cast, or if one loses their eyesight, they learn to use a cane or work with a seeing-eye dog (Dreikurs, 1950; Mosak & Maniacci, 1999). If we examine compensation in a more psychosocial realm, examples might include a college student who cannot find a suitable boyfriend or girlfriend so they focus on becoming a straight A student, a student who does not do well academically focuses their efforts on becoming a star athlete, or an only child who wished to have brothers and sisters has many children of their own (Lundin, 1989). In such instances, compensation leads to balance in one's life. A weakness, or at least a perceived weakness, is compensated for in other ways (Manaster & Corsini, 1982). **Overcompensation** involves taking compensation to extremes. For example, a person born with a bad foot strives to become a professional dancer, or a person born in poverty strives to become a millionaire and then continues to work 80 hours a week or more striving to become a billionaire. Generally speaking, the mechanisms of personality inferiority are more complex than those of organ inferiority. Likewise, compensation and overcompensation are more complex when they pertain to one's personality than when they involve physical challenges (Manaster & Corsini, 1982).

When a person finds it difficult to overcome their challenges in life, they can develop what Adler called an **inferiority complex** (Adler, 1928, 1929a, 1931a). Although feelings of inferiority are universal, as is the striving for superiority, people are not created equal. We all have different strengths and weaknesses. However, when an individual cannot compensate for their weaknesses, and their feelings of inferiority overwhelm them, the inferiority complex arises. According to Adler, the term complex is not really accurate, because the so-called inferiority complex is complicated, and it permeates the entire personality. And yet, it may not always be obvious. An individual with an inferiority complex may feel comfortable in situations in which they have enough experience to feel self-assured, although they may create those situations by avoiding competition that might expose their weaknesses (Adler, 1929a). The inferiority complex will show itself, however, in tense or difficult situations, and often takes the form of excuses as to why the individual can't pursue a certain course of action. For psychologists, according to Adler, the presence of an inferiority complex can typically be recognized by contradictions, by certain emotions such as doubt, and by generally hesitant behavior. The proper treatment, therefore, is to encourage people, never to discourage them, and to help them understand that they are capable of solving problems and facing the difficulties of life (Adler, 1929a).

When the intense feelings of inferiority associated with the inferiority complex become too much to bear, they can be transformed into a unique delusion that Adler described as the **superiority complex** (Adler, 1928, 1929a, 1931a). The superiority complex should not be viewed as an extension of the normal process of striving for superiority. The superiority complex arises out of the inferiority complex, and is actually an extension of the intense feelings of inferiority. Interestingly, such people typically do not present themselves as superior individuals, instead they may be arrogant, snooty, domineering, or they may cling to prominent and important people. In contrast, people who truly are superior often have a sense of modesty (Lundin, 1989; Mosak & Maniacci, 1999). The complexity of the superiority complex, and its origin in feelings of inferiority and the continued striving for superiority that is universal can be seen not only in neurotic symptoms and other forms of mental illness, but also in criminal behavior:

> We see children who start stealing suffering from the feeling of superiority. They believe they are deceiving others; that others do not know they are stealing. Thus they are richer with little effort. This same feeling is very pronounced among criminals who have the idea that they are superior heroes…he wants to arrange matters so that he escapes the solution of the problems of life. Criminality is thus, the result of a superiority complex and not the expression of fundamental and original viciousness. (pp. 80-81; Adler, 1929a)

Discussion Question: Adler believed that we all begin life with feelings of inferiority and then strive for superiority. What sort of things have you tried to be really good at in life? Can you remember times when you felt inferior trying to accomplish those same goals?

The Style of Life and the Life Plan

According to Adler, everyone faces difficulties in life, and they strive to overcome those difficulties. As each individual faces their unique difficulties, and strives to compensate in their own characteristic ways, given the environment (or culture) in which they live, the individual develops a sense of meaning for their life and they set a goal for their strivings. Initially Adler referred to the consistent movement toward this overriding goal as a **life plan**, but that term proved to be somewhat confusing. So, Adler chose instead to refer to the pursuit of one's goal as the **style of life**. The style of life unifies the personality, as it is based on one's early life experiences. However, Individual Psychology looks not to the past, but rather to the future. If we know a person's style of life, we can predict their future actions (Adler, 1929a, 1931a).

It is not always easy to recognize the style of life, however, particularly in a psychologically healthy person or during times of relative calm. It is when a person faces a new situation, or a new difficulty, that the style of life becomes clear to others. For the normal person, the style of life is a framework within which the person is adapted to their society in such a way that the society benefits from the work of the person and the person themselves has the energy and courage to face any problems and difficulties that arise (Adler, 1929a). The style of life encompasses our individual creativity, the ways in which we solve problems and compensate for inferiorities, our attitudes, opinions, and goals. It unifies and expresses our personality, provides consistency for how we live our life, and helps us to find our place in the world (Adler, 1931a; Dreikurs, 1950; Lundin, 1989; Mosak & Maniacci, 1999).

The style of life is established fairly early in childhood, which can be a serious problem when it proves to be a dysfunctional style of life. The inferiority complex is, of course, one faulty style of life. When an inferiority complex arises out of an actual organ inferiority it can be particularly troublesome. Robert Lundin (1989) described the case of a senior student he knew in college who was only 5' 3" tall (very short for a man, though this would really only be a perceived inferiority). He was extremely arrogant and hostile toward younger students, claiming to be intellectually superior in every regard. He even offered to be Lundin's roommate, since Lundin obviously needed his help to improve Lundin's deficient personality! Lundin declined the offer. Adler noted that organ inferiority is not always a negative situation, and given the advances in prosthetic devices that exist today, it is even truer now that organ inferiority does not necessarily diminish one's quality of life. However, Adler emphasized that what matters most is how the individual *experiences* the weakness of their organ inferiority. Some try to avoid or deny the problem, others constantly "wrestle and struggle" with their difficulties. In the end, it comes down to the creative power of the individual to adapt (see below; Adler, 1932a/1964).

In addition to the style of life of that can result from organ inferiority (or perceived organ inferiority), Adler discussed two other factors that commonly lead to dysfunctional styles of life, and which can be attributed primarily to parental influence: **pampering** and **neglect**. The pampered style of life was of particular concern to Adler. He was not referring to children who are loved and cared for intimately, but to children whose parents constantly hover over them, solve every problem, and relieve the child of any duties or responsibilities. As a result, the child never learns to take care of itself or to interact with others in a cooperative manner.

> The more deeply I have delved into the problem of neurosis and searched the cases presented, the more clearly have I come to see that in every individual with a neurosis some degree of pampering can be traced...Under such circumstances the child develops like a parasite… (pp. 88-89; Adler, 1932a/1964)

Extending this idea, Adler wrote that whether one is dealing with "difficult children, nervous or insane persons, suicides, delinquents, drug-addicts, or perverts, etc." there is a lack of social feeling (Adler, 1964). In other words, they simply do not function well in relationship to others because they have never had to. As for the neglected child, one who is unwanted, they have had no opportunity for social interaction whatsoever, since their own family fails to interact with them. In cases of suicide, Adler believed that even death can be desired as a means of revenge against those who have hurt or neglected a child by showing others what they have lost in the one they failed to love (Adler, 1967). Since feelings of neglect are relative, pampered children often find themselves in situations, later in life, where they feel neglected, since they may no longer receive the pampering to which they have become accustomed (Adler, 1932a/1964).

Discussion Question: How would you describe your style of life? Adler believed that dysfunctional styles of life often result from either pampering or neglect. Do you know anyone whose style of life clearly reflects how they were raised? Are they someone you like to spend time with, or someone you would rather avoid?

Social Interest and Cooperation

Adler believed that the right way to achieve superiority was through **social interest** and the **cooperation** that naturally follows. This is not some high-minded philosophy, however, but simple reality. According to Adler, "we are in the midst of the stream of evolution." As such, the human species as a whole has sought superiority, just as each individual seeks their own personal superiority (Adler, 1964). The individual's weakness causes them to seek support from others, by living within a society:

> All persons feel inadequate in certain situations. They feel overwhelmed by the difficulties of life and are incapable of meeting them single-handed. Hence one of the strongest tendencies in man has been to form groups in order that he may live as a member of a society and not as an isolated individual. This social life has without doubt been a great help to him in

> overcoming his feeling of inadequacy and inferiority. We know that this is the case with animals, where the weaker species always live in groups...On the other hand, gorillas, lions, and tigers can live isolated because nature has given them the means of self-protection. A human being has not their great strength, their claws, nor their teeth, and so cannot live apart. Thus we find that the beginning of social life lies in the weakness of the individual. (pp. 60-61; Adler, 1929a)

This evolutionary perspective provides an explanation for the paradox that Individual Psychology is focused largely on social relationships! Once again, we know (though perhaps unconsciously) that alone we are weak and inferior, but together we can accomplish great things. Adler's hopeful vision for the future is that someday humanity's social feeling will overcome everything that opposes it, and people will live in harmony. In the meantime, however, he acknowledges that many things still oppose it, and work to destroy the social feelings and social interest of children: sexism, racism, poverty, crime, the death penalty, suicide, greed, mistreatment of the poor, the handicapped, and the elderly, and all forms prejudice, discrimination, and intolerance (Adler, 1964). It is not an easy challenge facing humanity, but Adler suggested that the path toward harmony lies, in part, in recognizing the three main ties that every person must take into account. First, we are tied to this one world, the earth. We must learn how to survive here, given whatever advantages and disadvantages that means. Second, we are not the only member of the human race. Through cooperation and association we can find strength for all, and we can ensure the future of humanity. Finally, we must accept that there are two sexes. For Adler, this last tie is resolved primarily through love and marriage. While this may sound like a product of Adler's cultural upbringing, it also implies caring for and respecting members of the other sex. Otherwise, love is a word used without meaning. Adler proposed that if we give meaning to life through the recognition of these three ties to our environment, then others can share in our meaning of life, and the benefit will then return to us (Adler, 1931a).

Children often cooperate without any need for encouragement, especially when one of them has a skill that another lacks. [Image by Mark Kelland]

In more practical terms, social interest is evident in cooperation. In order for an individual to overcome their own feelings of inferiority they must know that they are valuable, which comes only from contributing to the common welfare. Adler felt that those who seek personal power are pursuing a false goal, and they will eventually disappear from life altogether. However, by contributing to family and society, either through raising children or contributing to the success of one's culture or society, one can claim a sense of immortality. Individual psychology is based on the premise that when a person realizes that the common good is essential to the development of humanity, then they will pursue personal development that is in accord with the greater good. They will recognize both the good and challenges that come their way as belonging to all, and they will cooperate in seeking to solve the challenges. They will not ask for anything in return, since they recognize that whatever they do to benefit others is ultimately to their own benefit as well (Adler, 1933/1964). This perspective is surprisingly close to Eastern philosophies and the concepts of interbeing and karma, though Adler's religious references are primarily Christian (though born Jewish, Adler later became a Christian).

In American society, work is often done by **teams**. The short definition of a team is two or more individuals, with different roles, who socially interact in order to pursue some common goal. Teams can lead to successful outcomes in a wide variety of settings, such as in software development, Olympic hockey, disease outbreak responses, or the unexpected damage to a spacecraft like Apollo 13 (for two excellent and entertaining movies on teamwork, see Miracle [O'Connor & Guggenheim, 2004] and Apollo 13 [Howard, Broyles, Jr., & Reinert, 1995]). However, teams can also lead to group failures, such as the international intelligence failures leading up to the 9/11 terrorist attack on the World Trade Center, the Space Shuttle Columbia accident, or the widely reported, storm-related deaths on Mt. Everest in 1997 (Kozlowski & Ilgen, 2006; Marks, 2006; for more on Mt. Everest see Boukreev & DeWalt, 1997; Krakauer, 1997). Given the importance of teamwork, both in personal settings and within organizations, there has been a great deal of research on teams, addressing cognitive, motivational, and behavioral factors, as well as information on effective team design, team training, and team leadership. Despite the wealth of information on both the positive and negative factors involved in teamwork, there is an interesting contradiction in the Western world:

> …We school our children as individuals. We hire, train, and reward employees as individuals. And, yet, we have great faith that individuals thrown together into a team with little thought devoted to team composition, training and development, and leadership will be effective and successful. (pg. 115; Kozlowski & Ilgen, 2006)

Discussion Question: Working in teams can turn out good or bad, depending on dynamics of the team and the individuals involved. Are you actively involved in any teamwork? Does your team work well together, or do the dynamics of the team cause problems and interfere with accomplishing your goals?

The Life Tasks - Work, Communal Life, and Love

Based on the three ties described above, our ties to earth, humanity, and the opposite sex, Adler described three **life tasks**: **work**, **communal life**, and **love**. Work relates to the earth in an evolutionary sense, dating back to when our ancient ancestors were hunter/gatherers dependent on the environment for food and shelter. According to Adler, all of the questions of life can be found within these three tasks, which challenge us continuously throughout our lives. They tasks are not unrelated, since each one depends upon the successful pursuit of the other two. Given this interrelationship, Adler believed that how a person approaches each of these tasks, through their style of life, reveals a great deal about what they view as the meaning of life. It is necessary, of course, for there to be balance. For example, a person in an unhappy marriage might spend a great deal of time at work. This represents a mistaken style of life (Adler, 1931a, 1964). Worse still, is someone who fails to pursue any of the life tasks:

> Suppose, for example, we consider a man whose love-life is incomplete, who makes no efforts in his profession, who has few friends and who finds contact with his fellows painful. From the limits and restrictions of his life we may conclude that he feels *being alive* as a difficult and dangerous thing, offering few opportunities and many defeats. (pg. 7; Adler, 1931a)

The importance of the work task is to be found in the fact that we must do *something* with our time. As people began to cooperate, they were able to divide their labors. Some would hunt, some would farm, some became craftsmen, some raised the young, and eventually others served in the armies that protected all the rest. In this manner, each person served a valuable role within society (even if the role was not prestigious), and everyone benefited from the ability of each person to become more of an expert in their role. Of course, this sort of social cooperation is the second task of life, the communal life or, as it is sometimes referred to, having friends. Working with others for the common good can be quite difficult if people are doing so only for their own benefit, and it they distrust or fear those they seem to be cooperating with. As societies became more advanced, and education became an important part of society, most societies encourage social interest as an aspect of education. In America, for example, we talk about children learning to be good citizens, and schools include many civics lessons. In addition, societies establish not only formal and informal guidelines and norms for acceptable behavior, but actual laws are written to punish those who act in defiance of the common good. Not that this is easy! The first amendment to the American constitution guarantees free speech, which includes the right to challenge the very existence of our form of government. However, it is generally recognized that the greater good is served by protecting the people from possible abuses of power by the government. Without getting into a discussion of politics, this balance, which seeks to serve the best interests of the community of citizens, has resulted in one of the longest lasting governments in the world today.

When Adler referred to the third task of life, love, he was primarily talking about choosing a partner to bear and raise children. When a child is first born, the love of its mother is the basis for the child's development of social feelings. If a child is neglected, they do not learn how to relate to others, or if they are spoiled, they do not need to relate to others. An early challenge for the child is found in the nature of the father, and then any siblings who may be a part of the family. They typically do not approach the child with the same tender love as the mother. If the mother protects the child from this, spoiling and coddling the infant, a disordered style of life develops, but if the mother leaves the child to face this new challenge on its own, they must rely on their creative powers to adapt to these different social relationships. Children readily have this capacity, if they are allowed to utilize it. Later in life, each person must choose a mate in order to have their own children, and their ability to adapt to relationships with love interests will, obviously, depend on their own development earlier in life. Active, friendly members of a community will have more opportunities to meet someone they are truly attracted to. Individuals who are successful and productive in their work will be better able to provide for a family. And of course, the ultimate existence of each member of the community depends on continued procreation of the species. Thus, work, communal life, and love come together within a healthy society for everyone's benefit (Adler, 1931a, 1964; Lundin, 1989; Mosak & Maniacci, 1999).

Connections Across Cultures: Randy Kearse and Using Prison as an Opportunity for Change

One of the challenges to social cooperation is the ability to communicate. Communication takes place in at least two important ways: language and shared experiences/goals. If we cannot understand what a person is saying, then communication is obviously difficult. But even if we speak the same language, if our entire perspective on life is different, particularly the direction in which we are headed (our style of life), it can be even more difficult to really communicate. Randy Kearse is a man who has lived outside of what many of us consider mainstream America. He grew up in a Brooklyn, NY ghetto, where he became well versed in street talk, or what he refers to as hip-hop and urban **slanguage** (Kearse, 2006a). Despite coming from a relatively stable family (his mother was a teacher and all of his brothers and his sister graduated from high school), he descended into a life of drugs and crime, eventually spending over 13 years in a federal prison for dealing illegal drugs. This introduced Kearse to a large, and growing, subculture in America: the prison population. Kearse learned one lesson very clearly in prison: he hated it! He hated people having such power over him, he hated the disrespect his mother had to endure when she visited him, he hated the food, he hated having the guards read his mail, etc., *ad infinitum*.

> With so many reasons to hate prison, there was no way I was gonna put myself back in the same situation again. Brothers complain about being locked up everyday all day while they're there, but when they get a chance to run the streets again their hatred for prison life fades away. That's crazy! (pg. 132; Kearse, 2006b)

But how does one stay out of prison? In *Changin' Your Game Plan!* (Kearse, 2006b), Kearse offers some very practical steps. But more importantly, he discusses why it matters, and how one needs to change their mindset in order to be successful. His advice fits well with Adler's emphasis on social interest and cooperation, as well as with Adler's three life tasks. As Kearse says, what good is street pride when you don't have the respect of your mother, your children, and other people who know what you're capable of accomplishing?

Kearse believes that everyone has a purpose in life. Even prisoners serving life sentences can preach to others about straightening out their lives so the ones who do get out of prison can stay out. For his own part, Kearse is trying to set a good example now that he is out. He talks about the misguided sense of pride that keeps people from working minimum wage jobs when they come home. Most people in prison do not want their children to live such a life, but can they really set the right example when they themselves get out of prison? One of the most important things to realize is that their style of life has helped to create the problems that exist in their community:

> We have a real obligation to make these changes while incarcerated because a lot of us are to blame for the condition our neighborhoods are in today. We were major contributors to the chaos, mayhem and destruction that have plagued our communities…The saddest thing you can see while incarcerated, is a youngster young enough to be your son walk through the doors. (pg. 133; Kearse, 2006b)

In order to help their communities and their families, Kearse emphasizes that individuals returning home from prison need to get a job and work for an honest living. Kearse tells New Yorkers exactly where to go and how to go about getting ID and a social security card. He recommends getting a job as a messenger, especially if you have a driver's license and can afford to buy a van (or if you save up the money to buy a van). For most of us, having these things is simply taken for granted, but not so for many poor people growing up in the city where such things may not be necessary (especially if one works illegally). One of the advantages of having a messenger/delivery job is that one gets to travel around, meet different people, and become aware of different opportunities. This proved very helpful to Kearse as he pursued his dream of publishing *Street Talk: Da Official Guide to Hip-Hop & Urban Slanguage* (Kearse, 2006a). Curiously, the book is not complete. In acceptance of his publisher's concerns (representing the community), the commercially available version left out the most derogatory slang pertaining to women, race, sexual preference, ethnicity, and religion. Kearse later published a supplemental version ("Da Grimy Version") through a private site. As Kearse became more experienced, he established his own publishing company for his second book, *Changin' Your Game Plan!*, and he is now working on an autobiography. Randy Kearse is working hard to make a better life for himself, set an example for his community, and to honor the mother who raised him to have ambition and dreams. His mother still loved Kearse when he was sent to prison, but her patience was limited:

> Once I received my sentence my mother told me straight up, *"I'll ride this time out with you, but if you get back out here and get caught up in them streets again don't call me,"* and I can't blame her for that. How much can a mother take seeing her child going back and forth to prison? (pg. 33; Kearse, 2006b)

It would be very difficult for most of us to imagine what prison life and culture is like, or even what it would be like to get caught up in the judicial system. But for people who live in difficult circumstances, it can be just as difficult to avoid getting caught up in a style of life that promises instant gratification, but which costs a lot of money. People who try to take shortcuts, such as stealing what they want, or selling drugs to make a lot of money, end up with little to show for their life except "a gang of years in prison." Escaping this style of life requires a plan, and even more so the motivation for making that plan work:

> Coming out of prison you have to have a plan. If you don't, the chance of you returning to prison is great and you and I both know *these people* aren't playing. They'll lock your ass up for a hun'ned years and not care…Shit is real. (pg. xxiii; Kearse, 2006b)

The Creative Power of the Individual and Fictional Finalism

> The science of Individual Psychology developed out of the effort to understand that mysterious creative power of life - that power which expresses itself in the desire to develop, to strive and to achieve - and even to compensate for defeats in one direction by striving for success in another. (pg. 32; Adler, 1929a)

Adler believed that we are all born with a creative force: the **creative power of the individual**. He did not reject the concepts of heredity, temperament, or disposition, but he emphasized that it not so important what we are born with, but rather what we do with it (Adler, 1932a/1964). As noted above, infants *are* inferior, so everyone begins life with feelings of inferiority. This leads to the striving for superiority, and the development of a style of life, which is aimed toward some goal. The nature of that style of life is unique because it is created by the child, and it is done very early in life. This is not a deterministic perspective, this creation of the style of life is just that, creative, and therefore it must be unique (hence, *Individual* Psychology). Since Adler believed that all thought and behavior was oriented toward some goal, there must be some goal that underlies the manner in which the style of life is created. Since a child cannot see into the future and create a specific goal in life, Adler proposed that we are guided by a fictional goal, the so-called **fictional finalism** (Adler, 1914/1963, 1928, 1929a, 1932a/1964; Lundin, 1989; Manaster & Corsini, 1982).

The fictional final goal involves the sentiment of superiority, or at least the elevation of the personality to an extent that makes life seem worth living (Adler, 1928). Thus, it does not need to be precisely defined, which is important for our consideration that it is created by a young child. And yet it exists within the child's mind, it provides the framework within which the style of life is creatively formed, and it serves as the child's goal in life (though it remains primarily unconscious). It is also important to recognize that although this goal is fictional, it is entirely positive, it is a healthy and natural motivational force (Lundin, 1989). The fictional finalism should definitely not be mistaken for **fictive superiority**. Fictive superiority is the imagination, or false belief, that one is actually superior. It is a typical neurotic symptom that stems, primarily, from having been pampered. A pampered child is superior, at least in the sense that everything is done for them. However, adult life no longer sustains that delusion, yet the child has never learned how to adapt to life's challenges, their style of life is set in the expectation of challenges being solved for them. A healthy child, on the other hand, has learned to face challenges, and to strive toward overcoming them. Thus, the healthy child develops a style of life that incorporates the process of facing and overcoming life's obstacles, and this carries over into a healthy adulthood (Adler, 1932b/1964).

Within his discussion of the creative power of the individual and the fictional finalism, Adler began to address what can be viewed as the foundation for cognitive psychology and cognitive therapy (see Chapter 12):

> In a word, I am convinced that *a person's behaviour springs from his idea.* We should not be surprised at this, because our senses do not receive actual facts, but merely a subjective image of them - a reflection of the external world. (pg. 19; Adler, 1964)

According to Adler, the prototype of the style of life, as it points toward the fictional finalism, is set in a particular orientation. Throughout the individual's life, their perceptions of the world are then constrained to "fall into a groove established by the line of direction" (Adler, 1929a). He referred to this phenomenon as the **scheme of apperception**. As a result of this scheme, the individual interprets experiences before they are accepted, and the interpretation always agrees with the original meaning that the individual has given to their life. When the individual has developed a mistaken meaning to life, or when experience cannot be reconciled with the meaning they hold, they may be forced to change their scheme of apperception. This is not easy, however, and only occurs when there is sufficient social pressure to do so (Adler, 1931a).

Discussion Question: Adler described fictive superiority as the mistaken belief that one *is* superior to others. What do you think about people who think they are great, who think they know everything about everything, and can do anything at all, but who really are no different than anyone else?

Child Development and Education

Adler agreed with Freud that personality is basically set in the early childhood years. Thus, Adler was particularly interested in child development, and also in the training of those responsible for raising children (typically, the parents, the rest of the family, and school teachers). The emphasis in much of his work was on ensuring that children are brought up in the best way possible from the very beginning of life. We have already examined the importance of the mother's role, and that she needs to be supportive but must not spoil her child. A child who is unable to resolve life's problem without the assistance of others will grow up into a neurotic person demonstrating a dysfunctional style of life (Adler, 1913a/1963). Since this is something that happens within the family, the parents obviously cannot serve as part of the solution for this problem. Thus, Adler turned his attention to school teachers.

Adler believed that a person is educated when it becomes clear that they have become more relevant to more people (Adler, 1958). In other words, they become a more active and involved member of their community, society, and perhaps even the whole world. School represents a new situation for a child. If they have been raised well, they pass this test rather easily. If not, the defects in their style of life become evident. School work requires cooperation with both the teacher and the other students, and the ability to cooperate is probably more important than the child's innate intellectual abilities. Adler did not dismiss the importance of I.Q. (though he did suggest that the child and the parents should never be told what it is), but he pointed out that a child's ability to concentrate on school subjects is primarily dependent on the child's interest in the teacher (Adler, 1930b). So once again, we see the three life tasks coming into play. School work is the child's work, and it must take place within a communal setting (the classroom). But what about love? Whether you want to call it support, encouragement, caring, motivation, or love, Adler was clear in terms of what he thought about the "peculiar position" held by teachers:

> The teacher, professional or amateur, must teach the simple thing: love, and call it by its simple name: love. Almost since the beginnings of recorded history, however, the teacher has been in a peculiar position: he is facing pupils, children or adults, who do not expect that the thing they ought to learn is so simple. (pg. 115; Adler, 1958)

According to Adler, it is the role of teachers to recognize the difficulties that children cannot overcome, and to "correct the mistakes of the parents." An essential aspect of this "correction," however, is that it must never be punitive. Adler believed that if teachers scold or criticize students who cannot connect with their teacher or their classmates, then the child will realize they were *right* to dislike school. Rather, teachers must help children to connect with themselves, and then reach out to connect with others (Adler, 1931a). But what about children who cannot redirect their style of life or face up to the challenges they encounter?

Discussion Question: Teachers play an important role in each person's development, according to Adler. Who were the teachers who really influenced you, and were they good teachers who helped you, or bad teachers who inspired you to be a better person than you saw in them?

Adler wrote a great deal about guiding children, and about helping them to avoid and recover from delinquency (Adler, 1918/1963, 1930a, 1931a, 1935/1964, 1963), and his daughter Alexandra joined him in this endeavor (Alexandra Adler, 1930a,b). Often the discussion addresses the primary problem in Adler's view: a lack of social interest due to having been pampered. In addition, both Adler and his daughter bring into consideration an interesting family dynamic that appears to play some role: the child's **birth order**. An **only child** is in an unfavorable situation. Although they certainly receive attention and support from their parents, since they receive all of it they tend to be pampered and they lack practice in being sociable. As they leave the pampered surroundings of the home, such as when they go to school, the child grows up fighting against their environment and trying to dominate it. Their solutions can be passive, such as being timid, anxious, or routinely getting "sick," or their solutions can be active, such as being excessively talkative, defiant, or combative (Alexandra Adler, 1930a; Adler, 1929/1964). They face the potential of becoming like parasites, people who do nothing but enjoy life while expecting others to take care of them (Adler, 1928). The situation can be much worse, however, for the **oldest child**. The oldest child was, for a time, an only child, and received all of the privilege and pampering associated with that position. With the arrival of the next child, however, they lose their privileged position, and the mother must be particularly attentive to the new infant. The oldest child is **dethroned**, and this can feel quite tragic, leading to consuming jealousy and a bitter struggle to regain the parent's attention (Adler, 1929/1964, 1931a, 1963). Dethroning is an experience that always leaves a great impression, and can lead to a critical attitude toward the mother and a turning away toward the father (Adler, 1929/1964). According to Adler, one often finds the experience of being dethroned in the past of problem children, neurotics, criminals, drunkards, and perverts (Adler, 1931a). Nonetheless, being the oldest child also has distinct advantages. Amongst the siblings, the first born is typically the biggest and more experienced child. They have a certain power over the other children, in that they are often given greater responsibility, including, perhaps, the responsibility of caring for their younger brothers and sisters. They tend to be guardians of law and order, and they have an especially high valuation of power (Adler, 1928). Adler was careful to point out, however, that too much is often made of his theories on birth order. It is not the birth order, per se, which determines the nature of development. For example, if the oldest child is not competitive, the second child may develop as if they were the first child. Similarly, if two children are born much later than their older siblings, the elder of those two may develop the characteristics of a first born.

In those cases where the challenges of adolescence become too much for a child, they begin to creatively protect themselves by doing things such as forging report cards, skipping school, etc. As they meet others doing the same things, they join with them, form gangs, and may well start out on a road that leads to a life of crime. Demonstrating his great concern for the individual, however, Adler wrote:

> All this can be avoided if we accept the point of view of Individual Psychology that no child should be thought hopeless. We must feel that a method can always be found to help a child. Even in the worst of circumstances there is always a particular way of approach - but this of course needs to be found. (pg. 179; Adler, 1930b)

In a recent special issue of the *American Psychologist*, a series of articles were presented focusing on effective, evidence-based prevention programs designed to increase the number of children and youth who will succeed and contribute both in school and in life (Weissberg, Kumpfer, & Seligman, 2003). In accordance with Adler's theories, effective parenting seems to be the best way to reduce adolescent problem behaviors, and the family can be strengthened through approaches such as behavioral parent training, family skills training, and family therapy (Kumpfer & Alvarado, 2003). School-based prevention programs can also be beneficial, but it is important that educational approaches coordinate social and emotional learning with more traditional academic learning (Greenberg, et al., 2003). Since the problems of adolescence are so variable, including such things as alcohol, tobacco, and other drug abuse, violence, delinquency, mental illness, etc., and since they affect so many children, approaches that attempt to intervene with one child at a time may not be adequate. Accordingly, community interventions become important, and may go so far as to require coordinated national efforts, such as Head Start or the combined efforts of the Department of Health and Human Services, Department of Housing and Urban Development, and the Environmental Protection Agency to reduce lead poisoning (Ripple & Zigler, 2003; Wandersman & Florin, 2003). And last but not least, health care providers can play an important role in ensuring the psychological well-being of their patients, as well as their physical health (Johnson & Millstein, 2003). Indeed, Adler quoted the renowned Rudolf Virchow (one of the founders of cellular pathology; who coined the terms thrombosis, embolism, and leukemia, among many other accomplishments) in saying: "Physicians will eventually become the educators of humanity" (pg. 317; Adler, 1918/1963; see also Knopf & Wexberg, 1930). Perhaps the most important aspect of these studies is the concerted effort to combine scientific research with clinical practice and experience, as well as doing so in socioculturally relevant ways (Biglan, et al., 2003; Nation, et al., 2003). Echoing Adler's call from 1930, and moving toward its answer:

> If researchers can foster increased use of scientific practices in these ways, it is possible to achieve a society in which the largest possible proportion of children experience healthy, happy, and successful development and arrive at adulthood with the social, emotional, and cognitive skills they need to lead healthy and successful lives. (pg. 438; Biglan et al., 2003)

The Psychology of Women

Adler's views on the psychology of women could not have been more different than those of Freud. As someone who questioned cultural discrimination long before most, Adler considered women to be equal to men, and he described the belief that they were inferior as a myth. A division of labor has always been an important part of the communal life of the human species. When neighboring groups came into conflict, it was the larger, stronger men who did most of the fighting to protect the group. According to Adler, men extended this conflict and feeling of power to the subjugation of women. Ever since, men have enjoyed privileges that were denied to women, and this has been maintained primarily through force, or the threat of force, but also through indoctrination and education (Adler, 1910/ 1978, 1927/1978, 1928). Adler himself avoided the use of the term "opposite sex," a term that implies an adversarial relationship, preferring instead to use the term "other sex" when referring to women (Manaster & Corsini, 1982).

Adler recognized that what women really desire is the privilege that men enjoy, but this is not unique to women. There are also men, or boys, who are not dominant, and they also strive for superiority and privilege. At birth, of course, both male and female infants are helpless and inferior, and must begin to strive for superiority. The form that this striving takes is something Adler called the **masculine protest**. It was not his intention to suggest that masculine traits of dominance and aggression make men better than women, but this was the nature of the times in which he lived. It is purely cultural that the male gender role includes strength, knowledge, physical activity, etc., whereas the female gender role includes submissiveness, weakness, the desire for physical and emotional closeness, etc. All children display some degree of these traits, but society directs boys toward the male role, and girls toward the female role (Adler, 1910/1978, 1912a/1963, 1928, 1929/1964). We can now recognize what many consider Freud's great mistake regarding the psychology of women. Women who display masculine traits were seen as neurotic by Freud, but Adler viewed them as protesting the cultural denigration of women. Still, it is not easy to challenge the nature of society, so Adler still acknowledged that women were more likely to be neurotic than men. However, Adler attributes the neurosis of most women to masculine protest, *not* to the inability to resolve a woman's penis envy! In 1910, just as Adler was about to break away from Freud's Psychoanalytic Society, Adler proposed that the great Oedipus complex is only a small part, just a stage, of the masculine protest, for both men and women (Adler, 1910/1978).

Discussion Question: Adler described masculine protest as a cultural phenomenon in which women, and even some men, strive to act masculine in order to ensure the privilege reserved only for men. Can you think of any strong women whose career or style of life fits into this theory? What about any men you know (or know of)?

Are strong women just that, or are they acting out their masculine protest? [Image by Mark Kelland]

Adlerian Psychotherapy

Adler's approach to psychotherapy has been the topic of numerous books and chapters (e.g., Dinkmeyer, Dinkmeyer, Jr., & Sperry, 1979; Mosak, 1995; Nikelly, 1971a; Watts & Carlson, 1999), including specific books on family therapy and lifestyle counseling for people with disabilities (Rule, 1984; Sherman & Dinkmeyer, 1987). It is generally accepted that Adlerian psychotherapists have no specific technique, but rather are eclectic in their approach. There are, however, a few key elements to Individual Psychology. First is the goal of understanding the style of life. Once the therapist understands the style of life, they can understand most everything the patient does. The therapist then helps the patient to strengthen their social interest. This involves a practical application of social interest: reorienting and readjusting the patient's style of life. Underlying the success of therapy in Individual Psychology is a supportive therapeutic relationship. Adler believed in facing his clients, on an equal basis. The therapist helps to educate the patient on the nature of therapy and the goals that might be pursued, which involves helping the client to recognize the mistaken style of life and goals they have been pursuing in the past. In this way, the therapist helps the client in their own creative process of personality change (Dinkmeyer, Dinkmeyer, Jr., & Sperry, 1979; Mosak, 1995). This approach shares many similarities with both the client-centered approach popularized by Carl Rogers and the behavioral-cognitive approaches developed by Albert Ellis and Aaron Beck.

Understanding the Style of Life

Psychotherapy is about helping people to change their lives for the better. Thus, it involves looking forward, despite whether or not we need to know what has happened in the past (and different theories consider the importance of the past in radically different ways). According to Adler, "in order to understand a person's future we must understand his style of life" (pg. 99; Adler, 1929a). The style of life, and the associated scheme of apperception, brings all experience into line with the person's fictional final goal. So, if we can understand how a person is living their life, if we understand their style of life, we can help them to understand it as well, and then perhaps make changes for the better. So, how might we go about understanding the style of life?

As Freud and Breuer had before him, one area of interest for Adler was the analysis of dreams. However, Adler did not distinguish between the conscious and unconscious, or between waking and sleep. He considered dreams to be a reflection of the style of life, and the individual's striving for superiority. Thus, dreams do not hold any special meaning (Adler, 1912b/1963, 1928, 1929a, 1932b/1964). As such, their interpretation can be relatively straight-forward:

> Take, for instance, our knowledge that mankind as a whole is really cowardly. From this general fact we can presuppose that the largest number of dreams will be dreams of fear, danger, or anxiety. And so if we know a person and see that his goal is to escape the solution of life's problems, we can guess that he often dreams that he falls down. Such a dream is like a warning to him: "Do not go on - you will be defeated." (pg. 155; Adler, 1929a)

Of greater interest to Adler was the analysis of **early memories**. He believed that the earliest childhood recollections provided valuable information, and he did not let a single patient go without having been asked about them:

> The information regarding memory is significant. Memory is an activity. It is based on the life style, which here steps in by selecting from old impressions a single one. This leads us to the question, why this single one? In it the entire life style resonates. (pg. 197; Adler, 1932b/1964)

It is not even important if the memory is, in fact, true. A "memory" may be created by a child based on their conscious experience in order to reflect an attitude, or an emotional tone, if that is necessary to pursue their unique, personal goal (Adler, 1928). Accordingly, if we can obtain a person's earliest memories, we make reasonable predictions regarding the future course of their life. However, early memories are not reasons for behavior, but they are hints. It is also true that some forgotten memories (or unconscious memories) may have played a role in the creation of the style of life, but they are obviously more difficult to obtain, so they defy analysis. But, Adler did not consider them to be any different in content and tone from the conscious memories; the unconscious psyche enacts the same style of life toward the same final goal (as with dreams; Adler, 1929a, 1931a, 1964). There may, however, be some interesting differences in early memories based on culture. For example, Wang (2006b) examined the earliest memories of European American and Taiwanese college students in response to five cue words: self, mother, family, friend, and surroundings. In both groups, memories for 'mother' came from an earlier time than memories for 'self,' and memories for 'mother,' 'family,' and 'friend' were more socially oriented. The European Americans typically had memories from earlier ages, and their memories tended to report more specific events and to focus on their personal roles and autonomy in those memories. Thus, early memories not only reflect one's style of life, but do so within a cultural context.

In two major case studies published by Adler, *The Case of Miss R.* (1929b) and *The Case of Mrs. A* (1931b), the subtitle of each book refers to the style of life. In the latter book, he concludes by saying: "I have simply wanted to show you the COHERENCE OF A LIFE-STYLE" (pg. 46; Adler, 1931b). Moving well beyond neurosis, both Adler and his son Kurt applied the study of the style of life to patients suffering from psychotic disorders, including schizophrenia and manic phase of bipolar disorder (Adler, 1929/1964; Kurt Adler, 1959). Kurt Adler does an excellent job of summarizing Individual Psychology, and he quotes his father's description of neurosis and psychosis as attempts by a person to avoid clashing with reality and exposing their weakness and inferiority. However, these are "failed" styles of life, because they lead to an avoidance of social interest, which is necessary for solving life's challenges in cooperation with others. In the case of a disorder such as schizophrenia, the child begins life with extreme feelings of inferiority, which lead to an exaggerated fictional goal. Subsequently, it is more difficult to achieve any success in life, which creates a vicious cycle of failure and greater distrust of others. Finally, as the individual fails to develop social-emotional capacities, common sense, or logic, they retreat into the private world that accommodates their exaggerated fictional personal goal. The subsequent treatment of psychotic patients is difficult, particularly if the therapist expects too much. Kurt Adler extends his father's caution that the therapist must be aware of their own style of life, set aside any personal expectations, and never *expect* anything of the patient (Kurt Adler, 1959). As we will see below, Harry Stack Sullivan also paid special attention to psychodynamic processes in schizophrenia.

Discussion Question: What are your earliest memories, especially of your mother, father, and sense of self? Can you see a clear relationship between the content of those memories and your style of life? How does your life plan fit with those memories?

<u>*Strengthening Social Interest and Reorienting the Style of Life*</u>

Adler believed that everyone has some degree of social interest, but in neurotic and psychotic patients there is relatively less. He described Freudian transference as an expression of the patient's social interest, directed toward the therapist. Resistance is simply the patient lacking the courage (i.e., feeling too inferior) to return to social usefulness and cooperation with others. The therapist must, therefore, help the patient to strengthen their social interest and reorient their style of life. Since the style of life is creatively formed, it becomes important to understand how and when the failed style of life began. Just as the individual took time and was selective in the formation of their failed style of life, the therapist must take time to understand it and educate the patient about it (Adler, 1913b/1963, 1929/1964, 1930c, 1932b/1964, 1958).

> Individual Psychology stresses enormously that the psychological development of a person can reach a normal condition only when he can achieve the necessary degree of ability to cooperate. (pg. 199; Adler, 1932b/1964)

> It is almost impossible to exaggerate the value of an increase in social feeling…The feeling of worth and value is heightened, giving courage and an optimistic view…The individual feels at home in life and feels his existence to be worthwhile just so far as he is useful to others… (pg. 79; Adler, 1929/1964)

There are numerous ways in which a therapist can help a client to increase their social interest. It begins with the therapist openly communicating with and accepting the patient, which is, of course, a social interaction. This is especially effective if the therapist displays social feeling themselves, while also helping the patient to recognize the patient's value as a human being (as well as the value of other people). The therapist can point out that if other people, including the therapist, had the same values, goals, and cognitive orientation as the patient then others would also have the same problems as the patient. The therapist can then nudge the patient toward their own niche, where they can feel comfortable with others without fearing being the loser in personal interactions. And finally, the therapist can encourage the patient to get involved in concerns outside themselves (Nikelly, 1971b). Each of these ways of encouraging social interest can be a part of the reorientation and readjustment process, the "working-through" phase of therapy, in which the patient gains insight into their style of life, confronts their goals, and realizes that they are capable of making choices and decisions (Nikelly & Bostrom, 1971). The patient must be encouraged to understand and believe that they have the power to implement their insights and change their life.

> The client must not be allowed to think of himself as the victim of past circumstances but must come to recognize that the problem is his alone and that he alone will solve it. In contrast, emphasis on past history may lead to rationalization and intellectualization without appropriate action. The client learns more and more about his problem and does less and less about it. (pg. 103; Nikelly & Bostrom, 1971)

Group Psychotherapy and Family Therapy

Our discussion of Adlerian psychotherapy would not be complete without mentioning **group psychotherapy**, and in the same breath, **family therapy**. Group psychotherapy probably has multiple origins, having been tried by a variety of independent therapists. In 1921, Adler began interviewing and counseling parents in front of a group of professionals. This fit well within his perspective on the three life tasks and social interest, since he felt that parents, family, and other important people, such as school teachers, needed to be involved in the development of children. Adler soon discovered that these settings led to personal growth in everyone present, establishing a form of group therapy that may be the oldest still in use. Strictly speaking, Individual Psychology does not prescribe any specific techniques for group psychotherapy, but rather, there is Individual Psychology for patients in a private setting as well as for patients receiving therapy in a group setting (Corsini, 1971).

Involving the parents in a child's therapy is, quite obviously, the beginning of family therapy. However, when Adler established his child guidance centers, they were open for parents, teachers, social workers, and other interested people to be able to observe the process of psychotherapy. Adler felt it was important for everyone involved in the development of children to be educated in the important process of Individual Psychology, and the same was true of Rudolf Dreikurs, a student of Adler who opened family education centers in the United States (the first in Chicago in 1937; see Dreikurs, 1950; Sherman & Dinkmeyer, 1987). This education may be particularly important for the parents, whose attitude can have a profound influence on whether psychotherapy for a child is successful or not. As for teachers, understanding Individual Psychology can help them to put a child's academic performance into a context that helps to explain it as a style of life aimed toward a particular goal, even if that goal is dysfunctional and interferes with schoolwork (Friedmann, 1930; Spiel & Birnbaum, 1930). Overall, the goal of family therapy is to improve communication and cooperation amongst all members of the family, and to help parents avoid the most difficult problems (Alexandra Adler, 1930a; Adler, 1930d).

> In our conversations with the parents we relentlessly try to make them realize that children must not be beaten. Beating can only lead to a discouragement of the child, and we know well enough that this can make the child worse and not better...We always dissuade parents from engaging in warfare with the child, since the child inevitably remains in the end the stronger party. (pp. 110-111; Alexandra Adler, 1930a)

Discussion Question: Have you ever experienced group psychotherapy, family therapy, or anything similar (or know anyone who has)? What advantages did you experience, or what do you think you might experience if you were to work on your relationships with family members or other people?

A Brief Biography of Harry Stack Sullivan

Several aspects of Harry Stack Sullivan's life history are quite strange, and so, according to some biographers, was Harry Stack Sullivan himself. He was born on February 21st, 1892, though his medical records say he was born in 1886, in the rural community of Norwich, New York. His father's name was Timothy Sullivan and his mother's name seems to have been Ella Stack, but it remains unclear whether her name was actually Ella. That is the name that appears on Sullivan's birth certificate and on her death certificate, but in the family records her name was listed as Ellen, and on Sullivan's baptismal certificate it was listed as Ellina. Timothy Sullivan was a hired-hand on the Stack farm (or another farm nearby), whose father had died when Timothy Sullivan was young, leaving the family quite poor. There was a great deal of discrimination against Irish Catholics at the time, and Timothy and Ella struggled. They lived in a poor part of town, where there was an improperly drained canal that was believed to be a breeding ground for "black diphtheria." The Sullivans had two children before Harry, both born in February, who died in terrible convulsions before reaching the fall of their first year. When Harry was born in February, his mother was terrified that he would die as well (Alexander, 1990; Evans, 1996; Perry, 1982).

When Sullivan was 2 ½ he was sent to Smyrna, New York to live with his maternal grandmother. Where his mother was for the next few years is unknown. It was rumored that she had a nervous breakdown, and may have been kept hidden away in the attic of the barn until she recovered. Although she eventually returned to public view, she was never really Sullivan's caretaker again. Neither was his father. When Sullivan's maternal grandfather died, there was no one to run the farm, which provided the support for him and his grandmother. Being poor himself, Timothy Sullivan was granted control of the farm. However, the Stack family had always considered Timothy Sullivan to be beneath them (the Stack family had a prestigious ancestry), so the legal documents were quite demeaning to Timothy Sullivan, and the farm's name remained the Stack farm. Timothy Sullivan worked hard, but withdrew into himself and had little contact with others (Alexander, 1990; Evans, 1996; Perry, 1982).

Sullivan did very well in school, but had few friends due to the common prejudice and discrimination. At one point, the Ku Klux Klan burned a cross in front of the Stack farm. His only friend was a boy who was 5 years older, Clarence Bellinger. The two were very close throughout school, and both went on to become psychiatrists. However, after high school, they never contacted one another again. Bellinger always spoke poorly of Sullivan, and Sullivan simply never spoke of Bellinger. The reasons why are unknown, but it may have something to do with the fact that neither one of them ever married, and Sullivan was widely regarded as a homosexual. When Sullivan was 35, he took in a foster son, who may also have been a psychotic patient. Late in life, Sullivan seems to have referred to the young man as a "lover" (Alexander, 1990). If this was their relationship when his companion was only 15, and if his companion was a former patient, it was both unethical and criminal. It is tempting to suggest that Sullivan's sexual development and alleged later actions may have been influenced by an inappropriate relationship with Bellinger while Sullivan was still quite young. However, the truth is not known, and there are other gaps in the history of Sullivan's life (Alexander, 1990; Evans, 1996; Perry, 1982).

Two family members helped Sullivan with his education during his school years. His mother's sister Margaret, a schoolteacher, brought him many books and introduced him to a wide range of intellectual ideas. His father's brother, Will, was a respected lawyer and then a judge who was influential in applying psychological issues to the law. He helped to foster Sullivan's interest in human problems. This aunt and uncle both later helped Sullivan with college finances, and they helped him to win a prestigious New York State Regents' Scholarship to Cornell University. However, Sullivan was not prepared for college. After a fair start, his grades dropped drastically. He became involved with a group of boys who were illegally obtaining and selling chemicals. Only Sullivan was caught, and he was convicted of mail fraud. His whereabouts for the next 2 years are unknown. He may have been in jail, but there is evidence to suggest that he was hospitalized at Bellevue Hospital following a psychotic break. Later in life he was friends with the renowned A. A. Brill (the psychiatrist who first translated many of Freud's books into English), and Brill was working at Bellevue at the time. Sullivan was also friends later in life with another employee who worked at Bellevue at that time, and no simple explanation can be given for his friendship with two men who worked at Bellevue Hospital during the time Sullivan's whereabouts are unknown (Alexander, 1990; Evans, 1996; Perry, 1982).

In 1911, Sullivan reappeared and entered the Chicago College of Medicine and Surgery. He finished his coursework in 1915, but did not receive a degree, possibly due to owing the school money. He worked briefly as an industrial surgeon in a steel mill, and in 1916 joined the Illinois National Guard. After only 5 months he was released on medical grounds, supposedly due to a broken jaw. He then disappeared for a while, later claiming that he received 75 hours of psychoanalysis during the disappearance. But where that occurred, or with whom, is again unknown. In 1917, he was finally awarded his medical degree, and he joined the U. S. Army. His application contained many inaccuracies and falsifications, including lying about his age. Nonetheless, he was commissioned as a lieutenant, promoted to captain at the end of World War I, and spent 2 years moving between Chicago and Washington, DC. In 1920, he left the Army, and again a year of his life seems to be missing. In November, 1921, he joined St. Elizabeth's Hospital in Washington, DC, and began his career in psychiatry (Alexander, 1990; Evans, 1996; Perry, 1982).

St. Elizabeth's Hospital was one of best psychiatric hospitals of the time (and remains so today), under the leadership of the renowned William Alanson White, a pioneer in applying dynamic psychotherapy to psychotic patients. After a year, however, there was no permanent position for Sullivan. So, he applied for a position at the Sheppard and Enoch Pratt Hospital in Baltimore (as prestigious as St. Elizabeth's both then and now). White's letter of recommendation for Sullivan was lukewarm and vague. He described Sullivan as "better equipped than the average State Hospital assistant," but he also acknowledged that he didn't really know Sullivan because of Sullivan's personal distance from other people (Alexander, 1990). Nonetheless, Sullivan was hired for his first clinical psychiatric position at Sheppard Pratt (as it is more commonly known - Note: The author's wife had the privilege of working at Sheppard Pratt early in her career), and he began an exciting and innovative period of eight years, during which he did the most important clinical work of his career, including innovative techniques for the treatment of schizophrenia in young patients (Alexander, 1990; Evans, 1996; Perry, 1982). Today, the Sheppard Pratt Health System includes the Harry Stack Sullivan Day Hospital, a partial hospitalization program assisting adults with severe mental illness, including psychotic disorders.

During his time at Sheppard Pratt, Sullivan became close friends with a young psychiatrist named Clara Thompson. They shared an interest in questioning Freud's concepts of the feminine psyche and other challenges to orthodox psychoanalysis. As Sullivan became particularly interested in the work of Sandor Ferenczi (who accompanied Sigmund Freud and Carl Jung on Freud's only trip to America, but later split with Freud), he encourage Thompson to go to Budapest and be psychoanalyzed by Ferenczi. She did so, and upon her return she was Sullivan's training analyst, and Sullivan was later admitted to the American Psychoanalytic Society. The two remained close throughout their lives, and supposedly agreed to marry one another, but both quickly broke off the engagement the very next morning (Alexander, 1990; Evans, 1996; Perry, 1982).

In 1930, Sullivan moved to New York City to establish a private practice and conduct research. However, he failed to make much money, incurred some family debts following his father's death, and he filed for bankruptcy in 1932. The next few years were interesting, but unstable. He was the driving force behind the establishment of the William Alanson White Foundation in 1933, and he actively collaborated with two colleagues at Yale University (where they likely had an influence on Erik Erikson's work). However, one of those colleagues died in 1939, and Sullivan immersed himself in a project studying Black adolescents in Tennessee and Mississippi. He then settled in Bethesda, Maryland, where he spent the rest of his career (Alexander, 1990; Evans, 1996; Perry, 1982).

The year 1939 marked the beginning of a highly productive period for Sullivan. Dexter Bullard, the director of a psychiatric hospital named Chestnut Lodge, provided Sullivan with steady consulting opportunities. This provided Sullivan financial security, and through Chestnut Lodge he met many influential psychiatrists in the Washington, DC area. William Alanson White had died in 1937, and Sullivan delivered a series of public lectures, which became the First William Alanson White Memorial Lectures, and which were released as Sullivan's only book published while he was still alive: *Conceptions of Modern Psychiatry* (Sullivan, 1940). The White Foundation established the journal *Psychiatry*, and the Washington School of Psychiatry. Sullivan also encouraged the White Foundation to establish a second training program in New York City, and the core faculty included Clara Thompson and Erich Fromm. The second program is known today as the William Alanson White Institute. When, in 1941, Karen Horney was disqualified as a training analyst by the New York Psychoanalytic Society, Clara Thompson walked out of the meeting, and helped to establish a rival Association for the Advancement of Psychoanalysis, with Horney as its dean. A series of political battles between opposing psychoanalytic societies followed, in many ways pitting followers of Freud against those whose interests and relationships were closer to Sullivan (Alexander, 1990; Evans, 1996; Perry, 1982).

In 1945, Sullivan became quite ill, and was urged to retire for his health. Instead, Sullivan accepted a new challenge. He was invited by Brock Chisholm, who was soon to become the first director of the World Health Organization, to serve as a consultant for the post-World War II International Congress on Mental Health. Sullivan focused on applying psychiatric principles to problems of world peace, including educating children on values for peace. He helped to establish the World Federation for Mental Health, and participated in the UNESCO Seminar on Childhood Education Toward World-Mindedness. In January 1949, following a particularly frustrating meeting of the World Federation for Mental Health, Sullivan died in a hotel room in Paris, France. He was cremated, as he had requested, and his ashes were buried at Arlington National Cemetery, honoring his service to the U. S. Army Medical Corps during World War I. A committee was established by the White Foundation to publish his papers. Between 1953 and 1972, the committee published seven books of Sullivan's work, ensuring that his theories remained available to the fields of psychiatry and psychology (Alexander, 1990; Evans, 1996; Perry, 1982).

Placing Sullivan in Context: America's Psychodynamic Theorist

Harry Stack Sullivan was an enigmatic character. His parents were poor and, apparently, both suffered from mental illness; his siblings died during their infancies. The region where he was raised was extremely prejudiced against Irish Catholics, and the KKK burned a cross in front of their home. As a student, Sullivan was very successful, but legal problems (due to his own bad choices) and presumed hospitalizations for his own mental illness delayed his success in college and medical school. And yet, he went on to become the most influential psychodynamic theorist born in America, worked at two highly prestigious psychiatric hospitals, co-founded an influential foundation, and has a hospital named after him. Like Adler, however, his contributions seldom receive proper recognition, and he remains somewhat obscure.

Sullivan's most interesting and enduring contributions relate to his relationship with William Alanson White. Although Sullivan only worked with White briefly, and White's letter of recommendation for Sullivan's next position admits that White considered Sullivan to be distant and hard to get to know, Sullivan vigorously pursued White's interest in the treatment of schizophrenia. Sullivan helped to found the William Alanson White Foundation, which established two psychiatric training institutes and the journal *Psychiatry*, and Sullivan delivered the First William Alanson White Memorial Lectures. Today, the Sheppard Pratt Health System includes the Harry Stack Sullivan Day Hospital (for the treatment of psychotic disorders).

Sullivan's Interpersonal Psychology

Sullivan shares two particular distinctions with Adler: his influence is extraordinarily wide ranging, and he is not very well known. It has been suggested that he was the most original and creative American-born psychiatrist (Chapman & Chapman, 1980). In Corsini & Wedding's *Current Psychotherapies* (1995), Sullivan is mentioned in ten of the fourteen chapters, including those written by Albert Ellis, Carl Rogers, Aaron Beck, and Rollo May, as well as the chapters written about Sigmund Freud, Alfred Adler, and Carl Jung. Due largely to his emphasis on interpersonal relationships, he is acknowledged by Jean Baker Miller and other founding members of the Stone Center (see Chapter 9; Jordan, et al., 1991; Miller, 1976). So how can he be relatively unknown? According to Evans (1996), there are a number of reasons for Sullivan's lack of popularity, but two seem to stand out. First, Sullivan did not publish much during his lifetime, and what he did publish was somewhat poorly written and difficult to understand. Second, Sullivan was apparently a very difficult and strange man, whose writings often included derogatory statements about psychiatry and psychiatrists (even though this was his own field). Whatever the reasons are for his lack of renown, Sullivan has had a significant influence on psychiatry and psychology nonetheless.

Whereas Adler considered relationships to be an obvious consequence of social interest, the primary factor in Individual Psychology is the striving for superiority. Social interest and interpersonal relationships, of course, make healthy superiority possible. For Sullivan, however, it was the interpersonal relationships themselves that were paramount:

> *One achieves mental health to the extent that one becomes aware of one's interpersonal relations*...It is part of the framework that supports all explanations of what is going on, what might be going on, and what will presently be going on...It is *the* necessary formula to which everything must be assimilable, if it is therapy. (pg. 207; Sullivan, 1940)

Euphoria, Tension, and Security

Sullivan believed that we exist somewhere between the states of absolute **euphoria** and absolute **tension**. Absolute euphoria is a state of utter well-being, which, unfortunately, is not really possible. The closest we can come to experiencing absolute euphoria is in the deep sleep of a newborn infant. Tension is the alternative state to euphoria, and tension is very much a part of our lives. It arises from two sources: **needs** and **anxiety**. There are two basic types of needs: those that arise from actual biological needs (food, water, air, etc.), and those that are cultural or learned. In real life, however, these types of needs cannot be separated. An infant cannot satisfy its biological needs, it must be cared for. Thus, Sullivan talked routinely about a mothering need, which is a need for an intimate, interpersonal relationship. When the mother does indeed care for the infant, the infant experiences this as **tenderness**, and the infant develops an ongoing need for tenderness. Thus, through the need for a mother and the need for tenderness, the infant finds itself in a world in which it needs interpersonal relationships for continued survival and psychological development (Chapman & Chapman, 1980; Lundin, 1979; Mullahy & Melinek, 1983; Sullivan, 1940, 1953).

Anxiety is the result of real or imagined threats, and can be experienced by the infant or caused by an anxious mother. In either case, it can be particularly intense in an infant because they cannot specifically do anything about it. Furthermore, unlike biological needs that can be met quite specifically (e.g., a hungry child can be fed), how can anxiety be satisfied? The answer, according to Sullivan, is through the pursuit of interpersonal **security**. In other words, a sense of security, the alternative to anxiety, can be obtained only through relationships that provide the child with tenderness and **empathy**. Sullivan used the term empathy to describe "the peculiar emotional linkage that subtends the relationship of the infant with other significant people - the mother or the nurse" (pg. 17; Sullivan, 1940). Long before infants show any sense of understanding emotional expressions, they seem to be able to share in emotional feelings, through what Sullivan considered an innate capacity for empathy. Even an infant is not, however, merely a recipient of the relationships in which it is involved, it is an active and engaged person. Likewise, children do not simply wait and hope for security, they actively engage in thoughts and behaviors that Sullivan called **security operations**. Security operations serve to maintain our sense of self-esteem, or self-respect, and they often begin with an emphatic sense of "I." Unfortunately, this leads to an odd paradox: the concept that we can have self-esteem without being in relationship with others:

> It is one's prestige, one's status, the importance which people feel one is entitled to, the respect that one can expect from people…that dominate awareness. *These things are so focal in interpersonal relations of our day and age that the almost unassailable conviction develops…that each of us, as defined by the animal organism that we were at birth, are unique, isolated individuals in the human world…* (pg. 219; Sullivan, 1964)

Dynamisms and the Self-System

Underlying Sullivan's emphasis on interpersonal relationships is the fundamental concept of **dynamism**. Similar to the physical universe, our psychological environment involves ongoing transfers of energy (in the psychological sense) between ourselves and the people we interact with, and this is a dynamic back-and-forth system (i.e., a relationship). A dynamism is a relatively enduring pattern of energy transformation that allows us to characterize a living organism. Each organism, or each person, has many dynamisms, but the ones of particular interest to psychiatrists, according to Sullivan, are those related to how we interact with others (Sullivan, 1953).

One of the most important dynamisms is the **self-system**. The self-system is somewhat unique, in that it integrates and provides meaning for all of the individual's interactions and experiences; Sullivan referred to it as a secondary dynamism (secondary here refers to a higher level of processing, not secondary in importance; Sullivan, 1953). The self-system also integrates the security operations, and serves to protect the individual from tension. Chapman & Chapman (1980) offer a useful description of various ways in which the self-system utilizes security operations in the actions of a 3-year-old child:

1. When faced with an emotionally threatening situation, the child may lapse into stubborn silence.
2. When there is tension between the child and the demands of older children, the child will obstinately resist the efforts of the older children to get the child to conform to their desires.
3. When stressful interpersonal situations arise, the child will withdraw into solitary play.
4. In new, anxiety-provoking environments the child will physically cling to a familiar adult.
5. When anxiety arises between the child and others, the child may engage in meticulous play with inanimate objects (toys, coloring books, etc.).
6. When the child's emotional needs are not met by others, they may regress into more immature behavior and speech.

By observing these behaviors, we can understand who this child is at this point in their life. For a 3-year-old, such behaviors are quite normal. However, such security operations would be considered less appropriate for an adult. And yet, sometimes these behaviors become part of the self-system of an adolescent, or an adult, and Sullivan referred to such instances as **dynamisms of difficulty** (Sullivan, 1956, 1972). When dynamisms of difficulty go into action, they fail to achieve a desired goal, or at best achieve only an unsatisfactory goal. Since they are relatively enduring, as are all dynamisms, they tend to characterize states of psychological illness, and would indicate the need for psychotherapy. As a curious side-note, while discussing the dynamism of the self-system, Sullivan appears to be the first person to have used the now well-known term **significant other** (Sullivan, 1953).

Another important type of dynamism is the **personification**. A newborn infant cannot really understand who their mother is, or who they themselves are, so the infant develops an image of the mother, the father, themselves, etc. These images, which can sometimes conflict with one another, are called personifications. For instance, when the mother feeds and comforts the infant, she is the "good" mother. But when she fails to display appropriate tenderness, or her own anxiety is expressed to and experienced by the infant, she is the "bad" mother. Later, as the child develops greater intellectual capacity and experience, these personifications are fused into a single mother. Similarly, the infant begins life with personifications of itself as sometimes "bad" and sometimes "good," and later in life fuses these personifications as the adolescent begins to establish a clear identity (Chapman & Chapman, 1980; Mullahy & Melinek, 1983; Sullivan, 1953, 1964). As with all of the concepts we have discussed here, the process of personification continues into adulthood. A mother will develop her own personifications of the infant, which, as mentioned above, may be experienced by the infant. For example, if a baby is colicky (cries constantly and cannot be soothed), it can be very frustrating for a mother, especially a new mother. Her anxiety may lead to a personification of her baby as inconsolable and of herself as a "bad" mother. Her discomfort, then, in caring for her baby can be experienced by the baby, leading to the baby's personification of her as a "bad" mother. The key here, according to Sullivan's theory, is that neither the mother nor the baby is in any way bad or good, inconsolable or tender, *except in relation to one another*!

Sullivan described the **personified self** as those aspects of personality about which one is consciously aware. This provides important information for a psychotherapist, and pursuing information about the personified self is an important part of the **psychiatric interview** (Sullivan, 1954). During the interview, Sullivan recommended that the psychotherapist examine four aspects of personified self: what does the patient esteem and/or disparage about themselves; to what experiences is the patient's self-esteem particularly and unreasonably vulnerable; what are the characteristic security operations employed when the patient is made anxious; and how great are the patient's reserves of security? In addition to these important points, Sullivan also considered it essential for a psychotherapist to gain an impression of the whole interview situation, particularly with regard to the patient's sense of proportion in terms of where they fit into life. By understanding the personified self, the patient's knowledge of themselves, and how they view themselves within the context of their life, the psychotherapist can gain an understanding of what is realistically possible for the patient during the course of therapy (Sullivan, 1954).

Discussion Question: Sullivan described the personified self as knowing what you like or dislike about yourself, what experiences are particularly damaging to your self-esteem, your characteristic security operations, and how deep your reserves of security are. Consider each of these points, and provide yourself with a self-evaluation. Overall, do you see yourself as a relatively healthy, secure person, or someone whose life is plagues by tension and anxiety?

Developmental Epochs

Sullivan considered an understanding of the course of human development to be essential to understanding individuals. He described seven **developmental epochs**: **infancy**, **childhood**, the **juvenile era**, **preadolescence**, **early adolescence**, **late adolescence**, and **adulthood** (Sullivan, 1953, 1954, 1964). These developmental stages represent a gradual unfolding of the individual's capacity for effective interpersonal relationships or, in other words, the individual's ability to fit into the social structure of their environment (Chrzanowski, 1977; Lundin, 1979). As we all know, children maintain very different relationships than adults do, and we would not expect children to have adult-like relationships. Thus, when attempting to evaluate a person's state of mental health, which Sullivan equated with their ability to form healthy relationships, we clearly need to understand something about what constitutes the developmentally appropriate possibilities.

Infancy begins at birth, and lasts until the acquisition of speech. It is the time of the most empathic connection between the infant and its caregivers, which can be characterized by tenderness and security, or by anxiety and tension. Childhood lasts through the remainder of the preschool years, and involves extending one's interpersonal relationships outside of the immediate family to peers (friends and playmates). In addition, language is incorporated into one's experiences of approval and disapproval. The juvenile era begins as one enters grade school. Once again, interpersonal relations are expanded to include a wider variety of people and situations, including competition with one's peers and subordination to authority figures (such as teachers and the school's principal).

Adolescence involves some very dramatic changes, particularly in the direction of the intensely intimate relationships of adulthood. During preadolescence, there is a marked increase in the closeness of friendships (e.g., "best friends forever!"), which is characterized by an intimate dynamism. Early adolescence is marked by an interest in the other sex, and an erotic dynamism is formed. Late adolescence, which Sullivan placed between the middle high school years the early college years, were a time of developing full and mature interrelationships, as well as understanding of the need for responsible citizenship within one's society. When these dynamisms, including the self-system, become stabilized, and society has transformed the individual into a completely social being, the person has attained adulthood (Chrzanowski, 1977; Lundin, 1979; Sullivan, 1953, 1954, 1964).

Sullivan provided ages for the transition of these developmental epochs, but he also acknowledged that they are based on experience. Thus, it is possible for the stages to occur at different times in unique individuals. The course, however, remains the same, unless the course fails to progress. If an individual is not provided with the opportunities to advance their interpersonal development, there can be an **arrest of development** (Sullivan, 1953, 1964). An arrest of development does not mean that the personality becomes static, but rather, the freedom and velocity of constructive changes becomes markedly reduced. Later, the arrested development becomes apparent through eccentricities in one's interpersonal relations. The individual does not simply continue to act like a normal child, there is an increased likelihood that this "warp" in personality development will also lead to malevolent dynamisms and the consequent social problems (such as delinquency and crime).

Discussion Question: Do you know anyone who demonstrates arrested development (someone who seems immature, especially in relationships)? Are you able to maintain a friendship with that person, or is the situation too stressful?

Final Notes on Harry Stack Sullivan

From his early days working with William Alanson White, Sullivan was particularly interested in the treatment of schizophrenia. One of the books published by the White Foundation was entitled *Schizophrenia as a Human Process* (Sullivan, 1962), in which his longtime friend Clara Thompson described him as having a "genuine liking and respect" for his patients. Later the White Foundation published a series of seminars Sullivan offered to the psychiatric residents at Sheppard Pratt, as well as members of the Chestnut Lodge and the Washington School of Psychiatry, on the treatment of a young, male schizophrenic. The text includes commentary by others some 25 years after the seminar (see Kvarnes & Parloff, 1976).

Like Alfred and Kurt Adler, Sullivan recognized the difficulty of treating psychotic patients. The prognosis, in Sullivan's opinion, depends to a large extent upon the patient's history of successful interpersonal relationships:

> ...let us consider the empirical fact that the schizophrenia which appears in the form of a sudden dramatic onset is usually considered to have a more favorable prognosis than the schizophrenia with more gradual onset. But in those cases of sudden onset in which satisfactory experience with significant persons in the past is totally lacking, the patient may be practically beyond redemption; he may manifest empirically trustworthy capacity for recovery to the extent of making excellent institutional recovery; but the psychiatrist is daft who expects that he can put the patient out into the world without prompt relapse. (pg. 197; Sullivan, 1956)

Returning to Sullivan's basic concept of personality, he offered the following definition:

> Personality is the relatively enduring configuration of life-processes characterizing all of the person's total activity pertaining to such other persons, real or fantastic, as become from time to relevant factors in his total situations. (pg. 47; Sullivan, 1972)

While this definition is rather sweeping in its coverage, it remains focused on interpersonal relationships. According to Thompson, Sullivan was very serious about his own relationships:

> The quality of his friendship showed the same genuineness and tolerance so characteristic of his relation to patients. He was slow in making friends. He tested them for a long time...Once a person had passed the test he could count on Harry for absolute loyalty. No matter what your mistakes - and he might point them out to you privately - before the world he was on your side...He had a characteristic phrase when parting form a friend - "God keep you." (pg. xxxiv; Clara Thompson in Sullivan, 1962)

Personality Theory in Real Life: Achieving Athletic Excellence Despite Physical Challenges

Adler's studies on inferiority began with physical problems, what he called organ inferiority (Adler, 1917). Most students of Adler look past that medical beginning, and focus instead on the psychological inferiorities that children experience during their development. However, there are many people with organ inferiority, or what we more commonly refer to as disabilities, handicaps, or "challenges." There may be some debate as to which term is preferred, but since the phrase "politically correct" is itself a contradiction in terms, I will use the terms **disability** and **handicap** as presented in Warren Rule's book *Lifestyle Counseling for Adjustment to Disability* (Rule, 1984). In his summary of previous research, Rule adopts the definition of a disability as a "relatively severe chronic impairment of function" that occurs as the result of a congenital defect, disease, or an accident. Accordingly, disability refers to actual physical, mental, or emotional impairments that become a handicap *only if* they cause lowered self-assessment, reduced activity, or limited opportunities. When disabilities become a handicap, they can affect the individual's entire style of life. Thus, Rule brought together a group of therapists trained in Individual Psychology, and published the aforementioned book on using lifestyle counseling for people with disabilities that have led to handicaps.

However, not everyone with a disability develops a handicap. Instead, some individuals become truly inspirational by the way in which they live their lives in spite of their disability, or rather, as if they simply were not disabled. Erik Weihenmayer (2001; see also Stoltz & Weihenmayer, 2006) was born with retinoscheses, a degenerative eye disease, which slowly destroyed his retinas, leaving him blind by the age of 13. In high school, Erik spent a month one summer at the Carroll Center for the Blind in Massachusetts. The summer camp included a weekend of rock climbing in N. Conway, New Hampshire (where the author has done a lot of rock-climbing). Weihenmayer's rock climbing experience altered his life. He continued climbing rock, and then moved on to ice-climbing and mountaineering. He didn't just followed more experienced climbers up the cliffs, he also learned to lead-climb: placing one's own protection along the climb and then clipping in the rope, what climbers call "the sharp end" of the rope. I had the pleasure of climbing with Erik in Michigan's Upper Peninsula a few years ago, while his seeing-eye dog slept in a sort of ice cave formed by the overhanging ice. It is truly extraordinary to watch him climb. He moves so smoothly, as he feels the ice above with his ice axe, and then sets the ice axe so deliberately when he finds the right spot, that you would not know he was climbing blind if you only watched for a little while. Eventually, Erik decided to pursue the Seven Summits, climbing the highest peak on each continent: Mt. McKinley (N. America), Aconcagua (S. America), Mt. Everest (Asia), Mt. Elbrus (Europe), Vinson Massif (Antarctica), Mt. Kosciusko (Australia), Kilimanjaro (Africa). He accomplished his goal in 2002.

Erik Weihenmayer is by no means the only well-known, disabled climber. In an amazing video,

Beyond the Barriers (Perlman & Wellman, 1998), Erik goes climbing with Mark Wellman and Hugh Herr. Wellman was paralyzed from the waist down in a climbing accident (Wellman & Flinn, 1992), and Herr lost both of his lower legs to frostbite after being caught in a vicious winter storm on Mt. Washington, NH (Osius, 1991; Note: The author has suffered a small patch of frostbite during a winter storm on Mt. Washington). In *Beyond the Barriers*, Herr leads the hike toward the climb, while Erik carries Wellman. Once on the climb, Herr leads the climb, Erik follows, and they set ropes for Wellman to do pull-ups up the cliff. It simply has to be seen to be believed. One of the surprising aspects is how they joke with each other about what they are doing. As Erik is carrying Wellman, Wellman says: "I don't know man. A blind man giving a para a piggyback ride? It's a pretty scary thing!" When Herr starts climbing on a day when it was snowing, he says his hands are getting numb from the cold. So, Erik asks him how his feet feel! Humor was always an important part of Adlerian psychotherapy (Scott, 1984), so perhaps it should not be surprising that a sense of humor is an aspect of their personalities. One of the funniest stories that Erik tells is about the time he accidentally drank out of his climbing partners piss bottle (a bottle used to urinate inside the tent during storms). Erik became quite upset that the bottle wasn't marked somehow, but his partner defended himself by saying he had clearly written on the bottle which one it was. It slowly dawned on Erik's partner that the writing was of no help to Erik. As another example of Erik's humor, consider the challenge he tried to avoid after having climbed the highest peaks in Africa and North and South America:

> Emma Louise Weihenmayer was born on June 21, year 2000, at 3:57 A.M. There is so much to learn about parenthood. Sometimes being a father is about as intense as climbing Denali, Kilimanjaro, and Aconcagua, all in a day. Because I'm blind, I tried to convince Ellie that I couldn't change diapers, but for some reason, she didn't buy it. (pg. 303; Weihenmayer, 2001)

In addition to his climbing, Erik Weihenmayer is a college graduate with a teaching certificate, and he spent some time as a middle school teacher. He also tried the sport of wrestling, and was a wrestling coach. Trevon Jenifer was also a wrestler.

Trevon Jenifer was born without legs. Perhaps even more challenging, however, was the fact that he was the fourth child of a poor, single mother living in a ghetto outside of Washington, DC. Obviously, Trey (the name he goes by) began life facing difficult obstacles, but little by little, things got better. His mother, Connie, made a conscious decision to take care of him the best she could. She soon met Eric Brown, who became Trey's step-father, providing a stable home for their family. He met a wonderful special education teacher named Bob Gray, who got Trey interested in sports, and who helped to make participating in sports a realistic possibility. He eventually joined a wheelchair track and basketball team named Air Capital, and he was very successful on the track, setting national records in the 100-, 200-, and 400-meter races. It was prior to his junior year in high school, however, that his step-father, who had been a wrestler, recommended that Trey try out for the wrestling team, the *regular* wrestling team.

What Trey wanted more than anything was to fit in, to have a normal social life at school. Being in a wheelchair, that was not likely to happen. However, he felt that sports might help him accomplish that goal, so he did try out for the wrestling team. He worked hard, learned as much as he could, and he made the varsity team as the 103-pound competitor (actually, there was no one else that light on the team, but he didn't know that). His coach, Terry Green, did all he could to help Trey find a wrestling style that would take advantage of his relative arm strength (he made weight without legs, so his upper body was relatively large) while overcoming the disadvantage of not being able to balance or leverage his body weight by spreading out his legs. Now it was up to Trey. He was nervous in his first match, didn't assert himself, and was easily pinned. In his second match he became the aggressor and earned his first victory. The rest of his junior year continued to be a series of wins and losses, and he ended the season 17-18. Of course, it had only been his first season of wrestling.

In anticipation of his senior year in high school, Trey continued to train hard. Outside of the ring he also received recognition, and became a part of the social network of the school. He received a *Medal of Courage* from the National Wrestling Hall of Fame, he attended his school's prom, and he was chosen as co-captain of the wrestling team. Once again, humor played a role, as he compared his strength to a teammate from the previous year. Trey had made significant strides in how much he could bench-press, so his former teammate asked him how much he could squat (a lift done entirely with the legs)! Both wrestlers enjoyed a good laugh at that one.

Trey was doing quite well in league wrestling, and he also began to do well in tournaments. Eventually, he won a tournament, ended his season at 26-6, and from there went on the state championship. He won his first match, but then had to face an undefeated wrestler. He lost, but in that loss there was a sense of accomplishment due to how far he had come:

> I lost 5-2…I was hurt less by the fact that I lost, and more by the closeness of it. This one hurt even more because of how close I was to beating the best wrestler in the state. Sharbaugh went on to win the state championship. In fact, he won his last two matches very convincingly, 6-0, and, 12-5. He told reporters afterward that my match was his toughest of the tournament. (pp. 171-172; Trevon Jenifer in Jenifer & Goldenbach, 2006).

The next morning he had to return to the championships to wrestle for a chance at third place in the state. He began with a vengeance, scoring victories of 9-1 and 9-2. His next match, and a shot at third place, was not so easy, but he won 3-1, earning his 30th victory of the season. He then won his final match, and earned third place in the state championship. However, an even more important challenge now loomed ahead of him: college.

Coming from a poor, Black family, there was no tradition of children going to college. However, a group of concerned philanthropists became interested in supporting his dreams. His old coach at Air Capital had talked to Jim Glatch, who coached wheelchair basketball at Edinboro College in Pennsylvania, a school with a large population (10 percent) of students with disabilities. Trevon Jenifer currently attends Edinboro College and plays on the wheelchair basketball team. He does not know if he will ever wrestle again, but it is interesting to note that Edinboro College has a famous wrestler as their athletic director: two-time Olympic gold medalist Bruce Baumgartner!

Recently, Trey was kind enough to respond to an email I sent him, and he provided me with an update on how things have gone during his first year of college. He misses wrestling very much, but he has really enjoyed his return to wheelchair basketball. It probably didn't hurt that the team is very good, and they came in second-place in the NCAA championship for wheelchair basketball. Trey maintained good grades, his family strongly supports him in pursuing his education, and he has made many new friends. But a few challenges remain. It has been a little difficult for him to get used to the weather in northwestern Pennsylvania, and he has been too busy to attend as many book signings as his publisher would like (but he says they have been very understanding). As for becoming the inspiration his mother thought he was born to be:

> I think that I have inspired some people, and I think that is great, but I don't think that it has reached all the people that I would like it too. My family says that I have done a good job, but I [think that I could do a lot better], and I will try until I feel that I have reached that. (Trevon Jenifer; personal communication, 2007)

The range of sports in which disabled individuals compete is extraordinary today. *Beyond the Barriers* also includes disabled individuals sailing, scuba diving, surfing, and hang gliding. A few years ago, I began practicing Tae Kwon Do, and I soon discovered that I had degenerative joint disease in both hips. I considered quitting Tae Kwon Do, but I was strongly encouraged to continue by my instructors, as well as by my orthopedic surgeon and physical therapist. I have since learned that Dirk Robertson, a former social worker turned actor and writer, has worked hard promoting martial arts training for people with disabilities (Robertson, 1991; see also McNab, 2003). Each person simply needs to be encouraged to do their best. Adler suggested that the best way to strive for superiority was through social interest. Whether it's a climbing partner, a wrestling team, a wheelchair basketball team, a martial arts school, whatever, when people work together to help each individual achieve their potential, it can prove to be a highly rewarding experience.

> Whilst it is important to be sensitive to their particular situation, their disability should not be the central focus all the time. Their *ability* to learn, listen and adapt should be built on and encouraged. Do not be over-protective or an instant expert on people with disabilities. The experts are the people themselves, so listen to what they have to say. (pp. 101-102; Robertson, 1991)

Review of Key Points

- Adler faced death numerous times as a child, including his brother's actual death. These events had a profound impact on the nature of his theories.
- Adler helped Freud gain recognition for Freud's personality theory. This lends credence to Adler's claim that he was never a student or follower of Freud, but rather a colleague interested in similar psychiatric/psychological questions.
- The fundamental aspect of Individual Psychology is that we are born inferior and spend our lives striving for superiority.
- Striving for superiority takes the form of compensating for our weaknesses, which, unfortunately, can sometimes lead to overcompensation.
- When individuals can not compensate, they may develop an inferiority complex. Extreme feelings of inferiority can lead to the paradoxical superiority complex.
- Adler believed that all thought and behavior was tied to some goal. Our overriding goal is the life plan, and we pursue it by living a characteristic style of life.
- Dysfunctional styles of life can result from pampering and neglect, both of which reduce our social interest.
- According to Adler, social interest is the best way to achieve superiority, and it can most easily be seen in cooperation.
- Formal examples of cooperation include teamwork, which can lead to either positive or negative outcomes, depending on the circumstances.
- Adler described three life tasks: work, communal life, and love.
- Important aspects of our ability to strive for superiority are the creative power of the individual and the goal we set as the fictional finalism.
- Each person exists within their own perception of the world, known as the scheme of apperception. This scheme guides all experience to fit into our style of life and our goals.
- Since child development is so important, Adler created child guidance centers to train both parents and schoolteachers in the principles of Individual Psychology.
- Adler was very interested in the effects of birth order and the family constellation. Being an only child is likely to result in pampering, whereas an oldest child must deal with being dethroned.
- In an attempt to understand the psychological motivation of women, and some men as well, Adler proposed the theory of masculine protest.
- The key to Adlerian psychotherapy is understanding the patient's style of life.
- An important technique for revealing the style of life is the early memories test.

- Once the style of life is understood, Adlerian psychotherapists work to strengthen social interest and reorient the style of life.
- Adler was an early innovator in terms of both family therapy and group psychotherapy.
- Sullivan began his formal psychiatric career at two prestigious hospitals: St. Elizabeth's and Sheppard Pratt.
- According to Sullivan, we are a constant state of tension, due to our needs and anxieties. We seek security, and we employ security operations to reduce our anxiety and tension.
- Sullivan referred to the energy transformation that underlies our personal interactions as dynamisms. Perhaps the most important dynamism is the self-system.
- When an individual develops dysfunctional security operations, Sullivan referred to them as dynamisms of difficulty.
- Before we can truly understand relationships, we develop images in our mind known as personifications. The personified self includes everything we can consciously describe about ourselves.
- Sullivan described seven developmental epochs, which provide a framework for our unfolding abilities to engage in healthy interpersonal relationships.

Review of Key Terms

adulthood	fictional finalism	pampering
anxiety	fictive superiority	personification
arrest of development	group psychotherapy	personified self
birth order	handicap	preadolescence
childhood	individual psychology	psychiatric interview
communal life	infancy	scheme of apperception
compensation	inferiority	security
cooperation	inferiority complex	security operations
creative power of the individual	juvenile era	self-system
	late adolescence	significant other
dethroned	life plan	slanguage
developmental epochs	life tasks	social interest
disability	love	style of life
dynamism	masculine protest	superiority
dynamisms of difficulty	needs	superiority complex
early adolescence	neglect	teams
early memories	oldest child	tenderness
empathy	only child	tension
euphoria	organ inferiority	unity of the individual
family therapy	overcompensation	work

Annotated Bibliography

Adler, A. (1929a). *The science of living*. New York, NY: Greenberg.
Adler, A. (1931a). *What life should mean to you*. New York, NY: Capricorn Books.
Adler, A. (1964). *Social interest: A challenge to mankind*. New York, NY: Capricorn Books.

These excellent books by Adler present all of the basic information on his theory of Individual Psychology. Each one by itself is fairly complete, but taken together, very little of importance is missing.

Adler, A. (1929/1964). *Problems of neurosis: A book of case histories*. New York, NY: Harper & Row.

A marvelous book filled with specific case studies demonstrating Adler's clinical use of the theory of Individual Psychology. Particularly interesting are the discussions on early memories and the superiority complex.

Adler, A. (1930b). *The education of children*. New York, NY: Greenberg.
Adler, A. (1963). *The problem child: The life style of the difficult child as analyzed in specific cases*. New York, NY: Capricorn. Books.

These books obviously focus on the psychology of children and their development, which includes the influence of education and techniques for educating parents. The second book contains nearly twenty specific cases from Adler's experience, and concludes with a discussion of the important of kindergarten and kindergarten teachers.

Adler, A. (Ed.). (1925/1963). *The practice and theory of Individual Psychology*. Paterson, NJ: Littlefield, Adams & Co.
Ansbacher, H. L. & Ansbacher, R. R. (Eds). (1964). *Alfred Adler - Superiority and social interest: A collection of later writings*. New York, NY: The Viking Press.

These books contain many of Adler's most important papers and lectures. Together, they provide an incomparable collection of Adler's thoughts on Individual Psychology. Indeed, Adler himself collected the papers presented in the first of these books.

Adler, A. (Ed.). (1930a). *Guiding the child: On the principles of Individual Psychology*. New York, NY: Greenberg.

This is another volume edited by Adler, with the individual chapters written by many of the people who worked in the Vienna Child Guidance Clinics. Adler contributed one chapter that presents a case study, and his daughter Alexandra wrote chapters on techniques of child guidance and the personality of the only child.

Dreikurs, R. (1950). *Fundamentals of Adlerian psychology*. New York, NY: Greenburg.

This book provides an excellent overview of Adler's theories, written by one of his best known students. After studying with Adler, Dreikurs began establishing family education centers in the United States (the first in Chicago in 1937).

Boukreev, A. & DeWalt, G. W. (1997). *The climb: Tragic ambitions on Everest*. New York, NY: St. Martin's Press.
Krakauer, J. (1997). *Into thin air: A personal account of the Mount Everest disaster*. New York, NY: Villard.

These two books tell the gripping tale of the deaths of six climbers on Mt. Everest on May 10, 1996. What made this event even more shocking was that the climbing parties were led by two of the most experienced and well-respected high-altitude mountain guides in the world. Although Krakauer's book was widely advertised and became well-known, Krakauer (an experienced mountaineer) was lying in his tent exhausted while Boukreev (one of the mountaineering guides) repeatedly went back out into the storm and rescued a number of the survivors.

Sullivan, H. S. (1940). *Conceptions of modern psychiatry*. New York, NY: W. W. Norton & Company.

This is the one book that Sullivan published himself, while he was still alive, and it serves as a tribute to William Alanson White (it contains the First William Alanson White Memorial

Lectures). In the book, Sullivan presents many of the basic ideas that came to form his theories. The second edition of the book includes a review of Sullivan's lectures by Patrick Mullahy.

Sullivan, H. S. (1953). *The interpersonal theory of psychiatry*. New York, NY: W. W. Norton & Company.
Sullivan, H. S. (1956). *Clinical studies in psychiatry*. New York, NY: W. W. Norton & Company.

These two books provide a thorough review of Sullivan's theories, with the first book emphasizing the developmental epochs and the second book providing extensive information on applying the principles of Interpersonal Psychology in clinical settings. *Clinical Studies...* also contains numerous examples of Sullivan's consultations on a variety of psychiatric cases (including, of course, schizophrenia).

Sullivan, H. S. (1972). *Personal psychopathology: Early formulations*. New York, NY: W. W. Norton & Company.

The last of Sullivan's books to be published by the White Foundation, this contains some very interesting chapters. Included are discussions on dynamisms of difficulty, male/female differences in development during adolescence, and the relationship between sleep, dreams, and schizophrenia. The final chapter presents a discussion on welfare programs.

Kearse, R. (2006b). *Changin' your game plan! - How to use incarceration as a stepping stone for success*. New York, NY: Big Mouth Street Media.

Randy "Mo Betta" Kearse spent over 13 years in a federal prison for dealing drugs. He does not want to go back. In this book, he offers practical suggestions for change and pursuing a positive direction in one's life and community. Kearse writes with an intensity that can only come from real-life experience.

Jenifer, T. & Goldenbach, A. (2006). *Trevon Jenifer: From the ground up*. Champaign, IL: Sports Publishing L. L. C.
Weihenmayer, E. (2001). *Touch the top of the world: A blind man's journey to climb farther than the eye can see*. New York, NY: Dutton.

Trevon Jenifer was born without legs, and he became a very successful high school wrestler. Erik Weihenmayer was born with a degenerative eye disease that left him blind by his early teenage years, yet he became a rock- and ice-climber, and then a serious mountaineer. Their books provide marvelously inspirational tales of overcoming challenges in ways that bring Adler's theories to life.

Chapter 6 - Neo-Freudian Perspectives

Who were the neo-Freudians, and what exactly does this term mean? Many early psychoanalysts remained basically true to Freud and his theories. These individuals are collectively known as either neo-Freudians or as ego psychologists, for their emphasis on the ego. Shifting from Freud's emphasis on the id to an emphasis on the ego is a major change, but it does not require rejecting the basic elements of Freud's theory. The shift also encourages the study of children. After all, it is during childhood that most of this dramatic psychological development occurs. The neo-Freudians stand in contrast to Alfred Adler and Carl Jung, who intentionally distanced themselves from Freud, and Karen Horney, who initially brought a female perspective to psychodynamic theory (a perspective in which she directly challenged some of Freud's ideas on women) but later shifted to a cultural perspective on the psychology of women. For an interesting introduction to a number of important neo-Freudians, see *Freud and Beyond* (Mitchell & Black, 1995), and for an introduction to some of their papers see *The First Freudians* (Ruitenbeek, 1973).

In this chapter, we will only be able to take a brief look at a handful of these theorists. Among the many neo-Freudians, there are some notable individuals we will not be covering. Karl Abraham was an active psychoanalyst in Berlin when the rest of Germany was largely mocking Freud's theory. Sándor Ferenczi accompanied Freud and Jung on their landmark trip to America. A. A. Brill was influential in the development of psychoanalysis in America, and an early translator of Freud's works into English. As important as these theorists were in their own right, they have not had quite the influence of those whom we will cover in this chapter.

First, we will examine Anna Freud's contributions on the defense mechanisms. Although her father had described many of the defense mechanisms, he left it to his daughter to literally write the book on them (A. Freud, 1936/1966). Anna Freud also moved beyond her father's work in at least one significant way: she contributed to the study of applying psychoanalysis to children. Two other early contributors to the application of psychoanalysis to children were Melanie Klein and D. W. Winnicott. Although Klein and Anna Freud shared an interest in studying children, they often did not agree. This conflict led to a split in the English school of psychoanalysis (Mitchell & Black, 1995). Winnicott had been trained in part by colleagues of Klein, and he was supervised by Klein personally for a time, but eventually his independence led him to develop his own theories. Having been a pediatrician before he became a psychoanalyst, he was able to draw on a wealth of experience observing children interacting with their mothers (Mitchell & Black, 1995). Finally, we will take a very brief look at the work of Heinz Kohut and Margaret Mahler, and their perspectives on how an individual finally becomes just that.

Placing the Neo-Freudians in Context - 1: Connecting Personality Theories

In one sense, it is not possible to put the neo-Freudians in context, because to do so would be to suggest that these theorists have concluded their work. As we will see, the process of modifying Sigmund Freud's theories toward some final, comprehensive theory accepted by all psychoanalysts continues today. So we must keep in mind that we are really just putting those theorists mentioned in this chapter in context, and this task is one that will continue into the future.

If you had been able to predict in 1910 what future perspectives on Freud's theory would become, you might have easily done it. Some theorists stayed true to Freud's basic principles, others took radically different approaches, and the rest fell somewhere in between. Not surprisingly, the strongest supporter of Freud's theory was his own daughter Anna. Although she shifted the focus of psychoanalysis from the id to the ego, and emphasized analyzing children, these were reasonable extensions of Freud's own work. And more importantly, she made these changes only within the constraints that her father's theory allowed.

In contrast, Melanie Klein made radical changes to psychoanalytic theory, and directly challenged the views of Anna Freud. This challenge led to a public battle, one in which Anna Freud seems to have been respectful toward Klein, but Klein did not return the courtesy. Subsequently a third group arose, a group of moderates who appreciated the direction Klein had taken, but who had their own differences of opinion with her. Following a series of open discussions during World War II, it was agreed by all to acknowledge the differences among those who followed Anna Freud, Klein, or their own independent paths.

Eventually, subsequent theorists began to recognize the value in each different approach to psychoanalysis. Today, theorists like Otto Kernberg have come a long way toward blending the different neo-Freudian approaches together. But there remained an important area of psychology that needed further study in its own right: the psychology of women. The object relations theorists had laid an interesting foundation for what became a relational-cultural approach to the study of women, and ultimately all people.

Anna Freud and Ego Psychology

Anna Freud (1895-1982) was the youngest of Sigmund and Martha Freud's six children, and the only one to pursue a career in psychoanalysis. However, this did not come about immediately, and Anna Freud never attended medical school as her father had. Therefore, she was one of the first lay psychoanalysts, which is an important consideration for all mental health practitioners today (since Freud and most other early psychoanalysts were actually psychiatrists who had attended medical school). In 1971, a survey conducted among psychiatrists and psychoanalysts identified Anna Freud as the most outstanding colleague among both groups (see Peters, 1985).

Anna Freud lived with her parents until Sigmund Freud's death in 1939. She was a lively child, with a reputation for being mischievous. Although she always enjoyed a good relationship with her father, it was her older sister Sophie who was her father's favorite daughter (Peters, 1985). She was quite intelligent, but never attended college. She did, however, attend private schools, eventually entering the Cottage Lyceum in Vienna during fifth grade. She soon entered the Cottage Lyceum's high school, graduating in 1912. Since she had not chosen a career, she traveled to England to improve her English, one of several languages she had learned. Upon returning to Vienna, she became a teacher at the Cottage Lyceum's elementary school. She was very popular among her students, one of whom described her as "such a marvelous and simple figure that I loved her deeply at that time" (cited in Peters, 1985). Her popularity likely resulted from her own love of teaching and for her students (Coles, 1992). Anna Freud considered this experience as a teacher to have been very valuable for her later career as a child psychoanalyst:

> The people who follow this line of thought hold that those who analyze children should possess not only the correct analytical training and mental attitude but something further: something which is called for by the idiosyncrasies of childhood, namely, the training and the mental attitude of the pedagogue… (pg. 130; A. Freud, 1973).

Even before she graduated, Anna Freud had begun reading her father's works. But it was not until 1918 that she entered into psychoanalysis. Such a situation, a father psychoanalyzing his own daughter, would be considered inappropriate today, but at that time the entire field was still quite new and many aspects of it were still experimental. In any case, Anna Freud subsequently became one of her father's most unwavering supporters and an important psychoanalyst in her own right. In 1920 she attended the International Psychoanalytical Congress with her father, and 2 years later she was a member of the Vienna Psychoanalytical Society and began presenting her own papers. In 1923 she began her own practice treating children.

As Anna Freud was developing her theories regarding the psychoanalysis of children, Melanie Klein was developing her theories in England. There were significant disagreements between them, including a symposium in 1927 organized specifically to provide an opportunity for Klein to publicly attack Anna Freud's theories (Peters, 1985). After Anna Freud arrived to stay in England with her family in 1938, the conflict between them threatened to split the British Psychoanalytic Society. However, during World War II, a series of discussion forums resulted in the establishment of parallel training courses for the two groups.

After the war began, Anna Freud helped to set up the Hampstead War Nursery to provide foster care for over 80 children, a number that rose to a total of 190 children over several years (Peters, 1985). In addition to simply providing care for the children, she hoped to provide the children with continuity in their relationships with staff and family. With long-time friend Dorothy Burlingham she studied the effects of stress on young children in wartime. This work continued after the war when she had an opportunity to help provide care for six orphans who had survived the Theresienstadt concentration camp (Coles, 1992; Peters, 1985).

Throughout the rest of her life, she remained devoted to her work at the Hampstead War Nursery. She helped to establish the Hampstead Child Therapy Course (in 1947) and a children's clinic. Eventually the nursery became known more simply as the Hampstead Clinic, and Anna Freud became one of the major figures in psychoanalysis. She often traveled to lecture in the United States, and in the 1970s she was a co-author, with two professors from Yale University, of two books about governmental involvement in the lives of children who have been emotionally deprived and socially disadvantaged (see below). She received many honors, including honorary doctorates from Clark University (where her father had lectured during his trip to America), Harvard University, and Vienna University. The honorary medical degree she received from Vienna University was awarded in 1972, only 1 year after she returned to visit her native city for the first time since the Freud's had escaped the Nazis in 1938.

Shortly after her death, the Hampstead Clinic was renamed the Anna Freud Centre, in her honor, and in 1986 her former home became the Freud Museum. Although she has been considered by some to have done little more than continue her father's work, she was a pioneer in both ego psychology and the psychoanalysis of children. Accordingly, she deserves to be considered one of the most influential neo-Freudians. Much of the information in this biography can be found on *The Anna Freud Centre* website, as well as much more information on the center itself (http://www.annafreudcentre.org).

Ego Psychology and the Defense Mechanisms

In 1936, Anna Freud published perhaps her most influential book: *The Ego and the Mechanisms of Defense* (A. Freud, 1936/1966). She began by stating a redefinition of the field of psychoanalysis. There was a general bias, in her opinion, among many psychoanalysts to focus on the deep instinctual impulses of the id at the expense of considering the ego. However, since the id is always unconscious, its processes can never be observed directly. It may also be difficult to observe the processes of the ego as well, but at least the ego exists partially within the conscious mind. Since it is the ego that observes both the impulses of the id and the restraints of the superego, and since the ego is available to the psychoanalyst, she concluded "this means that the proper field for our observation is always the ego." (A. Freud, 1936/1966)

Although the ego is observable, that doesn't mean that a person's thoughts and behaviors always make sense. As the id demands the satisfaction of its impulses, the ego attempts to restrain the id, in accordance with the external demands of society and the internal representation of those demands in the superego. When these factors come in conflict, and the ego cannot easily resolve the conflict, anxiety develops. In order to help alleviate that anxiety, and to continue restraining the impulses of the id, the ego resorts to defense mechanisms. In so doing, the ego transforms the conflict somewhat and attempts to keep both the conflict and the basis for the conflict unconscious. When an individual is suffering psychologically and has sought help from a therapist, according to Anna Freud, the psychoanalyst arrives on the scene as someone who disturbs this fragile peace. This is because "it is the task of the analyst to bring into consciousness that which is unconscious…" (A. Freud, 1936/1966).

In order to understand how the ego uses defense mechanisms, it is necessary to understand the defense mechanisms themselves and how they function. Some defense mechanisms are seen as protecting us from within, from the instinctual impulses of the id (e.g., repression); other defense mechanisms protect us from external threats (e.g., denial). When treating a patient, the goal of the psychoanalyst is to determine how much a given defense mechanism contributes to the symptoms and to the ego resistance of the patient (in other words, resistance to therapy). To help understand these issues, Anna Freud identified and discussed ten defense mechanisms as being commonly recognized in the field of psychoanalysis: **regression, repression, reaction-formation, isolation, undoing, projection, introjection, turning against the self, reversal**, and **sublimation.** See Table 6.1 for a description of some of the defense mechanisms most commonly discussed today.

The defense mechanisms are not all available to an individual at the same time. As originally proposed by her father, Anna Freud believed that the defense mechanisms develop with the structures of personality (the id, ego, and superego). For example, projection and introjection depend on the differentiation of the ego from the outside world, so they would not be available to the ego as defense mechanisms until the ego had sufficiently developed (and, perhaps, differentiated into the superego as well; A. Freud, 1936/1966). This became an important point of contention, however, with the English school of analysis that included Melanie Klein. Whereas Anna Freud and her colleagues believed that projection and introjection would not be available in early childhood, since the structures of personality have not adequately developed, members of the English school believed that projection and introjection were a necessary part of that development. Although this debate and others between Freudian and Kleinian theorists became rather bitter (Mitchell & Black, 1995), Anna Freud did acknowledge the following:

> These differences of opinion bring home to us the fact that the chronology of psychic processes is still one of the most obscure fields of analytic theory…So a classification of the defense mechanisms according to position in time inevitably partakes of all the doubt and uncertainty which even today attach to chronological pronouncements in analysis. It will probably be best to abandon the attempt so to classify them and, instead, to study in detail the situations which call for the defensive reactions. (pg. 53; A. Freud, 1936/1966)

The final outcome of personality development, whether primarily normal or abnormal, depends on the overall process of these defense mechanisms throughout development. It is natural that defense mechanisms are called upon by the ego during both waves of psychosexual development. Whether or not the ego develops as a yielding and flexible structure depends on the strength of the instincts during development and the environment in which the individual develops. If instinctual demands are excessively urgent during development, the ego will redouble its defensive activities. This can stiffen the resistance of the ego to the instinctual impulses, leading to symptoms and inhibitions that remain throughout life (A. Freud, 1936/1966). At least, they might remain until the patient is successfully analyzed by a qualified psychoanalyst.

What is the status of defense mechanisms in psychology today? Clinical psychologists have always found the concept of defense mechanisms useful, but for a period of time defense mechanisms did not receive much attention from academic psychologists (Cramer, 2000). The primary reason for this was that early studies aimed at demonstrating the existence of the defense mechanisms and their processes were not promising. However, these are particularly difficult processes to study, since much of the processing occurs unconsciously (Cramer, 2000; Kernberg, 2004). According to Cramer (2000), as the various fields of psychology developed, they began to examine psychological processes that received new names within the particular field, even though the processes being studied were actually defense mechanisms that had already been discovered within psychoanalysis. Just to cite a few examples: what cognitive psychologists describe as selective attention may involve the defenses of splitting and dissociation, in social psychology scapegoating is a form of displacement, and in developmental psychology a child's verbal report of positive emotion while their facial expression clearly represents negative emotion is a classic case of denial (for a variety of examples and references see Cramer, 2000). Therefore, one can conclude that defense mechanisms, and defensive processes, have remained an important aspect of psychology and psychotherapy since they were first described by Sigmund Freud and Josef Breuer in 1895 (Freud & Breuer, 1895/2004).

Discussion Question: Anna Freud believed that even normal personality development involved the common use of defense mechanisms. Consider your own personality. Are there situations that make you anxious and, if so, can you recognize the defense mechanisms you rely on? Do you have a common defense mechanism that you use more than any other?

Psychoanalysis with Children

As mentioned above, Anna Freud began her career as a school teacher. This interest in children never diminished, and as she began to devote her career to psychoanalysis and psychoanalytic research her focus remained on the psychological lives of children. In 1946 she published *The Psycho-Analytical Treatment of Children* (A. Freud, 1946). This book is a collection of works she had written mostly in 1926 and 1927, with the final portion having been written in 1945. The book begins with an interesting preface, an apology that the book had not been available in English at an earlier date, particularly in the country of England. The reason for this, according to Anna Freud (and many historians agree), is that in England the theories of Melanie Klein dominated the psychoanalytic community (see also Mitchell & Black, 1995). Klein and her colleagues believed that psychoanalysis could be conducted successfully with young children, and that the process of transference occurred in the same manner as it did with adult patients. Initially, Anna Freud believed that psychoanalysis could not be performed with young children. Later, she acknowledged that the efforts of her colleagues had helped to make that a possibility, but she steadfastly denied that she had ever seen the normal process of transference in anyone younger than adulthood (A. Freud, 1946).

Table 6.1: Common Defense Mechanisms	
Repression	Repression involves blocking an impulse from conscious expression. Examples include forgetting a traumatic event, such as sexual abuse, or being unaware of hostile feelings toward family members.
Regression	When faced with difficult situations that we cannot resolve, we may regress to behavior indicative of an earlier stage of development. For example, when we are very sick, we may act as helpless as if we were an infant and hope that someone will take care of us.
Denial	Denial refers to simply refusing to believe an unpleasant reality. For example, when someone is told they have a terminal illness, they may deny it and refuse to follow treatment recommendations.
Projection	Projection involves attributing our own negative impulses to another person. If, for example, we want to see another person fail, perhaps to make us feel superior, we may claim that they are trying to interfere with our success.
Reaction-Formation	A reaction-formation is the process of suppressing unacceptable impulses and adopting an opposite course of action. For example, a parent who resents having children may shower them with love.
Identification	We often model our behavior after people we admire, or adjust our behavior based on people we fear. Internalizing this process of identifying with others is primarily how the superego develops, how we adopt the rules and guidelines of our culture and make them our own.
Displacement	Sometimes we cannot respond directly to unpleasant situations, so we displace (or transfer) our impulses onto another object. For example, if your boss yells at you at work, you then go home and yell at people in your family.
Rationalization	Rationalization is the process of finding logical reasons for unacceptable behavior or thoughts. For example, a professor may constantly battle with administrators about policies, while claiming that he/she only has the best interests of their students in mind.
Isolation	Isolation involves separating the anxiety-provoking aspects of an event from one's other thoughts and behaviors. For example, following the death of a child, one parent may set aside their grief in order to be able to provide support for the other parent.
Sublimation	Sometimes referred to as the successful defense mechanism, sublimation is the process of channeling unacceptable impulses into socially acceptable forms. It is often said that great artists must suffer before they can find the inspiration to master their craft.

The importance of the analysis of children in terms of research is threefold, according to Anna Freud. It helps to confirm the theories develop by Sigmund Freud and others based on the analysis of adults, it leads to fresh conclusions and new conceptions (and she commends Melanie Klein on this point), and it serves as a point of transition to a field of applied analysis that she felt might become the most important of all: working with children as they develop (A. Freud, 1927/1973). What Anna Freud tried most to do in her writings was to point out the circumstances that make psychoanalysis with children different than psychoanalysis with adults. Fundamentally, there is no difference in the process. However, the results of the process must be viewed differently in order to understand what happens with children. Since Melanie Klein was actively pursuing the same goals, Anna Freud often wrote specifically about Klein, acknowledging her accomplishments, but also pointing out their differences.

The basic argument was aimed at the intellectual and psychological abilities of young children, and the extent to which the psychical apparatus (the id, ego, and superego) have developed. Since all three personality structures have developed in an adult, there is no need for the analyst to worry about that. All the analyst needs to do is to bring into consciousness the neurotic processes that have led to the patient's symptoms (granted, that may be easier said than done). In children, however, the ego and especially the superego are still developing. Therefore, the analyst must consider the role he/she may play in the development of the child. The analyst must consider the extent to which the superego has already developed, and the analyst may be able to take advantage of its continuing development and help to direct and/or instruct superego development. According to Anna Freud (1927/1973):

> ...In the analysis of the adult we are at a point where the superego has already established its independence - an independence which is unshakable by any influence from the outside world...But child analysis must include all those cases in which the superego has as yet not reached any true independence. Only too clearly it strives to please its taskmasters, the child's parents and others responsible for his training...we have to use our influence from without in an educational manner by changing the child's relation to those who are bringing him up... (pgs. 138-139)

As these processes are actually observed, Anna Freud believed that the child's symptoms could transform in the presence of the psychoanalyst, in a way that simply did not happen with adults. Thus, it was essential to observe children from a different point of view than one observes adults. She acknowledged that Melanie Klein had contributed to our understanding of how children might be observed, but she felt that Klein had attributed too much to what Klein and her colleagues observed. Klein allowed children the opportunity to play with toys in her office, a situation in which the child's imagination can run wild. Klein believed this was the same for a child as free association was for an adult. However, Anna Freud countered that an adult is aware of their goals in psychoanalysis, whereas a child at play is not aware of being in therapy. As a result, Anna Freud viewed the play of children as fundamentally different than an adult's free association:

> The play technique worked out by Mrs. Melanie Klein is certainly valuable for observing the child. Instead of taking the time and trouble to pursue it into its domestic environment we establish at one stroke the whole of its known world in the analyst's room, and let it move about in it under the analyst's eye but at first without his interference...
>
> Mrs. Klein however...assumes the same status for these play-actions of the child as for the free associations of the adult patient...if the child's play is not dominated by the same purposive attitude as the adult's free association, there is no justification for treating it as having the same significance. (pgs. 28-29; A. Freud, 1946)

Anna Freud's steadfast belief that children do not have the intellectual or psychological capacity for free association, in part because they simply can't relax and lie still for an hour on the psychoanalyst's couch, also raises questions for the use of the second most common psychoanalytic technique, dream analysis. Dream analysis depends on the patient's ability to freely associate about the manifest content of the dream. With children, it is necessary for the psychoanalyst to connect the manifest content with the latent content, and this process will always be somewhat suspect (A. Freud, 1946). These problems lead into another controversy, the age at which psychoanalysis can occur. Whereas Klein and her colleagues believed that psychoanalysis could occur at any age, since babies are involved in play as part of their earliest activities, Anna Freud believed that some amount of speech was necessary to form an adequate therapeutic relationship with a child (so the earliest reasonable age for psychoanalysis would be around two to three years of age; A. Freud, 1946).

In her conclusion to *The Psycho-Analytical Treatment of Children*, Anna Freud re-emphasizes the role that the developmental processes play as a child (and their id, ego, and superego) grows. As such, a child analyst needs to be "as intimately familiar with the normal sequence of child development as he is familiar with the neurotic or psychotic disturbances of it" (A. Freud, 1946). She specifically mentions academic psychology and the tests being created by psychologists for the measurement of personality as useful in this regard. She also mentions one test as being especially useful in examining libido development and its disturbances: the Rorschach test. Still, she acknowledges that our understanding of the developmental processes of the libido and of the ego is "very incomplete." Yet she cautions psychoanalytic investigators "not to confine examinations to short-cuts of any kind…" (A. Freud, 1946). Clearly her concern for children, and for a professional approach to psychoanalytic research and practice, were foremost in her mind.

So what does current research tell us about the effectiveness of psychoanalysis on children? As is often the case, the results are not clear. Although a number of studies have shown that children benefit from psychoanalysis, the degree of that benefit has been disappointing (see Jarvis, 2004). When children of different age groups were studied, the results showed that psychoanalysis was more effective for younger children than it was for adolescents, something that Anna Freud would probably not have predicted. An important problem in many of the studies providing positive results, however, is that the results are based on reports by the therapists. Such reports are highly subjective and open to bias (Jarvis, 2004). Also, as we might expect, the effectiveness of psychoanalysis is dependent on the experience and skill of the analyst. Typically, analysts who have experience teaching and supervising psychoanalysis, as well as those who are prepared to try a variety of psychoanalytic techniques, achieve significantly better outcomes with their patients (Kernberg, 2004). So we must consider the question of the effectiveness of child psychoanalysis as one that remains unanswered.

Discussion Question: Is a child at play engaging in the same mental activity as an adult engaged in free association? Melanie Klein believed yes, but Anna Freud disagreed. Do you think that children are capable of the same participatory role in psychoanalysis as adults, and is play the best way to observe children?

Late in her life and career, Anna Freud extended her work beyond the psychoanalytic treatment of children to larger issues of child advocacy. In collaboration with Joseph Goldstein, a professor of law at Yale University, and Albert Solnit, a professor of pediatrics and psychiatry at Yale's medical school and Director of the Child Study Center at Yale, she co-authored two books: *Beyond the Best Interests of the Child* (Goldstein, A. Freud, & Solnit, 1973) and *Before the Best Interests of the Child* (Goldstein, A. Freud, & Solnit, 1979). These books focus on the importance of placing the interests of children first when the government intervenes in cases involving the custody and placement of children. These situations arise is many circumstances, such as in the case of orphans or following a difficult divorce, but also in more extreme cases of abuse or when certain parents do not believe in allowing medical care for very sick children. Since these situations can pit one parent against another, or the parents against the interests of society, the authors addressed very clearly reasons why the interests of the child should be placed first:

> Some will assert that the views presented in this volume are so child-oriented as to neglect the needs and rights of the adults. In fact, this is not the case. There is nothing one-sided about our position, that the child's interests should be the paramount consideration once, but not before, a child's placement becomes the subject of official controversy. Its other side is that the law, to accord with the continuity guideline, must safeguard the rights of any adults, serving as parents, to raise their children as they see fit, free of intervention by the state, and free of law-aided and law-abetted harassment by disappointed adult claimants. To say that a child's ongoing relationship with a specific adult, the psychological parent, must not be interrupted, is also to say that this adult's rights are protected against intrusion by the state on behalf of other adults.
>
> As set out in this volume, then, a child's placement should rest entirely on consideration for the child's own inner situation and developmental needs… (Goldstein, A. Freud, & Solnit, 1973)

> So long as the child is part of a viable family, his own interests are merged with those of the other members. Only *after* the family fails in its function should the child's interests become a matter for state intrusion. (Goldstein, A. Freud, & Solnit, 1979)

Object Relations Theory

There are those who say that it is inappropriate to refer to **object relations theory** as if it were a single theory. It is more appropriate to refer to object relations theorists, a group of psychoanalysts who share a common interest in object relations, but whose theories tend to vary with each individual theorist. Sigmund Freud used the term object to refer to any target of instinctual impulses. In the current context, an object is a person, or some substitute for a person such as a blanket or a teddy bear, which is the aim of the relational needs of a developing child. Melanie Klein is generally recognized as the first object relations theorist, and her change in emphasis from Sigmund Freud's view was rather profound. Freud believed that a child is born more like an animal than a human, driven entirely by instinctual impulses. Only after the ego and the superego begin to develop is the child psychologically human. Klein, however, felt that a baby is born with drives that include human objects, and the corresponding need for relationships. In other words, the infant's instinctual impulses are designed to help the child adapt to the distinctly human world into which the child is born (Mitchell & Black, 1995).

Melanie Klein

Melanie Klein (1882-1960) was also born in Vienna, about 13 years before Anna Freud. However, she did not remain there. She moved first to Budapest, where Klein entered into psychoanalysis with Sándor Ferenczi. She then moved to Berlin, where she continued her psychoanalysis with Karl Abraham. Since the move to Berlin occurred in 1921, and since she credited this period with Abraham much more significantly than the time she spent with Ferenczi, the most significant portion of her psychoanalysis actually occurred shortly after that of Anna Freud (Mitchell, 1986). However, the time periods are so close that, despite the difference in age, they really should be considered contemporaries. But they certainly did not agree, as we have already seen.

There are two factors that contributed to the differences between Klein and Anna Freud. Since Klein underwent psychoanalysis with Ferenczi in Budapest, and then Abraham in Berlin, her exposure to multiple points of view likely gave her a unique perspective on psychoanalysis. Anna Freud, remember, never left her father's home while he was alive. Also, in 1925, just as the two women were embarking fully on their own careers, Klein moved to England following the death of her mentor Karl Abraham. This separation from the continent of Europe, in a country where analysts already shared ideas similar to Klein's, led to a freedom of thought that allowed Klein to develop her own theories without restraint (Mitchell, 1986).

As mentioned above, Klein believed that an infant is born with the capacity and drive to relate to others. An inherent problem with this reality, however, is that the infant must be prepared to deal with all types of people and relationships. Thus, Klein believed that the death-instinct and its aggressive energy are every bit as important as the life-instinct (Eros) and its libidinal energy:

> ...What then happens is that the libido enters upon a struggle with the destructive impulses and gradually consolidates its positions...the vicious circle dominated by the death-instinct, in which aggression gives rise to anxiety and anxiety reinforces aggression, can be broken through by the libidinal forces when these have gained in strength. As we know, in the early stages of development the life-instinct has to exert its power to the utmost in order to maintain itself against the death-instinct. But this very necessity stimulates the growth of the sexual life of the individual. (pgs. 211-212; Klein, 1932/1963)

As the child continues to develop, love becomes the manifestation of the life-instinct, and hate becomes the manifestation of the death-instinct (Mitchell, 1986). As for people in the child's life, the child will begin to recognize both good and bad elements of their support for and relationship to the child. The child will also recognize good and bad aspects of its own thoughts and behaviors. As a result, the child will begin a process known as **splitting**, in which the bad parts of an object are split off and not allowed to contaminate the good parts of the object. In simpler terms, a child can continue to love its parents, even though there may be times that the parents do not satisfy the impulses of the child. Similarly, the child can continue to feel a positive sense of self-esteem, even though they sometimes fail or do bad things. Such split attitudes can continue into adulthood, and we sometimes hear people talk about "love-hate" relationships.

Since the child is born with the life-instincts and death-instincts necessary to establish and maintain object relations, Klein did not focus on development as going through a series of stages. Instead, she suggested two basic developmental orientations that help the child to reconcile its emotions and feelings regarding the inner and outer worlds in which the child exists: the **paranoid-schizoid position** and the **depressive position** (Jarvis, 2004; Kernberg, 2004; Mitchell, 1986; Mitchell & Black, 1995). The means by which the child processes these emotions and orientations is based largely on fantasy. Klein believed that the child is capable at birth of an active fantasy-life. This fantasy emanates from within, and imagines what is without, and it represents the child's primitive form of thinking about the world and about the child's relationships (Jarvis, 2004; Kernberg, 2004; Mitchell, 1986). With regard to the mother, the child's first object:

> In the baby's mind, the 'internal' mother is bound up with the 'external' one, of whom she is a 'double', though one which at once undergoes alterations in his mind through the very process of internalization; that is to say, her image is influenced by his phantasies, and by internal stimuli and internal experiences of all kinds. (pgs. 148-149; Klein, 1940/1986)

Klein believed that object relations are present at birth, and the first object is the mother's breast (Klein, 1946/1986). Due, in part, to the trauma of birth, the child's destructive impulses are directed toward the mother's breast from the beginning of life. As the child fantasizes attacking and destroying its mother, it begins to fear retaliation. This leads to the paranoid position. Because of this fear, and in order to protect itself, the child begins the process of splitting the mother's breast and itself into good and bad parts (the schizoid position). The child then relies on two principle defense mechanisms to reduce this anxiety: introjection leads the child to incorporate the good parts of the object into itself, and projection involves focusing the bad parts of the object and the child onto the external object. This introjection and projection then provide the basis for the development of the ego and the superego (Klein, 1946/1986; Mitchell, 1986).

As the child continues to develop, it becomes intellectually capable of considering the mother, or any other object, as a whole. In other words, the mother can be both good and bad. With this realization, the child begins to feel guilt and sadness over the earlier fantasized destruction of the mother. This results in the depressive position, and it represents an advancement of the child's maturity (Jarvis, 2004; Kernberg, 2004; Klein, 1946/1986; Mitchell, 1986).

Discussion Question: Melanie Klein is unique in her emphasis on aggression and the death-instinct. Does it seem reasonable to consider aggression as important in human development as libido (and Eros)? Is it possible that aggression was an essential element in the development of the human species, but one that is no longer needed?

Another important contribution by Klein was the method of **play analysis**. She acknowledged that some psychoanalytic work had been done with children prior to 1920, particularly by Dr. Hug-Hellmuth (Klein, 1955/1986). Dr. Hug-Hellmuth used some drawings and play during psychoanalysis, but she did not develop a specific technique and she did not work with any children under the age of 6. Although Klein believed that even younger children could be psychoanalyzed in the same manner as adults, that doesn't mean they have the same ability to communicate as adults. Klein's interest in play analysis began with a 5 year-old boy known as 'Fritz.' Initially Klein worked with the child's mother, but when his symptoms were not sufficiently relieved, Klein decided to psychoanalyze him. During the course of psychoanalysis, she not only listened to the child's free associations, she observed his play and considered that to be an equally valuable expression of the child's unconscious mind (Klein, 1955/1986). In *The Psycho-Analysis of Children* (1932/1963), she described the basics of the technique:

> On a low table in my analytic room there are laid out a number of small toys of a primitive kind - little wooden men and women, carts, carriages, motor-cars, trains, animals, bricks and houses, as well as paper, scissors and pencils. Even a child that is usually inhibited in its play will at least glance at the toys or touch them, and will soon give me a first glimpse into its complexive life by the way in which it begins to play with them or lays them aside, or by its general attitude toward them. (pg. 40)

Klein believed that by watching children at play an analyst can gain a deep understanding of the psychodynamic processes taking place in the child's mind. [Image by Mark Kelland]

It is interesting to note that although Anna Freud often commented on Klein's work, Klein seldom mentioned Anna Freud. It may be that Anna Freud felt compelled to address the work of a leading figure whom Anna Freud considered to be incorrect, whereas Klein felt no such need to address the work of the younger Anna Freud. Klein certainly cited Sigmund Freud's work extensively, but when she mentioned Anna Freud she typically failed to give credit where credit is due. For example, in *The Psycho-Analysis of Children* (Klein, 1932/1963), she mentions Anna Freud only once, in the introduction to the book:

> Anna Freud has been led by her findings in regard to the ego of the child to modify the classical technique, and has worked out her method of analysing children in the latency period quite independently of my procedure…In her opinion children do not develop a transference-neurosis, so that a fundamental condition for analytical treatment is absent…My observations have taught me that children can quite well produce a transference-neurosis, and that a transference-situation arises just as in the case of grown-up persons…Moreover, in so far as it does so without having recourse to any educational influence, analysis not only does not weaken the child's ego, but actually strengthens it. (pg. 18-19)

This quote not only emphasizes a fundamental disagreement between Klein and Anna Freud, it also seems to dismiss the value Anna Freud placed on her educational background. Later in her career, Klein even went so far as to suggest that she herself was closer to Sigmund Freud's perspective than Anna Freud was:

> I do not know Anna Freud's view about this aspect of Freud's work. But, as regards the question of auto-eroticism and narcissism, she seems only to have taken into account Freud's conclusion that an auto-erotic and a narcissistic stage precede object relations, and not to have allowed for the other possibilities implied in some of Freud's statements such as the ones I referred to above. This is one of the reasons why the divergence between Anna Freud's conception and my conception of early infancy is far greater than that between Freud's views, taken as a whole, and my view. (pg. 206; Klein, 1952/1986)

Clearly, whereas Anna Freud felt that Klein was reading too much into her analysis of children, Klein felt that Anna Freud had failed to consider the wider perspectives allowed by the work of Sigmund Freud. Given the complexity of individual personality, it may be that the true answer to this question is different for each person undergoing psychoanalysis.

Placing the Neo-Freudians in Context - 2:
The Psychoanalysis of Children

Before continuing our examination of object relations theorists, it is important to stop and ask why the psychoanalysis of children received so much attention. Many people think of early childhood as a carefree time to run and play, a time when our parents take care of every need, and we have no responsibilities at all. However, for many children, life holds much more challenging problems than just the normal psychological processes of growing up. Abuse, neglect, being caught in the middle of a bitter divorce, these are just some of the things that occur in the lives of too many children. In considering situations where society is forced to intervene, Anna Freud and her colleagues believed that we should shift our focus from thinking about the "best interests" of the child and think instead about providing the "least detrimental available alternative for safeguarding the child's growth and development" (Goldstein, Freud, & Solnit, 1973). Their reasoning was that in cases of abuse, neglect, divorce, etc., the "best interests" of the child are no longer possible, and certainly cannot be restored by a judge. Therefore, the best that society can hope to do is to help the child as much as possible. Obviously, psychotherapy may play an important role in this process for those children who are emotionally disturbed.

The question remains, however: at how early an age can psychoanalysis be effective? The answer depends somewhat on your perspective. As we have already seen, Anna Freud did not consider children capable of fully participating in psychoanalysis as adults can; she did not consider their play behavior to be the same thing as free association. Melanie Klein, however, did consider children to be good subjects for psychoanalysis at very early ages. In fact, Klein took it one step further: she practically considered psychoanalysis necessary for normal development! Klein's childhood was not easy. Her father seemed to care only for her sister Emilie, and Emilie and their brother Emmanuel constantly harassed Klein. Her closest sister in age, Sidonie, took pity on Klein and taught her arithmetic and how to read. However, when Klein was only 4 years old, both she and Sidonie came down with tuberculosis. Sidonie died, and her death was very traumatic for Klein. Klein suffered from depression throughout her life, and even spent some time in a hospital being treated for it during her 20s (Sayers, 1991; Segal, 2004). This may have had a lot to do with Klein's focus on the death instinct and aggression during early childhood development. Her own descriptions of childhood can seem quite frightening:

> We get to look upon the child's fear of being devoured, or cut up, or torn to pieces, or its terror of being surrounded and pursued by menacing figures, as a regular component of its mental life; and we know that the man-eating wolf, the fire-spewing dragon, and all the evil monsters out of myths and fairy stories flourish and exert their unconscious influence in the fantasy of each individual child, and it feels itself persecuted and threatened by those evil shapes. (pgs. 254-255; Klein, 1930/1973)

Not only are such early childhood challenges frightening for individuals, Klein also believed that all attempts to improve humanity as a whole have failed because no one has understood "the full depth and vigor" of the aggressive instincts in each person. Klein believed that psychoanalysis could help both individuals and all humanity by alleviating the anxiety caused by the hatred and fear that she proposed all children experience during their psychodynamic development (Klein, 1930/1973). And so, Klein expressed the following desire for psychoanalysis:

> ...I hope, child analysis will become as much a part of every person's upbringing as school education is now. Then, perhaps, that hostile attitude, springing from fear and suspicion, which is latent more or less strongly in each human being, and which intensifies a hundredfold in him every impulse of destruction, will give way to kindlier and more trustful feelings toward his fellow men, and people may inhabit the world together in greater peace and goodwill than they do now. (pgs. 267-268; Klein, 1930/1973).

Donald W. Winnicott

Anna Freud and Melanie Klein represent two extremes in the debate over the development of personality in childhood and how psychoanalysis can help to understand that development and treat psychological disorders. Anna Freud strictly adhered to her father's theory, believing that young children lacked the psychological development necessary for participating fully in adult-like psychoanalysis. Klein, on the other hand, considered children quite advanced at birth, with the death-instinct and its aggressive impulses being every bit as important as Eros and the libido. In contrast to these extremes, an independent school of object relations theorists developed with more moderate views. Donald Winnicott was one of the most influential of these more moderate theorists, as were Margaret Mahler and Heinz Kohut. We will take a look at some of the ideas of Mahler and Kohut in the next section.

Winnicott (1896-1971) was a pediatrician before becoming an analyst, so he brought a wealth of experience in observing mother-infant interactions to psychoanalysis. Already well respected for his medical treatment of children, Winnicott became increasingly interested in their emotional disorders. So, he joined a group of psychoanalysts being formed in London under the guidance of Sigmund Freud (Winnicott, Shepherd, & Davis, 1986). His first analyst was James Strachey, the man responsible for translating much of Freud's work into English and who was also instrumental in bringing Klein to England. Winnicott continued his analysis with Joan Riviere, one of Klein's closest colleagues, and he was eventually supervised by Klein herself (Mitchell & Black, 1995). Due to his prior experience and independent spirit, however, he developed his own theories separately from those of Klein.

Winnicott saw the early years of life as being a time when the child must transition from a state of **subjective omnipotence** toward one of **objective reality**. When a newborn is hungry, the breast appears. When a newborn is cold, it is wrapped in a blanket and warmed. The baby believes that it has created these conditions through its own wishing, and so it feels omnipotent. The mother's responsibility during this time is to cater to the baby's every wish, to anticipate the needs of the child. As a result, the baby does indeed have its wishes granted almost immediately. This subjective sense of self, as an empowered individual, is crucial to the core of personality as the child grows and represents the **true self** (Kernberg, 2004; Mitchell & Black, 1995; Winnicott, 1967/1986).

For this development to proceed in a healthy manner, the child must have what Winnicott called a **good enough mother** (Winnicott, 1945/1996, 1968a,b/2002, 1968c/1986). The good enough mother at first fulfills the child's wishes immediately and completely, but then withdraws when not needed. This creates an environment in which the child is protected without realizing it is being protected. Over time, the mother slowly withdraws even from the immediate satisfaction of the child's needs. This allows the child to develop a sense of objective reality, the reality that the world does not immediately and completely satisfy anyone's desires and needs, and that wishing does not lead to satisfaction. So the good enough mother is not a perfect mother in the sense that she provides forever anything that the child wants. Instead, she does what is best for the development of the child, offering fulfillment and protection when needed, and withdrawing when the child must pursue its own development. Winnicott considered the unique condition of the good enough mother as something quite fascinating:

> A good enough mother starts off with a high degree of adaptation to the baby's needs. That is what "good-enough" means, this tremendous capacity that mothers ordinarily have to give themselves over to identification with the baby...The mother is laying down the basis for the mental health of the baby, and more than health - fulfillment and richness, with all the dangers and conflicts that these bring, with all the awkwardnesses that belong to growth and development. (pg. 234; Winnicott, 1968b/2002)

A good enough mother satisfies the needs of her child, but withdraws when the child does not need her, eventually no longer being available to the child in an instant. Over time, this allows the child to develop a realistic sense of the world. [Image by Mark Kelland]

Discussion Question: Donald Winnicott believed that healthy development required a child to have a good enough mother. Do you think you had a good enough mother (or father), and do you agree with this approach to raising an infant?

There is at least one big problem with discussing how extraordinary the good enough mother is: it seems to ignore the role of the father. However, this was not the case. Although Winnicott emphasized the biological reality that the father does not share the same physiological relationship that the mother and child share, he did acknowledge that in the course of development the father plays an important role (Winnicott, 1968b/2002, 1968c/1986). Thus, in considering the overall development of the child, he acknowledges the role of good enough parents:

> I must be careful. So easily in describing what very young children need I can seem to be wanting parents to be selfless angels, and expecting the world to be ideal…Of children, even of babies, it can be said that they do not do well on mechanical perfection. They need human beings around them who both succeed and fail.
>
> I like to use the words "good enough." Good enough parents can be used by babies and young children, and good enough means you and me. In order to be consistent, and so to be predictable for our children, we must be *ourselves*. If we are ourselves our children can get to know us. Certainly if we are acting a part we shall be found out when we get caught without our make-up. (pg. 179; Winnicott, 1969/2002)

Objective reality is not, however, the goal of development. It is just as extreme as subjective omnipotence. While it is true that wishing does not lead to satisfaction, it is also true that loved ones will help to satisfy our needs and desires to the best of their ability. An individual living entirely in the realm of objective reality lacks the subjective core of their true self and cannot connect with others. Instead, they live in expectation of what others will do, influenced entirely by external stimuli (Mitchell & Black, 1995). Such individuals develop what is called a **false self disorder** (Winnicott, 1964/1986, 1967/1986, 1971). Although Winnicott described the false self as a successful defense, within the context of ongoing development, he did not consider it to be a condition of psychological good health (Winnicott, 1964/1986, 1967/1986). However, it is part of normal development in every person's life. For example, children are taught to say "thank you" even when they may not be thankful for something. We actually teach them to lie, as part of the price for socialization. However, some children find it difficult because of the need to continually re-establish the importance of the true self relative to the false self (Winnicott, 1964).

For Winnicott, the process of transitioning from subjective omnipotence toward objective reality is crucial to development. The **transitional experience** is not just a concept, however, since it often involves **transitional objects**. A child's blanket, or a teddy bear, is very important to the child. They do not exist merely as a substitute for the mother, they are also an extension of the child's own self. This allows the child to experience a world that is neither entirely within its control nor entirely beyond its control (Kernberg, 2004; Mitchell & Black, 1995). Such a world is closer to the condition in which most of us actually live, and fits well with Winnicott's definition of the good enough parent: one who is honest and real in dealing with their children. The relationship between the child and its mother, as well as the relationships between the child and its larger family, are actively involved in this transitional experience. There is an intimate connection between a mother and a child when they are playing, and that connection exists in a common ground: the transitional space that is neither child nor mother. Because this is a shared and secret place, it is a symbol of the trust and union between them. Taken further, this space becomes an opportunity for the child to see itself **mirrored** in the mother's face. If the mother is loving and supportive, the child is able to develop a sense of feeling real (Winnicott, 1968a/2002). Although the relationship with the mother may be the most special, these phenomena do carry over to the father and the rest of the family as well (Winnicott, 1966/2002).

Discussion Question: Winnicott felt that transitional objects were important for helping children to develop without too much anxiety. Did you have a favorite transitional object, and do you still have it? Do you think it is healthy for children to have such objects, and what might you do with your own children if you have them? If you already have children, do they have transitional objects, and did you ever consciously expect them to have them?

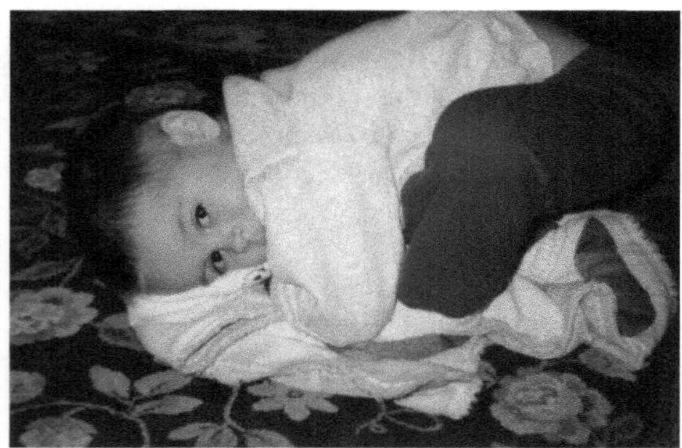

Winnicott proposed that the transition that occurs during early development, from subjective omnipotence to objective reality, is facilitated by transitional objects. In the picture on the left, John is cuddling his blanket. To the right is John's other important transitional object, his gorilla HaHas, and the author's old Teddy bear. [Image by Mark Kelland]

For Winnicott, the psychoanalytic process was an opportunity for the patient to re-experience the early subjective experiences of a relationship with the good enough mother. The therapist takes the role of the good enough mother, allowing the patient to spontaneously "be" in the relationship, while the analyst tries to anticipate and accommodate the patient's needs. The hope is that the analyst and the therapeutic environment will allow the patient's aborted development to be reanimated, with the patient's true self emerging as a result (Mitchell & Black, 1995). However, there can be no single technique in this process, as each case is different (Winnicott, 1971). More important than technique is the analyst's overall skill as an analyst, their ability to make use of various techniques within the psychoanalytic session. Perhaps the most important aspect of this overall view of what is necessary for effective psychoanalysis, according to Winnicott, is that the analyst needs to have been a good, healthy candidate in the first place. Winnicott believed that "it is not easy to turn a badly selected candidate into a good analyst…" (Winnicott, 1971).

Although Winnicott may have felt that technique was not some special trick to be used by anyone in performing psychoanalysis, he did have some favorite techniques. As described above, he watched the playful interaction between child and mother, in much the same way as Klein used her play technique. Winnicott also liked to use the **Squiggle Game**, a technique that makes use of drawings by the child and the analyst, including the opportunity for each to make changes in the other's drawings. Winnicott believed that this process provided a special opportunity to make contact with the child, in which it felt to him as if the child were alongside him helping to describe the case (Winnicott, 1971). In *Therapeutic Consultations in Child Psychiatry*, Winnicott (1971) offers many examples of such drawings along with brief descriptions and analyses of the corresponding cases.

In closing, Winnicott felt it was important to focus on psychological health, and he defined this as something much more than simply making it through each day, going to work, and raising a family. He believed that healthy individuals actually lived three different lives: 1) a life in the world, with interpersonal relationships being key; 2) a personal psychic reality, including creativity and dreams; and 3) their cultural experience. Winnicott admitted that it was difficult to incorporate the cultural experience into the life of an individual. However, he favored the transitional space between the child and its mother, and felt that it was dependent on the mother having been very supportive of the child during development (Winnicott, 1967/1986). In considering the overall purpose of life, in contrast to Freud's perspective, Winnicott wrote:

> …What is life about? I do not need to know the answer, but we can agree that it is more nearly about BEING than about sex…Being and feeling real belong essentially to health, and it is only if we can take being for granted that we can get on to the more positive things…the vast majority of people take feeling real for granted, but at what cost? To what extent are they denying a fact, namely, that there could be a danger for them of feeling unreal, of feeling possessed, of feeling they are not themselves, of falling for ever, of having no orientation, of being detached from their bodies, of being annihilated, of being nothing, nowhere? Health is not associated with *denial* of anything. (pgs. 34-35; Winnicott, 1967/1986)

The Final Development of Individuality: Margaret Mahler and Heinz Kohut

Margaret Mahler (1897-1985), was also a pediatrician before becoming a child analyst, and the early relationship between a child and its mother had a significant impact on her views of developmental ego psychology. At birth, according to Mahler, a child is focused entirely on itself, in a state of **primary narcissism** known as the **normal autistic phase**. In agreement with Sigmund Freud, Mahler believed that in the first few weeks of life there is very little cathexis of libido outside of the child itself. She borrowed Freud's analogy of a bird's egg to describe this period in which the child has minimal interaction with external stimuli. Through contact with the mother, however, the child slowly becomes aware that it cannot satisfy its needs by itself. As the child becomes dimly aware of the mother's activities, the child begins to think of itself and its mother as an inseparable system. This intimate connection between child and mother is called **normal symbiosis** (Kernberg, 2004; Mahler, Pine, & Bergman, 1975; Mitchell & Black, 1995). As important as this stage is for the development of the child, the child still needs to develop a sense of individuality. That process is known as **separation-individuation**:

> We refer to the psychological birth of the individual as the *separation-individuation process*: the establishment of a sense of separateness from, and relation to, a world of reality, particularly with regard to the experiences of *one's own body* and to the principal representative of the world as the infant experiences it, the *primary love object*. Like any intrapsychic process, this one reverberates throughout the life cycle. It is never finished; it remains always active...(pg. 3; Mahler, Pine, & Bergman, 1975)

Separation-individuation, therefore, refers to the two main tasks that a young child must accomplish in order to grow up. First, they must separate from their mother (including the psychological understanding that they and their mother are two separate beings), and then they must fully develop their individuality. According to Mahler, this process involves a series of four subphases: **differentiation, practicing, rapprochement**, and **consolidation**. The earliest subphase, differentiation, is signaled by the child's increasing alertness around the age of 4 to 5 months. Following a "hatching process", the child directs much of its attention outward, but this alternates with the child often turning back to the mother as its point of orientation. Transitional objects, as described by Winnicott, are also important during this period. As the child becomes old enough to start crawling, it moves out into the world and begins practicing its ability to interact with the environment. The practicing subphase enters full force as the child begins to walk, and an important aspect of this is a full, physical understanding of the child's separateness from its mother. Accordingly, its interests can now spill over into the many toys and other objects the child discovers in the world (Kernberg, 2004; Mahler, Pine, & Bergman, 1975; Mitchell & Black, 1995).

During the rapprochement subphase (approximately 1 ½ to 2 years of age), the child's psychological development catches up with its physical development, and the child potentially enters a state of confusion and anxiety. The child becomes aware that the mobility it gained during the practicing subphase has had the unfortunate effect of truly, and physically, separating the child from its mother. The distress this causes leads the child to regularly check in with its mother for security. This is a progressive stage, but is often seen as a regression by the parents (Mitchell & Black, 1995). Pushing the child away too early at this stage can lead to psychological problems later in life, and Mahler urged that one cannot emphasize too strongly the importance of the mother providing optimal emotional availability to the child (Mahler, Pine, & Bergman, 1975). If all goes well, the child will then enter the final subphase and consolidate a definite, and in some aspects lifelong, individuality. Mahler believed that this process indicated a far-reaching structuralization of the ego and definite signs that the child has internalized parental demands, an indication that the superego has developed as well (Mahler, Pine, & Bergman, 1975).

Louise Kaplan, who worked with Mahler for a time, was interested in applying the theory Mahler had developed to the full range of human life, both in terms of age and cultural differences. Although Kaplan agreed that the most profound development occurs during early childhood, she emphasized that the purpose of all this, from the point of view of society, is what sort of person will grow out of each child.

> In the first three years of life every human being undergoes yet a second birth, in which he is born as a psychological being possessing selfhood and separate identity. The quality of self

an infant achieves in those crucial three years will profoundly affect all of his subsequent existence. (pg. 15; Kaplan, 1978)

The conditions of these early years, however, are not always good. In many cultures women are oppressed, sometimes violently. This has an effect on the mothering these women are able to provide their children. Male children may be valued, but in a possessive way. Female children may be scorned, as they lack the male privileges the mother wishes she had herself (Kaplan, 1978). Of course, not all cultures are like this. Kaplan describes a wide variety of cultures, both primitive and modern, and considers some of the many factors that contribute to the nature of adulthood. She compared hunter/gatherer cultures such as the Zhun/twasi or the Ik, tribes found in southern Africa, as they are compelled to transition from old ways of life toward more modern ways. The increased aggressiveness and general life stress that Kaplan observed coinciding with these changes in culture suggests to her that our modern way of life has led to many of these psychological problems. She believed that in "every adult human there still lives a helpless child who is afraid of aloneness." When social conditions are competitive and/or abusive, adults are as alone and helpless as children. According to Kaplan, this would be true even if there were perfect babies and perfect mothers (Kaplan, 1978).

Discussion Question: Mahler believed that children develop through three stages. First the child focuses on itself, then the child becomes aware of their intimate relationship with their mother, and finally a sense of individuality develops. If you look at your relationship with your parents, which stage seems more dominant: your narcissism, your symbiosis, or your separation-individuation?

Heinz Kohut (1913-1981) continued and expanded on this perspective of the important and revealing relationship between childhood development and the life and psychological health (or not) of adults. Kohut was born in Vienna, and studied medicine at the University of Vienna, as Sigmund Freud had. Also similar to Freud, he took some time to study medicine in Paris. In 1937, Kohut's father died and he was deeply troubled. He first went to a psychologist for treatment, but later sought psychoanalysis from August Aichhorn. Aichhorn was a highly respected analyst, and a close personal friend of both Sigmund and Anna Freud. The success of his analysis greatly interested Kohut himself, and led to his becoming an analyst as well. After fleeing Nazi controlled Austria in 1939, Kohut eventually settled in America. He continued his psychoanalytic training at the Chicago Institute for Psychoanalysis (where Karen Horney had been the first associate director), but not without difficulty. Initially, Kohut was soundly rejected by the institute. He then entered into therapy with Ruth Eissler, a training and supervising analyst at the institute, and the wife of a protégé of the well-respected Aichhorn. Making these connections was an intentional effort at good networking, and Kohut was later accepted into training (Strozier, 2001).

In his theory, Kohut focused on the **self** and **narcissism**. Most theorists express a negative view of narcissism, but Kohut felt it served an essential role in the development of individuality. Early childhood is a time of vitality, children are exuberant, expansive, and creative. Kohut was interested in the fate of this vitality, and how it can be preserved into adulthood (Mitchell & Black, 1995). The development of a healthy self depends on three kinds of **selfobject** experiences. Selfobjects are the adults who care for the child, and they need to provide for both physiological and psychological needs. First, a child needs selfobjects who confirm the child's vitality, who look on the child with joy and approval. In this first basic narcissistic process, known as **mirroring**, the child is able to see itself as wonderful through the eyes of others. An important aspect of mirroring is empathy, a state in which the mother and child actually share their feelings as if they were one (Strozier, 2001). The second type of selfobject satisfies the child's need to be involved with powerful others, people the child can look up to as images of calmness, control, and omnipotence. This second basic narcissistic process, known as **idealizing**, allows the child to experience the wonder of others, and to consider itself special due to its relationship with them. Finally, the child needs to experience others who are open and similar to the child, allowing the child to sense an essential likeness between the child and the selfobject. Although this was not described as a basic narcissistic process, its lack of development can be seen in the twinship transference described below. These various relationships will help the child to develop a healthy narcissism, a realistic sense of self-esteem. Although reality will begin to chip away at this narcissism, in a healthy environment the child will survive the occasional frustration and disappointment and develop a secure, resilient self that maintains some kernel of the vitality of early childhood into adulthood (Mitchell & Black, 1995).

An important question, however, is how are the selfobjects incorporated into the child's sense of self? As suggested above, mirroring is the first important step. As the child observes the mother's joy and approval of the child, the child comes to believe that it must be wonderful. Why else would the mother be so happy to see the child? Similarly, as the child observes selfobjects that are powerful and calm, those selfobjects the child has idealized, the child projects the best part of itself onto those selfobjects. Accordingly, the child sees those selfobjects as wonderful and, since the child is with them, the child must be wonderful too. In these instances the child strengthens its own sense of self, its own narcissism, in comparison to others. These processes can be seen in the psychoanalytic session with patients who have not developed a healthy sense of self. They will exhibit three types of selfobject transference toward the analyst: **mirroring transference, idealizing transference**, and **twinship transference**. In mirroring transference, the attention of the analyst allows the patient to feel more real and more internally substantial. In idealizing transference, the patient comes to believe that the analyst is an important and powerful person, and the patient is to be valued by virtue of their association with the analyst. And finally, in twinship transference, the patient feels as if they are a companion to the analyst in the process of therapy (Mitchell & Black, 1995; Strozier, 2001).

Discussion Question: Heinz Kohut also considered a degree of narcissism to be necessary for a child to develop a sense of individuality. Are you more likely to choose friends who admire you (mirroring), or whom you admire (idealizing)? Or do you choose friends who are similar to you, and who help you to develop a realistic sense of self (twinship)? In each instance, is your choice an overwhelming desire, or just one aspect of choosing your friends?

Late in his career Kohut turned his attention to a topic that had also captured Sigmund Freud's attention late in his career: God and religion. Kohut felt that Freud had made a crucial error in evaluating religion. Freud believed that religion would be undone by the study of science, but Kohut felt that it was simply wrong to try evaluating religion in a scientific way. He did not consider God to be an internalized image of the frightening and all-powerful father, but rather an internalization of the earliest and most wonderful relationship in life: the love of a mother (Strozier, 2001). In keeping with his basic theory, he tried to outline the precise psychological needs that were being satisfied by religion. Most importantly, there is something uplifting about religion. The mirroring need is typically referred to as grace, the gifts freely given to us by God, something psychologically similar to the love shown by a mother holding and cuddling her beloved child. God is, of course, the ultimate in idealization, a perfect being, all-knowing and all-powerful. While an immense and ornate cathedral or temple may seem awesome to those who are religious, other spiritual people can be similarly impressed looking down from a mountaintop, walking along the ocean shore, or listening to beautiful music. As for the final selfobject need, twinship, one can easily relate the community of a religious congregation. Perhaps it is no coincidence that we often hear priests and ministers talking about a congregation as the children of God. Although it was never quite clear what Kohut's own religious or spiritual beliefs were, he did write:

> There is something about this world in our experience that does lift us up beyond the simplicity of an individual existence, that lifts us into something higher, enduring, or, as I would rather say, timeless. (pg. 332; quoted in Strozier, 2001)

Connections Across Cultures: Cultural Perspectives on Parent-Child Attachment

This is a true story. I was at our local gym while my older son was at gymnastics practice. There were some children attending a party at the gym, including a little boy about 2 years old who was running around on one of the gymnastics floors. He fell down and hurt himself, and he started crying. A couple of the coaches walked over to help him, but he just cried louder and roughly turned away from them. Then he heard his mother calling him. He ran over to his mother, crying all the way, and she scooped him up into her arms. Almost immediately he stopped crying, started squirming around, and when she put him down he raced back onto the floor and started running wildly in circles and yelling for joy! This is a marvelous example of what psychologists call a secure attachment.

Attachment theory was developed by John Bowlby and advanced by Mary Ainsworth (see Jarvis, 2004; Mitchell & Black, 1995; Rothbaum, Weisz, Pott, Miyake, & Morelli, 2000). Bowlby considered attachment theory to fit within an object relations approach to psychodynamic theory, but it was largely rejected by the psychodynamic community. He proposed an evolutionary basis for attachment, a basis that serves the species by aiding in the survival of the infant. In other words, the attachment between an infant and its primary caregivers helps to ensure both that the infant stays close to the parents (the objects, if we consider object relations theory) and the parents respond quickly and appropriately to the needs of the infant. Ainsworth studied the attachment styles of children using a technique called the **strange situation**. In the strange situation, one of the caregivers (let's say the mother) takes a child into an unfamiliar playroom, and allows the child to explore. A stranger enters, interacts with the mother, and then tries to interact with the child. The mother leaves, then returns, the stranger leaves, and then the mother leaves again. The stranger then returns, then leaves, and finally the mother returns. Throughout all of these events, the child is observed for evidence of having a secure base (feeling comfortable enough to explore the unfamiliar room), separation anxiety (due to the absence of the mother), stranger anxiety (due to the presence of the stranger), and, finally, for its attachment to its mother (when the mother returns at the end of the experiment) (Jarvis, 2004). A securely attached child, as in the story above, will feel free to explore a new environment. When hurt or frightened, however, the child will seek its mother for protection and comfort. Having found that comfort, having affirmed its secure base, the child will then venture out again. But is this true for children in all cultures?

It has been suggested that attachment theory and interpretations of the strange situation are embedded in Western perspectives and ideals, particularly those of middle-class White Americans. In particular, a secure attachment seems to promote the independence of the child, and its ability to separate from the mother and move out into the world. One of the key measures of a secure attachment is that child is comforted by the presence of its mother, particularly after the child has been in the presence of strangers. However, numerous cultural problems arise from these perspectives. For example, in many African American households children are raised by different members of an extended family, possible including individuals who are not related to the family. Thus, African American children raised in such an environment may respond quite differently to the strange situation, it may not be novel to them (Belgrave & Allison, 2006). As mentioned briefly in Chapter 1, Kenneth and Mamie Clark were two very important individuals who studied the development of African American children. Respectively, they were the first African American man and African American woman to receive Ph.D. degrees in psychology. In addition to studying racial identification in African American children during the 1940s (Clark & Clark, 1947), they established what became the Northside Center for Child Development in Harlem, New York. Primarily under Mamie Clark's guidance, the center provided a broad range of psychological services including consultations for behavioral and emotional problems, vocational guidance for adolescents, and child-rearing education for African American parents. In addition, the center provided the same services for a smaller number of White and Puerto Rican children from working-class families in Harlem. Mamie Clark's goal was to give the children of Harlem the same sense of emotional security that she had enjoyed as a child, a sense of security that was elusive in the poor neighborhoods of Harlem (Lal, 2002).

Rothbaum et al. (2000) compared American perspectives on attachment to those in Japan, a country with similar socioeconomic conditions but a very different history and culture. Attachment theory has been considered to have three, universal core hypotheses: sensitivity, competence, and the secure base. In order for a child to feel secure, the mother must respond quickly and appropriately when the child perceives a threat. In other words, she must be sensitive to the child's needs. When a child feels secure, and has a secure relationship with its primary caregivers, attachment theory predicts that the child will grow up socially and emotionally competent. And finally, the secure base is intimately linked with the child's exploration of the environment and the child's ability to respond appropriately to environmental stimuli.

If we compare Japan to the United States, and how we define each of the factors listed above, we come to very different conclusions. According to Rothbaum et al. (2000), so-called sensitive parents in the United States emphasize the child's autonomy. They expect their children to explore the environment, and they wait for their children to express their needs before responding. In Japan, however, mothers try to anticipate their children's needs, and they promote the child's dependence on its mother. In Japan, mothers emphasize emotion and social factors, as opposed to communication and physical objects. Similar differences are seen with regard to social competence. An American who grows up socially competent (assumed to be the result of secure attachments in childhood) is expected to be independent and self-sufficient, willing to express and defend their own opinions. In Japan, however, as in all typical collectivist cultures, a socially competent adult is expected to be dependent on the social in-group and emotionally restrained (Rothbaum et al., 2000). With regard to the secure base, in the United States it is expected to encourage the child's autonomy, exploration, and general orientation to the environment first. In contrast, Japanese children are encouraged to focus more on their mothers, in both distressing situations and in those involving positive emotions. Since the expectations of each aspect of attachment theory are so different in Japan and the United States, which are assumed to be representative of Western and Eastern societies, Rothbaum et al. (2000) question whether attachment theory itself is truly universal. They do not question that children and their parents form important and deeply meaningful attachments, but they do question whether attachment can be reasonably evaluated the same way in all cultures.

There are other researchers, however, who question whether the perspectives of Rothbaum et al. (2000) justify rejecting the universality of attachment theory. For example, Posada and Jacobs (2001) acknowledge differences in behavior among different cultures, but they emphasize that all children have the potential for developing secure base relations with their parents and the subsequent secure attachments. It is important to keep in mind that Bowlby's theory was originally proposed in an evolutionary context and humans are, after all, primates. Also, Ainsworth first coined the term *secure base relationship* after studying a rural, African community in Uganda, not in a Western culture (Posada and Jacobs, 2001). Rothbaum et al. (2000) also suggest that the relationship between Japanese mothers and their children is better expressed by ***amae***, a dependence on and presumption of another's love. Amae has been described as what a child feels when seeking his or her mother (consider the child in the story at the beginning of this section, as he ran crying to his mother). However, when the question is asked in the right way, Japanese mothers would prefer their children to fit a definition of a secure child as opposed to one experiencing amae (van IJzendoorn and Sagi, 2001). Indeed, the very meaning of amae is not clearly understood, and may not be easily compared to behaviors recognized in Western cultures (Gjerde, 2001). It may also be true that insecure relationships may be more adaptive in some cultures than secure attachments, and our misunderstanding of these concepts does not allow us to conclude which perspective on attachment theory, if any, should be preferred (Kondo-Ikemura, 2001).

Finally, since attachment problems do sometimes arise, and since attachment must be defined within a relational context, is an individual therapy such as psychoanalysis the best course? If family therapy might be a better option in some circumstances, is anything being done to address cultural issues there? Fortunately, the answer is yes. Psychologists have begun comparing and contrasting family therapy in such diverse cultures as Japan, Israel, and the U.S. Virgin Islands (Dudley-Grant, 2001; Halpern, 2001; Kameguchi & Murphy-Shigematsu, 2001; see also Kaslow, 2001). In keeping with the hopeful sentiments that Melanie Klein expressed regarding child psychoanalysis, Kaslow (2001) believes that family psychology has a role to play "in undertaking the challenges of working with and for families in creating a healthier, more peaceful, less violent world for all."

A Contemporary Perspective: Otto Kernberg

Otto Kernberg (1928-present) is one of the leading figures in psychodynamic theory today. Kernberg has focused on two major paths: trying to integrate the various psychodynamic, ego psychology, and object relations theories into a unified perspective and trying to provide a research-based methodology for the treatment of patients, particularly patients with **borderline personality organization** (a pathological identity formation that includes all of the major personality disorders; Kernberg, 2004, Kernberg & Caligor, 2005).

Despite seemingly significant differences between Freud's classical theory and the theories of the neo-Freudians we have examined above (as well as others we have not looked at), Kernberg has done an admirable job of bringing the theories into a cohesive framework. This was accomplished by setting up a hierarchical series of developmental levels at which failure to develop normally causes characteristic types of disorders, whereas successful development leads to a healthy individual. In contrast to Freud, Kernberg believes that an infant begins life as an emotional being unable to separate its own reality from others around it. As the child experiences object relations in this first stage of development, those emotions develop into the drives described by Freud: pleasant emotions lead to libidinal drives and unpleasant emotions lead to aggressive drives. During the second stage of development, the child's continued development in relation to others leads to an understanding that objects can be both negative and positive (the process of splitting described by Klein), and this leads to a reduction in the intensity of love and hate toward those objects. In other words, the child can love flawed individuals, since the child does not need to completely love or completely hate the important objects in their life. In simple terms, according to Kernberg, individuals who fail to accomplish the first stage of development, an understanding that they are separate from others, develop psychotic disorders. Individuals who fail to accomplish the splitting necessary in the second stage of development will develop borderline disorders, characterized by an exaggerated fixation on "bad" self and object representations (Kernberg, 2004). Completing these first two stages does not end the process, however, because the third level is the one described by Freud himself: the developmental stage in which unconscious id (emotional) impulses threaten the individual's sense of what is good and acceptable behavior. Thus, classic neurotic disorders still potentially face those who have moved beyond the more severe psychological pathologies of psychotic and borderline conditions (Kernberg, 2004; Mitchell & Black, 1995). We will examine Kernberg's theory in more detail at the end of the chapter, where we will examine his psychoanalytic theory of personality disorders.

In 2004, Kernberg published an excellent book entitled *Contemporary Controversies in Psychoanalytic Theory, Techniques, and Their Applications*. In this chapter we have seen that many disagreements arose between neo-Freudian theorists, and at first glance their theories seem to disagree more than they agree. Kernberg, however, has this to say:

> Psychoanalytic object relations theories constitute so broad a spectrum of approaches that it might be said that psychoanalysis itself, by its very nature, is an object relations theory: all psychoanalytic theorizing deals, after all, with the impact of early object relations on the genesis of unconscious conflict, the development of psychic structure, and the re-actualization or enactments of past pathogenic internalized object relations in transference developments in the current psychoanalytic situation. (pg. 26; Kernberg, 2004)

He offers an excellent summary of the basic elements of theorists we have examined (Klein, Winnicott, Sullivan, Mahler), as well as some we haven't (Fairbairn, Jacobson), and how their theories can be blended with classical Freudian psychoanalytic theory. He then examines how psychoanalysts today are addressing a wide variety of unresolved topics, including: Freud's dual-drive theory (libido and aggression), homosexuality and bisexuality, mourning and depression, social violence, and the resistance among many in the field of psychoanalysis to improved research and changes in psychoanalytic education and training (Kernberg, 2004).

In the final chapter of his book on *Contemporary Controversies…*, Kernberg examines the historical progression of psychoanalytic thought in English speaking countries (the so-called English schools). The "controversial discussions" of the 1940s led to a mutual agreement to disagree among three major lines of thought: the ego psychologists following Anna Freud, the object relations theorists following Melanie Klein, and the independent school that included D. W. Winnicott. Although the result of these discussion was to delineate the differences among these approaches, over time practicing psychoanalysts recognized the limitations of each approach (Kernberg, 2004). So, many theorists and clinicians began bringing together those elements of each approach that were most valuable. Along the way came some very different perspectives, such as those of Kohut and his self psychology and the culturalist views of Sullivan, and the field was changed dramatically. Kernberg also contrasts these developments to those within the French school of psychoanalysis, a somewhat more traditional approach that emphasizes psychoanalytic method over technique (Kernberg, 2004). He concludes by suggesting that the future of psychoanalytic thought may be a blending of the English and French schools (Kernberg, 2004). One notable early French psychoanalyst was Princess Marie Bonaparte, a personal friend of Sigmund and Anna Freud. We will briefly look at her contributions to psychoanalytic theory in a later chapter.

Personality Theory in Real Life: Kernberg's Psychoanalytic Theory of Personality Disorders

Otto Kernberg is one of the leading figures advocating a psychoanalytic theory of personality disorders, particularly within an object relations perspective (see Kernberg & Caligor, 2005). In important ways he has followed the model of Sigmund Freud, in that he has based much of this theory on experience psychoanalyzing patients. His theory has been developed in conjunction with the therapeutic approach that grew out of both that experience and his developing theory. Thus, Kernberg's work represents an applied approach to the study of personality disorders.

Kernberg's model of personality disorder emphasizes personality structures, which are derived from the interaction of constitutional (i.e., temperamental) and environmental factors during early childhood. These structures are relatively stable mental functions or processes that serve to organize an individual's behavior and subjective experiences. Psychological structures that are conscious and observable are typically referred to as **"surface" structures**, whereas those that are primarily unconscious are called **"deep" structures**. The basic building blocks of these personality structures are internalized object relations. Internalized object relations are particular emotional states linked to a specific image of a particular relationship (e.g., anxiety linked with an image of a confused and unsure self and a critical, judgmental parent). These internal object relations are integrated and hierarchically organized into the higher-order structures that form the personality. At the core of this personality organization is the individual's **"identity."** According to Kernberg and Caligor (2005), a healthy, consolidated identity corresponds with a stable and realistic sense of self and others. In contrast, a pathological identity stems from an unstable, polarized, and unrealistic sense of self and others. This pathology arises because the emotional states of the internalized object relations are predominately negative; they are crude, intense, and poorly modulated. There is also a preponderance of aggression and defensive mechanisms based on primitive dissociation (splitting).

A normal personality, according to Kernberg, is characterized by an integrated concept of self and an integrated concept of significant others. Individuals with a normal personality can express a wide range of emotions, and even intense emotions do not lead to a loss of impulse control. Normal individuals have an integrated and mature system of internalized values, and they can appropriately manage their sexual, dependent, and aggressive motivations. The development of the normal personality depends to a large extent on the relationship the child has with its mother (the primary caregiver). If the mother is successful in helping the child transform highly emotional states into integrated experiences, then the child's internalized object relations will be primarily positive. Erik Erikson first proposed this concept, and he believed that ego identity was not complete until adolescence (see Kernberg & Caligor, 2005).

The abnormal personality, in contrast, results from early childhood interactions with caregivers who do not help to transform highly emotional states into integrated experiences. On the contrary, caregiver's failure to help the child integrate its emotional experiences can intensify the child's anger and anxiety, perhaps leading to an increase in aggression. Consequently, a child who cannot integrate the good and bad aspects of its emotional states and object relations will come to depend on defense mechanisms that enhance continued splitting. The child becomes fixated at a poorly integrated level of development. One of the most important implications of this approach to personality disorders is the role that primary caregivers play. What constitutes a parent, or other caregiver, who cannot help the child to integrate its emotional states in a healthy, normal manner? Numerous studies in different countries have identified a high rate of physical and sexual abuse in patients with borderline disorders.

The level at which integration fails to occur results in the nature of the pathological personality organization. A psychotic personality organization occurs when the individual has not integrated a clear concept of self and significant others. They do not have a clear identity formation, they may not distinguish intrapsychic processes from external stimuli, and therefore there may be a lack of reality testing. According to Kernberg, psychotic personality organization represents an atypical form of psychosis (Kernberg & Caligor, 2005). Borderline personality organization is similar, but less severe. The individual has achieved a level of integration in which the self and others are seen as separate, but that integration is pathological. There is a great deal of defensive splitting, and the individual lacks a clearly developed set of internalized values (the superego). Emotion fluctuates from intense to superficial, emotion is generally negative, and there may be excessive aggression. There is also a lack of integration of the sense of others, making relationships particularly unstable and unrealistic. Curiously, achieving an integrated sense of self and others does not resolve all psychological problems associated with personality development. Even if an individual has moved beyond the stages of psychotic and borderline personality development, and developed an integrated sense of self and others, they may still be prone to neurotic personality organization. At this level, defenses are based primarily on repression and stable reality testing. This is the level at which Sigmund Freud studied personality and psychological disorders, according to Kernberg (2004).

With this perspective in mind, how then do we treat individuals with personality disorders? Kernberg's primary focus is an exploration of the patient's internal object relations. These pathological internal object relations play out in the patient's current interpersonal relationships, and through the process of transference they play out in the therapeutic relationship as well. In patients with neurotic personality disorganization these transferences are relatively stable and understandable within a psychoanalytic context. With more severe personality organizations, the transferences are poorly organized, unstable, unrealistic, and the activation of the internal object relations can be immediate and chaotic. There is also a rapid interchange between the roles played by the patient with regard to which object of an internal object relation they identify with, and, accordingly, which object they attribute as the analyst. With severe borderline patients special attention must always be paid to the strong tendency toward acting out, which can lead to suicide attempts, drug abuse, self-mutilation, and other aggressive behavior (Kernberg & Caligor, 2005).

Therapy with these patients is a long and difficult task. In order for psychoanalysis to be successful, it may require multiple sessions each week for 4 to 6 years. This is necessary because the goal is no less ambitious than modifying personality organization and the quality of the patient's internal object relations, all of which were laid down during the formative years of infancy and early childhood (Kernberg & Caligor, 2005). Within the context of this theory, the outcome for individuals with a neurotic personality organization is hopeful, whereas the outcome for those with a borderline personality organization remains challenging. Kernberg and Caligor (2005) do not propose an approach to the treatment of patients with a psychotic personality organization. Therefore, continued research and clinical application will be necessary if we hope to be able to treat all patients suffering from personality disorders.

Review of Key Points

- The neo-Freudians, also known as ego psychologists, remained true to much of Freud's original theory, but they shifted their focus from the id to the ego.
- Anna Freud began her career as a teacher. This concern for children continued throughout her career, much of which was spent caring for children at the Hampstead War Nursery (which later became the Hampstead Clinic, and is now called the Anna Freud Centre, as a tribute to the career of Anna Freud).
- Anna Freud established ego psychology, believing that it made more sense to focus on the conscious ego, which we can observe directly, than on the unconscious id.
- As her father had, Anna Freud described defense mechanisms as the means by which the ego avoids the anxiety associated with being unable to meet the demands of the id or the constraints of the superego.
- There are a wide variety of defense mechanisms, which are generally oriented toward protecting us from internal threats (id impulses) or external threats (the rules and expectations of society).
- Anna Freud was one of the first psychoanalysts to work with children, and she used the same basic approach that she did with adults.
- Later in her career, Anna Freud accepted that even very young children (under the age of 6) could benefit from psychoanalysis, but she insisted that they could not cooperate with the psychoanalyst in the same way as an adult.

- When working with children, Anna Freud felt it was important to fill in gaps that the child could not (such as connecting manifest and latent content in dreams). She also believed that the psychoanalyst should help to educate the child with regard to his/her relationships.
- Object relations theory emphasizes that children are born with the capacity and drive to relate to others.
- Since all aspects of relationships have importance, Melanie Klein proposed that the death-instinct and aggression are just as important as the life-instinct (Eros) and libido.
- Splitting is an important process that involves recognizing the good and bad aspects of objects.
- Klein proposed that an infant goes through two developmental orientations: the paranoid-schizoid position later develops into the depressive position.
- One of Klein's major contributions was the method of play analysis. She felt that observing the play of children could reveal as much unconscious material as free association by adults.
- Anna Freud and Melanie Klein disagreed about how fully the child could be psychoanalyzed, and how young they could be during psychoanalysis.
- According to Winnicott, a child must transition from a state of subjective omnipotence toward one of objective reality.
- In order for a child to develop a healthy personality and realize their true self, according to Winnicott, the child must have a good enough mother (and good enough parents).
- When development does not follow a healthy path, children can develop a false self disorder.
- The transitional experience that children must go through may be facilitated by transitional objects (such as a blanket or teddy bear).
- For Winnicott, the primary purpose of therapy is to provide an opportunity for the patient to re-experience the relationship of a good enough mother.
- Winnicott was an advocate of the Squiggle Game, a therapeutic technique that allows children to draw pictures to represent their thoughts and feelings.
- Mahler believed that children begin life in a state of primary narcissism known as the normal autistic phase. As they become aware of their mother they enter into normal symbiosis.
- In order for the child to develop a sense of individuality, according to Mahler, the child must go through a process known as separation-individuation.
- Louise Kaplan, a student and colleague of Mahler, suggested that much of the stress experienced during development is the result of societal changes, and that modern cultures exacerbate this stress.
- Kohut believed that a certain measure of narcissism was necessary for the development of individuality.
- According to Kohut, children need several types of selfobjects. They will see themselves mirrored in the eyes of others, they will idealize others, and they will develop a realistic sense of self-esteem through relationships with others.
- During psychoanalysis, the analyst can provide each of these types of relationships through mirroring transference, idealizing transference, and twinship transference. This allows the patient to feel more real and more substantial.
- Kohut questioned Freud's rejection of religion. He offered a point of view in which religion fulfills a variety of basic psychological needs for people.
- Otto Kernberg has offered a perspective that blends all of the neo-Freudian and object relations theories together, suggesting that they represent a continuum of stages in human development.

Review of Key Terms

Amae borderline personality organization consolidation deep structures denial depressive position differentiation	mirrored, mirroring mirroring transference narcissism normal autistic phase normal symbiosis object relations theory objective reality paranoid-schizoid position	repression reversal self selfobject separation-individuation splitting Squiggle Game strange situation

displacement false self disorder good enough mother idealizing idealizing transference identification identity introjection isolation	play analysis practicing primary narcissism projection rapprochement rationalization reaction-formation regression	subjective omnipotence sublimation surface structures transitional experience transitional object true self turning against the self twinship transference undoing

Annotated Bibliography

Freud, A. (1936/1966). *The ego and the mechanisms of defense.* Madison, CT: International Univ. Press.
Freud, A. (1946). *The psycho-analytical treatment of children.* New York, NY: International Univ. Press.

These two books are Anna Freud's major contributions to psychoanalysis. The first book laid the foundation for ego psychology, and the second, obviously, discusses her theories on the psychoanalysis of children. As the daughter of Sigmund Freud, and keeping true to his theories, Anna Freud advanced the theory of psychoanalysis in new directions while never directly challenging any of the theories of her father.

Klein, M. (1932/1963). *The psycho-analysis of children.* London, England: Hogarth Press Ltd.
Klein, M. (1955/1986). The psycho-analytic play technique: Its history and significance. In J. Mitchell (Ed.), *The selected Melanie Klein* (pp 35-54). New York, NY: The Free Press.

In the first book, Klein describes the major elements of her theory on the psychoanalysis of children. The chapter on her development of the play technique describes this particular approach in great detail. The rest of *The Selected Melanie Klein* also provides additional information on Klein's basic theories.

Winnicott, C., Shepherd, R., & Davis, M. (Eds.). (1986). *D. W. Winnicott: Home is where we start from - Essays by a psychoanalyst.* New York, NY: W. W. Norton & Company.
The Winnicott Trust (Eds.). (2002) *Winnicott on the child* (pp 221-231). Cambridge, MA: Perseus.

These books are both excellent collections of Winnicott's writings and lectures, many of which were unpublished when Winnicott died. It is interesting to note that the first book was edited, in part, by Winnicott's widow, Clare Winnicott.

Winnicott, D. W. (1971). *Therapeutic consultations in child psychiatry.* New York, NY: Basic Books.

This is a wonderful book focusing on psychoanalysis with children. It contains many examples of pictures drawn by Winnicott and the children he was analyzing with the therapeutic technique known as the Squiggle Game. Winnicott also describes how he and the children talked about and interpreted the pictures.

Kernberg, O. (2004). *Contemporary controversies in psychoanalytic theory, techniques, and their applications.* New Haven, CT: Yale University Press.

Kernberg has provided a well-written and comprehensive view of many of the controversial issues that continue to face psychodynamic theory and psychoanalysis today. Most importantly, he does not try to advocate one approach over another, but rather takes a balanced approach in which he attempts to integrate psychoanalysis, ego psychology, object relations, and other developments in the field.

Chapter 7 - Erik Erikson and Development Throughout Life

Erik Erikson is one of the few personality theorists from a Western perspective who addressed the entire lifespan. He shifted from Freud's emphasis on psychosexual conflicts to one of psychosocial crises, which have unique manifestations through adulthood and old age. Erikson's theory has always been popular, but as our society has become increasingly older the need has grown to understand the aged individual, making Erikson's perspective even more valuable and relevant today than it was when he first proposed it. If, indeed, Erikson's perspective on the personality changes occurring in adulthood and old age do become more relevant with time, it may result in an interesting change in Erikson's place in psychology. Although most personality textbooks devote a chapter to Erikson, and he is typically covered in lifespan developmental texts as well, he is not mentioned in most history of psychology textbooks, and those that do mention him do so only briefly. As popular as he is with students of psychology, and most psychology faculty as well, becoming a common topic in the history of his field would be a distinct honor.

It is also important to note that Erikson was first, and foremost, a psychoanalyst, and a child psychoanalyst at that. He did not neglect the importance of childhood as he pursued the psychosocial changes that accompany aging:

> One may scan work after work on history, society, and morality and find little reference to the fact that all people start as children and that all peoples begin in their nurseries. It is human to have a long childhood; it is civilized to have an ever longer childhood. Long childhood makes a technical and mental virtuoso out of man, but it also leaves a lifelong residue of emotional immaturity in him. (pg. 12; Erikson, 1950)

Brief Biography of Erik Erikson

The most curious aspect of Erik Erikson's life is certainly that his name was not Erikson. No one alive today knows the name of his real father, and he never learned it either. He implored his mother to tell him who his father was, as did his wife Joan, but Erikson's mother had promised her second husband, Theodor Homburger, the man who raised Erikson and whose name Erikson had been given, that she would never reveal the truth. And she kept that promise. When Erikson and his family moved to the United States, their son Kai was taunted by schoolmates, who called him "hamburger, hamburger." So, Erikson and his wife turned to the Scandinavian tradition of naming a son after his father, and they called their son Kai Erik's son, or Kai Erikson. They then adopted the surname themselves, becoming Erik and Joan Erikson. It is also surprising to note that Joan Erikson's name was not Joan. Her first name was Sarah, and as a child she was called Sally. According to her daughter Sue, she hated both names, and eventually chose to be called Joan (Sue Erikson Bloland, 2005).

Erik Homburger Erikson was born Erik Salomonsen on June 15, 1902, near Frankfurt, Germany. His mother, Karla Abrahamsen, was from a wealthy Jewish family in Copenhagen, Denmark. She had married a man named Valdemar Salomonsen, but her husband left Europe within a day of their marriage and went to North America; she never saw him again and he seems to have had no further relationship with her. A few years later she became pregnant, and in order to avoid scandal, she either left or was sent away from Denmark to Germany, where she would be near relatives. She settled near Frankfurt, and raised Erikson alone. Shortly after Erikson was born, they received word that Valdemar Salomonsen had died, making Erikson's mother a widow. When, at about the age of 3, Erikson became ill, his mother took him to the local pediatrician, Theodor Homburger. Karla Abrahamsen and Theodor Homburger fell in love, got married, and Homburger helped to raise Erikson as his own son. Erikson was 8 years old when he learned the truth that Homburger was not his father, but he still grew up as Erik Homburger, since his mother never revealed the truth about his actual father's name (Bloland, 2005; Coles, 1970; Friedman, 1999).

As a child, Erikson was never secure in his relationship with his mother. They were close, and his mother delighted in his intelligence and sensitivity. She shared her passion for philosophy and art with her son, but she had to pay special attention to her new and very proper husband Dr. Homburger. Erikson himself was, by all accounts, deeply traumatized by his mother shifting her attention to this new husband, and by the deception he eventually learned about regarding the fact that Homburger was not his father. Although he was eventually adopted by Homburger, it was more about proper appearances than any close relationship between step-father and step-son. Later in life, Erikson rarely ever mentioned him (Bloland, 2005; Coles, 1970; Friedman, 1999).

Erikson attended a primary school for 4 years, and then went to a very traditional *Gymnasium*. He studied Latin and Greek, German literature, ancient history, and art. He was not a particularly good student, but he excelled at history and art. Since the Homburger family was rather prestigious, and given his mother's interest in art, their home was often entertained by many regional artists. Erikson sought formal training as an artist, and was considered quite talented. So, rather than attending college, he spent a year wandering through Europe living a Bohemian lifestyle. However, he was still deeply troubled by his sense of having no identity, no heritage, and by his own account was marginally functional at best. He was able to make ends meet only because his mother secretly sent him money, something his step-father would have been very angry about, because Homburger was becoming openly intolerant of Erikson's avoidance of social and financial responsibility. After a year, Erikson returned home and entered an art school, and then went to Munich to study at another art school. After 2 years in Munich he moved to Florence, Italy, where he spent most of his time wandering around and studying people. He also made friends with other wandering artists, including a writer named Peter Blos, who had actually been in his graduating class at the *Gymnasium* and who later became a well-known child psychoanalyst. Eventually, however, Erikson realized he would not be successful as an artist, and he returned home, caught in the grip of a deep depression (Bloland, 2005; Coles, 1970; Friedman, 1999).

Then, in 1927, something most important happened in Erikson's life. His friend Peter Blos had been privately tutoring the children of Dorothy Burlingham, a wealthy American who had come to Vienna for psychoanalysis and to meet Sigmund Freud. Blos had been living with the Burlinghams, and he also came to know the Freud family well, but he had decided that the time had come to move on. However, Mrs. Burlingham and her close, personal friend Anna Freud did not want to lose a teacher they were so fond of. So, they offered Blos the opportunity to establish a school of his own, and he invited Erikson to help him develop the curriculum and to teach art and history. Blos and Erikson were given a free hand to develop a progressive curriculum, and the two men flourished. The results were astounding. The children had great freedom, and with Erikson they studied art, music, poetry, German history, ancient history, geography, they read about Eskimos and American Indians, and they made tools, toys, and exhibits. The environment in what came to be known as the Hietzing School also provided much food for thought for Anna Freud, as she was just developing her ideas on the psychoanalysis of children (Bloland, 2005; Coles, 1970; Friedman, 1999).

Through his relationship with the Burlingham family and Anna Freud, Erikson became well acquainted with the entire Freud family. He greatly impressed Anna Freud with how quickly he bonded with the children in the Hietzing School. So, he was accepted into psychoanalysis, both as a patient and a psychoanalyst in training. Since his interests in the school had shifted from teaching to studying and observing the children as they lived their lives, Erikson, like Anna Freud, was already interested in becoming a child psychoanalyst. As he pursued his psychoanalytic training, he also pursued training in the Montessori approach to education. He actually became one of only two men in the Vienna Montessori Women's Teacher Association. As if all this wasn't enough, in 1929 Erikson met Joan Serson. Born in a small town in Ontario, Canada, she had moved to Vienna to pursue her own studies (she had a Master's degree in Sociology, and had been working on a Ph.D.). The two met at a masked ball at a palace in Vienna, and before long were living together, and Serson was teaching at the Hietzing School with Erikson and Blos. In the spring of 1930, Serson went to Philadelphia, where her mother was very ill. While there she learned that she was pregnant. She returned to Vienna, only to find that Erikson balked at marrying her. However, a number of his friends urged him to avoid the mistakes of his own father, and that he should not abandon the woman who was carrying his child, let alone the child itself. So, Joan and Erik Erikson were married in 1930. She joined the faculty of the Hietzing School, and there were clearly some happy times:

> After our marriage we lived on the Kueniglberg, above the school. When our son Kai was born (after some time out for Joan) we daily carried him between us in a laundry basket to the tiny schoolyard or the Rosenfelds' back porch. It became routine that the children would tell us during class when he was crying ("Kai weint"), and in the intermission some watched him being nursed. It was enriching for us all to share this experience. (pg. 5; Erikson & Erikson, 1980).

In 1932, however, the Hietzing School closed, in part because some of the children returned to America with their families, and in part because of different opinions on how the school should be run between Mrs. Burlingham and Anna Freud on one hand and Erikson and Blos on the other. Not only did it seem appropriate that Erikson move on from the school in Vienna, the climate in Europe was becoming increasingly hostile as the Nazis took over Germany and the surrounding areas (including Austria). Erikson was concerned about his family (they had two sons by that point). So Erikson moved his young family to America, in order to escape the dangerous conditions brewing in Europe (Bloland, 2005; Coles, 1970; Friedman, 1999).

Considering his illustrious credentials, having been an acquaintance of Sigmund Freud and trained by Anna Freud, Erikson was welcomed into the American psychoanalytic community, despite never having graduated from college (let alone medical school). The Eriksons never really settled anywhere, in many ways his career was one of unending research and clinical experience. In 1933, the Eriksons moved to Boston, Massachusetts, and Erik received appointments at the Harvard Medical School, Massachusetts General Hospital, and the Judge Baker Guidance Center. He was associated with the Harvard Psychological Clinic, and came to know Henry Murray. In 1936, he accepted a position at Yale University's Institute of Human Relations, where he met John Dollard. Dollard encouraged Erikson's interests in cross-cultural research and in extending Freud's theories to the entire lifespan. Indeed, Dollard may have had a significant influence on Erikson's eight-stage theory of development (Coles, 1970; Friedman, 1999).

In the summer of 1938, the year that his daughter was born, Erikson joined anthropologist Scudder Mekeel on a trip to the Pine Ridge Reservation in South Dakota to study the children of the Sioux Indians. He was able to make extensive observations of mother-child interactions, and to talk with employees of the Bureau of Indian Affairs. In 1939 the Eriksons moved to California. Erikson practiced psychoanalysis in San Francisco, taught at the University of California, and continued his studies on Native Americans by visiting the Yurok tribe in Northern California. During this time he consolidated his major interests into his most significant book, *Childhood and Society* (Erikson, 1950), which includes sections on the influence of social life, culture (based on his Native American studies), the use of toys and playing when studying children, the evolution of identity, and the eight stages of development. Erikson also became an American citizen (Coles, 1970; Friedman, 1999).

In 1944, however, a disturbing and tragic event befell the Eriksons, one that they kept secret as much as possible. They had a fourth child, named Neil. When she went to deliver the child, Joan Erikson had been heavily sedated, because of a surgical procedure that had been planned ahead of time (as a result of an earlier pregnancy). Erikson was summoned by the doctors, who told him that his newborn child was a "Mongolian Idiot" (known today as a Down Syndrome child). The case was considered severe, and he was told it was unlikely that the child would live more than a year or two. The medical staff recommended having the child institutionalized. Erikson was not used to making such decisions, it was Joan who ran the household and supported him while he worked. He called a close friend, Margaret Mead. She assured him that the medical staff was right. Another friend, Joseph Wheelwright (a respected Jungian analyst) agreed. Erikson signed the necessary papers, and Neil Erikson was transferred before his mother ever woke up. The decision tormented both of them. Joan felt that she had never been given a chance to participate in the decision, but she also never made any effort to bring Neil home. They told their children that he had died, and many of their friends never knew he had even existed (no mention is made in the 1970 biography by Robert Coles). After a year or two they did tell their oldest son, Kai, but he was strictly forbidden to mention Neil. Making the situation even more tragic was the fact that Neil lived to be 21 years old. Since much less was known about mental retardation at the time, and this occurred well before the prevailing attitude had begun to change, what else might the doctors have been wrong about (Bloland, 2005; Friedman, 1999)?

In 1949, Erikson was appointed as a professor at the University of California at Berkeley. Within a year, however, as McCarthyism gripped America, Erikson refused to sign a loyalty oath. Erikson protested publicly, his statement was read at conferences and published in the journal *Psychiatry*. He was not a communist, and had never had any interest in communism, but he felt that signing the oath would have made him a hypocrite, as well as being a betrayal of junior colleagues who had refused to sign the oath and were promptly dismissed. Although the tenure committee recommended that he be allowed to remain at the University of California, due in large part to the dismissal of junior colleagues, Erikson resigned his position. He was quickly offered a position at the Austen Riggs Center in Stockbridge, Massachusetts (Coles, 1970; Friedman, 1999).

Erikson was something of a celebrity in Stockbridge. He spent 10 years in Stockbridge, during which he published *Young Man Luther* (Erikson, 1958), an historical/psychoanalytic biography that brought together two of Erikson's academic strengths, and that brought him a certain amount of acclaim. He also taught a graduate seminar at the Massachusetts Institute of Technology, using *Young Man Luther* as a model for the course. He was subsequently offered a professorship at Harvard, but not without some controversy. One of the faculty who protested Erikson's appointment, claiming that he came at too high a price (literally), was David McClelland. Others supported Erikson, and he was eventually appointed as a professor with no particular department. It proved to be a good decision. Erikson used his influence and personal connections to invite renowned guest speakers, ranging from pediatrician Benjamin Spock to anthropologist Margaret Mead and Beat poet Allen Ginsberg. He inspired students such as Howard Gardner, Carol Gilligan, and future congressman, senator, and Vice President of the United States Albert Gore, Jr. (Gore wrote a biography of his father for Erikson's class). Erikson also continued his interest in historical biography with the publication of *Gandhi's Truth* (Erikson, 1969), following a 3-month visit to India in 1962/1963. *Gandhi's Truth* won a Pulitzer Prize and the National Book Award. Always afraid that he would not be recognized for his accomplishments, Erikson hoped that he would also win the Nobel Prize for Literature, and he was disappointed when it did not happen (Bloland, 2005; Coles, 1970; Friedman, 1999).

Erikson retired in 1970, and he and Joan returned to California. Erikson continued writing for a number of years, focusing on issues related to personality changes that accompany old age. Eventually, however, time began to catch up with him. In 1987, as his health deteriorated, he and Joan returned to Cambridge, Massachusetts to live with two young professors who could help Joan care for her husband. He died in 1994 (Bloland, 2005; Coles, 1970; Friedman, 1999).

Joan Erikson missed her husband terribly, but managed to spend some time on her own writing. She wrote several chapters that were added as an addendum to *The Life Cycle Completed*, in which she proposed a ninth stage of development (Erikson & Erikson, 1997). She spoke to their daughter Sue regularly as Sue followed her father's footsteps and became a psychoanalyst. Sue Erikson Bloland was deeply concerned, however, since Lawrence Friedman was about to publish his biography on Erikson, which included extensive coverage of the Erikson's son Neil. Fortunately, perhaps, Joan Erikson died in 1997, and never had to face the public reaction to Friedman's biography (Bloland, 2005).

Special Biographical Note: While preparing his biography on Erikson, Lawrence Friedman tried his best to identify Erikson's father. He went to Copenhagen to review historical documents and interview relatives, particularly in the Abrahamsen family. There was a persistent rumor that Erik Erikson had been named after his real father, who had been a court photographer. According to historical records of the appropriate time period, there were two court photographers in Copenhagen named Erik: Erik Strom and Erik Bahnsen. However, little evidence supports that either of these men could have been Erikson's father. Thus, Friedman concluded that this mystery will never be solved (Friedman, 1999).

Discussion Question: Erikson never knew who his father was, so he never knew his heritage (at least on one side of his family). What do you know of your heritage? In what way, if any, has it influenced your personal development?

Placing Erikson in Context: Psychodynamic Challenges Across the Lifespan

Erik Erikson is well-known and popular, and he was highly respected by most of his colleagues. He knew Sigmund Freud personally, and he was trained in psychoanalysis by Anna Freud. And yet, it is difficult to place Erikson in context. He believed that he had remained true to Freud's theories, but his shift from psychosexual stages to psychosocial crises, and his extension of them throughout the lifespan, was something that Anna Freud found objectionable, and she dismissed his work as "not much… designed to make my father's work palatable to Harvard freshman" (cited in Bloland, 2005). Erikson was always bothered by this rejection, even when the importance of his place in psychoanalytic theory was assured by others.

Erikson also stands apart from most other theorists with his emphasis on the continuation of psychodynamic processes throughout the lifespan. Although Jung had discussed the importance of middle age, his theorizing was based on Eastern perspectives, not on psychodynamic theory. A number of other analysts emphasized sociocultural factors in adulthood, including Adler and Horney, but only Erikson proposed a continuous, single theory from birth to old age, a theory based on traditional psychodynamic perspectives.

Erikson was not unique in his emphasis on cross-cultural studies, but other theorists typically looked to confirm their psychodynamic theory after the fact. Erikson's studies on the childhood of the Sioux and the Yurok helped him form his psychosocial theory, since those studies were part of his experience during the time his theory was forming in his mind.

And finally, Erikson was one of the few theorists who addressed personality changes in old age. As life expectancy continues to rise in America, there are many more elderly people today than ever before. And they are healthier at older ages as well. Thus, our understanding of the unique aspects of the elderly person will become increasingly more relevant, not only to psychology, but to all of society as well.

Basic Concepts Underlying the Study of Development

Erikson is well known for his theory on the eight stages of development. He did not simply theorize these stages, of course. He drew upon Sigmund Freud's basic theories, Anna Freud's explorations in the psychological development of children, and his own experience as a teacher and, later, as a child psychoanalyst. In addition, he attempted to repeat many of his observations in different cultures, particularly in two Native American tribes, the Sioux and the Yurok. These basic principles and observations form the foundation upon which Erikson built his stage theory of development.

The Epigenetic Principle and Psychosocial Crises

Epigenesis is a biological term referring to the development of an embryo, and ultimately an adult organism, from an undifferentiated egg. Similarly, Erikson viewed psychological development as a series of predictable stages in each individual. We begin life without having faced or resolved any of these stages. Only the experience of our life can result in moving us along. This aspect of Erikson's theory is identical to Freud's. Where they differ, however, is on the matter of what are the critical factors that drive the process of these stages. For Sigmund Freud, it was psychosexual development, and each stage is based on the region of the body from which the child gains sexual satisfaction (first the mouth, then the anus, then the genitals, etc.). In contrast, Erikson proposed that the underlying framework for the developmental stages is a series of **psychosocial crises**. Erikson used the term psychosocial crises to refer to turning points, or crucial moments, in a person's development, which contain within them the potential for abnormal development and the failure to reach one's development.

In other words, we face predictable, yet critical, developmental tasks as we move through our lives. We cannot experience one aspect of a crisis without also experiencing the opposite aspect. Our goal, or task, is to achieve a greater degree of the favorable aspect of the crisis (such as being more trusting than distrusting; see below), within the context of our social and cultural environments (Erikson, 1950, 1954, 1968a).

Observing Children at Play

Erikson borrowed Freud's famous line regarding dreams as the royal road to the unconscious mind, saying instead that **play** is the royal road to understanding the young child's ego and identity development (Erikson, 1950). With very young children there is a unique challenge for both experimental psychologists and therapists: the child's limited language development. Not only does observing play allow for insight into ego development, it can also show us the capacity for the ego to find recreation and to cure itself, if necessary. This makes play useful in the therapeutic setting, as we saw when examining the contributions of Melanie Klein and Donald Winnicott.

Erikson studied childhood play extensively, publishing articles that included clinical notes on how and why children build things or choose the toys they play with (Erikson, 1937), psychological factors behind and effects of disruptions in play (Erikson, 1940), gender differences in play (Erikson, 1955), and ethnic, racial, nationality, and socioeconomic status differences in play (Erikson, 1972). Ultimately, Erikson published *Toys and Reasons* (Erikson, 1977), in which he argued that childhood play provides a basis for ritualizing our life experiences, and that ritualization continues throughout the stages of life. Whether play serves to help master and resolve traumatic experiences, or provides catharsis for pent-up emotion or surplus energy, or whether it has a functional role in which a child can exercise new faculties and potentials in preparation for the future, Erikson argued that play is an act of renewal and self-expression, one that can be an expression of inventiveness and abandon. Play provides a means for connecting with others, in order to cope with the challenges of life (Erikson, 1977).

Discussion Question: Have you ever watched children play? What has it told you about the individual child, and is it always consistent with who you think that child is? What sort of games or sports do you like to play, and do you like to play with children?

The Value of Cross-Cultural Studies

The value of studying other cultures was summarized rather succinctly by Erikson in an interview with Richard Evans:

> The interesting thing was that all the childhood problems which we had begun to take seriously on the basis of pathological developments in our own culture, the Indians talked about spontaneously and most seriously without any prodding. They referred to our stages as the decisive steps in the making of a good Sioux Indian or a good Yurok Indian…And "good" meant whatever seemed "virtuous" in a "strong" man or woman in that culture. I think this contributed eventually to my imagery of basic human strengths. (pg. 62; Erikson cited in Evans, 1964)

So, it was actually on the basis of cross-cultural comparisons that Erikson felt confident in proposing his eight stage theory of psychosocial development.

Erikson was deeply indebted to two anthropologists, H. Scudder Mekeel and Alfred Kroeber, who introduced him to the Sioux and Yurok tribes they had been studying. Through their introductions, Erikson was able to gain the confidence of the individual Sioux and Yurok who provided Erikson with invaluable evidence on their traditional ways of life and their child-rearing practices. But it is important to note that Native Americans were not the only other cultural groups that Erikson studied. He studied the childhood myths of Hitler and the Bolshevik myth of Maxim Gorky's youth, in an attempt to understand the terrible political events that occurred in Nazi Germany and Communist Russia. He also examined the factors influencing Black identity in America. He suggested that one of the greatest struggles for Blacks in this country, after the Civil War had ended slavery, was the mostly false promise of a better life in the North. As they left behind their successful identity as slaves (Note: successful only means that it was a clear identity, not that it was moral or justified) for a fragmented identity of supposedly free people, though prejudice and discrimination were still rampant, even in the North. Erikson made some interesting comparisons between Blacks and Native Americans in terms of their attempts to identify their place in American society:

> I have mentioned the fact that mixed-blood Indians in areas where they hardly ever see Negroes refer to their full-blood brothers as "niggers," thus indicating the power of the national imagery which serves to contrast the dominant ideal images and the dominant evil images in the inventory of available prototypes. No individual can escape this opposition of images which, in a great variety of syndromes, is all-pervasive in the men and in the women, in the majorities and in the minorities, and in all the classes of a given national or cultural unit. (pg. 215; Erikson, 1950)

Individuals try to resolve their identity crises in as simple and straightforward a way as possible. Every group within a society is somewhat familiar with the stereotypical identity attributed to other groups, and these factors play an important role, even when they are expressed in negative ways, such as mixed-blood Native Americans calling full-blooded Native Americans "niggers." Erikson later noted that full-blooded Sioux on the Pine Ridge Reservation turn around and call their half-blooded brothers "white trash" (Erikson, 1980a). These factors also tell us something about the place different groups occupy in the minds of members of other groups, and how that might influence the individuals within those groups. We will return to the concept of identity after examining Erikson's stages of development.

> **Discussion Question:** Erikson believed that his theories had been confirmed in different cultures, such as the Sioux and the Yurok. Do you think his theories apply to all cultures? If not, what problems do you see with his work?

Erikson's Eight Stages of Development

Many people are familiar with Erikson's eight stages of life, but what is less well known is that each stage is tied to specific, basic social institutions and is also associated with a particular strength, which Erikson believed gave the individual a "semblance of instinctive certainty in his social ecology" (Erikson, 1968a; see also Erikson, 1950). Each stage can also be viewed as awakening a specific sense of estrangement, which can become the basis for psychopathology. As we are about to see, the first stage is basic trust vs. basic mistrust. If a child develops basic trust, they will also develop the basic strength of hope. Then, as they progress through life, they will likely encounter situations in which people cannot be trusted, but the person can remain hopeful. In contrast, hopelessness is a term closely identified with depression, and it is easy to see how a person who learns from the beginning of life that the people around them, indeed the whole world (as they perceive it), is a threatening and untrustworthy place. As each of the eight stages is introduced, the title will begin with the general age at which the stage occurs, the psychosocial crisis experienced during that stage, and finally, the primary human strength that is associated with the successful resolution of the crisis.

Infancy - Basic Trust vs. Basic Mistrust - Hope: The primary relationship (or social institution) of this first stage is the mother. The infant needs to be fed (and traditionally this was only breast-feeding), comforted, and protected. As we have seen in earlier chapters, the child does not necessarily recognize that the mother is a separate person, so the bond between them is extraordinarily intimate. It is inevitable, however, that the child will experience discomfort and pain, and that the mother will not be able to immediately attend to every need. In such times of distress, the child who mostly trusts in the care of their mother will be able to hope that the care is coming.

As a young child develop a sense of autonomy, they begin to do more for themselves. [Image by Mark Kelland]

Early Childhood - Autonomy vs. Shame, Doubt - Will: At this stage, both parents become the primary social institution. As young children develop the ability to walk and talk they begin to do many things for themselves. However, their actions often lead to restrictions, as they experience the categorical rules of "yes and no," "right and wrong," or "good and bad." Shame is the consequence of being told that one is bad or wrong. Doubt arises when the child is unsure. As they develop their will power, i.e., their exercise of free will, they may not be sure what to do in a certain situation. A child who has been supported in exercising their autonomy will develop the will power to restrain themselves without experiencing shame or doubt. For example, they will learn not to run out into the busy street, and even feel good about their ability to take care of and protect themselves. It is often fascinating to watch a young child demonstrate this protectiveness when they interact with an even younger child. One can easily see the satisfaction in understanding rules and guidelines as, say, an eight-year old looks after a two-year old cousin.

Play Age - Initiative vs. Guilt - Purpose: The entire family (e.g., siblings, grandparents, etc.) provides the social context for this developmental stage. As the child of age three or four years old becomes able to do much more, and to do so more vigorously, they begin to realize something of what is expected of them as adults. So, they being to play with other children, older children, and to play games that mimic things done by adults. This helps them to develop a sense of purpose, and to pursue valued goals and skills. Excessive initiative, especially when combined with autonomy, can lead to problems such as rivalry and jealousy, especially with younger siblings. It can also lead to aggressive manipulation or coercion. Consequently, the child can begin to feel guilty about their actions, especially if they are punished.

As children grow a little older, they begin to mimic what they see being done by older children and adults. [Image by Mark Kelland]

School Age - Industry vs. Inferiority - Competence: The social institutions relevant to this stage now move outside the family, including the neighborhood, community, and schools. It is one thing to play adult roles, such as in the previous stage, but in this stage the child actually begins the process of preparing to be a caretaker and provider for others, such as their own children. In all cultures, according to Erikson, at this age (beginning at 5 to 6 years old) children receive some form of systematic training, and they also learn eagerly from older children. Unfortunately, some children are not as successful as others, particularly in the restrictive learning environment of schools. Keep in mind that Erikson was trained in the Montessori style of education, which emphasizes free exploration and active learning, at each child's own pace (Lillard & Jessen, 2003; Spietz, 1991). If children are indeed successful, if they are given the freedom to learn, they will develop a sense of competence, which will help them to persevere when faced with more challenging tasks.

Adolescence - Identity vs. Role Diffusion, Confusion - Fidelity: The family finally loses its place of primacy as a social institution, as peer groups and outgroups become the most significant social institutions. According to Erikson, childhood comes to an end when a person has developed the skills and tools to proceed into adulthood. First, however, there is the period in which one's body changes from a child to an adult: **puberty**. Known psychologically as adolescence, it is a period in which each person must determine how they will fit their particular skills into the adult world of their culture. This requires forming one's identity. The fidelity that Erikson speaks of refers to the ability to remain true to oneself, and to one's significant others. This period is easiest for children who are gifted and well trained in the pursuit of clear goals, and also for children who receive a good deal of affirmation from their peers.

The pursuit of one's identity can be quite challenging, and we will examine identity in more detail in the next section. But first, one way to cope with the challenge of forming one's identity is to stop doing it for a while, something Erikson called a psychosocial **moratorium** (Erikson, 1959). A moratorium is a break that one takes in life before committing oneself to a career. Some people serve in the military or the Peace Corps before coming home and taking their place in the community. Some travel, and try to "see the world," before starting college. Erikson considered the moratorium to be a natural and, in many cases, quite productive activity. To cite one of Erikson's examples, a young Charles Darwin, who had been training for the ministry, left England on a 5-year voyage on a ship called the Beagle in order to participate in geological studies (he was also studying geology). It was during that trip that he made the initial observations of animals and fossils that ultimately led to his theory of evolution.

Young Adulthood - Intimacy vs. Isolation - Love: With the onset of adulthood, the most significant social factors become partners in friendship, sex, competition, and cooperation. Once an individual has consolidated their own identity, they are capable of the self-abandonment necessary for intimate affiliations, passionate sexual unions, or inspiring encounters. According to Erikson, sexual encounters prior to fulfilling this stage are of the identity-confirming kind, rather than the truly intimate sexual relationships based on love. Love is the mutual devotion of two people. Individuals who are unsuccessful in making intimate contacts are at risk for exaggerating their isolation, which brings with it the danger of not making any new contacts that might lead to the very intimate relationship they are lacking.

Adulthood - Generativity vs. Stagnation, Self-Absorption - Care: The family household, including divided labor and shared household duties, becomes the primary social institution of adulthood. Erikson also referred to adulthood as **maturity**, and he considered this stage to be reciprocal. A mature person needs to be needed, and it is their very maturity that guides them to care for the needs of others. So, generativity is the concern with helping to establish and guide the next generation. It is psychosocial because it includes productivity and creativity, not just procreation. When the potential enrichment to be found in generativity fails, the consequences are often seen in the estrangements of the next generation. In other words, the children of stagnant, self-absorbed parents may have great difficulty forming their own identities and achieving intimacy in their relationships.

Old Age - Integrity vs. Despair - Wisdom: The social concerns for those approaching the end of life include "Humanity" and "Family." Wisdom allows one to maintain and convey the integrity of one's lifetime of experience, despite the gradual physical decline of the body. Wise people are able to pass on an integrated heritage to the next generation. For those who have failed to integrate their life's experiences, despair arises as the fear of death, death being the time limit on their opportunity to achieve integrity. Erikson described wisdom as "a detached and yet active concern with life in the face of death" (Erikson, 1968a).

Is there a ninth stage? After Erikson died, Joan Erikson wrote a few short chapters that were added to *The Life Cycle Completed* (Erikson & Erikson, 1997). Erikson had suggested that his wife was an important contributor to all of his theories, throughout his career, so it was not surprising that she offered these additions after his death. Indeed, they are most likely the result of her observations regarding his death, something he could then no longer write about.

Very Old Age - Despair vs. Gerotranscendence: Unlike the earlier stages, Joan Erikson felt that the negative aspect of this stage should be placed first. People who make it to 90 years old, and beyond, are close to death. Their bodies are steadily deteriorating, most, if not all, of their friends have died, some of their children may have died, their spouse has likely died, and the despair they face is quite real. The despair experienced in the eighth stage involves looking back at one's life, but in the ninth stage it involves looking squarely at one's present reality, and passing once again through life's stages. People who are very old can no longer trust their own capabilities, and they may need to be cared for, thus losing some of their autonomy. Their sense of purpose is dulled, and they lose the urgency and energy necessary to be industrious. Likewise, their identity may become unclear once again, and they can become isolated and self-absorbed. However, some very old people hold a special place in their families and/or communities, and may withdraw only by choice, in order to contemplate and be at peace with their life. Joan Erikson refers to this choice as a dance with life:

> With great satisfaction I have found that "transcendence" become very much alive if it is activated into "transcen*dance*," which speaks to soul and body and challenges it to rise above the dystonic, clinging aspects of our worldly existence that burden and distract us from true growth and aspiration.
>
> To reach for gerotranscen*dance* is to rise above, exceed, outdo, go beyond, independent of the universe and time. It involves surpassing all human knowledge and experience. How, for heaven's sake, is this to be accomplished? I am persuaded that only by doing and making do we become. (pg. 127; Erikson & Erikson, 1997)

Discussion Question: Joan Erikson proposed a ninth stage, when death is imminent. Do you agree with this stage; do you hope it is possible to achieve gerotranscendence? Have you known anyone who was very old and facing death, and what was it like for them?

The Importance of Identity

The developmental crisis that Erikson focused much of his career on was that of developing one's identity. From the beginning of publishing his theories, he emphasized that a lot of the psychological distress and pathological symptoms seen in childhood can be interpreted as the child expressing their *right* to find an identity in the world, and neurosis typically results from the loss of one's identity (Erikson, 1950). Erikson returned to this theme repeatedly in books such as *Identity and the Life Cycle* (Erikson, 1980a; originally published in 1959), *Identity: Youth and Crisis* (Erikson, 1968b), and *Dimensions of a New Identity* (Erikson, 1974). He also published *A Memorandum on Identity and Negro Youth* at the height of the Civil Rights Movement in America (Erikson, 1964). The importance of identity, and the stage of identity vs. role-diffusion and confusion, is that only upon completion of the first four stages of life is the ego fully mature, the point at which a person is ready to be an adult. But the entire period, the entire psychosocial crisis, is a critical time of transition:

> Adolescents have always been especially open to conversion or to what is now called consciousness-expansion in the direction of physical, spiritual, and social experience. Their cognitive capacities and social interests are such that they want to go to the limit of experience before they fit themselves into their culture and fit their culture to themselves. (pg. 37; Erikson cited in Evans, 1964)

A General Definition of Identity

Since Erikson labeled his fifth stage of development identity vs. role diffusion and/or confusion, it is common to think that identity formation is something that occurs during adolescence. Actually, identity formation begins at birth, and continues throughout the lifespan. It is only in adolescence that the individual finally has the material around which to form an integrated identity that can remain somewhat stable, hence the psychosocial crisis that arises during that process of integration and more stable identity formation. Thus, a child will have some sense of self, but it is not until adolescence that it becomes a crisis. So what is that sense of self that forms the identity? Erikson himself turned to two great men, whom he described as "bearded and patriarchal founding fathers of the psychologies on which our thinking on identity is based:" William James and Sigmund Freud (Erikson, 1968).

> A man's character is discernible in the mental or moral attitude in which, when it came upon him, he felt himself most deeply and intensely active and alive. At such moments there is a voice inside which speaks and says: "*This* is the real me!" (pg. 19; William James in a letter to his wife, cited in Erikson, 1968)

Moving beyond James' very personal description, Freud spoke of his Jewish identity as something that provided a cultural context in which he lived his life, even though he was never religious, and openly despised religion. He felt that he shared a Jewish cultural nature, which offered an explanation for, as well as a justification for, aspects of his personality that defied any other obvious explanation.

Based on these perspectives by James and Freud, Erikson described identity as a process rooted in the core of the individual, yet also rooted in the core of their communal culture. This complicated process involves both judging oneself in light of how others judge you, as well as judging the judgments others make about you. Eventually, the interplay between psychological and social factors results in an identity based on **psychosocial relativity** (Erikson, 1968). In other words, one's identity is very much influenced by where a person sees themselves fitting into their world. Consequently, a person may develop a healthy identity, or they can just as easily develop a negative identity (see below).

The term **identity crisis** was first used by Erikson during World War II, to describe a particular psychological disorder. They encountered patients, who had been fighting in the war, who had become severely disturbed. However, they could not be described in the typical ways, such as being "shell-shocked" or just faking mental illness to escape combat. Instead, they had lost a sense of personal sameness and historical continuity. Erikson proposed that they had lost the central control over that part of their self that psychoanalysts could only describe as the ego. Thus, he described these patients as having lost their "ego identity." Since World War II, Erikson felt that he and his colleagues were observing the same fundamental disorder in many severely conflicted young patients. These disturbed individuals were, in a sense, waging a war within themselves and against society. An identity crisis of this sort can affect groups as well as individuals (Erikson, 1968). In an interesting, and somewhat amusing example of group identity crisis, we can look at the reaction of the psychoanalytic community to the theories of Carl Jung. In Erikson's view, the psychoanalytic community reacted to Jung's proposal of the collective unconscious and archetypes as a threat to scientific approach advocated by Freud. Consequently, the majority of the psychoanalytic community ignored Jung's reasonable observations as well as his somewhat less scientific interpretations (Erikson, 1980a).

Obstacles to the Development of Identity

Erikson talked about two obstacles to the development of identity: **ratio** and **negative identity**. Ratio refers to the balance between the opposite poles of each psychosocial crisis: trust vs. mistrust, autonomy vs. shame, etc. Although it may be best for the ratio to favor trust, autonomy, and so on, it is unreasonable to expect a person to develop without any experience of trust being misplaced or without any feelings of shame. This helps to ground the person in the real world, particularly as it is appropriate to the customs of their culture (see Evans, 1964). Indeed, Erikson felt that identity could be viewed as being that subsystem within the ego that is closest to social reality, based on the integrated self-representations formed during the psychosocial crises of childhood. Thus, identity:

> …could be said to be characterized by the more or less *actually attained but forever-to-be-revised* sense of the reality of the self within social reality; while the imagery of the ego ideal could be said to represent a set of *to-be-strived-for but forever-not-quite-attainable ideal* goals for the self. (pg. 160; Erikson, 1980a)

Negative identity is often expressed as an angry and snobbish rejection of the roles expected by one's family, community, or even society. It is a profound reaction to the loss of identity that typically arises when identity development has lost the promise of wholeness that one expects to obtain from their identity. The consequences can be severe, for both individuals and groups of young people. Erikson worked with young people who were beginning to make choices in life that could easily lead them toward their vindictive fantasies of becoming prostitutes or drug addicts (an extreme way of rebelling against their parents). As such disturbed young people gather together, they can form gangs, drug rings, sex clubs, and the like (Erikson, 1968b, 1980a). Society, according to Erikson, often makes the mistake of enhancing this maladaptive behavior:

> If, for simplicity's sake or in order to accommodate ingrown habits of law or psychiatry, they diagnose and treat as a criminal, as a constitutional misfit, as a derelict doomed by his upbringing, or indeed as a deranged patient a young person who, for reasons of personal or social marginality, is close to choosing a negative identity, that young person may well put his energy into becoming exactly what the careless and fearful community expects him to be - and make a total job of it. (pg. 196; Erikson, 1968b)

Erikson believed that women and minorities (indeed, oppressed people in any situation) face special problems in the formation of their identity. Erikson considered men and women to be fundamentally different, but more importantly, he believed that only women could ensure the future of humanity. According to Erikson, men try to solve problems with "bigger and better wars." And now, with the advent of nuclear bombs, men have nearly reached the limit of their ability to destroy each other. The future, therefore, requires the feminine aspects of personality, including realistically caring for the home, responsibly raising the children, being resourceful in peacekeeping, and devotion to healing:

> The question arises whether such a potential for annihilation as now exists in the world should continue to exist without the representation of the mothers of the species in the councils of image-making and decision. (pg. 261; Erikson, 1968b)

For Blacks in America, the identity crisis has been one of being separated from their African heritage, and yet also separated from the White American heritage that surrounds them. Erikson recounts both clinical examples and folklore that emphasize the value placed on being White by Blacks themselves (Erikson, 1950, 1964, 1968, 1980a). The result is often psychological distress and depression, such as that seen in the classic study by Kenneth and Mamie Clark, in which Black children considered identification with their race as bad. Using Black and White dolls, some of the young Black children actually cried when asked to point to the doll they looked most like (Clark & Clark, 1947). Perhaps the most dramatic example of Erikson's theory in action occurred during the 1960s. Disenfranchised Blacks adopted a negative identity and opposed many aspects of the American society that had oppressed Black's for so long (Note: *Negative* identity is used here only as Erikson's term, not to imply that the fight for racial equality was, in any way, something negative). With Malcolm X and the Nation of Islam, and Huey Newton and the Black Panthers, some young Black men opposed both the Christianity and the Democracy that formed so much of the American national identity. Those who did not, found themselves at odds with their own people, as we will see with Brian Copeland, author of *Not a Genuine Black Man* (see Chapter 16; Copeland, 2006). It should be noted, however, that the seemingly contradictory perspective of rejecting a society that gives one the very right to oppose it is not alien to the African psyche:

> …the African gods south of the Sahara always had at least two heads, one for evil and one for good. Now people create God in their own image, what they think He - for God is always a "He" in patriarchal societies - what He is like or should be. So the African said, in effect: I am both good and evil; good and evil are the two parts of the thing that is me… (pg. 24; Huey Newton, recorded in Kai Erikson, 1973)

The idea that Black Americans might have been adopting a negative identity was more than just an academic theory for Erikson. In 1971, both Erikson and Huey Newton (who was then known as Supreme Commander of the Black Panther Party) presented talks to the students of Yale University. A short time later, they met again for a series of conversations in Oakland, California, which also included the Black sociologist J. Herman Blake and Erikson's son, Kai Erikson, also a sociologist (see K. Erikson, 1973). Among many topics, Newton described the revolutionary actions of Black activists at that time as a process, a contradiction between old ways and new ways. Any change, he argued, might be viewed as revolutionary at a particular point in time. Newton went on to describe how the Black community expected him to hate all White people, and how the Black community rejected many of its own because they had too many Caucasian features (such as relatively light skin). He rebelled against this discrimination, just as he did against the oppression that was so inherent in American society. Erikson, for his part, talked mostly about just how difficult it is for people of different backgrounds to understand each other's perspective. Most important, however, is the act of searching for some basis for understanding one another (K. Erikson, 1973).

In his autobiographical book *Revolutionary Suicide* (the preparation of which was assisted by J. Herman Blake; Newton, 1973), Newton begins with a tribute to a comrade who was killed in a shootout with the police, while seeking nothing more than what Newton considered the right of all men: dignity and freedom. He then offers a poem, which sounds very much like Taoist philosophy, as well as a search for a greater identity:

By having no family,
I inherited the family of humanity.
By having no possessions,
I have possessed all.
By rejecting the love of one,
I received the love of all.
By surrendering my life to the revolution,
I found eternal life.
Revolutionary suicide.

Huey P. Newton, in Revolutionary Suicide (1973)

Discussion Question: Erikson described the adoption of a negative identity as a serious rejection of one's expected place in life. Has there been a time in your life when you adopted a negative identity? Do you feel that sometimes it is necessary to adopt a negative identity in order to change the world we live in?

Identity and the Role of the Family - Perspectives from Around the World

Identity is not merely a personal phenomenon, it develops within a cultural context that is passed on through the family. The most important social institutions of the first three stages of development are the mother, then both parents, and finally, the family as a whole. As adults, individuals face not only their own psychosocial crises, but they serve as the parents of the next generation, as their children face the early development crises. Thus, it is important to consider the role that the family plays in general, and the perspectives that can be offered by **family psychology**.

It is difficult to define the word **family**, since it includes nuclear families (two-generations, with married parents and their own children), extended families (three or more generations), foster and adoptive families (which may be multi-racial and/or multi-cultural), single-parent families, gay or lesbian couples with or without children, remarried/step families, and others (Kaslow, 2001). Further complicating matters is the role the family plays as a microsystem of a given culture, especially when that culture is dramatically altered. For example, when the former Soviet Union collapsed, the entire economic and political structure of countries like Russia, Poland, East Germany, and Czechoslovakia were wiped out. When Yugoslavia broke apart, ancient ethnic hatred led to brutal, local wars. The role that women play in many cultures has changed in recent years, whereas in some cultures the patriarchal authority has aggressively retained its domination of the culture. The Nobel Peace Prize for 2006 was awarded to Muhammad Yunus and the Grameen Bank for developing micro-credit loans, most of which go to poor women in oppressive societies, in an effort to help these women and their children rise out of poverty.

Family psychology addresses issues as complex as families themselves, including male-female relationships, domestic violence, child-rearing and socialization practices, divorce, the search for identity in a dysfunctional family setting, spirituality, drug addiction, war, crime and violence, homelessness, kidnapping, immigration, etc. (Kaslow, 2001). When the members of a family face any of these problems, or perhaps a number of them, family psychologists can help the individuals to retain their own sense of identity, in part by focusing on reconstructing the social structure of the family (as opposed to focusing on diagnosing individual disorders). Unfortunately, the problems facing families are common throughout the world. However, since the family is the basic social structure within communities across all cultures, family therapy can play an important role in helping to solve these problems. For example, family therapy has been used to study and treat a variety of problems in different countries: conduct disorder in youth from the U.S. Virgin Islands (Dudley-Grant, 2001); community disasters, war stress, and the effects of immigration on Israeli families (Halpern, 2001); and the refusal of some children in Japan to attend school (Kameguchi & Murphy-Shigematsu, 2001). In each of these cultures the family is considered to play a particularly important role in identity formation.

Adulthood

Many theories on personality and cognitive development end with adolescence. As one enters into adulthood, it is assumed, one has accomplished all of the tasks necessary to be an adult, including one's identity. And yet, if adolescence ends sometime in the late teens, many people can reasonably expect to live another 60 to 80 years. Does it really make any sense to propose that nothing meaningful happens during those years? Of course, Erikson described development stages throughout adulthood and old age, but what about other psychologists? Srivastava, et al. (2003) examined changes in the Big Five personality traits across the years of adulthood. They found that conscientiousness and agreeableness increased through early and middle adulthood, whereas neuroticism decreased in women, but not in men. In other words, both men and women become more responsible and cooperative as they grow through adulthood, and women become more stable. One can speculate that these changes fit well within Erikson's model, in which most adults take on the tasks involved in raising a family. Self-esteem rises steadily throughout adulthood, before dropping sharply in old age (Robins & Trzesniewski, 2005). Similarly, the ability to integrate cognitive and affective components of the self, in order to maintain positive self-development, increases steadily during adulthood until beginning to decline with old age (Labouvie-Vief, 2003). Thus, adulthood does appear to be a time of personality change.

Adulthood, however, means different things in different cultures. In *Adulthood* (Erikson, 1978), Erikson brought together a collection of authors who examined adulthood from a variety of cultural perspectives. For a Christian adult, growth occurs primarily through social experiences. One encounters Christ in service to others, or in other words, by loving your neighbor. Christ himself serves as the model for adulthood (Bouwsma, 1978). Adulthood in Islam carries with it responsibility for the religious commands and obligations of Islam. One must reconcile the reality of the world with one's place in it, as willed by Allah. Adulthood then becomes an expression of the inner peace achieved by living in the world in accord with the divinely revealed reality (Lapidus, 1978). In the Confucian tradition, adulthood is the complete process of becoming a person. In this patriarchal model, first a man comes of age, then he marries and has children, then he begins a career as a scholar-official, and that career is expected to be served with distinction (Wei-Ming, 1978). In Japan, adulthood is a time of social responsibility, discipline, and perseverance, in preparation for the integrity and respect typically associated with old age (Rohlen, 1978). India presents a particularly difficult challenge, and it is not really possible to speak of a single adulthood model. The caste system inherent in the India of the past created vastly different life conditions for the people of India (Rudolph & Rudolph, 1978). The problems of language and multicultural populations create unique difficulties for understanding adulthood in Russia and America (Jordan, 1978; Malia, 1978). What is clear across cultures is that adulthood is a time of continued development, it can vary quite dramatically (even within a culture), and it often involves an aspect of anticipating old age. The anticipation of old age, however, can vary dramatically, based on individual and cultural attitudes about old age, as we will see in the next section.

Adulthood can be the most productive and, in some ways, most gratifying years of life. Some of the unique challenges of adulthood have become popular topics in psychology, such as the **midlife crisis** and the **empty nest** syndrome. And yet, adulthood is the least studied period of life. One possible explanation for this neglect, according to Smelser (1980a), is that most research is done by adults, and they tend to be more interested in stages of development other than their own. In a second collection of articles, entitled *Themes of Work and Love in Adulthood* (Smelser & Erikson, 1980), Smelser and Erikson brought together a variety of perspectives on what they viewed as two of the most important life phenomena that dominate the adulthood years. Sigmund Freud is alleged to have said that maturity is to be found in the capacity to love and to work. Throughout one's life, both of these phenomena follow certain paths, typically involving a period of growing interest and ability, followed by a fairly stable level (which typically lasts for decades), followed by a gradual (as in work) or sudden (as in the death of a spouse) decline (Smelser, 1980a). In examining the relationship between Sigmund Freud and Carl Jung, evident in their letters to one another, Erikson (1980b) found distinctly adult content related to such topics as mutual regard, confidence, affection, intimate concern for their families, both good and bad observations regarding their professional colleagues, and an ongoing debate regarding the important issues in psychodynamic theory and the psychoanalytic movement. There are similarities, but some interesting contrasts, between these letters and the ones Freud had written to Wilhelm Fliess years earlier. In that younger period of adulthood, Freud seemed more in need of a close friend, particularly since he was in the process of creating the field that was becoming well-established by the time Freud met Jung. Perhaps due to Freud being older when he met Jung, it seems that he interacted with Fliess and Jung in different ways: when Freud was young he interacted with his colleague Fliess as a colleague, but when he was older he interacted with Jung in a much more father-son type relationship (and Jung had lost his father years earlier).

Work and love interact, or don't, depending on the nature of individual cultures. For example, in America we compartmentalize our lives. We tend to have clearly defined career paths, and our personal relationships exist primarily outside of the workplace (Smelser, 1980b). In contrast, the Gusii in Kenya have not traditionally had "careers," but rather a domestically based economy. They also practice polygyny (each man having many wives, but *not* vice versa). Thus, a husband must balance the resources at his command between his different wives and their children. As such, although love plays some role in marriage, it can actually become a problem for that man who cannot maintain fair and equitable treatment of each wife and her children. This is handled by maintaining a certain distance from each wife, including having his own house, and visiting each wife on a rotating schedule that is acceptable to everyone (LeVine, 1980). Such a concept of love and marriage is extraordinarily alien to the symbolic and mythic nature of the love ideal that lies at the foundation of American culture: a man and a woman committed to one another in a way that ennobles and transforms them both (Swidler, 1980).

However, the romantic vision of love in American culture is not without its drawbacks. The romantic, passionate, committed love that Americans envision completes one's identity. In Erikson's terms, it stands in opposition to isolation. However, it is all too common that most marriages, as well as other long-term relationships, eventually come to an end. What then happens to each person's identity? Love also provides a basis for rebellion, such as when a person "marries for love" in spite of the objections of one's family and/or friends. Love can also lead to conformity, such as one sees in the term "settling down" or when women, in particular, are expected to take on the primary responsibility for the household as an expression of their love, even if they also have a job outside of the home as their husband does. When one partner, more so than the other, must engage in self-sacrifice, what happens to their opportunities for self-realization? If it is possible to find fulfillment through the love of another, then self-sacrifice can be self-realization (Swidler, 1980). If not, we might see high divorce rates. And a high divorce rate is the reality in America today.

So, whether love and work are intermingled or separate, whether simple or complex, whether fulfilling or a necessary social expectation, they dominate the years of early and middle adulthood. No one period in adulthood is more likely than another to result in change, as different stressors impact each age differently. Work related stress is particularly likely for the young adult, but older adults face the challenge of preparing (both financially and psychologically) for retirement, and unexpected changes can occur at any age. Love, particularly as it relates to marriage, causes stress throughout adulthood, but in different ways. Younger couples are more likely to experience separation and/or divorce, middle-aged adults experience their children leaving home and possible career transitions, and older couples are more likely to experience illness, disabilities, and perhaps the loss of a spouse. Each of these different forms of stress brings with it a need for coping mechanisms, and if those coping mechanisms fail, the likelihood for psychological distress becomes very real (Pearlin, 1980). Perhaps the most challenging stressor in our lives, one that ultimately cannot be overcome, but that may be transcended and accepted, is old age and our inevitable death.

Connections Across Cultures: Glorifying Youth vs. Valuing the Elderly

We hear a lot in our society about how we value youth, and consider the elderly to be of little worth. The obsession with youth and appearance is such that plastic surgery has become the subject of numerous television shows. But is our society really different than other societies, and if so, what factors might have contributed to the difference? The matter is particularly important today, since the world's older population is the fastest growing group. One estimate has suggested by the year 2020 the total population of people over 65 years of age will be 690 million (Hillier & Barrow, 1999). Thus, it won't be long before there are a billion people over the age of 65. But is 65 years old a valid point for declaring someone as old?

Old age can be defined functionally, as in whether or not a person can still do the things expected of them in their culture, it can be defined formally by some external event, such as the birth of the first grandchild, or it can be determined chronologically, as it typically is in the United States (we traditionally use the age of 65 years). Each measure has its advantages and disadvantages, but regardless, when a person is viewed by others as old, the question becomes one of how they will be treated. Generally speaking, the more industrialized a society is, the less likely it is to treat its elderly with respect and dignity. In non-industrialized societies, the elderly play a number of important roles in the traditions and ceremonies emphasized by such cultures, since they know the most about those traditions and ceremonies. Older members of the community function as historians, vocational instructors, and often as doctors and ministers. In agrarian societies they continue to work as long as they are able. As a result, the elderly are still vital, contributing members of the community, and as such, they are naturally treated with the respect they deserve (Hillier & Barrow, 1999).

There are, however, variations even within non-industrialized societies. For example, nomadic societies have few resources, and often live in harsh climates. Their geographic mobility favors youth and vigor, as well as individual autonomy, all elements that fade with advanced age. Even with minor advances in technology, the important roles that elders played in many cultures have faded with time. Among the Aleuts in Northern Russia there were always one or two old men who educated the children. However, the availability of printed material has largely eliminated the need for this type of education. In places such as Turkey and Nepal, the elderly have lost their place in the workforce with the urbanization and industrialization of the country. The Igbo of Nigeria once held their elders in high regard, but mass migrations have diminished their authority, and formal education in schools has supplanted their spiritual roles (Hillier & Barrow, 1999). Many more examples can be found of changes in how communities, societies, and cultures treat the elderly more poorly than they have in the past.

As a result, many older people want to look and feel younger. Studies have shown that one's attitude about their body image is positively correlated with their self-esteem, and that this holds true throughout the lifespan. In other words, people with high self-esteem feel good about their bodies, but people with low self-esteem feel bad about their bodies. People who are treated without respect or dignity, who feel that they are being discarded by society, are likely to experience lowered self-esteem, and with it a lower regard for their body image. These people become easy targets for fraudulent cures for arthritis, cancer, weight-loss, and sexual aids. It is estimated that Americans spend as much as $27 billion dollars a year on quack medical products or services (Hillier & Barrow, 1999). There are also many products that do help people look younger, so even more money is spent in a vain effort to pretend that people are younger than they actually are.

Consider your own relationships with people who are much older, or if you are a bit older yourself, with people who are younger than you. Do you even have relationships with people of different ages, or do such relationships tend to make you uncomfortable? How do you feel about the efforts of some people to try looking younger? Has there been an older person in your life, perhaps a grandparent, who has had a dramatic, positive influence on who you are today? Try to imagine your life at 60 or 70 years old, and how your children and grandchildren, or perhaps co-workers and friends, might treat you. Remember, your attitudes and actions toward older people today might have a significant effect on how your family and friends act toward you when the roles are reversed.

Old Age and Death

In Western culture most people seem to focus on youth. Old age and death are to be avoided, even feared. And yet, both are inevitable, unless we die young, something that is even less desirable than eventually dying of old age. What is most curious, however, is that there is nothing in our culture to suggest that death is something bad. Most people believe in life after death, and that good people go to Heaven. So why would we want to avoid that? In many other cultures, death is not viewed with the same finality as it is in Western culture, and ancestors are revered, and even worshipped. Even within Western culture, there are those who embrace the later years in life, and who do not fear death. These are the perspectives we will examine here.

<u>Growing Old: Or Older and Growing?</u>

The title for this section was taken from an essay written by Carl Rogers (1980). Rogers was 75 years old at the time, and he was looking back on the previous 10 years of his life. Rogers was experiencing a number of physical problems associated with the natural deterioration of his body due to advanced age, such as some loss of vision and arthritis in his right shoulder (making it impossible to enjoy playing Frisbee), but he still enjoyed 4 mile walks on the beach and felt physically strong in many ways. As for his career, from the age of 65 to 75 years old he had been very productive, publishing numerous books and articles. He also led many workshops and encounter groups, including some that required him to travel around the world. Professionally he began to take many risks, experimenting with his theories and workshops in ways he might never have considered earlier in his career. As it became necessary for him to rely on others for help, due to his slowing down with age, he also found that he was able to form far more intimate relationships with those colleague/friends who helped him. Even as his wife approached death during those years, he found that the struggle and pain led him to realize just how much he had loved her. Ten years later, as he turned 85 years old, Rogers wrote another essay, *On Reaching 85* (Rogers, 1989). Once again, he had been very productive during the 10 years between being 75 and 85 years old, most notably leading a number of peace conferences that led to his nomination for a Nobel Peace Prize. He felt deeply privileged to have lived long enough to see the great international influence of his work. There can be little doubt that when his life ended, which was actually before this essay was published (he wrote the essay, turned 85, and died 1 month later), he had experienced integrity and wisdom:

> I hope it is clear that my life at eighty-five is better than anything I could have planned, dreamed of, or expected. And I cannot close without at least mentioning the love relationships that nurture me, enrich my being, and invigorate my life. I do not know when I will die, but I do know that I will have lived a full and exciting eighty-five years! (pg. 58; Rogers, 1989)

Erikson, in contrast, knew something of the despair that contrasts the integrity one hopes for in old age. Never having known his own father, which resulted in an unending identity crisis, he struggled with feelings of having been an inadequate father himself. As famous as he was, he desired the ultimate recognition of a Nobel Prize, and was disappointed that *Ghandi's Truth* only won a Pulitzer Prize. He was also very sensitive to criticism in any form. As his own daughter pointed out, it is a tragic irony that individuals such as Erikson do not accept the vast majority of approval as commentary on their real self, but they do experience every shred of criticism as being very real (Bloland, 2005). Erikson himself said that even when a person developed a clear identity following adolescence, significant life events later on can precipitate a renewal of the identity crisis. One can only imagine the terrible psychological burden of sending away their baby Neil to die alone and secretly in a hospital, only to have him live for 21 years. Under such circumstances, Erikson described the search for a new identity as frantic (Evans, 1964).

One of the most interesting, important, and potentially enjoyable consequences of old age is the likelihood that one has grandchildren. All too often in American culture there are challenges to the relationships between grandparents and grandchildren. Families move across the country, they are broken apart by divorce, and, in general, our culture does not place value on the experiences of the elderly. However, only the elderly can provide generational continuity, which can be an important aspect of one's identity. For the grandparents, they can play a vital role in supporting the emotional development of their grandchildren, especially following a traumatic event such as divorce. They can provide adolescents with hope for continued development and purpose throughout life, a prospect that might seem quite difficult for an adolescent to comprehend on their own. And perhaps most importantly, they can simply spend quality time with their grandchildren, without the burden of being responsible for the day-to-day raising of the child (Erikson, 1959; Erikson & Erikson, 1997; Erikson, Erikson, & Kivnick, 1986). As shared by Joan Erikson, a grandmother and her grandchild can congratulate themselves for doing a marvelous job picking blueberries, while experiencing the reality of the life cycle:

> After a while I did need to sit down on a rock and rest a bit, but not he. He continued for a moment or so and then stood up very straight in front of me to clarify essentials. "Nama," he said, "you are old and I am new" - an unchallengeable pronouncement. (pg. 115; Erikson & Erikson, 1997)

Healthy relationships between grandparents and their grandchildren can benefit everyone in the family. In particular, grandparents provide a generational link that can help young people form their own identities. [Image by Mark Kelland]

While Carl Rogers and Joan Erikson seemed to accept old age and achieve integrity, Erik Erikson struggled with despair, despite his international acclaim and many obvious accomplishments. Thus, it should become clear that an individual's point of view is an important aspect of one's identity. In *Still Here* (Ram Dass, 2000), Ram Dass, a former Harvard University psychologist turned renowned guru of Bhakti Yoga and Kirtan (see Chapter 17), acknowledges the challenges of old age: physical problems, illness, loneliness, embarrassment, powerlessness, loss of role/meaning, depression, and even senility. The suffering associated with these conditions is, however, self-induced, and one can choose mindfully to *not* suffer. Whether or not one suffers, therefore, and whether or not one approaches the end of life with relative integrity or despair, is in many ways a choice. And that choice will have a dramatic effect on the final stage of life: death.

Death and Dying

It is important to begin by distinguishing between **death** and **dying**. Death is the end of life, and as far as scientific psychology is concerned, no one alive has been able to study death itself. Dying is a process that occurs when death is imminent, but does not come immediately. The dying process begins either with old age or the diagnosis of a terminal illness. Elisabeth Kubler-Ross is well-known for her research on the dying process, as are the five stages that she described in *On Death and Dying* (1969): **Denial and Isolation**; **Anger**; **Bargaining**; **Depression**; and **Acceptance**. When diagnosed with a terminal illness, most people naturally respond with the common defense mechanism of denial, but there is more to it. Many psychology textbooks do not address the second aspect of this first stage: isolation. Denial is usually temporary, but the dying person may still not be ready or even able to talk about their death, so they isolate themselves psychologically. Unfortunately, hospital staff members often foster this isolation, because of their own fears and discomfort regarding death. Kubler-Ross and her colleagues found it quite difficult to stop hospital staff members from encouraging the isolation of patients clinging to denial, including such simple tasks as keeping the patient's door open so that people passing by could look in and vice versa. The final stage of acceptance, according to Kubler-Ross, is one that many patients do not achieve. Many people fear death, and Western culture, due in part to its emphasis on science and medicine, and its movement away from religion, encourages people to challenge death. But for those who fight, struggle, and hope to the very end, even they eventually "just cannot make it anymore" (Kubler-Ross, 1969).

There are, however, many people who do come to accept the inevitability of death, either as a result of illness or old age. Erikson seemed to finally be at peace at the very end of his life, smiling whenever he recognized his wife or daughter:

> I was deeply touched on one visit to Dad when a flash of pleasure crossed his face as I entered the room, and he said faintly to himself, *Meine Tochter* ("my daughter" in his native tongue). (pg. 204; Bloland, 2005)

Carl Rogers was largely unconcerned about death, he seldom thought about it. He was, however, quite interested in the work of Kubler-Ross, particularly after he experienced his wife's dying process. One night, when his wife was near death, he told her that she should not feel obligated to live, all was well with her family, and that she should feel free to live or die, as she wished. After Rogers left that evening, his wife called for the nurses, thanked them for all they had done, and told them she was going to die. By the next morning she was in a coma, and by the next day she was dead (Rogers, 1980). This experience was profoundly moving for Rogers, and awakened a deep spirituality in him, but with a decidedly unscientific aspect to it. Kubler-Ross joined Carl Jung in believing in synchronicity and the possibility of out-of-body experiences, life after death, and the like (see Kubler-Ross, 1983, 1997). Rogers also came to believe in such possibilities. Helen Rogers reported seeing evil figures and the Devil by her hospital bed, as well as a white light that would come and begin to lift her from the bed. Earlier the two of them had attended sessions with a medium who claimed to be able to contact the dead. Rogers was thoroughly convinced that the medium's abilities were real, and that she had contacted Helen's deceased sister, and later Helen Rogers herself. According to Rogers, each event was "an incredible, and certainly non-fraudulent experience" (Rogers, 1980).

For the individual who is, indeed, about to die, what remains of life? Kubler-Ross, Joan Erikson, and Ram Dass all see death itself as a final stage of growth. For Joan Erikson, when hope and trust can no longer sustain the individual, "to face down despair with faith and appropriate humility is perhaps the wisest course," and one may then strive for gerotranscendence. Indeed, the ninth stage of development proposed by Joan Erikson seems quite similar to the stage of acceptance proposed by Kubler-Ross (Erikson & Erikson, 1997). Ram Dass talks about the different perspective on death in India, and how it helped him to believe that although the body and the mind, as well as their reflection in the ego/self, could die, the soul was something that would exist forever. Accordingly, it is more common in India, and in many other cultures, to prepare for death. The failure to do so in America can have painful consequences:

> When I was in my 30s, my mother was diagnosed with a terminal blood disorder. I went to visit her in the hospital, and all the people around her were saying things like, "You look great!" "You'll be home in no time!" But she looked terrible, and it was likely she'd never come home again. No one - not my father, her sister or the rabbi - would tell her the truth. In that moment I saw just how isolated she was. She was dying and no one would talk to her about death. We spoke about it, Soul to Soul, and she began to relax. (pg. 149; Ram Dass, 2000)

Kubler-Ross examined a variety of cultural perspectives on death, in a collection of essays entitled *Death: The Final Stage of Growth* (Kubler-Ross, 1975). Among Alaskan Indians the time of death was a choice. As death approaches, if it does not come suddenly, the dying person would call together relatives and friends for a time of storytelling and prayer. The dying person's life would be celebrated, and their death would be accepted as an inevitable matter of fact (Trelease, 1975). In the Jewish faith, tradition holds that the dying process should be met with efforts to alleviate distress as much as possible, but that death must also be accepted as the decree of human mortality by the Eternal and Righteous Judge (Rabbi Heller, 1975). In Hindu and Buddhist traditions, there is no death, but rather a common belief in rebirth. The circumstances of one's rebirth, however, are determined by how one lived their most recent life (based on karma). So, one's life, as well as the preparations preceding the death of one's body in this life, is an important factor in determining the nature of the next life. Of course, one can transcend this cycle of death and rebirth by attaining enlightenment. Thus, it is common in countries like India and China to practice Yoga or Buddhist meditation, as well as other spiritual practices, in order to either attain nirvana or, at least, a more favorable circumstance in the next life (Long, 1975). Each of these traditions, as well as others, considers death to be an important transition between this life and something beyond. It is in anticipation of something beyond that death and dying should be approached, both in terms of one's actions and one's state of mind. In conclusion:

> There is no need to be afraid of death. It is not the end of the physical body that should worry us. Rather, our concern must be to *live* while we're alive - to release our inner selves from the spiritual death that comes with living behind a façade designed to conform to external definitions of who and what we are. ...when you fully understand that each day you awaken could be the last you have, you take the time *that day* to grow, to become more of who you really are, to reach out to other human beings. (pg. 164; Kubler-Ross, 1975)

Discussion Question: People who have experienced the dying process often report strange occurrences, such as out-of-body experiences, visions of spirits (including angels and demons), or white lights shining down from above and beyond. Do you believe in any of these phenomena? Why do you think they only seem to occur with people who are, indeed, close to death?

Personality Theory in Real Life: ...and in Death!

Arthur Benjamin Niemoller was a fine example of a man who had achieved integrity in old age, which is not to say that his later years were entirely easy. As he prepared to travel from Ohio to Massachusetts for the first graduation of one of his grandchildren from college (me), his wife lapsed into a coma due to a serious blood infection. Knowing it was unlikely that she would survive, or that she would even know if he was there, he chose to attend my graduation. After the ceremony was over, and everyone returned to my mother's house for a party, the call had come from the doctor. My grandmother had died. I spent the next week in Ohio, helping my grandfather make the funeral arrangements for my grandmother. We had a service in Montgomery, Ohio where they had lived for many years, and then another in Putnam, Connecticut, where there is an old family graveyard. My grandfather made it very clear that he was glad he had attended my graduation, because he was proud of his family and wouldn't have wanted to miss it.

Arthur Benjamin Niemoller (1912-1998) lived a Long and full life. He exemplified dignity during his final years of life. [Image by Mark Kelland]

But the story doesn't end there. I attended graduate school at Wayne State University in Detroit, which isn't too far from the Cincinnati area, where Montgomery is located. I began visiting my grandfather regularly, which was quite interesting because I'd had very little contact with him before that (my family has never been close). He was a very active man. He as a Sunday School teacher and church council member at the local Presbyterian church, he belonged to a retired men's club, he had season tickets to the opera, and he regularly attended the symphony. He had many friends, some whom had also lost their spouses to old age. He was responsible for developing the computer programs that calculated the materials needed and the cost of those materials for building an isolated phase bus (something for carrying industrial strength electrical currents in power plants, I never really understood what he did). He was very proud of his work, and always eager to show me his new computer programs. I was just as proud of him, and I am very pleased to be able to say that he is the only person who attended all three of my college graduations (B.S., M.A., and Ph.D.). We developed a relationship I will always treasure.

The last time I saw my grandfather, he had been given 3 weeks to live. He had been suffering from dementia for several years, and typically wasn't sure who was visiting him. He thought I was his son Donny, and it didn't help that my wife and my aunt are both named Donna. On that last day I saw him, he was not the excited man of 80 years old who had a new computer program to show me. In fact, it took a while for me to convince myself he was actually still alive. It is frightening to see what can happen to the human body as a result of what is simply a natural process (old age, that is, dementia is certainly *not* a given with old age). Before I left, I prayed to God, deeply and sincerely, that my grandfather would finally just die. I was the last person in our family to see him alive. It is even more frightening, though merciful nonetheless, to think that my prayer was answered. I was satisfied that his life had been a good one, and content that his suffering was ended.

Has there been anyone in your life who meant a great deal to you but who has died? Were you able to participate in their dying process, and if so, how difficult was it? Imagine what it might be like to face death yourself, and think about how you might want others to treat you. Do your feelings and expectations fit within the cultural expectations and/or traditions of your family and community?

Review of Key Points

- Erikson never knew who his father was, and his relationship with his mother was never secure. This challenge to his own identity led him to focus much of his career on the development of identity.
- Erikson's theory was epigenetic, in that he believed people progress through a predictable series of psychological stages.
- At each stage, there is a unique and critical psychosocial crisis.
- Play is the royal road to understanding the young child's ego, according to Erikson.
- Before fully developing his theory, Erikson confirmed many of his observations in distinct cultures, including two Native American tribes (Sioux and Yurok).
- Erikson described eight stages of development: trust vs. mistrust; autonomy vs. shame/doubt; initiative vs. guilt; industry vs. inferiority; identity vs. role diffusion/confusion; intimacy vs. isolation; generativity vs. stagnation/self-absorption; and integrity vs. despair.
- Each of the eight stages is associated with a particular strength: hope, will, purpose, competence, fidelity, love, care, wisdom.
- Sometimes young adults will take a moratorium during their search for an identity.
- Joan Erikson proposed a ninth stage of development when death is imminent: despair vs. gerotranscendence.
- Identity develops in relation to one's environment and culture. Thus, it involves psychosocial relativity.
- Individuals who lose a sense of personal sameness and historical continuity may face an identity crisis.
- Both the ratio of where one falls on each continuum of a psychosocial crisis and the possibility of adopting a negative identity are challenges to healthy identity formation.
- Erikson believed that the significant challenges faced by young Blacks trying to find an identity in America, their disconnection from both their African heritage and the White majority in America, led them toward adopting a negative identity. Evidence can be found in the movement of some young Blacks toward the Nation of Islam and the Black Panthers during the 1960s.
- The family is an integral social institution in all cultures. Thus, family psychology can play an important role in helping individuals to recover from identity crises.
- Adulthood is a time of continued psychological development, with its own unique psychosocial crises. The form of these crises, however, varies dramatically from one culture to another.

- In all cultures, the primary activities of adulthood, around which the psychosocial crises revolve, are work and love.
- Very old individuals can still be productive and creative. Old age is also an important time for grandparents to communicate a sense of continuity, a generational link, to their grandchildren.
- Kubler-Ross described five stages that occur during the dying process: denial and isolation, anger, bargaining, depression, and acceptance. Unfortunately, many people never reach the stage of acceptance.
- When faced with death itself, those who have achieved acceptance can transcend life, and die in peace. Many non-Western cultures have different attitudes regarding death, and are able to facilitate acceptance much more readily.

Review of Key Terms

acceptance	epigenesis	love
anger	family	maturity
autonomy vs. shame, doubt	family psychology	midlife crisis
bargaining	fidelity	moratorium
basic trust vs. basic mistrust	generativity vs. stagnation, self-absorption	negative identity
care	hope	play
competence	identity vs. role diffusion, confusion	psychosocial crises
death	identity crisis	psychosocial relativity
denial and isolation	industry vs. interiority	puberty
depression	initiative vs. guilt	purpose
despair vs. gerotranscendence	integrity vs. despair	ratio
dying	intimacy vs. isolation	will
empty nest		wisdom

Annotated Bibliography

Erikson, E. H. (1950). *Childhood and Society*. New York, NY: W. W. Norton & Company.

In his first and, perhaps, most influential book, Erikson collected the observations of his early teaching career and clinical experience as a psychoanalyst. The book includes sections on the influence of social life and culture, the use of toys and playing when studying children, the evolution of identity, and his famous eight stages of development.

Erikson, E. H. (1968b). *Identity: Youth and crisis*. New York, NY: W. W. Norton & Company.
Erikson, E. H. (1980a). *Identity and the life cycle*. New York, NY: W. W. Norton & Company.

Although Erikson is best known for his eight stage theory of development, he really focused the majority of his career on the development of one's identity, something that continues throughout life. These are his two primary books on this topic. Each book offers examples of healthy and unhealthy identity formation, and the first one includes specific sections on identity formation in woman and in racial minorities.

Erikson, E. H. & Erikson, J. M. (1997). *The life cycle completed: Extended version - With new chapters on the ninth stage of development*. New York, NY: W. W. Norton & Company.

The first version of this book offered Erikson's perspective on the generational link provided by adults to all stages of life. The extended version includes three chapters by Joan Erikson on her proposed ninth stage of development, the role of older persons in the community, and gerotranscendence.

Schlein, S. (Ed.). (1987). ***A way of looking at things: Selected papers from 1930 to 1980 Erik H. Erikson*****. New York, NY: W. W. Norton & Company.**

This marvelous collection of Erikson's papers, including several co-authored by Joan Erikson and their son Kai, covers a wide range of personal reflections and professional topics.

Friedman, L. J. (1999). ***Identity's architect: A biography of Erik H. Erikson*****. New York, NY: Scribner.**
Bloland, S. E. (2005). ***In the shadow of fame: A memoir by the daughter of Erik H. Erikson*****. New York, NY: Viking.**

These are the definitive biographies of Erik Erikson. What sets Friedman's biography apart from others is the coverage of Neil Erikson, who was born with Down Syndrome, and information on Friedman's special effort to identify Erikson's father (an effort that failed). Sue Bloland was the Erikson's daughter, so she is able to provide unique, personal insights into the lives of both Erik and Joan Erikson.

Evans, R. I. (1964). ***Dialogue with Erik Erikson*****. New York, NY: Praeger Publishers.**

This book provides an interesting addition to the biographies on Erikson. In a conversion with Richard Evans, Erikson discusses a variety of personal and professional topics, offering his own perspective on the course of his life and his theories.

Kubler-Ross, E. (1969). ***On death and dying: What the dying have to teach doctors, nurses, clergy, and their own families*****. New York, NY: Scribner.**
Kubler-Ross, E. (Ed.). (1975). ***Death: The final stage of growth*****. New York, NY: A Touchstone Book.**
Kubler-Ross, E. (1983). ***On children and death: How children and their parents can and do cope with death*****. New York, NY: A Touchstone Book.**

Kubler-Ross is the person who most likely comes to mind when we think of studies on death and dying. Her first book describes the five stages of the dying process, as well as the challenges she faced in addressing this topic to a wider audience of health care professionals. The second book focuses more on the end of the dying process: death itself. In this second book, Kubler-Ross brought together colleagues who offer a variety of different cultural perspectives on death. In the third book listed above, Kubler-Ross addresses a most painful topic: the death of a child. She also delves into spiritual matters that she encountered time and time again while working with children who were close to death.

Ram Dass (2000). ***Still here: Embracing aging, changing, and dying*****. New York, NY: Riverhead Books.**

Ram Dass was a Harvard University psychology professor when Erikson arrived at Harvard (his name then was Richard Alpert). Ram Dass left Harvard and eventually became a guru of Bhakti Yoga. In this book, he offers an Eastern perspective on aging, dying, and death. The book is intended to help people prepare for and accept that which is inevitable, and which need not be feared.

Rogers, C. R. (1980). ***A way of Being*****. Boston, MA: Houghton Mifflin.**
Rogers, C. R. (1989). On reaching 85. In H. Kirschenbaum & V. L. Henderson (Eds.). ***The Carl Rogers Reader*** **(pp. 56-58). Boston, MA: Houghton Mifflin.**

In the fourth chapter of *A Way of Being*, and in the brief essay included in *The Carl Rogers Reader* (which was originally published in the *Person-Centered Review*), Carl Rogers reflects on his life at 75 years old, and then again at 85 years old. Each essay offers a marvelous view of the integrity that comes from living a fulfilling life.

Chapter 8 - Karen Horney and Erich Fromm

Karen Horney stands alone as the only women recognized as worthy of her own chapter in many personality textbooks, and the significance of her work certainly merits that honor. She did not, however, focus her entire career on the psychology of women. Horney came to believe that culture was more important than gender in determining differences between men and women. After refuting some of Freud's theories on women, Horney shifted her focus to the development of basic anxiety in children, and the lifelong interpersonal relationship styles and intrapsychic conflicts that determine our personality and our personal adjustment.

Personally, Horney was a complex woman. Jack Rubins, who knew Horney during the last few years of her life, interviewed many people who knew her and came away with conflicting views:

> She was described variously as both frail and powerful, both open and reticent, both warm and reserved, both close and detached, both a leader and needing to be led, both timid and awesome, both simple and profound. From these characterizations, the impression emerges that she was not only a complex personality but changeable and constantly changing. She was able to encompass and unify, though with struggle, many diverse attitudes and traits… (pg. 13; Rubins, 1972)

Erich Fromm, who was a lay-analyst with a Ph.D. (not an M.D. like most early psychoanalysts), focused even more than Horney on social influences, particularly one's relationship with society itself. He not only knew and worked with Horney personally, but the two were intimately involved for a number of years, and Fromm analyzed Horney's daughter Marianne. Both Horney and Fromm can be seen as extending Adler's emphasis on social interest and cooperation (or the lack thereof), and their belief that individuals pursue safety and security to overcome their anxiety is similar to Adler's concept of striving for superiority.

Brief Biography of Karen Horney

Karen Clementine Theodore Danielssen was born on September 16th, 1885, in Hamburg, Germany. Her father was Norwegian by birth, but had become a German national. A successful sailor, he had become the captain of his own ship, and his family accompanied him on a few of his voyages, including trips around Cape Horn, along the west coast of South America, and as far north as San Diego in the United States. Those trips established a life-long interest in travel, foreign customs, and diversity in the young Karen Horney. Although her father was a stern and repressive man, her mother, who was Dutch and 17 years younger than Horney's father, was a dynamic, intelligent, and beautiful woman who maintained a very happy home for the children (Kelman, 1971; Rubins, 1972, 1978).

From early childhood, Horney enjoyed reading, studying, and going to school. She was particularly interested in the novels of Karl May, who often wrote about the Native Americans, and Horney would play many games in which she pretended to be an Indian (usually, Chief Winnetou, a fictional character from May's novels). Her father believed that education was only for men, but her mother encouraged Horney's schooling, and in doing so, set an example of independence that greatly influenced Horney's life and career. Horney followed the traditional education of the day, covering science, math, French, Latin, English, and the humanities. She also took special classes in speech, and for a time was very interested in dancing, drama, and the theatre. Despite the challenging curriculum, she was an excellent student, and often placed first in her class. After being impressed by a friendly country doctor when she was 12, she decided to pursue a career in medicine. When she began college at the University of Freiburg-in-Breisgau, at the age of 20, her mother came along to get her settled in and care for her. Horney soon became good friends with Ida Grote, who moved in with Horney and her mother to help offset the costs of attending college. In 1906, Horney also met her future husband, Oskar Horney (Kelman, 1971; Rubins, 1972, 1978).

Over the next few years, she began her medical studies at the University of Gottingen, and then transferred to the University of Berlin, where she received her medical degree in 1911. In 1909 she had married Oskar Horney, who was described as a tall, slim, handsome man, a brilliant thinker, gifted organizer, and possessing great physical and emotional strength. He also attended the University of Berlin, eventually receiving doctorate degrees in Law, Economics, and Political Science! They soon had three daughters, Brigitte, Marianne, and Renate (between 1911 and 1915). Both Karen and Oskar Horney were successful in their careers during the beginning of their marriage. He worked as a lawyer for a munitions company, and did very well financially. She was actively developing her medical career, but had to work that much harder due to continued discrimination against women at the time. Still, the family spent time together on weekends, when her brother's family often visited, and vacations. Nonetheless, the Horneys grew apart during these years. In 1923, during the turmoil following World War I, Oskar's investments collapsed, and he eventually went bankrupt. A year later, he was stricken with severe encephalomeningitis, and spent 8 months in critical condition. These events radically altered his personality, as he became a broken and depressed person. In 1926 they separated, and never got back together. It was not, however, until 1939 that Karen Horney legally divorced her husband (Kelman, 1971; Rubins, 1972, 1978).

For Karen Horney's career, the years in Berlin were important and productive. She entered into psychoanalysis with Karl Abraham, and later she was also analyzed by Hanns Sachs for a brief time. Abraham appointed her as an instructor in the Berlin Psychoanalytic Poliklinik in 1919, and brought her to the attention of Sigmund Freud (with high praise). She came to know many of the candidates for psychoanalytic training, and also became friends with many of them, including Melanie Klein, Wilhelm Reich, and Erich Fromm. She also had many friends outside psychoanalytic circles, including the existential theologian Paul Tillich and the neurologist Kurt Goldstein (who coined the term self-actualization). The psychoanalytic scene in Berlin was active and dynamic, and Horney was very much in the middle of it all, never shy about expressing her own ideas and different opinions. One such issue was that of training lay-analysts (psychologists, as opposed to psychiatrists). She favored allowing the training for the purposes of research, but clearly favored medical training for those who would actually practice therapeutic psychoanalysis. This eventually led to conflict between Horney and her close friend Erich Fromm. Despite the many favorable circumstances in Berlin at the time, in the early 1930s Hitler was elected, and the Nazi regime began. Although Horney was not Jewish, psychoanalysis was considered a "Jewish" science. So, when Franz Alexander, who had been asked to come to Chicago to establish a new psychoanalytic training institute, asked her to be the Associate Director of the newly established Chicago Institute of Psychoanalysis, she accepted (Kelman, 1971; Rubins, 1972, 1978). This dramatic turn in the events of her life did not, however, occur without a bit of chance. Alexander had first asked Helene Deutsch, one of the first women to join Freud's psychoanalytic group (see Sayers, 1991), but Deutsch was not interested at the time. Thus, Horney was the second choice for the position that brought her to America for the rest of her life (Kelman, 1971; Rubins, 1972, 1978).

Once in Chicago, however, her theoretical differences with Alexander became a clear source of disagreement. Alexander was not willing, as Horney was, to discard significant elements of Freud's original theories. So, just 2 years later, in 1934, Horney moved to New York City and joined the New York Psychoanalytic Institute. A number of her friends from Berlin had also come to New York, including Erich Fromm and Paul Tillich, and Wilhelm Reich also visited her there. She soon met Harry Stack Sullivan and Clara Thompson, as they were establishing their new training institute in New York. She also began teaching at the New School for Social Research, and the American Institute for Psychoanalysis. Her private practice grew steadily, and Alvin Johnson, the president of the New School (as it is commonly known) introduced her to W. W. Norton, who established a well-known publishing house that produced all of Horney's books. Her first book was entitled *The Neurotic Personality of Our Time* (1937), which was followed by perhaps her two most radical books, *New Ways in Psychoanalysis* (1939) and *Self-Analysis* (1942). Horney had pursued new techniques in psychoanalysis and self-analysis, in part, because of her dissatisfaction with her own results as both a patient and a psychoanalyst. Later, she published *Our Inner Conflicts* (1945), *Are You Considering Psychoanalysis* (1946), and *Neurosis and Human Growth: The Struggle Toward Self-Realization* (1950). After her death, Harold Kelman (who was both a friend and colleague) brought together a number of her early papers in *Feminine Psychology* (Kelman, 1967), and, as a special tribute, Douglas Ingram published the transcripts of her final lectures, presented during a class she taught in the fall of 1952 (Ingram, 1987).

During the 1930s and 1940s, Horney's personal life was a social whirlwind. She entertained frequently, often cooking herself, and when her own home was in disarray she would arrange the party at a friend's home. She bought and sold vacation homes often, including one where Oskar Horney stayed for a time, and she traveled frequently. She enjoyed playing cards, and wanted to win so much that she would sometimes cheat! When caught, she would freely admit it, laugh, and say that her opponents should have stopped her sooner. Sometimes she would even gather her friends together and loudly sing German songs, in memory of their homeland (Kelman, 1971; Rubins, 1972, 1978).

At work, however, there was constant tension regarding theoretical and political issues in the psychoanalytic societies. In 1941, the New York Psychoanalytic Institute voted to disqualify Horney as a training analyst, due to her seemingly radical ideas on psychoanalytic techniques. Half the society did not vote, however, and they soon left to form a new institute. Immediately following the vote, Horney walked out, and a group of analysts led by Clara Thompson followed her. The very same month, twenty analysts joined Horney in forming the Association for the Advancement of Psychoanalysis, and Horney was asked to become the Dean of their soon to be established American Institute for Psychoanalysis. When Thompson suggested that Sullivan be granted honorary membership, and Horney recommended the same for Fromm, Fromm refused because he was not going to be recognized as a clinical psychoanalyst. The resulting controversy led to a committee review, which voted against Fromm's membership. Among others, Fromm, Thompson, and Sullivan left the society. There were other political battles as well, and Horney was routinely torn between her professional beliefs, her need to control the direction of the society and institute, and her personal friendships with the individuals involved. Through it all, although she held strong beliefs (such as opposing therapeutic psychoanalysis by lay-analysts like Fromm), she nonetheless encouraged challenging the original theories developed by Freud, as well as her own theories:

> I recall being impressed by her response at my first meeting with her, when I indicated my own curiosity and bent for research. She had warmly hoped I would continue this way, since her views needed further work and clarification. Indeed, during an interview in 1952, she stated that she knew her ideas would be changed, if not by herself by someone else. (pg. 37; Rubins, 1972)

By 1950, Horney seemed to be feeling lonely and isolated. Perhaps the political and theoretical battles had taken their toll, perhaps it was her strained relationships with her daughters (they were never really close), or perhaps it was the beginning of the cancer that would eventually take her life. Although Horney would not consult with her physician about the abdominal pains she was experiencing (thus she did not know that she had cancer), she did begin to develop strong spiritual interests. She occasionally attended Tillich's sermons at St. John the Divine Church, though she seemed more interested in the philosophical and ethical aspects of religion than the spiritual aspects. She kept a copy of Aldous Huxley's *The Perennial Philosophy* (1945/2004) by her bedside for over a year, reading daily on Huxley's interpretations of Eastern and Western mystics. A few years earlier she had met D. T. Suzuki, and she became particularly interested in Zen. She was especially impressed by a book he recommended entitled *Zen in the Art of Archery* (Herrigel, 1953; based on an article he wrote in 1936). In 1951, Suzuki led Horney on a trip to Japan, where she visited a number of Zen temples and had lengthy discussions with Zen monks. Although she seemed more interested in the practical aspects of being a student of Zen, she nonetheless endeavored to put Zen principles into a context she could understand (such as equating enlightenment with self-realization; Rubins, 1972, 1978). Late in 1952, her cancer became so advanced that she finally sought medical care. However, it was too late. On December 4, 1952, she died peacefully, surrounded by daughters.

Placing Horney in Context: Culture and the Female Psyche

Karen Horney's career intersected many areas of psychology, relevant both to the past and to the future. One of the first women trained in psychoanalysis, she was the first to challenge Freud's views on women. She did not, however, attempt to reject his influence, but rather, felt that she honored him by building upon his achievements. The most significant change that she felt needed to be made was a shift away from the biological/medical model of Freud to one in which cultural factors were at least as important. Indeed, she challenged Freud's fundamental belief that anxiety follows biological impulses, and instead suggested that our behaviors adapt themselves to a fundamental anxiety associated with the simple desire for survival and to cultural determinants of abnormal, anxiety-provoking situations.

Horney was also significant in the development of psychodynamic theory and psychoanalysis in America. She helped to establish psychoanalytic societies and training institutes in Chicago and New York. She was a friend and colleague to many influential psychoanalysts, including Harry Stack Sullivan and Erich Fromm. She encouraged cross-cultural research and practice through her own example, not only citing the work of anthropologists and sociologists, but also through her personal interest and support for the study of Zen Buddhism.

Although Horney herself abandoned the study of feminine psychology, suggesting instead that it represented the cultural effect of women being an oppressed minority group, her subsequent emphasis on the importance of relationships and interpersonal psychodynamic processes laid the foundation for later theories on the psychology of women (such as the relational-cultural model). Thus, her influence is still being felt quite strongly today.

Horney's Shifting Perspectives on Psychodynamic Theory

Horney did not establish a specific theory of personality. Rather, her career proceeded through a series of stages in which she addressed the issues that were of particular concern to her at the time. Accordingly, her theories can be grouped into three stages: feminine psychology, culture and disturbed human relationships, and finally, the mature theory in which she focused on the distinction between interpersonal and intrapsychic defenses (Paris, 1994).

Feminine Psychology

Horney was neither the first, nor the only, significant woman in the early days of psychodynamic theory and psychoanalysis. However, women such as Helene Deutsch, Marie Bonaparte, Anna Freud, and Melanie Klein remained faithful to Freud's basic theories. In contrast, Horney directly challenged Freud's theories, and offered her own alternatives. In doing so, she offered a very different perspective on the psychology of women and personality development in girls and women. Her papers have been collected and published in *Feminine Psychology* by her friend and colleague Harold Kelman (1967), and an excellent overview of their content can be found in the biography written by Rubins (1978).

In her first two papers, *On the Genesis of the Castration Complex in Women* (Horney, 1923/1967) and *The Flight from Womanhood* (Horney, 1926/1967), Horney challenged the Freudian perspective on the psychological development of females. Although she acknowledged Freud's pioneering theories, even as they applied to women, she believed that they suffered from a male perspective, and that the men who originally offered these theories simply did not understand the feminine perspective. Horney agreed that girls develop penis envy, but not that it is the only dynamic force influencing development during the phallic stage. Girls envy the ability of boys to urinate standing up, the fact that boys can see their genitals, and the relative ease with which boys can satisfy their desire for masturbation. More important for girls than penis envy, however, was the fear and anxiety young girls experience with regard to vaginal injury were they to actually have intercourse with their fathers (which, Horney agreed, they may fantasize). Thus, they experience a unique dynamic force called **female genital anxiety**. Another element of the castration complex in women, according to Horney, was the consequence of castration fantasies that she called **wounded womanhood** (incorporating the belief that the girl had been castrated).

Far more important than these basic processes, however, was the male bias inherent in society and culture. The very name *phallic* stage implies that only someone with a phallus (penis) can achieve sexual satisfaction and healthy personality development. Girls are repeatedly made to feel inferior to boys, feminine values are considered inferior to masculine values, even motherhood is considered a burden for women to bear (according to the Bible, the pain of childbirth is a curse from God!). In addition, male-dominated societies do not provide women with adequate outlets for their creative drives. As a result, many women develop a **masculinity complex**, involving feelings of revenge against men and the rejection of their own feminine traits. Thus, it may be true that women are more likely to suffer from anxiety and other psychological disorders, but this is not due to an inherent inferiority as proposed by Freud. Rather, women find it difficult in a patriarchal society to fulfill their personal development in accordance with their individual personality (unless they naturally happen to fit into society's expectations).

Perhaps the most curious aspect of these early studies was the fact that Horney turned the tables on Freud and his concept of penis envy. The female's biological role in childbirth is vastly superior (if that is a proper term) to that of the male. Horney noted that many boys express an intense envy of pregnancy and motherhood. If this so-called **womb envy** is the male counterpart of penis envy, which is the greater problem? Horney suggests that the apparently greater need of men to depreciate women is a reflection of their unconscious feelings of inferiority, due to the very limited role they play in childbirth and the raising of children (particularly breast-feeding infants, which they cannot do). In addition, the powerful creative drives and excessive ambition that are characteristic of many men can be viewed, according to Horney, as overcompensation for their limited role in parenting. Thus, as wonderful and intimate as motherhood may be, it can be a burden in the sense that the men who dominate society have turned it against women. This is, of course, an illogical state of affairs, since the children being born and raised by women are also the children of the very men who then feel inferior and psychologically threatened.

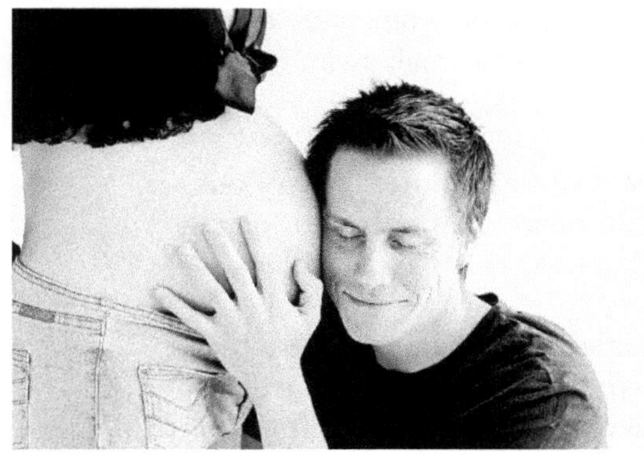

Womb envy can arise when men realize how little they are involved in the birth of a child. [Image by Tawny Nina]

In a later paper, Horney (1932/1967) carried these ideas a step further. She suggested that, during the Oedipus stage, boys naturally judge the size of their penis as inadequate sexually with regard to their mother. They dread this inadequacy, which leads to anxiety and fear of rejection. This proves to be quite frustrating, and in accordance with the frustration-aggression hypothesis, the boy becomes angry and aggressive toward his mother. For men who are unable to overcome this issue, their adult sexual life becomes an ongoing effort to conquer and possess as many women as possible (a narcissistic overcompensation for their feelings of inadequacy). Unfortunately, according to Horney, these men become very upset with any woman who then expects a long-term or meaningful relationship, since that would require him to then prove his manhood in other, non-sexual ways.

For women, one of the most significant problems that results from these development processes is a desperate need to be in a relationship with a man, which Horney addressed in two of her last papers on feminine psychology: *The Overvaluation of Love* (1934/1967) and *The Neurotic Need for Love* (1937/1967). She recognized in many of her patients an obsession with having a relationship with a man, so much so that all other aspects of life seem unimportant. While others had considered this an inherent characteristic of women, Horney insisted that characteristics such as this **overvaluation of love** always include a significant portion of tradition and culture. Thus, it is not an inherent need in women, but one that has accompanied the patriarchal society's demeaning of women, leading to low self-esteem that can only be overcome within society by becoming a wife and mother. Indeed, Horney found that many women suffer an intense fear of not being normal. Unfortunately, as noted above, the men these women are seeking relationships with are themselves seeking to *avoid* long-term relationships (due to their own insecurities). This results in an intense and destructive attitude of rivalry between women (at least, those women caught up in this neurotic need for love). When a woman loses a man to another woman, which may happen again and again, the situation can lead to depression, permanent feelings of insecurity with regard to feminine self-esteem, and profound anger toward other women. If these feelings are repressed, and remain primarily unconscious, the effect is that the woman searches within her own personality for answers to her failure to maintain the coveted relationship with a man. She may feel shame, believe that she is ugly, or imagine that she has some physical defect. Horney described the potential intensity of these feelings as "self-tormenting."

In 1935, just a few years after coming to America, Horney rather abruptly stopped studying the psychology of women (though her last paper on the subject was not published until 1937). Bernard Paris found the transcript of a talk that Horney had delivered that year to the National Federation of Professional and Business Women's Clubs, which provided her reasoning for this change in her professional direction (see Paris, 1994). First, Horney suggested that women should be suspicious of any general interest in feminine psychology, since it usually represents an effort by men to keep women in their subservient position. In order to avoid competition, men praise the values of being a loving wife and mother. When women accept these same values, they themselves begin to demean any other pursuits in life. They become a teacher because they consider themselves unattractive to men, or they go into business because they aren't feminine and lack sex appeal (Horney, cited in Paris, 1994). The emphasis on attracting men and having children leads to a "cult of beauty and charm," and the overvaluation of love. The consequence of this tragic situation is that as women become mature, they become more anxious due to their fear of displeasing men:

> …The young woman feels a temporary security because of her ability to attract men, but mature women can hardly hope to escape being devalued even in their own eyes. And this feeling of inferiority robs them of the strength for action which rightly belongs to maturity.
>
> Inferiority feelings are the most common evil of our time and our culture. To be sure we do not die of them, but I think they are nevertheless more disastrous to happiness and progress than cancer or tuberculosis. (pg. 236; Horney cited in Paris, 1994)

The key to the preceding quote is Horney's reference to culture. Having been in America for a few years at this point, she was already questioning the difference between the greater opportunities for women in America than in Europe (though the difference was merely relative). She also emphasized that when women are demeaned by society, this had negative consequences on men and children. Thus, she wanted to break away from any perspective that led to challenges between men and women:

> …First of all we need to understand that there are no unalterable qualities of inferiority of our sex due to laws of God or of nature. Our limitations are, for the greater part, culturally and socially conditioned. Men who have lived under the same conditions for a long time have developed similar attitudes and shortcomings.
>
> Once and for all we should stop bothering about what is feminine and what is not. Such concerns only undermine our energies…In the meantime what we can do is to work together for the full development of the human personalities of all for the sake of general welfare. (pg. 238; Horney cited in Paris, 1994)

In her final paper on feminine psychology, Horney (1937/1967) concludes her discussion of the neurotic need for love with a general discussion of the relationship between anxiety and the need for love. Of course, this is true for both boys and girls. This conclusion provided a clear transition from Horney's study of the psychology of women to her more general perspectives on human development, beginning with the child's need for security and the anxiety that arises when that security seems threatened.

Discussion Question: After a number of years studying feminine psychology, Horney came to believe that women are no different than any other minority group, and she began to pursue different directions in her career. Are the problems faced by women different than other minority groups? If so, how are they different?

Anxiety and Culture

In the introduction to *The Neurotic Personality of Our Time*, Horney (1937) makes three important points. First, she acknowledged that neuroses have their roots in childhood experiences, but she also considered the experiences of adulthood to be equally important. Second, she believed that neuroses can only develop within a cultural context. They may stem from individual experience, but their form and expression are intimately tied to one's cultural setting. And finally, she emphasized that she was not rejecting Freud's basic theory. Though she disagreed with many of his ideas, she considered it an honor to build upon the foundation of his "gigantic achievements." To do so, she wrote, helps to avoid the danger of stagnation. If any more evidence than her word was necessary to demonstrate her loyalty to Freud, in this introduction we also find mention of Alfred Adler. Although Horney acknowledges some similarities with Adler's perspective, she insists that her ideas are grounded in Freudian theory, and she describes Adler's work as having become sterile and one-sided.

Horney believed that anxiety was a natural state of all living things, something the German philosophers had called **Angst der Kreatur** (anxiety of the creature), a feeling that one is helpless against such forces as illness, old age, and death. We first experience this anxiety as infants, and it remains with us throughout life. It does not, however, lead to neurotic anxiety. But if a child is not cared for, if their anxiety is not alleviated by the protection of their parents, the child may develop **basic anxiety**:

> The condition that is fostered…is an insidiously increasing, all-pervading feeling of being lonely and helpless in a hostile world…This attitude as such does not constitute a neurosis but it

> is the nutritive soil out of which a definite neurosis may develop at any time. (pg. 89; Horney, 1937)

Thus, in contrast to Freud's belief that anxiety followed the threat of id impulses breaking free of the unconscious mind, Horney places anxiety before behavior. The child, through interactions with other people (particularly the parents), strives to alleviate its anxiety. If the child does not find support, then basic anxiety develops, and neurotic disorders become a distinct possibility. From that point forward, the child's drives and impulses are motivated by anxiety, rather than being the cause of anxiety as proposed by Freud. Basic anxiety is considered basic for two reasons, one of which is that it is the source of neuroses. The other reason is that it arises out of early, but disturbed, relationships with the parents. This leads to feelings of hostility toward the parents, and Horney considered there to be a very close connection between anxiety and hostility. And yet, the child remains dependent on the parents, so it must not exhibit that hostility. This creates a vicious circle in which more anxiety is experienced, followed by more hostility, etc. Unresolved, these psychological processes leave the child feeling not only basic anxiety, but also **basic hostility** (Horney, 1937; May, 1977). In order to deal with this basic anxiety and basic hostility, Horney proposed both interpersonal and intrapsychic strategies of defense (which we will examine in the next two sections). First, however, let's take a brief, closer look at Horney's views on culture and anxiety.

A neurotic individual, simply put, is someone whose anxiety levels and behavior are significantly different than normal. What is normal, of course, can only be defined within a cultural context. Horney cited a number of famous anthropologists and sociologists to support this claim, including Margaret Mead and Ruth Benedict. She cites H. Scudder Mekeel's somewhat famous example of Native Americans having high regard for individuals who have visions and hallucinations, since those visions are considered to be special gifts, indeed blessings, from the spirits. This is in sharp contrast to the standard Western view, which considers hallucinations to be a symptom of psychosis. And yet, Native Americans are not fundamentally different than Westerners. Only one year after Horney's book was published, Mekeel led Erik Erikson on the first of Erikson's studies of Native American development, which led Erikson to conclude that his stages of psychosocial crisis were valid, since they seemed to apply to Europeans, European-Americans, and Native Americans. After citing many such examples, from simple matters such as preferred foods to complex matters such as attitudes toward murder, Horney concluded that every aspect of human life, including personality, was intimately tied to cultural factors:

> It is no longer valid to suppose that a new psychological finding reveals a universal trend inherent in human nature…This in turn means that if we know the cultural conditions under which we live we have a good chance of gaining a much deeper understanding of the special character of normal feelings and attitudes. (pg. 19; Horney, 1937)

This emphasis on culture, however, should not be confused with the importance of individuality. Anxieties and neurotic symptoms exist within individuals, and present themselves within personal relationships. Culture, once again, merely guides the nature or form of those anxieties. In Western culture, we are driven primarily by economic and individual competition. Thus, other people are seen as competitors, or rivals. For one person to gain something, another must lose. As a result, according to Horney, there is a diffuse hostile tension pervading all of our relationships. For those who cannot resolve this tension, most likely due to having experienced the culturally determined anxieties in exaggerated form during a dysfunctional childhood, they become neurotic. Accordingly, Horney described the neurotic individual as "a stepchild of our culture" (Horney, 1937).

Interpersonal Strategies of Defense

Horney considered inner conflicts, and the personality disturbances they cause, to be the source of all psychological illness. In other words, calm, well-balanced individuals do not suffer psychological disorders (consider the stress-diathesis model of abnormal psychology). Although Freud approached this concept in his work, it was those who followed him, such as Franz Alexander, Otto Rank, Wilhelm Reich, and Harald Schultz-Nencke, who defined it more clearly. Still, Horney felt they all failed to understand the precise nature and dynamics of character structure, because they did not take into account the cultural influences. It was only during her own work on feminine psychology that Horney came to the full understanding of these psychodynamic processes (at least, in her own view; Horney, 1945).

At the core of these conflicts is a **basic conflict**, which Freud described as being between one's desire for immediate and total satisfaction (the id) and the forbidding environment, such as the parents and society (the superego). Horney generally agreed with Freud on this concept, but she did not consider the basic conflict to be basic. Rather, she considered it an essential aspect of only the neurotic personality. Thus, it is a basic conflict in the neurotic individual, one which expresses itself in the person's predominant style of relating to others. The three general attitudes that arise as neurotic attempts to solve conflict are known as **moving toward people**, **moving against people**, and **moving away from people** (Horney, 1945). Although they provide a way for neurotics to attempt solutions in their disturbed interpersonal relationships, they achieve only an artificial balance, which creates new conflicts. These new conflicts create greater hostility, anxiety, and alienation, thus continuing a vicious circle, which Horney believed could be broken by psychoanalysis.

Psychoanalysis is important for understanding neurotic individuals in part because they build a defensive structure around their basic conflict. Their behavior, according to Horney, reflects more of their efforts to solve conflicts, rather than the basic conflict itself. Thus, the basic conflict becomes so deeply embedded in the personality, that it can never be seen in its pure form. Nonetheless, when one of the basic character attitudes becomes predominant, we can observe characteristic behaviors that reflect the neurotic failure to resolve one's inner conflicts.

Moving toward people, also known as the **compliant personality**, incorporates needs for affection and approval, and a special need for a partner who will fulfill all of one's expectations of life. These needs are characteristic of neurotic trends: they are compulsive, indiscriminate, and they generate anxiety when they are frustrated. In addition, they operate independently of one's feelings toward or value of the person who is the object of those needs (Horney, 1945). In order to ensure the continued support of others, the compliant individual will do almost anything to maintain relationships, but they give themselves over so completely that they may enjoy nothing for themselves. They begin to feel weak and helpless, and they subordinate themselves to others, thinking that everyone is smarter, more attractive, and more worthwhile than they are. They rate themselves by the opinions of others, so much so that any rejection can be catastrophic. Love becomes the most compulsive desire, but their lack of self-esteem makes true love difficult. Accordingly, sexual relations become a substitute for love, as well as the "evidence" that they are loved and desired.

> Just as the compliant type clings to the belief that people are "nice," and is continually baffled by evidence to the contrary, so the aggressive type takes it for granted that everyone is hostile, and refuses to admit that they are not. To him life is a struggle of all against all, and the devil take the hindmost. (pg. 63; Horney, 1945)

As noted in the preceding quote, those who move against people, the **aggressive personality,** are driven by a need to control others. They view the world in a Darwinian sense, a world dominated by survival of the fittest, where the strong annihilate the weak. The aggressive person may seem polite and fair-minded, but it is mostly a front, put up in order to facilitate their own goals. They may be openly aggressive, or they may choose to manipulate others indirectly, sometimes preferring to be the power behind the throne. Love, which is such a desperate need for the compliant person, is of little consequence for the aggressive person. They may very well be "in love," and they may marry, but they are more concerned in what they can get out of the relationship. They tend to choose mates for their attractiveness, prestige, or wealth. What is most important is how their mate can enhance their own social position. They are keen competitors, looking for any evidence of weakness or ambition in others. Unfortunately, they also tend to suppress emotion in their lives, making it difficult, if not impossible, to enjoy life.

Those who move away from people, the **detached personality**, are not merely seeking meaningful solitude. Instead, they are driven to avoid other people because of the unbearable strain of associating with others. In addition, they are estranged from themselves, they do not know who they are, or what they love, desire, value, or believe. Horney described them as zombies, able to work and function like living people, but there is no life in them. A crucial element appears to be their desire to put emotional distance between themselves and others. They become very self-sufficient and private. Since these individuals seek negative goals, *not* to be involved, *not* to need help, *not* to be bothered, as opposed to having clear goals (needing a loving partner or needing to control others) their behavior is more subject to variability, but the focus remains on being detached from others in order to avoid facing the conflicts within their psyche (Horney, 1945).

Each of these three character attitudes has within it some value. It is important and healthy to maintain relationships with others (moving toward), ambition and a drive to excel have definite benefits in many cultures (moving against), and peaceful solitude, a chance to get away from it all, can be very refreshing (moving away). The healthy individual is likely able to make use of each of these solutions in the appropriate situations. When someone needs our help, we reach out to them. If someone tries to take advantage of us, we stand up for ourselves. When the daily hassles of life wear us down, we retreat into solitude for a short time, maybe exercising, going to a movie, or listening to our favorite music. As Horney attempted to make very clear, the neurotic individual is marked by a compulsion to use one style of relating to others, and they do so to their own detriment.

Connections Across Cultures: Cultural Differences in Interpersonal Relationship Styles

As Horney repeatedly pointed out, neurotic behavior can only be viewed as such within a cultural context. Thus, in the competitive and individualistic Western world, our cultural tendencies are likely to favor moving against and moving away from others. The same is *not* true in many other cultures.

Relationships can exist in two basic styles: exchange or communal relationships. **Exchange relationships** are based on the expectation of some return on one's investment in the relationship. **Communal relationships**, in contrast, occur when one person feels responsible for the well-being of the other person(s). In African and African-American cultures we are much more likely to find communal relationships, and interpersonal relationships are considered to be a core value amongst people of African descent (Belgrave & Allison, 2006). While there may be a tendency in Western culture to consider this dependence on others as somehow "weak," it provides a source of emotional attachment, need fulfillment, and the influence and involvement of people in each other's activities and lives.

Cultural differences also come into play in love and marriage. In America, passionate love tends to be favored, whereas in China companionate love is favored. African cultures seem to fall somewhere in between (Belgrave & Allison, 2006). When considering the divorce rate in America, as compared to many other countries, it has been suggested that Americans marry the person they love, whereas people in many other cultures love the person they marry. In a study involving people from India, Pakistan, Thailand, Mexico, Brazil, Japan, Hong Kong, the Philippines, Australia, England, and the United States, it was found that individualistic cultures placed greater importance on the role of love in choosing to get married, and also on the loss of love as sufficient justification for divorce. For intercultural marriages, these differences are a significant, though not insurmountable, source of conflict (Matsumoto & Juang, 2004). Attempting to maintain awareness of cultural differences when relationship conflicts occur, rather than attributing the conflict to the personality of the other person, can be an important first step in resolving intercultural conflict. However, it must also be remembered that different cultures acknowledge and tolerate conflict to different extents (Brislin, 2000; Matsumoto, 1997; Okun, Fried, & Okun, 1999; for a brief discussion of intergroup dialogue and conflict resolution options, see Miller & Garran, 2008).

These cultural differences are so fundamental, that even at the level of considering basic intelligence we see the effects of these contrasting perspectives. In a study on the Kiganda culture (within the country of Uganda, in Africa), Wober (1974) found that they consider intelligence to be more externally directed than we do, and they view successful social climbing and social interaction as evidence of intelligent behavior. This matches the attitude amongst Mediterranean cultures that notable people will be devoted to a life of public service (in contrast, the word "idiot" is derived from a Greek word meaning a private man).

Thus, moving toward others would be favored much more in other cultures than it might be in the Western world. Consequently, a significant attitude and the behavior of moving toward others would be less likely to be viewed as neurotic. Such issues are, of course, very important as we interact with people of other cultures, as we may consider their behavior to be odd according to our standards. Naturally, they may be thinking the same thing about us. What is probably most important is that we learn about and experience other cultures, so that differences in customs and behavior are not surprising when they occur.

There are two other mechanisms that Horney suggested are used by people in their attempts to resolve inner conflict: the **idealized image**, and **externalization** (Horney, 1945). The idealized image is a creation of what the person believes themselves to be, or what they feel they can or ought to be. It is always flattering, and quite removed from reality. The individual may see themselves as beautiful, powerful, saintly, or a genius. Consequently, they become quite arrogant. The more unrealistic their view is, the more compulsive their need for affirmation and recognition. Since they need no confirmation of what they know to be true, they are particularly sensitive when questioned about their false claims! The idealized image is not to be confused with authentic ideals. Ideals are goals, they have a dynamic quality, they arouse incentive to achieve those goals, and they are important for personal growth and development. Having genuine ideals tends to result in humility. The idealized image, in contrast, is static, and it hinders growth by denying or condemning one's shortcomings.

The idealized image can provide a temporary refuge from the basic conflict, but when the tension between the actual self and the idealized image becomes unbearable, there is nothing within the self to fall back on. Consequently, an extreme attempt at a solution is to run away from the self entirely. Externalization is the tendency to experience one's own psychodynamic processes as having occurred outside oneself, and then blaming others for one's own problems. Such individuals become dependent on others, because they become preoccupied with changing, reforming, punishing, or impressing those individuals who are responsible for their own well-being. A particularly unfortunate consequence of externalization is a feeling Horney described as a "gnawing sense of emptiness and shallowness" (pg. 117; Horney, 1945). However, rather than allowing themselves to feel the emotion, they might experience it as an empty feeling in the stomach, and attempt to satisfy themselves by, for example, overeating. Overall, the self-contempt they feel is externalized in two basic ways: either despising others, or feeling that others despise them. Either way, it is easy to see how damaged the individual's personal relationships would become. Horney described externalization as a process of self-elimination, which aggravates the very process with set it in motion: the conflict between the person and their environment.

Discussion Question: Horney described three basic attitudes regarding other people: moving toward, moving against, or moving away from them. Do you easily use all three styles of relating to others, or do you tend to rely on one more than the others? Does this create problems in your relationships?

Intrapsychic Strategies of Defense

In *Neurosis and Human Growth*, Horney (1950) addressed the psychodynamic struggle toward self-realization. She described a series of psychological events that occur in the development of a neurotic personality, and how they interfere with the healthy psychological growth of the **real self**. Indeed, neurotic symptoms arise out of the conflict between the real self, our deep source of growth, and the idealized image. She began this book with a simple statement as to why she focused so much of her work on neurotic personalities:

> The neurotic process is a special form of human development, and - because of the waste of constructive energies which it involves - is a particularly unfortunate one. (pg. 13; Horney, 1950)

Horney believed in an innate potentiality within all people, which she referred to as **growth toward self-realization**. The real self underlies this tendency toward self-realization, but it can be diverted by the development of basic anxiety. In order to overcome basic anxiety, the child adopts one of the strategies described above, attempting to solve its conflicts by moving toward, against, or away from others. Under adverse conditions, the child adopts one of these strategies in a rigid and extreme fashion, and begins the neurotic development. And yet, the tendency toward self-realization remains deep within the psyche, demanding that the neurotic development seek some higher level. Thus, the idealized image is formed, and a variety of intrapsychic processes begin an attempt to justify oneself based upon that idealized image.

The establishment of the idealized image involves self-glorification, and it reflects a need to lift oneself above others. The psychic energy associated with self-realization is shifted toward realization of the idealized image, establishing a general drive that Horney called the **search for glory** (Horney, 1950). The search for glory includes several elements, which are manifested as drives or needs. There is a **need for perfection**, which aims at the complete molding of the personality into the idealized self, and a drive for **neurotic ambition**, or striving for external success. The most damaging element of the search for glory, however, is the drive toward **vindictive triumph**. The aim of vindictive triumph is to put others to shame, or to defeat them, through one's own success. Horney considered this drive to be vindictive because its motivating source is the desire to take revenge for humiliations suffered in childhood (i.e., to pay others back for the circumstances that created basic anxiety).

The elements of the search for glory are not necessarily bad. Who wouldn't want to be perfect, ambitious, and triumphant? However, in their compulsive and neurotic form, Horney believed that people came to expect these elements, creating what she called the **neurotic claims**. When simple desires or needs become claims, individual feel they have a right to those things, they feel they are entitled. They fully expect to be satisfied in every way, and they also expect, indeed feel they are entitled, to never be criticized, doubted, or questioned (Horney, 1950). These claims are not only made on other people, but also on institutions, such as the workplace or society as a whole. The individual becomes highly egocentric, reminding others of a spoiled child, and they expect their needs to be satisfied without putting forth any effort of their own. Obviously, it is highly unlikely that such a person's needs are going to be fulfilled, creating a diffuse state of frustration and discontent, so all-encompassing that Horney suggested it can actually be viewed as a character trait in the neurotic individual. From the therapist's point of view, neurotic claims are particularly serious because they take the place of the patient's actual personality growth. In other words, the patient believes that merely wanting or intending to change is enough, and no effort is necessary. Indeed, the claims themselves are the neurotic's guarantee of future glory (Horney, 1950).

While these neurotic claims and the feelings of entitlement that accompany them may seem to be just a personal problem, the fact is that many people make seriously flawed self-assessments of their abilities, attributes, and future behavior. Indeed, the "average" person typically rates themselves as "above average" in many areas of their lives. These flawed self-assessments come into play in many aspects of our lives, and can easily affect others (Dunning, Heath, & Suls, 2004; Williams, 2004). For example, the United States spends more of its gross domestic product on health care than any other major industrialized country, and yet many people seriously underestimate the consequences of a wide range of unhealthy behaviors, such as smoking, drinking alcohol, overeating to the point of obesity, and avoiding exercise. The poor physical health of many Americans has become a regular topic in the mainstream media, as it threatens both individual lives (and, consequently, the family and friends of those who die) and our ability to fund healthcare for those who are poor or aged. In education, students dramatically overestimate the extent to which they have learned, limiting the likelihood that they will take fuller advantage of their education. And in business, the consequences can be severe for many employees, and therefore their families, when a President or CEO is so over-confident that they make poor decisions that bankrupt the company. As suggested above, these problems are common, not just confined to those who are neurotic. Thus, the problem of overconfidence, whether the result of an unreasonable trend in society to ensure everyone's self-esteem or the result of neurotic claims, as well as the extent to which individuals are able to know themselves and, therefore, function in the real world, is critical to everyone (Dunning, Heath, & Suls, 2004; Williams, 2004).

Whereas the neurotic claims are directed outward, the individual then turns their attention back into the self. They begin to tell themselves (though this may unconscious) to forget about the worthless creature they believe they *are*, and start behaving as they *should*. In order to match up with the idealized image, they *should* be honest, generous, and just, they *should* be able to endure any misfortune, they *should* be the perfect friend and lover, they *should* like everyone, they *should* never feel hurt, they *should* never be attached to anyone or anything, they *should* know, understand, and foresee everything, they *should* be able to overcome any difficulty, etc. Obviously, no one can be everything at all times. Horney described this tragic state as the **tyranny of the should**. Since it is virtually impossible for anyone to maintain such discipline in their life, rather than developing real self-confidence, the neurotic individual develops a questionable alternative: **neurotic pride**. However, the pride is not in who the individual is, but rather in who the individual believes they should be (Horney, 1950).

Sooner or later, it is inevitable that the neurotic individual will have their pride hurt in real life. When this happens, the other side of neurotic pride comes out: **self-hate**. Indeed, Horney believed that pride and self-hate are a single entity, which she called the **pride system**. As the neurotic individual becomes more aware of their failure to live up to the idealized self, they develop self-hate and self-contempt. According to Horney, the battle lines are now drawn between the pride system and the real self. It is not the real self that is hated, however, but the emerging constructive forces of the real self (the actual aim of psychotherapy!). This conflict, between the pride system and the constructive forces for change inherent in the real self, are so profound, that Horney named it the **central inner conflict**! In her earlier writings, Horney used the term neurotic conflict to refer to conflicts between incompatible compulsive drives. The central inner conflict is unique, in that it sets up a conflict between a neurotic drive (the pride system) and a healthy drive (the trend toward self-realization). Horney believed that individuals who have arrived at this psychological state of affairs were indeed in a difficult situation:

> Surveying self-hate and its ravaging force, we cannot help but see in it a great tragedy, perhaps the greatest tragedy of the human mind. Man in reaching out for the Infinite and Absolute also starts destroying himself. When he makes a pact with the devil, who promises him glory, he has to go to hell - to the hell within himself. (pg. 154; Horney, 1950).

Discussion Question: Horney defined the central inner conflict as the battle between the constructive forces for change inherent in the real self and the self-hate that arises out of the pride system. Have you ever found yourself giving up on something important because you feel incapable, unworthy, or overly self-critical? If you have ever been aware of these feelings at the time they occurred, what, if anything, did you do about them?

Horney's Challenge for Psychoanalysis

One of the actions that made Horney most controversial was her willingness to challenge how psychoanalysis should be conducted with patients. In *New Ways in Psychoanalysis* (Horney, 1939), Horney made it very clear why she thought that psychoanalysis needed to be questioned:

> My desire to make a critical re-evaluation of psychoanalytical theories had its origin in a dissatisfaction with therapeutic results. (pg. 7; Horney, 1939)

Simply put, she had asked many leading psychoanalysts questions about problems in treating her patients, and none of them could offer meaningful answers (at least, they had no meaning for Horney). In addition, a few of them, such as Wilhelm Reich, encouraged her to question orthodox psychoanalytic theory. As always, Horney did not see this as a rejection of Freud. Indeed, she felt that as she pursued new ideas, she found stronger reasons to admire the foundation that Freud had established. More importantly, she was upset that those who criticized psychoanalysis often simply ignored it, rather than looking more deeply into the valuable insights she believed it still had to offer for any therapist. As before, she saved her most serious critiques for the study of feminine psychology, though she still considered psychoanalysis with an emphasis on culture to be a valid therapeutic approach:

> The American woman is different from the German woman; both are different from certain Pueblo Indian women. The New York society woman is different from the farmer's wife in Idaho. The way specific cultural conditions engender specific qualities and faculties, in women as in men - this is what we may hope to understand. (pg. 119; Horney, 1939)

In her second book on therapy, Horney proposed something quite radical: the possibility of *Self-Analysis* (Horney, 1942). She considered **self-analysis** important for two main reasons. First, psychoanalysis was an important means of personal development, though not the only means. In this assertion, she was both emphasizing the value of psychoanalysis for many people, while at the same time saying that it wasn't *so* important that it had to conducted in the orthodox manner by an extensively trained psychoanalyst, since there are many paths to self-development (e.g., good friends and a meaningful career). Second, even if many people sought traditional psychoanalysis, there simply aren't enough psychoanalysts to go around. So, Horney provided a book to help those willing to pursue their own self-analysis, even if they do so only occasionally (which she believed could be quite effective for specific issues). She did not suggest that self-analysis was by any means easy, but more important was the realization that it was possible. With regard to the possible criticism that self-analysts might not finish the job, that they might not delve into the darkest and most repressed areas of their psyche, she simply suggested that no analysis is ever complete. What matters more than being successful is the desire to continue (Horney, 1942).

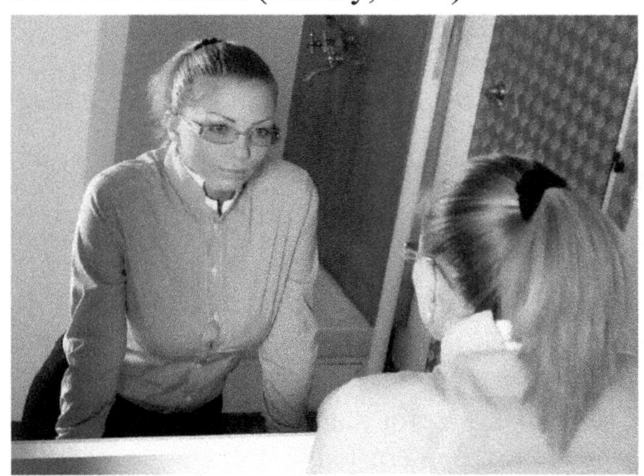

Horney advocated self-analysis, partly due to her own disappointment with psychoanalysis. [Image by Claudio Scott]

When the Association for the Advancement of Psychoanalysis was established, an important part of their mission was community education. One of the courses was entitled *Are You Considering Psychoanalysis?* This course was so popular, that the instructors decided to publish a book by the same name, and Horney was chosen the editor-in-chief (Horney, 1946). The chapters present very practical topics, such as: *What Are Your Doubts About Psychoanalysis?* (Kelman, 1946); *What Do You Do in Analysis?* (Kilpatrick, 1946); and *How Does Analysis Help?* (Ivimey, 1946). Perhaps reflecting her own concerns about the ability of psychoanalysis to "cure" a person's problems, Horney entitled the final chapter, which she wrote herself: *How Do You Progress After Analysis?* She begins the chapter by addressing the concern that many of her patients had: why would a person need more progress after psychoanalysis? Isn't psychoanalysis supposed to resolve all of a person's psychological problems? As noted above, however, Horney felt that no analysis is ever complete. But this time the reasoning is not based on questioning the effectiveness of psychoanalysis itself. Rather, it is based on the potential for human growth, a potential that is boundless:

> Your growth as a human being, however, is a process that can and should go on as long as you live...analytical therapy merely sets this process in motion... (pg. 236; Horney, 1946)

Discussion Question: Have you ever tried self-analysis, in either a formal or an informal way? If yes, were your efforts based on any personal experience or knowledge, and did it prove to be helpful?

Brief Biography of Erich Fromm

Erich Fromm was a colleague and long-time friend of Horney. He became interested in psychoanalysis at the beginning of World War I, when he was amazed at how readily so many people seemed eager for war. Unlike most other psychoanalysts, however, he earned a Ph.D., not an M.D. This eventually proved to be a source of conflict between Fromm and Horney, as she believed that lay-analysts should not be allowed to conduct therapy. Still, Fromm acknowledged Horney as influencing his career and sharing his own interests in culture and particularly in society itself (Evans, 1981a). Fromm also considered himself as remaining especially true to the theories of Sigmund Freud, though some authors consider him to be more of a philosopher than a psychologist (Evans, 1981a; Lundin, 1979; see also Funk, 1982, 2000).

Fromm was born on March 23, 1900, the only son of Orthodox Jewish parents, in Frankfurt, Germany. He studied the Talmud and law, but eventually switched from the University of Frankfurt to the University of Heidelberg and changed his major to sociology and economics. In 1922 he received his doctorate, and in 1924 he was psychoanalyzed by Frieda Reichmann. He turned away from Orthodox Judaism, married Frieda Reichmann (whom he later divorced), and became active in the Berlin psychoanalytic community (where he completed his psychoanalytic training). In 1933, Horney invited Fromm to guest lecture in Chicago. A year later, he moved to New York. There he collaborated with Horney, Harry Stack Sullivan (whom he also acknowledged as a significance influence on his thinking; see, e.g., Evans, 1981a and Fromm, 1941, 1955a), and Clara Thompson.

In 1940 he became a United States citizen, then in 1941 he published *Escape from Freedom* (Fromm, 1941) and began teaching at the New School (Funk, 1982, 2000).

After his break with Horney (both personally and professionally), Fromm married his second wife and spent some time teaching at Yale University. A few years later his wife died, Fromm soon married for the third time, and that marriage lasted until his death. Shortly after his third marriage, Fromm moved to Mexico City, Mexico, where he lived for the next 24 years. He joined the medical faculty at the National Autonomous University of Mexico, and co-founded a Mexican psychoanalytic society. In 1956, he published his acclaimed book *The Art of Loving* (Fromm, 1956). He taught a seminar with D. T. Suzuki, and their friendship led to the publication of *Zen Buddhism & Psychoanalysis* (Suzuki, Fromm, and De Martino, 1960). He also conducted important cross-cultural studies in a Mexican peasant village, resulting in the publication of *Social Character in a Mexican Village* (Fromm & Maccoby, 1970),

In 1966, Fromm suffered a heart attack and began spending more time back in Europe. In 1974, he sold his home in Mexico and settled permanently in Switzerland (where he had been spending his summers). After a series of three more heart attacks, Fromm died in 1980 (Funk, 1982, 2000).

Placing Fromm in Context: Individuality in Relation to Society

Erich Fromm was a colleague and close personal friend of Karen Horney for many years. He shared her interest in the role of culture in personality, and was even more interested in the interactions between the individual and society as a whole. Fromm viewed societies as forces that lead to alienation from a more natural, primitive way of life. As a result, freedom and individuality actually create psychological problems, as we become disconnected from our immediate social groups (such as the family or local community). This often leads to unfortunate consequences, such as seeking fellowship within a society at the expense of one's regard for self and others, providing a framework within which dictatorships can develop (as individuals completely surrender their freedom).

Fromm examined and combined many different interests in his career, including philosophy, economics, and psychology, and he felt that such a combination of interests was essential for the study of psychology to have real meaning. In one of the longest projects of his life, he and a number of colleagues applied a unique form of "psychoanalysis" to an entire village in rural Mexico. He then described how an understanding of social character can lead to an understanding of individual character, providing guidance for future considerations on planning social development during times of dramatic socioeconomic change.

Our Relationship to Society

Fromm was a prolific writer, whose interests included psychoanalysis, economics, religion, ethics, culture, and societal systems. He evaluated both Freud the man and Freud's theories in *Sigmund Freud's Mission* (Fromm, 1978) and *Greatness and Limitations of Freud's Thought* (Fromm, 1980). His religious works include such provocative titles as *The Dogma of Christ* (Fromm, 1955b) and *You Shall Be as Gods* (Fromm, 1966). He addressed the person's place within society in books such as *The Sane Society* (1955a) and *The Revolution of Hope* (1968). And a collection of his works on gender psychology, *Love, Sexuality, and Matriarchy*, was edited by Rainer Funk (1977). The unifying theme throughout Fromm's writings is each person's relationship to society, which he addressed most directly in *Escape from Freedom* (Fromm, 1941).

Fromm interpreted Freud's theories on the satisfaction of drives as necessarily involving other people, but for Freud those relationships are only a means to an end. Although hunger, thirst, and sex may be common needs, Fromm suggested that the needs that lead to differences in people's character, such as love and hatred, lusting for power or yearning to submit, or the enjoyment of sensuous pleasure as well as the fear of it, are all the result of social processes. One's very nature is a product of the interaction between the individual and their cultural setting. We are the creation and achievement of human history, and at the same time we influence the course of that history and culture. In modern times, particularly in the Western world, our pursuit of individuality has alienated us from others, from the very social structure that is inherent to our nature. Consequently, our **freedom** has become a psychological problem, it has isolated us from the connections necessary for our survival and development (Fromm, 1941). The danger with this situation, according to Fromm, is that when an entire society is suffering from feelings of isolation and disconnection with the natural order (from nature itself, in Fromm's view), the members of that society may seek connection with a societal structure that destroys their freedom and, thus, integrates their self into the whole (albeit in a dysfunctional way). The three ways in which individuals escape from freedom are **authoritarianism**, or giving oneself up to some authority in order to gain the strength that the individual lacks, **destructiveness**, in which the individual tries to destroy the object causing anxiety (e.g., society), and **automaton conformity**, in which the person renounces their individual integrity. Fromm believed that these phenomena provided an explanation for the development of dictatorships, such as the rise of Fascism in Europe during the 1920s and 1930s. For the leaders of these societies, these processes are such a deeply ingrained aspect of their character that Fromm actually described Adolf Hitler's destructiveness as evidence of a necrophilous character (a necrophiliac is someone sexually attracted to the dead; Fromm, 1973).

Fromm was interested in how so many people can support a dictator like Hitler. [Image from Wikimedia Commons]

In order to approach a solution for this problem, Fromm pursued an overall integration of the person and society. He believed that psychology cannot be divorced from philosophy, sociology, economics, or ethics. The moral problem facing people in the modern world is their indifference to themselves. Although democracy and individuality seem to offer freedom, it is only a promise of freedom. When our insecurities and anxieties lead us to submit to some source of power, be it a political party, church, club, whatever, we surrender our personal power (Fromm, 1947). Consequently, we become subject to the undue influence of others (and in extreme situations, to a Hitler or a Stalin). The solution may be as simple as love, but Fromm suggests that love is by no means an easy task, and it is not simply a relationship between two people:

> ...love is not a sentiment which can be easily indulged in by anyone, regardless of the level of maturity reached by him. It [Fromm's book] wants to convince the reader that all his attempts for love are bound to fail, unless he tries most actively to develop his total personality, so as to achieve a productive orientation; that satisfaction in individual love cannot be attained without the capacity to love one's neighbor, without true humility, courage, faith and discipline. (pg. xxi; Fromm, 1956)

An individual's capacity for love is a reflection of the extent to which their culture encourages the development of the capacity for love as part of the character of each person. Capitalist societies, according to Fromm, emphasize individual freedom and economic relations. Thus, a capitalist society values economic gain (amassed wealth) over labor (the power of people). And yet, such an economy needs large groups of people working together (the labor force). As individuals become anxious in their pursuit of life, they become psychologically invested in the capitalist system, they surrender themselves to capitalism, and become the labor force that leads to the wealth of those who own the company. Fromm believed this alienated us from ourselves, from others, and from nature (or, the natural order). In order to regain our connection to others in a healthy way, we need to practice the art of love, love both for ourselves and for others. Doing so requires discipline, concentration, and patience, personal strengths that are all taught in the practice of Zen. Indeed, Fromm recommends one of Horney's favorite books: *Zen in the Art of Archery* (Herrigel, 1953). We will examine the relationship between Zen and the approaches of Horney and Fromm to solving society's problems in more detail in "Personality Theory in Real Life." But first, Fromm chose to examine whether the principles of psychoanalysis could be used to examine the relationship between individuals and society. He and his colleagues addressed this question in a Mexican village, a study we will examine in the next section.

> **Discussion Question:** Fromm believed that the freedom we have in modern, Western societies actually separates and alienates us from others, becoming a source of great anxiety. Can you agree that freedom can become a problem? Can you agree that people within an entire society could become so anxious that they support the rise of a dictator?

Fromm's Cross-Cultural Studies in Mexico

Fromm believed that in addition to individual's having a certain character structure, there is also **social character**. Social character is common to groups or classes within a society, and provides a framework within which psychic energy in general is transformed into the specific psychic energy of each person within the group. From 1957 to 1963, Fromm, Michael Maccoby, and numerous colleagues interviewed every adult member of a Mexican village, and about half the children, with a focus on applying psychodynamic theory in order to understand the social character of the village and its role in determining the personality of each person. The village was chosen as representative of many small villages (this village had approximately 800 residents) in Mexico that underwent substantial changes in socioeconomic structure following the Mexican revolution. The primary, and most controversial, purpose of this study was to determine whether a society could be "psychoanalyzed" in order to understand the character of individual's within that society. Fromm & Maccoby also hoped that their study would provide information to help predict and plan social change during times of dramatic socioeconomic change, such as the transition from a non-democratic to a democratic society (Fromm & Maccoby, 1970).

While it took an entire book for Fromm and Maccoby to report their results, a few key findings can be summarized. First, although they began their study with a questionnaire that had been developed for a previous study, the level of interpretation needed for psychoanalytic theorizing required additional information. This was obtained by also having the participants take the Rorschach inkblot test. Second, the theory of social character, as an adaptation to the socioeconomic conditions of a society that serve to stabilize and maintain that society, was confirmed. Of particular interest were those individuals whose character was typically viewed as deviant, because they seek change and opportunity. When external socioeconomic conditions force changes upon a society, the previously "deviant" individuals are among those who flourish under this new opportunity for change. In other words, their so-called deviance now becomes advantageous, and they lead others toward new adaptive changes in social character (though this may occur slowly for most members of the society). In a manner similar to natural selection in evolution, Fromm and Maccoby referred to this type of change in a society as **social selection**. Unfortunately, if the individuals leading these changes are dysfunctional or cruel individuals, such as the leaders of the fascist groups in Europe during the 1920s and 1930s, the consequences can be tragic. It was for this very reason that Fromm sought to understand how people are drawn into groups following their alienation and anxiety due to changes in the course of society.

Personality Theory in Real Life: Feminine Psychology, Zen Mindfulness, Psychoanalysis, and Everyday Relationships

The ancient practice of mindfulness, which is associated with Buddhism but also has roots in other spiritual practices and religions, has become an important and fairly common psychotherapeutic technique (see, e.g., Germer, Siegel, & Fulton, 2005; Richards & Bergin, 2000; Sperry & Shafranske, 2005). There are also some interesting connections between the practice of Buddhist mindfulness and those who established feminine psychology. At the end of her life, Karen Horney went to Japan to study Zen Buddhism with the renowned Buddhist scholar D. T. Suzuki, and Janet Surrey, one of the founding members of the Stone Center (which will be introduced in the next chapter), has been practicing mindfulness and working to synthesize Buddhist practices with relational-cultural approaches to psychology for over 20 years (Surrey, 2005). Surrey is also on the faculty of the Institute for Meditation and Psychotherapy, and teaches seminars on the use of mindfulness in conjunction with relational-cultural therapy (and I can personally attest to the wonderful job she does).

Since Horney became interested in Zen near the end of her life, she wrote very little about it.

Indeed, most of what is recorded is in the book *Final Lectures* (Ingram, 1987), which was published by Douglas Ingram many years after Horney died. However, her close friend and colleague Erich Fromm also worked with Suzuki. Fromm mentions Yoga and Buddhism often in his books, and Suzuki and Fromm (along with another colleague) co-authored *Zen Buddhism & Psychoanalysis* in 1960.

Horney equated Zen mindfulness with living fully in each moment, with wholehearted concentration (Horney, 1945, 1950; Ingram, 1987). This general theme is expressed quite eloquently in one of Horney's favorite books, *Zen in the Art of Archery* (Herrigel, 1953), as well as in Herrigel's other book, *The Method of Zen* (Herrigel, 1960). In the latter book, Herrigel expresses the essence of Zen from his perspective, presenting a psychological view that fits well with the relational-cultural perspective we will examine in the next chapter:

> …the Zen Buddhist is far from limiting his feelings of joy and compassion to human beings and to every aspect of human existence. He embraces in these feelings everything that lives and breathes…The Zen Buddhist is constantly confirmed in his experience that there is a fundamental communication which embraces all forms of existence…He does not pass by the joys and sufferings of others without taking them to himself and reinforcing them with his own feelings… (pp. 119-120; Herrigel, 1960)

Fromm knew Suzuki at the same time as Horney, but the two men really got to know each other when Suzuki spent a week in Mexico in 1956, and Fromm then visited Suzuki in New York. In 1964, Fromm wrote to Suzuki that every morning he read a passage on Zen or something by Meister Eckhart (a well-known Christian mystic). In addition, Fromm was interested in Kabbalah and Sufism, as well as other spiritual approaches to understanding people (Funk, 2000). Fromm examined many of these diverse perspective in books such as *The Nature of Man* (Fromm & Xirau, 1968) and *Psychoanalysis and Religion* (Fromm, 1950), and he drew interesting connections between the physical activities of Yoga and Wilhelm Reich's somatic psychology (Fromm, 1992). He was by no means an unqualified supporter, however, suggesting that some self-proclaimed gurus can do more harm than good when seeking to serve their own selfish interests (usually in order to make money; Fromm, 1994).

In their work together, Suzuki provided a brief overview of the essentials of Zen practice, which focuses on living life:

> Zen may occasionally appear too enigmatic, cryptic, and full of contradictions, but it is after all a simple discipline and teaching:
>
> To do goods,
> To avoid evils,
> To purify one's own heart:
> This is the Buddha-Way.
>
> Is this not applicable to all human situations, modern as well as ancient, Western as well as Eastern? (pg. 76; Suzuki, Fromm, & DeMartino, 1960)

Fromm, for his part, identified ways in which Zen principles appeared to be compatible with psychoanalysis. He considered psychoanalysis to be the Western parallel to Zen, since Zen arose from Indian rationality and abstraction mixed with Chinese concreteness and realism, whereas psychoanalysis arose from Western humanism and rationalism. Fromm described the Western world as suffering from a spiritual crisis, resulting from a change in the pursuit of the perfection of humanity to the pursuit of the perfection of things (e.g., technology). Since we have lost our connection to nature, and to ourselves and our communities, we have become anxious and depressed. Psychoanalysis was developed to help us deal with these anxieties, as an alternative to the flawed ways in which we had been dealing with them in the past: religion (according to Freud). As described very simply in the quote above, Zen Buddhism also seeks to resolve human anxiety, simply by doing good and avoiding evil. In Freudian terms, doing good results from knowing oneself, and one can only know oneself through the process of psychoanalysis. Then, a person can act in accordance with reality, rather than being influenced by unconscious, repressed, and dysfunctional psychological processes. Therefore, Fromm considered the essential nature of psychoanalysis to be compatible with Zen (Suzuki, Fromm, & DeMartino, 1960), a perspective supported more recently by Mark Epstein in his comparison of Buddhist meditation and psychoanalysis, *Thoughts Without a Thinker* (Epstein, 1995).

Fitting even more closely with Fromm's perspective on human development and psychoanalysis, Zen art is intimately involved with nature, and with humanity's relationship with nature (Herrigel, 1953, 1960; Suzuki, Fromm, & DeMartino, 1960). Fromm used Zen perspectives to reform his views on psychoanalysis and development. He considered the development of the individual to be a re-enactment of the development of the species (i.e., ontogeny recapitulates phylogeny). Prior to birth there is no anxiety, following birth we must deal with anxiety. We can try to deal with our anxieties by regressing to our earliest state, or we can attempt to complete the process of birth, which Fromm described as a lifelong process:

> Birth is not one act; it is a process. The aim of life is to be fully born, though its tragedy is that most of us die before we are thus born. To live is to be born every minute. (pg. 88; Suzuki, Fromm, & DeMartino, 1960)

Fromm does not suggest that this is easy, but it is possible. However, which method is to be preferred: psychoanalysis or the practice of Zen Buddhism? That would appear to be a personal matter, since both psychoanalysis and Zen Buddhism aim toward the same goal:

> This description of Zen's aim could be applied without change as a description of what psychoanalysis aspires to achieve; insight into one's own nature, the achievement of freedom, happiness and love, liberation of energy, salvation from being insane or crippled…The aim of Zen transcends the goal of ethical behavior, and so does psychoanalysis. It might be said that both systems assume that the achievement of their aim brings with it an ethical transformation, the overcoming of greed and the capacity for love and compassion. (pp. 122-123; Suzuki, Fromm, & DeMartino, 1960)

Just as love is considered an essential element of being Christian, compassion is essential to Buddhism. In *The Art of Loving*, Fromm (1956) noted that a person cannot love themselves if they do not love others. Thus, love and compassion are intertwined, one must love and care for all people, indeed for all things, to be fulfilled. Zen teaches this peace in many ways, even sword fighting and archery become art when performed by a Zen master. Fromm acknowledged that a Zen master of sword fighting has no wish to kill and experiences no hate for his opponent. Although a classic psychoanalyst might insist that the sword master is motivated by some unconscious hatred or anger, Fromm says that such a psychoanalyst simply does not grasp the spirit of Zen. Likewise, citing Herrigel's *Zen in the Art of Archery* again, Fromm notes how archery has been transformed from a military skill into an exercise of spirituality, or in non-spiritual terms, a form of *playful* violence (as opposed to aggressive violence; Fromm, 1964, 1973).

Thus, the practice of mindfulness, the art of love, compassion, all play similar roles in helping people to be aware of who they are and of their relationships with others. In addition, they encourage and support a genuine desire to be connected to others, and to maintain healthy interpersonal connections, even in such diverse activities as eating breakfast, going to work, or practicing archery.

Karen Horney and Erich Fromm

Review of Key Points

- Horney was the first psychodynamic theorist to challenge Freud's perspective on the psychology of women.
- Horney did not deny that girls envy boys for certain anatomical advantages that boys have, but she suggested that another dynamic force comes into play: female genital anxiety.
- In addition to female genital anxiety, an important consequence of the castration complex in women is the experience of wounded womanhood.
- Because girls are repeatedly made to feel inferior to boys, and few outlets are available for their creative drives, many women develop a masculinity complex. This complex is manifested by a desire for revenge against men and the rejection of feminine traits.
- Horney suggested that boys are actually more envious of girls, since boys place such a minimal role in pregnancy, childbirth, and nurturing an infant. Indeed, they may feel so inadequate that they seek to conquer many women in relationships, but avoid any long-term or meaningful relationships.
- As the result of cultural pressure, Horney felt that many women overvalue love, and experience a desperate need to be with a man.
- Horney eventually moved away from studying feminine psychology, considering it more of a cultural issue than a gender issue. She believed that demeaning women also hurt children and men, and she did not want to further the conflict between men and women.
- Horney believed that all children are born with an anxiety related to survival. When they are not nurtured and cared for fully, they then develop a basic anxiety toward the seemingly unsafe world.
- Basic anxiety leads to basic hostility, and the child must then choose some strategy for dealing with other people. The three basic strategies are moving toward people, moving against people, and moving away from people.
- As the neurotic personality progresses, due to the continued failure to resolve one's conflicts, an idealized image is formed. In addition, the neurotic individual externalizes their anxiety.
- Horney suggested that the real self contains an innate trend toward self-realization. However, in the neurotic individual, this energy is turned toward realizing the idealized image.
- The neurotic individual then embarks on a search for glory, which includes neurotic claims. The neurotic claims then lead to a powerful compulsion known as the tyranny of the should.
- As this dysfunctional state continues, neurotic pride leads to self-hate, the two phenomena being opposite sides of the pride system. This conflict between the real self and the pride system is the central inner conflict.
- Horney felt that psychoanalysis needed to be re-evaluated because in many cases it was ineffective. Her most radical suggestion involved the possibility of teaching people about self-analysis.
- Fromm believed that the freedom associated with modern societies had alienated us from the natural order. Consequently, freedom had become a psychological problem, resulting in alienation and anxiety.
- Individuals who feel anxious and alienated seek connection by any means, according Fromm, including submitting themselves to authoritarian regimes.
- Fromm encouraged practicing the art of love, or a deep concern for others, as a way to feel connected without surrendering one's personal freedom.
- In his extensive study of a Mexican village, Fromm believed that psychodynamic principles could be used to study the social character of groups. He also felt that the evolution of groups, or societies, over time reflects a type of social selection.
- Both Horney and Fromm believed that Zen Buddhism and psychoanalysis shared common elements, and that each discipline could benefit from studying the other. They attempted to incorporate these ideas in ways that might enhance interpersonal relationships in our everyday lives.

Review of Key Terms

aggressive personality	externalization	neurotic pride
Angst der Kreatur	female genital anxiety	overvaluation of love
authoritarianism	freedom	pride system
automaton conformity	growth toward self-realization	real self
basic anxiety	idealized image	search for glory
basic conflict	masculinity complex	self-analysis
basic hostility	moving against people	self-hate
central inner conflict	moving away from people	social character
communal relationships	moving toward people	social selection
compliant personality	need for perfection	tyranny of the should
destructiveness	neurotic ambition	vindictive triumph
detached personality	neurotic claims	womb envy
exchange relationships		wounded womanhood

Annotated Bibliography

Horney, K. (1937). *The neurotic personality of our time*. New York, NY: W. W. Norton & Company.
Horney, K. (1945). *Our inner conflicts: A constructive theory of neurosis*. New York, NY: W. W. Norton & Company.
Horney, K. (1950). *Neurosis and human growth: The struggle toward self-realization*. New York, NY: W. W. Norton & Company.

Few authors have so clearly presented their theories in such a straightforward and easily comprehended fashion as Karen Horney has in these three books. More importantly, however, is the depth of understanding that she conveys. Always quick to complement Freud, she nonetheless takes his theories to new heights that even he was unlikely to envision. In my opinion, these three books demonstrate Horney's genius in the field of psychodynamic theory.

Horney, K. (1942). *Self-analysis*. New York, NY: W. W. Norton & Company.

Self-analysis is perhaps Horney's most radical book. The suggestion that a psychoanalyst is not necessary for psychoanalysis was probably viewed as quite threatening to many therapists at the time. However, Horney placed great value in psychoanalysis, and she knew that not every person could avail themselves of a properly trained analyst. Thus, she placed her concern for people above her concern for the profit of her fellow analysts.

Horney, K. (Ed.). (1946). *Are you considering psychoanalysis?* New York, NY: W. W. Norton & Company.

For those who are interested in the services of a trained analyst, Horney and her colleagues at the Association for the Advancement of Psychoanalysis offered this practical guide to understanding the entire psychoanalytic process. The book includes discussion on the responsibilities of the patient, as well as the limitations of psychoanalysis.

Kelman, H. (Ed.). (1967). *Feminine psychology*. New York, NY: W. W. Norton & Company.

Kelman's wonderful collection includes Horney's fifteen major publications on feminine psychology, presented in chronological order. In addition, Kelman provides an excellent introduction, which offers a brief biography of Horney, with special emphasis on her orientation to Freud's theories.

Kelman, H. (1971). *Helping people: Karen Horney's psychoanalytic approach*. New York, NY: Science House.
Rubins, J. L. (1978). *Karen Horney: Gentle rebel of psychoanalysis*. New York, NY: The Dial Press.

Harold Kelman was a friend and colleague of Horney for a number of years, following in her footsteps as Dean of the American Institute for Psychoanalysis. His book provides a brief biography, followed by an extensive evaluation of her views on psychoanalysis. Jack Rubins knew Horney for five years prior to her death, and his biography provides a particularly helpful review of her work on feminine psychology.

Fromm, E. (1941). *Escape from freedom*. New York, NY: Holt, Rinehart and Winston.

In what is likely Fromm's most significant work, he attempts to explain why totalitarian dictatorships seem to arise so easily from free societies. Using insight derived from a psychodynamic perspective, Fromm described how the people in a society might become anxious about the alienation that can be associated with freedom. Consequently, they seek connection and belonging by any means, even Fascism.

Fromm, E. (1956). *The art of loving*. New York, NY: Harper & Row.

This fairly brief book, which is partly academic and partly a self-help book, quickly became very popular, selling many millions of copies around the world. Clearly Fromm touched on a deep and universal need, and in so doing he offered practical advice on how to enrich one's life by learning to love both oneself and others.

Fromm, E. & Maccoby, M. (1970). *Social character in a Mexican village: A sociopsychoanalytic study*. Englewood Cliffs, NJ: Prentice-Hall.

In this amazing sociological/psychoanalytic study of an entire village in Mexico, Fromm and Maccoby provided support for Fromm's theories and the applicability of psychoanalysis to many people, even in diverse cultures. In addition, they demonstrated the interactive relationship between individuals, communities, and society as a whole, in the development of an individual's character.

Fromm, E. & Xirau, R. (1968). *The nature of man*. New York, NY: The Macmillan Company.

This extraordinary book includes many brief passages on the nature of man, written by some of the greatest minds in human history. To cite just a few: Gotama Buddha, Socrates, Plato, Lucretius, Meister Eckhart, Martin Luther, Rene Descartes, Friedrich Nietzsche, William James, and Jean-Paul Sartre.

Suzuki, D. T., Fromm, E., & De Martino, R. (1960). *Zen Buddhism & psychoanalysis*. New York, NY: Harper & Brothers.

In this classic text, D. T. Suzuki provides a very readable overview of the nature and focus of Zen. Fromm then compares Zen to psychoanalysis, and vice versa. Interestingly, Fromm considered psychoanalysis to be as uniquely Western as Zen is uniquely Eastern. He also believed that psychoanalysis could benefit from an understanding of Zen, a practice and philosophy that has existed much longer.

Funk, R. (1982). ***Erich Fromm: The courage to be human.*** **New York, NY: Continuum.**
Funk, R. (2000). ***Erich Fromm - His life and ideas: An illustrated biography.*** **New York, NY: Continuum.**

Rainer Funk was Fromm's assistant for the last six years of his life, and then became the literary executor of Fromm's estate. In *The Courage to be Human* he provides a brief biography of Fromm, followed by an extensive discussion of Fromm's theories and their relation to the philosophies and theories of others. The illustrated biography provides, of course, both an interesting biography and many wonderful photographs.

Herrigel, E. (1953). ***Zen in the Art of Archery.*** **New York, NY: Vintage Spiritual Classics.**

Eugen Herrigel was a German philosophy professor teaching in Tokyo. After spending six years studying archery as a path to understanding Zen, he wrote this marvelous book, which provides a very intimate look into the practice of Zen. The book is easy to understand, and fairly short, making for a quick and enjoyable read. It was a favorite of both Horney and Fromm, and the introduction was written by D. T. Suzuki.

Chapter 9 - The Psychology of Women, the Stone Center Group, and Human Relations

Although Karen Horney was the first female psychoanalyst to openly challenge Sigmund Freud's theories regarding the psychology of women, she abandoned this line of work when she came to the conclusion that culture was a more significant issue than gender in determining the psychology of women. Of course, that decision is based on separating gender from culture, which is not something that everyone would agree with. In the 1970s, the Stone Center was established, as a group of pioneering women began the work that led to a theory on the personality development and psychology of women based on a combination of seeking and forming relationships within a cultural context. This work continues today, and the theory is being expanded to include the personality development of all people, women and men.

However, not all female theorists have separated themselves so clearly from Freud's basic theories. One of those women holds a special place in the history of psychology, since she was instrumental in helping both Sigmund and Anna Freud escape Austria as the Nazi regime came to power. Her name was Marie Bonaparte. Bonaparte was a princess, a great-grandniece of Emperor Napoleon I of France, a patient and student of Sigmund Freud, and in 1953 she wrote *Female Sexuality* (Bonaparte, 1953). Her perspective on women closely followed a traditional Freudian view. In contrast, Nancy Chodorow's feminist perspective has significantly separated her perspective on the psychology women from that of Freud. Still, Chodorow has worked to combine feminist and psychoanalytic perspectives, in a manner similar to the object relations theories put forth by the Neo-Freudians, and she has focused on the unique female experience of mothering.

We will begin this chapter by examining the work of Princess Bonaparte, as an example of a female theorist who remained true to Freud's own theories. Then, we will examine the alternative presented by the members of the Stone Center group. Finally, this chapter will conclude with a brief look at Chodorow's efforts to combine the psychoanalytic and feminist perspectives.

Feminine Psychology in the Freudian Tradition

Although Sigmund Freud believed that female psychology was the result of an incomplete and frustrated male development, he also acknowledged that he did not fully understand the psychology of women. A particularly interesting passage can be found in his *New Introductory Lectures on Psycho-Analysis*:

> One might consider characterizing femininity psychologically as giving preference to passive aims. This is not, of course, the same thing as passivity; to achieve a passive aim may call for a large amount of activity...we must beware in this of underestimating the influence of social customs, which similarly force women into passive situations. All this is still far from being cleared up… (pgs. 143-144; Freud, 1933/1965)

So, Freud did suggest the possibility that cultural factors (social customs) play a role in the development of girls and women. Furthermore, he acknowledged that there was much more to learn about these developmental processes. Freud ended his lecture on femininity with the following:

> That is all I had to say to you about femininity. It is certainly incomplete and fragmentary and does not always sound friendly. But do not forget that I have only been describing women in so far as their nature is determined by their sexual function. It is true that that influence extends very far; but we do not overlook the fact that an individual woman may be a human being in other respects as well. If you want to know more about femininity, enquire from your own experiences of life, or turn to the poets, or wait until science can give you deeper and more coherent information. (pg. 167; Freud 1933/1965)

Published in 1933, this was one of the last times Freud wrote about femininity and the psychology of women. Always the scientist, Freud suggested that future research will provide a better understanding of this topic. The Stone Center group, whose work we will encounter shortly, is perhaps the most complete effort made toward fulfilling Freud's expectations. First, however, let's consider the interesting work of Princess Marie Bonaparte, as one of the female psychodynamic theorists who adhered closely to Freud's perspective.

Princess Marie Bonaparte

Marie Bonaparte (1882-1962), Her Royal Highness Princess George of Greece, was a patient, student, and dear friend of Sigmund Freud. She was the great-grandniece of Napoleon Bonaparte, Emperor of France, and she married Prince George of Greece in 1907. As a wealthy aristocrat, she was able to help both Freud himself and the financially struggling International Psychoanalytic Publishing House (known more commonly as the *Verlag*, from its name in German). It was Marie Bonaparte who paid a ransom to the Nazis in Austria in order to secure Freud's release as World War II approached. Earlier, she had used her wealth to help support the Verlag, which Freud had established to provide a means for publishing a variety of works on psychoanalysis (Gay, 1998; Jones, 1957). However, Bonaparte was far more than just a wealthy colleague.

Bonaparte shared Freud's interest in antiquities, and often helped him find the best pieces for his collection (M. Freud, 1983). She also loved dogs, particularly Chows, and Freud came to love that breed as well. As Freud, his wife Martha, and their daughter Anna waited to escape Austria in 1938, Freud and Anna spent some of their time translating books and articles into German. One of those books was entitled *Topsy*, written by Bonaparte about her favorite dog (M. Freud, 1983; Jones, 1957). But it was not just a simple matter of waiting to leave Austria. In a particularly poignant story, Martin Freud described the time when his sister Anna was arrested by the Gestapo. Bonaparte was with her, and demanded to be arrested as well. However, at that point in time the Nazis were still intimidated by members of the royal houses of Europe, and Anna Freud was taken alone. She was released later, but Freud is said to have paced all day in his house worrying about her (M. Freud, 1983). When the Freud family finally left Austria for England, only Bonaparte was able to safely transfer their gold out of the country. She did so by sending the gold to the king of Greece, who then sent it to the Greek embassy in London (Jones, 1957). Thus, Freud and his family were financially secure upon reaching London, and Freud was able to repay the ransom that Bonaparte had paid for his release.

Bonaparte also served the field of psychoanalysis in an important way other than her own work. Early in Freud's career, during the time when he underwent his own psychoanalysis, he had a very close friend named Wilhelm Fliess. So close were these friends, and at such a critical time in Freud's career, that their correspondence contained a great many intimate details. In addition to personal correspondence, Freud sent many scientific notes about his theory to Fliess. When Fliess died in 1931, his widow asked Freud to return the letters Fliess had written to Freud. However, Freud had destroyed all of them years earlier, and he wanted her to do the same to his letters. However, she chose to sell the letters to a bookseller. The bookseller then sold them to Bonaparte. When Bonaparte told Freud that she had them, he insisted that she destroy them. She refused, however, and those letters eventually became available to the fields of psychology and psychiatry (Gay, 1998; Jones, 1953).

As Bonaparte became involved in psychoanalysis professionally, Freud both admired and supported her work (Gay, 1998; Jones, 1957). In a letter to Bonaparte after Freud had reviewed her paper on psychoanalysis and time, Freud wrote "The work does you honor." (cited in Jones, 1957). She was also active in establishing the growing field as a whole. She had helped to establish a psychoanalytic society in France, and Freud later nominated her to be vice-president of the International Psychoanalytic Association. In nominating her, Freud considered her a worthy candidate:

> ...not "only because one can show her off to the outside world," but because she "is a person of high intelligence, of masculine capacity for work, has done fine papers, is wholly devoted to the cause, and, as is well known, also in a position to lend material aid. She has now become 50 years old, will probably turn away increasingly from her private interests and steep herself in analytic work. I need not mention that she alone keeps the Fr[ench] group together." (pg. 586; cited in Gay, 1998).

Female Sexuality

Bonaparte first met Freud as a patient seeking help with her **frigidity**. The psychoanalysis does not appear to have been successful, but the experience did provide Bonaparte with a new goal in life (Gay, 1998).

Given the nature of her own problems, it should not be surprising that her writings on psychoanalysis focused on sexuality. *Female Sexuality* is a wide-ranging book that draws heavily on Freud's work, but also relies on the works of Horney and Klein. In addition, she mentions Adler in a somewhat favorable light, though she concludes that both Freud and Adler failed to fully understand female sexuality (as they themselves acknowledged). Still, she bases most of her work on a paper of the same title written by Freud in 1931, although she attempts to describe the development of girls and women more thoroughly and with more consideration given to potential alternatives.

Bonaparte began by describing three types of women. The so-called "true women" are those who have succeeded in substituting the desire for a penis (penis envy) with a desire to have children (particularly a son); their sexuality is normal, vaginal, and maternal. They are known as **acceptives**. The second type, the **renouncers**, gives up all competition with men, fail to seek external love objects, and live largely unfulfilled lives. The **claimers**, however, deny reality and cling to both psychical and organic male elements present in all women. While it may appear to us today that the claimers are asserting themselves as being proud to be female, Bonaparte considered this position to cause an inability to adapt to one's erotic function. As Freud had described, in order for a girl to develop, she must transfer both her love object (from mother to father) and her erotogenic zone (from clitoris to vagina). According to Bonaparte, claimers who will not transfer their love object will become lesbians, those who do not transfer their erotogenic zone will never achieve fully satisfying sexual relationships as adults. In other words, they will be frigid. Evidence of the psychical nature of the problem of frigidity can be seen in the responsiveness of patients to psychoanalysis. Patients who are totally frigid, those who experience no pleasure in sexual activity, often respond well to psychoanalysis. However, women who are partially frigid, those who have more specifically not transferred their erotogenic zone from the clitoris to the vagina, tend to be very resistant to psychoanalysis. According to Bonaparte, partial frigidity is much more common than total frigidity. Partial frigidity is also much more common than men realize, since many women hide this reality by pretending to enjoy sexual activity.

In agreement with Freud, Bonaparte considers boys and girls to begin their sexual lives equally, in an oral erotic stage focused on the mother's breast. As they transition into the anal stage, there are the beginnings of a contrast between active and passive forces: the expulsion of feces vs. the retention of feces. The important activity of toilet training begins in this stage, and so social conditioning is also coming into play. Although Bonaparte, like Freud, continued to emphasize biological factors in sexual development, the acknowledgement that sociocultural factors related to toilet training come into play lays the foundation for girls being pushed toward the passive role that strict Freudians believe they must play.

In the transition from the anal stage to the phallic stage, the interplay between active and passive forces that were present during the anal stage takes a different direction in boys and girls. Very simply, since the boys penis actively protrudes, and his love object can continue to be his mother (or, later, other women as substitutes), the boy will develop an active relationship with the world around him. Girls, however, ultimately need to transfer their sexuality from the clitoris (which had been related to a small penis until this point) to the vagina, a passive organ with regard to sexuality. Girls must also transfer their love object to their father (or, later, to other men), and accept the physical penetration that is required for sexual intercourse. In this manner, according to Freud, Bonaparte, and others, boys grow into aggressive men and girls grow into passive women. Provided, of course, that women accept their role.

Adding to the complexity of this process for girls, who need to transfer the libidinal cathexes from both the clitoris and the love object of mother, is the consequence of when the girl first experiences an orgasm. Since this potentially can occur at any time during the dynamic processes of transferring these libidinal cathexes, the first orgasm can have a variety of either positive or negative effects. For boys it is simply easier, since the penis is the one obvious source of sexual pleasure, and the boy never has to transfer his love object away from women (though it should transfer from the mother to another woman). This difference in sexual development is summed up by Bonaparte:

> It is on these diverse superimposed courses that the edifice of female sexuality rises. Constitutional factors are its foundation, and life builds thereon. Finally, we see the feminine psychosexual structure in its main varieties, varieties more multiform even than those to which male sexuality is susceptible, centered as it is on the phallus, that highly differentiated organ developed to serve the male erotic function. (pg. 140; Bonaparte, 1953)

As an interesting side note, Bonaparte also discussed some of the research that had been done up to that point in time on female circumcision/mutilation, particularly in primitive cultures. She speculated on how psychoanalytic theories of sexuality might apply to those practices, and how societies today might compare to primitive cultures that have retained such practices. Can we really say that things have changed since Bonaparte wrote the following passage?

> It would appear that humans, living in communities, cannot dispense with sexual repression of some kind and that, if it has not succeeded in coming from within, it must go on coming from without. (pg. 157; Bonaparte, 1953)

Before we turn our attention to the Stone Center group, I would like to mention something that may have already entered your mind. This book is about personality, not sexuality. While it may be true that sexuality is an important part of life, it is certainly not the same thing as one's personality. Unless, of course, you happen to be a strict Freudian theorist, as was Bonaparte. She does tend to equate the psychology of women with their sexuality. The psychologists of the Stone Center group, however, have moved beyond this biased view of the psychology of women.

Discussion Question: In keeping with Freud's original theory, Bonaparte believed that sexual development is much more difficult for girls than it is boys. Do you agree with that, and if you do, what is it that makes things so much more difficult for girls? Are there any unique challenges that only boys face?

Placing the Psychology of Women in Context: Sexism vs. Feminism

Sigmund Freud developed a theory of female sexuality that helped to explain his observation that most people in psychoanalysis were women. Karen Horney agreed that women suffer more than men, but she placed the blame on men, and the patriarchal culture that maintains special privileges for men only. Despite the fact that Freud and Adler admitted that they did not fully understand women, and that there were many women among the neo-Freudians, it was a long time before a unique perspective on the psychology of women developed.

In contrast to women like Princess Bonaparte and Helene Deutsch, the first leading female member of the Vienna Psychoanalytic Society (the very first female member, Hermine von Hug-Hellmuth, was murdered in 1924; Deutsch, 1973, Sayers, 1991) and the first person to devote an entire book to the psychology of women (a two volume set published in consecutive years; Deutsch, 1944, 1945), Jean Baker Miller and her colleagues at the Stone Center developed a unique theory on the psychological development and personality of women. Although their theory, based on personal relationships and culture, developed in part as a result of increasing interest in feminist studies in the 1960s and 1970s, the work that continues today strives to include the personality development of all people (women and men).

There are some women, however, who believe that a feminist perspective can be combined more readily with Freud's basic ideas (see, e.g., Mitchell, 2000). Nancy Chodorow has worked to combine both psychodynamic and feminist ideas into a comprehensive theory. Although the result is basically an object relations theory, Chodorow's work has been reserved for this chapter due to her inclusion of the feminist side of the perspective.

It is also important to note that the work of the Stone Center group and Nancy Chodorow is much more contemporary than that of Bonaparte, Deutsch, and many of the neo-Freudians discussed in this book (most of whom are no longer alive). Thus, the development of feminist perspectives on the psychology of women continues today.

Human Relations and a Modern Perspective on the Psychology of Women

Despite the valuable contributions of women included among the neo-Freudians, and Horney's suggestion of womb envy as a powerful counterpart to penis envy, theories on the psychology of women remained framed within a psychodynamic perspective. Until, that is, the 1970s, when Jean Baker Miller and a group of women colleagues created a revolution in our potential understanding of the psychology of women.

Jean Baker Miller and the Stone Center Group

In 1974, Wellesley College in Massachusetts established the Center for Research on Women, and in 1981, the Stone Center for Developmental Services and Studies was established. Working in collaboration as the Wellesley Centers for Women (WCW), the Center for Research on Women conducts a variety of interdisciplinary studies on matters related to gender equity, while the Stone Center focuses on psychological well-being and a comprehensive understanding of human development, particularly the psychological development of women. A wide range of information on the WCW can be found on their website (http://www.wcwonline.org).

Jean Baker Miller (1927-present) was a practicing psychoanalyst who had already written one book on the psychoanalysis of women when she published *Toward a New Psychology of Women* (Miller, 1976). This book has been credited with nothing less than changing the very way in which we study the psychology of women. Since the earliest work of Sigmund Freud, women were seen as inferior, and so-called feminine attributes (e.g., vulnerability, weakness, emotionality, helping others; see Miller, 1976) were seen as psychologically weak. Miller and her colleagues at the Stone Center have worked hard to change that perspective. Typically working in collaboration, publishing collections of writing in books such as *Women's Growth in Connection* (Jordan, Kaplan, Miller, Stiver, & Surrey, 1991), *Women's Growth in Diversity* (Jordan, 1997b), and *The Complexity of Connection* (Jordan, Walker, & Hartling, 2004), they developed a relational model of human development that focuses on **connections, disconnections, mutuality,** and **empathy**. Examples of how relationships can be damaged when one person seeks connection but the other person seeks to disconnect are all around us. Miller presented an example from a patient she identified as Doris. Doris was trying to share with her husband how upset she was after a day of finding it very difficult to deal with her colleagues at work:

> He listened for about ten minutes. That's about his limit. Then he said, "Aw, don't let the bastards upset you." That's just the sort of thing I suspect. It sounds fine and even supportive. But it really means, "Shut up. I've heard enough." (pg. 100; Miller, 1976)

More recently, as members of the Stone Center became increasingly aware of the role of culture in development, the relational model evolved into the **relational-cultural theory** (RCT) of human development (Jordan & Walker, 2004). The inclusion of culture in the theory should not be underestimated or taken for granted. Psychological theories are not immune from the bias inherent in societies that seek to maintain their hierarchical power structures. Western societies are highly individualistic, and when individuality is favored in our theories the result can be unfortunate:

> In a culture that valorizes separation and autonomy, persons with cultural privilege can falsely appear more self-sufficient and so will be judged as healthier, more mature, more worthy of the privilege the society affords. Those who enjoy less cultural privilege (whether by virtue of race, ethnicity, sexual orientation, or economic status) will more likely be viewed as deficient and needy. They are more likely to be subject to systematic disadvantage and culture shaming. (pgs. 4-5; Jordan & Walker, 2004)

Relational-Cultural Theory

Miller established the foundation of RCT by addressing two fundamental differences in status and power that are part of human life: the differences between children and adults, and the differences between boys/men and girls/women. Children lack the privileges of adulthood, but this is temporary, and it is the role of parents and other adults (e.g., teachers) to help children grow up. In most modern cultures, women have typically lacked the privileges of men, and to a large extent that continues today. Since male/female differences are permanent, cultural phenomena usually develop in which men seek to maintain their power and status over women. This is the reason why psychology, a field traditionally dominated by men, has equated feminine attributes with psychological pathology (Miller, 1976). Curiously, not only men participate in this bias. Anna Freud did not challenge her father's views on girls and women, Melanie Klein claimed to be closer to Freud's point of view than even his daughter was, and Marie Bonaparte believed that women who do not accept the role defined for them by men would never be able to experience sexual satisfaction. It is not uncommon for a subordinate group to participate in this adaptive role, according to Miller, and as a result women may have gained their greatest advantage: the responsibility, and with it the privilege, of the intense emotional connection necessary to raise a child (Miller, 1976).

Considering the primary object relation necessary for a child to grow and thrive, the relationship between a mother and her infant, a relationship in which the mother serves the child first, many feminine attributes take on new meaning. Vulnerability, weakness, helplessness, emotionality, participating in the development of others, cooperation, and creativity are all essential to giving oneself over to others, which is necessary to care for a baby, while at the same time allowing that baby to develop its own sense of mastery over the world and its own sense of individuality. Should it be surprising that women want to relate to other adults in the same way? According to Miller, one of the greatest difficulties men face in relationships with women is that men actually want to reclaim those very same elements of personality that men have delegated to women, and that gave rise to the woman's defined role in society. In accomplishing this task, as women advance their own place within society, men will have to adapt their coping strategies (Miller, 1976).

Now let us consider the essential elements of RCT. In RCT, the concept of object relations is viewed in light of connections vs. disconnections. People seek connections: family, friends, clubs, church groups, neighbors, the list goes on. Very few people live in isolation, and fewer still want it that way. But this raises a question about the meaning of the word "self." If a woman's experience is based on connections, do women develop a sense of self, and what is the nature of that self? Miller (1991) suggests that we don't get caught up in technicalities regarding the words we use to define this construct, but simply accept an open-minded definition of self. It appears to her that boys do develop a more clearly delineated sense of self, whereas girls may develop a more encompassing sense of self. Women do talk more about relationships, but not because they want or need to be either dependent or independent. Women simply want to be in relationships with others, to be connected. Looking more closely at the meaning of being "dependent" in a relationship, Stiver (1991) suggests that women often adopt a role of apparent dependence in relationships with men in order to connect with them in a manner acceptable to the man's gender role perspective. It does not appear to her that women are any more dependent in relationships than men, but when they do seek connection they do so by whatever means necessary. So when it is necessary for forming connections, Stiver considers "to depend" on another as part of an interpersonal dynamic:

> I would like to define dependency as: A process of counting on other people to provide help in coping physically and emotionally with the experiences and tasks encountered in the world when one has not sufficient skill, confidence, energy, and/or time. I have defined it as a process to stress that it is not static but changes with opportunities, circumstances, and inner struggles. (pg. 160; Stiver, 1991)

Making successful connections involves two other important processes: mutuality and empathy. These closely related constructs come into play in meaningful relationships. Mutuality refers to both participants (or more, as the case may be) in a relationship being fully engaged in the connection. Each person is interested in and aware of the other, they are willing and able to share their thoughts, feelings, and needs, they do not manipulate each other, they value the connection, and they are open to change. Perhaps most importantly, they also experience empathy with other persons (Jordan, 1991a). Empathy, according to Jordan (1991b), is "an understanding of that aspect of the self that involves we-ness, transcendence of the separate, disconnected self." Jordan acknowledges a connection between her views and those of Kohut, who considered empathy an essential aspect of the mirroring that helps an infant to first see itself through the eyes of another as it plays with its mother (see also Mitchell & Black, 1995; Strozier, 2001). Empathy is a complex cognitive and emotional process necessary for a sense of separateness within connection, and self-empathy is an important therapeutic construct (Jordan, 1991b). Interactions of such intimacy are not new to object relations theory, but are usually only considered in the context of the earliest relationship between mother and child. RCT considers mutuality and empathy as essential attributes of connections made by adults, particularly connections made by women. An often overlooked consideration is that mutuality and empathy need to be taught and learned. For example, Winnicott's "good enough mother" does not simply appear when a child is born (Surrey, 1991).

> **Discussion Question:** Relational-cultural theory proposes that people seek connections in their lives, such as family, friends, church groups, clubs, etc. What groups do you consider yourself to be a member of, and how important to you is that membership? Do you, or people you know, consider the groups they belong to as more important than themselves?

According to relational-cultural theory (RCT), women seek connections in their lives, and support each other with mutuality and empathy. These attributes have helped women in their role as the primary caregivers for our children. However, as a cultural theory, RCT suggests that these so-called feminine attributes are the result of gender roles, not some inherent difference between males and females. [Image by Mark Kelland]

The source of most suffering in life, according to RCT, is disconnection. An acute disconnection can often be recognized by the loss of energy in the moment. This may be followed by negative emotions, such as sadness, anger, or depression. There may be a heightened sense of self-consciousness and relational awareness may slow down, we may even become immobilized (Jordan, 2004). After repeated disconnections we may become fearful of turning to others for help and support, even when we need it most. This has been referred to as the **central paradox of connection/disconnection**. When we hurt someone we love, or are hurt by someone we love, the conflict often leads to withdrawal and the development of **strategies of disconnection**. As a consequence of this ongoing process, although we all share a desire to connect with others, those who have been hurt by loved ones believe that they can connect with others only if they hold back part of themselves when they try to connect. Within the context of RCT, this desire for connection, while holding back from it, is also known as the **central relational paradox** (Miller et al., 2004).

This may very well be a significant factor in the fact that so many marriages end in divorce. Marriage is probably the most significant connection that adults in Western cultures choose to make, and so divorce would also be the most significant disconnection. There is certainly no easy answer for the high divorce rate, but an interesting possibility has been suggested by Harville Hendrix, who specializes in marital therapy. Hendrix (1988) believes that we choose a mate based on the unconscious recognition of characteristics they have in common with our parents, and that we hope through marriage to solve the psychological and emotional damage we suffered as children. In other words, we think we are connecting with our spouse, but we really want to reconnect with our parents. Unfortunately, this creates a false connection, a connection that cannot easily be resolved, especially given the apparently different communication styles of men and women (Gray, 1997, 1999, 2002, 2004; Vincent, 2006).

So how do we resolve problems of disconnection? Relational therapy is based on the idea that a therapist can provide a relationship in which the patient can experience connection, mutuality, and empathy. In looking at the therapeutic approaches of people like Sigmund Freud, Winnicott, and Kohut, Judith Jordan (1997a) argues that the actual engagement in the therapeutic relationship is aloof and disconnected. She feels that an obvious and overlooked aspect of therapy is that the more engaged the therapist is the more one enhances the self, the other, and the relationship. Consequently, the therapeutic relationship can enhance one's capacity to be more whole, real, and integrated in other relationships as well. This relational perspective, which provides the basis for relational therapy, is based on three principles:

1. That people grow in, through, and toward relationships.
2. For women in particular, connection with others is central to psychological well-being.
3. Movement toward relational mutuality can occur throughout life, through mutual empathy, responsiveness, and contribution to the growth of each individual and to the relationship. (Jordan, 1997a)

Once again we see the importance of empathy. Empathy involves more than just sharing the other person's feelings, it stresses the capacity to "feel into" the other person's experience (Jordan, 1997a; Mitchell & Black, 1995). Kohut emphasized the importance of empathy, as did the humanistic psychologist Carl Rogers. In contrast to empathy, the emphasis that has existed in therapy on the autonomous self as the "real self" can result in the creation of pathologically isolated individuals, individuals who feel self-sufficient, but who are really disconnected from others. Relational therapy does not focus on the self, but rather on relationships. To accomplish this goal, the therapist must be willing to respond to their patients in an authentic manner (Miller, Jordan, Stiver, Walker, Surrey, & Eldridge, 2004). If the therapist can convey to the patient that they are moved, the patient will be moved, knowing that her/his thoughts and feelings have reached another person, they do matter, and they can be part of a mutual experience. This is connection, and appears to be the key source of change in relational therapy (Miller et al., 2004).

Discussion Question: Relational therapy focuses on providing an environment for the patient to experience connection, empathy, and mutuality. It requires an engaged therapist. What are your ideas about how therapy should be conducted?

Connections Across Cultures: Janet Surrey and Eastern Perspectives on Human Relations

Janet Surrey is one of the founding members of the Stone Center group, and for over 20 years she has been working to synthesize Buddhist mindfulness with relational-cultural theory and relational therapy. Most people think of mindfulness meditation as a solitary activity, but at its core is a desire to connect with the universal spirit that we all share. So, from the latter perspective, mindfulness meditation fosters a deep connection with others. Connecting with others is also at the core of relational therapy (with disconnection seen as the primary cause of suffering in life). Thus, the practice of mindfulness meditation can enhance the connections sought in relational therapy, and relational therapy can enhance one's attention to the present moment in both relational therapy and in one's everyday relationships.

Of particular value for the therapist, the practice of mindfulness meditation can deepen one's empathic skills. According to Surrey, during a mindfulness-informed therapy session the skilled therapist is attentive to their own sensations, feelings, thoughts, and memories as the patient is describing the same psychological phenomena. This helps the therapist to both experience the patient and attend to the flow of the relationship. Thus, the therapist can be fully aware of the shifting qualities of the connections and disconnections within the therapeutic relationship. Although therapists typically rely on verbal interaction, the practice of mindfulness offers a unique opportunity to experience a conscious silence. Just such a rare opportunity for silence in one's busy life can be created in the genuine connection that results from a healthy and meaningful relationship (Surrey, 2005).

Surrey is by no means alone in drawing connections between Buddhist mindfulness and either the value of relationships or relational forms of therapy. His Holiness the Dalai Lama has emphasized that human beings cannot live in isolation, our very nature is that we are social animals. Our communities, indeed our entire society, require us to live cooperatively. This cooperation is best accomplished through love and compassion. It is not enough, however, to care only for those who care for us. When we harbor negative emotions toward those whom we do not like, those negative emotions harm ourselves. Thus, the Dalai Lama considers it essential to cultivate equanimity, the ability to care for everyone equally, no matter whom they may be (Dalai Lama, 2001, 2002). Likewise, the widely respected Buddhist monk Thich Nhat Hanh (nominated for a Nobel Peace Prize by Martin Luther King, Jr.) stresses the importance of practicing mindfulness within a supportive group, and then extending the compassion that arises to all others (Thich Nhat Hanh, 1995, 1999).

Within the field of psychology, the well-known therapist/authors Jon Kabat-Zinn, who developed the *Mindfulness Based Stress Reduction* program, and Steven Hayes, the founder of Acceptance and Commitment Therapy, have emphasized the importance of relationships with other people and the world around us, as well as how mindfulness can help to enhance those relationships (Hayes, 2004; Hayes et al., 1999; Kabat-Zinn, 1990). In addition, personal relationships appear to be particularly important for a variety of groups in American society, including: African Americans (Belgrave & Allison, 2006; Cook & Wiley, 2000; Taylor et al., 2004), Native Americans (Axelson, 1999; Trujillo, 2000), aged individuals (Belsky, 1999; Hillier & Barrow, 1999), and those who are dying (Kubler-Ross, 1969, 1983). Indeed, the ability to form and maintain healthy relationships has been identified as a vitally important human strength and an important aspect of well-being (Berscheid, 2003; Cantor, 2003; Cloninger, 2004; Sears, 2003). Thus, by examining cross-cultural factors that aid in developing and maintaining healthy relationships and, therefore, a healthy personality, we can continue to move toward a psychology that benefits us all.

Nancy Chodorow's Psychoanalytic Feminism and the Role of Mothering

In 1974, Juliet Mitchell suggested that Freudian psychoanalysis offered an important means for understanding the psychology of women, and that feminism should embrace Freud's theoretical perspective. She did not suggest that Freud was necessarily right about the psychological development of women, but she did emphasize the importance of object relations theory and the interactions between mothers, their children, and families as a whole (Mitchell, 2000). Some 50 years earlier, Helene Deutsch had suggested that women do not seek to become mothers due to penis envy, but rather they want to replace passive femininity with an active role as a woman and mother (Deutsch was analyzed and trained by Sigmund Freud himself; Deutsch, 1944, 1945, 1973, Sayers, 1991). Deutsch (1973) wrote that she had great admiration for Marie Bonaparte as a person and a scholar (Deutsch knew Bonaparte personally), but Deutsch found little of interest in Bonaparte's strict application of Freudian theory to the psychology of women. The person best known today for attempting to combine elements of Freud's theory with an objective perspective on a psychology of women is Nancy Chodorow (1944-present), a sociologist and psychoanalyst who has focused on the special relationship between mothers and daughters.

In 1978, Chodorow published *The Reproduction of Mothering*. Twenty years later, she wrote a new preface for the second edition, in which she had the advantage of looking back at both the success of her book and the criticism that it drew from some. Chodorow acknowledged that many feminists felt obliged to choose between a biologically-based psychology of women and mothering (the essential Freudian perspective) versus a view in which the psychology of women and their feelings about mothering were determined by social structure and cultural mandate. Chodorow believed that social structure and culture were important, but she insisted nonetheless that the biological differences between males and females could not be dismissed. Indeed, they lead to an essential difference in the mother-daughter relationship as compared to the mother-son relationship (Chodorow, 1999a).

According to Chodorow, when a woman becomes a mother, the most important aspect of her relationship with any daughter is the recognition that they are alike. Thus, her daughter can also become a mother someday. This special connection is felt by the daughter and incorporated into her psyche, or ego. It is important to remember that much of this is happening at an unconscious level. It is not as if women choose to favor their daughters over their sons, and it is not as if women reject their sons. Chodorow argues that it just simply happens, because of the biological similarity between females. As a consequence of this special relationship, daughters are subtly shaped in ways that lead to what we often think of as feminine attributes: a sense of **self-in-relation**, feeling connected to others, being able to empathize, and being embedded in or dependent on relationships. For

Chodorow, the internalization of the mother-daughter relationship, from the daughter's point of view, is the development of a most important object relation. As adults, many women feel a desire to have children, which is often described as a maternal instinct or a biological drive (the feeling that their "biological clock" is ticking). As an alternative, Chodorow suggests that these feelings have instead been shaped by the unconscious fantasies and emotions associated with the woman's internal relationship to her own mother (Chodorow, 1999a).

In contrast to the development of daughters, Chodorow suggests that sons are influenced by the essential feelings of difference conveyed by their mother. Consequently, and in contrast to women, men grow up asserting their independence, and they will be anxious about intimacy if it signals dependence on another. In addition, within the cultural framework of society, men develop a greater concern with being masculine than women are concerned with their femininity (Chodorow, 1999a).

The cultural differences between men and women, as well as the early childhood differences in their relationships with their parents, create problems for the typical family structure. Since men tend to avoid relationships, they are unlikely to fulfill the relational needs that women have. In addition, young girls most likely experience their relationship with their father within the context of their relationship with their mother, whereas young boys have a more direct two-person relationship with their mother (in terms of heterosexual relationships; Chodorow, 1999a). Therefore, in order for a woman to balance the relational triangle she experienced with her mother and father, and the subsequent intrapsychic object-relational structure she developed, she needs to have a child. In other words, by having children, women can "reimpose intrapsychic relational structure on the social world," and they can relate to the father of their child in terms of a family structure they were familiar with in childhood. Furthermore, having a child recreates the intimacy a woman shared with her own mother.

One critique of *The Reproduction of Mothering* that Chodorow agreed with was her emphasis on a universal mother-daughter experience, within a heterosexual nuclear family. In her later writings, Chodorow emphasized individual subjectivity, still in relation to others, but also within a wider range of family structures and individual situations (Chodorow, 1989, 1994, 1999b). She felt that a balance between the principles of psychoanalysis and an understanding of culture was the best overall approach:

> A psychoanalysis that begins with the immediacy of unconscious fantasy and feeling found in the clinical encounter illuminates our understanding of individual subjectivity and potentially transforms all sociocultural thought...At the same time, feminist, anthropological, and other cultural theories require that psychoanalysts take seriously the ways in which cultural meanings intertwine with and help to constitute psychic life. (pg. 274; Chodorow, 1999b)

Personality Theory in Real Life: The Experience of Mothering

When Helene Deutsch wrote the first books devoted entirely to the psychology of women, the second volume was devoted entirely to *Motherhood* (Deutsch, 1945). She described motherhood as providing a wonderful opportunity to directly experience a sense of immortality. She distinguished, however, between **motherhood** and **motherliness**. Motherhood, according to Deutsch, refers to the relationship between mother and child, which varies from individual to individual and from culture to culture. When Deutsch wrote of motherliness, she referred to both a quality of character that pervades a woman's whole personality and emotional phenomena related to a child's helplessness and need for care. In a motherly woman, one's own need for love is transferred from the ego to the child, and this maternal love has the chief characteristic of **tenderness** (Deutsch, 1945). Of course, no two women experience motherhood in exactly the same way. Deutsch recognized two primary types of mothers. The first type is the woman whose world is opened to a new reality by the birth of a child. She feels no loss, and she develops her own personality fully only after having a child. The second type of mother feels restricted and impoverished by her children. Such women, according to Deutsch, have spent their emotionality on other pursuits (such as sexuality, or a career), and they lack sufficient libido to withstand the emotional burden of children:

> The woman's relation to her husband and family, her economic situation, and the

> position of the child in her existence, give a personal color to each woman's motherliness. (pg. 55; Deutsch, 1945)

Deutsch had several miscarriages in the early years of her marriage, causing her a great deal of anxiety during the pregnancy that finally gave her a son named Martin. In her autobiography, she speaks both fondly and proudly of her only child, as well as of the wonderful relationship he shared with his father. With regard to being a busy, working woman during her son's childhood, Deutsch wrote that this could only be worked out on individual basis, and with some necessary compromise (Deutsch, 1973).

Although fathers play a role in parenting, only a woman can really understand what it's like to be a mother. Two entertaining books written by mothers about their relationships with their children are *good-enough mother* (Syler, 2007) and *Mother Shock: Loving Every (Other) Minute of It* (Buchanan, 2003). In addition to stories about the joys of raising children, they also discuss the trials and tribulations as well. In accordance with the work of the Stone Center group, they also talk about how important it is for mothers, as women, to have meaningful relationships with friends both in and beyond their families. In a chapter entitled *mommy needs a playdate*, Syler writes:

> …behind every good-enough mother is another good-enough mother with whom to commiserate, shop, or just hang out and have a crab-fest. It's a healthy dose of friendship that fuels us to fight another day. (pg. 189; Syler, 2007)

But what happens when a woman is not a good mother? Christine Lawson has studied the mothering abilities of women who suffer from borderline personality disorder. In *Understanding the Borderline Mother* (2000), Lawson has identified four types of borderline mother: the waif (characterized by helplessness and hopelessness), the hermit (characterized by perfectionism and worrying), the queen (characterized by demanding attention and feelings of emptiness), and the witch (characterized by a desire for power and the very real threat of being physically abusive). The tragic challenge for the children of borderline mothers, according to Lawson, is that our mother is the first thing any of must understand in our lives, and our survival depends on understanding her. Although borderline personality is highly resistant to treatment in therapy, as with any personality disorder, therapy can help women with borderline personality disorder to avoid passing on the condition to their children.

While it is understandable that mothering would be difficult for women suffering from psychological disorders, it also appears to be true that no such thing as a "maternal instinct" exists. Anthropologist Sarah Hrdy, who has been elected to both the National Academy of Sciences and the American Academy of Arts and Sciences, has studied infanticide in different cultures and other primate species. She found it quite surprising that some mothers (human, ape, and monkey) will contribute to the death of their own child (or children), and in some cases then mate with the male that killed them. While this is a complex issue, covered by Hrdy in a rather lengthy book entitled *Mother Nature* (Hrdy, 1999), she raises some profound questions. For example, if women instinctively love their children, why do so many women directly or indirectly contribute to their deaths? Since fathers contribute equally to the genetic makeup of the child, why haven't fathers evolved a greater interest in and commitment to caring for their children? And perhaps most interestingly, "just why did these little creatures evolve to be so plump, engaging, and utterly adorable?" (Hrdy, 1999).

Consider your own mother and your relationship with her. Do you consider her to have been a good-enough mother? Whether you are a man or a woman, how has your relationship with your mother affected your relationships with others (especially if you have children)?

Discussion Question: Chodorow proposed that women desire to have children in order to recreate the intimacy they had with their mother when they were a baby, and to balance their relationship with their husband in a manner similar to how they first experienced their father. Does this suggestion seem reasonable, or do you think there may be a more fundamental biological drive

toward bearing offspring?

Review of Key Points

- Sigmund Freud acknowledged that he really did not fully understand female psychology.
- Within a strict Freudian paradigm, Marie Bonaparte described three types of women. There are women who accept their proper role in society, those who give up on meaningful relationships, and those who fight society. Bonaparte believed that the women who fight their role in society can never be fulfilled sexually.
- Bonaparte suggested that psychological development in boys is easier than it is for girls, since all children begin by loving a women (their mother), which is appropriate for boys. She also believed the physical structure of the penis made understanding sexuality easier for boys.
- Jean Baker Miller began addressing the differences in power and status that exist between boys/men and girls/women, and the cultural system that develop to maintain those differences.
- Since a woman must make major sacrifices to raise an infant, Miller believed that so-called feminine attributes are essential to accomplish that goal.
- According to Miller, and other theorists at the Stone Center, a woman's experience is based on connections with others. This led to the formation of relational-cultural theory.
- Empathy and mutuality are essential to forming successful connections.
- Problems arise when people become disconnected. Repeated disconnection can make individuals afraid to form connections, resulting in the central paradox of connection/disconnection.
- Relational therapy seeks to provide an opportunity for patients to experience empathy, mutuality, and connection. It requires therapists to become fully engaged in the therapeutic process.
- According to Chodorow, the mother-daughter relationship is special because the mother experiences her daughter(s) as similar to herself. The daughter incorporates this special relationship as a primary object relation.
- A woman's development of the special object relation regarding her mother leads to a need to balance her relational world by becoming a mother herself.
- Chodorow believed that since mothers experience their sons as different, boys begin to develop as more independent individuals.

Review of Key Terms

acceptives	disconnections	Relational-Cultural Theory
central paradox of connection/disconnection	empathy	renouncers
central relational paradox	frigidity	self-in-relation
claimers	motherhood	strategies of disconnection
connections	motherliness	tenderness
	mutuality	

Annotated Bibliography

Bonaparte, M. (1953). *Female sexuality*. New York, NY: Grove Press.

Some women today may find this book offensive, but it should still be an interesting book to read. It is an example of a very traditional Freudian perspective on sexuality, even though it was written by a woman. Bonaparte does devote substantial attention to how much more difficult it is for girls to develop sexually, and she examines cultural factors associated with female mutilation among primitive peoples. With regard to the latter, she was clearly addressing issues that have come to the forefront of women's rights in the world today.

Miller, J. B. (1976). *Toward a new psychology of women*. Boston, MA: Beacon Press.

This is the landmark book in which Jean Baker Miller reoriented psychology's perspectives on gender. This book laid the foundation for a great deal of the research on gender psychology that followed.

Jordan, J. V., Kaplan, A. G., Miller, J. B., Stiver, I. P., & Surrey, J. L. (Eds.). (1991). *Women's growth in connection: Writings from the Stone Center*. New York, NY: The Guilford Press.
Jordan, J. V. (Ed.). (1997b). *Women's growth in diversity: More writings from the Stone Center* (pp 138-161). New York, NY: The Guilford Press.

These two books are the first major collections of works by Jean Baker Miller and her colleagues at the Stone Center for Development Services and Studies, part of the Wellesley Centers for Women (WCW). Miller's basic theories are expanded, clarified, and described in well-written chapters providing the theoretical basis for relational-cultural theory.

Hendrix, H. (1988). *Getting the love you want: A guide for couples*. New York, NY: HarperPerennial.

This is a wonderful book by a well-known therapist who specializes in marriage and couples therapy. He addresses both unconscious and conscious factors that affect relationships from the very beginnings of our initial attraction to another person. Since marriage is one of the deepest connections that most people make, which can later lead to a most devastating disconnection, this book is a valuable resource for anyone in the field of psychology (and others as well).

Chodorow, N. J. (1999a). *The reproduction of mothering – With a new preface*. Berkeley, CA: University of California Press.
Deutsch, H. (1945). *The psychology of women: A psychoanalytic interpretation, Volume Two: Motherhood*. New York, NY: Grune & Stratton.

Both Helene Deutsch and Nancy Chodorow have offered a woman's perspective on the psychology of women within a psychoanalytic framework. Deutsch was trained by Freud himself, and remained somewhat faithful to his perspective. In contrast, Chodorow was influenced by sociology, anthropology, and feminism, leading her to present a quite different perspective on women and the role of mothering in personality development.

Buchanan, A. J. (2003). *Mother shock: Loving every (other) minute of it*. Emeryville, CA: Seal Press.
Syler, R. (2007). *Good-enough mother: The perfectly imperfect book of parenting*. New York, NY: Simon Spotlight Entertainment.

Each of these books contains a variety of insightful and entertaining essays/stories on the experience of being a mother. Given the brief length of each chapter, these books are ideal for casual reading, although the heartfelt meaningfulness with which each woman writes in anything but superficial.

Chapter 10 - B. F. Skinner, John Dollard, and Neal Miller

While psychodynamic theory was developing in Europe, American psychology was largely under the influence of behaviorism. The American psychologist John B. Watson (of "Little Albert" fame) is considered to be the father of behaviorism. Although he is not known for addressing issues of personality development, he did feel it was important for behaviorists to do so. His approach involved reducing personality to smaller and smaller units of behavior referred to as habit systems, suggesting that personality was very consistent. Nonetheless, through further conditioning the personality of an individual could change, leading Watson to make the bold statement that if he was given a dozen healthy infants he could take any one at random and train him or her for any career, including "doctor, lawyer, artist, merchant-chief and yes, even beggar-man and thief" (cited in Stagner, 1988; see also Lundin, 1979).

As the scientific study of behavior continued, it became common to try determining behavior on the basis of mathematical models. This work led to an era of grand learning theories, which culminated in the highly complex models of behavior proposed by Clark Hull (see Bower & Hilgard, 1981). This research took the behavioral study of personality in a very different direction than psychodynamic theory. The direction in which B. F. Skinner took personality theory, however, was so different that it became known as **"radical behaviorism."** Skinner rejected anything he could not directly observe, so concepts such as consciousness, thought, reasoning, and the "mind," were all considered irrelevant to the study of individuals. Only the specific behaviors performed by the individual were open to being examined in Skinner's form of behaviorism.

In contrast, John Dollard and Neal Miller tried to find some common ground between psychodynamic theory and learning theory. Dollard was a true generalist, with interests in anthropology and sociology in addition to psychology. Miller studied with two renowned learning theorists, Edwin Guthrie and Clark Hull, and was psychoanalyzed by Heinz Hartman in Vienna, while studying in Europe in the 1930s. Together, Dollard and Miller tried to develop a theory that would encompass psychodynamic theory, learning theory, and the influence of sociocultural factors. Their effort to develop what might be called a unified theory of personality stands in stark contrast to the constraints of radical behaviorism. Most importantly, they set the stage for the social learning theorists who followed.

B. F. Skinner and the Behavioral Analysis of Personality Development

Many psychology students find it difficult to apply the strict principles of radical behaviorism to personality development. And yet, psychologists generally consider our discipline to be objective and scientific. Thus, it would seem essential that we acknowledge those psychologists who apply a strict scientific approach to the study of behavior. Skinner represents the extreme conditions under which some psychologists control the study of behavior, and his contributions to understanding the basic underlying principles of reward and punishment, and their consequences, rank him among the most influential psychologists of all time.

A Brief Biography of B. F. Skinner

Burrhus Frederic Skinner was born on March 20, 1904 in Susquehanna, Pennsylvania. He lived there for 18 years, and graduated from the same high school as his mother and father. By his own account he had a happy childhood, though it was somewhat chaotic in the rough and tumble coal town that was Susquehanna. Skinner roamed the hillsides, invented and built all sorts of gadgets, and developed a love for the wide variety of experiences that life has to offer a child living in a "warm and stable" home. He constantly satisfied his curiosity and imagination:

> I was always building things. I built roller-skate scooters, steerable wagons, sleds, and rafts…I made seesaws, merry-go-rounds, and slides. I made slingshots, bows and arrows, blow guns and water pistols…and from a discarded water boiler a steam cannon with which I could shoot plugs of potato and carrot over the houses of our neighbors. (Skinner, 1970).

Skinner's father, a lawyer, bought many books and maintained a large library in their home. Skinner enjoyed school and, under the guidance of an influential teacher named Mary Graves, eventually chose to major in English Literature in college and then to pursue a career in writing. While still at home, Skinner played the piano and the saxophone, and during high school he played in a jazz band. He also became quite interested in spirituality, particularly under the conflicting views of Miss Graves and his grandmother Skinner. Miss Graves was a devout Christian, who had taught Skinner's Sunday school class, but held fairly liberal views on the Bible. Grandmother Skinner took a more fire-and-brimstone approach, showing Skinner the burning coals in the stove to make sure he understand the dangers of Hell! Ultimately Skinner came to his own perspective, and from that point forward he no longer believed in God (Bjork, 1997; Skinner, 1970, 1976).

Skinner attended Hamilton College, where he majored in English and minored in Romance languages. He felt that he never quite fit in at college, largely because he was no good at sports and because Hamilton College required students to attend daily chapel. By his senior year, he and his friends became involved in some serious pranks, ultimately being threatened with not being allowed to graduate. He did graduate, however, and began a brief attempt at a career as an author. A professor with whom Skinner had taken a summer course introduced him to the renowned poet Robert Frost. Frost offered to review some of Skinner's stories, and he sent a favorable reply that greatly encouraged Skinner (the letter is reprinted in Skinner, 1976). However, Skinner had only one success as an author. His father had always hoped Skinner would practice law with him, and together they published a private book on legal decisions in the ongoing battles between the coal companies and the unions. Skinner then spent 6 months living a bohemian lifestyle in New York's Greenwich Village, followed by some time in Paris, France. Ultimately, however, he gave up his career as an author because he simply "had nothing important to say" (Bjork, 1997; Skinner, 1970, 1976).

As a child, Skinner had always been interested in the behavior of animals and kept many wild pets. In high school he was very interested in philosophy, and in college a professor had introduced him to comparative psychology and Pavlov's work on classical conditioning. He began reading Pavlov and Watson while living in Greenwich Village, and eventually went to Harvard University to study psychology. At Harvard Skinner developed the rigorous work schedule that was to become one of his personal hallmarks. After leaving Harvard he taught at the University of Minnesota, where, during World War II, he conducted research on using pigeons as the guidance system for missiles. He then moved on for a brief period as the chairman of the psychology department at Indiana University. In 1948 he was asked to return to Harvard, where he worked for the remainder of his career (Bjork, 1997; Skinner, 1970).

Throughout the rest of his career, Skinner attempted to apply aspects of his radical behaviorism to a variety of issues, including child care, education, and the very nature of society itself. His influence has been substantial, particularly with regard for his emphasis on psychology as a science. However, his views on scientific methodology and other fields of psychology have been controversial. For example:

> …I suppose it was only my extraordinary luck which kept me from becoming a Gestalt or (so help me) a cognitive psychologist. (pg. 8; Skinner, 1970)

> The Freudian mental apparatus doesn't make much sense to me…I don't believe that he devised a useful conceptual system… (pp. 5-7; Evans, 1968)

> Dreaming…is almost always weak behavior and hence determined by trivia. (pg. 193; Epstein, 1980)

> New, deep, real, growth, harmony, understanding potential, unfoldment - an opiate soothing syrup for humanistic psychologists, hashish for the searchers for identity. (an informal review of a new journal for transpersonal psychology; pg. 291; Epstein, 1980)

> I'm not at all impressed by the model builders, the information theory analysts, the systems analysts, and so on. They still haven't shown me that they can do anything important. (pg. 82; Evans, 1968)

> In general, scientific methodology is not an accurate reflection of what the scientist really does…it doesn't reflect the actual behavior of the scientist. Fortunately for science, scientific method and statistics weren't formulated until the middle of the nineteenth century. (pg. 89; Evans, 1968)

In Skinner's defense, however, he often felt that his position was misunderstood. One of the most important approaches to the study of behavior that he emphasized was to focus on individuals, not on average measures of behavior that show "none of the characteristic individuality of the organism you're studying" (pg. 92; Evans, 1968). Despite harsh criticism, Skinner did not take attacks on his scientific perspectives personally. As he described it, he simply reported the facts that arose from his research, and chose not to debate those who disagreed. One exception, however, was Carl Rogers. On several occasions he debated Rogers, whom he described as a friend, about the dignity of man and the control of men (Bjork, 1997; Evans, 1968). He also sent a letter to E. L. Thorndike, who described the Law of Effect after studying cats escaping from puzzle-boxes well before Skinner was born (published in 1898; see Bower & Hilgard, 1981), apologizing for perhaps having failed to give Thorndike proper recognition for establishing the basic concepts that led to the study of **operant conditioning**. Thorndike replied that he was more honored to have been of service to new scientists than if he were to have received credit for founding a new "school" of psychology (Skinner, 1970).

In 1970, *American Psychologist* listed Skinner second only to Freud in his influence on twentieth-century psychology, and in 1989 Skinner seemed to express some pride in being cited more often than Freud (Bjork, 1997). Near the end of 1989, however, Skinner was diagnosed with leukemia. He continued to work as best he could, and expressed no anxiety about his approaching death. In August, 1990 he spoke for 20 minutes to a standing-room only audience at the annual meeting of the American Psychological Association. Eight days later he died (Bjork, 1997).

Placing B. F. Skinner in Context: Radical Behaviorism

B. F. Skinner shares at least one thing in common with Sigmund Freud: he provided a target for the behavioral and cognitive theorists who followed him. Freud, of course, was a target for everyone in psychiatry and psychology, including Skinner. Although some might say that Skinner established the experimental analysis of behavior, as far as personality is concerned, Freud also thought that he was being very scientific in his studies of human behavior and the human mind. In order to absolutely define his understanding of behavioral principles, Skinner rejected anything he could not observe. Although this allowed him to claim a level of precision never before possible in the study of behavior, it disallowed the study of the mind, consciousness, thinking, emotion, the very things that most people consider to be the domain of psychology! It also disallowed doing many types of research on humans, and so Skinner, his students, and his colleagues focused much of their effort on studying rats and pigeons.

Like Freud before him, Skinner faced his critics and defended his theories. He certainly had solid scientific data to support his position, but when he went so far as to propose that he could solve the problems of society (in his novel *Walden Two*), perhaps he was asking for criticism. Nonetheless, in psychology today, behavioral and cognitive approaches to understanding mental illness and conducting psychotherapy are popular and effective. Although behavioral and cognitive theorists incorporate the very things Skinner rejected (emotions, thought, etc.), they have built upon the unquestioned behavioral principles studied first by Skinner. In addition, the application of many of Skinner's theories, such as reinforcement and punishment, has had a major influence on child rearing and education, or at least in our understanding of those processes.

Although Skinner was not the first behaviorist, that honor goes primarily to John B. Watson (since Pavlov was first and foremost a physiologist), his name is typically the first that comes to mind when recognizing behaviorism as one of three great forces in psychology (the others being psychodynamic and humanistic psychology). Thus, Skinner stands with Freud and with Rogers and Maslow as a giant in the history of psychology.

Scientific Analysis of Behavior and Personality

Late in Skinner's life (in 1988 to be exact), his former graduate student A. Charles Catania had this to say:

> Of all contemporary psychologists, B. F. Skinner is perhaps the most honored and the most maligned, the most widely recognized and the most misrepresented, the most cited and the most misunderstood. (pg. 3; Catania & Harnad, 1988)

Skinner emphasized, above all else, approaching human behavior scientifically. However, he acknowledged that human behavior is complex, and that our familiarity with it makes it difficult for us to be truly objective. In addition, he recognized that many people find it offensive to suggest that human behavior can be understood and predicted in terms of environmental stimuli and their consequences. Still, Skinner took the scientific approach very seriously, and he knew that science is about more than just determining a set of facts or principles. In Science and Human Behavior (Skinner, 1953), Skinner wrote that:

> Science is concerned with the general, but the behavior of the individual is necessarily unique. The "case history" has a richness and flavor which are in decided contrast with general principles…A prediction of what the *average* individual will do is often of little or no value in dealing with a particular individual…The extraordinary complexity of behavior is sometimes held to be an added source of difficulty. Even though behavior may be lawful, it may be too complex to be dealt with in terms of law. (pp. 20-21; Skinner, 1953)

Given this complexity, Skinner focused on **"cause"** and **"effect"** relationships in behavior. In common use, these terms have come to carry a meaning far beyond the original intention. For Skinner, a cause is a change in an independent variable, whereas an effect is a change in a dependent variable. Skinner argued that the terms cause and effect say nothing about how a cause leads to an effect, but rather, only that there is a specific relationship in specific order. If we can discover and analyze the causes, we can predict behavior; if we can manipulate the causes, then we can control behavior (Skinner, 1953). By focusing entirely on observable behavior, Skinner felt that psychologists have an advantage, in that they will not waste time and effort pursuing either inner psychic forces or external social forces that may not even exist. Focusing on actual behavior is simply more direct and practical. Before examining some of the larger implications of this approach, however, let's review the basic principles of operant conditioning as defined by Skinner.

> **Discussion Question:** Skinner emphasized a scientific approach to the study of behavior, in part, because individual behavior is so unique. Understanding what the average person might do may tell us nothing about a certain individual. However, a science of personality that treats everyone as unique seems to become hopelessly complex, because we must study everyone individually. Does this really seem like a scientific approach, and whether it is or not, can it really help us to understand other people?

Principles of Operant Conditioning

Operant conditioning begins with a response, known as an operant, which has some effect in the organism's environment. These responses have consequences that determine whether or not the probability of the response will increase or decrease in the future. **Reinforcers** increase the probability of a given response that precedes them, whereas **punishers** decrease the probability of a response that precedes them. In common terms we might say that good consequences increase behaviors, or that the behavior is rewarded. However, Skinner avoids words like reward due to their psychological implications, preferring instead to use the technical term reinforcer (Holland & Skinner, 1961; Skinner, 1953).

Both reinforcement and punishment come in two forms: positive and negative. **Positive reinforcement** involves the application, or administration, of a favorable consequence to a response. For example, when a child cleans their room, they receive some money as an allowance. The response of cleaning the room results in the application of a tangible reinforcer: money. **Negative reinforcement** involves the removal of an **aversive** or **noxious** stimulus. We are commonly told not to scratch itchy bug bites, because we might get them infected. However, an itch is a very noxious stimulus, and it is not easy to ignore them. When we finally give in and scratch, the itching goes away (at least for a while). The response of scratching is negatively reinforced by the removal of the noxious stimulus (no more itching). In both of these examples, the response (the operant of room cleaning or scratching) is followed by a consequence (reinforcement) that increases the likelihood that we will clean our room or scratch our itchy bug bite.

Punishment can also be positive or negative. If a child misbehaves and is spanked, that is a **positive punishment**. In other words, an aversive consequence is applied (the spanking) as a result of the misbehavior. With **negative punishment**, favorable stimuli are withdrawn. For example, a child who misbehaves receives a time-out, thus removing them from toys, playmates, snacks, etc. Other common examples of a negative punishment are being grounded or losing privileges (such as television or video games). Once again, in positive punishment the response (misbehavior) results in the application of an aversive stimulus (a spanking), whereas in negative punishment the response misbehaving results in the removal of favorable consequences (loss of privileges). One of the most common mistakes that psychology students make is to confuse negative reinforcement with punishment. This is understandable, because of the use of the word "negative." So it is essential to determine first whether a consequence is a reinforcer or a punisher. Then determine whether the reinforcer is positive or negative, or whether the punisher is positive or negative. It is also generally accepted that punishment is not as effective as reinforcement, and it is more difficult to precisely control the cause-effect relationship (Skinner, 1953, 1974, 1987). This is partly due to **discriminative stimuli,** which signal the contingencies that may be in effect at a given time. In other words, the presence or absence of a parent (a discriminative stimulus) may determine whether one will be punished for a given response (if the cat's away, the mice will play). In addition, the possibility always exists that punishment can cross the line into abuse (physical and/or emotional). As Skinner noted, science is not just about the facts, there is always something more. In theory punishment may seem equivalent to reinforcement, but in practical matters, such as raising children, every situation may require a more detailed analysis.

In order to reliably measure the behavior of animals (typically rats or pigeons) in his laboratory, Skinner built a special piece of equipment commonly known as a **Skinner box** (though its technical name is an **operant conditioning chamber**). This apparatus allowed for the precise measurement of how subjects responded over time under varying conditions, and produced a special measure of behavior known as a **cumulative record**. Although continuous reinforcement is certainly effective for increasing behavior, in most situations we are not reinforced every time we engage in a certain behavior. Skinner identified four basic **schedules of reinforcement**, based on variations in the number of responses necessary for reinforcement, so-called **ratio schedules**, or the time intervals between making reinforcers available, so-called **interval schedules**. Both ratio and interval schedules can be either fixed or variable.

By using rats and pigeons as his subjects, Skinner was able to conduct extensive and precisely controlled experiments on operant behavior and its consequences. [Rat image by Kira Hoffman; Pigeon image by George Hodan]

Although the principles of reinforcement may seem relatively straightforward, they can lead to either complex or odd behavior. Complex behavior can be developed with operant conditioning through the process of **shaping**. Shaping involves reinforcing chains of behavior in a specific sequence, with each change being relatively small and, therefore, relatively simple. As a result, complex behavior can be explained in terms of shaping a series of simple changes in behavior. As Skinner describes it:

> Operant conditioning shapes behavior as a sculptor shapes a lump of clay. Although at some point the sculptor seems to have produced an entirely novel object, we can always follow the process back to the original undifferentiated lump, and we can make the successive stages by which we return to this condition as small as we wish. At no point does anything emerge which is very different from what preceded it. (pg. 91, Skinner, 1953)

Sometimes, however, this process goes awry. When an individual accidentally associates a consequence with a response, even though no actual relationship existed, **superstitious behavior** can result. For example, if you provide a few seconds of access to food for a hungry pigeon every 20 seconds, regardless of what the pigeon is doing at the time, the pigeon will develop some form of food-getting ritual. Since the food is delivered regardless of what the pigeon does, the ritual that develops is superstitious. The development of superstition in humans is believed to follow the same principles (Skinner, 1953, 1987). For a straightforward description of the principles of operant conditioning, and the prime example of how Skinner believed these principles might be applied to education, see the programmed instruction book entitled *The Analysis of Behavior* by Holland and Skinner (1961).

Discussion Question: It has become commonly accepted, at least in psychology, that children should never receive positive punishment (e.g., a spanking). Instead, parents should use negative punishment (e.g., a timeout) and then redirect their child's behavior in positive ways. How does this compare to how you were punished, and do you agree that this is *always* true?

Personality Development

Based upon the principles of operant conditioning, Skinner proceeded to address the full range of human behavior, including personality development, education, language, mental illness and psychotherapy, and even the nature of society itself.

Skinner believed that the terms "self" and "personality" are simply ways in which we describe the characteristic patterns of behavior engaged in by an individual. Skinner also referred to the self as "a functionally unified system of responses" (Skinner, 1953), or "at best a repertoire of behavior imparted by an organized set of contingencies" (Skinner, 1974). Skinner acknowledges that critics of the science of behavior claim that behaviorists neglect the person or the self. However, Skinner claims that the only thing neglected is a vestige of **animism**, which in its crudest form attributes behavior to spirits. If behavior is disruptive, the spirit is a demon; if behavior is creative, the spirit is a muse or guiding genius (Skinner, 1974). Indeed, Skinner's arguments describing the self sound quite similar to the Buddhist perspective we will examine later in this book:

> When a man jams his hands into his pockets to keep himself from biting his nails, *who* is controlling *whom*? When he discovers that a sudden mood must be due to a glimpse of an unpleasant person, *who* discovers *whose* mood to be due to *whose* visual response? Is the self which works to facilitate the recall of a name the same as the self which recalls it? When a thinker teases out an idea, is it the teaser who also eventually has the idea? (pg. 283; Skinner, 1953)

If the self, or the personality, does not exist, but is instead simply a collection of behavioral attributes and functions, then it is an irrelevant concept that needs to be discarded. Skinner did not discount the value of Freud's explanation of human behavior, since Skinner acknowledged that many sciences take time to develop. But now that behavioral science was advancing, according to Skinner, it became time to discard Freudian concepts of an unconscious mind and mental functioning. Curiously, this is very similar to the way in which Freud addressed religion: as something that had served its purpose in the course of human development, but which should now be discarded in favor of the science of psychoanalysis.

Since no two people have exactly the same experiences (not even identical twins, who do share an identical genetic make-up), each individual is truly unique. When any one of us seems to have an experience of identity, a feeling of self, it always exists within the unique circumstances of our experiential contingencies, the reinforcers, punishers, discriminative stimuli, etc. that have determined our behavioral patterns. Thus, Skinner argues that we do have a unique individuality, but we are not an originating agent, not a self that decides to act a certain way. Instead, we are a **locus**, a point of convergence for genetic and environmental conditions which have come together and that will determine our next act (Skinner, 1974).

Education

Skinner's theories have direct applications to education, particularly with regard to controlling classroom behavior and motivating students to learn. Indeed, when looking at the big picture, the challenges facing educators that Skinner wrote about in the 1970s sound very much like the challenges in education today (Skinner, 1978). Teachers are being asked to do more, to address new and different material in their classrooms, and schools face dwindling budgets and rising costs. A reasonable solution: make education more efficient.

Skinner's approach to increasing the efficiency of teaching was to rely on programmed instruction, either through teaching machines (see, e.g., Skinner, 1959) or specially designed books (e.g., Holland & Skinner, 1961). When I was a teaching assistant at Wayne State University in Detroit, we used *The Analysis of Behavior* by Holland and Skinner for laboratory sections of the learning course. It proved to be both efficient and effective. Unfortunately, however, programmed instruction is just that, a systematic program, and it takes up time that might otherwise allow for meaningful and stimulating relationships between professors and students. Interestingly, one of the strongest trends in higher education today is to shift from lecture-based classes to learner-centered education. But this is done with the intent of increasing the active participation of students within the classroom, not to isolate them in programmed instruction.

In defense of Skinner's approach, it is true that his simple teaching machines and books were only a start. Today we have access to marvelous educational programs on computer, and most of them are anything but boring. Some of the educational programs available for children are fascinating and fun games, and that may be wonderful for children. But is the same approach appropriate for college-level students? In time, perhaps, technology will bring us yet other innovative approaches that combine the best of programmed instruction and human interaction.

> **Discussion Question:** Skinner proposed that education could be made more efficient and effective through the use of programmed learning and teaching machines. Have you ever experienced either of these approaches? Did you feel that you were getting the most out of your education in these situations?

Language

One of the most controversial areas to which Skinner applied his behavioral theories was that of language. It took Skinner over 20 years to write *Verbal Behavior* (Skinner, 1957), but in the end he presented an analysis of language in which he argued that even our most complex verbal behavior could be understood in terms of simple behavioral contingencies. Skinner began by considering whether there is any difference between speech and any other behavior. For example, what is the difference between using the word water when asking for a glass of water and using the arm to reach for that glass of water? In looking at the beginnings of verbal behavior in childhood, Skinner emphasized the simplicity of a young child's early use of single words to convey meaning far beyond the particular word. For example, when a 2-year old says "cookie," they are asking for, and expecting to receive, a cookie that they cannot get for themselves. Skinner referred to such simple one word utterances as a **mand**, which he said was short for several related concepts: command, demand, countermand, etc. When the child says "cookie," they will then receive one (reinforcement) or they will not. If it is too close to dinner, or if the child has already been told no, the child may receive a loud "No!" (punishment). To make a long story short, all complex verbal behavior develops from this simple beginning, taking its more complex variations from the process of shaping, just like any other behavior.

Perhaps even more controversial, Skinner assigned "thought" to the role of subaudible speech. In other words, thinking was nothing more than talking to one's self, or behaving in the roles of both the speaker and the listener, but doing so without making any sounds out loud. As strange as it may sound to consider thought as nothing more than another behavior subject to reinforcement or punishment, if one is willing to accept Skinner's theory on verbal behavior in the first place, he then makes a compelling argument:

> ...speech is only a special case of behavior and subaudible speech a further subdivision. The range of verbal behavior is roughly suggested, in descending order of energy, by shouting, loud talking, quiet talking, whispering, muttering "under one's breath," subaudible speech with

> detectable muscular action, subaudible speech of unclear dimensions, and perhaps even the "unconscious thinking" sometimes inferred in instances of problem solving. There is no point at which it is profitable to draw a line distinguishing thinking from acting on this continuum. (pg. 438; Skinner, 1957).

There are those, of course, who do not accept Skinner's theory on verbal behavior. The renowned linguist Noam Chomsky published critical reviews of both *Verbal Behavior* and, later, *Beyond Freedom & Dignity* (Skinner, 1971). Bower and Hilgard (1981) consider Chomsky's critiques to be perhaps the most effective in challenging Skinner's viewpoint. Chomsky argued that our knowledge of a series of input-output relationships tells us nothing of behavior in general, but rather we should be examining the internal structure, states, and organization of the organism that produced these unique input-output relationships (the very concepts that Skinner rejected). Most importantly, rather than accepting that Skinner had taken an appropriate scientific approach, Chomsky felt that Skinner had placed unnecessary fetters on the scientific process. Chomsky also adopted the cognitive perspective that addresses whether a stimulus in the environment really exists in isolation from the individual. In other words, is the nature of a stimulus affected by the perception of the individual (e.g., how might a paranoid person react to a friendly greeting)? Attempts at supporting Skinner's view and answering Chomsky's critique have, according to Bower and Hilgard, simply failed to be effective or persuasive. And so, experimental psycholinguistics has remained with the general disciplines of linguistics and cognitive psychology, rather than becoming a branch of behavioral learning theory (Bower & Hilgard, 1981).

Old Age and Walden Two

Although much of our conditioning takes place during the early years of life, Skinner did not neglect the later years. However, he addressed issues of aging in a decidedly unscientific way, mostly by describing ways in which he had personally dealt with the intellectual challenges of aging. Skinner wrote about a variety of techniques he had found useful in dealing with forgetfulness, fatigue, and a lack of motivation (see Skinner, 1987). More importantly, however, was the need to prepare for old age when young. By preparing for old age, we can meet its challenges in the best possible health and frame of mind. In *Enjoy Old Age*, co-authored with Dr. Margaret Vaughan, one finds the following advice:

> Nevertheless, it is probably easier to be happy when you are young...We do not live in order to be old, and for young people to expect that "the best is yet to be" would be a great mistake. But what comes can be enjoyed if we simply take a little extra thought. (pg. 28; Skinner & Vaughan, 1983)

In this relatively brief book, Skinner and Vaughan recommend a series of practical steps that one might take: do something about old age, keep in touch with the world, keep in touch with the past, think clearly, keep busy, have a good day, get along with people, feel better, recognize death as a necessary end, and play the role of old age with dignity. An important part of the latter step is to have a sense of humor. The realities of old age can be frustrating, but when you can laugh at the lighter side of these challenges, then everyone around you has the chance to feel better too (Skinner & Vaughan, 1983).

Having addressed the full range of human life, Skinner also addressed the very nature of society itself. Actually, it was rather early in Skinner's career that he wrote the controversial novel *Walden Two* (Skinner, 1948). And yes, this book was a novel, not a scientific study, though it certainly addresses Skinner's scientific endeavors. *Walden Two* is about a utopia, a society based entirely on behavioral principles. Similar to the challenges Skinner faced in his failed attempt at a career as an author, Walden Two was rejected by two publishers, and it was accepted by Macmillan only when Skinner agreed to also write an introductory textbook for them. Few critics were impressed by the book, and it failed to sell for a dozen years. But eventually it did sell, and became a well known, if still controversial, book (Skinner, 1978). Skinner himself has written interesting reflections on *Walden Two* and its implications, including a fictional conversation between one of the characters and the late George Orwell (author of *1984*; Skinner, 1978, 1987).

Perhaps the most interesting aspect of Skinner's behavioral, utopian society is that it has not remained fictional. At least two communities have been established based on the ideas presented in *Walden Two*. The first, established in 1967, is the Twin Oaks Intentional Community, located in rural Virginia (www.twinoaks.org). The second, established in 1973, is Los Horcones, located in Sonora, Mexico (www.loshorcones.org.mx). Los Horcones has, among its many interesting programs, developed special education programs for developmentally delayed children, particularly those suffering from autism. Although both communities have been successful, they have found it difficult to expand.

Mental Illness and Behavior Therapy

Although the topics of mental illness and behavior therapy are better left to a course in abnormal psychology, let's take a brief look at some of the more dramatic applications of Skinner's theories to this important topic. Today, an important trend in psychology is community mental health, in which it is common for a team of mental health practitioners, including psychologists, psychiatrists, social workers, and mental health nurses, to come together and combine their unique specialties in the treatment of a variety of mental health issues. Following two conferences in 1953 and 1954, on the development and causes of mental disease, Skinner wrote that it is important for psychology to maintain a narrow focus, not an interdisciplinary one.

Specifically, Skinner believed that psychologists should focus on the significant properties of "mental disease." He describes the organism (or person) as being under the influence of hereditary and environmental influences, and engaging in behaviors. How we define these variables depends on our perspective. We can refer to genetic influences as instincts or, in humans, as traits and abilities. We can refer to environmental variables, both past and present, as memories, needs, emotions, perception, etc. But we do not have to interpret those factors we cannot observe, and Skinner felt it was not useful to do so (Skinner, 1959).

Skinner did not actually reject the possibility of the existence of a mental apparatus, as described by Freud, but he did consider it outside the realm of psychological *science*. And as with complex verbal behavior, Skinner believed that if we could sufficiently break down the behavioral contingencies that underlie psychotic behavior, then we would be able to describe its significant properties in behavioral terms. This analysis may someday involve a more detailed understanding of what happens in the nervous system (and in the brain), but that analysis may appropriately belong in psychiatry and/or neurology, not in psychology (Skinner, 1959).

Skinner felt that mental illness centered on issues of control, and the development of abnormal contingencies in the control of behavior. Most people fear control, and Skinner posed the somewhat amusing question: How often do psychotics have delusions about benevolent controllers? (pg. 234; Epstein, 1980). When faced with being controlled, under excessive conditions, individuals may attempt to escape, revolt, or resist passively. Given the complexity of human life, these behaviors can take many forms and can result in many emotional by-products, such as fear, anxiety, anger or rage, or depression (Skinner, 1953). When these conditions become maladaptive or dangerous, a need for psychotherapy arises. Skinner viewed psychotherapy as yet another form of control, but one in which the therapist creates a non-punishing situation that allows the patient to address problematic behaviors. The therapist and the patient can then work out programs that reduce occasions of punishment and increase occasions of reinforcement in the patient's life. As such, Skinner considered psychotherapy to be somewhat the opposite of religion and governmental agencies, both of which tend to rely on punitive measures to control the behavior of people (Skinner, 1953).

Through it all, Skinner was optimistic about the future of humanity, and he felt that behaviorism would help people to achieve their full potential. In this regard, he was similar to Freud, who felt that psychoanalysis was a fully scientific endeavor, which would also help to advance the development of humanity. The difference between these two great scientists of human behavior lies in how this might come about:

> An experimental analysis shifts the determination of behavior from autonomous man to the environment - an environment responsible both for the evolution of the species and for the repertoire acquired by each member...but we must remember that it is an environment largely of his own making. The evolution of a culture is a gigantic exercise in self-control...But no theory changes what it is a theory about; man remains what he has always been. And a new theory may change what can be done with its subject matter. A scientific view of man offers exciting possibilities. We have not yet seen what man can make of man. (pp. 214-215; Skinner, 1971)

Connections Across Cultures: Personality within Society

John Dollard was one of three theorists whom we will cover in this book who made significant contributions to studying racial issues and minority groups. However, unlike Erik Erikson (see Chapter 7) and Gordon Allport (see Chapter 13), both of whom addressed these issues later in their careers, Dollard (trained in sociology and anthropology) began these studies before he made his significant contributions to psychology. This fact had an important influence on his later approach to how personality is learned, and the use he and Miller made of cross-cultural examples in the books they published together. Indeed, as something of a prelude to his work with Miller, Dollard ends the book *Caste and Class in a Southern Town* (Dollard, 1937) with the following passage:

> …It is one of the urgent needs of social psychology to see the life-history problem against the background of class structure and to get life records from persons who are also described from the sociological standpoint. (pg. 459; Dollard, 1937)

Dollard made an important distinction between **class** and **caste**, as it applies to Blacks and Whites living in the Southern United States in the 1930s. Class generally refers to a group of people of similar economic and political status, such as lower (or working) class, middle class or upper class. A caste is a group defined by some social and/or hereditary factor, such as being ethnically Black or White. There are lower class Blacks and Whites, and there are middle class Blacks and Whites. However, in our society it has been the Blacks who were most dramatically oppressed, through the institution of slavery. Thus, Blacks have been relegated to a lower caste, regardless of whether their economic success qualifies them for middle class status, or even whether they are wealthy. This has had a detrimental influence on family structure in the Black community, and with it an important influence of personality development:

> Personality formation must be intelligible in terms of patterns in the family. The study of the family as a formal unit has been slighted in this research, but some things are known. One is that the lower-class Negro family differs from the middle-class white family and seems by comparison to be "disorganized." This is undoubtedly a result of the fact that during slavery days it was impossible for Negroes to approximate white family structure. (pp. 413-414; Dollard, 1937)

Dollard discusses a variety of ways in which White plantation owners worked to eliminate all trace of the African family structure and culture among their slaves, not the least of which was the dramatic removal of them from Africa to America. In many ways the slave owners encouraged pleasure-seeking, lack of discipline, and independence from family. These values helped to keep male slaves somewhat satisfied in spite of their conditions, and they encouraged the independence of children so that they might begin working at a young age (Dollard, 1937). These values slowly established a new culture for Blacks in America, often with negative consequences. After the Civil War, some Blacks also began to adopt the values of the White culture, but they were not accepted by many people in America. This conflict is what ultimately led the Supreme Court of the United States, in the 1954 ruling *Brown v. Board Education*, to declare that separate is *not* equal.

Dollard also co-authored *Children of Bondage*, with a social anthropologist named Allison Davis (Davis & Dollard, 1940). Davis was one of the first Black professors to receive tenure at a university that was not an historically Black institution (the University of Chicago). He successfully challenged the racial bias in IQ tests of the past, helping to eliminate their use in the school systems of many cities, and he was recognized by the U. S. government with a postage stamp in a series that included Dr. Martin Luther King, Jr. and Jackie Robinson. In their work together, Davis and Dollard focus on describing the personalities and socialization of eight adolescent Blacks in the deep south. They emphasize the demands placed on these youth by both their particular caste position and the social class into which they were born. Individuals may attempt to rebel against their feelings of inferiority with regard to class, and class mobility is possible, but not so with one's racial identity:

> In studying the status controls operating upon an individual one finds that most persons in our society are disposed to conceal, even from themselves, any inferiority in their social rank...Refusal to acknowledge one's inferior status, and the building of defenses to decrease anxiety on this score are especially complex with regard to class status...Color caste, however, is so clearly and so rigidly defined that persons in the lower-caste society (as well as the general American reader of this book) will exhibit much less psychological resistance to the fact of caste status than to that of class position. (pg. 17; Davis & Dollard, 1940)

It was within this context, recognizing caste and class as socializing factors influencing personality development, that Dollard went on to study learning theories related to personality development:

> "But what," one may ask, "is the practical use of studying these class patterns of behavior?"...what good is such knowledge to the student of human nature, and to our society?...is it a valuable tool which will help us to *predict* behavior in any given situation and in the end to change it?
>
> The writers' studies of the class conditioning of Negro children have convinced them...that when properly understood the sanctions of the class position, as enforced by the family, the clique, and the larger class environment, are among the most important controls in the formation of human habits. In order to understand the powerful grip of this class behavior, we must first examine the social environment in which Negro children learn their habits and the specific methods by which this learning is reinforced. (pg. 259; Davis & Dollard, 1940)

John Dollard and Neal Miller: Psychodynamic Learning Theory

Sigmund Freud felt that only his approach to psychodynamic theory and psychoanalysis would allow for an understanding of human behavior. B. F. Skinner felt the same way about radical behaviorism. But very few psychologists have felt so strongly about one, and only one, approach to psychology. John Dollard and Neal Miller attempted to blend psychodynamic theory with learning theory, and the results were quite successful. Their theories on the relationship between frustration and aggression, social learning (developed more fully by Bandura, Rotter, and Mischel, whom we will cover in the next chapter), and conflict are standard topics in introductory psychology textbooks.

Brief Biographies of John Dollard and Neal Miller

John Dollard (1900-1980) and Neal Miller (1909-2002) were born just a few years and a few miles apart in Wisconsin, though Miller's family soon moved to Washington. Dollard was a generalist, with interests in psychology, anthropology, and sociology, who conducted important research on racial discrimination in the American south. Miller was particularly interested in physiological psychology, and his pioneering work on biofeedback is as famous as anything we will discuss in this chapter. Though pursuing very different careers, their paths crossed at Yale University's Institute of Human Relations.

Dollard received his bachelor's degree from the University of Wisconsin in 1922, and then went to the University of Chicago, where he earned his M.A. and Ph.D. degrees in sociology in 1931. His interests at the time were primarily in sociology and anthropology, and he accepted an assistant professorship in anthropology at Yale University. A year later he became an assistant professor of sociology at Yale's newly formed Institute of Human Relations. Dollard remained at Yale throughout his career, earning the status of professor emeritus in

1969. In addition to his work with Miller, Dollard studied the effects of racial segregation and discrimination in the southern United States, resulting in two landmark books. Dollard also traveled to Germany between completing graduate school and beginning his position at Yale. While there, he studied psychoanalysis and was psychoanalyzed at the Berlin Institute.

Miller received his bachelor's degree from the University of Washington in 1931, where he studied with the well-known learning theorist Edwin Guthrie. He received an M.A. from Stanford University, and his Ph.D. from Yale in 1935. While a graduate student at Yale he studied with Clark Hull, one of the most influential learning theorists. Like Dollard, Miller traveled to Europe after graduate school, and was psychoanalyzed at the Vienna Institute for Psychoanalysis (reportedly he could not afford to be analyzed by Freud himself). Upon returning, Miller joined the faculty at Yale's Institute of Human Relations. He remained there from 1936 to 1941, and it was during these years that worked closely with Dollard.

During World War II Miller conducted psychological research for the Army Air Force, while Dollard remained at Yale and studied the effects of combat on fear. Miller returned to Yale as a professor of psychology, and remained there until 1966. He then left Yale to establish the Laboratory of Physiological Psychology at Rockefeller University, where he retired as professor emeritus. Among his many honors, Miller served as president of the American Psychological Association, he received an award for Outstanding Lifetime Contribution to Psychology from APA, and he received a National Medal of Science from President Johnson in 1964.

Placing Dollard and Miller in Context: Learning Theory in Moderation

Dollard and Miller brought important perspectives into the study of learning and personality. Dollard was a sociologist with strong interests in anthropology. Miller was trained as a learning theorist with a future in physiological psychology. Although two such men might seem an unlikely pairing, their combined perspective opened the door for eclectic approaches to psychology. Both Dollard and Miller had also studied psychoanalysis. This combination of psychoanalysis, sociology, and learning led to some of the most famous theories in psychology: the frustration-aggression hypothesis, social learning, and a theoretical basis for understanding behavior in conflict situations. These studies laid the foundation for social learning and cognitive personality theorists.

In addition, Dollard studied cultural effects on personality development, particularly under oppressive conditions. Once again, his work laid the foundation for an appreciation of cross-cultural studies in psychology. However, despite occasional studies by noted theorists, such as Erik Erikson and Gordon Allport, the field of psychology has only recently begun to make a concerted effort to study cross-cultural issues (Sue, 1999). Thus, in some ways, the fulfillment of Dollard and Miller's legacy remains to be realized.

Learning Theory and the Influence of Clark Hull

As mentioned above, Miller was a student of Clark Hull, one of the most influential learning theorists. As an example of just how influential Hull was, five theorists who advanced his ideas (including Miller, Orval Mowrer [a co-author on Dollard and Miller's first book together], and Ernest Hilgard [whose learning theories text, co-authored with Gordon Bower, is cited in this chapter]) went on to the presidency of the American Psychological Association and also received distinguished scientific contribution awards from APA (Stagner, 1988). Hull's theory is not easy to understand, as it is a complex mathematical model of the variables impinging upon an organism's behavior. Unlike Skinner, Hull focused on the organism that exists between the input and output that were the sole focus of radical behaviorists.

According to Hull, the strength of a response (**net response strength**; E), or its probability of occurring, is determined by the strength of an internal **drive** (D) and the strength of relevant **habits** (H), all within the context of **conditioned inhibition (extinction**; $_sI_r$) and the organisms overall level of response inhibition (e.g., fatigue; I_r). Hull expressed this relationship by using a formula:

$$E = (H \times D) - ({}_sI_r + I_r).$$

Hull later modified his theory to take into account non-learning factors, such as the effectiveness of an evoking stimulus (V) and the incentive motivation of stimuli (K), resulting in the modified formula:

$$E = H \times D \times V \times K.$$

For a more detailed discussion of learning theory see *Theories of Learning* by Bower and Hilgard (1981). Clearly, Hull's consideration of psychological factors, such as the quality of stimuli, their value as motivators, internal drives and habits, all of which influence the nature of input-output relationships stands in stark contrast to Skinner's theories. It was within this context that Dollard and Miller attempted to blend learning theory with psychodynamic phenomena.

Discussion Question: Clark Hull proposed a mathematical formula for understanding behavior, based in part on habit and the incentive of rewards. Look at the formula E = H x D x V x K, and consider whether you agree that human behavior can be reduced to mathematics.

Dollard and Miller's Psychodynamic Learning Perspective: Frustration-Aggression; Social Learning and Imitation; Conflict

Dollard and Miller collaborated on three books, in which they attempted to apply Hull's principles of learning theory to Freudian psychoanalysis: *Frustration and Aggression* (Dollard, Doob, Miller, Mowrer, & Sears, 1939), *Social Learning & Imitation* (Miller & Dollard, 1941), and *Personality and Psychotherapy* (Dollard & Miller, 1950). Like Hull before them, Dollard and Miller emphasized drives and habits. They also addressed theoretical differences in the strength of reinforcers and punishers, and they equated Freud's concept of displacement to the behavioral concept of generalization. Rather than considering psychoanalysis and behaviorism as fundamentally opposed, as Skinner had, Dollard and Miller allowed for a synthesis of these two major schools of psychology. Their vision led to influential and popular perspectives (Bower & Hilgard, 1981; Lundin, 1979; Stagner, 1988).

Dollard, Miller, and their colleagues believed that the relationship between **frustration** and **aggression** is absolute. In other words, aggression is always the result of frustration. Equally true, but not always as obvious, is the fact that frustration always leads to some form of aggression. While it may appear that some people very quickly accept situations in which they do not get their own way (i.e., they are frustrated), it is also true that we learn early in life to restrain our aggressive impulses. Although we may appear to be successful in not responding to frustration with aggression, this restraint is most likely only temporary. We may then aggressively respond after some delay, or toward some other target, but there will eventually be an aggressive response as a result of the initial frustration (Dollard et al., 1939). In addition, such aggression does not have to involve active responses, since passive-aggressive behavior is all too common. Indeed, a **passive-aggressive personality disorder** (identified by Theodore Millon as the **negativistic personality disorder** [Millon, 1996; Millon and Grossman, 2005]; see the Appendix) was included in the DSM-IV-TR for further study, although it did not make it into the DSM-V (American Psychiatric Association, 2000, 2013). This is an essential contrast to the view of Skinner. Radical behaviorism does not do a very satisfying job of relating responses and stimuli following long delays, not does it easily address the displacement of aggression. However, by accepting internal psychological processes, more flexible learning theories can incorporate factors such as memory, reasoning, emotion, etc. into the relationships between us and our environments.

Aggression comes in many forms, and Dollard, Miller, and their colleagues addressed a wide variety of social factors, including child and adolescent development, criminality, differences between democracy, fascism, and communism, and the nature of aggression amongst the Ashanti. The Ashanti are a West African tribe of people who were considered powerful and warlike. Their fierceness in intertribal battle was said to strike terror into their enemies. Based on anthropological records (primarily the writings of a Captain Rattray), Dollard, Miller, et al. (1939) described a variety of aspects of the Ashanti culture within the framework of the **frustration-aggression hypothesis**. For example, being captured during war was considered treason, and treason was punishable by death. Thus, it was expected that a warrior would never surrender, but rather would fight to the death. However, a warrior's primary goal during war was to win, and then return home to the family and way of life they were fighting for. If it became clear to a warrior that he was going to lose, his desire to survive should be foremost in his mind. However, surrendering was punishable by death, so it was not an option. This created profound frustration! The response might then be an aggressive rejection of the culture that demanded his death, and he might go ahead and surrender (as often happened). Another shocking example involved the claiming of infants. In Ashanti culture children were cherished. For the first eight days after birth, an infant was kept in very simple conditions, hidden from any outside observers. Then, after the 8 days, the parents would claim the child in a public ceremony. The child would be named, dressed in fine clothes, given a special sleeping mat, and brought out into the community. If the child died during those first 8 days, while the family was making its preparations for the celebration, the result was a very painful frustration. Consequently, the custom was to violently abuse the body, whipping and mutilating it, and finally burying it in the women's latrine! As shocking as this may seem, it represents an extreme example of the frustration-aggression hypothesis in a culture where aggression plays an important role.

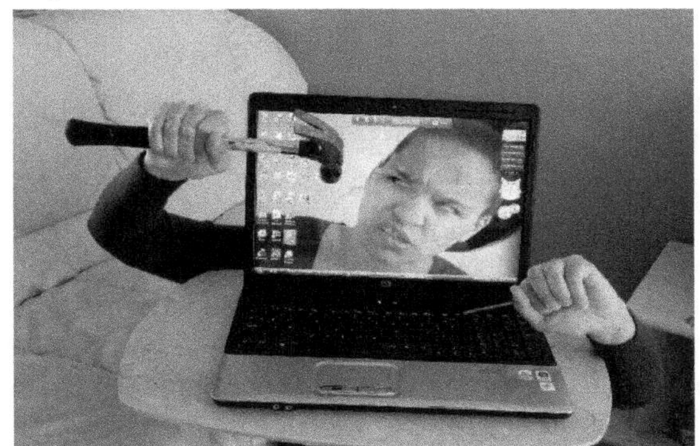

According to do Dollard and Miller, frustration leads to aggression. Many people are frustrated by the computers that were designed to make life more convenient. [Image by fluffster (Jeanie)]

In a study relating Freud's defense mechanism of displacement to the behavioral concept of generalization, Miller conducted a study in which rats were trained to strike each other (see Lundin, 1979). Very simply, a mild electrical shock was applied to the floor of a cage containing two rats, and as soon as the rats bumped into each other the shock was turned off. The rats quickly learned to strike each other as soon as the electrical current was turned on. A white, plastic doll was then added to the cage, and when the electrical current was turned on the rats quickly struck each other. Then, when one of the rats was placed in the cage alone, and the electrical current was turned on, the rat struck the doll. Whether this is displacement or generalization depends simply on whether it is defined by a Freudian or a behaviorist, respectively. Although Dollard, Miller, et al. defined the frustration-aggression hypothesis as we know it today, they credit Freud with "the most systematic and extensive use of the frustration-aggression hypothesis," which led to Freud's proposal of the death instinct and its underlying aggressive energy (Dollard, et al., 1939).

In their second book together, *Social Learning & Imitation* (Miller & Dollard, 1941), Miller and Dollard addressed the roles of culture and society in the learning process:

> ...To understand thoroughly any item of human behavior - either in the social group or in the individual life - one must know the psychological principles involved in its learning and the social conditions under which this learning took place. It is not enough to know either principles or conditions of learning; in order to predict behavior both must be known. The field of psychology describes learning principles, while the various social science disciplines describe the conditions. (pg. 1; Miller & Dollard, 1941)

Given Dollard's background in sociology and anthropology, it should not be surprising that they gave such emphasis to the social conditions surrounding learning. Indeed, in the preface to this book they discuss the difficulty they had communicating with one another, since they each brought very different backgrounds into this combined effort. They then defined learning theory as the study of the circumstances under which responses and cue stimuli become connected, and they focused their studies on **imitation** and **copying**.

According to Miller and Dollard (1941), there are four essential factors involved in learning: the cue, the response, drive, and reward. In simple terms, in the presence of an appropriate signal (the cue), the person responds with a particular behavior, if there is an adequate reward (based on learning). The entire process will not take place, however, if the individual does not want a reward (drive). The normal order, after learning has taken place, would then be: drive → cue → response → reward; when we want something, and we see a signal that it is available, we try to get it, and are rewarded for our actions. Another important aspect of social learning is that both drives and rewards can be acquired. For example, food choices are highly cultural. Would you enjoy a dinner of grubs, whale blubber, and sheep entrails, followed by a few crunchy grasshoppers for dessert? And yet, each of these items is commonly eaten in some cultures, so they must be reinforcers for hungry people there.

As an additional example of the importance of social learning, Dollard and Miller once again turned to the anthropological literature. The Semang people of the Malay Peninsula are quite different than the Ashanti described above. The Semang are known as excessively shy and timid people. When faced with hostility they never respond in kind. Instead, they just retreat farther into the jungle. Dollard and Miller questioned whether this behavior was due to some personality trait or to learning. The Semang often dealt with the more powerful Malay tribe. The Malay often cheated the Semang, stole their land, and enslaved some of their people. When the Semang resisted, they were severely punished by the Malay. As a result, escape behavior among the Semang was rewarded, whereas aggression was severely punished. As this became engrained within the culture of the Semang, it was no longer necessary for each generation to re-learn these contingencies, withdrawal and escape became the cultural norm for the Semang people (Dollard & Miller, 1941). To put it in the terms used above, there is a drive for survival. In the presence of aggressive Malays (a cue), escape (the response) is rewarded with safety (drive → cue → response → reward).

In perhaps their most influential book, *Personality and Psychotherapy*, Dollard and Miller (1950) advocated an eclectic approach to psychology. They believed that the "ultimate goal is to combine the vitality of psychoanalysis, the rigor of the natural-science laboratory, and the facts of culture" (Dollard & Miller, 1950). They also felt it was important for all psychologists, even experimental psychologists, to understand psychotherapy, since it provides a window to higher mental life. They proposed that psychiatric clinics are full of patients showing three common signs: misery, stupidity (in some ways), and neurotic symptoms. Basically, Dollard and Miller believed that **conflict** produces the misery, that repression produces the stupidity (perhaps we should say "unconsciousness" or "unaware"), and that neurotic symptoms reduce conflict. However, neurotic symptoms do not solve conflicts, they only mitigate the conflict. In order to better understand these conflicts, Dollard and Miller presented a detailed analysis of conflict, which became the best-known portion of their final book together (Dollard & Miller, 1950).

Psychotherapy may take place in a therapist's office, but misery and conflict can only be relieved in real life. Dollard and Miller give credit to Freud for making this observation, but there is a distinct difference between how Freud viewed conflict, as something primarily intrapsychic (between the id, ego, and superego), and how Dollard and Miller viewed conflict, as a choice between opposing options. Conflict arises when we must make a choice. Some stimuli are rewarding, some are punishing, and some can be both. We tend to approach a rewarding stimulus, and that tendency grows stronger as we get closer to it. Likewise, we tend to move away from a punishing stimulus, and our tendency to move away is stronger if we are close to it. Two other important differences, according to Dollard and Miller (1950), are that the strength of avoidance increases more rapidly as we get closer to punishing stimuli than does the strength of approaching a rewarding stimulus, and the strength of both varies with their associated drives. These relationships are easier to understand when viewed graphically.

Three types of conflict are most commonly discussed. In **approach-approach conflicts**, the individual must make a choice between two rewarding stimuli, such as having ice cream or cookies for dessert. This type of conflict is easily resolved, since one reward is likely to be more inviting (perhaps you haven't had ice cream for a while). A much more difficult situation is an **approach-avoidance conflict**. In this situation, from a distance the rewarding aspect of the stimulus is stronger, so we approach the stimulus. As we approach, however, the drive to avoid the stimulus grows rapidly, until we move away. For example, when an abusive parent tries to comfort a child (something an abused child cannot trust), there is a drive to move toward the parent for comfort (approach) as well as a drive to avoid further abuse (avoidance). Thus, the child may begin to approach the parent, but as they move closer they become more fearful and anxious, so they back away. This type of conflict can clearly create the sort of misery that Dollard and Miller were writing about. Finally, we have **avoidance-avoidance conflicts**, where both of our choices will result in punishment. For example, if a child has misbehaved, and their parent is going to punish them, the natural response is to run away. With young children this situation can be very easy to observe. However, many parents will then yell: "Don't you dare run away from me!" Now the child must choose between being punished (avoidance) or running away and being punished worse (avoidance). In this situation, the typical response is to freeze, and make no choice at all. The child may still be punished, but they will not have chosen the punishment.

Addressing the nature of an individual patient and their levels of approach and avoidance in conflicting situations is critical. According to Dollard and Miller, neurotic patients generally have high levels of avoidance. The key here is that these people have become patients. Many people suffer, and are urged by their friends to work on improving their situation. When those individuals have relatively low levels of avoidance motivation, they may well be successful in taking care of their problems. It is the ones who cannot overcome their avoidance issues who end up in therapy. Thus, if the therapist attempts to encourage the patient to approach their feared goals, the therapist will only increase the patient's fear and conflict, and the resulting misery will drive the patient out of therapy (Dollard & Miller, 1950). Instead, the therapist must focus on reducing the fears that motivated the patient's avoidance in the first place.

Overall, Dollard and Miller emphasized that psychotherapists must be well-trained, open-minded, stable individuals who put the interests of their patients first.

> We have emphasized the precautions important to psychologists who work as psychotherapists. In the same connection we stress that the ability to treat organic disease does not automatically carry with it a skill at psychotherapy. Nor does the possession of any degree such as Ph.D. or M.D. routinely confer such skill. Only the knowledge of theory, the kind of character, and the supervised training discussed here can make a man a psychotherapist. Anyone who undertakes psychotherapy without such training is exposing his patient to real danger and committing a moral, if not yet a legal, fraud. (pg. 422; Dollard & Miller, 1950)

Discussion Question: Dollard and Miller described how the Semang culture seems to lack aggression, as a result of their learning the danger of challenging the Malay. Can you recognize examples in your own life where a certain group seems to act in a predictable way as the result of how another group acts? If yes, how has one group reinforced or punished the behavior of the other in consistent ways, in keeping with the predictable behavioral outcomes?

Psychoanalysis, Behavior Therapy, and Relational Models

Paul Wachtel has continued studying the relationship between psychoanalysis and behavior therapy, following in the footsteps of Dollard and Miller, and he has also extended this comparison into the "relational world" (Wachtel, 1977, 1997). Wachtel emphasized that psychotherapy should be understood in terms of the theory that guides it, and that the practice of therapy provides the true test of any psychological theory related to personality and/or mental illness. Behavior therapy is appealing in terms of being direct and practical, but Wachtel feels that it can gain in several ways from being blended with psychoanalysis. He questions whether pure behavior therapists can really assess psychological conditions, whether they achieve narrow gains at the expense of broader psychological change, and he addresses the ethical implications of being involved in specifically changing another person's behavior. He also addresses several problems that behaviorists see for psychoanalysis, such as the focus on internal states that cannot be observed, whether underlying causes are really treated instead of symptoms, and the application of the medical model to psychological processes.

> It is my general premise that psychodynamic and behavioral approaches to psychotherapy, and to the understanding of personality, are far more compatible than is generally recognized, and that an integration of the concepts and observations accumulated by these two approaches can greatly enrich our clinical work and our understanding of human behavior...It is my experience that workers guided by either of these two broad frames of reference tend to have only a rather superficial knowledge (and sometimes none at all) of the important regularities observed by those guided by the other viewpoint. (pg. 5; Wachtel, 1977)

In *Psychoanalysis, Behavior Therapy, and the Relational World*, Wachtel (1997) discusses advances in the recognition of object relations theory in American psychology, and how object relations theory fits into connections between traditional psychodynamic perspectives and learning theory. Although it was not necessarily the intent of object relations theorists, object relations theory has shifted the focus of psychoanalysis from internal psychological conflicts to relationships with other people. Thus, there has been a shift from an internal focus to an external focus, which is more compatible with learning theory (and the input-output contingencies that are essential to learning). Wachtel also considers this shift as favorable for connections between psychoanalysis and family systems approaches to therapy. Surprisingly, Wachtel makes no mention of relational-cultural theory and the work of the Stone Center Group, which seems ideally suited to the integration of approaches proposed by Wachtel. Regardless of the nature and extent to which these various approaches might be integrated, it remains of the utmost importance that the focus of the therapist remains on helping the patient (Wachtel, 1997).

Cultural Effects on Learning

As shown above, Dollard and Miller regularly incorporated interesting cultural examples in their work relating learning theory to psychodynamic processes. Though it may not be obvious, Skinner's radical behaviorism is as intercultural as any theory. A detailed analysis of environmental influences on behavior, including past contingencies and present cues, *must* incorporate an examination of the unique cultural factors that are part and parcel of those contingencies in different cultural groups. In addition, of course, some psychologists today continue to study relationships between culture and learning.

Tweed and Lehman (2002) compared Western and Chinese learning styles by using two extraordinary teachers from ancient times as examples of these potentially different styles: Confucius and Socrates. Their article begins with an attempt to address the likely controversy that accompanies such a study. They carefully and thoughtfully point out that one can easily misunderstand any contrast between cultures that are difficult to define. For example, what does "Western" mean? Does it really mean European-Americans, or does that leave out Canadians, Australians, and non-European Westerners? So, Tweed and Lehman prefer the terms **culturally Western** and **culturally Chinese**, openly admitting that another important issue is that some Western people may be culturally Chinese and vice versa. They also point out their study was meant to be descriptive, not judgmental. Having presented such caveats, they proceeded with their study, and yet received some criticism nonetheless (Gurung, 2003; Li, 2003; see also the response to these critiques by Tweed & Lehman, 2003).

Tweed and Lehman offer the following generalizations about culturally Western and culturally Chinese learning: culturally Western learning focuses on overt and private questioning, expressing personal hypotheses, and a desire for self-directed tasks, whereas culturally Chinese learning emphasizes effort-focused learning, pragmatic orientations, and acceptance of behavior reform as an academic goal (Tweed & Lehman, 2002). In keeping with their non-judgmental attitude, they suggest that these disparate approaches both have their place in education, and that the ideal situation for students would be one that is academically bicultural, an environment that offers the opportunity for the strengths of each approach to learning to come out:

> ...These students would be in a sense academically bicultural and could operate adaptively within environments requiring Confucian or Socratic approaches...Educators...would encourage both thoughtful acquisition (Confucian) and inquiry (Socratic) such that students acquire knowledge and thinking skills that become fully understood, active, and elicited in many domains beyond the academic context. (pg. 97; Tweed & Lehman, 2002)

One of the individuals who commented on Tweed and Lehman's article, Jin Li, has focused more directly on how cultural factors influence learning itself. As essential difference between culturally Western and culturally Chinese learning is that Socrates proposed that the best learners develop and use their minds to inquire into the world, whereas the great Chinese tutor Mencius taught that becoming a better, more virtuous person is the most essential quality for a learner (Li, 2005). This perspective is reminiscent of Wober's study on intelligence amongst the Baganda people in Africa. They consider intelligence to be something closer to what we would call wisdom, and their educational system is focused on an individual's ability to succeed by conforming to the expectations of society, rather than on the ability to solve new and independent problems (Wober, 1974). Since cultural attitudes and beliefs develop early in life (Ferraro, 2006a; Matsumoto & Juang, 2004), a valuable educational objective would be to emphasize the strengths of each approach to learning as early as possible in the school years (or even during the preschool years).

In addition to broad-based effects of culture on learning in general, culture also comes into play for many of the aspects of learning we have examined in this chapter. Henrich et al. (2006) recently demonstrated that a wide variety of societies are willing to participate in costly punishment in order to encourage cooperation among groups. In other words, each party to an agreement is motivated to abide by the agreement because the consequences of breaking it are severe. This study involved fifteen different cultural groups from Africa, North America, South America, Asia, and Oceania, suggesting that willingness to cooperate as a function of severe punishment is universal. Language, which Skinner believed is learned just like any other behavior, appears to be essential for the development of autobiographical memory, which serves primarily social and cultural functions and is intimately related to social and cultural development (Fivush & Nelson, 2004). Presenting an interesting perspective on conflict, Eidelson and Eidelson (2003) have identified five belief domains that propel groups toward conflict. When individuals experience feelings of superiority, injustice, vulnerability, distrust, or helplessness, there is a good chance they will feel frustrated. When their individual-level core beliefs parallel the group-level worldview, the situation may trigger or constrain conflict or, possibly, trigger violent struggle (Eidelson & Eidelson, 2003). In such situations, the worldview of the larger group may be serving as a discriminative stimulus that it is acceptable to act out on one's individual frustration, since the society in which one lives is likely to reinforce any subsequent aggression (since they share the individual's frustration). In the next two chapters, we take a closer look at how the social environment and cognitive processes contribute to the development of our personality.

Personality Theory in Real Life: Positive Reinforcement Keeps Us Behaving!

The presence of positive reinforcement in our lives can be seen in a multitude of ways. We use it to encourage our children and train our pets, it is quite common in education, from the earliest grades through college, and it enters into our lives as adults in many ways. Often the application of reinforcement is not intentional, we give it out of habit, and partly because it leads to reinforcement for us as well. Although learning theorists may disagree about the nature of reinforcement, no one can deny it.

There are many ways in which positive reinforcement is given to children. Infants respond favorably to attention, and as they coo and smile back, that attention is itself reinforced. This helps to create an essential bond between the child and its caregivers. In the case of premature infants, gentle physical contact (massaging or stroking) by the parents is typically reinforced as a result of the babies gaining weight more rapidly and being more active (Field, 1993). In other words, caring for an at-risk infant is reinforced, and thus the caring behavior continues. Infant massage is quite popular in many countries around the world, and it is part of the total approach to therapy recommended by Wilhelm Reich (Field, 2000, 2001).

As children grow a little older, **secondary reinforcers** such as encouraging words ("You can do it!") or clapping are commonly used to reinforce taking first steps or solving a simple puzzle. Of course, **primary reinforcers** (e.g., crackers or juice) remain very popular as well. Such simple examples of reinforcement are certainly not unique to humans. Small pieces of food are often used to train dogs, and the reinforced behavior increases as a result, just like it does with children. While this demonstrates the basic universality of behavioral principles, it does not suggest that dogs have a personality. However, if you were to ask most pet owners, they will tell you that their animals do have personalities. And junk yard dogs don't become vicious as a result of being treated with loving kindness.

In educational settings, positive reinforcement is used quite intentionally, and can be a lot of fun with young children. Teachers can use a wide variety of stars, smiley face stickers, student of the week awards, and other little treats that children find very rewarding. Sometimes children receive "good citizen" awards when their teachers observe an occasion of **prosocial behavior** (such as helping another child who was hurt on the playground). Each of these reinforcers is intended to increase those behaviors that are viewed favorably in the educational environment (completed assignments, good grades, and good citizenship). As students get older, the reinforcers come less often (as with schedules of reinforcement). Grades are given out at the end of a term or semester (reinforcing, of course, only if they are good grades). Measures such as being Valedictorian, in the top 10 of the class, being on the Dean's List in college, or graduating summa cum laude are the pinnacles of this positive reinforcement hierarchy, yet they depend on long time intervals (some as long as the typical four years of high school or college).

As adults, our reinforcement often becomes more complicated. Based on Hull's formula H x D x V x K, consider the effect of being offered chocolate for dessert. After eating dinner, our drive for food should decrease, and we should not be likely to eat more. However, chocolate is a powerful incentive, so we may go ahead and eat it even if we are no longer hungry. Skinner's radical behaviorism cannot account for the phenomenon of eating something we really like when we have already eaten our fill. And yet many of us have experienced that desire to continue eating something we really like, even after we feel uncomfortably stuffed with food! One might also consider Dollard and Miller's frustration-aggression hypothesis, and the problem many people face when trying to lose weight. It is extremely difficult to stay on a low calorie diet, especially if we cannot eat the foods we like. Very simply, this is frustrating. According to Dollard and Miller, frustration always leads to aggression. How might this aggression be manifested? We return to overeating, even though it is bad for us. In other words, we are harming ourselves and/or rebelling against a culture that seems to demand being thin in order to be attractive. Interestingly, many diet programs have responded to this problem (whether or not they understood it this way) by providing either tantalizing recipes or by offering the food itself in prepackaged form. The hope is that the meals will themselves be reinforcing, thus eliminating the frustration caused by munching endless amounts of celery and rice cakes. Of course, these days you can buy quite an interesting variety of flavored rice cakes, so even they can be reinforcing for some people!

Review of Key Points

- Skinner emphasized the experimental analysis of human behavior, despite its complexity. He addressed causes and effects, but was very precise in describing a cause as a change in an independent variable and an effect as a change in a dependent variable.
- Reinforcers increase the likelihood of behaviors that precede them; punishers decrease the likelihood of behaviors that precede them.
- Positive reinforcement involves giving a reinforcer, negative reinforcement involves removing an aversive or noxious stimulus.
- Positive punishment involves applying a punisher, negative punishment involves removing reinforcers.
- Discriminative stimuli signal the behavioral contingencies in effect at a given time.
- Skinner automated much of his research, inventing the operant conditioning chamber (aka, the Skinner box). The data were typically collected in the form a cumulative record.
- The operant conditioning chamber was designed to control the schedule of reinforcement. These schedules could be either fixed or variable, and based on either ratios (number) or intervals (time).
- Operant conditioning can lead to complex behavior by shaping the behavior in a series of small steps.
- When a subject accidentally forms an inappropriate association, superstitious behavior can result.
- Skinner claimed that our typical idea of the person, or the self, is a vestige of animism, the belief that we are inhabited by spirits. Instead, he believed we are simply a locus for the convergence of genetic and environmental conditions.
- According to Skinner, education can be made more efficient by using programmed instruction and teaching machines.
- Language, according Skinner, begins with the association of simple word elements known as mands.
- Skinner believed that behavioral principles could be applied to improve life in old age as well as to improve society itself.
- In attempting to address mental illness, Skinner did not rule out the possibility of a disordered mind. However, he felt that such a construct served no useful purpose in understanding abnormal behavior. He also believed that mental illness focused on issues of control.
- Clark Hull, a major influence on Dollard and Miller, proposed a mathematical model of learning that included the nature of the mind and experience.
- Dollard and Miller believed that frustration always led to aggression, and that aggression could always be traced back to frustration. They applied their frustration-aggression hypothesis to a variety of cultural groups.

B. F. Skinner, John Dollard, and Neal Miller

- Dollard and Miller began the field of social learning, with an emphasis on the learning processes of imitation and copying.
- When addressing psychological disorders, Dollard and Miller emphasized conflict. They provided a theoretical basis for understanding approach-approach conflicts, approach-avoidance conflicts, and avoidance-avoidance conflicts.
- By incorporating an appreciation for the contribution of object relations theory, Wachtel has advanced our understanding of how learning theory and psychodynamic theory can be combined in an eclectic approach to psychotherapy.
- Tweed and Lehman caution against regional stereotypes when examining cultural aspects of learning. They propose using the terms "culturally Western" and, for their particular study, "culturally Chinese."
- Since culture is learned early in life, any attempt to incorporate the best aspects of different cultural approaches to education must begin early.

Review of Key Terms

aggression animism approach-approach conflict approach-avoidance conflict aversive avoidance-avoidance conflict caste cause class conditioned inhibition conflict copying culturally Chinese culturally Western cumulative record discriminative stimuli drive	effect extinction frustration frustration-aggression hypothesis habit imitation interval schedules locus mand negative punishment negative reinforcement negativistic personality disorder net response strength noxious operant conditioning	operant conditioning chamber passive-aggressive personality disorder positive punishment positive reinforcement primary reinforcer prosocial behavior punisher radical behaviorism ratio schedules reinforcer schedules of reinforcement secondary reinforcer Skinner box shaping superstitious behavior

Annotated Bibliography

Skinner, B. F. (1953). *Science and human behavior.* New York, NY: The Free Press.

This is perhaps the most thorough report of Skinner's work. It contains many of the basic principles that define operant conditioning, including how they apply to human behavior (as opposed to just rats and pigeons).

Skinner, B. F. (1974). *About behaviorism.* New York, NY: Alfred A. Knopf.
Skinner, B. F. (1987). *Upon further reflection.* Englewood Cliffs, NJ: Prentice-Hall.

These two books, written late in Skinner's career, reflect upon his theories and their implications. Skinner offers both analysis and insight, and he defends his radical behaviorist position.

Holland, J. G. & Skinner, B. F. (1961). *The analysis of behavior.* New York, NY: McGraw-Hill.

This book is the classic example of applying Skinner's theories to education. It offers a programmed instruction approach to learning the basic principles of operant conditioning and human development. This book may also be considered the forerunner to today's educational computer games.

Bjork, D. W. (1997). *B. F. Skinner: A life*. Washington, D.C.: American Psychological Association.

Bjork presents a thorough biography of Skinner's life. Although several autobiographical works have been written by Skinner himself, they tend to be brief and selective. This biography, however, covers both the entire life and the enduring influence of Skinner.

Dollard, J., Doob, L. W., Miller, N. E., Mowrer, O. H., & Sears, R. R. (1939). *Frustration and aggression*. New Haven, CT: Yale University Press.

Dollard, J. & Miller, N. E. (1950). *Personality and psychotherapy: An analysis in terms of learning, thinking, and culture*. New York, NY: McGraw-Hill.

Dollard and Miller's first book together, *Frustration and Aggression*, combines classic learning theory and psychodynamic theory in a most interesting way. Given the violence that exists in the world today, and understanding how frustration leads to aggression is essential to working toward safety and peace. In their last and perhaps most influential book together, *Personality and Psychotherapy*, they present their famous theory on conflict. In all three of their books, Dollard and Miller routinely use fascinating examples from a wide variety of cultures.

Wachtel, P. L. (1997). *Psychoanalysis, behavior therapy, and the relational world*. Washington, DC: American Psychological Association.

Wachtel has furthered the association between learning theory, behavior therapy, and psychodynamic theory begun by Dollard and Miller. Although much of the book was published previously, this book includes new material based on advances in American psychology's appreciation of object relations theory. Wachtel makes a compelling argument for adopting an eclectic approach to diagnosis and therapy, drawing on the strengths of psychodynamic theory and learning theory.

Interesting Websites

www.loshorcones.org.mx ...and... **www.twinoaks.org**

Los Horcones and Twin Oaks are communities based on Skinner's vision of how his behavioral principles might be used to create an ideal society. Skinner presented these ideas in his novel *Walden Two*.

Chapter 11 - Albert Bandura, Julian Rotter, and Walter Mischel

The social learning theorists observed that the complexity of human behavior cannot easily be explained by traditional behavioral theories. Bandura recognized that people learn a great deal from watching other people and seeing the rewards and/or punishments that other people receive. Social learning theorists do not deny the influence of reinforcement and punishment, but rather, they suggest that it can be experienced through observation and does not require direct, personal experience as Skinner would argue. In addition, observational learning requires cognition, something that radical behaviorists consider outside the realm of psychological research, since cognition cannot be observed. Bandura took a broad theoretical perspective on social learning, whereas Rotter and Mischel focused more closely on specific cognitive aspects of social learning and behavior.

It is also important to point out an artificial distinction that is difficult to avoid in the chapters of this section. Chapters 10, 11, and 12 are roughly set up as chapters on radical behaviorism and formal learning theory, followed by social learning, and then concluding with cognitive theories on personality development. However, as will be evident, the chapters overlap a great deal. For example, Dollard and Miller's attempt to find a middle ground between Freud and Skinner led to their initial descriptions of social learning, which provided a prelude to this chapter. Bandura, Rotter, and Mischel address a number of aspects of cognition in their theories, but they are not as completely focused on cognition as are Kelly, Beck, and Ellis, hence the separation of this chapter from the following one. In *Social Learning Theory*, Bandura had this to say:

> A valid criticism of extreme behaviorism is that, in a vigorous effort to avoid spurious inner causes, it has neglected determinants of behavior arising from cognitive functioning...Because some of the inner causes invoked by theorists over the years have been ill-founded does not justify excluding all internal determinants from scientific inquiry...such studies reveal that people learn and retain behavior much better by using cognitive aids that they generate than by reinforced repetitive performance...A theory that denies that thoughts can regulate actions does not lend itself readily to the explanation of complex human behavior. (pg. 10; Bandura, 1977).

Albert Bandura and Social Learning Theory

Bandura is the most widely recognized individual in the field of **social learning theory**, despite the facts that Dollard and Miller established the field and Rotter was beginning to examine cognitive social learning a few years before Bandura. Nonetheless, Bandura's research has had the most significant impact, and the effects of **modeling** on aggressive behavior continue to be studied today (see "Personality Theory in Real Life" at the end of the chapter). Therefore, we will begin this chapter by examining the basics of Bandura's social learning perspective.

Brief Biography of Albert Bandura

Albert Bandura was born in 1925, in the small town of Mundare, in northern Alberta, Canada. His parents had emigrated from Eastern Europe (his father from Poland, his mother from the Ukraine), and eventually saved enough money to buy a farm. Farming in northern Canada was not easy. One of Bandura's sisters died during a flu pandemic, one of his brothers died in a hunting accident, and part of the family farm was lost during the Great Depression. Nonetheless, the Bandura family persevered, and maintained a lively and happy home.

Although Bandura's parents lacked any formal education, they stressed its value. Despite having only one small school in town, which lacked both teachers and academic resources, the town's children developed a love of learning and most of them attended universities around the world. Following the encouragement of his parents, Bandura also sought a wide variety of other experiences while he was young. He worked in a furniture manufacturing plant, and performed maintenance on the Trans-Alaska highway. The latter experience, in particular, introduced Bandura to a variety of unusual individuals, and offered a unique perspective on psychopathology in everyday life.

When Bandura went to the University of British Columbia, he intended to major in biology. However, he had joined a carpool with engineering and pre-med students who attended classes early in the morning. Bandura looked for a class to fit this schedule, and happened to notice that an introductory psychology course was offered at that time. Bandura enjoyed the class so much that he changed his major to psychology, receiving his bachelor's degree in 1949. Bandura then attended graduate school at the University of Iowa, in a psychology department strongly influenced by Kenneth Spence, a former student of Clark Hull. Thus, the psychology program at the University of Iowa was strongly behavioral in its orientation, and they were well versed in the behavioral research conducted in the psychology department at Yale University.

As we saw in the previous chapter, John Dollard and Neal Miller had established the field of social learning at Yale in the 1930s, but they had done so within the conceptual guidelines of Hullian learning theory. Bandura was not particularly interested in Hull's approach to learning, but he was impressed by Dollard and Miller's concepts of modeling and imitation. Bandura received his Ph.D. in clinical psychology in 1952, and then began a postdoctoral position at the Wichita Guidance Center. Bandura was attracted to this position, in part, because the psychologist in charge was not heavily immersed in the Freudian psychodynamic approach that was still so prevalent in clinical psychology.

Following his postdoctoral training, Bandura became a member of the faculty at Stanford University, where he spent the rest of his career. The chairman of Bandura's department had been studying frustration and aggression, and this influenced Bandura to begin his own studies on social learning and aggression. This research revealed the critical role that modeling plays in social learning, and soon resulted in the publication of *Adolescent Aggression* (co-authored by Richard Walters, Bandura's first graduate student; Bandura & Walters, 1959). This line of research also led to the famous "Bobo" doll studies, which helped to demonstrate that even young children can learn aggressive behavior by observing models. Bandura then became interested in self-regulatory behavior in children, and one of the colleagues he collaborated with was Walter Mischel, whose work we will address later in this chapter. During his long and productive career, Bandura became more and more interested in the role played by cognition in social learning, eventually renaming his theory to reflect his social cognitive perspective on human learning. He also examined the role of the individual in influencing the nature of the environment in which they experience life, and how their own expectations of self-efficacy affect their willingness to participate in aspects of that life.

Bandura has received numerous honors during his career. Included among them, he has served as president of the American Psychological Association and received a *Distinguished Scientific Contribution Award* from APA. He received the *William James Award* from the American Psychological Society (known today as the Association for Psychological Science), a Guggenheim Fellowship, the *Distinguished Contribution Award* from the International Society for Research in Aggression, and a *Distinguished Scientist Award* from the Society of Behavioral Medicine. Bandura has also been elected to the American Academy of Arts and Sciences, to the Institute of Medicine of the National Academy of Sciences, and he has received numerous honorary degrees from universities around the world. The list goes on, not the least of which is his *Outstanding Lifetime Contribution to Psychology Award*, received from APA in 2004.

Placing Bandura in Context: Social Learning Theory Establishes Its Independence

Although social learning theory has its foundation in the work of Dollard and Miller, they addressed social learning in the context of Hullian learning theory (complete with mathematical formulae). Bandura shifted the focus of social learning away from traditional behavioral perspectives, and established social learning as a theory on its own. Bandura also freely acknowledged cognition in the learning process, something that earlier behaviorists had actively avoided. By acknowledging both the external processes of reinforcement and punishment and the internal cognitive processes that make humans so complex, Bandura provided a comprehensive theory of personality that has been very influential.

Although Bandura criticized both operant conditioning and Pavlovian conditioning as being too radical, he relied on a procedure that came from Pavlovian conditioning research for one of his most influential concepts: the use of modeling. The modeling procedure was developed by Mary Cover Jones, a student of John B. Watson, in her attempts to counter-condition learned phobias. Subsequent to the infamous "Little Albert" studies conducted by Watson, Jones used models to interact in a pleasant manner with a rabbit that test subjects had been conditioned to fear. After a few sessions, the test subjects were no longer afraid of the rabbit (see Stagner, 1988). This may have been the first use of behavior therapy, and Bandura's use of the procedure helped to bring together different behavioral disciplines.

Perhaps one of Bandura's most significant contributions, however, has been the application of his theory to many forms of media. Congressional committees have debated the influence of modeling aggression through violent television programs, movies, and video games. We now have ratings on each of those forms of media, and yet the debate continues because of the levels of aggression seen in our schools, in particular, and society in general. Bandura's Bobo doll studies are certainly among of the best known studies in psychology, and they are also among the most influential in terms of practical daily applications. The long list of awards that Bandura has received is a testament to both his influence on psychology and the respect that influence has earned for him.

Reciprocal Determinism

One of the most important aspects of Bandura's view on how personality is learned is that each one of us is an agent of change, fully participating in our surroundings and influencing the environmental contingencies that behaviorists believe affect our behavior. These interactions can be viewed three different ways. The first is to consider behavior as a function of the person and the environment. In this view, personal dispositions (or traits) and the consequences of our actions (reinforcement or punishment) combine to cause our behavior. This perspective is closest to the radical behaviorism of Skinner. The second view considers that personal dispositions and the environment interact, and the result of the interaction causes our behavior, a view somewhat closer to that of Dollard and Miller. In each of these perspectives, behavior is caused, or determined, by dispositional and environmental factors, the behavior itself is not a factor in how that behavior comes about. However, according to Bandura, social learning theory emphasizes that behavior, personal factors, and environmental factors are all equal, interlocking determinants of each other. This concept is referred to as **reciprocal determinism** (Bandura, 1973, 1977).

Early theories considered behavior to be a function of the person and their environment, or a function of the interaction between the person and their environment. Bandura believed that behavior itself influences both the person and the environment, each of which in turn affects behavior and each other. The result is a complex interplay of factors known as reciprocal determinism. [Image by Mark Kelland]

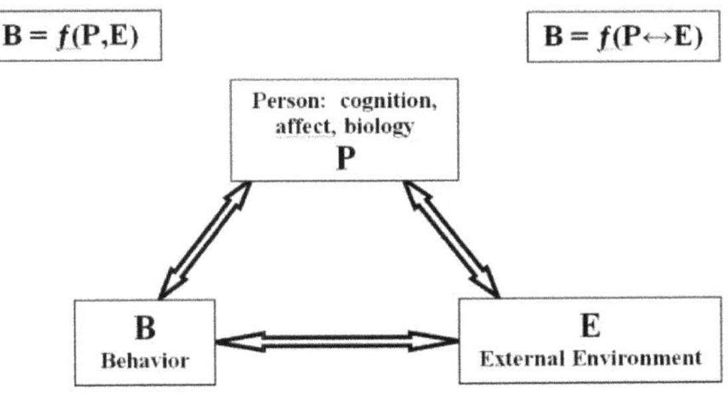

Reciprocal determinism can be seen in everyday observations, such as those made by Bandura and others during their studies of aggression. For example, approximately 75 percent of the time, hostile behavior results in unfriendly responses, whereas friendly acts seldom result in such consequences. With little effort, it becomes easy to recognize individuals who create negative social climates (Bandura, 1973). Thus, while it may still be true that changing environmental contingencies changes behavior, it is also true that changing behavior alters the environmental contingencies. This results in a unique perspective on freedom vs. determinism. Usually we think of determinism as something that eliminates or restricts our freedom. However, Bandura believed that individuals can intentionally act as agents of change within their environment, thus altering the factors that determine their behavior. In other words, we have the freedom to influence that which determines our behavior:

> ...Given the same environmental constraints, individuals who have many behavioral options and are adept at regulating their own behavior will experience greater freedom than will individuals whose personal resources are limited. (pg. 203; Bandura, 1977)

> **Discussion Question:** According to the theory of reciprocal determinism, our behavior interacts with our environment and our personality variables to influence our life. Can you think of situations in which your actions caused a noticeable change in the people or situations around you? Remember that these changes can be either good or bad.

Observational Learning and Aggression

Social learning is also commonly referred to as **observational learning**, because it comes about as a result of observing **models**. Bandura became interested in social aspects of learning at the beginning of his career. Trained as a clinical psychologist, he began working with juvenile delinquents, a somewhat outdated term that is essentially a socio-legal description of adolescents who engage in antisocial behavior. In the 1950s there was already research on the relationships between aggressive boys and their parents, as well as some theoretical perspectives regarding the effects of different child-rearing practices on the behavior and attitudes of adolescent boys (Bandura & Walters, 1959). Much of the research focused, however, on sociological issues involved in the environment of delinquent boys. Choosing a different approach, Bandura decided to study boys who had no obvious sociological disadvantages (such as poverty, language difficulties due to recent immigration, low IQ, etc.). Bandura and Walters restricted their sample to boys of average or above average intelligence, from intact homes, with steadily employed parents, whose families had been settled in America for at least three generations. No children from minority groups were included either. In other words, the boys were from apparently typical, White, middle-class American families. And yet, half of the boys studied were identified through the county probation service or their school guidance center as demonstrating serious, repetitive, antisocial, aggressive behavior (Bandura & Walters, 1959).

Citing the work of Dollard and Miller, as well as others who paved the way for social learning theory, Bandura and Walters began their study on adolescent aggression by examining how the parents of delinquents train their children to be socialized. Working from a general learning perspective, emphasizing cues and consequences, they found significant problems in the development of socialization among the delinquent boys. These boys developed dependency, a necessary step toward socialization, but they were not taught to conform their behavior to the expectations of society. Consequently, they began to demand immediate and unconditional gratification from their surroundings, something that seldom happens. Of course, this failure to learn proper socialization does not necessarily lead to aggression, since it can also lead to lifestyles such as the hobo, the bohemian, or the "beatnik" (Bandura & Walters, 1959). Why then do some boys become so aggressive? To briefly summarize their study, Bandura and Walters found that parents of delinquent boys were more likely to model aggressive behavior and to use coercive punishment (as opposed to reasoning with their children to help them conform to social norms). Although parental modeling of aggressive behavior teaches such behavior to children, these parents tend to be effective at suppressing their children's aggressive behavior at home. In contrast, however, they provide subtle encouragement for aggression outside the home. As a result, these poorly socialized boys are likely to displace the aggressive impulses that develop in the home, and they are well trained in doing so. If they happen to associate with a delinquent group (such as a gang), they are provided with an opportunity to learn new and more effective ways to engage in antisocial behavior, and they are directly rewarded for engaging in such behaviors (Bandura & Walters, 1959; also see Bandura, 1973).

Having found evidence that parents of aggressive, delinquent boys had modeled aggressive behavior, Bandura and his colleagues embarked on a series of studies on the modeling of aggression (Bandura, Ross, & Ross, 1961, 1963a,b). Initially, children were given the opportunity to play in a room containing a variety of toys, including the 5-foot tall, inflated Bobo doll (a toy clown). As part of the experiment, an adult (the model) was also invited into the room to join in the game. When the model exhibited clear aggressive behavior toward the Bobo doll, and then the children were allowed to play on their own, they children demonstrated aggressive behavior as well. The children who observed a model who was not aggressive seldom demonstrated aggressive behavior, thus confirming that the aggression in the experimental group resulted from observational learning. In the second study, children who observed the behavior of aggressive models on film also demonstrated a significant increase in aggressive behavior, suggesting that the physical presence of the model is not necessary (providing an important implication for violent aggression on TV and in movies; see "Personality in Theory in Real Life" at the end of the chapter). In addition to confirming the role of observation or social learning in the development of aggressive behavior, these studies also provided a starting point for examining what it is that makes a model influential.

One of the significant findings in this line of research on aggression is the influence of models on behavioral restraint. When children are exposed to models who are not aggressive and who inhibit their own behavior, the children also tend to inhibit their own aggressive responses and to restrict their range of behavior in general (Bandura, Ross, & Ross, 1961). Thus, children can learn from others, in particular their parents, how to regulate their behavior in socially appropriate ways. When the inappropriate behavior of others is punished, the children observing are also vicariously punished, and likely to experience anxiety, if not outright fear, when they consider engaging in similar inappropriate behavior. However, when models behave aggressively and their behavior is rewarded, or even just tolerated, the child's own tendency to restrict aggressive impulses may be weakened. This weakening of restraint, which can then lead to acting out aggressive impulses, is known as **disinhibition**:

> Modeling may produce disinhibitory effects in several ways. When people respond approvingly or even indifferently to the actions of assailants, they convey the impression that aggression is not only acceptable but expected in similar situations. By thus legitimizing aggressive conduct, observers anticipate less risk of reprimand or loss of self-respect for such action. (pg. 129; Bandura, 1973)

Discussion Question: The concept of disinhibition is based on the belief that we all have aggressive tendencies, and our self-control is diminished when we see models rewarded for aggressive behavior. Have you ever found yourself in situations where someone was rewarded for acting aggressively? Did you then adopt an aggressive attitude, or act out on your aggression?

Characteristics of the Modeling Situation

When one person matches the behavior of another, there are several perspectives on why that matching behavior occurs. Theorists who suggest that matching behavior results from simple **imitation** don't allow for any significant psychological changes. Dollard and Miller discussed imitation in their attempts to combine traditional learning theory with a psychodynamic perspective, but they did not advance the theory very far. A more traditional psychodynamic approach describes matching behavior as the result of **identification**, the concept that an observer connects with a model in some psychological way. However, identification means different things to different theorists, and the term remains somewhat vague. In social learning, as it has been advanced by Bandura, modeling is the term that best describes and, therefore, is used to characterize the psychological processes that underlie matching behavior (Bandura, 1986).

Observational learning through modeling is not merely an alternative to Pavlovian or operant conditioning:

> Learning would be exceedingly laborious, not to mention hazardous, if people had to rely solely on the effects of their own actions to inform them what to do. Fortunately, most human behavior is learned observationally through modeling: from observing others one forms an idea of how new behaviors are performed, and on later occasions this coded information serves as a guide for action. (pg. 22; Bandura, 1977)

Individuals differ in the degree to which they can be influenced by models, and not all models are equally effective. According to Bandura, three factors are most influential in terms of the effectiveness of modeling situations: the characteristics of the model, the attributes of the observers, and the consequences of the model's actions. The most relevant characteristics of an influential model are high status, competence, and power. When observers are unsure about a situation, they rely on cues to indicate what they perceive as evidence of past success by the model. Such cues include general appearance, symbols of socioeconomic success (e.g., a fancy sports car), and signs of expertise (e.g., a doctor's lab coat). Since those models appear to have been successful themselves, it seems logical that observers might want to imitate their behavior. Individuals who are low in self-esteem, dependent, and who lack confidence are not necessarily more likely to be influenced by models. Bandura proposed that when modeling is used to explicitly develop new competencies, the ones who will benefit most from the situation are those who are more talented and more venturesome (Bandura, 1977).

Despite the potential influence of models, the entire process of observational learning in a social learning environment would probably not be successful if not for four important component processes: **attentional processes**, **retention processes**, **production** (or reproduction) **processes**, and **motivational processes** (Bandura, 1977, 1986). The fact that an observer must pay attention to a model might seem obvious, but some models are more likely to attract attention. Individuals are more likely to pay attention to models with whom they associate, even if the association is more cognitive than personal. It is also well-known that people who are admired, such as those who are physically attractive or popular athletes, make for attention-getting models. There are also certain types of media that are very good at getting people's attention, such as television advertisements (Bandura, 1977, 1986). It is a curious cultural phenomenon that the television advertisements presented during the National Football League's Super Bowl have become almost as much of the excitement as the game itself (and even more exciting for those who are not football fans)!

The retention processes involve primarily an observer's memory for the modeled behavior. The most important memory processes, according to Bandura, are visual imagery and verbal coding, with visual imagery being particularly important early in development when verbal skills are limited. Once modeled behavior has been transformed into visual and/or verbal codes, these memories can serve to guide the performance of the behavior at appropriate times. When the modeled behavior is produced by the observer, the so-called production process, the re-enactment can be broken down into the cognitive organization of the responses, their initiation, subsequent monitoring, and finally the refinement of the behavior based on informative feedback. Producing complex modeled behaviors is not always an easy task:

> ...A common problem in learning complex skills, such as golf or swimming, is that performers cannot fully observe their responses, and must therefore rely upon vague kinesthetic cues or verbal reports of onlookers. It is difficult to guide actions that are only partially observable or to identify the corrections needed to achieve a close match between representation and performance. (pg. 28; Bandura, 1977)

Finally, motivational processes determine whether the observer is inclined to match the modeled behavior in the first place. Individuals are most likely to model behaviors that result in an outcome they value, and if the behavior seems to be effective for the models who demonstrated the behavior. Given the complexity of the relationships between models, observers, the perceived effectiveness of modeled behavior, and the subjective value of rewards, even using prominent models does not guarantee that they will be able to create similar behavior in observers (Bandura, 1977, 1986).

Producing complex behaviors that cannot be readily observed by the performer can prove quite difficult. John cut behind the defender to drive the ball with his knee over the goalie's head and into the goal (above). Samuel scores a round kick in a Taekwondo tournament (right). [Images by Mark Kelland]

A common misconception regarding modeling is that it only leads to learning the behaviors that have been modeled. However, modeling can lead to innovative behavior patterns. Observers typically see a given behavior performed by multiple models; even in early childhood one often gets to see both parents model a given behavior. When the behavior is then matched, the observer will typically select elements from the different models, relying on only certain aspects of the behavior performed by each, and then create a unique pattern that accomplishes the final behavior. Thus, partial departures from the originally modeled behavior can be a source of new directions, especially in creative endeavors (such as composing music or creating a sculpture). In contrast, however, when simple routines prove useful, modeling can actually stifle innovation. So, the most innovative individuals appear to be those who have been exposed to innovative models, provided that the models are not so innovative as to create an unreasonably difficult challenge in modeling their creativity and innovation (Bandura, 1977, 1986; Bandura, Ross, & Ross, 1963b).

Discussion Question: Two of the components necessary for modeling to be effective, according to Bandura, are attention and retention. What aspects of commercial advertisements are most likely to catch your attention? What do you tend to remember about advertisements? Can you think of situations in which the way an advertiser gets your attention also helps you to remember the product?

Connections Across Cultures: Global Marketing and Advertising

Although we are constantly surrounded by modeling situations, the most obvious and intentional use of models and modeling is in advertising. As our world becomes increasingly global, the use of advertisements that work well in one place may be entirely inappropriate in a different culture. Marieke de Mooij, the president of a cross-cultural communications consulting firm in the Netherlands, and a visiting professor at universities in the Netherlands, Spain, Finland, and Germany, has undertaken the challenging task of studying how culture affects consumer behavior and the consequences of those effects for marketing and advertising in different societies around the world (de Mooij, 2000, 2004a,b, 2005).

To some, increasing globalization suggests that markets around the world will become more similar to one another. De Mooij (2000), however, contends that as different cultures become more similar in economic terms, their more personal cultural differences will actually become more significant! Thus, it is essential for global businesses to understand those cultural differences, so that marketing and advertising can be appropriately adjusted. The challenge is in recognizing and dealing with the "global-local paradox." People in business are taught to think global, but act local. This is because most people throughout the world tend to prefer things that are familiar. They may adopt and enjoy global products, but they remain true to their own culture (de Mooij, 2005). Thus, it is important to understand local culture and consumer behavior in general before beginning an advertising campaign in a foreign country.

In her studies on culture and consumer behavior, de Mooij (2004b, 2005) addresses a wide variety of topics, including several that are covered in this chapter. In terms of the characteristics of models, many countries do not emphasize physical attractiveness and/or fashionable clothes the way we do in America. However, the overall aesthetic appeal of advertising can be more important in many Asian markets, focusing on preferences for values such as nature and harmony. Given that America is generally an individualistic culture and most Asian cultures are collectivistic, it should be no surprise that Americans tend to focus on the appeal of the model whereas Asians tend to focus on the appeal of the overall scene and relationships amongst the various aspects depicted within it. In a similar way, cultures differ in terms of their general perspective on locus of control. In cultures that tend to believe that their lives are determined by external forces, the moral authorities (such as the church and the press) are typically trusted. People in such cultures might not be responsiveness to advertisements that call for individual restraint, such as efforts to reduce cigarette smoking for better health, since they rely on their doctors (external agents) to take care of their health.

There are also significant differences in how people in different cultures think and process information, and cognitive processes underlie all aspects of social learning. Involvement theory suggests differences in how individuals and cultures differ in their approach to purchasing, and how advertising must take those differences into account. For example, amongst American consumers considering a "high involvement" product (such as a car), those who are likely to buy something respond to advertising in which they learn something, develop a favorable attitude toward the product, and then buy it (learn-feel-do). For everyday products, which are considered "low involvement," consumers respond to advertising in which they learn something, then buy the product, and perhaps afterward they tend to prefer that brand (learn-do-feel). There is now evidence that in typically more collectivist cultures such as Japan, China, and Korea, it is important to first establish a relationship between the company and the consumer. Only then does the consumer purchase the particular product, and then they become more familiar with it (feel-do-learn). Thus, the very purpose of advertising changes from culture to culture (de Mooij, 2004b). Naturally, a number of other approaches to advertising exist, based on concepts such as: persuasion, awareness, emotions, and likeability (de Mooij, 2005). Each of these techniques relies on a different psychological approach, taking into account the observers that the advertiser hopes to influence (the so-called target demographic).

One of the most important aspects of advertising, when it is being carried from one culture to another, is the translation of verbal and written information. Different languages have different symbolic references. They rely on different myths, history, humor, and art, and failing to tap into such differences is likely to result in bland advertising that does not appeal to the local audience (de Mooij, 2004a). Other languages are simply structured differently as well, perhaps requiring meaning in a name, and this sometimes makes direct translation impossible. Thus, an international advertiser must choose a different name for their product. For example, Coca-Cola is marketed in China as the homonym *kekou kele*, which means "tasty and happy" (de Mooij, 2004a). Visual references also have cultural meanings. A Nokia ad, shown in Finland, used a squirrel in a forest to represent good reception and free movement in a deep forest. A Chinese group, however, understood it as depicting an animal that lives far away from people. They simply did not understand the intent of the commercial. Research on interpersonal verbal communication styles suggests that certain countries can be grouped into preferred styles. Based on a comparison of multiple dimensions of preferred verbal style, some of the countries that share similar styles are: 1) the United States, the United Kingdom, Norway, the Netherlands, Sweden, and Denmark; 2) Austria, Finland, and Germany; 3) India, China, and Singapore; and 4) Italy, Spain, Belgium, France, Argentina, Brazil, and the Arab world (de Mooij, 2004a).

As challenging as it might seem to address these issues (and the many more we have not covered), it is essential for individuals involved in global marketing and advertising:

> The cultural variety of countries worldwide as well as in Europe implies that success in one country does not automatically mean success in other countries…finding the most relevant cultural values is difficult, especially because many researchers are based in Western societies that are individualistic and have universalistic values. Western marketers, advertisers, and researchers are inclined to search for similarities, whereas understanding the differences will be more profitable…There are global products and global brands, but there are no global buying motives for such brands because people are not global. Understanding people across cultures is the first and most important step in international marketing. (pg. 314; de Mooij, 2004b)

Finally, none of these approaches to international marketing and advertising is going to be successful if business relationships are not established in the first place. In *The Cultural Dimension of International Business*, Ferraro (2006b) offers a comprehensive guide to understanding cultural differences. In addition to the importance of being aware of such factors, which the very existence of the books and articles in this section belies, Ferraro emphasizes cultural differences in communication. For individuals working in a foreign country where English is not the first language, good communication becomes a matter of intent:

> Because communication is so vitally important for conducting business at home, it should come as no surprise that it is equally important for successful business abroad. The single best way to become an effective communicator as an expatriate is to learn the local language...Besides knowing how to speak another language, expatriate candidates should demonstrate a willingness to use it. For a variety of reasons, some people lack the motivation, confidence, or willingness to throw themselves into conversational situations. *[Authors note: see the section on self-efficacy below]* ...Thus, communication skills must be assessed in terms of language competency, motivation to learn another language, and willingness to use it in professional and personal situations. (pg. 170; Ferraro, 2006b)

Self-Regulation and Self-Efficacy

Self-regulation and **self-efficacy** are two elements of Bandura's theory that rely heavily on cognitive processes. They represent an individual's ability to control their behavior through internal reward or punishment, in the case of self-regulation, and their beliefs in their ability to achieve desired goals as a result of their own actions, in the case of self-efficacy. Bandura never rejects the influence of external rewards or punishments, but he proposes that including internal, **self-reinforcement** and **self-punishment** expands the potential for learning:

> ...Theories that explain human behavior as solely the product of external rewards and punishments present a truncated image of people because they possess self-reactive capacities that enable them to exercise some control over their own feelings, thoughts, and actions. Behavior is therefore regulated by the interplay of self-generated and external sources of influence... (pg. 129; Bandura, 1977)

Self-regulation is a general term that includes both self-reinforcement and self-punishment. Self-reinforcement works primarily through its motivational effects. When an individual sets a standard of performance for themselves, they judge their behavior and determine whether or not it meets the self-determined criteria for reward. Since many activities do not have absolute measures of success, the individual often sets their standards in relative ways. For example, a weight-lifter might keep track of how much total weight they lift in each training session, and then monitor their improvement over time or as each competition arrives. Although competitions offer the potential for external reward, the individual might still set a personal standard for success, such as being satisfied only if they win at least one of the individual lifts. The standards that an individual sets for themselves can be learned through modeling. This can create problems when models are highly competent, much more so than the observer is capable of performing (such as learning the standards of a world-class athlete). Children, however, seem to be more inclined to model the standards of low-achieving or moderately competent models, setting standards that are reasonably within their own reach (Bandura, 1977). According to Bandura, the cumulative effect of setting standards and regulating one's own performance in terms of those standards can lead to judgments about one's self. Within a social learning context, negative self-concepts arise when one is prone to devalue oneself, whereas positive self-concepts arise from a tendency to judge oneself favorably (Bandura, 1977). Overall, the complexity of this process makes predicting the behavior of an individual rather difficult, and behavior often deviates from social norms in ways that would not ordinarily be expected. However, this appears to be the case in a variety of cultures, suggesting that it is indeed a natural process for people (Bandura & Walters, 1963).

As noted above, "*perceived self-efficacy refers to beliefs in one's capabilities to organize and execute the courses of action required to produce given attainments*" (Bandura, 1997). The desire to control our circumstances in life seems to have been with us throughout history. In ancient times, when people knew little about the world, they prayed in the hope that benevolent gods would help them and/or protect them from evil gods. Elaborate rituals were developed in the hope or belief that the gods would respond to their efforts and dedication. As we learned more about our world and how it works, we also learned that we can have a significant impact on it. Most importantly, we can have a direct effect on our immediate personal environment, especially with regard to personal relationships. What motivates us to try influencing our environment is specific ways is the belief that we can, indeed, make a difference in a direction we want. Thus, research has focused largely on what people think about their efficacy, rather than on their actual ability to achieve their goals (Bandura, 1997).

Self-efficacy has been a popular topic for research, and Bandura's book *Self-Efficacy: The Exercise of Control* (1997) is some 600 pages long. We will address two key issues on this fascinating topic: the relationships between (1) efficacy beliefs and outcome expectancies and (2) self-efficacy and **self-esteem**. In any situation, one has beliefs about one's ability to influence the situation, and yet those beliefs are typically balanced against realistic expectations that change can occur. Each side of the equation can have both negative and positive qualities. Suppose, as a student, you are concerned about the rising cost of a college education, and you would like to challenge those rising costs. You may believe that there is nothing you can do (negative) and tuition and fees will inevitably increase (negative). This dual negative perspective leads to resignation and apathy, certainly not a favorable situation. But what if you believe you can change the college's direction (positive), and that the college can cut certain costs in order to offset the need for higher tuition (positive). Now you are likely to engage the college community in productive discussions, and this may lead to personal satisfaction (Bandura, 1997). In the first scenario, you are not likely to do anything, in the second scenario you will most likely be highly motivated to act, even energized as you work toward productive changes. Of course, there are two other possible scenarios. You may believe there is nothing you can do (negative), but that change is possible (positive). In this case, you are likely to devalue yourself, perhaps feeling depressed about your own inability to accomplish good. Conversely, you may believe there is something you can do (positive), but that external forces will make change difficult or impossible (negative). This may lead some people to challenge the system in spite of their lack of expected change, resulting in protests and other forms of social activism (Bandura, 1997). Since all of these scenarios are based on beliefs and expectations, not on the unknown eventual outcome that will occur, it becomes clear that what we think about our ability to perform in various situations, as well as our actual expectations of the consequences of those actions, has both complex and profound effects on our motivation to engage in a particular behavior or course of action.

As for self-efficacy and self-esteem, these terms are often used interchangeably, and on the surface that might seem appropriate. Wouldn't we feel good about ourselves if we believed in our abilities to achieve our goals? In fact, self-efficacy and self-esteem are entirely different:

> …There is no fixed relationship between beliefs about one's capabilities and whether one likes or dislikes oneself. Individuals may judge themselves hopelessly inefficacious in a given activity without suffering any loss of self-esteem whatsoever, because they do not invest their self-worth in that activity. (pg. 11; Bandura, 1997)

For example, my family was active in the Korean martial art Taekwondo. Taekwondo emphasizes powerful kicks. Because I suffer from degenerative joint disease in both hips, there are certain kicks I simply can't do, and I don't do any of the kicks particularly well. But I accept that, and focus my attention on areas where I am successful, such as forms and helping to teach the white belt class. Likewise, Bandura notes that his complete inefficacy in ballroom dancing does not lead him into bouts of self-devaluation (Bandura, 1997). So, though it may improve our self-esteem to have realistic feelings of self-efficacy in challenging situations, there is not necessarily any corresponding loss of self-esteem when we acknowledge our weaknesses. And even positive self-efficacy might not lead to higher self-esteem when a task is simple or unpleasant. To cite Bandura's example, someone might be very good at evicting people from their homes when they can't pay their rent or mortgage, but that skill might not lead to positive feelings of self-esteem. This concept was the basis for the classic story *A Christmas Carol,* featuring the character Ebenezer Scrooge (Charles Dickens, 1843/1994).

The Development of Self-Efficacy

Young children have little understanding of what they can and cannot do, so the development of realistic self-efficacy is a very important process:

> ...Very young children lack knowledge of their own capabilities and the demands and potential hazards of different courses of action. They would repeatedly get themselves into dangerous predicaments were it not for the guidance of others. They can climb to high places, wander into rivers or deep pools, and wield sharp knives before they develop the necessary skills for managing such situations safely...Adult watchfulness and guidance see young children through this early formative period until they gain sufficient knowledge of what they can do and what different situations require in the way of skills. (pg. 414; Bandura, 1986)

During infancy, the development of perceived causal efficacy, in other words the perception that one has affected the world by one's own actions, appears to be an important aspect of developing a sense of self. As the infant interacts with its environment, the infant is able to cause predictable events, such as the sound that accompanies shaking a rattle. The understanding that one's own actions can influence the environment is something Bandura refers to as **personal agency**, the ability to act as an agent of change in one's own world. The infant also begins to experience that certain events affect models differently than the child. For example, if a model touches a hot stove it does not hurt the infant, so the infant begins to recognize their uniqueness, their actual existence as an individual. During this period, interactions with the physical environment may be more important than social interactions, since the physical environment is more predictable, and therefore easier to learn about (Bandura, 1986, 1997). Quickly, however, social interaction becomes highly influential.

Not only does the child learn a great deal from the family, but as they grow peers become increasingly important. As the child's world expands, peers bring with them a broadening of self-efficacy experiences. This can have both positive and negative consequences. Peers who are most experienced and competent can become important models of behavior. However, if a child perceives themselves as socially inefficacious, but does develop self-efficacy in coercive, aggressive behavior, then that child is likely to become a bully. In the midst of this effort to learn socially acceptable behavior, most children also begin attending school, where the primary focus is on the development of cognitive efficacy. For many children, unfortunately, the academic environment of school is a challenge. Children quickly learn to rank themselves (grades help, both good and bad), and children who do poorly can lose the sense of self-efficacy that is necessary for continued effort at school. According to Bandura, it is important that educational practices focus not only on the content they provide, but also on what they do to children's beliefs about their abilities (Bandura, 1986, 1997).

As children continue through adolescence toward adulthood, they need to assume responsibility for themselves in all aspects of life. They must master many new skills, and a sense of confidence in working toward the future is dependent on a developing sense of self-efficacy supported by past experiences of mastery. In adulthood, a healthy and realistic sense of self-efficacy provides the motivation necessary to pursue success in one's life. Poorly equipped adults, wracked with self-doubt, often find life stressful and depressing. Even psychologically healthy adults must eventually face the realities of aging, and the inevitable decline in physical status. There is little evidence, however, for significant declines in mental states until very advanced old age. In cultures that admire youth, there may well be a tendency for the aged to lose their sense of self-efficacy and begin an inexorable decline toward death. But in societies that promote self-growth throughout life, and who admire elders for their wisdom and experience, there is potential for aged individuals to continue living productive and self-fulfilling lives (Bandura, 1986, 1997).

Discussion Question: Self-efficacy refers to our beliefs regarding our actual abilities, and self-esteem refers to how we feel about ourselves. What are you good at? Do others agree that you are good at that skill? When you find yourself trying to do something that you are NOT good at, does it disappoint you (i.e., lower your self-esteem)?

Behavior Modification

In *Principles of Behavior Modification* (Bandura, 1969), Bandura suggests that behavioral approaches to psychological change, whether in clinical settings or elsewhere, have a distinct advantage over many of the other theories that have arisen in psychology. Whereas psychological theories often arise first, become popular as approaches to psychotherapy, but then fail to withstand proper scientific validation, behavioral approaches have a long history of rigorous laboratory testing. Thus, behavioral techniques are often validated first, and then prove to be applicable in clinical settings. Indeed, behavioral and cognitive approaches to psychotherapy are typically well respected amongst psychotherapists (though some might consider their range somewhat limited).

Bandura made several points regarding the application of social learning theory to behaviorally-oriented psychotherapy. For example, Bandura notes that the labeling of psychological disorders, indeed the definition of what constitutes abnormal behavior, is made within a social context. While it has been demonstrated that common categories of mental illness are seen throughout a wide variety of cultures (Murphy, 1976), we still view those with psychological disorders based on sociocultural norms and, in the case of too many observers, with unreasonable prejudice. Bandura also opposed the medical model of categorizing and treating psychopathology, believing that the desire to identify and utilize medications has hindered the advancement of applying appropriate psychotherapies. The application of an appropriate therapy involves issues of ethical concern and goal-setting. Therapy cannot be successful, according to Bandura, if it does not have clear goals characterized in terms of observable behaviors. Choosing goals means that one must make value judgments. In making these decisions it is important that the client and the therapist share similar values (or at least that the therapist work with values appropriate for their client), and that the therapist does not try to impose their own values on the client (Bandura, 1969).

Overall, Bandura presents behavioral approaches to psychotherapy as non-judgmental applications of learning principles to problematic behavior, behavior that is not to be viewed as psychological "illness:"

> …From a social-learning perspective, behaviors that may be detrimental to the individual or that depart widely from accepted social and ethical norms are considered not as manifestations of an underlying pathology but as ways, which the person has learned, of coping with environmental and self-imposed demands. (pg. 62; Bandura, 1969)

Cognitive Aspects of Social Learning Theory: The Contributions of Julian Rotter and Walter Mischel

Julian Rotter deserves at least as much credit as Albert Bandura for the establishment of social learning theory. Indeed, his book *Social Learning & Clinical Psychology* (Rotter, 1954) was published five years before Bandura's *Adolescent Aggression* (Bandura & Walters, 1959). In addition, Rotter always focused on cognitive aspects of social learning, something Bandura gave more consideration to only later in his career. But their careers were by no means separated from one another. Walter Mischel was Rotter's graduate student, and later joined the faculty of Stanford University where he was a colleague of Bandura. Mischel and Bandura collaborated on some of Mischel's best known research: delayed gratification.

Brief Biographies of Julian Rotter and Walter Mischel

Julian Rotter was born in 1916 in Brooklyn, NY. The son of successful Jewish immigrants, his childhood was quite comfortable. During the Great Depression, however, the family business failed, and for a few years the family struggled (as many people did). This time of struggle instilled in Rotter a profound sense of social justice, as well as an interest in the effects of situational environments.

As a child Rotter was an avid reader, and eventually he read most of the novels in the local library. He then turned to reading books on psychology, taking a particular interest in works by Freud and Adler. During his senior year in high school he was interpreting people's dreams and he wrote a paper based on Freud's *Psychopathology of Everyday Life* (Freud, 1904/1995). He attended Brooklyn College, but chose to major in chemistry instead of psychology, as it seemed more likely to provide a promising career. During college, however, he learned that Adler was teaching at the Long Island College of Medicine. He began attending Adler's seminars, became Adler's friend, and was invited to meetings of the Society for Individual Psychology. Another well-known psychology professor who influenced Rotter was Solomon Asch. When he graduated from Brooklyn College, he actually had more credits in psychology than in chemistry.

Rotter attended the University of Iowa, where he earned a Master's Degree in 1938, and then took a clinical internship at the Worcester State Hospital in Massachusetts. A year later he began working on his Ph.D. at Indiana University, because a professor there, C. M Louttit, had published one of the first books advocating clinical psychology as a career. Rotter received his Ph.D. in Clinical Psychology in 1941. After a short period of time at Norwich State Hospital in Connecticut, Rotter was drafted into the Army. He spent World War II working as a military psychologist. After the war he briefly returned to Norwich, but soon Rotter accepted a position at Ohio State University.

It was during his time at Ohio State University that Rotter developed his ideas on social learning theory. He and George Kelly were the two most prominent members of the psychology department, each of them having a lasting influence in the fields of social and cognitive learning theory. Rotter attracted many excellent graduate students, including Walter Mischel. Rotter was also keenly interested in the training of clinical psychologists, and he helped to outline the training model that became the basis for how doctoral level clinical psychologists are trained today.

As much as he enjoyed his time at Ohio State University, Rotter left in 1963 to direct the rebuilding of the clinical psychology training program at the University of Connecticut. He retired as professor emeritus in 1987. One year later he received an American Psychological Association's *Distinguished Scientific Contribution Award*, and one year after that he was recognized by the Council of University Directors of Clinical Psychology with their *Distinguished Contribution to Clinical Training Award*. He has also worked with the Peace Corps. Rotter included a brief autobiography in his self-edited compendium entitled *The Development and Applications of Social Learning Theory* (Rotter, 1982).

Walter Mischel was born in 1930, into a comfortable home, where he enjoyed a pleasant childhood. They lived in Vienna, a short distance from Sigmund Freud's house. However, when the Nazis invaded Austria at the beginning of World War II, the Mischel family moved to the United States, eventually settling in New York City. In college, Mischel studied to become a social worker. While working as a social worker in the Lower East Side slums, Mischel attended City College of New York and pursued a graduate degree in clinical psychology. He had been taught that Freud's theory offered the best explanation of human behavior, but he did not find this to be true in his work with juvenile delinquents (the same practical conclusion occurred to Carl Rogers in his first clinical position).

He then attended Ohio State University, where he was a graduate student of both Julian Rotter and George Kelly. Rotter and Kelly helped to firmly establish Mischel as a member of the general social learning/cognitive learning camp, and later Mischel became a faculty member at Stanford University, alongside Albert Bandura (from 1962-1983). He then returned to New York as a faculty member at Columbia University, where he continued his work on delayed gratification and the effects of situations on personal behavior. Mischel has been recognized with a *Distinguished Scientific Contribution Award* by the American Psychological Association.

Placing Rotter and Mischel in Context: Cognitive Social Learning Theory

The distinction between Bandura as a social learning theorist, and Rotter and Mischel as cognitive learning theorists, is not entirely accurate. As Bandura's career progressed, he focused more and more on cognitive factors, and Mischel collaborated with Bandura while both were at Stanford University. What distinguishes Rotter and Mischel is that cognitive factors were always the most important aspect of their learning theories. Although humans are capable of learning simply by watching a model, their expectations regarding the outcome of a situation, and the value the place on the potential reward (or punishment), determines their course of action. According to Mischel, these variables can lead to seemingly inconsistent behavior, but when examined in closer detail individuals demonstrate consistent patterns of variation, a form of consistency in itself.

Rotter and Mischel can also be seen as having encompassed Bandura's career. Although all three men were active during the same general time frame, Rotter's first book on social learning theory preceded Bandura's first book by 5 years. Mischel, a student of Rotter, and then a colleague of Bandura for a while, has continued to modify his most influential theory quite recently, in the 1990s and 2000s.

Rotter and Mischel can also be considered as providing a bridge between the more traditional social learning theory of Bandura and the full-fledged cognitive theory of George Kelly. Kelly was

Rotter's colleague at Ohio State University, and Mischel studied under both men while in graduate school. Thus, social learning theory, cognitive social learning theory, and cognitive theories of personality development all occurred in close relationship to one another, and they all offered a dramatic alternative to radical behaviorism, an alternative that helped to fulfill the vision of John Dollard and Neal Miller.

Basic Constructs in Rotter's Social Learning Theory

Rotter's early research focused on the need to understand human behavior and personality so that clinical psychologists might effectively help their patients. In the preface to *Social Learning & Clinical Psychology*, Rotter wrote:

> …the practice of clinical psychology in many instances is unsystematic and confused when viewed from logical or rigorous scientific viewpoints. This confusion, however, is not a necessary condition but the result of the failure of the clinical psychologists' training program to translate and relate the basic knowledge of experimental and theoretical psychology into the practical situations of the clinic, the hospital, and the school… (pg. viii; Rotter, 1954)

Given his emphasis on clinical psychology, Rotter focused on the clinician's ability to predict behavior. According to Rotter, social learning theory assumes that the unit of investigation for the study of personality is the interaction between the individual and their meaningful environment. Although personality has unity, the individual's experiences influence each other. As a result, personality is continuously changing, since each person is always having new experiences. However, personality is also stable in some respects, since previous experiences influence new learning. Given the complexity of each individual, Rotter believed that in order to make reasonable predictions about behavior it was necessary to examine four kinds of variables: **behavior potential**, **expectancy**, **reinforcement value**, and the **psychological situation** (Rotter, 1954, 1964, 1972; Rotter & Hochreich, 1975).

Behavior potential refers to the likelihood of a certain behavior occurring in the context of specific potential reinforcement. For example, in order to earn good grades a student can rely on any number of possible behaviors, such as studying, cheating, skipping class to avoid a bad grade, etc. Each potential behavior can only be described as more or less likely than other potential behaviors, and included as potential behaviors are psychological reactions such as thoughts, emotions, and even defense mechanisms. Expectancy is defined as the probability held by the individual that reinforcement will follow one's chosen behavior. Although Rotter preferred to avoid the concept that expectancy is subjective, he acknowledged that an element of subjectivity is involved. Regardless, it is the individual's point of view, their expectations in a given situation, that are more important for predicting behavior than the realistic probability of a chosen behavior resulting in an expected reinforcement. Reinforcement value, quite simply, refers to the preference for a given reinforcer. To use Rotter's own example, most people would consistently choose to be paid $10 dollars an hour rather than $1 an hour, if it were simply their choice. Finally, there is the psychological situation. According to Rotter, it is not enough to say that to each individual a given situation might seem different. In order to address the situation in more objective terms, psychologists need to identify a variety of cues within the situation. In an objective sense, consequently, different people can be described as attending to different specific cues in the environment (Rotter, 1954, 1972; Rotter & Hochreich, 1975).

Although Rotter broke new ground in this approach to the study of social learning theory, he did not entirely abandon the use of mathematical formulae similar to those of Dollard and Miller. Rotter proposed the following basic formula for predicting goal-directed behavior:

$$BP_{x,S1Ra} = f(E_{x,RaS1} \ \& \ RV_{a,S1})$$

Although this formula appears complicated at first glance, it is relatively straightforward. The potential for behavior x (BPx) to occur in situation 1 with potential reinforcement a (S1Ra) is a function (f) of the expectancy (E) that reinforcement a will follow behavior x in situation 1 (x,RaS1) and the reinforcement value (RV) of reinforcement a in situation 1 (a,S1) (Rotter, 1954; Rotter & Hochreich, 1975). In other words, we are most likely to choose the behavioral option that we realistically expect will result in the most favorable outcome in our current situation.

> **Discussion Question:** Rotter believed that both the expectancy of reward and the perceived value of that reward were essential in determining whether an individual engaged in a particular behavior. Have you ever found yourself doing something even though you did not expect to get anything for your efforts? Have you ever had a job where you felt that you weren't being paid what you deserved? In such situations, how long did you continue your behavior, and how did you feel about it?

Locus of Control

One of the most important generalized expectancies underlying behavior, and perhaps Rotter's best known concept, is referred to as **internal versus external control of reinforcement** (commonly known as **locus of control**):

> People are known to differ in their belief that what happens to them is the result of their own behaviors and attributes (internal control) versus the result of luck, fate, chance, or powerful others (external control). Clearly, persons who believe or expect that they can control their own destinies will behave differently, in many situations, than those who expect that their outcomes are controlled by other people or determined by luck. (pg. 105; Rotter & Hochreich, 1975)

Rotter pointed out that almost all psychologists recognize the role that reinforcement or reward plays in determining future behavior, but that this is not a "simple stamping-in process." For beings as complex as humans, the effects of reinforcement depend upon an individual's perception of a causal relationship between their behavior and the potential reward (Rotter & Hochreich, 1975).

A number of scales have been developed to measure locus of control (for an early review see Lefcourt, 1976), including one developed by Rotter himself (Rotter, 1966). Rotter's scale, simply referred to as the **I-E scale** (for internal-external), consists of 29 forced-choice statements. For example:

1.a. Children get into trouble because their parents punish them too much.
1.b. The trouble with most children nowadays is that their parents are too easy with them.

In each instance, the person taking the test must choose one or the other option. After taking all 29, the person's score is the total number of external choices. Does it seem difficult to determine whether 1.a. or 1.b. is the external choice? Good! Question 1 is actually a filler question, designed to interfere with the test taker's ability to understand what the test is about! So, consider question 2:

2.a. Many of the unhappy things in people's lives are partly due to bad luck.
2.b. People's misfortunes result from the mistakes they make.

For question 2 it is quite obvious that choice a is the external choice, and if it wasn't clear, the test has choice a marked for you! There are a total of six filler questions, leaving the test itself with 23 choices (Rotter, 1966).

Locus of control appears to arise from two primary sources: the family, and **contingency awareness** (Lefcourt, 1976). The role of the family in the development of locus of control is complex, and appears to be somewhat different based on the behavior of mothers and fathers. The most reliable finding appears to be that individuals with an internal locus of control had mothers who pushed them to achieve independence at an early age. This motherly push, however, must be a careful one. Children need support, guidance and nurturance, but they must not be smothered to the point of being pampered. Lefcourt (1976) cites Adler's concern regarding two extremes in child-rearing, pampering and neglect, neither of which is conducive to the healthy psychological growth of a child. Contingency awareness refers to an understanding of instrumentality, the conception that one's actions are indeed related to certain outcomes. In order for a child to repeat a behavior with purpose, the child must be able to recall that their prior actions resulted in a given outcome, and they must know that their actions were related to the expected outcomes. It would appear that children as young as two months old are capable of this type of social learning, and it tends to result in positive emotional reactions (Lefcourt, 1976).

Early studies on locus of control also focused on some interesting cultural questions. It is generally accepted that social class and ethnic group are important determinants of personality. Battle and Rotter (1963) found that lower class Blacks were significantly more external in their locus of control than were middle class Whites. Interestingly, middle class Blacks were closer to middle class Whites than lower class Whites were to middle class Whites, suggesting that social class may have been the primary factor in these results, rather than the race or ethnicity of the subjects. Furthermore, IQ seems to have exacerbated these results in that the most external individuals were high IQ lower class Blacks (i.e., individuals aware of social injustice in American society) and the most internal individuals were low IQ middle class Whites (who may be blaming themselves for failing to live up to their expected potential; Battle & Rotter, 1963). During the civil rights movement, Gore & Rotter (1963) examined whether locus of control might be a useful measure of social action. They found that students at a southern Black college who expressed interest in attending a civil rights rally or marching on the state capitol scored significantly more internal on the I-E scale. In other words, those who believed they could personally make a difference were more willing to try making that difference. In a study that followed soon after, Strickland (1965) compared Blacks who were indeed active in the civil rights movement to those who were not (but who were matched for sex, age, education, etc.). As predicted, the individuals who were active in the civil rights movement scored significantly more internal on the I-E scale than those who were not active. Strickland did note, however, that the individuals she studied were pioneers in the civil rights movement, and had become active, in part, because others groups had failed to demonstrate an adequate degree of commitment to the civil rights movement. Strickland's concern seems to contradict earlier results of Mischel (1958a), who found that when individual's make public commitments, they are less likely to change their expectancies (i.e., individuals publicly involved in the civil rights movement should have remained committed to the cause even when faced with initial failure). Still, as Mischel himself noted, one cannot rely entirely on inferences from research when considering the complexities of real-life (and, at the time, dangerous) behavior.

Discussion Question: Do you consider yourself to have an internal or an external locus of control? Do you feel that locus of control is an important influence on personality; might it be good or bad?

Rotter's Emphasis on Clinical Psychology

As noted above, Rotter was actively involved in developing the model that provided the basis for how clinical psychologists are typically trained today. Accordingly, much of Rotter's career was devoted to clinical applications of his work, In addition to writing two books that emphasized clinical psychology (Rotter, 1954, 1964) and developing the I-E scale (Rotter, 1966), Rotter and one of his research assistants published *The Rotter Incomplete Sentences Blank: College Form* (Rotter and Rafferty, 1950). The book was intended to formalize the **sentence completion method**, particularly for use with college students. The test consists of forty simple statements that require the subject to finish the sentence. For example, one beginning is simply "My father…" The subjects responses are then scored in terms of whether they demonstrate conflict (on a scale of 1-3), are neutral, or whether they are positive (also on a scale of 1-3). The manual offers examples of possible answers for both males and females. For example, conflicted responses for males include breaking promises or being a fool (level 3), or never had much of a chance or is proud (level 1). A neutral response might simply be that the father is a salesman, or is a hard worker. Positive responses for females include that the father is quite a character or is a good man (level 1), or that he has a great sense of humor or is a lot of fun (level 3). Interpreting this test requires a great deal of experience, and an understanding of personality and human nature. Fortunately, Rotter and Rafferty include a number of individual cases as examples of how the **Rotter Incomplete Sentences Blank** can be used to evaluate individuals. Both the Rotter Incomplete Sentences Blank and the I-E scale have proven useful in evaluating patients, as well as normal individuals, in a variety of settings and cultures, including Africa, Sri Lanka, American Indians, Brazil, Black and White college students in America, Ukrainian doctors training in Canada, and amongst military personnel (Janzen, Paterson, Reid, & Everall, 1996; Lefcourt, 1976; Logan & Waehler, 2001; Nagelschmidt & Jakob, 1977; Niles, 1981; Picano, Roland, Rollins, & Williams, 2002; Rossier,

Dahourou, & McCrae, 2005; Rotter, 1960, 1966; Trimble & Richardson, 1982). In a particularly interesting study, a unique version of the Sentence Completion Test was developed by Herbert Phillips and provided the basis for a major study on the personality of Thai peasants living in the village of Bang Chan, Thailand (Phillips, 1965). The Rotter Incomplete Sentences Blank, and other variations of the sentence completion method, remain very popular today (Holaday, Smith, & Sherry, 2000), ranking with the Rorschach Inkblot Test and the Thematic Apperception Test as the most popular projective tests for personality assessment.

Overall, Rotter emphasized the value of training clinical psychologists for just that responsibility, with a particular emphasis on the realities that will face the psychologist in an actual clinical setting (Rotter, 1954, 1964). In 1972, Rotter edited a volume including both original and previously published papers in which social learning theory was applied to psychopathology in general (Phares, 1972) and to such diverse topics as drinking amongst college students, excessively needy individuals, working with mentally retarded children, and electroconvulsive shock therapy (Cromwell, 1972; Dies, 1968; Jessor, Carman, & Grossman, 1968; Jessor, Liverant, & Opochinsky, 1963). A particularly important aspect of therapy also addressed in this volume is the issue of terminating therapy. Strickland & Crowne (1963) found that defensiveness and avoiding self-criticism are common signs in individuals who are likely to end therapy abruptly, whereas Piper, Wogan, & Getter (1972) found that the patient's expectancy regarding improvement, and the value they place on improving, are useful predictors of terminating therapy. Although helping patient's to achieve a level of psychological health that allows terminating therapy should be the goal of every therapist, premature termination might prove even more detrimental to the patient. For Rotter, the proper training of clinical psychologists is not an easy task. In the preface to *Clinical Psychology*, Rotter wrote:

> ...Yet psychology itself is a relatively new science and its areas of application are in rapid transition. Neither theory nor "facts" are always agreed upon, and in clinical psychology there is no single set of orthodox, approved skills for which a person can be certified as a trained practitioner...The goal is to gain comprehension without resorting to an oversimplification of the complex nature of man or of the problem of understanding him. (pg. xi; Rotter, 1964).

Behavioral Specificity and Consistency

In 1968, Walter Mischel challenged both state and trait theories of personality. Psychological states typically fall with the domain of psychodynamic theory, whereas trait theories are a perspective unto themselves. According to Mischel (1968), although state and trait theorists use very different language, they tend to approach personality in the same general way: they use responses to infer pervasive, underlying mental structures that exert enduring causal effects on behavior. Thus, both state and trait theorists emphasize consistency in behavior. However, there is a wealth of data that individuals do not act consistently from situation to situation. Instead, Mischel argues, behavior can best be predicted only when one takes into account the specific situation in which the behavior occurs:

> Progress in the area of personality psychology and assessment has been hindered by the failure to apply relevant principles about the conditions that produce, maintain, and modify social behavior. The principles that emerge from basic research too often have not been seen as directly relevant to the understanding of the determinants of test responses in the clinic or the assessment project. It is as if we live in two independent worlds: The abstractions and artificial situations of the laboratory and the realities of life. (pg. 1; Mischel, 1968).

In order to support his argument, Mischel examined which aspects of behavior are or are not consistent. Generally, intellect is consistent, including academic ability, achievement, and cognitive style. In contrast, there is little evidence to support consistency of behavior across situations when examining personality variables such as attitudes, moral behavior, sexual identification, dependency, aggression, tolerance, conditionability, etc. (Mischel, 1968). How, then, might we predict behavior? Mischel suggests a dynamic perspective on how persons interact with their situations. If the environment has not changed much, we can expect past behavior to be a reasonable predictor of current behavior (and state and trait theories would seem to hold true as well). However, if the environment changes dramatically, the individual may act in unpredictable ways. In addition, the individual may begin to learn new social conditions, thus allowing for considerable change in behavior over time:

> Global traits and states are excessively crude, gross units to encompass adequately the extraordinary complexity and subtlety of the discriminations that people constantly make. Traditional trait-state conceptions of man have depicted him as victimized by his infantile history, as possessed by unchanging rigid trait attributes, and as driven inexorably by unconscious irrational forces…A more adequate conceptualization must take full account of man's extraordinary adaptiveness and capacities for discrimination, awareness, and self-regulation…and that an understanding of how humans can constructively modify their behavior in systematic ways is the core of a truly dynamic personality psychology. (pg. 301; Mischel, 1968)

Delayed Gratification

Perhaps Mischel's most famous contribution to psychology is his research on **delayed gratification**. In a series of studies, begun in the late 1950s, Mischel examined the conditions under which children choose immediate gratification or whether they can delay gratification in order to obtain a larger reinforcer at a later time. The ability to delay gratification, according to Mischel, is essential for the development of self-control. From early childhood throughout the lifespan, achieving long-term goals often requires setting aside tempting distractions. Conversely, many personal and social problems result from failures of self-control, such as dropping out of school, poor job performance, and even violent and criminal behavior (Mischel & Mischel, 1980). In an amazing longitudinal study, Mischel and his colleagues offered 4 year-old children the opportunity to grab a marshmallow. But, if the child could wait until the researcher ran an errand, the child could then have two marshmallows! Some children grabbed the marshmallow as soon as the experimenter left, but others were able to wait 15-20 minutes. It was not easy, however. The children who waited demonstrated a variety of behaviors to distract themselves from the marshmallow: they would play, sing, cover their eyes so they didn't have to look at the marshmallow, etc. The most striking results from this study were actually obtained years later. Mischel and his colleagues tracked down the former 4 year-old subjects as they were graduating from high school. The individuals who had delayed gratification as 4 year-olds were significantly more personally effective and self-assertive, and they were better able to cope with life's frustrations (Mischel, Shoda, & Rodriguez, 1989; Shoda, Mischel, & Peake, 1990). In addition, the 4 year-old children who had been able to delay gratification were more successful as students in a variety of ways, including eventually earning significantly higher SAT scores (210 points higher, on the combined score), and the ability to delay gratification proved to be a better predictor of SAT scores than IQ (Peake, cited in Goleman, 1994).

Although the famous marshmallow-grabbing study was conducted at a preschool on the campus of Stanford University, Mischel began this research with very different groups: Black and East Indian children on the islands of Trinidad and Grenada (Mischel, 1958b, 1961). On these relatively poor, Caribbean islands, Mischel not only compared the Black and East Indian children, he also compared the children of Trinidad to the children of Grenada. The main purpose of the second study, however, was to examine the effect of fathers being absent from the home on the preference of children for immediate or delayed gratification. Overall, when fathers are absent from the home, both young boys and young girls (ages 8 to 9 years old) demonstrated a preference for immediate gratification. Mischel suggests that the inability to delay gratification amongst children who lack a father may be related to immaturity or poor psychological adjustment (Mischel, 1961).

While Mischel was at Stanford University, he also collaborated with Bandura. Blending the interests of both men, they examined whether observing models would affect children's choices regarding immediate vs. delayed gratification. They identified two groups of children (both boys and girls) as preferring either immediate gratification (a small candy bar now) or delayed gratification (a larger candy bar later). The children were then exposed to either a live model choosing the alternative strategy, a symbolic model (a description of an adult choosing the alternative), or no model. As expected, exposure to a model choosing the alternative strategy dramatically affected the behavior of the children, and a live model was more effective than the symbolic model. The effects of this modeling appeared to be quite persistent (Bandura & Mischel, 1965). Considering the importance that modeling can play in developing the ability to delay gratification, it is perhaps easy to see why children in families lacking a complete and stable family structure don't develop self-control as well as other children.

Sometimes, delaying gratification can be very difficult for children. [Image by Danielle MacInnes]

Discussion Question: Mischel's most famous contribution is the concept of delayed gratification. How good are you at waiting for gratification? Are some rewards easier to wait for than others? If you know anyone who is significantly different than you, either wanting immediate gratification or being able to delay it without much trouble, does the difference between you create any problems or interesting situations?

The Cognitive-Affective Processing System (CAPS)

More recently, Mischel has turned his attention to solving what has been called the "**personality paradox**:" How do we reconcile our intuition and theories that personality is relatively stable with the overwhelming evidence that personality varies across different situations? Mischel proposes a dynamic personality system that takes into account both: (1) the behavioral consistency that accounts for specific scores on trait tests and indicates what the individual is like in general; and (2) the consistency in how an individual varies across different situations. This consistency of variation is recognized by distinct patterns of *if...then...* relationships, which are characteristic of the individual's overall personality (Mischel, 2004).

In 1995, Mischel and Shoda first presented this dynamic approach to understanding personality, referring to it then as the cognitive-affective personality system, but now preferring the term **cognitive-affective processing system** (CAPS; Mischel, 2004; Mischel & Shoda, 1995/2000; Shoda, Leetiernan, & Mischel, 2002). Over a number of years, Mischel, his students, and his colleagues studied children extensively in a residential summer camp. They observed both behaviors and the situations in which they occurred. Over time, they were able to identify patterns of *if...then...* situation-behavior relations that reflected distinctive and stable characteristics of each child's behavior organization. These observations, therefore, gave rise to **situation-behavior profiles** for each child. It is essential to recognize, however, that the term "situation" in these studies does not refer to simple environmental stimuli, as they might for a behaviorist such as B. F. Skinner. Instead, these situations activate a whole set of internal reactions, including cognitive and emotional elements. They are also not limited to the external world; they can be generated in thought, fantasy, planning, etc. Accordingly, Mischel and Shoda referred to these personality variables as **cognitive-affective units** (or CAUs). These CAUs include encodings, expectancies and beliefs, affects, goals and values, and competencies and self-regulatory plans.

Mischel and Shoda (1995/2000) did not neglect the individual's development in this theory. Our ability to recognize distinct aspects of the environment are influenced by genetic/biological factors, cultural factors, and the interactions between them. These genetic/biological/cultural factors also influence the CAPS, as does our social learning history. In a sense, bringing all of these factors together begins to move us beyond the person-situation debate, since both sides of the debate are correct in the proper context. The future of personality theory may lie in an as yet undetermined synthesis of these perspectives (Fleeson, 2004). For now, according to Mischel, this dynamic approach to understanding personality has at least helped to bring together the major aspects of different schools of personality theory:

> The two goals - dispositions and dynamics - that have so long been pursued separately do not require two fields from this perspective. In this theory, dispositions are conceptualized not in semantic terms but as processing structures characterized by stable cognitive affective

organizations in the processing system that becomes activated when the individual encounters relevant situational features. (pg. 170; Mischel & Shoda, 1995/2000)

The Impact of Social Learning Theory

It would be difficult to overestimate the impact of social learning theory on psychology, because the human species is so inherently social. Social life seems to come automatically, mediated via mental processes that are largely unconscious (Bargh & Williams, 2006), and our social norms appear to arise from social behavior that is adaptive within local ecologies (Kameda, Takezawa, & Hastie, 2005). It is important to note, however, that social organization is by no means unique to the human species. There are many animal species that live in social groups, some demonstrating a surprising degree of intelligence, suggesting that social living itself may have helped to foster the development of intelligence (Pennisi, 2006). Further evidence for the impact of social learning theory on psychology can be found in the simple name recognition enjoyed by Bandura, certainly one of the most famous psychologists.

There are also interesting lines of research within the field of neuroscience that provide support for Mischel and Shoda's cognitive-affective processing system. Utilizing functional magnetic resonance imaging (fMRI), Decety & Jackson (2006) have found that empathy appears to involve activation of the same brain regions involved in experiencing the situation about which one is feeling empathy toward another person. For example, there is significant activation of brain regions involved in pain when an individual views pictures of someone else in a clearly painful situation. This would seem to provide neurobiological evidence in support of Mischel and Shoda's cognitive-affective units, the functional components of the cognitive-affective processing system. Similarly, Knoblich & Sebanz (2006) have demonstrated that perceptual, cognitive, and motor processes are enhanced by social interaction, and that such interactions can be measured using event-related potentials that measure brain electrical activity. Some of the data presented in the study by Knoblich & Sebanz are essentially situation-behavior profiles for the individuals in their study.

Finally, let's address the role of expectancy in one of the most challenging social issues facing the world today: diversity. We hear more and more about the value of diversity in higher education and in the workplace, but pursuing diversity is often challenged by prejudice. Expectations of prejudice enhance attention to social cues that threaten one's social identity. In other words, when individuals expect that engaging in diversity will lead to prejudice, and perhaps then to discriminatory behavior, they are more likely to notice evidence of that very outcome (Kaiser, Vick, & Major, 2006). In addition, contact between diverse groups does less to displace feelings of prejudice among members of minority groups than it does among members of the majority group (likely due to the minority group members' recognition of the ongoing effects of prejudice and discrimination; Tropp & Pettigrew, 2005). These represent difficult situation-behavior circumstances, since it can obviously be very difficult for team members to predict the behavioral responses likely to follow the artificial establishment of diversity. In making recommendations to the leaders of organizational teams, Mannix & Neale (2005) suggest clearly defining the team's tasks and goals, providing bridges across diversity, and enhancing the influence of the minority. Perhaps most importantly, there is a need to provide incentives for change. Taken together, these approaches both increase the expectancy of success and raise the reinforcement value of working toward successfully diversifying the team. As such, principles that have arisen from social learning theory can clearly play a positive role is reshaping society.

The Future of Psychology: Bandura's Vision as Compared to Freud

In *Toward a Psychology of Human Agency*, Bandura (2006) agrees with Freud that religion played a significant role in the advancement of civilization, and that the scientific revolution that began with Darwin's Theory of Evolution shifted our focus toward natural and scientific approaches to understanding and improving human life. However, evolution emphasizes random effects on genetically determined structures and traits, and does not allow for the choices made by individuals, though sociobiologists argue that genetics can exert influences on those choices. Rather than relying on psychoanalysis in order to understand the impulses of the id that drive us to survive, as Freud proposed (1927/1961, 1930/1961), Bandura believes that people are agents of change in their own lives, and that they can choose the direction that change takes.

Being an agent involves intentionally influencing one's functioning and life circumstances, and there are four core properties of human agency. **Intentionality** refers to our ability to form action plans and the strategies necessary for accomplishing them. **Forethought** is the temporal extension of agency, in which we set goals for ourselves and anticipate likely outcomes of our actions to both guide and motivate our behavior. Once having chosen a course of action, of course, we do not simply sit back and wait for the right things to happen. Agency also involves both **self-reactiveness** and **self-reflectiveness**, processes in which we regulate our behavior, monitor our courses of action, and examine whether we are capable of being successful in our various endeavors (Bandura, 2006). As much as human agency involves our own thoughts, goals, motivation, and expectations, however, we do not exist autonomously. All human behavior occurs within social structures, and there is a reciprocal interplay between personal, behavioral, and environmental determinants (reciprocal determinism). This means that human agency, the exercise of self-influence, is part of the causal structure of our lives. As Bandura points out, this is not "free will," which would be a throwback to medieval theology, but rather a matter of acting as an agent, the role of an individual in making causal contributions to the course of events in their life (Bandura, 2006).

> ...Social cognitive theory rejects a duality of human agency and a disembodied social structure. Social systems are the product of human activity, and social systems, in turn, help to organize, guide, and regulate human affairs. However, in the dynamic interplay within the societal rule structures, there is considerable personal variation in the interpretation of, adoption of, enforcement of, circumvention of, and opposition to societal prescriptions and sanctions...freedom is conceived not just passively as the absence of constraints, but also proactively as the exercise of self-influence... (pg. 165; Bandura, 2006)

Personality Theory in Real Life: Media Violence and Its Effects on Children

The second Bobo doll study conducted by Bandura and his colleagues presented videotapes of the models behaving aggressively toward the Bobo doll (Bandura, Ross, & Ross, 1963a). The observation in this study that children did, indeed, imitate the aggressive behavior of models seen on film, but not in person, has become one the most influential articles in history, both in terms of stimulating further research on the modeling of aggression and in terms of practical applications (e.g., ratings on television programs, video games, and CDs with controversial lyrics). In their introduction to an issue of *Psychological Science in the Public Interest* (*PSPI*) on media violence and its effects on children, Ceci and Bjork (2003) describe how the authors of this particular *PSPI* issue were a collection of experts brought together to prepare a portion of the U.S. Surgeon General's report on youth violence. However, political concerns led the Surgeon General's office to radically alter the report. The authors protested, and attempted to satisfy the concerns of the politicians. Ultimately, however, this portion of the report was dropped from the final version. So, the editors of PSPI chose to publish this valuable psychological information, which clearly causes political concerns for some, so that psychologists, psychiatrists, law enforcement officials, teachers and school administrators, government policy makers, parents, indeed anyone who has a vested interest in youth violence, might have the most current information available on the effects of media violence on America's youth. I would also like to acknowledge an important point made by the authors themselves. This issue of PSPI was a collaborative project by eight experts on the effects of media violence. The authors decided that the fairest way to list their names was alphabetical order. Thus, as I refer to the article as Anderson, et al. (2003), please note that the "et al." includes widely respected experts, chosen by the National Institute of Mental Health for this project, each of whom contributed significantly to this article.

It would be difficult to do justice to this report by summarizing it here, since the report, which is a review itself, is nearly thirty pages long and cites 245 research studies. Clearly, the attention drawn by this question, the role of media violence in affecting violent behavior among children, provides a testament to the significance of this research. Anderson, et al. (2003) provide an overview of the empirical research, offer theoretical explanations, they address moderating effects, media use and content, and they examine research on interventions.

Empirical research on media violence and aggression has covered of wide variety of media types, including dramatic television and movies, television news violence, music videos and their lyrics, video games, and the internet. The review of this extensive body of research has shown a statistically significant association between exposure to media violence and aggression and violence among youth. Exposure to media violence, and the findings are consistent across the various types of media, increases the likelihood that children have aggressive thoughts and, indeed, engage in aggressive behavior. Most importantly, longitudinal studies have consistently shown that exposure to media violence in childhood, even beginning in late adolescence, are predictors of increased aggression and violent behavior in adulthood. Although the effects are at best small to medium, the authors note that they are as high as other problems that are considered significant public health issues, such as cigarette smoking and exposure to asbestos.

Several theories have been put forth to explain the manner in which exposure to media violence increases aggression in children, not the least of which is Bandura's theory of observational learning. Observational learning appears to be so important to the humans, and other primate species, that we have developed a specific neurological system to learn from watching others: the **mirror-neuron system** (see Rizzolatti & Craighero, 2004). Additional theories suggest that exposure to media violence prepares an individual to engage in aggressive behavior. This can occur either because the media violence primes the individual by activating aggressive thoughts and scripts or by generally arousing the individual, and that arousal then carries over into heightened aggressive behavior in situations that provoke aggressive actions. Finally, there is the widely used, and often misunderstood, term "**desensitization**." Anderson et al. (2003) prefer the term **emotional desensitization** to refer to a reduction in distress-related reactions to observing or thinking about violence. Although emotional desensitization may result in an individual being more willing to engage in aggressive or violent behavior, there is no evidence that it stimulates aggression. Thus, although emotional desensitization may be related to the disinhibition discussed in the chapter (it may even be the same thing), its role remains unclear.

Not all children are affected by media violence in the same way, and not all examples of media violence are equally effective in enhancing aggression. Thus, there must be moderating factors that come into play in the relationship between exposure to media violence and subsequent aggressive behavior. For example, the effects of media violence decline as children grow older, media violence is less likely to affect children who are less aggressive to begin with, and, although there is not a direct effect of intelligence, children of lower intelligence are more likely to watch television and to be at risk for other factors enhancing aggressiveness. The way in which the violence is presented in the media is also important, as is any portrayed justification for the violence as well as its consequences. However, all of these relationships are complex, and have not been studied in great detail. Thus, there is much more work to be done. Finally, one of the most important moderating factors is parental control. When parents discuss the content of media violence with their children, when they comment regularly on the reality of violence, children are much less likely to demonstrate aggressive tendencies.

This entire discussion would be moot, if not for the prevalence of media in our society and the content of that media. Data reported by Anderson, et al. (2003) from three national surveys provide an amazing view of media availability in America. Virtually all families with children have a television set, most have at least one VCR or DVD player, and about three quarters of those families subscribe to cable or satellite television. Approximately 70 percent of families with children have a video game system and a computer, and most American children have a television in their room (including 30 percent of children age 0 to 3 years old!). Watching television is the third most common activity for children, after sleeping and going to school. A significant number of children watch more than 40 hours of television a week, and children ages 0 to 6 years spend more time engaged in media entertainment than engaged in reading, being read to, and playing outside combined! And what's included in that media content? Plenty of violence: 61 percent of programs contain violence, and only 4 percent of programs contain an anti-violence theme:

> ...put in another way, 96% of all violent television programs use aggression as a narrative, cinematic device for simply entertaining the audience...Moreover, most aggression on television is glamorized and trivialized...and nearly 75% of all violent scenes feature no immediate punishment or condemnation for violence. (pg. 101; Anderson, et al., 2003)

Similar findings have been reported for violence in video games, both in America and in Japan. Parents seldom recognize the popularity of those violent games, and only about one third of parents even knew the name of their child's favorite video game (Anderson, et al., 2003).

Despite the wealth of information on the relationship between exposure to media violence and aggressive behavior, and a number of potential approaches for intervention, there has been little empirical research on potential interventions. In general, there are three approaches to reducing the influence of violent media: changing attitudes to counter violent messages, encouraging parental monitoring and guidance, and providing education on the content and effects of various forms of media. But once again, none of these potential interventions has been studied in detail. It must also be remembered that this is only one of many factors that contribute to aggressive and violent behavior amongst youth, though it may be the least expensive to address, since it involves little more than making choices about the media children are exposed to:

> ...However, the troubling truth is that violent media are entering the home and inviting active participation of even very young children - often with little parental supervision...Although additional research to address unresolved questions is needed, it is clear that media violence is a causal risk factor that should be addressed in thoughtful ways...parents can reduce and shape their children's consumption of violent media...from a public-health perspective, today's consumption patterns are far from optimal. And for many youths, they are clearly harmful. (pgs. 105-106; Anderson, et al., 2003)

Research on this important issue certainly did not end with the publication of the *PSPI* issue in 2003. In a more recent study, Carnagey and Anderson (2005) had college students play one of three versions of a race-car video game: one version rewarded all violence, one punished all violence, and one was non-violent. Overall, rewarding violent actions in the game increased hostile emotion, aggressive thinking, and aggressive behavior. In contrast, punishing violence still increased hostile emotion, but did not increase aggressive thoughts or behaviors. The authors suggest that an important mechanism through which violent media increases aggressive behavior is to first increase aggressive thoughts and states of mind. Another interesting result in this study was that the non-violent game did not result in as much violence as the game in which violence was rewarded, suggesting that the violent behavior in the game was not simply the result of competitiveness by the players. Of course, not everyone responds aggressively when aggression is modeled. It appears that individuals who score high on the trait of agreeableness (one of the "Big Five" traits, see Chapter 13) are able to short-circuit the effects of aggression-related cues and curb their aggression (Meier, Robinson, & Wilkowski, 2006). Meier, et al. go on to suggest that teaching other people to associate aggression-related cues with prosocial behavior might become a valuable intervention in continued efforts to reduce aggression and violence in our society. First, however, it might prove important to reduce the number of weapons present in American society (or at least our relationship with them). Klinesmith, Kasser, and McAndrew (2006) recently demonstrated that when male college students were exposed to a gun there was an increase in both their testosterone levels and their aggressive behavior. Media violence is clearly not the only aggression-related cue present for most people. However, as noted above, it may well be one area in which a distinct reduction in such cues can easily be accomplished without substantial financial costs (but certainly with substantial benefits) to society.

Albert Bandura, Julian Rotter, and Walter Mischel

Review of Key Points

- Reciprocal determinism refers to the concept that behavior, personal factors, and environmental factors are equal, interlocking determinants of each other.
- Observational learning is a specific type of social learning in which observers view the behavior of models.
- Highly aggressive children appear to learn this behavior at home, having experienced their parents modeling aggressive behavior.
- When models are rewarded for aggressive behavior, the result can be the disinhibition of aggression that had previously been restrained.
- Social learning is different than either simple imitation or identification, in that social learning implies underlying psychological processes (cognition).
- In order for social learning to occur, conditions must be met that support the components of this process: attention, retention, production, and motivation.
- Since observers do not copy behavior perfectly, and since they may choose to mix and match the behavior of different models, observational learning can lead to new and different behaviors.
- Self-regulation refers to the processes of self-reinforcement and self-punishment. Self-reinforcement works primarily through its motivational effects.
- Self-efficacy is the belief in one's capabilities to perform specific behaviors in order to accomplish specific outcomes.
- Self-efficacy and self-esteem are separate concepts. An individual may lack a certain ability and be well aware of it, but if one's concept of self-worth is not tied to that skill, there will be no corresponding loss of self-esteem.
- Bandura referred to the ability to act as an agent of change in one's environment as personal agency.
- Bandura believed that behavioral approaches have an advantage over other methods of therapy because of their basis in rigorous, scientific testing.
- Behavioral therapies can only be successful if they focus on goals characterized by clear and observable behaviors.
- Rotter proposed that one must understand four kinds of variables in order to make reasonable predictions about behavior: behavior potential, expectancy, reinforcement value, and the psychological situation.
- Internal versus external control of reinforcement (aka, locus of control) may be the most important generalized expectancy underlying behavior, according to Rotter.
- Rotter developed the I-E scale in order to measure locus of control.
- A key element in locus of control is contingency awareness, the knowledge that one's behavior is capable of producing specific outcomes.
- Rotter also developed the Rotter Incomplete Sentences Blank, specifically designed to measure the personality and psychological adjustment of college students.
- Delayed gratification refers to the concept of working (or restraining oneself) at the present time for a reward that will be granted only at a later time.
- Working together, Mischel and Bandura showed that modeling can alter the preference of children for delayed or immediate gratification.
- Mischel addressed what is known as the personality paradox, the appearance that behavior is inconsistent, while our intuition suggests that behavior is consistent.
- Mischel and Shoda proposed the Cognitive-Affective Processing System (CAPS) in order to address the personality paradox. By developing situation-behavior profiles, it is possible to identify patterns in the apparent inconsistency of individual behavior.
- fMRI studies have demonstrated specific brain activity that appears to correspond to the cognitive-affective units that underlie the CAPS.
- Situation-behavior characteristics have helped to address some of the problems that arise in situations in which diverse groups do not come together easily.

Albert Bandura, Julian Rotter, and Walter Mischel

Review of Key Terms

attentional processes behavior potential cognitive-affective processing system cognitive-affective units contingency awareness delayed gratification desensitization disinhibition emotional desensitization expectancy forethought I-E scale identification imitation	intentionality internal vs. external control of reinforcement locus of control mirror-neuron system models/modeling motivational processes observational learning personal agency personality paradox production processes psychological situation reciprocal determinism reinforcement value	retention processes Rotter Incomplete Sentences Blank self-efficacy self-esteem self-punishment self-reactiveness self-reflectiveness self-regulation self-reinforcement sentence completion method situation-behavior profiles social learning theory

Annotated Bibliography

Bandura, A. (1986). ***Social foundations of thought & action: A social cognitive theory.*** **Upper Saddle River, NJ: Prentice-Hall.**
Bandura, A. (1997). ***Self-efficacy: The exercise of control.*** **New York, NY: W. H. Freeman and Company.**

These substantial books, written late in Bandura's career, summarize his theories and much of the research supporting them. Although his earlier books make for some very interesting reading, especially his first book on adolescent aggression, these two provide an updated and comprehensive overview of social learning theory from Bandura's perspective.

Bandura, A., Ross, D., & Ross, S. A. (1961). Transmission of aggression through imitation of aggressive models. ***Journal of Abnormal and Social Psychology, 63*****, 575-582.**
Bandura, A., Ross, D., & Ross, S. A. (1963a). Imitation of film-mediated aggressive models. ***Journal of Abnormal and Social Psychology, 66*****, 3-11.**

These classic research articles are probably included in every introductory psychology textbook. Since they provide the empirical basis for a line of research that has had a significant impact on society, they are an ideal example of the role research psychologists can play in helping to understand and improve our world.

Anderson, C. A., Berkowitz, L., Donnerstein, E., Huesmann, L. R., Johnson, J. D., Linz, D., Malamuth, N. M., & Wartella, E. (2003). The influence of media violence on youth. ***Psychological Science in the Public Interest, 4*****, 81-110.**

Originally written for inclusion in a U.S. Surgeon General's report on youth violence, this special section of PSPI offers a thorough and excellent review of the influence of violent media on children, the leading theories attempting to explain those effects, and various interventions that may prove useful in mediating the effects of exposure to media violence.

De Mooij, M. (2004b). ***Consumer behavior and culture: Consequences for global marketing and advertising.*** **Thousand Oaks, CA: Sage Publications.**
De Mooij, M. (2005). ***Global marketing and advertising: Understanding cultural paradoxes, 2nd Ed.*** **Thousand Oaks, CA: Sage Publications.**

The most obvious, practical application of the factors that determine the influence of a model is advertising. As more companies, brands, and products become global, it is essential to understand how culture and psychology interact in determining the effectiveness of marketing campaigns and advertisements. De Mooij is a leading expert in this field, and her books are both readable and engaging.

Rotter, J. B. (1954). ***Social learning and clinical psychology*****. New York, NY: Prentice-Hall.**
Rotter, J. B. & Hochreich, D. J. (1975). ***Personality*****. Glenview, IL: Scott, Foresman and Company.**

In these two books Rotter covers the essential elements of his theories on cognitive social learning theory. Of particular interest in the second book is Rotter's own evaluation of a variety of theories on personality development, with his own theory included for comparison.

Lefcourt, H. M. (1976). ***Locus of control: Current trends in theory & research*****. Hillsdale, NJ: Lawrence Earlbaum Associates.**

Lefcourt offers an extensive review of the research on locus of control conducted by the mid-1970s. Of particular interest, Lefcourt also includes a number of tests that had been developed to measure locus of control. This offers significant insight into how other psychologists viewed Rotter's concept of locus of control.

Mischel, W. (1968). ***Personality and assessment*****. Mahwah, NJ: Lawrence Erlbaum Associates.**

In Michsel's only theoretical book, he challenged the prevailing attitudes in psychology, and sought instead to move toward and then beyond an integration of state and trait perspectives. Mischel argues that behavior is not consistent, and that we need to examine the dynamic manner in which people interact with their environments.

Mischel, W. & Shoda, Y. (1995/2000). A cognitive-affective system theory of personality: Reconceptualizing situations, dispositions, dynamics, and invariance in personality structure. In E. T. Higgins & A. W. Kruglanski (Eds.), ***Motivation Science: Social and Personality Perspectives*** **(pp. 150-176). Philadelphia, PA: Psychology Press.**
Mischel, W. (2004). Toward an integrative science of the person. ***Ann. Rev. Psych., 55*****, 1-22.**

Mischel and Shoda presented a theoretical perspective on personality theory, the cognitive-affective processing system (CAPS), which attempts to explain the consistency that can be seen in patterns of behavior that vary across situations. Mischel continues to advance this theory in his efforts to explain the "personality paradox."

Decety, J. & Jackson, P. L. (2006). A social-neuroscience perspective on empathy. ***Current Directions in Psychological Science, 15*****, 54-58.**
Rizzolatti, G. & Craighero, L. (2004). The mirror-neuron system. ***Annual Review of Neuroscience, 27*****, 169-192.**

In two fascinating studies from the field of behavioral neuroscience, these authors offer neurobiological evidence for the brain mechanisms underlying the theories presented in this chapter. Rizzolatti and Craighero have helped to identify brain regions that are inherently involved in observational learning in primates (including humans). Decety and Jackson have offered evidence of a brain mechanism underlying empathy, which looks very much like a potential cognitive-affective unit (the basis for Mischel and Shoda's CAPS).

Chapter 12 - George Kelly, Albert Ellis, and Aaron Beck

George Kelly's personal construct theory goes beyond the cognitive elements addressed by social learning theorists and provides a full-fledged cognitive theory. Kelly believed that individuals act very much like scientists studying personality: they create constructs, or expectations about the environment and people around them, and then they behave in ways that "test" those beliefs and expectations. For Kelly, the personal constructs are more important than actual reality, since it is the construct that guides cognition and behavior, not the actual situation. His theory was unique, and quite unrelated to others that came before and after. This was, in part, Kelly's very intention:

> It is only fair to warn the reader about what may be in store...the term *learning*, so honorably embedded in most psychological texts, scarcely appears at all. That is wholly intentional; we are for throwing it overboard altogether. There is no *ego*, no *emotion*, no *motivation*, no *reinforcement*, no *drive*, no *unconscious*, no *need*...all this will make for periods of strange, and perhaps uncomfortable, reading. Yet, inevitably, a different approach calls for a different lexicon... (pg. x; Kelly, 1955a)

Albert Ellis and Aaron Beck are best known for developing therapeutic techniques that are based on a cognitive perspective of personality and behavior. Although they are not known for developing actual theories of personality, their clinical approaches are based on underlying theoretical perspectives, which shed light on how they view the nature of personality. Thus, their influential work is naturally connected to that of Kelly, whose theory of personality was entirely cognitive (as compared to the cognitive social learning theorists Bandura, Rotter, and Mischel). More recently, there have been cognitive approaches to therapy put forth that are connected to much older approaches to human understanding. Acceptance and Commitment Therapy (ACT) takes an experiential approach to changing behavior that shares many similarities to Buddhist approaches (Hayes & Smith, 2005; Hayes, Strosahl, & Wilson, 1999), whereas Radical Acceptance relies directly on Buddhist teachings to encourage people to embrace their own lives (Brach, 2003).

Personal Construct Theory

Kelly's **personal construct theory** departs from cognitive social learning in that he proposes it is not simply enough to know what a person is likely to do in a given situation, even when your predictions are correct. More importantly, we need to know what a person might have done (Kelly, 1966). Thus, unlike the cognitive social learning theorists who consider cognitive processes as an aspect of the environmental circumstances associated with behavior, Kelly focused on the cognitive constructs first and foremost.

Kelly presented his personal construct theory in a two volume set, which was published in 1955 (Kelly, 1955a,b). In the mid-1960s Kelly was preparing a new book that was to include talks and papers he had presented around the world, many of which were never published. Unfortunately, he did not survive to complete this task, but the project was later completed by Brendan Maher (Maher, 1969), thus furthering the information available on this unique theory.

Brief Biography of George Kelly

Not much is known about George Kelly as a person, particularly regarding his childhood. Later in life he instructed his wife to destroy all of his personal correspondence. Thus, it has been somewhat difficult to piece together a picture of how this fascinating individual became the man he was. He was born in 1905 on a farm near Perth, Kansas. His father had been educated for the Presbyterian ministry, but after getting married his parents moved to the farm in Kansas, where they had their only child. The Kelly family moved around from farm to farm, including a failed farm in Colorado on some of the last free land given to settlers in the West. Kelly's education was erratic, and he learned what he could when the family would occasionally spend a few weeks in town. He attended four different high schools, and apparently never established any long-term relationships. He was, however, favorably influenced by the exciting stories told by his maternal grandfather, who had been the captain of a sailing ship in the North Atlantic (Fransella, 1995).

Despite his erratic education, Kelly attended college at Friends University and then Park College, where he received a Bachelor's degree in physics and mathematics. Despite studying math and science, the collegiate debates he experienced had sparked a keen interest in social problems. So, he entered the University of Kansas to earn a Master's degree in educational sociology, and in 1927 he completed his thesis on the distribution of leisure time activities of workers in Kansas City. He then moved to Minneapolis and supported himself by teaching one night a week in each of three different night schools. He began studying sociology and biometrics at the University of Minnesota, but when the university found out that he couldn't pay his tuition he was told to leave. He was then hired to teach psychology and speech at Sheldon Junior College in Iowa, where he spent a year and a half. He then returned to the University of Minnesota for a semester of studying sociology, but then went back to Wichita, Kansas and worked as an aeronautical engineer for a few months. He then received an exchange scholar fellowship to study at the University of Edinburgh in Scotland, where he earned a Bachelor's degree in education in 1930, having written his thesis on predicting teaching success. He then returned to the United States, attended the State University of Iowa, and in 1931 he received a Ph.D. in psychology, with a focus on reading and speech disabilities. Two days later he married Gladys Thompson (Fransella, 1995; Maher, 1969).

As uncharacteristic as it may seem, Kelly finally settled down. He spent the next ten years teaching at Fort Hays Kansas State College. His research and writings during this time focused on the practical aspects of providing clinical psychological services for schools. Much like Alfred Adler had in Austria, he developed traveling clinics to provide training around the state of Kansas, and his model had a dramatic influence on the future of rural school psychology. With the advent of World War II, however, Kelly entered the Navy as an aviation psychologist. At first he helped to train local civilian pilots, but then he transferred to the Bureau of Medicine and Surgery of the Navy in Washington to help select naval air cadets. After the war he spent a year at the University of Maryland, but in 1946 he was appointed Professor and director of Clinical Psychology at Ohio State University, where he spent the next 20 years (Fransella, 1995; Maher, 1969).

During his first few years at Ohio State he focused on making their clinical psychology training program into one of the best in the country. One of his colleagues in the department was Julian Rotter, also known for his role in shaping the training programs used in psychology today, and one of their students was Walter Mischel (who admired both Rotter and Kelly). Kelly then turned his attention to the theory that made him famous, the two volume work entitled *The Psychology of Personal Constructs* (Kelly, 1955a,b). Kelly's theory gained immediate recognition as both unique and significant, and he was invited to teach and lecture around the United States and in Europe, the Soviet Union, South America, Asia, and the Caribbean. He was elected president of both the Clinical Division and the Consulting Division of the American Psychological Association, and he served as president of the American Board of Examiners in Professional Psychology. In 1965, Kelly left Ohio State for Brandeis University, where he was appointed to the Riklis Chair of Behavioral Science. He began working on a collection of his papers and lectures from the past decade, but he died unexpectedly in March, 1966. As mentioned above, that collection of works was completed by the man who succeeded Kelly as Riklis Professor of Behavioral Science, and was published under the title *Clinical Psychology and Personality: The Selected Papers of George Kelly* (Maher, 1969).

Placing Kelly in Context: A Cognitive Theory of Personality

Simply put, Kelly's personal construct theory represents the culmination of the shift from animalistic behaviorism to humanistic cognition. In American psychology, behaviorism was a powerful force, and began with the very traditional approach of theorists such as John B. Watson and B. F. Skinner. Alongside the experimental behaviorists were the learning theorists, such as Clark Hull. As Dollard and Miller tried to find some common ground between psychodynamic theory and traditional learning approaches, they were inevitably led to consider the role of social factors in human learning. Bandura, Rotter, and Mischel built on the legacy of Dollard and Miller, but added to it the active role of cognition in the human species. Finally, Kelly moved to a purely cognitive description of how individuals become who they are.

However, we must address an important caveat. Just as Skinner's radical behaviorism was an extreme position of ignoring cognitive processes, perhaps Kelly's position is equally extreme for attributing significant cognitive processing to all aspects of personality and personality development. Although the man-the-scientist concept may hold a certain curious appeal for some, who doesn't sometimes knowingly try acting in different ways to see what effect it has on others? Likewise, who isn't attracted to a theory that says we desire the ability to both predict and control the events in our lives? However, as Kelly the therapist was keenly aware, many people cannot predict or control the events surrounding them. Is this always the result of failed construct systems, or is it possible that sometimes we just aren't thinking? Regardless of the answer, Kelly is the recognized leader of a significant development in the field of personality, a development that contributed to the highly regarded cognitive therapies of Ellis and Beck.

It is also interesting to note that the basis for his theory of constructive alternativism questions the reality of the self in a manner similar to Eastern/Buddhist concepts of consciousness and self. Carl Jung was dramatically influenced by the ancient Vedic traditions of India, and Carl Rogers, the founder of humanistic psychology, was influenced by the spiritual traditions of China. And now we have Kelly, whose theory represents the culmination of behavioral-cognitive theories, sharing a fundamental similarity with Buddhist psychology. Clearly, throughout the history of personality theory, there have been important theorists who looked beyond the constraints of their own training and their own culture.

Constructive Alternativism

Kelly begins by questioning the role that psychologists have assigned to themselves. Psychologists consider themselves to be scientists, engaged in the systematic study of human behavior and thought. Kelly questions why we, as psychologists, don't extend the same perspective to all people. According to Kelly, doesn't every person seek to predict and control the course of events in their lives? Doesn't every person have their own theories about situations in life, don't they test their own hypotheses, and weigh the experimental evidence gained through experience?

> …it is as though the psychologist were saying to himself, "I, being a *psychologist*, and therefore a *scientist*, am performing this experiment in order to improve the prediction and control of certain human phenomena; but my subject, being merely a human organism, is obviously propelled by inexorable drives welling up within him, or else he is in gluttonous pursuit of sustenance and shelter." (pg. 5; Kelly, 1955a)

Since Kelly proposes that each individual is theorizing about and testing their own life circumstances, he suggests the term **man-the-scientist** for understanding how all people (including, of course, women) approach the world around them.

In trying to understand the world around us, using arguments that sound either existential or like Eastern philosophy, Kelly questions the existence of the universe. Of course it exists, he says, but so do the thoughts of each individual, and the correspondence between what people think exists and what does, in fact, exist is constantly changing. Thus, Kelly suggests that it is better to say that the world around us is *existing*, rather than to say it exists. Likewise, life can only be understood in the context of time, if it is to make sense. However, life is not simply the changes that occur over time. Rather, it is a relationship between living things and their environment. Kelly emphasizes the creative capacity of living things to represent their environment, as opposed to simply reacting to it. These representations are known as **constructs**, patterns that we create in our mind and attempt to fit over the realities of the world. Since our constructs don't always fit with reality, we are constantly modifying them, as well as trying to increase our repertoire of constructs. Over time, we test our constructs for the ability to predict what will happen in our lives. With sufficient time and experience, and if we are willing to learn from our mistakes, we can evaluate all of our interpretations of the world in which we live (Kelly, 1955a).

Kelly believes that all of our present interpretations of the environment are open to revision or replacement; there are always alternative constructs that may help us deal with new or difficult situations. It is this philosophical position that Kelly refers to as **constructive alternativism**. It is important to keep in mind, of course, that not just any alternative will work in a given situation. Therefore, each potential alternative construct must be evaluated in terms of its specific predictive efficiency, as well as in terms of overall predictive efficiency of the system it would become part of, if that alternative construct were adopted (Kelly, 1955a).

> **Discussion Question:** According to Kelly, it is more important to know what a person might have done, and he believed that people act as scientists, testing their constructs in order to become better at predicting and controlling their lives. Can you think of situations in which someone did what you expected, but you really wanted to know what they had thought about doing as alternatives?

Basic Theory of Personal Constructs

Personal construct theory begins with a **fundamental postulate**, which is then elaborated with eleven corollaries. The fundamental postulate states that "*a person's processes are psychologically channelized by the ways in which he anticipates events*" (Kelly, 1955a). The carefully chosen words in this postulate define the nature of personal construct theory. The words *person* and *he* emphasize the individuality of this theory, the unique nature of each person's constructs. Each person is then recognized as a *process*. The mind does not stop and start, simply reacting to stimuli, but rather it is constantly in motion, constantly experimenting with constructs. These processes operate through a network of pathways, or *channels*, according to the devices, or *ways*, a person constructs in order to achieve their goals. Since these processes, ways, and channels have not been identified as specific physiological mechanisms or anatomical structures, Kelly emphasizes that this is a *psychological* theory. So when we discuss this mechanism we are not necessarily addressing neuroscience on one hand or sociology on the other hand, we are working within the constraints of the field of psychology. We then have *anticipation*, the "push and pull of the psychology of personal constructs" (Kelly, 1955a). Being man-the-scientist, each of us seeks to predict the future and choose our actions accordingly. Finally, we have real-life *events*. Kelly was always very practical about both his personality theory and his approach to psychotherapy. Thus, the psychology of personal constructs is not an ethereal theory. Psychological processes, according to Kelly, are tied down to reality, and anticipation is carried forward in order to better represent future reality. Having established the fundamental postulate, Kelly then described eleven corollaries, or propositions, which both follow from the postulate and amplify his system by elaborating on the fundamental idea (Kelly, 1955a).

Construction Corollary: *A person anticipates events by construing their replications.* Construing refers to placing an interpretation upon an event. Since a new event will not occur exactly as a past event, our anticipation involves interpreting what the new event will be like. Kelly uses the example of a day. Today is not the same as yesterday, tomorrow will not be the same as today, but each day follows something of a similar pattern. Thus, our anticipation of tomorrow involves constructs based on both the similarities and differences between days we have experienced in the past. It is important to note that this process is not the same as cognition, it is not simply thinking about tomorrow. Much of this process is preverbal, or unconscious, and in that sense occurs automatically.

Individuality Corollary: *Persons differ from each other in their construction of events.* No matter how closely associated two people are, they cannot play exactly the same role in any situation. Therefore, they will interpret events differently. Although Kelly acknowledges that people often share similar experiences, particularly as they attend to the experiences of others in the same or similar situations, this corollary emphasizes the unique, subjective nature of interpreting and anticipating events.

Organization Corollary: *Each person characteristically evolves, for his convenience in anticipating events, a construction system embracing ordinal relationships between constructs.* When faced with conflict, there may be solutions that contradict one another. Thus, the constructs we develop may contradict each other. Kelly suggested that we develop our constructs in a systematic and organized way, with some constructs being ranked more highly than others. For example, some constructs may be good vs. bad, or stupid vs. intelligent. A stupid construct might work in a given solution, but an intelligent one would probably be preferred. For instance, suppose you have an electric garage door opener, and the power is out. You could put your car in the garage by driving through the garage door. However, it might be preferable to get out of the car, go into the garage through the house or side door, and then disconnect the garage door from the opener and open it by hand.

Dichotomy Corollary: *A person's construction system is composed of a finite number of dichotomous constructs.* Every construct has both positive and negative aspects. In the example used above, both ways of putting your car in the garage have advantages and disadvantage. Driving through the garage door is quick and easy in the short term, but results in needing a new garage door. Getting out of the car and using another entrance takes more time and effort, and may be unpleasant in a bad storm, but it protects your property (and saves time and money in the long run). The essential nature of contrast was eloquently described some 2,600 years ago by Lao Tsu:

> Under Heaven all can see beauty as beauty only because there is ugliness.
> All can know good as good only because there is evil.
>
> Therefore having and not having arise together.
> Difficult and easy complement each other.
> Long and short contrast each other;
> High and low rest upon each other;
> Voice and sound harmonize each other;
> Front and back follow one another.
>
> Lao Tsu, c600 B.C.
> (pg. 4; Lao Tsu, c600 B.C./1989)

Choice Corollary: *A person chooses for himself that alternative in a dichotomized construct through which he anticipates the greater possibility for extension and definition of his system.* Simply put, since each situation requires us to choose between the options we construct, Kelly believed we choose the alternative that serves us best (at least within our system of constructs, which may be different than the reality of the best choice). But what about situations in which the best choice is not so obvious? Kelly believed that the choice corollary allowed for shades of gray when a decision is not clearly a choice between black and white alternatives. He did not view this as a contradiction, but rather, he proposed that the choice becomes one between options that are more gray or less gray. Thus, we can maintain the dichotomy of the choice while still also allowing the choice itself.

Range Corollary: *A construct is convenient for the anticipation of a finite range of events only.* Every personal construct has a range or focus, and few, if any, are relevant to all events. As Kelly points out, the construct *tall vs. short* may apply well to descriptions of people, trees, and buildings. But what would we mean by tall weather, or short light? Clearly, the construct *tall vs. short* is limited to certain types of discrete, physical objects.

Experience Corollary: *A person's construction system varies as he successively construes the replications of events.* As we apply constructs in our efforts to predict what happens in our lives, we sometimes experience unexpected outcomes. As a result, we reconstruct our constructs, and learn from our experiences. In other words, man-the-scientist is by definition a work in process, and that process is ongoing.

Modulation Corollary: *The variation in a person's construction system is limited by the permeability of the constructs within whose range of convenience the variants lie.* This corollary addresses the ease with which the experience corollary can occur. Although all individuals modify the constructs that guide their anticipation of events, some constructs are modified more easily, and some people are more open to changing their perspectives (and, hence, reconstructing their constructs). This is one area where Kelly re-emphasizes the difference between psychological processes and the process of science. Scientists seek hypotheses, theories, and laws that are not likely to change. Indeed, there is a continuum from hypothesis to law based on how likely it is that a scientific observation is true. People, however, are constantly testing and retesting their constructs, and reconstructing them as necessary and appropriate. Therefore, people may act like scientists, but their psychological processes serve to facilitate the individual's life, not the lives of others (as scientific theories and laws are meant to apply to the whole universe).

Fragmentation Corollary: *A person may successively employ a variety of construction subsystems which are inferentially incompatible with each other.* This corollary extends from the previous one, but with a twist. As an individual encounters unexpected events, they modify their constructs to the extent that they are able. Thus, their behavior may change slowly, or more quickly, depending on the nature of the constructs that guide their openness to change. The twist comes into play when individuals are either resisting change, or in the process of change, and it involves the dichotomy corollary. If an individual is failing to predict and control events in their life, they may choose an incompatible construct, essentially reversing the course of their behavior. One of the advantages of Kelly's personal construct theory is that these dramatic changes in behavior can now be seen as reasonable progressions in one's ongoing desire for predictability and control.

Commonality Corollary: *To the extent that one person employs a construction of experience which is similar to that employed by another, his psychological processes are similar to those of the other person.* This corollary is important for interpersonal relations. Even though two people cannot experience the same event in exactly the same way, their ability to share their experiences is facilitated by the similarity of their experiences. This raises important implications for therapists working with clients of different cultures, since they might not share similar constructs based on certain events. It also raises an important distinction between cognitive and behavioral approaches to understanding personality. In behavioral perspectives, simple stimulus-response relationships are the same for everyone who experiences them. However, in the cognitive perspective, each person necessarily experiences any event in a unique way.

Sociality Corollary: *To the extent that one person construes the construction processes of another, he may play a role in a social process involving the other person.* Humans are social creatures. Our ability to predict and control our lives is largely based on our ability to predict and either control or work with other people. Thus, it is important for individuals to construe to thoughts and behaviors of others, and in so doing we can each play a role in the lives of others. Kelly suggests that this provides a natural connection between personal construct theory and social psychology, as well as a connection between personal construct theory and cross-cultural psychology.

Dimensions of Transition

Since life is an ongoing process, there are regular transitions in one's personal constructs. According to the organizational and modulation corollaries, individuals have certain preferences amongst their constructs and differences in their ability to reconstruct them. Problems in life arise when individuals find it difficult to transition from an ineffective construct, one that does not allow for predicting or controlling events, to an effective construct. According to Kelly (1955a), the major problems are seen as the psychological phenomena of **threat**, **fear**, **guilt**, and **anxiety**. Kelly defines these terms as follows:

Threat is the awareness of imminent comprehensive change in one's core structures.
Fear is like threat, except that, in this case, it is a new incidental construct, rather than a comprehensive construct, that seems about to take over.
Perception of one's apparent dislodgment from his core role structure constitutes the experience of guilt.
Anxiety is the recognition that the events with which one is confronted lie outside the range of convenience of one's construct system.

In each case, the psychological phenomenon is based on either the failure of one's constructs to provide courses of action or a direct challenge to the system of constructs available to the individual. Given that the individual's personal construct systems define the larger construct of self, these psychological phenomena represent a challenge to the very self experiencing them. In defense of the individual, aggressiveness is seen as *the active elaboration of one's perceptual field.* In other words, aggressive individuals try to control events in ways that force decisions favorable to the individual. Similarly, hostility is viewed as *the continued effort to extort validational evidence in favor of a type of social prediction which has already proved itself a failure.* In this case, the individual tries to find confirmation of success following failed constructs, and this can only be done at the expense of others (Kelly, 1955a).

As people live their everyday lives, there are two typical cycles of transition, the **C-P-C Cycle** and the **Creativity Cycle**. The C-P-C Cycle involves circumspection, preemption, and control. Being circumspect refers to being wary, not taking risks. Thus, as we construe events we try to be precise in the development of our constructs. We then preempt these constructs for membership in an exclusive realm, one that best fits the event we are trying to predict and control. Finally, the first two steps have control as their natural consequence. Still, the individual must make the choice of that course of action, so Kelly suggests that the final C could just as well stand for choice as it does for control. In contrast, the Creativity Cycle begins with loose constructions, and then leads to tightened and validated constructions. What makes the Creativity Cycle meaningful is the individual's ability to quickly experiment with various constructs and then seize upon the most promising, which is then tightened up and tested. Since much of this process is preverbal, the thought processes of creative individuals may not be apparent to others. According to Kelly, although individuals who begin with tight constructions might be productive, they cannot be creative. Creativity requires beginning with loose constructions (Kelly, 1955a). The value of creativity is not simply to be found as a distinction between the types of cycles experienced by individuals in their daily lives. Creativity is an important component of well-being, and a common topic in books on positive psychology and human strengths and virtues (Aspinwall & Staudinger, 2003; Cloninger, 2004; Compton, 2005; Peterson & Seligman, 2004; Snyder & Lopez, 2005). Indeed, Carl Rogers identified creativity as a significant aspect of the personality of a fully functioning person (Rogers, 1961).

Discussion Question: Many psychologists, including Kelly and Carl Rogers, consider creativity to be an essential aspect of healthy psychological development. Have you ever entered into an unfamiliar situation and tried to be creative in how you handled it? Was it difficult to set aside preconceived notions about how to act, or do you find it easy to try different things in new situations?

The Role of the Psychotherapist

Kelly was first and foremost a clinical psychologist, and his writings are full of practical examples related to clinical work. Theories are of little value unless they are rooted in the values of the psychologists using them. Kelly considered this to be particularly true of clinical psychologists, since they are routinely dealing with clients (Kelly, 1955b). Kelly believed that the role of the psychotherapist involves not only the training and perspectives of the therapist, but also a need to understand the client, and essential ethical considerations:

> The role of the psychotherapist involves keen alertness to what the client expects from psychotherapy and the initial acceptance of a wide variety of client misperceptions of what psychotherapy is…it involves certain ethical obligations that transcend mere legal status. (pg. 618; Kelly, 1955b)

In his typically practical style, Kelly provides lengthy lists of what psychotherapy means to the client, the client's conceptualization of the therapist, the clinician's conceptualization of their role, and basic approaches to revising the client's constructs. At the beginning of therapy, it is unlikely that the client has a good concept of what therapy is and what it can accomplish. Nonetheless, the client has some construction of what will take place in therapy. The complaint presented by the client says something about what he or she thinks therapy can accomplish, and some see therapy as an end in itself. However, the reality is that therapy is a means to an end, and that end should be generating movement forward on the part of the client. In contrast, some clients are so ready for change that the therapist must be cautious in interpreting the client's state of mind (Kelly, 1955b). Just as the client makes predictions about therapy, they will also have an initial conceptualization of the therapist. They may construe the therapist as a parent, an absolver of guilt, a companion, or even a threat. Hopefully, according to Kelly, the client may construe the therapist as a representative of reality. In this case, the client may feel free to experiment with his or her constructs without fear of failure. Most importantly, how the client construes the therapist will have a dramatic effect on their relationship:

> From the client's conceptualization of psychotherapy comes the role he expects to play and the role he expects the therapist to play…He may be bitterly disappointed in the therapist's enactment of the expected role. He may stretch his perceptions of the therapist in order to construe him in the manner he expected to construe him rather than in the manner the therapist seeks to be construed….The client may then feel lost and insecure in the psychotherapeutic relationship. (pg. 575; Kelly, 1955b)

As the client is engaging in these processes, the clinician is also conceptualizing their own role. Overall, the goal of any therapist should be to assist in the continuous reconstruction of the client's construct system, and the changes that take place in therapy should set the stage for continued reconstruction after therapy has been discontinued. Initially, the therapist may rely on a variety of techniques to accomplish superficial reconstructions.

The therapist needs to be patient, and initially must accept the client's construct systems as they are. The latter point is quite similar to the empathy described by Carl Rogers in humanistic, client-centered therapy, and Kelly does indeed use the word "empathize" in his own writings. As therapy progresses, the therapist needs to help the client select new conceptual elements, accelerate the tempo of the client's experience, and design and implement experiments. Finally, the therapist serves to validate the client's experiments as they attempt to reconstruct their construct systems (Kelly, 1955b).

Psychological Assessment within Personal Construct Theory

Kelly believed that therapy was a joint effort between the therapist and the client, and since the goal was the ongoing reconstruction of the client's psychological systems (even after therapy), the client ultimately needs to become his own therapist. Therefore, the **psychotherapeutic interview** (Note: by "interview," Kelly means what we would commonly call a therapy session) becomes an essential part of therapy. Throughout the process of the interview, the therapist makes decisions regarding the course of the interchange between the therapist and the client. Overall, the decisions made by the therapist are tailored to the specific client, but still the therapist must remain in control of the interview. This requires that the therapist plan for the interview. Those plans include how often to interview the client, how long the interviews should last, the tempo of the interview, and when to terminate the interview. Since the client continues to live their life outside of the interview room, the therapist must also consider whether special circumstances will require special interview plans (Kelly, 1955b, 1958). One of the most practical aspects of the interview is that the client can simply provide information needed by the therapist, to a point:

> …there is a useful adage for clinical psychologists to follow on occasion: if you do not know what is wrong with a person, ask him; he may tell you. (pp. 322; Kelly, 1955a)

The **Role Construct Repertory Test** (Rep Test) was developed by Kelly in order to understand how a client's personal constructs influence their personal-social behavior. The client begins with a **Role Title List**, on which they list the names of important people in their lives (see Table 10-1). The names are then grouped three at a time, and the client is asked to describe in what *important way* two of the three individuals are alike but different than the third person. A more organized form of the Rep Test, particularly useful for research purposes, involves creating the **Repertory Grid**. Once again the client is asked to identify significant people in their life. The grid provides three-person pairings that address various relational factors (family, intimate friends, conflicted relationships, authority figures, and values), and as before the client provides a construct that associates two of the people yet distinguishes them from the third. The common factor is listed as the **emergent pole**, the distinguishing factor is listed as the **implicit pole**. The Rep Test does not result in specific outcomes, so its interpretation is also subject to different methods. If the Rep Test is interpreted formally, it will provide results on the number and range of constructs present within the client's construct systems. In the hands of an experienced and skilled examiner, information can be gleaned on the equivalence of constructs, thus providing deeper detail on the effective range of the client's construct system. As more information is obtained from the Rep Test, the better able the therapist will be to guide the therapeutic process (Kelly, 1955a).

Fixed-role therapy is a technique derived from personal construct theory. First, the client prepares a **self-characterization sketch**, a technique in which the client is asked to write a character sketch about themselves as if they were the principal character in a play, but written as if by a friend who knows the client well. Using information from the self-characterization sketch, as well as from interviews and perhaps the Rep Test, the therapist then writes a **fixed-role sketch**. The client is asked to act out the fixed-role sketch over a period of weeks. Initially, Kelly and his colleagues emphasized minor changes in the client's construct systems. However, they later found that it is often easier for a client to play out roles that are the opposite of their usual constructs, rather than making only minor changes in their behavior. Over time, it is expected that the client will learn that the new construct systems are more predictive than their old construct systems, and the fixed-role therapy will establish an ongoing process of reconstruction within the client (Kelly, 1955a).

Table 12.1: The Role Title List Used for the Personal Construct Repertory Test

1. A teacher you liked. (Or the teacher of a subject you liked.)
2. A teach you disliked. (Or the teacher of a subject you disliked.)
3. Your wife or present girl friend.

3a. (for women) Your husband or present boy friend.

4. An employer, supervisor, or officer under whom you worked or served and whom you found hard to get along with. (Or someone under whom you worked in a situation you did not like.)
5. An employer, supervisor, or officer under whom you worked or served and whom you liked. (Or someone under whom you worked in a situation you liked.)
6. Your mother. (Or the person who has played the part of a mother in your life.)
7. Your father. (Or the person who has played the part of a father in your life.)
8. Your brother nearest your age. (Or the person who has been most like a brother.)
9. Your sister nearest your age. (Or the person who has been most like a sister.)
10. A person with whom you have worked who was easy to get along with.
11. A person with whom you have worked who was hard to understand.
12. A neighbor with whom you get along well.
13. A neighbor whom you find hard to understand.
14. A boy you got along well with when you were in high school. (Or when you were 16.)
15. A girl you got along well with when you were in high school. (Or when you were 16.)
16. A boy you did not like when you were in high school. (Or when you were 16.)
17. A girl you did not like when you were in high school. (Or when you were 16.)
18. A person of your own sex whom you would enjoy having as a companion on a trip.
19. A person of your own sex whom you would dislike having as a companion on a trip.
20. A person with whom you have been closely associated recently who appears to dislike you.
21. The person whom you would most like to be of help to. (Or whom you feel most sorry for.)
22. The most intelligent person whom you know personally.
23. The most successful person whom you know personally.
24. The most interesting person whom you know personally.

Discussion Question: Kelly's fixed-role therapy requires the client to write a script for how they want to live their life. He found that sometimes it was easier for his clients to act out the opposite of their typical behavior. Would you find it easier to make minor changes in your behavior, or easier to make dramatic changes?

Connections Across Cultures: Understanding Culture's Effects on Cognitive Style as a Prerequisite for Effective Cognitive-Behavioral Therapy

An essential element of all cognitive therapies is the desire to identify and challenge a client's underlying dysfunctional cognitions, whether they are mistaken beliefs, schemas, automatic thoughts, cognitive distortions, whatever the case may be. To do so, requires that the therapist knows when cognitions are dysfunctional, and to some extent, what would be a reasonable cognition in the client's personal situation. While it may seem obvious that any psychologically healthy person, particularly a trained therapist, would be able to recognize the difference between functional and dysfunctional thoughts, feelings, and behaviors, this assumes that the therapist and the client come from similar environments. This may very well NOT be the case when the client and the therapist come from dramatically different cultures. Furthermore, as G. Morris Carstairs noted regarding psychiatric interviews (1961), it makes a significant difference whether it is the therapist or the client who is outside of their familiar culture. For example, when a psychologist conducts research in a foreign country, particularly in small towns or villages, local people may simply fear and avoid strangers.

Kelly discussed culture at length in *The Psychology of Personal Constructs* (Kelly, 1955a,b). Both the commonality corollary and the sociality corollary are directly influenced by our understanding of culture. We, and by "we" I mean to include therapists, tend to expect that people from similar cultures have experienced basically similar upbringings and environments. We also tend to believe that people from a given culture share their expectations regarding the behavior of others from that culture. Thus, in order for a therapist to gain access to the personal constructs of their client, it is important for the therapist to learn as much as possible about the client's cultural heritage. Failure to do so may interfere with the therapist's ability to understand some of the client's disruptive anxieties about either therapy itself or their life in general. Indeed, Kelly shares an example in which a White therapist (whom Kelly was supervising) found it difficult to help a Black client, because the Black client was overly anxious about discussing racially charged feelings regarding interracial sexual relationships. Since the client had discussed sexual issues before, the White therapist did not readily recognize the discomfort with which the Black client addressed his attraction to White women (remember, this was in the 1950s!).

Kelly goes on to discuss cultural differences in mannerisms, language, expectations regarding mental illness, the influence of religion, and how a therapist might go about learning more about a client's cultural experiences. He does caution, however, that one should not attribute too much value to the influence of culture:

> …It is important that the clinician be aware of cultural variations. Yet, from our theoretical view, we look upon the "influence" of culture in the same way as we look upon other events. The client is not merely the product of his culture, but it has undoubtedly provided him with much evidence of what is "true" and much of the data which his personal construct system has had to keep in systematic order. (pg. 688; Kelly, 1955b)
>
> For example, it is often considered the mark of a sophisticated clinician that he considers all of his clients in terms of the culture groups to which they belong. Yet, in the final analysis, a client who is to be genuinely understood should never be confined to the stereotype of his culture. (pg. 833; Kelly, 1955b)

Albert Ellis and Aaron Beck, originators of the best known cognitive-behavioral therapies (see Beck & Weishaar, 1995; Ellis, 1995), also discussed cultural influences, though not as extensively as Kelly had. Ellis emphasized that each individual develops a belief system which helps them make judgments and evaluate situations. Although each person's belief system is unique, they share many beliefs with other members of their society and/or culture. Perhaps more importantly, different cultures can have very different belief systems. To complicate the situation even further, cultural beliefs can change, either due to gradual evolution of the culture or in a more dramatic fashion when an influential thinker or leader offers a different perspective on life (Ellis, 1977). Beck has discussed how culturally-determined schemas can be so fundamental that they contribute to how and who we both love and hate (Beck, 1988, 1999).

Today, studies on the relationship between culture and cognition continue, both in clinical and non-clinical settings. There are at least two handbooks focusing on cross-cultural and multicultural factors in personality assessment (Dana, 2000; Suzuki, Ponterotto, & Meller, 2001). According to Suzuki, et al. (2001), these handbooks are necessary due to "the growing number of racial and ethnic minorities in the United States and in recognition of the multitude of variables that affect performance on cognitive and personality tests…" As assessment transitions to therapy, it becomes quite a challenge for any therapist to be familiar with the wide variety of cultures in America. Axelson (1999) has identified six basic cultural groups in America: native Americans, Anglo-Americans, European ethnic Americans, African Americans, Hispanic Americans, and

Asian Americans. This list obviously does not include the many immigrants living in this country who are not considered to be American. When faced with such cross-cultural challenges, the essential skills for a therapist include careful and active listening, genuine verbal and nonverbal responses that indicate successful communication, being honest about what you do not understand, respecting and caring about the client, and being patient and optimistic (Axelson, 1999).

Additional studies have suggested that cultural knowledge influences the interpretation of stimuli in a dynamic, constructivist fashion (Hong, Morris, Chiu, & Benet-Martinez, 2000), that these processes occur automatically (Bargh & Williams, 2006), and that experiencing a wider variety of cultures in one's education may actually lead to more complex cognitive processing (Antonio, Chang, Hakuta, Kenny, Levin, & Milem, 2004). When considering fundamental cultural differences, what some consider the **core values** that distinguish amongst cultures, most psychology students are familiar with the distinction between individualistic and collectivistic cultures (cultures in which one favors one's own goals as compared to subordinating one's own goals in favor of group goals). However, Laungani (1999) suggests that there are three other common dimensions: free will vs. determinism, materialism vs. spiritualism, and cognitivism vs. emotionalism. According to Laungani, Western cultures tend to be work- and activity-centered. Thus, they operate in a cognitive mode that emphasizes rational, logical, and controlled thought and behavior. Non-Western cultures, in contrast, tend to be relationship-centered, operating in an emotional mode. Public displays of feelings and emotions, both positive and negative, are not frowned upon (Laungani, 1999). These core values carry over into cognitive styles. For example, the cognitive style prevalent in Africa tends toward synthesis, as opposed to analysis. Africans tend to integrate their experiences into an inclusive whole, and they view such tendencies as more natural than the typical Western alternative (Okeke, Draguns, Sheku, & Allen, 1999). Thus, one can imagine a therapeutic situation in which the client resists analyzing their problems, and the therapist considers that resistance to be a specific problem unique to the client. Any subsequent attempts by the therapist to break down that resistance would be flawed, since the therapist has not understood the underlying cognitive style of the client. The failure of therapists to properly address the significance of cultural factors in therapy, regardless of whether or not their failure was unintentional, has been described as **cultural malpractice** (Iijima Hall, 1997).

Cognitive-Behavioral Therapy and Acceptance Therapy

Albert Ellis and Aaron Beck are not known as personality theorists, but both are well-known therapists and prolific authors. Their unique approaches to therapy are, of course, based on their theoretical perspectives, each of which emphasizes cognitive processes. Thus, we will take a brief look at how they have applied cognitive aspects of personality theory to the treatment of psychological disorders.

Pretzer and Beck (2005) have suggested that cognitive therapies are truly integrative approaches that treat the individual within a **phenomenological** perspective. Beck was trained as psychoanalyst, and began examining his patients' thought processes carefully in an attempt to prove that Freud was right about depression being the result of anger turned inward. However, Beck instead discovered that his patient's thoughts focused more on themes such as despair and defeat, and that their appraisals of situations in life and their consistently negative biases in processing information were better predictors of their mood and behavior. Thus, Beck began to develop a cognitive approach to working with his patients. At the same time Ellis was developing rational-emotive therapy, and the two theories have influenced each other in many ways (Pretzer & Beck, 2005). In addition, cognitive therapy has been influenced by many other developments in the field of psychology, including the work of Freud, Adler, Horney, Rogers, Bandura, and, of course, Kelly. The integration of these various approaches, in order to truly understand the individual, requires the therapist to work actively with the client:

> …The idea of "collaborative empiricism" is central to the practice of cognitive therapy. In the course of therapy, the cognitive therapist works with his or her client to collect detailed information regarding the specific thoughts, feelings, and actions that occur in problem situations. These observations are used as a basis for developing an individualized understanding of the

> client which provides a basis for strategic intervention…For the cognitive therapist to intervene effectively, he or she must endeavor both to understand the individual's subjective experience and to perceive objective reality accurately. (pp. 46-47; Pretzer & Beck, 2005)

More recent developments in cognitive therapy have focused on accepting the circumstances of one's life, doing so not as an excuse, but in order to facilitate moving forward from that point. **Acceptance and Commitment Therapy** (ACT) acknowledges the presence of suffering in human life, and focuses on using mindfulness to re-orient one's relational framework to the circumstances of one's life (Eifert & Forsyth, 2005; Hayes & Smith, 2005; Hayes, Strosahl, & Wilson, 1999). ACT has many elements in common with the traditional practice of Buddhist mindfulness, an approach that is taken directly in Radical Acceptance (Brach, 2003).

Brief Biographies of Albert Ellis and Aaron Beck

Albert Ellis was born in 1913 in Pittsburgh, Pennsylvania. When he was 4 years old his family moved to New York City, and Ellis has remained there ever since. Although Ellis considered his childhood to have had no significant effect on his subsequent career in psychology, there were some rather dramatic factors that influenced the person he became. His father was a traveling salesman who was seldom home, and when he was home he paid little attention to his children. After his parents were divorced, Ellis seldom saw his father again. His mother wasn't much more attentive, doing very little for the children, and often leaving them home alone. Ellis later wrote: "As for my nice Jewish mother, a hell of a lot of help she was!" (cited in Yankura & Dryden, 1994). Ellis was also very sick following tonsillitis and a strep infection. He needed emergency surgery, and then developed nephritis. Over the next 2 years, from 5 to 7 years old, he was hospitalized eight times, once for 10 months. Yet his parents remained uncaring, and he would sometimes go weeks without anyone from the family visiting him in the hospital. The illness kept him from playing sports or other games even when he was home from the hospital. Perhaps as a result of all of these circumstances, or perhaps because of his temperament, Ellis was painfully shy. He dreaded public activities, such as when he won an award for his excellent academic work, and he avoided making social overtures toward any girl he had a crush on (Yankura & Dryden, 1994).

Surprisingly, Ellis grew strong from these experiences. He thrived on his independence and autonomy, and turned his attention toward his schoolwork. He obtained praise from adults other than his parents, and at one point became something of a leader amongst the children in the hospital. Although his shyness plagued him for many years, he developed a strong sense of self-esteem based on his success in academics. Most importantly, he developed a sense of choosing to overcome his adverse childhood. He did not become a strong-willed individual because of his bad childhood, for example he describes his sister as never really being happy, but in spite of it, due largely to being born with an innate capacity for rational thinking (Yankura & Dryden, 1994).

Much like B. F. Skinner, Ellis hoped to become a writer. Having finished high school at the age of 16, he decided to attend business school at the City College of New York so he might make enough money to support his writing career. However, the Great Depression was just beginning, so there was little opportunity for a young man to make money in business. Nonetheless, he wrote a great deal. He wrote a 500,000-word autobiographical novel. By the age of 28 he had written twenty full-length novels, plays, and books of poetry. None of them were published. He also wrote numerous non-fiction works on sex, philosophy, and politics. None of them were published. However, his research on the topics of sex, love, and marriage made him a popular source of advice amongst his friends. And so he decided to pursue professional training in psychology (Yankura & Dryden, 1994).

Ellis began his studies in the psychology program at Columbia University, and then transferred to the clinical psychology program at Teachers College of Columbia University, receiving a Ph.D. in clinical psychology in 1947. That year he also began training as a psychoanalyst at the Karen Horney Institute for Psychoanalysis. His training analyst was Dr. Charles Hulbeck, who had been analyzed by Hermann Rorschach. One of the personal issues Ellis addressed during his training analysis was whether or not to marry the women he had begun dating. He eventually decided not to marry her (he was later married twice, one marriage ended in annulment, the other in divorce). Ellis was successful as a psychoanalyst, but many patients couldn't afford to come as often as was recommended in traditional psychoanalytic theory. Curiously, Ellis noticed that patients who came less often seemed to fare better in therapy, especially when the constraints of limited time caused Ellis to be more proactive in therapy. He pursued this active-directive approach to therapy, and by the mid-1950s he had developed rational emotive behavior therapy to the point where he published his first articles and began describing the technique at professional conferences (Yankura & Dryden, 1994).

Ellis devoted the rest of his career to establishing rational emotive behavior therapy as a significant force in psychotherapy. In 1959 he established the Institute for Rational Living, and by the 1980s there were similar institutes in Australia, Britain, Canada, Germany, Israel, Italy, Mexico, and the Netherlands. He has written over 75 books, beginning with *How to Live with a Neurotic* (Ellis, 1957), hundreds of articles, and he has received many distinguished awards. After 60 years as a psychotherapist, marriage and family counselor, and sex therapist, Ellis has been honored as a fellow of five major associations. He was recognized with the *Humanist of the Year Award* by the American Humanist Association, the *Distinguished Psychologist Award* of the Academy of Psychologists in Marital and Family Therapy, the *Distinguished Practitioner Award* of the American Association of Sex Educators, Counselors and Therapists, and the American Psychological Association has recognized him for *Distinguished Professional Contributions to Knowledge*. In a 1991 survey ranking the "Most Influential Psychotherapist," Canadian psychologists ranked Ellis #1, whereas American psychologists ranked him second to Carl Rogers, but ahead of third-place Sigmund Freud (Ellis, 1994, 2005; Yankura & Dryden, 1994)!

In most ways, Aaron Beck's childhood couldn't have been more different than that of Ellis. Born in 1921, he was the youngest child of loving and supportive parents. His parents were particularly supportive of education: his brother Irving became a physician, and his brother Maurice entered social work after earning a Master's degree in psychology (the other two children had died in childhood, his only sister dying in the worldwide influenza epidemic of 1919). Like Ellis, however, Beck was extremely ill as a child. When he was seven years old, Beck broke his arm at a playground. An infection set in, which then developed into septicemia (a generalized blood infection). At the time, septicemia was 90 percent fatal, and his brother Irving overheard the doctor tell their mother that Beck would die. Although he obviously survived, he missed so much school that he had to be held back a year. As often happens when young children are held back in school, the effect on his self-esteem was devastating, and Beck came to believe that he was stupid and inept (Weishaar, 1993; for more information on the negative effects of grade retention visit the National Association of School Psychologists' website at www.nasponline.org).

However, with the help of his brothers, Beck was able to catch up to and eventually surpass his classmates, graduating first in his high school class. Along the way he belonged to the Audubon Society, worked as a camp counselor, became the youngest Eagle Scout in his Boy Scout troop, and was editor of the high school newspaper. He followed his brothers to Brown University, but was unsure of a career path. He majored in English and Political Science, but he took a wide variety of courses, eventually taking the courses necessary to go on to medical school. He graduated *magna cum laude*, Phi Beta Kappa, and won awards for oratory and essay writing. Despite his dramatic successes, Beck suffered a great deal of anxiety, particularly a blood/injury phobia that most likely resulted from his frightening experiences related to the emergency surgery necessary when he broke his arm. Having been accepted to the Yale School of Medicine, his surgery rotation was very difficult in light of his fear of blood. However, he worked through his fears cognitively (an obvious foreshadowing of the work that would make him famous), and successfully completed his medical degree (Weishaar, 1993).

Beck never intended to study psychiatry, and thought little of psychoanalysis. However, having graduated in 1946, there were many veterans returning from World War II. In 1949, he began a residency in neurology at a veteran's administration hospital in Massachusetts. Due to a pressing need for psychiatrists, the director of the program began requiring everyone to complete a rotation is psychiatry. The psychiatry program at the hospital was primarily influenced by the Boston Psychoanalytic Institute, and Beck protested that psychoanalytic formulations seemed far-fetched, but he eventually decided to stay in psychiatry and to study psychoanalysis in greater detail. He first studied psychoanalysis at the Austin Riggs Center in Massachusetts, where one of his supervisors was Erik Erikson. After completing his training in psychiatry, he joined the faculty of the University of Pennsylvania Medical School (in 1954), where he has remained ever since. As he began his research career, Beck intended to confirm Freud's hypothesis that depression was the result of hostility turned inward. However, he began to recognize that his patients were greatly influenced by underlying patterns of cognition, the so-called automatic thoughts that are so well-known today. About this same time, Beck learned of Kelly's work on personal constructs (which Beck later referred to as schemas). As a result of these ideas and experiences coming together, Beck's own cognitive theory began to take shape. Then, in 1963, Ellis read an article written by Beck. Ellis sent copies of his own work to Beck, and reprinted Beck's article in the journal *Rational Living*. Beck then invited Ellis to speak to the psychiatry residents at Penn, and from that point forward the two maintained close contact. Beck has credited Ellis as being an excellent spokesperson for cognitive approaches to psychotherapy (Weishaar, 1993).

During his career, Beck has received many awards, including the *Distinguished Scientific Award for the Applications of Psychology* from the American Psychological Association. He has also received major awards from the American Psychiatric Association, the American Psychopathological Association, and the American Association of Suicidology. He received an honorary doctorate in medical science from his alma mater, Brown University, in 1987 he was elected a Fellow of the Royal College of Psychiatrists (England), and he is a senior member of the Institute of Medicine. Perhaps the most meaningful tribute, however, is that his daughter, Dr. Judith Beck, has followed in his footsteps. She is currently the Director of the Beck Institute for Cognitive Therapy and Research, and a Clinical Associate Professor at the University of Pennsylvania. She has written a number of books on cognitive therapy and, with her father, developed the *Beck Youth Inventories* (for more information visit the website for the Beck Institute for Cognitive Therapy and Research at www.beckinstitute.org).

Placing Ellis and Beck in Context: Cognitive Therapy

In one sense, Ellis and Beck do not belong in a book about personality theory. They are not known for their theoretical contributions to our understanding of personality development. In another sense, they are among the most important theorists covered, since the practical application of cognitive theories to psychotherapy has had a dramatic influence on the effectiveness of psychotherapy in treating psychological disorders. Remember that Freud, as well as most of the other well-known psychodynamic theorists, began conducting therapy first and later developed theoretical perspectives which helped to explain what they saw in their patients and what worked in therapy. Similarly, Ellis and Beck focused on the development of their therapeutic approaches, and to a large extent their theoretical perspective is inferred from the techniques they use in therapy.

In addition, one could argue that the cognitive therapies of Ellis and Beck stand at the pinnacle of the behavioral and cognitive theories of personality that have been so influential in American psychology. As evidence of their significance, Beck received an Albert Lasker Clinical Medical Research Award in 2006. Often called the American Nobel Prize (some seventy recipients have gone on to win a Nobel Prize), in the 60 years that the Lasker prizes have been awarded, Beck is the first psychotherapist to be honored. This award is a testament both to the respect that cognitive psychotherapy has earned in the medical community and to Beck for the honor he has earned amongst many ground-breaking psychotherapists.

Although cognitive therapies may seem highly specialized, both Ellis and Beck drew upon many different areas of psychology and psychiatry, as well as Eastern philosophies, while developing their techniques. Their psychoanalytic training exposed them to the directive approach of Adler and to Horney's emphasis on the (which can be viewed as a neurotic belief or a type of automatic thought). In addition, they cited theorists, authors, and spiritual leaders such as Bandura, Frankl, Rogers, Piaget, the Dalai Lama, D. T. Suzuki, Lao Tsu, Jesus of Nazareth, and many others. The range of ideas that Ellis and Beck synthesized into a cohesive and direct approach to psychotherapy is unparalleled in the fields of psychology and psychiatry.

Rational Emotive Behavior Therapy

In order to understand Ellis' perspective on therapy, one must first understand his perspective on the basis of psychological disturbances, whether they are minor problems with personal adjustment or more serious forms of mental illness. Individuals with problems typically have a long history related to the disorder. Using the same example as Ellis (1957), suppose a woman is chronically depressed because she has been rejected by men she really liked and with whom she wanted to have long-term relationships. She understandably concludes that the activating event of being rejected leads to the consequence of being depressed. However, this conclusion is wrong! According to Ellis, it is not the rejection that causes her depression, it is the belief system that arises within her, particularly irrational beliefs, that cause her depression. For example, if she rationally believed that it was unfortunate that someone she liked rejected her, or that it was frustrating that she was rejected, she might not become depressed. However, if she irrationally believes that it is *awful* that she has been rejected, or that she *should* have been more beautiful so that he wouldn't have rejected her, then she is quite likely to become depressed. This is what Ellis referred to as the A-B-C's of emotional disturbance or self-defeating behaviors and attitudes. A refers to the **activating event** (being rejected), B refers to the person's beliefs (this is awful, I'm not pretty), and C is the consequence of the beliefs: depression. The basis for therapy in such situations can be found by extending the A-B-C's to the D-E's: disputing (D) the irrational beliefs, which hopefully leads to the cognitive effect (E - effective new philosophies, emotions, and behaviors) of disrupting the self-defeating patterns of behavior (Ellis, 1957, 1973, 1996). More recently, Ellis has proposed one more letter for his **ABC theory of personality**, the letter G for goals (*note: there is no "F"). Goals consist of a person's purposes, values, standards, and hopes. When these goals are thwarted by an activating event, the person can respond by choosing healthy or unhealthy alternatives, and the nature of that choice is based on one's beliefs (Ellis, 1994). Ellis considered the ABC theory to be so straightforward that it could prove helpful to anyone.

When an individual has become trapped by unhealthy belief systems and the corresponding self-defeating behavior patterns that accompany them, the potential need for psychotherapy arises. The therapy that Ellis developed has come to be known as **rational emotive behavior therapy**, or **REBT** (the name went through several permutations over Ellis' career, and he finally settled on REBT). The primary task of the therapist using REBT is to challenge the client's irrational beliefs and, in so doing, to help the client change their belief systems. In essence, when the client believes that it would be catastrophic for a certain negative outcome to occur, the therapist tries to help them by disputing the irrational belief with questions such as: "Why would a certain outcome be catastrophic?" While trying to dispute the irrational beliefs, the therapist also searches for underlying philosophies that support the irrational belief system, philosophies that can then also be disputed. In addition to the cognitive aspect of REBT, the therapist often encourages the client to act against their irrational fears. If the client is willing, they have the opportunity to experience anxiety-ridden situations without the catastrophic consequences they have feared (although the help of the therapist may prove necessary along the way). Throughout this process, REBT does not intend to ignore the person's feelings. However, when a client is suffering from unhealthy and self-defeating feelings, such as anxiety, depression, or anger, REBT can help to minimize those unhealthy feelings. In addition, REBT encourages healthy, positive emotions, and recognizes that sometimes a strong negative response, such as sadness or grief, to a tragic activating event may be healthy or constructive. When utilized effectively, REBT offered what Ellis believed was a better, deeper, and more enduring therapy, which could achieve those results in a fairly brief amount of time (Ellis, 1962, 1973, 1994, 1995, 1996). Ellis also believed that REBT was applicable to a wider range of clients than any other psychotherapy:

> RET [later known as REBT], on the contrary, seems to be almost the only major kind of psychotherapy (aside, perhaps, from Zen Buddhism, if this is conceptualized as psychotherapy…) that holds that the individual does not need *any* trait, characteristic, achievement, purpose, or social approval in order to accept himself. In fact, he does not have to rate himself, esteem himself, or have any self-measurement or self-concept whatever. (pg. 65; Ellis, 1973)

First and foremost, Ellis focused on practical applications of psychotherapy, and he considered his approach to be humanistic in its emphasis on the whole person. He acknowledged that REBT shared important elements with the approaches of other classic theorists who had emphasized the value of individuals, including Alfred Adler, Viktor Frankl, Rollo May, Carl Rogers, Abraham Maslow, and Karen Horney (Ellis, 1973, 1995). Ellis' discussion of the practice of REBT seems to focus on what Horney addressed in her concepts of neurotic needs and the tyranny of the should. Taken together, the desire to focus on practical applications and helping individuals has led to a wide variety of self-help books based on REBT (Yankura & Dryden, 1994). Naturally, this list includes many books by Ellis himself, including titles such as *How to Live With a Neurotic* (Ellis, 1957), *A New Guide to Rational Living* (Ellis & Harper, 1975), *How to Live With - and Without - Anger* (Ellis, 1977), *How to Cope With a Fatal Illness* (Ellis & Abrams, 1994), *How to Keep People from Pushing Your Buttons* (Ellis & Lange, 1994), *How to Control Your Anxiety Before It Controls You* (Ellis, 1998), and *Sex Without Guilt in the 21st Century* (Ellis, 2003). REBT has also been applied to a wide variety of other problems that have been covered in Ellis' books, such as marriage counseling, personality disorders, depression, and even schizophrenia, and REBT has proved successful in both individual and group settings (Ellis, 1962, 1973, 2001; Ellis & Dryden, 1987).

> **Discussion Question:** Rational emotive behavior therapy is based on the ABC theory of personality. Can you think of situations in which activating events led you to specific consequences, even though your beliefs, if you thought about them enough, were the real reason for the consequence you experienced?

Ellis, as well as other therapists using REBT, has also addressed addictive disorders, including alcoholism (Ellis, 2001; Ellis, McInerney, DiGuiseppe, & Yeager, 1988; Trimpey, Velten, & Dain, 1993; Yeager, Yeager, & Shillingford, 1993). In the early 1990s, **Rational Recovery (RR)** was developed by Jack Trimpey as an alternative to the Alcoholics Anonymous (AA) approach to treating alcohol abuse. Both Ellis and Trimpey challenge the basic principles of AA: that the addict has no control over their alcohol cravings, that they must turn over control to a higher power (such as God), that they can never drink alcohol again, and that only AA works for alcoholics. Objective research simply does not support these assertions, and practitioners of REBT and RR have great faith in the ability of individuals to take control of their own lives (though they may need some help from a therapist to get on the right path). RR also does not include the strong religious overtones of AA, which may be an impediment to recovery for anyone required to attend AA meetings but who does not believe in God:

> …The core of these methods is learning to recognize and dispute self-defeating thinking that RR frequently labels "the Beast" or "the addictive voice." In addition to its treatment purposes, RR has a political purpose in advocating for people who are mandated to attend spiritual healing groups but who find that approach useless or offensive. Furthermore, RR attempts to educate professionals about available options and sensitize them to the ethical and possible legal issues involved in overriding client's objections to spiritual healing approaches. (pg. 271; Trimpey, Velten, & Dain, 1993)

Since REBT focuses on the choices that individuals make for themselves, what role is there for religion within such a perspective? Ellis maintains that there is a significant positive correlation between devout religious beliefs and a variety of emotional disturbances. However, he has argued that the problem is not religion *per se*, but rather highly restrictive, dogmatic religiosity that causes problems for an individual (Ellis, 2004; also see Yankura & Dryden, 1994). Ellis studied the works of Lao Tsu (author of the *Tao Te Ching*), Gotama Buddha (known by most people simply as the Buddha), and the existential theologian Paul Tillich, finding helpful perspectives for working with his clients and on his own problems (Ellis, 2004). He overcame his early objections to religion and spirituality by recognizing that when one's religious beliefs contribute to good psychological health the belief itself, regardless of whether or not God exists, is helpful. Similarly, Zen Buddhism is not actually a religion, but has significant religious overtones. Nonetheless, Ellis was impressed by the effectiveness of Zen meditation for many clients, so he incorporated various Eastern perspectives into the development of REBT.

> **Discussion Question:** Alcoholics Anonymous has helped many people, but it doesn't help everyone, especially those who are opposed to religiosity or are simply atheists. Nonetheless, the AA approach has become a standard recommendation in many legal jurisdictions when someone commits a crime such as drunk driving. What do you think about Rational Recovery (based on REBT) as an alternative to AA?

Is Self-Esteem a Sickness?

The heading for this section is the title of the first chapter in a fascinating book by Ellis: *The Myth of Self-Esteem* (Ellis, 2005). Ellis believed that self-esteem is defined by psychologists in a way that requires individuals to rate, or judge, themselves. This may work fine when everything is going well for the person, but people are not perfect. Thus, they will eventually fail at something, perhaps at many things, and they must then judge themselves as bad, or unworthy. If, however, you accept yourself as imperfect, and rate only your behaviors and thoughts, not your self, then you need not suffer from the effects of low self-esteem. In other words, Ellis advocates unconditional self-acceptance, a very old philosophy known to the Greeks, Romans, Buddhists, Daoists, and others (Ellis, 2005). Ellis considers many different approaches to the concepts of self-esteem and self-acceptance, including the perspectives of Solomon, Jesus of Nazareth, the existential philosophers Kierkegaard, Heidegger, and Sartre, Carl Rogers, the Eastern philosophers Lao Tsu, D. T. Suzuki, and the Dalai Lama, and Steven Hayes (founder of Acceptance and Commitment Therapy, see below). Ellis concludes that one must seek not only to unconditionally accept oneself, but also to unconditionally accept others and the nature of life itself. But this is not a pie-in-the-sky philosophy. Ellis recognizes that there are sad and unfortunate events in life (we are fallible, and we are mortal). He strongly recommends that we do not avoid normal sadness and regret, since these emotions provide the motivation for trying to prevent unfortunate events and for seeking new relationships. The choice is yours:

> Both self-esteem and self-acceptance, then, can be had definitionally - for the asking, for the choosing. Take one or the other. Choose! Better yet, take no *global* rating. Choose your goals and values and rate how you experience them - well or badly. Don't rate yourself, being, entity, personality at all. Your totality is too complex and too changing to measure. Repeatedly acknowledge *that*.
>
> Now stop farting around and get on with your *life*! (pg. 16; Ellis, 2005)

Discussion Question: Ellis opposes the concept of self-esteem because he believes it requires a person to judge themselves. He advocates instead that we unconditionally accept ourselves, faults included. Does this make sense to you?

Beck's Cognitive Model of Depression

Having begun his research in an attempt to examine Freud's theory on the cause of depression, Beck continued studying depression and suicide throughout his career. The reason for this continued focus was the prevalence of depression in society:

> Depression is the most common psychiatric disorder treated in office practice and in outpatient clinics. Some authorities have estimated that at least 12 per cent of the adult population will have an episode of depression of sufficient clinical severity to warrant treatment. (pg. vii; Beck, 1967)

Relying on an interplay between clinical work and research, Beck proposed a cognitive model based on **automatic thoughts**, **schemas**, and **cognitive distortions** (Beck, 1967; Beck & Freeman, 1990; Beck, Rush, Shaw, & Emery, 1979; Beck & Weishaar, 1995; Pretzer & Beck, 2005). Automatic thoughts are an individual's immediate, spontaneous appraisals of a given situation. They shape and elicit a person's emotional and behavioral responses to that situation. Since they are automatic, they are rarely questioned. Even when they are predominantly negative, the individual accepts them as true and can be overwhelmed by constant questions and images that hurt one's self-esteem (questions such as "Why am I such a failure," or seeing oneself as ugly). The reason that even highly negative automatic thoughts are accepted, even when they might be objectively untrue, is that these thoughts do not arise spontaneously. Rather, they are the result of the person's schemas. Every situation is comprised of many stimuli, and when confronted with an unfamiliar situation a person tends to conceptualize it. Although different people will conceptualize the situation differently, each individual will be consistent. These stable cognitive patterns of interpreting situations are known as schemas. An individual's schemas then determine how they are likely to respond, automatically, to many situations.

People are also prone to a variety of cognitive distortions, which can amplify the effects of one's schemas, thus helping to confirm maladaptive schemas even when contradictory evidence is available. Over time, Beck and his colleagues have identified a growing number of such distortions, such as: **dichotomous thinking**, or seeing things as only black or white, without the possibility of shades of gray; **personalization**, the tendency to interpret external events as being related directly to oneself; **overgeneralization**, the application of isolated incidents to either all or at least many other situations; and **catastrophizing**, treating actual or anticipated negative events as intolerable catastrophes, even though they may be relatively minor problems. Overall, these cognitive distortions lead the individual into extreme, judgmental, global interpretations of the situations they experience, which establish general schemas, which lead to automatic thoughts and feelings that support the idiosyncratic experience of the world (Beck, Rush, Shaw, & Emery, 1979; Beck & Weishaar, 1995; Pretzer & Beck, 2005). The goal of cognitive therapy, therefore, is to help the individual break out of this self-supporting, maladaptive pattern of cognition.

Depression can become an ongoing cognitive process that is difficult to escape. [Image by Naomi August].

Another important aspect of the depressive syndrome is known as the **cognitive triad**, three cognitive patterns that cause the person to view themselves in a negative manner. First, the individual has a negative view of themselves. Primarily, the depressed individual sees themselves as defective in some psychological, moral, or physical way, and because of the presumed defects they are undesirable and worthless. Second, the depressed person has a tendency to interpret their ongoing experiences in negative ways. These negative misinterpretations persist even in the face of incompatible evidence. And finally, they tend to hold a negative view of the future. They anticipate continued difficulty, failure, emotional suffering. As a result, they lack motivation, they become paralyzed by pessimism and hopelessness. According to Beck, suicide can be viewed as an extreme attempt to escape problems that depressed individuals believe cannot be solved and the unbearable suffering that the future holds! These negative cognitive patterns are not something that the depressed person plans or has much control over, since they typically occur in the form of automatic thoughts (Beck, 1967; Beck, Rush, Shaw, & Emery, 1979; Beck & Weishaar, 1995; also see Beck, Resnick, & Lettieri, 1974).

Discussion Question: Beck described a number of common cognitive distortions, including dichotomous thinking, personalization, overgeneralization, and catastrophizing. Think about situations in your own life when you made these distortions. What sort of problems resulted from these cognitive errors, and how often do you make them?

Beck's Cognitive Therapy

Cognitive therapy, according to Beck, "is an active, directive, time-limited, structured approach used to treat a variety of psychiatric disorders" (Beck, Rush, Shaw, & Emery, 1979). With regard to depression, it is most effective after a major depression has lifted somewhat, though it can also be helpful for some patients during depression, particularly if the depression is of the reactive type (as opposed to endogenous depression; Beck, 1967). As mentioned above, the basic procedure is to help the individual break out of the trap of negative schemas, automatic thoughts, and cognitive distortions that support the client's problem. The techniques employed are designed to identify, test the reality of, and correct the cognitive distortions and schemas that lead to dysfunctional automatic thoughts. It involves an active collaboration between the therapist and the client, such that the client learns to reduce their symptoms by thinking and acting more realistically.

Beck referred to the constant interaction between the client and the therapist as **collaborative empiricism**, and contrasted this approach to both psychoanalysis and client-centered therapy. His intention was to provide the client with a series of specific learning experiences that would teach the patient the following skills: (1) monitoring their own negative, automatic thoughts; (2) recognizing the connections between thought, emotion, and behavior; (3) examining evidence for and against their cognitive distortions; (4) substituting reality-based interpretations for their cognitive distortions; and (5) learning to identify and alter the dysfunctional schemas that lead to the cognitive distortions (Beck, Rush, Shaw, & Emery, 1979). The interaction with the client is not superficial, as it involves discussing the very rationale of the therapy to the patient and, ultimately, providing the client with techniques to monitor their dysfunctional thoughts on their own. The therapist teaches the client to recognize the nature of cognition, particularly the client's dysfunctional cognitions, all with the goal of eventually neutralizing the automatic thoughts. Somewhat related to collaborative empiricism is the concept of **guided discovery**. Guided discovery is the process by which the therapist serves as a guide for the client, in order to help them recognize their problematic cognitions and behaviors and also help them design new experiences (behavioral experiments) in which they might acquire new skills and perspectives (Beck & Weishaar, 1995). In addition, the therapeutic relationship provides an opportunity for the client to begin to make progress:

> If the patient begins to feel better after the expression of feeling, this may then set up a favorable cycle. Since the depressed patient may have lost hope that he would ever be able to feel better again, this positive experience helps to restore his morale and also his motivation to cooperate in the therapy. Any evidence of feeling better is likely to increase the patient's motivation for therapy and thus contribute to its efficacy. (pp. 43-44; Beck, Rush, Shaw, & Emery, 1979)

Although Beck focused much of his research on depression, cognitive therapy can be used to treat a wide variety of psychiatric and psychological disorders, including anxiety disorders, phobias, substance abuse disorders, anger and violence, and personality disorders (Beck, 1999; Beck & Emery, 1985; Beck & Freeman, 1990; Beck & Weishaar, 1995; Beck, Wright, Newman, & Liese, 1993; Pretzer & Beck, 2005). In *Love is Never Enough* (Beck, 1988), Beck extended cognitive therapy to working with couples. He had observed that many of his depressed client's were in troubled relationships, and in other cases his client's depression and/or anxiety had led to relationship problems. As Beck began working with couples, he found that couples were capable of the same cognitive distortions that individuals make, as each party within the relationship began focusing on the negative aspects of the relationship. As conflict grows, the partners blame each other, rather than seeing the conflict as a problem that can be resolved. Just as with individuals, cognitive therapy offers a means for breaking the cycle of conflict and miscommunication.

Discussion Question: Collaborative empiricism and guided discovery both suggest that the client must be an active member of the therapeutic team. In your opinion, is it possible for someone who needs therapy to help in their own recovery? Do you think there is a point at which the therapist must take over in order to ensure that therapy is successful?

Acceptance and Commitment Therapy (ACT) and Radical Acceptance

A recent development in cognitive therapy shares an ancient tradition with Eastern philosophies: mindfulness. Mindfulness training involves learning to accept one's emotional realities, and one of the most significant realities is that much of human life involves suffering. Starting with these basic observations, Steven Hayes and his colleagues have developed **Acceptance and Commitment Therapy** (ACT; Hayes & Smith, 2005; Hayes, Strosahl, & Wilson, 1999; see also Eifert & Forsyth, 2005; Hayes, Follette, & Linehan, 2004). Hayes and his colleagues do not mean acceptance in the sense of resigning oneself to suffering, but rather in the sense of accepting life as it comes. Then, one must commit oneself to moving forward and living a values-based life, regardless of the presence of challenges:

> The constant possibility of psychological pain is a challenging burden that we all need to face…This doesn't mean that you must resign yourself to trudging through your life suffering. Pain and suffering are very different. We believe that there is a way to change your relationship to pain and to then live a good life, perhaps a great life, even though you are a human being whose memory and verbal skills keep the possibility of pain just an instant away. (pg. 12; Hayes & Smith, 2005)

Although Hayes and his colleagues make passing reference to mindfulness as a Buddhist teaching, they do not take a spiritual approach with ACT. They do, however, acknowledge that psychologists often make the mistake of ignoring spiritual practices that might prove helpful to their clients (Hayes, Strosahl, & Wilson, 1999). Many people in psychology today, including Ellis and Beck, recognize that cognitive psychology began with the

Buddha some 2,500 years ago (Ellis, 2005; Pretzer & Beck, 2005; see also Olendzki, 2005). Dr. Tara Brach, a clinical psychologist and teacher of mindfulness meditation (also known as **vipassana**, which means "to see clearly"), makes no qualms about following a Buddhist approach to therapy. In *Radical Acceptance: Embracing Your Life with the Heart of a Buddha* (Brach, 2003), Brach talks about living in a trance of unworthiness. Plagued by beliefs of their own inadequacies, some individuals limit their ability to live a full life. Consequently, they cannot trust that they are lovable, and they live with an undercurrent of depression or helplessness. They then embark on a series of strategies designed to protect themselves: they attempt self-improvement projects, they hold back and play it safe, they withdraw from the present moment, they keep busy, they criticize themselves, and they focus on other's faults. **Radical Acceptance** as a therapeutic approach involves both mindfulness meditation and Buddhist teachings on compassion as a basis for teaching people to accept themselves as they are:

> Radical Acceptance reverses our habit of living at war with experiences that are unfamiliar, frightening or intense. It is the necessary antidote to years of neglecting ourselves, years of judging and treating ourselves harshly, years of rejecting this moment's experience. Radical Acceptance is the willingness to experience ourselves and our life as it is. A moment of Radical Acceptance is a moment of genuine freedom. (pg. 4; Brach, 2003)

Mindfulness as a therapeutic technique has also been used by a variety of other therapists: in couples therapy (Christensen, Sevier, Simpson, & Gattis, 2004; Fruzzetti & Iverson, 2004), following traumatic experiences (Follette, Palm, & Rasmussen Hall, 2004), and for the treatment of eating disorders (Wilson, 2004) and substance abuse (Marlatt, et al., 2004). Janet Surrey, one of the founding members of the Stone Center Group, has favorably compared relational psychotherapy to mindfulness (Surrey, 2005), and Trudy Goodman, who studied child development with Jean Piaget, uses mindfulness in therapy with children (Goodman, 2005). Thus, whether in the more structured approach of ACT or Radical Acceptance, or in more informal ways in the hands of therapists familiar with mindfulness meditation, paying attention to the mind in a calm and careful way is becoming an important trend in psychotherapy. According to Steven Hayes (2004), this approach represents a third wave in behavioral-cognitive therapy, following traditional behavior therapy and then the cognitive therapies of Ellis and Beck. This third wave is also the basis for the popular and influential work of Jon Kabat-Zinn (1990, 1994, 2005; see also Germer et al., 2005) and connects behavioral and cognitive theories to the rapidly growing field of **social neuroscience** (the study of the interactive influences between the structure/function of the brain and social behavior; see, e.g., Begley, 2007; Cacioppo et al., 2006; Cozolino, 2002; Harmon-Jones & Winkielman, 2007; Siegel, 1999, 2007).

Personality Theory in Real Life: Beck's Cognitive Therapy and the Treatment of Personality Disorders

Aaron Beck and a number of his colleagues, as well as others, have attempted to apply cognitive therapy to the treatment of personality disorders. It is widely accepted that personality disorders are highly resistant to treatment, but aside from the problems they present by themselves, there is another important reason to continue trying to address these serious psychological disorders. Personality disorders often co-occur with other psychological conditions (Axis I disorders), and they may be the primary reason why psychotherapy does not work well with certain patients (Pretzer & Beck, 2005). Since cognitive therapy in particular requires that the therapist gain an understanding of what the client is thinking, in order to then help the client recognize their own dysfunctional cognitions so that the client may work toward change, it is necessary for the therapist to have a complete understanding of the client's psychological make-up. As a prelude to treating personality disorders with cognitive therapy, one needs to understand personality disorders in cognitive-behavioral terms.

As with depression, or any other psychological disorder, the cognitive-behavioral perspective suggests that individuals suffering from personality disorders have formed dysfunctional schemas that create an attributional bias, which then causes the person to interpret life's experiences in dysfunctional ways, but in ways that nonetheless support and maintain the dysfunction of the personality disorder. If this theory is accurate, one should be able to identify typical patterns of dysfunctional schemas that match the characterization of different personality disorder diagnoses. Indeed, Beck and Freeman (1990) have offered those patterns in *Cognitive Therapy of Personality Disorders*. What distinguishes the negative schemas that characterize personality disorders from schemas that characterize other psychological disorders reflects the basic difference between Axis II and Axis I in the DSM system:

> The typical schemas of the personality disorders resemble those that are activated in the symptom syndromes, but they are operative on a more continuous basis in information processing. In dependent personality disorder, the schema "I need help" will be activated whenever a problematic situation arises, whereas in depressed persons it will be prominent only during the depression. In personality disorders, the schemas are part of normal, everyday processing of information. (pg. 32; Beck & Freeman, 1990)

What might the typical schemas associated with other personality disorders be? Beck and his colleagues offer detailed examples for all ten of the personality disorders listed in the DSM, as well as for the passive-aggressive (negativistic) personality disorder (Beck & Freeman, 1990; Pretzer & Beck, 2005). To cite just a few examples, the antisocial individual thinks that "people are there to be taken," the narcissistic individual thinks "I am special," and the histrionic individual believes "I need to impress." As a result of these basic beliefs and attitudes, these individuals adopt corresponding behavioral strategies. The dependent person seeks attachment, the antisocial person attacks, the narcissist engages in self-aggrandizement, and the histrionic person performs dramatically (Beck & Freeman, 1990).

How does a personality disorder arise, according to the cognitive-behavioral perspective? First, there are inherited predispositions that may represent primeval strategies. For example, Beck has suggested that the antisocial personality reflects a predatory strategy, whereas in contrast, the paranoid personality reflects a defensive strategy (see Pretzer & Beck, 2005). Second, the characteristics of personality disorders can result from social learning, especially when the social environment enhances genetic predispositions. A child born with a shy disposition, in a household that seems threatening and/or confusing, may naturally withdraw. That withdrawal, taken to its extreme, is a strategy compatible with the avoidant personality disorder. And finally, there is the possibility of traumatic experiences during development. Personality becomes well established during childhood. If one's experiences during this important time are dysfunctional and traumatic, the individual is likely to develop a personality that has ingrained dysfunctional schemas, thus affecting the individual's life from that point forward. In this model, personality disorders are not necessarily any different in form than other psychological conditions, but since they directly involve one's relationship with others, they become significant, problematic features of one's daily life:

> …The cognitive view of "personality disorder" is that this is simply the term used to refer to individuals with *pervasive, self-perpetuating cognitive-interpersonal cycles* which are dysfunctional enough to come to the attention of mental health professionals. (pg. 61; Pretzer & Beck, 2005)

The basic approach to treating personality disorders with cognitive therapy is not different than usual, but does require some special attention to detail:

> Personality disorders are among the most difficult and least understood problems faced by therapists regardless of the therapist's orientation. The treatment of clients with these disorders can be just as complex and frustrating for

> cognitive therapists as it is for other therapists…For cognitive therapy to live up to its promise as an approach to understanding and treating personality disorders, it is necessary to tailor the approach to the characteristics of individuals with personality disorders rather than simply using "standard" cognitive therapy without modification. (pp. 44-45; Pretzer & Beck, 2005)

Based on this concern, Pretzer and Beck (2005) have offered a list of twelve key elements that require attention when using cognitive therapy to treat an individual with a personality disorder:

1. Interventions are most effective when based on an individualized conceptualization of the client's problems.
2. It is important for therapist and client to work collaboratively toward clearly identified, shared goals.
3. It is important to focus more than the usual amount of attention on the therapist-client relationship.
4. Consider beginning with interventions which do not require extensive self-disclosure.
5. Interventions that increase the client's sense of self-efficacy often reduce the intensity of the client's symptomatology and facilitate other interventions.
6. Do not rely primarily on verbal interventions.
7. Try to identify and address the client's fears before implementing changes.
8. Help the client deal adaptively with aversive emotions.
9. Anticipate problems with compliance.
10. Do not presume that the client exists in a reasonable environment.
11. Attend to your own emotional reactions during the course of therapy.
12. Be realistic regarding the length of therapy, goals for therapy, and standards for therapist self-evaluation.

Despite these straight-forward steps toward effective cognitive therapy, it seems clear from looking at them that there are going to be challenges when dealing with clients who have a personality disorder. Indeed, the very process of collaborative empiricism can be quite difficult with these clients. Beck & Freeman (1990) have identified nineteen problems associated with establishing an effective collaboration with clients who have a personality disorder:

1. The patient may lack the skill to be collaborative.
2. The therapist may lack the skill to develop collaboration.
3. Environmental stressors may preclude changing or reinforce dysfunctional behavior.
4. Patients' ideas and beliefs regarding their potential failure in therapy may contribute to noncollaboration.
5. Patients' ideas and beliefs regarding effects of the patients' changing on others may preclude compliance.
6. Patients' fears regarding changing and the "new" self may contribute to noncompliance.
7. The patient's and therapist's dysfunctional beliefs may be harmoniously blended.
8. Poor socialization to the model may be a factor in noncompliance.
9. A patient may experience secondary gain from maintaining the dysfunctional pattern.
10. Poor timing of interventions may be a factor in noncompliance.
11. Patients may lack motivation.
12. Patients' rigidity may foil compliance.

13. The patient may have poor impulse control.
14. The goals of therapy may be unrealistic.
15. The goals of therapy may be unstated.
16. The goals of therapy may be vague and amorphous.
17. There may have been no agreement between therapist and patient relative to the treatment goals.
18. The patient or therapist may be frustrated because of a lack of progress in therapy.
19. Issues involving the patient's perception of lowered status and self-esteem may be factors in noncompliance.

Although Beck and his colleagues offer more details and specific clinical examples in their writings (Beck & Freeman, 1990; Pretzer & Beck, 2005), the preceding lengthy list of problems a therapist is like to encounter clearly suggests that working with these clients is difficult at best. So, is cognitive therapy effective in the treatment of personality disorders? Numerous uncontrolled clinical reports suggest that it is, but the small number of controlled studies have offered equivocal results. More important, however, is the reality of "real-life" clinical practice:

> In clinical practice, most therapists do not apply a standardized treatment protocol with a homogenous sample of individuals who share a common diagnosis. Instead, clinicians face a variety of clients and take an individualized approach to treatment. A recent study of the effectiveness of cognitive therapy under such "real world" conditions provides important support for the clinical use of cognitive therapy with clients who are diagnosed as having personality disorders… (pg. 102; Pretzer & Beck, 2005)

So what can we conclude from this discussion? There is consensus that personality disorders are prevalent in our society and they are resistant to treatment. Cognitive therapy, and the theory underlying it, has offered a promising avenue for further research. Given the significant impact of personality disorders on both individuals and society as a whole, any promising line of research deserves to be pursued vigorously.

Review of Key Points

- Personal construct theory emphasizes the cognitions that precede behavior, even more than one's ability to accurately predict behavior.
- Kelly used the term man-the-scientist to describe how each person creates and tests representations of the world, in an effort to predict and control their environment.
- Our representations, or constructs, are open to revision, and there are always alternatives. The process by which we test and modify our constructs is called constructive alternativism.
- Personal construct theory begins with a fundamental postulate, which is then elaborated with eleven corollaries.
- Personal constructs regularly undergo transition, from ineffective constructs to more effective constructs. Problems with these transitions may result in feelings of threat, fear, guilt, or anxiety.
- There are two typical cycles of transition: the C-P-C Cycle and the Creativity Cycle. The first involves circumspection, preemption, and control. The Creativity Cycle requires beginning with loose constructions and then rapidly testing and pursuing new and effective constructs.
- Creativity appears to be an important component of healthy psychological functioning.
- Both the therapist and the client bring their own conceptualizations about therapy into the therapeutic process. The ultimate goal is to help the client generate movement forward, such that the process can continue after therapy has ended.

George Kelly, Albert Ellis, and Aaron Beck

- In order to facilitate cognitive-behavioral therapy within his theoretical framework, Kelly developed an assessment tool known as the Role Construct Repertory Test and a therapeutic procedure known as fixed-role therapy.
- In diverse settings, it is essential for therapists to be familiar with cross-cultural issues related to therapy in order to understand the nature of a client's constructs and schemas.
- Ellis proposed an ABC theory of personality: activating events lead to beliefs about a situation, and those beliefs lead to the consequences of the event.
- Rational emotive behavior therapy was designed to dispute the client's irrational beliefs, thus leading to effective new philosophies, emotions, and behaviors.
- The straightforward nature of rational emotive behavior therapy, and Ellis' willingness to write for a popular audience, was a major factor in establishing the self-help genera.
- Rational Recovery, based on rational emotive behavior therapy, was developed as an alternative to Alcoholics Anonymous. In particular, it does not include the religious requirements of AA.
- Rational emotive behavior therapy was challenged as being atheistic. Ellis later wrote that he is not opposed to spirituality, but he is opposed to dysfunctional, dogmatic religious beliefs that hinder one's personal growth.
- Ellis openly challenged the value placed on self-esteem, suggesting instead that what is important is acceptance of ourselves, including our flaws and mistakes.
- Beck developed his cognitive therapy while conducting research on depression.
- Beck's cognitive model is based on automatic thoughts, schemas, and cognitive distortions. Depression in particular results from a cognitive triad: a negative view of past, present, and future.
- Cognitive therapy offers an active, directive, time-limited, and structured approach to psychotherapy.
- Cognitive therapy involves collaborative empiricism and guided discovery. Hopefully, the client is able to learn skills that will allow them to continue improving their life even after therapy has ended.
- Acceptance and Commitment Therapy incorporates mindfulness into a modern therapeutic process, emphasizing the acceptance of one's suffering in life followed by moving forward and living a values-based life. Radical Acceptance incorporates traditional Buddhist mindfulness practice (vipassana) into the therapeutic process.

Review of Key Terms

ABC theory of personality	cultural malpractice	phenomenological
Acceptance and Commitment Therapy	dichotomous thinking	psychotherapeutic interview
activating event	dichotomy corollary	Radical Acceptance
anxiety	emergent pole	range corollary
automatic thoughts	experience corollary	rational emotive behavior therapy (REBT)
catastrophizing	fear	Rational Recovery (RR)
choice corollary	fixed-role sketch	Repertory Grid
cognitive distortions	fixed-role therapy	Role Construct Repertory Test
cognitive triad	fragmentation corollary	Role Title List
collaborative empiricism	fundamental postulate	schemas
commonality corollary	guided discovery	self-characterization sketch
constructive alternativism	guilt	social neuroscience
construction corollary	implicit pole	sociality corollary
constructs	individuality corollary	threat
core values	man-the-scientist	vipassana
C-P-C Cycle	modulation corollary	
Creativity Cycle	organization corollary	
	overgeneralization	
	personal construct theory	
	personalization	

Annotated Bibliography

Kelly, G. A. (1955a). ***The psychology of personal constructs - Vol. 1: A theory of personality.*** **New York, NY: W. W. Norton & Company.**

Kelly, G. A. (1955b). ***The psychology of personal constructs - Vol. 2: Clinical diagnosis and psychotherapy.*** **New York, NY: W. W. Norton & Company.**

This two volume work was Kelly's major contribution to the field of cognitive psychology. Approximately 1,200 pages in length, Kelly attends to every detail in describing his theory, how to apply it in therapy, and how to use the Rep Test to evaluate the personal constructs of clients. In addition to the technical details, Kelly uses many examples from actual cases involving his clients.

Ellis, A. (1973). ***Humanistic psychotherapy: The rational-emotive approach.*** **New York, NY: McGraw-Hill.**

In this extraordinary book, Ellis addresses the value of each person, and how he believes rational emotive behavior therapy makes a contribution to society by offering a practical and effective approach to psychotherapy. Of particular interest is the chapter devoted to Alfred Adler, in which Ellis demonstrates great respect and admiration for the contributions of Adler to psychotherapy.

Ellis. A. (1994). ***Reason and emotion in psychotherapy: A comprehensive method of treating human disturbances - Revised and Updated.*** **New York, NY: A Birch Lane Press Book.**

In this substantial text, which updates one of Ellis' first books, he covers every detail regarding rational emotive behavior therapy. From an historical perspective on the origins of REBT and the theory underlying it to the limitations of and objections to REBT, Ellis uses many practical examples to defend the therapy he developed.

Ellis, A. (2005). ***The myth of self-esteem: How rational emotive behavior therapy can change your life forever.*** **Amherst, NY: Prometheus Books.**

Self-esteem may be one of the best-recognized terms in psychology, and it is almost universally considered essential to good psychological health (at least amongst non-psychologists). Ellis challenges the value of self-esteem as a myth, and in one of the most extraordinarily diverse books in the history of psychology, he draws upon many different perspectives to support his case, including: Solomon, Jesus of Nazareth, Lao Tsu, both religious and atheistic existential philosophers, the Dalai Lama and other Buddhist monks, Stephen Hayes, Carl Rogers, and Aaron Beck.

Beck, A. T., Rush, A. J., Shaw, B. F., & Emery, G. (1979). ***Cognitive therapy of depression.*** **New York, NY: Guilford Press.**

Described by some as a landmark text, Beck and his colleagues cover the full range of practical and theoretical aspects of cognitive therapy and its application in the treatment of depression. This book offers clear and practical advice to therapists who would adopt Beck's techniques, as well as offering great insight to those with an academic interest in these topics.

Beck, A. T. & Freeman, A. (1990). ***Cognitive therapy of personality disorders.*** **New York, NY: Guilford Press.**

With nine other leading cognitive therapists contributing to the development of this text (including Beck's daughter), Beck and Freeman present the definitive work on applying cognitive therapy to the treatment of personality disorders. After covering the theoretical and clinical issues relevant to cognitive therapy and personality disorders in general, chapter by chapter they address each of the well-defined personality disorders. Each chapter typically contains a cognitive conceptualization of the specific personality disorder, case histories or examples, and specific treatment recommendations for working with clients suffering from the particular personality disorder.

Hayes, S. C., Strosahl, K. D., & Wilson, K. G. (1999). ***Acceptance and Commitment Therapy: An experiential approach to behavior change.*** **New York, NY: The Guilford Press.**

Brach, T. (2003). ***Radical acceptance: Embracing your life with the heart of a Buddha.*** **New York, NY: Bantam Books.**

These books are representative of some of the current trends in cognitive-behavioral therapy, with a healthy dose of ancient Eastern philosophy thrown in (mindfulness). Hayes and his colleagues have developed this approach within the tradition of modern psychotherapy, and tend to avoid the religious overtones of the Eastern approach. Brach represents many therapists who are familiar with Buddhist approaches to mindfulness, though she has presented a more fully developed approach to mindfulness therapy.

Lao Tsu (c600 B.C./1989) ***Tao Te Ching.*** **New York, NY: Vintage Books.**

The Tao Te Ching, loosely translated as "The Way of Virtue Book," may be the most widely read book in the world. Written some 2,600 years ago, it offers a strange perspective on how we might view the world and our place in it. Lao Tsu challenges our normal way of thinking with such gems as: "…he who knows that enough is enough will always have enough" (pg. 48), and "When wisdom and intelligence are born, the great pretence begins" (pg. 20).

Chapter 13 - Trait Theories

Gordon Allport is considered the founder of trait theory. Trait theory is sometimes viewed as dry, inflexible, and devoid of paying attention to the rich and interesting developmental aspects of personality that so many students enjoy studying. Those same students would probably be quite surprised to learn that Allport is generally considered to have been humanistic in his approach. It was within his effort to understand the individual, however, that Allport focused on traits, psychological phenomena that allow some ability to predict the behavior of an individual. Allport was also concerned about factors that negatively affect people, such as prejudice. Indeed, in 1954, he published a classic study on prejudice in which he argued that despite all of humanity's scientific advances we remain "in the Stone Age so far as our handling of human relationships is concerned" (Allport, 1979). This concern for all people likely grew out of his profound spiritual faith (for a collection of Allport's daily prayer reflections see Bertocci, 1978). Thus, the trait approach to psychology, as envisioned by Allport, was anything but dry and inflexible, and it paid careful attention to the unique value of each individual.

Raymond Cattell provides a dramatic contrast to Allport. His approach to trait theory was purely scientific and mathematical. He focused on psychological testing, and made extraordinary contributions to psychology in this regard. Unfortunately, he was also quite different than Allport with regard to his views on racial, ethnic, and other forms of diversity. Cattell was a staunch advocate of **eugenics**, the controlled interbreeding of people to enhance desired human traits. He believed that the government should decide how to control the eugenic breeding, that rich people should be encouraged and allowed to have more children than other people, there should be genetic experiments to pursue new and more favorable traits, and once we can identify such favorable traits we should provide prenatal screening and abort those children who will not be good enough (Cattell, 1972).

Hans Eysenck, followed by Paul Costa and Robert McCrae, attempted to identify a smaller number of traits that could be used to provide a reasonable description of an individual's personality. The Five-Factor Model of personality, identified by Costa & McCrae (see, e.g., McCrae & Costa, 2003), is considered by many to be the culmination of this area of psychology. However, there are many personality traits that are significant factors for certain individuals, but which do not comprise one the five major factors. One example is the sensation-seeking trait described by Marvin Zuckerman (see, e.g., Zuckerman, 1994). As such, Zuckerman represents the approach of many trait theorists today: take a trait of interest, such as sensation-seeking or religiosity, and study it in great detail. In this chapter, we will examine the approaches taken by these theorists, as well as the form of the theories they subsequently presented.

Brief Biography of Gordon Allport

Gordon Willard Allport was born on November 11, 1897, in Montezuma, Indiana. His father had been a businessman, but then decided to go into medicine and become a country doctor. It was in Indiana that Allport's father set up his first medical practice shortly before Allport was born, the youngest of four brothers. The family soon moved to Ohio, eventually settling in Glenville, where Allport spent his school years. His brothers were considerably older, causing him to feel like an outsider. Despite feelings of isolation, he worked hard to be the star of a small group of friends. He also did well in school, though he was uninspired and not curious about much outside of routine adolescent concerns (Allport, 1968).

His home life was marked by trust and affection, but it was not one of leisure. Rather, it was marked by "plain Protestant piety and hard work" (pg. 379; Allport, 1968). His mother had been a schoolteacher, and she encouraged philosophical and religious interests among her children. Also, the family home doubled as his father's medical clinic and hospital, so there was always much work to be done around the house. Family vacations were rare, and his father liked it that way. According to Allport, his father believed that everyone should work as hard as they could and accept as pay only what their family needed to survive, so that there might be enough wealth to go around for everyone. In many ways, the Allport children were taught the importance of being concerned with the welfare of others (Allport, 1968).

After graduating from high school, in 1915, Allport followed his brother Floyd to Harvard University. Floyd Allport had graduated from Harvard in 1913, and then continued in the graduate program in psychology. Floyd Allport encouraged his younger brother to study psychology, and he was the teaching assistant for Allport's first psychology course. At the beginning of his first semester Allport received poor grades, but after redoubling his efforts, he ended his first year with all As. What Allport found most interesting was the distinction between "causal" psychology and "purposive" psychology, and he wondered if the two couldn't be reconciled. During World War I he was a member of the Students' Army Training Corps, but the war ended before he had to serve in Europe. Allport also studied in the Department of Social Ethics, and he engaged in extensive community service. He ran a boys' club in Boston, Massachusetts, did volunteer work for the Family Society and as a probation officer, and he spent a summer working at the Humane Society in Cleveland, Ohio. Allport found this community service to be very rewarding, partly because he enjoyed it, and partly because it helped him to feel competent (offsetting his general feelings of inferiority). He became convinced that effective social service could only be provided if one first had a sound understanding of human personality. At the 1919 Harvard commencement, he received his bachelor's degree and his brother Floyd received a Ph.D. (Floyd Allport is considered one of the founders of the discipline of social psychology).

After graduating, Allport spent a year teaching English and sociology at Robert College in Constantinople, Turkey. He was then offered a fellowship for the graduate program in psychology at Harvard. On the way back to the United States, Allport had an extraordinarily influential meeting with Sigmund Freud. He stopped in Vienna to visit his brother Fayette, and while there he requested a meeting with Freud. He received a kind invitation, and when he arrived Freud sat silently waiting for Allport to state the purpose of their meeting. Unprepared for silence, Allport quickly chose to relate a story of a young boy he had seen who was terribly afraid of dirt. The boy's mother was so dominant and proper that Allport thought the source of the boy's anxiety was clear. Freud, however, looked at Allport and asked "And was that little boy you?" Freud had entirely misinterpreted Allport's reason for visiting him, assuming that it was a therapeutic encounter. Allport became convinced that depth psychology might plunge too deeply, and that psychologists should consider manifest motives before digging into the unconscious (Allport, 1968).

Allport found graduate school quite easy, and in 1922 he received his Ph.D. However, he was unable to find any colleagues who shared his interest in a humanistic approach to the study of personality. Thus, he had to chart his own path. His first paper, published with his brother, was on classifying and measuring personality traits. His course entitled *Personality: Its Psychological and Social Aspects*, first taught at Harvard in 1924, was probably the first personality course in America. Allport then received a fellowship that allowed him to spend 2 years studying in Germany and England. In 1925 he married Ada Lufkin Gould, who had a masters' degree in clinical psychology, and in 1927 they had a son named Robert. Allport also moved to Dartmouth College that year. In 1928 he and Floyd published a test for measuring dominant and submissive tendencies, but they never collaborated again. Although they helped each other from time to time, their psychological perspectives were simply too different as their careers progressed (Allport, 1968).

In 1930 Allport returned to Harvard, where he remained for the rest of his career. His first book, *Studies in Expressive Movement*, included a section on handwriting analysis and personality, known as graphology (Allport & Vernon, 1933). This was followed by *The Psychology of Radio* (Cantril & Allport, 1935), and then the landmark *Personality: A Psychological Interpretation* (Allport, 1937). It was in the latter book that Allport outlined the majority of the theory for which he is recognized, and it was the culmination of ideas that had been "cooking" in his head since graduate school. It was his ambition at the time to give a psychological definition to the field of personality. He certainly helped to accomplish that task, but it should also be noted that another landmark personality text, with a similar goal, was published the same year by Ross Stagner, entitled *Psychology of Personality* (Stagner, 1937; for a discussion of the significance of these two books see Craik, 1993; Stagner, 1993). Somewhat unfairly, Allport is often recognized for having published the first personality textbook, and Stagner is overlooked. However, Stagner was quite young at the time (only 28 years old). Accordingly, Allport was well-established in his field, and Stagner cites earlier work by both Gordon and Floyd Allport numerous times in his textbook.

During World War II, Allport worked with the Emergency Committee in Psychology under the American Psychological Association. He spent some time working on the problem of morale among the American people, and he wrote a daily column for the Boston *Traveler* that focused, in part, on rumors. An important aspect of rumors was those rumors designed to enhance prejudice and group antagonism. This work led to a series of seminars on race relations for the Boston Police Department, a book entitled *The Psychology of Rumor* (Allport & Postman, 1947), and ultimately to Allport's classic study *The Nature of Prejudice* (first published in 1954; Allport, 1979). Another factor facilitating Allport's work on social issues was the establishment of a new department at Harvard shortly after WWII: the Department of Social Relations. Given his lifelong interest in social ethics, Allport flourished in this new environment, remaining active in its administration throughout his career. Later in his career Allport continued to refine his personality and social psychological theories, he pursued his interest in social and religious development, with books such as *The Individual and His Religion* (Allport, 1950) and *Becoming* (Allport, 1955), and the application of trait theory to the analysis of an individual's historical documents. With regard to the latter, Allport had published *The Use of Personal Documents in Psychological Science* in 1942, and after using a collection of personal letters reflecting a mother-son relationships as lecture aids for many years, he eventually published *Letters from Jenny* in 1965. In 1966, as Allport was entering into semiretirement, Harvard University appointed him the first Richard Clarke Cabot Professor of Social Ethics. Cabot, a wealthy Boston philanthropist, was also a professor of cardiology and social ethics at Harvard. Cabot had been a professional friend and mentor to Allport for many years, and Allport credited him with having a great influence on Allport's career. As early as 1919, when Allport was just earning his bachelor's degree, Cabot was commenting on the poor state of the study of personality. Thus, it is perhaps no surprise that he mentored and supported Allport, who went on to become the "patron saint" of personality psychology (Nicholson, 2003).

Allport died in 1967, 1 month shy of his seventieth birthday, leaving behind many unfinished books, articles, and two psychological tests. He had received many honors, including a *Gold Medal Award for Life Achievement* from the American Psychological Foundation in 1963 (an award his older brother Floyd won five years later) and a *Distinguished Scientific Contribution Award* from the American Psychological Association in 1964 (Maddi & Costa, 1972). He was the first personality psychologist elected president of APA, and a 1951 survey placed him second only to Freud as a personality theorist whose work was directly applicable to clinical practice. However, one award stood out for him, and it is the only one he mentions in his autobiography. At the XVII International Congress of Psychology, fifty-five of his former doctoral students gave him a two-volume set of their own writings, with an inscription thanking him for respecting their individuality. In Allport's own words, this was "an intimate honor, and one I prize above all others" (pg. 407; Allport, 1968). In that same autobiography, which was actually published after his death, he acknowledged a small number of personality theorists whom he felt were on the right path toward understanding human life, including Carl Rogers, Abraham Maslow, and Henry Murray.

Placing Allport in Context: The Beginning of Trait Theory

Gordon Allport is viewed by many as the founder of trait theories of personality. In addition, because of his specific focus on personality itself, he is also viewed as the founder of personality psychology as a distinct discipline. His entire approach to psychology, and more specifically to personality, was born of his strong devotion to social ethics. He was a profoundly spiritual man, who challenged the negative aspects of religious dogma and championed the positive aspects of having a spiritual direction in one's life. Because his psychology carried with it that devotion to social ethics, he wrote one of the most famous books on prejudice, in which he suggested that the future role of psychology in understanding this disturbing inclination of people everywhere must be based on values.

Since his approach to studying and teaching psychology emphasized the value and uniqueness of each person, he is considered to have been a humanistic psychologist, even though he is seldom grouped with Carl Rogers and Abraham Maslow (instead, he is grouped with other trait theorists). Always aware of the future challenges facing those who would study personality, Allport hoped that movements toward individual, humanistic, and existential psychology would continue:

> I'm quite certain there will be a strong movement toward what is called a third force which will be neither behavioristic nor psychoanalytic. But I wouldn't be willing to predict that it will dominate the field, though I can say I do hope it will develop sturdily and result in fruitful new methods to approach molar and complex levels of personality structure and social behavior...Human nature is such a hard nut to crack that no one should be denied a chance to contribute to it at any level. (pg. 112; Allport cited in Evans, 1981b)

Trait Theories

Allport's Psychology of Personality

> As a rule, science regards the individual as a mere bothersome accident. Psychology, too, ordinarily treats him as something to be brushed aside so the main business of accounting for the uniformity of events can get under way...With the intention of supplementing this abstract portrait by one that is more life-like, a new movement within psychological science has gradually grown up. It attempts in a variety of ways and from many points of view to depict and account for the manifest individuality of mind. This new movement has come to be known (in America) as the *psychology of personality*. (pg. vii; Allport, 1937)

With these words, in the preface to *Personality: A Psychological Interpretation*, Allport "officially" established the study of personality as a discipline in the field of psychology. His goal was two-fold: (1) to gather together the most important research on personality to date, and (2) to provide a framework within which the study of personality might then proceed toward understanding this "endlessly rich subject-matter" (Allport, 1937).

What Is Personality and What Are Traits?

Allport provides an interesting history of the use of the term **persona**, including a set of definitions written by Cicero (106-43 B.C.): as one appears to others (but not as one really is); the part one plays in life; the collection of personal qualities that fits one's career (or place in life); and distinction and dignity. These and other definitions of persona represent a contradiction, that persona, or personality in psychological terms, is both something vital and internal and yet also something external and false. Although psychologists came to favor definitions that emphasized an assemblage of personal qualities, Allport noted that no two psychologists could easily agree on one definition for the term "personality." So Allport offered a definition of his own:

> Personality is the dynamic organization within the individual of those psychophysical systems that determine his unique adjustments to his environment. (pg. 48; Allport, 1937)

Dynamic Organization: According to Allport, personality involves active organization, which is constantly evolving and changing, and which involves motivation and self-regulation. Thus, it is dynamic, not static. Organization also brings with it the possibility of disorganization, and the resulting abnormalities associated with personality disorders and/or mental illness.

Psychophysical Systems: The term "psychophysical" is meant to remind us that personality reflects both mind and body, the total organism. The systems include habits, attitudes, sentiments, and dispositions of various kinds. Most important, however, are the traits, which may be either latent or active.

Determine: In Allport's view, "personality *is* something and *does* something." Personality is not synonymous with behavior, it underlies it, and it comes from within the individual. The systems mentioned above can be viewed as determining tendencies.

Unique: Naturally, each adjustment by an individual is unique in time, space, and quality. However, Allport mentioned this aspect in anticipation of his later discussion of individual vs. common traits (see below).

Adjustments to His Environment: Personality, according to Allport, is a mode of survival, it has functional and evolutionary significance. For humans, we are not simply reactive, as plants and animals are, because we can be spontaneous and creative. We can, and do, seek mastery over our environment (both behavioral and geographic). Unfortunately, once again the possibility exists for maladaptive behavior that arises under abnormal conditions (such as an abusive home environment).

In 1961, Allport wrote an updated and substantially revised version of his personality text entitled *Pattern and Growth in Personality*. He made only one significant change to his definition of personality, which reflected a greater emphasis on cognitive processes. He changed the phrase "unique adjustments to his environment" to "characteristic behavior and thought" (pg. 28; Allport, 1961). He described "characteristic" in essentially the same way as he had described "unique" so that change was insignificant. However, the phrase "behavior and thought" was intended to indicate that individuals do more than simply adjust to their environment, they also reflect on it. Thus, the human intellect is an important factor in the manner in which we seek mastery over our environment and, indeed, over our lives.

So now we turn our attention to **traits**, those special psychophysical systems that are at the center of Allport's theory of personality. In 1936, Allport and Odbert had examined the 1925 edition of *Webster's New International Dictionary* and identified 17,953 words (4½ percent of the English language) that described aspects of distinctive and personal behavior that would commonly be described as traits (see Allport, 1937). Allport viewed a trait as both a form of readiness and a determining tendency. There are a number of other concepts that share some similarity with traits, such as **habits**, **attitudes**, **needs**, **types**, and **instincts**. In each case, however, these other forms of readiness to engage in certain responses or activities are different than traits, particularly with regard to their specificity and external focus or, as in the case of types, they describe a collection of correlated attributes. After describing the differences, Allport arrived at the following definition of a trait:

> We are left with a concept of trait as *a generalized and focalized neuropsychic system (peculiar to the individual), with the capacity to render many stimuli functionally equivalent, and to initiate and guide consistent (equivalent) forms of adaptive and expressive behavior.* (pg. 295; Allport, 1937)

The essential aspect of this definition is equivalence, both perceptually and behaviorally. As the result of a trait, different stimuli are perceived as similar, and responded to in similar ways. This occurs regardless of the nature of the stimuli themselves. Suppose, for example, an individual is paranoid. If someone walks by and says "Hi, how are you today?" the paranoid individual might wonder "What is that supposed to mean? Why are they pretending to be so nice? What are they really up to?" As illogical as this response might seem, a paranoid trait has the ability to render even a simple hello as a threat.

Allport also made an important distinction between **individual traits** and **common traits**. Underlying this discussion was another important topic in Allport's approach to psychology: the distinction between the **idiographic** and **nomothetic** approaches to studying psychology. As psychologists attempted to define their discipline as a scientific endeavor, they pursued a nomothetic approach, one that emphasizes general rules that apply to all. However, the psychology of personality that Allport was pursuing is inherently idiographic, an approach that emphasizes individuality. Strictly speaking, no two people can have exactly the same trait. Thus, all traits are inherently individual traits. However, this creates an extraordinary challenge for psychologists, both experimental psychologists who would measure traits and clinical psychologists who would describe an individual as possessing a certain trait (at some level) in order to provide a framework for communication and therapy. Allport agreed that is was logical to assume the existence of common traits, since normal people in a given culture would naturally tend to develop comparable modes of adjustment. However, Allport cautioned that developing clinical or experimental measures of such traits would at best be approximations of the individual traits present in each person (Allport, 1937, 1961).

Discussion Question: Allport described the persona as something vital and internal, yet external and false. How can this be? Can you think of different aspects of your personality that fit both perspectives, and if so, how do those aspects of your personality fit together?

Personal Dispositions

Having acknowledged that there is logic to examining common traits as opposed to individual traits, Allport then returned to each individual's unique personality by addressing **personal dispositions**. A personal disposition is based on traits, but somewhat more complex, such as in a unique combination of traits (e.g., someone who is tentatively aggressive, as opposed to someone who is belligerently aggressive). In another important change between the 1937 and 1961 editions of Allport's general personality text, the latter book discusses cardinal, central, and secondary dispositions, rather than cardinal, central, and secondary traits.

A **cardinal disposition** is one that dominates an individual's entire life. It cannot remain hidden, and the individual will be known by it. Historically, some commonly used terms have adopted the reputation of famous figures, including at least one that appears in the DSM-V: the Narcissistic Personality Disorder (named after

Narcissus, from Greek mythology). Another example would be to describe someone as Christ-like. Personalities that posses one cardinal disposition, however, are quite unusual.

Much more common are **central dispositions**. If you were asked to describe a good friend, you would most likely offer a handful of distinguishable central dispositions. The interesting question, of course, is how many central dispositions does a typical personal have? Allport suggested that a person's central dispositions would be those things one would mention in a carefully written letter of recommendation, a response that might make sense to someone like a professor, who often writes such letters.

Of lesser importance, according to Allport, are the **secondary dispositions**. These are less conspicuous, less consistent, and are less often called into play. In concluding his discussion of cardinal, central, and secondary dispositions, Allport acknowledged that these gradations are arbitrary, and presented primarily for convenience. In reality, he said, there are many degrees of personality organization, from the most loosely structured and unstable to the most pervasive and firmly structured. The value of these distinctions is to provide a relative measure of the influence of traits and dispositions when discussing personality.

Personality Development, Functional Autonomy, and the Mature Personality

According to Allport, a newborn infant has no personality, for it has not experienced the world in which it will live and it has had no opportunity to develop its distinctive modes of adjusting to that environment. Personality exists only later, after the common elements of human nature have interacted and produced the unique, self-continuing, and evolving systems that form the individual's personality. The basic aspects of growth, following the infant's initial random and diffuse behavior, involve **differentiation**, **integration**, **maturation**, and **learning**. As the child's nervous system develops, it gradually gains finer control over its movement. Little by little, the young child differentiates more efficient and adaptive patterns of behavior, including vocal behavior. Psychologically, this differentiation involves more than just behaviors themselves, it also includes the ability to control the initiation of those behaviors. Very young children have little capacity for delaying their actions; they want to do things now! As the child's behavioral repertoire increases, it becomes just as necessary and adaptive to begin integrating some of those behaviors into coordinated actions. Once again, if applied to psychological and cognitive processes, the development of traits and dispositions begins with the integration of life's experiences. As these processes are occurring, the child is also maturing physically. Allport did not view maturation as something that contributed directly to personality, but it does indirectly by bringing out every inherited feature of the individual, including temperament, intellectual capacity, physical features, etc. All of these factors, plus the extensive contribution of different types of learning, contribute to the manner in which the individual experiences their environment (Allport, 1937). However, we can never truly know the personality that develops:

> Of the whole of our own natures we are never directly aware, nor of any large portion of the whole. At any single moment the range of consciousness is remarkably slight. It seems only a restless pencil point of light entirely insufficient to illuminate the edifice of personality…It is through…temporal reference and content, that we arrive at the conviction that we do somehow possess consistent personalities surrounding the momentary conscious core. (pg. 159; Allport, 1937)

As a sense of self develops, these developmental processes of childhood progress through a series of stages: (1) a sense of bodily self, (2) a sense of continuing identity, (3) a sense of self-esteem or pride, (4) the extension of self, (5) a self-image, (6) a sense of self as rationally able to cope, and finally, in adolescence, (7) a sense of "directedness" or "intentionality." Allport described these seven aspects of selfhood as a sense of self-relevance that we feel. When combined, they create the "me" as felt and known. In order to identify this sense of "me" or "I" Allport recommended the term **proprium**. Proprium is derived from the Latin term proprius, and it refers to a property common to the members of some class, but which is not part of the definition of that class. In other words, everyone has a personality, but no one's personality is part of the definition of what it means to be a person. But why not simply use the word "self?" Allport felt that many psychologists use the words "self" and "ego" to mean only one or two aspects of the entire proprium. Also, Allport wanted to distinguish between the self as an object, and the self as the "knower" of that object. The proprium refers specifically to the self as an object, whereas self refers both to the object and the "knower." We can be directly aware of the proprium in a way that we can never be fully aware of the "knower" (Allport, 1961).

As the child matures, both physically and psychologically, the individual's interests and motives become stable and predictable. A special type of psychological maturity (as opposed to genetic/biological maturity) takes place, which Allport termed **functional autonomy**. Functional autonomy regards adult motives as varied, and as self-sustaining systems that are unique to the individual. They may have arisen out of developmental processes and experiences, but they are independent of them. This means that any tie between adult motives and early childhood experience is historical, not functional. This is a radically different view than that of Sigmund Freud and most psychodynamic theorists, who considered early childhood experiences to be the driving force behind adult behavior, especially neurotic behavior. Allport offers the example of a good workman. Such a workman feels compelled to do his best work, even though his income no longer depends on maintaining high standards. Indeed, doing his very best on every job may actually hurt him financially, but his personal standards, his motivation, demand nothing less (Allport, 1937, 1961). When viewed a different way, functional autonomy serves another important motivational role. If one considers early childhood experiences to be the determining factors in personality, then all adult motives must have some infantile source. However, by separating adult motives from their childhood antecedents, then there does not need to be anything childish about what motivates adults. This allows for entirely new sources of motivation to be relevant during adulthood, motives that might have been completely beyond the intellectual and cognitive capacities of children.

In considering what constitutes a mature personality, Allport considered the writings of Sigmund Freud, Richard Clarke Cabot, Erik Erikson, and Abraham Maslow. He also considered the length of each man's list. Allport settled on a list of six ideal characteristics of the mature personality. He described the list as an ideal, because he freely acknowledged that no one is perfect, even the "sturdiest of personalities have their foibles and their regressive moments; and to a large extent they depend on environmental supports for their maturity" (pp. 282-282; Allport, 1961).

Extension of the Sense of Self: The mature person focuses on more than simple needs or drive-reduction; they develop strong interests outside of themselves. By truly participating in life, they give direction to their life.

Warm Relating of Self to Others: The mature person is marked by two kinds of warmth. On one hand, through self-extension they are capable of great intimacy in their capacity for love, whether it involves family members or friends. On the other hand, they avoid gossipy, intrusive, or possessive relationships with other people. They respect other persons as persons, they express tolerance and the so-called "democratic character structure."

Emotional Security (Self-Acceptance): Mature individuals demonstrate emotional poise; they have the ability to avoid overreacting. Especially important, according to Allport, is that they possess the quality of "frustration tolerance."

Realistic Perception, Skills, and Assignments: Generally speaking, the mature person is in close contact with what we call the "real world." They see things, including people, for what they really are.

Self-Objectification - Insight and Humor: In describing this characteristic, Allport quoted Socrates: "know thyself." In Allport's psychology classes, 96 percent of his students thought they had average or better than average insight (by definition, only 50 percent can be above the average). So people *think* they have good insight, but this is often not the case. There does appear to be a high correlation between insight and humor. People who truly know themselves are able to look at themselves objectively, and to laugh at their own failings and mistakes.

The Unifying Philosophy of Life: According to Allport, humor may be essential, but it is never sufficient. Maturity requires a sense of life's purpose. This sense of purpose can be found in having a clear direction to one's life, in a strong orientation to values, within one's religious sentiment, or through a generic conscience. Allport found it quite interesting that many people consider their desire to serve society was a more important generic motive than the fulfillment of any sense of religious or spiritual duty. He concluded that an integrated sense of moral obligation can provide a unifying philosophy of life regardless of whether or not it is tied to one's religious sentiments.

Discussion Question: Consider Allport's definition of a mature personality. Do you know anyone who fits all of the criteria? What are they like as a person, and do you consider them a friend (or, do they consider you a friend)?

The Assessment of Personality

> Personality is so complex a thing that every legitimate method must be employed in its study. (pg. 369; Allport, 1937)

In Chapter 1 we examined the common procedures used to assess personality today, and Allport reviewed similar concepts, as well as procedures that were available at the time. It is interesting to note that, in his 1937 text, the very first topic in Allport's survey of assessment methods is the importance of evaluating the cultural setting. Two other topics were also of particular interest to Allport: the study of **expressive behavior** and the use of **personal documents**.

Allport's first two books, *Studies in Expressive Movement* (Allport & Vernon, 1933) and *The Psychology of Radio* (Cantril & Allport, 1935), both addressed what Allport considered to be the second level at which personality is evaluated (the first level consists of the traits, interests, attitudes, etc., that compose the "inner" personality). He considered the study of expressive movement to be a more direct analysis of personality, since it is based on observation, and does not require the use of tests that only indirectly address the inner dispositions revealed in the first level of analysis. For example, what a patient says or writes while taking the Rorschach test is *projective*, but how they say or write it, the tone of their voice or the style of their handwriting, is *expressive* (Allport, 1961). Perhaps the primary value of expressive behavior is that it is freely emitted by the person being observed. It can include all aspects of behavior, including walking, talking, handwriting, gesturing, shaking hands, sketching, doodling, etc. Cantril and Allport examined a variety of curious aspects of radio voices. For example, a natural voice is more revealing of personality than a voice transmitted over the radio. They also found that blind people are *not* better at judging personality from voices than other people, perhaps dispelling the common belief that when people lose one sense they enhance their ability to rely on other senses. Much of what they found was difficult to interpret, however. Voice definitely conveyed accurate measures of personality, but there are no characteristics of personality that are always revealed correctly. Most people preferred to hear a male voice on the radio, but no one could actually explain why, and there were a variety of differences based on the specific aspects of the message or its content (Cantril & Allport, 1935). As for handwriting analysis, Allport felt that through careful research it could become a valid tool for personality analysis. He acknowledged that this was a difficult and complex task, but he concluded that both handwriting and gestures reflect essentially stable and consistent individual styles (Allport & Vernon, 1933).

There are many types of personal documents, including letters, diaries, recorded interviews, and autobiographies. Perhaps the richest of these sources, personal letters, may well become a thing of the past. Letter writing has become much less formal with the advent of phone calls and email. Today, text messages don't even rely on whole words. Politicians often rely on speech writers, so even their written words aren't necessarily their own. Of greater concern, according to Allport, is that personal documents are not representative samples and they are not objective (Allport, 1942, 1961). However, if they can still provide insight into the nature of an individual's personality, then why shouldn't they be used with caution? Allport had a unique set of letters that had been written over a number of years by a woman, between the ages of 58 and 70, to a young married couple. The young husband had been her son's college roommate. Seeing value in the letters as a source of psychological material, the couple made them available for publication, and they came into Allport's possession to be published. For many years he used the letters to provide examples in his own classes, and eventually Allport published them again, along with his analysis of the woman's personality, in *Letters from Jenny* (Allport, 1965). Of particular interest, is that Allport interpreted the letters in a variety of ways, including existential, Jungian, Adlerian, and Freudian perspectives. Allport concluded by addressing whether or not Jenny was normal, a point on which some people disagreed. Using his six characteristics of a mature personality, he assigned relatively low scores to Jenny based on her letters, but he also found some strengths within each characteristic. Thus, although Jenny appears to have been troubled, Allport concludes that it is not a simple matter to say she is normal or abnormal, but "her tangled life has contributed stimulus and challenge to posterity" (pg. 223; Allport, 1965).

Religion and Prejudice

> Two contrary sets of threads are woven into the fabric of all religion - the warp of brotherhood and the woof of bigotry. I am not speaking of religion in any ideal sense, but, rather, of religion-in-the-round as it actually exists historically, culturally, and in the lives of individual

> men and women, the great majority of whom (in our land) profess some religious affiliation and belief. Taken in-the-round, there is something about religion that makes for prejudice, and something about it that unmakes prejudice. It is this paradoxical situation that I wish to explore here. (pg. 218; Allport, 1968)

Allport was a deeply spiritual man, and he often wrote about the role of religion in personality. Religion is such an important factor in so many people's lives, that Allport considered it "thoroughly ridiculous" that psychologists had paid so little attention to it (see Evans, 1981b). Although Allport acknowledged that there were useful and logical reasons for psychology to establish itself as a scientific endeavor, he felt it was just as illogical to reject religion. Allport made neither assumptions nor denials regarding the claims of revealed religion, and he felt that as a scientist he had no right to do so. Still, he believed that psychology must examine subjective religion in the structure of personality whenever and wherever religion is involved. So he delivered a series of six lectures on religion, and published them as *The Individual and His Religion* (Allport, 1950). The book takes a positive perspective on the role of religion. Allport acknowledged that religion seems primarily symptomatic of fear and frustration in many people's live, but he preferred to focus on the psychology, not the psychopathology, of religion. What he found was that the religious sentiment, as it pertains to personality, is as varied and unique as each individual. His findings echoed those of William James, whose own foray into this area of psychology was published in *The Varieties of Religious Experience* (James, 1902/1987).

The relation between religion and prejudice seems to stem from a dichotomy within religion itself. There appears to be an intrinsic value and an extrinsic value associated with religion. The extrinsic or outwardly directed attitude, one that the individual uses for their own purposes, is correlated with prejudice, whereas the intrinsic attitude is correlated with very low prejudice (Evans, 1981b). In focusing on the positive aspects of the intrinsic religious sentiment, Allport suggested that it was attached to the most elusive facets of becoming, enhancing one's unifying philosophy of life and a sense of direction, intentionality, and good conscience (Allport, 1955). When fully developed, the religious sentiment is distinct from its developmental origins (it has functional autonomy). In other words, it is not simply the following of family tradition, or the practice of meaningless rituals, but rather it becomes a unique part of the individual. It becomes morally true for the person, as it engages reason, faith, and love. This was particularly true for Allport. From 1938 to 1966, about twice a year, Allport offered a prayerful meditation during the daily prayers in Appleton Chapel at Harvard University (collected in Bertocci, 1978). In a meditation offered on *The Virtues and Social Science*, Allport wrote:

> We have much to learn about industrial relations, about the resolution of conflict (personal, national, international); about the control of prejudice, the strengthening of brotherhood and compassion. In such areas as these we have yet to make vital discoveries; we have yet "to think God's thoughts after Him." (pp. 89-90; Allport cited in Bertocci, 1978)

Unfortunately, however, there remains the extrinsic attitude toward religion that is correlated with prejudice. In many ways, religions encourage bigotry, most commonly through doctrines of revelation or election. Revealed truth is not to be tampered with, and certain people are chosen, or cursed, above all others. However, these attitudes often follow a very selective reading of the religious texts, and even disagree with other writings. Nonetheless, one cannot deny the horrifying impact that religion can have when perverted for purposes of those who wield power. Allport relates stories such as the Nazi Propaganda Minister Goebbels declaring that Hitler was the intermediary between the German people and God's throne, or the member of the Ku Klux Klan (an allegedly Christian organization) who justified killing Black children by saying that when you kill rattlesnakes you don't care if they are young or old (Allport, 1960, 1968). Allport described such people as using religion as they would use any social group, for their own purposes: making friends, influencing people, furthering business pursuits, gaining prestige, etc. It becomes exclusionistic so that only the members of the group benefit, not anyone else. However, although this is a common outcome of religious activity, there remains a minority of people for whom this does not occur. They serve their religion, not the other way around. They have adopted the creeds and doctrines as an important component of their value system, but included within that value system is the doctrine of human brotherhood (see Evans, 1981b). Religion is, of course, only one factor that leads to prejudice and discrimination. Allport studied those factors in great detail in his classic work on prejudice.

Connections Across Cultures: The Nature of Prejudice

Since Allport was committed to social ethics throughout his life, his classic study on prejudice did not arise suddenly. During World War II, one of his projects was to study the effects of **rumor**. A rumor, according to Allport's definition, is a specific proposition for belief, passed from person to person, without any secure standards of evidence. When a rumor follows some event, the information that people report is based on memory. Important aspects of those memories are often false, and they are false in conjunction with negative stereotypes. Interestingly, this is much less likely to occur with children, who often fail to identify the racial aspects of scenes they have observed (at least in a research setting). Rumors are particularly dangerous when they incite riots, and Allport and Postman wrote that "no riot ever occurs without rumors to incite, accompany, and intensify the violence" (pg. 193; Allport & Postman, 1947). In 1943 there were major riots in Harlem and Detroit, in which negative racial rumors played an important role. In Detroit in particular, according to Allport, if the authorities had listened to the rumors the violence might have been avoided.

The following year, Allport taught a course on minority group problems to the police captains for the city of Boston, Massachusetts. In 1947 he repeated the course for police officers in Cambridge, Massachusetts. One year later, he presented some of his material in a *Freedom Pamphlet* entitled *ABC's of Scapegoating* (Allport, 1948). This pamphlet later grew (rather dramatically, from 36 pages to 537 pages) into his book *The Nature of Prejudice*, which was published in 1954 (Allport, 1979). Despite this preparation, the challenge of a major study on prejudice was still daunting. The problem of the causes of prejudice was so large that it took Allport several years to work out the table of contents, which ended up being eight pages long, including sections on preferential thinking, group differences, perceiving and thinking about group differences, sociocultural factors, acquiring prejudice, the dynamics of prejudice, character structure, and reducing group tensions.

Despite being over 500 pages long, *The Nature of Prejudice* is concise. In part, this indicates the magnitude of the problem of prejudice, and also makes it extremely difficult to summarize the book. Allport begins by asking "What is the problem?" He describes five levels at which people act on prejudice. Most people will only talk about their prejudice with like-minded friends. If the prejudice is strong, they may actively avoid members of another group, and then they may discriminate against them, engaging in detrimental activities toward the disliked group. More extreme prejudice may actually lead to physical attacks, and ultimately, to extermination, such as lynchings or genocide. Is this behavior to be expected? According to Allport, the essential ingredients of prejudice, erroneous generalization and hostility, are natural and common capacities of the human mind. What is necessary, however, is the formation of in-groups, and the rejection of out-groups. We form in-groups naturally as we develop; we learn to like the things we are familiar with. This does not require hostility toward out-groups, but it is an unfortunate reality that many people define their loyalty to the in-group in terms of rejecting the values and customs of the out-group. For those people, rejecting the out-group becomes a powerful need.

Although many differences exist between groups, why has race been emphasized? The answer is, in part, disturbingly simple: we can see race. In addition, most people don't know the difference between race and ethnic group, or race and social caste. Thus, it is simply easier to identify out-groups on the basis of race. Making matters worse, of course, is the reality that we can't even define race that well. Allport discusses research that has suggested as many as thirty different human races or types, yet most of us think in terms of three basic races: White, Black, and Asian (more recently the number would be four, including Hispanics). Discriminating against one "race," such as Blacks in America, without even beginning to understand individual character (i.e., personality) or other aspects of culture, such as religion, customs, or national character (which can also be quite complex), is simply an ignorant act. Yet a point that Allport returns to, as an explanation regarding how natural it is to be prejudice, is that people who are different seem strange, and strangeness is something that makes most people uncomfortable, and it may actually be aversive to many people.

Unfortunately, the victimization of minority groups can enhance the differences and discomfort that exist between groups. As Allport noted:

> Ask yourself what would happen to your own personality if you heard it said over and over again that you were lazy, a simple child of nature, expected to steal, and had inferior blood. Suppose this opinion were forced on you by the majority of your fellow-citizens. And suppose nothing that you could do would change this opinion - because you happen to have black skin. (pg. 142; Allport, 1979)

Minorities can become obsessively concerned about everything they do and everywhere they go in public. They develop a basic feeling of insecurity. The simplest response to prejudice is to deny one's membership in the minority group. For example, some very light-skinned Blacks have passed as White people. But this can lead to great personal conflict, and the feeling that one is a traitor. Huey Newton, co-founder of the Black Panthers, had to fight against prejudice within the Black community itself against those Blacks whose skin was viewed as too light. Oppressed minority group members might also become withdrawn, passive, or they might act like clowns, trying to make fun of their circumstances. Worse, they may identify with the majority group, leading to self-hate and acting out against members of their own group. Of course, there are those who will also fight back aggressively, such as Huey Newton and the members of the Black Panthers.

How might we begin to combat prejudice? Allport discussed an interesting study that addressed the sociological theory of contact between groups. During the Detroit riots of 1943, both Black and White students at Wayne University (which later became Wayne State University) attended class peacefully during what became known as Bloody Monday. It has been suggested that when groups of humans meet they go through a four-stage process: contact itself, followed by competition, then accommodation, and finally assimilation. Thus, the initial contact naturally leads to a peaceful progression of the inter-group relationship. While this is not always the case, there are many examples where it has been. But, it cannot occur without the initial contact. Thus, encouraging contact between groups is an important step in combating prejudice. Allport notes, however, that it is important for the contact to be of equal status and to be in the pursuit of common goals.

Allport also addressed the issue of using legislation to fight prejudice. Unfortunately, as he points out, laws can only have an indirect effect on personal prejudice. They cannot affect one's thoughts and feelings, they can only influence behavior. However, it is also known that behavior can influence one's thoughts, opinions, and attitudes. Thus, Allport encourages the continued use of legislation as a significant method for reducing public discrimination and personal prejudice. More important, however, is the need to take positive action toward reducing prejudice, including the use of intercultural education.

In a fascinating study published one year after *The Nature of Prejudice*, Gillespie & Allport presented the results of a study entitled *Youth's Outlook on the Future* (Gillespie & Allport, 1955). What made the study remarkable was that it included students from the United States, New Zealand, South Africa (both Black and White students), Egypt, Mexico, France, Italy, Germany, Japan, and Israel. Included among the questions was the issue of racial equality, whether students desired greater racial equality and whether they expected greater racial equality. A large majority of college students reported that they desired greater racial equality, ranging from 83 to 99 percent. The notable exceptions were Germany (65 percent), and English speaking South Africans (75 percent) and Afrikaners in South Africa (14 percent - this was during Apartheid). As for the expectation that there would be greater racial equality in the future, students in most of the countries studied said yes between 67 to 73 percent of the time, with notable exceptions being Black South Africans (57 percent), Japanese (53 percent), and Mexicans (87 percent). Thus, most college students around the world (in 1955) desired racial equality, but a significant portion of them did not expect to see it in the future. Considering the state of the world today, we are far from learning the final outcome of this crucial social issue.

If it were possible to achieve a world in which people were not prejudice, what attitude should replace it? This question was recently addressed by Whitley and Kite (2006), and they identify the two most commonly raised options: color-blindness and multiculturalism. The **color-blind perspective** suggests that people should ignore race and ethnicity, acting as if they simply don't exist, whereas the

multicultural perspective considers ethnic/racial identity as cognitively inescapable and fundamental to self-concept. Color-blind proponents argue that as long as race is an issue, there will be some forms of discrimination. Multicultural proponents argue in favor or retaining one's cultural heritage, thus preserving integrity, while also encouraging group interaction and harmonious coexistence. Does one approach appear to be more effective at reducing prejudice? To date, the evidence favors the multicultural approach. Whitley and Kite suggest that reducing prejudice is most likely to occur as a result of individuals both changing their own attitudes and working to help others change their attitudes as well. It is important to reflect on one's own thoughts and behaviors, and to help others become aware of their attitudes and behaviors. In addition, it is important to learn more about other groups, and to actively participate in inter-group contact (Whitley & Kite, 2006). In other words, multiculturalism works best when it actually exists; people need to associate with people of other races, religions, and cultures. Only then can ignorance, as in simply not knowing about other people and their cultural differences, be replaced by knowledge and acceptance.

When Allport published his study on prejudice, it was important that the topic was even being addressed. Today, it is more common to examine the nature of cultural differences and to pursue positive aspects of the value of multicultural settings. A number of recent studies have emphasized various aspects of the differences between people from various cultures, the importance of not feeling so different, and how interaction between groups can prove valuable. For example, the Chinese tend to anticipate change more readily than Americans, they predict greater levels of change when it begins, and they consider those who predict change to be wise (Ji, Nisbett, & Su, 2001). Asian Americans, South Koreans, and Russians are more likely than Americans to adopt avoidance goals, but the adoption of those goals is not a negative predictor of subjective well-being in those collectivist cultures, as it is in individualistic cultures (Elliot et al., 2001). The Japanese appear to be subject to cognitive dissonance effects in a "free" choice paradigm, but only in the presence of important others. Americans, in contrast, are less affected by social-cue manipulations in a "free" choice situation (Kitayama et al., 2004). Although social stereotyping typically results in an over-generalized tendency to include people in groups, under certain circumstance it can also lead to excluding certain individuals from their apparent in-group (Biernat, 2003). Particularly for young people, in-group connection is very important. Low-income, high risk African American and Latino teens who do not "look" like other members of their in-group are at a much higher risk for dropping out of school, but the ability to fit in has a protective effect (Oyserman et al., 2006). Even when significant contact between groups does occur, it may only reduce certain aspects of prejudice, and may do so only for the minority group (as opposed to any change in the majority group; Henry & Hardin, 2006). So how can contact between different cultural groups begin to reduce prejudice and discrimination in such a complex issue? It has been shown that when college students are placed in racially diverse groups, they actually engage in more complex thinking, and they credited minority members with adding to the novelty of their discussions (Antonio et al., 2004). Perhaps most importantly, multiculturalism can also foster the development of a character strength described by Fowers and Davidov (2006) as **openness to the other**.

However, multiculturalism is not without its challenges. Working in diverse teams can lead to social divisions, increasing the likelihood of negative performance teams. Accordingly, it is essential to examine the types of diversity that come into play, since some favor and exploit a wider variety of perspectives and skills, whereas others more readily lead to conflict and division (Kravitz, 2005; Mannix & Neale, 2005). Within the field of psychology, a discipline actively encouraging the growth of minority group membership, there has been a lag in successfully moving students beyond the bachelor's degree to the doctoral level (Maton et al., 2006). The challenges faced by minority graduate students and faculty are, not surprisingly, as diverse as the individuals themselves (see Vasquez et al., 2006). Thus, we have a long way to go in understanding and overcoming prejudice and discrimination. However, within a framework first established in detail by Allport, our examination and understanding of the major issues is rapidly growing.

Discussion Question: Are you prejudiced? Now that you have probably answered no, think again. Are there times, or situations, where you find yourself having thoughts that make you uncomfortable when you stop to really think about them? What do you think is more important, eliminating prejudice, or enacting laws against discrimination?

Brief Biography of Raymond Cattell

Raymond Bernard Cattell was born on March 20, 1905, in the seaside town of Staffordshire, England. Cattell developed a great love for the sea, and his first book was actually about sailing. His father was a mechanical engineer who worked on projects such as innovations for WWI military equipment, the steam engine, and the new internal combustion engine. Cattell was an excellent student, and he earned a scholarship to attend London University. He majored in chemistry, and he received his bachelor's degree in 1924, with first class honors.

The years following World War I were a time of great change in Europe, and Cattell decided that studying psychology would provide him with the opportunity to address the political and economic issues facing society. He entered University College in London, where he worked on his Ph.D. with Charles Spearman, the renowned statistician and expert on intelligence testing (a student of Wilhelm Wundt, and advisor to David Wechsler as well). During his studies, he was involved in the development of factor analysis, a new statistical method that was to have a profound effect on the development of psychological tests (including the MMPI). He completed his Ph.D. in 1929, after which he both worked and continued his education. He spent six years as the director of the City Psychological Clinic, a child guidance center in Leicester, earned a master's degree in education, and a doctorate of science degree.

In 1937, he came to America to work with E. L. Thorndike at Columbia University, where he continued his work on theories of intelligence. In 1939, he moved to Clark University, where his research interests turned to developing objective measures of personality. In part, this work led to his theory on fluid vs. crystallized intelligence. Then, in 1941, at the invitation of Allport, Cattell joined the faculty at Harvard University. While at Harvard, he was influenced by Allport and Henry Murray, and Cattell became even more strongly interested in the study of personality. It was in this stimulating environment that be began to consider applying factor analysis to the study of personality.

In 1945, Cattell accepted a research professorship at the University of Illinois, where he remained for nearly 30 years. The University of Illinois soon became the site of the first electronic computer, providing Cattell with the technology necessary to conduct large-scale factor-analytic studies on personality (factor analysis is a math intensive statistical technique, even relative to other statistical techniques). He established the Laboratory of Personality Assessment and Group Behavior, where he and his colleagues were highly productive and produced a number of influential books advancing psychological science, including *Description and Measurement of Personality* (Cattell, 1946), *An Introduction to Personality Study* (Cattell, 1950a), *Personality: A Systemic Theoretical and Factual Study* (Cattell, 1950b), *Factor Analysis* (Cattell, 1952), and *Personality and Motivation Structure and Measurement* (Cattell, 1957). In these books, Cattell gathered together extensive data from a methodologically sophisticated program of research on the development and organization of personality. In 1960, he called for an international meeting of researchers in the scientific study of personality, which resulted in the foundation of the Society of Multivariate Experimental Psychology, and in 1966 he co-wrote and edited the influential *Handbook of Multivariate Experimental Psychology* (Cattell, 1966).

After retiring in 1973, Cattell continued his research in Colorado. In 1978, he moved to Hawaii, where he taught at the University of Hawaii and the Hawaii School of Professional Psychology (which later became the American School of Professional Psychology). During his career, Cattell received many honors, including the *Wenner-Gren* Prize from the New York Academy of Sciences, and in 1972 the Society of Multivariate Experimental Psychology established the *Cattell Award* for young psychologists. In 1997, he was chosen to receive a *Gold Medal Award for Life Achievement* (the same honor received by both Gordon and Floyd Allport). However, the announcement resulted in objections that Cattel should not be honored, because he had used his psychological theories to support eugenics. Essentially, he was accused of using his research to support racism, and, therefore, he was a racist. In an open letter to the American Psychological Association, Cattell claimed that his views had been misinterpreted, and that he was being held accountable for statements made as a young man in the 1930s. However, he continued to publish these controversial ideas in the 1970s and 1980s. Regardless,

Cattell asked that his name be withdrawn from consideration. Less than two months after writing the letter, Cattell died at his home in Honolulu on February 2, 1998 (Cattell & Horn, 2007; Gale Reference Team, 2004).

Placing Cattell in Context: Statistical Analysis of Trait Dimensions

Raymond Cattell stands alongside Allport as one the two principal founders of the trait approach to understanding personality. As his unique contribution, Cattell brought a level of precision to the scientific and statistical analysis of personality factors that was not available beforehand. Indeed, Cattell helped to develop the factor analysis method that revolutionized objective psychological testing. His 16-PF test was the forerunner of the research that led to today's highly regarded conception of the Big Five personality traits.

In addition, although he is not generally known for it, Cattell was one of the few early personality theorists who considered the continuation of personality development throughout the lifespan. His publication of these ideas coincides with Erik Erikson's publication of his first major book, so Cattell was not simply echoing the work of someone who came before him, but rather had developed this interest on his own.

Unfortunately, Cattell also provided the basis for one of the most controversial topics in psychology today. Specifically, he advocated directing the efforts and support of society toward those already advantaged within it. In contrast, the discipline of psychology, as a social science, is held by the vast majority of its members to expectations of ethics and morality that emphasize improving the good of *all* people. Thus, most psychologists would agree that our discipline, as well as our society, should focus most of its support on those who need it most, even if that approach does not stand up well to a cost-benefit analysis. After all, how does one apply the concept of costs and benefits to the value of a human being?

Basic Concepts of Cattell's Theory

Cattell studied a variety of personality types and personality traits. Of particular interest to Cattell was how to assess personality, and his work is heavily influenced by the systematic collection of scientific data. This is quite different than many of the psychodynamic and humanistic theorists, who based their theories on clinical observation, but it is similar to the learning theorists, who also value careful, objective observation and the collection of scientific data. Neither approach is inherently better, since they each serve a different purpose. Cattell's approach, however, has had a dramatic effect on psychological testing.

Types and Traits

A psychological type refers to a broader description of personality than a psychological trait, and is often associated with abnormal psychology. According to Cattell, a type can only be understood in terms of personality traits. For example, a villain is a type based on a pattern of associated traits such as immorality, cruelty, and disregard for the law and the rights of others. Cattell considered types to fall into one of five principal categories: temperamental characteristics, interests and character, abilities, disposition, and disintegration and disease processes. As further examples, and in accordance with Cattell's type categories, we can include the ancient personality types of Hippocrates (sanguine, choleric, melancholic, phlegmatic), the oral-erotic and anal-erotic types of Sigmund Freud, musical vs. mathematical geniuses, unrestrained vs. restrained personalities, and various neurotic and psychotic syndromes (Cattell, 1946, 1950a,b, 1965).

Cattell believed that clinical psychologists always took personality traits for granted, but focused their attention on the patterns of traits that defined clinical syndromes (or types). However, if one wishes to conduct a thorough description and measurement of personality, traits must be the target of that investigation. Thus, Cattell focused his attention on the details of understanding and describing traits. He agreed with Allport's description of individual vs. common traits, though he preferred the use of the term **unique traits** to describe the former. Cattell described a trait as a collection of reactions or responses bound by some sort of unity, thus allowing the responses to be covered by one term and treated similarly in most situations. The challenge lies in identifying the nature of the unity, which has been done in different ways throughout the history of studying personality. For Cattell:

> ...the unity of a set of parts is established by their moving - i.e., appearing, changing, disappearing - together, by their exercising an effect together, and by an influence on one being an influence on all. (pg. 71; Cattell, 1946)

Thus, a trait guides behavior in a specific direction, by connecting all aspects of that trait into a unit (whether the process is directed outward, a response, or the result of external stimuli, a reaction). Since an understanding of an individual's traits would allow us to predict the nature of such responses or reactions, Cattell offered a rather simple definition of personality:

> Personality is that which permits a prediction of what a person will do in a given situation. (pg. 2; Cattell, 1950b)

According to Cattell, traits and types are not fundamentally different, but rather opposite extremes of the same statistical measures. The fundamental, underlying traits are known as **source traits**. Source traits often combine and/or interact in ways that appear, on the surface, to indicate a single trait. For example, in the area of abilities, a unitary intelligence shows itself in good academic performance, such a child who does well in school. Of course, children who do well in school typically do well in most areas, such as math, English, social studies, etc. What may now appear to be a type, a "good student," can also be described as a **surface trait** (Cattell, 1950b). As useful as surface traits, or types, may be descriptively, in order to truly understand personality, one must address the source traits. First, however, they must be identified.

Source Traits and Factor Analysis

Cattell used the factor-analytic technique to identify sixteen source traits. He often uses the terms source trait and **factor** interchangeably. **Factor analysis** is a statistical technique that determines a number of factors, or clusters, based on the intercorrelation between a number of individual elements. Cattell considered factor analysis to be a radical departure from the personality research that preceded his, because it is *not* based on an arbitrary choice as to which variables are the most important. Instead, the factor-analytic technique determines the relevant variables, based on the available data:

> ...the trouble with measuring traits is that there are too many of them!...The tendency in the past has been for a psychologist to fancy some particular trait, such as 'authoritarianism', 'extraversion', 'flexibility-*vs*-rigidity', 'intolerance of ambiguity', etc., and to concentrate on its relations to all kinds of things...individual psychologists lead to a system which tries to handle at least as many traits as there are psychologists! (pg. 55; Cattell, 1965)

When Cattell applied factor analysis to the list of words identified by Allport and Odbert, he identified 16 personality factors, more or less. The reason for saying more or less is that any statistical technique is subject to known probabilities of error. Thus, Cattell considered his sixteen factors to be only an estimate of the number of source traits (Cattell, 1952). As potential source traits were identified that Cattell found difficult to put into words, he assigned them a Universal Index (U.I.) number, so that they could be kept for consideration until they could be studied and explained. Cattell identified as many as forty-two personality factors (see Cattell, 1957). By 1965, when Cattell wrote *The Scientific Analysis of Personality*, he had included three additional factors to his primary list, giving him nineteen personality factors, and kept thirteen of the remaining factors on his list as yet to be confirmed (though each one had a tentative name).

In the late 1940s, Cattell and his colleagues developed the **Sixteen Personality Factor Questionnaire** (commonly known as the 16-PF), based on the 15 factors they considered best established by their data, plus general intelligence as the sixteenth factor (see Cattell, 1956). The sixteen factors are described in Table 13.1. In a very interesting chapter written by Heather Cattell (Cattell's third wife), the 16-PF profiles are presented, and compared, for a married couple in which the husband was undergoing therapy with Heather Cattell (see H. Cattell, 1986). She described how the profiles offer insight into the problems occurring for Mr. A (as the husband is identified in the chapter), both in his personal life and in his marriage. Although the marriage ended in divorce, a subsequent follow-up found both Mr. A and Mrs. A seemingly doing well in their separate lives.

Table 13.1: The Sixteen Personality Factor Questionnaire Dimensions		
Factor	*Low Score Description*	*High Score Description*
A	***Reserved*** - detached, critical, aloof, stiff	***Outgoing*** - warmhearted, easy-going, participating
B	***Less Intelligent*** - concrete-thinking	***More Intelligent*** - abstract-thinking, bright
C	***Affected By Feelings*** - emotionally less stable, easily upset, changeable	***Emotionally Stable*** - mature, faces reality, calm
E	***Humble*** - mild, easily led, docile, accommodating	***Assertive*** - aggressive, stubborn, competitive
F	***Sober*** - taciturn, serious	***Happy-Go-Lucky*** - enthusiastic
G	***Expedient*** - disregards rules	***Conscientious*** - persistent, moralistic, staid
H	***Shy*** - timid, threat-sensitive	***Venturesome*** - uninhibited, socially bold
I	***Tough-Minded*** - self-reliant, realistic	***Tender-Minded*** - sensitive, clinging, overprotected
L	***Trusting*** - accepting conditions	***Suspicious*** - hard to fool
M	***Practical*** - "down-to-earth" concerns	***Imaginative*** - bohemian, absent-minded
N	***Forthright*** - unpretentious, genuine but socially clumsy	***Astute*** - polished, socially aware
O	***Self-Assured*** - placid, secure, complacent, serene	***Apprehensive*** - self-reproaching, insecure, worrying, troubled
Q_1	***Conservative*** - respecting traditional ideas	***Experimenting*** - liberal, free-thinking
Q_2	***Group-Dependent*** - a "joiner" and sound follower	***Self-Sufficient*** - resourceful, prefers own decisions
Q_3	***Undisciplined Self-Conflict*** - lax, follows own urges, careless of social rules	***Controlled*** - exacting will power, socially precise, compulsive
Q_4	***Relaxed*** - tranquil, unfrustrated, composed	***Tense*** - frustrated, driven, overwrought
For examples of 16-PF profiles used in a therapy setting see H. Cattell (1986).		

The Types of Data Used in the Assessment of Personality

In a rather obvious statement, Cattell noted that in order for a psychologist to study correlations there must be two measures available to be correlated. The systematic measure of various aspects of the mind, including personality, has led to the development of a specific branch of psychology known as **psychometry**. In order for a psychometrist to get a complete and unbiased measure of personality, they must have a concept of the individual's total behavior, what Cattell called the **personality sphere**. Cattell believed this could best be accomplished by taking a sample 24-hour period in the person's life and collecting three types of data: measures of the individual's "life-record," or **L-data**; information provided by questionnaires, or **Q-data**; and data on their personality structure provided by objective tests, or **T-data** (Cattell, 1965).

L-data deals with the individual's actual everyday situations. Ideally, L-data can be collected without the need for the judgment of a trained psychometrist. Examples of specific behaviors include things such as their grades in school, the number of automobile accidents a person has had, the number of times they have been arrested by the police, how many organizations they belong to, etc. Sometimes these data are not so easy to obtain, and must be gathered from someone who knows the person well. For example, we may ask friends or family members to rate the person in terms of how sociable they are in school, how emotionally stable they are when playing sports, or how responsible they are (Cattell, 1965).

Q-data is obtained by having the person fill out a questionnaire, such as the information sheet you fill out when waiting to see a doctor for a medical exam. Unfortunately, these data are subject to a number of problems, such as distortions due to poor self-knowledge, delusions about the self, or the deliberate intention to fake the outcome of the questionnaire. Therefore, it is very important that a psychologist choose the right words when developing a questionnaire:

> Although a questionnaire looks like a simple series of questions to which a person underlines a brief answer, such as 'yes', 'no', 'generally', [sic] etc., actually a great deal of art enters into the psychologist's choice of words, the direction of the question, the use of adjectives to ensure that all alternatives are well used, and so on. (pg. 61; Cattell, 1965)

As noted above, T-data is obtained from objective tests. According to Cattell, questionnaire may seem objective, since their scoring is objective, but the process involves having the individual evaluate themselves. In truly objective tests the individual's specific behaviors or thoughts are directly and precisely measured. It is essential that only **closed-ended questions** are used, such as multiple choice or Yes-No options. If **open-ended questions** are used, such as "How do you feel when you wake up in the morning?" it is possible that two psychologists will interpret the answer quite differently. If there is a possibility of different interpretations, obviously the test cannot be objective.

In comparing the three types of data, Cattell made some interesting observations regarding L-data. Although it occurs naturally, measuring it is artificial and somewhat arbitrary. Although it is objective in the sense that it is real behavior, it is neither created nor controlled, it is simply observed. It is also subject to cultural differences much more so than Q-data and T-data. Of particular concern to Cattell, however, was the commonplace nature of L-data:

> Much of the irresponsible theorizing on personality criticized in Chapter 1 happens to have grown up in the realm of L-data, for this has been the traditional field of observation of the philosopher, the armchair observer, and the clinician, whereas Q- and T-data have been developed by the psychometrist concerned with the more disciplined methods. L-data is, indeed, the field of behavior that is the common property of everyone...there arises at this point the need for a proper development of measurement techniques particularly as they apply to L-data... (pp. 54-55; Cattell, 1957)

Discussion Question: Cattell believed that personality assessment worked best when the psychologist understood a person's entire personality sphere. To accomplish this, one needs to measure L-data, Q-data, and T-data. Do these data provide a complete picture of the person? What data do you think might be the most difficult to obtain, and how might that affect the overall personality picture?

Stages of Development

Cattell described six principal life stages: **infancy**, **childhood**, **adolescence**, **maturity**, **middle age**, and **old age**. Infancy, from birth to 6 years old, is the "great formative period for personality" (pg. 211; Cattell, 1950a). In relation to its family members, the infant develops its basic social attitudes, sense of security or insecurity, the strength of various defense mechanisms (which determine whether the individual will be prone to neuroses), and the general strength of the ego and super-ego. Childhood, the period from age six to fourteen years old, is, according to Cattell, a relatively easy period of consolidation. The child grows toward independence, moving from its family to relationships with peers. Children are primarily realists, but they may have an active day dream life as they long for the status and privilege of adult life (Cattell, 1950a,b).

Adolescence is, of course, a period of psychological storm and stress, requiring many adjustments and readjustments in one's life. Covering the ages of approximately 14 to 23 years old, Cattell believed that the stress experienced by normal individuals could best be illustrated by its consequences in extreme personalities. Adolescence is the time when some individuals become delinquents, whereas others show the initial signs of mental illness and neurotic behavior. While many of the changes occurring during adolescence are due to the physiological changes associated with puberty, external factors are also critical. All cultures appear to have some ritual associated with the break between childhood and adulthood, and many arrange for an initiation or formal ritual to take place. Of course, there are also positive changes associated with adolescence, such as increased interest in the arts of emotionality and love: poetry, religion, and drama (Cattell, 1950a,b).

> Indeed adolescence is the time when even the dullest clod knows that he possesses a soul; and it has been said of the genius that he lives in a perpetual adolescence. (pg. 215; Cattell, 1950a)

Adulthood brings with it maturity, and the pursuit of a career, a mate, a family, and a home. From age 23 to 46 years old, personality becomes set, and the chosen habits of adolescence become settled. Cattell considered it a busy and happy time for most people, but not for those few who failed to resolve their adolescence. They become, in Cattell's words, shipwrecked in physical disease, mental illness, and the persistent inability to solve the questions of work and wife (or husband, as the case may be; Cattell, 1950a). Middle age is characterized by the beginning of certain physical and mental changes that begin the inevitable decline toward old age and death. Thus, middle age demands a reevaluation of one's life values, and often leads to the search for some philosophy to make sense of life. Positive changes include an increase in leisure. First, the responsibilities for raising children lessen as the children move out on their own, and later, one approaches the age of retirement.

Old age requires further adjustment, as one begins to question one's place and value in society. This can cause the frustration of ego needs and a sense of insecurity, which can lead to a restricted range of interests, "crabbiness," and constant worry about one's financial state and physical health. However, many people retain their general intellectual capacity and positive attitude toward life unimpaired until death. Even in 1950, Cattell took note of the growing number of people who were living longer and doing so in better health, thus making our understanding of the psychology of old age an increasingly important issue (Cattell, 1950a,b). That trend not only continues today, but may actually be increasing as our knowledge of medicine and interests in health psychology continue to grow.

National Character and Intelligence

Cattell was interested in measuring intelligence throughout his career. Just before coming to the United States, he published *A Guide to Mental Testing* (Cattell, 1936), which covered topics as diverse as the measurement of intelligence, aptitudes (mechanical, musical, artistic, etc.), scholastic attainment, temperament, interests, and character. Much later in his career, Cattell confirmed his controversial interest in the relationship between intelligence and national achievement (see Cattell, 1983). What made this research controversial was the apparent racist overtones of the research. As noted above, Cattell claimed that his views were taken out of context, and that the most controversial claims were made in the 1930s, before he even came to the United States. However, consider some of the following statements written by Cattell in 1983!

> In the state of Hawaii, where I happen to be writing, there are at least a dozen ethnic groups of good sample size and differing in racial composition and life style. The lack of seriousness about

> education, and lack of concern with conversations on things of the mind, can be well brought into relief by comparing some low groups (which shall be nameless) with say, high groups such as the Japanese, the Chinese, and the Jews, whose literacy, school achievement, and employment rates are high. (pg. 12; Cattell, 1983)

> …a 15 point difference in average tells us nothing immediately about an *individual*, White or Black. It does tell us that there will be considerable overlap of the two groups…It also tells us, however, that if we look for persons with I.Q.s of above, say, 130…the chances of finding a Black among 1,000 or of a White among 1,000 to exceed 130 is far higher in the second group. (pg. 41; Cattell, 1983)

> …regarding special educational expenditure. Should it be on the top, say, 10% of highly gifted children or on the lagging 10% of dull and backward children?...A eugenist is compelled to argue that the social conscience should, in terms of family planning have shifted the higher birth rate in the first place from the I.Q. 70-80 range to the I.Q. 120-130 range. (pg. 59; Cattell, 1983)

> Incidentally one would expect most effect on both productivity and potency of national defense to derive from the magnitude of the supply *in the topmost ranges* of intelligence, from which, given appropriately more advanced education, resourceful management and beneficial invention result. The numbers in that range depend both on their birth rates and the assortiveness of mating, and a rise in the latter could admittedly *temporarily* offset a decline in the former. Surely *everyone* will agree that the schools should turn to giving appropriate education to these much brighter individuals, but it will take *a more far-sighted public* to encourage measures for their greater production. (pp. 14-15; Cattell, 1983)

Taken together, these suggestions lead to very clear impression of Cattell's opinions and goals: there are "low" groups and "high" groups of people, Blacks in America are a "low" group, special education spending should not be wasted on people of low intelligence, the families who produced those children should not have any more children, and "resourceful management" should be used to ensure that "high" groups have more children and "low" groups do not! What makes these views most disturbing is not that one person has them, but rather, that Cattell has colleagues who agree with him. Most notorious, in recent times, was the publication of *The Bell Curve* by Herrnstein & Murray (1994; for a discussion of some of the problems associated with *The Bell Curve* see Belgrave & Allison, 2006).

The suggestion of people like Cattell, Herrnstein, & Murray, that society should discard whole groups of people is unconscionable to many people, and should have no place in a psychology that emphasizes the improvement of the human condition. Another somewhat controversial figure, Arthur Jensen, also argues that general intelligence, or *g* as it was first described by Spearman, is largely inherited, but at the same time he acknowledges that there is an environmental component to even this most basic aspect of intelligence (Jensen, 1998). Considering any role for environmental factors in intelligence, we must then take into serious consideration the discriminatory practices that denied adequate education to minorities throughout history, both in America and elsewhere. When provided with good education, Blacks have demonstrated an equal ability to learn as compared to Whites (see Belgrave & Allison, 2006; Miller & Garran, 2008). Thus, rather than seeking to exclude people from opportunities to advance within our society, we should be encouraging, as much as possible, equal access to educational support systems.

In a somewhat related article, Robert McCrae (whose research on the Big Five personality traits will be examined below) and Antonio Terracciano examined whether or not there is a valid basis for determining national character based on personality traits. People in all cultures have shared perceptions of what people are like in both their own culture and in other cultures, perceptions which form the basis of stereotypes. After examining data from nearly fifty different countries, McCrae & Terracciano concluded that national character stereotypes are unfounded, even when examining people's impressions of their own country (McCrae & Terracciano, 2006)! Clearly, if stereotypes based on personality are not accurate reflections of personality, how can stereotypes based on measures of intelligence have a meaningful bearing on our decisions regarding social programs?

> **Discussion Question:** Cattell created a great deal of controversy with his views on nationality, race, intelligence, and achievement. What effect, if any, do you think it has on the field of psychology when one of its leading scientists makes an issue of such controversy? How much worse, if at all, did it make it when he claimed he was being persecuted for comments made in the 1930s as a young man, when in fact, he had continued to publish these ideas as late as 1983!

Hans Eysenck's Dimensions of Personality

Hans Eysenck offered a theory of personality that was much more concise than that of Cattell, suggesting that there were only three major factors. He also emphasized the importance a hereditary basis for personality and intelligence, and he applied his research to some important everyday life circumstances. Accordingly, he was a very popular and widely acknowledged researcher. In 1997, he was identified as the most widely cited living person, second only to Sigmund Freud and Karl Marx amongst the most cited individuals of all time (Jensen, 1997). In addition, he was honored with not one, but two *Festschriften*, the first on his sixty-fifth birthday (Lynn, 1981), and the second in honor of his eightieth birthday (Nyborg, 1997).

Eysenck was born in Berlin, Germany, in 1916. His parents divorced when he was 2, and he was raised by his grandmother, seeing his parents only once or twice a year. He was a star athlete, including being a nationally ranked tennis player. He left Germany to escape the Nazis in 1934, and spent a brief period of time studying literature and history in France and England. His grandmother, however, died in a concentration camp around 1941 or 1942. He eventually began studying psychology at University College in London, under the renowned Cyril Burt. He earned his Ph.D. in 1940, and during World War II he worked as a research psychologist using factor analysis to study personality. After the war he became a psychologist at Maudsley Hospital, where he became friends with Philip Vernon (who completed his Ph.D. with Allport; see, e.g., Allport & Vernon, 1933), then helped to form a psychiatry institute at the hospital and affiliated with the University of London. He spent the rest of his career there, though he spent some time as a visiting professor in the United States (Eysenck, 1982, 1997). Eysenck received numerous awards during his career, including a *Distinguished Scientist Award* from the American Psychological Association. He died in 1997.

The Structure of Personality

According to Eysenck, the sixteen primary personality factors identified by Cattell in the 16-PF test were unreliable and could not be replicated. Eysenck chose instead to focus on higher order factor analysis, and he identified three "**superfactors**:" **extraversion**, **neuroticism**, and **psychoticism** (Eysenck, 1982). According to Eysenck, higher order factors are similar to types, and they represent combinations of primary personality traits. Thus, he considered the sixteen factors that Cattell included in the 16-PF as primary factors, whereas extraversion, neuroticism, and psychoticism were second-order factors (or types). Actually, even the primary factors are comprised of lower level responses that result in a hierarchical model of personality: specific responses, habitual responses, traits (or factors), and finally, types (or superfactors). Similarly, *g*, or general intelligence, is a higher order factor than its component intelligences (e.g., verbal, numerical, memory, visuo-spatial, and reasoning). Thus, Eysenck's theory does not contradict that of Cattell, but rather looks at a higher level of personality structure (Eysenck, 1952, 1967, 1970).

An extravert is commonly described as an outgoing, expressive person, but the technical definition described by Eysenck is more complex. Extraversion is a combination of sociability, impulsiveness, frivolity, general activity, and overt sexuality. The complex nature of each higher order factor may lead to some of the differences in personality theory. According to Eysenck, the impulsiveness associated with extraversion is most likely hereditary (a temperamental trait), whereas the sociability aspect of extraversion is more likely to be influenced by one's environment. Thus, perhaps, it is not surprising that Eysenck finds support for hereditary influences on personality whereas others, like Cattell, find support for environmental influences. Depending on how one designs their questions and experiments, the component traits within a higher order factor can support different perspectives (Eysenck, 1982).

Neuroticism refers to one's emotional stability, or lack thereof. It incorporates mood swings, poor emotional adjustment, feelings of inferiority, a lack of social responsibility, a lack of persistence, issues of trust vs. suspiciousness, social shyness, hypochondria, and the lack of relaxed composure. Neuroticism raises the intensity of emotional reactions. Since it is a function of the reactivity of the autonomic nervous system, it is an inherited characteristic. Individuals who measure high in neuroticism are more likely to suffer from neuroses, but high neuroticism is not necessarily less desirable than low levels of neuroticism. For example, aesthetic appreciation and creativity can benefit from an individual being highly emotional. On the clearly negative side, high levels of neuroticism have routinely been found in criminals, perhaps because whenever an individual has antisocial tendencies, a high level of neuroticism enhances their fear/anxiety responses and functions as a powerful, albeit dysfunctional, drive (Eysenck, 1977, 1982; Kendrick, 1981). Cattell also studied neuroticism, and his findings were very similar to those of Eysenck (Cattell & Scheier, 1961).

Psychoticism was added to Eysenck's theory well after identifying extraversion and neuroticism, and it is the least clearly defined or heritable of the three superfactors. It incorporates traits of dominance-leadership, dominance-submission, sensation seeking, and the lack of a superego. Children who score high on a measure of psychoticism tend to have behavior problems and learning difficulties, they become loners, skip school, commit crimes, and are generally disliked by teachers and peers. Whether as children or as adults, they do not typically benefit from traditional psychotherapies or counseling, as there tends to be a paranoid, suspicious barrier. There is some evidence, however, for successful treatment with intensive behavioral techniques. Interestingly, whether or not these children become criminals as adults seems to depend on how they score on the other two superfactors. High neuroticism seems to be the factor which makes juvenile delinquency a habit that persists into a life of crime (S. Eysenck, 1997).

Discussion Question: In contrast to Cattell's sixteen primary factors, Eysenck proposed just three superfactors. Can a reasonable evaluation of personality be conducted along just three dimensions? If not, do you think these are still the three most essential dimensions?

The Role of Heredity in Personality

Eysenck believed strongly in the inheritance of personality and intelligence. If it is true that genetics plays a major role in personality, then evolution should provide us with an interesting test: do other primate species demonstrate the same superfactors that we see in humans? Eysenck examined this question in conjunction with Harry Harlow. After conducting factor analysis on the social behavior of rhesus monkeys, they found three clear behavior factors: affectionate, fearful, and hostile social behavior. These factors match well with the human factors of extraversion, neuroticism, and psychoticism, respectively. Of course, there were marked differences between animals, but those differences were characteristic and reliable for each monkey. Thus, it would appear that the biological basis for personality superfactors can be confirmed in comparative psychological studies (Chamove, Eysenck, & Harlow, 1972).

Whether heredity or learning is more important in personality development remains unclear. [Image by Mark Kelland]

Reviews of Eysenck's overall contribution to the field of behavior genetics have, however, been the subject of debate. Whereas some praise Eysenck for identifying the significant role that genetic determinants play in personality factors (see Martin & Jardine, 1986), others argue that Eysenck's own data provide evidence that he overstated the significance of genetics (see Loehlin, 1986). Indeed, Loehlin suggests that the data in Eysenck's own publications can be interpreted to suggest that genetics account for about half of the variance in personality factors, which leaves the other half subject to the environment. Still, Loehlin acknowledges Eysenck's primary role in bringing these issues into the realm of science, and he commends Eysenck for providing his data openly, so that others, like Loehlin, might be able to evaluate and debate those results (Loehlin, 1986). Eysenck, for his part, acknowledged the points made by Loehlin, and expressed hope that continued research in the future would help to better clarify the role of genetics in determining behavior, intelligence, and personality (Eysenck, 1986).

Personality and Real Life Issues

Although Eysenck's approach to personality focused on group differences and genetics, he was not without concern for the individual and her or his daily life. He also challenged the way in which psychologists are pursuing their discipline, and the effect it has on the public's view of psychology. In 1972, he published *Psychology is About People*, which included jokes about psychology and psychiatry, as well as topics as diverse as sex, socialism, education, pornography, and behaviorism (Eysenck, 1972). In *Uses and Abuses of Psychology* he challenged the stereotypes associated with views on national character, and urged the learning of facts about other cultures (numerous other topics are covered as well; Eysenck, 1953). In *Sense and Nonsense in Psychology* he examined such things as hypnosis, lie detectors, telepathy, interpreting dreams, and politics:

> If it be true that there are more things in heaven and earth than are dreamed of in our philosophy, it is surely equally true that things are dreamed of in our philosophy which do not appear in heaven or on earth. Among these figments of the imagination appear such varied objects as the philosopher's stone, which was supposed to transmute base metals into gold, the Oedipus complex, which was supposed to transmute a normal person into a gibbering neurotic…and the Jungian archetypes, which are supposed to haunt our modern minds with mystical reminders of the inherited wisdom, or otherwise, of our race. (pg. 71; Eysenck, 1957)

Eysenck wrote extensively about sex and personality, and the role that violence and the media may play in distorting sexuality (e.g., Eysenck, 1976; Eysenck & Nias, 1978). He also wrote about the relationship between personality and criminal behavior (e.g., Eysenck, 1964; Eysenck & Gudjonsson, 1989), and the role that personality and stress play in the lives of people who smoke cigarettes (Eysenck, 1991). Like Cattell, Jensen, and others, Eysenck was very much caught up in the controversy over racial differences in intelligence testing (see, e.g., Eysenck, 1973a,b, 1995; Eysenck & Kamin, 1981; Pearson, 1991). Eysenck, however, offered something for the average person, two books on how to measure your own I.Q. (Eysenck, 1962, 1966). Late in his career, Eysenck offered an interesting reflection on his decision to focus most of his career on differences between people, as opposed to the uniqueness of each person:

> Gordon Allport and I did not always see eye to eye on theoretical matters. I remember very well him telling me that he thought every psychologist should write his autobiography at the end of his life, to see the unities that emerged in his conduct over a lengthy period of time. This idiographic point of view contrasted very much with my own nomothetic one, and at the time I paid little attention to it. Now, half a life-time later, I can see what he was driving at, and can also see the possible importance of such consistencies of behaviour in one's own life. (pg. 375; Eysenck, 1986)

Discussion Question: Eysenck wrote two books that challenged the field of psychology: *Uses and Abuses of Psychology* and *Sense and Nonsense* in Psychology. What advantages do you think it has for the field when someone of Eysenck's stature questions the scientific validity of certain areas of study or certain procedures?

Paul Costa and Robert McCrae and the Five-Factor Model of Personality

Costa and McCrae followed in the footsteps of Eysenck, but they expanded slightly upon the number of second order factors. The result of their efforts became one the most widely respected perspectives on personality structure today: the **Five-Factor Model** of personality. Indeed, the Five-Factor Model has been so well researched, research that has supported and expanded the original conception, that Costa and McCrae believe it now deserves to be referred to as the **Five-Factor Theory** (see McCrae & Costa, 2003).

Paul Costa earned a Ph.D. in human development from the University of Chicago in 1970. He taught for 2 years at Harvard University, and then joined the faculty of the University of Massachusetts at Boston. In 1978 he joined the National Institute on Aging, a branch of the National Institutes of Health. Since 1985, he has been the Chief of the Laboratory of Personality and Cognition, Gerontology Research Center. He also holds appointments at the University of Maryland, Duke University Medical Center, The Johns Hopkins University School of Medicine, and the Georgetown University School of Medicine. Among numerous awards, he has been elected as a Fellow of the Gerontological Society of America, the American Psychological Association, and the Society of Behavioral Medicine. He has published hundreds of research articles, many of them in collaboration with Robert McCrae. McCrae earned his Ph.D. in personality psychology at Boston University in 1976. After teaching and conducting research at Boston University, the Veteran's Administration Outpatient Clinic in Boston, and the University of Massachusetts at Boston, in 1978 he joined the Gerontology Research Center at the National Institute on Aging, where he continues to conduct research today. He is also a Fellow of the Gerontological Society of America, as well as a Fellow of the American Psychological Society and Division 20 (Adult Development and Aging) of the American Psychological Association (for more information visit the National Institute on Aging website at www.grc.nia.nih.gov).

The Five-Factor Theory of Personality

Costa and McCrae acknowledged the important role that Eysenck played when he identified extraversion and neuroticism as second-order personality factors, and for developing the Maudsley Personality Inventory, the Eysenck Personality Inventory, and the Eysenck Personality Questionnaire (the latter test, developed with his wife Sybil, was the first to include psychoticism; see S. Eysenck, 1997) as tools for measuring these factors. However, they disagreed with Eysenck regarding psychoticism. They initially proposed a different factor called **openness**. When they discussed this issue with Eysenck, he felt that openness might be the opposite pole of psychoticism, but McCrae and Costa believed the factors were significantly different (see Costa & McCrae, 1986). Since that time, Costa and McCrae have moved beyond the third factor of openness, and added two more second-order factors: **agreeableness** and **conscientiousness** (see Costa & McCrae, 1989; Costa & Widiger, 1994; McCrae & Allik, 2002; McCrae & Costa, 2003). Together, Costa and McCrae developed the **NEO Personality Inventory** (or NEO-PI) to measure neuroticism, extraversion, and openness, and later they developed the **Revised NEO-PI**, or NEO-PI-R, which also measures agreeableness and conscientiousness (see McCrae & Costa, 2003).

Table 13.2: The Five-Factor Model of Personality

Factor	*Low Score Description*	*High Score Description*
Neuroticism	Calm, Even-tempered, Self-satisfied, Comfortable, Unemotional, Hardy	Worrying, Temperamental, Self-pitying, Self-conscious, Emotional, Vulnerable
Extraversion	Reserved, Loner, Quiet, Passive, Sober, Unfeeling	Affectionate, Joiner, Talkative, Active, Fun-loving, Passionate
Openness to Experience	Down-to-earth, Uncreative, Conventional, Prefer routine, Uncurious, Conservative	Imaginative, Creative, Original, Prefer variety, Curious, Liberal
Agreeableness	Ruthless, Suspicious, Stingy, Antagonistic, Critical, Irritable	Softhearted, Trusting, Generous, Acquiescent, Lenient, Good-natured
Conscientiousness	Negligent, Lazy, Disorganized, Late, Aimless, Quitting	Conscientious, Hardworking, Well-organized, Punctual, Ambitious, Persevering

Taken from McCrae and Costa (2003).

The general descriptions of extraversion, neuroticism, openness, agreeableness, and conscientious are listed in Table 13.2. It is important to note that these five factors are distinct, and neither low nor high scores are necessarily better or 'good' or 'bad:'

> ...all traits have passed the evolutionary test of survival, and from society's point of view all kinds of people are necessary: those who work well with others and those who can finish a task on their own; those who come up with creative new ways of doing things and those who maintain the best solutions of the past. There are probably even advantages to found [sic] in Neuroticism, since a society of extremely easygoing individuals might not compete well with other societies of suspicious and hostile individuals. Cultures need members fit for war as well as peace, work as well as play... (pp. 51-52; McCrae & Costa, 2003)

As a basis for studying personality, the Five-Factor Model has proven quite comprehensive. The five factors stand up well when measured with a variety of other tests and within other theoretical perspectives, including a thorough comparison with the list of human needs proposed by Henry Murray. Particularly important in psychology today, the Five-Factor Model has also stood up very well when examined across cultures, a topic we will examine in more detail in *Connections Across Cultures*.

Connections Across Cultures: The Big Five Across Cultures

In order to evaluate the cross-cultural application of the Five-Factor Model, Robert McCrae has suggested that we need to address the issue in three ways. **Transcultural** analyses look for personality factors that transcend culture. In other words, personality factors that are universal, or common to all people. **Intracultural** analyses look at the specific expression of traits within a culture. And finally, **intercultural** analyses compare trait characteristics between cultures (see Allik & McCrae, 2002). In 2002, McCrae and Allik published *The Five-Factor Model of Personality Across Cultures*, a collection of research in which a variety of investigators examined the applicability of the Five-Factor Model (FFM) in a wide variety of cultures. The various studies contained in this book examine personality structure, as well as the validity and generalizability of using the NEO-PI-R to measure personality, in some forty cultures spread across five continents. McCrae and Allik acknowledge that there is much more to personality than just traits, but the traits identified in the FFM appear to offer a robust cross-cultural foundation for understanding personality worldwide.

The potential validity of translating the NEO-PI-R and studying the FFM in different cultures is based on the idea that the most important factors in human interaction would be encoded in the languages of most, if not all, cultures (see Pervin, 1999). Given concerns regarding this lexical hypothesis and the challenges of translation, Peabody (1999) used trait descriptions with contrasting terms to help clarify matters in a study on the judgment of national character. He had judges from 12 different European countries, plus America, the Philippines, Japan, and China rate one another. Upon examining the data from a FFM perspective, Peabody found strong support for the utility of this model in cross-cultural studies. Other investigators have had significant success using the NEO-PI-R in direct translation. Rolland (2002) collected data from studies in which the NEO-PI-R was administered to people in cultures speaking 16 different languages (including Sino-Tibetan, Indo-European, Uralic, Hamito-Semitic, and Austronesian languages, and one unclassified language [Korean]). Overall, he confirmed the generalizability of the personality structure identified by the FFM in these varied cultures. Similar favorable results pertaining to personality structure have been identified with both adults and adolescents in Czeck, Polish, and Slovak groups (Hrebickova, et al., 2002) and amongst the Shona in Zimbabwe (Piedmont, et al., 2002), as well as for the relationship between personality and emotion amongst Canadian, Spanish, Chinese, Japanese, and Korean subjects (Yik, et al., 2002) and the relationship between personality and cultural goals in Americans and Vietnamese (Leininger, 2002). These studies, as well as numerous others that are not mentioned, provide substantial support for the consistency of the FFM across a wide variety of cultures, at least as far as personality structure is concerned. However, it remains unclear whether the scores obtained from two different cultural groups are equivalent (see Poortinga, Van de Vijver, & Van Hemert, 2002). In other words, if Culture A scored higher than Culture B on, say, agreeableness, it may be that the translation used for Culture A is more responsible for the result than an actual difference between Cultures A and B. Further research will be necessary in order to address issues such as this.

Despite the numerous studies that support the cross-cultural application of the FFM, there are psychologists, generally favorable to the FFM, who nonetheless emphasize caution. The fundamental question is whether or not trait descriptions are how people in other cultures describe another person. While it is true that using abstract trait names is common practice in American culture, in other cultures, such as India and China, it is more common to describe people in terms of context dependent actions. To fit such data into a FFM requires some manipulation, which leaves the validity of the work open to some debate (see Pervin, 1999). However, when comparing Chinese and American students, the FFM does provide an adequate measure of each group's stereotypes regarding one another (Zhang, et al., 1999). What is clear is the need for continued research on cross-cultural perspectives, as well as a need for cross-cultural training programs. In that regard, Brislin (1999) has offered ways in which the FFM can be used as one basis for developing such programs, in part by telling us something about each person in a cross-cultural training program and, therefore, which type of program might work best for them (see also McCauley, Draguns, & Lee, 1999). Whether one favors the FFM or some other model of personality structure, the importance of cross-cultural studies is clear:

> Human nature cannot be independent of culture. Neither can human personality. Human beings do share certain social norms or rules within their cultural groups. More than 2000 years ago, Aristotle held that man is by nature a social animal. Similarly, Xun Kuang (298-238 B.C.), a Chinese philosopher, pointed out that humans in social groups cannot function without shared guidance or rules. Therefore, each culture or cultural group establishes its own norms. Constantly, these norms and rules are connected with the behavior and personality of members within a culture and society. (pg. vii; Lee, McCauley, & Draguns, 1999)

In proposing a Five-Factor *Theory* of personality, McCrae and Costa addressed the nature of personality theories themselves:

> A theory of personality is a way of accounting for what people are like and how they act; a good theory explains a wide range of observations and points researchers in the right direction for future research. Freudian theory pointed researchers toward the study of dreams, but decades of research have yielded very little by way of supportive evidence…Trait theory pointed researchers toward general styles of thinking, feeling, and acting, and has resulted in thousands of interesting and useful findings. That is why most personality psychologists today prefer trait theory to psychoanalysis…But…there is more to human personality than traits. (pp 184-185; McCrae & Costa, 2003)

They propose that there are three central components to personality: **basic tendencies** (which are the five personality factors), **characteristic adaptations**, and **self-concept** (a highly adapted and extensively studied form of characteristic adaptation). The basic tendencies interact with three peripheral components that mark the interface with systems outside personality. There are the biological inputs to the basic tendencies, the external environment, and **objective biography** (all that a person does and experiences). Connecting all of these components are **dynamic processes**, such as perception, coping, role playing, reasoning, etc. Although this theory is newer, it does account for one of the most important issues challenging trait theories in general: how does one account for the general consistency of traits, yet the potential for, and occasional observation of, change in personality? Simply, the basic tendencies are consistent, whereas the characteristic adaptations are subject to change, both as a result of dramatic environmental influences and due to changes associated with aging (McCrae & Costa, 2003).

Consistency Across the Lifespan

In over 25 years of teaching, it has been my experience that most college students *want* to believe that adult personality can readily change. Likewise, most psychologists, particularly clinical psychologists helping people to change their dysfunctional lives, *want* to believe that personality can change. However, trait theorists have repeatedly shown that traits are highly resistant to change once adulthood has been reached (see, e.g., Costa & McCrae, 1989; McCrae & Costa, 2003). This is particularly true for Neuroticism, Extraversion, and Openness, for both men and women, and for Blacks and Whites. While Costa and McCrae acknowledge that individuals sometimes change dramatically, as a general rule, consistency is clearly more important. They also suggest that this should be an opportunity for optimism. As individuals age, they should not fear becoming a different person, such as someone isolated or depressed. If, however, an individual of younger age is isolated, depressed, or suffers from some other psychological malady, they should also realize that time or aging alone is not likely to change them, but rather, psychotherapy may be a desirable and effective course of action. Once again, Costa & McCrae emphasize the newness of these theories, and suggest the need for systematic prospective studies of the Five-Factor Theory over the entire adult lifespan. Fortunately, the NEO-PI-R provides the tool necessary to evaluate the Five-Factor Theory throughout life and in different cultures. Given the steady increase in life expectancy in Western societies, and the growing percentage of elderly people within our society, this research is likely to become a priority in the field of personality.

Marvin Zuckerman and the Sensation Seeking Personality Trait

Marvin Zuckerman represents the current approach taken by many psychologists who study traits. He developed an interest in one particular trait, and he has studied that trait in great detail. He called it **sensation seeking**, and in order to study it carefully he also developed the **Sensation Seeking Scale**. The study of this trait has enjoyed a certain popular appeal, exemplified by the success of the *X Games* and, more recently, the popularity of televised mixed martial arts competitions.

Zuckerman was the son of a mechanical engineer who came to America from Russia. His mother's father had also come from Russia, and both sides of the family had a tradition of their sons becoming rabbis. As a boy, Zuckerman enjoyed playing football, but most of his sensation seeking centered on reading adventure books. He first became interested in psychology when he encountered a book about graphology. When he entered the University of Kentucky, he experienced the "disinhibitory joys of drinking, sex, and hitchhiking around the country" (pg. 46; Zuckerman, 1993). He then suffered a period of depression, during which he discovered the work of Sigmund Freud. He decided to become a psychoanalyst, so, after serving his duty in the army (following World War II), attended New York University. Unfortunately, a bad grade in chemistry made it impossible to get into the medical school of his choice, so he chose to begin the graduate program in clinical psychology at NYU.

Zuckerman found it difficult to find an area of psychology that appealed to him, except for a vague interest in experimental studies that suggested an "exploratory drive," something we might also call curiosity, in a variety of animal species. Zuckerman also found clinical work unfulfilling, so he began to focus more on conducting research. He spent a few years at a hospital and then a psychiatric research institute in Indiana, where he began studying sensory deprivation (see, e.g., Zuckerman et al., 1962). In contrast to sensory deprivation, he also began to study sensation seeking, its apparent counterpart. After several moves, including the threat of being fired from Adelphi University due to newspaper photos of the college professor arrested and lying in the local jail (following his involvement in a protest against racism), in 1968 he joined the faculty of the University of Delaware. Since he found it difficult to find continued funding for sensory deprivation research, he began to focus on sensation seeking itself. In 1975, Zuckerman took a sabbatical to work with Hans Eysenck, leading to the publication of some joint papers, and Zuckerman's eventual contribution to Eysenck's second *festschrift* (see Zuckerman, 1997). His work on sensation seeking, and his relationship with Eysenck, have led Zuckerman to become one of today's leading proponents of the biological basis of personality. He retired in 2002, but has remained busy enjoying life, giving talks, writing, and conducting research (Zuckerman, 1983, 1991, 2006).

The Sensation Seeking Trait

Sensation seeking is a trait defined by the need for varied, novel, and complex sensations and experiences and the willingness to take physical and social risks for the sake of such

> experience…The high-sensation seeker is sensitive to his or her internal sensations and chooses external stimuli that maximize them. (pg. 10; Zuckerman, 1979)

All people seem to seek an optimal level of stimulation and/or arousal. For some, that level of arousal is quite high, for others, it is rather low. The concept was not new when Zuckerman began to study **sensory deprivation** and sensation seeking. Indeed, the examination of **optimal levels of arousal** dates back to the very beginning of psychology: the experimentalist Wilhelm Wundt was studying it as early as 1893 (see Zuckerman, 1979), as were Sigmund Freud and Josef Breuer in 1895 (Freud and Breuer, 1895/2004). Following the **"brainwashing"** techniques used by the Chinese during the Korean War, the Canadian government pursued research on sensory deprivation, work led by D. O. Hebb. Following this early research, Zuckerman began his own investigations. Generally, sensory deprivation leads to increased anxiety, somatic discomfort, and thinking and concentration difficulties. In addition, many of the subjects experienced both auditory and visual hallucinations. None of the effects of sensory deprivation seemed to correlate with any personality variables (Zuckerman et al., 1962). It was because of these profound effects of sensory deprivation that Zuckerman began to pursue the underlying variable that leads individuals to their optimal level of arousal.

The Sensation Seeking Scale has been revised a number of times. The fifth version was developed in collaboration with Hans and Sybil Eysenck, and included comparisons of males to females and American students to English students (see Zuckerman, 1979, 1994). Using factor analysis, Zuckerman and his colleagues have identified four subscales within the sensation seeking trait:

Thrill and Adventure Seeking: Many people enjoy engaging in risky sports and other potentially dangerous experiences that produce unique sensations related to speed or defying gravity, such as rock climbing, BASE jumping, or drag racing. This factor is exemplified by the sports included in the X Games.

Experience Seeking: This factor encompasses novel sensations and experiences, such as arousing music, art, and travel. It also incorporates social nonconformity, particularly associated with belonging to groups on the fringes of conventional society.

Disinhibition: This factor covers sensation seeking that focuses on social activities, such as parties, drinking, illegal drugs, and sex.

Boredom Susceptibility: Individuals who score high on this factor cannot tolerate any kind of repetitive experience, including routine work and boring people.

Sensation seeking comes in many forms. Here, the author is hanging from two ice screws about 800 or 900 feet up the alpine route Pinnacle Gulley on Mt. Washington in New Hampshire. The temperature was an invigorating -15° F. [Image by Mark Kelland]

Sensation seeking should not be confused with being reckless. For example, individuals who are high sensation seekers are more likely to have varied sexual experiences, but they are not more likely to avoid using condoms. They may be more inclined to drive fast, but they are not less likely to use their seatbelts. And rock and ice climbers take full advantage of safety gear, they study self-rescue techniques, and they check their gear carefully before each trip. However, adolescence may be a particularly risky time, since there is a temporal gap between the onset of puberty, during which adolescents are highly thrill seeking, and the slow maturation of the cognitive-control systems that govern such behavior in adulthood (Steinberg, 2007). It is also important to note that it is neither good nor bad to score high or low on this scale:

> In this sociobiological sense, the high sensation seeker is a hunter and the low sensation seeker is a farmer. Hunters are positively excited by change, danger, and the variety and unpredictability of the hunt. They need a strong capacity to focus attention on the prey while remaining alert to other factors like the direction of the wind and the movements of other hunters. Farmers, in contrast, depend on stability of the environment (rainfall, sun, and other seasonal regularities of climate). Plants grow slowly and require patience and tedious kinds of labor to insure their survival. (pp. 384-385; Zuckerman, 1994)

During the course of his research, Zuckerman found a close relationship between sensation seeking and **impulsivity**. If he limited his factor analysis to five factors, as Costa and McCrae had, impulsivity and sensation seeking always combined to form a factor that he called **impulsive sensation seeking**. This proved to be rather curious, since impulsivity was a substrate of neuroticism, whereas "excitement seeking" was a substrate of extraversion. Another problem that Zuckerman expressed with regard to the Five-Factor Model was his belief that words like "conscientiousness" have no meaning in species other than humans. Since Zuckerman favors a biological/genetic basis for personality, there should be evolutionary correlates of any personality structure in other animals, particularly the closely related apes. Thus, Zuckerman examined his data, conducted a factor analysis, and offered an alternative to the Five-Factor Model. His five factors are sociability, neuroticism-anxiety, impulsive sensation seeking, aggression-hostility, and activity (Zuckerman, 2006). While Zuckerman did not intend for his five factors to match those of Costa and McCrae exactly, it is easy to see a relationship between sociability and agreeableness, activity and extraversion, sensation seeking and openness, and neuroticism and neuroticism. Aggression-hostility, however, seems to relate more to Eysenck's factor psychoticism. Thus, there remains a need for continued research into this field, particularly as it pertains to the evolutionary basis for personality factors, but Eysenck, Costa, McCrae, and Zuckerman have provided an excellent and coherent basis for further research.

The author is highly susceptible to boredom, so he likes to travel to interesting places. Here we see the author in Mt. Washington's alpine garden (NH) in winter (top left) and above the clouds on Mt. Rainier, Washington (bottom right), and the author's son walking in the Great Salt Lake in Utah's desert (top right). [Images by Mark Kelland]

Discussion Question: Which areas of Zuckerman's sensation seeking trait do you find most interesting, and which subscales do you think you would score high on (they may not be the same)? If there are any subscales on which you think you would score either low or high, what impression do you have of people who have an opposite score on those same scales?

Grit - Getting Things Done!

Another specific trait that has become somewhat popular recently in higher education has been called **grit** by Angela Duckworth and her colleagues (see Duckworth et al., 2007). Grit is defined as the perseverance and passion necessary to accomplish long-term goals. In particular, it refers to the ability to continue striving toward those goals despite temporary failure, adversity, and plateaus in one's progress. Although much of the research on grit has focused on academic goals, grit does not correlate well with intelligence. Rather, it correlates highly with the Big-Five trait of conscientiousness.

We used to believe that individuals who become experts in a particular area (whether it's math, playing a musical instrument, playing chess, or competing in athletic events, etc.) had some innate ability or talent for their skill. However, Anders Ericsson proposed and studied a different theoretical framework. Although an individual may show some early talent in a particular domain, what resulted in their becoming an expert, or a star athlete, was the intensive **deliberate practice** that followed, often taking many years before the individual truly excelled (Anders Ericsson, 2004; Anders Ericsson et al., 1993). Working together, Duckworth, Ericsson, and a few of their colleagues showed that deliberate practice is the key to success in an academic competition that tends to fascinate many people because of just how difficult it is: the National Spelling Bee (Duckworth et al., 2010).

Whether it's grit, consciousness, or the associated behavior of deliberate practice, those who continue to strive toward their goals tend to succeed not only in school, but also in most aspects of life, including life satisfaction and earning a good income (Duckworth & Carlson, 2013; Duckworth et al., 2012). But what can, perhaps, interfere with one's ability and/or motivation to continue striving toward one's goals? It appears that life stress in early adolescence can significantly impair one's ability to strive toward a positive and fruitful future (Duckworth et al., 2013). It's quite possible that since adolescence is the time of developing one's identity, according to Erik Erikson, and identity associated with negative life events and stress is incompatible with maintaining grit.

As I mentioned above, this is an area only recently becoming well-known (i.e., popular) in the field of higher education. It is likely to become an increasingly significant factor in how we work toward helping students achieve their goals, whether academic or in other aspects of their lives.

Final Note: Moving Toward a New "Big Five"?

In 2006, Dan McAdams and Jennifer Pals argued that personality psychology has failed to provide a comprehensive framework in which we can understand the whole person. Since this was a guiding principle of many of the founders of this field, an effort to combine recent research with early principles would help the field of personality psychology move toward maturity. In a manner similar to Costa and McCrae's Five-Factor Theory, McAdams and Pals suggest that those who study personality should be guided by five fundamental principles: evolutionary design, dispositional traits, characteristic adaptations, integrative life narrative, and culture. Their examination of these principles led them to the following definition of personality:

> Personality is an individual's unique variation on the general evolutionary design for human nature, expressed as a developing pattern of dispositional traits, characteristic adaptations, and integrative life stories complexly and differentially situated in culture. (pg. 212; McAdams & Pals, 2006)

If personality psychologists use these principles in their ongoing efforts to understand each individual, they should be able to achieve an understanding of an old paradox offered to explain personality: every person is like every other person, like some other persons, and like no other person (see McAdams & Pals, 2006).

Personality Theory in Real Life: Reconceptualizing Personality Disorders within the Context of the Five-Factor Model

There remains debate as to exactly how personality disorders should be classified (see the Appendix). This issue is more than just a matter of curiosity, since our entire conception of personality disorders is an essential factor in how we approach their treatment. As perhaps the most widely accepted and scientifically validated trait perspective on normal personality, it stands to reason that the Five-Factor Model (FFM) ought to also provide a basis for classifying abnormal personality and, in particular, the personality disorders. Thus, Costa and Widiger (1994) brought together a group of experts, including Theodore Millon, to address personality disorders within the context of the FFM.

The *DSM-III* thru *DSM-V* use diagnostic categories for the personality disorders, whereas the FFM suggests a dimensional approach. The categorical approach has several advantages. It is relatively easier to conceptualize disorders as either having them or not, clinicians are familiar with the current categories, and when clinical decisions are categorical they tend to be consistent. However, the dimensional approach offers the advantages of not being arbitrary in defining specific symptom cut-off points for a diagnosis, they allow for retaining information on those patients who just miss the cut-off point for a diagnosis (and could, therefore, simply be classified as *not* having the disorder), and the dimensions are more flexible than a categorical diagnosis. More importantly than just speculating on advantages and disadvantages, however, is that the majority of empirical data seems to support the dimensional approach (Widiger & Frances, 1994). For example, borderline personality disorder patients do not show a specific profile on the MMPI, but rather a nonspecific elevation across most scales. Diagnosis is typically made following a clinical evaluation including an interview. A similar challenge faces clinicians using the NEO-PI (the assessment tool specifically designed for the FFM), but useful and relevant data are available from looking at the specific trait scores within factors, particularly within the factor neuroticism (Trull & McCrae, 1994). In addition, factor analysis on the dimensions of personality disorder yielded results that fit very well with the FFM, with several aspects of personality disorder (but not all) again being linked to neuroticism (Schroeder, Wormworth, & Livesley, 1994). It is important to remember, however, that the very idea of using a dimensional approach is based, in part, on an assumption:

> …If one assumes that disordered personality is qualitatively different from normal personality, then the inclusion of a dimensional model of personality may be insufficient or inappropriate for investigation. If one assumes that disordered personality reflects quantitative differences in the manifestation or severity of normal personality traits (i.e., a dimensional approach), then the adoption of a personality taxonomy for use as a structural referent becomes a necessary or even fundamental conceptual task. (pp. 73-74; Wiggins & Pincus, 1994)

What, then, might personality disorders look like in terms of a dimensional description? Clark, Vorhies, and McEwen (1994) take an integrated approach based on two basic propositions pertaining to traits: first, that they are continuously distributed and exhibit wide individual variation; and second, that they are not fixed, but rather they are adaptations to the environment that are consistent within one's individual range. These two points lead to the notions that a single trait structure can represent both normal and abnormal personality, that within the normal range there is great individual difference in each person's characteristic and adaptive styles of thinking, feeling, and behaving, and that personality disorders are characterized by extreme and inflexible expressions of the normal personality structure. When examining data from individuals diagnosed with personality disorder, they have identified symptom clusters that form dimensions, or factors, which once again fit well with the FFM (Clark, et al., 1994). Widiger and several colleagues have actually offered five-factor translations of the standard categories of DSM-III and DSM-IV personality disorders (see Widiger, et al., 1994). The purpose of these translations is to take the personality disorder categories that psychologists are familiar with and put them in terms of the FFM. Consider two examples:

> **Paranoid Personality Disorder:** Paranoid personality disorder (PAR) involves interpreting the actions of others as threatening or deliberately demeaning. These individuals tend to be suspicious, mistrustful, hypervigilant, and argumentative. According to the FFM, PAR is characterized primarily by excessively low agreeableness, particularly on the suspiciousness facet (a facet is one of the traits that makes up a factor). They are also characterized by the low agreeableness facets of very low straightforwardness and compliance, which represent the PAR tendencies to be secretive and oppositional. PAR is also characterized by the angry hostility facet of neuroticism, low extraversion, and low openness.
>
> **Antisocial Personality Disorder:** Antisocial personality disorder (ATS) is characterized by irresponsible and antisocial behavior, and often involves criminal activity and a lack of regard for the rights of others. Within the FFM, they score

excessively low on conscientiousness and agreeableness (particularly low on the facets of straightforwardness, altruism, compliance, and tendermindedness). They score high on the neuroticism facets of hostility, anxiety, depression, and impulsivity. However, so-called "successful" psychopaths may be characterized by very low levels of anxiety and self-consciousness.
(see Widiger, et al., 1994)

So, given the possibility of reconceptualizing personality disorders within the FFM, is it something we should do? Millon suggests that we view personality as the psychological equivalent of the body's biological systems. Personality is, in this conception, a psychic system of structures and functions that lead to characteristic patterns of thought, feeling, and behavior. These characteristics cannot be viewed as simply normal or abnormal, since any specific element of the personality might be adaptive in one situation but maladaptive in another. Thus, the dimensional approach to describing personality provides a comprehensive picture in which little information of potential significance is lost (Millon, 1994). McCrae questions the very validity of Axis II of the *DSM* system, which appears to have little empirical support. He suggests that clinicians include in their diagnosis of patients a global assessment of the five personality factors. Thus, the diagnostic report would provide the necessary information on personality pertaining to the common symptoms and problems associated with either high or low scores on each factor (McCrae, 1994; Widiger, 1994). For example:

High Neuroticism: chronic negative affects, difficulty in inhibiting impulses, irrational beliefs
Low Neuroticism: lack of appropriate concern for potential problems in health or social adjustment, emotional blandness
High Agreeableness: gullibility, excessive candor and generosity, inability to stand up to others, easily taken advantage of
Low Agreeableness: cynicism and paranoid thinking, inability to trust, quarrelsomeness, too ready to pick fights, exploitative and manipulative, lying, rude and inconsiderate
(see McCrae, 1994)

Perhaps the most valuable aspect of any model used for classifying the personality disorders is its ability to provide guidelines for conceptualizing a treatment strategy. Sanderson and Clarkin (1994) have indeed found the NEO-PI useful in differential treatment planning. For example, the NEO-PI, in conjunction with a clinical interview, helps describe the typical interpersonal patterns of the patient, suggesting areas of difficulty needing treatment regardless of whether the therapy format is individual, family, or a group setting. In addition, the NEO-PI can help to identify which therapy format might be best suited to each particular patient. Although Sanderson and Clarkin (1994) caution that such conceptions still await empirical confirmation, they do offer some examples from their own supportive clinical experience. Likewise, MacKenzie (1994) offers numerous specific examples from cases in which factor scores provided clear target areas for focusing therapy. For example, a women who scored high in agreeableness acknowledged that she repeatedly got into relationships in which she felt used, a teacher who scored very high on openness was overly stimulated in new situations and felt overwhelmed with creative ideas, and a man who scored low on conscientiousness felt stuck in life, having worked only itinerant construction jobs despite having earned a graduate degree in college. In each case, the NEO-PI data matched the clinical presentation quite well, suggesting that the FFM would indeed be an effective conceptualization of treatment strategies for personality disorder issues (as well as, presumably, for other psychological and adjustment disorders).

The diagnosis of personality disorders, whether categorical or dimensional, remains a controversial topic. Of even greater concern, is the resistance of these disorders to treatment. However, the FFM appears to offer an advantageous way of describing personality disorder as an extreme extension of normal personality dimensions, and the NEO-PI scales offer practical direction with regard to treatment strategies. Change, however, may not come easily:

> Some observers have said that what is at issue here is the American Psychiatric Association "versus" the American Psychological Association. In other words, the potential conflict between psychiatric/categorical and psychological/dimensional models could stall progress in this field. It has been suggested that the American Psychological Association should issue a rival *DSM* that uses a dimensional approach. We believe a far better solution would be cooperation between the two approaches, which would lead to more coordinated research and shared clinical experience. (pg. 325; Costa & Widiger, 1994).

Review of Key Points

- Allport's approach to the study of personality emphasized the individual above all else.
- In defining personality, Allport proposed a dynamic interaction between traits and how they affect the individual's adjustment to his or her environment.
- Allport defined traits as neuropsychic systems that had the effect of rendering different aspects of the environment as the same, thus guiding behavior in consistent ways (in keeping with the traits, not the environment per se).
- Individual traits provide the basis for an idiographic approach to personality, whereas common traits relate more to the nomothetic approach.
- Each person's unique personality is influenced by their dispositions. An individual can be influenced by cardinal, central, or secondary dispositions.
- As the various stages of development influence one's personality, the unique sense of "me" or "I" that develops should be referred to as the proprium, according to Allport.
- An adult's motives are independent of their development, something Allport referred to as functional autonomy.
- Allport proposed six aspects of a mature personality: an extended sense of self, personal warmth, emotional security, realistic perceptions, insight and humor, and a unifying philosophy of life.
- In addition to personality tests, Allport valued the observation of expressive behavior and the review of personal documents (when available).
- Allport was a deeply spiritual man, emphasizing the positive role that religion can play in peoples' lives.
- Allport's personal faith, and his lifelong commitment to social ethics, led him to write one of the most significant works on prejudice ever published.
- Cattell distinguished between traits and types, the latter being a broader term. Similarly, he distinguished between source traits and surface traits, respectively.
- Using factor analysis, Cattell settled on sixteen factors, or source traits. He developed the 16-PF Questionnaire to measure these factors in individuals.
- Cattell helped to establish the field of psychometry, emphasizing the need for L-data, Q-data, and T-data.
- About the same time as Erikson, Cattell offered a lifespan theory of personality development. He proposed six stages: infancy, childhood, adolescence, maturity, middle age, and old age.
- Eysenck used a second-order factor analysis to identify three superfactors: extraversion, neuroticism, and psychoticism.
- In support of his belief in the biological/evolutionary basis for personality, Eysenck joined Harry Harlow in demonstrating that monkeys appear to have three similar factors underlying their "personalities."
- Some authors have suggested that Eysenck overstated the role of genetics, even based on his own data. Eysenck acknowledged such concerns, and hopefully anticipated future research that might help clarify the issue.
- Eysenck, like Allport, was interested in practical applications of personality research. He also addressed a wide variety of controversial topics that have, at best, highly questionable evidence supporting them.

Trait Theories

- Costa and McCrae expanded on Eysenck's theory, and proposed five superfactors: extraversion, neuroticism, openness, agreeableness, and conscientiousness.
- They also developed the NEO-PI-R to measure these factors. The NEO-PI-R has proven robust across cultures, and research using the NEO-PI-R has supported the universality of the Five-Factor Model.
- Despite arguments to the contrary, the majority of research shows that personality, as measured by trait theories, is highly consistent throughout adulthood.
- Zuckerman identified a sensation seeking trait, comprised of four aspects: thrill and adventure seeking, experience seeking, disinhibition, and boredom susceptibility.
- Zuckerman offered an alternative to the Five-Factor Model, which is quite similar, but more applicable to a wider variety of species. Once again, this supports a genetic/evolutionary perspective on the development of personality.

Review of Key Terms

adolescence	grit	persona
agreeableness	habits	personal dispositions
attitudes	idiographic	personal documents
basic tendencies	impulsive sensation seeking	personality sphere
Boredom Susceptibility	impulsivity	proprium
brainwashing	individual traits	psychometry
cardinal disposition	infancy	psychoticism
central dispositions	instincts	Q-data
characteristic adaptations	Intracultural	rumor
childhood	integration	Revised NEO-PI
closed-ended questions	intercultural	secondary dispositions
color-blind perspective	L-data	self-concept
common traits	learning	sensation seeking
Conscientiousness	maturation	Sensation Seeking Scale
deliberate practice	maturity	sensory deprivation
differentiation	middle age	Sixteen Personality Factor Questionnaire
Disinhibition	multicultural perspective	source traits
dynamic processes	needs	superfactors
eugenics	NEO Personality Inventory	surface traits
Experience Seeking	neuroticism	T-data
expressive behavior	nomothetic	Thrill and Adventure Seeking
extraversion	objective biography	traits
factor	old age	transcultural
factor analysis	open-ended questions	types
Five-Factor Model	openness	unique traits
Five-Factor Theory	openness to the other	
functional autonomy	optimal levels of arousal	

Annotated Bibliography

Allport, G. W. (1937). *Personality: A psychological interpretation*. New York, NY: Henry Holt and Company.

Allport, G. W. (1961). *Pattern and growth in personality*. New York, NY: Holt, Rinehart and Winston.

The first of these two books is often identified as the first personality textbook, and it lays out many of Allport's basic ideas. The second book is something of a revised version of the first book, but the revisions are substantial, and the research providing evidence in favor of his theories had been advanced by more than two decades.

Allport, G. W. (1979). ***The nature of prejudice - 25th Anniversary edition.*** **Reading, MA: Addison-Wesley Publishing Company.**

Miller, J. & Garran, A. M. (2008). ***Racism in the United States: Implications for the helping professions.*** **Belmont, CA: Thomson Brooks/Cole.**

Allport's book is *the* classic study on prejudice. The breadth of topics covered is extraordinary, from defining the issues to proposing how we might eliminate prejudice altogether. The 25th Anniversary edition includes a new introduction by Kenneth Clark.

Race and ethnicity are important cultural phenomena to the extent that people see them and react to them. Racism is a problem that has existed throughout human history. This valuable book, aimed at those in helping professions such as psychology, addresses a wide variety of topics pertaining to racism, including the history of racism and how to begin combating it.

Bertocci, P. A. (Ed.). (1978). ***Waiting for the Lord: 33 Meditations on God and man - Gordon W. Allport.*** **New York, NY: Macmillan Publishing.**

This book is a wonderful collection of the meditations on God offered by Allport at the daily worship service in Harvard University's Appleton Chapel. Allport offered prayers approximately twice a year from 1938 to 1967.

Cattell, R. B. (1950a). ***An introduction to personality study.*** **London, England: Hutchinson's University Library.**

Cattell, R. B. (1965). ***The scientific analysis of personality.*** **Baltimore, MD: Penguin Books.**

These fairly concise books cover the relevant details of Cattell's personality theory, including his perspective on the stages of life, and the relative roles of genetic and environmental factors in personality development.

Craik, K. H., Hogan, R., & Wolfe, R. N. (1993). Fifty years of personality psychology. New York, NY: Plenum Press.

This marvelous book was published following the fiftieth anniversary of the publication of Allport's personality textbook. As noted in the chapter, there was another personality textbook published that year by a young professor named Ross Stagner. Stagner contributed a chapter to this book, still active in a career that had spanned over fifty years by that time.

Eysenck, H. J. (1952). ***The scientific study of personality.*** **New York, NY: The Macmillan Company.**

Eysenck, H. J. (1967). ***The biological basis of personality.*** **Springfield, IL: Charles C. Thomas, Publisher.**

These books provide the essential ideas behind Eysenck's personality theory and his approach to the dimensions of personality structure. The second book emphasizes his belief that personality is determined primarily by biological/genetic factors.

Eysenck, H. J. (1972). ***Psychology is about people.*** **New York, NY: The Library Press.**

This book exemplifies Eysenck's interest in the practical applications of personality theory. It is also presented in a somewhat light-hearted way, including a chapter entitled *Don't Shoot the Behaviorist: He is Doing His Best.*

Eysenck, H. J. (1953). ***Uses and abuses of psychology*****. Baltimore, MD: Penguin Books.**
Eysenck, H. J. (1957). ***Sense and nonsense in psychology*****. Baltimore, MD: Penguin Books.**

In these two entertaining books, Eysenck questions the validity of psychology, and various topics that some appreciate and others do not. Together they would help anyone to put the field of psychology into context, particularly with regard to the historic development of psychology as a scientific discipline.

McCrae, R. R. & Costa, Jr., P. T. (2003). ***Personality in adulthood: A Five-Factor Theory perspective, 2nd Ed.*** **New York, NY: The Guilford Press.**
McCrae, R. R. & Allik, J. (Eds.). (2002). ***The Five-Factor Model of personality across cultures*****. New York, NY: Kluwer Academic/Plenum Publishers.**
Costa, Jr., P. T. & Widiger, T. A. (Eds.). (1994). ***Personality disorders and the Five-Factor Model of personality*****. Washington, DC: American Psychological Association.**

Taken together, these three books solidly establish the Five-Factor Model as one of the leading, if not *the* leading, perspectives on personality today. The first book provides the essential information on the Five-Factor Model, as well as McCrae and Costa's extension of that model to a Five-Factor Theory of personality. The second book confirms the applicability of this theory to a wide variety of cultural groups, and the third book addresses the utility of conceptualizing personality disorders (a perplexing problem within abnormal psychology) within the Five-Factor Model. These books also represent the culmination of decades of work by Allport, Cattell, and Eysenck.

Zuckerman, M. (1994). ***Behavioral expressions and biosocial bases of sensation seeking*****. Cambridge, England: Cambridge University Press.**

This is Zuckerman's principal book on the sensation seeking trait, including the history behind developing the Sensation Seeking Scale. As the title suggests, the book also includes substantial information on the biological basis of this trait, as well as social factors that influence its expression.

Zuckerman, M. (2006). The shaping of personality: Genes, environment, and chance encounters. In S. Strack & B. N. Kinder (Eds.), ***Pioneers of personality science: Autobiographical perspectives*** **(pp. 387-412). New York, NY: Springer Publishing Company.**

Zuckerman's chapter in this book provides an autobiography of his life, as well as information of his sensation seeking research. The book as a whole provides autobiographies of many groundbreaking personality scientists, including Theodore Millon.

Chapter 14 - Biology and Personality; Sociobiology; Mindfulness and the Martial Arts

During the evolution of the human species, we appear to have lost the ability to rely on instinctive behavior as we developed extraordinary abilities to learn and adapt to the conditions facing us in our environment. In addition, we can pass on that learning to other members of our social group. This is the basis for culture, and the success of the human species is a testament to the advantages of this approach to survival. However, this transition from instinct to learning and culture has not resulted in the elimination of biological influences on our behavior. Certain groups of people, usually a minority of the population, retain biological predispositions to behave and react in certain distinct ways. To a lesser extent, all of us have some degree of these biological predispositions.

The purpose of the first half of this chapter is to examine those biological predispositions that are directly reflected in aspects of individual personality. In the second half of the chapter, we will examine the connection between the mind and the body, and some of the ways in which individuals train the mind/body connection in order to achieve a more balanced and healthy lifestyle.

Over 2,500 years ago, Gotama Buddha came to a fascinating understanding of the human mind. The Buddha taught a series of **mindfulness** exercises to train the mind, and these mindfulness exercises form the basis for many styles of meditations. Today, cutting-edge neurobiologists are using functional magnetic resonance imaging (fMRI) and other brain imaging techniques to examine brain activity during deep meditation. The goal of these studies is to understand the nature of the human mind, and to examine whether the Buddha (as well as the Rishis and Yogis of ancient India) had discovered a way to actually alter the state of the mind. However, too much time spent in meditation can lead to a weak body. So, the founder of Zen Buddhism, Bodhidharma, when he arrived at the Shao-Lin temple, developed techniques of physical training to strengthen the monks and to help them both defend themselves from bandits and prepare for extended periods of meditation. This was the legendary beginning of the martial arts, formal techniques to train the body and mind. Since the martial arts were developed with noble goals, they have throughout their history had a reputation for developing strong, admirable character traits. In other words, those who practice martial arts with proper discipline also train themselves to conform to a personality style marked by a calm, humble, yet confident demeanor.

Placing Biological and Mind/Body Theories of Personality in Context: Testing Personality Theories Across the Full Range of Human History

This chapter has the broadest context of any chapter in this book. Some 2,500 years ago, Gotama Buddha presented what can be considered the first psychological theory, a theory on the nature of the human mind and how one can work to control it in a mindful way. Doing so can help to lead one toward a more peaceful life, both individually and in relation to others. Today, neurobiologists using cutting edge technology are trying to determine what actually happens to the state of the human mind during the techniques of meditation taught by the Buddha. In addition, the usefulness of meditation and mindfulness in psychotherapy is a popular area of clinical practice and research, as well as a means toward enhancing the cross-cultural perspectives of psychology in general.

Wilhelm Reich, a student and highly respected colleague of Sigmund Freud, was one of the first Western psychologists to consider the connection between body and mind as essential for psychology health. According to Reich, we can be psychologically healthy only if we are able to fully express and satisfy our biological, sexual needs. Reich devoted his career to helping individuals do just that, and in recognizing the role of the body, he anticipated the field of sociobiology. Sociobiology addresses the ways in which our behavior might have been shaped by evolution. In other words, behaviors are naturally selected if they provide an advantage for our genetic reproduction (having children, grandchildren, etc.).

Whereas Reich and the sociobiologists focus on the expression and pursuit of our biological desires, Eastern tradition taught ways to train the body and mind to control these desires. Indeed, the Buddha taught that through mindfulness training we could detach ourselves from these needs, and live a life in which we acknowledge desires, but feel no attachment to them. Such mental discipline, however, requires practice. As monks became physically weak from spending all their time meditating, the founder of Zen Buddhism, Bodhidharma, developed the first formal techniques of Kung Fu. Since the martial arts arose out of the desire to remain healthy during meditation practice, they have always been associated with a spirituality devoted to nonviolence and mental discipline.

The popularity of martial arts, meditation, Yoga, and a variety of Eastern philosophies and practices in the United States today tells us that there is a strong interest in combing the traditions of East and West. The interest of cognitive neuroscientists in the brain's changes during meditation shows us that Eastern philosophy need not stand in opposition to our tradition of formal scientific inquiry in the West. And so, Buddhist mindfulness, somatic psychology, behavior genetics, sociobiology, evolutionary psychology, and the martial arts all seem to fit together as a grand theory of the nature of body and mind and their inherent connection.

Biology and Personality

When talking about the role of biology in behavior, the natural starting point is the genetic makeup of each person. Our specific genetic blueprint is what distinguishes each of us as a unique individual, except for identical twins. However, since humans no longer rely on instinctive behavior, there are no aspects of personality that are specifically determined by genetics. Instead, it is more appropriate to say that our genetic makeup determines ranges within which we might develop, and our environment then determines where we fall within that range. The topics of greatest interest in the biology of personality are those topics that appear to be under a relatively greater influence of genetics than environment. But how do we determine the relative contributions of genetics and environment? Psychologists have relied mostly on twin and adoption studies.

Twin Studies, Adoption Studies, Family Studies

Twin studies have a long and interesting history in the field of psychology. Sir Francis Galton (1822-1911) studied mental abilities and is recognized as being the first to utilize twin studies. His use of identical twins, in the mid to late 1800s, is generally recognized as the first use of an experimental control group (Diamond, 1977/1997; Jensen, 1998), and the use of identical vs. fraternal twins continues to be recognized as a natural control condition by psychologists and sociobiologists (Kagan, Kearsley, & Zelazo, 1978; Wilson, 1978). Twin studies were also of interest to psychologists in the former Soviet Union (Cole & Maltzman, 1969). While Anna Freud and Melanie Klein were applying psychoanalysis to the study and treatment of children, the American physician and psychologist Arnold Gesell was comparing the achievement of fundamental developmental milestones between twins (Lomax, Kagan, & Rosencrantz, 1978), and Wayne Dennis was conducting an astonishing experiment on a pair of twins. Dennis and his wife raised the twins under conditions of minimal social and sensory stimulation. This research had a noble goal: to understand the basis for the detrimental effects of institutionalized care that was being recognized in overcrowded orphanages. However, one of the twins ended up showing signs of mental retardation (though this was attributed to an early head injury; Lomax, Kagan, & Rosencrantz, 1978). Obviously such an experiment would never be approved today, due to the ethical guidelines and oversight that have become a common part of psychological research, but twin studies done in reasonable and ethical ways continue to be an important part of psychological research.

What makes identical twins important is that they share 100 percent of their genetic material, whereas fraternal twins (like any other siblings) share an average of 50 percent of their genetic material. By extending this to families, and finally to people who have no biological relationship, we have a continuum of genetic relatedness from complete to none. This allows us to address the issue of **heritability**, or the degree of individual variance on some measure of behavior or personality that can be attributed to genetics. It is important to remember, however, that heritability is measured in populations (see Kagan, 1994; Sternberg, Grigorenko, & Kidd, 2005). It makes no sense to suggest, for example, that a 5-foot tall person is 54 inches tall due to genetics and then grew another 6 inches thanks to good nutrition. **Adoption studies** add an interesting twist to this research, since adopted children take the genetic contributions of their parents into different environmental situations, making adoption studies a useful tool for comparing the environmental contributions to the genetic contributions. However, these studies remain challenging. For example, intelligence is perhaps the most widely studied trait in terms of whether and how much it is genetic. Some of this research has been very controversial. Sir Francis Galton, who was mentioned above, believed that his research confirmed that certain races were superior to others, and that superior races had an obligation to selectively breed their best individuals for the good of future generations, as had been done (and continues to be done today) with certain breeds of dogs and horses (Galton, 1869/1997). Despite this controversial beginning to the study of genetics and intelligence, the topic has remained widely studied, but elusive nonetheless. Estimates on the heritability of intelligence range from approximately 65 to 85 percent (Gould, 1982; Jensen, 1998). However, at very early ages the genetic and environmental influences are closer to 50-50, decrease with age, and by adulthood the genetic component is almost entirely responsible for the correlation of intelligence between related individuals (Gould, 1982; Jensen, 1998). Further complicating the situation for studying children, when a wider range of extended family members are considered and cultural factors are separated from non-transmissible environmental factors, it appears that genetics, culture, and environment all play roughly equal roles (Boyd & Richerson, 1985). Indeed, culture can have profound effects on intelligence, including our definition of intelligence itself (Sternberg, 2004). Finally, returning to the controversial perspective of Galton and other proponents of the **eugenics** movement (the belief that superior races and classes should not mix with inferior groups), research today has demonstrated that no legitimate connection can be made between race and intelligence (Sternberg, Grigorenko, & Kidd, 2005; also see Loehlin, 1997; Williams & Ceci, 1997), and when it comes to education, IQ isn't even the best predictor of academic performance (Duckworth & Seligman, 2005).

Another important point is the issue of **family studies**. Usually, we think of the family as providing genetic similarity, since children inherit their genes from their parents. Second, we tend to think that families provide a common environmental situation for each of their children, particularly in small families. However, this is not always true. In the Russian literature there was a well-known case in which the first-born girl was always treated as the elder sister, even though her younger identical twin was only minutes younger. The result of the differential treatment was that the "older" girl reached most developmental milestones before her sister (Bozhovich, 1969). In a case described by the renowned Russian neuropsychologist A. R. Luria, identical twins with retarded speech had begun to develop their own autonomous language. Once separated into different classes in nursery school, however, the autonomous language disappeared (Luria, 1969). Thus, the family can have a very dramatic environmental influence, whether intentional or not, that goes against the genetic similarity due to biological relationships or even identical twinship. What then, can we conclude regarding the heritability of personality traits in humans? Certainly genetic factors play an important role, but the complexity of the human organism and its sociocultural environment makes it difficult to draw definite conclusions about exactly how much of an influence our unique genetic profile has on our individual personality. Nonetheless, psychologists have continued to pursue this important question.

Genetically Determined Dispositions

Behavior genetics is the term most commonly used to refer to studies on the influence of genetics on behavior. Most of these studies have relied on comparing identical twins to fraternal twins, other siblings, and unrelated individuals, including when possible twins who have been reared apart. These studies are often conducted in European countries that have thorough records of family histories, but one major, longitudinal study ongoing here in the United States has been the Minnesota Twin Family Study conducted at the University of Minnesota since 1983. These various sources of data, in addition to other research procedures, have helped psychologists come to some understanding of the role played by genetics in determining behavior and personality.

Psychologist Jerome Kagan is well known for his early studies on the nature of **temperament**. Temperament is perhaps the most salient characteristic of personality. It has been loosely described as the emotional component of our personality, as stable behavioral and emotional reactions that appear early in life and are influenced by genetic factors (Kagan, 1994). Kagan further describes temperamental categories as qualities that (1) vary among individuals, (2) are moderately stable over time and in different situations, (3) are partly determined by genetics, and (4) appear early in life. In part because they were easy to observe, the most popular temperamental qualities that have been studied are activity, irritability, and fearfulness, or as Kagan describes them: watchful inhibition vs. fearless exploration. About 10 percent of children exhibit extreme inhibition to nonthreatening, but unfamiliar, events (Kagan, 1984). Although this behavior can seemingly be altered by parental influence, subtle signs of the behavioral inhibition can be seen as the child grows, and they tend to continue into adulthood. Similarly, with uninhibited children, it is extremely unlikely that they will ever become inhibited children. Further studies on twins have helped to confirm that being inhibited or outgoing is influenced by genetics (Kagan, Kearsley, & Zelazo, 1978). Similar results have also been found with Guatemalan and Chinese children (Kagan, Kearsley, & Zelazo, 1978). As important as our emotional reactions are (see, e.g., the work of Daniel Goleman, 1995, 1998), they still do not necessarily dominate our personality:

An even temperament leads to stable behavioral and emotional reactions. [Image by Mark Kelland]

> ...it is wise to state explicitly that many differences among children may have little to do with temperament...Our current knowledge indicates that the motivation to perform well in school, the willingness to help a friend, loyalty to family, tolerance toward others, and a host of other motives and beliefs are minimally influenced by temperament. (pg. 77; Kagan, 1994)

Recently, Thomas Bouchard, Jr. (2004) offered a concise review of the heritability of psychological traits. With regard to the "Big Five" personality traits, they all exhibit heritability in the range of 42 to 57 percent. If one considers the alternative known as the "Big Three," the range is 44 to 52 percent (Bouchard, 2004). Thus, genetics make a significant contribution to the nature of basic personality, but at the same time there is at least as much of an environmental contribution (though that certainly includes a variety of factors). There is also significant heritability of psychological interests (such as being realistic, artistic, social, etc.), social attitudes, and psychiatric illness (especially schizophrenia; Bouchard, 2004; see also Bouchard, 1994; Bouchard & McGue, 1990; Bouchard et al., 1990; Kety, 1975; Mendlewicz, Fleiss, & Fieve, 1975; Shields, Heston, & Gottesman, 1975). Even such complex personality variables as well-being, traditionalism, religiosity, and criminality have been found to be highly influenced by our genetic make-up (Crowe, 1975; Kagan, 1994; Kessler, 1975; Tellegen et al., 1988; Waller et al., 1990). To put it simply, virtually all psychological factors are significantly influenced by our genetic makeup, but none are specifically determined by genetics. This led Danielle Dick and Richard Rose (2002) to question whether the field of behavior genetics has completed what it can reasonably hope to accomplish. They argue that there is much more to be studied, particularly in the area of **gene-environment interactions**. In such interactions, individuals experience the same environment in different ways due to their genetic predispositions.

In *Galen's Prophecy*, Kagan (1994) describes the role that he believes the **amygdala** plays in mediating responses to anxiety-producing stimuli. Eight percent of children demonstrate highly reactive responses to such stimuli, which animal research has shown is associated with increased activity in the amygdala and, consequently, a **behavioral inhibition system**. As a result, these children either freeze or withdraw from unfamiliar people and situations. In other words, they seem shy and withdrawn. Approximately 18 percent of children demonstrate low reactivity, their amygdala and the behavioral inhibition system are not activated, and they are likely to approach unfamiliar people and situations with curiosity. These simple patterns of behavior can have profound effects on personality. Kagan (1994) has found that **high reactive infants**, those who become anxious as a result of unfamiliarity, tend to become dour, serious, and fearful as they grow. In contrast, the **low reactive infants**, those who may respond to unfamiliarity with curiosity and interest, become more joyful and fearless as they grow up. However, these tendencies are by no means guarantees, because the environment plays a significant role. If mothers are firm and set strict limits on the child's behavior, if they are supportive but do not always hold the child when it is upset (i.e., they hold the child when it *needs* help, but not when the child does *not need* help), then a high reactive child has a much better chance of overcoming its tendency to become an anxious and withdrawn person. One explanation, according to Kagan, is that these mothers require their children to meet her socialization demands; they must learn to deal with the uncertainty of unfamiliar situations. As for overprotective parents:

> ...It appears that mothers who protect their high reactive infants from frustration and anxiety in the hope of effecting a benevolent outcome seem to exacerbate the infant's uncertainty and produce the opposite effect. This result is in greater accord with the old-fashioned

behavioristic view than with the modern emphasis on the infant's need for a sensitive parent. (pg. 205; Kagan, 1994)

In support of Kagan's studies, Fox and his colleagues have demonstrated a specific gene-environment interaction that predicts behavioral inhibition in children aged 14 and 84 months (young 1 year-olds and 7 year-olds; Fox et al., 2005). Although it is difficult to describe such studies in simple terms, suffice it to say that children with a combination of the short 5-HTT allele (a gene for the molecule that transports the neurotransmitter serotonin) and low social support are at an increased risk for behavioral inhibition. When the children were 1 year old, behavioral inhibition was measured in terms of the latency to approach novel objects and unfamiliar adults, and when the children were 7 years old it was measured in terms of their disconnection from a group of children at play. The short allele of the 5-HTT gene has been associated with increased anxiety, negative emotionality, and relatively strong coupling with the amygdala. Therefore, in the absence of social support, children with the short allele are more likely to experience stress in the presence of novelty and strangers (Fox et al., 2005). Moffitt, Caspi, and Rutter have written an excellent review of how psychologists and other scientists approach this important new field of gene-environment interactions, and in that review they suggest that it is most likely that such interactions are common in psychopathology (Moffitt et al., 2006).

Discussion Question: Jerome Kagan studied temperament, and found that approximately 10% of children are shy and inhibited and approximately 20 percent of children are curious and adventurous, and these temperaments are most likely to continue into adulthood. Consider the people you know. Have their basic temperaments remained constant throughout their lives? What about you?

Sociobiology and Evolutionary Influences on Behavior

Sociobiology is a relatively new field of study that applies evolutionary biology to social behavior (Barash, 1977; Wilson, 1975). Although much of the research underlying sociobiology has been conducted with non-human animals, the value of this research and its applications to understanding human behavior and personality should not be underestimated. Samuel Gosling and his colleagues have demonstrated that a wide variety of other animal species have personality traits similar to those of humans (Gosling, 2001; Gosling & John, 1999; Gosling, Kwan, & John, 2003; Gosling & Vazire, 2002; Jones & Gosling, 2005; Mehta & Gosling, 2006). When the **ethologists** Nikolaas Tinbergen, Konrad Lorenz, and Karl von Frisch shared the Nobel Prize in 1973 it was the first Nobel Prize awarded for the study of behavior. Sociobiology, a field similar to ethology, has offered valuable new perspectives on human behavior, perspectives on behaviors that do not always seem logical at first. As an aside, sociobiology also allows us to address an exciting variety of human behaviors, including the apparent evolutionary and neurobiological bases for laughter (see Panksepp, 2005).

The fundamental concept underlying sociobiology is that of **inclusive fitness**. Inclusive fitness refers to the advantages of behaviors that increase the likelihood of an individual's genetic survival through the survival of genetically related **kin** (Barash, 1977; Wilson, 1975). Therefore, in looking at the evolution of human social behavior, we must not consider only the ways in which behaviors contribute to individual survival (which is a traditional Darwinian perspective on survival of the fittest), but rather on how behaviors contribute to the survival of our children, family, and perhaps even our community.

Sociobiologists have looked at several major topics regarding the evolution of human behavior, but we will only take a brief look at three behaviors: mate selection, parenting, and religion. In Chapter 2 we discussed male/female differences as a matter of fact. This has become commonly accepted in the popular media, and evidence suggests that men and women are inclined to essentialize their differences (Prentice & Miller, 2006). In contrast, Janet Shibley Hyde has provided compelling evidence that men and women are actually much more alike than they are different (Hyde, 1996, 2005; also see Spelke, 2005; Stewart & McDermott, 2004). So which is it? When it comes to mate selection, sociobiology suggests that men and women should be different, because the roles they will need to play in eventual child rearing require them to be different. It is a biological fact that men need to contribute very little to the birth of a child, whereas women become pregnant for nine months and, from an evolutionary perspective, must then breast-feed the child for one or two years. Thus, a man can improve his inclusive fitness by seeking multiple relationships with women in their prime child-bearing years and exhibiting physical characteristics indicative of good reproductive health. Unfortunately, other men are looking for the same women, so competition can become fierce. Women, on the other hand, should be inclined to seek men who have already won those competitions, demonstrating that they can provide and protect resources for their offspring, usually by commanding a territory or a privileged place in society (Barash, 1977; Wilson, 1975, 1978). So it is not uncommon for women to be inclined to marry older men, particularly men who are above them on the socioeconomic scale (Barash, 1977). Women would also be inclined to select men who make some commitment in terms of child rearing (Barash, 1979). So, men who were inclined to make only the minimum commitment necessary to the sexual act did not improve their inclusive fitness, since they were not selected by discriminating females.

When parenting is discussed in introductory psychology courses, the most common topic is parenting styles and their influence on personality development. In sociobiology, however, the most relevant issues are the survival of the offspring and how taxing it is on the parents to help their offspring survive. We are just beginning to understand some aspects of the biological basis for attachment from the offspring's perspective (Hofer, 2006), but understanding the attachment of the parent to the offspring remains elusive. Obviously, raising a child requires a considerable amount of effort on the parent's part, but typically more on the part of the mother. Thus, close social bonding is important, and this may form the basis of love as an added emotional component to sex, as well as the growing love that parents feel for their children (Barash, 1977; Wilson, 1978). Older women are particularly more sensitive to the needs of first-born children, since the child may well represent the only opportunity for the mother to reproduce. Nature is full of well-known examples of female animals vigorously defending their young, even if their own life is endangered (Barash, 1977, 1979). Of peculiar interest is the behavior of grandparents, since a parent is really only successful in reproducing if they eventually become grandparents. Barash (1977) discusses two interesting situations. When a child is born, it is most likely that the mother's parents come to help. But if a young couple chooses to live with parents, it is most likely the father's parents. These may simply seem to be cultural artifacts, but they have a basis in biological fitness. Only a mother can be sure that she has made a genetic contribution to a child (at least in the past, when our behaviors were evolving). So, when a woman has a baby, only her parents are sure that they have become grandparents. The man's parents serve their own interests best if they can watch over the woman, to make sure that she does not stray from her relationship with their son (Barash, 1977). All of this may sound cold and calculating, but it is logical nonetheless, and if we believe in an unconscious mind, then people don't need to be aware of exactly what they are doing.

Religion has been a profound influence throughout the history of the human species. It has been suggested that children naturally seek a divine explanation for the existence of a world they cannot comprehend (Kelemen, 2004). According to sociobiologist E. O. Wilson:

> The predisposition to religious belief is the most complex and powerful force in the human mind and in all probability an ineradicable part of human nature...It is one of the universals of social behavior, taking recognizable form in every society from hunter-gatherer band to socialist republics...At Shanidar, Iraq, sixty thousand years ago, Neanderthal people decorated a grave with seven species of flowers having medicinal and economic value, perhaps to honor a shaman. Since that time, according to the anthropologist Anthony F. C. Wallace, mankind has produced on the order of 100 thousand religions. (pg. 169; Wilson, 1978).

But what evolutionary advantage might religion serve? This question is difficult to answer, in part because religion appears to be unique to the human species. Many of the principles of sociobiology were determined by working with lower animals, especially the social insects. Without other species to use for comparison, it is not easy to understand our own species. According to Wilson, the best avenue for understanding the advantage conferred by religion to inclusive fitness is the ability to conform to the expectations of society. Humans seem to seek indoctrination. As we became more intelligent, more capable of making individual choices, perhaps we evolved the behavioral predispositions necessary to continue remaining within our tribe. As a result, the rules and rituals that developed to codify this behavior enhance the survival of our group, and it is this group-selection that sociobiologists recognize as the evolutionary advantage resulting from religion (Boyd & Richerson, 1985; Wilson, 1975, 1978). This is not unlike the role ascribed to religion by Sigmund Freud, except that sociobiologists propose an underlying genetic basis, whereas Freud proposed an underlying psychodynamic basis.

One of the most common negative reactions to sociobiology is resistance to the idea that we are still animals being driven by our genes and evolution. The simple logic provided by sociobiologists, and the clear parallels between human behavior and the behavior of other animals is not enough to sway the minds of some people. Culture definitely plays a significant role in our lives, gene-culture co-evolution may underlie human cooperation and altruism (Henrich, et al., 2006), and separating genetics from culture on a topic such as mate selection is difficult (Buss, 2003; Miller, Putcha-Bhagavatula, & Pedersen, 2002). But is culture something different than evolution? Richard Dawkins, in his profound book *The Selfish Gene* (1976), has proposed that the human mind has evolved to a point where it can create self-replicating units of culture, which he called **memes**. Memes can be transmitted from person to person, and they can evolve faster than genes. Thus, human culture has been able to outpace genetic evolution, creating many of the challenges we face today when we try to separate culture from genetics in order to understand complex human behaviors. As examples, let us consider two potential memes: belief in God, and belief in life after death. As mentioned above, children appear to be inclined to believe in a supernatural creator of the world that they, as children, simply cannot understand. And religion is a cultural universal. Not every religion, however, believes in life after death, and even fewer believe in heaven or hell. So religion appears to be a very successful meme, whereas belief in life after death is somewhat less successful, but successful enough to still be prevalent. One of the most fascinating aspects of memes is that they may actually increase the likelihood that you can have a very long lasting effect on the world. As Dawkins points out, Queen Elizabeth II of England is a direct descendant of William the Conqueror, but the odds are very low that she has even a single gene descended from him. So, immortality cannot really be achieved through reproduction:

> But if you contribute to the world's culture, if you have a good idea, compose a tune, invent a sparking plug, write a poem, it may live on, intact, long after your genes have dissolved in the common pool. Socrates may or may not have a gene or two alive in the world today…but who cares? The meme-complexes of Socrates, Leonardo, Copernicus, and Marconi are still going strong. (pg. 214; Dawkins, 1976)

Discussion Question: According to Richard Dawkins, the true path to immortality is found through cultural contributions to society, by virtue of cultural units he called memes. What memes do you think are important in your life and in your community? Has that changed during your life and, if so, why?

Evolutionary Psychology

The field of **evolutionary psychology** is a direct application of sociobiology to psychology, and appears to have begun with the publication of *The Adapted Mind* (Barkow et al., 1992). In this landmark book, a collection of authors were brought together with the purpose of addressing three major premises: (1) that there is a universal human nature, but that it is based on evolved psychological mechanisms as opposed to culture, (2) that these psychological mechanisms were adaptations constructed by natural selection, and (3) that these adaptations fit the way of life of our ancient ancestors, and may not fit our modern circumstances. Similar to the sociobiologists, evolutionary psychologists examine how evolution shaped human behavior and cognition in ways that helped individuals to pass on their genes to future generations, covering topics such as cooperation, mate preference, parental care, the development of language and perceptual abilities, the individual need to belong, helping and altruism, and the universality of emotions (Barkow et al., 1992; Buss, 1999; Larsen & Buss, 2005).

One of the best known psychologists studying evolutionary phenomena is David Buss, and he has paid particular attention to how we choose and attempt to keep our mates. In *The Evolution of Desire*, Buss (2003) describes how biological differences between males and females leads to different mating strategies, and that this should lead to inevitable conflict. Thus, according to Buss, conflict in a marriage is the norm, not the result of choosing the wrong person. As a result of this conflict, and for a variety of reasons underlying it, the possibility always exists that a man or woman in a marriage (or other committed relationship) will engage in other sexual relationships outside of the marriage. In order to defend against this potential loss of a committed mate, it was an advantage for people to evolve the emotion of jealousy. In *The Dangerous Passion*, Buss (2000b) argues that jealousy is just as important as love and sex. Passion is necessary for us to have motivation (consider Jung's description of the shadow archetype). But with jealousy:

> …Jealousy can keep a couple committed or drive a man to savagely beat his wife. An attraction to a neighbor's spouse can generate intoxicating sexual euphoria while destroying two marriages. (pg. 2; Buss, 2000b)

Indeed, the competition that accompanied the desire to obtain and hold onto a mate in our distant past was so intense that we also evolved the psychological mechanisms necessary to kill people. Although this psychological mechanism may be maladaptive in our society today, its effectiveness in the prehistoric past remains hidden just below the surface of our minds. As a result, it can come out suddenly, explaining why the majority of murderers seem to be normal individuals until the day they kill someone (often someone they know and care about; Buss, 2005).

We have a tendency to think of things such as marital conflict, marital infidelity, jealousy, and murder as abnormal situations. Evolutionary psychologists suggest instead that such behaviors are the result of natural adaptations. However, as noted above, these adaptations were appropriate for our ancient ancestors, and may not fit within our society today (murder is illegal). Yet, these behaviors and emotions are common, suggesting that we can't simply dismiss them. Since evolution typically takes a very long time, it is hard to say whether different adaptations will occur in the future of our species, given the cultural changes that have occurred through history. Perhaps the best we can hope for now is a continued development of our understanding of personality, through a variety of theoretical perspectives.

Connections Across Cultures: The Somatic Psychology of Wilhelm Reich

Wilhelm Reich (1897-1957) was a respected student and colleague of Sigmund Freud, a political activist, and eventually a convicted criminal in the United States whose books and journals were burned by the American government. But he left behind a legacy of focusing on the body and mind as deeply interrelated. In Germany in the 1930s, Reich devoted extraordinary effort to programs addressing sex education, sex hygiene, access to birth control, etc. He gave up his psychoanalytic practice, because he felt that sex education programs had the potential to be more helpful to more people by preventing sexual and psychological difficulties. Despite the so-called sexual revolution of the 1960s, many of these issues still plague society today. Reich's description of the phases involved in the experience of an organism (first studied in the 1920s and 1930s) anticipated the famous research of Masters and Johnson (1966), and incorporated a psychoanalytic view of mindsets occurring during sexual activity (Reich, 1973). His work on **somatic psychology** relates to physical approaches to psychotherapy that continue today. These contributions and controversies earned Reich a place in the marvelous history of the study of mental illness entitled *Masters of the Mind* (Millon, 2004).

Raised on a farm, Reich was interested in animal husbandry, and conducted extensive studies of animal sexual behavior. As a young child, he witnessed one of the family's maids having intercourse with her boyfriend. When he asked the maid if he could "play" the lover, she obliged. When he was 12 years old, he caught his mother having an affair with one of his tutors. In a classic example of the Oedipus complex, he considered using the information to blackmail his mother into allowing him to have sexual intercourse with her! Instead, he turned again to one of the family maids. He then told his father, whom Reich had witnessed beating his mother in the past, and shortly thereafter his mother committed suicide. For the rest of his life, Reich was tormented by the thought that he may have been responsible for his mother's death. His father died when Reich was 17 years old, and Reich took over the family farm until it was destroyed in World War I.

While attending medical school at the University of Vienna, Reich joined the Vienna Psychoanalytic Society, where he began studying with Sigmund Freud. Reich and Freud were deeply impressed with one another. Reich eventually held several important positions in Freud's training clinic, including Director of the Seminar for Psychoanalytic Therapy, and his work on character analysis was widely respected. Indeed, Reich was so involved with the society, Freud, and the clinic that many people thought of him as "Freud's pet" (Higgins, 1973; Sharaf, 1983).

However, Reich fell out of favor with the psychoanalytic society. In 1930, he moved to Germany, joined the communist party, and became active in a variety of sex education and sex hygiene programs.

But the communists opposed progressive sex education, because they hoped to gain the favor of the Catholic Church, in opposition to the growing threat of the Nazis. Reich stepped right into this dangerous controversy, often relating one particular story of how moved he was when a young pregnant girl sought his help, help she had not received from the Hitler Youth (Sharaf, 1983). In 1933, he published *The Mass Psychology of Fascism*, a book subsequently banned by the Nazis (Reich, 1933/1970). Eventually, Reich was excluded from both the Communist Party and the psychoanalytic society.

Reich left Germany for Denmark, and then moved to Norway, where his life and work began to take a strange turn. He became convinced that he had discovered a primordial cosmic energy, **orgone energy**, which provided the underlying energy for all life. He believed that orgone energy streams created hurricanes and galaxies. He built orgone energy accumulators, and began studying how it might be used for such diverse goals as treating cancer and controlling the weather. He was compelled to leave Norway, and in 1939 moved to the United States. Eventually, however, the U.S. Food and Drug Administration (FDA) sought an injunction in federal court to put an end to Reich's work on orgone energy. Reich refused to appear in court, and the injunction was issued in default (see Greenfield, 1974). Reich was accused and found guilty of criminal contempt, and sentenced to two years in federal prison. The FDA destroyed much of Reich's equipment, and burned tons of his papers and books. In 1957, Reich suffered a heart attack and died in the Federal Penitentiary at Lewisburg, Pennsylvania.

Somatic Psychology

Reich's psychoanalytic work emphasized three important topics: the intimate relationship between body and mind, the character of the individual, and the value of precise diagnosis. By the 1920s, Freud and his colleagues had stopped paying much attention to the concept of libido. In contrast, Reich became more and more interested in this sexual energy, which he associated directly with sexual activity. While working with his patients, Reich was impressed by their descriptions of feeling an "emptiness" in their genitals. This was an especially interesting point regarding women, since Reich himself considered the sexual inhibition experienced by many women as something appropriate to their development. However, as Reich pursued these ideas, he began to question the completeness and accuracy of Freud's theories. Reich developed what became known as the **orgasm theory**, and he proposed the concept of **orgastic potency**:

> Orgastic potency is the capacity to surrender to the streaming of biological energy, free of any inhibitions; the capacity to discharge completely the dammed-up sexual excitation through involuntary, pleasurable convulsions of the body… (pg. 29; Reich, 1973)

Reich considered the ability to enjoy sexual release as a critical aspect of normal and healthy personal development. This perspective demands a direct link between the body and the mind, since only through physical satisfaction can psychological and emotional satisfaction be achieved. When discussing neurotic symptoms, he described orgastic impotence as the "somatic core of the neurosis…" (Reich, 1933/1972). To further emphasize the point, Reich did not merely consider the *ability* to have meaningful sexual relations as important, he believed that they needed regular satisfaction:

> …I maintain that every person who has succeeded in preserving a certain amount of naturalness knows that those who are psychically ill need but one thing - complete and repeated sexual gratification… (pp. 23; Reich, 1973)

Reich's most widely respected work within the psychoanalytic community centered on character analysis, in which he emphasized **character armoring** and **character resistance**. Both of these constructs can be viewed as defense mechanisms, but they are deep and secondary fragmentations of the ego. Thus, they define the very character of the patient, and must be removed before traditional psychoanalysis can be effective. In keeping with the term somatic psychology, Reich addressed the physical manifestation of character armoring as **muscular armor**. Individuals who are actively character armoring demonstrate what Reich described as a chronic, frozen, muscular-like bearing. He believed that the visible muscular rigidity was the natural consequence of inhibiting aggression, and that it could be understood on the basis of only one principle: "the armoring of the periphery of the biopsychic system" (Reich, 1933/1972). In other words, the body physically responds to what the mind is doing; if the mind is defending itself, the body prepares to defend itself. This muscular tension is by no means easy to remove. If the analyst tries to get the patient to relax, the muscular tension is replaced by restlessness. Based on his theories, Reich described two basic types of character: the **genital character** and the **neurotic character**. The genital character refers to individuals who are relatively healthy in terms of their psychological development, and their capacity to enjoy life is uninhibited. The neurotic character is governed by rigid armor of both body and mind.

Many psychologists and a variety of practitioners in other areas have made the connection between body and mind an important part of their studies and their lifestyle. For example, we often "talk" with our hands (Goldin-Meadow, 2006), forced stereotypic movement leads to stereotypic thoughts about others (Mussweiler, 2006), young infants integrate their body movement and their attention (Robertson, Bacher, & Huntington, 2001), physical movement is more important than visual information for effective navigation (Ruddle & Lessels, 2006), and members of different cultures actually perceive the physical environment in different ways (Miyamoto, Nisbett, & Masuda, 2006). Yoga has become very popular in the United States, particularly the physical aspect of Hatha Yoga, and Yoga practitioners talk about understanding and respecting the body (e.g., Scaravelli, 1991; Stewart, 1994). This is particularly true as we age, since "we all die sooner or later, but what we must do is not allow the body to degenerate while living" (Scaravelli, 1991).

Reich referred to a "genetic differentiation of character types" and the "genetic-dynamic theory of the character" long before other psychologists were talking about the heritability of personality or gene-environment interactions. Reich went on to say that the social and economic/political factors that play such an important cultural role in personality development would not be as influential as they are if not for the likelihood that they "must first have impinged upon and changed human needs before these transformed drives and needs could begin to have an effect as historical factors" (Reich, 1932/1972). This sounds very much like sociobiology: the selection of behaviors, behaviors that are determined genetically, as adaptable to the relevant human condition. If indeed this idea does reflect the same basic premise as sociobiology, then Reich was thinking about a new field of research into human behavior that was still over 40 years in the future. In his discussion of muscular armor, Reich referred to three primary emotions that influence human behavior: sexuality, anxiety, and anger or hate (Reich, 1932/1972). Gotama Buddha (who most people think of as *the* Buddha) described three root causes of human suffering: desire, delusion, and hatred. What is sexuality but the greatest desire in human life? According to sociobiologists, particularly Dawkins (1976), life is about ensuring the propagation of individual genes, and in our case that means sexual reproduction. In addition, both Reich and the Buddha acknowledged hatred as key, and Buddhists typically see hatred as the antithesis of desire. Thus, Wilhelm Reich, once regarded as Freud's "pet," had incorporated both ancient Eastern philosophies and the as-yet unknown field of sociobiology into a cohesive theory of human character, while still in his mid-thirties. One can only imagine what he might have accomplished had he not pursued the odd theory of orgone energy, which led to his being ostracized and, ultimately, to the federal prison where he died.

Discussion Question: Wilhelm Reich believed that an active and uninhibited sexual life was essential for healthy development. He also believed that one's ability to experience that healthy sexuality, their orgastic potency, was in important measure of psychological health. Do you agree with this perspective, and do you think society agrees with this perspective?

Ancient and Modern Approaches to Training the Mind/Body Connection

Wilhelm Reich was by no means the first person to consider the connection between the body and the mind as something of essential importance to understanding the nature of the human experience. Gotama Buddha had developed just such a system approximately 500 years B.C. (see Chapter 17 for a more detailed discussion of Buddhism). The Buddha did more, however, than simply describe the nature of the human mind. He offered a few ways to begin quieting the mind, so that one could become a more peaceful, aware, and content individual. In the following section, we will consider his four techniques of **mindfulness meditation**.

Buddhism and Mindfulness

Andrew Olendzki (2003, 2005), a scholar of early Buddhist tradition and executive director of the Barre Center for Buddhist Studies in Massachusetts, has done a marvelous job of trying to put the teachings of the Buddha into a perspective understandable to Western psychologists. In *very* simple terms covering only a small part of what the Buddha taught, when a sense object that we are capable of detecting is, indeed, detected by one of our sensory systems, we become aware of the experience. For example, when a sound is detected by our ear, we become aware of hearing a sound. Consciousness is an emergent phenomenon of each of these individual moments of **contact**, i.e., the moment of contact between the sense object, the sensory organ, and the awareness of the object. Since we are constantly encountering different moments of contact that arise and then fall out of consciousness, from all of our various senses, the Buddhist concept of consciousness is not a continuous one (this is in contrast to the stream of consciousness perspective of America's preeminent psychologist William James). Since consciousness is not continuous, neither is the self. Our sense of self as continuous and real is an illusion, and it is because we cling to that illusion that we inevitably suffer (the first noble truth in Buddhism). In order to alleviate our suffering, and to understand the true nature of our self, the Buddha taught a series of mindfulness meditations to help us see ourselves as we really are.

There are **four mindfulness trainings: mindfulness of body, mindfulness of feeling, mindfulness of mind**, and **mindfulness of mental objects** (Olendzki, 2005; Thanissaro Bhikkhu, 1996). When meditating mindfully on the body, it is common to focus on the breath. This can be done in a variety of positions: sitting, standing, lying down, or walking. One can also become very mindful of the body by performing certain **martial arts** as moving meditation, particularly **Tai Chi Chuan** or **Qigong** (Khor, 1981). When meditating mindfully on feelings, one considers the pleasant or unpleasant quality of each experience. For example, after sitting for a while, pain or discomfort may arise in a knee or hip. There is nothing wrong with this pain, and with practice one can experience it as a sensation without the negative or unpleasant feeling that we describe as pain. This is, of course, not easy. All forms of meditation require time and practice. Still, it is important to remember that if there is a real problem, such sitting on a sharp rock, you may want to move in a slow and mindful manner until comfortable again. When meditating mindfully on the mind itself, one takes notice of the thoughts arising during meditation. One should pay particular attention to whether the thoughts are related to one of the three root causes of suffering: greed, hatred, or delusion.

> …In any given moment, the mind is either caught up by one or more of these or it is not, and this is something of which one can learn to be aware. Greed and hatred are the two polarities of desire, the intense wanting or not wanting of an object, while delusion is a strong form of the basic misunderstanding that gives desire its power over us. (pg. 255; Olendzki, 2005)

One does not pass judgment on these thoughts, mindfulness teaches us only to become aware of our thoughts and to recognize their presence and reality. Finally, there is mindfulness of mental objects (or mental qualities), a deep understanding of the content of mental experience that arises as one masters mindfulness meditation (Olendzki, 2005; Thanissaro Bhikkhu, 1996). Mindfulness of mental objects involves focusing on the nature of desires as they arise in relation to the five hindrances: desire, aversion, indolence, restlessness and doubt.

This conservative and traditional understanding of mindfulness may seem rather esoteric, but it is proving to be very influential in psychology today. To be sure, meditation has been described as "now one of the most enduring, widespread, and researched of all psychotherapeutic methods" (Walsh & Shapiro, 2006). A **mindfulness-based stress reduction** program has been developed and popularized by Jon Kabat-Zinn (1990,

1994, 2005), and a similar therapeutic technique, called **Focusing**, had previously been developed in the late 1970s (Gendlin, 1990). Mindfulness has also been incorporated into psychotherapeutic approaches to dealing with anxiety, depression, and feelings of unworthiness and insecurity (Brach, 2003; Brantley, 2003; McQuaid & Carmona, 2004), and it has provided new perspectives on the treatment of addiction and anger issues (Aronson, 2004; Dudley-Grant, 2003). Of particular interest to students, mindfulness has proven to be helpful in alleviating the stress associated with studying psychology in graduate school (Borynski, 2003)! In addition, Janet Surrey, one of the founding members of the Stone Center group, has studied comparisons between mindfulness and relational therapy (Surrey, 2005). Likewise, Trudy Goodman, who studied with Jean Piaget and now also teaches insight meditation, has utilized mindfulness in therapy with children (Goodman, 2005).

This traditional approach to mindfulness is usually associated with Southeast Asia, particularly the Thai forest monks. Jack Kornfield, a former Buddhist monk and currently a clinical psychologist, practiced with the renowned Ajahn Chah. Ajahn Chah's teachings have been translated into English (Ajahn Chah, 2001), and another of his students has written two books in English (Ajahn Sumedho, 1987; 1995). Thanissaro Bhikku is another interesting individual dedicated to offering the teachings of the Buddha, known as the Dhamma. In conjunction with Dhamma Dana Publications, he has written his own book (Thanissaro Bhikkhu, 1993), translated the works of Buddhist monks and nuns (Ajaan Fuang Jotiko, 2005; Upasika Kee Nanayon, 1995), and translated with commentary some of the Pali Canon, the first written record of the teachings of the Buddha (Thanissaro Bhikkhu, 1996). Dhamma Dana Publications is committed to the free dissemination of these teachings and their books, sending many copies to people in prison who wish to better their lives. This is, of course, an active application of the Buddha's teachings, and a way to help improve our society.

Discussion Question: The Buddha proposed a method for alleviating the suffering associated with our desires and distresses: the four mindfulness trainings. Have you ever tried meditating, particularly the form of mindfulness meditation taught in the Theravadan tradition? Has it been helpful, or if you haven't tried it, do you think it might be helpful?

The Neurobiology of Mindfulness

We began this chapter by looking at genetics and biology. We then transitioned into Buddhist mindfulness techniques that are thousands of years old. Today, these two disciplines have come together in some fascinating research. Neurobiologists and psychologists are working together with advanced meditators and respected Buddhist monks (including His Holiness the Dalai Lama) to study the activity of the brain, in real time, during meditation. These studies may also help to advance our understanding of the nature of the mind, but that may still be somewhat beyond our technical abilities. The interest of the field of psychology, and academia in general, is clearly evidenced by articles that have been written about these studies in venues such as the prestigious journal *Science* (Barinaga, 2003), the popular *The Chronicle of Higher Education* (Monastersky, 2006), and the *Monitor on Psychology* published by the American Psychological Association (Winerman, 2006).

Cognitive neuroscience has taken advantage of many technical advances in brain imaging, such as **functional magnetic resonance imaging (fMRI)**, **single photon emission computed tomography (SPECT)**, and **positron emission tomography (PET)** to study the activity of the brain during mental tasks. Initially, these studies focused on identifying brain regions involved in very specific tasks. More recently, however, some investigators have become interested in using these techniques to study broad questions, such as the nature of the mind. Since we don't know what the nature of the mind is, we don't exactly know what to look for in these brain imaging studies. So, the investigators pursuing this research must creatively examine the brain during meditation (as well as under other conditions). It has been shown that meditation activates neural structures involved in attention and arousal (Lazar et al., 2000, 2005a; Newberg, 2001), alterations in sensory processing and the sense of space (Lazar, 2005a; Newberg, 2001), and a dramatic increase in synchronization of neural activity (Lutz et al., 2004). In perhaps the most striking of these studies, Lazar and her colleagues have demonstrated that long-term meditation practice is associated with increased cortical thickness in brain regions associated with attention and sensory processing (Lazar, 2005a). These effects were most pronounced in the older subjects, suggesting that meditation may have beneficial effects in terms of offsetting age-related declines in cortical thickness. Given these dramatic changes in brain function as a result of meditation, perhaps it should come as no surprise that meditation and mindfulness have proven to be useful adjuncts to therapy for a wide variety of psychological and medical disorders (for reviews see Lazar, 2005b and Newberg & Lee, 2005; see also Cozolino, 2002; Germer et al., 2005; Siegel, 2007).

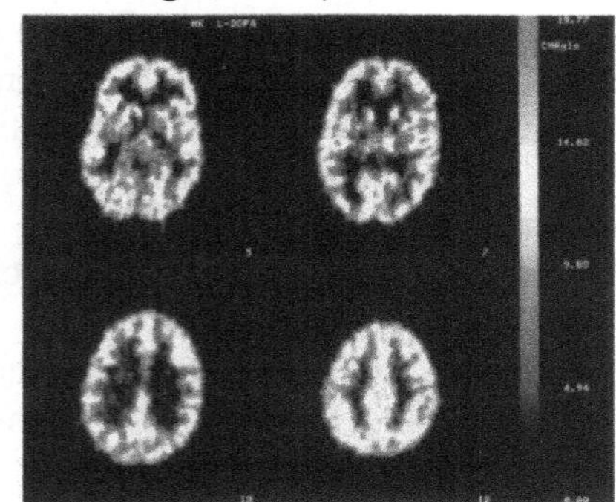

PET scan images of the author's brain on the anti-Parkinson's Disease drug l-DOPA (for research). [Image by Mark Kelland]

The use of these brain imaging techniques to study the mind during meditation raises the possibility that they may be useful in studying other altered states of consciousness. Indeed, Amir Raz and his colleagues (2005) have utilized fMRI and electrical scalp recording of **event-related potentials** to demonstrate that **hypnotic suggestion** reduces the activity of cortical regions in the brain that have been associated with conflict monitoring. In other words, when hypnosis is used to alter the behavior and cognition of individuals, there are recognizable changes in brain function. When the study of hypnosis is combined with the data obtained on alterations in brain function during meditation and under the influence of mind-altering drugs (see Mathew, 2001), it seems clear that the mind, either in its normal state or in various altered states, is reflected in unique states of neural activity. We may be a long way from fully understanding the details of the relationship between the mind and neural activity, and there may indeed be more to the mind than simply the neural activity itself, but this is certainly a fascinating field of study on the nature of who we are as individuals.

Discussion Question: Cognitive neuroscientists have begun to identify changes in brain activity associated with meditation, and similar changes occur during hypnosis. What do you think this says about the mind?

Martial Arts

When we think of the martial arts, most of us think of East Asia. The different forms are typically associated with the countries where they developed: **Kung Fu** in China, **Taekwondo** in Korea, and **Karate** and **Judo** in Japan. Actually, Karate was developed on the island of Okinawa, and, although it is part of Japan today, its martial arts history has been influenced more by Chinese settlers than by the Japanese (Chesterman, 2003; Hornsey, 2002; Johnson, 2003a; Lewis, 1993; Ribner & Chin, 1978). Today, however, the martial arts are popular worldwide. There are many forms in addition to those listed above, including **Capoeira**, a martial art developed in Brazil by African slaves (Atwood, 1999). Capoeira is a particularly complex martial art, involving play, dance, and music. As some slaves escaped, they banded together to fight Portuguese soldiers and help other slaves to escape. More recently, Capoeira was one of the inspirations for break dancing, an African American dance style that developed in the 1970s and 1980s (Atwood, 1999). Although the Western world certainly has its equivalent forms of armed and unarmed combat, such as wrestling, boxing, and fencing (e.g., see Styers, 1974), they are not typically thought of as belonging to the Asian forms of fighting known as the martial arts.

It is estimated that as many as 18 million people in America alone practice some form of the martial arts (Nathan, 2005), and martial arts films have proven very popular. From Bruce Lee to Jackie Chan, and more recently Chow Yun Fat (star of *Crouching Tiger, Hidden Dragon*, which won four Academy Awards [Lee, Ling, Schamus, & Jung, 2000]), we have seen examples of the classic good-guy, an honorable individual defending those who are abused by others. The famous American martial artist and movie star Chuck Norris, in cooperation with former President George H. W. Bush, has established a national program called KICKSTART to introduce martial arts to "at risk" middle school students to raise their self-esteem (Nathan, 2005). Although the martial arts are often seen as an opportunity for athletic young men to engage in disciplined and/or ritualized combat, there are also programs for children of all ages, general physical conditioning, and people with disabilities (Chaline, 2003; Johnson, 2003b; McNab, 2003). There is also a rich history of women practicing the martial arts (Atkinson, 1983; Chaline, 2003b). Indeed, Bruce Lee first studied the Wing Chun style of Kung Fu, a style developed some 400 years ago by a Buddhist nun named Ng Mui and her student Yim Wing Chun, who was also a nun. It was later that Lee developed his own technique, known as Jeet Kune Do or "the way of the intercepting fist" (Lee, 1975; see also Johnson, 2003a; Lewis, 1993; Little, 1998; Ribner & Chin, 1978).

What sets the martial arts apart is the balanced approach to both physical exercise and spiritual/mental discipline. Although the martial arts certainly existed farther back in ancient times, it is accepted by many that they were first formalized in the **Shao-Lin temple** by the founder of Zen Buddhism, Bodhidharma. When Bodhidharma first arrived at the Shao-Lin temple in China, after leaving his home in India, he found the monks in very poor physical condition. He developed a series of eighteen exercises that helped the monks to achieve a good level of physical fitness, something necessary for their self-defense as well as for extended periods of sitting in meditation (Johnson, 2003a; Lewis, 1993; Red Pine, 1987; Ribner & Chin, 1978). These exercises established the first formal practice of Kung Fu. It is important to note the role of Bodhidharma, a highly spiritual monk who had left his home to help spread the teachings of the Buddha. Since one of the basic tenets of Buddhism is to not harm any other living being, the martial arts have always emphasized mental discipline and the intention that the fighting skills should only be used in self-defense or in the defense of others who cannot defend themselves. Non-combative forms of the martial arts have developed around the concept of mindfulness of the body, which can be used as forms of moving meditation. Examples of such forms are Tai Chi Chuan and Qigong (Johnson, 2003a,c; Lewis, 1993; Khor, 1981; Ribner & Chin, 1978). There are also more traditional forms of martial arts, such as **Aikido** and **Hapkido** (Hapkido being "the way of harmony"; Chesterman, 2003), which emphasize the soft style of defending oneself that is advocated in the *Tao Te Ching* (Lao Tsu, c600 B.C./1989). As with the regular martial arts, these soft, meditative, defensive martial arts originated in the countries with the strongest histories in the more aggressive forms: Tai Chi Chuan and Qigong originated in China, Aikido in Japan, and Hapkido in Korea.

Samuel demonstrating an excellent side kick on the way to earning his black belt in Taekwondo. [Image by Mark Kelland]

When the martial arts are approached properly, as a means to health, strength, and a calm state of mind, we can refer to the practice as the **martial Way**, a means to living one's life in a virtuous manner (Chu, 2003). Because martial arts training can prepare one to injure others it must be approached with the right attitude:

> This concept of power as the cornerstone of personal freedom lies at the bottom of all martial arts philosophy. The recognition that power emanates from physical force and martial capability cuts both ways; it can be channeled toward constructive uses or abused as a means of destruction. This is the reason why martial arts training must always be directed toward the cultivation of the higher ideals of discipline, humility, benevolence and responsibility. (pg. 29; Chu, 2003)

Continuing to emphasize the role that the martial arts can play in helping people to live a more satisfying life, Chu goes on to say:

> The demands of work, family, finances, as well as fatigue, neglect and health all distract the martial artist from his best intentions. Even the devoted student may be disappointed if he expects martial arts training to neatly bring his physical and spiritual condition into working order. Nevertheless, regular training can serve as a constant, to discipline him to develop his best self even as the daily routine pulls him in different directions. The strategies underlying training can be effectively applied not just in life threatening situations but to daily life. (pgs. 44-45; Chu, 2003)

In order to help martial artists pursue and maintain this virtuous Way, various codes and tenets have been devised. My family practices Taekwondo, so we have been taught to follow the **five tenets of Taekwondo**: courtesy, integrity, perseverance, self-control, and indomitable spirit. These principles were set forth by General Choi Hong Hi, who re-established the modern forms of Taekwondo when Korea regained its independence after World War II. He believed that if Taekwondo students lived their lives according to these principles they would become better people and help to make the world a better place (Chesterman, 2003; Lewis, 1993). Perhaps the most famous of the martial arts codes is the **Bushido code** of the Japanese **Samurai**. It can sometimes be difficult to translate Asian languages into English, but generally the Bushido code contains seven essential principles: making right decisions, bravery, compassion, taking right actions, honesty, honor, and loyalty. Although these principles seem to include states of mind, or conscious intentions, it is through the physical practice, through the body and the unconscious mind, that Bushido becomes a way of life (Deshimaru, 1982). Only after many years of practice does this become a natural way of life, without the need for continued attention to one's practice. Then many more years of practice are necessary before one finally becomes a true master. The consciousness, or mindfulness, necessary for this combined practice of body and mind can be found in Zen Buddhism, which is closely intertwined with **Budo**, the Japanese way of the warrior (Deshimaru, 1982). As with the tenets of Taekwondo, the principles of the Bushido code helped warriors to restrain themselves from violent aggression in their daily lives (Chu, 2003). According to Chu (2003), it is the higher ideals of spirituality in codes like Bushido and the tenets of Taekwondo that separates the warrior from the predator.

Despite having emphasized the balance between physical and spiritual aspects of the martial arts, we must still consider that they can play a most important role in self-defense. It is an unfortunate reality that there are many people in this world who don't follow virtuous principles such as the tenets of Taekwondo or the Bushido code. I am fortunate to know a martial artist and special education teacher named David Schied, who wrote a most interesting book combining martial arts, Eastern philosophy, and basic techniques of self-defense in all aspects of one's life (Schied, 1986). Many people live timid lives, some live in outright fear. It has been suggested that as many as 160,000 children miss school every day out of fear that they will be bullied by other students (Nathan, 2005). This fear can seriously disrupt our ability to function in our daily world:

> Most of us don't see ourselves as unified human beings (people who can call forth all our resources and use our total capabilities at will). We tend not to give our all to the situation at hand (even when nothing less will do). Instead of giving our best we give "enough" which rarely is enough. Left to our own means most of us respond to life's demands in a fragmented fashion. Instead of reacting to the challenges of everyday life by focusing and directing our energies to the task at hand, we respond haphazardly and incompletely. (pg. iv; Schied, 1986)

By studying the martial arts and other techniques of self-defense and security, and by learning strategies to become aware of and deal with our emotional responses to danger, we can not only resolve our fears in those dangerous situations, but we can also remain calm and in control of other aspects or our lives (Schied, 1986). In addition to simply preparing for danger by learning how to avoid it or how to fight when one can't avoid it, the age-old Eastern techniques of meditation and mindfulness can help to calm one's nerves before, during, and after facing a crisis. As peace of mind becomes your usual emotional state, you become more open to living your own life and enjoying your relationships with others in a loving and compassionate way. Then, when faced with danger from another:

> The opening of yourself to life with love will enable you not only to take proper measures for the extension of your life (surviving) in an attack, but also to greet your attacker as everyone else you meet - with an open hand and an open mind. You will begin to see an infinite number of ways to share love with those who mean you bodily harm. By giving to another that love which is so plentiful within you, you will help instead of hurt him. *This is the ultimate self-defense.* (pg. 208; Schied, 1986)

Discussion Question: The martial Way refers to integrating the physical, spiritual, and mental aspects of the martial arts into your daily life. Have you ever practiced a martial art? If yes, how seriously did you take the spiritual philosophy of your particular martial art or the martial arts in general?

Final Note

This chapter may seem to have an odd assortment of topics, but if we look closely we can better understand the meaningful connections. We have covered: 2,500 year-old Buddhist teachings on mindfulness, 1,500 year-old techniques in the martial arts, 100-year-old Victorian era theories on somatic psychology, recent theories in sociobiology and evolutionary psychology, and cutting-edge brain imaging of real-time changes in mental states! How can all of this possibly fit together? The answer is actually quite simple. For as long as people have been able to wonder, they have wondered about the two things in our lives that cannot be denied: the fact that we have a body, and the fact that we are aware of it. Conscious awareness of our own existence, and the body that is the physical manifestation of that existence, is something that all people, all races and all nationalities, have shared throughout time. These topics are the most thoroughly cross-cultural topics in psychology.

Finally, when Bruce Lee's famous movie *Enter the Dragon* was first released in the United States, they cut one of the opening scenes in which he is tested by his master on his understanding of fundamental Buddhist/Daoist philosophy as it pertains to the martial arts. In the twenty-fifth anniversary special edition, Warner Brothers studios apparently decided that American audiences would now appreciate this dialogue, so they put the scene back into the movie (Clouse & Allin, 1998).

Personality Theory in Real Life: An Evolutionary Perspective on the Development of Pathological Personality Patterns

In the Appendix, there is a brief presentation of Theodore Millon's alternative classification scheme for personality disorders, as compared to the DSM-V (Millon, 1996; Millon & Grossman, 2005). This perspective is based on Millon's belief that personality disorders represent patterns of thought and behavior that are adaptive, albeit under abnormal conditions, and therefore have been selected for through the process of evolution. Millon believes that it is necessary for psychology to draw upon related fields of science in order to strengthen the entire discipline:

> Much of psychology as a whole remains adrift, divorced from broader spheres of scientific knowledge, isolated from deeper and more fundamental, if not universal, principles…we have failed to draw on the rich possibilities that may be found in both historic and adjacent realms of scholarly pursuit. (pg. 333; Millon & Grossman, 2005)

Millon and Grossman acknowledge the contributions of sociobiology to our understanding of human behavior, and they offer a sociobiological perspective on personality. Personality, they argue, can be thought of as the distinctive style of adaptive functioning that an individual exhibits as they relate to their typical range of environments. Personality development is healthy when the individual encounters average or relatively normal environments and is effective in adapting to them. Personality disorders arise when the individual relies on maladaptive functioning that can be traced to psychic deficiencies, trait imbalances, or internal conflicts that occur when relating to their environment. In other words, when individuals adapt to abnormal environments (e.g., an abusive home), their personality style may then prove to be maladaptive in situations outside of their typical environment.

Millon proposes that every person, indeed every organism, must accomplish four basic goals, each of which has two polarities: they must exist (seek pleasure and avoid pain), they must adapt (respond actively or remain passive), they must reproduce (focus on self or focus on others), and they must deal with unexpected or abstract situations (rely on thinking or react to feelings). These four demands correspond to four neurodevelopmental stages: sensory attachment associated with life enhancement (seeking pleasure) or life preservation (avoiding pain), sensorimotor autonomy associated with modifying the environment (active) or accommodating to the environment (passive), pubertal genital identity associated with propagating oneself (self-oriented) or nurturing children (other-oriented), and finally intracortical integration associated with intellect (thinking-oriented) or emotion (feeling-oriented). It should be clear that these stages cover the range of development from birth to young adulthood. In contrast to theories that focus on critical points in development as key times when psychological problems occur:

> …the *quality* or *kind of stimulation* the youngster experiences is often of greater importance. The impact of parental harshness or inconsistency, of sibling rivalry or social failure, is more than a matter of stimulus volume and timing. Different dimensions of experience take precedence as the meaning conveyed by the source of stimulation becomes clear to the growing child. (pg. 361; Millon & Grossman, 2005)

While it is difficult to clearly define what constitutes normal vs. abnormal personalities, in simple terms individuals who are relatively normal are able to shift between and balance the demands of each of these polarities as appropriate to the situations they encounter. When examining individuals with pathological personality patterns (a term preferred by Millon & Grossman, since personality *disorder* implies a medical condition that might be cured), their behavioral constraints arise primarily from within themselves, due to the abnormal conditions in which they developed. The traits associated with these abnormal personality patterns take on an inner momentum and autonomy, so they are expressed regardless of the external situation. In other words, individuals with pathological personality patterns are not able to appropriately adapt their behaviors to different situations in which they find themselves.

The following is a description of one abnormal personality type, the self-defeating (masochistic) personality:

> This disorder stems largely from a reversal of the pain-pleasure polarity. These persons interpret events and engage in relationships in a manner that is not only at variance with this deeply rooted polarity but is contrary to the associations these life-promoting emotions usually acquire through learning. To the self-defeating personality, pain may be a preferred experience, tolerantly accepted if not encouraged in intimate relationships. It is often intensified by purposeful self-denial, and blame acceptance may be aggravated by acts that engender difficulties as well as by thoughts that exaggerate past misfortunes and anticipate future ones. (pp. 376-377; Millon & Grossman, 2005)

As strange as this condition seems, how might it arise? How does a person develop an adaptive strategy that seeks pain, and how can such a strategy actually be adaptive? Imagine an abused child, whose only source of love is the parents who abuse them! In such a terrible situation, the best strategy for the child to adapt might be to reverse the pleasure-pain polarity. This is clearly an extreme response, but one that might make the child's world easier to endure and less likely to create further abuse. However, when the child grows up and moves on to other relationships, the deeply embedded characteristics of this pathological personality pattern make healthy relationships all but impossible. An important point to make here is that the term adaptive is not always synonymous with our ideas of good psychological health. Adaptation can only be considered within its particular context. And that is exactly the consideration that Millon proposes in his evolutionary perspective on personality development. Each person develops adaptively to their own environment, and as a result they establish persistent characteristics (personality patterns) along the polarities of pain-pleasure, active-passive, self-other, and thinking-feeling. Whether these adaptations are healthy or unhealthy is a matter to be determined after the fact. However, by recognizing how they develop, as psychologists we can attempt to educate others on how to avoid causing these conditions.

Review of Key Points

- Twin studies, adoption studies, and family studies allow us to examine the heritability of personality traits. Identical twins share 100 percent of the genetic material, and siblings raised in different families following adoption allow for an ideal comparison between genetic and environmental factors.

Biology and Personality; Sociobiology; Mindfulness and the Martial Arts

- As important as genetics are, the environment also plays a significant role in development. Studies on intelligence have shown a strong degree of heritability, but culture also makes a significant contribution.
- Behavior genetics is the term used for the study of the influence of genetics on behavior. Kagan has demonstrated that temperament, the emotional component of personality, appears to be the most salient of inborn characteristics. According to Kagan, approximately 10 percent of children are naturally inhibited, whereas approximately 20 percent of children are naturally more outgoing and adventurous.
- Studies on the heritability of personality traits consistently show that genetics is responsible for approximately 50 percent of the nature of our personality. Genetic factors also play a role in a wide variety of other psychological factors, such as attitudes, interests, and psychological disorders.
- Current studies on the role of genetics in personality tend to focus on gene-environment interactions. Kagan's research has identified the amygdala, and its role in emotional reactivity to novel situations, as an important neurological structure in the development of a behavioral inhibition system in some people.
- Sociobiology examines the role of evolution in the behavior of humans. Sociobiologists focus on inclusive fitness, the advantage that a given behavior confers on the likelihood of specific genes being passed on to an individual's offspring or the offspring of their close kin.
- Sociobiology allows for new perspectives on behavior that might otherwise seem illogical or, at least, difficult to explain. Patterns of mate selection, parenting and grandparenting, and religion all offer biological advantages when viewed from this perspective.
- Evolutionary psychology is the field of study in which sociobiology is specifically applied to psychology.
- Richard Dawkins has suggested that cultural units, which he calls memes, are subject to the same rules of evolution as are genes. The transmission of these cultural units may play a critical role in the development of individuals and the human species as a whole.
- Evolutionary psychology is the specific application of sociobiology to the field of psychology.
- Reich's somatic psychology is focused on the intimate interrelationship between the body and the mind. He believed that psychological health required the fulfillment and release of biological energy through the orgasm. Reich also described the physical presentation of individuals demonstrating muscular armoring, which he considered to be the natural consequence of inhibiting aggression.
- The Buddha described consciousness as arising from moments of contact, the contact between a sense object (stimulus), a sense organ, and awareness of the object.
- Being mindful of these moments of contact involves practicing the four mindfulness trainings: mindfulness of body, mindfulness of feeling, mindfulness of mind, and mindfulness of mental objects.
- Mindfulness training has had a significant impact on Western psychology. Examples include the influential mindfulness-based stress reduction program developed by Jon Kabat-Zinn and Focusing. Mindfulness training has also been extended to working with children and to relational-cultural therapy.
- Cognitive neuroscientists are beginning to demonstrate changes in brain function as a result of deep meditation. Similar changes occur during hypnosis, suggesting the possibility of some inherent function for altered states of consciousness.
- The martial arts provide methods for training the body and mind together. The first formal martial arts program appears to have been developed by the founder of Zen Buddhism, Bodhidharma. He intended to help the monks at the Shao-Lin temple keep their bodies fit as they devoted their lives to meditation. These concepts of keeping body and mind fit together leads to a lifestyle that can be called the martial Way.
- The martial arts include guidelines for balancing physical discipline with spiritual/mental discipline. Examples of these guidelines include the five tenets of Taekwondo and the Bushido code of the Samurai warriors.

Review of Key Terms

adoption studies Aikido amygdala behavior genetics	functional magnetic resonance imaging (fMRI) gene-environment	mindfulness of body mindfulness of feeling mindfulness of mental objects

behavioral inhibition system	interactions	mindfulness of mind
Budo	genital character	muscular armor
Bushido Code	Hapkido	neurotic character
Capoeira	heritability	orgasm theory
character armoring	high reactive infants	orgastic potency
character resistance	hypnotic suggestion	orgone energy
cognitive neuroscience	inclusive fitness	positron emission tomography (PET)
contact	Judo	Qigong
ethology	Karate	Samurai
eugenics	kin	Shao-Lin Temple
event-related potentials	Kung Fu	single photon emission computed tomography (SPECT)
evolutionary psychology	low reactive infants	sociobiology
family studies	martial arts	somatic psychology
Five Tenets of Taekwondo	Martial Way	Taekwondo
Focusing	memes	Tai Chi Chuan
four mindfulness trainings	mindfulness	temperament
	Mindfulness-Based Stress Reduction	twin studies
	mindfulness meditation	

Annotated Bibliography

Kagan, J. (1994). *Galen's prophecy: Temperament in human nature.* New York, NY: BasicBooks.

Jerome Kagan is a renowned psychologist who has focused his career on the heritability of personality traits. This book summarizes decades of research on the influence of temperament at birth on personality development into adulthood. However, Kagan does not believe that our inherited temperament determines who we become. Instead, he discusses the balance between temperament and environment, and how parents can influence the growth of their children.

Wilson, E. O. (1975). *Sociobiology: The new synthesis.* Cambridge, MA: The Belknap Press.
Dawkins, R. (1976). *The selfish gene.* New York, NY: Oxford University Press.
Barash, D. P. (1977). *Sociobiology and behavior.* New York, NY: Elsevier.

These three books provided the foundation for the field of sociobiology. Whereas the books by Dawkins and Barash are relatively short, Wilson's book is a tour de force that can keep the most avid reader busy for a quite while. Each of these books provides fascinating new insights into human behavior and how certain behavioral patterns and ways of thinking and feeling might actually have been selected for during our genetic evolution. Dawkins, in particular, suggests that our evolution as a species is not likely over. Certain characteristics of culture seem to be as capable, if not more capable, of evolution as our genetic blueprints.

Barkow, J. H., Cosmides, L., & Tooby, J. (Eds.). (1992). *The adapted mind: Evolutionary psychology and the generation of culture.* New York, NY: Oxford University Press.
Buss, D. M. (1999). *Evolutionary psychology: The new science of the mind.* Boston, MA: Allyn and Bacon.

These two books present the foundation of evolutionary psychology. The book by Barkow et al. is a collection of chapters from the early leaders in this field (including Buss). Buss then prepared the first textbook on evolutionary psychology, making for an excellent and readable overview of this recent discipline.

Reich, W. (1933/1972). *Character Analysis, 3rd, Enlarged Edition*. New York, NY: Farrar, Straus and Giroux.
Higgins, M. B. (Ed.). (1973). *Wilhelm Reich selected writings: An introduction to orgonomy*. New York, NY: Farrar, Straus and Giroux.

Character Analysis was Wilhelm Reich's most important work in the field of psychoanalysis. Upon reading it, it is easy to see why Reich was held in such high regard early in his career. The collection edited by the executrix of Reich's estate, Mary Boyd Higgins, fills in the gaps, particularly with regard to Reich's early work on orgasm theory and orgastic potency.

Sharaf, M. (1983). *Fury on Earth: A biography of Wilhelm Reich*. New York, NY: Da Capo Press.

This is a well-written and engaging biography of Wilhelm Reich by someone who knew him personally and worked with him for about 10 years. Thanks to that personal relationship, Sharaf is able to provide fascinating insights into the remarkable man who was Wilhelm Reich.

Germer, C. K., Siegel, R. D., & Fulton, P. R. (Eds.). (2005). *Mindfulness and psychotherapy*. New York, NY: Guilford Press.

An excellent reference for relationships between Eastern and Western thought. In addition to material used in this chapter on the historical roots of mindfulness (Olendzki) and the neurobiology of mindfulness (Lazar), there is also valuable information on mindfulness and children, mindfulness and relational therapy, and positive psychology.

Ajahn Chah (2001). *Being Dharma: The essence of the Buddha's teachings*. Boston, MA: Shambhala.
Ajahn Sumedho (1987). *Mindfulness: The path to the deathless*. Hertfordshire, England: Amaravati Publications.
Ajahn Sumedho (1995). *The mind and the way: Buddhist reflections on life*. Boston, MA: Wisdom Publications.
Thanissaro Bhikkhu (1993). *The mind like fire unbound*. Barre, MA: Dhamma Dana Publications.

These books represent a wonderful collection of readings on the traditional teachings of the Buddha and mindfulness meditation. Ajahn Chah was a revered Buddhist monk in Thailand who influenced many notable Western students, including Ajahn Sumedho and Jack Kornfield. His book includes student questions and the insightful answers of this wonderful teacher. Ajahn Sumedho offers additional depth and insight to the teachings of his teacher and the Buddha. Thanissaro Bhikku also relies on traditional teachings of the Buddha in this marvelous description of the mind being like fire that cannot be extinguished.

Kabat-Zinn, J. (1990). *Full catastrophe living: Using the wisdom of your body and mind to face stress, pain, and illness*. New York, NY: Delta Trade Paperbooks.

This wonderful book stands out even among the others cited in this bibliography. Dr. Kabat-Zinn addresses an amazingly wide range of topics while writing in a casual and comfortable manner, offering many practical, real-life examples on how to apply mindfulness to the difficulties of our daily life. His program on mindful-based stress reduction has been very influential among clinical psychologists and other medical practitioners.

Chu, F. J. (2003). ***The martial Way and its virtues: Tao De Gung*****. Boston, MA: YMAA Publication Center.**
Schied, D. (1986). ***Streetwise: An introduction to self-defense*****. Los Angeles, CA: Peter Brooks.**

These two books combine the philosophy of the martial arts with the practicalities of living one's daily life. The book by Chu focuses on philosophy and spirituality, whereas as the book by Schied includes many illustrations of practical self-defense techniques (drawn by a professional sports illustrator). Mr. Schied has been working on a second edition to his book.

Clouse, R. (Director), & Allin, M. (Screenwriter). (1998). ***Enter the dragon*** **[25th Anniversary Special Edition Motion Picture]. United States: Warner Brothers.**
Lee, A. (Director), Ling, W. H., Schamus, J., & Jung, T. K. (Screenwriters). (2000). ***Crouching tiger, hidden dragon*** **[Motion Picture]. China: United China Vision & Columbia Pictures Film Production Asia.**

These are two of the greatest martial arts films ever made. *Enter the Dragon* was first released in the United States in 1973, and it made a star of Bruce Lee. *Crouching Tiger, Hidden Dragon*, a more recent film, won four Academy Awards. Both films do a marvelous job of portraying the honor and discipline of a true martial artist, while not shying away from the pain and misfortune that so often accompanies real life (indeed, always accompanies it according to Buddhists).

Lenzenweger, M. F. & Clarkin, J. F. (Eds.). (2005). ***Major theories of personality disorder, 2nd ed.*** **New York, NY: Guilford Press.**

This book contains the chapter by Millon and Grossman that was the primary source for the discussion of the evolutionary theory of personality disorders. This valuable and informative text also contains the psychoanalytic perspective of Kernberg and Caligor, the cognitive perspective of Pretzer and Beck, and the attachment perspective of Meyer and Pilkonis on personality disorders that we have reviewed earlier in this textbook.

Chapter 15 - Carl Rogers, Abraham Maslow, and Henry Murray

In contrast to both the often dark, subconscious emphasis of the psychodynamic theorists and the somewhat cold, calculated perspectives of behavioral/cognitive theorists, the humanistic psychologists focus on each individual's potential for personal growth and self-actualization. Carl Rogers was influenced by strong religious experiences (both in America and in China) and his early clinical career in a children's hospital. Consequently, he developed his therapeutic techniques and the accompanying theory in accordance with a positive and hopeful perspective. Rogers also focused on the unique characteristics and viewpoint of individuals.

Abraham Maslow is best known for his extensive studies on the most salient feature of the humanistic perspective: self-actualization. He is also the one who referred to humanistic psychology as the third force, after the psychodynamic and behavioral/cognitive perspectives, and he specifically addressed the need for psychology to move beyond its study of unhealthy individuals. He was also interested in the psychology of the work place, and his recognition in the business field has perhaps made him the most famous psychologist.

Henry Murray was an enigmatic figure, who seemingly failed to properly acknowledge the woman who inspired much of his work, and who believed his life had been something of a failure. Perhaps he felt remorse as a result of maintaining an extramarital affair with the aforementioned woman, thanks in large part to the advice and help of Carl Jung! Murray extended a primarily psychodynamic perspective to the study of human needs in normal individuals. His Thematic Apperception Test was one of the first psychological tests applied outside of a therapeutic setting, and it provided the basis for studying the need for achievement (something akin to a learned form of self-actualization).

Carl Rogers and Humanistic Psychology

Carl Rogers is the psychologist many people associate first with humanistic psychology, but he did not establish the field in the way that Freud established psychoanalysis. A few years older than Abraham Maslow, and having moved into clinical practice more directly, Rogers felt a need to develop a new theoretical perspective that fit with his clinical observations and personal beliefs. Thus, he was proposing a humanistic approach to psychology and, more specifically, psychotherapy before Maslow. It was Maslow, however, who used the term humanistic psychology as a direct contrast to behaviorism and psychoanalysis. And it was Maslow who contacted some friends, in 1954, in order to begin meetings that led to the creation of the American Association for Humanistic Psychology. Rogers was included in that group, but so were Erich Fromm and Karen Horney, both of whom had distinctly humanistic elements in their own theories, elements that shared a common connection to Alfred Adler's Individual Psychology (Stagner, 1988). In addition, the spiritual aspects of humanistic psychology, such as peak experiences and transcendence, have roots in the work of Carl Jung and William James, and go even further back in time to ancient philosophies of Yoga and Buddhism.

In at least one important way, Rogers' career was similar to that of Sigmund Freud. As he began his clinical career, he found that the techniques he had been taught were not very effective. So, he began experimenting with his own ideas, and developing his own therapeutic approach. As that approach developed, so did a unique theory of personality that aimed at explaining the effectiveness of the therapy. Rogers found it difficult to explain what he had learned, but he felt quite passionately about it:

> …the real meaning of a word can never be expressed in words, because the real meaning would be the thing itself. If one wishes to give such a real meaning he should put his hand over his mouth and *point*. This is what I should most like to do. I would willingly throw away all the words of this manuscript if I could, somehow, effectively *point* to the experience which is therapy. It is a process, a thing-in-itself, an experience, a relationship, a dynamic… (pp. ix; Rogers, 1951)

Brief Biography of Carl Rogers

Carl Ransom Rogers was born on January 8, 1902, in Chicago, Illinois. His parents were well-educated, and his father was a successful civil engineer. His parents loved their six children, of whom Rogers was the fourth, but they exerted a distinct control over them. They were fundamentalist Christians, who emphasized a close-knit family and constant, productive work, but approved of little else. The Rogers household expected standards of behavior appropriate for the 'elect' of God: there was no drinking of alcohol, no dancing, no visits to the theater, no card games, and little social life at all (DeCarvalho, 1991; Thorne, 2003).

Rogers was not the healthiest of children, and his family considered him to be overly sensitive. The more his family teased him, the more he retreated into a lonely world of fantasy. He sought consolation by reading books, and he was well above his grade level for reading when he began school. In 1914 the family moved to a large farm west of Chicago, a move motivated primarily by a desire to keep the children away from the temptations of suburban city life. The result was even more isolation for Rogers, who lamented that he'd only had two dates by the end of high school. He continued to learn, however, becoming something of an expert on the large moths that lived in the area. In addition, his father encouraged the children to develop their own ventures, and Rogers and his brothers raised a variety of livestock. Given these interests, and in keeping with family tradition, Rogers enrolled in the University of Wisconsin-Madison to study scientific agriculture (DeCarvalho, 1991; Thorne, 2003).

During his first year of college, Rogers attended a Sunday morning group of students led by Professor George Humphrey. Professor Humphrey was a facilitative leader, who refused to be conventional and who encouraged the students to make their own decisions. Rogers found the intellectual freedom very stimulating, and he also began to make close friends. This increased intellectual and emotional energy led Rogers to re-examine his commitment to Christianity. Given his strong religious faith, he decided to change his major to history, in anticipation of a career as a Christian minister. He was fortunate to be chosen as one of only twelve students from America to attend a World Student Christian Federation conference in Peking, China. He traveled throughout China (also visiting Korea, Hong Kong, Japan, the Philippines, and Hawaii) for 6 months, surrounded by other intelligent and creative young people. He kept a detailed journal, and wrote lengthy letters to his family and Helen Elliott, a childhood friend whom he considered to be his "sweetheart." His mind was stretched in all directions by this profound cross-cultural experience, and the intellectual and spiritual freedom he was embracing blinded him to the fact that his fundamentalist family was deeply disturbed by what he had to say. However, by the time Rogers was aware of his family's disapproval, he had been changed, and he believed that people of very different cultures and faiths can all be sincere and honest (Kirschenbaum, 1995; Thorne, 2003). As a curious side note, Rogers' roommate on the trip was a Black seminary professor. Rogers was vaguely aware that it was strange at that time for a Black man and a White man to room together, but he was particularly surprised at the stares they received from the Chinese people they met, who had never seen a Black person before (Rogers & Russell, 2002). After his return from China, Rogers graduated from college, and 2 months later he married Helen. Again his family disapproved, believing that the young couple should be more established first. But Rogers had been accepted to the Union Theological Seminary in New York City, and both he and Helen wanted to be together. His family may have wanted them to wait because Union Theological Seminary was, perhaps, the most liberal seminary in America at the time (DeCarvalho, 1991; Rogers & Russell, 2002; Thorne, 2003).

Rogers spent 2 years at the seminary, including a summer assignment as the pastor of a small church in Vermont. However, his desire not to impose his own beliefs on others, made it difficult for him to preach. He began taking courses at nearby Teachers' College of Columbia University, where he learned about clinical and educational psychology, as well as working with disturbed children. He then transferred to Teachers' College, and after writing a dissertation in which he developed a test for measuring personality adjustment in children, he earned his Ph.D. in Clinical Psychology. Then, in 1928, he began working at the Rochester Society for the Prevention of Cruelty to Children (DeCarvalho, 1991; Thorne, 2003).

Rogers was immersed in his work in Rochester for 12 years. He found that even the most elaborate theories made little sense when dealing with children who had suffered severe psychological damage after traveling through the courts and the social work systems. So Rogers developed his own approach, and did his best to help them. Many of his colleagues, including the director, had no particular therapeutic orientation:

> When I would try to see what I could do to alter their behavior, sometimes they would refuse to see me the next time. I'd have a hard time getting them to come from the detention home to my office, and that would cause me to think, "What is it that I did that offended the child?" Well, usually it was overinterpretation, or getting too smart in analyzing the causes of behavior...So we approached every situation with much more of a question of "What can we do to help?" rather than "What is the mysterious cause of this behavior?" or "What theory does the child fit into?" It was a very good place for learning in that it was easy to be open to experience,

and there was certainly no pressure to fit into any particular pattern of thought. (pg. 108; Rogers & Russell, 2002)

Eventually Rogers wrote a book outlining his work with children, *The Clinical Treatment of the Problem Child* (Rogers, 1939), which received excellent reviews. He was offered a professorship at Ohio State University. Beginning as a full professor gave Rogers a great deal of freedom, and he was frequently invited to give talks. It has been suggested that one such talk, in December 1940, at the University of Minnesota, entitled "Newer Concepts in Psychotherapy," was the official birthday of client-centered therapy. Very popular with his students, Rogers was not so welcome amongst his colleagues. Rogers believed that his work was particularly threatening to those colleagues who believed that only their own expertise could make psychotherapy effective. After only 4 years, during which he published *Counseling and Psychotherapy* (Rogers, 1942), Rogers moved on to the University of Chicago, where he established the counseling center, wrote *Client-Centered Therapy* (Rogers, 1951) and contributed several chapters to *Psychotherapy and Personality Change* (Rogers & Dymond, 1954), and in 1956 received a *Distinguished Scientific Contribution Award* from the American Psychological Association. Then, in 1957, he accepted a joint appointment in psychiatry and psychology at the University of Wisconsin to study psychotic individuals. Rogers had serious doubts about leaving Chicago, but felt that the joint appointment would allow him to make a dramatic contribution to psychotherapy. It was a serious mistake. He did not get along with his colleagues in the psychology department, whom he considered to be antagonistic, outdated, "rat-oriented," and distrustful of clinical psychology, and so he resigned. He kept his appointment in the psychiatry department, however, and in 1961 published perhaps his most influential book, *On Becoming a Person* (Rogers, 1961).

In 1963, Rogers moved to California to join the Western Behavioral Sciences Institute, at the invitation of one of his former students, Richard Farson. This was a non-profit institute dedicated to the study of humanistically-oriented interpersonal relations. Rogers was leery of making another major move, but eventually agreed. He became very active in research on encounter groups and educational theory. Five years later, when Farson left the institute, there was a change in its direction. Rogers was unhappy with the changes, so he joined some colleagues in leaving and establishing the Center for Studies of the Person, where he remained until his death. In his later years, Rogers wrote books on topics such as personal power and marriage (Rogers, 1972, 1977). In 1980, he published *A Way of Being* (Rogers, 1980), in which he changed the terminology of his perspective from "client-centered" to "person-centered." With the assistance of his daughter Natalie, who had studied with Abraham Maslow, he held many group workshops on life, family, business, education, and world peace. He traveled to regions where tension and danger were high, including Poland, Russia, South Africa, and Northern Ireland. In 1985 he brought together influential leaders of seventeen Central American countries for a peace conference in Austria. The day he died, February 4, 1987, without knowing it, he had just been nominated for the Nobel Peace Prize (DeCarvalho, 1991; Kirschenbaum, 1995; Thorne, 2003).

Placing Rogers in Context: A Psychology 2,600 Years in the Making

Carl Rogers was an extraordinary individual whose approach to psychology emphasized individuality. Raised with a strong Christian faith, exposed to Eastern culture and spirituality in college, and then employed as a therapist for children, he came to value and respect each person he met. Because of that respect for the ability of each person to grow, and the belief that we are innately driven toward actualization, Rogers began the distinctly humanistic approach to psychotherapy that became known as client-centered therapy.

Taken together, client-centered therapy and self-actualization offer a far more positive approach to fostering the growth of each person than most other disciplines in psychology. Unlike the existing approaches of psychoanalysis, which aimed to uncover problems from the past, or behavior therapies, which aimed to identify problem behaviors and control or "fix" them, client-centered therapy grew out of Rogers' simple desire to help his clients move forward in their lives. Indeed, he had been trained as a psychoanalyst, but Rogers found the techniques unsatisfying, both in their goals and their ability to help the children he was working with at the time. The seemingly hands-off approach of client-centered therapy fit well with a Taoist perspective, something Rogers had studied, discussed, and debated during his trip to China. In *A Way of Being*, Rogers (1980) quotes what he says is perhaps his favorite saying, one which sums up many of his deeper beliefs:

> If I keep from meddling with people, they take care of themselves,
> If I keep from commanding people, they behave themselves,
> If I keep from preaching at people, they improve themselves,
> If I keep from imposing on people, they become themselves.
>
> *Lao Tsu, c600 B.C.*; Note: This translation differs somewhat from the one cited in the References. I have included the translation Rogers quoted, since the difference likely influenced his impression of this saying.

Rogers, like Maslow, wanted to see psychology contribute far more to society than merely helping individuals with psychological distress. He extended his sincere desire to help people learn to really communicate, with empathic understanding, to efforts aimed at bringing peace to the world. On the day he died, he had just been nominated for the Nobel Peace Prize. Since a Nobel Prize cannot be awarded to someone who has died, he was not eligible to be nominated again. If he had lived a few more years, he may well have received that award. His later years were certainly committed to peace in a way that deserved such recognition.

Basic Concepts

Rogers believed that each of us lives in a constantly changing private world, which he called the **experiential field**. Everyone exists at the center of their own experiential field, and that field can only be fully understood from the perspective of the individual. This concept has a number of important implications. The individual's behavior must be understood as a reaction to their experience and perception of the field. They react to it as an organized whole, and it is their reality. The problem this presents for the therapist is that only the individual can really understand their experiential field. This is quite different than the Freudian perspective, in which only the trained and objective psychoanalyst can break through the defense mechanisms and understand the basis of the patient's unconscious impulses. One's perception of the experiential field is limited, however. Rogers believed that certain impulses, or sensations, can only enter into the conscious field of experience under certain circumstances. Thus, the experiential field is not a true reality, but rather an individual's potential reality (Rogers, 1951).

The one basic tendency and striving of the individual is to actualize, maintain, and enhance the experiencing of the individual or, in other words, an **actualizing tendency**. Rogers borrowed the term **self-actualization**, a term first used by Kurt Goldstein, to describe this basic striving.

> The tendency of normal life is toward activity and progress. For the sick, the only form of self-actualization that remains is the maintenance of the existent state. That, however, is not the tendency of the normal...Under adequate conditions the normal organism seeks further activity. (pp. 162-163; Goldstein, 1934/1995).

For Rogers, self-actualization was a tendency to move forward, toward greater maturity and independence, or self-responsibility. This development occurs throughout life, both biologically (the differentiation of a fertilized egg into the many organ systems of the body) and psychologically (self-government, self-regulation, socialization, even to the point of choosing life goals). A key factor in understanding self-actualization is the experiential field. A person's needs are defined, as well as limited, by their own potential for experience. Part of this experiential field is an individual's emotions, feelings, and attitudes. Therefore, who the individual is, their actual **self**, is critical in determining the nature and course of their self-actualization (Rogers, 1951). We will examine Maslow's work on self-actualization in more detail below.

What then, is the self? In Rogers' (1951) initial description of his theory of personality, the experiential field is described in four points, the self-actualizing tendency in three points, and the remaining eleven points attempt to define the self. First and foremost, the self is a differentiated portion of the experiential field. In other words, the self is that part of our private world that we identify as "me," "myself," or "I." Beyond that, the self remains somewhat puzzling. Can the self exist in isolation, outside of relationships that provide some context for the self? Must the self be synonymous with the physical body? As Rogers' pointed out, when our foot "goes to sleep" from a lack of circulation, we view it as an object, not as a part of our self! Despite these challenging questions, Rogers tried to define and describe the self.

Rogers believed the self is formed in relation to others; it is an organized, fluid, yet consistent conceptual pattern of our experiential interactions with the environment and the values attached to those experiences. These experiences are symbolized and incorporated into the structure of the self, and our behavior is guided largely by how well new experiences fit within that structure. We may behave in ways inconsistent with the structure of our self, but when we do we will not "own" that behavior. When experiences are so inconsistent that we cannot symbolize them, or fit them into the structure of our self, the potential for psychological distress arises. On the other hand, when our concept of self is mature enough to incorporate all of our perceptions and experiences, and we can assimilate those experiences symbolically into our self, our psychological adjustment will be quite healthy. Individuals who find it difficult to assimilate new and different experiences, those experiences that threaten the structure of the self, will develop an increasingly rigid **self-structure**. Healthy individuals, in contrast, will assimilate new experiences, their self-structure will change and continue to grow, and they will become more capable of understanding and accepting others as individuals (Rogers, 1951).

The ability of individuals to make the choices necessary for actualizing their self-structure and to then fulfill those choices is what Rogers called **personal power** (Rogers, 1977). He believed there are many self-actualized individuals revolutionizing the world by trusting their own power, without feeling a need to have "power over" others. They are also willing to foster the latent actualizing tendency in others. We can easily see the influence of Alfred Adler here, both in terms of the creative power of the individual and seeking superiority within a healthy context of social interest. **Client-centered therapy** was based on making the context of personal power a clear strategy in the therapeutic relationship:

> …the client-centered approach is a conscious renunciation and avoidance by the therapist of all control over, or decision-making for, the client. It is the facilitation of self-ownership by the client and the strategies by which this can be achieved…based on the premise that the human being is basically a trustworthy organism, capable of…making constructive choices as to the next steps in life, and acting on those choices. (pp. 14-15; Rogers, 1977)

Discussion Question: Rogers claimed that no one can really understand your experiential field. Would you agree, or do you sometimes find that close friends or family members seem to understand you better than you understand yourself? Are these relationships congruent?

Personality Development

Although Rogers described personality within the therapist-client relationship, the focus of his therapeutic approach was based on how he believed the person had arrived at a point in their life where they were suffering from psychological distress. Therefore, the same issues apply to personality development as in therapy. A very important aspect of personality development, according to Rogers, is the parent-child relationship. The nature of that relationship, and whether it fosters self-actualization or impedes personal growth, determines the nature of the individual's personality and, consequently, their self-structure and psychological adjustment.

A child begins life with an actualizing tendency. As they experience life, and perceive the world around them, they may be supported in all things by those who care for them, or they may only be supported under certain conditions (e.g., if their behavior complies with strict rules). As the child becomes self-aware, it develops a need for **positive regard**. When the parents offer the child **unconditional positive regard**, the child continues moving forward in concert with its actualizing tendency. So, when there is no discrepancy between the child's **self-regard** and its positive regard (from the parents), the child will grow up psychologically healthy and well-adjusted. However, if the parents offer only **conditional positive regard**, if they only support the child according the desires and rules of the parents, the child will develop **conditions of worth**. As a result of these conditions of worth, the child will begin to perceive their world selectively; they will avoid those experiences that do not fit with its goal of obtaining positive regard. The child will begin to live the life of those who set the conditions of worth, rather than living its own life.

As the child grows older, and more aware of its own condition in the world, their behavior will either fit within their own self-structure or not. If they have received unconditional positive regard, such that their self-regard and positive regard are closely matched, they will experience **congruence**. In other words, their sense of self and their experiences in life will fit together, and the child will be relatively happy and well-adjusted. But, if their sense of self and their ability to obtain positive regard do not match, the child will develop **incongruence**. Consider, for example, children playing sports. That alone tells us that parents have established guidelines within which the children are expected to "play." Then we have some children who are naturally athletic, and other children who are more awkward and/or clumsy. They may become quite athletic later in life, or not, but during childhood there are many different levels of ability as they grow. If a parent expects their child to be the best player on the team, but the child simply isn't athletic, how does the parent react? Do they support the child and encourage them to have fun, or do they pressure the child to perform better and belittle them when they can't? Children are very good at recognizing who the better athletes are, and they know their place in the hierarchy of athletics, i.e., their athletic self-structure. So if a parent demands dominance from a child who knows they just aren't that good, the child will develop incongruence. Rogers believed, quite understandably, that such conditions are threatening to a child, and will activate defense mechanisms. Over time, however, excessive or sudden and dramatic incongruence can lead to the breakdown and disorganization of the self-structure. As a result, the individual is likely to experience psychological distress that will continue throughout life (Rogers, 1959/1989).

Discussion Question: Conditions of worth are typically first established in childhood, based on the relationship between a child and his or her parents. Think about your relationship with your own parents and, if you have children, think about how you treat them. Are most of the examples that come to mind unconditional positive regard, or conditional positive regard? How has that affected your relationship with your parents and/or your own children?

Sometimes parents create conditions of worth by overemphasizing the importance of competition. Even a trip to the pumpkin patch can be a challenge to get the biggest, best pumpkin. [Image by Mark Kelland]

Another way in which Rogers approached the idea of congruence and incongruence was based on an individual's dual concept of self. There is, of course, the actual self-structure, or **real self**. In addition, there is also an **ideal self**, much like the fictional finalism described by Adler or the idealized self-image described by Horney. Incongruence develops when the real self falls far short of the accomplishment expected of the ideal self, when experience does not match the expectations of the self-structure (Rogers, 1951, 1959/1989). Once again, the relationship between parents and their children plays an important role in this development. If parents expect too much, such as all A's every marking period in school, but the child just isn't academically talented, or if the parents expect their child to be the football team's quarterback, but the child isn't a good athlete, then the ideal self will remain out of reach. Perhaps even worse, is when a child is physically or emotionally abused. Such a child's ideal self may remain at a relatively low standard, but the real self may be so utterly depressed that incongruence is still the result. An important aspect of therapy will be to provide a relationship in which a person in this unfortunate condition can experience the unconditional positive regard necessary to begin reintegrating the self-structure, such that the gap between the real self and the ideal self can begin to close, allowing the person to experience congruence in their life.

What about individuals who have developed congruence, having received unconditional positive regard throughout development or having experienced successful client-centered therapy? They become, according to Rogers (1961), a **fully functioning person**. He also said they lead a good life. The good life is a process, not a state of being, and a direction, not a destination. It requires psychological freedom, and is the natural consequence of being psychologically free to begin with. Whether or not it develops naturally, thanks to a healthy and supportive environment in the home, or comes about as a result of successful therapy, there are certain characteristics of this process. The fully functioning person is increasingly open to new experiences, they live fully in each moment, and they trust themselves more and more. They become more able and more willing to experience all of their feelings, they are creative, they trust human nature, and they experience the richness of life. The fully functioning person is not simply content, or happy, they are *alive*:

> I believe it will become evident why, for me, adjectives such as happy, contented, blissful, enjoyable, do not seem quite appropriate to any general description of this process I have called the good life, even though the person in this process would experience each one of these feelings at appropriate times. But the adjectives which seem more generally fitting are adjectives such as enriching, exciting, rewarding, challenging, meaningful. This process…involves the courage to be. …the deeply exciting thing about human beings is that when the individual is inwardly free, he chooses as the good life this process of becoming. (pp. 195-196; Rogers, 1961)

Discussion Question: Rogers described self-actualized people as fully functioning persons who are living a good life. Do you know anyone who seems to be a fully functioning person? Are there aspects of their personality that you aspire to for yourself? Does it seem difficult to be fully functioning, or does it seem to make life both easier and more enjoyable?

Connections Across Cultures: Self-Realization as the Path to Being a Fully Functioning Person

Rogers described an innate drive toward self-actualization, he talked about an ideal self, and he said that a fully functioning person lived a good life. But what does this actually mean? In the Western world we look for specific, tangible answers to such questions. We want to know what the self-actualization drive is, we want to know which ideals, or virtues, are best or right, and we want to define a "good life." All too often, we define a good life in terms of money, power, and possessions. The Eastern world has, for thousands of years, emphasized a very different perspective. They believe there is a natural order to life, and it is important that we let go of our need to explain the universe, and it is especially important that we let go of our need to own pieces of the universe. In the *Tao Te Ching*, Lao Tsu (c. 600 B.C./1989) writes:

> Something mysteriously formed,
> Born before heaven and earth.
> In the silence and the void,
> Standing alone and unchanging,
> Ever present and in motion.
> Perhaps it is the mother of ten thousand things.
> I do not know its name,
> Call it Tao.
> For lack of a better word, I call it great…
>
> The greatest Virtue is to follow Tao and Tao alone…
> Tao follows what is natural.

At about the same time, some 2,600 years ago, the *Bhagavad Gita* was also written down (Mitchell, 2000). In the second chapter one finds:

> When a man gives up all desires
> That emerge from the mind, and rests
> Contented in the Self by the Self,
> He is called a man of firm wisdom…

> In the night of all beings, the wise man
> Sees only the radiance of the Self;
> But the sense-world where all beings wake,
> For him is as dark as night.

In each of these sacred books, we are taught that there is something deeper than ourselves that permeates the universe, but it is beyond our comprehension. It is only when we stop attempting to explain it, our way of trying to control it, and be content to just be ourselves, that we can actually attain that goal. To achieve this goal seems to require the absence of conditions of worth. If someone has been given unconditional positive regard throughout their life, they will be content to live that life as it is. Rogers was well aware of this challenge, and he described the good life as a process, not something that you could actually get, but something that you had to "Be." Still, is it possible that a fully functioning person might have the insight necessary to understand the essence of the universe? Not according to Swami Sri Yukteswar:

> Man possesses eternal faith and believes intuitively in the existence of a Substance, of which the objects of sense - sound, touch, sight, taste, and smell, the component parts of this visible world - are but properties. As man identifies himself with his material body, composed of the aforesaid properties, he is able to comprehend by these imperfect organs these properties only, and not the Substance to which these properties belong. The eternal Father, God, the only Substance in the universe, is therefore not comprehensible by man of this material world, unless he becomes divine by lifting his self above this creation of Darkness or *Maya*. See Hebrews 11:1 and John 8:28.
>
> "Now faith is the substance of things hoped for, the evidence of things not seen."
>
> "Then said Jesus unto them, When ye have lifted up the son of man, then shall ye know that I am he."
>
> *Jnanavatar Swami Sri Yukteswar Giri, 1894/1990*

So whether we believe in God, Tao, an eternal Self, a mortal Self, or merely an actualizing tendency, for thousands of years there has been the belief, amongst many people, that our lives are about more than just being alive for a limited period of time. And it is in the recognition and acceptance, indeed the embracing, of that something more, even if we can't conceive it in our conscious mind, that we find and live a good life. When Paramahansa Yogananda, a direct disciple of Swami Yukteswar, came to the United States in 1920 to establish a permanent Yoga society, it was suggested that he name his society God-Realization. However, since he believed life is about realizing (or actualizing, in psychological terms) our selves, he established his organization as the Self-Realization Fellowship (Yogananda, 1946).

Self-realization, in the context of Yoga, refers to becoming aware of one's connection to the spark of divinity that exists within us, which may well be the source of our actualizing tendency. It is not the same as the sense of "I" or "me" that we normally think of. After all, are we our body or our mind? Consider the body. Is it the body we were born with, or the body we have now? Is our mind what we are thinking now, or what we were thinking 2 years ago? Both the body and the mind are transient, but the Self continues. It is that Self that Yogis, Buddhists, and Taoists seek to realize, and it may well be that Self which seeks its own actualization (separate from the consciousness created by the brain underlying our mind; see Feuerstein, 2003; Kabat-Zinn, 1994). This is also the Self of Being and transcendence, as described by Maslow.

Social Relationships and Marriage

Social and personal relationships were very important to Rogers, both in therapy and in everyday life. During each moment, we have our awareness (or consciousness), our experience (our perception of what is happening), and our communication (our relational behavior). For the fully functioning person, there is congruence between each of these phenomena. Unfortunately, we tend to be a poor judge of our own congruence. For example, if someone becomes angry with another person at a meeting or in a therapy group, they may remain unaware of their anger, even though it may be quite obvious to everyone else in the room. Thus, our relationship with others can reflect the true nature of our own personality, and the degree to which we are congruent. If others are congruent, and therefore are willing to talk to us openly and honestly, it will encourage us to become more congruent and, consequently, more psychologically healthy (Rogers, 1961, 1980). Curiously, the reason this became so important to Rogers was the lack of such meaningful relationships in his own life. Because his family followed strict, fundamentalist rules, they discouraged relationships with people outside their family. The consequences were rather disturbing for Rogers:

> …the attitudes toward persons outside our large family can be summed up schematically in this way: "Other persons behave in dubious ways which we do not approve in our family. Many of them play cards, go to movies, smoke, dance, drink, and engage in other activities, some unmentionable. So the best thing to do is to be tolerant of them, since they may not know better, but to keep away from any close communication with them and to live your life within the family…"
>
> I could sum up these boyhood years by saying that anything I would today regard as a close and communicative interpersonal relationship with another was completely lacking during that period…I was peculiar, a loner, with very little place or opportunity for a place in the world of persons. I was socially incompetent in any but superficial contacts. My fantasies during this period were definitely bizarre, and probably would be classed as schizoid by a diagnostician, but fortunately I never came in contact with a psychologist. (pp. 28-30; Rogers, 1980)

As noted above, the development of healthy relationships takes place whenever one person in the relationship is congruent. Their congruence encourages the other person to be more congruent, which supports the continued open communication on behalf of the first person. This interplay goes back and forth, encouraging continued and growing congruence in the relationship. As we will see below, this is basically the therapeutic situation, in which the therapist is expected to be congruent. However, it certainly does not require a trained therapist, since it occurs naturally in any situation in which one person is congruent from the beginning of the relationship.

One of the most important, and hopefully meaningful, relationships in anyone's life is marriage. Rogers was married for 55 years, and as the end of his wife's life approached he poured out his love to her with a depth that astonished him (Rogers, 1980). As relationships became more and more meaningful to him, he wanted to study the extraordinary relationships that become more than temporary. Although this is not necessarily synonymous with marriage, it most typically is. So he conducted a series of informal interviews with people who were, or had been, in lengthy relationships (at least 3 years). In comparing the relationships that seemed successful, as compared to those that were unhappy or had already come to an end, Rogers identified four factors that he believed were most important for long-term, healthy relationships: dedication or commitment, communication, the dissolution of roles, and becoming a separate self (Rogers, 1972).

Dedication, Commitment: Marriage is challenging: love seems to fade, vows are forgotten or set aside, religious rules are ignored (e.g., "What therefore God has joined together, let no man put asunder."; Matthew 19:6; Holy Bible, 1962). Rogers believed that in order for a relationship to last, each person must be dedicated to their partnership. They must commit themselves to working together throughout the changing process of their relationship, which is enriching their love and their life.

Communication: Communication encompasses much of human behavior, and it can be both subtle and complex. Communication itself is not a good thing, since many negative and hurtful things can be communicated. However, Rogers believed that we need to communicate persistent feeling, whether positive or negative, so that they don't overwhelm us and come out in inappropriate ways. It is always important to express such communication in terms of your own thoughts and feelings, rather than projecting those feelings onto others (especially in angry and/or accusatory ways). This process involves risk, but one must be willing to risk the end of a relationship in order to allow it to grow.

Dissolution of Roles: Culture provides many expectations for the nature of relationships, whether it be dating or something more permanent like marriage. According to Rogers, obeying the cultural rules seems to contradict the idea of a growing and maturing relationship, a relationship that is moving forward (toward actualization). However, when individuals make an intentional choice to fulfill cultural expectations, because they *want* to, then the relationship can certainly be actualizing for them.

Becoming a Separate Self: Rogers believed that "a *living* partnership is composed of two people, each of whom owns, respect, and develops his or her own selfhood" (pg. 206; Rogers, 1972). While it may seem contradictory that becoming an individual should enhance a relationship, as each person becomes more real and more open they can bring these qualities into the relationship. As a result, the relationship can contribute to the continued growth of each person.

Discussion Question: Consider Rogers' criteria for a successful marriage, which begins with commitment to the marriage. Given the divorce rate (which studies now place at over 60%), and ongoing political debates about what marriage is or is not, what is your opinion of the status of marriage in society today?

Client-Centered and Person-Centered Therapy

Central to Rogers' view of psychotherapy is the relationship between the therapist and the client, and we must again emphasize the distinction between a client and a patient. This involves shifting the emphasis in therapy from a psychologist/psychiatrist who can "fix" the patient to the client themselves, since only the client can truly understand their own experiential field. The therapist must provide a warm, safe environment in which the client feels free to express whatever attitude they experience in the same way that they perceive it. At the same time, the client experiences the therapist as someone temporarily divested of their own self, in their complete desire to understand the client. The therapist can then accurately and objectively reflect the thoughts, feelings, perceptions, confusions, ambivalences, etc., of the client back to the client. In this open, congruent, and supportive environment, the client is able to begin the process of reorganizing and reintegrating their self-structure, and living congruently within that self-structure (Rogers, 1951).

In 1957, Rogers published an article entitled *The Necessary and Sufficient Conditions of Therapeutic Personality Change* (Rogers, 1957/1989). The list is fairly short and straightforward:

1. The client and the therapist must be in psychological contact.
2. The client must be in a state of incongruence, being vulnerable or anxious.
3. The therapist must be congruent in the relationship.
4. The therapist must experience unconditional positive regard for the client.
5. The therapist must experience empathic understanding of the client's frame of reference and endeavor to communicate this experience to the client.
6. The client must perceive, at least to a minimal degree, the therapist's empathic understanding and unconditional positive regard.

According to Rogers, there is nothing else that is required; if these conditions are met over a period of time, there will be constructive personality change. What Rogers considered more remarkable are those factors that do *not* seem necessary for positive therapeutic change. For example, these conditions do not apply to one type of client, but to all clients, and they are not unique to client-centered therapy, but apply in all types of therapy. The relationship between the therapist and client is also not unique, these factors hold true in any interpersonal relationship. And most surprisingly, these conditions do not require any special training on the part of therapist, or even an accurate diagnosis of the client's psychological problems! Any program designed for the purpose of encouraging constructive change in the personality structure and behavior of individuals, whether educational, military, correctional, or industrial, can benefit from these conditions and use them as a measure of the effectiveness of the program (Rogers, 1957).

Can any one of these conditions be considered more important than the others? Although they are all necessary, Rogers came to believe that the critical factor may be the therapist's **empathic understanding** of the client (Rogers, 1980). The Dalai Lama (2001) has said that empathy is an essential first step toward a compassionate heart. It brings us closer to others, and allows us to recognize the depth of their pain. According to Rogers, empathy refers to entering the private world of the client, and moving about within it without making any judgments. It is essential to set aside one's own views and values, so that the other person's world may be entered without prejudice. Not just anyone can accomplish this successfully:

> In some sense it means that you lay aside your self; this can only be done by persons who are secure enough in themselves that they know they will not get lost in what may turn out to be the strange or bizarre world of the other, and that they can comfortably return to their own world when they wish. (pg. 143; Rogers, 1980)

Finally, let us consider group therapy situations. Within a group, all of the factors described above hold true. Rogers, who late in his career was becoming more and more interested in the growth of all people, including those reasonably well-adjusted and mature to begin with, became particularly interested in **T-groups** and **encounter groups**. These groups were developed following the proposition by Kurt Lewin that modern society was overlooking the importance of training in human relations skills (the "T" in T-group stands for "training"). Encounter groups were quite similar to T-groups, except that there was a greater emphasis on personal growth and improved interpersonal communication through an experiential process. Each group has a leader, or facilitator, who fosters and encourages open communication. The group serves as a reflection of the congruence, or lack thereof, in the communication of whoever is currently expressing themselves. As a result, the group hopefully moves toward congruence, and the subsequent personal growth and actualization of the individual (Rogers, 1970).

Given the usefulness of T-groups and encounter in a variety of settings, as well as the importance of continued personal growth and actualization for the well-adjusted as well as those suffering psychological distress, Rogers shifted his focus from simply client-centered therapy to a more universal **person-centered approach**, which encompasses client-centered therapy, student-centered teaching, and group-centered leadership (Rogers, 1980; see also Rogers & Roethlisberger, 1952/1993). Rogers believed that all people have within them vast resources for self-understanding and for changing their self-concepts, attitudes, and behaviors. In all relationships, whether therapist-client, parent-child, teacher-student, leader-group, employer-employee, etc., there are three elements that can foster personal growth: genuineness or congruence, acceptance or caring, and empathic understanding. When these elements are fostered in any setting, "there is greater freedom to be the true, whole person." The implications go far beyond individual relationships. We live in what seems to be an increasingly dangerous world. Globalism has brought with it global tension and conflict. However, Rogers argued that a person-centered approach would help to ease intercultural tension, by helping each of us to learn to appreciate and understand others. Whether the cultural differences are political, racial, ethnic, economic, whatever, as more leaders become person-centered there is the possibility for future growth of intercultural understanding and cooperation (Rogers, 1977).

Abraham Maslow and Holistic-Dynamic Psychology

Maslow stands alongside Rogers as one of the founders of humanistic psychology. Although he began his career working with two of the most famous experimental psychologists in America, he was profoundly influenced by the events that led into World War II. He became devoted to studying the more virtuous aspects of personality, and he may be viewed as one of the founders of positive psychology. Well-known primarily for his work on self-actualization, Maslow also had a significant impact on the field of management. His fame in both psychology and business makes him a candidate for being, perhaps, the best-known psychologist of all time (Freud is certainly more famous, but remember that he was a psychiatrist). According to Maslow, his **holistic-dynamic theory** of personality was a blend of theories that had come before his:

> This theory is, I think, in the functionalist tradition of James and Dewey, and is fused with the holism of Wertheimer, Goldstein, and Gestalt psychology, and with the dynamicism of

> Freud, Fromm, Horney, Reich, Jung, and Adler. This integration or synthesis may be called a holistic-dynamic theory. (pg. 35; Maslow, 1970)

Brief Biography of Abraham Maslow

Abraham H. Maslow was born on April 1, 1908 in Brooklyn, New York, the first of seven children. His father, Samuel, had left Kiev, Russia at just 14 years old. When Samuel Maslow arrived in America he had no money and did not speak English. Samuel Maslow spent a few years in Philadelphia, doing odd jobs and learning the language, before moving to New York City, where he married his first cousin Rose and began a cooperage business (a cooper builds and repairs barrels). Samuel and Rose Maslow did not have a happy marriage, and Abraham Maslow was particularly sensitive to this fact. Maslow resented his father's frequent absences, and apparently hated his mother. His mother was a superstitious woman, who severely punished Maslow for even minor misbehavior by threatening him with God's wrath. Maslow developed an intense distrust of religion, and was proud to consider himself an atheist (Gabor, 2000; Hoffman, 1988; Maddi & Costa, 1972).

Maslow's childhood was no better outside the home. Anti-Semitism was rampant in New York. Many teachers were cruel, and he overheard them say nasty things about him. He had no friends, and there were anti-Semitic gangs that would find and beat up Jewish children. At one point he decided to join a Jewish gang for protection, but he didn't have the "right" attitude:

> I wanted to be a member of the gang, but I couldn't: they rejected me because I couldn't kill cats...We'd stake out a cat on a [clothesline] and stand back so many paces and throw rocks at it and kill it.
>
> And the other thing was to throw rocks at the girls on the corner. Now I knew that the girls liked it, and yet I couldn't throw rocks at girls and I couldn't kill cats, so I was ruled out of the gang, and I could never be the gangster that I wanted to become. (pg. 4; Maslow, cited in Hoffman, 1988)

With six more children joining the family, one every couple of years, the family was constantly moving and, following the troubling death of one of his little sisters (Maslow blamed her illness, in part, on their mother's neglect), Maslow became a very unhappy and shy child. He also thought he was terribly ugly, something his father said openly at a large family gathering! Perhaps worst of all, he felt profoundly strange and different than other children, largely because he was so intellectual. Maslow reconciled with his father later in life. During the depression, Samuel Maslow lost his business. By that time he had divorced Maslow's mother, Rose, and he moved in with his son. The two became close, and after Samuel Maslow died, his son remembered him fondly. Maslow never forgave his mother, however. Some of the childhood stories he related were shockingly cruel. Once, he had searched through second-hand record shops for some special 78-RPM records. When he failed to put them away soon after returning home, his mother stomped them into pieces on the living room floor. Another time, Maslow brought home two abandoned kittens he had found. When his mother caught him feeding them a saucer of milk, she grabbed the kittens and smashed their heads against a wall until they were dead! Later in life, he refused to even attend her funeral.

> What I had reacted to and totally hated and rejected was not only her physical appearance, but also her values and world view...I've always wondered where my utopianism, ethical stress, humanism, stress on kindness, love, friendship, and all the rest came from. I knew certainly of the direct consequences of having no mother-love. But the whole thrust of my life-philosophy and all my research and theorizing also has its roots in a hatred for and revulsion against everything she stood for. (pg. 9; Maslow cited in Hoffman, 1988)

Maslow spent much of his childhood reading, and despite the treatment he received from many of his prejudiced teachers, he loved to learn. After high school Maslow won a scholarship to Cornell University, but encountered pervasive anti-Semitism throughout his first year. So he transferred to City College, where he first studied the work of behavioral scientists like John B. Watson. He was impressed by Watson's desire to use the newly created science of behaviorism to fight social problems, such as racial and ethnic discrimination. At the same time, however, Maslow had fallen in love with his first cousin Bertha Goodman, a relationship his parents strongly opposed. So Maslow left for the University of Wisconsin (Gabor, 2000; Hoffman, 1988; Maddi & Costa, 1972). Bertha Goodman followed, and they were soon married. Marriage boosted Maslow's self-esteem, and provided him with a sense of purpose in life. He later said that "life didn't really start for me until I got married and went to Wisconsin" (pg. 128; cited in Maddi & Costa, 1972).

In Wisconsin, Maslow studied the behavior of primates under the supervision of the renowned Harry Harlow (most famous for his studies on **contact comfort**). One day, while watching some monkeys seemingly enjoy munching on peanuts and other treats, Maslow recognized that appetite and hunger are two different things. Thus, motivation must be comprised of separate elements as well. In another study, Maslow tried to address the different aspects of Freud and Adler's psychodynamic perspectives by observing dominance behavior amongst the monkeys. His colleagues and professors, however, had little interest in the psychoanalytic science that they considered to be a European endeavor. Maslow completed his Ph.D. at Wisconsin in 1934, and then returned to New York. He earned a position at Columbia University with the renowned Edward Thorndike, and began studying the relative contributions of heredity and environment on social behavior, as part of a project to study factors involved in poverty, illiteracy, and crime. As a curious side note, Thorndike had also developed an IQ test; Maslow scored 195 on this test, one of the highest scores ever recorded. During this time at Columbia University, Maslow also began relationships with many of the psychologists, sociologists, and anthropologists who had fled Nazi Germany. He was very impressed with Max Wertheimer, one of the founders of Gestalt psychology, and who helped to lay the foundation for positive psychology:

> "Are there not tendencies in men and in children to be kind, to deal sincerely [and] justly with the other fellow? Are these nothing but internalized rules on the basis of compulsion and fear?" he asked rhetorically. (pg. 159; Wertheimer, cited in Gabor, 2000)

Maslow was one of the first students to study with Alfred Adler in America, being particularly impressed with Adler's work helping academically-challenged children to succeed despite their low IQ scores. Maslow also studied with Erich Fromm, Karen Horney, and Ruth Benedict. Benedict was an anthropologist who encouraged Maslow to gain some field experience. She sponsored a grant application that Maslow received to study the Blackfoot Indians. During the summer of 1938, Maslow examined the dominance and emotional security of the Blackfoot Indians. He was impressed by their culture, and recognized what he believed was an innate need to experience a sense of purpose in life, a sense of meaning. A few years later, shortly after the beginning of World War II, Maslow had an epiphany regarding psychology's failure to understand the true nature of people. He devoted the rest of his life to the study of a hopeful psychology (Gabor, 2000; Hoffman, 1988; Maddi & Costa, 1972).

Maslow taught for a few years at Brooklyn College, and also served as the plant manager for the Maslow Cooperage Corporation (from 1947-1949). In 1951 he was appointed Professor and Chair of the Department of Psychology at Brandeis University, where he conducted the research and wrote the books for which he is most famous. By the late 1960s, Maslow had become disillusioned with academic life. He had suffered a heart attack in 1966, and seemed somewhat disconnected from the very department he had helped to form. In 1969, however, he accepted a four year grant from the Laughlin Foundation, primarily to study the philosophy of democracy, economics, and ethics as influenced by humanistic psychology. He had been troubled by what he viewed as a loss of faith in American values, and he was greatly enjoying his time working in California. He also attended management seminars at the Saga Corporation, urging the participants to commit themselves to humanistic management. One day in June, 1970, he was jogging slowly when he suffered a massive heart attack. He was already dead by the time his wife rushed over to him (Gabor, 2000; Hoffman, 1988; Maddi & Costa, 1972). He was only 62 years old. Shortly after his death, the *International Study Project* of Menlo Park, CA published a memorial volume in tribute to Abraham Maslow (International Study Project, 1972).

Placing Maslow in Context: Beyond Humanistic Psychology

Whereas Carl Rogers is often thought of as the founder of humanistic psychology, in large part because of his emphasis on psychotherapy, it was Maslow who studied in great detail the most significant theoretical aspect of it: self-actualization. In addition to studying self-actualization, he applied it both in psychology and beyond. His application of self-actualization to management continued the classic relationship between psychology and business (which began with John B. Watson and his application of psychological principles to advertising). Unfortunately, Maslow died just as he was beginning to study his proposed fourth force: transpersonal psychology. Transpersonal psychology offered a connection between psychology and many of the Eastern philosophies associated with Yoga and Buddhism, and also provided a foundation for the study of positive psychology.

Maslow's interest in business and management has quite possibly led to his being the most famous psychologist of all time, since he is well-known in both psychology and business. If he had continued being a vocal advocate for transpersonal psychology (if not for his untimely death at an early age), given today's growing interest in Eastern philosophy and psychology and the establishment of positive psychology as a goal for the field of psychology by former APA President Martin Seligman, Maslow may well have become even more famous. It is interesting to note that someone so truly visionary seems to have become that way as a result of studying people whom he felt were themselves self-actualized. If positive psychology, the psychology of virtue and values, becomes the heir of Maslow's goal, it should become a significant force in the field of psychology. That will be Maslow's true legacy.

The Importance of Values in the Science of Psychology

A common criticism leveled against many personality theorists is that they have not confirmed their theories in a strict, scientific manner. When one goes so far as to consider **values**, which are typically associated with religious morality, there is even greater resistance on the part of those who would have psychology become "truly" scientific to consider such matters worthy of examination. However, Maslow felt that:

> Both orthodox science and orthodox religion have been institutionalized and frozen into a mutually excluding dichotomy...One consequence is that they are both pathologized, split into sickness, ripped apart into a crippled half-science and a crippled half-religion...As a result...the student who becomes a scientist automatically gives up a great deal of life, especially its richest portions. (pg. 119; Maslow, 1966)

Consequently, Maslow urged that we need to be fully aware of our values at all times, and aware of how our values influence us in our study of psychology. Although people approach the world in common ways, they also pay selective attention to what is happening, and they reshuffle the events occurring around them according to their own interests, needs, desires, fears, etc. Consequently, Maslow believed that paying attention to human values, particularly to an individual's values, actually helps the psychological scientist achieve the goal of clearly understanding human behavior (Maslow, 1970). In a similar vein, when Maslow co-authored an abnormal psychology text early in his career, he included a chapter on normal psychology. His description of the characteristics of a healthy, normal personality provides an interesting foreshadowing of his research on self-actualization (Maslow & Mittelmann, 1941).

Maslow felt so strongly about the loss of values in our society that he helped to organize a conference and then served as editor for a book entitled *New Knowledge in Human Values* (Maslow, 1959). In the preface, Maslow laments that "...the ultimate disease of our time is valuelessness...this state is more crucially dangerous than ever before in history..." (pg. vii; Maslow, 1959). Maslow does suggest, however, that something can be done about this loss of values, if only people will try. In the book, he brought together an interesting variety of individuals, including: Kurt Goldstein, a well-known neurophysiologist who studied the holistic function of healthy vs. brain-damaged patients and who coined the term self-actualization; D. T. Suzuki, a renowned Zen Buddhist scholar; and Paul Tillich, a highly respected existential theologian (who had a direct and significant influence on the career of Rollo May). There are also chapters by Gordon Allport and Erich Fromm. In his own chapter, Maslow concludes:

> If we wish to help humans to become more fully human, we must realize not only that they try to realize themselves but that they are also reluctant or afraid or unable to do so. Only by fully appreciating this dialectic between sickness and health can we help to tip the balance in favor of health. (pg. 135; Maslow, 1959)

Discussion Question: Maslow believed that values are very important, not only in the study of psychology, but in society as well. Do you agree? When politicians or religious leaders talk about values, do you think they represent meaningful, true values, or do they just support the values that are an advantage to their own goal or the goals of their political party or church?

The Hierarchy of Needs

Maslow's is undoubtedly best known for his **hierarchy of needs**. Developed within the context of a theory of human motivation, Maslow believed that human behavior is driven and guided by a set of **basic needs**: **physiological needs, safety needs, belongingness and love needs, esteem needs,** and the **need for self-actualization**. It is generally accepted that individuals must move through the hierarchy in order, satisfying the needs at each level before one can move on to a higher level. The reason for this is that lower needs tend to occupy the mind if they remain unsatisfied. How easy is it to work or study when you are really hungry or thirsty? But Maslow did not consider the hierarchy to be rigid. For example, he encountered some people for whom self-esteem was more important than love, individuals suffering from antisocial personality disorder seem to have a permanent loss of the need for love, or if a need has been satisfied for a long time it may become less important. As lower needs are becoming satisfied, though not yet fully satisfied, higher needs may begin to present themselves. And of course there are sometimes multiple determinants of behavior, making the relationship between a given behavior and a basic need difficult to identify (Maslow, 1943/1973; Maslow, 1970).

The physiological needs are based, in part, on the concept of **homeostasis**, the natural tendency of the body to maintain critical biological levels of essential elements or conditions, such as water, salt, energy, and body temperature. Sexual activity, though not essential for the individual, is biologically necessary for the human species to survive. Maslow described the physiological needs as the most **prepotent**. In other words, if a person is lacking everything in life, having failed to satisfy physiological, safety, belongingness and love, and esteem needs, their consciousness will most like be consumed with their desire for food and water. As the lowest and most clearly biological of the needs, these are also the most animal-like of our behavior. In Western culture, however, it is rare to find someone who is actually starving. So when we talk about being hungry, we are really talking about an appetite, rather than real hunger (Maslow, 1943/1973; Maslow, 1970). Many Americans are fascinated by stories such as those of the ill-fated Donner party, trapped in the Sierra Nevada mountains during the winter of 1846-1847, and the Uruguayan soccer team whose plane crashed in the Andes mountains in 1972. In each case, either some or all of the survivors were forced to cannibalize those who had died. As shocking as such stories are, they demonstrate just how powerful our physiological needs can be.

The safety needs can easily be seen in young children. They are easily startled or frightened by loud noises, flashing lights, and rough handling. They can become quite upset when other family members are fighting, since it disrupts the feeling of safety usually associated with the home. According to Maslow, many adult neurotics are like children who do not feel safe. From another perspective, that of Erik Erikson, children and adults raised in such an environment do not trust the environment to provide for their needs. Although it can be argued that few people in America seriously suffer from a lack of satisfying physiological needs, there are many people who live unsafe lives. For example, inner city crime, abusive spouses and parents, incurable diseases like HIV/AIDS, all present life threatening dangers to many people on a daily basis.

One place where we expect our children to be safe is in school. However, as we saw in the last chapter (in the section on the martial arts), 160,000 children each day are too frightened to attend school (Nathan, 2005). Juvonen et al. (2006) looked at the effects of ethnic diversity on children's perception of safety in urban middle schools (Grade 6). They surveyed approximately 2,000 students in 99 classrooms in the greater Los Angeles area. The ethnicity of the students in this study was 46 percent Latino (primarily of Mexican origin), 29 percent African American, 9 percent Asian (primarily East Asian), 9 percent Caucasian, and 7 percent multiracial. When a given classroom, or a given school, is more ethnically diverse, both African American and Latino students felt safer, were harassed less by peers, felt less lonely, and they had higher levels of self-worth (even when the authors controlled for differences in academic engagement). Thus, it appears that ethnic diversity in schools leads toward satisfaction of the need for safety, at least in one important area of a child's life. Unfortunately, most minority students continue to be educated in schools that are largely ethnically segregated (Juvonen, et al., 2006).

Throughout the evolution of the human species we found safety primarily within our family, tribal group, or our community. It was within those groups that we shared the hunting and gathering that provided food. Once the physiological and safety needs have been fairly well satisfied, according to Maslow, "the person will feel keenly, as never before, the absence of friends, or a sweetheart, or a wife, or children" (Maslow, 1970). Although there is little scientific confirmation of the belongingness and love needs, many therapists attribute much of human suffering to society's thwarting of the need for love and affection. Most notable among personality theorists who addressed this issue was Wilhelm Reich. An important aspect of love and affection is sex. Although sex is often considered a physiological need, given its role in procreation, sex is what Maslow referred to as a multidetermined behavior. In other words, it serves both a physiological role (procreation) and a belongingness/love role (the tenderness and/or passion of the physical side of love). Maslow was also careful to point out that love needs involve both giving and receiving love in order for them to be fully satisfied (Maslow, 1943/1973; Maslow, 1970).

Maslow believed that all people desire a stable and firmly based high evaluation of themselves and others (at least the others who comprise their close relationships). This need for self-esteem, or self-respect, involves two components. First is the desire to feel competent, strong, and successful (similar to Bandura's self-efficacy). Second is the need for prestige or status, which can range from simple recognition to fame and glory. Maslow credited Adler for addressing this human need, but felt that Freud had neglected it. Maslow also believed that the need for self-esteem was becoming a central issue in therapy for many psychotherapists. However, as we saw in Chapter 12, Albert Ellis considers self-esteem to be a sickness. Ellis' concern is that self-esteem, including efforts to boost self-esteem in therapy, requires that people rate themselves, something that Ellis felt will eventually lead to a negative evaluation (no one is perfect!). Maslow did acknowledge that the healthiest self-esteem is based on well-earned and deserved respect from others, rather than fleeting fame or celebrity status (Maslow, 1943/1973; Maslow, 1970).

When all of these lower needs (physiological, safety, belongingness and love, and esteem) have been largely satisfied, we may still feel restless and discontented unless we are doing what is right for ourselves. "What a man *can* be, he *must* be" (pg. 46; Maslow, 1970). Thus, the need for self-actualization, which Maslow described as the highest of the basic needs, can also be referred to as a **Being-need**, as opposed to the lower **deficiency-needs** (Maslow, 1968). We will examine self-actualization in more detail in the following section.

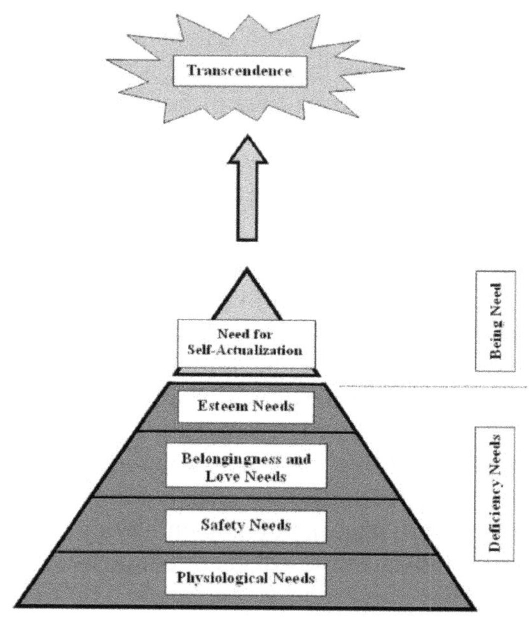

Maslow's hierarchy of needs is based on a theory of motivation. Individuals must essentially satisfy the lower deficiency needs before they become focused on satisfying the higher Being needs. Beyond even the Being needs there is something more, a state of transcendence that ties all people and the whole of creation together. [Image by Mark Kelland]

Although Maslow recognized that humans no longer have instincts in the technical sense, we nonetheless share basic drives with other animals. We get hungry, even though how and what we eat is determined culturally. We need to be safe, like any other animal, but again we seek and maintain our safety in different ways (such as having a police force to provide safety for us). Given our fundamental similarity to other animals, therefore, Maslow referred to the basic needs as **instinctoid**. The lower the need the more animal-like it is, the higher the need, the more human it is, and self-actualization was, in Maslow's opinion, uniquely human (Maslow, 1970).

In addition to the basic needs, Maslow referred to **cognitive needs** and **aesthetic needs**. Little is known about cognitive needs, since they are seldom an important focus in clinic settings. However, he felt there were ample grounds for proposing that there are positive impulses to know, to satisfy curiosity, to understand, and to explain. The eight-fold path described by the Buddha, some 2,600 years ago, begins with right knowledge. The importance of mental stimulation for some people is described quite vividly by Maslow:

> I have seen a few cases in which it seemed clear to me that the pathology (boredom, loss of zest in life, self-dislike, general depression of the bodily functions, steady deterioration of the intellectual life, of tastes, etc.) were produced in intelligent people leading stupid lives in stupid jobs. I have at least one case in which the appropriate cognitive therapy (resuming part-time studies, getting a position that was more intellectually demanding, insight) removed the symptoms.
>
> I have seen many women, intelligent, prosperous, and unoccupied, slowly develop these same symptoms of intellectual inanition. Those who followed my recommendation to immerse themselves in something worthy of them showed improvement or cure often enough to impress me with the reality of the cognitive needs. (pg. 49; Maslow, 1970)

There are also classic studies on the importance of environmental enrichment on the structural development of the brain itself (Diamond et al., 1975; Globus, et al., 1973; Greenough & Volkmar, 1973; Rosenzweig, 1984; Spinelli & Jensen, 1979; Spinelli, Jensen, & DiPrisco, 1980). Even less is known about the aesthetic needs, but Maslow was convinced that some people need to experience, indeed they crave, beauty in their world. Ancient cave drawings have been found that seem to serve no other purpose than being art. The cognitive and aesthetic needs may very well have been fundamental to our evolution as modern humans.

Self-Actualization

Maslow began his studies on self-actualization in order to satisfy his own curiosity about people who seemed to be fulfilling their unique potential as individuals. He did not intend to undertake a formal research project, but he was so impressed by his results that he felt compelled to report his findings. Amongst people he knew personally and public and historical figures, he looked for individuals who appeared to have made full use of their talents, capacities, and potentialities. In other words, "people who have developed or are developing to the full stature of which they are capable" (Maslow, 1970). His list of those who clearly seemed self-actualized included Abraham Lincoln, Thomas Jefferson, Albert Einstein, Eleanor Roosevelt, Jane Addams, William James, Albert Schweitzer, Aldous Huxley, and Baruch Spinoza. His list of individuals who were most-likely self-actualized included Goethe (possibly the great-grandfather of Carl Jung), George Washington, Benjamin Franklin, Harriet Tubman (born into slavery, she became a conductor on the Underground Railroad prior to the Civil War), and George Washington Carver (born into slavery at the end of the Civil War, he became an agricultural chemist and prolific inventor). In addition to the positive attributes listed above, Maslow also considered it very important that there be no evidence of psychopathology in those he chose to study. After comparing the seemingly self-actualized individuals to people who did not seem to have fulfilled their lives, Maslow identified fourteen characteristics of self-actualizing people (Maslow, 1950/1973, 1970), as follows:

More Efficient Perception of Reality and More Comfortable Relations with It: Self-actualizing people have an ability to recognize fakers, those who present a false persona. More than that, however, Maslow believed they could recognize hidden or confused realities in all aspects of life: science, politics, values and ethics, etc. They are not afraid of the unknown or people who are different, they find such differences to be a pleasant challenge. Although a high IQ may be associated with this characteristic, it is not uncommon to find those who are seemingly intelligent yet unable to be creative in their efforts to discover new phenomena. Thus, the perception of reality is not simply the same as being smart.

Acceptance (Self, Others, Nature): Similar to the approach Albert Ellis took with REBT (and his hypothesized dangers inherent in self-esteem), Maslow believed that self-actualizing people accept themselves as they are, including their faults and the differences between their personal reality and their ideal image of themselves. This is not to say that they are without guilt. They are concerned about personal faults that can be improved, any remaining habits or psychological issues that are unhealthy (e.g., prejudice, jealousy, etc.), and the shortcomings of their community and/or culture.

Spontaneity: The lives of self-actualizing people are marked by simplicity and a natural ease as they pursue their goals. Their outward behavior is relatively spontaneous, and their inner life (thoughts, drives, etc.) is particularly so. In spite of this spontaneity, they are not always unconventional, because they can easily accept the constraints of society and find their own way to fit in without being untrue to their own sense of self.

Problem-Centering: Self-actualizing individuals are highly problem-centered, not ego-centered. The problems they focus on are typically not their own, however. They focus on problems outside themselves, on important causes they would describe as necessary. Solving such problems is taken as their duty or responsibility, rather than as something they want to do for themselves.

The Quality of Detachment; the Need for Privacy: Whereas social withdrawal is often seen as psychologically unhealthy, self-actualizing people enjoy their privacy. They can remain calm as they separate themselves from problematic situations, remaining above the fray. In accordance with this healthy form of detachment, they are active, responsible, self-disciplined individuals in charge of their own lives. Maslow believed that they have more free will than the average person.

Self-actualized individuals need their privacy. This may help them put life in perspective and prepare for each day. [Image by Mark Kelland]

Autonomy, Independence of Culture and Environment: As an extension of the preceding characteristics, self-actualizing individuals are growth-motivated as opposed to being deficiency-motivated. They do not need the presence, companionship, or approval of others. Indeed, they may be hampered by others. The love, honor, esteem, etc., that can be bestowed by others has become less important to someone who is self-actualizing than self-development and inner growth.

Continued Freshness of Appreciation: Self-actualizing people are able to appreciate the wonders, as well as the common aspects, of life again and again. Such feelings may not occur all the time, but they can occur in the most unexpected ways and at unexpected times. Maslow offered a surprising evaluation of the importance of this characteristic of self-actualization:

> I have also become convinced that getting used to our blessings is one of the most important nonevil generators of human evil, tragedy, and suffering. What we take for granted we undervalue, and we are therefore too apt to sell a valuable birthright for a mess of pottage, leaving behind regret, remorse, and a lowering of self-esteem. Wives, husbands, children, friends are unfortunately more apt to be loved and appreciated after they have died than while they are still available. Something similar is true for physical health, for political freedoms, for economic well-being; we learn their true value after we have lost them. (pp. 163-164; Maslow, 1970)

The "Mystic Experience" or "Oceanic Feeling;" Peak Experiences: The difference between a **mystic experience** (also known as an **oceanic feeling**) and a **peak experience** is a matter of definition. Mystic experiences are viewed as gifts from God, something reserved for special or deserving (i.e., faithful) servants. Maslow, however, believed that this was a natural occurrence that could happen for anyone, and to some extent probably did. He assigned the psychological term of peak experiences. Such experiences tend to be sudden feelings of limitless horizons opening up to one's vision, simultaneous feelings of great power and great vulnerability, feelings of ecstasy, wonder and awe, a loss of the sense of time and place, and the feeling that something extraordinary and transformative has happened. Self-actualizers who do not typically experience these peaks, the so-called "**non-peakers**," are more likely to become direct agents of social change, the reformers, politicians, crusaders, and so on. The more transcendent "**peakers**," in contrast, become the poets, musicians, philosophers, and theologians.

Maslow devoted a great deal of attention to peak experiences, including their relationship to religion. At the core of religion, according to Maslow, is the private illumination or revelation of spiritual leaders. Such experiences seem to be very similar to peak experiences, and Maslow suggests that throughout history these peak experiences may have been mistaken for revelations from God. In his own studies, Maslow found that people who were spiritual, but not religious (i.e., not hindered by the doctrine of a specific faith or church), actually had more peak experiences than other people. Part of the explanation for this, according to Maslow, is that such people need to be more serious about their ethics, values, and philosophy of life, since their guidance and motivation must come from within. Individuals who seek such an appreciation of life may help themselves to experience an extended form of peak experience that Maslow called the **plateau experience**. Plateau experiences always have both noetic and cognitive elements, whereas peak experiences can be entirely emotional (Maslow, 1964). Put another way, plateau experiences involve serene and contemplative **Being-cognition**, as opposed to the more climactic peak experiences (Maslow, 1971).

Gemeinschaftsgefuhl: A word invented by Alfred Adler, **gemeinschatfsgefuhl** refers to the profound feelings of identification, sympathy, and affection for other people that are common in self-actualization individuals. Although self-actualizers may often feel apart from others, like a stranger in a strange land, becoming upset by the shortcomings of the average person, they nonetheless feel a sense of kinship with others. These feelings lead to a sincere desire to help the human race.

Interpersonal Relations: Maslow believed that self-actualizers have deeper and more profound personal relationships than other people. They tend to be kind to everyone, and are especially fond of children. Maslow described this characteristic as "compassion for all mankind," a perspective that would fit well with Buddhist and Christian philosophies.

The Democratic Character Structure: Self-actualizing people are typically friendly with anyone, regardless of class, race, political beliefs, or education. They can learn from anyone who has something to teach them. They respect all people, simply because they are people. They are not, however, undiscriminating:

> The careful distinction must be made between this democratic feeling and a lack of discrimination in taste, of an undiscriminating equalizing of any one human being with any other. These individuals, themselves elite, select for their friends elite, but this is an elite of character, capacity, and talent, rather than of birth, race, blood, name, family, age, youth, fame, or power. (pg. 168; Maslow, 1970)

Discrimination Between Means and Ends, Between Good and Evil: Self-actualizers know the difference between right and wrong. They are ethical, have high moral standards, and they do good things while avoiding doing bad things. They do not experience the average person's confusion or inconsistency in making ethical choices. They tend to focus on ends, rather than means, although they sometimes become absorbed in the means themselves, viewing the process itself as a series of ends.

Philosophical, Unhostile Sense of Humor: The sense of humor shared by self-actualizers is not typical. They do not laugh at hostile, superior, or rebellious humor. They do not tell jokes that make fun of other people. Instead, they poke fun at people in general for being foolish, or trying to claim a place in the universe that is beyond us. Such humor often takes the form of poking fun at oneself, but not in a clown-like way. Although such humor can be found in nearly every aspect of life, to non-self-actualizing people the self-actualizers seem to be somewhat sober and serious.

Creativeness: According to Maslow, self-actualizing people are universally creative. This is not the creativity associated with genius, such as that of Mozart or Thomas Edison, but rather the fresh and naive creativity of an unspoiled child. Maslow believed that this creativity was a natural potential given to all humans at their birth, but that the constraints on behavior inherent in most cultures lead to its suppression.

As desirable as self-actualization may seem, self-actualizing individuals still face problems in their lives. According to Maslow, they are typically not well adjusted. This is because they resist being enculturated. They do not stand out in grossly abnormal ways, but there is a certain inner detachment from the culture in which they live. They are not viewed as rebels in the adolescent sense, though they may be rebels while growing up, but rather they work steadily toward social change and/or the accomplishment of their goals. As a result of their immersion in some personal goal, they may lose interest in or patience with common people and common social practices. Thus, they may seem detached, insulting, absent-minded, or humorless. They can seem boring, stubborn, or irritating, particularly because they are often superficially vain and proud only of their own accomplishments and their own family, friends, and work. According to Maslow, outbursts of temper are not rare. Maslow argued that there are, in fact, people who become saints, movers and shakers, creators, and sages.

However, these same people can be irritating, selfish, angry, or depressed. No one is perfect, not even those who are self-actualizing (Maslow, 1950/1973, 1970).

> **Discussion Question:** Consider Maslow's characteristics of self-actualizing people. Which of those characteristics do you think are part of your personality? Are there any characteristics that you think may be particularly difficult for you to achieve?

Obstacles to Self-Actualization

In *The Farther Reaches of Human Nature* (Maslow, 1971), which was completed by Maslow's wife and one of his colleagues shortly after Maslow's death, Maslow described self-actualization as something that one does not obtain or fulfill at a specific point in time. Rather, it is an ongoing process of self-actualizing, characterized for some by brief periods of self-actualization (the peak experiences, for example). Maslow also described two major obstacles to achieving self-actualization: **desacralizing** and the **Jonah complex**. The Jonah complex, a name suggested by Maslow's friend Professor Frank Manuel, refers to being afraid of one's own greatness, or evading one's destiny or calling in life. Maslow specifically described this as a non-Freudian defense mechanism in which a person is as afraid of the best aspects of their psyche as they are afraid of the worst aspects of their psyche (i.e., the socially unacceptable id impulses). He described the process of this fear as a recognition, despite how much we enjoy the godlike possibilities revealed by our finest accomplishments, of the weakness, awe, and fear we experience when we achieve those accomplishments. According to Maslow, "great emotions after all can in *fact* overwhelm us" (Maslow, 1971). Nonetheless, he encouraged people to strive for greatness, within a reasonable sense of their own limitations.

A very important defense mechanism, which affects young people in particular, is what Maslow called desacralizing. The source of this problem is usually found within the family:

> These youngsters mistrust the possibility of values and virtues. They feel themselves swindled or thwarted in their lives. Most of them have, in fact, dopey parents whom they don't respect very much, parents who are quite confused themselves about values and who, frequently, are simply terrified of their children and never punish them or stop them from doing things that are wrong. So you have a situation where the youngsters simply despise their elders - often for good and sufficient reason. (pg. 49; Maslow, 1971)

As a result, children grow up without respect for their elders, or for anything their elders consider important. The values of the culture itself can be called into question. While such a situation may sometimes be important for changing social conventions that unfairly discriminate against some people, can we really afford to live in a society in which *nothing* is sacred? Indeed, can such a society or culture continue to exist? Thus, Maslow emphasized a need for **resacralizing**. Maslow noted that he had to make up the words desacralizing and resacralizing "because the English language is rotten for good people. It has no decent vocabulary for the virtues" (Maslow, 1971). Resacralizing means being willing to see the sacred, the eternal, the symbolic. As an example, Maslow suggested considering a medical student dissecting a human brain. Would such a student see the brain simply as a biological organ, or would they be awed by it, also seeing the brain as a sacred object, including even its poetic aspects? This concept is particularly important for counselors working with the aged, people approaching the end of their lives, and may be critical for helping them move toward self-actualization. According to Maslow, when someone asks a counselor for help with the self-actualizing process, the counselor had better have an answer for them, "or we're not doing what it is our job to do" (Maslow, 1971).

> **Discussion Question:** Maslow believed that desacralizing was particularly challenging for young people. Do you think our society has lost its way, have we lost sight of meaningful values? Is nothing sacred anymore? Is there anything that you do in your life to recognize something as sacred in a way that has real meaning for your community?

Maslow had something else interesting to say about self-actualization in *The Farther Reaches of Human Nature*: "What does self-actualization mean in moment-to-moment terms? What does it mean on Tuesday at four o'clock?" (pg. 41). Consequently, he offered a preliminary suggestion for an operational definition of the process by which self-actualization occurs. In other words, what are the behaviors exhibited by people on the path toward fulfilling or achieving the fourteen characteristics of self-actualized people described above? Sadly, this could only remain a preliminary description, i.e., they are "ideas that are in midstream rather than ready for formulation into a final version," because this book was published after Maslow's death (having been put together before his sudden and unexpected heart attack).

> What does one do when he self-actualizes? Does he grit his teeth and squeeze? What does self-actualization mean in terms of actual behavior, actual procedure? I shall describe eight ways in which one self-actualizes. (pg. 45; Maslow, 1971)

- They experience full, vivid, and selfless *concentration* and total absorption.
- Within the ongoing process of self-actualization, they make *growth choices* (rather than fear choices; progressive choices rather than regressive choices).
- They are aware that there is a *self* to be actualized.
- When in doubt, they choose to be *honest* rather than dishonest.
- They trust their own *judgment,* even if it means being different or unpopular (being courageous is another version of this behavior).
- They put in the effort necessary to improve themselves, working regularly toward *self-development* no matter how arduous or demanding .
- They embrace the occurrence of *peak experiences*, doing what they can to facilitate and enjoy more of them (as opposed to denying these experiences as many people do).
- They identify and *set aside their ego defenses* (they have "the courage to give them up"). Although this requires that they face up to painful experiences, it is more beneficial than the consequences of defenses such as repression.

Being and Transcendence

Maslow had great hope and optimism for the human race. Although self-actualization might seem to be the pinnacle of personal human achievement, he viewed Humanistic Psychology, or **Third Force Psychology**, as just another step in our progression:

> I should say also that I consider Humanistic, Third Force Psychology to be transitional, a preparation for a still "higher" Fourth Psychology, transpersonal, transhuman, centered in the cosmos rather than in human needs and interest, going beyond humanness, identity, self-actualization, and the like…These new developments may very well offer a tangible, usable, effective satisfaction of the "frustrated idealism" of many quietly desperate people, especially young people. These psychologies give promise of developing into the life-philosophy, the religion-surrogate, the value-system, the life-program that these people have been missing. Without the transcendent and the transpersonal, we get sick, violent, and nihilistic, or else hopeless and apathetic. We need something "bigger than we are" to be awed by and to commit ourselves to in a new, naturalistic, empirical, non-churchly sense, perhaps as Thoreau and Whitman, William James and John Dewey did. (pp. iii-iv; Maslow, 1968)

Although Maslow wrote about this need for a **Fourth Force Psychology** in 1968, it was not until the year 1998 that APA President Martin Seligman issued his call for the pursuit of positive psychology as an active force in the field of psychology. Maslow believed that all self-actualizing people were involved in some calling or vocation, a cause outside of themselves, something that fate has called them to and that they love doing. In so doing, they devote themselves to the search for **Being-values** (or B-values; Maslow, 1964, 1967/2008, 1968). The desire to attain self-actualization results in the B-values acting like needs. Since they are higher than the basic needs, Maslow called them **metaneeds**. When individuals are unable to attain these goals, the result can be

metapathology, a sickness of the soul. Whereas counselors may be able to help the average person with their average problems, metapathologies may require the help of a **metacounselor**, a counselor trained in philosophical and spiritual matters that go far beyond the more instinctoid training of the traditional psychoanalyst (Maslow, 1967/2008). The B-values identified by Maslow (1964) are an interesting blend of the characteristics of self-actualizing individuals and the human needs described by Henry Murray: truth, goodness, beauty, wholeness, dichotomu-transcendence, aliveness, uniqueness, perfection, necessity, completion, justice, order, simplicity, richness, effortlessness, playfulness, self-sufficiency.

Transcendence is typically associated with people who are religious, spiritual, or artistic, but Maslow said that he found transcendent individuals amongst creative people in a wide variety of vocations (including business, managers, educators, and politicians), though there are not many of them in any field. Transcendence, according to Maslow, is the very highest and most holistic level of human consciousness, which involves relating to oneself, to all others, to all species, to nature, and to the cosmos as an end rather than as a means (Maslow, 1971). It is essential that individuals not be reduced to the role they play in relation to others, transcendence can only be found within oneself (Maslow, 1964, 1968). Maslow's idea is certainly not new. Ancient teachings in Yoga tell us that there is a single universal spirit that connects us all, and Buddhists describe this connection as **interbeing**. The Abrahamic religions teach us that the entire universe was created by, and therefore is connected through, one god. It was Maslow's hope that a transcendent Fourth Force in psychology would help all people to become self-actualizing. In Buddhist terms, Maslow was advocating the intentional creation of psychological Bodhisattvas. Perhaps this is what Maslow meant by the term metacounselor.

Connections Across Cultures: Is Nothing Sacred?

Maslow described some lofty ambitions for humanity in *Toward a Psychology of Being* (1968) and *The Farther Reaches of Human Nature* (1971), as well as some challenges we face along the way. Transcendence, according to Maslow, is a loss of our sense of Self, as we begin to feel an intimate connection with the world around us and all other people. But transcendence is exceedingly difficult when we are hindered by the defense mechanism of desacralization. What exactly does the word "sacred" mean? It is not easily found in psychological works. William James often wrote about spiritual matters, but not about what is or is not sacred. Sigmund Freud mentioned sacred prohibitions in his final book, *Moses and Monotheism* (Freud, 1939/1967), but he felt that anything sacred was simply a cultural adaptation of all children's fear of challenging their father's will (and God was created as a symbol of the mythological father). A dictionary definition of sacred says that it is "connected with God (or the gods) or dedicated to a religious purpose and so deserving veneration." However, there is another definition that does not require a religious context: "regarded with great respect and reverence by a particular religion, group, or individual" (The Oxford American College Dictionary, 2002). Maslow described desacralization as a rejection of the values and virtues of one's parents. As a result, people grow up without the ability to see anything as sacred, eternal, or symbolic. In other words, they grow up without meaning in their lives.

The process of resacralization, which Maslow considered an essential task of therapists working with clients who seek help in this critical area of their life, requires that we have some concept of what is sacred. So, what is sacred? Many answers can be found, but there does seem to be at least one common thread.

> Christians have long believed that forgiveness lies at the heart of faith. Psychologists have recently found that forgiveness may also lie at the heart of emotional and physical well-being.
>
> *David Myers & Malcolm Jeeves (2003)*
>
> ...Compassion is the wish that others be free of suffering. It is by means of compassion that we aspire to attain enlightenment. It is compassion that inspires us to engage in the virtuous practices that lead to Buddhahood. We must therefore devote

ourselves to developing compassion.

The Dalai Lama (2001)

I have been engaged in peace work for more than thirty years: combating poverty, ignorance, and disease; going to sea to help rescue boat people; evacuating the wounded from combat zones; resettling refugees; helping hungry children and orphans; opposing wars; producing and disseminating peace literature; training peace and social workers; and rebuilding villages destroyed by bombs. It is because of the practice of meditation - stopping, calming, and looking deeply - that I have been able to nourish and protect the sources of my spiritual energy and continue this work.

Thich Nhat Hanh (1995)

...Our progress is the penetrating of the present moment, living life with our feet on the ground, living in compassionate, active relationship with others, and yet living in the awareness that life has been penetrated by the eternal moment of God and unfolds in the power of that moment.

Fr. Laurence Freeman (1986)

Keep your hands busy with your duties in this world, and your heart busy with God.

Sheikh Muzaffer (cited in *Essential Sufism* by Fadiman & Frager, 1997)

Forgiveness is a letting go of past suffering and betrayal, a release of the burden of pain and hate that we carry.

Forgiveness honors the heart's greatest dignity. Whenever we are lost, it brings us back to the ground of love.

Jack Kornfield (2002)

And he said to him, "You shall love the Lord your God with all your heart, and with all your soul, and with all your mind. This is the great and first commandment. And a second is like it, You shall love your neighbor as yourself..."

Jesus Christ (The Holy Bible, 1962)

In examining self-actualizing people directly, I find that in all cases, at least in our culture, they are dedicated people, devoted to some task "outside themselves," some vocation, or duty, or beloved job. Generally the devotion and dedication is so marked that one can fairly use the old words vocation, calling, or mission to describe their passionate, selfless, and profound feeling for their "work."

The spiritual life is then part of the human essence. It is a defining-characteristic of human nature, without which human nature is not full human nature. It is part of the Real Self, of one's identity, of one's inner core, of one's specieshood, of full humanness.

Abraham Maslow (1971)

Christians, Buddhists, Muslims, as well as members of other religions and humanists, all have some variation of what has been called *The Golden Rule*: treating others as you would like to be treated. If that is sacred, then even amongst atheists, young people can evaluate the values and virtues of their parents, community, and culture, and then decide whether those values are right or wrong, whether they want to perpetuate an aspect of that society based on their own thoughts and feelings about how they, themselves, may be treated someday by others. This resacralization need not be religious or spiritual, but it commonly is, and some psychologists are comfortable embracing spirituality as such.

Kenneth Pargament and Annette Mahoney (2005) wrote a chapter entitled *Spirituality: Discovering and Conserving the Sacred*, which was included in the *Handbook of Positive Psychology* (Snyder & Lopez, 2005). First, they point out that religion is an undeniable fact in American society. Some 95 percent of Americans believe in God, and 86 percent believe that He can be reached through prayer and that He is important or very important to them. Spirituality, according to Pargament and Mahoney, is the process in which individuals seek both to discover and to conserve that which is sacred. It is interesting to note that Maslow and Rogers consider self-actualization and transcendence to be a process as well, not something that one can get and keep permanently. An important aspect of defining what is sacred is that it is imbued with divinity. God may be seen as manifest in marriage, work can be seen as a vocation to which the person is called, the environment can been seen as God's creation. In each of these situations, and in others, what is viewed as sacred has been sanctified by those who consider it sacred. Unfortunately, this can have negative results as well, such as when the Heaven's Gate cult followed their sanctified leader to their deaths. Thus, spirituality is not necessarily synonymous with a good and healthy lifestyle.

Still, there is research that has shown that couples who sanctify their marriage experience greater marital satisfaction, less marital conflict, and more effective marital problem-solving strategies. Likewise, mothers and fathers who sanctify the role of parenting report less aggression and more consistent discipline in raising their children. For college students, spiritual striving was more highly correlated with well-being than any other form of goal-setting (see Pargament & Mahoney, 2005). So there appear to be real psychological advantages to spiritual pursuits. This may be particularly true during challenging times in our lives:

> …there are aspects of our lives that are beyond our control. Birth, developmental transitions, accidents, illnesses, and death are immutable elements of existence. Try as we might to affect these elements, a significant portion of our lives remains beyond our immediate control. In spirituality, however, we can find ways to understand and deal with our fundamental human insufficiency, the fact that there are limits to our control… (pg. 655; Pargament & Mahoney, 2005)

Eupsychian Management and Theory Z

It is not merely a coincidence that Maslow is well-known in the field of business. He spent 3 years as the plant manager for the Maslow Cooperage Corporation, and later he spent a summer studying at an electronics firm in California (Non-Linear Systems, Inc.) at the invitation of the company's president. He became very interested in industrial and managerial psychology, and the journal he kept in California was published as *Eupsychian Management* (Maslow, 1965). **Eupsychia** refers to real possibility and improvability, and a movement toward psychological health, as opposed to the vague fantasies of proposed Utopian societies. More precisely, though this is something of a fantasy itself, Maslow described Eupsychia as the culture that would arise if 1,000 self-actualizing people were allowed to live their own lives on a sheltered island somewhere. Maslow applied his psychological theories, including both the hierarchy of needs and self-actualization, to a management style that takes advantage of this knowledge to maximize the potential of the employees in a company (also see the collection of Maslow's unpublished papers by Hoffman, 1996).

Maslow introduced a variety of terms related to his theories on management, one of the most interesting being **synergy**. Having borrowed the term from Ruth Benedict, synergy refers to a situation in which a person pursuing their own, selfish goals is automatically helping others, and a person unselfishly helping others is, at the same time, helping themselves. According to Maslow, when selfishness and unselfishness are mutually exclusive, it is a sign of mild psychopathology. Self-actualizing individuals are above the distinction between selfishness and unselfishness; they enjoy seeing others experience pleasure. Maslow offered the personal example of feeding strawberries to his little daughter. As the child smacked her lips and thoroughly loved the strawberries, an experience that thrilled Maslow, what was he actually giving up by letting her eat the strawberries instead of eating them himself? In his experience with the Blackfoot tribe, a member named Teddy was able to buy a car. He was the only one who had one, but tradition allowed anyone in the tribe to borrow it. Teddy used his car no more often than anyone else, but he had to pay the bills, including the gas bill. And yet, everyone in the tribe was so proud of him that he was greatly admired and they elected him chief. So, he benefited in other ways by following tradition and letting everyone use his car (Maslow, 1965). In the business field, when managers encourage cooperation and communication, everyone benefits from the healthy growth and continuous improvement of the company. And this leads us to **Theory Z** (which is Eupsychian management).

Douglas McGregor, a professor of industrial relations at the Massachusetts Institute of Technology, was greatly impressed with Maslow's work, and McGregor had used *Motivation and Personality* as a textbook in his business classes. Based on Maslow's theories, McGregor published a book in 1960 in which he outlined two managerial models, **Theory X** and **Theory Y** (Gabor, 2000; Hoffman, 1996). Maslow described the two theories as follows:

> ...To put it succinctly, *Theory Y* assumes that if you give people responsibilities and freedom, then they will like to work and will do a better job. Theory Y also assumes that workers basically like excellence, efficiency, perfection, and the like.
>
> *Theory X*, which still dominates most of the world's workplace, has a contrasting view. It assumes that people are basically stupid, lazy, hurtful, and untrustworthy and, therefore, that you have got to check everything constantly because workers will steal you blind if you don't. (pg. 187; Maslow, 1996a)

The Theory X/Theory Y strategy was intentionally put into practice at Non-Linear Systems, hence Maslow's invitation to study there. Maslow concluded, however, that even Theory Y did not go far enough in maximizing people's potential. People have metaneeds (the need for B-values), needs that go beyond simply offering higher salaries. When employees have their basic needs met, but recognize inefficiency and mismanagement in the company, they will still complain, but these higher level complaints can now be described as **metagrumbles** (as opposed to the lower level grumbles about lower level needs). Theory Z attempts to transcend Theory Y and actively facilitate the growth of a company's employees toward self-actualization (Hoffman, 1996; Maslow, 1971; Maslow 1996b).

Discussion Question: How's your job (or any job you have had)? Would you describe your supervisor or boss as someone who uses Eupsychian or Theory Z management? Does the workplace foster synergy amongst the employees? If not, can you imagine how the job would be different if they did?

Henry Murray and Personology

Henry Murray was primarily psychodynamic in his orientation. However, the fundamental aspect of his theory is the presence of needs in our lives, and there was a distinctly humanistic aspect to his theories as well (Maddi & Costa, 1972). Thus, it seems appropriate to include Murray alongside Maslow's discussion of human needs. In addition, Murray developed a practical application of his famous test, the **Thematic Apperception Test** (or **TAT**), for screening candidates for special work assignments. Once again, this is similar to Maslow's forays into the field of industrial/organizational psychology. Although it is common to present different fields as fundamentally opposed, such as humanistic psychology **vs.** psychodynamic psychology, Murray and Maslow provide an ideal opportunity to see the commonalities that often exist between different areas in psychology. It must also be remembered that Murray was no strict adherent to the dogmatic view of psychoanalysis presented by Freud:

> ...psychoanalysis stands for a conceptual system which explains, it seems to me, as much as any other. But this is no reason for going in blind and swallowing the whole indigestible bolus,

> cannibalistically devouring the totem father in the hope of acquiring his genius, his authoritative dominance, and thus rising to power in the psychoanalytic society, that battle-ground of Little Corporals. No; I, for one, prefer to take what I please, suspend judgment, reject what I please, speak freely. (pg. 31; Murray, 1940/2008).

Brief Biography of Henry Murray

Henry Alexander Murray, Jr. was born in 1893 in New York City. He had many nicknames, and typically asked his friends to call him Harry. His family was quite wealthy, and had a noble history. He was a descendant of John Murray, the fourth Earl of Dunmore, the last Royal Governor of Virginia, and his mother's great-grandfather, Colonel Harry Babcock, had served on General George Washington's staff during the Revolutionary War. Murray lived a life of luxury, spending the summers on Long Island and often traveling throughout Europe. He was educated at exclusive private schools. However, his childhood was not without challenges. He felt abandoned by his mother, who suffered from depression much of her life, when Murray was quite young. He stuttered, and was cross-eyed. The operation to help cure his internal strabismus accidentally left him with an external strabismus. This created problems for Murray when it came to competing in athletics, but Murray worked hard to overcome his difficulties and he excelled at sports. He became the quarterback of his football team and won a featherweight boxing championship at school. In college, he made the rowing team at Harvard University (Maddi & Costa, 1972; Robinson, 1992).

In spite of his athletic success at Harvard, or perhaps because of it, he did not do well academically, receiving below average grades. Nonetheless, he earned a degree in history in 1915. While at Harvard he also married Josephine Rantoul, after a lengthy courtship. Despite his mediocre grades at Harvard, Murray was accepted into the Columbia College of Physicians and Surgeons, and graduated first in his class in 1919. He then completed a surgical internship at Presbyterian Hospital in New York, where he once treated the future president Franklin D. Roosevelt, followed by a period of research at the Rockefeller Institute for Medical Research and Cambridge University, which culminated in a Ph.D. in biochemistry in 1927. He then accepted a position as assistant to Morton Prince, and became the director of Harvard University's psychology clinic. Murray had never taken a psychology course, but he had some interesting experience (Maddi & Costa, 1972; Robinson, 1992).

Murray had a psychiatry course in medical school, and had read Freud's *Interpretation of Dreams*. He also had a research assistant from Vienna, Alma Rosenthal, who had been a long-time friend of Anna Freud. While both working together and having an intimate love affair, Rosenthal introduced Murray to the deeper dimensions of the unconscious mind. However, it was Murray's lifelong mistress, Christiana Morgan, who introduced him to Jung's book *Psychology Types*. Murray was deeply impressed by Jung's book, but even more by Jung himself. Murray was troubled by the intense love affair he had developed with Morgan, so he went to Zurich in order to be psychoanalyzed by Jung. Jung managed to help Murray understand his stuttering and accept having his affair with Morgan. After all, Jung had maintained a mistress of his own for many years. Jung also managed to convince Murray's wife and Morgan's husband to accept the affair as well, and Christiana Morgan remained a very important colleague throughout Murray's life. It has been suggested that she played a far more important role in his theories, and in the development of the TAT, than she has been given credit for (Maddi & Costa, 1972; Robinson, 1992). Partly because Jung had directly helped him with a psychological problem, and partly because of the extraordinary range of ideas that Jung was open to, Murray always spoke highly of Jung (though he believed that Jung tended toward being psychotic, just as Freud tended toward being neurotic; see Brian, 1995).

Initially, Murray's reappointment as clinic director was challenged by the experimental psychologists Edwin Boring and Karl Lashley, but he was supported by the clinical psychologists, who were led by Gordon Allport (Stagner, 1988). As his work continued he was quite productive (it was during this time that he developed the TAT), and many important clinicians passed through the clinic. Included among them was Erik Erikson, who came to the clinic after having been psychoanalyzed by Anna Freud in Vienna. Murray also spent a great deal of time traveling and studying in Europe, and enjoyed a memorable evening with Sigmund and Anna Freud. As he was preparing to return to the clinic, World War II began. Murray joined the Army Medical Corps, and eventually worked for the Office of Strategic Services (OSS). Of particular interest was his use of the TAT to screen OSS agents for sensitive missions (the OSS was the precursor to the CIA, so in peacetime these agents would be called spies). He was in China studying errors they had made in their assessments when the atomic bomb was dropped on Hiroshima. Murray was shocked, and devoted the rest of his life to seeking alternatives to war (Maddi & Costa, 1972; Robinson, 1992).

As his career and life approached their ends, Murray received the *Distinguished Scientific Contribution Award* from the American Psychological Association, and the *Gold Medal Award* from the American Psychological Foundation. He received numerous honorary degrees, and collections of papers have been published in his honor (e.g., White, 1963; Zucker, Rabin, Aronoff, & Frank, 1992). In June, 1988, Murray told his nurse that he was dead. She disagreed with him, and pinched him gently on the cheek to prove her point. He curtly disagreed with her, declaring that he was the doctor, she was the nurse, and he was dead. A few days later he was right (Robinson, 1992).

Placing Murray in Context: A Challenging Task

There does not seem to be a consensus on where Murray fits within the field of personality theory. Trained as a Freudian psychoanalyst, he is often grouped with the neo-Freudians. However, he has also been placed with the trait theorists, and he was a colleague of Gordon Allport. However, many personality theory textbooks don't consider Murray worthy of significant attention. He is included alongside Maslow in this textbook because his work focused primarily on needs. In addition, the practical application of his Thematic Apperception Test in screening candidates for OSS assignments was similar to Maslow's application of psychological principles in the business field.

The Thematic Apperception Test is certainly Murray's claim to fame. It remains one of the best-known tests in psychology, having been applied in research, business, and therapeutic settings. Since Murray used the TAT in combination with the Rorschach Inkblot Test, he maintained his ties to traditional psychoanalysis and helped to advance the fame of the other renowned projective test. As such, his practical contributions to psychology seem to outweigh his theoretical contributions.

It has been said that the value of a theory can be measured by the research that follows. David McClelland's use of the TAT to study the need for achievement is a common topic in introductory psychology textbooks. Thus, Murray's contributions have inspired classic research in psychology. That alone should ensure a place of significance for Murray in the history of personality theory.

Human Needs

In *Explorations in Personality* (Murray, 1938), Murray describes people as "today's great problem". What can we know about someone, and how can we describe it in a way that has clear meaning? Nothing is more important in the field of psychology:

> The point of view adopted in this book is that personalities constitute the subject matter of psychology, the life history of a single man being a unit with which this discipline has to deal… Our guiding thought was that personality is a temporal whole and to understand a part of it one must have sense, though vague, of the totality. (pgs. 3-4; Murray, 1938)

Thus, Murray and his colleagues sought to understand the nature of personality, in order to help them understand individuals. He referred to this direct study of personality as **personology**, simply because he considered it clumsy to refer to "the psychology of personality" instead.

Murray described the very elegant process by which the Harvard Clinic group systematically approached their studies, and then presented a lengthy series of propositions regarding a theory of personality. The primary focus of these propositions came down to what Murray called a press-need combination. A **need**, according to Murray, is a hypothetical process that is imagined to occur in order to account for certain objective and subjective facts. In other words, when an organism reliably acts in a certain way to obtain some goal, we can determine that the organism had a need to achieve that goal. Needs are often recognized only after the fact, the behavior that satisfies the need may be a blind impulse, but it still leads toward satisfying the needed goal. **Press** is the term Murray applied to environmental objects or situations that designate directional tendencies, or that guide our needs. Anything in the environment, either harmful or beneficial to the organism, exerts press. Thus, our current needs, in the context of current environmental press, determine our ongoing behavior (Murray, 1938).

Like Maslow, Murray separated needs into biological and psychology factors based on how essential they were to one's survival. The primary, or **viscerogenic needs**, include air, water, food, sex, harm-avoidance, etc. The secondary or **psychogenic needs**, which are presumed to derive from the primary needs, are common reaction systems and wishes. Although Murray organizes the psychogenic needs into groups, they are not rank-ordered as was Maslow's hierarchy, so we will not consider the groups any further. Individually, there are a total of twenty-eight human needs (Murray, 1938). A partial list, with definitions, includes the following:

- Acquisition: the need to gain possessions and property
- Retention: the need to retain possession of things, to refuse to give or lend
- Order: the need to arrange, organize, put away objects, to be tidy and clean
- Construction: the need to build things
- Achievement: the need to overcome obstacles, to exercise power, to strive to do something difficult as well and as quickly as possible
- Recognition: the need to excite praise and commendation, to demand respect
- Exhibition: the need to attract attention to oneself
- Defendance: the need to defend oneself against blame or belittlement
- Counteraction: the need to proudly overcome defeat by restriving and retaliating, to defend one's honor
- Dominance: the need to influence or control others
- Deference: the need to admire and willingly follow a superior
- Aggression: the need to assault or injure another, to harm, blame, accuse, or ridicule a person
- Abasement: the need to surrender, to comply and accept punishment
- Affiliation: the need to form friendships and associations, to greet, join, and live with others, to love
- Rejection: the need to snub, ignore, or exclude others
- Play: the need to relax, amuse oneself, seek diversion and entertainment
- Cognizance: the need to explore, to ask questions, to satisfy curiosity

According the Murray, in the course of daily life these needs are often interrelated. When a single action can satisfy more than one need, we can say that the needs are fused. However, needs can also come into conflict. For example, an individual's need for dominance may make it difficult to satisfy their need for affiliation, unless they can find someone with a powerful need for abasement. Such a situation is one of the ways in which psychologists have tried to understand abusive relationships. In other words, when someone with a strong need for affiliation and debasement becomes involved with someone with a strong need for affiliation and dominance (particularly in a pathological sense), the results can be very unfortunate.

Anyone who has children is often reminded of their need for playing, and most any setting can provide an opportunity for play. Here, the author's children are playing cards. [Image by Mark Kelland]

Any object, or person, that evokes a need is said to "be cathected" by the person being studied. In other words, they have invested some of their limited psychic energy (libido) into that object. Murray believed that an individual's personality is revealed by the objects to which that person is attached by the cathexis of libido, especially if you can recognize the intensity, endurance, and rigidity of the cathexis. This process not only applies to individuals, but institutions and cultures also have predictable patterns in terms of their cathected objects. Put more simply, we can strive to understand individuals, including doing so from a cross-cultural perspective, by examining the nature and pattern of needs they seek to satisfy in their daily lives (Murray, 1938).

Morris Stein, who worked with Murray in the OSS and then earned a Ph.D. at the Harvard Clinic, combined Murray's work on identifying human needs and Jung's concept of psychological types. By looking at patterns in the rank-order of needs among industrial chemists and Peace Corps volunteers, Stein was able to divide each group into separate psychological types (Stein, 1963). For example, there were five basic types of industrial chemists: Type A was achievement oriented but still worked well with others; Type B focused on pleasing others, often at the expense of their own ideas; Type C was achievement oriented, but more driven and hostile than Type A; Type D was motivated by achievement and affiliation, but with an emphasis on order that protected them from criticism or blame; and Type E was particularly focused on relationships marked by cooperation and trust. As interesting as these types may be, they are quite different than the personality types identified amongst the Peace Corps volunteers (Stein, 1963). Thus, although Stein's investigation suggests that personality types can be identified based on patterns of need, this approach probably would not provide a general theory of personology that could be applied to anyone.

Discussion Question: Consider Murray's list of psychogenic needs. Which needs are the ones that affect you the most? Are you able to fulfill those needs?

The TAT and the OSS

Murray is typically credited with the development the TAT. However, the original article has Christiana Morgan as the first author (Morgan & Murray, 1935), and in *Explorations in Personality* most of the TAT work is described by Morgan (Murray, 1938). Apparently, when the test was revised and republished in 1943, Murray did most of the revision, partly because Morgan was quite ill at the time. The TAT consists of a series of pictures depicting potentially dramatic events (although the pictures are actually rather vague). The person taking the test is asked to provide a story that relates events preceding the picture to some final outcome of the situation. It is expected that the subject will project their own thoughts and feelings into the picture as they create their story. In order for this to be possible, Morgan and Murray made sure that in most pictures there was at least one person with whom the subject could easily empathize and identify themselves. The TAT became one of the most popular projective tests ever developed, and continues to be widely used today.

The TAT has been used in two particularly interesting settings outside of clinical psychology: to study the need for achievement (see the next section), and to screen agents for the Office of Strategic Services during World War II. Murray used the TAT as part of a program to help select members of the OSS for critical, dangerous missions. Even before joining the OSS, Murray worked for the government in support of the war effort. In conjunction with Gordon Allport, he provided an analysis of the personality of Adolf Hitler, along with predictions as to how Hitler might react after Germany was defeated. He also helped to develop a series of questions for the crew of a captured German U-boat. The OSS program involved assessing candidate's responses to highly stressful situations. In addition to psychological testing, using instruments such as the TAT, the candidates were put into highly stressful situations. For example, they were told to pick two men to help them put together a five-foot cube with wooden poles, blocks, and pegs. However, the available men were all secretly on Murray's staff. One of them would act helpless and passive, whereas the other made stupid suggestions and constantly criticized the recruit. The task was, of course, never completed, but it provided Murray with the information he needed on how the candidate performed under stress (Brian, 1995; Robinson, 1992).

In the next chapter we will see that the existential psychologist Rollo May talked about our need for myths, in order to make sense out of our often senseless world. Although this was not a need included by Murray, he did have an interest in mythology. The imagination that is necessary to create a story around a picture in the TAT often involves symbolism that arises from the depths of the whole self (Murray, 1960). In this regard, Murray sounds quite similar to Jung and his theory of archetypes, and Murray discussed some classic images from our historical mythology. Of particular interest to Murray, however, is whether or not we will establish new myths in the future. There are older myths that remain oriented to our future, such as the apocalyptic myths or the myth of the Promised Land (Murray, 1960). The existential philosopher Jean-Paul Sartre lamented the demythologizing of the universe by science, and he advocated a remythologizing of the self (see McAdams, 1992). Given that Murray did include a need for cognizance, the need to explore, to ask questions, and to satisfy curiosity, perhaps there will be new myths created in our future. If so, psychologists will need to keep current with the cultural phenomena that influence people's unconscious projections onto the TAT and other projective tests.

David McClelland and the Need for Achievement

David McClelland, who joined the faculty of Harvard University a few years before Murray retired, conducted some well-known research utilizing the TAT to examine the **need for achievement**. The research began shortly after World War II, and was supported by the Office of Naval Research. McClelland and his colleagues made an interesting point, in the preface to their book *The Achievement Motive* (McClelland, Atkinson, Clark, & Lowell, 1953), about studying just one of Murray's needs: "concentration on a limited research problem is not necessarily narrowing; it may lead ultimately into the whole of psychology." Indeed, they felt that they learned a great deal about personality by studying one of the most important of human needs.

McClelland and his colleagues used the TAT and borrowed heavily from Murray's procedures and scoring system. However, they made a number of modifications. They used additional pictures of their own, they often presented the pictures on a screen to a group of subjects, those subjects were all male college students, and some of their experimental conditions were designed to evoke achievement-oriented responses, or responses based on success or failure. An important aspect of this study was that the TAT (and similar pictures developed by McClelland) requires writing imaginative stories of what the subject projects onto the picture. Therefore, situations that stimulate achievement-oriented imagination can result in higher scores on the need for achievement, something that McClelland and his colleagues confirmed in Navaho children during the course of their research (suggesting it is a universal phenomenon). Overall, they found that individuals who are high in their need for achievement perform more tasks during timed tests, improve more quickly in their ability to perform those tasks, set higher levels of aspirations, remember more of the tasks they failed to perform, and they are more future-oriented and recognize achievement-oriented situations (McClelland et al., 1953). In addition, they found a positive correlation between the need for achievement and cultures and families in which there is an emphasis on the individual development of children, with early childhood being of particular importance. After examining eight Native American cultures (Navaho, Ciricahua-Apache, Western Apache, Hopi, Comanche, Sanpoil, Paiute, and Flatheads), McClelland and his colleagues determined that the need for achievement in each culture (measured from classic legends involving the archetypal trickster "coyote") correlates highly with both an early age onset and the severity of independence training (McClelland et al., 1953). In summary, the need for achievement is a motivational force that develops in early childhood, and which pushes individuals toward accomplishing life's tasks.

An excellent essay on the need for achievement, which addresses some of the criticism this concept has endured, was written by McClelland in a new introduction for the second printing of his book *The Achieving Society* (McClelland, 1976). This book also adds to the cross-cultural reach of McClelland's work, since as he extends his theory on the need for achievement to the societies in which individuals live he also extends his theory to other societies around the world. First, the concept itself has typically been misunderstood:

> …the word "achievement" cues all sorts of surplus meanings that the technically defined *n* Achievement variable does not have. It refers specifically to the desire to do something better, faster, more efficiently, with less effort. It is not a generalized desire to succeed… (pg. A; McClelland, 1976)

In studying the role of need for achievement within societies, McClelland focused on business and economic development as one of the most easily compared aspects of different cultures. He believed that nations possess something like a "group mind," which can lead the nation in certain directions. Again using literary sources as examples of cultural perspectives on the need for achievement, McClelland found support for his theory that high need for achievement preceded dramatic societal development in ancient Greece, pre-Incan Peru, Spain in the late middle ages, England leading up to the industrial revolution, and during the development of the United States (particularly in the 1800s). Once again, McClelland cautions against over-generalizing the meaning of need for achievement:

> It is a very specific, rather rare, drive which focuses on the goal of efficiency and which expresses itself in activities available in the culture which permit or encourage one to be more efficient; and across cultures the most common form such activity takes is business. (pg. B; McClelland, 1976)

The question of where the need for achievement comes from continued to perplex McClelland. Although early childhood appears to be when a lasting need for achievement develops, the need for achievement can be enhanced in adults through training seminars. More importantly, however, is the question of where need for achievement comes from in the first place, how does it develop within a society? When McClelland was working in Ethiopia with the Peace Corps, he studied the Gurage. This small tribal group was treated with disdain by both the dominant Christian Amhara and the Muslim Galla tribes. And yet the Gurage were recognized for their clever business strategies, and their children wrote stories filled with imagery indicative of a high need for achievement. Since the Gurage had developed without contact with Western Christian, Muslim, or Greco-Roman cultures, they seemed to have developed their own need for achievement. Unfortunately, so little is known about their history, that McClelland was unable to identify the source of their motivation (McClelland, 1976).

In support of the contention that studying the need for achievement could provide insights into many aspects of personality, McClelland pursued a number of interesting topics throughout his career, including how societies can motivate economic growth and identify talent (McClelland, Baldwin, Bronfenbrenner, & Strodtbeck, 1958; McClelland & Winter, 1969), the power motive (McClelland, 1975), the development of social maturity and values (McClelland, 1982a; McClelland, 1982b), and a cross-cultural study on the role of alcohol in society (McClelland, Davis, Kalin, & Wanner, 1972). Moving in a quite different direction, McClelland also wrote a book entitled *The Roots of Consciousness* (McClelland, 1964), in which he argues that Sigmund Freud's psychoanalysis is really an expression of Jewish spiritual mysticism known as Kabbalah. We will examine Kabbalah, as well as Christian and Islamic mysticism, as a positive approach to one's lifestyle in Chapter 18.

Discussion Question: McClelland found support for his ideas on the development of the need for achievement amongst Native Americans, but he did not find that same support among the Gurage tribe in Ethiopia (they had a strong need for achievement, but the source was unclear). How important do you think it is for us to re-examine psychological theories in multiple cultures, and what would it mean for psychology if we often find contradictions?

A Final Note: Humanistic or Existential?

In this chapter we have examined the humanistic theories of Carl Rogers and Abraham Maslow. In the next chapter we will examine the existential theories of Viktor Frankl and Rollo May. What really is the difference? The distinction is subtle, based on definition, and may seem nonexistent at first glance. Indeed, both the humanistic and existential theorists have been influenced by the likes of Adler, Horney, Fromm, and Otto Rank, and Rogers in particular often writes about existential choices in his books. Even the cognitive therapist Albert Ellis, himself profoundly influenced by Adler, considered Rational Emotive Behavior Therapy to be distinctly humanistic (see *Humanistic Psychotherapy*; Ellis, 1973). In 1986, the Saybrook Institute republished a series of essays, which had appeared in the *Journal of Humanistic Psychology*, under the title *Politics and Innocence: A Humanistic Debate* (May, Rogers, Maslow, et al., 1986). In this volume, Rogers refers to May as "the leading scholar of humanistic psychology." May, for his part, concluded an open letter to Rogers in which he expressed "profound respect for you and your contribution in the past to all of us." May also maintained a friendship and correspondence with Maslow (May, 1991). Clearly, the humanistic and existential psychologists have much in common, and the important figures here in America communicated actively and with respect for the contributions of each other.

Personality Theory in Real Life: Seeking Self-Actualization

Carl Rogers described the actualizing tendency as something that exists within every living organism. It is a tendency to grow, develop, and realize one's full potential. It can be thwarted, but it cannot be destroyed without destroying the organism itself. His person-centered approach was based on this belief, and the resulting trust that one can place in each person. In other words, we can trust that each person is driven forward by this actualizing tendency, and that under the right conditions it will flourish (Rogers, 1977, 1986/1989).

According to Abraham Maslow, life is a process of choices. At each point, we must choose between a progression choice and a regression choice. Although many people make safe, defensive choices, self-actualizing people regularly make **growth choices** (Maslow, 1971). Each growth choice moves the person closer to self-actualization, and the process continues throughout life.

So, consider your own life. Do you feel the actualizing tendency within you? Do you aspire to accomplish something great, or simply to be a good person in whatever path you choose? Think about your educational and/or career plans. Think about your life plans, and whether they include a family or special friends. Do you feel a calling that is pulling in one direction or another? The drive to accomplish, to make a contribution to your community or society, the belief that you are meant for great things, or simply that you are meant to be a source of support for others, all of these might be aspects of your actualizing tendency. Or are you moving through life without a plan, without goals? Do you skate along from day to day, with no destination in mind?

If you do feel your actualizing tendency, consider how you are living your life. Are you pursuing the steps necessary to accomplish your goals? Have you made choices, perhaps difficult choices, which have moved you forward toward those goals?

Basically, do you feel that you are on a path toward self-actualization, and do you think you should be? Is it reasonable to expect, or hope, that everyone might become self-actualized?

What might it be like to live a fully transcendent, self-actualized life? Although there are many different, and individual, answers to that question, we can find one example in the remarkable life of Peace Pilgrim (Friends of Peace Pilgrim, 1982). No one knows her original name, or exactly where or when she was born (other than it was on a small farm in the Eastern United States in the early 1900s). Her family was poor, but happy, and she enjoyed her childhood. Her life was fruitful, but eventually she found the world's focus on self-centeredness and material goods to be unfulfilling. In 1953, she chose to leave her life behind. She adopted the name Peace Pilgrim, and began walking across America as a prayer for peace.

> A pilgrim is a wanderer with a purpose…Mine is for peace, and that is why I am a Peace Pilgrim…My pilgrimage covers the entire peace picture: peace among nations, peace among groups, peace within our environment, peace among individuals, and the very, very important inner peace - which I talk about most often because that is where peace begins…I have no money. I do not accept any money on my pilgrimage. I belong to no organization…I own only what I wear and carry. There is nothing to tie me down. I am as free as a bird soaring in the sky.
>
> I walk until given shelter, fast until given food. I don't ask - it's given without asking. Aren't people good! There is a spark of good in everybody, no matter how deeply it may be buried, it is there. It's waiting to govern your life gloriously. (pg. 25; Peace Pilgrim cited in Friends of Peace Pilgrim, 1982)

Between 1953 and her death in 1981, she walked, and walked, and walked. By 1964, she had walked 25,000 miles, including walking across the United States twice and through every Canadian province. After that, she no longer kept track of her mileage, but she completed at least four more pilgrimages, including Alaska, Hawaii, and a pilgrimage in Mexico. Among the many friends and admirers she met along the way, there are two notable people (whom psychology students should be familiar with) who provided comments for the cover of her book: Elisabeth Kubler-Ross called her "a wonderful lady," and the popular author/counselor Wayne Dyer said "she is my hero." As for your own life, Peace Pilgrim has some simple advice:

> There is no glimpse of the light without walking the path. You can't get it from anyone else, nor can you give it to anyone. Just take whatever steps seem easiest for you, and as you take a few steps it will be easier for you to take a few more. (pg. 91; Peace Pilgrim cited in Friends of Peace Pilgrim, 1982).

Carl Rogers, Abraham Maslow, and Henry Murray

Review of Key Points

- Rogers began his clinical career searching for effective ways of conducting psychotherapy, since the techniques he had been taught were not providing adequate results.
- Rogers believed that each person exists in their own, unique experiential field. Only they can see that field clearly, although even they may not perceive it accurately (incongruence).
- Everyone has an actualizing tendency, according to Rogers. The term commonly applied to this tendency is self-actualization.
- The self is that portion of the experiential field that is recognized as "I" or "me." It is organized into a self-structure.
- Rogers used the term personal power to describe each person's ability to make choices necessary for the actualization of their self-structure and to then fulfill those choices or goals.
- In order for a person to grow, they must fulfill a need for positive regard. This can only come from receiving unconditional positive regard from important family members and friends (typically beginning with the parents).
- When people receive only conditional positive regard, they develop conditions of worth. Their self-regard then becomes tied to those conditions of worth.
- When an individual's self-regard and positive regard are closely related, the person is said to be congruent. If not, they are said to be incongruent.
- Congruence and incongruence can be measured by understanding the gap between a person's real self and their ideal self.
- Rogers described individuals who are congruent and continuing to grow as fully functioning persons.
- Relationships can serve to mirror our true personality, and to reveal incongruence we are unaware of ourselves.
- Successful marriages, according to Rogers, seem to be based on dedication/commitment, communication, dissolution of roles, and maintaining each person's separate self.
- Rogers identified six necessary and sufficient conditions for positive therapeutic change, conditions that can exist in any interpersonal relationships (not just in therapy). The key factor in these relationships may be empathic understanding.
- Rogers extended his study of clinical psychology into other groups designed to help all people grow and self-actualize, such as T-groups and encounter groups. He described his shift from purely clinical work to fostering growth in all people as a person-centered approach.
- Maslow worked with an amazing range of people, from the renowned experimental psychologists Harry Harlow and Edward Thorndike, to the Gestalt psychologist Max Wertheimer and the personality theorists/clinicians Alfred Adler, Karen Horney, and Erich Fromm.
- Values were very important to Maslow in his approach to psychology. He did not, however, advocate his own values. He reached beyond humanistic psychology to include areas of study such as existential psychology, existential theology, and Zen Buddhism.
- Maslow described a hierarchy of needs, as follows: physiological needs, safety needs, belongingness and love needs, esteem needs, and the need for self-actualization. Lower needs must be largely satisfied before the individual begins to focus on higher needs.
- The lower needs can be described as deficiency-needs, whereas self-actualization is a Being-need.
- In addition to the basic needs, there are also cognitive needs and aesthetic needs.
- Maslow described fourteen characteristics of self-actualizing people. He developed his list by studying both contemporary and historical people who seemed to him to be self-actualizing.
- Perhaps the best know characteristic of self-actualizing is the peak experience. This experience is often described in mystical terms, and Maslow believed it may have provided a basis for the creation of religion in the early history of the human species.
- Maslow described two defense mechanisms that interfere with the process of self-actualizing: desacralizing and the Jonah complex.

- Maslow proposed a Fourth Force Psychology based on Being-values and metaneeds. He felt that some people could suffer from a sickness of the soul, a so-called metapathology, and Maslow suggested a need for metacounselors.
- Some individuals experience profound peak experiences, which Maslow described as transcendent. His concept of transcendence seems very close to the Buddhist perspective of interbeing.
- Maslow proposed that organizations should seek Eupsychia, a realistically attainable environment in which the actualizing tendency of all the organization's members are supported.
- When Eupsychian management does support self-actualization, the actualization of each person benefits the others around them. The process is known as synergy.
- Based on a management model that described Theory X and theory Y management styles, Maslow proposed Theory Z. Theory Z management seeks a transcendent management style that encourages and maximizes self-actualization and synergy in the work place.
- Murray based "personology" on the study of needs. He distinguished between viscerogenic needs and psychogenic needs.
- Christiana Morgan and Murray developed the Thematic Apperception Test, a famous projective psychological test. Murray used the test during World War II to select special agents for highly sensitive, dangerous missions.
- Murray believed that a person's ability to create a story around a picture in the TAT was based in large part on their personal mythology. He shared this interest in myth, and its role in psychology, with Carl Jung and Rollo May.
- McClelland used the TAT to study the need for achievement. Initially, McClelland considered parental influence very important for the development of the achievement need, a finding he confirmed in Native Americans. However, he found contradictory evidence when he studied the Gurage tribe in Ethiopia. Thus, he considered the true source of the achievement need as something needing further research.
- The distinction between humanistic psychology and existential psychology is not clear, and there is significant overlap in the thinking of representatives from both fields. In addition, there is a distinct humanistic element in the psychodynamic theories of Adler, Horney, Fromm, Murray, and others.

Review of Key Terms

actualizing tendency	hierarchy of needs	physiological needs
aesthetic needs	holistic-dynamic theory	positive regard
basic needs	homeostasis	prepotent
Being-cognition	ideal self	press
Being-needs	interbeing	psychogenic needs
Being-values	incongruence	real self
belongingness and love needs	instinctoid	resacralizing
client-centered therapy	Jonah complex	safety needs
cognitive needs	metacounselor	self
conditional positive regard	metagrumbles	self-actualization
conditions of worth	metaneeds	self-regard
congruence	metapathology	self-structure
contact comfort	mystic experience	synergy
growth choices	need	T-groups
deficiency-needs	need for achievement	Thematic Apperception Test (TAT)
desacralizing	need for self-actualization	Theory X
empathic understanding	non-peakers	Theory Y
encounter groups	oceanic feeling	Theory Z
esteem needs	peak experience	Third Force Psychology
eupsychia	peakers	unconditional positive regard
experiential field	personal power	
	person-centered approach	

Fourth Force Psychology fully functioning person gemeinschaftsgefühl	personology plateau experience	values viscerogenic needs

Annotated Bibliography

Rogers, C. R. (1951). *Client-centered therapy*. Boston, MA: Houghton Mifflin Company.

This is the classic text in which Rogers presented the major ideas behind client-centered therapy and the theoretical basis for personality development and change. Rogers included numerous clinical examples in support of his ideas.

Rogers, C. R. (1961). *On becoming a person*. Boston, MA: Houghton Mifflin Company.
Rogers, C. R. (1980). *A way of Being*. Boston, MA: Houghton Mifflin Company.

In these books Rogers presented a more mature perspective on client-centered therapy and his developing person-centered approach. The first book includes his ideas on the nature of helping relationships and the fully functioning person. The second book emphasizes the person-centered approach and empathic understanding.

Rogers, C. R. (1977). *On personal power: Inner strength and its revolutionary impact*. New York, NY: Delacorte Press.

This is Rogers' major work on the person-centered approach and its implications for society. Throughout the book Rogers describes the movement toward a person-centered approach as a quiet revolution.

Kirschenbaum, H. & Henderson, V. L. (Eds.). (1989). *The Carl Rogers reader*. Boston, MA: Houghton Mifflin Company.

This is an excellent collection of Rogers' work, including autobiographical essays written in 1961, 1972, 1980, and 1987. The collection also includes Rogers' 1957 article *The Necessary and Sufficient Conditions of Therapeutic Personality Change*.

Maslow, A. H. (1970). *Motivation and Personality, 2nd Ed*. New York, NY: Harper & Row, Publishers.
Maslow, A. H. (1968). *Toward a psychology of Being, 2nd Ed*. New York, NY: D. Van Nostrand Company.

These are Maslow's two major books. In the first, he collects his perspectives on human motivation, including his work on the hierarchy of needs and self-actualization. In the second book, he emphasizes growth, values, and the future of psychology.

Maslow, A. H. (1964). *Religions, values, and peak-experiences*. New York, NY: The Viking Press.

In this thought-provoking book, Maslow questions whether religious experiences, such as the revelations described by prophets of many religions, might in fact have been peak experiences. In addition, he discusses the relationship between peak experiences and Being-values.

Maslow, A. H. (1965). *Eupsychian management: A journal*. Homewood, IL: Richard D. Irwin, Inc. & The Dorsey Press.

This wonderful book is an actual journal that Maslow kept during his time as a Visiting Fellow at Non-Linear Systems in Del Mar, California in 1962. Maslow speculates on a wide variety of social psychological factors as they pertain to the working conditions and management styles present at Non-Linear Systems, as well as the implications of management style for the future of the company.

McClelland, D. C., Atkinson, J. W., Clark, R. A., & Lowell, E. L. (1953). *The achievement motive*. New York, NY: Appleton-Century-Crofts.

McClelland, D. C. (1976). *The achieving society - With a new introduction*. New York, NY: Irvington Publishers.

These are the two major books on the need for achievement as studied by McClelland and his colleagues. *The Achievement Motive* outlines the basic concepts and the research done to support this theory. *The Achieving Society* was first published in 1961, but the new introduction to the later printing is an excellent summary in which McClelland responds to several critiques of his research. This book also extends the concept of achievement motivation to whole societies.

Murray, H. A. (1938). Explorations in personality: A clinical study of fifty men of college age. New York, NY: Oxford University Press.

Murray describes the combined effort of twenty-seven members of the Harvard Psychological Clinic, working under Murray's direction, in this remarkable book. He clearly describes the systematic approach they followed in collecting their data and validating their theoretical proposals regarding personology. Murray then thoughtfully describes the underlying needs that influence personality. Included are a number of actual responses to the TAT by subjects in this study.

Chapter 16 - Viktor Frankl, Rollo May, and Existential Psychology

> Man is nothing else but what he makes of himself. Such is the first principle of Existentialism...For we mean that man first exists, that is, that man first of all is the being who hurls himself toward a future and who is conscious of imagining himself as being in the future...Thus, Existentialism's first move is to make every man aware of what he is and to make the full responsibility of his existence rest on him. (pg. 456; Jean-Paul Sartre, 1947/1996)

Existential psychology is the area within psychology most closely linked to the field of philosophy. Curiously, this provides one of the most common complaints against existential psychology. Many historians identify the establishment of Wilhelm Wundt's experimental laboratory in Germany in 1879 as the official date of the founding of psychology. Sigmund Freud, with his strong background in biomedical research, also sought to bring scientific methodology to the study of the mind and mental processes, including psychological disorders and psychotherapy. Shortly thereafter, Americans such as Edward Thorndike and John Watson were establishing behaviorism, and its rigorous methodology, as the most influential field in American psychology. So, as existential psychology arose in the 1940s and 1950s it was viewed as something of a throwback to an earlier time when psychology was not distinguished from philosophy (Lundin, 1979).

However, as with those who identify themselves as humanistic psychologists, existential psychologists are deeply concerned with individuals and the conditions of each unique human life. The detachment that seems so essential to experimental psychologists is unacceptable to existential psychologists. The difference can easily be seen in the titles of two influential books written by the leading existential psychologists: *Man's Search for Meaning* by Viktor Frankl (1946/1992) and *Man's Search for Himself* by Rollo May (1953). Existential psychology differs significantly from humanistic psychology, however, in focusing on present existence and the fear, anguish, and sorrow that are so often associated with the circumstances of our lives (Lundin, 1979).

Understanding the Philosophy of Existentialism

The roots of **existentialism** as a philosophy began with the Danish philosopher Søren Kierkegaard (1813-1855). Kierkegaard was intensely interested in man's relationship with God, and its ultimate impossibility. Man is finite and individual, whereas God is infinite and absolute, so the two can never truly meet. In pursuing the relationship, however, man goes through three stages or modes of existence: the **aesthetic mode**, the **ethical mode**, and the **religious mode**. The aesthetic mode is concerned with the here and now, and focuses primarily on pleasure and pain. Young children live primarily in this mode. The ethical mode involves making choices and wrestling with the concept of responsibility. An individual in the ethical mode must choose whether or not to live by a code or according to the rules of society. This submission to rules and codes may prove useful in terms of making life simple, but it is a dead end. In order to break out of this dead end, one must live in the religious mode by making a firm commitment to do so. While this may lead to the recognition that each of us is a unique individual, it also brings with it the realization of our total inadequacy relative to God. As a result, we experience loneliness, anxiety, fear, and dread. All of this anguish, however, allows us to know what is really true, and for Kierkegaard truth was synonymous with faith (in God). However, as important as man's relationship to God was for Kierkegaard, he was adamantly opposed to organized religion. Kierkegaard rejected objective, so-called **"truth"** in the form of religious dogma in favor of the subjective "truth" that each person "knows" within themselves. While this subjective, personal truth brings with it the responsibility that leads to anxiety, it can also elevate a person to an authentic existence (Breisach, 1962; Frost, 1942).

Another philosopher considered essential to the foundation of existentialism was the enigmatic German philosopher Friedrich Nietzsche (1844-1900). A key element of Nietzsche's philosophy is the **will-to-power**. He believed this will-to-power is the fundamental force in the universe (Alfred Adler considered it fundamental to personality development). Ironically, according to Nietzsche, the universe has no regard for humanity. Natural forces (such as disaster and disease) destroy people, life is extremely difficult, and even those who struggle on attempting to realize their will eventually succumb to death. There is no hope to be found in an afterlife, since Nietzsche is famous for declaring that God is dead! Neither is there much hope within society for many people. Nietzsche believed that inequality was the natural state of humanity, so he considered slavery to be perfectly understandable and he felt that women (who are physically weaker than men) should never expect the same rights as men. Nonetheless, Nietzsche saw a great future for humanity, in the belief, indeed the faith, that we would create a **superman** (or superwoman, as the case may be). It is the creation of the superman that gives purpose to existence. Although the concept of the superman helped to fuel Nazi views on creating a German master race, it also made its way into American comic books as the great hero Superman (Fritzsche, 2007; Frost, 1942; Jaspers, 1965). In perhaps Nietzsche's most famous work, *Thus Spoke Zarathustra*, the would-be prophet Zarathustra encouraged people to seek a better future for humanity:

> *I will teach you about the superman.* Man is something that should be overcome. What have you done to overcome him? (pg. 81, Nietzsche, quoted in Fritzsche, 2007)

The German existentialists Martin Heidegger (1889-1976) and Karl Jaspers (1883-1969) focused on human existence itself and our role in the world. In a sense, Heidegger trivialized the nature of God, equating God with little more than the greatest being in the world, but a being nonetheless (just as humans are). Jaspers was not an atheist, but still his existential theory focused on the human journey toward a **freedom** that has meaning only when it reveals itself in union with God (Breisach, 1962; Lescoe, 1974). Heidegger considered individuals as beings who are all connected in **Being**, thus distinguishing between mere beings (including other animals) and the nature of truth or Being. Only humans are capable of understanding this connection between all beings, and Heidegger referred to this discovery as **Dasein** ("being here," or existence). On one level, Dasein is common to all creatures, but the possibility of being aware of one's connection to Being is uniquely human. For those who ask the big questions, Dasein can become authentic existence. This experience comes in the fullness of life, but only if one adopts the mode of existence known as **being-in-the-world**. Heidegger insisted that Dasein and being-in-the-world are equal. Being-in-the-world is an odd concept, however, since Heidegger believed that Being can only arise from nothingness, and so we ourselves arise as **being-thrown-into-this-world**. Having been thrown into this mysterious world we wish to make it our own, but our desire for connection with Being leads to anxiety. This anxiety cannot be overcome, because we are aware that we will die! Surprisingly, however, Heidegger considers death to be something positive. It is only because we are going to die that some of us strive to experience life fully. If we can accept that death will come, and nothing will follow, we can be true to ourselves and live an authentic life (Breisach, 1962; Lundin, 1979).

Finally we come to the French existentialist Jean-Paul Sartre (1905-1980). Sartre was an extraordinary author and one of the most important philosophers of the twentieth century. He was awarded the Nobel Prize in Literature in 1964, but chose to reject it. More importantly for us, however, is the fact that he carried existential philosophy directly into psychology, with books such as *The Transcendence of the Ego* (Sartre, 1937/1957) and a section entitled "Existential Psychoanalysis" in his extraordinary work *Being and Nothingness* (Sartre, 1943). Whereas Kierkegaard believed that man could never truly be one with God, and Heidegger trivialized God, Sartre simply stated that God does not exist. But this is not inconsequential:

> The Existentialist, on the contrary, thinks it very distressing that God does not exist, because all possibility of finding values in a heaven of ideas disappears along with Him; there can no longer be an *a priori* Good, since there is no infinite and perfect consciousness to think it. (pg. 459; Sartre, 1947/1996).

If one looks at the title of Sartre's most famous philosophical work, *Being and Nothingness* (Sartre, 1943), you might get the impression that Sartre followed in the footsteps of Heidegger. However, Sartre did not agree with Heidegger (see Sartre, 1943). Sartre divided the world into **en-soi** (the in-itself) and **pour-soi** (the for-itself). Pour-soi can be defined as conscious beings, of which there is only one kind: human beings. Everything else is en-soi, things (including non-human animals) that are silent and dead, and from which come no meaning, they only are (Breisach, 1962). For Sartre, there is no mystery, no Being, tying all of creation together. Man's consciousness is not a connection to God that can be realized, it is simply a unique characteristic of the human species. The nothingness to which Sartre refers is a shell around the pour-soi, the individual, which separates it from the en-soi. People who try to deny living authentically, those who try to deny the responsibility that comes with being conscious and settle into being nothing more than en-soi will have a shattering experience and be totally destroyed (since there is no Being, as described by Heidegger, beyond the shell surrounding the pour-soi; Breisach, 1962). This establishes critical ethical implications for the individual, since their life will be what they make of it, and nothing more.

Unfortunately, many people do reject their unique consciousness and desire to be en-soi, just letting life happen around them. As the en-soi closes in around them, they begin to experience nausea, forlornness, anxiety, and despair. Herein lays the need for **existential psychoanalysis**:

> Existential psychoanalysis is going to reveal to man the real goal of his pursuit, which is being as a synthetic fusion of the in-itself with the for-itself; existential psychoanalysis is going to acquaint man with his passion…Many men, in fact, know that the goal of their pursuit is being; and … they refrain from appropriating things for their own sake and try to realize the symbolic appropriations of their being-in-itself…existential psychoanalysis…must reveal to the moral agent that he is *the being by whom values exist.* It is then that his freedom will become conscious of itself… (pg. 797; Sartre, 1943)

Sartre proposed that individuals become conscious, and through that consciousness create the world itself, but also that we are "condemned to despair" and "doomed to failure" when we realize that all human activities are merely equivalent. This philosophical approach leads into Sartre's criticism of the psychology of his time. Sartre believed that psychologists, and even most philosophers, stopped short of really understanding people:

> For most philosophers the ego is an "inhabitant" of consciousness...Others - psychologists for the most part - claim to discover its material presence, as the center of desires and acts, in each moment of our psychic life. We should like to show here that the ego is neither formally nor materially *in* consciousness: it is outside, *in the world.* It is a being of the world, like the ego of another. (pg. 31; Sartre, 1937/1957)

So, Sartre believed that an existential psychoanalysis was needed to go beyond the limits of Freudian psychoanalysis. It is not enough, according to Sartre, to stop at describing mere patterns of desires and tendencies (Sartre, 1943). In critiquing the psychoanalytic biography of a famous author named Flaubert, Sartre asked very meaningful questions about this individual's life: why did Flaubert become a writer instead of a painter, why did he come to feel exalted and self-important instead of gloomy, why did his writing emphasize violence, or amorous adventures, etc.? Sartre's point is a common criticism of Freudian psychoanalytic theory. If most any result can come from an individual's experiences, then what does psychoanalysis really tell us about anyone? Sartre proposed a deeper form of psychoanalysis:

> This comparison allows us to understand better what an existential psychoanalysis must be if it is entitled to exist. It is a method destined to bring to light, in a strictly objective form, the subjective choice by which each living person makes himself a person; that is, makes known to himself what he is. Since what the method seeks is a *choice of being* at the same time as a *being,* it must reduce particular behavior patterns to fundamental relations - not of sexuality or of the will-to-power, but *of being* - which are expressed in this behavior. It is then guided from the start toward a comprehension of being and must not assign itself any other goal than to discover being and the mode of being of the being confronting this being. It is forbidden to stop before attaining this goal…This psychoanalysis has not yet found its Freud. (pp. 733-734; Sartre; 1943)

Placing Existential Psychology in Context: Height Psychology Goes Deeper Than Depth Psychology

The two theorists highlighted in this chapter were truly extraordinary individuals. Both Viktor Frankl (who coined the term "height psychology") and Rollo May were well immersed in existential thought and its application to psychology when they faced seemingly certain death. For Frankl, who was imprisoned in the Nazi concentration camps, death was expected. For May, who was confined to a sanitarium with tuberculosis, death was a very real possibility (and indeed many died there). But Frankl and May were intelligent, observant, and thoughtful men. They watched as many died, while some lived, and they sought answers that might explain who was destined for each group. Both men observed that for those who resigned themselves to death, death came soon. But for those who chose to live, they had a real chance to survive despite the terrible conditions in which they existed.

Frankl and May also shared their training in traditional psychoanalysis, and both had studied with Alfred Adler, at least somewhat. However, they found the so-called depth psychology as lacking, since it did not address the true potential for humans to rise above their conditions. In this regard, existential psychologists have typically been viewed as belonging within the humanistic psychology camp. However, both Frankl and May considered humanistic psychology to also be lacking, in that it neglected the true potential for humans to make bad choices, and to harm both themselves and others. So for existential psychologists, the center of their focus is on the immediate existence of the individual, in the context of their relationship to others. It is this seeming paradox, and the drive to resolve it, that provides the motivation and energy for life.

There is also a natural connection between existentialism and Eastern schools of thought, including yoga, Buddhism, and Taoism. Some of the comparisons are so striking that, shortly after discussing Taoism, May wrote "one gets the same shock of similarity in Zen Buddhism" (May, 1983). And so, this chapter should provide an interesting transition to the final section of this text, in which we will examine both Eastern and Western spiritual approaches to making positive choices in one's life.

Viktor Frankl and Logotherapy

Viktor Frankl (1905-1997) was truly an extraordinary man. His first paper was submitted for publication by Sigmund Freud; his second paper was published at the urging of Alfred Adler. Gordon Allport was instrumental in getting Frankl's book *Man's Search for Meaning* (Frankl, 1946/1992) published in English, a book that went on to be recognized by the Library of Congress as one of the ten most influential books in America. He lectured around the world, and received some thirty honorary doctoral degrees in addition to the medical degree and the Ph.D. he had earned as a student. He was invited to a private audience with Pope Paul VI, even though Frankl was Jewish. All of this was accomplished in spite of, and partly because of, the fact that he spent several years in Nazi concentration camps during World War II, camps where his parents, brother, wife, and millions of other Jews died.

A Brief Biography of Viktor Frankl

Viktor Frankl was born in Vienna, Austria on March 26, 1905. Although his father had been forced to drop out of medical school for financial reasons, Gabriel Frankl held a series of positions with the Austrian government, working primarily with the department of child protection and youth welfare. He instilled in his son the importance of being intensely rational and having a firm sense of social justice, and Frankl became something of a perfectionist. Frankl described his mother Elsa as a kindhearted and deeply pious woman, but during his childhood she often described him as a pest, and she even changed the words of Frankl's favorite childhood lullaby to include calling him a pest. This may have been due to the fact that Frankl was often asking questions, so much so that a family friend nicknamed him "The Thinker" (Frankl, 1995/2000). From his mother, Frankl inherited a deep emotionality. One aspect of this emotionality involved a deep attachment to his childhood home, and he often felt homesick as his responsibilities kept him away. And those responsibilities began at an early age (Frankl, 1995/2000; Pattakos, 2004).

Even in high school Frankl was developing a keen interest in existential philosophy and psychology. At the age of 16 he delivered a public lecture "On the Meaning of Life" and at 18 he wrote his graduation essay "On the Psychology of Philosophical Thought." Throughout his high school years he maintained a correspondence with Sigmund Freud (letters that were later destroyed by the Gestapo when Frankl was deported to his first concentration camp). When Frankl was just 19, Freud submitted one of Frankl's papers for publication in the *International Journal of Psychoanalysis*, afterward hoping that Frankl would agree and give his belated consent. Despite having impressed Freud, Frankl himself was already impressed by Alfred Adler. Frankl became active in

Adler's individual psychology group, and as he began medical school he was urged by Adler to publish a paper in the *International Journal of Individual Psychology*. It is hard to imagine that many people could have come into the favor of both Freud and Adler by such a young age, even before having begun medical school or a career in psychiatry. Despite Frankl's young age and somewhat limited experience, the paper published by Adler was dealing with difficult material, specifically the "border area that lies between psychotherapy and philosophy, with special attention to the problems of meanings and values in psychology" (Frankl, 1995/2000). Eventually, however, Frankl fell out of favor with Adler. Frankl had been impressed with two men, Allers and Schwarz, whose views were at odds with Adler. On the evening when Allers and Schwarz announced to the society that they could not agree with Adler, Adler challenged Frankl and a friend to speak up. Frankl chose to do so, and he defended Allers and Schwarz, believing that a middle ground could be found. Adler never spoke to Frankl again, even when Frankl said hello in the local coffee shop. For a few months Adler had other people suggest to Frankl that he should quit the society. When Frankl did not, he was expelled by Adler (Frankl, 1995/2000; Pattakos, 2004).

Frankl proceeded to develop his own practice and his own school of psychotherapy, known as **logotherapy** (the therapy of meaning, as in finding meaning in one's life). As early as 1929, Frankl had begun to recognize three possible ways to find meaning in life: a deed we do or a work we create; a meaningful human encounter, particularly one involving **love**; and choosing one's attitude in the face of unavoidable suffering. Logotherapy eventually became known as the third school of Viennese psychotherapy, after Freud's psychoanalysis and Adler's individual psychology. During the 1930s Frankl did much of his work with suicidal patients and teenagers. He had extensive talks with Wilhelm Reich in Berlin, who was also involved in youth counseling by that time. As the 1930s came to an end, and Austria had been taken over by the Nazis, Frankl sought a visa to emigrate to the United States, which was eventually granted. However, Frankl's parents could not get a visa, so he chose to remain in Austria with them. He also began work on his first book, eventually published in English under the title *The Doctor and the Soul* (Frankl, 1946/1986), which provided the foundation for logotherapy. He fell in love with Tilly Grosser, and they were married in 1941, the last legal Jewish marriage in Vienna under the Nazis.

Shortly thereafter, the realities of Nazi Germany overcame what little privilege Frankl had enjoyed as a doctor at a major hospital. Since it was illegal for Jews to have children, Tilly Frankl was forced to abort their first child. Frankl later dedicated *The Unheard Cry for Meaning* "To Harry or Marion an unborn child" (Frankl, 1978). Then the entire Frankl family, except for his sister who had gone to Australia, was deported to the Theresienstadt concentration camp (the same camp from which Anna Freud cared for orphans after the war). As they marched into the camp with hundreds, perhaps thousands, of other prisoners, his father tried to calm those who panicked by saying again and again: "Be of good cheer, for God is near." Frankl's parents, his only brother, and his wife Tilly died in the concentration camps. Most tragically, Frankl believed that his wife died after the war, but before the liberating Allied forces could care for all of the many, many suffering people (Frankl, 1995/2000).

When Frankl was deported, he tried to hide and save his only copy of *The Doctor and the Soul* by sewing it into the lining of his coat. However, he was forced to trade his good coat for an old one, and the manuscript was lost. While imprisoned, he managed to obtain a few scraps of paper on which to make notes. Those notes later helped him to recreate his book, and that goal gave such meaning to his life that he considered it an important factor in his will to survive the horrors of the concentration camps. It would be difficult to adequately describe the conditions of the concentration camps, or how they affected the minds of those imprisoned, especially since the effects were quite varied. Frankl describes those conditions in *Man's Search for Meaning*. The book is rather short, but its contents are deep beyond comprehension. Frankl himself, however, might take exception to referring to his book as "deep." Depth psychology was a term used for psychodynamically-oriented psychology. In 1938 Frankl coined the term **"height psychology"** in order to supplement, but not replace, depth psychology (Frankl, 1978).

After the war, Frankl's life was nothing less than amazing. He returned to his home city of Vienna, married Eleonore Katharina, née Schwindt, and raised a daughter named Gabriele, whose husband and the Frankl's grandchildren all lived in Vienna. He lectured around the world, received many honors, wrote numerous books, all while continuing to practice psychiatry and teach at the University of Vienna, Harvard, and elsewhere. He had a great interest in humor and in cartooning. Throughout his life, Frankl steadfastly refused to acknowledge the validity of collective guilt toward the German people. When asked repeatedly how he could return to Vienna, after all that happened to him and his family, Frankl replied:

> …I answered with a counter-question: "Who did what to me?" There had been a Catholic baroness who risked her life by hiding my cousin for years in her apartment. There had been a Socialist attorney (Bruno Pitterman, later vice chancellor of Austria), who knew me only casually and for whom I had never done anything; and it was he who smuggled some food to me whenever he could. For what reason, then, should I turn my back on Vienna? (pp. 101-102; Frankl, 1995/2000)

Viktor Frankl died peacefully on September 2, 1997. He was 92 years old. During his life, his work influenced many people, from the ordinary to the famous and influential. "Viktor Frankl, to be sure, leaves a profound legacy" (pg. 24; Pattakos, 2004).

Viktor Frankl and his family were deported to the Nazi Concentration Camps. His parents, wife, and only brother died there. Yet he remembered the people in Vienna who tried to help. [Image by Gabe Fuson]

The Theoretical Basis for Logotherapy

While Frankl was in medical school, he considered specializing in dermatology or obstetrics. A fellow student who was aware of Frankl's wide-ranging interests, however, introduced Frankl to the works of Kierkegaard. This friend had been reminded of Kierkegaard's emphasis on living an authentic life, and he urged Frankl to pursue his interest in psychiatry. While still in medical school Frankl delivered a lecture to the Academic Society for Medical Psychology, of which Frankl was the founding vice-president, and used the term logotherapy for the first time (a few years later he first used the alternative term existential analysis; Frankl, 1995/2000). The word logos is Greek for "meaning," and this third Viennese school of psychotherapy focuses on the meaning of human existence and man's search for such a meaning. Logotherapy, therefore, focuses on man's **will-to-meaning**, in contrast to Freud's **will-to-pleasure** (the drive to satisfy the desires of the id, the pleasure principle) or Adler's **will-to-power** (the drive to overcome inferiority and attain superiority; adopted from Nietzsche) (Frankl, 1946/1986, 1946/1992).

The will-to-meaning is, according to Frankl, the primary source of one's motivation in life. It is not a secondary rationalization of the instinctual drives, and meaning and values are not simply defense mechanisms. As Frankl eloquently points out:

> …as for myself, I would not be willing to live merely for the sake of my "defense mechanisms," nor would I be ready to die merely for the sake of my "reaction formations." Man, however, is able to live and even to die for the sake of his ideals and values! (pg. 105; Frankl, 1946/1992)

Unfortunately, one's search for meaning can be frustrated. This **existential frustration** can lead to what Frankl identified as a **noogenic neurosis** (a neurosis of the mind or, in other words, the specifically human dimension). Frankl suggested that when neuroses arise from an individual's inability to find meaning in their life, what they need is logotherapy, not psychotherapy. More specifically, they need help to find some meaning in their life, some reason to be. When reading Frankl's examples of how he helps such people, and Frankl offers many of these examples in his writings, it seems so simple. But it must be remembered that it takes a great deal of experience, knowledge, and maturity, as well as an ability to put oneself in another's shoes, in order to creatively think of how another person can find meaning in their life. It would be safe to say that many of us find it difficult to find meaning in our own lives, and research has indeed shown that the will-to-meaning is a significant concern throughout the world (Frankl, 1946/1992). In order to make sense of this problem, Frankl has suggested that we should not ask what we expect from life, but rather, we should understand that life expects something from us:

> A colleague, an aged general practitioner, turned to me because he could not come to terms with the loss of his wife, who had died two years before. His marriage had been very happy, and he was now extremely depressed. I asked him quite simply: "Tell me what would have happened if you had died first and your wife had survived you?" "That would have been

> terrible," he said. "How my wife would have suffered?" "Well, you see," I answered, "your wife has been spared that, and it was you who spared her, though of course you must now pay by surviving and mourning her." In that very moment his mourning had been given a meaning - the meaning of a sacrifice. (pg. xx; Frankl, 1946/1986)

The latter point brings us back to Frankl's discussion of how one can find meaning in life: through creating a work or doing a deed; by experiencing something or encountering someone, particularly when love is involved; or by choosing one's attitude toward unavoidable suffering. Those of us who have lost someone dear know how easily it leads to deep suffering. Frankl had already written the first version of *The Doctor and the Soul* when he entered the Theresienstadt concentration camp, so his views on how one should choose their attitude toward unavoidable suffering were put to a test that no research protocol could ever hope to achieve! His observations form the basis for much of *Man's Search for Meaning*. Both his observations of others and his own reactions in this unimaginably horrible and tragic situation are quite fascinating:

> ...as we stumbled on for miles, slipping on icy spots, supporting each other time and again, dragging one another up and onward, nothing was said, but we both knew: each of was thinking his wife...my mind clung to my wife's image...Real or not, her look was then more luminous than the sun...A thought transfixed me: for the first time in my life I saw the truth as it is set into song by so many poets, proclaimed as the final wisdom by so many thinkers. The truth - that love is the ultimate and the highest goal to which man can aspire. Then I grasped the meaning of the greatest secret that human poetry and human thought and belief have to impart: *The salvation of man is through love and in love*. (pp. 48-49; Frankl, 1946/1992)
>
> ...One evening, when we were already resting on the floor of our hut, dead tired, soup bowls in hand, a fellow prisoner rushed in and asked us to run out to the assembly grounds and see the wonderful sunset. Standing outside we saw sinister clouds glowing in the west and the whole sky alive with clouds of ever-changing shapes and colors, from steel blue to blood red...Then, after minutes of moving silence, one prisoner said to another, "How beautiful the world *could* be!" (pg. 51; Frankl, 1946/1992)
>
> ...The experiences of camp life show that man does have a choice of action. There were enough examples, often of a heroic nature, which proved that apathy could be overcome, irritability suppressed. Man *can* preserve a vestige of spiritual freedom, of independence of mind, even in such terrible conditions of psychic and physical stress.
>
> We who lived in concentration camps can remember the men who walked through the huts comforting others, giving away their last piece of bread. They may have been few in number, but they offer sufficient proof that everything can be taken from a man but one thing: the last of the human freedoms - to choose one's attitude in any given set of circumstances, to choose one's own way. (pp. 74-75; Frankl, 1946/1992)

Discussion Question: Frankl considered the most important aspect of survival to be the ability to find meaning in one's life. Have you found meaning in your life? Are there goals you have that you believe might add meaning to your life? Do you know anyone personally whose life seems to be filled with meaning, and if so, how does it appear to affect them?

Logotherapy as a Technique

Unfortunately, as noted by Frankl, not everyone can successfully accomplish the will-to-meaning. Those who rapidly declined toward death itself had lost the ability to have faith in the future; they could not identify any goal that provided meaning for their future. Such individual's exist in what Frankl called an existential vacuum. We have no instincts that tell us what we have to do, fewer and fewer traditions that tell us what we should do, and we often don't even know what we want to do. Therein lays the need for logotherapy. As a technique, logotherapy relies primarily on **paradoxical intention** and **dereflection** (Frankl, 1946/1986, 1946/1992).

Paradoxical intention is based on a simple trap in which neurotic individuals often find themselves. When a person thinks about or approaches a situation that provokes a neurotic symptom, such as fear, the person experiences **anticipatory anxiety**. This anticipatory anxiety takes the form of the symptom, which reinforces their anxiety. And so on… In order to help people break out of this negative cycle, Frankl recommends having them focus intently on the very thing that evokes their symptoms, even trying to exhibit their symptoms more severely than ever before! As a result, the patient is able to separate themselves from their own neurosis, and eventually the neurosis loses its potency.

Similar to anticipatory anxiety, people often experience a compulsive inclination to observe themselves, resulting in hyper-reflection. For example, people who suffer from insomnia focus on their efforts to sleep, or people who cannot enjoy a sexual relationship often focus on their physical, sexual responses. Because of this intense focus on sleep, or having an orgasm, these very things are unattainable. In dereflection, patients are taught not to pay attention to what they desire. A person who cannot sleep might read in bed, they will eventually fall asleep. A person who cannot enjoy intimate sexuality could focus on their partner, and as a result they should experience satisfaction that they did not expect. In essence, whereas paradoxical intention teaches the patient to ridicule their symptoms, dereflection teaches the patient to ignore his or her symptoms (Frankl, 1946/1986).

Discussion Question: Logotherapy relies on paradoxical intention and dereflection to break the anticipatory anxiety that often leads to failure (and then, more anxiety). Are there situations where you find yourself getting anxious or nervous even before the situation begins? What steps, if any, have you taken to break out of that pattern?

The Search for Ultimate Meaning

Kierkegaard believed that man could never truly be in contact with the infinite and absolute God. Similarly, Frankl talked about a **super-meaning** to life, something that goes far deeper than logic. When Frankl told his daughter that the *good* Lord had cured her measles, his daughter reminded him that the *good* Lord had given her the measles in the first place. Since children may not benefit from the challenges of suffering as adults might, and even adults find it difficult to find meaning in truly horrible situations like the concentration camps of Nazi Germany or the gulags of the former Soviet Union, the meaning of life in the greater context of human societies is often not readily apparent. But as Frankl says:

> This ultimate meaning necessarily exceeds and surpasses the finite intellectual capacities of man; in logotherapy, we speak in this context of a super-meaning. What is demanded of man is not, as some existential philosophers teach, to endure the meaninglessness of life, but rather to bear his incapacity to grasp its unconditional meaningfulness in rational terms. *Logos* is deeper than logic. (pg. 122; Frankl, 1946/1992)

In discussing the value of logotherapy, Frankl offered critiques of other popular fields in psychology and psychiatry. His most serious critique was of the deterministic nature of psychoanalysis. Frankl fervently believed in an individual's freedom to transcend their self and choose to make the best of any situation. And he had plenty of experience to back up his opinion: "…I am a survivor of four camps - concentration camps, that is - and as such I also bear witness to the unexpected extent to which man is capable of defying and braving even the worst conditions conceivable" (pg. 47; Frankl, 1978). He did not, however, reject determinism entirely. Instead, he attributed determinism to the psychological dimension, whereas freedom exists within the noölogical dimension. He acknowledged Freud and Adler for teaching us to "unmask the neurotic." As for behaviorism, Frankl acknowledged that it helped to "demythologize" neurosis, by pointing out that not every psychological problem is due to unconscious forces from early childhood, and he included Pavlov, Watson, and Skinner as great pioneers. Still, both psychoanalysis and behaviorism ignore the essential humanness of the individual.

Despite his emphasis on the individual human, Frankl did not consider logotherapy as belonging within humanistic psychology (or at least not within what he called pseudo-humanism; Frankl, 1978). He believed that humanistic psychology focused so much on the humanity of individuals, that they did not quite appreciate the uniqueness of each person. It is not enough to merely encounter another person. In order to be moved on the personal level there must be an element of love (love for another person, if not a more intimate and personal love as for a spouse or a child). As we will see below, Rollo May also considered love to be of great importance to our lives. The emphasis that Frankl placed on love may have something to do with his deep spirituality. Frankl believed in a spiritual unconscious, separate from the instinctual unconscious described by Freud (Frankl, 1948/2000). In order for an individual to experience an authentic existence, they must determine whether a given phenomenon (thoughts, feelings, impulses, etc.) is instinctual or spiritual, and then freely choose how to behave or respond. Frankl returned to Heidegger's concept of Dasein, living according to the understanding that one is connected to Being. Although this concept may seem reminiscent of Jung's collective unconscious, nothing could be further from the truth:

> …It cannot be emphasized strongly enough that not only is the unconscious neither divine nor omniscient, but above all man's unconscious relation to God is profoundly personal. The "unconscious God" must not be mistaken as an impersonal force operant in man. This understanding was the great mistake to which C. G. Jung fell prey. Jung must be credited with having discovered distinctly religious elements within the unconscious. Yet he misplaced this unconscious religiousness of man, failing to locate the unconscious God in the personal and existential region. Instead, he allotted it to the region of drives and instincts, where unconscious religiousness no longer remained a matter of choice and decision. According to Jung, something within me is religious, but it is not I who then is religious; something within me drives me to God, but it is not I who makes the choice and takes the responsibility. (pg. 70; Frankl, 1948/2000)

Those who live authentic lives often have a transcendent quality that leads them toward a will-to-ultimate-meaning. [Image by Cristian Newman]

According to Frankl, the most human of all human phenomena is the will-to-meaning. Religion, or spirituality, seeks a **will-to-ultimate-meaning**. Once again, Frankl believed that Freudian psychoanalysis and Adlerian individual psychology had failed to sufficiently credit the self-transcendent quality of individuals who live authentic lives. It is in the study of authentic lives that "height psychology," as Frankl called it, can address the higher aspirations of the human psyche. In other words, beyond seeking pleasure and/or power, there is man's search for meaning (Frankl, 1948/2000).

Discussion Question: Frankl was a very spiritual man. He talked about super-meaning and a will-to-ultimate-meaning. Are you a spiritual and/or religious person? If yes, does your faith help to give meaning to your life?

Rollo May and Existential Psychology

Rollo May (1909-1994) introduced existentialism to American psychologists, and has remained the best known proponent of this approach in America. Trained in a fairly traditional format as a psychoanalyst, May considered the detachment with which psychoanalysts approached their patients as a violation of social ethics. For example, if a psychoanalyst helps a patient to be the best they can be, and the person happens to earn their living in an unseemly or criminal way, it hardly seems proper (Stagner, 1988). On the other hand, who is to decide which values should be preferred in a particular society? In the pursuit of freedom, May suggested that sometimes individuals might reasonably oppose the standards or morality of their society. Politics, a wonderful topic for lively debates, is dependent on opposing viewpoints. Only when an individual lives an authentic life, however, should their opinion be considered valid, and existential psychology seeks to help individuals live authentic lives.

A Brief Biography of Rollo May

Rollo Reese May was born on April 21, 1909, in Ohio, and grew up in Marine City, Michigan. He attended Oberlin College in Ohio, graduating in 1930. Having always been interested in art and artistic creativity, he joined with a small group of artists and traveled to Europe, where they studied the local art of Poland. In order to remain in Europe, May took a teaching position with the American College at Salonika in Greece. When not teaching, he traveled widely throughout Greece, Poland, Romania, and Turkey. He attended the summer school taught by Alfred Adler. Deeply impressed by Adler (as Frankl had been), he nonetheless considered Adler's theories overly simplistic and too general. This may well have been due to his awakening awareness of the tragic side of human life, keeping in mind that much of Europe suffered greatly during the depression between World War I and World War II (Reeves, 1977).

Upon returning to the United States, May worked as a student advisor and the editor of a student magazine at Michigan State University. In 1936, he enrolled at Union Theological Seminary in New York, with the intention of asking, and most likely hoping to find answers to, the ultimate questions about human life. Despite having no particular desire to become a minister, he did serve in a parish in Montclair, New Jersey for a while. While at the seminary, he became a lifelong friend of Paul Tillich, a well-known existential theologian. Tillich, whose classes May regularly attended, introduced May to the works of Kierkegaard and Heidegger. May also met Kurt Goldstein during this time, and became acquainted with Goldstein's theories of self-actualization and anxiety as a reaction by organisms to catastrophic events. Regarding his time as a minister, May reflected that the only events which seemed to include an element of reality were the funerals (Reeves, 1977).

Shortly after graduating from the seminary, May began writing books on counseling and creative living. He worked as a counselor at the College of the City of New York, and trained as a psychoanalyst at the William Alanson White Institute of Psychiatry, Psychoanalysis, and Psychology in New York. His time at the training institute overlapped with Harry Stack Sullivan being the president of the William Alanson White Foundation, and Erich Fromm as a fellow associate. In 1946, May began a private practice in psychoanalysis, in 1948 he became a faculty member at the institute, and in 1949 he received the first Ph.D. in clinical psychology at Columbia University. His doctoral dissertation was published as *The Meaning of Anxiety* (May, 1950), a book that heavily cites the work of Freud and Kierkegaard on anxiety, as well as Fromm, Horney, and Tillich (May, 1950; Reeves, 1977).

Similar to Viktor Frankl, May's life had taken a dramatic turn during this time, an uncontrollable event that threatened his life: May contracted tuberculosis. At the time, there were no effective treatments for this contagious disease, many people died from it, and like many others May had to spend several years at a sanitarium (Saranac Sanitarium in upstate New York). It was during his time in the sanitarium that May theorized about anxiety and came to one of the most important conclusions in his career. He determined that although Freud had done a masterful job of characterizing the effects of anxiety on the individual, it was Kierkegaard who had truly identified what anxiety is: the threat of becoming nothing. From this point on May could clearly be identified as an existential psychologist. He collaborated with Abraham Maslow, Carl Rogers, and Gordon Allport to present a symposium on existential psychology, in conjunction with the 1959 annual convention of American Psychological Association, which led to the publication of a book on the subject (Reeves, 1977).

As May's career continued, he became a supervisory and training analyst at the William Alanson White Institute, and an adjunct professor of psychology in the graduate school at New York University. He gave a series of radio talks on existential psychology on a Canadian Broadcasting Corporation show, he served as a visiting professor at Harvard and Princeton, and he continued writing. His later books include works on dreams, symbolism, religion, and love. He eventually settled in California, where he died in 1994.

Anxiety

May considered **anxiety** to be the underlying cause of nearly every crisis, whether domestic, professional, economic, or political. He described the world we live in as an age of anxiety. Even though May published *The Meaning of Anxiety* in 1950, it is safe to say that his concerns are even more relevant today, particularly with the advent of the depersonalization of our world due to the computer age (Reeves, 1977). May considered a wide range of theories on anxiety, including philosophers, neurologists (Kurt Goldstein), and the major psychodynamic theorists (including Freud, Adler, Jung, Horney, Sullivan, and Fromm). He came to the conclusion that Freud had done the best job of explaining anxiety, but it was Kierkegaard who best understood anxiety. May was particularly impressed by Kierkegaard's idea that anxiety must be understood in the context of an orientation toward freedom. Freedom is the goal of personality development, and although this freedom brings with it anxiety, it is through facing this anxiety that the possibility of freedom arises (May, 1950). In praise of Kierkegaard, May wrote:

> …Kierkegaard is proclaiming that "self-strength" develops out of the individual's successful confronting of anxiety-creating experiences; this is the way one becomes educated to maturity as a self. What is amazing in Kierkegaard is that despite his lack of the tools for interpreting unconscious material - which tools have been available in their most complete form only since Freud - he so keenly and profoundly anticipated modern psychoanalytic insight into anxiety; and that at the same time he placed these insights in the broad context of a poetic and philosophical understanding of human experience. (pg. 45; May, 1950)

In defining anxiety, May distinguished between anxiety and fear, and between **normal anxiety** and **neurotic anxiety**. According to May, "anxiety is the apprehension cued off by a threat to some value which the individual holds essential to his existence as a personality" (pg. 191; May, 1950). The threat may be either physical or psychological, such as facing death from tuberculosis or being imprisoned in a concentration camp (which, of course, brought the threat of death in addition to the loss of freedom), or the threat may challenge some other value that the individual identifies with their existence or personal identity (such as the loss of a career, a divorce, a challenge to patriotism in time of war, etc.). What differentiates anxiety from fear, is that fear is a reaction to a specific event, whereas anxiety is vague and diffuse. For example, during a robbery you may fear a man with a gun, but in America today many people are anxious about terrorism. No one can tell when or where terrorists may strike, or even whether they will be foreign terrorists (such as in the World Trade Center attacks) or American terrorists (such as the bombing of the federal building in Oklahoma City or the D.C. sniper killings). May carefully pointed out that using the terms "vague" and "diffuse" to describe anxiety should in no way diminish our understanding of the intensity and painfulness that anxiety can bring. Therein lies the difference between normal vs. neurotic anxiety (May, 1950).

Everyone faces challenges in life, but not everyone sees the same challenges as actual threats. Losing one's job can be an opportunity to begin a new career, perhaps to go back to school to pursue that new career. However, the transition is often difficult, especially when one is used to being the primary wage earner in the family, and also if the family has to cut back on items they can no longer afford. So anxiety would be a reasonable reaction. That anxiety is considered normal if it is 1) not disproportionate to the objective threat, 2) does not involve mechanisms of intrapsychic conflict, and 3) does not require defense mechanisms for its management (May, 1950). Normal anxiety is often overlooked in adults since it is not particularly intense, especially compared to neurotic anxiety, and it can be managed constructively. It does not show itself in panic or other dramatic symptoms. Neurotic anxiety is, simply, the opposite of normal anxiety. It is disproportionate to the objective threat, it does require intrapsychic defense mechanisms, and it results in neurotic symptoms in spite of those defense mechanisms. It is important to keep in mind that we should not consider individuals who suffer from neurotic anxiety as suffering from objective weaknesses, but rather they suffer from inner psychological patterns and conflicts that prevent them from using their powers to cope.

True to his training in psychodynamic theory, May believed that the psychological patterns resulting in the inability to cope have their origin in childhood, particularly due to poor early relations between the infant and its parents, since an infant's essential values arise from the security patterns established between the infant and its caregivers (as in Erikson's first psychosocial crisis: trust vs. mistrust, see Chapter 7). One of the most important factors seems to be the infant's subjective interpretation of rejection by its primary caregiver, and that subjectivity is influenced by expectations that form later in life (e.g., middle- and upper-class children, who expect more support from their parents, are especially prone to react to rejection with neurotic anxiety; May, 1950).

Discussion Question: May felt that we must understand anxiety in relation to freedom, or rather, as the fear that we will lose our freedom. He said that some of this anxiety is normal, and only in extreme cases does it become neurotic anxiety. What are some of the situations in your life that make you anxious, and how might they be a threat to your personal freedom? Do you think the level of these anxieties is normal, or is it severe enough to perhaps be considered neurotic?

Culture, Anxiety, and Hostility

May also addressed the effects of culture on anxiety, and the close interrelationship between anxiety and **hostility**. Culture affects both the kinds and the quantities of anxiety experienced by individuals. Beyond the essential relationship between infant and caregiver, the determinants of personality that each of us consider essential to our existence as a personality are largely cultural. Indeed, even the nature of the infant/caregiver relationship is subject to cultural influence. The amount of anxiety most people are likely to experience is determined, in part, by the stability of the culture. For example, if a culture is relatively stable and unified, there will be less anxiety throughout that culture (May, 1950). Today, however, many societies are in dramatic flux, due in large part to the powerful trend toward globalization.

As psychologists have begun to examine anxiety in different groups around the world, a variety of interesting, and sometimes disturbing, results have been found. Keep in mind, however, that these are generalities, and do not necessarily apply to each individual within any group. Generally, Asians are more anxious than Europeans and White Americans, who are more anxious than Black Americans and Africans, and there may be a neurological basis for these relative anxiety levels (Rushton, 1999). However, when looking at the specific form of anxiety related to taking academic tests, Black Americans and Chilean students demonstrate higher levels of test anxiety than White Americans (Clawson, Firment, & Trower, 1981; Guida & Ludlow, 1989). One suggestion for the higher levels of anxiety among Blacks in America is that our society is much less sociocentric than most African cultures. Thus, Blacks in America, even if they have lived here for generations, still experience the effects of their displacement from Africa when the culture they carried with them is at odds with Western cultural expectations (Okeke at al., 1999), and even more so when an individual seems to be at odds with most members of their own cultural group (Copeland, 2006). Indeed, the greater the discrepancy between one's individual cultural expectations and the cultural expectations of the majority of society, the greater the anxiety an individual experiences. This is particularly true during attempts at intercultural communication (Matsumoto & Juang, 2004). Any subsequent breakdown of intercultural communication, which is more likely during periods of high anxiety, can either lead to or enhance pre-existing hostility, prejudice, discrimination, and scapegoating (Whitley & Kite, 2006). One important challenge to intercultural communication in psychology is the need for clinical psychologists to recognize the growing number of anxiety disorders unique to non-Western cultures, such as: **hwa-bung** (Korea), **koro** (Malaysia and Southern China), **nervios** (Latin America), **dhat syndrome** (India), **susto** (Latin America), and **taijin kyofusho** (Japan) (Castillo, 1997).

Culture can influence individuals in a wide variety of ways. May (1950) used the example of competitive individual success in the Western world as his main example, which he considered to be *the* dominant goal in America. There are many negative effects of this competition, including the high incidences of gastric ulcers and heart disease in our society. Less than a decade later, Freidman and Rosenman (1959) published their classic study on the relationship between Type A behavior (studied in highly competitive businessmen) and cardiovascular disease. Subsequent studies have shown that the key component of Type A behavior predictive of heart disease is hostility, which we will discuss in more detail below (Dembrowski et al., 1985; Lachar, 1993; MacDougal et al., 1985). There has also been a great deal of discussion in our society about media influences on body image, the relationship between unreasonable expectations for women to be thin and the incidence of eating disorders in girls and women, and the repression of female sexuality in many cultures. Goldenberg (2005) recently presented an existential perspective on the body itself as a threat. Cultural beliefs often help to overcome fears of mortality by convincing individuals that they are of greater value than other, lower animals. However, despite the beliefs of many that only humans have a soul, our body is still a mortal animal. As a reaction to the anxiety presented by the reality of our mortal body, many people act in a hostile fashion toward their own bodies, ranging from denying themselves healthy physical relationships with others (e.g., sexual repression) to outright self-destructive behavior (e.g., anorexia nervosa). The problem reaches its extreme, however, when one powerful group directs its hostility in an organized fashion toward another group.

The relationship between anxiety and hostility, according to May, involves a vicious circle. Anxiety gives rise to hostility, and hostility gives rise to increased anxiety. But which comes first? May believed that it was anxiety that underlies hostility, and the evidence can be found in clinical cases involving repressed hostility:

> Granted the interrelation between hostility and anxiety, which affect is generally basic? There is ground for believing that, even though hostility may be the specific affect present in many situations, anxiety is often present below the hostility…For one example, in some of the

> psychosomatic studies of patients with hypertension…it has been found that the reason the patients repressed their hostility was that they were anxious and dependent...The hostility would not have to be repressed in the first place except that the individual is anxious and fears counter-hostility or alienation… (pg. 223; May, 1950)

In Reeves' analysis of May's theory (1977), Reeves discusses one of the most important social issues to have faced the United States: the civil rights movement of the 1960s. When an individual's sense of selfhood is challenged by dramatic changes in society, it can be a very painful experience. And one is likely to resent those responsible for those changes. While it is true that many White people in America supported the civil rights movement, White people in the Deep South (and elsewhere, of course) turned their anxiety, and its associated hostility, toward Blacks. It should not be necessary here to describe the many terrible acts of violence that followed. Suffice it to say that the federal government had to use military troops to intervene in some of the worst cases. Today, we face a similar problem in the war on terrorism. Given the often unequal and unfair manner in which globalization brings vastly different cultures into conflict, and the ease with which so many people can travel the globe, perhaps we should not be surprised at the dramatic level of terrorism in the world today.

Connections Across Cultures: Terrorists and Terrorism

Since September 11, 2001, when agents of the terrorist organization Al Qaeda destroyed the World Trade Center in New York City and killed some 3,000 people, the United States has been involved in what has been called an international war on terrorism. As the war on terrorism developed, it had two main goals: to capture Osama bin Laden, leader of Al Qaeda and mastermind of the World Trade Center bombings, and to overthrow Saddam Hussein, the dictator of Iraq (for his alleged role in supporting international terrorism). To date, this war has lasted *much* longer than World War II, we have spent hundreds of billions of dollars, and thousands more young American men and women have died fighting in Afghanistan and Iraq. Many Iraqi and Afghan civilians, as well as additional coalition military personnel, have also died. Saddam Hussein was removed from power in Iraq; he was also tried, convicted, and executed. It took nearly 10 years, but Osama bin Laden was finally tracked down and killed in a raid in Pakistan by U.S. Navy Seals. However, Al Qaeda is still committing acts of terrorism, Iraq is descending once again into bitter sectarian violence (rising to the level of civil war), and Americans continue to die fighting in Afghanistan as our intended date for withdrawal slowly draws near (after 13 years!). One thing that will not be addressed in this section, because it does not exist, is an easy answer to these problems.

Please allow me to share a little personal history here. When the Iranian revolution under Ayatollah Khomeini overthrew the Shah of Iran, and the revolutionaries captured the American embassy in Tehran and took sixty-six people hostage (fifty-two of those hostages were held for well over a year before being released), I was in the United States Marine Corps Reserve. I received a phone call at 2:00 a.m. on a Friday morning at my apartment in Cambridge, MA. By midnight, that same day, my reserve unit was in Camp Lejeune, NC, with full combat gear, ready to go to war in Iran. We spent the weekend preparing, though President Carter ultimately chose not to send us overseas. Approximately 10 years later, when the first Gulf War erupted after Iraq invaded Kuwait, my sister took part in Operation Desert Storm. As an Air Force nurse, she was sent to England to help prepare a hospital for wounded military personnel being evacuated from the Middle East (fortunately casualties were minimal). I considered re-enlisting in the Marine Corps at that time, since I certainly wasn't going to sit at home while my own sister "fought" for our country and our allies. Thankfully, that first Gulf War was brief and, seemingly, simple. So I have followed events in the Middle East carefully ever since, and when Al Qaeda attacked us in New York, I saw it as the latest in a continuation of events in my own life since 1979. For people in the Middle East, however, it was a continuation of events that have lasted for thousands of years.

What I believe matters most for Americans today is to begin to make an honest effort to understand terrorism, its causes, its goals, and how best to deal with it around the world. First, we must dispense with misconceptions. Terrorism and Islam are **not** one and the same. In an insightful and easily readable book entitled *Islam versus Terrorism*, Firooz Zadeh (2002) discusses how Islam opposes violence and murder, especially of innocent women and children. He also attempts to identify what is and is not terrorism, and in that effort he identifies eight types of terrorism: state terrorism, religious terrorism, criminal terrorism, terrorism by those who are mentally sick, political terrorism, oppositional terrorism, copy cat terrorism, and victim terrorism. According to Zadeh, the highest cost to society results from state terrorism. When the United States supports corrupt, terrorist governments in other parts of the world, our credibility as a nation fighting terrorism is suspect at best. Has this been the case? Yes, and in the worst possible way: we switch sides as it serves our political and economic interests. The United States helped to train Osama bin Laden and the Taliban fighters in Afghanistan when we wanted them to fight the Russians. Now we call them enemies. We provided weapons and training to Saddam Hussein's army when they were fighting the Iranians, because of the hostages taken in Tehran. Now we have deposed Hussein. We also sold weapons to Iran, and used the money to help support the Contras (freedom fighters or terrorists, depending on your point of view) trying to overthrow the leftist Sandinista government of Nicaragua. Zadeh proposes that people in the Middle East cannot trust the United States, except in one area: our support of Israel. And since other Middle Eastern countries see Israel as the one obstacle to a Palestinian homeland, they disapprove of that support. It does not matter whether the actions of the United States were right or wrong, whether they really were in our best interests or not. What matters is how the rest of the world sees us now, and whether our top government officials are willing to consider how we are viewed globally and to act responsibly in terms of foreign policy in order to ensure what is best for all people around the world. In addressing the Middle East in particular, Fathali Moghaddam wrote:

> Islamic communities in many parts of the world are experiencing a profound and historic identity crisis, one tragic manifestation of which is terrorism. In order to understand and avert this destructive trend, we must come to grips with the monumental crisis of identity that is paralyzing moderate movements but energizing fanatic forces in Islamic communities.
>
> ...Why do we need to understand how the terrorists see the world? Because this is the best way for us to find an effective means to end terrorism...Seeing the world from the terrorists' point of view does not mean condoning terrorism; rather, it means better understanding terrorism so as to end it. (pg. ix; Moghaddam, 2006)

As mentioned above, there are many different forms of terrorism, so it is difficult to define exactly what it is. Nevertheless, in an effort to do so, Moghaddam (2005) defines terrorism as "politically motivated violence, perpetrated by individuals, groups, or state-sponsored agents, intended to instill feelings of terror and helplessness in a population in order to influence decision making and to change behavior." Moghaddam suggests that psychologists need to play an important role in understanding terrorism for two main reasons: the basis for terrorist actions is typically subjectively interpreted values and beliefs, and the actions of terrorists are designed to cause specific psychological experiences, i.e., terror and helplessness. Moghaddam (2005, 2006) proposes a metaphor for how one becomes a terrorist, based on climbing a staircase, in which options are perceived to become more and more limited as one climbs the stairs. The most significant factor is the condition in which many people live on the ground floor, before they even consider climbing that staircase. Many people in this world live in abject poverty, under repressive governments that are unjust. When individuals see no hope within the system, and they lack any political means to effect change, then a path toward terrorism becomes perhaps the only reasonable possibility. Still, very few people are likely to become suicide bombers.

Individuals living in desperate conditions may move to the first floor on the staircase toward terrorism, where they evaluate their perceived options to fight unfair treatment. If there appear to be no options for justice within one's society, no opportunity to be heard, and no opportunity for personal mobility, the individual may then move to the second floor. Here the individual begins to displace their aggression. This often involves education/propaganda that identifies a clear target, for example the United States, also known as the "Great Satan." This is the important beginning of an us-versus-them mentality. On the third floor, individuals become morally engaged with the terrorist organization. While we may see terrorists as immoral, they are beginning to believe that they are fighting for a just cause, against the immoral repression of their chosen target. As they move to the fourth floor, they solidify their categorical thinking (the us-versus-them mentality) and begin to see the terrorist organization, and terrorist acts, as legitimate. At this point there is little chance that they can leave the terrorist organization alive. For specific individuals, the training necessary to carry out a terrorist act takes place, often very quickly. Not only does a terrorist need to learn about weapons and tactics, they must also be trained to sidestep the natural, biological inhibition against killing other human beings. Two factors in helping to prepare people to kill are the intense indoctrination in the belief that their actions are for a greater good and secrecy. If an attack is done suddenly and without warning, victims have no opportunity to submit or to beg for mercy. The act occurs before the terrorist might become compassionate as he or she faces their intended victims (Moghaddam, 2005, 2006). Based on this model, Moghaddam proposes four steps that are necessary to stop terrorism by interrupting the formation of new terrorists. First, there must be prevention. Unfortunately, our government has a long history of choosing short-term fixes, rather than long-term preventative measures. Case in point: America's failure in the war on drugs. Aggressive responses aimed at individuals only provide an opening for someone new to step in and continuing using and/or selling drugs, and the same is true of terrorists. We need to work toward eliminating the pathway to terrorism, so we will not need to use the military and/or FBI to track down individuals (except, of course, in extreme cases such as terrorism that results from psychological disorder - e.g., consider the case of Theodore Kaczynski, the Unabomber). In addition, Moghaddam suggests supporting contextualized democracy, educating against categorical thinking, and promoting interobjectivity and justice. In order for there to be a long-term solution, there must be international dialogue and improved intercultural understanding (Moghaddam, 2005).

Returning to the misconception in the minds of many Americans that terrorism is synonymous with Islam, let's examine where known terrorist organizations are located around the world. Fairly notorious organizations have come from Northern Ireland (e.g., the Irish Republican Army and the Ulster Defense Association), throughout mainland Europe (e.g., the Red Army Faction in Germany, the Red Brigades in Italy, and Action Directe in France), throughout the Middle East (e.g., Hezbollah in Lebanon, the Palestinian group Hamas, the Stern Gang that fought for the establishment of Israel, and Al Qaeda), Africa, Asia, Latin America, Canada, and the United States (e.g., the Animal Liberation Front, Aryan Nations, the Black Panthers, and the Ku Klux Klan). As of 1999, at least twenty-eight well-organized terrorist groups existed, and when one takes into account factions within those groups and smaller, yet still identifiable, groups, as many as eighty-three terrorists groups have been identified around the world (Henderson, 2001). Some are primarily political, and some are primarily religious. Some are global, and some are more local. They include people and cultures of great diversity: Black, White, Asian, Latin, Catholic, Protestant, Muslim, Hindu, etc. Although terrorism appears to arise out of poverty and desperation, terrorists themselves, or at least the leaders, tend to be better educated than most and they are well versed in propaganda and well trained in weapons and tactics (Moghaddam, 2005; Zadeh, 2002). The only characteristic that all terrorists seem to share is an extreme commitment to violence, which arises out of desperation and perceived injustice, and is viewed as the only means to be heard and to effect change.

So can terrorism effect change, is terrorism effective? One can easily find authors who argue that it does indeed work (Dershowitz, 2002) or that it always fails (Carr, 2002). Alan Dershowitz (2002) argues that the very reason terrorism works is everything we have looked at so far: an effort to understand the root causes of terrorism and the terrorists themselves. Accordingly, he says:

> We must take precisely the opposite approach to terrorism. We must commit ourselves *never to try to understand or eliminate its alleged root causes*, but rather to place it beyond the pale of dialogue and negotiation. Our message must be this: even if you have legitimate grievances, if you resort to terrorism as a means toward eliminating them we will simply not listen to you, we will not try to understand you, and we will certainly never change any of our policies toward you. Instead, we will

> hunt you down and destroy your capacity to engage in terror. (pp. 24-25; Dershowitz, 2002)

As a case in point, Dershowitz cites the awarding of observer status at the United Nations to the Palestinian Liberation Organization only after Palestinian terrorists began hijacking commercial airliners. Prior to the hijackings, 20 years of pleading their case to the United Nations had little effect. Dershowitz then offers a timeline that appears to clearly establish an effective relationship in which terrorism became more and more effective over time (from 1968-1999) in eliciting international recognition and support for the Palestinian cause. In contrast, Caleb Carr (2002) views terrorism entirely within the discipline of military history. He considers today's terrorism to be nothing more than a modern permutation of warfare against civilians in order to break their support for either leaders or policies that the terrorists oppose, the origins of which are as old as human conflict itself. Viewing terrorism as warfare has certain interesting implications. Throughout history, those who wage war against civilians ultimately defeated themselves by turning sentiment against them. On 9/11, Al Qaeda attacked civilians to a degree that has not been seen in ages:

> …In so doing, the organizers, sponsors, and foot soldiers of every terrorist group involved in the September 11 attacks have unwittingly ensured that their extremist cause will be discredited among many of their sympathizers, disowned by most of their former sponsors, and finally defeated by their enemies: two thousand years of the lessons of terror dictate that this is the ultimate fate that awaits the attackers, no matter how many noncombatants they manage to kill along the way. (pp. 223-224; Carr, 2002).

Carr also addresses the other most important implication of treating terrorism as warfare: it must be met with warfare, but that warfare must not be excessive, such that it might also be viewed as terrorism. If our response to terrorism is excessive military might, then the tide of public opinion can swing back in favor of Al Qaeda, especially in Muslim countries where the United States is not trusted.

Echoing Carr's concerns about the extent and nature of our military actions in the war on terror, one way in which terrorism might work against us, without seeming to have gained what was intended (if we can even know what was intended), is if our fundamental democratic principles change. In *The Lesser Evil: Political Ethics in an Age of Terror*, Michael Ignatieff (2004) argues that terrorism must be met with force, and that such force is a lesser evil than the terrorism that necessitated the response. The danger lies in succumbing to the greater evil of seeking revenge. Dershowitz (2002) provides a compelling case for how an amoral society could control and possibly eliminate all terrorism, but America is not an amoral society. Our responses are constrained by the constitution and by the political debate that forms the very basis of our democracy. When we respond to terrorist acts, we must consider what we want that response to accomplish:

> Terrorism requires us to think carefully about who we are as free peoples and what we need to do in order to remain so. When we are confronted with terrorist violence, we cannot allow the claims of national security to trump the claims of liberty, since what we are trying to defend is our continued existence as a free people. Freedom must set a limit to the measures we employ to maintain it. (pg. 145; Ignatieff, 2004)

Finally, can the ultimate answer to terrorism be found in promoting democratic governments in every nation? The war on terror has led us to depose both Saddam Hussein in Iraq and the Taliban in Afghanistan, and to replace them with democratically elected governments. Only time will tell whether those governments will survive, but there is reason for caution. Religious turmoil continues in the Middle East. In America, our constitution provides for separation of church and state, and that separation has become an important tradition. But for Muslims, the idea of a secular democracy, one that is not guided by Allah, is simply inconceivable. They are not opposed to democracy per se, indeed it has been argued that Islam is likely to eventually lead to pluralist democracies (Aslan, 2005). But to pressure Islamic countries into accepting the secular democracy that we hold so dear is, according to Robert Shedinger (2004), equivalent to declaring war on Islam. So what appears to be essential to promoting stability in the Middle East, and elsewhere, is an effort to support contextual democracy, that is, forms of democracy that fit with the culture of the people who will create and participate in that democracy (Aslan, 2005; Moghaddam, 2005, 2006; Shedinger, 2004; Zadeh, 2002).

Integration and the Human Dilemma

In the preface to *Man's Search for Himself* (May, 1953), May presents the existential philosophy that there is meaning to be found in challenges and suffering, and that psychologists in particular may find a special opportunity in such circumstances:

> When our society, in its time of upheaval in standards and values, can give us no clear picture of "what we are and what we ought to be,"...we are thrown back on the search for ourselves. The painful insecurity on all sides gives us new incentive to ask, Is there perhaps some important source of guidance and strength we have overlooked?...How can anyone undertake the long development toward self-realization in a time when practically nothing is certain, either in the present or the future?...The psychotherapist has no magic answers...But there is something in addition to his technical training and his own self-understanding...This something is the wisdom the psychotherapist gains in working with people who are striving to overcome their problems. He has the extraordinary, if often taxing, privilege of accompanying persons through their intimate and profound struggles to gain new integration. (pg. 7; May, 1953)

Integration, according to May, is similar to Heidegger's concept of Dasein (being-in-the-world). As conscious, free, and responsible beings our goal should be to separate ourselves from the conformist, automaton masses (the en-soi, according to Sartre) and progressively integrate with others in freely chosen love and creative work (May, 1953), or as Clement Reeves puts it: "To understand and elucidate the specific, distinguishing characteristics of the human being, and to grasp what it is to achieve courageous, decisive, integrated response to the challenge inherent in existence..." (Reeves, 1977). The process of integration is lifelong, and should be appropriate for whatever age each one of us happens to be right now. May suggests that a healthy child of eight, who is fulfilling his capacity of self-conscious choice for a child of eight years old, is more of a person than a neurotic adult who is 30 years old. Likewise, a person who can face death courageously at the age of thirty is more mature than someone 80 years old who "cringes and begs still to be shielded from reality" (May, 1953). Thus, it is important to live each moment with freedom, honesty, and responsibility. If each of us lives within the present moment, working to fulfill our potential, being true to whom we are and the situations within which we live, May proposes that we will experience joy and gratification:

> ...*Does not the uncertainty of our time teach us the most important lesson of all - that the ultimate criteria are the honesty, integrity, courage and love of a given moment of relatedness?* If we do not have that, we are not building for the future anyway; if we do have it, we can trust the future to itself. (pg. 276; May, 1953)

One of the challenges to living an integrated life is seen in what May described as the **human dilemma** (May, 1967). Are we the subject of our lives, or are we an object in our world? When we become absorbed in the details of our responsibilities and actions, when we allow ourselves to be controlled and directed in order to accomplish our assigned tasks, when we become slaves to the clock, doing this and that, going here and there, as others expect us to, we are viewing ourselves as objects. This is reminiscent of what Karen Horney called the tyranny of the should. On the other hand, when we consider our feelings, wishes, and desires, when we are true to ourselves, or living authentically, then we are viewing ourselves as subjects, as active participants in our own lives. According to May (1967), the human dilemma arises out of our capacity to experience ourselves as *both* subject and object at the same time. But how can opposite poles of the human experience both be true? It is in the process between the two poles that development of human consciousness develops, both deepening and widening that consciousness. This is essentially the same idea, though in different form, used by Heidegger and Sartre in describing the unique nature of human beings. For Heidegger this nothingness was the undefined distinction between Being and beings, for Sartre it was the shell that surrounded the pour-soi.

May believed that existential psychology occupied a space somewhere between the two extremes that existed, and continue to exist, in psychology: behaviorism vs. humanism. May rejected Skinner's arguments that all human behavior can be understood in terms of stimuli and responses, declaring that there is ample evidence in both clinical practice and everyday life of people being active participants in their view of, actions in, and reactions to their world. He was equally critical of Carl Rogers, believing that humanistic psychologists no longer recognized very real irrational behavior, as well as aggression and hostility (May, 1967). He believed that psychology had become trapped in a misguided desire to define everything scientifically, and according to rules that then determined each psychologist's view of the world and their patients. As a caution to those psychologists who cannot see beyond their theories, May wrote:

> Now I am certainly aware, if I may say so without sounding patronizing, that the compelling need for honesty is one of the motives which leads psychologists to seek quantitative measures…I am also aware that research in our day has to be carefully set up so that the results are teachable and can be built upon by others. The compelling drive to get at the truth is what improves us all as psychologists, and is part and parcel of intellectual integrity. But I do urge that we not let the drive for honesty put blinders on us and cut off our range of vision so that we miss the very thing we set out to understand - namely, the living human being. (pg. 14; May, 1967)

Discussion Question: May suggested that we need to separate ourselves from the conformist masses, and then integrate ourselves with others in free and responsible ways. Are you a follower, or a leader? Either way, do you consciously choose the role you play, thereby living an authentic life?

Love and Intentionality

Love was a very important topic for May. Simply put, "To be capable of giving and receiving mature love is as sound a criterion as we have for the fulfilled personality" (May, 1953). He was certainly not alone. Harry Harlow, best known for his studies on **contact comfort**, described love as "a wondrous state, deep, tender, and rewarding," and Abraham Maslow said "We *must* understand love; we must be able to teach it, to create it, to predict it, or else the world is lost to hostility and to suspicion" (Harlow, 1975; Maslow, 1975). However, there are "a million and one" types of relationships that people call love, so it remains a perplexing issue (May, 1953).

May talked about four types of love in Western tradition: **sex, eros, philia**, and **agape** (May, 1969). Sex and eros are closely related, but they are different. Sex is what we also call lust or libido, whereas eros is the drive of love to procreate or create. As changes in society allowed the more open study of sex, prompted by the work of people like Sigmund Freud and Wilhelm Reich, May noted three particular paradoxes. First, our so-called enlightenment has not removed the sexual problems in our culture. In the past, an individual could refrain from sexual activity using the moral guidelines of society as an explanation. As casual sex became common, even expected, individuals had to face expressing their own morality as just that: their own! This also created a new source of anxiety for some, namely the possibility that their personal relationships might carry an expectation of sexual activity, and that if they did not comply they might not be able to continue dating someone they liked. The second paradox is that "*the new emphasis on technique in sex and love-making backfires*" (May, 1969). Emphasizing technique (or prowess) can result in a mechanistic attitude toward making love, possibly leading to alienation, feelings of loneliness, and depersonalization. This can lead to the anticipatory anxiety described by Frankl. Finally, May believed that our sexual freedom was actually a new form of Puritanism. There is a state of alienation from the body, a separation of emotion from reason, and the use of the body as a machine. Whereas in the Victorian era people tried to be in love without falling into sex, today many people try to have sex without falling in love.

Philia and agape are also related to one another, as with sex and love. Philia refers to feelings of friendship or brotherly love, whereas agape is the love devoted to caring for others. Friendship during childhood is very important, and May believed it was essential for meaningful and loving relationships as adults, including those involving eros. Indeed, the tension created by eros in terms of continuous attraction and continuous passion would be unbearable if philia did not enter into the equation and allow one to relax in the pleasant and friendly company of the object of one's desires. Harry Harlow, once again, showed that the opportunity to make friends was as essential in the development of young monkeys as it appears to be in humans (cited in May, 1969). In the West, however, given our highly individualistic and competitive society, deep, meaningful friendships seem to be something of the past, especially among men. May cautions, however, that since the evidence shows the importance of friendship during development perhaps we should remember the value of having good friends.

Finally we have agape, a selfless love beyond any hope of gain for oneself. May compared this love to the biological aspect of nature in which a parent will fight to the death in defense of their offspring. With agape, we run the risk of being like God, in the sense that we know others never act without some degree of their own interests in mind. Similarly, we don't want to be loved in an ethereal sense, or on the other hand only for our body. We want to be loved completely. So, all true love involves some element of the other types of love, no matter how little or how obscured it may be (May, 1969).

Agape is exemplified in the bond between a parent and their child. [Image by Mark Kelland]

In the foreword to *Love and Will* (May, 1969) May acknowledged that some of his readers might find it odd that he combined the two topics in one book, but he felt strongly that the topics belong together. He considered both love and will to be interdependent, they are processes in which people reach out to influence others, to help to mold and create the consciousness of others. Love without will is sentimental and experimental, whereas will without love is manipulative. Only by remaining open to the influence of others can we likewise influence them, so love must have an honest purpose, and purpose must be taken with care.

Will, or **will power** as it is more commonly known, was one of the earliest subjects in American psychology, having been examined in detail by William James as early as 1890 (see James, 1892/1992) and again in 1897 in *The Will to Believe* (James, 1897/1992). May considered Sigmund Freud's greatest discovery to be the uncovering of unconscious desires and motives. Although many people may believe themselves to be acting out of higher ideals, most of us are, in reality, acting according to psychologically determined factors of which we are unaware. Nonetheless, May considered this to be one of the most unfortunate results of Freud's work. By accepting determinism, we undermine the influence of will and making decisions. As May put it, Freud's theory suggests that we are "not *driving* any more, but *driven*" (May, 1969).

The suggestion that we are no longer in charge of our own lives, that we are driven by psychological determinism, seems strange to those who believe that never before have people had such power, both in terms of individual freedom and in the collective conquest of nature. But May referred to a **contradiction in will**, the contrast between our feelings of powerlessness and self-doubt and the societal assurances that we can do anything we set our minds to. May believed that we exist in a "curious predicament," in that the technical wonders that make us feel so powerful are the very same processes that overwhelm us (May, 1969):

> Thus, the crisis in will does not arise from either the presence or absence of power in the individual's world. It comes from the contradiction between the two - the result of which is a paralysis of will. (pg. 189; May, 1969)

Will alone is not the driving force that leads us to responsible and authentic lives. Underlying will is something May called **intentionality**. Intentionality is the structure that gives meaning to experience, it is both how we perceive the world and how the world can be perceived by us. In other words, through our perceptual processes we influence the world around us; we affect the very things that we perceive. Intentionality is a bridge between subject and object (May, 1969). Compare this once again to the nothingness between beings and Being (à la Heidegger), or between the en-soi and the pour-soi (à la Sartre). Still, our ability to reach and form the very objects that we perceive, in other words, to participate actively in our lives, can be dramatically curtailed by the problem addressed by May early in his career, anxiety:

> Overwhelming anxiety destroys the capacity to perceive and conceive one's world, to reach out toward it to form and re-form it. In this sense, it destroys intentionality. We cannot hope, plan, promise, or create in severe anxiety; we shrink back into a stockade of limited consciousness hoping only to preserve ourselves until the danger is past. (pp. 244; May, 1969)

Discussion Question: Consider the different loves in your life. How do they differ? How have they brought meaning to your life? Has your view of what love is changed during your life, in either good or bad ways?

The Daimonic: Source of Violence and Creativity

The **daimonic**, according to May, is "any natural function which has the power to take over the whole person" (May, 1969). It can be either destructive or creative, and is often both. In this way it is similar to Jung's concept of the shadow, and May himself made that comparison (May, 1991; see also Diamond, 1996, Reeves, 1977). In fact, it is the mixture of good and evil in the daimonic that protects us from the dangers of excess, whether excess good or the passivity of feeling powerless. When May did not know whether he would live or die from tuberculosis, he realized that his feelings of helplessness were turning into passivity, and that this was sure to lead to his death (as he had seen with others). He described this experience as the product of his innocence, and that because he was innocent he allowed the bacteria infecting his body to do violence to him. However, when he chose to fight the disease, when he asserted his will to live, he began to make steady progress and, indeed, he recovered. In this sense, May had chosen to allow the daimonic to take over his self in the interest of self preservation. In each instance, how one allows the daimonic to take over is influenced by personal responsibility (Reeves, 1977).

When the daimonic takes over without one having made a responsible choice, however, it can lead to violence toward others. Our lives often involve conflict between those who have power and those who do not. When a person feels powerless, helpless, insignificant, they can lash out under the control of the daimonic. According to May, violence is bred in impotence and apathy (May, 1972). This can be particularly important for those who have little or no advantage in our society. In *Power and Innocence* (May, 1972), May described a patient who was a young, Black woman. Being both Black and female, born before the civil rights movement, she was about as powerless as one could be in America. Her stepfather had forced her to serve as a prostitute for years. Although quite intelligent, and successful in school and college, she felt so helpless that May described her as having "no active belief that she deserved to be helped." An important aspect of therapy for this patient was to get in touch with her anger, to get in touch with the violence that had been done to her and that she wished to do to others.

In considering the case of this young woman, May concluded that we must not simply condemn all violence and try to eliminate even the possibility of it. To do so would be to take away a part of full humanity. In this context, May criticizes humanistic psychology and its emphasis on fulfilling self-actualization, an emphasis that May felt moved toward greater moral perfection. However, the recognition that we are not perfect, that each of us has good and evil within, prohibits us from moral arrogance. Recognizing this leads to the restraint necessary for making forgiveness possible.

Our ability to achieve good is dependent on who we are, and who we are is based partly on our own **creativity**. Since humans are not simply driven by instinct and fixed action patterns, in contrast to every other creature on earth we must create ourselves. This creation must take place within the world that exists around us, and must take into account all of the emotions and predispositions that we do carry with us as biological organisms.

> Art - and creative activities of all kinds - can provide comparatively healthy outlets for the constructive expression of anger and rage. Creativity cannot, however, always substitute for psychotherapy. Nevertheless, creativity is at the very core of the psychotherapeutic project: The patient is encouraged to become more creative in psychologically restructuring his or her *inner*

> world, and then to continue this creative process in the *outer* world, not only by accepting and adjusting to reality, but, whenever possible, by reshaping it…
>
> "Creativity" can be broadly defined as *the constructive utilization of the daimonic.* Creativity is called forth from each one of us by the inevitable conflicts and chaos inherent in human existence… (pp. 255-256; Diamond, 1996)

Pursuing this creativity is not easy, however. We live in a world that is rapidly changing. Since May's death in 1994 change in the world has probably even accelerated. May asked whether we would withdraw in anxiety and panic as our foundations where shaken, or would we actively choose to participate in forming the future (May, 1975). Choosing to live in the future requires leaping into the unknown, going where others have not been, and therefore cannot guide us. It involves what existentialists call the anxiety of nothingness (May, 1975). Making this bold choice requires **courage**. One of the reasons we need to be courageous is that we must fully commit ourselves to pursuing a responsible creation of the future, but at the same time we must recognize that sometimes we will be wrong. Those who claim they are absolutely right can be dangerous, since such an attitude can lead to dogmatism, or worse, fanaticism (May, 1975).

Finally, not only must we accept that we might make bad choices, we must also recognize that our creativity is limited. In *The Courage to Create* (May, 1975), May described having attended a conference where the introductory speaker declared that there is no limit to the possibilities of the human being. Following this statement, the discussion at the conference was a flop. May realized that if there is no limit to what we can accomplish, then there really aren't any problems any more, we only need to wait until our potentiality catches up with our situation and the problem solves itself. May offered a rather amusing example to clarify this point:

> …it is like putting someone into a canoe and pushing him out into the Atlantic toward England with the cheery comment, "The sky's the limit." The canoer is only too aware of the fact that an inescapably real limit is also the bottom of the ocean. (pg. 113, May, 1975)

Another inescapable limit is our death. There is no creative act that can change the fact that we will die someday, and that we cannot know when or how it will happen. May believed, however, that these limits are valuable, that creativity itself needs limits. He proposed that consciousness arises from our awareness of these limits, and from the struggle against these limits. May compared this concept to Adler's theory that much of what we as individuals, and also society as a whole, are arises from our efforts to compensate for inferiority. Thus, our limits lead to what May called a **passion for form**. In its passion for form, the mind is actively forming and re-forming the world in which we live (May, 1975).

Discussion Question: May believed that creatively taking charge of your life required courage. Have you ever had to make a really difficult decision? Did you take the easy way out, or the safe path, or did you make a bold decision that offered great opportunity?

The Cry for Myth

> As a practicing psychoanalyst I find that contemporary therapy is almost entirely concerned, when all is surveyed, with the problems of the individual's search for myths. The fact that Western society has all but lost its myths was the main reason for the birth and development of psychoanalysis in the first place. (pg. 9; May, 1991)

The preceding quote is how May began *The Cry for Myth*, the last book of his career (May, 1991). According to May, the definition of a **myth** is quite simple: it "is a way of making sense in a senseless world." In addition, myths give substance to our existence. In a healthy society the myths provide relief from neurotic guilt and excessive anxiety, and so a compassionate therapist will not discourage them. In the twentieth century, especially in Western culture, we have lost our myths, and with them we have lost our sense of existence and our direction or purpose in life. The danger in this is that people are then susceptible to cults, drugs, superstition, etc., in a vain effort to replace that purpose (May, 1991).

As we pass through the experiences of our lives, our memory is dependent mainly upon myth. It is well accepted today that human memory is constructive, and influenced by our expectations of memory. As May describes it, the formation of a memory, regardless of whether it is real or fantasy, is molded like clay. We then retain it as a myth, and rely on that myth for future guidance in similar situations. For example, an infant is fed three times a day and put to bed 365 days a year, and yet they remember only one or two of these events from their years of early childhood. For whatever reason, good or bad, these specific events take on mythic proportions and greatly influence the course of our lives. May acknowledges the contribution of Alfred Adler in recognizing the value of these early memories, describing Adler as "a perceptive and humble man, he was gifted with unusual sensitivity for children" (May, 1991). As we have seen, Adler considered the basis for neurosis to be a lack of social interest. In therapy, Adler focused on the "guiding fiction" of a child's life, something May considered to be synonymous with a "myth." Since "memory is the mother of creativity," and memory depends upon myth, May believed that the myths that form the identity of our culture are essential for the formation of our self.

May ends his final book with a chapter entitled *The Great Circle of Love*. Having covered a variety of famous myths in the book, including Dante's *Divine Comedy*, Marlow's *Faust*, Captain Ahab in *Moby Dick*, and Poe's *The Raven*, May concludes:

> In each of these dramas the liberation of both woman and man is possible only when each achieves a new myth of the other sex, leading to a new significant psychological relationship. They are both then liberated from their previous empty and lonely existence. The woman and the man find their true selves only when they are fully present to each other. They find they both need each other, not only physically but psychologically and spiritually as well. (pg. 288; May, 1991)

Existential Psychotherapy

Existential psychotherapy is not so much a technique as it is an overall approach to understanding the nature of the human being. By asking deep questions about the nature of anxiety, loneliness, isolation, despair, etc., as well as about creativity and love, existential psychotherapists seek to avoid the "common error of distorting human beings in the very effort of trying to help them" (May & Yalom, 1995). May believed that American psychology has had both an affinity for and an aversion to existential psychotherapy. The affinity arises from an historical place in American psychology that was very similar to existentialism: William James' emphasis on the immediacy of experience, the importance of will, and the unity of thought and action. The aversion arises from the Western tendency to dehumanize people through strict adherence to scientific principles of research, i.e., to reform humans in the image of machines (May, 1983).

An essential aspect of existential psychotherapy is to help individuals realize their own being, their own role in choosing the form that their life will take. This is known as the **"I-Am" experience**. It is all too common for us to associate ourselves with external factors: I am a professor, I am a student, I work at a store, I run a business, etc. We repress our own sense of being. To use an example similar to a case described by May: I am a professor, but that is not really who I am. I am a father and a husband, but that isn't all that I am. I have a family and a career, but that isn't quite it either. What is left, or what is common in each of these statements? I am! And as May put it, if I am, I have a right to be (example cited in May & Yalom, 1995). This realization is not the solution to my problems, but it is a necessary precondition to finding the courage to pursue the rest of my life.

Once an individual finds the courage to recreate their life, the existential therapist will address a variety of issues. As discussed above, May placed a great deal of emphasis on anxiety. Guilt is also an important issue to be addressed, since we may feel guilty about poor ethical choices or instances when we failed to be responsible with our actions. As with anxiety, guilt can be normal (after actually doing something bad) or neurotic (when we fantasize some transgression). Both anxiety and guilt affect how we experience Kierkegaard's concept of being-in-the-world. Our world can be viewed in several different ways, however. There is the **Umwelt** (the world around), the **Mitwelt** (the with-world), and the **Eigenwelt** (the own-world). The Umwelt is the world around us, the natural environment. It encompasses our biological needs, and the unavoidable reality that we will die one day. The Eigenwelt refers to our self-awareness and our ability to relate to our selves, and it is uniquely human (May & Yalom, 1995).

The Mitwelt bears a special relationship to another important concept in existential psychotherapy: **time**. Because we tend to think about ourselves spatially, as objects within our life, we tend to focus on the past. In other words, we focus on what we have become, as opposed to what we might be. Moments when we truly encounter ourselves are rare, but it is only when we grasp the moment that we truly experience life. Those moments can be positive, such as the experience of love, or negative, such as the experience of depression, but they are real nonetheless. The Mitwelt contains the inner meaning of the events that occur in our lives. Individuals who suffer from brain damage often cannot think in terms of abstract possibilities, they become trapped in concrete time. In order to be fully healthy, and something essential to the growth of humans, is our ability to transcend time:

> If we are to understand a given person as existing, dynamic, at every moment becoming, we cannot avoid the dimension of transcendence. Existing involves a continual emerging, in the sense of emergent evolution, a transcending of one's past and present in order to reach the future. (pg. 267; May & Yalom, 1995)

Although the content described above might seem very different from the type of psychoanalysis described by Freud, the general process of existential psychotherapy is similar to psychoanalysis. It is accepted that the client experiences anxiety, that some of this anxiety is unconscious, and that the client is relying on defense mechanisms in order to cope with the anxiety. A fundamental difference, however, is the focus of the therapy. Rather than digging into the deep, dark past, the existential psychotherapist strives to understand the meaning of the client's current experiences, the depth of experience in the given moment. For this reason, the therapist-client relationship remains important, but the emphasis is not on transference. Rather, the emphasis is on the relationship itself as fundamentally important (May & Yalom, 1995).

Discussion Question: Have you ever had an "I-Am" experience?

Buddhism and Existentialism: The Completion of a Circle?

Buddhism is by far the oldest theory of psychology that we will cover in this book. Applied existentialism, particularly the work of Rollo May, is one of the more recent developments in psychology. And yet, these two approaches share a great deal in common, a fact readily acknowledged by May:

> ...The likenesses between these Eastern philosophies and existentialism go much deeper than the chance similarity of words. Both are concerned with ontology, the study of being. Both seek a relation to reality which cuts below the cleavage between subject and object. Both would insist that the Western absorption in conquering and gaining power over nature has resulted not only in the estrangement of man from nature but also indirectly in the estrangement of man from himself. The basic reason for these similarities is that Eastern thought never suffered the radical split between subject and object that has characterized Western thought, and this dichotomy is exactly what existentialism seeks to overcome. (pp. 58-59; May, 1983)

In Japan there is a form of psychotherapy, known as **Morita**, which emphasizes the treatment of anxiety. The treatment consists of acceptance, reattribution, dereflection, and active engagement. The dereflection mentioned is the same technique developed by Viktor Frankl. The active engagement continues this effort at distracting the client from their anxiety, hopefully breaking them out of the circle of anticipatory anxiety and subsequent failure described by Frankl. This procedure has proven both successful and, consequently, influential amongst Japanese psychotherapists. A second Japanese technique, **Naikan**, combines a more traditional Buddhist approach with elements of existential psychology. The client is directed to reflect intensely on their past relationships, and then to consider what they have done for others, what others have done for them, and the difficulties they have caused for others. The goal is to help the client recognize the interdependence of humans, and to appreciate whether or not they, as well as others, have acted responsibly within the relationships. By confronting feelings of guilt and unworthiness, it is hoped that the client will realize that they have been loved and appreciated nonetheless (Walsh, 1995).

Belinda Siew Luan Khong (2003) has examined the role of responsibility in a particular form of existential psychotherapy known as **daseinsanalysis** (developed by the Swiss psychiatrist Medard Boss and grounded in the philosophy of Heidegger) and compared it to Buddhist practice in the Theravadan tradition. She found that daseinsanalysis and Buddhist practices share much in common, and that both have something to offer to each other:

> ...An integration of these two disciplines will make their ideas and practices more accessible to communities outside their traditional domains. The daseinsanalytic and Buddhist perspectives relating to personal and social responsibility provide us with valuable philosophical and psychological insights into this very important human phenomenon and show us practically how individuals can be assisted in taking responsibility for every moment of their existence, and to develop a sense of respond-ability to different situations. (pg. 158; Khong, 2003)

Stephen Batchelor, a former Buddhist monk turned author and teacher, has presented existentialism as an interesting approach to the primary problem facing Buddhism in America today (Batchelor, 1983). According to Batchelor, Buddhism in the west is split between those who wish to follow a traditional path (emphasizing meditation and practice) and those who insist upon an academic approach to the analysis and understanding of Buddhism. Between the two approaches lies a great chasm. As we have seen, existentialism draws its deepest and most meaningful philosophy from nothingness, be it the distinction between Being and beings (Dasein, according to Heidegger) or the shell separating the pour-soi from the en-soi (as proposed by Sartre). Drawing primarily from his Buddhist training and the philosophy of Heidegger and Tillich (see below), Batchelor contrasts **being-alone** and **being-with**. We are essentially alone at birth and at death, in that we cannot share the experience with others, and this leads to unavoidable anxiety throughout our lives (though not necessarily overwhelming anxiety for most people). As we will see in the next chapter, the first noble truth of Buddhism is that human life is suffering. But just as much as we are alone, we are unavoidably linked to others as well. What matters then, is that we experience authentic **being-with-others**, and the root of authentic being-with is concern for others (as opposed to the inauthentic distortion of self-concern; Batchelor, 1983).

> The genuine welfare of man, of both oneself and others, is found in the optimum actualization of the potentialities of his being. To exist in the fullest possible way in our aloneness as well as in our relations with others is the fulfillment of the inner aim of human life...(pg. 88; Batchelor, 1983)

Some Final Thoughts on Existentialism and Existential Psychology

Jean-Paul Sartre's *Being and Nothingness* (1943) is considered the defining text of modern existentialism. Sartre was an atheist, so the brief introduction to existentialism in this chapter went in the direction of atheism. However, Frankl and May were not atheists, and one of May's most influential mentors, as well as a close personal friend, was Paul Tillich. Tillich remains a well-known and respected existential philosopher in the spiritual tradition. May went so far as to say that Tillich' book *The Courage to Be* might be the best and most understandable presentation of existentialism as an approach to life that has been written in English (May, 1983).

It is also interesting to note that both Frankl and May were significantly influenced by Alfred Adler. Frankl worked closely with Adler for a time, and May took a summer course with Adler. Both cite Adler regularly in their writings. Adler's focus on the childhood struggle against one's own inferiority, his emphasis on social interest as a responsible means to superiority, and his recognition of the dangers inherent in seeking superiority at the expense of others, all fit well with the existential perspective on making responsible choices in living one's life. This point emphasizes, once again, the profound influence that Adler has had on psychology, and that he is in all probability the most under-recognized figure in the history of psychology.

In 1897, William James published an essay entitled *Is Life Worth Living?* (James, 1897/1992). James begins by describing how some people see the value in life, indeed they fully enjoy life, no matter what happens to them or around them. However, for most people this is not the case, and there is no magic way to give everyone such an optimistic point of view. So, James presents a series of arguments that one might use with suicidal people (that is the term he uses) in order to convince them that life is worth living. He relies heavily on religious faith, though not on any particular religion, but also leads into a discussion of existential thought. Approximately a decade before Frankl and May were even born, James wrote the following words:

> ...Suppose, however thickly evils crowd upon you, that your unconquerable subjectivity proves to be their match, and that you find a more wonderful joy than any passive pleasure can bring in trusting ever in the larger whole. Have you not now made life worth living on these terms?...This life *is* worth living, we can say, *since it is what we make it, from the moral point of view*, and we are determined to make it from that point of view, so far as we have anything to do with it, a success...These, then, are my last words to you: Be not afraid of life. Believe that life *is* worth living, and your belief will help create the fact. (pp. 501-503; James, 1897/1992)

The challenges that we all face in trying to live authentic lives, the challenges of making responsible and ethical choices that are true to who we ourselves are, can be difficult. In a fascinating book entitled *Not a Genuine Black Man*, Brian Copeland (2006) talks about his family's racial struggles during the civil rights movement and the difficulties he faces today as a Black man who has adopted many so-called "White" cultural values. Copeland insists, however, that we cannot so easily claim that any given value or personal interest belongs only to one group of people:

> ...When all is said and done, I AM indeed a Genuine Black Man - because I am resilient. That's what being black in America is truly about: resilience...I stayed on my feet through taunts and harassment, through police intimidation and bigoted nuns, through schoolyard bullies and Sylvester, through my mother's death and bouts of sometimes crippling depression. I am still standing.
>
> I am black because, as my friend Mr. Wilkins once told me, people should be called what they *want* to be called. I have the right and the ability to determine my identity regardless of what other blacks *or* whites say. I am not an "oreo," nor am I "still a nigger." I am a man. I am a black man.
>
> No one person or group of individuals holds the monopoly on what in this society is the "true" black experience. My world is as "black" as that of Malcolm X, Colin Powell, Snoop Dogg, Jesse Jackson, Usher, Bill Cosby, or Diddy. As their experiences in America are unique, mine is unique - yet it is the same. It is as valid as that of the poor African American living in "the 'hood," the rich black rapper balancing a lifestyle of fame and violence, and the black scholar working to better this world through academic dissertation. It is as authentic as the experiences of those who marched with Dr. King for civil rights and those who defy the black community by arguing the conservative point of view.
>
> It is the "true" black experience because it is *my* experience... (pp. 243-244; Copeland, 2006)

Discussion Question: Brian Copeland talked about how difficult it can be to live an authentic life when you don't meet the expectations of others. Have you ever gone against the advice of family or friends? Did it prove to be the right decision, or did it at least help you to feel better about your own confidence in yourself?

Personality Theory in Real Life: The Application of Frankl's Theories to the Workplace and Everyday Life

In 1989, Stephen Covey published *The 7 Habits of Highly Effective People*. Covey's book became very popular, selling millions of copies on the way to becoming a #1 New York Times bestseller. If you were to read the first chapter of that book now, it would seem very familiar. Covey presents a very existential approach to understanding our lives, particularly with regard to the problems we experience every day. Perhaps it should not be surprising, then, that in the chapters describing the first two of these seven habits he cites and quotes Viktor Frankl numerous times. Indeed, Covey cites Frankl's first two books as being profoundly influential in his own life, and how impressed Covey was having met Frankl shortly before Frankl's death (see Covey's foreword in Pattakos, 2004).

The first two habits, according to Covey, are: 1) be proactive, and 2) begin with the end in mind.

He briefly describes Frankl's experiences in the concentration camps, and refers to Frankl's most widely quoted saying, that Frankl himself could decide how his experiences would affect him, and that no one could take that freedom away from Frankl! People who choose to develop this level of personal freedom are certainly being proactive, as opposed to responding passively to events that occur around them and to them. It is not necessary, of course, to suffer such tragic circumstances in order to become proactive in one's own life:

> ...It is in the ordinary events of every day that we develop the proactive capacity to handle the extraordinary pressures of life. It's how we make and keep commitments, how we handle a traffic jam, how we respond to an irate customer or a disobedient child. It's how we view our problems and where we focus our energies. It's the language we use. (pg. 92; Covey, 1989)

Covey compares his habit of beginning with the end in mind to logotherapy, helping people to recognize the meaning that their life holds. Covey works primarily in business leadership training, so the value of working toward a greater goal than simply keeping a company in business from day to day is clear, especially for those who care about employee morale and quality control (see also *Principle-Centered Leadership*; Covey, 1990). When employees share a sense of purpose in their work, they are likely to have higher intrinsic motivation. Think about it for a moment. Have you ever had a job you didn't really understand, and didn't care about? Have you ever been given that sort of homework in school or college? So, how much effort did you really put into that job or assignment?

Covey's remaining habits are: 3) put first things first, 4) think win/win, 5) seek first to understand, then to be understood, 6) synergize, and 7) sharpen the saw. At first glance these principles seem reasonably straight forward, emphasizing practical and responsible actions. However, what does "sharpen the saw" mean? Sharpening the saw refers to keeping our tools in good working order, and we are our most important tool. Covey considers it essential to regularly and consistently, in wise and balanced ways, to exercise the four dimensions of our nature: physical, mental, social/emotional, and spiritual. By investing in ourselves, we are taking care to live an authentic life.

More recently, Covey has examined his principles beyond the business world. In 1997 he published *The 7 Habits of Highly Effective Families*, a book in which he applies the same 7 habits to family life. Covey certainly has solid credentials as a family man, as father of 9 and grandfather of 43 children, and he won the 2003 Fatherhood Award from the National Fatherhood Initiative. Drawing in large part on his own extensive, personal experience, Covey uses many stories, anecdotes, and examples of real-life situations to help provide context to the challenges of raising a family and how we might best work with them. But first, he introduces a simple process: have a clear vision of what you want to accomplish, have a plan of how you might accomplish it, and use a compass (your own unique gifts that enable you to be an agent of change in your family). In essence, Covey is recommending that you prepare yourself to develop the seven habits. We all know how difficult it is to establish a new habit or break a bad habit; how is your New Year's resolution going?

Just as families change, so does the world we live in. Recently, Covey addressed this change by proposing an eighth habit (Covey, 2004). He says that this was not simply an important habit he had overlooked before, but one that has risen to new significance as we have fully entered the age of information and technology in the twenty-first century. As communication has become much easier (e.g., email), it has also become less personal and meaningful. Thus the need for the eighth habit: find your voice and inspire others to find theirs. According to Covey, "voice is unique personal significance." Essentially, it is the same as finding meaning in one's life, and then helping others to find meaning in their own lives. It is through finding a mission or a purpose in life that we can move "from effectiveness to greatness" (Covey, 2004).

Whereas Covey presented an approach to personal and professional effectiveness (and later to greatness as well) that parallels the principles set forth by Viktor Frankl, Alex Pattakos very directly applies Frankl's theories to both the workplace and one's everyday life in *Prisoners of Our Thoughts: Viktor Frankl's Principles at Work* (with a foreword by Stephen Covey; Pattakos, 2004). Frankl himself urged Pattakos to publish his book during a meeting in 1996. Pattakos, like Covey, has been profoundly influenced by Frankl's writings throughout Pattakos' career. According to Pattakos, we are creatures of habit, and we prefer a life that is both predictable and within our comfort zone. As the world is changing in the twenty-first century, so the conditions under which we work are changing. Pattakos believes there is a need for humanizing work. More than just balancing one's personal life and career, humanizing work is an attempt to honor our own individuality and to fully engage our human spirit at work. Simply put, it is an effort to apply Frankl's will-to-meaning in our workplace (Pattakos, 2004).

Like Covey, Pattakos presents seven core principles. They are similar to Covey's seven habits, but in keeping with Pattakos' intentions they are aligned more directly with the principles of logotherapy and existential psychology described by Frankl. The seven core principles are: 1) exercise the freedom to choose your attitude, 2) realize your will-to-meaning, 3) detect the meaning of life's moments, 4) don't work against yourself, 5) look at yourself from a distance, 6) shift your focus of attention, and 7) extend beyond yourself. These principles include not only the ideas of personal freedom and will-to-meaning, but also dereflection (principles 4 and 6) and the will-to-ultimate-meaning (principle 7). Clearly Pattakos has accomplished his goal of applying logotherapy to the workplace, but how well does this application work in real life?

Pattakos describes the case of a probation officer with the state department of corrections. Rick, as Pattakos identifies him, was raised in foster care and orphanages. However, rather than developing a sense of caring and concern for others who have difficulties in their lives, Rick refers to his clients as "maggots." Rick has become insensitive and unforgiving, he has also become deeply depressed and anxious. Overall, he feels lost, unhappy, and unfulfilled, and he doesn't know what to do about it. According to Pattakos, he has become a prisoner of his own thoughts, and only he has the key to his own freedom. Very simply put, he needs to find a new job or find meaning in the one he has now. One possibility is for Rick to consider his own life circumstances in relationship to his clients:

> ...Whenever we stop long enough to connect to ourselves, to our environment, to those with whom we work, to the task before us, to the extraordinary interdependence that is always part of our lives, we experience meaning. Meaning is who we are in this world. And it is the world that graces us with meaning. (pg. 157; Pattakos, 2004)

By making a responsible choice to seek meaning in our lives, to not work against ourselves, we can put ourselves on a path we had not seen before:

> When we live and work with meaning, we can choose to make meaning, to see meaning, and to share meaning. We can choose our attitudes to life and work; we can choose how to respond to others, how to respond to our jobs, and how to make the very best of difficult circumstances. We can transcend ourselves and be transformed by meaning. We can find connection to meaning at work, in the most unusual places and with the most unexpected people. Meaning is full of surprises. (pg. 159; Pattakos, 2004)

And finally, it does not matter what sort of job we have. It is our choice, our freedom:

> No matter what our specific job might be, it is the *work* we do that represents who we are. When we meet our work with enthusiasm, appreciation, generosity, and integrity, we meet it with meaning. And no matter how mundane a job might seem at the time, we can transform it with meaning. Meaning is life's legacy, and it is as available to us at work as it is available to us in our deepest spiritual quests. We breathe, therefore we are - spiritual. Life is; therefore it is - meaningful. We do, therefore we work.

Viktor Frankl's legacy was one of hope and possibility. He saw the human condition at its worst, and human beings behaving in ways intolerable to the imagination. He also saw human beings rising to heights of compassion and caring in ways that can only be described as miraculous acts of unselfishness and transcendence. There is something in us that can rise above and beyond everything we think possible… (pg. 162; Pattakos, 2004)

Discussion Question: Stephen Covey and Alex Pattakos have applied Frankl's theories to both the workplace and our everyday lives. How well do you think the principles of existential psychology can address the problems that you face at work, home, school, etc.? Is it ever really as simple as applying one's will and choosing to act responsibly? Do you live an authentic life?

Review of Key Points

- Existentialism focuses on an individual's subjective "truth." The freedom and responsibility that come with personal truth lead to anxiety, but they can also elevate the individual to lead an authentic life.
- Heidegger believed that all creatures are connected, but that only humans can become aware of this connection. Dasein, the realization of this connection, allows us to connect with Being. Awareness of our impending death, however, leads to anxiety, but if we accept that truth we can live an authentic life.
- Sartre believed that humans were unique, something he called en-soi. Awareness of the nothingness that separates the en-soi from the pour-soi is what drives some individuals to make something significant of their lives. For those who cannot, Sartre expressed a need for existential psychoanalysis.
- Viktor Frankl developed his ideas for logotherapy (an existential psychoanalysis) during his impressive early career. He had an extraordinary opportunity to put his ideas to the test while imprisoned in the Nazi concentration camps.
- Recognized as the third Viennese school of psychotherapy, logotherapy focuses on one's will-to-meaning, the desire to find meaning and purpose in one's life.
- People who cannot find meaning experience existential frustration, which can lead to a noogenic neurosis.
- Logotherapy itself relies primarily on the techniques of paradoxical intention and dereflection. These techniques are designed to break the cycle of anticipatory anxiety and failure that plague individuals who suffer from existential crises.
- Going beyond ordinary, everyday life, Frankl proposed a super-meaning to life, and he suggested that there is also a will-to-ultimate-meaning that can be pursued through religion or spirituality. In this light, Frankl referred to logotherapy as "height psychology" (in contrast to depth psychology, another term for psychoanalysis).
- Rollo May believed that anxiety underlies nearly every crisis. He proposed that anxiety must be understood in terms of freedom, and he distinguished between normal anxiety and neurotic anxiety.
- Culture has significant effects on the nature and amount of anxiety that people are likely to experience in their lives. Since anxiety can lead to hostility, these cultural factors are, and have been throughout history, very important issues (e.g., opposition to the civil rights movement in the United States, and the recent dramatic rise in international terrorism).
- A critical factor in life, according to May, is our ability to integrate into our world. One of the challenges to integration is the human dilemma: whether we are the subject or the object in our lives. As self-aware beings we can know that we are both subject and object, and so, in psychological terms, we exist in a world between either behaviorism or humanistic psychology.
- There are different types of love, all of which are very important to our lives. Love can give meaning to our lives, but it must be honest and responsible love.
- Through will and intentionality we can give structure to our lives and meaning to our actions. However, overwhelming anxiety can destroy our ability to participate actively in our own lives.

- The daimonic is any function that can take over the whole person. It can be a source of violence, but also a source of creativity. We can choose how the daimonic takes over, and whether that choice is responsible or not determines whether our actions are violent or creative.
- Being creative requires that we live in the future and actively participate in shaping our lives. Such bold choices require courage, especially in light of the inescapable reality that we will die.
- May felt that myth provides an important cultural framework within which we can form our lives. Unfortunately, the Western world has lost many of its myths, making people susceptible to cults, drugs, superstition, etc.
- According to May, the primary goal of existential psychotherapy is to help the client realize their own being, to have an "I-Am" experience. Time is an important aspect of this procedure. The client must be helped to shift their focus from the past to the future, and even more so, to transcend time altogether.
- Although existential psychology is younger than most other schools of psychology, it has much in common with ancient Eastern philosophies, such as Yoga, Buddhism, and Taoism.
- Terrorism is not the result of Islam. Terrorists are found all over the world, from many different races, religions, and nationalities. Islam opposes violence and murder.
- Terrorism is based on psychological factors (a perception that there are no alternatives, and that terrorism is legitimate), and seeks to cause psychological effects (feelings of terror and helplessness). Thus, psychologists have an important role to play in understanding and eliminating terrorism.
- One can easily find those who believe that terrorism either never works or always works. Some believe that we must respond with understanding to eliminate the root causes of terrorism, whereas others believe we must use force (but not too much force, lest we become terrorists as well). Clearly there are no easy answers for dealing with terrorists themselves or terrorism in general.

Review of Key Terms

agape	eros	neurotic anxiety
aesthetic mode	ethical mode	noogenic neurosis
anticipatory anxiety	existential frustration	normal anxiety
anxiety	existential psychoanalysis	paradoxical intention
Being	existential psychology	passion for form
being-alone	existentialism	philia
being-in-the-world	freedom	pour-soi
being-thrown-into-this-world	height psychology	religious mode
being-with	hostility	sex
being-with-others	human dilemma	superman
contact comfort	hwa-bung	super-meaning
contradiction in will	"I-Am" experience	susto
courage	integration	taijin kyofusho
creativity	intentionality	time
daimonic	koro	truth
Dasein	logotherapy	Umwelt
daseinsanalysis	love	will
dereflection	Mitwelt	will power
dhat syndrome	Morita	will-to-meaning
Eigenwelt	myth	will-to-pleasure
en-soi	Naikan	will-to-power
	nervios	will-to-ultimate-meaning

Annotated Bibliography

Sartre, J.-P. (1943). *Being and nothingness*. New York, NY: Washington Square Press.

Subtitled *A Phenomenological Essay on Ontology*, this book is **not** light reading. It is approximately 800 pages of heavy and perplexing philosophy. However, it is also fascinating, and considered one of the great works in philosophy, by a man who went on to win a Nobel Prize for Literature. If philosophy is what you like, and if you enjoy reading, this book will keep you enthralled for some time.

Frankl, V. E. (1946/1992). *Man's search for meaning: An introduction to Logotherapy*. Boston, MA: Beacon Press.

Considered by many to be one of the most influential books of all time, this classic work packs unimaginable wisdom into only a very few pages. The book must be read, it cannot be adequately described. I recommend a recent printing, one that includes the essay *Logotherapy in a Nutshell*, which offers exactly what it advertises.

Frankl, V. E. (1946/1986). *The doctor and the soul: From psychotherapy to logotherapy*. New York, NY: Vintage Books.
Frankl, V. E. (1995/2000). *Viktor Frankl - Recollections: An autobiography*. Cambridge, MA: Perseus Publishing.

The Doctor and the Soul was Frankl's first book, though it was published at the same time as *Man's Search for Meaning* due to Frankl's imprisonment in the concentration camps. It provides much of the theory behind logotherapy, which Frankl had developed early in his career. *Recollections...* is a brief and compelling autobiography, which covers much more of Frankl's life than just his time in the concentration camps.

May, R. (1950). *The meaning of anxiety*. New York, NY: The Ronald Press Company.
May, R. (1953). *Man's search for himself*. New York, NY: W. W. Norton & Company.

In *The Meaning of Anxiety*, May clearly established the value of existentialism for psychology, by recognizing (rightfully, I believe) that Kierkegaard understood something deeper about anxiety than even Sigmund Freud. In *Man's Search for Himself*, May also relates the philosophy of Heidegger to psychological theories. Taken together, these books provide a direct connection between European existential philosophy and American psychology.

May, R. (1991). *The cry for myth*. New York, NY: A Delta Book.

For anyone who enjoys classic literature, this book provides an application of existential psychology to those stories. With so much media bombarding us today, it is hard to recognize the myths that may be arising now. By examining the nature of our myths from the past, perhaps we can more easily recognize the stories of today that will last far enough into the future to become myths themselves.

Copeland, B. (2006). *Not a genuine black man: Or, how I claimed my piece of ground in the lily-white suburbs*. New York, NY: Hyperion.

Mr. Copeland's family was embroiled in the civil rights movement, when his mother sued their landlord in a virtually all-White California community to fight their eviction. Today, Mr. Copeland lives in that same suburb, and shares many of the cultural values that are generally associated with White people. In this engaging and often surprising autobiography, Mr. Copeland takes us along his path toward realizing who he is and what he needs to do in order to live an authentic life.

Covey, S. R. (1989). *The 7 habits of highly effective people: Restoring the character ethic.* New York, NY: Free Press.

Pattakos, A. (2004). *Prisoners of our thoughts: Viktor Frankl's principles at work.* San Francisco, CA: Berrett-Koehler Publishers.

The value of each of these books is to be found in their practical application of existential psychology and closely related topics. Existentialism as a philosophy is a curiosity, existential psychology finds its primary application in therapy, but when these principles make their way into everyday life, then psychology can serve to benefit everyone. Perhaps this is what Frankl meant when he used the term "height psychology" to describe logotherapy.

Moghaddam, F. M. (2005). The staircase to terrorism: A psychological exploration. *American Psychologist, 60*, 161-169.

Moghaddam, F. M. (2006). From the terrorists' point of view: What they experience and why they come to destroy. Westport, CT: Praeger Security International.

Fathali Moghaddam was born in Iran, educated in England, and then returned to Iran and taught there for several years after the revolution in 1979. He is currently a professor at Georgetown University and studies culture and justice. As someone who has lived in both the Western world (England, Canada, and the U.S.A.) and in an Islamic country during the establishment of a fundamentalist government, he is uniquely qualified to address the complex issues of terrorism and becoming a terrorist.

Zadeh, F. E. (2002). *Islam versus terrorism: Understanding Islam and the culture of the Middle East.* Twin Lakes, CO: Twin Lakes Publishing.

This is an insightful and readable description of Islam, terrorism, and the relationships between countries of the Middle East and the West. Zadeh was also born and raised in Iran (like Moghaddam), during the reign of the Shah, but has lived and taught in the United States for over a quarter of a century. He has an excellent perspective on both sides of these issues, and presents his ideas clearly and logically.

Chapter 17 - Yoga: A Purpose for Personal Development, and Buddhism: Zen and the Middle Way

Yoga and Buddhism are vast subjects, spanning many thousands of years, and they are amazing philosophies. But, are they philosophy or religion? They both certainly have significant religious overtones, and are considered to be religions by many people. Actually, however, they are styles of life that developed in order to help people be more in tune with their religion and with God. Yoga, which means unity, was a practice that developed within the Hindu religion to help Hindus achieve unity with God. So it developed as a practice in one's daily life that led to religious fulfillment. The **Buddha** was a Yogi, and did not consider himself to be different than other people. His followers, however, have so fervently held to his teachings that the practice of Buddhism is often viewed as a religion, and over time it became mixed with religious stories and myths, as people tried to fit Buddhism into their traditional culture.

We will look at Yoga and Buddhism as lifestyles, which lead individuals toward a healthy psychological development. We will not be able to avoid the obvious religious and metaphysical overtones, nor should we try. It will actually be quite interesting to compare Yoga and Buddhism to the lifestyle philosophies of Judaism, Christianity, and Islam (which cover at least the traditional religions of most American students), since Judaism, Christianity, and Islam certainly have no shortage of guidelines for living one's daily life in the service of God. Indeed, Alice Bailey (1927), who has offered an inspiring commentary on the earliest teachings on Yoga, suggests that in order for students to have a complete picture of the fulfillment of the soul they need to have read three books: the ***Yoga Sutras*** and the ***Bhagavad Gita***, the philosophy of which will be covered briefly in this chapter, and the *New Testament*, covered in the next chapter.

Before beginning this chapter and the next one, however, it should be noted that there are many translations of the classic books on Yoga and Buddhism and terminology varies from translation to translation. One must simply accept this, since the only alternative is for each one of us to learn all of the languages in which these books were written. In this chapter, we will only be exploring the basic concepts of these different perspectives on human nature and intentional personality development.

Toward the end of each section we will take a look at how Yoga and Buddhism have influenced America and Western psychology. Quite a lot has been written on this topic, including works by some of the most famous personality theorists (Freud, Jung, Fromm, James, etc.). However, only recently has there been sufficient interest in the field of personality for these discussions to start becoming more common. Since religion and spirituality are important aspects of positive psychology, which is itself a rapidly growing force in psychology, it is likely that knowledge of the overlap between Yoga, Buddhism, and other spiritual aspects of human nature and personality theory will continue to grow.

Historical Description of Yoga

Yoga dates back thousands of years. Yoga as we know it today stems primarily from the writings of Patanjali. Patanjali was one of the first to write down an ancient oral tradition, in his *Yoga Sutras* (the rules of Yoga), sometime between 800 B.C. and 300 A.D. (though some claim it is much older). Divided into four short books, they contain a profound philosophy that continues to have significant influence today. There are many branches of Yoga now, but the type that was brought to the West, specifically to the United States by Paramahansa Yogananda in the 1920s (Yogananda, 1946), traces its roots directly to the Yoga of Patanjali.

The Yoga Sutras of Patanjali

An early translation of the *Yoga Sutras* lists 195 sutras in the four books, totaling only sixteen pages (Bailey, 1927). And yet, the philosophy contained within them is amazing, although somewhat difficult to understand without having prepared oneself for this very different Eastern philosophy. A more Americanized version of the *Yoga Sutras* has recently been provided by Hartranft (2003), along with a section by section interpretation of the text.

The first verse of the first book states very clearly what Yoga is about. "Aum. The following instruction concerneth the Science of Union." (*Yoga Sutras* I:1; Bailey, 1927). Aum, or **Om**, is the sound of creation, which many Christians may relate to the Word of God in the New Testament (John 1:1; Holy Bible, 1962). The union refers to the union of the individual with the divine creator. Don't be confused by the fact that Hindus believe in many gods. In reality, they view those lesser gods as aspects or manifestations of the one true God, much as Christians believe in one God but refer often to Father, Son, and Holy Spirit (the Holy Trinity) and the angels and demons (including Satan).

The second and third verses then set the stage for the purpose of practicing Yoga: restraining one's inquisitive nature and controlling the mind, so that we might see ourselves realistically. The primary way in which we control the mind is to meditate. The remaining verses describe the nature of man, the universe, and the divine, the proper practice of Yoga through **meditation**, the challenges one is likely to face along the way, and the marvelous benefits of Yoga. Thousands of books, describing many different approaches to Yoga, have followed these simple and straightforward guidelines. No matter which type of Yoga one may choose to study, it would be valuable for anyone to return to this primary source of information to be reminded of the basic goal and purpose of Yoga.

The Bhagavad Gita

The *Bhagavad Gita*, or "Song of the Blessed One," is a fascinating story, with great religious significance if one accepts it at face value (Mitchell, 2000). It consists primarily of a conversation between **Krishna**, a great **Avatar** or divine incarnation, and Arjuna, a great warrior, on the eve of a battle. The battle is a civil war, with noble warriors and relatives split between both sides. Arjuna decides that no good can come of killing so many people in this battle, and he decides not to fight. Krishna, who is driving Arjuna's chariot, instructs Arjuna in Yoga as he discusses what is right both for Arjuna and for all people. Many of the principles of Yoga derive from what Krishna told Arjuna, thus it is believed by many that these Yoga principles come from the mouth of God. This is similar to what Jews, Christians, and Muslims believe about the Torah, the Bible, and the Qur'an: that they are divinely inspired texts.

My favorite quote from the *Bhagavad Gita* refers directly to the self:

> The Self is a friend for him who masters himself by the Self;
> but for him who is not self-mastered, the self is the cruelest foe.
> (pg. 89; Mitchell, 2000)

This quote suggests that we can be our own best friend, or our own worst enemy. Indeed, Krishna tells Arjuna that what he must do is to be himself. It is only through his own actions that Arjuna can fulfill his potential. However, Arjuna must not remain attached to the consequences of his actions; he must simply act and allow the universe to move forward as it will. Only by truly understanding the nature of the universe, and the nature of ourselves, can we properly make this choice. The practice of Yoga helps us to see this reality, and the *Bhagavad Gita* helps to describe the essential practices.

The altar prepared for the ceremony when the author was initiated into Kriya Yoga. [Image by Mark Kelland]

Together, the *Bhagavad Gita* and the *Yoga Sutras* contain all of the basic information on Yoga we will explore in this chapter. There is actually a fair amount of overlap between the books, but it is unclear which one may have been written first. Most scholars believe that the *Bhagavad Gita* was written between 500 B.C. and 100 A.D. (Mitchell, 2000), which falls right in the middle of when Patanjali is believed to have written down the *Yoga Sutras*. Since both philosophies seem to come from much older sources, it may well be that they owe their commonalities to some older tradition that can no longer be specifically identified.

Placing Yoga in Context: An Ancient Plan for Self Development

Yoga is much older than any other theory described in this book, with the exception of those parts of other theories that were borrowed from Yoga and Buddhism. The ancient **Vedas**, which provide much of the mythological and philosophical basis for Hinduism, are 4,000 to 5,000 years old (placing them amongst the oldest recorded literature in the world). The *Yoga Sutras* of Patanjali and the *Bhagavad Gita*, which provide the basic teachings of traditional Yoga, were written as early as 600 B.C. (though there is little consensus on exactly when). Kriya-Yoga, the yoga believed by many to be the original Yoga of Patanjali, was lost to the world for many centuries, until it was reintroduced by Lahiri Mahasaya in 1861. Yoga continues to evolve today, with many different styles being introduced and revised, both in the East and the West.

Although this ancient philosophy may not seem relevant to modern personality theory, it has actually been part of psychology from the very beginning. Most notably, Jung and Rogers were clearly influenced by their travels to India and China, respectively. The knowledge of Yoga and Buddhism they developed as a result of those and other experiences helped to shape their personality theories. Fromm also examined how psychoanalysis and Buddhist meditation compare to each other. Today, as positive psychology examines topics such as happiness and well being, and as spiritual psychotherapists examine the important role that spirituality plays in the lives of many people, those practices that Yoga, Buddhism, and other spiritual disciplines have in common are being examined more closely by psychologists. In the next chapter we will examine similar spiritual disciplines that exist within the Jewish, Christian, and Muslim traditions.

The Concept of Self from a Yogic Perspective

Spirit, Nature, and Consciousness

In the metaphysics of Yoga there is believed to be a duality between spirit and nature. Spirit is pure consciousness; nature is the opposite of spirit. Human beings are a combination of spirit and nature. The body and mind come from nature, but the transcendental self comes from spirit. A key point here is that it is the *transcendental* self that comes from spirit, not the self we are aware of every day. Our thoughts, feelings, sensations, indeed our mind itself, are all the result of neural activity in our brain, and our brain is part of our body. Thus, our awareness is not our consciousness.

Our true self, the transcendental self, is a temporary manifestation of Spirit in essence. The great mistake in our lives is to confuse our body and mind with who we really are, to believe that this body and this mind are our self. The practice of Yoga, however, teaches us to still our minds, to eliminate all thought and sensation, so that we might be in union with our transcendental self and the universal spirit. Once we have accomplished this task, by subjugating our natural tendency to think and restraining our mind itself, we will know who and what we really are (*Yoga Sutras* I:2,3 [Bailey, 1927]). This is not an easy task, but it has a great reward. As Sri Yukteswar told Yogananda:

> The soul expanded into Spirit remains alone in the region of lightless light, darkless dark, thoughtless thought, intoxicated with its ecstasy of joy in God's dream of cosmic creation (Yogananda, 1946; pgs. 489-490).

William James, America's foremost psychologist, is best known for his theory on the stream of consciousness. According to James, it is the continuity of consciousness that defines our self. This is in direct contradiction to Eastern philosophies, which consider the conscious mind to be derived from the natural world, and therefore only an illusion. Eastern philosophies consider the transcendental self to be real, but obscured from us by the distraction of the so-called conscious mind. Can we find some compromise between these points of view? No! However, such a contradiction would probably not bother James. James (1892) did talk about the soul, the transcendental ego, and spirit as possible sources for the conscious self, but considered that possibility to be outside the realm of psychological study.

> **Discussion Question:** Do you believe in a transcendental self (whether you call it self, spirit, soul…whatever)? What does this make you feel about your physical body? As for all of nature can you really believe it is just an illusion?

Karma

Karma is a difficult concept to grasp. We generally think of karma as the consequences of things we have done wrong, but karma does not apply simply to our misbehavior, it applies to all of our actions. An easy to understand discussion of karma has been written by Goldstein and Kornfield (2001). The law of karma can be understood on two levels. First, karma refers to cause and effect. Whenever we perform an action, we experience some consequence at a later time. The second level of karma may be more important, as it refers to our state of mind at the time when we performed the action in question. Our intentions, or the motives behind an action, determine the nature of the consequences we experience. The importance of this point is that we control the nature of our karma. This, of course, has important implications for personality development. Once we understand the karmic law, it is only natural that we should begin to plant the seeds of healthy karma. In other words, we should be inclined to act only in ways that are healthy and socially beneficial, so that the consequences we then experience will lead to greater well-being for ourselves.

The second level of karma, that it is our intentions and motivation that affect the outcome of our lives, seems quite similar to cognitive theories in psychology. Cognitive psychology focuses on the nature of our thought, and problems often arise when we are trapped in a series of automatic thoughts that create problems for us. In other words, when we view the world negatively, we react in negative and maladaptive ways. Similarly, our past karma influences the karma we create for the future. If we think and act in negative ways, we create negative karma, but it is also true that if we think and act in positive ways we create positive karma. Cognitive therapy resembles much of what is written in the East about recognizing the cause-and-effect pattern that our karma traps us within. Successful cognitive therapy is something like enlightenment: when we realize the truth of what we are doing we have a chance to break that pattern and move in a healthy direction.

> **Discussion Question:** Karma refers to the cosmic law of cause and effect, the idea that our past actions will someday affect our current and future lives. Do you believe this, and can you provide any examples of this happening to you?

The Three Principles of Creation

Would it be possible for us to avoid or circumvent the law of karma by remaining inactive? Sometimes many of us do just want to get away from everything and everyone. However, social withdrawal is often an early sign of psychological distress or mental illness, suggesting that this is generally not a healthy action. According to Yoga, all nature is composed of three aspects called the **gunas**: **rajas**, **tamas**, and **sattva**. According to Krishna, as recorded in the *Bhagavad Gita*, the three gunas "bind to the mortal body the deathless embodied Self" (pg. 158; Mitchell, 2000). Rajas (born of craving) binds us to action, tamas (born of ignorance) binds us to dullness, and sattva (untainted and luminous) binds us to knowledge and joy. Only through faithful Yoga practice can an individual transcend the gunas and achieve unity with God. Only then will the individual be free from any attachment to action and free from the law of karma.

Another important and practical question that arises from an understanding of the three gunas is: what should we eat? In America we generally associate being vegetarian with practicing Yoga or being a Buddhist. But is there a good reason for this? Everything is made from the three gunas, but in different proportions. So we might say that a hot, spicy dish like Gang Garee from Thailand (a personal favorite) is predominantly rajas. Heavy food, with a thick sauce or gravy is predominantly tamas. Fruits and vegetables, however, are lighter and more refreshing; they are predominantly sattva. So a vegetarian diet should increase the relative amount of sattva in our body, thus making us a better person. This is just like the old saying: "You are what you eat!" This goes beyond diet, however, since diet only directly affects the body. What about the mind? Everything we take in is comprised of the three gunas: words and ideas that we hear, music, the emotions expressed by people we spend time with, and so on (Vivekananda, 1955a). It is important not only that we eat well, but also that we spend time in relaxing and healthy environments, associate with good people, and generally try to cultivate a life that moves more toward sattva than the other gunas.

The Guru or Teacher

Spirit vs. nature, consciousness, karma, the three gunas, it can all seem very strange to those of us who did not grow up with these concepts. Another common source of confusion is the distinction between the terms **yogi** and **guru**. A yogi is anyone who practices Yoga. A guru is a teacher, someone advanced in Yoga and capable of leading others on the path. A true guru is typically revered in the East, and in English they are often referred to as prophets, or saints.

Many believe that a guru is essential to the practice of Yoga. The practice of Yoga can be difficult, and the principles can be confusing. Some argue that only through initiation by a guru can an individual truly and correctly use **mantras** such as Om. Otherwise, the would-be student of Yoga will not know the correct frequency or nature of the mantra. Perhaps most important, though, is the spiritual consciousness provided by the guru. As described by Yogananda:

> ...If I entered the hermitage in a worried or indifferent frame of mind, my attitude imperceptibly changed. A healing calm descended at the mere sight of my guru. Each day with him was a new experience in joy, peace, and wisdom. Never did I find him deluded or emotionally intoxicated with greed, anger, or human attachment. (pg. 137; Yogananda, 1946)

Another aspect involved in the importance of a guru is his or her lineage. In Western culture we are very individualistic, so it is common for each new teacher or leader to try establishing a new beginning. In the collectivist cultures of the East, however, they pay more attention to the earlier teachers of current teachers. Establishing this lineage is very important, not to suggest that one line of Yoga is better than another, but to connect the past to the present and, presumably, the present to the future. Recent research in the field of positive psychology has suggested that such a balanced time perspective, emphasizing the past, present, and future, is an important facet of psychological well-being (Boniwell, 2005; Boniwell & Zimbardo, 2003).

> **Discussion Question:** In Eastern cultures they talk about gurus, in Western cultures we often hear about mentors. Do the words "guru" and "mentor" mean the same thing to you? Have you ever been inspired by someone you thought of as a guru or mentor?

Pathways to Personal Growth: Schools of Yoga

There are many schools of Yoga, and the styles depend somewhat on which translations and which authors you happen to read. In her discourse accompanying the translation of Patanjali's *Yoga Sutras*, Bailey refers to four types of Yoga that developed as humanity developed (1927). In chronological order they are **Hatha-Yoga**, **Laya-Yoga**, **Bhakti-Yoga**, and **Raja-Yoga** (also known as **Kriya-Yoga**, see Yogananda [1946]). Feuerstein (2003) adds three more to what he describes as the seven major branches of the tree of Hindu Yoga: **Jnana-Yoga**, **Karma-Yoga**, and **Mantra-Yoga**.

The purpose of each of these schools of Yoga, in their own way, is to guide the individual toward the fulfillment of their life. This fulfillment is not necessarily **enlightenment**, or what we in the West may think of as heaven, but may instead be preparation for steadily improving lives over subsequent reincarnations. In accordance with the concept of karma, if we do our best to live this life as a good and faithful person, then in our future lives we will benefit from the seeds of good karma we have planted in this life. As humans we can achieve enlightenment in this life, but we are not doomed to eternal damnation if we don't quite make it. So, Yoga offers us a hopeful guide toward being a good person, and teaches ways in which to continue our personal growth.

Hatha-Yoga

Hatha-Yoga is the Yoga of power, referring primarily to the **Kundalini energy** and **prana** (vital energy) within the body. The practices of Hatha-Yoga are intended to strengthen and prepare the body for controlling the life forces within. An important aspect is the practice of **asanas**, the postures that are often misidentified as being Hatha-Yoga itself. However, traditional Hatha-Yoga also involves celibacy, a vegetarian diet, breathing and concentration exercises (meditation), and cleansing the nasal passages and the alimentary canal.

Laya-Yoga

Laya-Yoga focuses on meditative absorption of the psyche or mind to the point of ecstatic realization, or **samadhi**. As an advancement from Hatha-Yoga, Laya-Yoga leaves behind the physical focus of Hatha-Yoga for a highly developed state of meditation in which one's sense of self dissolves into transcendental self-realization (i.e., realization of the true self, the transcendental spirit).

Bhakti-Yoga

Bhakti-Yoga is the Yoga of devotion or love, in which the force of human emotion is channeled toward the Divine. This devotion develops along nine stages, the first being to listen to the names of God. The second is to chant praises in honor of the Lord, which is why chanting is so common in the practice of Yoga and Buddhism. The remaining stages involve a variety of practices or rituals. As simple as the first two stages may seem, together they have given rise to a special form of musical prayer: **Kirtan**, the practice of singing the many names of God (see the section on spiritual music below).

Bakti-Yoga is more than just a simple devotion to **atman** (the Supreme Soul that is God). It is a deep, genuine searching for the Lord that begins, continues, and ends in love (Vivekananda, 1955a). The secret of Bhakti-Yoga is that the great sages of ancient India realized that passionate human emotions are not wrong in themselves, they are not to be avoided and repressed, but rather they should be carefully harnessed and turned toward a higher spiritual direction. This is the direction of God, and the true nature of Bhakti-Yoga. However, there can also be dark side to Bhakti-Yoga, among those who have not turned toward a higher direction. Individuals who become trapped in the lowest level of Bhakti-Yoga can become religious fanatics. The only way they see to truly love one ideal is to hate all others (Vivekananda, 1955a). Religious fanaticism has caused great torment throughout the history of the human race, but it should never be confused with the true ideals of religion or spirituality.

Raja-Yoga or Kriya-Yoga

Raja-Yoga, or Royal Yoga, combines the principles, though not necessarily the practices, of other forms of Yoga and thus supersedes them all (Bailey, 1927). Raja-Yoga is that which was originally taught by Patanjali in the *Yoga Sutras*. It is also known by the name Kriya-Yoga, and it is this term that Yogananda used when bringing Yoga to the United States in 1920. According to Yogananda, this form of Yoga is more than just a practice developed by a great man. Patanjali is believed to be one of the ancient avatars of India, making this form of Yoga a direct divine inspiration (Yogananda, 1946). Furthermore, this form of Yoga was lost to humanity for centuries, until another avatar named Babaji revealed it again to the Indian guru named Lahiri Mahasaya in 1861 (Yogananda, 1946). Of particular interest to Americans may be the fact that Babaji inspired Yogananda to come to America, through Babaji's disciples Lahiri Mahasaya and Sri Yukteswar. Thus, Yoga came to the United States, as well as the rest of the Western world, at the behest of Babaji, a divine incarnation believed by many to be as significant as Gotama Buddha or Jesus Christ!

Jnana-Yoga

Jnana-Yoga is the Yoga of wisdom or knowledge. It is a rigorous discipline in which one uses the intellect to discern reality from **maya**. Maya is often misunderstood, and described as the cosmic delusion that our Self is this body in this life. However, Swami Vivekananda has offered an excellent explanation of what maya really is: simply a matter of fact statement about the nature of the world and of man (Vivekananda, 1955b).

The philosophy from which our understanding of maya comes is neither optimistic nor pessimistic, but it does challenge our basic understanding of everything we believe is real. There is no good without evil, no happiness without misery, no beauty without ugliness. Consequently, there will never be a perfect world, a world in which there is no suffering or death. Even the basic existence of the world must be considered in the context of no-existence. This strange and challenging philosophy is described by Vivekananda in the following passage:

> What, then, does the statement that the world exists mean? It really means that the world has no existence. What, again, does the statement that the world has no existence mean? It means that it has no absolute existence: it exists only in relation to my mind, to your mind, and to the mind of everyone else. We see this world with the five senses, but if we had another sense, we would see in it something more. If we had yet another sense, it would appear as something still different. It has, therefore, no real existence; it has no unchangeable, immovable, infinite existence. Nor can it be said to have non-existence, since it exists and we have to work in and through it. It is a mixture of existence and non-existence. (pg. 27-28).

As you can see from this passage, Jnana-Yoga requires not only a keen intellect, but an open-minded willingness to embrace a different perspective. This perspective had a strong influence on the development of Chinese religion and philosophy, and similar concepts can be found in the famous *Tao Te Ching* of Lao Tsu, which provides the basis for Taoism (Lao Tsu, c. 600 B.C.).

The question of whether or not we recognize the reality of our world is central to cognitive psychology. In cognitive therapy, it is taken for granted that an individual does not view their environment realistically, that automatic thoughts of a maladaptive nature turn each situation into another instance of the person's typical problem. With the help of an objective therapist, the individual may come to realize the nature of their maladaptive thought processes, and learn to control and re-evaluate their thoughts and feelings, so that they can react appropriately to other people and to new situations. In a similar way, the principles of Yoga, under the guidance of a guru, can help us to understand our world and the role we play in determining our future (creating good or bad karma).

Karma-Yoga

Because we are inseparably compelled by the gunas (the three aspects of existence), existence involves action. Karma-Yoga teaches us to act without attachment to the consequences of our actions and without any expectations. But it is not enough to control our actions, we must understand why we are controlling our mind. As Krishna tells Arjuna in the third chapter of the *Bhagavad Gita*:

> He who controls his actions, but lets his mind dwell on sense-objects, is deluding himself and spoiling his search for the deepest truth. The superior man is he whose mind can control his senses; with no attachment to results, he engages in the yoga of action (pgs. 62-63).

The practical values of Karma-Yoga are many. According to Vivekananda (1955a), the true character of a person can be seen by watching their actions. Those who work for work's sake, just because good will come of it, and who have given up any sense of self or attachment to their works, has achieved the ideal of Karma-Yoga. As difficult as it may be to take control of one's life, in other words to direct one's own karma, it can be done. If we learn to look at our past and present bad circumstances simply as facts that have happened, it is really our own opinion that allows those circumstances to affect our self-image (Schied, 1986). If we can look past those negative circumstances, indeed even look for the positive aspects in all situations, we can begin to act in positive ways that will create good karma for our future.

"In the end, these things matter most: How well did you love?
How fully did you live? How deeply did you learn
To let go?" – Kornfield, 1994

Mantra-Yoga

Mantra-Yoga is the Yoga of sound or vibration. The universe is believed to be in constant vibration. **Om**, the most sacred mantra, is believed to be the word representing the fundamental vibration of the universe. As such, meditating while chanting Om is believed to have almost magical transformative powers over the body and mind (Feuerstein, 2003). It is also common to chant short prayer phrases, such as Om Namah Shivaya (I bow to Shiva), the Hare Krishna mantra (the mahamantra, or great mantra), and Om Mani Padme Hum (a Tibetan Buddhist chant that has no direct translation). The CD *Pilgrim Heart,* by Krishna Das (2002), offers both insightful description and a modern musical presentation of some of these chants.

Connections Across Cultures: Franchised Yoga Centers in America

If you take a look at the magazine section of a major bookstore, you will find several magazines devoted to the practice of Yoga. In those magazines, you can find dozens of Yoga training centers and retreats. Many colleges and universities in America offer courses in Yoga. Yoga is very much a part of life for many Americans. But has it made its way into the mainstream? There is some interesting evidence to suggest that if it hasn't yet, it will very soon. The days when Yoga centers were only individual operations, run by a small group of devoted yogis, appear to be over.

In 2003, internet entrepreneurs George Lichter and Rob Wrubel (formerly with the search engine Ask Jeeves International) were looking to move into a new business venture. When the two men realized that both were practicing Yoga (primarily the physical aspects of Hatha-Yoga), they decided to create a chain of Yoga centers across America. Beginning with the purchase of an established yoga center in Los Angeles, they have plans to expand to a variety of major cities, and ultimately to smaller locations around the country. Although a business model may fit well with American capitalism, can such an approach fit with Yoga? They hope that by having the company focus on the business aspects of running a Yoga studio, the instructors can be freed to focus on teaching Yoga to their students.

Many Americans still view Yoga as an odd curiosity and, primarily, as a form of exercise. Before I first began going to a Yoga retreat center I wondered if it would be too strange for me (even though I knew someone who had been going there for years). I had a wonderful time, and have returned there many times. But, like so many others, it is a retreat center all by itself. As Yoga centers based on the model of chain stores, with some consistency in terms of the services and environment they offer, spread across America, I think more people will take a chance on beginning to examine this curious path toward relaxation and peace of mind.

Obstacles to Personal Growth: Patanjali's Five Hindrances

Patanjali's five hindrances refer to conditions that block our personal development. The hindrances are identified as: **avidya** (ignorance), sense of personality, desire, hate, and sense of attachment. It may seem confusing to us that a sense of personality is a hindrance to personal development. Isn't the goal in life to become aware of and comfortable with our true selves? Unfortunately, from the perspective of Yoga, that belief is the result of the single most challenging hindrance, the one that is the source of all other difficulties: ignorance. The problem, according to Patanjali, is that our sense of personality is a mistaken identification of our mental awareness, a product of our brain (nature), with our true and transcendental self (spirit). Specifically, the fifth Sutra of Book II states that "avidya is the condition of confusing the permanent, pure, blissful and the Self with that which is impermanent, impure, painful and the not-Self" (Bailey, 1927; pg. 115). The latter point refers specifically to the duality between our true self, that temporary manifestation of spirit in nature, with the body/mind of this world that will cease to exist when we die (though death does not really exist in the same sense in the perspective of Yoga).

It is also something of a problem to use the term attachment in a negative way. In Western psychology attachment is typically used to refer to the bonding between parent and child. Thus, we consider attachment to be a necessary condition of healthy development. In Yoga, however, any form of attachment is a delusion in which we consider elements of the natural world to be of importance. Only the universal spirit is perspective, even the love of a parent for a child is a delusion that keeps us attached to this world, and would therefore be a hindrance to our union with God. Actually, things are not as bleak as that might make them seem at first. Since there is only one universal spirit, we and our children, indeed everyone everywhere, is one and the same universal spirit, both past and present (hence the meaninglessness of death). So it is not wrong to love, it is only a mistake to think that love for a person or love for a thing is the most important thing in life. What is important is to practice Yoga in order to overcome these hindrances, to escape the laws of karma, to quiet the mind and transcend the natural world. Then one will know their union with God and all creation.

Discussion Question: According to Patanjali, the single greatest obstacle to personal growth is avidya (ignorance). How has your education helped you to grow as a person? Have you taken any courses specifically designed to help you with personal development? What plans, if any, do you have for continuing your education after you finish school?

Classic Indian Stages of Life

According to the Vedic teaching of ancient India, each Hindu male should progress through four stages of life: student, householder, hermit or forest-dweller, and finally renunciant. At a young age the child would be sent to live with a guru, so that he might devote himself to spiritual development, studying the **Vedas** (ancient Indian texts that provide much of the philosophy, practices, rituals and other guides for Hindu life), and mastering Yoga. Then the young man returns home, takes a wife (usually an arranged marriage), runs the family business, and basically takes care of the business of maintaining the Indian society. As the man grows older, and his children become ready to take over as the householders, he becomes a hermit, once again devoting himself to Yoga. Finally, the old man leaves society completely behind and focuses himself entirely on unity with God. For Hindu females all that can be said is that, unfortunately, this philosophy comes from an old and patriarchal society. There are no classic stages of life for women in the Vedic teachings.

These four stages are an ideal of the traditional Hindu life. As in our own culture, both personal and family values change over time. Many Hindus do not follow these ancient ways. Though this style of life is certainly not necessary for the practice of Yoga, one can see the advantage of beginning and ending one's life with the sole purpose of practicing and mastering Yoga. Another interesting issue raised by these stages of life is the importance of middle age. In America we often hear about the so-called midlife crisis. There is some debate as to whether the midlife crisis exists, and whether it exists for both men and women, but in traditional Indian culture there is a profound difference: middle age is not the beginning of a decline toward old age and death, but rather a time to focus on the future and one's enlightenment. Therefore, middle age should be a particularly hopeful and peaceful time.

Yoga in America: The Self-Realization Fellowship and Transcendental Meditation

Although many different gurus have come to America, teaching many different types of Yoga, perhaps the two most influential have been Paramahansa Yogananda and Maharishi Mahesh Yogi. Yogananda established the Self-Realization Fellowship (SRF) in 1920 (Yogananda, 1946). Yogananda was one of the first gurus to come to America, and the SRF may be the oldest continuing school of Yoga in the West. Headquartered in California, SRF is dedicated to combining the Yoga of old with the predominant religion of the new world: Christianity. One of Yogananda's most important works is *The Second Coming of Christ*, a two volume discussion of the Christian Gospels viewed from a Yogic perspective (Yogananda, 2004a,b). The basic premise of this work is that God is within us as the Christ consciousness, it is His presence that gives us life, and when we realize that He is within our selves (thus, the name Self-Realization) we cannot help but lead a better life. As strange as this may seem to many Christians, blending religious and philosophical beliefs is commonly accepted in Eastern cultures. They seek the best points of view in a variety of perspectives, and try to live according to those beliefs that are common and which benefit everyone in their community. More information on the SRF can be found on their website (listed at the end of the chapter).

In 1958, a guru named Maharishi Mahesh Yogi began formally teaching **Transcendental Meditation** (TM; Maharishi Mahesh Yogi, 1963). TM became a very popular meditation technique in America, and as many as 6 million people around the world have learned the TM technique (this website is also listed at the end of the chapter). Yogi's first book on TM was originally entitled *The Science of Being and the Art of Living*, and he stated very clearly the purpose of life: "Expansion of happiness is the purpose of life…" (pg. 64) and "When one does not live a normal life or a life using his full potential, he feels miserable and tense and suffers in many ways" (pg. 69). This reference to the necessity of using one's full potential sounds very similar to Roger's and Maslow's concept of self-actualization (or perhaps self-realization as described in the preceding paragraph). As is true of the SRF, the TM program does not advocate or reject any organized religion. Instead, TM is presented as a means to fulfill one's life, regardless of the situation in which one is living.

Connections with Western Religious Practice

Contemplative Prayer

Consider the following quote: "Listen carefully, my son, to the master's instructions, and attend to them with the ear of your heart. This is advice from a father who loves you; welcome it, and faithfully put it into practice. The labor of obedience will bring you back to him from whom you had drifted through the sloth of disobedience. This message of mine is for you, then, if you are ready to give up your own will…" This sounds like the words of a guru, especially the part about giving up your own will. Doesn't that sound like the Yoga philosophy of transcending the mind in order to be in union with the spirit? Actually, this was written by St. Benedict, a Catholic monk who lived from 480-547 (Fry, 1982). In fact, this is the very beginning of the Rule of St. Benedict, and it is interesting to note that the very first word is "Listen…" Remember the first stage of devotion in Bhakti-Yoga? It is not easy to listen, and listening intently with our whole being is something that takes a lifetime to master (deWaal, 1984). Naturally, it is easier to listen when we are focused, and either the practice of Yoga or contemplative prayer can help to still our mind, to tune out the distractions of our daily lives, so that we can listen to and/or be in union with God.

During the twentieth century, a Benedictine monk named John Main (1926-1982) tried to help the Christian world rediscover meditation and contemplative prayer. In addition to his own efforts, he inspired the creation of the *World Community for Christian Meditation*, an international community that practices and teaches meditation in the Christian tradition (see the website list at the end of the chapter). As is true of many practitioners of meditation, Fr. Main recommended meditating twice a day, once in the morning and once in the evening. A marvelous collection of Fr. Main's writings has been compiled by Paul Harris (2003). The readings are quite short, and there is one for each day of the year. They can be used as a starting point for contemplation and prayer on the day assigned for each reading (if one chooses to follow that pattern). We will cover Christian mysticism, meditation, and contemplative prayer in more detail in the next chapter.

Spiritual Music

Another interesting comparison between Eastern and Western spiritualism is the use of music and song. The importance of chanting was mentioned above, but now we will take a closer look at the importance of music. The Yoga of Patanjali focuses on withdrawing from all sensory experience. The goal of meditation is to focus and then clear the mind, so that one is no longer distracted by the events of this world. However, in Bhakti-Yoga, the Yoga of devotion, some yogis embrace the fullness of refined human emotion (Mandala Publishing Group, 2000). Music is one of the best ways to fully express our emotional connection with all that is around us. A special type of musical prayer called Kirtan grew out of the first two stages of Bhakti-Yoga. Kirtan refers to the practice of singing the many names of God (including Goddess names). In the practice of Kirtan, the words that are sung are typically short mantras, and a wide variety of emotional states can be accommodated. Regardless of how one feels when beginning Kirtan, the practice of Kirtan can lead to a transformational, meditative state that "creates a safe, calm haven for the flower of the heart to unfold" (Jai Uttal, 2003). A wonderful CD of Kirtan, including an explanation of this practice in English, has been recorded by Jai Uttal (2003). If you would like to learn more about Kirtan, especially if you are interested in reducing stress in your life, this CD is highly recommended.

Although most Christian church services include some music, few are thought of as profoundly inspirational and emotionally moving as the gospel choirs associated with Black churches, especially those in the Southern United States. Much of this music is rooted in the **spirituals** sung by American slaves. Much like

Kirtan as a practice within Yoga, the spirituals helped to hold onto an identity shared by Africans brought to America as slaves. The music was not strictly religious, but religious themes were common. More importantly, the spirituals helped to connect the slaves to their African ancestry, and to provide a context within which they could share the lives they had come to know in a new country (Cone, 1972; Lovell, Jr., 1972). As slavery came to an end in the United States, prejudice and discrimination certainly did not. On one hand the spirituals gave rise to the blues, but on the other hand they gave rise to distinctly religious gospel music (Boyer and Yearwood, 1995; Broughton, 1985). Gospel music can be so passionate that it has been described as "hinting at a vocal imperative which was said to induce religious convulsions in their audiences…" (Broughton, 1985). Perhaps it should not be surprising that Black gospel music is so deeply emotional, since it arose from a group of people who had been slaves, and were still suffering from rampant discrimination in a country that claimed to hold freedom above all else. Although such raw emotion is not common to Kirtan, it is still deeply passionate for those who feel its intimate connection to the universal spirit.

Discussion Question: Using music during prayer or religious services has a long and rich history. Many of our social gatherings are centered on music. How has music influence your life? Do you listen to inspirational music when you feel a need to clear your mind and relax, or do you listen to lively and entertaining music to enhance the enjoyment of being with family and/or friends?

Historical Description of Buddhism

Siddhattha Gotama

Siddhattha Gotama is recognized as the Buddha, but this is technically incorrect. Anyone can be a Buddha, there were many before Gotama Buddha, many after, and more to come. Indeed, Siddhattha Gotama had lived many lives before he was born into that earthly identity (if, of course, you believe in such things), and this had an important impact on his life. According to legend, Dipankara Buddha foretold that Siddhattha Gotama would be born as a prince in the kingdom of the Shakyas (so he is also referred to as Prince Shakyamuni and as Shakyamuni Buddha), and that in that lifetime he would become a Buddha. Sometime around the fifth or sixth century B.C., Prince Shakyamuni was born. Not wanting his son to leave the kingdom, the king indulged his son with every sensual pleasure known to man. The king also protected his son from knowing the unpleasant realities of life (disease, death, etc.). However, the prince's destiny was set. Prince Shakyamuni decided he wanted to see the kingdom. In order to prevent the prince from seeing the reality of life, the king ordered that everything in the city should be cleaned and decorated and everyone should be on their best behavior. However, four heavenly beings appeared to Prince Shakyamuni: the first as someone suffering the ravages of old age, the second as someone stricken with disease, the third as a corpse, and the fourth as a wandering monk. These visitors made a profound impression on the young prince, who left his wife, child, and home to seek enlightenment.

Siddhattha Gotama, aka the Buddha, lived in India some 2,500 years ago. [Image by Mark Kelland]

Living in India, the path to spiritual enlightenment that he followed was to become a yogi. He studied meditation, he became an accomplished ascetic (it is said he lived for a time on one grain of rice a day), but he failed to achieve anything satisfying. So finally he had a nice lunch and sat down under a Bodhi tree, vowing to remain seated until he achieved enlightenment. Finally, he was "awakened," which is the meaning of the word Buddha. In his first sermon, Gotama Buddha revealed the **Four Noble Truths** and the **Middle Way**, the latter also being known as the **Eightfold Path**. Those who have followed his teachings have come to be known as Buddhists. For more on the life of the Buddha, an excellent chapter has been written by Goldstein and Kornfield (2001). The sayings of the Buddha have also been collected, and are readily available (e.g., see Byrom, 1993). In his own words, we can see the relationship between Buddhism and psychology, and how these teachings were meant to guide people toward a healthy and happy life. In the teaching entitled "Choices," the Buddha says:

> We are what we think.
> All that we are arises with our thoughts.
> With our thoughts we make the world.
> Speak or act with a pure mind
> And happiness will follow you
> As your shadow, unshakable. (pgs. 1-2)

Bodhidharma

Bodhidharma (c. 440-528) is recognized as the monk responsible for bringing **Zen** Buddhism from India into China. He was also present during the construction of the Shaolin Temple, and was one of the first monks there. During his time at Shaolin Temple he is most famous for spending nine years in meditation, staring at the wall of a cave. He is also credited with developing kung-fu, the well-known martial arts technique, so that the temple monks could protect themselves from bandits. Although Bodhidharma may have spent a great deal of time in meditation, his Zen teaching was based more on a sword of wisdom (Red Pine, 1987). Some of the strange practices in Zen that we will examine in this chapter can be described as almost surprising people into enlightenment. Of course, many years of practice and discipline are necessary in order to be ready for this enlightenment. Some of Bodhidharma's writings are still available to us today (e.g., Red Pine, 1987), and in his own words (translated, of course) we can get a glimpse of just how strange a Zen understanding of the truth can be:

> If you use your mind to study reality, you won't understand either your mind or reality. If you study reality without using your mind, you'll understand both. Those who don't understand, don't understand understanding. And those who understand, understand not understanding. People capable of true vision know that the mind is empty. They transcend both understanding and not understanding. The absence of both understanding and not understanding is true understanding. (pg. 55)

His Holiness the Dalai Lama

Unlike the historical figures Gotama Buddha and Bodhidharma, the Dalai Lama is alive today. Although his home is Tibet, where he was born in 1935, he lives in exile in India. He is believed to be the 14th Dalai Lama, a reincarnation of the previous Dalai Lamas, the first of whom is believed to have been the reincarnation of a boy who lived during the time of Gotama Buddha. That boy was an incarnation of Chenrezig (also known as Avalokiteshvara), the Bodhisattva of Compassion (a Bodhisattva is like a Buddha – see below), and the Dalai Lamas have served for over 650 years as the religious leader of the Tibetan people. Due to political circumstances in Tibet today, it is unclear what may happen to Tibetan culture. The Dalai Lama himself does not know whether he will be the last of the Dalai Lamas, but he hopes that choice will someday be made by a free and democratic Tibetan society (Dalai Lama, 2002).

Placing Buddhism in Context: The First Psychology?

Both Buddhism and Yoga share roots in ancient traditions among the Vedic people. Siddhattha Gotama was a yogi seeking enlightenment, and it was his followers who established Buddhism as the practice of his new path: the Middle Way. Since most people think of Buddhism and Yoga as separate, it makes things easier to treat them separately.

Buddhism is as old as the Yoga of Patanjali, perhaps even older, and like Yoga had a profound influence on some well-known personality theorists (such as Rogers and Fromm). Since Yoga is usually thought of as a form of exercise in America, because of the popularity of Hatha Yoga, when people think of meditation they often think first of Buddhism. Zen Buddhism emphasizes meditation, and Zen has been the most popular and best-known form of Buddhism in America, largely due to the arrival of D. T. Suzuki in 1897.

There are two major schools of Buddhism in the world today. The Theravada tradition is most popular in southeast Asia. It emphasizes self-discipline and seeking nirvana. The Mahayana tradition is most popular in China, Tibet, Korea, and Japan. The Mahayana tradition emphasizes compassion, and is the school within which Zen developed. Tibetan Buddhism, which also developed within the Mahayana tradition, enjoys something of a celebrity status due to the renown of the Dalai Lama, who is recognized as the spiritual leader of the Tibetan people.

In many ways one can find connections between Buddhism and psychology today. As an interesting example, the well-known author and spiritual leader Jack Kornfield became a Thai Buddhist monk before returning to the United States and becoming a clinical psychologist. Many of the books comparing Eastern philosophy to Western psychology have focused on Zen Buddhism. Zen emphasizes meditation, which in one form or another has become a common element of many types of psychotherapy, particularly in humanistic and cognitive approaches. Since Buddhism shares the same tradition as Yoga, it would make no sense to say that Buddhism has influenced psychology more than Yoga. They are fundamentally the same, and their influence continues to grow.

The Four Noble Truths of Human Life

Following his enlightenment, the Buddha began to teach what he had realized. In his first lesson, he described the Four Noble Truths: 1) suffering is an unavoidable reality in human life; 2) the source of suffering is craving or desire, and the bad karma it creates; 3) the craving that leads to suffering can be destroyed; 4) the Middle Way is the path to eliminate craving and suffering (Suzuki, 1960; World's Great Religions, 1957; Wilkins, 1967). People often ask why there is so much suffering in the world. When this question is asked, there is usually an unspoken desire to remove this suffering from the world. The Buddha, however, taught us that we cannot escape from reality. Who has never been sick? Who never dies? Who can live without desiring something? The problem is that when our cravings are satisfied, we typically find that we want something else, or something more, we never seem to be really satisfied. And so this cycle of craving, temporary satisfaction, craving again, and so on, continues throughout our life, unless we consciously do something to break the pattern. The Buddha taught us how to do that: by following the Middle Way.

The Middle Way is also known as the Eightfold Path, because there are eight aspects to it: 1) right knowledge, 2) right intention, 3) right speech, 4) right conduct, 5) right livelihood, 6) right effort, 7) right mindfulness, and 8) right concentration. Some believe that each step depends on what goes before it, so that in order to reach higher levels of this discipline one must accomplish the lower levels (Wilkins, 1967). A hierarchical series of steps like this is reminiscent of Maslow's hierarchy of needs. In Buddhism, we must begin with an understanding of how things really are, an understanding of the four noble truths, impermanence, and **interbeing** (right knowledge). We must then develop the right intentions, to want to be compassionate, selflessly detached, loving, and non-violent. Once we have developed a conducive state of mind, we can choose to refrain from lying, gossiping, swearing, and other misuse of language (right speech). We can avoid doing things that are immoral, irresponsible, cruel, or illegal (right conduct), and we would not choose a career which required us to do any such things (right livelihood). Then we would be able to focus our will on avoiding any unhealthy states of mind, and on eliminating them quickly should they arise (right effort). Finally we could become more aware of our sensations, feelings, minds, and bodies (right mindfulness), so that we might focus on the discipline necessary to continue our practice of the Middle Way (right concentration).

These principles provide the basis for a practical code of conduct, which all Buddhists must follow, known as the **Five Precepts**. They are: 1) to abstain from killing, 2) to abstain from stealing, 3) to abstain from sexual misconduct, 4) to abstain from lying, and 5) to abstain from mind-altering intoxicants (World's Great Religions, 1957). The first four seem to follow naturally from the Eightfold Path, but the last one is somewhat more interesting. The problem with intoxicating drugs, such as alcohol, is that they cloud the mind. They make it difficult for us to make responsible choices, which is what the Middle Way is all about. Also, if you think back to our discussion of karma, the intentions behind your actions are as important, if not more important, than the actions themselves. When you have made a choice to use intoxicating drugs, and then violate any of the other precepts, it is the consequence of your earlier choice. And who needs bad karma on top of bad karma?

"Calm and compassion are so precious. Make sure not to lose them through intoxication." – Kornfield, 1994

Characteristics of Existence

Impermanence

The Buddha said that "everything arises and passes away…existence is illusion" (in Byrom, 1993). The idea that nothing is permanent is a central belief in Buddhism. People are born, grow up, grow old, and die. Buildings wear down, cars break down, and enormous trees wither away. Even mountains are eventually worn down by erosion. However, children are born, new cars and buildings are built, new plants grow, and life goes on. The implications for Buddhism are quite interesting. If everything, and everyone, changes, then even someone who is enlightened will change! One cannot *be* a Buddha, for they will change. We must always continue to grow. Likewise, Buddhism itself will change, so most of their doctrines are not seen as static. They anticipate change over time.

For psychology, this has both good and not so good implications. For people who are depressed or anxious, they might take heart in impermanence, since things should eventually get better. Indeed, studies on the effects of psychotherapy often show that some people get better over time without treatment. However, if things seem to be going great, if you are happy and having lots of fun, those things will change too. But knowing this, we can prepare ourselves for it. An important aspect of coping with life's challenges is a sense of being in control. Although there are a wide variety of variables that contribute to individual resilience, maintaining a positive state of mind can help, and knowledge can help to maintain that positive state of mind (Bonnano, 2004, 2005; Folkman and Moskowitz, 2000; Ray, 2004).

If we practice **mindfulness** and meditation, we can begin to see the impermanence of our lives. As we let go of our attachments to our self-image, our life will flow by like the pictures of a movie, each one a separate image, which only appears to flow smoothly when viewed at high speed. As we observe these fleeting images, we see how our sensations, thoughts, feelings, every aspect of our lives, change so quickly. We might then embrace the change that is truly our life. This process of letting go can be very difficult, but also very liberating (Goldstein and Kornfield, 2001).

"Do not seek perfection in a changing world. Instead, perfect your love." – Kornfield, 1994

Suffering

As we learned with the first of the Four Noble Truths, suffering is an integral part of the human experience. It is easy for us to think of suffering in terms of big pictures: war, famine, natural disasters, and the like. But how often do we think of suffering as an inherent part of our daily lives? Life is difficult, it is a struggle, especially the way most of us live it. A struggle can only lead to suffering. The ultimate outcome of life's struggle, should we lose the battle, is death. If we could defeat death we would end up alone, and that loneliness might be even worse than the original suffering itself (Suzuki, 1962). Still, we do not even need to look at suffering in terms of a lifetime battle against aging and death, we can see suffering in every moment of the day. Goldstein and Kornfield offer a marvelous description of the daily challenge to be satisfied (2001). It goes something like this. Suppose we woke up on a day when we had no obligations at all. It might be tempting to stay in bed all day, but eventually we become uncomfortable because we have to go to the bathroom. Finally we go, and then crawl back into bed to get warm. But then we get hungry, so finally we get up to get something to eat. Then we get bored, so maybe we watch TV. Then we get uncomfortable, and have to change positions. Even each pleasurable moment is brief, and fails to bring lasting satisfaction. So on, and so forth. We just keep suffering!

The source of this suffering is attachment. We are attached to pleasurable things because we crave them. We are also attached to things that are not pleasant, because they occupy our mind and we cannot be free. The

Buddha says, "Free yourself from pleasure and pain. For in craving pleasure or in nursing pain, there is only sorrow" (in Byrom, 1993). It may seem strange that we would be attached to our pain, but the word is used differently here than in most of Western psychology. Traditionally, psychologists think of attachment in a positive way, such as the attachment a child feels toward his or her parents. And yet, some cognitive psychologists do talk about individuals whose automatic thoughts lead them into consistently negative states of mind by disqualifying positive events, catastrophizing events, taking everything too personally, etc. (Pretzer and Beck, 2005). In Buddhism, attachment is neither positive nor negative, it is simply anything that reflects our illusion that the natural world is real. Only when we let go of our attachments to this world can we be one with the universal spirit, and only then can we end our suffering. There is also something hopeful in suffering. Bodhidharma taught that every suffering is a Buddha-seed, because suffering leads us to seek wisdom (in Red Pine, 1987). In this analogy, he describes the body and mind as a field. Suffering is the seed, wisdom the sprout, and Buddhahood the grain.

Discussion Question: Gotama Buddha taught that suffering is the result of craving or desire. Many of us have heard the saying that money is the root of all evil. Is our society excessively focused on buying more and bigger things? Do you ever find yourself obsessed with some material purchase? What problems, if any, have you experienced because people were more concerned with getting things than caring about the people around them?

Selflessness

In keeping with its origins in Yoga, Buddhism teaches that there is no immortal, unchanging soul. All that we are is a temporary collection of attributes, made up of the body, the feelings, the perceptions, the reactions, and the consciousness of the mind (which, coming from the brain, is really part of the body). It is because we confuse our true self (the transcendental self) with this temporary collection of illusory things that we crave satisfaction, and ultimately suffer as a result. Now it may seem illogical to reject everything we are familiar with, including our own physical body, as an illusion, but Buddhists would suggest that there is a danger in choosing intellectual logic over faith. According to D.T. Suzuki (1962), "Faith lives and the intellect kills." Try the following exercise. Consider your body. Is it real? How much food have you eaten in your life, and where is it now? How many times have you gone to the bathroom, and where did all of that come from? It certainly isn't the same as when you ate it! Your body has been replaced many, many times. It is being replaced right now. It isn't real, it is only temporary, ever changing. The same is true with your mind. Even when William James discussed the stream of consciousness, he described a constantly changing awareness, one in which you cannot have the same thought twice. It just isn't possible. James (1892) realized that we cannot establish a *substantial* identity continuing from day to day, but concluded that our sense of continuity must reveal a *functional* identity. Arriving at a very different conclusion, Buddhists consider this to be maya, our inability to see things as they truly are (Suzuki, 1960).

These three characteristics of existence (impermanence, suffering, and selflessness) can be somewhat unsettling. It is not very appealing to believe that we don't really exist, that we will suffer as long as we believe we do exist, and all of it will just eventually pass away anyway. So, how does one continue in this practice? It is important to keep as our goal a true understanding of the way things are, and the practice of meditation and other aspects of Yoga and Buddhism will help to deepen our realization of these basic truths (Goldstein & Kornfield, 2001). The practice remains challenging, however, because as we deepen our understanding the characteristic most often occupying the center of our greatest realization is that of suffering (Goldstein & Kornfield, 2001; Suzuki, 1962). We must then put aside our intellectualizing, we must slay it and throw it to the dogs, experiencing what Buddhists call the "Great Death" (Suzuki, 1962). Only then will we know the greatest wisdom and compassion. This is the beginning of our transcendence. It is not a separation from others, but a realization that we are all one. In other words, we are all in this together.

Interbeing – A Connection Between All People and All Things

Many people are familiar with the golden rule: do unto others as you would have others do unto you! This Christian saying also has great implications when considered from a Buddhist perspective. Based on the same philosophical/cosmological perspective as Yoga, Buddhists believe that there is one universal spirit. Therefore, we are really all the same, indeed the entire universe of living creatures and even inanimate objects in the physical world come from and return to the same, single source of creation. Thus, we could alter the golden rule to something like: as you do unto others you are doing unto yourself! This concept is not simply about being nice to other people for your own good, however. Much more importantly, it is about appreciating the relationships between all things. For example, when you drink a refreshing glass of milk, maybe after eating a few chocolate chip cookies, can you taste the grass and feel the falling rain? After all, the cow could not have grown up to give milk if it hadn't eaten grass, and the grass would not have grown if there hadn't been any rain. When you enjoy that milk do you remember to thank the farmer who milked the cow, or the grocer who sold the milk to you? And what about the worms that helped to create and aerate the soil in which the grass grew? Appreciating the concept of interbeing helps us to understand the importance of everyone and everything.

The value of this concept of interbeing is that it can be much more than simply a curious academic topic. The Vietnamese Buddhist monk Thich Nhat Hanh writes very eloquently about interbeing and its potential for promoting healthy relationships, both between people and between societies (Thich Nhat Hanh, 1995):

> "Looking deeply" means observing something or someone with so much concentration that the distinction between observer and observed disappears. The result is insight into the true nature of the object. When we look into the heart of a flower, we see clouds, sunshine, minerals, time, the earth, and everything else in the cosmos in it. Without clouds, there could be no rain, and there would be no flower. Without time, the flower could not bloom. In fact, the flower is made entirely of non-flower elements; it has no independent, individual existence. It "inter-is" with everything else in the universe. ... When we see the nature of interbeing, barriers between ourselves and others are dissolved, and peace, love, and understanding are possible. Whenever there is understanding, compassion is born. (pg. 10)

Having understood this concept, how might it apply to personality? One of the best known cross-cultural topics in psychology today is the distinction between collectivistic vs. individualistic cultures (Triandis & Suh, 2002; Triandis et al., 1988). It is generally accepted that Western cultures focus on the individual, whereas Eastern cultures focus on society as a collective group. One can easily imagine how people whose religious and cultural philosophy focus on a single, universal spirit (the basis of interbeing) would focus more on their family and societal groups than on the individual. Both individualistic and collectivistic cultures seem to have advantages. People living in individualistic cultures report higher levels of subjective well-being and self-esteem, whereas people in collectivistic cultures have tend to have lower levels of stress and correspondingly lower levels of cardiovascular disease (Triandis & Suh, 2002; Triandis et al., 1988). In collectivistic cultures people tend to view the environment as relatively fixed, and themselves as more flexible, more ready to fit in (Triandis & Suh, 2002). The collectivistic perspective supports the value of social cooperation and social interest (something Alfred Adler would likely appreciate). Still, even within cultures there are individual differences. There are idiocentric persons (those who favor individuality) living in collectivistic cultures, and allocentric persons (those who favor ingroups) living in individualistic cultures. The best relationship between personality and culture may be the "culture fit" model, which suggests that it is best to live in the culture that matches your personal inclinations.

Discussion Question: The concept of interbeing suggests that all things are ultimately connected. Have you ever taken the time to think about all the things that had to happen, and all the people who were involved, in producing anything you hold in your hand? What about all the things that had to happen, and all the people who were involved, in your creation? And if we are all connected in some way, if we are all interbeing, what have you done to value those relationships?

Connections Across Cultures: The Non-Violent Struggles of Mahatma Gandhi, Thich Nhat Hanh, Martin Luther King, Jr., and the 14th Dalai Lama

The four men listed above are famous in a variety of ways, but they are probably best known for their commitment to nonviolence as a way to achieve political and social justice. Most importantly, they vowed non-violence while those around them were committed to terrible violence in order to deny justice to others. The two who are not alive today were both assassinated, and the other two were forced to live in exile. Gandhi was a Hindu who practiced Yoga, Thich Nhat Hanh and the Dalai Lama are Buddhists, and M. L. King, Jr. was a Christian, and it was their spiritual beliefs that so profoundly determined those aspects of their personalities that demanded peace.

Gandhi (1869-1948) is considered the father of modern India. He was born when the British ruled India, and spent much of his life fighting for the independence of his homeland. Twice he was imprisoned by the government, even though he insisted that all protests should be nonviolent. Indeed, he had established a movement of nonviolence known as **Satyagraha**. Ultimately this movement was successful, and India achieved its independence. Gandhi, however, was assassinated less than a year later. As he died, he spoke the name of God: Rama (Easwaran, 1972; Wilkinson, 2005).

Thich Nhat Hanh (1926-present) was born in Vietnam, and saw his country dominated first by the French and then by communists. During those difficult times he helped to develop what he and his friends called "engaged Buddhism." Rather than sitting in the temple meditating, they went out into the villages and tried to help the poor people of Vietnam. When confronted by soldiers they did their best to remain mindful, and to feel compassion for the soldiers who threatened them. After all, it was clear to Thich Nhat Hanh that many of those young soldiers were frightened themselves, and so their behavior was very hard to predict. Thus, the calm and peace that accompany mindfulness was often essential for protecting everyone in those terrifying encounters. After being exiled from Vietnam in 1966, he established a community called Plum Village in France, where he still resides today (Thich Nhat Hanh, 1966, 2003).

Martin Luther King, Jr. (1929-1968) was a major figure in America's civil rights movement of the 1950s and 60s. The King children learned at an early age about the realities of racism in America. Coming from an educated and socially active family, both his father and grandfather were ministers, he vowed at an early age to work against racial injustice. According to his sister, he said he would turn the world upside down (Farris, 2003). However, he always insisted on doing so in a nonviolent fashion. For this commitment to nonviolence, in 1964 he became the youngest person to ever receive the Nobel Peace Prize. Despite the peace prize and the passage of both the 1964 Civil Rights Act and the Voting Rights Act in 1965, discrimination continued in America. So did the nonviolent protests led by Dr. King. Then, in 1968, Martin Luther King, Jr. was assassinated (Burns, 2004; Hansen, 2003; Patrick, 1990).

The Dalai Lama (1935-present) lives in exile in India, though he also spends a great deal of time in America. When China invaded Tibet in 1950, he appealed to the United Nations, other countries, and even tried to reach an agreement with the Chinese leadership. Eventually, however, he was forced to leave Tibet in 1959. Today, nearly 50 years later, he continues to seek a peaceful resolution resulting in freedom for Tibet. He also works to deliberately cultivate feelings of compassion for the Chinese, believing that someday those who have harmed the people of Tibet will have to face the consequences of their actions (Dalai Lama, 2002). The Dalai Lama received the Nobel Peace Prize in 1989.

These men have more in common than simply their shared belief in nonviolence. In addition to M. L. King, Jr. and the Dalai Lama receiving the Nobel Peace Prize, as Nobel Laureates are entitled to do, Dr. King nominated Thich Nhat Hanh for the same award. Dr. King had received a letter from Thich Nhat Hanh asking for help in protesting the Vietnam war, which by the 1960s involved the United States. Dr. King was impressed by the Buddhist monk, and once appeared with him at a press conference in Chicago (Burns, 2004). Dr. King was also familiar with and impressed by the teachings of Gandhi. In 1959 he traveled to India to learn firsthand about Gandhi's Satyagraha, the basis for Gandhi's nonviolent independence movement (King, 2000). In 1966, Dr. King delivered the Gandhi Memorial Lecture at Howard University (Hansen, 2003). Since both the Dalai Lama and Thich Nhat

Hanh are alive today, they have met one another and the Dalai Lama has written several forewords for books by Thich Nhat Hanh. If these men from different countries and different cultures can share so much through the simple (though not easy) practice of nonviolence, perhaps there is something special here for everyone to learn more about.

Meditation

Meditation Techniques

Meditation is the means by which we control our mind and guide it in a more virtuous direction (Dalai Lama, 2001). Modern brain imaging techniques have even begun to identify the brain regions involved in these processes (Barinaga, 2003). There are many different meditation techniques in Yoga and Buddhism, and no one technique is necessarily better than another. What is most important is to pick one type of meditation and stick with it. Meditation takes practice. Most of us find it very difficult to relax and clear our mind. Even when we do, it is difficult to stay relaxed and keep our mind clear. We are distracted by constant thoughts, getting uncomfortable, we have itches and sneezes and whatever… But over time we can get better at relaxing. It helps to have a well-described procedure, and it can be very helpful to meditate in a group (especially if they offer classes or lessons on how to meditate). If you try meditation, don't get discouraged the first few times. Keep it up. As with all paths toward self-improvement, it takes time to progress in your ability to meditate.

Some of the writings of Master Dogen (1200-1253), the monk who founded Japanese Soto Zen, have survived during the 800 years since he lived (in Cook, 2002). Master Dogen recommends a very traditional form of seated meditation. Basically, sit straight up on a comfortable cushion with your legs crossed. Place your right hand in your lap, palm up, and your left hand on your right hand in the same manner, so that your thumbs touch slightly. Keep the eyes slightly open, the mouth closed, and breathe softly. Next comes the hard part: "Think about the unthinkable. How do you think about the unthinkable? Non-thinking."

Meditation can be performed in a variety of different ways. [Image by Kosal Ley]

Non-thinking may sound strange, but it is a fascinating experience for those who achieve it. It can actually make a 3- or 6-hour mediation seem to go by more quickly than a shorter meditation in which you never quite clear your mind. If it sounds a little too strange, don't worry, it isn't the goal of every form of meditation. Some forms of meditation focus on a mantra, or in Christian mediation a short prayer. Trying to focus on God through the celestial eye (in the middle of the forehead) is also a common technique. The Dalai Lama describes several different approaches in one of his books (Dalai Lama, 2001), and Thich Nhat Hanh discusses being reasonable in one's approach to longer meditations (Thich Nhat Hanh, 1991). Once again, there is not a right or wrong method of meditation. Whatever technique you try, whether from a book, a guru, a teacher, or a group, it is whatever works for you on your path to personal development.

Soto Zen and Zazen

Soto Zen is one of the two forms of Zen popular in Japan. Soto Zen emphasizes **zazen**, which translates loosely as "sitting meditation." It is believed that this form of meditation, common to the way most Americans envision meditation, is a tribute to the legend of Zen founder Bodhidharma spending nine years meditating while staring at a wall (Suzuki, 1962). However, there is a problem in the literature on zazen. For those who believe that zazen can help to achieve Buddhahood, the masters have taught that it cannot work. Still, it remains the essential core practice. How can this be? According to Alan Watts (1957), it may be better to consider an alternative translation of zazen, in which it translates as "sitting just to sit." In this view, zazen results in a clear mind, the condition necessary for enlightenment. A wonderful resource for practicing basic meditation of this type has been provided by Jack Kornfield, a clinical psychologist who trained as a Buddhist monk. *Meditation* *for Beginners* (Kornfield, 2004) not only briefly describes the history, purpose, and benefits of meditation, but it also includes a CD with guided meditations led by the author.

Rinzai Zen and the Koan

The other form of Zen popular in Japan is Rinzai Zen, founded by the monk Eisai (1141-1215). Buddhists in the Rinzai school practice zazen, but they also emphasize the curious practice of meditating on a koan, a riddle that has no answer. The Soto school of Zen frowns upon the use of the koan, considering it to be superficial and possibly misguided, something of a gimmick. But within the Rinzai school the Zen masters became concerned about what they saw as problems within the communities practicing Zen. One of the chief concerns of the Rinzai masters was the reliance on absolute quietude, pure meditation purely for the sake of meditation. They believed that Zen comes from life, and therefore must grow out of life (Suzuki, 1962). They were also concerned about the intellectualization of Zen, the belief that discerning logic could lead to enlightenment (again, concerned that the pursuit of logical ideas became its own pursuit). And so they developed the **koan**. The purpose of these unsolvable riddles is to put an end to logical thinking, to stop the wandering minds of students and to create a profound sense of doubt in the student's mind (Reps and Senzaki, 1994; Suzuki, 1960, 1962; Watts, 1957). The presentation of the student's views on a koan to the Zen master is an important time, and advanced students may even challenge whether the master appreciates how deeply the student understands Zen. These periodic visits to the Zen master to present an answer to a koan are known as **sanzen** (Suzuki, 1962; Watts, 1957).

Although koan are considered unsolvable, they do have answers. Certainly the most famous koan is the one in which the monk Joshu is asked: Does a dog have Buddha-nature? Joshu replied, "Mu!" Mu is the Chinese symbol for "no thing" or "not." The understanding of this koan is not found in the odd answer, or in Joshu's apparent refusal to provide a straight answer, "Mu" is Buddha-nature! If you find this particularly difficult to understand, I suggest you back up to the quote I gave you from the writings of Bodhidharma. I doubt it will make it any more clear, but perhaps it will help to illuminate the philosophy of non-attachment: don't worry too hard about understanding, just understand.

A student of the Rinzai school of Zen will actually study many koan, and the process is kept quite secret. Obviously if the answers to these koan were known, then students could offer the apparent answers. I say apparent answers because a Zen master would clearly recognize the mindless answer of one who really does not understand the koan. Since the process is kept secret, not many koan are publicly known, but there are some available. Not all koan are quite as odd as Joshu's "Mu;" some are seemingly easier to understand, but challenge our concepts of defining aspects of the natural world. For example, the monk Daie used to carry a short bamboo stick, and he would say, "If you call this a stick, you affirm; if you call it not a stick, you negate. Beyond affirmation and negation, what would you call it?" (Suzuki, 1962) This is clearly a challenge to move beyond logic, beyond the normal way of thinking about things. Enlightenment, of course, does not come from normal ways. Through the use of meditation to clear our minds, and the use of koan to challenge our perspectives, Rinzai Zen seeks to offer a path toward enlightenment that will be successful.

Discussion Question: Have you ever practiced meditation, or perhaps contemplative prayer? If you have, how does it make you feel? If you haven't, does it sound attractive? Were you surprised to learn that the practice of meditation is so old, and that it has counterparts in all of the major religions?

Mindfulness

Mindfulness is a form of meditation that occurs throughout every moment of the day. Indeed, it is very important to live fully in every moment, and to look deeply into each experience (Thich Nhat Hanh, 1991, 1995). By being mindful, we can enter into awareness of our body and our emotions. Thich Nhat Hanh relates a story in which the Buddha was asked when he and his monks practiced. The Buddha replied that they practiced when they sat, when they walked, and when they ate. When the person questioning the Buddha replied that everyone sits, walks, and eats, the Buddha replied that he and his monks *knew* they were sitting, *knew* they were walking, and *knew* they were eating (Thich Nhat Hanh, 1995). Mindfulness can also be applied to acts as simple as breathing. According to Thich Nhat Hanh, conscious breathing is the most basic Buddhist technique for touching peace (Thich Nhat Hanh, 1991, 1995). He suggests silently reciting the following lines while breathing mindfully:

> Breathing in, I calm my body.
> Breathing out, I smile.
> Dwelling in the present moment,
> I know this is a wonderful moment!

The concept of mindfulness, viewed in its traditional way, is also being used today in psychotherapy. Two recent books address the use of mindfulness either in combination with cognitive behavioral therapy to treat depression (McQuaid and Carmona, 2004) or as its own approach to the treatment of anxiety (Brantley, 2003). McQuaid and Carmona (2004) discuss how combining cognitive behavioral therapy and mindfulness together can provide a much stronger approach to treatment than either technique alone. Since the approaches have much in common, they amplify the effectiveness of each, and given their differences, they offer a complete path to moving beyond simple recovery toward more positive self development. Dr. Brantley (2003) moves more completely into the practice of mindfulness, emphasizing that it must become a way of life. It is not simply a clever therapeutic technique or gimmick.

Discussion Question: Mindfulness refers to maintaining a meditative state throughout the day. A similar approach is essential to cognitive/behavioral therapy. Are you aware of what you do during the day, or are you overwhelmed with being too busy? Could you see the practice of mindfulness as a helpful way to deal with your hectic life, and perhaps reduce stress at the same time?

Enlightenment and the Ideal Person

Concepts of Enlightenment

There are a wide variety of different concepts of enlightenment. One concept that is somewhat familiar in America is **nirvana**. Nirvana refers to the extinction of all ideas and concepts, thus resulting in the end of suffering due to the craving that results from being attached to anything in the natural world. In the Theravada tradition this should be the goal of all Buddhists, and a person who achieves nirvana is referred to as an **Arhat**. Other Buddhists, however, seek to avoid nirvana, because it leaves all others behind.

In the Mahayana tradition, an ideal person would be a Bodhisattva, one who vows to forego complete enlightenment until all other beings have been enlightened. According to Thich Nhat Hanh (1995), such individuals touch mindfulness, and as a result of living mindfully they can touch the Buddha and shine their light of awareness on everything they do. The desire to help others achieve enlightenment comes from the deep compassion developed by **Bodhisattvas**. Mindfulness leads to this compassion, as it leads one to develop **Bodhicitta**. Bodhicitta, which means "mind of enlightenment" or "mind of love," is an inner drive to fully realize oneself and to work for the well-being of all (in other words, it is the driving force of being a Bodhisattva; Dalai Lama, 2001; Thich Nhat Hanh, 1995, 1999).

Curiously, some Buddhists distinguish between "bodhi" as a temporary flash of enlightenment, which can even occur following arduous meditation or by accident, and "nirvana" or true liberation, which can only result from proper knowledge and dedicated practice (Mathew, 2001). This concept is similar to what Maslow described as the difference between a peak experience and a plateau experience. A peak experience is a brief period of fulfillment, usually associated with a particular event. A plateau experience, on the other hand, is a lasting feeling of oneness with the world around us. What is of particular importance for the study of personality is the recognition that individuals with certain personality characteristics, such as being kind-hearted and open-minded, can more easily accomplish long-term fulfillment, whether we call it nirvana or self-actualization.

Compassion and Loving-Kindness

"Just as compassion is the wish that all sentient beings be free of suffering, loving-kindness is the wish that all may enjoy happiness" (Dalai Lama, 2001). With these simple words about Buddhism, His Holiness the Dalai Lama has captured the history of psychology briefly presented in the introductory chapter: that psychology focused for many years on helping to identify and treat mental illness (hopefully freeing people from suffering), whereas now there is a strong movement toward positive psychology (hoping to improve well-being for all). This recognition of compassion as the strong feeling or wish that others be freed from suffering comes from mindfulness. As one becomes truly aware of the suffering involved in human life, and if one is able to feel genuine empathy for others, then compassion naturally arises (Chappell, 2003; Dalai Lama, 2001; Goldstein & Kornfield, 2001; Thich Nhat Hanh, 1995). Compassion has described as the ideal emotional state (Bankart et al., 2003; Cook, 2002; Dockett & North-Schulte, 2003; Ragsdale, 2003), and Carl Rogers considered genuine empathy to be essential for client-centered therapy to be successful. Aside from Rogers, however, have other psychologists begun to examine the value of compassion and loving-kindness? The answer is an unequivocal "Yes" (Bankart et al., 2003; Batson et al., 2005; Cassell, 2005; Dockett & North-Schulte, 2003; Keyes & Lopez, 2005; Khong, 2003; Ragsdale, 2003; Schulman, 2005; Young-Eisendrath, 2003)!

"Life is so hard, how can we be anything but kind?"
- Kornfield, 1994

Obstacles to Personal Growth: The Three Poisons of Buddhism

Buddhists believe in **three poisons**, the great obstacles to personal development. They are greed, anger, and delusion. These poisons, or realms as they are often called, have no nature of their own, they are created by us and they depend on us. Greed flows from attachment, anger flows from our emotions, and delusion flows from maya. By following the practices of Buddhism, we can free ourselves from these poisons as did the Buddha. According to Bodhidharma, the Buddha made three vows. He vowed to put an end to all evil, by practicing moral prohibitions to counter the poison of greed. He vowed to cultivate virtue by practicing meditation to counter the poison of anger. And he vowed to liberate all beings by practicing wisdom to counter the poison of delusion (in Red Pine, 1987). Likewise, we can devote ourselves to the three pure practices of morality, meditation, and wisdom.

It is interesting to note how well this philosophy fits with the growing field of positive psychology (e.g., see Compton, 2005; Peterson, 2006). Indeed, whole books have been written on the study of virtue in psychology (Fowers, 2005; Peterson & Seligman, 2004). Note, however, that these books are quite recent. Although the seeds of positive psychology, studies on virtue and similar topics have been around since the earliest days of psychology in the Western world, we seem to be just starting to "discover" concepts that have been well established in Eastern philosophy/psychology for thousands of years. As we recognize more similarities between traditional Eastern perspectives and current Western perspectives, it may help to guide these developing areas of psychological research in the Western world.

Zen Buddhism in America

Zen Buddhism is probably the best-known school of Buddhism in America due to the influence of D. T. Suzuki, who first visited America in the year 1897. Suzuki was a renowned Buddhist scholar, who wrote extensively on Zen Buddhism and its relationships to such diverse topics as Christian mysticism (Suzuki, 1957) and psychoanalysis, the latter book being co-authored by Erich Fromm (Suzuki et al., 1960). Zen Buddhism has also made its way into popular literature in the United States. The famous "Beat generation" author Jack Kerouac, who had many discussions with D. T. Suzuki (Suzuki taught for a few years at Columbia University, which happened to be Kerouac's alma mater), wrote a most entertaining book about his own pursuits on the path of Zen called *The Dharma Bums* (Kerouac, 1958). And there was the immensely popular classic entitled *Zen and the Art of Motorcycle Maintenance*, first published in 1974 (Pirsig, 1999), which opened the eyes of a whole new generation of Americans to the philosophy of the Far East.

Buddhism, and Zen Buddhism in particular, is also beginning to have more and more influence on psychotherapy in America today. Although a discussion of therapy techniques is beyond the scope of this chapter, it is becoming easy to find such material. There are books on Zen and psychotherapy (Brazier, 1995; Mruk and Hartzell, 2003), Buddhism and well-being (Brach, 2003), comparisons of psychoanalysis and Buddhism (Epstein, 1995; Suzuki et al., 1960), and a variety of chapters in spiritually oriented handbooks on psychotherapy (e.g., Cooper, 2005; Corbett & Stein, 2005; Crawford, 2005; Finn & Rubin, 2000; Lukoff & Lu, 2005; Roland, 2005; Sharma, 2000; Tan & Johnson, 2005). Not only does this blending of Eastern and Western philosophy promise to expand the horizons and potential effectiveness of psychotherapy, learning more about the different cultural perspectives that led to these different lifestyles will help to prepare psychologists to recognize more quickly and easily the culturally-related issues that are affecting their patients or clients.

Sangha: A Community Practicing Together

The concepts of togetherness, friendship, social support, etc. are certainly well known in the West, despite the fact that Western cultures are generally considered to be individualistic. Adler identified developing friendships as one of three main tasks in life, and the value of social support during times of stress and grief has been well documented. In Yoga and Buddhism these concepts have been central for thousands of years. Buddhists refer to the **Three Jewels** (also known as the Three Gems or the Three Refuges): the Buddha, the **Dharma**, and the **Sangha**. A Buddha is one who is fully enlightened (not just Gotama Buddha), and the Dharma is the way of understanding and love taught by Gotama Buddha. A Sangha is a community of Buddhists who practice the Dharma and seek enlightenment together (Suzuki, 1960; Thich Nhat Hanh, 1995). The Sangha is not, however, just a get-together of companions with similar interests. The Sangha can renew our inspiration and energy, and it can help us to keep practicing when our own motivation wanes (Goldstein & Kornfield, 1987). The energy and motivation we gain from being part of a Sangha can help us to develop Bodhicitta, the altruistic desire to help all people achieve enlightenment. The ceremony to actively generate Bodhicitta within us begins with a series of visualizations in which we imagine Gotama Buddha being with us, surrounded by other Buddhas, great sages, and all sentient beings (Dalai Lama, 2001). Being filled with Bodhicitta makes us a Bodhisattva right away (Thich Nhat Hanh, 1999). This is not simply a belief or devotion, however. Taking refuge in the Sangha is a practice, one that can only take place in the company of others and with their support (Thich Nhat Hanh, 1995).

The Sangha is by no means unique to Buddhism. In Yoga they refer to Satsanga, associating with the truth or with someone virtuous such as a guru (Feuerstein, 2003; Yogananda, 1946). I remember when a monk, and a monk in training, from the Self Realization Fellowship visited the Yoga retreat center I visit. During the evening they offered Satsanga, a brief lesson followed by a question and answer discussion. In this semi-formal setting we were all able to expand our understanding of Yoga and share our interests and experiences. Indeed, some people practicing traditional Yoga or Buddhism consider the guru (or lama, in Tibetan) to be a fourth jewel in which to seek refuge (Feuerstein, 2003).

Discussion Question: Buddhists strongly support a Sangha, a community of believers. Can you imagine practicing Buddhism alone? What about your own personal groups, whether church groups, clubs, friends, family, etc.? Are they supportive? How important are those groups to the way you live your life, and could you imagine your life without them?

A Final Note

This chapter and the one that follows have very religious overtones. So I would like to say a little more about the importance of covering these topics in a personality textbook. Alfred Adler said that if you want to understand someone, look at their style of life. As stated at the outset of this chapter, I have tried to present this material as guides for one's lifestyle that have developed within different cultures. There are three basic moral codes that influence our lives: community, autonomy, and divinity (see Triandis & Suh, 2002). In collectivistic cultures there is an emphasis on community moral codes, whereas autonomy codes are more influential in individualistic cultures. Both cultures emphasize moral codes related to divinity (as religion or spirituality). If we tried to separate religious culture absolutely from our study of personality, we might very well end up with an academic discipline that misses the richness and wonder of human life. More importantly, what happens to people who ignore spirituality in their own development? Abraham Maslow lamented the defense mechanism of desacralization, the failure of people to consider anything to be truly important and meaningful. Yehudi Menuhin, in his introduction to *Light on Yoga* by B. K. S. Iyengar (1966), offers a striking impression of those who do not seek harmony with the universe:

> What is the alternative? Thwarted, warped people condemning the order of things, cripples criticizing the upright, autocrats slumped in expectant coronary attitudes, the tragic spectacle of people working out their own imbalance and frustration on others. (pg. 12)

I don't know whether Maslow considered desacralization to be this frightening a possibility, but it certainly gives one reason to consider the value of spiritual aspects of human development, especially since spirituality is one of the cultural universals (Ferraro, 2006a; Murdock, 1945). And given that spirituality is universal, these matters are certainly not unique to Eastern culture. In the next chapter we will consider spiritually guided lifestyle recommendations as they apply to cultures influenced by the Abrahamic religions: Judaism, Christianity, and Islam.

Personality Theory in Real Life: Are You Really You?

We ended the first chapter in this book by asking an interesting question: Who are you? In this chapter, we have addressed the possibility that everything you know about yourself is an illusion, and that even knowing is an illusion. How can this be? The answer may be found, or perhaps not found, in the mystery that is God. The Christian Bible teaches that God's ways are not Man's ways. Paramahansa Yogananda provides a marvelous image of the mystery of the Godhead being so far beyond our comprehension that it defies description (Yogananda, 1946); and Dante's awesome description of the appearance of the divine essence in *Paradiso* is difficult to envision, even as one reads Dante's words (in Milano, 1947). Perhaps some things are beyond our comprehension.

How then, should we proceed to live our life? Based on the concept of Karma, our past actions will influence our future experiences. Consider things you have done in your life. Have you regretted some of them? Did they seem out of character for you? Try to determine if unfortunate events followed those actions you regret. On the positive side, are there things you have done that make you proud or happy? Have those things involved other people, or were they done for other people? Try to determine whether those good things you have done resulted in favorable consequences for you and for others.

Now, here comes the tricky part. When you have done good things, do they feel more like you than the bad things did? If the answer is yes, it may be that you have begun to touch something special within yourself. You are responsible for both the good things and the bad things you have done in this life. But perhaps the good things feel better, feel more like you, because they begin to connect you with your transcendental self, that spark of the divine within you, which may be called spirit or soul. Thinking this way is a deep and powerful challenge, which requires you to have some faith in yourself. Meditate on this, and see what happens!

Review of Key Points

- Although Yoga and Buddhism have significant religious overtones, they are actually lifestyle guidelines that promote psychological well-being.
- The principles of Yoga are outlined in the *Yoga Sutras* of Patanjali and in the *Bhagavad Gita*, both of which are approximately 2,500 years old.
- In Yoga there is a dichotomy between spirit and nature, with spirit being pure consciousness. Our belief that we are actually our physical selves (our natural self) is an illusion.
- Karma refers to the cosmic law of cause and effect. Our past actions, both good and bad, affect our future.
- Everything in the natural world is composed of three gunas: rajas (craving and action), tamas (ignorance and dullness), and sattva (light and joy).

Yoga: A Purpose for Personal Development, and Buddhism: Zen and the Middle Way

- A guru is a teacher, someone who is advanced in their practice of Yoga. The guru is essential for a student to properly follow the complex teachings and practices of Yoga.
- There are a wide variety of schools within Yoga, including Hatha-Yoga (which is popular in America), Bhakti-Yoga (devotional Yoga), Kriya-Yoga (believed to be the original Yoga of Patanjali), and Mantra-Yoga (which emphasizes the chanting of mantras, such as the sacred Om).
- Patanjali described five hindrances to personal development: avidya (ignorance), sense of personality, desire, hate, and sense of attachment.
- The ancient Vedic teachings propose four stages in the ideal life: student, householder, hermit or forest-dweller, renunciant.
- Yoga is well established in America, having been taught formally for over 85 years. This mixing of cultures has been possible, in part, because of similarities between Yoga and Christian practices. Two such common practices are contemplative prayer (which is similar to meditation) and singing to God.
- Buddhism is based on the 2,500 year-old teachings of Siddhattha Gotama, who is also known as Gotama Buddha. Bodhidharma brought Zen Buddhism to China some 1,500 years ago, and the Dalai Lama is a very famous Tibetan Buddhist leader alive today.
- The Buddha taught that there are four noble truths: suffering is a reality in human life, suffering comes from craving, the craving that leads to suffering can be destroyed, the path to destroy craving is the Middle Way (aka, the Eightfold Path).
- Buddhists believe in three basic characteristics of existence: nothing is permanent, suffering is an integral part of human life, and we have no immortal, unchanging soul.
- The Buddhist concept of interbeing emphasizes the connection between all living things, and even inanimate objects, because there is only one single source of all creation.
- Meditation, the common element in all forms of Yoga and Buddhism, is a means for controlling our mind and moving it in a more virtuous direction. Soto Zen emphasizes sitting meditation alone, whereas Rinzai Zen adds to seated meditation the practice of meditating on a koan, an unsolvable riddle.
- Mindfulness is the practice of maintaining a meditative state throughout our daily routine.
- In a very general sense, enlightenment refers to transcending this life, thus eliminating craving and suffering and escaping from the cause and effect of karma. In the Mahayana tradition, some Buddhists forego complete enlightenment so that they might remain in the world to help others achieve enlightenment.
- The ideal emotional state for Buddhists is compassion. Both compassion and loving-kindness flow naturally from mindfulness, since mindful individuals recognize the reality of our existence.
- Buddhists believe in three poisons, or obstacles to personal growth: greed, anger, and delusion.
- Zen Buddhism has been taught in the United States for over 100 years. It has found its way into popular literature and has had a clear influence on psychology.
- Buddhists refer to the Three Jewels: the Buddha, the Dharma (the teachings of the Buddha), and the Sangha (a community of Buddhists). The importance of community is by no means unique to Eastern thought, but certainly takes on great significance in a culture that is generally recognized as collectivistic.

Review of Key Terms

Arhat	Jnana-Yoga	prana
atman	Karma-Yoga	rajas
Avatar	koan	Raja-Yoga
avidya	Krishna	samadhi
asanas	Kriya-Yoga	Sangha
Bhagavad Gita	Kundalini energy	sanzen
Bhakti-Yoga	Laya-Yoga	sattva
Bodhicitta	interbeing	Satyagraha
Bodhisattva	karma	spirituals
Buddha	Kirtan	tamas
Dharma	mantra	Three Jewels

Eightfold Path	Mantra-Yoga	three poisons
enlightenment	maya	Transcendental Meditation
Five Precepts	meditation	Vedas
Four Noble Truths	Middle Way	Yoga Sutras
gunas	mindfulness	yogi
guru	nirvana	zazen
Hatha-Yoga	Om	Zen

Annotated Bibliography

Bailey, A. A. (1927). *The light of the soul: The Yoga Sutras of Pantanjali.* New York, NY: Lucis Publishing.
Hartranft, C. (2003). *The Yoga-Sutra of Patanjali.* Boston, MA: Shambala.
Mitchell, S. (2000). *Bhagavad Gita: A new translation.* New York, NY: Three Rivers Press.

These three books contain translations with commentary of the *Yoga Sutras* of Patanjali and the *Bhagavad Gita*, the two books that outline the discipline of Yoga. Each translation of the *Yoga Sutras* has its own advantages, depending on the interests of the reader. Mitchell's translation of the *Bhagavad Gita* contains a wonderful introduction.

Byrom, T. (1993). *Dhammapada: The Sayings of the Buddha.* Boston, MA: Shambala.
Reps, P. & Senzaki, N. (1994). *Zen flesh, Zen bones.* Boston, MA: Shambala.

These two pocket books are very short, but contain marvelous collections of the Buddha's own teaching and famous stories from or about Zen masters.

Dalai Lama, His Holiness the (2001). *An open heart: Practicing compassion in everyday life.* Boston, MA: Little Brown and Company.
Dalai Lama, His Holiness the (2002). *The spirit of peace.* London, England: Thorsons.

These two marvelous books were written by perhaps the most influential Buddhist teacher alive today. The first book presents the essence of the Dalai Lama's teaching, and the second book includes a brief autobiographical story of his early life.

Epstein, M. (1995). *Thoughts without a thinker.* New York, NY: Basic Books.

This book is a marvelous comparison of Buddhist meditation to Western psychotherapy. Surprisingly, one of the effects of this book for me was a renewed appreciation for psychoanalysis. This is a must-read for those who are interested in blending Eastern philosophy and Western psychology.

Feuerstein, G. (2003). *The deeper dimension of Yoga.* Boston, MA: Shambala.

This is by far the best general reference book on Yoga I have seen. It is quite thorough, but still readable, since each topic is broken down into short sections. I have recommended this book to students who have come back and agreed that it was very helpful for them.

Goldstein, J. & Kornfield, J. (2001). *Seeking the heart of wisdom: The path of insight meditation.* Boston, MA: Shambala.

This book provides an excellent overview of Buddhism, meditation, and how meditation can lead one in a positive direction. Kornfield's experiences as both a Buddhism monk and a clinical psychologist probably make him unique. Like Kornfield, Goldstein was a Peace Corps volunteer in Thailand in the 1960s. Their deep understanding of Buddhism, coupled with an

American education, help them to write in a very understandable fashion on topics that are often difficult for some of us to understand. This book is definitely a must-read.

Kerouac, J. (1959). *The Dharma bums*. London, England: Penguin Books.
Pirsig, R. M. (1999). *Zen and the art of motorcycle maintenance: An inquiry into values* [CD]. New York, NY: Audio Renaissance.

These books provide wonderful entertainment in which Yoga/Buddhist philosophy is worked into American stories. Kerouac, who is recognized as one of the best authors of the "Beat generation," was very interested in Buddhism and worked it into this novel. Pirsig was also well versed in Eastern philosophy, having studied in India, and his book is based on an actual motorcycle trip taken with his son and friends in 1968. *Zen and the Art of Motorcycle Maintenance* remains a classic.

Suzuki, D. T. (1962). *The essentials of Zen Buddhism*. New York, NY: Dutton & Co.

D. T. Suzuki is the Zen master best known for bringing this discipline to America. His writing can be difficult to follow, but this book presents the essentials of Zen in a fairly readable way. One of the most intriguing sections is his thorough presentation of the process of meditating on a koan. On this topic his insight is invaluable.

Thich Nhat Hanh (1991). *Peace is every step: The path of mindfulness in everyday life*. New York, NY: Bantam Books.
Thich Nhat Hanh (1995). *Living Buddha, living Christ*. New York, NY: Riverhead Books.

These two books are among the best writings of Thich Nhat Hanh, probably the second most influential Buddhist teacher alive today (after the Dalai Lama). The first book includes brief passages on the role that mindfulness can serve in living a good life. The second book, perhaps his best known, discusses how easily Buddhism and Christianity can blend together.

Watts, A. (1957) *The way of Zen*. New York, NY: Vintage Books.

This book is an excellent overview of Zen Buddhism, by one of the most renowned scholars of Eastern philosophy to have lived in the Western world. It includes a fair amount of historical information, and is presented in a very readable style.

Yogananda, Paramahansa (1946). *Autobiography of a yogi*. Los Angeles, CA: Self-Realization Fellowship.

As the title indicates, this is the autobiography of the yogi who brought formal Yoga training to America. It has many marvelous stories from Yogananda's own life, as well as a wide variety of general information on Yoga.

Some Interesting Websites

www.yogananda-srf.org is the official website for the Self Realization Fellowship, founded by Paramahansa Yogananda in 1920.
www.kriyayogalahiri.com is the official website for "Kriya Yoga in the Lahiri Mahasaya family tradition."
www.wccm.org is the official website for the World Community for Christian Meditation, founded by Fr. John Main, OSB.
www.tm.org is the official website for learning about "The Transcendental Meditation Program" established by Maharishi Mahesh Yogi.
www.yogaworks.com is the official website for Yoga Works, the company that hopes to bring consistency to Yoga instruction across America.

Chapter 18 - Kabbalah, Christian Mysticism, and Sufism

In the previous chapter, Yoga and Buddhism were presented as lifestyle choices, but it was acknowledged that they developed within a religious context. In this chapter we continue that trend, but for **Kabbalah**, **Christian mysticism**, and **Sufism**, we cannot separate the lifestyle from the religion. However, one can easily make the argument that we should not ignore the influence of religion on psychology. After all, both spirituality and formal religion are significant factors in the lives of many people, regardless of whether some may not believe in the existence of God, or any other divine being(s). It is also true that religion was a significant factor in the lives of many of the theorists we have examined in this book, and as a result, their spiritual beliefs helped to shape the nature of their personality theories.

We will examine the mystical approaches that have developed within the Jewish, Christian, and Muslim religions. These are the three Abrahamic religions, in the order in which they were established, and together they cover an extraordinary range of cultural groups, including some 3½ billion people (55 percent of the world's population; Haviland, Prins, Walrath, & McBride, 2005). Mysticism refers to the belief that one can know the spiritual truths of life and the universe that are beyond the intellect by being absorbed into the **Deity** through contemplation and self-surrender. In practice, they share common elements with Yoga and Buddhism (particularly meditation), and by bringing these five practices together, we have truly begun to take a look at the personalities, within a cultural context, of people around the entire world.

Abraham is the patriarch of Judaism, Christianity, and Islam. [Image by Fr. Lawrence Lew, O.P.]

It is important to keep in mind, however, that any of the theories we have examined so far might play a role in personality development in any cultural group, in conjunction with the cultural influences of spirituality and religion. Thus, the ideas presented in these last two chapters are *not* meant to offer alternatives to what we have discussed within traditional Western psychology. In addition, there are other significant cultural factors beside spirituality and religion, though few of them have been studied or contemplated as deeply as religion. And undoubtedly, no other cultural phenomenon has been actively promoted and spread around the world by missionaries of many different faiths, as has been the case with religion. It is important to be open-minded and aware of some of the major factors underlying the dramatic cultural differences that exist around the world. Only then can we honestly connect with other people in a global community.

Judaism and Kabbalah

We will begin our examination of spiritual/religious guidelines for living one's life with the oldest, but smallest, of the Abrahamic religions. **Judaism** holds a special place in the history of psychology, since nearly all of the early and most significant psychodynamic theorists were Jewish (even if they did not practice their faith). In addition, since many of those Jewish psychoanalysts came to America during the 1930s, they then had a significant effect on the continued development of psychodynamic theory and psychoanalysis here in the United States.

<u>*The Foundation of the Jewish Faith*</u>

Judaism is one of the oldest religions in the world, and today some 14 million people practice this faith. It is a monotheistic religion, thus believing that there is only one god: **Yahweh**. They believe that Yahweh called **Abraham** out of his homeland to establish a new home, in the general area of modern-day Israel. This occurred in approximately the year 1900 B.C. However, the formal foundation of Judaism involved the establishment of Yahweh's laws, known as the **Torah**. The Torah is not merely a set of laws or cultural guidelines, but rather, they are a pattern for living that transforms the Jewish people into Yahweh's people (Wilkins, 1967). The Torah is quite long, consisting of five books, which include many complex rules for both the people and the priesthood.

However, the rules were greatly simplified in Yahweh's special revelation to Moses on Mt. Sinai, around the year 1300 B.C., and these simplified guidelines for how to live one's life are known as the **Ten Commandments**:

> I am the Lord your God…You shall have no other gods before me.
> You shall not make for yourself a graven image…you shall not bow down to them or serve them…
> You shall not take the name of the Lord your God in vain…
> Remember the sabbath day, to keep it holy.
> Honor your father and your mother…
> You shall not kill.
> You shall not commit adultery.
> You shall not steal.
> You shall not bear false witness against your neighbor.
> You shall not covet your neighbor's house…your neighbor's wife…or anything that is your neighbor's.
> *from Exodus, Chapter 20; Holy Bible*

As simple as it might seem to follow these ten guidelines for living one's life, it is just as easy to ignore them. Unfortunately, ignoring them has often been the case, even among some of the most famous people in Jewish history. Thus, the mystical practice of Kabbalah has arisen, to both help people live a righteous life, and to help them do so without having to guide their behavior by simple, yet strict, commandments. In other words, there was, and is, a need to transform people's minds. In order to effect real change, we cannot simply expect people to follow the rules, we need to help them make the rules a part of their life. In this sense, Kabbalah, like Yoga, Buddhism, and as we shall see for Christian mysticism and Sufism, can be viewed as a sort of cognitive psychology, a redirection of one's conscious personality development.

Discussion Question: If the Ten Commandments are simply rules, as opposed to being an inherent part of our lives, is anything missing? Are there things we would still be allowed to do that would harm other people, or harm ourselves? What can we do to make the Ten Commandments a way of life, how can we be mindful of them?

Kabbalah

Kabbalah is a path designed to teach people about their place in life and in the universe, particularly with regard to the divine. It emphasizes that one's daily life should not be separated from one's spiritual life. In more practical terms, Kabbalah deals with the everyday experience that we have unlimited desires, but only limited resources to satisfy them. Thus, there will always be some degree of suffering in our lives if we focus only on the material world. Kabbalah teaches a pathway toward experiencing something beyond simple materialism. And yet, that path remains obscured in a certain degree of secrecy. The principal books are available only in the Hebrew and Aramaic languages, and some believe that Kabbalists who are qualified to teach Kabbalah are all in the country of Israel (Besserman, 1997; Laitman, 2005). Accordingly, a distinct degree of difficulty in the study of Kabbalah is to be expected:

> Whoever delves into mysticism cannot help but stumble, as it is written: "This stumbling block is in your hand." You cannot grasp these things unless you stumble over them. (pg. 163; Matt, 1995)

Kabbalah is as old as Judaism itself, perhaps older. Kabbalistic legend suggests that it may have begun with Enoch, the great-grandfather of Noah (as in Noah's Ark; Halevi, 1986), but its formal practice recognizes a few key historical events. In the sixth century B.C., a collection of manuals called *Maaseh Merkavah* emerged, and these manuals included a formal practice. For those who engaged in this practice, the goal was to directly experience the Deity by concentrating on mandala-like images that showed a path to the Throne of God (remember that Carl Jung also meditated on Mandala images). Their emphasis on out-of-body experiences distinguished them from similar Babylonian schools of spirituality that emphasized inner-directed visualizations and, therefore, were not as mystical as the Kabbalists. In the second century A.D., Rabbi Shimon Bar Yochai wrote an important Kabbalist text called the *Zohar* (translated as the *Book of Splendor* or the *Book of Radiance*), which was hidden in a cave in Israel and studied in secret until, around the year 1280 A.D., a Spanish Kabbalist named Moses de Leon published the *Zohar*. In the late 1500s, Rabbi Yitzhak Luria began teaching Kabbalah, and he contributed a number of additional influential books, such as *Etz Hachayim* (*The Tree of Life*), *Sha'ar HaKavanot* (*The Gateway on Intentions*), and *Sha'ar Hagilgulim* (*The Gateway of Reincarnation*). Known as the Ari (the Lion), he established a basic system for studying Kabbalah, which remains in use today (Besserman, 1997; Hoffman, 2007; Laitman, 2005).

The primary aspects of practicing Kabbalah are quite similar to what we saw with Buddhism. Surrendering oneself to Yahweh, and in the process annihilating one's ego (or concept of self), in order to release one's emotions is one of the main goals (Hoffman, 2007; Weiss, 2005). Meditation is a key practice, attempting to immerse oneself in Yahweh manifested as self, thus fulfilling the self. A common technique is to meditate on some Kabbalah teaching or a passage from the Bible. It is also highly recommended that Kabbalah be practiced within a group of other seekers, and under the guidance of a Rabbi (or teacher). Similar to Buddhist mindfulness, Kabbalists also attempt to incorporate their practice into every moment of their daily lives. As a result, the basic teachings of Judaism, such as the Ten Commandments, should become an individual's way of life, rather than a distant set of rules merely to be obeyed (or not).

> When you desire to eat or drink, or to fulfill other worldly desires, and you focus your awareness on the love of God, then you elevate that physical desire to spiritual desire…wherever you go and whatever you do - even mundane activities - you serve God. (pg. 151; Matt, 1995)

Kabbalah and Psychology

The mystical approach to understanding life and individuals has an interesting history in the field of psychology, with William James, Carl Jung, and Abraham Maslow being among those most interested in the study of spirituality and spiritual phenomena. As the meditation practices within Yoga and Buddhism have gained popularity in psychology, other spiritual/mystical traditions are being re-examined as well. Accordingly, Kabbalah is becoming more popular, both in Judaism and in psychology, and the links between Kabbalah and psychology are being actively explored (e.g., Halevi, 1986; Hoffman, 2007; Weiss, 2005).

Kabbalah seems to compare most favorably with a cognitive approach to understanding personality and healing broken relationships. Kabbalah describes a complex arrangement of elements that underlie our relationship with God, the universe, and consequently, ourselves and other people. Understanding these relationships is the key to balancing our emotions, thoughts, and styles of relating to others. Unhappiness is viewed as the result of a serious imbalance in our understanding of the true nature of our place in our community, society, and life itself. While many different forms of psychotherapy help people to develop insight into their personality and relationships, Kabbalah proposes to go beyond insight. Once again, for those people who live life with a deep spiritual faith, ignoring one's faith makes it all but impossible to find balance in one's life. Only a spiritual path, perhaps augmented by a traditional psychotherapeutic emphasis on everyday problems and stressors, can help to balance the entire life of the spiritual person. Thus, Kabbalah need not be viewed as an alternative to psychotherapy, but rather as a bridge between psychology and spirituality (Weiss, 2005).

There is, however, a problem facing most psychologists when it comes to the study of Kabbalah. Being based on spirituality and the unquestioned belief in Yahweh, Kabbalists are willing to examine questions that are decidedly unscientific, such as Jung's concept of synchronicity. They also study the higher dimensions of human existence, such as awakening ecstasy (Hoffman, 2007). In this regard their goals are similar to those of Maslow, and his desire to understand self-actualization and its relationship to spiritual experiences, and to the whole field of positive psychology, and its emphasis on doing more for people than simply addressing the adjustment disorders and/or mental illness of those suffering psychological distress. Yet Kabbalah goes even further into the realm of parapsychology, fully believing in reincarnation (Besserman, 1997; Hoffman, 2007; Laitman, 2005; Weiss, 2005). In 1988, psychiatrist Brian Weiss, Chairman Emeritus of Psychiatry at the Mount Sinai Medical Center in Miami, published *Many Lives, Many Masters*. In this book, he described a case in which he was able to help a young woman through the use of **past-life therapy**. Since the Kabbalistic view of reincarnation suggests an explanation for Jung's concept of the collective unconscious (see also, Halevi, 1986), the use of past-life therapy may not be as strange as many would insist it must be. In continuing to study this phenomenon, Dr. Weiss does not suggest simply accepting anyone's word that reincarnation is real or that past-life therapy will help:

> It is vital to carry your logical, rational mind on this journey. To accept everything without reflection, contemplation, and thoughtfulness would be just as foolish as rejecting everything in the same manner. Science is the art of observing carefully with an unbiased, non-prejudicial eye. (pg. 7; Weiss, 2000)

Similar thoughts occurred to Carl Jung and Elisabeth Kubler-Ross, both of whom were nervous about discussing their experiences with patients who reported near-death experiences. However, they were so common that Jung and Kubler-Ross felt compelled to discuss them. Carl Rogers also reported similar experiences as his wife was dying. Thus, the Kabbalists are not simply a group of spiritualists reporting events that are not considered real by any well-known psychologists or psychiatrists. The truth, however, is likely to remain elusive for those who do not accept the evidence on faith.

Discussion Question: Whether or not you actually believe in reincarnation, *can* you believe in it? Can past-life therapy be helpful even if it isn't real, or is it always a harmful delusion? Could reincarnation be the explanation for Jung's collective unconscious, and if not, is there a conceivable middle ground?

Christianity and Christian Mysticism

Although there are many denominations within **Christianity**, at times generating significant conflict between each other, Christianity as a whole has been a profoundly successful and influential religion. Approximately one-third of the world's population, over 2.2 billion people, are Christian, and it has spread around the entire world. At its heart, Christianity is a simple religion, and those who live a truly Christian life are guided by one simple philosophy: love your neighbor.

The Foundation of the Christian Faith

Approximately 2,000 years ago a man named **Jesus of Nazareth** was born. For 30 years he lived a simple life, but then embarked on a religious crusade that lasted for only 3 short years. At the end of those three years, he was crucified for having challenged the right of the religious and political authorities to lead the people, as well as their decency in so doing. However, he never outright challenged anyone, always teaching love, mercy, and peace. Following his death and resurrection he has been called the **Christ** (meaning **Messiah**, or anointed), hence the term Christianity.

Christians believed that Jesus was no ordinary man, but rather the son of God (Yahweh, the God of Judaism). They also believe that he was born of a virgin, through the power of the Holy Spirit. Thus, although Christians believe in one God, they view God in a Trinitarian way: **Father**, **Son**, and **Holy Spirit** (Wilkins, 1967). Although Judaic prophecy had foretold of the coming of a Messiah, they do not believe that Jesus was that person. Yet, having arisen out of Judaism, Christians believe much of the Jewish faith, including the importance of the Ten Commandments. However, when Jesus was challenged to identify the most important of the commandments, he surprised those listening:

> "The first is, 'Hear, O Israel: The Lord our God, the Lord is one; and you shall love the Lord your God with all your heart, and with all your soul, and with all your mind, and with all your strength.'
>
> The second is this, 'You shall love your neighbor as yourself.' There is no other commandment greater than these."
>
> *from Mark, Chapter 12; Holy Bible*

Jesus of Nazareth is believed by Christians to be the son of God. [Image by the More Good Foundation]

What is surprising about this answer is that Jesus simplified the Ten Commandments even further, emphasizing just two, but those two commandments encompass both the spiritual and the social worlds - love God, and love all people (the famous Good Samaritan parable teaches that all people are one another's neighbors). Thus, it seems appropriate for us to address the social and psychological aspects of loving and/or caring for other people, as well as for ourselves, as something separate from religious/spiritual pursuits. And yet at the same time, we cannot, and need not, separate our psychological studies from a religious/spiritual context (at least when trying to understand those people for whom religion and spirituality are important daily factors).

Discussion Question: Love God, and love your neighbor as yourself. Is it really that simple?

Christian Mysticism

Christian Mysticism is as old as Christianity itself, for Jesus led a mystic life (Walker, 2003). Since that time there have been many Christian mystics, but two particular groups stand out: the desert fathers and the women mystics (Chervin, 1992; Clement, 1993; Waddell, 1998). As the Christian faith became legal, following the conversion of the Roman emperor Constantine the Great late in the third century, Christianity became caught up in the politics of the empire. Soon enough, a group of spiritual men sought to escape worldly politics and secular distractions by becoming hermits. They traveled out into the Egyptian desert and began monastic lives. In order to be with God, they did not merely seek solitude, but they also sought to eliminate their sense of ego. This was attempted through what we might call contemplative prayer, or simply meditation. However, the sense of ego does not go away easily:

> The ego doesn't want us looking for God because when we find God, the illusion of being an ego will be destroyed. It will mean the end of our self-centered existence and all of its negative emotions…One cannot see God and continue to live as a separate person. (pg. 49; Walker, 2003).

Thus, a battle arises between the sense of ego and one's efforts to immerse oneself in the Deity. This spiritual combat, essentially the battle between good and evil, exists because of our freedom to choose our path in life (Clement, 1993). It was in recognition of this challenge that the desert fathers sought the solitude of the desert. There they were able to pursue the ecstasy of unknowing, that which is beyond the boundaries of any human ability to comprehend or rationalize the experience:

> At one time Zachary went to his abbot Silvanus, and found him in an ecstasy, and his hands were stretched out to heaven. And when he saw him thus, he closed the door and went away: and coming back about the sixth hour, and the ninth, he found him even so: but toward the tenth hour he knocked, and coming in found him lying quiet…the young man held his fee saying, "I shall not let thee go, until thou tell me what thou hast seen." The old man answered him: "I was caught up into heaven, and I saw the glory of God. And I stood there until now, and now am I sent away." (pg. 130; Sayings of the Fathers, in Waddell, 1998)

Although there have been many mystics who were men, including the desert fathers, Meister Eckhart (a favorite of Erich Fromm), and the anonymous author of *The Cloud of Unknowing* (see Kirvan, 1996a), there have also been a number of well-known women mystics, such as Blessed Julian of Norwich (see Chilson, 1995), Saint

Teresa of Avila (see Kirvan, 1996b), Saint Therese of Lisieux (Kirvan, 1996c), and most famous of them all, Saint Joan of Arc (see Chervin, 1992). Given the patriarchal history of the Roman Catholic Church, and the beginning of mysticism with the desert *fathers*, it is enlightening to see that so many women were blessed by God's grace and presence in a profound mystical fashion, and that this was recognized by the Catholic Church (as many of these women became saints). Thus, God does not discriminate based on gender. Indeed, in one mystical experience, St. Hildegard of Bingen (who lived from 1098-1179 A.D.) was instructed to use the majesty of her mystical gift to instruct men in the true meaning of faith:

> ...as I was gazing with great fear and trembling attention at a heavenly vision, I saw a great splendor in which resounded a voice from Heaven, saying to me, "O fragile human...Cry out and speak of the origin of pure salvation until those people are instructed, who, though they see the inmost contents of the Scriptures, do not wish to tell them or preach them, because they are lukewarm and sluggish in serving God's justice...Burst forth into a fountain of abundance and overflow with mystical knowledge, until they who now think you contemptible because of Eve's transgression are stirred up by the flood of your irrigation." (pp. 17-18; St. Hildegard of Bingen, cited in Chervin, 1992)

Christian Meditation

The practice of meditation as a form of contemplative prayer has continued to the present day, thanks in part to two influential monks who lived during the twentieth century: Thomas Merton, OCSO (1915-1968) and John Main, OSB (1926-1982). Fr. Merton was a Trappist monk who wrote extensively on the monastic life, contemplation and silence, and connections between Western and Eastern spiritual philosophies (e.g., Merton, 1948, 1951, 1977; Montaldo, 2001; Nouwen, 1972). Always supportive of these various approaches to life, Fr. Merton adopted one of Jung's objections to Freud's discounting of religion: the observation that many people in psychoanalysis (whether Catholic, Protestant, or Jewish) had at the core of their dysfunction a religious crisis. Whereas Freud blamed this problem on the failure of religion, Fr. Merton blamed the problem on a failure of faith:

> The real religious problem exists in the soul of those of us who in their hearts believe in God, and who recognize their obligation to love Him and serve Him - yet do not! (pg. 4; Merton, 1951)

While a monastic life may have allowed Fr. Merton to serve God with all his heart and soul, not everyone can be a monk or a nun. The Benedictine monk John Main sought to offer an easy path to meditation practice for the average person. Having become interested in mantra meditation following his early career in the Far East and his study of the writings of the desert fathers, Fr. Main began leading meditation groups at a monastery in London. He continued these meditation groups in Montreal after establishing the Benedictine priory there, and he also began sharing his interest in meditation through the publication of books such as *Word Into Silence* (Main, 1980), *Moment of Christ* (Main, 1984), and *The Way of Unknowing* (Main, 1989). Following Fr. Main's death, his devoted student Laurence Freeman, OSB continued teaching Christian Meditation. In 1991, Fr. Freeman helped to establish the World Community for Christian Meditation, with its headquarters in London, England, and he continues to serve as its director. Fr. Freeman has written his own books on Christ as the inner source teaching us about life (Freeman, 1986, 2000), as well as some very practical books on meditation practice and establishing a meditation group (Freeman, 1994, 2002, 2004). Both Fr. Main and Fr. Freeman recommended a simple mantra meditation, using the Aramaic word "**Maranatha**," one of the oldest Christian prayers, which means simply "Come Lord." This simple, yet spiritually deep, form of meditation comes quite easily to those who are willing to pursue this silent path to contentment and being one with God.

Discussion Question: There is a long and ongoing history of Christian meditation. Were you aware of this, or did you think that meditation and Christianity were unrelated? Does it seem appropriate to compare meditation to contemplative prayer?

Islam and Sufism

The last of the Abrahamic religions to be established, **Islam** has also been a profoundly successful religion. It ranks second in numbers only to Christianity, with some 1.5 billion followers around the world. **Muslims**, those who practice the Islamic faith, consider Jesus Christ to have been a great prophet, but they do not consider him to be the Son of God. They follow the teachings of the one whom they believe to be the last and greatest prophet: **Muhammad** (Wilkins, 1967).

The Foundation of the Islamic Faith

Muhammad was born around 571 A.D., in Mecca (in modern-day Saudi Arabia). An upright and honest man, Muhammad used to take refuge in a cave at Mount Hera, where he would contemplate (meditate?) good and evil. The religion of his time and region worshipped many spirits in the desert, including one called **Allah**. Muhammad came to believe that Allah was the one and only God, the creator of the universe. Muhammad devoted the rest of his life to preaching Allah's message, and was soon literally run out of town by the authorities. He fled to the city of Medina, in the year 622 A.D., a date which marks the beginning of Muhammad's formal efforts to establish the religion of Islam. Muhammad became a great leader, in the name of Allah, and when he died in the year 632 he controlled most of Arabia. Within one hundred years, Islam had spread around the Mediterranean to Europe, throughout North Africa, and to India in the East (Wilkins, 1967).

Muslims believe that Muhammad was directly descended from Abraham, through Abraham's son Ishmael. Ishmael was the half-brother of Isaac, through whom the Jewish people trace their heritage to Abraham. He received his revelation from Allah through the angel Gabriel, and wrote it down in the **Holy Qur'an**, the holy book of Islam (the first English translation by a Muslim generally available in the West was originally published in 1917, and has seen numerous new editions since then; Ali, 2002). Like Judaism and Christianity, Islam has a fairly simple set of guidelines for living one's life (Fadiman & Frager, 1997; Wilkins, 1967), known as the **Five Pillars of Islam**:

1. *Bearing Witness*, or the Confession of Faith, to Allah and to his chosen prophet Muhammad.
2. *Daily Prayer*, which occurs five times a day (dawn, noon, midafternoon, dusk, and night).
3. *Fasting*, for those who are able, during the month of **Ramadan** (the ninth month of the Muslim calendar).
4. *Charity*, or almsgiving, which involves giving one fourtieth (2½%) of one's accumulated wealth to the poor at the end of the month of Ramadan.
5. *Pilgrimage to Mecca*, once during the lifetime for those who are able and can afford to do so.

Two elements seem to stand out from the Five Pillars. First, Islam requires an active demonstration of one's faith in Allah. Second, every Muslim must follow through on that faith with good works, particularly the fasting during Ramadan and the giving of charity to the poor. Thus, neither faith nor good works alone are adequate for those who claim to be Muslim, they must incorporate both into their lives.

Discussion Question: The Five Pillars of Islam seem to be much more directly related to demonstrating one's faith in God than we saw with Judaism or Christianity. Do Muslims seem more religious than other religions? Is your answer just an impression, or is it based on real experience? In your opinion, how do the Five Pillars of Islam compare to the Ten Commandments or Jesus' two commandments?

**Connections Across Cultures: Islamic Faith,
Jihad, Ascesis, and Democracy**

When considering the Five Pillars of Islam, it is hard to imagine why there is such a negative view of the Islamic religion in the Western world, particularly in the United States. The answer is actually quite simple, but it is based on a terrible misunderstanding: radical Islamic fundamentalism, and its common element of terrorism, is viewed in the West as being synonymous with Islam itself. As noted in the main text, Maulana Muhammad Ali was the first Muslim to translate the Holy Qur'an into English (originally in 1917; see Ali, 2002). In addition, Ali published another lengthy book entitled *The Religion of Islam* (originally in 1936; see Ali, 1990).

Many Americans believe that Muslims have a religious duty to wage **jihad**, a holy war, on all people who do not follow Islam and put their faith in Allah. This belief is mistaken. First, the word jihad is not synonymous with war, but rather it means to *exert* oneself, or to have the *ability* to resist one's enemies. The enemies that must be resisted include the devil and one's self (our weaknesses and our ignorance, which keep us from the path toward truth). This striving for the truth is reflected, of course, in the verses of the *Holy Qur'an*:

> And those who strive hard for Us, We shall certainly guide them in
> Our ways. And Allah is surely with the doers of good.
> *Chpt. 29:69; Holy Qur'an (Ali, 2002)*

What might come as a surprise to many Christians is that this internal battle between oneself and evil is by no means unique to Muslims. In Christianity the same need to strive for God exists, and the word used to describe this striving is **ascesis**, a word with essentially the same meaning as jihad (Clement, 1993). In St. Paul's letter to the Ephesians he tells them to put on the armor of God and do battle with the devil. As for whom this striving is valuable, even Jesus makes it clear that one does *not* have to be Jewish or Christian. In a passage quite similar to the quote above from the Qur'an:

> John said to him, "Teacher, we saw a man casting out demons in your name, and we forbade him because he was not following us."
> But Jesus said, Do not forbid him, for no one who does a mighty work in my name will be able soon after to speak evil of me. For he that is not against us is for us. For truly I say to you, whoever gives you a cup of water to drink because you bear the name of Christ, will by no means lose his reward."
> *Mark 6:38-41; Holy Bible*

There are times, nonetheless, when one must fight in order to defend oneself. When this occurs, the Qur'an makes it clear that Muslims should prepare to accept peace when it is possible to do so:

> And if they incline to peace, incline thou also to it, and trust in Allah.
> Surely He is the Hearer, the Knower.
> *Chpt. 8:61; Holy Qur'an*

So if the Islamic and Christian faiths are not so different, and both are supposed to seek peace, why have we become so deeply involved with repeated military conflicts in the Middle East? The problem may simply lie with democracy, and our belief that it should be the basis for all government. In America we purport to believe in separation of church and state, though the reality of this is quite debatable. In Islam, however, every aspect of one's life must involve submission to Allah's will. Thus, any attempt to spread democracy to Islamic countries, particularly with the American emphasis on separation of church and state, is an act of war against Islam (Shedinger, 2004; see also Esack, 1999; Moghaddam, 2006). No matter how much we might want to disagree with this perspective, if it *is* their perspective, then we are the aggressors, and they are justified, according to the Qur'an, in fighting back.

We believe that we are fighting back, and so the vicious circle of politics continues.
However, there are those who believe that democracy is inevitable in Islamic societies. The critical difference is that they will be pluralistic democracies, not the secular democracy of America (Aslan, 2005, 2006; see also Manji, 2003). The Qur'an makes it clear that "There is no compulsion in religion…" (Chpt. 2:256; *Holy Qur'an*). Thus, the key to peace in the Middle East may lie in learning to understand one another, and in accepting the guidance of Yahweh, God, Christ, Allah, or whatever name you prefer for the Deity. The mystics sought to avoid the politics of the world, and to place themselves entirely within the presence of God.

Sufism

Keep your hands busy with your duties in this world,
and your heart busy with God.
Sheikh Muzaffer (pg. 35; in Fadiman & Frager, 1997)

This simple expression of the Sufi way demonstrates how one can seek Allah while remaining actively engaged in life, allowing for continued spiritual growth and opportunities to practice awareness, generosity, nonattachment, and love (Fadiman & Frager, 1997). The beginning of Sufism, as with the other mystical approaches, is somewhat shrouded in mystery. Since Islam is a continuation of the monotheistic religion of Judaism and Christianity, the Judaic and Christian mystics might be viewed as early Sufis. Sufism in its proper sense, however, exists within Islam. When the prophet Muhammad died, there was conflict between the primarily Arab and the primarily non-Arab followers of Islam. The primarily Arab Muslims emphasized the teachings of Muhammad's colleagues, and became known as **sunni**, whereas the primarily non-Arab Muslims followed Ali, the son of Muhammad, and became known as **shi'ah**. These two groups drifted apart, and their disagreements became serious, to say the least (Nurbakhsh, 1990). Those sociopolitical differences continue today, and provide much of the basis for the continuing violence in the Middle East. However, a third group also arose, a group that ignored the sociopolitical arguments of the sunni and shi'ah, and focused instead on inner prayer and devotion to Allah. These were the first Sufis.

Practice and understanding in Sufism goes through four stages, with each one building upon the others: understanding the teachings of Islam, practicing Sufism by making the teachings part of one's everyday life, discovering the Truth (or realizing the inner meaning of the teachings and practices), and finally, having the deep level of inner knowing, or superior wisdom, that transcends the Truth. The great Sheikh Ibn El-Arabi has described these stages as a progression from "yours and mine" through "mine is yours and yours is mine" and then there is "no mine and no yours," and finally there is "no me and no you" (Fadiman & Frager, 1997; see also Shah, 1971). This perspective is reminiscent of a combination of Kohlberg's stages of moral development (Kohlberg, 1963) and Eastern perspectives on nonattachment and selflessness.

The Whirling Dervishes attempt to achieve a state of religious ecstasy. [Image by Saaleha Bamjee]

Similar to Christianity, Sufism considers love to be of utmost importance in transforming the self. As we pursue a path of love in our lives, God begins to reach out and draw us in toward the divine presence. If we are willing to surrender to God, we will awaken and be taken in by Him. To assist with this loving pursuit of God, a number of great Sufi teachers have also been poets. Most notable among these Sufi teachers are Jalaluddin Rumi and Omar Khayyam (see Fadiman & Frager, 1997; Hall, 1975; Khan, 1999; Shah, 1971; Yogananda, 1994). In addition to his poetry, Rumi is recognized as the founder of the Order of the **Whirling Dervishes**. The whirling dance that distinguishes this group of Sufis is intended to help the Dervish achieve religious ecstasy, and it is far more ritualized than might be apparent at first sight. As strange as such a practice may seem in the Western world, the practice was apparently used on at least one occasion by the renowned St. Francis of Assisi, who lived at the same time as Rumi (Shah, 1971). Omar Kayyam is most famous for a collection of verses known as *The Rubaiyat* (see Yogananda, 1994). This strange and deeply symbolic poem almost defies interpretation, particularly for those raised in the Western world, unfamiliar with Sufi mysticism. The renowned Indian guru Paramahansa Yogananda, who also made an extensive study of the relationship between Christian gospel and Yoga (Yogananda, 2004a,b), has provided a marvelous interpretation of *The Rubaiyat*. For example, consider verse VII:

> Come, fill the Cup, and in the Fire of Spring
> The Winter Garment of Repentance fling:
> The Bird of Time has but a little way
> To fly - and Lo! the Bird is on the Wing.
> *Translation by Edward Fitzgerald, reprinted in Yogananda, 1994*

In this verse, *fill the cup* refers to filling one's consciousness (as one does during meditation), in the warmth of spiritual enthusiasm (*the fire of spring*). One should set aside regret caused by unfulfilled desires and disillusioning sensory indulgences (*the winter garment of repentance fling*). The *bird of time* represents fleeting, ever-changing human life, and it is flying away, leaving little time to establish purpose in one's life. In other words, don't waste your life worrying about, or punishing yourself for, either the past or your own shortcomings. Life is short, and there is a great spiritual truth to be discovered!

As with the Christian mystics, there have been many well-known Sufi women, including a number of Black women (Nurbakhsh, 1990). The following is an amusing story that both teaches a Sufi lesson and demonstrates that a woman can be every bit as faith-filled and wise as any man:

> Maymuna was reputed to be her brother's equal in asceticism, piety and reliance on God. Ahmad Ebn Salem recounts the story of a man who went to see Ebrahim Khawass. When he knocked on the door, he was met by Maymanu, Ebrahim's sister, who asked his name and what he wanted. He introduced himself and asked for Ebrahim Khawass.
>
> "He has gone out," she told him.
>
> "When will he return?"
>
> Maymuna replied, "How can someone who has surrendered his life to another know when he is returning?"
>
> (pg. 182; Nurbakhsh, 1990)

Discussion Question: What impression have you had of the whirling dervishes? Can you think of any religious groups within Christianity that demonstration such fervent, physical worship in their churches? What effect might this have on the sense of community within the church?

Connections Between Mystical and Eastern Perspectives

One of the most pleasing aspects of studying Yoga, Buddhism, Kabbalah, Christian mysticism, and Sufism is the recognition that all of these spiritual approaches to life respect one another. An examination of the works of many authors, representing each of these mystical approaches, suggests that there is but one God of the mystics (Armstrong, 1993). Sufi, Kabbalistic, and Zen practices often seem quite similar, as do select Hindu, Yogic, Buddhist, Judaic, Taoist, and Christian teachings (Holy Bible; Khan, 1999; Lao Tsu, c. 600 B.C./1989; Mitchell, 2000; Walker, 2003). Renowned Buddhist teachers, such as His Holiness the Dalai Lama (1996) and Thich Nhat Hahn (1995, 1999), have offered extensive comparisons of Buddhism to Christianity, as Paramahansa Yogananda has compared Yoga to Christianity (Yogananda, 2004a,b). Two of Fr. Laurence Freeman's books on Christian mysticism have forewords written by the Dalai Lama and Sir Yehudi Menuhin. Menuhin, who was Jewish, was also a personal friend of the guru B. K. S. Iyengar, and wrote the foreword for one of his books (Iyengar, 1966). Fr. Freeman has written an introduction for one of the Dalai Lama's books. Fr. Thomas Merton was friends with D. T. Suzuki, wrote *Mystics & Zen Masters* (Merton, 1967), traveled extensively throughout the Far East (Burton, Hart, & Laughlin, 1973), and the Dalai Lama praised Merton as having a more profound understanding of Buddhism than any other Christian he had known. In addition, Merton had a keen interest in Sufism, and taught a course on it, though he claimed not to understand it very well (Baker & Henry, 2005).

Similar to the importance of a guru, Sufis also emphasize the importance of a teacher, or **sheikh**. The sheikh must be someone who practices what they preach, in order to be an example for their students. A Sufi sheikh understands not only the complexity of Sufism, but also the complexity of the individual seeking Allah. In Sufism there are no self-appointed sheikhs, and all orders can trace their heritage to the prophet Muhammad (Fadiman & Frager, 1997). In Judaism, a priest is typically called **Rabbi**, which means teacher, and Jesus was often called Rabbi as well. Rabbis often believed that the whole of Israel (as in the Jewish people), were called to be Rabbis (Armstrong, 1993), and most Christians have heard that they are all called to be **evangelists**, or those who teach the faith and try to convert others to Christianity. As confusing as the mystical approach to the Deity can be, it should hardly be surprising that mystics believe in the need for a teacher to help others understand this path. When it is done sincerely, for those who are indeed seeking the Deity, it is a wonderful gift to be able to give, and even more so to be able to receive.

Discussion Question: Does the fact that mystics from so many different faiths can come together and share their faith offer hope to the future of humanity? Or will human nature always be a source of prejudice, discrimination, conflict, and war? If religion and/or spirituality cannot help, can psychology surpass them in the service of peace and contentment?

A Final Thought

One of the great challenges facing the world today, as it has been for thousands of years, is the belief that one religion is *right*, and all others are *wrong*. A Jesuit priest named Fr. Anthony de Mello, SJ (1931-1987), who lived in Poona, India, compared Christian contemplative prayer to a variety of Eastern practices, and wrote marvelous stories to convey this message of diversity (de Mello, 1978, 1982, 1990). The following story, from *The Song of the Bird*, exemplifies the folly of insisting upon a single religion being the only way to God:

> A Christian once visited a Zen master and said, "Allow me to read you some sentences from the Sermon on the Mount." "I shall listen to them with pleasure," said the master. The Christian read a few sentences and looked up. The master smiled and said, "Whoever said those words was truly enlightened." This pleased the Christian. He read on. The master interrupted and said, "Those words come from a savior of mankind." The Christian was thrilled. He continued to read to the end. The master then said, "That sermon was pronounced by someone who was radiant with divinity." The Christian's joy knew no bounds. He left, determined to return and persuade the master to become a Christian.
>
> On the way back home he found Jesus standing by the roadside. "Lord," he said enthusiastically, "I got that man to confess that you are divine!" Jesus smiled and said, "And what good did it do you except to inflate your Christian ego?"

Unfortunately, Fr. de Mello's writings led to him being censured by the Roman Catholic Church. Regardless, Fr. de Mello continued to consider the Catholic Church his spiritual home, and he dedicated *The Song of the Bird* to the church. Clearly, he believed and practiced what he was teaching to others.

Personality Theory in Real Life: Completing the Personality Theory Journey

At the end of Chapter 1 you were given an exercise to explore who you think you are, and whether other people see you as you see yourself. In the various chapters of this book, you have been introduced to many different ways of viewing personality and its development. You have probably been able to see elements of each major perspective in your own personality, which can make it difficult to think of one theory as being the right one. In these final chapters, you have been introduced to mystical approaches that suggest that there is no real personality or ego; it is an illusion, which separates us from the reality that we have within us an essence of divinity, a soul if you will. In order to help us realize our soul, and to be one with the divine reality, these mystical approaches suggest paths for personal development designed to help be at peace with who we are, and with our place in the universe.

So, have you ever contemplated, or have you practiced, actively developing your personality in a way that will lead to contentment in your life and peaceful, friendly relationships with other people? If you have, was your religious faith an essential element, and do you think that such a "spiritual" approach can also be effective if done "humanistically" by people who are atheists? And now the big question: Do you believe this topic belongs in the field of psychology, or should it only be considered by theologians and philosophers?

As before, there is no right or wrong answer to this last question. The mystics emphasized that the divine is divine, and the physical world is the world in which we live. Sometimes the two come together without conflict, but other times the conflict that arises from religious/political differences leads to terrible tragedies. Consider this: you have not completed your personality journey, despite the title of this section. Your life continues, your education continues, and you have significant control over the direction that both of those endeavors follow. How does that make you and your classmates feel?

Review of Key Points

- The Abrahamic religions include over 3.5 billion people around the world. Thus, they are an essential cultural consideration when examining the factors that influence personality.
- Judaism offers a simple set of guidelines for living one's life, known as the Ten Commandments.
- Kabbalah is the mystical form of Judaism, which emphasizes blending one's daily, worldly life with one's spiritual life.
- Kabbalists encourage a way of incorporating the Ten Commandments into one's life, in a manner reminiscent of Buddhist mindfulness. The meaningless alternative is to simply view the commandments as a static set of rules to be obeyed.
- Kabbalah, as an approach to the problems of daily life, compares favorably with cognitive psychotherapy.
- Past-life therapy relies on accepting the Kabbalistic belief in reincarnation, and using that knowledge to help people reconnect with their past lives.
- Christianity is the largest religion in the world, with over 2.2 billion followers.
- Jesus simplified the Ten Commandments to just two: love God, and love your neighbor as yourself.
- The early Christian mystics were desert hermits, who helped to establish both Christian mysticism and the monastic life.
- In Christian mysticism there have been many influential women saints, including some who challenged the patriarchal attitudes of men and one who became a great military leader (St. Joan of Arc).
- Fr. John Main, and his student Fr. Laurence Freeman, have actively worked to help bring simple Christian meditation techniques to people all around the world.
- Islam is the world's second largest religion, with over 1.5 billion followers.
- Muslims follow a set of guidelines known as the Five Pillars of Islam.
- Sufism arose amongst those Muslims who did not wish to be drawn into the political and social battles that continue today between the sunni and shi'ah. Instead, Sufis seek to be drawn into Allah.
- Sufism has developed some most interesting practices, including sheikhs who became renowned poets and the whirling dervishes.
- In contrast to the conflicts between organized religions, and their supposed followers, there is extraordinary peace and both spiritual and intellectual interaction between mystics of many paths (Hindu, Taoist, Jewish, Christian, Muslim, etc.).
- Mystics recognize the difficulty that often arises in the form of confusion regarding their ways. Accordingly, they routinely emphasize the need for a teacher (guru, rabbi, sheikh, master, etc.) for those who wish to pursue a mystic path.
- Jihad is neither a holy war nor a requirement of Muslims. It is an urging to strive for faith, especially in the presence of those who are unfaithful. Christianity shares the same element, and it is known as ascesis.

Kabbalah, Christian Mysticism, Sufism

Review of Key Terms

Abraham	Holy Spirit	Rabbi
Allah	Islam	Ramadan
ascesis	Jesus of Nazareth	sheikh
Christ	jihad	shi'ah
Christian mysticism	Judaism	Son
Christianity	Kabbalah	Sufism
Deity	Maranatha	sunni
evangelists	Messiah	Ten Commandments
Father	Muhammad	Torah
Five Pillars of Islam	Muslims	Whirling Dervishes
Holy Qur'an	past-life therapy	Yahweh

Annotated Bibliography

Besserman, P. (1997). *The Shambhala guide to Kabbalah and Jewish mysticism.* Boston, MA: Shambhala.
Laitman, R. M. (2005). *Kabbalah for beginners: A beginner's guide to the hidden wisdom.* Thornhill, Ontario, Canada: Laitman Kabbalah Publishers.

These two books provide a concise overview of the history and nature of Kabbalah. The book by Besserman is more complete, but the book by Laitman is a very quick and easy read.

Halevi, Z. (1986). *Psychology & Kabbalah.* York Beach, ME: Samuel Weiser, Inc.
Hoffman, E. (2007). *The way of splendor: Jewish mysticism and modern psychology - Updated 25th Anniversary Edition.* Lanham, MD: Rowman & Littlefield.
Weiss, A. (2005). *Connecting to God: Ancient Kabbalah and modern psychology.* New York, NY: Bell Tower.

As presented in any of these books, there have been active efforts to blend the teachings of Kabbalah with modern psychology. Each book brings a different emphasis to bear on this curious area of study.

Matt, D. C. (1995). *The essential Kabbalah: The heart of Jewish mysticism.* New York, NY: HarperSanFran.

Through a series of short passages and stories, this book provides an entertaining introduction to the spiritual philosophy of Kabbalistic mysticism.

Weiss, B. L. (1988). *Many lives, many masters: The true story of a prominent psychiatrist, his young patient, and the past-life therapy that changed both their lives.* New York, NY: A Fireside Book.

For those willing to set aside disbelief and explore the fringes of psychology and religion, this book offers a case study in past-life therapy. Dr. Weiss is a respected psychiatrist. If you accept this case as true, you will be exploring the farthest reaches of Jung's visionary theories.

Clement, O. (1993). *The roots of Christian mysticism.* Hyde Park, NY: New City Press.
Waddell, H. (1998). *The desert fathers.* New York, NY: Vintage Books.
Walker III, E. (2003). *The mystic Christ: The light of non-duality and the path of love as revealed in the life and teachings of Jesus.* Norman, OK: Devi Press.

These three excellent books provide a thorough overview of Christian mysticism, as well as its relationship to other religions. Taken together they represent a substantial amount of information, but they will not disappoint the interested student.

Kabbalah, Christian Mysticism, Sufism

Chervin, R. (1992). *Prayers of the women mystics.* Ann Arbor, MI: Servant Publications.

This book provides a marvelous overview of many of the best-known women mystics in Christian history. Chervin blends a brief biography of each woman with passages from their works, providing a meaningful introduction to each of them in a limited amount of space (making it easy to pick up the book and read about one or two mystics at a time).

de Mello, A. (1978). *Sadhana - A way to God: Christian exercises in Eastern form.* New York, NY: Image Books.
Main, J. (1984). *Moment of Christ: The path of meditation.* New York, NY: Continuum.
Merton, T. (1948). *The seven storey mountain.* New York, NY: Harcourt Brace Jovanovich.

Each of these inspired and holy monks wrote a number of books, and I have chosen one from each of them simply to save space. I could easily have chosen a different book for each of them. If you find a particular writing style more appealing than another, then there are more books by that person to choose from. They all do a marvelous job of presenting the joy that can come from pursuing a mystical path within the Christian religion.

Freeman, L. (2002). *A pearl of great price: Sharing the gift of meditation by starting a group.* Tucson, AZ: Medio Media.
Freeman, L. (2004). *A simple way: The path of Christian meditation.* Tucson, AZ: Medio Media.

Fr. Freeman has written some more substantial books that are worth reading, but these short guides provide simple and practical steps to begin making Christian meditation part of your daily life. Both include contact information for Christian meditation centers around the world.

Ali, M. M. (1990). *The religion of Islam.* Dublin, OH: Ahmadiyya Anjuman Isha'at Islam Lahore Inc.

This is an excellent overview of the Islamic faith, written by one of the first Muslims to bring the Western world a clear understanding of Islam. He spent seven years providing the first English translation of the Qur'an by a Muslim, and he quotes it extensively in this book, in order to support the truth of his presentation of Islam.

Nurbakhsh, J. (1990). *Sufi women, Revised 2nd Ed.* New York, NY: Khaniqahi-Himatullahi Publications.
Shah, I. (1971). *The Sufis.* New York, NY: Anchor Books.

Together, these two books offer a wonderful overview of the history of Sufism and the men and women who have helped to guide this mystical tradition. Shah takes a somewhat more historical/academic approach, whereas Nurbakhsh offers many stories and sayings to exemplify the teachings of the women Sufis.

Fadiman, J. & Frager, R. (1997). *Essential Sufism.* New York, NY: HarperSanFrancisco.

The brief quotations and stories presented in this book, taken from many of the greatest Sufi sheikhs, provide a wonderful introduction to the spiritual philosophy of Sufism.

Yogananda, Paramahansa. (1994). *Wine of the mystic: The Rubaiyat of Omar Khayyam - A spiritual interpretation.* Los Angeles, CA: Self-Realization Fellowship.

The renowned guru and author Paramahansa Yogananda extends his extraordinary spiritual knowledge into this interpretation of The Rubaiyat, by the equally renowned eleventh century poet and Sufi sheikh Omar Khayyam. Yogananda not only offers a spiritual interpretation, but also practical applications for one's daily life.

Appendix A - Personality Disorders

Many students begin a personality course hoping to learn about personality disorders. As fascinating and disturbing as personality disorders can be, this topic is best covered in an abnormal psychology course. However, many instructors also like to discuss personality disorders, in part to address the importance of developing a healthy personality. Thus, this appendix has been included to briefly present this topic, for those students and instructors who want to include it within their overall examination of personality development.

A Complex Problem

When I first wrote this appendix I approached the complexity of personality disorders by including two sections: the DSM criteria for diagnosing personality disorders and an alternative way of categorizing these disorders proposed by Theodore Millon. With the advent of the DSM-V (American Psychiatric Association, 2013) things have gotten even more complex. The DSM-V continues with the same categories as were used in the DSM-IV (American Psychiatric Association, 2000), but then it offers a completely different set of criteria for diagnosing personality disorders. No other DSM edition has done this, suggesting that personality disorders are proving to be the most complex group of psychological disorders.

So, I have now kept the same two first sections, since the official diagnostic criteria are essentially the same (only some changes in the wording of the text) and Theodore Millon's alternative theory is particularly interesting. Then, I briefly describe the new alterntive being offered in the DSM-V (leaving it up to you to explore them in more detail).

DSM-V Categories of Personality Disorder

The *Diagnostic and Statistical Manual of Mental Disorders, 5th Ed.* (DSM-V; American Psychiatric Association, 2013) defines personality disorders as "an enduring pattern of inner experience and behavior that deviates markedly from the expectations of the individual's culture, is pervasive and inflexible, has an onset in adolescence or early adulthood, is stable over time, and leads to distress or impairment." The consideration of cultural context is perhaps the most significant change in this definition from the earlier DSM-III. The DSM-V suggests that the personality disorders can be grouped into three clusters, plus a "not otherwise specified" category, for a total of 11 specific diagnoses, the authors caution that the identified clusters have not been consistently validated and that individuals may present combinations of personality disorders from different clusters. Nonetheless, the DSM-V still presents the three clusters of personality disorders (plus the "not otherwise specified" classification). **Cluster A, the odd or eccentric types**, are paranoid, schizoid, and schizotypal personality disorders. **Cluster B, the dramatic, emotional, or erratic types**, are antisocial, borderline, histrionic, and narcissistic personality disorders. And finally, **Cluster C, the anxious or fearful types**, are the avoidant, dependent, and obsessive-compulsive personality disorders.

The odd or eccentric personality disorders represent several of the typical symptoms of schizophrenia (paranoia, emotional detachment, and social withdrawal), leading some to suggest that they represent mild forms of the most widely recognized form of psychosis. However, distinct differences suggest that these personality disorders are not part of a continuum between normal personality and schizophrenia. For example, in individuals with an odd or eccentric personality disorder who also exhibit psychotic symptoms, the personality disorder can be recognized prior to the onset of psychotic symptoms and persists when the psychotic symptoms are in remission. Also, these disorders are not characterized by a pronounced thought disorder, which appears to be the defining characteristic of schizophrenia.

The dramatic, emotional, or erratic personality disorders include the most well-known, due in no small part to their dramatization in movies and television. Most serial killers suffer from antisocial personality disorder (they are often referred to as psychopaths), as do many people in prison. People with antisocial personality disorder demonstrate a complete lack of regard for the rights of others, and will routinely violate those rights. The other personality disorders in this cluster involve various forms of unstable interpersonal relationships, excessive emotions, and a distorted self-image. Interestingly, this cluster appears to involve a significant gender factor, in that antisocial personality disorder is diagnosed more frequently in men, whereas the borderline and histrionic personality disorders are diagnosed more frequently in women.

Probably the least recognized group of personality disorders, among students and the general public are the anxious or fearful personality disorders. The first two, avoidant personality disorder and dependent personality disorder, both involve pervasive patterns of anxiety relating to interpersonal relationships. Finally, obsessive-compulsive personality disorder involves a pervasive preoccupation with neatness, perfectionism, and interpersonal control.

Although the DSM-IV-TR made a point of adding cultural context to the definition of personality disorders, it wasn't until the publication of the DSM-V that much was said in the manual about culture. Not only is there limited research regarding the influence of culture on personality disorders, there is likewise only limited research on cultural influences on normal personality. The notable exception to this may be the well-known research on fundamental differences between individualistic vs. collectivist cultures, which are generally associated with Western vs. Eastern approaches to life. There are also fundamental religious associations that match these basic distinctions, since Western cultures are typically associated with the Abrahamic religions (Judaism, Christianity, and Islam), whereas Eastern cultures are typically associated with Yoga, Buddhism, Taoism, etc.

Discussion Question: What sort of impression do you have of people with personality disorders (it's OK to consider things you have seen on television and in movies)? Is this what you think of when you typically think of mental illness or psychological disorders?

An Alternative Perspective on Categorizing Personality Disorders

Theodore Millon has presented a different perspective on the categorization of personality disorders based upon an **evolutionary model** of personality development. In this model, personality is seen within the same context as any other factor contributing to the evolutionary survival of a species (and, therefore, individuals representing that species). As with other species, humans need to succeed in four areas: **existence** (a person must continue to live as an individual), **adaptation** (if the species cannot adapt it will become extinct), **replication** (individuals can "survive" over time by having offspring), and **abstraction** (the ability to plan and make good choices). According to Millon, we can now describe four polarities on which the personality develops to accommodate these evolutionary needs: the **pleasure-pain polarity** (existence), the **active-passive polarity** (adaptation), the **self-other polarity** (replication), and the **thinking-feeling polarity** (abstraction). Personality disorders can be viewed as adaptive forms of development under abnormal conditions, and they can be classified in accordance with these four dimensions (as opposed to the three clusters proposed in the DSM system). Millon cautions, however, that the complexity of individual personality and the developmental processes involved make it difficult to define in any simple terms how the development of anyone's individual personality might have occurred (Millon, 1996; Millon & Grossman, 2005).

The first category in this schema describes the **pleasure-deficient personalities**, individuals who lack the ability to experience the joys, rewards, and positive experiences of life. Individuals with schizoid personality disorder appear to lack the intrinsic capacity to experience the pleasurable aspects of life. Those with avoidant personality disorder show an excessive preoccupation with, and an oversensitivity to, life's stresses. And finally, people with depressive personality disorders have a pervasive sense of hopelessness and futility in their lives. So although these disorders arise for different reasons, they all arrive at a common point at which individuals suffering from these disorders do not find pleasure in their lives.

The second category includes those disorders that are characterized as **interpersonally-imbalanced personalities**, a condition in which disordered individuals are either overly disposed to orient themselves toward fulfilling the needs of others or overly inclined to meet their own selfish needs. The first two disorders in this group, dependent and histrionic personality disorders, are characterized by their need for social approval and affection, and by their willingness to live according to the desires of others. Individuals with dependent personality disorder do so by taking a passive stance, whereas those with histrionic personality disorder take an active stance. Those with narcissistic and antisocial personality disorders turn inward for gratification. For narcissistic types, their self-esteem is based on an inflated assumption of their own personal worth and superiority, and they expect others to behave accordingly. Antisocial types are fundamentally distrusting of others, and use aggressive self-determination as a protective maneuver.

The third category describes **intrapsychically-conflicted personalities**, individuals whose internal orientations move in opposite directions. Thus, these individuals remain at war with themselves. In both the sadistic personality disorder and the masochistic personality disorder the pleasure-pain polarity is transposed, such that normally pleasurable stimuli are experienced as painful and vice versa. For the compulsive personality disorder and the negativistic personality disorder it is the self-other polarity that is disordered. Individuals with compulsive personality disorder are caught within a conflict between obedience and defiance, but they suppress the conflict in order to appear well controlled and single-minded. In contrast, those with negativistic personality disorder fail to resolve their conflicts, resulting in indecisiveness, inconsistent attitudes, oppositional behavior and emotions, and they become generally erratic and unpredictable.

The three categories of disordered personality described above are primarily stylistic. Style, in this context, refers to the functional manner in which individuals relate to their internal and external worlds. The final category defines **structurally-defective personalities**, much more deeply embedded disorders that affect the function of the mind itself. Thus, the disorders in this final category are considered more severe than those in the categories described above. Schizotypal personality disorder involves eccentric thoughts, behaviors, and perceptions that mirror those found in schizophrenia. Individuals with borderline personality disorder exhibit deep and variable moods, including extended periods of dejection and disillusionment, occasional periods of euphoria, and frequent episodes of irritability, self-destructive acts, and impulsive anger. The paranoid personality disorder is characterized by suspicion and hostility, and the tendency to misread others and respond with anger to perceived deception and betrayal. And finally, the decompensated personality disorder, likely the most profoundly deteriorated personality type, involves consistent and pervasive impairment that is rarely broken by clear thoughts or normal behavior. Individuals with decompensated personality disorder typically require institutionalization, since they simply cannot function in society.

As you can see, the personality disorders described by Millon include the disorders listed in the DSM classification scheme, though the categories he uses are different than the three clusters in the DSM system. Millon also describes five disorders not included in the DSM system. For the most thorough discussion of the categories and disordered personality types described above, see Millon's *Disorders of Personality: DSM-IV and Beyond, 2nd Ed.* (1996). For a number of different perspectives on the development of personality disorders, including cognitive, psychoanalytic, attachment, and neurobehavioral models (among others), see *Major Theories of Personality Disorder, 2nd Ed.*, edited by Lenzenweger and Clarkin (2005).

Discussion Question: Millon has suggested that people with personality disorders have adapted in predictable ways to abusive/neglectful environments. Do you know anyone who seems to have *serious* personality problems that appear to reflect how they were raised or the environment in which they grew up?

Treating Personality Disorders

It is generally accepted that personality disorders are highly resistant to treatment. Personality is well-established in childhood, or at least by adolescence. Since many theorists consider it difficult to significantly change personality once it is established, even in a normal individual, by the time an adult is diagnosed with a personality disorder it has become a deeply embedded aspect of their personality. Thus, individuals suffering from personality disorders, individuals who typically lack insight into their problems, are simply unlikely to realize a need for change or to put any effort into making changes. And since change can only come from the individual, it cannot be forced by the therapist, if the individual suffering from a personality disorder does not cooperate with or put any effort into therapy, there can be no possibility for change. The evolutionary perspective on personality disorders offers another possible reason why they would be resistant to change. Personality disorders may be adaptations to abnormal, most likely abusive, conditions present during personality development. Therefore, even though they are viewed as abnormal, they have served an adaptive purpose for the individual suffering from the disorder.

Nonetheless, progress is being made. There is evidence to support the efficacy of some therapeutic approaches in the treatment of personality disorders, including cognitive, behavioral, interpersonal/psychosocial, and psychoanalytic treatments (Benjamin, 2005; Fonagy, 2006; Kernberg & Caligor, 2005; Leichsenring, 2006; Pretzer & Beck, 2005). Perhaps the most thoroughly studied and effective approach to the treatment of personality disorders is **dialectical behavior therapy** (DBT), developed by Marsha Linehan specifically for the treatment of borderline personality disorder and its commonly associated element of suicidal behavior (Linehan, 1987, 1993; Robins et al., 2004). DBT emphasizes the complete process of change, incorporating both the acceptance of the patient's real suffering and the desire for change. Since a natural conflict arises between acceptance and the desire/need for change, a conflict that can arouse intense negative emotion, DBT involves teaching patients mindfulness skills necessary to "allow" experiences without the need to either suppress or avoid them. These mindfulness skills were drawn primarily from Zen principles, but are similar to and compatible with Western contemplative practices (Robins et al., 2004).

Discussion Question: Does it surprise you to learn that the most promising treatment for personality disorders is based largely on the practice of Zen? What might this say about the importance of therapists being versed in a variety of techniques and being well-educated in cross-cultural perspectives?

A New Alternative in the DSM-V

The purpose for adding a second approach to the diagnosis of personality disorders is twofold: first, the APA Board of Trustees wanted to provide continuity in the diagnoses being offered by clinicians, but second, they recognised that few individuals with a personality disorder clearly fit into the criteria for just one personality disorder. Thus, an alternative method has been proposed that considers assessing both "impairments in personality *functioning* and pathological personality *traits*" (pg. 761; APA, 2013).

After listing general criteria for personality disorder that are quite similar to the traditional general criteria, the alternative approach addresses personality functioning in terms of two dimensions: self and interpersonal. The healthy vs. unhealthy aspects of the self involve one's sense of identity and one's self-direction, whereas the interpersonal component addresses empathy and intimacy. The individual is then assessed (as appropriate to the presumed, primary personality disorder) on 25 specific **trait facets** as they apply within five broad **trait domains**. The trait domains and associated facets are as follows:

Negative Affectivity: emotional lability, anxiousness, separation insecurity, submissiveness, hostility, perseveration, depressivity, suspiciousness, restricted affectivity (lack of)

Detachment: withdrawal, intimacy avoidance, anhedonia, depressivity, restricted affectivity, suspiciousness

Antagonism: manipulativeness, deceitfulness, grandiosity, attention seeking, callousness, hostility

Disinhibition: irresponsibility, impulsivity, distractibility, risk taking, rigid perfectionism (lack of)

Psychoticism: unusual beliefs and experiences, eccentricity, cognitive and perceptual dysregulation

The DSM-V then offers examples of diagnostic criteria according to this methodology for antisocial PD, avoidant PD, borderline PD, narcissistic PD, obsessive-compulsive PD, and schizotypal PD, as well as a new diagnosis of *Personality Disorder - Trait Specified.* Personality Disorder - Trait Specified is diagnosed based on two criteria. First there must be moderate or greater impairment in the functioning of personality, as manifested in two or more of the areas identified above as identity, self-direction, empathy, and intimacy. Second, there must be one or more pathological traits as defined by the 5 domains/25 facets.

So, with three different, utilitarian approach to the diagnosis of personality disorders, it is clear that disordered personality development is every bit as complex and fascinating as normal personality development. This should not be surprising, since individuals are unique and complex, and we all experience different lives. It *will* be quite interesting to see how the DSM-VI handles this issue.

A Final Note

This brief appendix on personality disorders merely scratches the surface of this complex set of psychological disorders. For example, it might appear as if Millon's classification system for personality disorders is at odds with the DSM-IV/DSM-V classification system, and, therefore, Millon himself may be at odds with the DSM-IV/DSM-V system. Actually, Millon was a member of the DSM-IV Personality Disorders Work Group. In addition, the DSM-IV included among its "criteria sets and axes provided for further study" two of the personality disorders contained within Millon's classification system: the depressive personality disorder and the passive-aggressive (negativistic) personality disorder. Accordingly, the classification systems continue to be the subject of ongoing research and potential modification, so much so that the DSM-V actually has two systems included. It will be years before we begin the hear about the DSM-VI, but it will be very interesting to see how personality disorders are handled then.

Likewise, although DBT has been very promising in the treatment of borderline personality disorder, there is less research on specific treatments for other personality disorders. Thus, continued research is necessary, perhaps including the development of new therapies specific to certain other personality disorders.

Review of Key Points

- Personality disorders are enduring patterns of deviant behavior that differ markedly from an individual's culture.
- The DSM classification system identifies three clusters of personality disorder: odd/eccentric, dramatic/emotional/erratic, and anxious/fearful.
- The odd/eccentric personality disorders bear some resemblance to the symptoms of schizophrenia.
- The personality disorders within Cluster B appear to involve a significant gender factor.
- Millon has proposed an alternative classification scheme based on an evolutionary model of personality disorders. He suggests that these disorders represent individual efforts to exist, adapt, replicate, and abstract within an abnormal developmental environment.
- Millon's model results in personality disorder clusters based on four factors: pleasure-deficiency, interpersonal-imbalance, intrapsychic-conflict, and structure-defectiveness.
- Personality disorders have traditionally been resistant to psychotherapeutic interventions.
- Linehan's dialectical behavior therapy has been quite promising in the treatment of borderline personality disorder. This treatment incorporates Zen mindfulness as an approach to balancing the acceptance of the individual with the desire/need for change.

Review of Key Terms

abstraction active-passive polarity adaptation Cluster A - odd or eccentric types Cluster B - dramatic, emotional, erratic types Cluster C - anxious or fearful types	dialectical behavior therapy evolutionary model existence interpersonally-imbalanced personalities intrapsychically-conflicted personalities pleasure-deficient personalities	pleasure-pain polarity replication self-other polarity structurally-defective personalities thinking-feeling polarity trait domains trait facets

Personality Disorders

Annotated Bibliography

Millon, T. (1996). ***Disorders of Personality: DSM-IV and Beyond*** **(2nd Ed.). New York, NY: Wiley & Sons.**

The sheer length of this tour-de-force description of Millon's theory on the adaptive nature of personality and how it can develop abnormally seems intimidating. However, the book is surprisingly readable, and the basic elements of the theory are presented clearly in well-identified sections. Any student who is seriously interested in understanding personality disorders should consider this alternative view to DSM-based descriptions, so that they might have a broader perspective on these very troubling psychological conditions.

Linehan, M. M. (1993). ***Cognitive-behavioral treatment of borderline personality disorder.*** **New York, NY: The Guilford Press.**

Linehan's widely cited book on her approach to treating borderline personality disorders has been translated from English into German, French, Italian, Dutch, and Polish. The accompanying manual has also been translated into Swedish and Spanish.

Robins, C. J., Schmidt III, H., & Linehan, M. M. (2004). Dialectical behavior therapy: Synthesizing radical acceptance with skillful means. In S. C. Hayes, V. M. Follette, & M. M. Linehan (Eds.), ***Mindfulness and acceptance: Expanding the cognitive-behavioral tradition*** **(pp. 30-44). New York, NY: The Guilford Press.**

This brief chapter provides an easily-read description of the philosophy of dialectics and the application of Zen mindfulness to treating patients with borderline personality. Indeed, the entire book is quite valuable for anyone interested in, as the title suggests, expanding their perspective on cognitive-behavioral approaches.

Appendix B – African Perspectives on Personality

To suggest that there is such a thing as an African personality may be misleading. Africa is the second largest continent, with just over 1 billion people spread out among over fifty different countries. It has been the target of extensive colonization over the centuries, and the struggle for liberation from European countries has surely left an indelible mark on the nature of the people there. In addition, the Sahara Desert creates a significant natural division of the people in the north from those in the south. The people of **North Africa** are primarily Arab-Berber Muslims, with ready access to southern Europe across the Mediterranean Sea. This region can rightly be viewed as an extension of Western Asia, in terms of culture, spirituality, and race/ethnicity (Chatterji, 1960; Senghor, 1971). In contrast, the Black Africans live south of the Sahara Desert, and they are the people usually referred to when we think about Africans. Indeed, for the remainder of this section I will use the term African to refer to Blacks living in **Sub-Saharan Africa**. Though many people in Africa identity themselves in terms of their unique ethnicity, history, and geography, this book would be incomplete if *no* effort was made to address the people of this continent. Keep in mind, however, that there is a great deal more work to do regarding our understanding of indigenous people around the entire world.

Africa is a large and diverse continent, with many different people. [Image by Rosario Fiore]

In 1999, James Lassiter wrote a very helpful article covering many of the historical problems that have affected the study of personality in Africa. Unfortunately, many studies sought to identify the nature of personality among Africans in terms of Western ideals, values, and socioeconomic and technological advancement. This biased view created a very negative attitude toward the people of Africa, a negative attitude that the people of Africa often adopted themselves. Thus, the study of personality fell into disrepute, and largely came to a halt. However, a number of professionals from other disciplines, such as sociology and anthropology, continued to examine whether or not there were characteristics common to the people of Africa, a unique and valuable personality distinct from other regions of the world. Though some controversy remains, and the definitions of what personality is from an African perspective are quite different than those we might recognize in traditional Western psychology, this work has led to some interesting insights. Fundamentally, these perspectives are summarized by the following simple proverb:

Umuntu ngumuntu ngabantu (a person is a person through other persons)
- Xhosa proverb (cited in Lassiter, 1999 and Tutu, 1999)

The African Worldview and Spirituality

For many authors, a common African personality derives from a common African **worldview**. According to Khoapa (1980), an African's existential reality is one of collective being, they seek to understand the world through their intersection with all aspects of the world and other people. This worldview is holistic and humanistic, and it focuses on interdependence, collective survival, harmony, an important role for the aged, the oral tradition, continuity of life, and rhythm. In addition, there is a fundamental belief in a metaphysical connection between all that exists within the universe, through an all-pervasive energy or "**spirit**" that is the essence of all things (Chatterji, 1960; Grills, 2002; Grills & Ajei, 2002; Khoapa, 1980; Mwikamba, 2005; Myers, 1988; Obasi, 2002; Parham et al., 1999; Senghor, 1965, 1971; Sofola, 1973).

At the center of the African worldview is spirit, or life itself, a vital force that animates the universe and that imparts *feeling* to all things from God down to the smallest grain of sand. Although this spirit pervades all things, there is a distinct hierarchy among the things that make up the universe. At the top of the hierarchy is God, followed by the ancestors (including the founders of the tribes, aka the "god-like ones") and the living. Then come the animals, plants, and minerals. Being in the center, humans hold a privileged position. As living beings, people are able to increase their **being** (using this term in the same context as in existentialism). The source of spirit, and the **spiritness** within each person, is divine, and transcends both the physical universe and time. Thus, it can connect us to any person, place, or thing. This is part of the basis for African veneration of their ancestors. In order for the ancestors to avoid becoming "completely dead," they must devote themselves to strengthening the lives of the living. As a result, they can still participate in life. When a person recognizes that through spirit all things become one, and if they adhere to this realization, they lose all sense of individual ego/mind. Instead, they experience the harmony of collective identity and a sense of extended self that includes ancestors, those not yet born, all nature, and their entire community (Busia, 1972; Grills, 2002; Grills & Ajei, 2002; Jahn, 1972; Myers, 1988; Obasi, 2002; Parham, 2002; Parham et al., 1999; Senghor, 1965).

Based on the previous paragraph, it should be clear that religion and spirituality are very important to Africans. We share a biological connection with animals, and an inherent spiritual connection with plants and minerals, but our privileged position at the junction of spirit and nature allows us to participate in a spiritual life that separates us from the animals, plants, and minerals. This is how Africans believe they are able to increase their being. According to Khoapa (1980), we link the universe with God, we awaken it, we speak to it, listen to it, and try to create harmony. This leads to a profound connection with the rhythm of the universe. Senghor (1965) describes rhythm as the "architecture of being…the pure expression of the life-force." Rhythm has become an important aspect of African life, particularly in art, music, and poetry (also see Busia, 1972; Chatterji, 1960; Jahn, 1972; Mwikamba, 2005; Senghor, 1971; Sofola, 1973).

> African music, like sculpture, is rooted in the nourishing earth, it is laden with rhythm, sounds and noises of the earth. This does not mean that it is descriptive or impressionist. It expresses feelings. (pg. 86; Senghor, 1965)

As noted above, the transcendent aspect of spirit leads to connections between past, present, and things that have not yet happened. This has led to a distinct relationship to time, one that differs dramatically from the Western world. Africans believe there is a rhythmic, cyclical pattern to life set in place by God, and God knows what is right. This includes the seasons, the rising and setting of the sun, and stages of life (birth, adolescence, adulthood, old age, and death). Events in the past are typically referred to in terms of reference points, such as a marriage or a birth. As for the future, in most African languages there is no word for the distant future, and plans for the near future are once again typically made around events rather than a specific time on a clock. Accordingly, time is something to be shared with others, there isn't really any such thing as wasting time. Tribal elders are respected for the wisdom they have accumulated over a lifetime, and the "living" dead are kept alive by the tribe's oral historian (Jahn, 1972; Parham et al., 1999; Sofola, 1973; Tembo, 1980).

Discussion Question: The African worldview focuses on the universe and all the people within it as an interconnected whole, and seeks harmony and rhythm. Do you see life in a holistic way, do you try to relate to others as if we are all part of one creation? Do you think the world would be a better place if everyone tried to relate to others in this way?

Family and Community

For Africans, the basic unit is the **tribe**, not the individual. Since the tribe seeks collective survival, cooperation is valued over competition and individualism. Since close, personal interconnections are so fundamental, aggression toward others is considered an act of aggression against oneself, and the concept of alienation doesn't exist. This concern for the community is reflected in the family structure. For Africans, family includes parents, children, brothers, sisters, cousins, aunts, uncles, etc. All relatives have the responsibility to care for one another, and when parents become old it is the responsibility of their children to care for them (Khoapa, 1980; Kithinji, 2005; Lambo, 1972; Parham et al., 1999).

According to Khoapa (1980), Westerners are surprised when they observe Africans in normal conversation. There is a great deal of spontaneity, laughter, and the conversation goes on and on. They do not wait to be introduced before engaging in conversation. No reason is necessary for someone to drop by and engage in a conversation. Every gathering is an extension of the family, so there is no reason for inhibiting one's behavior. Simply being together is reason enough to engage others. Khoapa suggests that the "deafening silence" observed when traveling in the Western world is very strange and confusing to Africans.

The cultural institution of marriage provides an interesting example of these principles in action. Marriage is a unifying link in the rhythm of life: past, present, and future generations are all represented. Having children is an obligation, and marriage provides the accepted opportunity to fulfill that obligation. Indeed, since the purpose of marriage is to have children, a marriage is not considered complete until children have been born (Khoapa, 1980; Kithinji, 2005; Lambo, 1972; Parham et al., 1999; Wanjohi, 2005). Marriages can also be a profound source of connection between people that goes far beyond the basic family unit (two parents and their children). The spirit that underlies and provides energy for the fulfillment of being experienced in a family unites that family with other families around the world. In a more practical sense, when a man and a woman from different tribes are married, the members of each tribe see themselves as all becoming one extended family through that marriage (Parham, et al., 1999; Samkange & Samkange, 1980).

The belief that we are all interconnected extends beyond one's family and tribe to all people. **Hospitality** is an important characteristic that Africans expect will be extended to all visitors, including strangers. Different than in the West, however, is the expectation that hospitality will precede asking any questions. Thus, when a visitor is met at the door, they will be invited in, offered something to eat and/or drink, and friendly conversation may ensue, all before asking anything about the visit or even who the person is (if they aren't known). Being benevolent to everyone is seen as a sign of good character or good reputation. African myth and folklore often includes stories about gods or spirits who travel in disguise, rewarding people in kind for how the god or spirit is treated. Selfishness does not promote the well being of the tribe, so a selfish person is likely to be held in contempt and stigmatized. The responsibility for becoming caring people begins with the family (Kithinji, 2005; Lambo, 1972; Sofola, 1973).

> Every Yoruba, the stranger inclusive, is expected to demonstrate that he was well brought up by his parents whose emblem he carries about by the virtue of his existence and former socialisation. A good home to the Yoruba African is a place where good training and nurturing in character and good behaviour including good mode of addressing people are imparted to the young…The good child is supposed not only to accept and show good character in the home but should show the glory of the home outside through his own good behaviour… (pp. 97-98; Sofola, 1973)

Discussion Question: In African culture, marriage and family are very important. How important are they to you? How has your personal history affected your feelings about marriage and family?

Ubuntu

The traditional African concept of ***ubuntu*** is one that encompasses the best that the people of Africa have to offer in terms of social harmony. It has come into play several times during difficult periods of nation building as African countries have gained independence and moved toward democracy. Archbishop Desmond Tutu, winner of the Nobel Peace Prize in 1984, served as Chairman of the Truth and Reconciliation Commission as the nation of South Africa transitioned from Apartheid to democracy. Rather than seeking revenge and the punishment of those who had supported Apartheid, or attempting to achieve some sort of national amnesia through blanket amnesty, the South Africans chose a third alternative. Amnesty would be granted only to those who admitted what had been done in the past. While some were concerned that such an option would allow crimes to go unpunished, the deep spirit of humanity that is *ubuntu* can lead to being magnanimous and forgiving.

> *Ubuntu*…speaks of the very essence of being human. When we want to give high praise to someone we say, "*Yu, u nobuntu*"; "Hey, so-and-so has *ubuntu*." Then you are generous, you are hospitable, you are friendly and caring and compassionate. You share what you have. It is to say, "My humanity is caught up, is inextricably bound up, in yours." We belong in a bundle of life. (pg. 31, Tutu, 1999)

Samkange and Samkange (1980) discuss how extensively *ubuntu* (aka, *hunhu*, depending on the language) is intertwined with life amongst the people of Zimbabwe. It leads to a sense of deep personal relationship with all members of different tribes related by the marriage of two individuals. It has influenced the development of nations as they achieved freedom from colonial governments, and it encourages amicable foreign policies. *Ubuntu* can help to guide judicial proceedings, division of resources, aid to victims of war and disaster, and the need to support free education for all people. The special characteristic that *ubuntu* imparts on African people can also be seen among the African **diaspora**, those Africans who have been displaced from their homeland. For example, Black Americans typically have something unique that distinguishes them from White Americans, something called "**soul**." According to Samkange and Samkange (1980) "soul is long suffering ("Oh Lord, have mercy"); soul is deep emotion ("Help me, Jesus") and soul is a feeling of oneness with other black people." As a result of the Black American's experience with slavery, we now have **soul food**, **soul music**, and **soul brothers**.

Discussion Question: It has been suggested that the essence of personality among African people has given something special to members of the African diaspora known as "soul." However, this may be a characteristic of all dispossessed people. Have you seen examples of this sort of "soul?" If yes, what was the experience like, and how did it affect your own views of life?

Although *ubuntu* is uniquely African, the peace and harmony associated with it can be experienced by all people. According to Archbishop Tutu it is the same spirit that leads to worldwide feelings of compassion and the outpouring of generosity following a terrible natural disaster, or to the founding of an institution like the United Nations, and the signing of international charters on the rights of children and woman, or trying to ban torture, racism, or the use of antipersonnel land mines (Tutu, 1999). Though *ubuntu* itself may belong to Africa, the essence of it is something shared by all dispossessed groups around the world (Mbigi & Maree, 1995). It embodies a group solidarity that is central to the survival of all poor communities, whether they are inner city ghettos in the West, or poor rural communities in developing countries. According to Mbigi and Maree (1995), the key values of *ubuntu* are group solidarity, conformity, compassion, respect, human dignity, and collective unity. They believe that African organizations need to harness these *ubuntu* values as a dynamic transformative force for the development of African nations and the African people. Samkange and Samkange share that view:

> …*ubuntuism* permeates and radiates through all facets of our lives, such as religion, politics, economics, etc…Some aspects of *hunhuism* or *ubuntuism* are applicable to the present and future as they were in the past…It is the duty of African scholars to discern and delineate *hunhuism* or *ubuntuism* so that it can, when applied, provide African solutions to African problems. (pg. 103; Samkange & Samkange, 1980)

Negritude and Nigrescence

Leopold Senghor (1965) has defined **Negritude** as "the awareness, defence and development of African cultural values…the sum total of the values of the civilization of the African world." For Senghor this is not a racial phenomenon, but a cultural one, based primarily on cooperation. He distinguished this cooperation from the collectivist idea we typically associate with Asian cultures by focusing more on a communal perspective. In other words, collectivist cultures may be seen as an aggregate of individuals, but in the truly communal society, whether in the family, the village, or the tribe, there is a connection from the center of each person in their heart (see also Grills, 2002; Senghor, 1971). This is what Senghor believes has always been held in honor in Africa, and it ultimately encourages dialogue with others in Africa (the White Africans, the Arab-Berbers in North Africa) and beyond, so that we can assure peace and build the "Civilization of the Universal."

> Negritude, then, is a part of Africanity. It is made of human warmth. It is democracy quickened by the sense of communion and brotherhood between men. More deeply, in works of art, which are a people's most authentic expression of itself, it is sense of image and rhythm, sense of symbol and beauty. (pg. 97; Senghor, 1965)

Abiola Irele has discussed the history of Negritude as a literary and ideological movement among Black, French-speaking intellectuals in Africa. It was initially a reaction to, and in opposition to, the colonial oppression of the African people. As such, it has been criticized by some as its own form of racism (see, e.g., Irele, 1981, 2001; Tembo, 1980), or as something unique to intellectuals, as opposed to more common people in Africa. However, as noted above, Negritude is about culture, not race *per se*. In addition, a small but nonetheless interesting study by Tembo (1980) provided evidence that scores on an **African Personality Scale** did not differ based on sex, marital status, having been educated in rural or urban schools, or whether they wished to pursue higher education in Africa or England. Irele compared Senghor's view of Negritude to that of the existential philosopher Jean-Paul Sartre. Sartre viewed Negritude as a stage in the development of Black consciousness, a stage that would be transcended by the ultimate realization of a human society without racism. In contrast, according to Irele, Senghor's Negritude is an inner state of Black people. It is a distinctive mode of being, which can be seen in their way of life, and which constitutes their very identity (Irele, 1981). Irele finds value in the concept of Negritude "insofar as it reflects a profound engagement of African minds upon the fundamental question of the African being in history…"

> At a time when Africans are trying to experiment with new ideas and institutions, adapt them to their needs in the light of their traditional value systems, there is the need for a sustained belief in oneself, and this belief can be generated and kept alive by an ideology. This has been, and still is, the function of Negritude. (pg. 86; Ghanaian scholar P. A. V. Ansah, cited in Irele, 1981)

Although the concept of Negritude is not without its critics, if one accepts its premise there are important implications for people of the Black diaspora (Irele, 2001). **Nigrescence** has been described as the process of converting from Negro to Black, i.e., rejecting the deracination imposed by Whites and embracing traditional African values and a Black identity (Parham, 2002; Parham et al., 1999; Tembo, 1980). This process of searching for one's identity can be very powerful, leading perhaps to a positive self-identity or, at least, serving as a buffer against racism and oppression (Parham & Parham, 2002). For additional information on the importance of identify formation and the development of negative identity, I refer you back to the discussion of negative personality development among Black Americans in the chapter on Erik Erikson. But what triggers this critical search for one's identity?

For people of African descent in places such as the United States, the process of nigrescence seems to follow four stages: **pre-encounter**, **encounter**, **immersion-emersion**, and **internalization** (Parham, 2002; Parham et al., 1999). In the pre-encounter stage, the indivdiual views the world from a White frame of reference. They think, act, and behave in ways that devalue and/or deny their Black heritage. Then, however, they encounter personal and/or social events that do not fit with their view of society. Muhammad Ali (formerly Cassius Clay) described in vivid and shocking detail how he was refused service at a restaurant because he was Black, after he had won the Olympic gold medal in boxing and been given the key to the city by the mayor of Louisville, Kentucky (Ali & Ali, 2004)! The individual then becomes immersed in Black culture. This can be a psychologically tumultuous time. For some, everything of value must reflect some aspect of Black and/or African heritage. They withdraw from contact with other racial/ethnic groups, and strong anti-White attitudes and feelings can emerge. Eventually, however, the individual internalizes their Black identity and becomes more secure. The tension, emotionality, and defensiveness of the previous stage is replaced with a calm and secure demeanor. The individual becomes more open minded, more ideologically flexible, and although Black values move to and remain at the forefront, there is a general trend toward being more pluralistic and nonracist, and anti-White attitudes and feelings decline (Parham et al., 1999; see also Mbalia, 1995).

Some Issues for Modern Africa

In a fascinating book entitled *Education for Self-Reliance*, Julius Nyerere (1967) discussed the importance of building the post-colonial educational system in Tanzania. A fundamental premise, according to Nyerere, is that the educational system needed to serve the goals of Tanzania (see also Gichuru, 2005; Khoapa, 1980). Therefore, they had to decide what kind of society they were building. He said their society was based on three principles: equality and respect for human dignity, sharing of resources, and work by everyone and exploitation by none. Interestingly, these principles do not focus on academic content. The successful community life of the village was more important. Social goals, the common good, and cooperation were all emphasized over individual achievement. Nyerere considered it particularly important to avoid intellectual arrogance, so that those who became well educated would not despise those whose skills were non-academic. "Such arrogance has no place in a society of equal citizens" (pg. 8; Nyerere, 1967).

The aim of education in Tanzania became one in which students were to realize they were being educated by the community in order to become intelligent and active members of the community. Since education is provided at the expense of the community, the community is well within its rights to expect those students to become leaders and innovators, to make significantly greater contributions to the community than if they had not received an education (Bennaars, 2005; Sanyal & Kinunda, 1977). To this end, the training of teachers places ideology ahead of content. Student-teachers are taught: 1) the true of meaning of the Tanzanian concept of *ujamaa* (familyhood and socialism; a basis for planned, self-contained villages), 2) to be dedicated and capable teachers who understand and care for the children in their charge, and 3) to deepen the students' general education. Since colonial rulers exploited, humiliated, and ignored the people of Africa for so long, it was believed that teachers should be of sound mind and sound body. Thus, admission into a teacher training program requires a good academic background, sound character, physical fitness, and a good all-around background (Mmari, 1979). Thus, teachers were trained to be good role models for the development of Tanzania and her people (see also Bennaars, 2005; Mbalia, 1995).

Discussion Question: In post-colonial Africa, some countries trained their teachers to educate children in being good citizens, and to be role models for how children should live their lives. Do you agree that teachers should play such an intentional role in helping to raise children? If not, does it seem that this was necessary for a time, given the history of colonization in Africa?

Although most of the work covered in this section has been done by writers, anthropologists, and sociologists, is there a role for more formalized personality testing in Africa? While this may not be the ideal approach for studying personality in African, it would allow us to compare this work with our Western concepts of personality (which constitutes the large majority of this book). There is preliminary evidence that the Five-Factor Model applies well when measuring the personality traits of Africans in Zimbabwe and South Africa (McCrae, 2002; Piedmont et al., 2002). Tembo (1980) developed an African Personality Scale on which Zambian college freshman did indeed demonstrate pro-African personality views (as opposed to anti-African personality views that would have indicated negative effects as the result of colonization; see, however, Mwikamba, 2005). Thomas Parham (2002) has used two personality tests designed to focus more specifically on the concept of an African personality: the **Racial Identity Attitude Scale** (RIAS; which Parham helped develop) and the **African Self-Consciousness Scale**. The RIAS measures the nigrescence construct, whereas the African Self-Consciousness Scale is grounded in Afrocentric theory (closer to the concept of Negritude). However, Parham has come to the conclusion that both of these tests fall short of measuring the core elements of what might be a common African personality, particularly spiritness and the potential biogenetic nature of African people (Parham, 2002). Thus, if this is an appropriate field of study, there certainly needs to be further investigation to determine whether Western concepts of personality assessment apply to the essence of African personality.

A Final Thought

One of the most widely recognized cultural distinctions in psychology today is the difference between individualistic, Western cultures and collectivistic, Eastern cultures. In Western societies, such as the United States of America, the individual not only has the freedom to seek purely personal advancement, it is expected of them. In contrast, the individual in countries such as China is expected to subordinate their own desires and ambitions for the good of the family and their community. With regard to a broad view of the African personality, we find a middle ground. There is significant individual freedom, but individuals are expected to serve their family and community. As a result, the individual also benefits from the overall success of the family and community. Thus, there is an ongoing interplay between the value of the individual and the values of family and community.

When this system works to its best potential, the results are people who flourish and can be proud of themselves. In the words of Dr. J. A. Sofola:

> ...the philosophy, the world-view, values and thought-patterns that form the ingredients or the building-blocks of the African Personality are live-and-let-live; the emphasis on wholesome human relations; the belief of the universality of man and communality of the people in the community; the historic sense of the unity of the human society as consisting of the ancestors, the living and the future generations yet unborn; spiritual attitude to life and attachment to communal life with communal responsibilities; a keen sense of rhythm; the conception of man as one roaming spirit in the chain of spirits in the universe...This is the personality which in its expression of an inward peace and stillness maintains an external composure and gait, head and chin raised high, and with deliberate, calculated dignified steps proclaims to the world: "Black is beautiful" and "I am black and proud of being so." (pp. 143-144; Sofola, 1973)

Review of Key Points

- Roughly speaking, African can be divided into two distinct regions: North Africa and sub-Saharan Africa.
- Black Africans are the people of sub-Saharan Africa.
- The African worldview focuses on interdependence, rhythm, harmony, and spirit.
- Religion and spirituality are very important to Africans, and humans hold a privileged position at the junction of spirit and nature.
- Time is part of the cyclical rhythm of life, set by God, who knows what is right.
- The tribe is the basic unit of life, not the individual. The family includes a broad range of relatives, and caring for one's family, especially the aged, is an important obligation.
- Marriage is an important institution, providing a rhythmic link between past, present, and future. A marriage is only complete when the couple has children.
- Hospitality to all people, including strangers, is expected, and a sign of good character.
- *Ubuntu* encompasses the social harmony that is valued in African life.
- Among the people of the African diaspora, *ubuntu* may be seen in action as the soul referred to in soul food, soul music, and soul brothers.
- Negritude represents the active claiming of those best elements of a common African personality by the people of Africa.
- Nigrescence is the process of converting from Negro to Black among the people of the African diaspora. It appears to follow four stages: pre-encounter, encounter, immersion-emersion, and internalization.
- In post-colonial African countries, educational systems were developed based on the ideals of the new nations. Teachers were trained to embody those ideals.
- There is some evidence for the usefulness of traditional approaches to studying personality in Africa with formalized testing. However, significantly more work needs to be done.
- Common elements of personality across Africa seem to represent a middle ground between the individualistic personalities seen in the West, and the collectivistic personalities seen in the East.

Review of Key Terms

African Personality Scale	Negritude	soul music
African Self-Consciousness Scale	nigrescence	spirit
being	North Africa	spiritness
diaspora	pre-encounter	Sub-Saharan Africa
encounter	Racial Identity Attitude Scale	tribe
hospitality	soul	*ubuntu*
immersion-emersion	soul brother	*ujamaa*
internalization	soul food	worldview

Annotated Bibliography

Chatterji, S. K. (1960). ***Africanism: The African personality*****. Calcutta, India: Bengal Publishers Private Ltd.**

This is a wonderful book written by a professor from India. Chatterji had been a student of African culture since 1919, and finally had occasion to visit Ghana, Nigeria, and Liberia in 1954. His writing is very engaging.

Irele, A. (1981). ***The African experience in literature and ideology*****. London, England: Heinemann.**
Irele, A. (2001). ***The African imagination: Literature in African and the Black Diaspora*****. New York, NY: Oxford University Press.**

As noted in the titles, these books offer Irele's perspective on the experience of being African, as it is presented in African literature. The first book includes an extensive discussion of Negritude.

Khoapa, B. A. (1980). ***The African personality*****. Tokyo, Japan: The United Nations University.**

This brief report contains a concise, yet surprisingly broad overview of African life and culture. It also offers a direct comparison of African culture to two styles of Western culture, and the roles of Christianity and Islam in African religion.

Nyerere, J. K. (1967). ***Education for self-reliance*****. Dar es Salaam, Tanzania: Ministry of Information and Tourism.**

Again, the depth of this book is not readily apparent when one sees how short it is. Nonetheless, it describes the intentional development of a post-colonial educational system in Tanzania based on the philosophical and political ideals of the new nation. In describing this vision, Nyerere conveys in clear and simple terms what it means to be African.

Parham, T. A., White, J. L., & Ajamu, A. (1999). ***The psychology of Blacks: An African-centered perspective*****. Upper Saddle River, NJ: Prentice Hall.**
Parham, T. A. (Ed.). (2002). ***Counseling persons of African descent: Raising the bar of practitioner competence*****. Upper Saddle River, NJ: Prentice Hall.**

Thomas Parham is a leading African American scholar in the field of psychology. These books cover a wide range of African and African American psychology, with special attention being paid to issues of education, development, mental health, and psychotherapy.

Samkange, S. & Samkange, T. M. (1980). ***Hunhuism or Ubuntuism: A Zimbabwe indigenous political philosophy*****. Salisbury, England: Graham Publishing.**

This very readable and entertaining book gives a wonderful perspective on life in Africa and the role that human relationships (in the spirit of *ubuntu*) have played in the development of African nations.

Senghor, L. S. (1965). ***Prose and poetry*** **(J. Reed & C. Wake, Trans.). London, England: Heinemann.**
Sofola, J. A. (1973). ***African culture and the African personality (What makes an African person African)*****. Ibadan, Nigeria: African Resources Publishers Co.**

These very insightful books were written by African scholars. Senghor was a poet, philosopher, and statesman. He was the first president of Senegal. This book offers a sampling of both his scholarly writings (including Negritude and rhythm) and his poetry. Likewise, Sofola offers a wide variety of perspectives on his view of what it means to be African.

References

Adler, Alexandra (1930a). Technique of educational guidance. In A. Adler (Ed.), *Guiding the child: On the principles of Individual Psychology* (pp. 102-118). New York, NY: Greenberg.

Adler, Alexandra (1930b). The only child. In A. Adler (Ed.), *Guiding the child: On the principles of Individual Psychology* (pp. 195-209). New York, NY: Greenberg.

Adler, A. (1910/1978). Masculine protest and a critique of Freud. In H. L. Ansbacher & R. R. Ansbacher (Eds.), *Co-operation between the sexes: Writings on women and men, love and marriage, and sexuality* (pp. 32-74). New York, NY: W. W. Norton & Company.

Adler, A. (1912a/1963). Psychical hermaphrodism and the masculine protest - The cardinal problem of nervous diseases. In A. Adler (Ed.), *The practice and theory of Individual Psychology* (pp. 17-22). Paterson, NJ: Littlefield, Adams & Co.

Adler, A. (1912b/1963). Dreams and dream-interpretation. In A. Adler (Ed.), *The practice and theory of Individual Psychology* (pp. 214-226). Paterson, NJ: Littlefield, Adams & Co.

Adler, A. (1913a/1963). The study of child psychology and neurosis. In A. Adler (Ed.), *The practice and theory of Individual Psychology* (pp. 59-77). Paterson, NJ: Littlefield, Adams & Co.

Adler, A. (1913b/1963). Individual-Psychological treatment of neuroses. In A. Adler (Ed.), *The practice and theory of Individual Psychology* (pp. 32-50). Paterson, NJ: Littlefield, Adams & Co.

Adler, A. (1914/1963). Individual Psychology, its assumptions and its results. In A. Adler (Ed.), *The practice and theory of individual psychology* (pp. 1-15). Paterson, NJ: Littlefield, Adams & Co.

Adler, A. (1917). *Study of organ inferiority and its psychical compensation: A contribution to clinical medicine.* New York, NY: The Nervous and Mental Disease Publishing Company.

Adler, A. (1918/1963). Individual-psychological education. In A. Adler (Ed.), *The practice and theory of Individual Psychology* (pp. 317-326). Paterson, NJ: Littlefield, Adams & Co.

Adler, A. (Ed.). (1925/1963). *The practice and theory of Individual Psychology*. Paterson, NJ: Littlefield, Adams & Co.

Adler, A. (1927/1978). The myth of women's inferiority. In H. L. Ansbacher & R. R. Ansbacher (Eds.), *Co-operation between the sexes: Writings on women and men, love and marriage, and sexuality* (pp. 3-31). New York, NY: W. W. Norton & Company.

Adler, A. (1928). *Understanding human nature*. London, England: George Allen & Unwin.

Adler, A. (1929a). *The science of living*. New York, NY: Greenberg.

Adler, A. (1929b). *The case of Miss R.: The interpretation of a life story*. New York, NY: Greenberg.

Adler, A. (1929/1964). *Problems of neurosis: A book of case histories*. New York, NY: Harper & Row.

Adler, A. (Ed.). (1930a). *Guiding the child: On the principles of Individual Psychology*. New York, NY: Greenberg.

Adler, A. (1930b). *The education of children*. New York, NY: Greenberg.

Adler, A. (1930c). *The pattern of life*. New York, NY: Cosmopolitan Book Corporation.

Adler, A. (1930d). A case from guidance practice. In A. Adler (Ed.), *Guiding the child: On the principles of Individual Psychology* (pp. 127-147). New York, NY: Greenberg.

Adler, A. (1931a). *What life should mean to you*. New York, NY: Capricorn Books.

Adler, A. (1931b). *The case of Mrs. A (the diagnosis of a life-style)*. London, England: The C. W. Daniel Company.

Adler, A. (1932a/1964). The structure of neurosis. In H. L. Ansbacher & R. R. Ansbacher (Eds.), *Superiority and social interest: A collection of later writings* (pp. 83-95). New York, NY: The Viking Press.

Adler, A. (1932b/1964). Technique of treatment. In H. L. Ansbacher & R. R. Ansbacher (Eds.), *Superiority and social interest: A collection of later writings* (pp. 191-201). New York, NY: The Viking Press.

Adler, A. (1933/1964). Religion and Individual Psychology. In H. L. Ansbacher & R. R. Ansbacher (Eds.), *Superiority and social interest: A collection of later writings* (pp. 271-308). New York, NY: The Viking Press.

Adler, A. (1935/1964). The structure and prevention of delinquency. In H. L. Ansbacher & R. R. Ansbacher (Eds.), *Superiority and social interest: A collection of later writings* (pp. 253-268). New York, NY: The Viking Press.

Adler, A. (1958). *The education of the individual*. New York, NY: Philosophical Library.

Adler, A. (1963). *The problem child: The life style of the difficult child as analyzed in specific cases*. New York, NY: Capricorn Books.

Adler, A. (1964). *Social interest: A challenge to mankind.* New York, NY: Capricorn Books.

Adler, A. (1967). On suicide. In P. Freidman (Ed.), *On suicide: With particular reference to suicide among young students* (pp. 109-121). New York, NY: International Universities Press.

Adler, K. A. (1959). Life style in schizophrenia. In K. A. Adler & D. Deutsch (Eds.), *Essays in Individual psychology: Contemporary applications of Alfred Adler's theories* (pp. 45-55). New York, NY: Grove Press.

References

Ahmed, M. & Boisvert, C. M. (2006). Using positive psychology with special mental health populations. *American Psychologist, 61*, 333-335.

Ajaan Fuang Jotiko (2005). *Awareness itself.* Barre, MA: Dhamma Dana Publications.

Ajahn Chah (2001). *Being Dharma: The essence of the Buddha's teachings*. Boston, MA: Shambhala.

Ajahn Sumedho (1987). *Mindfulness: The path to the deathless*. Hertfordshire, England: Amaravati Publications.

Ajahn Sumedho (1995). *The mind and the way: Buddhist reflections on life*. Boston, MA: Wisdom Publications.

Alexander, I. E. (1990). *Personology: Method and content in personality assessment and psychobiography*. Durham, NC: Duke University Press.

Ali, M. & Ali, H. Y. (2004). *The soul of a butterfly: Reflections on life's journey* [CD]. New York, NY: Simon & Schuster.

Ali, M. M. (1990). *The religion of Islam*. Dublin, OH: Ahmadiyya Anjuman Isha'at Islam Lahore Inc.

Ali, M. M. (2002). *The Holy Qur'an*. Dublin, OH: Ahmadiyya Anjuman Isha'at Islam Lahore Inc.

Allik, J. & McCrae, R. R. (2002). A Five-Factor Theory perspective. In R. R. McCrae & J. Allik (Eds.), *The Five-Factor Model of personality across cultures* (pp. 303-322). New York, NY: Kluwer Academic/Plenum Publishers.

Allport, G. W. (1937). *Personality: A psychological interpretation*. New York, NY: Henry Holt and Company.

Allport, G. W. (1942). *The use of personal documents in psychological science*. New York, NY: Social Science Research Council.

Allport, G. W. (1948). *ABC's of scapegoating*. New York, NY: Anti-Defamation League of B'nai B'rith.

Allport, G. W. (1950). *The individual and his religion.* New York, NY: The Macmillan Company.

Allport, G. W. (1955). *Becoming: Basic considerations for a psychology of personality*. New Haven, CT: Yale University Press.

Allport, G. W. (1960). *Personality & social encounter*. Boston, MA: Beacon Press.

Allport, G. W. (1961). *Pattern and growth in personality*. New York, NY: Holt, Rinehart and Winston.

Allport, G. W. (1965). *Letters from Jenny*. New York, NY: A Harvest/HBJ Book.

Allport, G. W. (1968). *The person in psychology*. Boston, MA: Beacon Press.

Allport, G. W. (1979). *The nature of prejudice - 25th Anniversary edition*. Reading, MA: Addison-Wesley Publishing Company.

Allport, G. W. & Postman, L. (1947). *The psychology of rumor*. New York, NY: Russell & Russell.

Allport, G. W. & Vernon, P. E. (1933). *Studies in expressive movement*. New York, NY: The Macmillan Company.

American Psychiatric Association. (2000). *Diagnostic and statistical manual of mental disorders* (4th Ed.) *Text Revision*. Washington, DC: Author.

American Psychiatric Association. (2013). *Diagnostic and statistical manual of mental disorders* (5th Ed.). Washington, DC: Author.

Anders Ericsson, K. (2004). Deliberate practice and acquisition and maintenance of expert performance in medicine and related domains. *Academic Medicine, 79*, S70-S81.

Anders Ericsson, K., Krampe, R. T., & Tesch-Romer, C. (1993). The role of deliberate practice in the acquisition of expert performance. *Psychological Review, 3*, 363-406.

Anderson, C. A., Berkowitz, L., Donnerstein, E., Huesmann, L. R., Johnson, J. D., Linz, D., Malamuth, N. M., & Wartella, E. (2003). The influence of media violence on youth. *Psychological Science in the Public Interest, 4*, 81-110.

Ansbacher, H. L. & Ansbacher, R. R. (Eds). (1964). *Alfred Adler - Superiority and social interest: A collection of later writings*. New York, NY: The Viking Press.

Antonio, A. L., Chang, M. J., Hakuta, K., Kenny, D. A., Levin, S., & Milem, J. F. (2004). Effects of racial diversity on complex thinking in college students. *Psychological Science, 15*, 507-510.

Arber, S., Davidson, K., & Ginn, J. (Eds.). (2003). *Gender and ageing: Changing roles and relationships*. Maidenhead, England: Open University Press.

Armstrong, K. (1993). *A history of God: The 4,000-year quest of Judaism, Christianity, and Islam*. New York, NY: Ballantine Books.

Arnett, J. J. (2002). The psychology of globalization. *American Psychologist, 57*, 774-783.

Aronson, H. B. (2004). *Buddhist practice on Western ground: Reconciling Eastern ideals and Western psychology*. Boston, MA: Shambhala.

Aslan, R. (2005). From Islam, pluralist democracies will surely grow. *The Chronicle of Higher Education, 51*, B6.

Aslan, R. (2006). *No god but God: The origins, evolution, and future of Islam*. New York, NY: Random House Trade Paperbacks.

Aspinwall, L. G. & Staudinger, U. M. (Eds.). (2003). *A psychology of human strengths: Fundamental questions and future directions for a positive psychology*. Washington, DC: American Psychological Association.

Atkinson, L. (1983). Women in the martial arts: A new spirit rising. New York, NY: Dodd, Mead & Company.

Atwood, J. (1999). *Capoeira: A martial art and a cultural tradition*. New York, NY: Rosen Publishing Group.

Axelson, J. A. (1999). *Counseling and development in a*

multicultural society, 3rd Ed. Pacific Grove, CA: Brooks/Cole.

Bailey, A. A. (1927). *The light of the soul: The Yoga Sutras of Pantanjali.* New York, NY: Lucis Publishing.

Baker, R. & Henry, G. (2005). *Merton & Sufism: The untold story.* Louisville, KY: Fons Vitae.

Baltes, P. B. & Staudinger, U. M. (2000). Wisdon: A metaheuristic (pragmatic) to orchestrate mind and virtue toward excellence. *American Psychologist, 55*, 122-136.

Bandura, A. (1969). *Principles of behavior modification.* New York, NY: Holt, Rinehart and Winston.

Bandura, A. (1973). *Aggression: A social learning analysis.* Englewood Cliffs, NJ: Prentice-Hall.

Bandura, A. (1977). *Social learning theory.* Englewood Cliffs, NJ: Prentice-Hall.

Bandura, A. (1986). *Social foundations of thought & action: A social cognitive theory.* Upper Saddle River, NJ: Prentice-Hall.

Bandura, A. (1997). *Self-efficacy: The exercise of control.* New York, NY: W. H. Freeman and Company.

Bandura, A. (2006). Toward a psychology of human agency. *Perspectives on Psychological Science, 1*, 164-180.

Bandura, A. & Mischel, W. (1965). Modification of self-imposed delay of reward through exposure to live and symbolic models. *Journal of Personality and Social Psychology 2*, 698-705.

Bandura, A., Ross, D., & Ross, S. A. (1961). Transmission of aggression through imitation of aggressive models. *Journal of Abnormal and Social Psychology, 63*, 575-582.

Bandura, A., Ross, D., & Ross, S. A. (1963a). Imitation of film-mediated aggressive models. *Journal of Abnormal and Social Psychology, 66*, 3-11.

Bandura, A., Ross, D., & Ross, S. A. (1963b). A comparative test of the status envy, social power, and secondary reinforcement theories of identificatory learning. *Journal of Abnormal and Social Psychology, 67*, 527-534.

Bandura, A. & Walters, R. H. (1959). *Adolescent aggression: A study of the influence of child-training practices and family interrelationships.* New York, NY: The Ronald Press Company.

Bandura, A. & Walters, R. H. (1963). *Social learning and personality development.* New York, NY: Holt, Rinehart and Winston.

Bankart, C. P., Dockett, K. H., & Dudley-Grant, G. R. (2005). On the path of the Buddha: A psychologists' guide to the history of Buddhism. In K. H. Dockett, G. R. Dudley-Grant, & C. P. Bankart (Eds.), *Psychology and Buddhism: From individual to global community* (pp. 13-44). New York, NY: Kluwer Academic/Plenum Publishers.

Barash, D. P. (1977). *Sociobiology and behavior.* New York, NY: Elsevier.

Barash, D. (1979). *The whisperings within: Evolution and the origin of human nature.* New York, NY: Harper & Row, Publishers.

Bargh, J. A. & Williams, E. L. (2006). The automaticity of social life. *Current Directions in Psychological Science*, 15, 1-4.

Bar-Haim, Y., Ziv, T., Lamy, D., & Hodes, R. M. (2006). Nature and nurture in Own-race face processing. *Psychological Science, 17*, 159-163.

Barinaga, M. (2003). Studying the Well Trained Mind. *Science, 302*, 44-46.

Barker, R. G., Wright, B. A., Meyerson, L., & Gonick, M. R. (1953). *Adjustment to physical handicap and illness: A survey of the social psychology of physique and disability.* New York, NY: Social Science Research Council.

Barkow, J. H., Cosmides, L., & Tooby, J. (1992). *The adapted mind: Evolutionary psychology and the generation of culture.* New York, NY: Oxford University Press.

Barnett, S. M. (2007). Complex questions rarely have simple answers. *Psychological Science in the Public Interest, 8*, i-ii.

Barrow, G. M. (1986). *Aging, the individual, and society, 3rd Ed.* St. Paul, MN: West Publishing Company.

Batchelor, S. (1983). *Alone with others: An existential approach to Buddhism.* New York, NY: Grove Press.

Batson, C. D., Ahmad, N., Lishner, D. A., & Tsang, J.-A. (2005). Empathy and altruism. In C. R. Snyder & S. J. Lopez (Eds.), *Handbook of positive psychology* (pp. 485-498). New York, NY: Oxford University Press.

Battle, E. S. & Rotter, J. B. (1963). Children's feelings of personal control as related to social class and ethnic group. *Journal of Personality, 31*, 482-490.

Bauer, J. J. & McAdams, D. P. (2004a). Growth goals, maturity, and well-being. *Developmental Psychology, 40*, 114-127.

Bauer, J. J. & McAdams, D. P. (2004b). Personal growth in adults' stories of life transitions. *Journal of Personality, 72*, 573-602.

Bauer, J. J., McAdams, D. P., & Sakaeda, A. R. (2005a). Crystallization of desire and crystallization of discontent in narratives of life-changing decisions. *Journal of Personality, 73*, 1181-1214.

Bauer, J. J., McAdams, D. P., & Sakaeda, A. R. (2005b). Interpreting the good life: Growth memories in the lives of mature, happy people. *Journal of Personality and Social Psychology, 88*, 203-217.

Beck, A. T. (1967). *The diagnosis and management of depression.* Philadelphia, PA: University of Pennsylvania Press.

Beck, A. T. (1988). *Love is never enough: How couples can overcome misunderstandings, resolve conflicts, and solve relationship problems through cognitive therapy*. New York, NY: Harper & Row Publishers.

Beck, A. T. (1999). *Prisoners of hate: The cognitive basis of anger, hostility, and violence*. New York, NY: HarperCollins Publishers.

Beck, A. T. & Emery, G. (1985). *Anxiety disorders and phobias: A cognitive perspective*. New York, NY: Basic Books.

Beck, A. T. & Freeman, A. (1990). *Cognitive therapy of personality disorders*. New York, NY: Guilford Press.

Beck, A. T., Resnik, H. L. P., & Lettieri, D. J. (Eds.). (1974). *The prediction of suicide*. Bowie, MD: The Charles Press Publishers.

Beck, A. T., Rush, A. J., Shaw, B. F., & Emery, G. (1979). *Cognitive therapy of depression*. New York, NY: Guilford Press.

Beck, A. T. & Weishaar, M. E. (1995). Cognitive therapy. In R. J. Corsini & D. Wedding (Eds.), *Current psychotherapies, 5th Ed.* (pp. 229-261). Itasca, IL: F. E. Peacock Publishers.

Beck, A. T., Wright, F. D., Newman, C. F., & Liese, B. S. (1993). *Cognitive therapy of substance abuse*. New York, NY: The Guilford Press.

Beck, R. C. (1978). *Motivation: Theories and principles*. Englewood Cliffs, NJ: Prentice-Hall.

Begley, S. (2007). *Train your mind, change your brain: How a new science reveals our extraordinary potential to transform ourselves*. New York, NY: Ballantine Books.

Belgrave, F. Z. & Allison, K. W. (2006). *African American psychology: From Africa to America*. Thousand Oaks, CA: Sage Publications.

Belsky, J. (1999). *The psychology of aging, 3rd Ed.* Pacific Grove, CA: Brooks/Cole.

Benchley, P. (1974). *Jaws*. Garden City, NJ: Doubleday.

Benjamin, L. S. (2005). Interpersonal theory of personality disorders. In M. F. Lenzenweger & J. F. Clarkin (Eds.), *Major theories of personality disorder, 2nd Ed.* (pp. 157-230). New York, NY: The Guilford Press.

Benjamin, L. T., Jr. (1993). *A history of psychology in letters*. Dubuque, IA: Brown & Benchmark.

Benjamin, Jr., L. T. & Crouse, E. M. (2002). The American Psychological Association's response to *Brown v. Board of Education*: The case of Kenneth B. Clark. *American Psychologist, 57*, 38-50.

Bennaars, G. A. (2005). Toward a pedagogy of hope. In G. J. Wanjohi & G. W. Wanjohi (Eds.), *Social and religious concerns of East Africa: A Wajibu anthology* (pp. 167-174). Nairobi, Kenya: Wajibu: A Journal of Social and Religious Concern.

Berscheid, E. (2003). The human's greatest strength: Other humans. In L. G. Aspinwall & U. M. Staudinger (Eds.), *A psychology of human strengths: Fundamental questions and future directions for a positive psychology* (pp. 37-47). Washington, DC: American Psychological Association.

Bertocci, P. A. (Ed.). (1978). *Waiting for the Lord: 33 Meditations on God and man - Gordon W. Allport*. New York, NY: Macmillan Publishing.

Besserman, P. (1997). *The Shambhala guide to Kabbalah and Jewish mysticism*. Boston, MA: Shambhala.

Biernat, M. (2003). Toward a broader view of social stereotyping. *American Psychologist, 58*, 1019-1027.

Biglan, A., Mrazek, P. J., Carnine, D., & Flay, B. R. (2003). The intregration of research and practice in the prevention of youth problem behaviors. *American Psychologist, 58*, 433-440.

Bjork, D. W. (1997). *B. F. Skinner: A life*. Washington, D.C.: American Psychological Association.

Bloland, S. E. (2005). *In the shadow of fame: A memoir by the daughter of Erik H. Erikson*. New York, NY: Viking.

Bonanno, G. A. (2004). Loss, trauma, and human resilience: Have we underestimated the human capacity to thrive after extremely aversive events? *American Psychologist, 59*, 20-28.

Bonanno, G. A. (2005a). Resilience in the face of potential trauma. *Current Directions in Psychological Science, 14*, 135-138.

Bonanno, G. A. (2005b). Clarifying and extending the construct of adult resilience. *American Psychologist, 60*, 265-267.

Bonaparte, M. (1953). *Female sexuality*. New York, NY: Grove Press.

Boniwell, I. (2005). Beyond time management: How the latest research on time perspective and perceived time use can assist clients with time-related concerns. *International Journal of Evidence Based Coaching and Mentoring, 3*, 61-74.

Boniwell, I. & Zimbardo, P. (2003). Time to find the right balance. *The Psychologist, 16*, 129-131.

Borynski, M. L. (2003). Waking up: Using mindfulness meditation in graduate school. *APS Observer, 16*, 33-34.

Bottome, P. (1957). *Alfred Adler: A portrait from life*. New York, NY: The Vanguard Press.

Bouchard, Jr., T. J. (1994). Genes, environment, and personality. *Science, 264*, 1700-1701.

Bouchard, Jr., T. J. (2004). Genetic influence on human psychological traits: A survey. *Current Directions in Psychological Science, 13*, 148-151.

Bouchard, Jr., T. J. & McGue, M. (1990). Genetic and rearing environmental influences on adult personality: An analysis of adopted twins reared apart. *Journal of Personality, 58*, 263-292.

Bouchard, Jr., T. J., Lykken, D. T., McGue, M., Segal, N. L., & Tellegen, A. (1990). Sources of human psychological differences: The Minnesota Study of Twins Reared Apart. *Science, 250*, 223-228.

Boukreev, A. & DeWalt, G. W. (1997). *The climb: Tragic*

ambitions on Everest. New York, NY: St. Martin's Press.

Bouwsma, W. J. (1978). Christian adulthood. In E. H. Erikson (Ed.), *Adulthood* (pp. 81-96). New York, NY: W. W. Norton & Company.

Bower, G. H. & Hilgard, E. R. (1981). *Theories of learning, 5th Ed.* Englewood Cliffs, NJ: Prentice-Hall.

Boyd, R. & Richerson, P. J. (1985). *Culture and the evolutionary process*. Chicago, IL: The University of Chicago Press.

Boyer, H. C. & Yearwood, L. (1995). *How sweet the sound: The golden age of gospel*. Washington, DC: Elliott and Clark Publishing.

Bozhovich, L. I. (1969). The personality of school children and problems of education. In M. Cole & I. Maltzman (Eds.), *A handbook of contemporary Soviet psychology* (pp. 209-248). New York, NY: Basic Books.

Brach, T. (2003). *Radical acceptance: Embracing your life with the heart of a Buddha*. New York, NY: Bantam Books.

Brantley, J. (2003). *Calming your anxious mind: How mindfulness and compassion can free you from anxiety, fear, and panic*. Oakland, CA: New Harbinger Publications.

Brazier, D. (1995). *Zen therapy: Transcending the sorrows of the human mind*. New York, NY: Wiley & Sons.

Breisach, E. (1962). *Introduction to modern Existentialism*. New York, NY: Grove Press.

Brian, D. (1995). *Genius talk: Conversations with Nobel scientists and other luminaries*. New York, NY: Plenum Press.

Brislin, R. (1999). Communicating information about culture and personality in formal cross-cultural training programs. In Y.-T. Lee, C. R. McCauley, & J. G. Draguns (Eds.), *Personality and person perception across cultures* (pp. 255-277). Mahway, NJ: Lawrence Erlbaum Associates, Publishers.

Brislin, R. (2000). *Understanding culture's influence on behavior, 2nd Ed.* Belmont, CA: Wadsworth Thomson.

Broughton, V. (1985). *Black gospel: An illustrated history of the gospel sound.* Poole, UK: Blandford Press.

Buchanan, A. J. (2003). *Mother shock: Loving every (other) minute of it*. Emeryville, CA: Seal Press.

Burns, S. (2004). *To the mountaintop: Martin Luther King Jr.'s sacred mission to save America: 1955-1968*. New York, NY: Harper San Francisco.

Burston, D. (2001). Sampson among the Philistines. *American Psychologist, 56*, 1175-1176.

Burton, N, Hart, P., & Laughlin, J. (1973). *The Asian Journal of Thomas Merton*. New York, NY: A New Directions Book.

Busia, K. A. (1972). The African world-view: A comparative approach. In S. H. Irvine & J. T. Sanders (Eds.), *Cultural adaptation within modern Africa* (pp. 77-80). New York, NY: Teachers College Press.

Buss, D. M. (1999). *Evolutionary psychology: The new science of the mind.* Boston, MA: Allyn and Bacon.

Buss, D. M. (2000a). The evolution of happiness. *American Psychologist, 55*, 15-23.

Buss, D. M. (2000b). *The dangerous passion: Why jealousy is as necessary as love and sex*. New York, NY: Free Press.

Buss, D. M. (2003). *The evolution of desire: Strategies of human mating, Revised Ed.* New York, NY: Basic Books.

Buss, D. M. (2005). *The murderer next door: Why the mind is designed to kill.* New York, NY: Penguin Press.

Byrom, T. (1993). *Dhammapada: The Sayings of the Buddha*. Boston, MA: Shambala.

Cacioppo, J. R., Visser, P. S., & Pickett, C. L. (Eds.). (2006). *Social Neuroscience: People thinking about thinking people.* Cambridge, MA: The MIT Press.

Calasanti, T. M. & Slevin, K. F. (2001). *Gender, social inequalities, and aging*. Walnut Creek, CA: AltaMira Press.

Callaghan, T., Rochat, P., Lillard, A., Claux, M. L., Odden, H., Itakura, S., Sombat, T., & Singh, S. (2005). Synchrony in the onset of mental-state reasoning: Evidence from five cultures. *Psychological Science, 16*, 378-384.

Campbell, D. T. & Stanley, J. C. (1963). *Experimental and quasi-experimental designs for research.* Chicago, IL: Rand McNally.

Cantor, N. (2003). Constructive cognition, personal goals, and the social embedding of personality. In L. G. Aspinwall & U. M. Staudinger (Eds.), *A psychology of human strengths: Fundamental questions and future directions for a positive psychology* (pp. 49-60). Washington, DC: American Psychological Association.

Cantril, H. & Allport, G. W. (1935). *The psychology of radio*. New York, NY: Harper & Brothers Publishers.

Carnagey, N. L. & Anderson, C. A. (2005). The effects of reward and punishment in violent video games on aggressive affect, cognition, and behavior. *Psychological Science, 16*, 882-889,

Carr, C. (2002). *The lessons of terror - A history of warfare against civilians: Why it has always failed and why it will fail again.* New York, NY: Random House.

Carstairs, G. M. (1961). Cross-cultural psychiatric interviewing. In B. Kaplan (Ed.), *Studying personality cross-culturally* (pp. 533-548). Evanston, IL: Row, Peterson and Company.

Cassell, E. J. (2005). Compassion. In C. R. Snyder & S. J. Lopez (Eds.), *Handbook of positive psychology* (pp. 434-445). New York, NY: Oxford University Press.

Castillo, R. J. (1997). *Culture & mental illness: A client-centered approach.* Pacific Grove, CA: Brooks/Cole.

Catania, A. C. & Harnad, S. (Eds.). (1988). *The selection of behavior - The operant conditioning of B. F. Skinner: Comments and consequences.* New York, NY: Cambridge University Press.

Cattell, H. B. (1986). The art of clinical assessment by the 16 P.F., CAQ, and MAT. In R. B. Cattell & R. C. Johnson (Eds.), *Functional psychological testing: Principles and Instruments* (pp. 377-424). New York, NY: Brunner/Mazel.

Cattell, H. E. P. & Horn, J. (2007). A short biography - Raymond Bernard Cattell. Retrieved April 25, 2007, www.cattell.net/devon/rbcbio.htm

Cattell, R. B. (1936). *A guide to mental testing.* London, England: University of London Press, Ltd.

Cattell, R. B. (1946). *Description and measurement of personality.* Yonkers-on-Hudson, NY: World Book Company.

Cattell, R. B. (1950a). *An introduction to personality study.* London, England: Hutchinson's University Library.

Cattell, R. B. (1950b). *Personality: A systematic theoretical and factual study.* New York, NY: McGraw-Hill Book Company.

Cattell, R. B. (1952). *Factor analysis: An introduction and manual for the psychologist and social scientist.* New York, NY: Harper & Brothers, Publishers.

Cattell, R. B. (1956). Second-order personality factors in the questionnaire realm. *Journal of Consulting Psychology, 20,* 411-418.

Cattell, R. B. (1957). *Personality and motivation structure and measurement.* Yonkers-on-Hudson, NY: World Book Company.

Cattell, R. B. (1965). *The scientific analysis of personality.* Baltimore, MD: Penguin Books.

Cattell, R. B. (Ed.). (1966). *Handbook of multivariate experimental psychology.* Chicago, IL: Rand McNally & Company.

Cattell, R. B. (1972). *A new morality from science: Beyondism.* New York, NY: Pergamon Press.

Cattell, R. B. (Ed.). (1983). *Intelligence and national achievement.* Washington, DC: The Cliveden Press.

Cattell, R. B. & Scheier, I. H. (1961). *The meaning and measurement of neuroticism and anxiety.* New York, NY: The Ronald Press Company.

Ceci, S. J. & Bjork, R. A. (2003). Science, politics, and violence in the media. *Psychological Science in the Public Interest, 4,* i-iii.

Chaline, E. (2003a). *Martial arts for athletic conditioning.* Broomall, PA: Mason Crest Publishers.

Chaline, E. (2003b). *Martial arts for women.* Broomall, PA: Mason Crest Publishers.

Chamove, A. S., Eysenck, H. J., & Harlow, H. F. (1972). Personality in monkeys: Factor analyses of rhesus social behavior. *Quarterly Journal of Experimental Psychology, 24,* 496-504.

Chao, R. (2001). Integrating culture and attachment. *American Psychologist, 56,* 822-823.

Chapman, A. H. & Chapman, M. C. M. S. (1980). *Harry Stack Sullivan's concepts of personality development and psychiatric illness.* New York, NY: Brunner/Mazel.

Chappell, D. W. (2005). Buddhist social principles. In K. H. Dockett, G. R. Dudley-Grant, & C. P. Bankart (Eds.), *Psychology and Buddhism: From individual to global community* (pp. 259-274). New York, NY: Kluwer Academic/Plenum Publishers.

Chatterji, S. K. (1960). *Africanism: The African personality.* Calcutta, India: Bengal Publishers Private Ltd.

Chervin, R. (1992). *Prayers of the women mystics.* Ann Arbor, MI: Servant Publications.

Chesterman, B. (2003). *Taekwondo.* Broomall, PA: Mason Crest Publishers.

Chilson, R. (1995). *All will be well: Based on the classic spirituality of Julian of Norwich.* Notre Dame, IN: Ave Maria Press.

Chodorow, N. J. (1989). *Feminism and psychoanalytic theory.* New Haven, CT: Yale University Press.

Chodorow, N. J. (1994). *Femininities, masculinities, sexualities: Freud and beyond.* Lexington, KY: The University Press of Kentucky.

Chodorow, N. J. (1999a). *The reproduction of mothering – With a new preface.* Berkeley, CA: University of California Press.

Chodorow, N. J. (1999b). *The power of feelings: Personal meaning in psychoanalysis, gender, and culture.* New Haven, CT: Yale University Press.

Christensen, A., Sevier, M., Simpson, L. E., & Gattis, K. S. (2004). Acceptance, mindfulness, and change in couple therapy. In S. C. Hayes, V. M. Follette, & M. M. Linehan (Eds.), *Mindfulness and acceptance: Expanding the cognitive-behavioral tradition* (pp. 288-309). New York, NY: The Guilford Press.

Chrzanowski, G. (1977). *Interpersonal approach to psychoanalysis: Contemporary view of Harry Stack Sullivan.* New York, NY: Gardner Press.

Chu, F. J. (2003). *The martial Way and its virtues: Tao De Gung.* Boston, MA: YMAA Publication Center.

Clark, K. B. & Clark, M. P. (1947). Racial identification and preference in Negro children. In T. N. Newcomb & E. L. Hartley (Eds.), *Readings in Social Psychology* (pp 169-178). New York, NY: Henry Holt.

Clark, L. A., Vorhies, L., & McEwen, J. L. (1994). Personality disorder syptomatology from the

Five-Factor Model perspective. In P. T. Costa, Jr. & T. A. Widiger (Eds.), *Personality disorders and the Five-Factor Model of personality* (pp. 95-116). Washington, DC: American Psychological Association.

Clawson, T., Firment, C., & Trower, T. (1981). Test anxiety: Another origin for racial bias in standardized testing. *Measurement and Evaluation in Guidance, 13*, 210-215.

Clement, O. (1993). *The roots of Christian mysticism.* Hyde Park, NY: New City Press.

Cloninger, C. R. (2004). *Feeling good: The science of well-being.* New York, NY: Oxford University Press.

Clouse, R. (Director), & Allin, M. (Screenwriter). (1998). *Enter the dragon* [25th Anniversary Special Edition Motion Picture]. United States: Warner Brothers.

Cohen, D. & Gunz, A. (2002). As seen by the other…: Perspectives on the self in the memories and emotional perceptions of Easterners and Westerners. *Psychological Science, 13*, 55-59.

Cohen, S. & Pressman, S. D. (2006). Positive affect and health. *Current Directions in Psychological Science, 15*, 122-125.

Cole, M. & Maltzman, I. (Eds.). (1969). *A handbook of contemporary Soviet psychology.* New York, NY: Basic Books.

Coles, R. (1970). *Erik H. Erikson: The growth of his work.* Boston, MA: Little, Brown and Company.

Coles, R. (1992). *Anna Freud: The dream of psychoanalysis.* Reading, MA: Addison-Wesley.

Compton, W. C. (2005). *An introduction to positive psychology.* Belmont, CA: Thomson Wadsworth.

Cone, J. H. (1972). *The spirituals & the blues.* New York, NY: Seabury Press.

Cook, D. A. & Wiley, C. Y. (2000). Psychotherapy with members of African American churches and spiritual traditions. In P. S. Richards & A. E. Bergin (Eds.), *Handbook of psychotherapy and religious diversity* (pp. 369-396). Washington, DC: American Psychological Association.

Cook, F. D. (2002). *How to raise an ox.* Boston, MA: Wisdom Publications.

Cool, L. & McCabe, J. (1983). The "scheming hag" and the "dear old think": The anthropology of aging women. In J. Sokolovsky (Ed.), *Growing old in different societies: Cross-cultural perspectives* (pp. 56-68). Belmont, CA: Wadsworth.

Cooper, P. C. (2005). The formless self in Buddhism and psychotherapy. In M. B. Weiner, P. C. Cooper, & C. Barbre (Eds.), *Psychotherapy and religion* (pp. 17-56). Lanham, MD: Aronson.

Copeland, B. (2006). *Not a genuine black man: Or, how I claimed my piece of ground in the lily-white suburbs.* New York, NY: Hyperion.

Corbett, L. & Stein, M. (2005). Contemporary Jungian approaches to spiritually oriented psychotherapy. In L. Sperry & E. P. Shafranske (Eds.), *Spiritually oriented psychotherapy* (pp. 51-73). Washington, DC: American Psychological Association.

Corsini, R. J. (1971). Group psychotherapy. In A. G. Nikelly (Ed.), *Techniques for behavior change: Applications of Adlerian therapy* (pp. 111-115). Springfield, IL: Charles C Thomas.

Costa, Jr., P. T. & McCrae, R. R. (1986). Major contributions to the psychology of personality. In S. Mogdil & C. Modgil (Eds.), *Hans Eysenck: Consensus and controversy* (pp. 63-72). Philadelphia, PA: The Falmer Press.

Costa, Jr., P. T. & McCrae, R. R. (1989). Personality continuity and the changes of adult life. In M. Storandt & G. R. VandenBos (Eds.), *The adult years: Continuity and change* (pp. 45-77). Washington, DC: American Psychological Association.

Costa, Jr., P. T. & Widiger, T. A. (Eds.). (1994). *Personality disorders and the Five-Factor Model of personality.* Washington, DC: American Psychological Association.

Corsini, R. J. & Wedding, D. (Eds.). (1995). *Current psychotherapies, 5th Ed.* Itasca, IL: F. E. Peacock Publishers.

Covey, S. R. (1989). *The 7 habits of highly effective people: Restoring the character ethic.* New York, NY: Free Press.

Covey, S. R. (1990). *Principle-centered leadership.* New York, NY: Summit Books.

Covey, S. R. (1997). *The 7 habits of highly effective families: Building a beautiful family culture in a turbulent world.* New York, NY: Golden Books.

Covey, S. R. (2004). *The 8th habit: From effectiveness to greatness.* New York, NY: Free Press.

Cozolino, L. (2002). *The neuroscience of psychotherapy: Building and rebuilding the human brain.* New York, NY: W. W. Norton & Company.

Craik, K. H. (1993). The 1937 Allport and Stagner texts in personality psychology. In K. H. Craik, R. Hogan, & R. N. Wolfe (Eds.), *Fifty years of personality psychology* (pp. 3-20). New York, NY: Plenum Press.

Craik, K. H., Hogan, R., & Wolfe, R. N. (1993). Fifty years of personality psychology. New York, NY: Plenum Press.

Cramer, P. (2000). Defense mechanisms in psychology today: Further processes for adaptation. *American Psychologist, 55*, 637-46.

Crawford, J. S. (2005). The delicacy of being. In M. B. Weiner, P. C. Cooper, & C. Barbre (Eds.), *Psychotherapy and religion* (pp. 77-102). Lanham, MD: Aronson.

Cromwell, R. L. (1972). Success-failure reactions in mentally retarded children. In J. B. Rotter, J. E. Chance, & E. J. Phares (Eds.), *Applications of a Social Learning Theory of Personality* (pp. 500-

509). New York, NY: Holt, Rinehart and Winston.

Crowe, R. R. (1975). An adoptive study of psychopathy: Preliminary results from arrest records and psychiatric hospital records. In R. R. Fieve, D. Rosenthal, & H. Brill (Eds.), *Genetic research in psychiatry* (pp. 95-103). Baltimore, MD: The Johns Hopkins University Press.

Dalai Lama, His Holiness the. (1996). *The good heart: A Buddhist perspective on the teachings of Jesus.* Boston, MA: Wisdom Publications.

Dalai Lama, His Holiness the (2001). *An open heart: Practicing compassion in everyday life.* Boston, MA: Little Brown and Company.

Dalai Lama, His Holiness the (2002). *The spirit of peace.* London, England: Thorsons.

Daley, T. C., Whaley, S. E., Sigman, M. D., Espinosa, M. P., & Neumann, C. (2003). IQ on the rise: The Flynn Effect in rural Kenyan children. *Psychological Science, 14*, 2003.

Dana, R. H. (Ed.). (2000). *Handbook of Cross-Cultural and Multicultural Personality Assessment.* Mahwah, NJ: Erlbaum Associates.

Davis, A. & Dollard, J. (1940). *Children of bondage: The personality development of Negro youth in the urban South.* New York, NY: Harper & Row, Publishers.

Dawkins, R. (1976). *The selfish gene.* New York, NY: Oxford University Press.

DeCarvalho, R. J. (1991). *The growth hypothesis in psychology: The humanistic psychology of Abraham Maslow and Carl Rogers.* San Francisco, CA: The Edwin Mellen Press.

Decety, J. & Jackson, P. L. (2006). A social-neuroscience perspective on empathy. *Current Directions in Psychological Science, 15*, 54-58.

Dembroski, T. M., MacDougall, J. M., Williams, R. B., Haney, T. L., & Blumenthal, J. A. (1985). Components of type A, hostility, and anger-in: Relationship to angiographic findings. *Psychosomatic Medicine, 47*, 219-233.

de Mello, A. (1978). *Sadhana - A way to God: Christian exercises in Eastern form.* New York, NY: Image Books.

de Mello, A. (1982). *The song of the bird.* New York, NY: Image Books.

de Mello, A. (1990). *Awareness: The perils and opportunities of reality.* New York, NY: Image Books.

De Mooij, M. (2000). The future is predictable of international marketers: Converging incomes lead to diverging consumer behaviour. *International Marketing Review, 17*, 103-113.

De Mooij, M. (2004a). Translating advertising: Painting the tip of an iceberg. *The Translator, 10*, 179-198.

De Mooij, M. (2004b). *Consumer behavior and culture: Consequences for global marketing and advertising.* Thousand Oaks, CA: Sage Publications.

De Mooij, M. (2005). *Global marketing and advertising: Understanding cultural paradoxes, 2nd Ed.* Thousand Oaks, CA: Sage Publications.

Dershowitz, A. M. (2002). *Why terrorism works: Understanding the threat, responding to the challenge.* New Haven, CT: Yale University Press.

Deshimaru, T. (1982). *The Zen way to the martial arts.* New York, NY: Compass.

Deutsch, H. (1944). *The psychology of women: A psychoanalytic interpretation, Volume One.* New York, NY: Grune & Stratton.

Deutsch, H. (1945). *The psychology of women: A psychoanalytic interpretation, Volume Two: Motherhood.* New York, NY: Grune & Stratton.

Deutsch, H. (1973). *Confrontations with myself: An epilogue.* New York, NY: W. W. Norton & Company.

DeWaal, E. (1984). *Seeking God: The way of St. Benedict.* Collegeville, MN: The Liturgical Press.

Diamond, M. C., Lindner, B., Johnson, R., Bennett, E. L., & Rosenzweig, M. R. (1975). Differences in occipital cortical synapses from environmentally enriched, impoverished, and standard colony rats. *Journal of Neuroscience Research, 1*, 109-119.

Diamond, S. (1977/1997). Francis Galton and American psychology. In L. T. Benjamin, Jr. (Ed.), *A history of psychology: Original sources and contemporary research, 2nd* Ed. (pp. 231-239). New York, NY: McGraw-Hill.

Diamond, S. A. (1996). *Anger, madness, and the daimonic: The psychological genesis of violence, evil, and creativity.* Albany, NY: State University of New York Press.

Dick, D. M. & Rose, R. J. (2002). Behavior genetics: What's new? What's next? *Current Directions in Psychological Science, 11*, 70-74.

Dickens, C. (1843/1994). *A Christmas Carol.* New York, NY: A Watermill Classic.

Diener, E. (2000). Subjective well-being: The science of happiness and a proposal for a national index. *American Psychologist, 55*, 34-43.

Diener, E. & Seligman, M. E. P. (2004). Beyond money: Toward an economy of well-being. *Psychological Science in the Public Interest, 5*, 1-31.

Dies, R. R. (1968). Electroconvulsive therapy: A social learning theory interpretation. *Journal of Nervous and Mental Disease, 146*, 334-340.

Dinkmeyer, D. C., Dinkmeyer, Jr., D. C., & Sperry, L. (1987). *Adlerian counseling and psychotherapy, 2nd Ed.* Columbus, OH: Merrill Publishing Company.

Dobel, C., Diesendruck, G., & Bolte, J. (2007). How writing system and age influence spatial representations of actions. *Psychological Science, 18*, 487-491.

Dockett, K. H., Dudley-Grant, G. R. & Bankart, C. P. (Eds.). (2003). *Psychology and Buddhism: From individual to global community*. New York, NY: Kluwer Academic/Plenum.

Dockett, K. H. & North-Schulte, D. (2005). Transcending self and other: Mahayana principles of integration. In K. H. Dockett, G. R. Dudley-Grant, & C. P. Bankart (Eds.), *Psychology and Buddhism: From individual to global community* (pp. 215-238). New York, NY: Kluwer Academic/Plenum Publishers.

Dolan, P. & White, M. P. (2007) How can measures of subjective well-being be used to inform public policy? *Perspectives on Psychological Science, 2*, 71-85.

Dollard, J. (1937). *Caste and class in a southern town*. Garden City, NY: Doubleday & Company.

Dollard, J. & Miller, N. E. (1950). *Personality and psychotherapy: An analysis in terms of learning, thinking, and culture*. New York, NY: McGraw-Hill.

Dollard, J., Doob, L. W., Miller, N. E., Mowrer, O. H., & Sears, R. R. (1939). *Frustration and aggression*. New Haven, CT: Yale University Press.

Douglas, C. (1995). Analytical psychotherapy. In R. J. Corsini & D. Wedding (Eds.), *Current Psychotherapies, 5th Ed.* (pp. 95-127). Itasca, IL: F. E. Peacock Publishers.

Dreikurs, R. (1950). *Fundamentals of Adlerian psychology*. New York, NY: Greenburg.

Duckworth, A. L., & Carlson, S. M. (2013). Self-regulation and school success. In B. W. Sokol, F. M. E. Grouzet, & U. Müller (Eds.), *Self-regulation and autonomy: Social and developmental dimensions of human conduct* (pp. 208-230). New York: Cambridge University Press.

Duckworth, A. L., Kim, B., & Tsukayama, E. (2013). Life stress impairs self-control in early adolescence. *Frontiers in Developmental Psychology, 3*, 1-12.

Duckworth, A. L., Kirby, T., Tsukayama, E., Berstein, H., Ericsson, K. (2010). Deliberate practice spells success: Why grittier competitors triumph at the National Spelling Bee. *Social Psychological and Personality Science, 2*, 174-181.

Duckworth, A. L., Peterson, C., Matthews, M. D., & Kelly, D. R. (2007). Grit: Perseverance and passion for long-term goals. *Journal of Personality and Social Psychology, 92*, 1087-1101.

Duckworth, A. L. & Seligman, M. E. P. (2005). Self-discipline outdoes IQ in predicting academic performance of adolescents. *Psychological Science, 16*, 939-944.

Duckworth, A. L., Weir, D., Tsukayama, E., & Kwok, D. (2012). Who does well in life? Conscientious adults excel in both objective and subjective success. *Frontiers in Personality Science and Individual Differences, 3*, 1-8.

Dudley-Grant, G. R. (2001). Eastern Caribbean family psychology with conduct-disordered adolescents from the Virgin Islands. *American Psychologist, 56*, 47-57.

Dudley-Grant, G. R. (2003). Buddhism, psychology, and addiction theory in psychotherapy. In K. H. Dockett, G. R. Dudley-Grant, & C. P. Bankart (Eds.), *Psychology and Buddhism: From individual to global community* (pp. 105-124). New York, NY: Kluwer Academic/Plenum Publishers.

Dunning, D., Heath, C., & Suls, J. M. (2004). Flawed self-assessment: Implications for health, education, and the workplace. *Psychological Science in the Public Interest, 5(3)*, 69-106.

Easwaran, E. (1972). *Gandhi the man: The story of his transformation*. Tomales, CA: Nilgiri Press.

Ekman, P., Davidson, R. J., Ricard, M., & Wallace, B. A. (2005). Buddhist and psychological perspectives on emotions and well-being. *Current Directions in Psychological Science, 14*, 59-63.

Eidelson, R. J. & Eidelson, J. I. (2003). Dangerous ideas: Five beliefs that propel groups toward conflict. *American Psychologist, 58*, 182-192.

Eifert, G. H. & Forsyth, J. P. (2005). *Acceptance & commitment therapy for anxiety disorders: A practitioner's treatment guide to using mindfulness, acceptance, and values-based behavior change strategies*. Oakland, CA: New Harbinger Publications.

Elfenbein, H. A. & Ambady, N. (2003). Universals and cultural differences in recognizing emotions. *Current Directions in Psychological Science, 12*, 159-164.

Elliot, A. J., Chirkov, V. I., Kim, Y., & Sheldon, K. M. (2001). A cross-cultural analysis of avoidance (relative to approach) personal goals. *Psychological Science, 12*, 505-510.

Ellis, A. (1957). *How to live with a "neurotic": At home and at work*. New York, NY: Crown Publishers.

Ellis, A. (1962). *Reason and emotion in psychotherapy*. New York, NY: Lyle Stuart.

Ellis, A. (1973). *Humanistic psychotherapy: The rational-emotive approach*. New York, NY: McGraw-Hill.

Ellis, A. (1977). *How to live with - and without - anger*. New York, NY: Reader's Digest Press.

Ellis. A. (1994). *Reason and emotion in psychotherapy: A comprehensive method of treating human disturbances - Revised and Updated*. New York, NY: A Birch Lane Press Book.

Ellis, A. (1995). Rational emotive behavior therapy. In R. J. Corsini & D. Wedding (Eds.), *Current psychotherapies, 5th Ed.* (pp. 162-196). Itasca, IL: F. E. Peacock Publishers.

References

Ellis, A. (1996). *Better, deeper, and more enduring brief therapy: The rational emotive behavior therapy approach*. New York, NY: Brunner/Mazel, Publishers.

Ellis, A. (1998). *How to control your anxiety before it controls you*. Secaucus, NJ: A Birch Lane Press Book.

Ellis, A. (2001). *Overcoming destructive beliefs, feelings, and behaviors: New directions for rational emotive behavior therapy*. Amherst, NY: Prometheus Books.

Ellis, A. (2003). *Sex without guilt in the 21st century*. Fort Lee, NJ: Barricade Books.

Ellis, A. (2004). *The road to tolerance: The philosophy of rational emotive behavior therapy*. Amherst, NY: Prometheus Books.

Ellis, A. (2005). *The myth of self-esteem: How rational emotive behavior therapy can change your life forever*. Amherst, NY: Prometheus Books.

Ellis, A. & Abrams, M. (1994). *How to cope with a fatal illness: The rational management of death and dying*. New York, NY: Barricade Books.

Ellis, A. & Dryden, W. (1987). *The practice of rational-emotive therapy (RET)*. New York, NY: Springer Publishing Company.

Ellis, A. & Harper, R. A. (1975). *A new guide to rational living*. Englewood Cliffs, NJ: Prentice-Hall.

Ellis, A. & Lange, A. (1994). *How to keep people from pushing your buttons*. New York, NY: A Birch Lane Press Book.

Ellis, A., McInterney, J. F., DiGiuseppe, R., & Yeager, R. J. (1988). *Rational-emotive therapy with alcoholics and substance abusers*. New York, NY: Pergamon Press.

Epstein, M. (1995). *Thoughts without a thinker: Psychotherapy from a Buddhist perspective*. New York, NY: Basic Books.

Epstein, R. (1980). *Notebooks, B. F. Skinner*. Englewood Cliffs, NJ: Prentice-Hall.

Erikson, E. H. (1937). Configurations in play - Clinical notes. In S. Schlein (Ed.), *A way of looking at things: Selected papers from 1930 to 1980 Erik H. Erikson* (pp. 77-138). New York, NY: W. W. Norton & Company.

Erikson, E. H. (1940). Studies in the interpretation of play: Clinical observation of play disruption in young children. In S. Schlein (Ed.), *A way of looking at things: Selected papers from 1930 to 1980 Erik H. Erikson* (pp. 139-236). New York, NY: W. W. Norton & Company.

Erikson, E. H. (1950). *Childhood and Society*. New York, NY: W. W. Norton & Company.

Erikson, E. H. (1954). The dream specimen of psychoanalysis. In S. Schlein (Ed.), *A way of looking at things: Selected papers from 1930 to 1980 Erik H. Erikson* (pp. 237-279). New York, NY: W. W. Norton & Company.

Erikson, E. H. (1955). Sex differences in the play configurations of American preadolescents. In S. Schlein (Ed.), *A way of looking at things: Selected papers from 1930 to 1980 Erik H. Erikson* (pp. 280-310). New York, NY: W. W. Norton & Company.

Erikson, E. H. (1958). *Young man Luther: A study in psychoanalysis and history*. New York, NY: W. W. Norton & Company.

Erikson, E. H. (1959). Late adolescence. In S. Schlein (Ed.), *A way of looking at things: Selected papers from 1930 to 1980 Erik H. Erikson* (pp. 631-643). New York, NY: W. W. Norton & Company.

Erikson, E. H. (1964). A memorandum on identity and Negro youth. In S. Schlein (Ed.), *A way of looking at things: Selected papers from 1930 to 1980 Erik H. Erikson* (pp. 644-659). New York, NY: W. W. Norton & Company.

Erikson, E. H. (1968a). The human life cycle. In S. Schlein (Ed.), *A way of looking at things: Selected papers from 1930 to 1980 Erik H. Erikson* (pp. 595-610). New York, NY: W. W. Norton & Company.

Erikson, E. H. (1968b). *Identity: Youth and crisis*. New York, NY: W. W. Norton & Company.

Erikson, E. H. (1969). *Gandhi's truth: On the origins of militant nonviolence*. New York, NY: W. W. Norton & Company.

Erikson, E. H. (1972). Play and actuality. In S. Schlein (Ed.), *A way of looking at things: Selected papers from 1930 to 1980 Erik H. Erikson* (pp. 311-338). New York, NY: W. W. Norton & Company.

Erikson, E. H. (1974). *Dimensions of a new identity: The 1973 Jefferson Lectures in the Humanities*. New York, NY: W. W. Norton & Company.

Erikson, E. H. (1977). *Toys and reasons: Stages in the ritualization of experience*. New York, NY: W. W. Norton & Company.

Erikson, E. H. (Ed.). (1978). *Adulthood*. New York, NY: W. W. Norton & Company.

Erikson, E. H. (1980a). *Identity and the life cycle*. New York, NY: W. W. Norton & Company.

Erikson, E. H. (1980b). Themes of adulthood in the Freud-Jung correspondence. In N. J. Smelser & E. H. Erikson (Eds.), *Themes of work and love in adulthood* (pp. 43-74). Cambridge, MA: Harvard University Press.

Erikson, E. H. & Erikson, J. M. (1980). Dorothy Burlingham's school in Vienna. In S. Schlein (Ed.), *A way of looking at things: Selected papers from 1930 to 1980 Erik H. Erikson* (pp. 2-13). New York, NY: W. W. Norton & Company.

Erikson, E. H. & Erikson, J. M. (1997). *The life cycle completed: Extended version - With new chapters on the ninth stage of development*. New York, NY: W. W. Norton & Company.

Erikson, E. H., Erikson, J. M., & Kivnick, H. Q. (1986).

Vital involvement in old age. New York, NY: W. W. Norton & Company.

Erikson, K. T. (1973). *In search of common ground: Conversations with Erik H. Erikson and Huey P. Newton*. New York, NY: W. W. Norton & Company.

Esack, F. (1999). *On being a Muslim: Finding a religious path in the world today*. Oxford, England: Oneworld Publications.

Evans, III, F. B. (1996). *Harry Stack Sullivan - Interpersonal theory and psychotherapy*. New York, NY: Routledge.

Evans, R. I. (1964). *Dialogue with Erik Erikson*. New York, NY: Praeger Publishers.

Evans, R. I. (1968). *B. F. Skinner: The man and his ideas*. New York, NY: E. P. Dutton & Co.

Evans, R. I. (1981a). *Dialogue with Erich Fromm*. New York, NY: Praeger.

Evans, R. I. (1981b). *Dialogue with Gordon Allport*. New York, NY: Praeger.

Evans-Wentz, W. Y. & Jung, C. G. (1975). *The Tibetan book of the great liberation: Or the method of realizing nirvana through knowing the mind*. New York, NY: Oxford University Press.

Eysenck, H. J. (1952). *The scientific study of personality*. New York, NY: The Macmillan Company.

Eysenck, H. J. (1953). *Uses and abuses of psychology*. Baltimore, MD: Penguin Books.

Eysenck, H. J. (1957). *Sense and nonsense in psychology*. Baltimore, MD: Penguin Books.

Eysenck, H. J. (1962). *Know your own I.Q.* Middlesex, England: Penguin Books.

Eysenck, H. J. (1964). *Crime and personality*. Boston, MA: Houghton Mifflin Company.

Eysenck, H. J. (1966). *Check your own I.Q.* Middlesex, England: Penguin Books.

Eysenck, H. J. (1967). *The biological basis of personality*. Springfield, IL: Charles C. Thomas, Publisher.

Eysenck, H. J. (1970). *The structure of human personality*. London, England: Methuen & Co. Ltd.

Eysenck, H. J. (1972). *Psychology is about people*. New York, NY: The Library Press.

Eysenck, H. J. (1973a). *The inequality of man*. San Diego, CA: EdITS Publishers.

Eysenck, H. J. (Ed.). (1973b). *The measurement of intelligence*. Lancaster, England: Medical and Technical Publishing Co. Ltd.

Eysenck, H. J. (1976). *Sex and personality*. Austin, TX: University of Texas Press.

Eysenck, H. J. (1977). *You and neurosis*. London, England: Maurice Temple Smith Ltd.

Eysenck, H. J. (1982). *Personality, genetics, and behavior*. New York, NY: Praeger.

Eysenck, H. J. (1986). Consensus and controversy: Two types of science. In S. Mogdil & C. Modgil (Eds.), *Hans Eysenck: Consensus and controversy* (pp. 375-398). Philadelphia, PA: The Falmer Press.

Eysenck, H. J. (1991). *Smoking, personality, and stress: Psychosocial factors in the prevention of cancer and coronary heart disease*. New York, NY: Springer-Verlag.

Eysenck, H. J. (1995). *Genius: The natural history of creativity*. Cambridge, England: Cambridge University Press.

Eysenck, H. J. (1997). *Rebel with a cause*. New Brunswick, NJ: Transaction Publishers.

Eysenck, H. J. & Gudjonsson, G. H. (1989). *The causes and cures of criminality*. New York, NY: Plenum Press.

Eysenck, H. J. & Kamin, L. (1981). *The intelligence controversy*. New York, NY: John Wiley and Sons.

Eysenck, H. J. & Nias, D. K. B. (1978). *Sex, violence, and the media*. London, England, Maurice Temple Smith Ltd.

Eysenck, S. (1997). Psychoticism as a dimension of personality. In H. Nyborg (Ed.), *The scientific study of human nature: Tribute to Hans J. Eysenck at eighty* (pp. 109-121). Oxford, England: Pergamon.

Fadiman, J. & Frager, R. (1997). *Essential Sufism*. New York, NY: HarperSanFrancisco.

Farris, C. K. (2003). *My brother Martin: A sister remembers growing up with the Rev. Dr. Martin Luther King Jr.* New York, NY: Simon & Schuster.

Feng, J., Spence, I., & Pratt, J. (2007). Playing an action video game reduces gender differences in spatial cognition. *Psychological Science, 18*, 850-855.

Ferraro, G. (2006). *Cultural anthropology: An applied perspective, 6th Ed.* Belmont, CA: Thomson Wadsworth.

Ferraro, G. P. (2006b). *The cultural dimension of international business, 5th Ed.* Upper Saddle River, NJ: Pearson Prentice Hall.

Feuerstein, G. (2003). *The deeper dimension of Yoga: Theory and practice*. Boston, MA: Shambala.

Field, T. M. (1993). The therapeutic effects of touch. In G. G. Brannigan & M. R. Merrens (Eds.), *The Undaunted Psychologist: Adventures in Research* (pp. 2-11). New York, NY: McGraw-Hill.

Field, T. (2000). *Touch therapy*. Philadelphia, PA: Churchill Livingstone.

Field, T. (2001). *Touch*. Cambridge, MA: MIT Press.

Finger, S. (1994). *Origins of neuroscience: A history of explorations into brain functions*. New York, NY: Oxford University Press.

Finn, M. & Rubin, J. B. (2000). Psychotherapy with Buddhists. In P. S. Richards & A. E. Bergin (Eds.), *Handbook of psychotherapy and religious diversity* (pp. 317-340). Washington, DC: American Psychological Association.

Fivush, R. & Nelson, K. (2004). Culture and language in the emergence of autobiographical memory. *Psychological Science, 15*, 573-577.

References

Fleeson, W. (2004). Moving personality beyond the person-situation debate: The challenge and the opportunity of within-person variability. *Current Directions in Psychological Science, 13*, 83-87.

Folkman, S. & Moskowitz, J. T. (2000). Positive affect and the other side of coping. *American Psychologist, 55*, 647-654.

Follette, V. M., Palm, K. M., & Rasmussen Hall, M. L. (2004). Acceptance, mindfulness, and trauma. In S. C. Hayes, V. M. Follette, & M. M. Linehan (Eds.), *Mindfulness and acceptance: Expanding the cognitive-behavioral tradition* (pp. 192-208). New York, NY: The Guilford Press.

Fonagy, P. (2006). Evidence-based psychodynamic psychotherapies. In PDM Task Force (Eds.), *Psychodynamic Diagnostic Manual* (pp 765-818). Silver Spring, MD: Alliance of Psychoanalytic Organizations.

Fowers, B. J. (2005). *Virtue and psychology: Pursuing excellence in ordinary practices*. Washington, DC: American Psychological Association.

Fowers, B. J. & Davidov, B. J. (2006). The virtue of multiculturalism: Personal transformation, character, and openness to the other. *American Psychologist, 61*, 581-594.

Fox, N. A., Nichols, K. E., Henderson, H. A., Rubin, K., Schmidt, L., Hamer, D., et al. (2005). Evidence for a gene-environment interaction in predicting behavioral inhibition in middle childhood. *Psychological Science, 16*, 921-926.

Frankl, V. E. (1946/1986). *The doctor and the soul: From psychotherapy to logotherapy*. New York, NY: Vintage Books.

Frankl, V. E. (1946/1992). *Man's search for meaning: An introduction to Logotherapy*. Boston, MA: Beacon Press.

Frankl, V. E. (1948/2000). *Man's search for ultimate meaning*. Cambridge, MA: Perseus Publishing.

Frankl, V. E. (1978). *The unheard cry for meaning: Psychotherapy and humanism*. New York, NY: Simon and Schuster.

Frankl, V. E. (1995/2000). *Viktor Frankl - Recollections: An autobiography*. Cambridge, MA: Perseus Publishing.

Fransella, F. (1995). *Key figures in counseling and psychotherapy: George Kelly*. Thousand Oaks, CA: Sage Publications.

Fredrickson, B. L. (2001). The role of positive emotions in positive psychology: The broaden-and-build theory of positive emotions. *American Psychologist, 56*, 218-226.

Fredrickson, B. L. & Joiner, T. (2002). Positive emotions trigger upward spirals toward emotional well-being. *Psychological Science, 13*, 172-175.

Fredrickson, B. L. & Losada, M. F. (2005). Positive affect and the complex dynamics of human flourishing. *American Psychologist, 60*, 678-686.

Freeman, L. (1986). *Light within: The inner path of meditation*. London, England: Darton, Longman and Todd Ltd.

Freeman, L. (1994). *Christian meditation: Your daily practice*. Tucson, AZ: Medio Media.

Freeman, L. (2000). *Jesus: The teacher within*. New York, NY: Continuum.

Freeman, L. (2002). *A pearl of great price: Sharing the gift of meditation by starting a group*. Tucson, AZ: Medio Media.

Freeman, L. (2004). *A simple way: The path of Christian meditation*. Tucson, AZ: Medio Media.

Freud, A. (1927/1973). On the theory of analysis of children. In H. M. Ruitenbeek (Ed.), *The first Freudians* (pp 129-143). New York, NY: Jason Aronson.

Freud, A. (1936/1966). *The ego and the mechanisms of defense*. Madison, CT: International Universities Press.

Freud, A. (1946). *The psycho-analytical treatment of children*. New York, NY: International Universities Press.

Freud, M. (1983). *Sigmund Freud: Man and father*. New York, NY: Jason Aronson.

Freud, S. (1900/1995). The interpretation of dreams. In A. A. Brill (Ed.), *The basic writings of Sigmund Freud* (pp 147-517). New York, NY: The Modern Library.

Freud, S. (1904/1995). Psychopathology of everyday life. In A. A. Brill (Ed.), *The basic writings of Sigmund Freud* (pp 1-146). New York, NY: The Modern Library.

Freud, S. (1905/1995). Three contributions to the theory of sex. In A. A. Brill (Ed.), *The basic writings of Sigmund Freud* (pp 519-597). New York, NY: The Modern Library.

Freud, S. (1905/1995). Wit and its relation to the unconscious. In A. A. Brill (Ed.), *The basic writings of Sigmund Freud* (pp 599-771). New York, NY: The Modern Library.

Freud, S. (1913/1995). Totem and taboo. In A. A. Brill (Ed.), *The basic writings of Sigmund Freud* (pp 773-898). New York, NY: The Modern Library.

Freud, S. (1914/1995). The history of the psychoanalytic movement. In A. A. Brill (Ed.), *The basic writings of Sigmund Freud* (pp 899-945). New York, NY: The Modern Library.

Freud, S. (1917/1966). *Introductory lectures on psycho-analysis*. New York, NY: W. W. Norton & Company.

Freud, S. (1920/1961). *Beyond the pleasure principle*. New York, NY: W. W. Norton & Company.

Freud, S. (1923/1960). *The ego and the id*. New York, NY: W. W. Norton & Company.

Freud, S. (1926/1959). *Inhibitions, symptoms and anxiety*. New York, NY: W. W. Norton & Company.

Freud, S. (1927/1961). *The future of an illusion*. New York, NY: W. W. Norton & Company.

References

Freud, S. (Freud, 1930/1961). *Civilization and its discontents*. New York, NY: W. W. Norton & Company.

Freud, S. (1933/1965). *New introductory lectures on psycho-analysis*. New York, NY: W. W. Norton & Company.

Freud, S. (1938/1949). *An outline of psycho-analysis*. New York, NY: W. W. Norton & Company.

Freud, S. (1939/1967). *Moses and monotheism*. New York, NY: Vintage Books.

Freud, S. (1952). *An autobiographical study*. New York, NY: W. W. Norton & Company.

Freud, S. & Breuer, J. (1895/2004). *Studies in Hysteria*. New York, NY: Penguin Books.

Friedman, L. J. (1999). *Identity's architect: A biography of Erik H. Erikson*. New York, NY: Scribner.

Friedman, M. & Rosenman, R. H. (1959). Association of specific overt behavior pattern with blood and cardiovascular findings. *Journal of the American Medical Association, 169*, 1286-1296.

Friedmann, A. (1930). The family and educational guidance. In A. Adler (Ed.), *Guiding the child: On the principles of Individual Psychology* (pp. 53-65). New York, NY: Greenberg.

Friends of Peace Pilgrim. (1982). *Peace Pilgrim: Her life and work in her own words*. Santa Fe, NM: Ocean Tree Books.

Frijda N.H & Sundararajan, L. (2007). Emotion refinement: A theory inspired by Chinese poetics. *Perspectives on Psychological Science, 2*, 227-241.

Fritzsche, P. (2007). *Nietzsche and the death of God: Select writings*. Boston, MA: Bedford/St. Martin's.

Fromm, E. (1941). *Escape from freedom*. New York, NY: Holt, Rinehart and Winston.

Fromm, E. (1947). *Man for himself: An inquiry into the psychology of ethics*. Greenwich, CN: A Fawcett Premier Book.

Fromm, E. (1950). *Psychoanalysis and religion*. New Haven, CN: Yale University Press.

Fromm, E. (1955a). *The sane society*. New York, NY: Henry Holt and Company.

Fromm, E. (1955b). *The dogma of Christ - and other essays on religion, psychology and culture*. New York, NY: Holt, Rinehart and Winston.

Fromm, E. (1956). *The art of loving*. New York, NY: Harper & Row.

Fromm, E. (1964). *The heart of man: Its genius for good and evil*. New York, NY: Harper & Row.

Fromm, E. (1966). *You shall be as gods: A radical interpretation of the old testament and its tradition*. New York, NY: Holt, Rinehart and Winston.

Fromm, E. (1968). *The revolution of hope*. New York, NY: Harper & Row.

Fromm, E. (1973). *The anatomy of human destructiveness*. New York, NY: Holt, Rinehart and Winston.

Fromm, E. (1978). *Sigmund Freud's mission: An analysis of his personality and influence*. Gloucester, MA: Peter Smith.

Fromm, E. (1980). *Greatness and limitations of Freud's thought*. New York, NY: Harper & Row.

Fromm, E. (1992). *The revision of psychoanalysis*. Boulder, CO: Westview Press.

Fromm, E. (1994). *The art of being*. New York, NY: Continuum.

Fromm, E. & Maccoby, M. (1970). *Social character in a Mexican village: A sociopsychoanalytic study*. Englewood Cliffs, NJ: Prentice-Hall.

Fromm, E. & Xirau, R. (1968). *The nature of man*. New York, NY: The Macmillan Company.

Frost, Jr., S. E. (1942). *Basic teachings of the great philosophers: A survey of their basic ideas*. New York, NY: A Dolphin Book.

Fruzzetti, A. E. & Iverson, K. M. (2004). Mindfulness, acceptance, validation, and "individual" psychopathology in couples. In S. C. Hayes, V. M. Follette, & M. M. Linehan (Eds.), *Mindfulness and acceptance: Expanding the cognitive-behavioral tradition* (pp. 168-191). New York, NY: The Guilford Press.

Fry, T. (Ed.). (1982). *The rule of St. Benedict in English*. Collegeville, MN: The Liturgical Press.

Funk, R. (1982). *Erich Fromm: The courage to be human*. New York, NY: Continuum.

Funk, R. (Ed.). (1997). *Love, sexuality, and matriarchy: About gender*. New York, NY: Fromm International Publishing Corporation.

Funk, R. (2000). *Erich Fromm - His life and ideas: An illustrated biography*. New York, NY: Continuum.

Gabor, A. (2000). *The capitalist philosophers: The geniuses of modern business - their lives, times, and ideas*. New York, NY: Times Books.

Gale Reference Team (2004). Biography - Cattell, Raymond Bernard (1905-1998). *Contemporary Authors*, Retrieved April 25, 2007, from http://media-server.amazon.com/exec/drm/amzproxy.cgi/...

Galton, F. (1869/1997). Natural abilities and the comparative worth of races. In L. T. Benjamin, Jr. (Ed.), *A history of psychology: Original sources and contemporary research, 2nd* Ed. (pp. 226-231). New York, NY: McGraw-Hill.

Gay, P. (1998). *Freud: A life for our time*. New York, NY: Norton & Co.

Gendlin, E. T. (1990). *Focusing: More than meditation or visualization* [Casette Tape]. New York, NY: Audio Renaissance.

German, T. P. & Barrett, H. C. (2005). Functional fixedness in a technologically sparse culture. *Psychological Science, 16*, 1-5.

Germer, C. K., Siegel, R. D., & Fulton, P. R. (Eds.). (2005). *Mindfulness and Psychotherapy*. New York, NY: The Guilford Press.

References

Gichuru, F. X. (2005). Basic education for all. In G. J. Wanjohi & G. W. Wanjohi (Eds.), *Social and religious concerns of East Africa: A Wajibu anthology* (pp. 158-166). Nairobi, Kenya: Wajibu: A Journal of Social and Religious Concern.

Gillespie, J. M. & Allport, G. W. (1955). *Youth's outlook on the future*. Garden City, NY: Doubleday & Company.

Ginges, J., Hansen, I., & Norenzayan, A. (2009). Religion and support for suicide attacks. *Psychological Science, 20*, 224-230.

Gjerde, P. F. (2001). Attachment, culture, and *amae*. *American Psychologist, 56*, 826-827.

Globus, A., Rosenzweig, M. R., Bennett, E. L., & Diamond, M. C. (1973). Effects of differential experience on dendritic spine counts in rat cerebral cortex. *Journal of Comparative and Physiological Psychology, 82*, 175-181.

Goldenberg, J. L. (2005). The body stripped down: An existential account of the threat posed by the physical body. *Current Directions in Psychological Science, 14*, 224-228.

Goldin-Meadow, S. (2006). Talking and thinking with our hands. *Current Directions in Psychological Science, 15*, 34-39.

Goldin-Meadow, S. & Saltzman, J. (2000). The cultural bounds of maternal accommodation: How Chinese and American mothers communicate with deaf and hearing children. *Psychological Science, 11*, 307-314.

Goldstein, G. & Hersen, M. (Eds.). (1990). *Handbook of Psychological Assessment*. New York, NY: Pergamon.

Goldstein, J., Freud, A., & Solnit, A. J. (1973). *Beyond the best interests of the child.* New York, NY: The Free Press.

Goldstein, J., Freud, A., & Solnit, A. J. (1979). *Before the best interests of the child.* New York, NY: The Free Press.

Goldstein, J. & Kornfield, J. (2001). *Seeking the heart of wisdom: The path of insight meditation.* Boston, MA: Shambala.

Goldstein, K. (1934/1995). *The organism.* New York, NY: Zone Books.

Goldston, D. B., Molock, S. D., Whitbeck, L. B., Murakami, J. L., Zayas, L. H, Hall, G. C. N. (2008). Cultural considerations in adolescent suicide prevention and psychosocial treatment. *American Psychologist, 63*, 14-31.

Goleman, D. (1988). *The meditative mind: The varieties of meditative experience.* New York, NY: G. P. Putnam's Sons.

Goleman, D. (1995). *Emotional intelligence: Why it can matter more than IQ*. New York, NY: Bantam Books.

Goleman, D. (1998). *Working with emotional intelligence.* New York, NY: Bantam Books.

Goleman, D. (2003). *Destructive emotions: How can we overcome them?* New York, NY: Bantam Books.

Goodley, D. & Lawthorn, R. (Eds.). (2006). *Disability and psychology: Critical introductions and reflections*. New York, NY: Palgrave Macmillan.

Goodman, T. A. (2005). Working with children: Beginner's mind. In C. K. Germer, R. D. Siegel, & P. R. Fulton (Eds.), *Mindfulness and psychotherapy* (pp. 197-219). New York, NY: The Guilford Press.

Gore, P. M. & Rotter, J. B. (1963). A personality correlate of social action. *Journal of Personality, 31*, 58-64.

Gosling, S. D. (2001). From mice to men: What can we learn about personality from animal research? *Psychological Bulletin, 127*, 45-86.

Gosling, S. D. & John, O. P. (1999). Personality dimensions in nonhuman animals: A cross-species review. *Current Directions in Psychological Science, 8*, 69-75.

Gosling, S. D., Kwan, V. S. Y., & John, O. P. (2003). A dog's got personality: A cross-species comparative approach to personality judgements in dogs and humans. *Journal of Personality and Social Psychology, 85*, 1161-1169.

Gosling, S. D. & Vazier, S. (2002). Are we barking up the right tree? Evaluating a comparative approach to personality. *Journal of Research in Personality, 36*, 607-614.

Gould, J. L. (1982). *Ethology: The mechanisms and evolution of behavior*. New York, NY: W. W. Norton & Company.

Graham, S. (2006). Peer victimization in school: Exploring the ethnic context. *Current Directions in Psychological Science, 15*, 317-321.

Greenberg, M. T., Weissberg, R. P., O'Brien, M. U., Zins, J. E., Fredericks, L., Resnik, H. & Elias, M. J. (2003). Enhancing school-based prevention and youth development through coordinated social, emotional, and academic learning. *American Psychologist, 58*, 466-474.

Greenfield, J. (1974). *Wilhelm Reich vs. the U.S.A.* New York, NY: W. W. Norton & Company.

Greenough, W. T. & Volkmar, F. R. (1973). Pattern of dendritic branching in occipital cortex of rats reared in complex environments. *Experimental Neurology, 40*, 491-504.

Groth-Marnat, G. (2003). *Handbook of Psychological Assessment* (4th Ed.). Hoboken, NJ: Wiley & Sons.

Gray, J. (1992). *Men are from Mars, women are from Venus*. New York, NY: Quill.

Gray, J. (1997). *Mars and Venus on a date: A guide for navigating the 5 stages of dating to create a loving and lasting relationship.* New York, NY: HarperCollins.

Gray, J. (1999). *Children are from Heaven: Positive parenting skills for raising cooperative, confident, and compassionate children.* New York, NY: HarperCollins.

Gray, J. (2002). *Mars and Venus in the workplace: A practical guide for improving communication and getting results at work.* New York, NY: HarperCollins.

Gray, J. (2004). *Men are from Mars, women are from Venus: The classic guide to understanding the opposite sex.* New York, NY: Quill.

Grills, C. (2002). African-centered Psychology: Basic principles. In T. A. Parham (Ed.), *Counseling persons of African descent: Raising the bar of practitioner competence* (pp. 10-24). Upper Saddle River, NJ: Prentice Hall.

Grills, C. & Ajei, M. (2002). African-centered conceptualizations of self and consciousness. In T. A. Parham (Ed.), *Counseling persons of African descent: Raising the bar of practitioner competence* (pp. 75-99). Upper Saddle River, NJ: Prentice Hall.

Guida, F. & Ludlow, L. (1989). A cross-cultural study of test anxiety. *Journal of Cross-Cultural Psychology, 20,* 178-190.

Gurung, R. A. R. (2003). Comparing cultural and individual learning tendencies. *American Psychologist, 58,* 145-146.

Gutmann, D. (1987). *Reclaimed powers: Toward a new psychology of men and women in later life.* New York, NY: Basic Books.

Gutmann, D. (1997). *The human elder in nature, culture, and society.* Boulder, CO: Westview Press.

Guyll, M. & Madon, S. (2000). Ethnicity research and theoretical conservatism. *American Psychologist, 55,* 1509-1510.

Halevi, Z. (1986). *Psychology & Kabbalah.* York Beach, ME: Samuel Weiser, Inc.

Hall, L. E. (2005). *Dictionary of multicultural psychology: Issues, terms, and concepts.* Thousand Oaks, CA: Sage Publications.

Hall, M. P. (1975). *The adepts: In the Eastern esoteric tradition - The mystics of Islam.* Los Angeles, CA: The Philosophical Research Society.

Halpern, D. F., Benbow, C. P., Geary, D. C., Gur, R. C., Hyde, J. S., & Gernsbacher, M. A. (2007). The science of sex differences in science and mathematics. *Psychological Science in the Public Interest, 8,* 1-51.

Halpern, E. (2001). Family psychology from an Israeli perspective. *American Psychologist, 56,* 58-64.

Hampson, S. E. (2008). Mechanisms by which childhood personality traits influence adult well-being. *Current Directions in Psychological Science, 17,* 264-268.

Hansen, D. D. (2003). *The dream: Martin Luther King, Jr. and the speech that inspired a nation.* New York, NY: ECCO.

Harlow, H. F. (1975). The nature of love. In A. Montagu (Ed.), *The practice of love* (pp. 17-31). Englewood Cliffs, NJ: Prentice-Hall.

Harmon-Jones, E. & Winkielman, P. (2007). *Social Neuroscience: Integrating biological and psychological explanations of social behavior.* New York, NY: The Guilford Press.

Harris, P. (2003). *Silence and stillness in every season.* New York, NY: Continuum.

Hartranft, C. (2003). *The Yoga-Sutras of Patanjali.* Boston, MA: Shambala.

Haviland, W. A., Prins, H. E. L., Walrath, D. & McBride, B. (2005). *Anthropology: The Human Challenge* (11th Ed.). Belmont, CA: Thomson Wadsworth.

Hayes, S. C. (2004). Acceptance and commitment therapy and the new behavior therapies: Mindfulness, acceptance, and relationship. In S. C. Hayes, V. M. Follette, & M. M. Linehan (Eds.), *Mindfulness and acceptance: Expanding the cognitive-behavioral tradition* (pp. 1-29). New York, NY: The Guilford Press.

Hayes, S. C., Follette, V. M., & Linehan, M. M. (Eds.). (2004). *Mindfulness and acceptance: Expanding the cognitive-behavioral tradition.* New York, NY: The Guilford Press.

Hayes, S. C. & Smith, S. (2005). *Get out of your mind & into your life: The new Acceptance & Commitment Therapy.* Oakland, CA: New Harbinger Publications.

Hayes, S. C., Strosahl, K. D., & Wilson, K. G. (1999). *Acceptance and commitment therapy: An experiential approach to behavior change.* New York, NY: The Guilford Press.

Hedden, T., Ketay, S., Aron, A., Markus, H. R., & Gabrieli, J. D. E. (2008). Cultural influences on neural substrates of attentional control. *Psychological Science, 19,* 12-17.

Heine S. J., Buchtel, E. E., & Norenzayan, A. (2008). What do cross-national comparisons of personality traits tell us? The case of conscientiousness. *Psychological Science, 19,* 309-313.

Heine S. J. & Norenzayan, A. 2006 Toward a psychological science for a cultural species. *Perspectives on Psychological Science, 1,* 251-269.

Hejmadi, A., Davidson, R. J., & Rozin, P. (2000). Exploring Hindu Indian emotion expressions: Evidence for accurate recognition by Americans and Indians. *Psychological Science, 11,* 183-187.

Heller, Z. I. (1975). The Jewish view of death: Guidelines for dying. In E. Kubler-Ross, Ed., *Death: The final stage of growth* (pp. 38-43). New York, NY: A Touchstone Book.

Helminiak, D. A. (2005). *Meditation without myth: What I wish they'd taught me in church about prayer, meditation, and the quest for peace.* New York, NY: Crossroad Publishing.

Henderson, G. & Bryan, W. V. (1984). *Psychosocial aspects of disability.* Springfield, IL: Charles C. Thomas · Publisher.

Henderson, H. (2001). *Terrorism*. New York, NY: Facts on File.

Hendrix, H. (1988). *Getting the love you want: A guide for couples*. New York, NY: HarperPerennial.

Henrich, J., McElreath, R., Barr, A., Ensminger, J., Barrett, C., Bolyanatz, A., et al. (2006). Costly punishment across human societies. *Science, 312*, 1767-1770.

Henry, P. J. & Hardin, C. D. (2006). The contact hypothesis revisited: Status bias in the reduction of implicit prejudice in the United States and Lebanon. *Psychological Science, 17*, 862-868.

Herrigel, E. (1953). *Zen in the Art of Archery*. New York, NY: Vintage Spiritual Classics.

Herrigel, E. (1960). *The method of Zen*. New York, NY: Vintage Books.

Herrnstein, R. J. & Murray, C. (1994). *The bell curve: Intelligence and class structure in American life*. New York, NY: The Free Press.

Higgins, M. B. (Ed.). (1973). *Wilhelm Reich selected writings: An introduction or orgonomy*. New York, NY: Farrar, Straus and Giroux.

Hill, P. C. & Pargament, K. I. (2003) Advances in the conceptualization and measurement of religion and spirituality: Implications for physical and mental health research. *American Psychologist, 58*, 64-74.

Hillier, S. & Barrow, G. M. (1999). *Aging, the individual, and society, 7th Ed.* Belmont, CA: Wadsworth.

Hofer, M. A. (2006). Psychobiological roots of early attachment. *Current Directions in Psychological Science, 15*, 84-88.

Hoffman, E. (1988). *The right to be human: A biography of Abraham Maslow*. Los Angeles, CA: Jeremy P. Tarcher, Inc.

Hoffman, E. (Ed.). (1996). *Future visions: The unpublished papers of Abraham Maslow*. Thousand Oaks, CA: SAGE Publications.

Hoffman, E. (2007). *The way of splendor: Jewish mysticism and modern psychology - Updated 25th Anniversary Edition*. Lanham, MD: Rowman & Littlefield.

Holaday, M., Smith, D. A., & Sherry, A. (2000). Sentence completion tests: A review of the literature and results of a survey of members of the Society for Personality Assessment. *Journal of Personality Assessment, 74*, 371-383.

Holland, J. G. & Skinner, B. F. (1961). *The analysis of behavior*. New York, NY: McGraw-Hill.

Holmes, L. D. (1983). *Other cultures, elder years: An introduction to cultural gerontology*. Minneapolis, MN: Burgess Publishing Company.

Holy Bible: Revised standard version. (1962). Cleveland, OH: World Publishing.

Hong, Y., Morris, M. W., Chiu, C., & Benet-Martinez, V. (2000). Multicultural minds: A dynamic constructivist approach to culture and cognition. *American Psychologist, 55*, 709-720.

Horney, K. (1923/1967). On the genesis of the castration complex in women. In H. Kelman (Ed.), *Feminine Psychology* (pp. 37-53). New York, NY: W. W. Norton & Company.

Horney, K. (1926/1967). The flight from womanhood: The masculinity-complex in women as viewed by men and by women. In H. Kelman (Ed.), *Feminine Psychology* (pp. 54-70). New York, NY: W. W. Norton & Company.

Horney, K. (1932/1967). The dread of woman: Observations on a specific difference in the dread felt by men and by women respectively for the opposite sex. In H. Kelman (Ed.), *Feminine Psychology* (pp. 133-146). New York, NY: W. W. Norton & Company.

Horney, K. (1934/1967). The overvaluation of love: A study of a common present-day feminine type. In H. Kelman (Ed.), *Feminine Psychology* (pp. 182-213). New York, NY: W. W. Norton & Company.

Horney, K. (1937/1967). The dread of woman: Observations on a specific difference in the dread felt by men and by women respectively for the opposite sex. In H. Kelman (Ed.), *Feminine Psychology* (pp. 245-258). New York, NY: W. W. Norton & Company.

Horney, K. (1937). *The neurotic personality of our time*. New York, NY: W. W. Norton & Company.

Horney, K. (1939). *New ways in psychoanalysis*. New York, NY: W. W. Norton & Company.

Horney, K. (1942). *Self-analysis*. New York, NY: W. W. Norton & Company.

Horney, K. (1945). *Our inner conflicts: A constructive theory of neurosis*. New York, NY: W. W. Norton & Company.

Horney, K. (Ed.). (1946). *Are you considering psychoanalysis?* New York, NY: W. W. Norton & Company.

Horney, K. (1950). *Neurosis and human growth: The struggle toward self-realization*. New York, NY: W. W. Norton & Company.

Hornsey, K. (2002). *Taekwondo: A step-by-step guide to the Korean art of self-defense*. Boston, MA: Tuttle.

Howard, R. (Director), Broyles, Jr., W. & Reinert, A. (Screenwriters). (1995). *Apollo 13* [Motion Picture]. United States: Universal City Studios.

Howard-Hamilton, M. F. & Frazier, K. (2005). Identity development and the convergence of race, ethnicity, and gender. In D. Comstock (Ed.), *Diversity and development* (pp 67-90). Belmont, CA: Thomson Brooks/Cole.

Hrdy, S. B. (1999). *Mother nature: A history of mothers, infants, and natural selection*. New York, NY: Pantheon Books.

Hrebickova, M., Urbanek, T., Cermak, I., Szarota, P., Fickova, E., & Orlicka, L. (2002). A Five-Factor Theory perspective. In R. R. McCrae & J. Allik (Eds.), *The Five-Factor Model of personality across cultures* (pp. 53-78). New York, NY: Kluwer Academic/Plenum Publishers.

Hsee, C. K., Hastie, R., & Chen, J. (2008). Hedonomics: Bridging decision research with happiness research. *Perspectives on Psychological Science, 3*, 224-243.

Huppert, F. A. (2009). A new approach to reducing disorder and improving well-being. *Perspectives on Psychological Science, 4*, 108-111.

Huxley, A. (1945/2004). *The perennial philosophy*. New York, NY: Perennial Classics.

Hyde, J. S. (1996). Where are the gender differences? Where are the gender similarities? In D. M. Buss & N. M. Malamuth (Eds.) *Sex, power, conflict: Evolutionary and feminist perspectives* (pp. 107-118). New York, NY: Oxford University Press.

Hyde, J. S. (2005). The gender similarities hypothesis. *American Psychologist, 60*, 581-592.

Ignatieff, M. (2004). *The lesser evil: Political ethics in an age of terror*. Princeton, NJ: Princeton University Press.

Iijima Hall, C. C. (1997). Cultural malpractice: The growing obsolescence of psychology with the changing U. S. population. *American Psychologist, 52*, 642-651.

Inglehart, R., Foa, R., Peterson, C., & Welzel, C. (2008). Development, freedom, and rising happiness: A global perspective (1981-2007). *Perspectives on Psychological Science, 3*, 264-285.

Ingram, D. H. (Ed.). (1987). *Final Lectures - Karen Horney*. New York, NY: W. W. Norton & Company.

International Study Project, Inc. (1972). *Abraham H. Maslow: A memorial volume*. Monterey, CA: Brooks/Cole Publishing Company.

Irele, A. (1981). *The African experience in literature and ideology*. London, England: Heinemann.

Irele, A. (2001). *The African imagination: Literature in African and the Black Diaspora*. New York, NY: Oxford University Press.

Irwin, M. H., Schafer, G. N., & Feiden, C. P. (1974). Emic and unfamiliar category sorting of Mano farmers and U.S. undergraduates. *Journal of Cross-Cultural Psychology, 5*, 407-423.

Ivimey, M. (1946). How does analysis help? In K. Horney (Ed.). *Are you considering psychoanalysis?* (pp. 211-233). New York, NY: W. W. Norton & Company.

Iyengar, B. K. S. (1966). *Light on Yoga*. New York, NY: Schocken Books.

Jacobi, J. & Hull, R. F. C. (1970). *C. G. Jung - Psychological reflections*. New York, NY: Harper & Brothers.

Jaffé, A. (1979). *C. G. Jung - Word and image*. Princeton, NJ: Princeton University Press.

Jahn, J. (1972). African systems of thought. In S. H. Irvine & J. T. Sanders (Eds.), *Cultural adaptation within modern Africa* (pp. 81-90). New York, NY: Teachers College Press.

Jai Uttal (2003). *Kirtan: The art and practice of ecstatic chant* [CD]. Boulder, CO: Sounds True.

James, W. (1892/1992). Psychology: Briefer course. In G. E. Myers (Ed.), *William James: Writings 1878-1899* (pp. 1-443). New York, NY: The Library of America.

James, W. (1897/1992). The will to believe: And other essays in popular philosophy. In G. E. Myers (Ed.), *William James: Writings 1878-1899* (pp. 445-704). New York, NY: The Library of America.

James, W. (1899/1992). Talks to teachers on psychology and to students on some of life's ideals. In G. E. Myers (Ed.), *William James: Writings 1878-1899* (pp. 705-887). New York, NY: The Library of America.

James, W. (1902/1987). The varieties of religious experience: A study in human nature. In B. Kuklick (Ed.), *William James: Writings 1902-1910* (pp. 1-477). New York, NY: The Library of America.

Janzen, H. L., Paterson, J. G., Reid, D., & Everall, R. (1996). Osvita Medical Project: Psychological assessment of Ukrainian physicians training in Canada. *International Journal for the Advancement of Counseling, 19*, 343-360.

Jarvis, M. (2004). *Psychodynamic psychology: Classical theory & contemporary research*. London, England: Thomson.

Jaspers, K. (1965). *Nietzsche: An introduction to the understanding of his philosophical activity*. South Bend, IN: Regnery/Gateway, Inc.

Jenifer, T. & Goldenbach, A. (2006). *Trevon Jenifer: From the ground up*. Champaign, IL: Sports Publishing L. L. C.

Jensen, A. R. (1997). Eysenck as teacher and mentor. In H. Nyborg (Ed.), *The scientific study of human nature: Tribute to Hans J. Eysenck at eighty* (pp. 543-559). Oxford, England: Pergamon Press.

Jensen, A. R. (1998). *The g factor: The science of mental ability*. Westport, CT: Praeger.

Jessor, R., Carman, R. S., & Grossman, P. H. (1968). Expectations of need satisfaction and drinking patterns of college students. *Quarterly Journal of Studies in Alcohol, 29*, 101-116.

Jessor, R., Liverant, S., & Opochinsky, S. (1963). Imbalance in need structure and maladjustment. *Journal of Abnormal and Social Psychology, 66*, 271-275.

Ji, L-J., Nisbett, R. E., & Su, Y. (2001). Culture, change, and prediction. *Psychological Science, 12*, 450-456.

Johnson, N. (2003a). *Kung Fu*. Broomall, PA: Mason Crest Publishers.

Johnson, N. (2003b). *Martial arts for children*. Broomall, PA: Mason Crest Publishers.

Johnson, N. (2003c). *Martial arts for the mind*. Broomall, PA: Mason Crest Publishers.

Johnson, P. & Thane, P. (Eds.) (1998). *Old age from antiquity to post-modernity*. New York, NY: Routledge.

Johnson, S. B. & Millstein, S. G. (2003). Prevention opportunities in health care settings. *American Psychologist, 58*, 475-481.

Jones, A. C. & Gosling, S. D. (2005). Temperament and personality in dogs (Canis familiaris): A review and evaluation of past research. *Applied Animal Behaviour Science, 95*, 1-53.

Jones, E. (1953). *The life and work of Sigmund Freud, Vol. 1: The formative years and the great discoveries, 1856-1900*. New York, NY: Basic Books.

Jones, E. (1957). *The life and work of Sigmund Freud, Vol. 3: The last phase, 1919-1939*. New York, NY: Basic Books.

Jordan, J. V. (1991a). The meaning of mutuality. In J. V. Jordan, A. G. Kaplan, J. B. Miller, I. P. Stiver, & J. L. Surrey (Eds.), *Women's growth in connection: Writings from the Stone Center* (pp 81-96). New York, NY: The Guilford Press.

Jordan, J. V. (1991b). Empathy and self boundaries. In J. V. Jordan, A. G. Kaplan, J. B. Miller, I. P. Stiver, & J. L. Surrey (Eds.), *Women's growth in connection: Writings from the Stone Center* (pp 67-80). New York, NY: The Guilford Press.

Jordan, J. V. (1997a). Relational development: Therapeutic implications of empathy and shame. In J. V. Jordan (Ed.), *Women's growth in diversity: More writings from the Stone Center* (pp 138-161). New York, NY: The Guilford Press.

Jordan, J. V. (Ed.). (1997b). *Women's growth in diversity: More writings from the Stone Center*. New York, NY: The Guilford Press.

Jordan, J. V. (2004). Relational awareness: Transforming disconnection. In J. V. Jordan, M. Walker, & L. M. Hartwig (Eds.), *The complexity of connection: Writings from the Stone Center's Jean Baker Miller Training Institute* (pp. 47-63). New York, NY: The Guilford Press.

Jordan, J. V., Kaplan, A. G., Miller, J. B., Stiver, I. P., & Surrey, J. L. (1991). *Women's growth in connection: Writings from the Stone Center*. New York, NY: The Guilford Press.

Jordan, J. V. & Walker, M. (2004). Introduction to the complexity of connection. In J. V. Jordan, M. Walker, & L. M. Hartling (Eds.), *The complexity of connection: Writings from the Stone Center's Jean Baker Miller Training Institute* (pp 1-8). New York, NY: The Guilford Press.

Jordan, J. V., Walker, M., & Hartling, L. M. (Eds.). (2004). *The complexity of connection: Writings from the Stone Center's Jean Baker Miller Training Institute*. New York, NY: The Guilford Press.

Jordan, W. D. (1978). Searching for adulthood in America. In E. H. Erikson (Ed.), *Adulthood* (pp. 189-199). New York, NY: W. W. Norton & Company.

Joseph, S. & Linley, P. A. (2006). Positive psychology versus the medical model?: Comment. *American Psychologist, 61*, 332-333.

Jung, C. G. (1916/1963). *Psychology of the unconscious: A study of the transformations and symbolisms of the libido*. New York, NY: Dodd, Mead and Company.

Jung, C. G. (1933). *Modern man in search of a soul*. New York, NY: Harcourt, Brace, Jovanovich.

Jung, C. G. (1940). *The integration of the personality*. London, England: Kegal Paul, Trench, Trubner & Co., Ltd.

Jung, C. G. (1954). *Answer to Job*. New York, NY: Meridian Books.

Jung, C. G. (1956). Symbols of transformation: An analysis of the prelude to a case of schizophrenia, 2nd Ed. In Sir H. Read, M. Fordham, G. Adler, & W. McGuire (Eds.), *The collected works of C. G. Jung, Vol. 11* (690 pp.). Princeton, NJ: Princeton University Press.

Jung, C. G. (1957). *The undiscovered self*. New York, NY: A Mentor Book.

Jung, C. G. (1958). Psychology and religion: West and East, 2nd Ed. In Sir H. Read, M. Fordham, G. Adler, & W. McGuire (Eds.), *The collected works of C. G. Jung, Vol. 11* (690 pp.). Princeton, NJ: Princeton University Press.

Jung, C. G. (1959a). On the nature of dreams. In V. S. de Laszlo (Ed.), *The basic writings of C. G. Jung* (pp. 363-379). New York, NY: The Modern Library.

Jung, C. G. (1959b). The relations between the ego and the unconscious. In V. S. de Laszlo (Ed.), *The basic writings of C. G. Jung* (pp. 105-182). New York, NY: The Modern Library.

Jung, C. G. (1959c). Aion: Researches into the phenomenology of the self, 2nd Ed. In Sir H. Read, M. Fordham, G. Adler, & W. McGuire (Eds.), *The collected works of C. G. Jung, Vol. 9* (333 pp.). Princeton, NJ: Princeton University Press.

Jung, C. G. (1961). *Memories, dreams, reflections*. New York, NY: Vintage Books.

Jung, C. G. (1964). Civilization in Transition. In Sir H. Read, M. Fordham, & G. Adler (Eds.), *The collected works of C. G. Jung, Vol. 10* (618 pp.). New York, NY: Pantheon Books.

Jung, C. G. (1968). *Analytical psychology: Its theory and practice - The Tavistock lectures*. New York, NY: Pantheon Books.

Jung, C. G. (1970). Mysterium coniunctionis: An inquiry into the separation and synthesis of psychic opposites in alchemy, 2nd Ed. In Sir H. Read, M. Fordham, G. Adler, & W. McGuire (Eds.), *The collected works of C. G. Jung, Vol. 14* (702 pp.). Princeton, NJ: Princeton University Press.

Jung, C. G. (1971). Psychological types. In Sir H. Read, M. Fordham, G. Adler, & W. McGuire (Eds.), *The collected works of C. G. Jung, Vol. 6* (608 pp.). Princeton, NJ: Princeton University Press.

Jung, C. G., von Franz, M.-L., Henderson, J. L., Jacobi, J., & Jaffé, A. (1964). *Man and his symbols*. Garden City, NY: Doubleday & Company.

Jung, C. G. & Pauli, W. (1959). *The interpretation of nature and the psyche*. New York, NY: Pantheon Books.

Juvonen, J., Nishina, A., & Graham, S. (2006). Ethnic diversity and perceptions of safety in urban middle schools. *Psychological Science, 17*, 393-400.

Kabat-Zinn, J. (1990). *Full catastrophe living: Using the wisdom of your body and mind to face stress, pain, and illness*. New York, NY: A Delta Book.

Kabat-Zinn, J. (1994). *Wherever you go, there you are: Mindfulness meditation in everyday life*. New York, NY: Hyperion.

Kabat-Zinn, J. (2005). *Coming to our senses: Healing ourselves and the world through mindfulness*. New York, NY: Hyperion.

Kagan, J. (1984). *The nature of the child*. New York, NY: Basic Books.

Kagan, J. (1994). *Galen's prophecy: Temperament in human nature*. New York, NY: BasicBooks.

Kagan, J., Kearsley, R. B., & Zelazo, P. R. (1978). *Infancy: Its place in human development*. Cambridge, MA: Harvard University Press.

Kaiser, C. R., Vick, S. B., & Major, B. (2006). Prejudice expectations moderate preconscious attention to cues that are threatening to social identity. *Psychological Science, 17*, 332-338.

Kameda, T., Takezawa, M., & Hastie, R. (2005). Where do social norms come from? The example of communal sharing. *Current Directions in Psychological Science, 14*, 331-334.

Kameguchi, K. & Murphy-Shigematsu, S. (2001). Family psychology and family therapy in Japan. *American Psychologist, 56*, 65-70.

Kaplan, L. J. (1978). *Oneness and separateness: From infant to individual*. New York, NY: Simon and Schuster.

Kardiner, A. (1939). *The individual and his society: The psychodynamics of primitive social organization*. New York, NY: Columbia University Press.

Kardiner, A., Linton, R., DuBois, C., & West, J. (1945). *The psychological frontiers of society*. New York, NY: Columbia University Press.

Kardiner, A. & Preble, E. (1961). *They studied man*. New York, NY: A Mentor Book.

Kaslow, F. W. (2001). Families and family psychology at the millennium: Intersecting crossroads. *American Psychologist, 56*, 37-46.

Kaufmann, W. (1992). *Discovering the mind, Vol. 3: Freud, Adler, and Jung*. New Brunswick, NJ: Transaction Publishers.

Kearse, R. (2006a). *Street talk: Da official guide to hip-hop & urban slanguage*. Fort Lee, NJ: Barricade Books.

Kearse, R. (2006b). *Changin' your game plan! - How to use incarceration as a stepping stone for success*. New York, NY: Big Mouth Street Media.

Keirsey, D. (1987). *Portraits of Temperament*. Del Mar, CA: Prometheus Nemesis Book Company.

Kelemen, D. (2004). Are children "intuitive theists"? *Psychological Science, 15*, 295-301.

Kelland, M. D., Freeman, A. S., & Chiodo, L. A. (1989). (±)-3,4-Methylenedioxymethamphetamine-induced changes in the basal activity and pharmacological responsiveness of nigrostriatal dopamine neurons. *European Journal of Pharmacology, 169*, 11-21.

Kelland, M. D. (2009). Psychology, physical disability, & the application of Buddhist mindfulness to martial arts programs. *Journal of Asian Martial Arts, 18(3)*, 8-17.

Kelland, M. (2010). *Psychological and spiritual factors in martial arts programs for people with physical disabilities*. Charleston, SC: Booksurge.

Keller, L. S., Butcher, J. N., & Slutske, W. S. (1990). Objective personality assessment. In G. Goldstein & M. Hersen (Eds.), *Handbook of psychological assessment, 2nd Ed.* (pp. 345-386). New York, NY: Pergamon.

Kelley, T. M. (2005). Natural resilience and innate mental health. *American Psychologist, 60*, 265.

Kelly, G. A. (1955a). *The psychology of personal constructs - Vol. 1: A theory of personality*. New York, NY: W. W. Norton & Company.

Kelly, G. A. (1955b). *The psychology of personal constructs - Vol. 2: Clinical diagnosis and psychotherapy*. New York, NY: W. W. Norton & Company.

Kelly, G. A. (1958/1969). Personal construct theory and the psychotherapeutic interview. In B. Maher (Ed.), *Clinical psychology and personality: The selected papers of George Kelly* (pp. 224-264). New York, NY: John Wiley & Sons.

Kelly, G. A. (1966/1969). Ontological Acceleration. In B. Maher (Ed.), *Clinical psychology and personality: The selected papers of George Kelly* (pp. 7-45). New York, NY: John Wiley & Sons.

Kelman, H. (1946). What are your doubts about analysis? In K. Horney (Ed.). *Are you considering psychoanalysis?* (pp. 93-133). New York, NY: W. W. Norton & Company.

Kelman, H. (Ed.). (1967). *Feminine psychology*. New York, NY: W. W. Norton & Company.

Kelman, H. (1971). *Helping people: Karen Horney's psychoanalytic approach*. New York, NY: Science House.

Kendrick, D. C. (1981). Neuroticism and extraversion as explanatory concepts in clinical psychology. In R. Lynn (Ed.), *Dimensions of personality:*

Papers in honour of H. J. Eysenck (pp. 253-261). Oxford, England: Pergamon.

Keppel, B. (2002). Kenneth B. Clark in the patterns of American culture. *American Psychologist, 57*, 29-37.

Kernberg, O. (2004). *Contemporary controversies in psychoanalytic theory, techniques, and their applications*. New Haven, CT: Yale University Press.

Kernberg, O. F. & Caligor, E. (2005). A psychoanalytic theory of personality disorders. In M. F. Lenzenweger & J. F. Clarkin (Eds.), *Major theories of personality disorder, 2nd Ed.* (pp. 114-156). New York, NY: The Guilford Press.

Kerouac, J. (1959). *The Dharma bums*. London, England: Penguin Books.

Kesebir, P. & Diener, E. (2008). In pursuit of happiness: Empirical answers to philosophical questions. *Perspectives on Psychological Science, 3*, 117-125.

Kessler, S. (1975). Extra chromosomes and criminality. In R. R. Fieve, D. Rosenthal, & H. Brill (Eds.), *Genetic research in psychiatry* (pp. 65-73). Baltimore, MD: The Johns Hopkins University Press.

Kety, S. S., Rosenthal, D., Wender, P. H., Schulsinger, F., & Jacobsen, B. (1975). Mental illness in the biological and adoptive families of adopted individuals who have become schizophrenic: A preliminary report based on psychiatric interviews. In R. R. Fieve, D. Rosenthal, & H. Brill (Eds.), *Genetic research in psychiatry* (pp. 147-165). Baltimore, MD: The Johns Hopkins University Press.

Keyes, C. L. M. & Lopez, S. J. (2005). Toward a science of mental health: Positive directions in diagnosis and interventions. In C. R. Snyder & S. J. Lopez (Eds.), *Handbook of positive psychology* (pp. 45-59). New York, NY: Oxford University Press.

Khan, P. V. I. (1999). *Awakening: A Sufi experience*. New York, NY: Jeremy P. Tarcher/Putnam.

Khoapa, B. A. (1980). *The African personality*. Tokyo, Japan: The United Nations University.

Khong, B. S. L. (2005). Role of responsibility in Daseinsanalysis and Buddhism. In K. H. Dockett, G. R. Dudley-Grant, & C. P. Bankart (Eds.), *Psychology and Buddhism: From individual to global community* (pp. 139-159). New York, NY: Kluwer Academic/Plenum Publishers.

Khor, G. (1981). *An introduction to: Tai Chi and Taoist Energy Meditation*. Balgowlah, New South Wales, Australia: Boobook Publications.

Kier, F. J. & Davenport, D. S. (2004). Unaddressed problems in the study of spirituality and health. *American Psychologist, 59*, 53-54.

Kilpatrick, E. (1946). What do you do in analysis? In K. Horney (Ed.). *Are you considering psychoanalysis?* (pp. 159-185). New York, NY: W. W. Norton & Company.

Kim, J. E. & Moen, P. (2001). Is retirement good or bad for subjective well-being? *Current Directions in Psychological Science, 10*, 83-86.

King, C. S. (19). The impact of King's India trip. In T. Siebold (Ed.), *People who made history: Martin Luther King Jr.* (pp. 66-74). San Diego, CA: Greenhaven Press.

Kirschenbaum, H. (1995). Carl Rogers. In M. M. Suhd (Ed.), *Positive regard: Carl Rogers and other notables he influenced* (pp. 1-102). Palo Alto, CA: Science and Behavior Books.

Kirvan, J. (1996a). *Where only love can go: A journey of the soul into The Cloud of Unknowing*. Notre Dame, IN: Ave Maria Press.

Kirvan, J. (1996b). *Let nothing disturb you: A journey to the center of the soul with Teresa of Avila*. Notre Dame, IN: Ave Maria Press.

Kirvan, J. (1996c). *Simply surrender: Based on the little way of Thérèse of Lisieux*. Notre Dame, IN: Ave Maria Press.

Kitayama, S., Duffy, S., Kawamura, T., & Larsen, J. T. (2003). Perceiving an object and its context in different cultures. *Psychological Science, 14*, 201-106.

Kitayama, S., Snibbe, A. C., Markus, H. R., & Suzuki, T. (2004). Is there and "free" choice?: Self and dissonance in two cultures. *Psychological Science, 15*, 527-533.

Kithinji, C. (2005). The individual in society: Focus on the African family. In G. J. Wanjohi & G. W. Wanjohi (Eds.), *Social and religious concerns of East Africa: A Wajibu anthology* (pp. 273-278). Nairobi, Kenya: Wajibu: A Journal of Social and Religious Concern.

Klein, M. (1930/1973). The early development of conscience in the child. In H. M. Ruitenbeek (Ed.), *The first Freudians* (pp 253-269). New York, NY: Jason Aronson.

Klein, M. (1932/1963). *The psycho-analysis of children.* London, England: Hogarth Press Ltd.

Klein, M. (1940/1986). Mourning and its relation to manic-depressive states. In J. Mitchell (Ed.), *The selected Melanie Klein* (pp 146-174). New York, NY: The Free Press.

Klein, M. (1946/1986). Notes on some schizoid mechanisms. In J. Mitchell (Ed.), *The selected Melanie Klein* (pp 175-200). New York, NY: The Free Press.

Klein, M. (1952/1986). The origins of transference. In J. Mitchell (Ed.), *The selected Melanie Klein* (pp 201-210). New York, NY: The Free Press.

Klein, M. (1955/1986). The psycho-analytic play technique: Its history and significance. In J. Mitchell (Ed.), *The selected Melanie Klein* (pp 35-54). New York, NY: The Free Press.

Klinesmith, J., Kasser, T., & McAndrew, F. T. (2006).

Guns, testosterone, and aggression. *Psychological Science, 17*, 568-571.

Knoblich, G. & Sebanz, N. (2006). The social nature of perception and action. *Current Directions in Psychological Science, 15*, 99-104.

Knopf, O. & Wexbert, E. (1930). The physician and educational guidance. In A. Adler (Ed.), *Guiding the child: On the principles of Individual Psychology* (pp. 28-46). New York, NY: Greenberg.

Kohlberg, L. (1963). The development of children's orientations toward a moral order: I. Sequence in the development of moral thought. *Vita Humana, 6*, 11-33.

Kondo-Ikemura, K. (2001). Insufficient evidence. *American Psychologist, 56*, 825-826.

Kornfield, J. (1994). *Buddha's little instruction book.* New York, NY: Bantam Books.

Kornfield, J. (2002). *The art of forgiveness, lovingkindness, and peace.* New York, NY: Bantam Books.

Kornfield, J. (2004). *Meditation for beginners.* Boulder, CO: Sounds True.

Kozlowski, S. W. J. & Ilgen, D. R. (2006). Enhancing the effectiveness of work groups and teams. *Psychological Science in the Public Interest, 7*, 77-124

Krakauer, J. (1997). *Into thin air: A personal account of the Mount Everest disaster.* New York, NY: Villard.

Kravitz, D. A. (2005). Diversity in teams: A two-edged sword requires careful handling. *Psychological Science in the Public Interest, 6*, i-ii.

Krippner, S. C. (2002). Conflicting perspectives on shamans and shamanism: Points and counterpoints. *American Psychologist, 57*, 962-977.

Krishna Das (2002). *Pilgrim heart* [CD]. New York, NY: Karuna.

Kroeger, O, Thuesen, J. M., & Rutledge, H. (2002). *Type talk at work: How the 16 personality types determine your success on the job.* New York, NY: Dell Publishing.

Krogman, W. M. (1945). The concept of race. In R. Linton (Ed.), *The science of man in the world crisis* (pp. 38-62). New York, NY: Columbia University Press.

Kubler-Ross, E. (1969). *On death and dying: What the dying have to teach doctors, nurses, clergy, and their own families.* New York, NY: Scribner.

Kubler-Ross, E. (Ed.). (1975). *Death: The final stage of growth.* New York, NY: A Touchstone Book.

Kubler-Ross, E. (1983). *On children and death: How children and their parents can and do cope with death.* New York, NY: A Touchstone Book.

Kubler-Ross, E. (1997). *The wheel of life: A memoir of living and dying.* New York, NY: A Touchstone Book.

Kumpfer, K. L. & Alvarado, R. (2003). Family-strengthening approaches for the prevention of youth problem behaviors. *American Psychologist, 58*, 457-465.

Kvarnes, R. G. & Parloff, G. H. (Eds.). (1976). *A Harry Stack Sullivan case seminar: Treatment of a young male schizophrenic.* New York, NY: W. W. Norton & Company.

Lachar, B. L. (1993). Coronary-prone behavior. Type A behavior revisited. *Texas Heart Institute Journal, 20*: 143-151.

Laitman, R. M. (2005). *Kabbalah for beginners: A beginner's guide to the hidden wisdom.* Thornhill, Ontario, Canada: Laitman Kabbalah Publishers.

Lal, S. (2002). Giving children security: Mamie Phipps Clark and the racialization of child psychology. *American Psychologist, 57*, 20-28.

Lambo, T. A. (1972). Early childhood experience and adult personality. In S. H. Irvine & J. T. Sanders (Eds.), *Cultural adaptation within modern Africa* (pp. 117-128). New York, NY: Teachers College Press.

Lao Tsu (c600 B.C./1989) *Tao Te Ching.* New York, NY: Vintage Books.

Larsen, R. J. & Buss, D. M. (2005). *Personality psychology: Domains of knowledge about human nature, 2nd Ed.* New York, NY: McGraw-Hill.

Larson, R. W. (2000). Toward a psychology of positive youth development. *American Psychologist, 55*, 170-183.

Labouvie-Vief, G. (2003). Dynamic integration: Affect, cognition, and the self in adulthood. *Current Directions in Psychological Science, 12*, 201-206.

Lapidus, I. M. (1978). Adulthood in Islam: Religious maturity in the Islamic tradition. In E. H. Erikson (Ed.), *Adulthood* (pp. 97-112). New York, NY: W. W. Norton & Company.

Lassiter, J. E. (1999). African culture and personality: Bad social science, effective social activism, or a call to reinvent ethnology? *African Studies Quarterly, 3(2)*, 1. Retrieved March 26, 2010 from the World Wide Web: http://web.africa.ufl.edu/asq/v3/v3i3a1.htm

Laungani, P. (1999). Cultural influences on identity and behavior: India and Britain. In Y.-T. Lee, C. R. McCauley, & J. G. Draguns (Eds.), *Personality and person perception across cultures* (pp. 191-212). Mahwah, NJ: Lawrence Erlbaum Associates.

Lawson, C. A. (2000). *Understanding the borderline mother: Helping her children transcend the intense, unpredictable, and volatile relationship.* Northvale, NJ: Jason Aronson Inc.

Lazar, S. W., Bush, G., Gollub, R. L., Fricchione, G. L., Khalsa, G., & Benson, H. (2000). Functional brain mapping of the relaxation response and meditation. *NeuroReport, 11*, 1581-1585.

Lazar, S. W., Kerr, C. E., Wasserman, R. H., Gray, J. R. Greve, D. N., Treadway, M. T., et al. (2005a). Meditation experience is associated with increased cortical thickness. *NeuroReport, 16*, 1893-1897.

Lazar, S. W. (2005b). Mindfulness research. In C. K. Germer, R. D. Siegel, & P. R. Fulton (Eds.), *Mindfulness and psychotherapy* (pp. 220-2238). New York, NY: Guilford Press.

Lee, A. (Director), Ling, W. H., Schamus, J., & Jung, T. K. (Screenwriters). (2000). *Crouching tiger, hidden dragon* [Motion Picture]. China: United China Vision & Columbia Pictures Film Production Asia.

Lee, B. (1975). *Tao of Jeet Kune Do*. Valencia, CA: Ohara Publications.

Lee, Y.-T., McCauley, C. R., & Draguns, J. G. (Eds.). (1999) *Personality and person perception across cultures*. Mahwah, NJ: Lawrence Erlbaum Associates.

Lefcourt, H. M. (1976). *Locus of control: Current trends in theory & research*. Hillsdale, NJ: Lawrence Earlbaum Associates.

Leichsenring, F. (2006). Review of meta-analyses of outcome studies of psychodynamic therapy. In PDM Task Force (Eds.), *Psychodynamic Diagnostic Manual* (pp. 819-837). Silver Spring, MD: Alliance of Psychoanalytic Organizations.

Leininger, A. (2002). Vietnamese-American personality and acculturation. In R. R. McCrae & J. Allik (Eds.), *The Five-Factor Model of personality across cultures* (pp. 197-225). New York, NY: Kluwer Academic/Plenum Publishers.

Lenzenweger, M. F. & Clarkin, J. F. (Eds.). (2005). *Major theories of personality disorder, 2nd Ed.* New York, NY: The Guilford Press.

Leong, F. T. L. (2007). Cultural accommodation as method and metaphor. *American Psychologist, 62*, 916-927.

Lescoe, F. J. (1974). *Existentialism: With or without God.* New York, NY: Alba House.

Leung, A. K.-y. & Cogen, D. (2007). The soft embodiment of culture: Camera angles and motion through time and space. *Psychological Science, 18*, 824-830.

Leung, A. K.-y., Maddux, W. W. Galinsky, A. K., & Chiu, C.-y. (2008). Multicultural experience enhances creativity: The when and how. *American Psychologist, 63*, 169-181.

Levey, M., Blanco, M., & Jones, W. T. (1998). *How to succeed on a majority campus: A guide for minority students*. Belmont, CA: Wadsworth.

LeVine, R. A. (1973). *Culture, Behavior, and Personality*. Chicago, IL: Aldine Publishing Company.

LeVine, R. A. (Ed.). (1974). *Culture and personality: Contemporary readings*. Chicago, IL: Aldine Publishing Company.

LeVine, R. A. (1980). Adulthood among the Gusii of Kenya. In N. J. Smelser & E. H. Erikson (Eds.), *Themes of work and love in adulthood* (pp. 77-104). Cambridge, MA: Harvard University Press.

Lewis, C. S. (1952) *Mere Christianity*. New York, NY: HarperCollins.

Lewis, P. (1993). *Martial arts of the Orient.* London, England: Multimedia Books Ltd.

Li, J. (2003). The core of Confucian learning. *American Psychologist, 58*, 146-147.

Li, J. (2005). Mind or virtue: Western and Chinese beliefs about learning. *Current Directions in Psychological Science, 14*, 190-194.

Lillard, P. P. & Jessen, L. L. (2003). *Montessori from the start: The child at home, from birth to age three.* New York, NY: Schocken Books.

Linehan, M. M. (1987). Dialectical behavior therapy: A cognitive behavioral approach to parasuicide. *Journal of Personality Disorders, 1*, 328-333.

Linehan, M. M. (1993). *Cognitive-behavioral treatment of borderline personality disorder*. New York, NY: The Guilford Press.

Linley, P. A. & Joseph, S. (2005). The human capacity for growth through adversity. *American Psychologist, 60*, 262-264.

Linton, R. (1936). *The study of man: An introduction.* New York, NY: D. Appleton-Century Company.

Linton, R. (1945). *The cultural background of personality*. New York, NY: Appleton-Century-Crofts.

Linton, R. (Ed.). (1949). *Most of the world: The peoples of Africa, Latin America, and the East today.* New York, NY: Columbia University Press.

Linton, R. (1955). *The tree of culture*. New York, NY: Alfred A. Knopf.

Little, J. (Ed.). (1998). Bruce Lee: The art of expressing the human body. Rutland, VT: Tuttle Publishing.

Litz, B. T. (2005). Has resilience to severe trauma been underestimated? *American Psychologist, 60*, 262.

Loehlin, J. C. (1986). H. J. Eysenck and behaviour genetics: A critical view. In S. Mogdil & C. Modgil (Eds.), *Hans Eysenck: Consensus and controversy* (pp. 49-61). Philadelphia, PA: The Falmer Press.

Loehlin, J. C. (1997). Dysgenesis and IQ: What evidence is relevant? *American Psychologist, 52*, 1236-1239.

Logan, R. E. & Waehler, C. A. (2001). The Rotter Incomplete Sentences Blank: Examining potential race differences. *Journal of Personality Assessment, 76*, 448-460.

Lomax, E. M. R., Kagan, J., & Rosenkrantz, B. G. (1978). *Science and patterns of child care.* San Francisco, CA: W. H. Freeman and Company.

Long, J. B. (1975). The death that ends death in Hinduism and Buddhism. In E. Kubler-Ross, Ed., *Death: The final stage of growth* (pp. 52-72). New York, NY: A Touchstone Book.

Lonner, W. J. & Malpass, R. S. (Eds.). (1994).

Psychology and culture. Boston, MA: Allyn and Bacon.

Lovell, Jr., J. (1972). *Black song: The forge and the flame*. New York, NY: Macmillan Company.

Lubinski, D. & Benbow, C. P. (2000). States of excellence. *American Psychologist, 55*, 137-150.

Lukoff, D. & Lu, F. (2005). A transpersonal-integrative approach to spiritually oriented psychotherapy. In L. Sperry & E. P. Shafranske (Eds.), *Spiritually oriented psychotherapy* (pp. 177-205). Washington, DC: American Psychological Association.

Lundin, R. W. (1979). *Theories and systems of psychology, 2nd ed.* Lexington, MA: D. C. Heath and Company.

Lundin, R. W. (1989). *Alfred Adler's basic concepts and implications*. Muncie, IN: Accelerated Development.

Luria, A. R. (1969). Speech development and the formation of mental processes. In M. Cole & I. Maltzman (Eds.), *A handbook of contemporary Soviet psychology* (pp. 121-162). New York, NY: Basic Books.

Lutz, A., Greischar, L. L., Rawlings, N. B., Ricard, M., & Davidson, R. J. (2004). Long-term meditators self-induce high-amplitude gamma synchrony during mental practice. *Proceedings of the National Academy of Sciences, 101*, 16369-16373.

Lynch, C. (2001). Individualism and Christianity. *American Psychologist, 56*, 1176.

Lynch Jr., M. (2001). Religion's influence on culture and psychology. *American Psychologist, 56*, 1174-1175.

Lynn, R. (1981). *Dimensions of personality: Papers in honour of H. J. Eysenck*. Oxford, England: Pergamon Press.

Lyubomirsky, S. (2001). Why are some people happier than others?: The role of cognitive and motivational processes in well-being. *American Psychologist, 56*, 239-249.

Maass, A. & Russo, A. (2003). Directional bias in the mental representation of spatial events: Nature or culture? *Psychological Science, 14*, 296-301.

MacDougall, J. M., Dembroski, T. M., Dimsdale, J. E., & Hackett, T. P. (1985). Components of type A, hostility, and anger-in: Further relationships to angiographic findings. *Health Psychology, 4*, 137-152.

MacKenzie, K. R. (1994). Using personality measurements in clinical practice. In P. T. Costa, Jr. & T. A. Widiger (Eds.), *Personality disorders and the Five-Factor Model of personality* (pp. 237-250). Washington, DC: American Psychological Association.

Maddi, S. R. (2005). On hardiness and other pathways to resilience. *American Psychologist, 60*, 261-262.

Maddi, S. R. & Costa, P. T. (1972). *Humanism in personology: Allport, Maslow, and Murray*. Chicago, IL: Aldine · Atherton.

Maharishi Mahesh Yogi (1963). *Transcendental meditation*. New York, NY: The New American Library.

Maher, B. (Ed.). (1969). *Clinical psychology and personality: The selected papers of George Kelly*. New York, NY: John Wiley & Sons.

Mahler, M. S., Pine, F., & Bergman, A. (1975). *The psychological birth of the human infant: Symbiosis and individuation*. New York, NY: Basic Books.

Main, J. (1980). *Word into silence*. New York, NY: Continuum.

Main, J. (1984). *Moment of Christ: The path of meditation*. New York, NY: Continuum.

Main, J. (1989). *The way of unknowing: Expanding spiritual horizons through meditation*. New York, NY: Crossroad.

Malia, M. E. (1978). Adulthood refracted: Russia and Leo Tolstoi. In E. H. Erikson (Ed.), *Adulthood* (pp. 173-187). New York, NY: W. W. Norton & Company.

Manaster, G. J. & Corsini, R. J. (1982). *Individual psychology: Theory and practice*. Itasca, IL: F. E. Peacock Publishers.

Manaster, G. J., Painter, G., Deutsch, D., & Overholt, B. J. (1977). *Alfred Adler: As we remember him*. Chicago, IL: North American Society of Adlerian Psychology.

Mandala Publishing Group. (2000). *Darshan: Sweet sounds of surrender*. San Rafael, CA: Author.

Mannix, E. & Neale, M. A. (2005). What differences make a difference? The promise and reality of diverse teams in organizations. *Psychological Science in the Public Interest, 6*, 31-55.

Manji, I. (2003). *The trouble with Islam today: A Muslim's call for reform in her faith*. New York, NY: St. Martin's Griffin.

Margolis, E. T. (2001). Sampson at last and applied. *American Psychologist, 56*, 1173-1174.

Marks, D. (1999). *Disability: Controversial debates and psychosocial perspectives*. New York, NY: Routledge.

Marks, M. (2006). The science of team effectiveness. *Psychological Science in the Public Interest, 7(3)*, i.

Markus, H. R., Uchida, Y., Omoregie, H., Townsend, S., & Kitayama, S. (2006). Going for the gold: Models of agency in Japanese and American contexts. *Psychological Science, 17*, 103-112.

Marlatt, G. A., Witkiewitz, K., Dillworth, T. M., Bowen, S. W., Parks, G. A., Macpherson, L. M., Lonczak, H. S., Larimer, M. E., Simpson, T., Blume, A. W., & Crutcher, R. (2004). Vipassana meditation as a treatment for alcohol and drug use disorders. In S. C. Hayes, V. M. Follette, & M. M. Linehan (Eds.), *Mindfulness and acceptance: Expanding the cognitive-behavioral tradition* (pp. 261-287). New York, NY: The Guilford Press.

Martin, N. & Jardine, R. (1986). Eysenck's contributions to behaviour genetics. In S. Mogdil & C. Modgil (Eds.), *Hans Eysenck: Consensus and controversy* (pp. 13-47). Philadelphia, PA: The Falmer Press.

Maslow, A. H. (1943/1973). A theory of human motivation. In R. J. Lowry (Ed.), *Dominance, self-esteem, self-actualization: Germinal papers of A. H. Maslow* (pp. 153-173). Monterey, CA: Brooks/Cole Publishing Company.

Maslow, A. H. (1950/1973). Self-actualizing people: A study of psychological health. In R. J. Lowry (Ed.), *Dominance, self-esteem, self-actualization: Germinal papers of A. H. Maslow* (pp. 177-201). Monterey, CA: Brooks/Cole Publishing Company.

Maslow, A. H. (Ed.). (1959). *New knowledge in human values*. Chicago, IL: Henry Regnery Company.

Maslow, A. H. (1964). *Religions, values, and peak-experiences*. New York, NY: The Viking Press.

Maslow, A. H. (1965). *Eupsychian management: A journal*. Homewood, IL: Richard D. Irwin, Inc. & The Dorsey Press.

Maslow, A. H. (1966). *The psychology of science: A reconnaissance*. New York, NY: Harper & Row.

Maslow, A. H. (1967/2008). Self-actualization and beyond. In M. W. Schustak & H. S. Friedman (Eds.), *The personality reader, 2nd Ed* (pp. 255-262). Boston, MA: Pearson Education.

Maslow, A. H. (1968). *Toward a psychology of Being, 2nd Ed.* New York, NY: D. Van Nostrand Company.

Maslow, A. H. (1970). *Motivation and Personality, 2nd Ed.* New York, NY: Harper & Row, Publishers.

Maslow, A. H. (1971). *The farther reaches of human nature*. New York, NY: The Viking Press.

Maslow, A. H. (1975). Love in healthy people. In A. Montagu (Ed.), *The practice of love* (pp. 89-113). Englewood Cliffs, NJ: Prentice-Hall.

Maslow, A. H. (1996a). The dynamics of American management. In E. Hoffman (Ed.), *Future visions: The unpublished papers of Abraham Maslow*. (pp. 184-194). Thousand Oaks, CA: SAGE Publications.

Maslow, A. H. (1996b). What is the essence of human nature? In E. Hoffman (Ed.), *Future visions: The unpublished papers of Abraham Maslow*. (pp. 83-87). Thousand Oaks, CA: SAGE Publications.

Maslow, A. H. & Mittelmann, B. (1941). *Principles of abnormal psychology: The dynamics of psychic illness*. New York, NY: Harper & Brothers Publishers.

Massimini, F. & Fave, A. D. (2000). Individual development in a bio-cultural perspective. *American Psychologist, 55*, 24-33.

Masten, A. S. (2001). Ordinary magic: Resilience processes in development. *American Psychologist, 56*, 227-238.

Masters, W. H. & Johnson, V. E. (1966). *Human sexual response*. Boston, MA: Little and Brown.

Mathew, R. J. (2001). *The true path: Western science and the quest for Yoga.* Cambridge, MA: Perseus.

Matlin, M. W. (2004). *The psychology of women, 5th Ed.* Belmont, CA: Thomson Wadsworth.

Maton, K. I., Kohout, J. L., Wicherski, M., Leary, G. E., & Vinokurov, A. (2006). Minority students of color and the psychology graduate pipeline: Disquieting and encouraging trends, 1989-2003. *American Psychologist, 61*, 117-131.

Matsumoto, D. (1994). *People: Psychology from a cultural perspective*. Pacific Grove, CA: Brooks/Cole.

Matsumoto, D. (1997). *Culture and modern life*. Pacific Grove, CA: Brooks/Cole.

Matsumoto, D. & Juang, L. (2004). *Culture and psychology, 3rd Ed.* Belmont, CA: Wadsworth/Thomson Learning.

Matsumoto, D. & Yoo, S. H. (2006). Toward a new generation of cross-cultural research. *Perspectives on Psychological Science, 1*, 234-250.

Matt, D. C. (1995). *The essential Kabbalah: The heart of Jewish mysticism*. New York, NY: HarperSanFrancisco.

May, R. (1950). *The meaning of anxiety*. New York, NY: The Ronald Press Company.

May, R. (1953). *Man's search for himself.* New York, NY: W. W. Norton & Company.

May, R. (1967). *Psychology and the human dilemma.* Princeton, NJ: D. Van Nostrand Company.

May, R. (1969). *Love and will*. New York, NY: W. W. Norton & Company.

May, R. (1972). *Power and innocence: A search for the sources of violence*. New York, NY: W. W. Norton & Company.

May, R. (1975). *The courage to create*. New York, NY: W. W. Norton & Company.

May, R. (1977). *The meaning of anxiety - Revised Edition*. New York, NY: W. W. Norton & Company.

May, R. (1983). *The discovery of being: Writings in existential psychology*. New York, NY: W. W. Norton & Company.

May, R. (1991). *The cry for myth*. New York, NY: A Delta Book.

May, R., Rogers, C., Maslow, A, et al. (1986). *Politics and innocence: A humanistic debate*. Dallas, TX: Saybrook Publishers.

May, R. & Yalom, I. (1995). Existential psychotherapy. In R. J. Corsini & D. Wedding (Eds.), *Current Psychotherapies, 5th Ed.* (pp. 262-292). Itasca, IL: F. E. Peacock Publishers.

Mbalia, D. D. (1995). *John Edgar Wideman: Reclaiming*

the African personality. Cranbury, NJ: Associated University Presses.

Mbigi, L. & Maree, J. (1995). *Ubuntu: The spirit of African transformation management*. Randburg, South Africa: Knowledge Resources.

McAdams, D. P. (1985). *Power, intimacy, and the life story: Personological inquiries into identity*. Homewood, IL: The Dorsey Press.

McAdams, D. P. (1992). Unity and purpose in human lives: The emergence of identity as a life story. In R. A. Zucker, A. I. Rabin, J. Aronoff, & S. J. Frank (Eds.), *Personality structure in the life course: Essays on personology in the Murray tradition* (pp. 323-375). New York, NY: Springer Publishing Company.

McAdams, D. P. (2006). *The redemptive self: Stories Americans live by*. New York, NY: Oxford University Press.

McAdams, D. P., Josselson, R., & Lieblich, A. (2001). *Turns in the road: Narrative studies of lives in transition*. Washington, DC: American Psychological Association.

McAdams, D. P. & Pals, J. L. (2006). A new big five: Fundamental principles for an integrative science of personality. *American Psychologist, 61*, 204-217.

McBride-Chang, C. & Treiman, R. (2003). Hong Kong Chinese kindergartners learn to read English analytically. *Psychological Science, 14*, 138-143.

McCauley, C., Draguns, J., & Lee, Y.-T. (1999). Person perception across cultures. In Y.-T. Lee, C. R. McCauley, & J. G. Draguns (Eds.), *Personality and person perception across cultures* (pp. 279-296). Mahway, NJ: Lawrence Erlbaum Associates, Publishers.

McCormick, D. J. (2004). Galton on spirituality, religion, and health. *American Psychologist, 59*, 52.

McCrae, R. R. (1994). A reformulation of Axis II: Personality and personality-related problems. In P. T. Costa, Jr. & T. A. Widiger (Eds.), *Personality disorders and the Five-Factor Model of personality* (pp. 303-309). Washington, DC: American Psychological Association.

McCrae, R. R. (2002). NEO-PI-R data from 36 cultures. In R. R. McCrae & J. Allik (Eds.), *The Five-Factor Model of personality across cultures* (pp. 105-125). New York, NY: Kluwer Academic/Plenum Publishers.

McCrae, R. R. & Allik, J. (Eds.). (2002). *The Five-Factor Model of personality across cultures*. New York, NY: Kluwer Academic/Plenum Publishers.

McCrae, R. R. & Costa, Jr., P. T. (2003). *Personality in adulthood: A Five-Factor Theory perspective, 2nd Ed.* New York, NY: The Guilford Press.

McCrae, R. R. & Terracciano, A. (2006). National Character and Personality. *Current Directions in Psychological Science, 15*, 156-161.

McDaniel, J. W. (1976). *Physical disability and human behavior, 2nd Ed.* New York, NY: Pergamon Press.

McClelland, D. C. (1964). *The roots of consciousness*. Princeton, NJ: D. Van Nostrand Company.

McClelland, D. C. (1975). *Power: The inner experience*. New York, NY: Irvington Publishers.

McClelland, D. C. (1976). *The achieving society - With a new introduction*. New York, NY: Irvington Publishers.

McClelland, D. C. (Ed.). (1982a). *The development of social maturity*. New York, NY: Irvington Publishers.

McClelland, D. C. (Ed.). (1982b). *Education for values*. New York, NY: Irvington Publishers.

McClelland, D. C., Atkinson, J. W., Clark, R. A., & Lowell, E. L. (1953). *The achievement motive*. New York, NY: Appleton-Century-Crofts.

McClelland, D. C., Baldwin, A. L., Bronfenbrenner, U., & Strodtbeck, F. L. (1958). *Talent and society: New perspectives in the identification of talent*. Princeton, NJ: D. Van Nostrand Company.

McClelland, D. C., Davis, W. N., Kalin, R., & Wanner, E. (Eds.). (1972). *The drinking man*. New York, NY: The Free Press.

McClelland, D. C. & Winter, D. G. (1969). *Motivating economic achievement*. New York, NY: The Free Press.

McNab, C. (2003). *Martial Arts for People with Disabilities: Essential Tips, Drills, and Combat Techniques*. Broomall, PA: Mason Crest Publishers.

McQuaid, J. R. & Carmona, P. E. (2004). *Peaceful mind: Using mindfulness & cognitive behavioral psychology to overcome depression*. Oakland, CA: New Harbinger Publications.

Mehta, P. H. & Gosling, S. D. (2006). How can animal studies contribute to research on the biological bases of personality? In T. Canli (Ed.), *Biology of personality and individual differences* (pp. 427-448). New York: Guilford.

Meier, B. P., Robinson, M. D., & Wilkowski, B. M. (2006). Turning the other cheek: Agreeableness and the regulation of aggression-related primes. *Psychological Science, 17*, 136-142.

Mendlewicz, J., Fleiss, J. L., & Fieve, R. R. (1975). Linkage studies in affective disorders: The Xg blood group and manic-depressive illness. In R. R. Fieve, D. Rosenthal, & H. Brill (Eds.), *Genetic research in psychiatry* (pp. 219-232). Baltimore, MD: The Johns Hopkins University Press.

Merton, T. (1948). *The seven storey mountain*. New York, NY: Harcourt Brace Jovanovich.

Merton, T. (1951). *The ascent to truth*. New York, NY: Harcourt, Brace and Company.

Merton, T. (1967). *Mystics & Zen masters*. New York, NY: Farrar, Straus and Giroux.

References

Merton, T. (1977). *The monastic journey*. Kansas City, KS: Sheed Andrews and McMeel.

Milano, P. (Ed.). (1947). *The portable Dante*. New York, NY: Penguin Books.

Miller, J. & Garran, A. M. (2008). *Racism in the United States: Implications for the helping professions*. Belmont, CA: Thomson Brooks/Cole.

Miller, J. B. (1976). *Toward a new psychology of women*. Boston, MA: Beacon Press.

Miller, J. B. (1991). The development of women's sense of self. In J. V. Jordan, A. G. Kaplan, J. B. Miller, I. P. Stiver, & J. L. Surrey (Eds.), *Women's growth in connection: Writings from the Stone Center* (pp 11-26). New York, NY: The Guilford Press.

Miller, J. B., Jordan, J. V., Stiver, I. P., Walker, M., Surrey, J. L., & Eldridge, N. S. (2004). Therapists' authenticity. In J. V. Jordan, M. Walker, & L. M. Hartling (Eds.), *The complexity of connection: Writings from the Stone Center's Jean Baker Miller Training Institute* (pp 64-89). New York, NY: The Guilford Press.

Miller, L. C., Putcha-Bhagavatula, A., & Pedersen, W. C. (2002). Men's and women's mating preferences: Distinct evolutionary mechanisms? *Current Directions in Psychological Science, 11*, 88-93.

Miller, N. E. & Dollard, J. (1941). *Social learning and imitation*. New Haven, CT: Yale University Press.

Miller, W. R. & Thoresen, C. E. (2003). Spirituality, religion, and health: An emerging research field. *American Psychologist, 58*, 24-35.

Miller, W. R. & Thoresen, C. E. (2004). Spirituality, health, and the discipline of psychology. *American Psychologist, 59*, 54-55.

Millon, T. (1994). Personality disorders: Conceptual distinctions and classification issues. In P. T. Costa, Jr. & T. A. Widiger (Eds.), *Personality disorders and the Five-Factor Model of personality* (pp. 279-301). Washington, DC: American Psychological Association.

Millon, T. (1996). *Disorders of Personality: DSM-IV and Beyond, 2nd Ed.* New York, NY: Wiley & Sons.

Millon, T. (2004). *Masters of the Mind: Exploring the story of mental illness from ancient times to the new millennium*. Hoboken, NJ: Wiley & Sons.

Millon, T. & Grossman, S. D. (2005). Personology: A theory based on evolutionary concepts. In M. F. Lenzenweger & J. F. Clark (Eds.), *Major theories of personality disorder* (pp. 332-390). New York, NY: The Guilford Press.

Mischel, W. (1958a). The effect of the commitment situation on the generalization of expectancies. *Journal of Personality, 26*, 508-516.

Mischel, W. (1958b). Preference for delayed reinforcement: An experimental study of a cultural observation. *Journal of Abnormal and Social Psychology, 56*, 57-61.

Mischel, W. (1961). Father-absence and delay of gratification: Cross-cultural comparisons. *Journal of Abnormal and Social Psychology, 63*, 116-124.

Mischel, W. (1968). *Personality and assessment*. Mahwah, NJ: Lawrence Erlbaum Associates.

Mischel, W. (2004). Toward an integrative science of the person. *Ann. Rev. Psychol., 55*, 1-22.

Mischel, W. & Mischel, H. N. (1980). *Essentials of Psychology, 2nd Ed.* New York, NY: Random House.

Mischel, W. & Shoda, Y. (1995/2000). A cognitive-affective system theory of personality: Reconceptualizing situations, dispositions, dynamics, and invariance in personality structure. In E. T. Higgins & A. W. Kruglanski (Eds.), *Motivation Science: Social and Personality Perspectives* (pp. 150-176). Philadelphia, PA: Psychology Press.

Mischel, W., Shoda, Y., & Rodriguez, M. I. (1989). Delay of gratification in children. *Science, 244*, 933-938.

Mitchell, J. (Ed.). (1986). *The selected Melanie Klein*. New York, NY: The Free Press.

Mitchell, J. (2000). *Psychoanalysis and feminism: A radical reassessment of Freudian psychoanalysis*. New York, NY: Basic Books.

Mitchell, S. (2000). *Bhagavad Gita: A new translation*. New York, NY: Three Rivers Press.

Mitchell, S. A. & Black, M. J. (1995). *Freud and beyond*. New York, NY: BasicBooks.

Miyamoto, Y., Nisbett, R. E., & Masuda, T. (2006). Culture and the Physcial Environment: Holistic Versus Analytic Perceptual Affordances. *Psychological Science, 17*, 113-119.

Mmari, G. R. V. (1979). Teacher training in Tanzania. In H. Hinzen & V. H. Hundsdörfer (Eds.), *The Tanzanian experience: Education for liberation and development* (pp. 119-131). Hamburg, Germany: Unesco Institute for Education.

Moffitt, T. E., Caspi, A., & Rutter, M. (2006). Measured gene-environment interactions in psychopathology: Concepts, research strategies, and implications for research, interventon, and public understanding genetics. *Perspectives on Psychological Science, 1*, 5-27.

Moghaddam, F. M. (2005). The staircase to terrorism: A psychological exploration. *American Psychologist, 60*, 161-169.

Moghaddam, F. M. (2006). *From the terrorists' point of view: What they experience and why they come to destroy*. Westport, CN: Praeger Security International.

Molden, D. C., Lucas, G. M., Finkel, E. J., Kumashiro, M., & Rusbult, C. (2009). Perceived support for promotion-focused and prevention-focused goals: Associations with well-being in unmarried and married couples. *Psychological Science, 20*, 787-793.

References

Monastersky, R. (2006). Religion on the brain. *The Chronicle of Higher Education, LII*, A14-A19.

Montaldo, J. (Ed.). (2001). *Dialogues with Silence: Prayers & Drawings - Thomas Merton*. New York, NY: HarperSanFrancisco.

Morgan, C. D. & Murray, H. A. (1935). A method of investigating fantasies: The Thematic Apperception Test. *Archives of Neurology and Psychiatry, 34*, 289-306.

Mosak, H. H. (1995). Adlerian psychotherapy. In R. J. Corsini & D. Wedding (Eds.), *Current psychotherapies, 5th Ed.* (pp. 51-94). Itasca, IL: F. E. Peacock Publishers.

Mosak, H. H. & Maniacci, M. P. (1999). *A primer of Adlerian psychology: The analytic-behavioral-cognitive psychology of Alfred Adler*. Philadelphia, PA: Brunner/Mazel.

Mruk, C. J. & Hartzell, J. (2003). *Zen and psychotherapy: Integrating traditional and nontraditional approaches*. New York, NY: Springer Publishing.

Mullahy, P. & Melinek, M. (1983). *Interpersonal psychiatry*. New York, NY: SP Medical & Scientific Books.

Murdock, G. P. (1945). The common denominator of cultures. In R. Linton (Ed.), *The science of man in the world crisis* (pp. 122-142). New York, NY: Columbia University Press.

Murphy, J. (1976). Psychiatric Labeling in Cross-Cultural Perspective. *Science, 191*, 1019-1028.

Murray, H. A. (1938). *Explorations in personality: A clinical and experimental study o fifty men of college age*. New York, NY: Oxford University Press.

Murray, H. A. (1940/2008). What should psychologists do about psychoanalysis? In M. W. Schustak & H. S. Friedman (Eds.), *The personality reader, 2nd Ed* (pp. 31-35). Boston, MA: Pearson Education.

Murray, H. A. (1960). The possible nature of a "mythology" to come. In H. A. Murray (Ed.), *Myth and mythmaking* (pp. 300-353). New York, NY: George Braziller.

Mussweiler, T. (2006). Doing is for thinking!: Stereotype activation by stereotypic movements. *Psychological Science, 17*, 17-21.

Mwikamba, C. M. (2005). In search of an African identity. In G. J. Wanjohi & G. W. Wanjohi (Eds.), *Social and religious concerns of East Africa: A Wajibu anthology* (pp. 3-15). Nairobi, Kenya: Wajibu: A Journal of Social and Religious Concern.

Myers D.G. (2000). The funds, friends, and faith of happy people. *American Psychologist, 55*, 56-67.

Myers, D. G. & Jeeves, M. A. (2003). *Psychology: Through the eyes of faith*. New York, NY: HarperCollins.

Myers, I. B. (1993). *Introduction to type: A guide to understanding your results on the Myers-Briggs Type Indicator, 5th Ed.* Palo Alto, CA: Consulting Psychologists Press.

Myers, I. B. & McCaulley, M. H. (1985). *A guide to the development and use of the Myers-Briggs Type Indicator*. Palo Alto, CA: Consulting Psychologists Press.

Myers, I. B. & Myers, P. B. (1980). *Gifts differing: Understanding personality type*. Palo Alto, CA: CPP Books.

Myers, L. J. (1988). *Understanding an Afrocentric world view: Introduction to an optimal psychology*. Dubuque, IA: Kendall/Hunt.

Nagelschmidt, A. M. & Jakob, R. (1977). Dimensionality of Rotter's I-E scale in the process of modernization. *Journal of Cross-Cultural Psychology, 8*, 101-112.

Napier, J. L. & Jost, J. T. (2008). Why are conservatives happier than liberals? *Psychological Science, 19*, 565-572.

Nardo, D. (1994). *The physically challenged*. New York, NY: Chelsea House Publishers.

Nathan, L. (2005). Karate, kids, and the culture: Your child and the martial arts. Retrieved June 10, 2006, www.crossroad.to/articles2/05/karate.htm

Nation, M., Crusto, C., Wandersman, A., Kumpfer, K. L., Seybolt, KD., Morrissey-Kane, E., & Davino, K. (2003). What works in prevention: Principles of effective prevention programs. *American Psychologist, 58*, 449-456.

Newberg, A., Alavi, A., Baime, M., Pourdehnad, M., Santanna, J., & d'Aquili, E. (2001). The measurement of regional cerebral blood blow during the complex cognitive task of meditation: A preliminary SPECT study. *Psychiatry Research: Neuroimaging Section, 106*, 113-122.

Newberg, A. B. & Lee, B. Y. (2005). The neuroscientific study of religious and spiritual phenomena: Or why God doesn't use biostatistics. *Zygon, 40*, 469-489.

Newton, H. P. (1973). *Revolutionary suicide*. New York, NY: Harcourt Brace Jovanovich.

Nicholi, A. M. (2002). *The question of God: C. S. Lewis and Sigmund Freud debate God, love, sex, and the meaning of life*. New York, NY: Free Press.

Nicholson, I. A. M. (2003). *Inventing personality: Gordon Allport and the science of selfhood*. Washington, DC: American Psychological Association.

Nikelly, A. G. (Ed.). (1971a). *Techniques for behavior change: Applications of Adlerian theory*. Springfield, IL: Charles C. Thomas.

Nikelly, A. G. (1971b). Developing social feeling in psychotherapy. In A. G. Nikelly (Ed.), *Techniques for behavior change: Applications of Adlerian therapy* (pp. 91-95). Springfield, IL: Charles C Thomas.

Nikelly, A. G. & Bostrom, J. A. (1971). Psychotherapy as reorientation and readjustment. In A. G. Nikelly (Ed.), *Techniques for behavior change:*

Applications of Adlerian therapy (pp. 103-107). Springfield, IL: Charles C Thomas.

Niles, F. S. (1981). Dimensionality of Rotter's I-E scale in Sri Lanka. *Journal of Cross-Cultural Psychology, 12*, 473-479.

Norenzayan, A. & Nisbett, R. E. (2000). Culture and causal cognition. *Current Directions in Psychological Science, 9*, 132-135.

Nouwen, H. J. M. (1972). *Pray to live - Thomas Merton: A contemplative critic*. Notre Dame, IN: Fides Publishers.

Nurbakhsh, J. (1990). *Sufi women, Revised 2nd Ed.* New York, NY: Khaniqahi-Himatullahi Publications.

Nyborg, H. (1997). *The scientific study of human nature: Tribute to Hans J. Eysenck at eighty*. Oxford, England: Pergamon Press.

Nyerere, J. K. (1967). *Education for self-reliance*. Dar es Salaam, Tanzania: Ministry of Information and Tourism.

Obasi, E. M. (2002). Reconceptualizing the notion of self from the African deep structure. In T. A. Parham (Ed.), *Counseling persons of African descent: Raising the bar of practitioner competence* (pp. 52-74). Upper Saddle River, NJ: Prentice Hall.

O'Connor, G. (Director), & Guggenheim, E. (Screenwriter). (2004). *Miracle* [Motion Picture]. United States: Walt Disney Pictures.

Oishi, S., Diener, E., & Lucas, R. E. (2007). The optimum level of well-being: Can People be too happy? *Perspectives on Psychological Science, 2*, 346-360.

Okeke, B.I., Draguns, J. G., Sheku, G., & Allen, W. (1999). Culture, self, and personality in Africa. In Y.-T. Lee, C. R. McCauley, & J. G. Draguns (Eds.), *Personality and person perception across cultures* (pp. 139-162). Mahwah, NJ: Lawrence Erlbaum Associates.

Okun, B. F., Fried, J., & Okun, M. L. (1999). *Understanding diversity: A learning-as-practice primer*. Pacific Grove, CA: Brooks/Cole.

Olendzki, A. (2003). Buddhist psychology. In S. R. Segall (Ed.), *Encountering Buddhism: Western psychology and Buddhist teachings* (pp. 9-30). Albany, NY: State University of New York Press.

Olendzki, A. (2005). The roots of mindfulness. In C. K. Germer, R. D. Siegel, & P. R. Fulton (Eds.), *Mindfulness and psychotherapy* (pp. 241-261). New York, NY: Guilford Press.

Osius, A. (1991). *Second ascent: The story of Hugh Herr*. Harrisburg, PA: Stackpole Books.

Oxford University Press. (2002). *The Oxford American college dictionary*. New York, NY: G. P. Putnam's Sons.

Oyersman, D., Brickman, D., Bybee, D., & Celious, A. (2006). Fitting in matters: Markers of in-group belonging and academic outcomes. *Psychological Science, 17*, 854-861.

Pack-Brown, S. P., Whittington-Clark, L. E., & Parker, W. M. (1998). *Images of me: A guide to group work with African-American women*. Boston, MA: Allyn & Bacon.

Panksepp, J. (2005). Beyond a joke: From animal laughter to human joy? *Science, 308*, 62-63.

Pargament, K. I. & Mahoney, A. (2005). Spirituality. In C. R. Snyder & S. J. Lopez (Eds.), *Handbook of positive psychology* (pp. 646-659). New York, NY: Oxford University Press.

Parham, T. A. (2002). Understanding personality and how to measure it. In T. A. Parham (Ed.), *Counseling persons of African descent: Raising the bar of practitioner competence* (pp. 38-51). Upper Saddle River, NJ: Prentice Hall.

Parham, T. A. & Parham, W. D. (2002). Understanding African American mental health. In T. A. Parham (Ed.), *Counseling persons of African descent: Raising the bar of practitioner competence* (pp. 25-37). Upper Saddle River, NJ: Prentice Hall.

Parham, T. A., White, J. L., & Ajamu, A. (1999). *The psychology of Blacks: An African-centered perspective*. Upper Saddle River, NJ: Prentice Hall.

Paris, B. J. (1994). *Karen Horney: A psychoanalyst's search for self-understanding*. New Haven, CT: Yale University Press.

Patrick, D. (1990). *Martin Luther King, Jr.* New York, NY: Franklin Watts.

Pattakos, A. (2004). *Prisoners of our thoughts: Viktor Frankl's principles at work*. San Francisco, CA: Berrett-Koehler Publishers.

PDM Task Force. (2006). *Psychodynamic Diagnostic Manual*. Silver Spring, MD: Alliance of Psychoanalytic Organizations.

Peabody, D. (1999). National characteristics: Dimensions for comparison. In Y.-T. Lee, C. R. McCauley, & J. G. Draguns (Eds.), *Personality and person perception across cultures* (pp. 65-84). Mahway, NJ: Lawrence Erlbaum Associates, Publishers.

Pearlin, L. I. (1980). Life strains and psychological distress among adults. In N. J. Smelser & E. H. Erikson (Eds.), *Themes of work and love in adulthood* (pp. 174-192). Cambridge, MA: Harvard University Press.

Pearson, R. (1991). *Race, intelligence and bias in academe*. Washington, DC: Scott-Townsend Publishers.

Pennisi, E. (2006). Social animals prove their smarts. *Science, 312*, 1734-1738.

Perlman, E. & Wellman, M. (Co-Directors & Co-Screenwriters). (1998). *Beyond the barriers* [Motion Picture]. United States: No Limits.

Perry, H. S. (1982). *Psychiatrist of America: The life of Harry Stack Sullivan*. Cambridge, MA: The Belknap Press.

Perunovic, W. Q. E., Heller, D., & Rafaeli, E. (2007). Within-person changes in the structure of emotion: The role of cultural identification and language. *Psychological Science, 18*, 607-613.

Pervin, L. A. (1999). The cross-cultural challenge to personality. In Y.-T. Lee, C. R. McCauley, & J. G. Draguns (Eds.), *Personality and person perception across cultures* (pp. 23-41). Mahway, NJ: Lawrence Erlbaum Associates, Publishers.

Peters, U. H. (1985). *Anna Freud: A life dedicated to children.* New York, NY: Schocken Books.

Peterson, C. (2000). The future of optimism. *American Psychologist, 55*, 44-55.

Peterson, C. (2006). *A primer in positive psychology*. New York, NY: Oxford University Press.

Peterson, C. & Seligman, M. E. P. (2004). *Character strengths and virtues: A handbook and classification.* New York, NY: Oxford University Press.

Phares, E. J. (1972). A social learning theory approach to psychopathology. In J. B. Rotter, J. E. Chance, & E. J. Phares (Eds.), *Applications of a Social Learning Theory of Personality* (pp. 436-469). New York, NY: Holt, Rinehart and Winston.

Phillips, H. P. (1965). *Thai peasant personality: The patterning of interpersonal behavior in the village of Bang Chan.* Berkeley, CA: University of California Press.

Picano, J. J., Roland, R. R., Rollins, K. D., & Williams, T. J. (2002). Development and validaton of a sentence completion test measure of defensive responding in military personnel assessed for nonroutine missions. *Military Psychology, 14*, 279-298.

Pickren, W. E. (2000). A whisper of salvation: American psychologists and religion in the popular press, 1884-1908. *American Psychologist, 55*, 1022-1024.

Pickren, W. E. & Tomes, H. (2002). The legacy of Kenneth B. Clark to the APA: The Board of Social and Ethical Responsibility for Psychology. *American Psychologist, 57*, 51-59.

Piedmont, R. L., Bain, E., McCrae, R. R., & Costa, Jr., P. T. (2002). The applicability of the Five-Factor Model in a sub-Saharan culture. In R. R. McCrae & J. Allik (Eds.), *The Five-Factor Model of personality across cultures* (pp. 155-173). New York, NY: Kluwer Academic/Plenum Publishers.

Pintner, R., Eisenson, J., & Stanton, M. (1941). *The psychology of the physically handicapped.* New York, NY: F. S. Crofts & Co.

Piper, W. E., Wogan, M., & Getter, H. (1972). Social learning theory predictors of termination in psychotherapy. In J. B. Rotter, J. E. Chance, & E. J. Phares (Eds.), *Applications of a Social Learning Theory of Personality* (pp. 548-553). New York, NY: Holt, Rinehart and Winston.

Pirsig, R. M. (1999). *Zen and the art of motorcycle maintenance: An inquiry into values* [CD]. New York, NY: Audio Renaissance.

Poe, E. A. (1844/1990). The Raven. In Classics Illustrated, G. Wilson (Illustrator), *The Raven and other poems* (pp. 2-11). New York, NY: Berkley/First Publishing.

Poortinga, Y. H., Van de Vijver, F. J. R., & van Hemert, D. A. (2002). Cross-cultural equivalence of the Big Five. In R. R. McCrae & J. Allik (Eds.), *The Five-Factor Model of personality across cultures* (pp. 281-303). New York, NY: Kluwer Academic/Plenum Publishers.

Posada, G. & Jacobs, A. (2001). Child-mother attachment relationships and culture. *American Psychologist, 56*, 821-822.

Powell, L. H., Shahabi, L., & Thoresen, C. E. (2003) Religion and spirituality: Linkages to physical health. *American Psychologist, 58*, 36-52.

Prentice, D. A. & Miller, D. T. (2006). Essentializing differences between women and men. *Psychological Science, 17*, 129-135.

Pretzer, J. L. & Beck, A. T. (2005). A cognitive theory of personality disorders. In M. F. Lenzenweger & J. F. Clarkin (Eds.), *Major theories of personality disorder, 2nd Ed.* (pp. 43-113). New York, NY: The Guilford Press.

Price, W. F. & Crapo, R. H. (2002). *Cross-cultural perspectives in introductory psychology, 4th Ed.* Belmont, CA: Wadsworth.

Progoff, I. (1973). *Jung, synchronicity, & human destiny.* New York, NY: The Julian Press.

Ragsdale, E. S. (2005). Value and meaning in Gestalt psychology and Mahayana Buddhism. In K. H. Dockett, G. R. Dudley-Grant, & C. P. Bankart (Eds.), *Psychology and Buddhism: From individual to global community* (pp. 71-101). New York, NY: Kluwer Academic/Plenum Publishers.

Ram Dass (2000). *Still here: Embracing aging, changing, and dying.* New York, NY: Riverhead Books.

Ray, O. (2004). How the mind hurts and heals the body. *American Psychologist, 59*, 29-40.

Rayburn, C. A. (2004). Religion, spirituality, and health. *American Psychologist, 59*, 52-53.

Raz, A., Fan, J., & Posner, M. I. (2005). Hypnotic suggestion reduces conflict in the human brain. *Proceedings of the National Academy of Sciences, 102*, 9978-9983.

Red Pine (1987). *The Zen teaching of Bodhidharma.* New York, NY: North Point Press.

Reeves, C. (1977). *The psychology of Rollo May.* San Francisco, CA: Jossey-Bass Publishers.

Reich, W. (1933/1970). *The mass psychology of fascism.* New York, NY: Farrar, Straus & Giroux.

Reich, W. (1933/1972). *Character Analysis, 3rd, Enlarged Edition.* New York, NY: Farrar, Straus and Giroux.

Reich, W. (1973). The orgasm theory. In M. B. Higgins (Ed.), *Wilhelm Reich selected writings: An introduction to orgonomy* (pp. 13-41). New York, NY: Farrar, Straus and Giroux.

Reps, P. & Senzaki, N. (1994). *Zen flesh, Zen bones.* Boston, MA: Shambala.

Ribner, S. & Chin, R. (1978). *The martial arts*. New York, NY: Harper & Row.

Richards, P. S. & Bergen, A. E. (Eds.). (2000). *Handbook of psychotherapy and religious diversity*. Washington, DC: American Psychological Association.

Richards, P. S. & Bergen, A. E. (Eds.). (2004). *Casebook for a spiritual strategy in counseling and psychotherapy*. Washington, DC: American Psychological Association.

Richards, R. S. & Bergen, A. E. (2005). *A spiritual strategy for counseling and psychotherapy* (2nd Ed.). Washington, DC: American Psychological Association.

Richmond, L. J. (2004). Religion, spirituality, and health: A topic not so new. *American Psychologist, 59*, 52.

Ripple, C. H. & Zigler, E. (2003). Research, Policy, and the federal role in prevention initiatives for children. *American Psychologist, 58*, 482-490.

Rizzolatti, G. & Craighero, L. (2004). The mirror-neuron system. *Annual Review of Neuroscience, 27*, 169-192.

Robins, C. J., Schmidt III, H., & Linehan, M. M. (2004). Dialectical behavior therapy: Synthesizing radical acceptance with skillful means. In S. C. Hayes, V. M. Follette, & M. M. Linehan (Eds.), *Mindfulness and acceptance: Expanding the cognitive-behavioral tradition* (pp. 30-44). New York, NY: The Guilford Press.

Robins, R. W. & Trzesniewski, K. H. (2005). Self-esteem development across the lifespan. *Current Directions in Psychological Science, 14*, 158-162.

Robinson, M. D., Vargas, P. T., Tamir, M., & Solberg, E. C. (2004). Using and being used by categories: The case of negative evaluations and daily well-being. *Psychological Science, 15*, 521-526.

Robinson, F. G. (1992). *Love's story told: A life of Henry A. Murray*. Cambridge, MA: Harvard University Press.

Robertson, D. (1991). *Martial Arts for People with Disabilities: An Introduction.* London, England: Souvenir Press Ltd.

Robertson, S. S., Bacher, L. F., & Huntington, N. L. (2001). The integration of body movement and attention in young infants. *Psychological Science, 12*, 523-526.

Robinson Jr., F. M., West, D., & Woodworth Jr., D. (1995). *Coping + Plus: Dimensions of Disability*. Westport, CT: Praeger.

Roessler, R. & Bolton, B. (1978). *Psychosocial adjustment to disability*. Baltimore, MD: University Park Press.

Rogers, C. R. (1939). *The clinical treatment of the problem child.* Boston, MA: Houghton Mifflin Company.

Rogers, C. R. (1942). *Counseling and psychotherapy: Newer concepts in practice*. Boston, MA: Houghton Mifflin Company.

Rogers, C. R. (1951). *Client-centered therapy*. Boston, MA: Houghton Mifflin Company.

Rogers, C. R. (1957/1989). The necessary and sufficient conditions of therapeutic personality change. In H. Kirschenbaum & V. L. Henderson (Eds.), *The Carl Rogers reader* (pp. 219-235). Boston, MA: Houghton Mifflin Company.

Rogers, C. R. (1959/1989). A theory of therapy, personality, and interpersonal relationships, as developed in the client-centered framework. In H. Kirschenbaum & V. L. Henderson (Eds.), *The Carl Rogers reader* (pp. 236-257). Boston, MA: Houghton Mifflin Company.

Rogers, C. R. (1961). *On becoming a person: A therapist's view of psychotherapy*. Boston, MA: Houghton Mifflin Company.

Rogers, C. R. (1970). *Carl Rogers on encounter groups*. New York, NY: Harper & Row.

Rogers, C. R. (1972). *Becoming partners: Marriage and its alternatives*. Delacorte Press.

Rogers, C. R. (1977). *On personal power: Inner strength and its revolutionary impact*. New York, NY: Delacorte Press.

Rogers, C. R. (1980). *A way of Being*. Boston, MA: Houghton Mifflin Company.

Rogers, C. R. (1986/1989). A client-centered/person-centered approach to therapy. In H. Kirschenbaum & V. L. Henderson (Eds.), *The Carl Rogers reader* (pp. 135-152). Boston, MA: Houghton Mifflin Company.

Rogers, C. R. (1989). On reaching 85. In H. Kirschenbaum & V. L. Henderson (Eds.). *The Carl Rogers Reader* (pp. 56-58). Boston, MA: Houghton Mifflin.

Rogers, C. R. & Dymond, R. F. (1954). *Psychotherapy and personality change*. Chicago, IL: University of Chicago Press.

Rogers, C. R. & Roethlisberger, F. J. (1952/1993). Barriers and gateways to communication. In The Harvard Business Review Book Series (Eds.), *The articulate executive: Orchestrating effective communication* (pp. 31-43). Boston, MA: A Harvard Business Review Book.

Rogers, C. R. & Russell, D. E. (2002). *Carl Rogers - The quiet revolutionary: An oral history*. Roseville, CA: Penmarin Books.

Rohlen, T. P. (1978). The promise of adulthood in Japanese spiritualism. In E. H. Erikson (Ed.), *Adulthood* (pp. 129-147). New York, NY: W. W. Norton & Company.

Roisman, G. I. (2005). Conceptual clarifications in the study of resilience. *American Psychologist, 60*, 264-265.

Roland, A. (2005). The spiritual self in psychoanalytic therapy. In M. B. Weiner, P. C. Cooper, & C.

Barbre (Eds.), *Psychotherapy and religion* (pp. 1-16). Lanham, MD: Aronson.

Rolland, J.-P. (2002). The cross-cultural generalizability of the Five-Factor Model of personality. In R. R. McCrae & J. Allik (Eds.), *The Five-Factor Model of personality across cultures* (pp. 7-28). New York, NY: Kluwer Academic/Plenum Publishers.

Rosenzweig, M. R. (1984). Experience, memory, and the brain. *American Psychologist, 39*, 365-376.

Rossier, J., Dahourou, D., & McCrae, R. R. (2005). Structural and mean-level analyses of the five-factor model and locus of control: Further evidence from Africa. *Journal of Cross-Cultural Psychology, 36*, 227-246.

Rothbaum, F., Weisz, J., Pott, M., Miyake, K., & Morelli, G. (2000). Attachment and culture: Security in the United States and Japan. *American Psychologist, 55*, 1093-1104.

Rothbaum, F., Weisz, J., Pott, M., Miyake, K., & Morelli, G. (2001). Deeper into attachment and culture. *American Psychologist, 56*, 827-829.

Rotter, J. B. (1954). *Social learning and clinical psychology*. New York, NY: Prentice-Hall.

Rotter, J. B. (1960). Some implications of a social learning theory for the prediction of goal directed behavior from testing procedures. *Psychological Review, 67*, 301-306.

Rotter, J. B. (1964). *Clinical psychology*. Englewood Cliffs, NJ: Prentice-Hall.

Rotter, J. B. (1966). Generalized expectancies for internal versus external control of reinforcement. *Psychological Monographs, 80*, 1-28.

Rotter, J. B. (1982). *The development and applications of social learning theory: Selected papers*. New York, NY: Praeger.

Rotter, J. B., Chance, J. E., & Phares, E. J. (1972). *Applications of a social learning theory of personality*. New York, NY: Holt, Rinehart and Winston.

Rotter, J. B. & Hochreich, D. J. (1975). *Personality*. Glenview, IL: Scott, Foresman and Company.

Rotter, J. B. & Rafferty, J. E. (1950). *The Rotter incomplete sentences blank: College form*. New York, NY: The Psychological Corporation.

Rubins, J. L. (Ed.). (1972). *Developments in Horney psychoanalysis: 1950...1970*. Huntington, NY: Robert E. Krieger Publishing Company.

Rubins, J. L. (1978). *Karen Horney: Gentle rebel of psychoanalysis*. New York, NY: The Dial Press.

Ruddle, R. A. & Lessels, S. (2006). For efficient navigational search, humans require full physical movement, but not a rich visual scene. *Psychological Science, 17*, 460-465.

Rudolph, S. H. & Rudolph, L. I. (1978). Rajput adulthood: Reflections on the Amar Singh diary. In E. H. Erikson (Ed.), *Adulthood* (pp. 149-171). New York, NY: W. W. Norton & Company.

Ruitenbeek, H. M. (Ed.). (1973). *The first Freudians*. New York, NY: Aronson.

Rule, W. R. (Ed.). (1984). *Lifestyle counseling for adjustment to disability*. Rockville, MD: An Aspen Publication.

Rushton, J. P. (1999). Ethnic differences in temperament. In Y.-T. Lee, C. R. McCauley, & J. G. Draguns (Eds.), *Personality and person perception across cultures* (pp. 45-63). Mahwah, NJ: Lawrence Erlbaum Associates.

Ryan, R. M. & Deci, E. L. (2000). Self-determination theory and the facilitation of intrinsic motivation, social development, and well-being. *American Psychologist, 55*, 68-78.

Salovey, P., Rothman, A. J., Detweiler, J. B., & Steward, W. T. (2000). Emotional states and physical health. *American Psychologist, 55*, 110-121.

Samkange, S. & Samkange, T. M. (1980). *Hunhuism or Ubuntuism: A Zimbabwe indigenous political philosophy*. Salisbury, England: Graham Publishing.

Sampson, E. E. (2000). Reinterpreting individualism and collectivism: Their religious roots and monologic versus dialogic person-other relationship. *American Psychologist, 55*, 1425-1432.

Sanderson, C. & Clarkin, J. F. (1994). Use of the NEO-PI personality dimensions in differential treatment planning. In P. T. Costa, Jr. & T. A. Widiger (Eds.), *Personality disorders and the Five-Factor Model of personality* (pp. 219-235). Washington, DC: American Psychological Association.

Sanyal, B. C. & Kinunda, M. J. (1977). *Higher education for self-reliance: The Tanzanian experience*. Paris, France: International Institute for Educational Planning.

Sartre, J.-P. (1943). *Being and nothingness: A phenomenological essay on ontology*. New York, NY: Washington Square Press.

Sartre, J.-P. (1947/1996). Free will, self construction, and anguish. In J. Feinberg (Ed.), *Reason and responsibility: Readings in some basic problems of philosophy, 9th Ed.* (pp. 456-463). Belmont, CA: Wadsworth.

Sartre, J.-P. (1937/1957). *The transcendence of the ego: An existentialist theory of consciousness*. New York, NY: Farrar, Straus and Giroux.

Sayers, J. (1991). *Mothers of Psychoanalysis: Helene Deutsch, Karen Horney, Anna Freud, Melanie Klein*. New York, NY: W. W. Norton & Company.

Scaravelli, V. (1991). *Awakening the spine: The stress-free Yoga that works with the body to restore health, vitality and energy*. New York, NY: HarperSanFrancisco.

Schied, D. (1986). *Streetwise: An introduction to self-defense*. Los Angeles, CA: Peter Brooks.

Schlein, S. (Ed.). (1987). *A way of looking at things: Selected papers from 1930 to 1980 Erik H. Erikson*. New York, NY: W. W. Norton & Company.

Schneider, S. L. (2001). In search of realistic optimism: Meaning, knowledge, and warm fuzziness. *American Psychologist, 56*, 250-263.

Schroeder, M. L., Wormworth, J. A. & Livesley, W. J. (1994). Dimensions of personality disorder and the Five-Factor Model of personality. In P. T. Costa, Jr. & T. A. Widiger (Eds.), *Personality disorders and the Five-Factor Model of personality* (pp. 117-127). Washington, DC: American Psychological Association.

Schulman, M. (2005). How we become moral: The sources of moral motivation. In C. R. Snyder & S. J. Lopez (Eds.), *Handbook of positive psychology* (pp. 499-512). New York, NY: Oxford University Press.

Schweitzer, M. M. (1983). The elders: Cultural dimensions of aging in two American Indian communities. In J. Sokolovsky (Ed.), *Growing old in different societies: Cross-cultural perspectives* (pp. 168-178). Belmont, CA: Wadsworth.

Scott, G. F. (1984). Lifestyle approaches and resistance to change. In W. R. Rule (Ed.), *Lifestyle counseling for adjustment to disability* (pp. 119-134). Rockville, MD: Aspen Systems Corporation.

Sears, D. O. (2003). Political symbols and collective moral action. In L. G. Aspinwall & U. M. Staudinger (Eds.), *A psychology of human strengths: Fundamental questions and future directions for a positive psychology* (pp. 289-303). Washington, DC: American Psychological Association.

Seeman, T. E., Dubin, L. F., & Seeman, M. (2003) Religiosity/spirituality and health: A critical review of the evidence for biological pathways. *American Psychologist, 58*, 53-63.

Segal, J. (2004). *Melanie Klein, 2nd Ed.* Thousand Oaks, CA: Sage Publications.

Segal, R. A. (1992). *The Gnostic Jung*. Princeton, NJ: Princeton University Press.

Segall, M. H., Dasen, P. R., Berry, J. W., & Poortinga, Y. H. (1990). *Human behavior in global perspective: An introduction to cross-cultural psychology*. Boston, MA: Allyn and Bacon.

Seligman, M. E. P. (1994). *What you can change & what you can't: The complete guide to successful self-improvement*. New York, NY: Knopf.

Seligman, M. E. P. (2002). *Authentic happiness: Using the new positive psychology to realize your potential for lasting fulfillment*. New York, NY: The Free Press.

Seligman, M. E. P. & Csikszentmihalyi, M. (2000). Positive psychology: An introduction. *American Psychologist, 55*, 5-14.

Seligman, M. E. P., Steen, T. A., Park, N., & Peterson, C. (2005). Positive psychology progress: Empirical validation of interventions. *American Psychologist, 60*, 410-421.

Senghor, L. S. (1965). *Prose and poetry* (J. Reed & C. Wake, Trans.). London, England: Heinemann.

Senghor, L. S. (1971). *The foundations of "Africanite" or "Negritude" and "Arabite."* Paris, France: Presence Africaine.

Seybold, K. S. & Hill, P. C. (2001). The role of religion and spirituality in mental and physical health. *Current Directions in Psychological Science, 10*, 21-24.

Shah, I. (1971). *The Sufis*. New York, NY: Anchor Books.

Shapiro, S. L., Schwartz, G. E. R., & Santerre, C. (2005). Meditation and positive psychology. In C. R. Snyder & S. J. Lopez (Eds.), *Handbook of positive psychology* (pp. 632-645). New York, NY: Oxford University Press.

Sharaf, M. (1983). *Fury on Earth: A biography of Wilhelm Reich*. New York, NY: Da Capo Press.

Sharma, A. R. (2000). Psychotherapy with Hindus. In P. S. Richards & A. E. Bergin (Eds.), *Handbook of psychotherapy and religious diversity* (pp. 341-365). Washington, DC: American Psychological Association.

Shedinger, R. F. (2004). Are we at war with Islam? Traditional Islamic resistance to American democracy. *Agora, 16*, 25-33.

Sheldon, K. M. & King, L. (2001). Why positive psychology is necessary. *American Psychologist, 56*, 216-217.

Sherman, R., & Dinkmeyer, D. (1987). *Systems of family therapy: An Adlerian integration*. New York, NY: Brunner/Mazel.

Shields, J., Heston, L. L., & Gottesman, I. I. (1975). Schizophrenia and the schizoid: The problem for genetic analysis. In R. R. Fieve, D. Rosenthal, & H. Brill (Eds.), *Genetic research in psychiatry* (pp. 167-197). Baltimore, MD: The Johns Hopkins University Press.

Shoda, Y., Leetiernan, S., & Mischel, W. (2002). Personality as a dynamical system: Emergence of stability and distinctiveness from intra- and interpersonal interactions. *Personality and Social Psychology Review, 6*, 316-325.

Shoda, Y., Mischel, W., & Peake, P. K. (1990). Predicting adolescent cognitive and self-regulatory competencies from preschool delay of gratification. *Developmental Psychology, 26*, 978-986.

Siegel, D. J. (1999). *The developing mind: How relationships and the brain interact to share who we are*. New York, NY: The Guilford Press.

Siegel, D. J. (2007). *The mindful brain: Reflection and attunement in the cultivation of well-being*. New York, NY: W. W. Norton & Company.

References

Simonton, D. K. (2000). Creativity: Cognitive, personal, developmental, and social aspects. *American Psychologist, 55*, 151-158.

Skinner, B. F. (1948). *Walden two*. New York, NY: The Macmillan Company.

Skinner, B. F. (1953). *Science and human behavior*. New York, NY: The Free Press.

Skinner, B. F. (1957). *Verbal behavior*. New York, NY: Appleton-Century-Crofts.

Skinner, B. F. (1959). *Cumulative Record*. New York, NY: Appleton-Century-Crofts.

Skinner, B. F. (1970). B. F. Skinner…An autobiography. In P. B. Dews (Ed.), *Festschrift for B. F. Skinner* (pp. 1-21). New York, NY: Irvington Publishers.

Skinner, B. F. (1971). *Beyond freedom & dignity*. New York, NY: Alfred A. Knopf.

Skinner, B. F. (1974). *About behaviorism*. New York, NY: Alfred A. Knopf.

Skinner, B. F. (1976). *Particulars of my life*. New York, NY: Alfred A. Knopf.

Skinner, B. F. (1978). *Reflections on behaviorism and society*. Englewood Cliffs, NJ: Prentice-Hall.

Skinner, B. F. & Vaughan, M. E. (1983). *Enjoy old age: A program of self-management*. New York, NY: W. W. Norton & Company.

Skinner, B. F. (1987). *Upon further reflection*. Englewood Cliffs, NJ: Prentice-Hall.

Smelser, N. J. (1980a). Issues in the study of work and love in adulthood. In N. J. Smelser & E. H. Erikson (Eds.), *Themes of work and love in adulthood* (pp. 1-26). Cambridge, MA: Harvard University Press.

Smelser, N. J. (1980b). Vicissitudes of work and love in Anglo-American society. In N. J. Smelser & E. H. Erikson (Eds.), *Themes of work and love in adulthood* (pp. 105-119). Cambridge, MA: Harvard University Press.

Smelser, N. J. & Erikson, E. H. (Eds.). (1980). *Themes of work and love in adulthood*. Cambridge, MA: Harvard University Press.

Smith, D. M., Langa, K. M., Kabeto, M. U., & Ubel, P. A. (2005). Health, wealth, and happiness: financial resources buffer subjective well-being after the onset of a disability. *Psychological Science, 16*, 663-666.

Smith, G. T., Spillane, N. S., & Annus, A. M. (2006). Implications of an emerging integration of universal and culturally specific psychologies. *Perspectives on Psychological Science, 1*, 211-233.

Snyder, C. R. & Lopez, S. J. (Eds.). (2005). *Handbook of positive psychology*. New York, NY: Oxford University Press.

Sobsey, D. (1994). *Violence and Abuse in the Lives of People with Disabilities: The End of Silent Acceptance?* Baltimore, MD.

Sofola, J. A. (1973). *African culture and the African personality (What makes an African person African)*. Ibadan, Nigeria: African Resources Publishers Co.

Sorokin, P. A. (1947). *Society, culture, and personality: Their structure and dynamics – A system of general sociology*. New York, NY: Cooper Square Publishers.

Spelke, E. S. (2005). Sex differences in intrinsic aptitude for mathematics and science?: A critical review. *American Psychologist, 60*, 950-958.

Sperber, M. (1974). *Masks of loneliness: Alfred Adler in perspective*. New York, NY: Macmillan Publishing.

Sperry, L. & Shafranske, E. P. (Eds.). (2005). *Spiritually oriented psychotherapy*. Washington, DC: American Psychological Association.

Spiel, O. & Birnbaum, F. (1930). The school and educational guidance. In A. Adler (Ed.), *Guiding the child: On the principles of Individual Psychology* (pp. 66-83). New York, NY: Greenberg.

Spietz, H. (1991). *Montessori at home*. Rossmoor, CA: American Montessori Consulting.

Spinelli, D. H. & Jensen, F. E. (1979). Plasticity: The mirror of experience. *Science, 203*, 75-78.

Spinelli, D. H., Jensen, F. E., & DiPrisco, G. V. (1980). Early experience effect on dendritic branching in normally reared kittens. *Experimental Neurology, 62*, 1-11.

Srivastava, S., John, O. P., Gosling, S. D., & Potter, J. (2003). Development of personality in early and middle adulthood: Set like plaster or persistent change? *Journal of Personality and Social Psychology, 84*, 1041-1053.

Stagner, R. (1937). Psychology of personality. New York, NY: McGraw-Hill.

Stagner, R. (1988). *A history of psychological theories*. New York, NY: Macmillan Publishing.

Stagner, R. (1993). Fifty years of the psychology of personality. In K. H. Craik, R. Hogan, & R. N. Wolfe (Eds.), *Fifty years of personality psychology* (pp. 23-38). New York, NY: Plenum Press.

Stein, M. (1963). Explorations in typology. In R. W. White (Ed.), *The study of lives: Essays on personality in honor of Henry A. Murray* (pp. 280-303). New York, NY: Atherton Press.

Steinberg, L. (2007). Risk taking in adolescence: New perspectives from brain and behavioral science. *Current Directions in Psychological Science, 16*, 55-59.

Sternberg, R. J. (2004). Culture and intelligence. *American Psychologist, 59*, 325-338.

Sternberg, R. J., Grigorenko, E. L., & Kidd, K. K. (2005). Intelligence, race, and genetics. *American Psychologist, 60*, 46-59.

Stevens, J. (2007). *Zen bow, Zen arrow: The life and teachings of Awa Kenzo*. Boston, MA: Shambhala.

Stewart, A. J. & McDermott, C. (2004). Gender in psychology. *Annual Review of Psychology, 55*, 519-544.

Stewart, M. (1994). *Yoga over 50: The way to vitality, health and energy in the prime of life*. New York, NY: FIRESIDE.

Stiver, I. P. (1991). The meanings of "dependency" in female-male relationships. In J. V. Jordan, A. G. Kaplan, J. B. Miller, I. P. Stiver, & J. L. Surrey (Eds.), *Women's growth in connection: Writings from the Stone Center* (pp 143-161). New York, NY: The Guilford Press.

Stoltz, P. G. & Weihenmayer, E. (2006). *The adversity advantage: Turning everyday struggles into everyday greatness*. New York, NY: A Fireside Book.

Storr, A. (1983). *The essential Jung*. Princeton, NJ: Princeton University Press.

Strickland, B. R. (1965). The prediction of social action from a dimension on internal-external control. *Journal of Social Psychology, 66*, 353-358.

Strickland, B. R. & Crowne, D. P. (1963). Need for approval and the premature termination of psychotherapy. *Journal of Consulting Psychology, 27*, 95-101.

Strozier, C. B. (2001). *The making of a psychoanalyst*. New York, NY: Farrar, Straus and Giroux.

Stubbins, J. (Ed.). (1977). *Social and psychological aspects of disability*. Baltimore, MD: University Park Press.

Styers, J. (1974). *Cold steel: Technique of close combat*. Boulder, CO: Paladin Press.

Sue, D. W. (2004). Whiteness and ethnocentric monoculturalism: Making the "invisible" visible. *American Psychologist, 59*, 761-769.

Sue, S. (1999). Science, ethnicity, and bias: Where have we gone wrong? *American Psychologist, 54*, 1070-1077.

Sue, S. (2000). The practice of psychological science. *American Psychologist, 55*, 1510-1511.

Sue, S. (2003). In defense of cultural competency in psychotherapy and treatment. *American Psychologist, 58*, 964-970.

Sullivan, H. S. (1940). *Conceptions of modern psychiatry*. New York, NY: W. W. Norton & Company.

Sullivan, H. S. (1953). *The interpersonal theory of psychiatry*. New York, NY: W. W. Norton & Company.

Sullivan, H. S. (1954). *The psychiatric interview*. New York, NY: W. W. Norton & Company.

Sullivan, H. S. (1956). *Clinical studies in psychiatry*. New York, NY: W. W. Norton & Company.

Sullivan, H. S. (1962). *Schizophrenia as a human process*. New York, NY: W. W. Norton & Company.

Sullivan, H. S. (1964). *The fusion of psychiatry and social science*. New York, NY: W. W. Norton & Company.

Sullivan, H. S. (1972). *Personal psychopathology: Early formulations*. New York, NY: W. W. Norton & Company.

Surrey, J. L. (1991). The self-in-relation: A theory of women's development. In J. V. Jordan, A. G. Kaplan, J. B. Miller, I. P. Stiver, & J. L. Surrey (Eds.), *Women's growth in connection: Writings from the Stone Center* (pp 51-66). New York, NY: The Guilford Press.

Surrey, J. L. (2005). Relational psychotherapy, relational mindfulness. In C. K. Germer, R. D. Siegel, & P. R. Fulton (Eds.), *Mindfulness and psychotherapy* (pp. 91-110). New York, NY: The Guilford Press.

Suzuki, D. T. (1957). *Mysticism: Christian and Buddhist*. New York, NY: Routledge Classics.

Suzuki, D. T. (1960). *Manual of Zen Buddhism*. New York, NY: Grove Press.

Suzuki, D. T. (1962). *The essentials of Zen Buddhism*. New York, NY: Dutton & Co.

Suzuki, D. T., Fromm, E., & De Martino, R. (1960). *Zen Buddhism & psychoanalysis*. New York, NY: Harper & Brothers.

Suzuki, L. A., Ponterotto, J. G. & Meller, P. J. (Eds.) (2001). *Handbook of Multicultural Assessment: Clinical, psychological, and educational applications*. San Francisco, CA: Jossey-Bass.

Swidler, A. (1980). Love and adulthood in American culture. In N. J. Smelser & E. H. Erikson (Eds.), *Themes of work and love in adulthood* (pp. 120-147). Cambridge, MA: Harvard University Press.

Syler, R. (2007). *Good-enough mother: The perfectly imperfect book of parenting*. New York, NY: Simon Spotlight Entertainment.

Tan, S.-Y. & Johnson, W. B. (2005). Spiritually oriented cognitive-behavioral therapy. In L. Sperry & E. P. Shafranske (Eds.), *Spiritually oriented psychotherapy* (pp. 77-103). Washington, DC: American Psychological Association.

Taylor, R. J., Chatters, L. M., & Levin, J. (2004). Religion in the lives of African Americans: Social, psychological, and health perspectives. Thousand Oaks, CA: Sage Publications.

Taylor, S. E., Kemeny, M. E., Reed, G. M., Bower, J. E., & Gruenewald, T. L. (2000). Psychological resources, positive illusions, and health. *American Psychologist, 55*, 99-109.

Taylor, S. E., Welch, W. T., Kim. H. S., & Sherman, D. K. (2007). Cultural differences in the impact of social support on psychological and biological stress responses. *Psychological Science, 18*, 831-837.

Taylor, R. J., Chatters, L. M., & Levin, J. (2004). *Religion in the lives of African Americans: Social, psychological, and health perspectives*. Thousand Oaks, CA: Sage Publications.

Tebes, J. K. (2000). External validity and scientific psychology. *American Psychologist, 55*, 1508-1509.

References

Tellegen, A., Lykken, D. T., Bouchard, T. J., Wilcox, K. J., Segal, N. L., & Rich, S. (1988). Personality similarity in twins reared apart and together. *Journal of Personality and Social Psychology, 54*, 1031-1039.

Tembo, J. S. (1980). *A sociological analysis of the African personality among Zambian students.* Unpublished Master's Thesis, Michigan State University, Lansing, MI.

Thanissaro Bhikkhu (1993). *The mind like fire unbound.* Barre, MA: Dhamma Dana Publications.

Thanissaro Bhikkhu (1996). *The wings to awakening: An anthology from the Pali Canon.* Barre, MA: Dhamma Dana Publications.

Thich Nhat Hanh (1966). *Fragrant palm leaves: Journals 1962-1966.* New York, NY: Riverhead books.

Thich Nhat Hanh (1991). *Peace is every step: The path of mindfulness in everyday life.* New York, NY: Bantam Books.

Thich Nhat Hanh (1995). *Living Buddha, living Christ.* New York, NY: Riverhead Books.

Thich Nhat Hanh (1999). *Going home: Jesus and Buddha as brothers.* New York, NY: Riverhead Books.

Thich Nhat Hanh (2003). *Creating true peace: Ending violence in yourself, your family, your community, and the world* [CD]. New York, NY: Simon & Schuster.

Thorne, B. (2003). *Carl Rogers, 2nd Ed.* Thousand Oaks, CA: SAGE Publications.

Tieger, P. D. & Barron-Tieger, B. (2001). *Do what you are: Discover the perfect career for you through the secrets of personality type, 3rd Ed.* Boston, MA: Little, Brown and Company.

Tomasello, M. (2000). Culture and cognitive development. *Current Directions in Psychological Science, 9*, 37-40.

Trelease, M. L. (1975). Dying among the Alaskan Indians: A matter of choice. In E. Kubler-Ross, Ed., *Death: The final stage of growth* (pp. 33-37). New York, NY: A Touchstone Book.

Triandis, H. C., Bontempo, R., Villareal, M. J., Asai, M., & Lucca, N. (1988). Individualism and collectivism: Cross-cultural perspectives on self-ingroup relationships. *Journal of Personality and Social Psychology, 54*, 323-338.

Triandis, H. C. & Suh, E. M. (2002). Cultural influences on personality. *Annual Review of Psychology, 53*, 133-160.

Trimble, J. E. & Richardson, S. S. (1982). Locus of control measures among American Indians: Cluster structure analytic characteristics. *Journal of Cross-Cultural Psychology, 13*, 228-238.

Trimpey, J., Velten, E., & Dain, R. (1993). Rational recovery from addictions. In W. Dryden & L. K. Hill (Eds.), *Innovations in Rational-Emotive Therapy* (pp. 253-271). Newbury Park, CA: SAGE Publications.

Tropp, L. R. & Pettigrew, T. F. (2005). Relationships between intergroup contact and prejudice among minority and majority status groups. *Psychological Science, 16*, 951-957.

Trujillo, A. (2000). Psychotherapy with Native Americans: A view into the role of religion and spirituality. In P. S. Richards & A. E. Bergin (Eds.), *Handbook of psychotherapy and religious diversity* (pp. 445-466). Washington, DC: American Psychological Association.

Trull, T. J. & McCrae, R. R. (1994). A five-factor perspective on personality disorder research. In P. T. Costa, Jr. & T. A. Widiger (Eds.), *Personality disorders and the Five-Factor Model of personality* (pp. 59-71). Washington, DC: American Psychological Association.

Tsai, J. L. (2007) Ideal affect: Cultural causes and behavior consequences. *Perspectives on Psychological Science, 2*, 242-259.

Tweed, R. G. & Lehman, D. R. (2002). Learning considered within a cultural context: Confucian and Socratic approaches. *American Psychologist, 57*, 89-99.

Tweed, R. G. & Lehman, D. R. (2003). Confucian and Socratic learning. *American Psychologist, 58*, 148-149.

Tucker, C. M. & Herman, K. C. (2002). Using culturally sensitive theories and research to meet the academic needs of low-income African American children. *American Psychologist, 57*, 762-773.

Tutu, D. (1999). *No future without forgiveness.* New York, NY: Doubleday.

Upasika Kee Nanayon (1995). *An unentangled knowing.* Barre, MA: Dhamma Dana Publications.

Vaillant, G. E. (2000). Adaptive mental mechanisms: Their role in a positive psychology. *American Psychologist, 55*, 89-98.

van Ijzendoorn, M. H. & Sagi, A. (2001) Cultural blindness or selective inattention? *American Psychologist, 56*, 824-825.

van Vugt, M., De Cremer, D., & Janssen, D. P. (2007). Gender differences in cooperation and competition: The male-warrior hypothesis. *Psychological Science, 18*, 19-23.

Vash, C. L. (1981). *The psychology of disability.* New York, NY: Springer Publishing Company.

Vasquez, M. J. T. (2007). Cultural difference and the therapeutic alliance: An evidence-based analysis. *American Psychologist, 62*, 878-885.

Vasquez, M. J. T., Lott, B., Garcia-Vazquez, E., Grant, S. K., Iwamasa, G. Y., Molina, L. E., Ragsdale, B. L., & Vestal-Dowdy, E. (2006). Personal reflections: Barriers and strategies in increasing diversity in psychology. *American Psychologist, 61*, 157-172.

Vincent, N. (2006). *Self-made man: One woman's journey into manhood and back again.* New York, NY: Viking.

Vivekananda, Swami (1955a). *Karma-Yoga and Bhakti-*

Yoga. New York, NY: Ramakrishna-Vivekananda Center.

Vivekananda, Swami (1955b). *Jnana-Yoga*. New York, NY: Ramakrishna-Vivekananda Center.

Wachtel, P. L. (1977). *Psychoanalysis & behavior therapy: Toward and integration*. New York, NY: Basic Books.

Wachtel, P. L. (1997). *Psychoanalysis, behavior therapy, and the relational world*. Washington, DC: American Psychological Association.

Waddell, H. (1998). *The desert fathers*. New York, NY: Vintage Books.

Wade, C. & Tavris, C. (1994). The longest war: Gender and culture. In W. J. Lonner & R. S. Malpass (Eds.), *Psychology and culture* (pp. 121-126). Boston, MA: Allyn and Bacon.

Walker III, E. (2003). *The mystic Christ: The light of non-duality and the path of love as revealed in the life and teachings of Jesus*. Norman, OK: Devi Press.

Wallace, B. A. & Shapiro, S. L. (2006). Mental balance and well-being: Building bridges between Buddhism and Western psychology. *American Psychologist, 61*, 690-701.

Waller, N. G., Kojetin, B. A., Bouchard, T. J., Lykken, D. T., & Tellegen, A. (1990). Genetic and environmental influences on religious interests, attitudes, and values. *Psychological Science, 1*, 138-142.

Walsh, R. (1995). Asian psychotherapies. In R. J. Corsini & D. Wedding (Eds.), *Current Psychotherapies, 5th Ed.* (pp. 387-398). Itasca, IL: F. E. Peacock Publishers.

Walsh, R. & Shapiro, S. L. (2006). The meeting of meditative disciplines and Western psychology: A mutually enriching dialogue. *American Psychologist, 61*, 227-239.

Wandersman, A. & Florin, P. (2003). Community interventions and effective prevention. *American Psychologist, 58*, 441-448.

Wang, Q. (2006a). Culture and the development of self-knowledge. *Current Directions in Psychological Science, 15*, 182-187.

Wang, Q. (2006b). Earliest recollections of self and others in European American and Taiwanese young adults. *Psychological Science, 17*, 708-714.

Wanjohi, G. J. (2005). African marriage, past and present. In G. J. Wanjohi & G. W. Wanjohi (Eds.), *Social and religious concerns of East Africa: A Wajibu anthology* (pp. 38-42). Nairobi, Kenya: Wajibu: A Journal of Social and Religious Concern.

Watts, A. (1957) *The way of Zen*. New York, NY: Vintage Books.

Watts, R. E. (1999). The vision of Adler: An introduction. In R. E. Watts & J. Carlson (Eds.), *Interventions and strategies in counseling and psychotherapy* (pp. 1-13). Philadelphia, PA: Accelerated Development.

Watts, R. E. & Carlson, J. (Eds.). (1999). *Interventions and strategies in counseling and psychotherapy*. Philadelphia, PA: Accelerated Development.

Wehr, G. (1989). *An illustrated biography of C. G. Jung*. Boston, MA: Shambhala.

Weihenmayer, E. (2001). *Touch the top of the world: A blind man's journey to climb farther than the eye can see*. New York, NY: Dutton.

Wei-Ming, T. (1978). The Confucian perception of adulthood. In E. H. Erikson (Ed.), *Adulthood* (pp. 113-127). New York, NY: W. W. Norton & Company.

Weiner, M. B., Cooper, P. C., & Barbre, C. (Eds.). (2005). *Psychotherapy and religion*. Lanham, MD: Aronson.

Weishaar, M. E. (1993). *Key figures in counseling and psychotherapy: Aaron T. Beck*. Thousand Oaks, CA: SAGE Publications.

Weiss, A. (2005). *Connecting to God: Ancient Kabbalah and modern psychology*. New York, NY: Bell Tower.

Weiss, A., Bates, T. C., & Luciano, M. (2008). Happiness is a personal(ity) thing: The genetics of personality and well-being in a representative sample. *Psychological Science, 19*, 205-210.

Weiss, B. L. (1988). *Many lives, many masters: The true story of a prominent psychiatrist, his young patient, and the past-life therapy that changed both their lives*. New York, NY: A Fireside Book.

Weiss, B. (2000). *Messages from the masters: Tapping into the power of love*. New York, NY: Warner Books.

Weissberg, R. P., Kumpfer, K. L., & Seligman, M. E. P. (2003). Prevention that works for children and youth: An introduction. *American Psychologist, 58*, 425-432.

Wellman, M. & Flinn, J. (1992). *Climbing back*. Merrillville, IL: ICS Books.

Westen, D., Novotny, C. M., & Thompson-Brenner, H. (2006). The empirical status of empirically supported psychotherapies: Assumptions, findings, and reporting in controlled clinical trials. In PDM Task Force (Eds.), *Psychodynamic Diagnostic Manual* (pp 691-764). Silver Spring, MD: Alliance of Psychoanalytic Organizations.

Whaley, A. L. & Davis, K. E. (2007). Cultural competence and evidence-based practice in mental health services: A complementary perspective. *American Psychologist, 62*, 563-574.

White, R. W. (1963). *The study of lives: Essays on personality in honor of Henry A. Murray*. New York, NY: Atherton Press.

Whitley Jr., B. E. & Kite, M. E. (2006). *The psychology of prejudice and discrimination*. Belmont, CA: Thomson Wadsworth.

References

Widiger, T. A. (1994). Conceptualizing a disorder of personality from the Five-Factor Model. In P. T. Costa, Jr. & T. A. Widiger (Eds.), *Personality disorders and the Five-Factor Model of personality* (pp. 311-317). Washington, DC: American Psychological Association.

Widiger, T. A. & Frances, A. J. (1994). Toward a dimensional model for the personality disorders. In P. T. Costa, Jr. & T. A. Widiger (Eds.), *Personality disorders and the Five-Factor Model of personality* (pp. 19-39). Washington, DC: American Psychological Association.

Widiger, T. A., Trull, T. J., Clarkin, J. F., Sanderson, C, & Costa, Jr., P. T. (1994). A description of the *DSM-III-R* and *DSM-IV* personality disorders with the Five-Factor Model of personality. In P. T. Costa, Jr. & T. A. Widiger (Eds.), *Personality disorders and the Five-Factor Model of personality* (pp. 41-56). Washington, DC: American Psychological Association.

Wiggins, J. S. & Pincus, A. L. (1994). Personality structure of the structure of personality disorders. In P. T. Costa, Jr. & T. A. Widiger (Eds.), *Personality disorders and the Five-Factor Model of personality* (pp. 73-93). Washington, DC: American Psychological Association.

Wikipedia. (2006). Freudian slip. Retrieved March 13, 2006, en.wikipedia.org/wiki/Freudian_slip

Wilhelm, R. (Translator). (1950). *The I Ching - or Book of Changes*. Princeton, NJ: Princeton University Press.

Wilkins, R. J. (1967) *The Religions of Man*. Dubuque, IA: Brown Co. Publishers.

Wilkinson, P. (2005). *Gandhi: The young protester who founded a nation*. Washington, DC: National Geographic Society.

Williams, M., Teasdale, J., Segal, Z., & Kabat-Zinn, J. (2007). *The mindful way through depression: Freeing yourself from chronic unhappiness*. New York, NY: The Guilford Press.

Williams, W. M. (2004). Blissfully incompetent. *Psychological Science in the Public Interest, 5(3)*, i-ii.

Williams, W. M. & Ceci, S. J. (1997). Are Americans becoming more or less alike?: Trends in race, class, and ability differences in intelligence. *American Psychologist, 52*, 1226-1235.

Wilson, G. T. (2004). Acceptance and change in the treatment of eating disorders. In S. C. Hayes, V. M. Follette, & M. M. Linehan (Eds.), *Mindfulness and acceptance: Expanding the cognitive-behavioral tradition* (pp. 243-260). New York, NY: The Guilford Press.

Wilson, E. O. (1975). *Sociobiology: The new synthesis*. Cambridge, MA: The Belknap Press.

Wilson, E. O. (1978). *On human nature*. Cambridge, MA: Harvard University Press.

Winerman, L. (2006). From the stage to the lab: Neuroimaging studies are helping hypnosis shed its 'occult' connotations by finding that its effects on the brain are real. *Monitor on Psychology, 37*, 26-27.

Winner, E. (2000). The origins and ends of giftedness. *American Psychologist, 55*, 159-169.

Winnicott, D. W. (1945/1996). Toward an objective study of human nature. In R. Shepherd, J. Johns, & H. T. Robinson (Eds.), *D. W. Winnicott: Thinking about Children* (pp 3-12). Reading, MA: Addison-Wesley.

Winnicott, D. W. (1964/1986). The concept of the false self. In C. Winnicott, R. Shepherd, & M. Davis (Eds.), *D. W. Winnicott: Home is where we start from - Essays by a psychoanalyst* (pp 65-70). New York, NY: W. W. Norton & Company.

Winnicott, D. W. (1966/2002). The child in the family group. In The Winnicott Trust (Eds.), *Winnicott on the child* (pp 221-231). Cambridge, MA: Perseus.

Winnicott, D. W. (1967/1986). The concept of a healthy individual. In C. Winnicott, R. Shepherd, & M. Davis (Eds.), *D. W. Winnicott: Home is where we start from - Essays by a psychoanalyst* (pp 21-38). New York, NY: W. W. Norton & Company.

Winnicott, D. W. (1968a/2002). Communication between infant and mother, and mother and infant, compared and contrasted. In The Winnicott Trust (Eds.), *Winnicott on the child* (pp 70-81). Cambridge, MA: Perseus.

Winnicott, D. W. (196b/2002). Children learning. In The Winnicott Trust (Eds.), *Winnicott on the child* (pp 232-238). Cambridge, MA: Perseus.

Winnicott, D. W. (1968c/1986). Adolescent immaturity. In C. Winnicott, R. Shepherd, & M. Davis (Eds.), *D. W. Winnicott: Home is where we start from - Essays by a psychoanalyst* (pp 150-166). New York, NY: W. W. Norton & Company.

Winnicott, D. W. (1969/2002). The building up of trust. In The Winnicott Trust (Eds.), *Winnicott on the child* (pp 178-187). Cambridge, MA: Perseus.

Winnicott, D. W. (1971). *Therapeutic consultations in child psychiatry*. New York, NY: Basic Books.

Winnicott, C., Shepherd, R., & Davis, M. (Eds.). (1986). *D. W. Winnicott: Home is where we start from - Essays by a psychoanalyst*. New York, NY: W. W. Norton & Company.

Withers, S. & Sims, S. (2007). *Broken Wing: You can't quit. Not ever. A true story of courage and inspiration*. Belfast, ME: Mystic Wolf Press.

Wober, M. (1974). Toward an understanding of the Kiganda concept of intelligence. In J. W. Berry & P. R. Dasen (Eds.), *Culture and Cognition* (pp. 261-280). London, England: Methuen.

Wong, R. Y-m. & Hong, Y-y. (2005). Dynamic influences of culture on cooperation in the prisoner's dilemma. *Psychological Science, 16*, 429-434.

References

World's Great Religions, The. (1957) New York, NY: Time.

Wright, B. A. (1983). *Physical Disability - A psychosocial approach, 2nd Ed.* New York, NY: Harper & Row.

Wu, S. & Keysar, B. (2007). The effect of culture on perspective taking. *Psychological Science, 18*, 600-606.

Yamagishi, T., Hashimoto, H., & Schug, J. (2008). Preferences versus strategies as explanations for culture-specific behavior. *Psychological Science, 19*, 579-584.

Yamaguchi, S., Greenwald, A. G., Banaji, M. R., Murakami, F., Chen, D., Shiomura, K., Kobayashi, C., Cai, H., & Krendl, A. (2007). Apparent universality of positive implicit self-esteem. *Psychological Science, 18*, 498-500.

Yankura, J. & Dryden, W. (1994). *Key figures in counseling and psychotherapy: Albert Ellis*. Thousand Oaks, CA: Sage Publications.

Yeager, R. J., Yeager, C. M., & Shillingford, J.-A. (1993). Treating adult children of alcoholics. In W. Dryden & L. K. Hill (Eds.), *Innovations in Rational-Emotive Therapy* (pp. 33-71). Newbury Park, CA: SAGE Publications.

Yik, M. S. M., Russell, J. A., Ahn, C.-K., Dols, J. M. F., & Suzuki, N. (2002). Relating the Five-Factor Model of personality to a circumplex model of affect. In R. R. McCrae & J. Allik (Eds.), *The Five-Factor Model of personality across cultures* (pp. 79-104). New York, NY: Kluwer Academic/Plenum Publishers.

Yogananda, Paramahansa (1946). *Autobiography of a yogi*. Los Angeles, CA: Self-Realization Fellowship.

Yogananda, Paramahansa. (1994). *Wine of the mystic: The Rubaiyat of Omar Khayyam - A spiritual interpretation*. Los Angeles, CA: Self-Realization Fellowship.

Yogananda, Paramahansa (2004a). *The second coming of Christ: The resurrection of the Christ within you, Vol. I.* Los Angeles, CA: Self-Realization Fellowship.

Yogananda, Paramahansa (2004b). *The second coming of Christ: The resurrection of the Christ within you, Vol. II.* Los Angeles, CA: Self-Realization Fellowship.

Young-Eisendrath, P. (2005). Suffering from biobabble: Searching for a science of subjectivity. In K. H. Dockett, G. R. Dudley-Grant, & C. P. Bankart (Eds.), *Psychology and Buddhism: From individual to global community* (pp. 125-138). New York, NY: Kluwer Academic/Plenum Publishers.

Yukteswar Giri, Jnanavatar Swami Sri (1894/1990). *The holy science*. Los Angeles, CA: Self-Realization Fellowship.

Zadeh, F. E. (2002). *Islam versus terrorism: Understanding Islam and the culture of the Middle East*. Twin Lakes, CO: Twin Lakes Publishing.

Zhang, K., Lee, Y.-T., Liu, Y., & McCauley, C. (1999). Chinese-American differences: A Chinese view. In Y.-T. Lee, C. R. McCauley, & J. G. Draguns (Eds.), *Personality and person perception across cultures* (pp. 127-138). Mahway, NJ: Lawrence Erlbaum Associates, Publishers.

Zimbardo, P. G. (2004). Does psychology make a significant difference in our lives? *American Psychologist, 59*, 339-351.

Zucker, R. A., Rabin, A. I., Aronoff, J., & Frank, S. (1992). *Personality structure in the life course: Essays on Personology in the Murray tradition.* New York, NY: Springer Publishing Company.

Zuckerman, M. (1979). *Sensation seeking: Beyond the optimal level of arousal*. Hillsdale, NJ: Lawrence Erlbaum Associates.

Zuckerman, M. (Ed.). (1983). *Biological bases of sensation seeking, impulsivity, and anxiety*. Hillsdale, NJ: Lawrence Erlbaum Associates.

Zuckerman, M. (1991). *Psychobiology of personality*. Cambridge, England: Cambridge University Press.

Zuckerman, M. (1993). Out of sensory deprivation and into sensation seeking: A personal and scientific journey. In G. G. Brannigan & M. R. Merrens (Eds.), *The undaunted psychologist: Adventures in research* (pp. 44-57). New York, NY: McGraw-Hill.

Zuckerman, M. (1994). *Behavioral expressions and biosocial bases of sensation seeking*. Cambridge, England: Cambridge University Press.

Zuckerman, M. (1997). The psychobiological basis of personality. In H. Nyborg (Ed.), *The scientific study of human nature: Tribute to Hans J. Eysenck at eighty* (pp. 3-16). Oxford, England: Pergamon Press.

Zuckerman, M. (2006). The shaping of personality: Genes, environment, and chance encounters. In S. Strack & B. N. Kinder (Eds.), *Pioneers of personality science: Autobiographical perspectives* (pp. 387-412). New York, NY: Springer Publishing Company.

Zuckerman, M., Albright, R. J., Marks, C. S., & Miller, G. L. (1962). Stress and hallucinatory effects of perceptual isolation and confinement. *Psychological Monographs: General and Applied, 76*, 1-15.

Index

Index

About the Author

[Image by Mark Kelland]

Mark Kelland has a Bachelor of Science (Summa Cum Laude) degree in Psychology from Northeastern University, and a Doctor of Philosophy degree in Physiological Psychology from Wayne State University. For a number of years he conducted biomedical research on Parkinson's Disease, Tourette Syndrome, and Schizophrenia. He worked at Sinai Hospital (Detroit), the National Institutes of Health, the Wayne State University School of Medicine, and Saint Anselm College (NH). Over time he made the transition from research to teaching, and is now a Professor of Social Science at Lansing Community College in Michigan. He has taught a wide variety of psychology courses and a few education courses, and his current interests focus on cross-cultural perspectives on the development of personality. His professional and personal interests have led to an active involvement in and study of Yoga, Buddhism, and Daoism. Among his awards and honors, Prof. Kelland is particularly proud to have won a Michigan Campus Compact Community Service-Learning Award and to have been nominated by a former student for Who's Who Among America's Teachers. In 2017 he was elected president of the academic senate at LCC.

Professor Kelland has been active in community service in a variety of ways. He established new service-learning programs in NH and MI. He has taught religious education, been a guest reader at several schools, tutored 1st-graders who were struggling to read, and coached youth soccer. He was a founding faculty member of the Adult Center for Enrichment of Livingston County (MI), and currently teaches spirituality, psychology, and self-defense classes at the Hartland (MI) Senior Center, the Howell (MI) Parks and Recreation Department, the Capitol Area Center for Independent Living (MI). He has taught Taekwondo to Little Dragons (4-5 year old children) and white/yellow belts (children and adults), and he is currently studying Brazilian Jiu Jitsu (and still teaching children's classes and helping adult beginners).

In high school, Prof. Kelland was crushed by a horse. Not knowing the extent of the damage to his hips, he became a highly competitive runner in his mid-20s. Years later, as he began practicing Taekwondo, the damage to his legs started to catch up with him. On a bad day, he almost could not walk. Shortly after earning his black belt in Taekwondo, he had the first of two total hip replacements. Prof. Kelland began actively studying the American Cane System (Cane Masters International Association), and then Defense-Ability (a wheelchair-based self-defense program; International Disabled Self-Defense Association). He is now certified in the C.R.I.T.I.C.A.L. Approach™ to teaching martial arts to people with physical challenges (Natural Motion Martial Arts), has his black belt and instructor's license in Defense-Ability, his black belt in the Amerian Cane System, and his 2nd degree black belt in Taekwondo. Prof. Kelland established Real-Life Self-Defense, LLC, a program for teaching martial arts and self-defense to people with physical disabilities. He has served on the Capital Area Business Leadership Network Disability Council in Lansing, MI.

Since first publishing this textbook, Prof. Kelland has published another OER textbook (*Tao of Positive Psychology*) and fourteen shorter books, ranging from a book on the psychology of disability and martial arts programs for people who are disabled (written on sabbatical) to two books including academic journals from his students and two children's books.

CPSIA information can be obtained
at www.ICGtesting.com
Printed in the USA
LVHW021155180122
708698LV00010B/561